FIND, RENOVATE, &
FINANCE THE
NON-TRADITIONAL
PERFORMANCE
SPACE

WILL IT MAKE A THEATRE?

ELDON ELDER
MICHELE LARUE, *Associate Writer*
Drawings by Eldon Elder

aca BOOKS

AMERICAN COUNCIL FOR THE ARTS
New York, New York

Published in cooperation with the Alliance of Resident Theatres/New York, Inc.

This book is made possible with public funds from the National Endowment for the Arts, Design Arts Program; the New York State Council on the Arts; and the City of New York through the Department of Cultural Affairs. Private funding from the AT&T Foundation is gratefully acknowledged. The chapter on Energy Conservation was funded by the New York State Energy Conservation Program sponsored by the New York State Energy Office and administered in New York City by The New York Community Trust.

Published by the American Council for the Arts in cooperation with the Alliance of Resident Theatres/New York, Inc.

Copyright © 1993 by Alliance of Resident Theatres/New York, Inc.

No part of this publication may be reproduced by any means without the written permission of the publisher. For information, contact: American Council for the Arts, 1 East 53rd Street, New York NY 10022.

Edited by Mindy N. Levine
Book and jacket design by Celine Brandes, Photo Plus Art.
Typesetting by The Desktop Shop.
Director of Publishing: Robert Porter.
Assistant Director of Publishing: Jill MacKenzie.

Library of Congress Cataloging-in-Publication data:

Elder, Eldon.
Will it make a theater : find, renovate,
and finance the non-traditional performance
space / compiled and written by Eldon Elder ; associate writer,
Michele LaRue ; drawings by Eldon Elder ; editor, Mindy N. Levine.
— 2nd ed.
p. cm.
ISBN 1-879903-02-4 : $26.95
1. Theater architecture—United States. 2. Theaters—United States—
Remodeling. 3. Theaters—United States—Law and legislation. 4. Buildings—
United States—Remodeling for other use. 5. Amateur theater—
United States—Production and direction.
I. LaRue, Michele. II. Levine, Mindy N. 1955- . III. Title.
NA6830.E43 1993
725'.8722—dc20
92-36871
CIP

Contents

Introduction 1

PART ONE

THE SEARCH FOR A SPACE 3

1 DEVELOPING GUIDELINES 4

The Purpose and the Program 4

2 SHAPE AND SIZE 9

Basic Theatre Configurations 9
Size Requirements 11

3 WHAT TO LOOK FOR 22

General Characteristics of the Potential Space 22
Types of Buildings 26
Offbeat Places to Consider 36

4 HOW TO FIND IT 42

Where to Look 42
Gathering Information 44

5 EVALUATING A SPACE 48

The Neighborhood 48
Transportation and Accessibility 49
Noise 49
Inspection of the Building 49

Can It Be Brought Up to Code?   52
Is It Worth the Rent?   53
Costs of Renovation and Conversion   54
Evaluation   55
    Profile: VICTORY GARDENS/BODY POLITIC, CHICAGO   56
    Profile: FORT MASON CENTER, SAN FRANCISCO   60

PART TWO
HOW TO GET IT   65

6 NEGOTIATING FOR A SPACE   66

Buying or Renting   66
Commercial Leases   67
Space Purchase   69
Legal Assistance   70
Neighborhood Assistance   70

7 RESOURCES FOR MAKING IT HAPPEN   72

Government Funding   72
Corporations   75
Foundations   75
    Profile: THE THEATRE ROW STORY   76
Loans   84
Individuals   84
Organizing the Campaign   86
Service Organizations   86

PART THREE
DESIGN AND PLANNING STRATEGIES   87

The Theatre Consultant and the Architect   88

8 THE STAGE SPACE   91

Stage Floor   91

Stage Walls 95
Stage Size 96
Access to the Stage 96
Overhead and Rigging 97
    Profile: LYRIC STAGE COMPANY, BOSTON 105

9 THE AUDIENCE SPACE 110

Sightlines 110
Seats and Seating Layout 112
Acoustics 116
Lighting 118
    Profile: BRIAR STREET THEATRE, CHICAGO 119

10 THE SUPPORT SPACES 121

Technical Control Booth 121
Dressing Rooms 122
Shops 124
Storage 126
Rehearsal Space 126
Box Office 128
Lobby and Lounge 129
Office Space 130
    Profile: LATINO CHICAGO THEATRE COMPANY, CHICAGO 131
    Profile: STEPPENWOLF THEATRE, CHICAGO 132

11 SOURCES OF MATERIALS AND EQUIPMENT 134

Donations 134
Scavenging 134
Auctions 135
Federal Surplus Property 135
Wholesale Buying and Other Sources 135
Renting vs. Buying 136
Buying Stage Lighting Equipment 136

12 GENERAL EQUIPMENT INSTALLATIONS 138

Portable vs. Permanent Installations 138

Sound Systems   138
Electrical Installations   139
Security Systems   140

13 ENERGY EFFICIENCY   141

Evaluating Space for Energy Efficiency   141
Designing Space for Energy Efficiency   142
Creating an Energy Management Plan   143
    Profile: TWO SUCCESSFUL CONVERSIONS:
       OPEN EYE THEATRE, NEW YORK CITY, AND STUDIO THEATRE, WASHINGTON, D.C.   144

PART FOUR

MAKING IT LEGAL: AN INTERPRETATION OF REGULATIONS AND CODES   153

Implications of Zoning and the Codes   154
Routine On-Site Inspections   154

14 ZONING   156

Use Groups and Zoning Districts   156
Getting a Zoning Variance   157

15 THE BUILDING CODE   159

Definitions   159
Old Code or New Code   161
Old Code Requirements   162
   Building Classification   162
   Means of Egress   163
   Seat and Row Spacing   164
   Live Load   164
   Exit Lighting   165
   Emergency Lighting   165
   Ventilation   165
   Plumbing and Sanitary Requirements   165
   Sprinklers   166
   Fire-Retardant or Flameproof   166

New Code Requirements 166
   Occupancy Classification 166
   Building Classification 167
   Means of Egress 168
   Exit Lighting 174
   Emergency Lighting 174
   Ventilation 174
   Plumbing and Sanitary Requirements 175
   Seat and Row Spacing 175
   Steps 175
   Live Load 175
   Sprinklers 176
   Fire Protection and Finish Materials 176

16 The Electrical Code 178

Stage Lighting Equipment and Installations 178
Dressing Rooms 179
House Lights and Work Lights 179
Emergency Lighting 179
Grounding 180

17 The Fire Prevention Code 181

Inspection Checklist 181
Permits 182

18 Application Procedures 189

Preliminary Procedures 189
Application Procedures for Permits and Licenses 190
Violations 199

19 Other Cities, Other Codes 202

Atlanta 202
Boston 205
Chicago 207
Los Angeles 209
San Francisco 211

APPENDIX: RESOURCE DIRECTORY   213

   National Service Organizations   213
   Atlanta Resource Directory   215
   Boston Resource Directory   216
   Chicago Resource Directory   218
   Los Angeles Resource Directory   219
   New York Resource Directory   221
   San Francisco Resource Directory   224

APPENDIX: SIX CITIES AGENCY CHART   226

APPENDIX: EVALUATION CHECKLIST   235

PUBLICATIONS OF INTEREST   237

INDEX   240

ABOUT A.R.T./NY   248

ABOUT ACA   248

Introduction

This book addresses the needs and problems of small, nonprofit theatre companies and those other performing arts groups looking for spaces to turn into permanent theatres. It contains information of value both to the new company looking for a non-traditional space in which to create its first theatre and to the established company planning to remodel or relocate in a new space.

This book will tell you where to look, what kinds of space to look for, what spaces to avoid, and what types of lease arrangements to negotiate. It explains resourceful ways that some arts groups have found to convert non-traditional spaces into performing arts facilities. Although *Will It Make a Theatre* will help you assess your needs, it will not be your lawyer, architect, or consultant. It will help you understand what is involved in finding, acquiring, designing and constructing theatre space, and assist you in making wise decisions. It will introduce you to agencies, neighborhoods, and non-traditional buildings where innovative possibilities exist. It will also help you interpret the building, fire and electrical codes.

Since survival for the small, not-for-profit theatre depends on getting more for less, it is the intention of this book to provide as many recommendations and approaches to this perpetual problem as possible.

Will It Make a Theatre is intended as a humanistic handbook—practical, down-to-earth, drawing on the experience of many, but tempered with the awareness that not all the recommended guidelines are applicable to every group's requirements.

The book is intended to be a survey. As such, some chapters will be more informative than others, depending on your areas of concern and level of expertise. Once you have read the book, go back and use applicable sections as a manual while planning your theatre. Feel free to copy the Evaluation Checklist and use it during your search for a space. Make notes in the book's margins. Tab the chapters of special concern to you.

It has been over a decade since the first version of *Will It Make a Theatre* was published in 1979. The alternative theatre community has changed substantially in those years and this thoroughly revised edition reflects those changes. Resource data has been completely updated and information in all chapters has been expanded to reflect the growing sophistication of the theatre community as well as new rules and regulations that influence theatre acquisition, design, and renovation—from code changes to smoking laws to regulations for the disabled. Most important, whereas the first edition of *Will It Make a Theatre* focused largely on New York City, this volume is national in scope.

Throughout the book, examples have been chosen largely from six major urban centers with a long history of theatre producing—Atlanta, Boston, Chicago, New York, Los Angeles, and San Francisco. Additionally, part 4, "Making It Legal: An Interpretation of Regulations and Codes," highlights the significant ways codes differ from city to city. The appendices list vital resources and city agencies that can be invaluable to individuals and groups working in each of these six cities. For companies located in other cities and towns across the country, the lists and information are meant to be suggestive of where you might turn in your locale for assistance. (While every effort has been made to ensure that this information is as up to date and accurate as possible, readers should keep in mind that organizations go out of business, addresses and phone numbers change, and organizational mandates and missions shift.)

The six cities highlighted throughout the pages that follow have been chosen because each contains vigorous and active theatre communities, and because their similarities and differences—in terms of basic building stock available, codes and regulations, climate, geography, municipal organization, and history of arts patronage—offer illuminating comparisons and contrasts. From Boston, where there is a substantial amount of university-based activity, to Los Angeles, a comparatively young city with a sprawling urban landscape; from Atlanta, where the arts community has taken an activist stance in the face of gentrification, to Chicago, where unique ties exist between the nonprofit and commercial theatre companies; from New York to San Francisco, where ambitious cooperative projects have been developed to address the space needs of arts groups; those involved in finding, renovating, designing, and bringing up to code the non-traditional performance space—wherever they may live—will find much to draw upon in these pages.

With a resourceful spirit, but in infinitely varied ways, theatre centers throughout the country have found creative solutions to their own unique problems. In Atlanta, old schools have proved particularly congenial homes for theatres. In Los Angeles, lacking the high-ceilinged old warehouses that so often serve as theatre spaces in New York, theatres have turned to storefronts. In Chicago, theatres must grapple with particularly stringent fire regulations, the legacy of the Great Chicago Fire of 1871 and the Iroquois Theatre fire in 1903. On the West Coast, seismic conditions—and the resulting code requirements to address them—present a special challenge to theatres.

Whatever the challenge, across the country, despite all odds, theatre is alive, well, and growing in spaces as diverse as the art itself.

PART ONE

THE SEARCH FOR A SPACE

1
Developing Guidelines

Probably no theatre has ever been created according to a strict set of rules, perhaps none will ever be; but there can be no doubt that it is worth the effort to develop a set of guidelines that presents a clear image of what you are looking for in a theatre before you begin the search for an appropriate space. To do this you must first develop an identity, a clear sense of who you are, what kind of theatre you are, how your company is unique, what you want to accomplish in your theatre and how you intend to do it—in short, a purpose and a program.

When starting out, it is difficult to think beyond the immediate goal—producing a play or a season of plays. But making some projections with regard to short- and long-term goals can save you from irreparable mistakes in the choice and conversion of space. The days of Judy Garland and Mickey Rooney and "Gee, wouldn't it be fun to put on a play!" are long gone.

The search for space must be constantly related to available money, materials and muscle power. While pinpointing your artistic space needs, you must always maintain a parallel, hard-nosed consideration of how costs will be met. For the small, not-for-profit theatre, there are three types of potential resources: money, materials, and "sweat" (i.e., free or low-cost labor). Assess your potential to tap all three areas. More imaginative solutions are possible when all three resources are combined.

It is reassuring to know that theatre people love to talk about what they are doing and what they have done. They are generous with help, advice, and tips on dos and don'ts, and can provide a compatriot's comfort when you most need it. Producers, artistic directors, designers, and technicians are exceedingly accessible to anyone who is serious; so talk to them. Networks of service organizations with local agencies have evolved in most cities; turn to them for help and advice. (See Resource Directory.)

THE PURPOSE AND THE PROGRAM

The most unique quality that any small, not-for-profit theatre offers its audience is its commitment to a particular artistic point of view. Without defining this point of view or purpose, and translating it into space requirements, you cannot intelligently choose a space.

Developing Guidelines

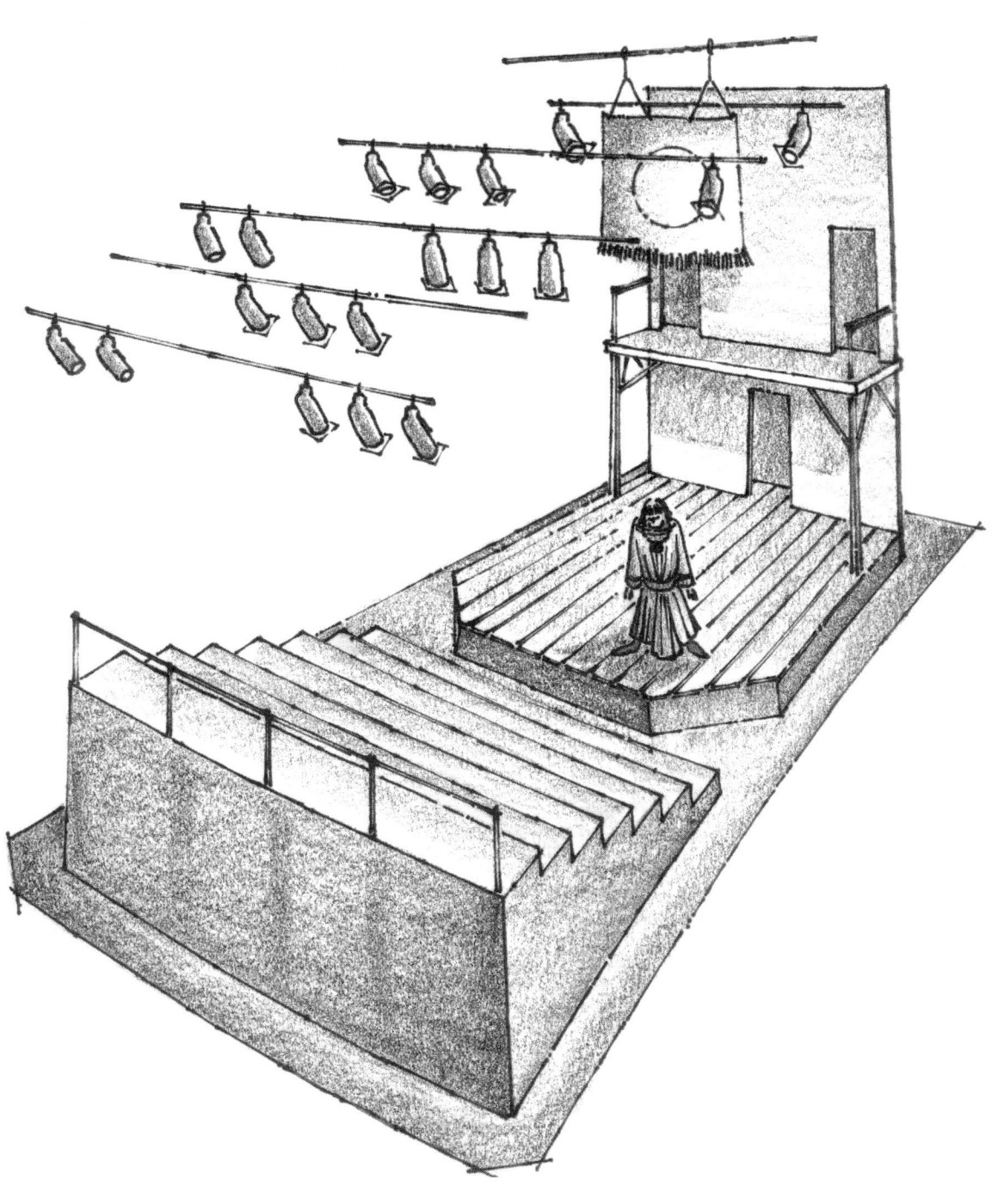

Begin by articulating an artistic purpose, a clearly focused statement of your mission. This artistic purpose, stated as a manifesto if you like, is the heart of your producing program and ultimately the foundation of your building plan.

Develop the statement of purpose with a summary of your goals. Ask what kind of plays you want to present. What kind of audience do you hope to address? Where do you hope to be in three years' time? In ten years' time?

- Assess your space needs. Begin with a list of the types of plays you plan to present. Will you do staged readings, workshops, or full productions? Spectacles with music and dance, or intimate drama? Do you want to do classics, which usually mean large casts; or revivals, which are often best served by a conventional proscenium form; or experimental and contemporary plays, which require the greatest possible flexibility and versatility in stage size and configuration?

- Narrow the list by re-examining your purpose and goals. At the same time, keep in mind desirable secondary functions such as dance, poetry, cabaret, children's theatre, classes, and musical events. Analyze how these activities will affect the size and shape of your stage, auditorium, and support spaces. None of these activities, however, should be pursued if they weaken the theatre's capacity to serve its primary function.

- Determine what size audience you want to reach. Allow for reasonable expansion in the future. Consider how the audience relates to the performers. Do you want intimacy or alienation, contact or separation?

- Clarify the specific audience you want to reach. How will that affect the size and shape of the auditorium? What type of building will this dictate? Where should the theatre be located to attract your desired audience?

- Evaluate production requirements. Will there be minimal scenery or a great deal? Will you build your own? If so, where—on stage, in the lobby, or in a scene shop? Will the shop be on or off the premises? Will productions make extensive use of lights and sound? And how about projections?

- Define cast requirements. Will they be large or small? What dressing room and costume handling facilities will you need? Will you build costumes? Will this require a costume shop? If so, where will it be located?

- Analyze administrative needs. Support spaces for these functions are as important as the performance space. Calculate the number of persons who will be involved in administration, not only at present, but also in future years. Keep in mind the needs of both staff and volunteers. Be careful not to underestimate the space needed for administration.

- Decide what ticket system will be used. Will tickets be handled by mail, phone, subscription, box office—or a combination of all four? Consider computerized systems (even if not a part of your initial plan), taking into account the equipment's space, power, and cooling requirements.

- Consider where your audience will assemble before a performance and during intermission. In short, take into account the lobby needs, plus lounge, public toilets, and concessions.

- Review rehearsal requirements, present and future. Can you rehearse on the stage? Will you need separate rehearsal spaces? How many productions or projects will be in rehearsal at the same time?

- Evaluate storage needs. Will you need storage for scenery, props, and costumes you plan to reuse? What types of equipment and materials will you store?

- Consider scheduling and how it will impact on the amount and kinds of space you will need. Productions in rotating repertory, for example, need more rehearsal space as well as adequate active storage space to

Developing Guidelines

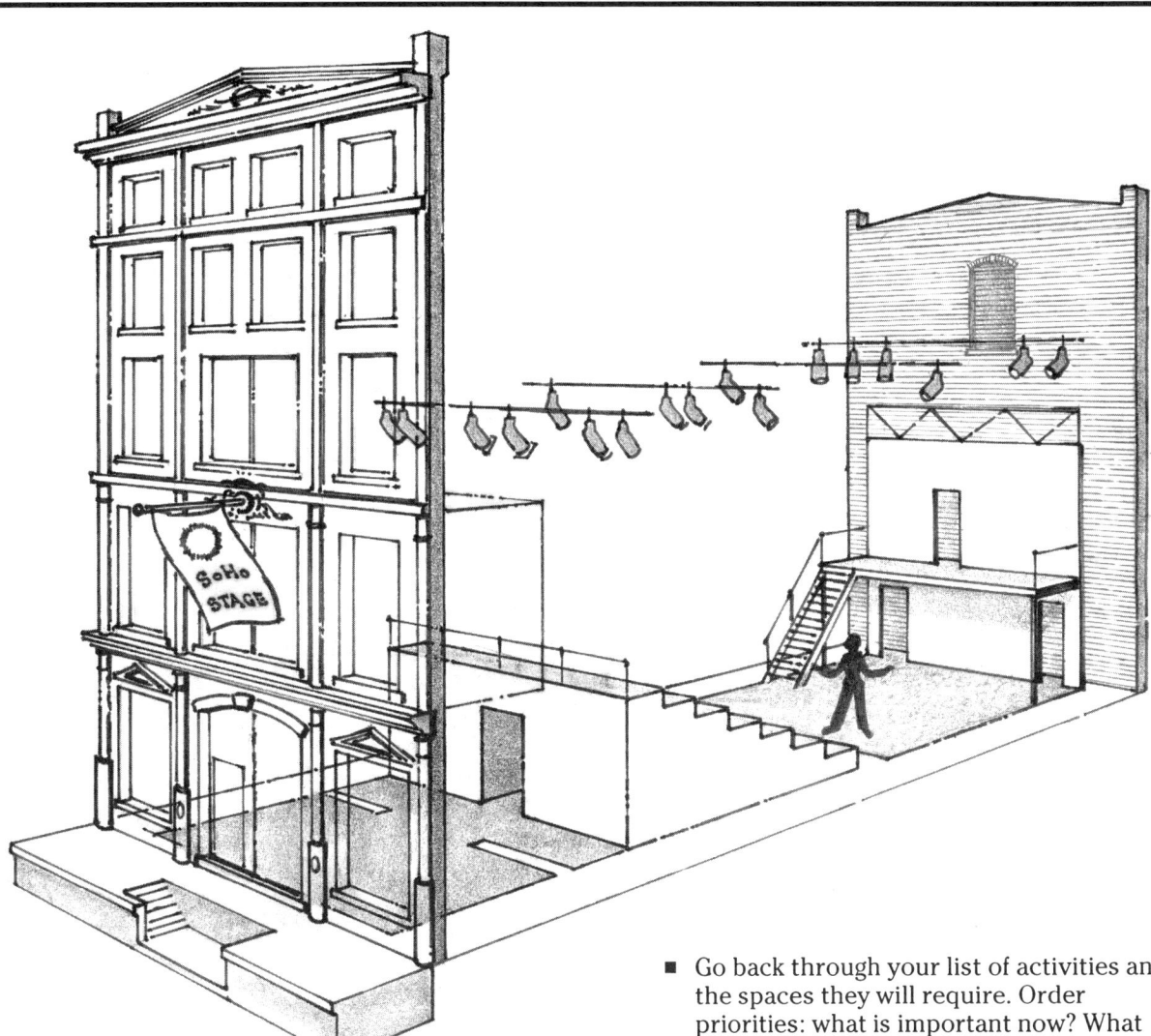

handle scenery, props, and costumes not in use while another production is on stage. The more storage space, the faster you can strike one show and mount another.

- Can you schedule rehearsal times for new productions that will allow you to use your own theatre for rehearsals while another show is playing? How would sharing space with other groups affect your programming and scheduling? (Support space is detailed in chapter 10.)

- Go back through your list of activities and the spaces they will require. Order priorities: what is important now? What can wait until later? Look for ways to consolidate programs. It may look great on paper to do two workshops, three readings, and one full production simultaneously, but some activities may need to be deferred until your organization is firmly established and you can accommodate them all. If necessary, consider a plan that allows you to grow over a period of time, phasing in activities gradually.

- Realistically evaluate your financial situation. How much money do you have on hand? How much do you need? How much can you raise? What is the shortfall?

- The gap between the money you have and the money you need can be at least partially closed by material and labor resources. Check within your company (both staff and board of directors) to determine what people are skilled in designing, building, or electrical and plumbing work. Do you have friends who might contribute professional advice? Obviously, the more donated labor and materials you can get, the further you can stretch the dollars you have.
- Some city, state, and federal agencies offer assistance that can stretch your labor resources. (See chapter 7 and Resource Directory and Agency Chart.)

This list of self-examining questions may look somewhat simplistic and will, to some, seem unnecessary. However, too many beginning producers and artistic directors organize a company and commit themselves to a space without asking and answering these basic questions. As a result, they make expensive, avoidable mistakes. Once you commit to a space and convert it, making further alterations may be difficult and costly, and you may be forced to select and schedule plays around the theatre's limitations.

You will not be able to stick dogmatically and rigidly to every detail of your artistic and building program. Don't expect to. Circumstances will force you to modify it. But, if clearly expressed, it will remain as a guide and a measuring stick throughout the lifespan of your theatre.

2 Shape and Size

Almost everyone wants an "all-purpose" space in the beginning—a space in which to present *any* kind of theatre. But as the hunt for the all-purpose space goes on and on, it invariably becomes clear that such a space is either not available, not affordable, or, perhaps, not even desirable. Then it becomes necessary to set priorities.

BASIC THEATRE CONFIGURATIONS

Before looking for space, examine all the possible theatre forms in order to determine the configuration and size that is right for you. The following survey of configurations will help you clarify exactly what kind of theatre best suits your artistic program.

Before you decide on a specific space configuration, visit a variety of small theatres in converted spaces. Study them under performance and nonperformance conditions to see how they function. Take notes on each space based on features discussed in this chapter. Talk to the people who chose these forms. This will direct you toward the right space.

PROSCENIUM STAGE. The proscenium arch encloses the performance area, and the audience faces the performance from one side only. A useful form if elaborate scenic effects are part of your plan. More than any other configuration, the proscenium creates actual and esthetic distance. Not practical in small, narrow, low-ceilinged spaces.

WILL IT MAKE A THEATRE?

END STAGE. Again the audience faces the performance area from one side only, but there is no proscenium arch. The end stage can provide intimacy and contact. Most often found in storefront and brownstone conversions, an end stage works well in long, narrow spaces. Height is desirable, but not absolutely essential. Actor access is often available from one end of the space only—the rear wall of the stage—which can be limiting.

OPEN OR THRUST STAGE—THREE-SIDED ARENA. A stage extends into the center of the audience with seating around three sides, which can provide intimacy. Requires a wide building. Can be useful where there are lower ceilings, for working around columns or other structural irregularities. Actor access from all sides is desirable.

THEATRE-IN-THE-ROUND—FOUR-SIDED ARENA. The audience completely surrounds the performance space. Not good for large-scale scenery. Can be useful for working around columns. Provides intimacy. Actor access from four sides. A squarish space is needed.

CENTER STAGE—TWO-SIDED ARENA. The audience faces the performance area from two opposite sides. Not good for large scale scenery. Can provide intimacy. Audience and actor access from both sides is needed. Works for a rectangular space.

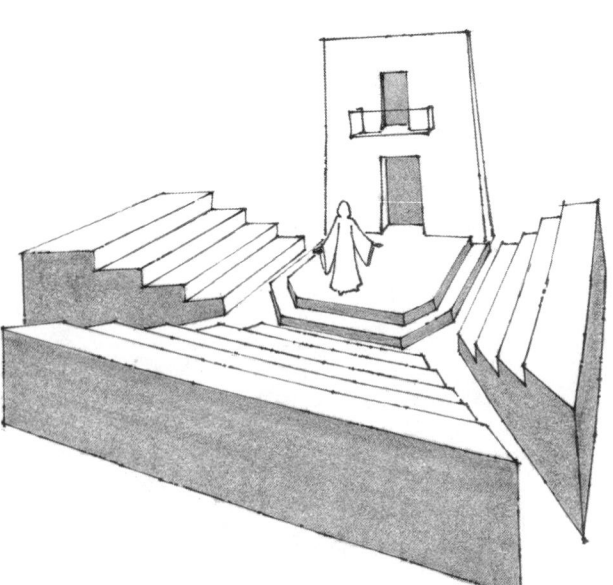

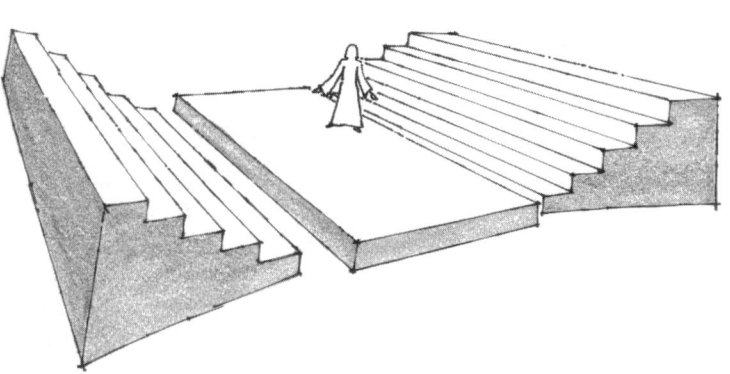

FLEXIBLE AND MULTIFORM THEATRE. The ambitious artistic director frequently begins by wanting "total flexibility"—a multiform space that can convert to any configuration. This is difficult, though not impossible, to achieve. Some forms and spaces convert more easily than others: end stage into center stage, or open stage (thrust) into theatre-in-the-round. Be aware that change-overs are not only time-consuming, but can also be expensive. They require a great deal of careful planning.

While the cliché that the "all-purpose theatre" is frequently the "no-purpose theatre" is true, almost all theatres are multipurpose in that they are sometimes used for events and performances other than their primary function. Most theatre configurations can serve more than one type of performance. Without compromising your theatrical vision, it's worthwhile to consider what secondary purposes your theatre space can serve. This should be assessed in the frame of full utilization of the space and possible sources of income through rental.

SIZE REQUIREMENTS

Small theatres are known for their ingenious use of small spaces, but there are limits as to how small a space can be and still function properly as a theatre. This section will deal with the *minimum* amounts of square footage in the various areas of a theatre. These square footage figures are derived from the building code minimum requirements and from the minimum standards used by consultants and architects. The New York City Building Code, which serves as a guideline for building codes throughout the country, is used as a reference in this book. (For important deviations in other city codes, see chapter 19.) The resulting dimensions are, practically speaking, the *absolute* minimum amount of space needed for an area to function in its intended use.

The areas discussed are broken down into two categories: necessary and optional. *Necessary* areas are those that are considered to be absolutely essential to the running of a theatre, no matter what its size. They include acting area, backstage area, seating and aisles, dressing rooms, technical control area, lobby, box office, administrative office, and rest rooms.

In some small theatres even these necessary areas are sometimes not affordable and spaces must serve multiple functions. Anyone who has worked Off-Off-Broadway can relate tales of the leading lady dressing in the public rest room, or of a bulk mailing to potential subscribers cluttering the lobby. But the functions of these spaces are necessary to the performance, even if spaces may have to serve double or triple duty.

The *optional* areas facilitate the operation of a theatre and include rehearsal space, additional offices, workshops (scenic and costume), lounge area, and storage areas. Like the necessary areas, the optional ones can do double duty: many alternative theatres without rehearsal rooms rehearse on stage; those with rehearsal rooms use them for informal play readings as well. Optional areas can also be housed in a building separate from the performance space, in a part of the city where rents are more affordable. West Hollywood's 99-seat Coast Playhouse supplements its small on-site office with a larger one five blocks away; Manhattan Theatre Club's offices on West 16th Street serve its two performance spaces on West 55th Street.

NECESSARY AREAS

Operating a small theatre encompasses many different facets of theatre activity, each needing its own specialized area.

The Acting Area

Consider the size of the stage in relation to the type of productions you envision within the space. A stage can be as small as 240 sq. ft.: 20' x 12' or 15' x 16', for example.

WILL IT MAKE A THEATRE?

Below is a sampling of sizes of a few very small New York City stages:

Theatre	Stage Space	Sq. Ft.
Writers Theatre	16' x 12'	192
York Theatre Co.	15' x 17'	255
Pearl Theatre Co.	20' x 20'	400
Theatre Off Park	20' x 22'	440

Some productions have been successfully mounted on even less space. For example, *Ain't Misbehavin'* opened at the Manhattan Theatre Club's original home, in the Cabaret, a 6' x 14' stage—84 sq. ft. Truly two planks and a passion!

An average sized stage in a small theatre is about 525 sq. ft.: 25' x 21' or 35' x 15'. In New York, the Ensemble Studio Theatre's stage is exactly 25' x 21'. Remember scenery and props will decrease the actual amount of space available to actors.

Musicals require a larger space to accommodate movement: 300 sq. ft. may be comfortable for a solo dancer but makes a very tight squeeze for a full company.

A more workable stage size for a small theatre would be around 1,000 sq. ft.: 40' x 25'. Playwright's Horizons' stage is 30' x 35'—1,050 sq. ft. In San Francisco, The Magic Theatre's Southside proscenium stage measures 30' x 40'—1,200 sq. ft., while its Northside three-quarter thrust stage is 700 sq. ft.

Off-Stage Spaces

In calculating the amount of square footage needed off-stage, try for at least 50% of the stage space. Therefore, if an acting area is 240 sq. ft., 120 sq. ft. will be a rough estimate of the off-stage space needed. Depending on a theatre's configuration, this space may be broken up into small areas or may be one space.

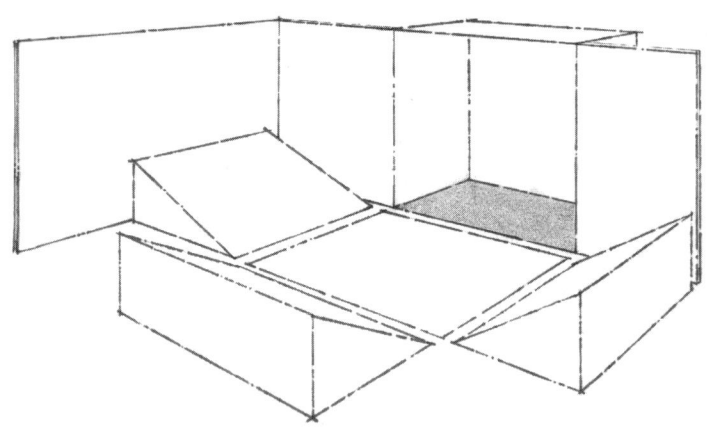

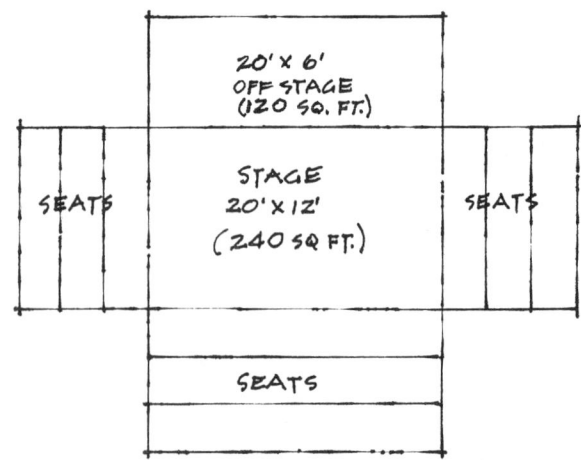

Minimum stage with off-stage space.

Shape and Size

Estimate the amount of space needed for the following, with relation to anticipated productions:

- the quantity of scenery or props to be stored off-stage
- the number of actors waiting for entrances
- space needed for cross-overs
- the stage manager (if not in the control booth)
- the technicians waiting for a scene change
- space needed for lighting equipment
- musicians and musical instruments when required

All of these should be considered in estimating the total off-stage space required.

Seating Area

This area comprises two parts: the seats and the aisles that lead to the seats.

SEATS. 18" wide seats with a back-to-back measurement of 31" complies with the Unified Building Code, a standard national code used in many cities, but the resulting seat plan is so tight that it should not even be considered.

A more realistic and comfortable dimension can be obtained by using 21" as the minimum seat width and 34" as the minimum back-to-back measurement. The result is 4.9 sq. ft. minimum per seat (for "rule of thumb" estimates: 5 sq. ft. per seat).

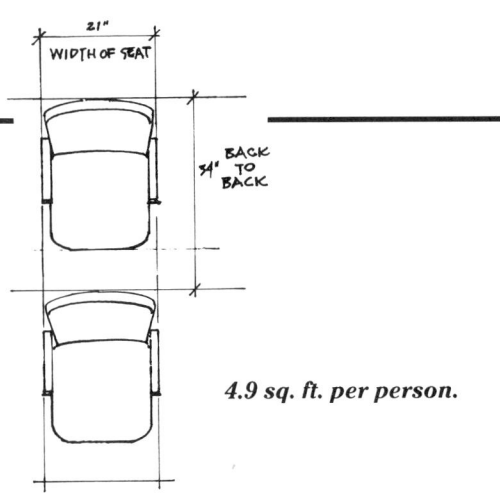

4.9 sq. ft. per person.

Square footage requirements can be computed as follows:

99 seats x 5 sq. ft. = 495 sq. ft.

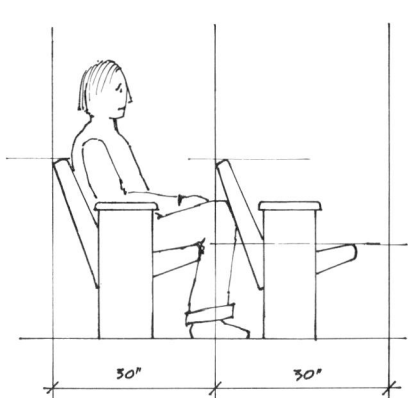

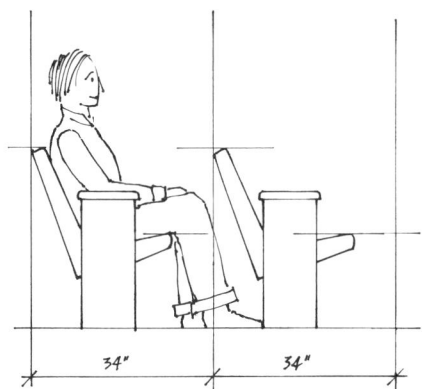

31" back-to-back—minimum building code requirement; 34" back-to-back—minimum allowance for comfort.

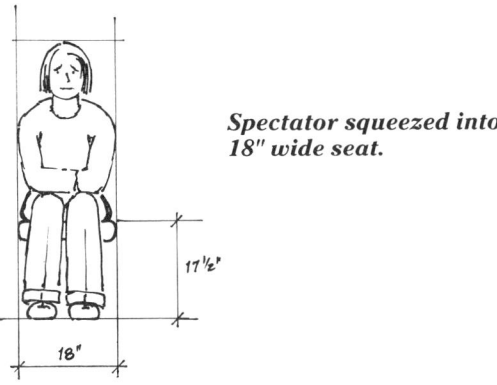

Spectator squeezed into 18" wide seat.

A more generous seating arrangement may be created by using a 22" seat width and a 36" back-to-back measurement, 5.5 sq. ft. per seat:

99 seats x 5.5 sq. ft. = 544.5 sq. ft.

AISLES. The minimum New York City Building Code requirement for width of an aisle is 36" in most situations. (Similar minimums apply in Chicago, San Francisco, and Los Angeles; in Atlanta and Boston minimums are 42" in most situations.) For a rough estimate of minimum aisle space needed, use 23% of the total seating square footage. Using the example of seating square footage given above, you can compute as follows:

23% of 495 sq. ft. (99 seats) = 113.8 sq. ft. *

23% of 1094.5 sq. ft. (199 seats) = 251.7 sq. ft. **

Obviously, to estimate total footage needed within the seating area, simply add the seating square footage and the aisle square footage:

495 + 113.8 = 608.8 sq. ft. needed for 99 seats *

1094.5 + 251.7 = 1346.2 sq. ft. for 199 seats **

Bear in mind that these figures are rough estimates only, and are the absolute minimum needed.

SEATING FOR THE DISABLED. Accessibility and seating spaces for the disabled are mandated by federal law 504. The New York City Code local law 58, which is typical, requires spaces for three wheelchairs for 75 to 100 seats, and up to nine spaces for 401 to 500 seats. (See chapter 19 for variations in other cities.) A wheelchair occupies the space of one and one-half seats. (See chapter 9 for details.)

---

* Based on 21" x 34" back-to-back seating

** Based on 22" x 36" back-to-back seating

The Americans with Disabilities Act (ADA) passed in July 1990 is concerned with physical and programmatic accessibility as well as employment practices. In New York City, local law 58 is more stringent than the ADA on physical accessibility, but the spirit of the ADA and programmatic accessibility will affect New York City theatres, as well as those around the country. (For more information about the ADA, contact the Job Accommodation Network's hotline toll-free at 1-800-ADA-WORK.)

Public Rest Rooms

All building codes have public rest room requirements. The New York City building code, for example, requires only one toilet for 100 persons and one urinal for every 200 persons plus one sink for every 200 persons. Although it is possible to comply with this requirement by providing only one facility, two should be considered the minimum to allow for handling men and women separately. You will need a minimum of 24 sq. ft. per facility, so allow at least 48 sq. ft. total.

Rest rooms for the disabled also must be included. (Space requirements are detailed on p. 21.)

Actors' Dressing and Lavatory Space

Although actors have changed costumes in public lavatories, dusty offices, and damp cellars, this can hardly be considered a viable solution to dressing room requirements.

The minimum amount of dressing space needed should be computed at 16 sq. ft. per person. For example, for six persons you will need 96 sq. ft. The type of shows you plan to produce and their cast sizes should serve as a guide to the amount of space required for dressing rooms.

Actors Equity contracts and agreements require that there be, separate from audience facilities, a minimum of one toilet and one washbasin with hot and cold water for all performers, plus one dressing room each for men and women.

Separate from its contractual demands, AEA also publishes renovation guidelines for backstage facilities, known as "Safe and Sanitary." Minimum

Shape and Size

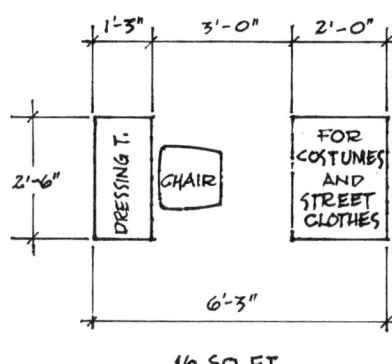

Minimum dressing space for one person allows for a 1'3" x 2'6" counter space, 1 chair, and 2' x 2'6" for hanging costumes and street clothes. Actors Equity Association recommends 3' minimum hanging space for costumes plus space for street clothes.

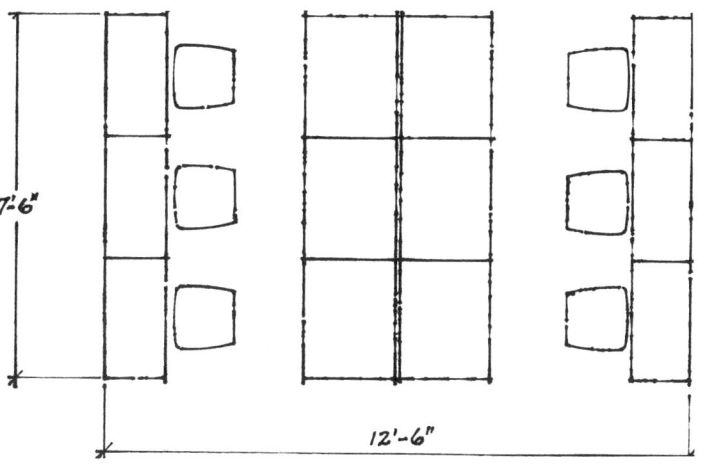

Dressing space for 6 persons.

recommendations include one toilet for men and one for women on each floor for every six performers, one washbasin for every four performers, one shower for every eight to ten performers.

And don't forget to provide space for the required Equity cot somewhere in your theatre.

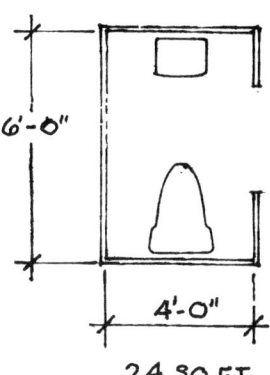

Minimum lavatory space.

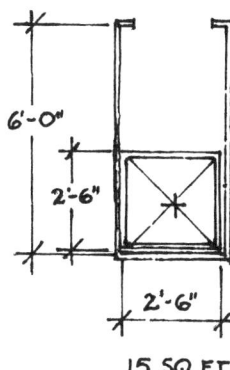

Minimum shower space.

Technical Control Space

Consider the number of people who will use this space at one time: lighting technician, sound technician, and stage manager. Depending on the amount and size of your equipment, this square footage will vary. The minimum space needed is approximately 61.6 sq. ft.

In some small theatres with very limited control room space, the stage manager doubles as the sound technician, reducing the space to two-person capacity—not a recommended compromise if it can be avoided. At the Lyric Stage's tiny original space in Boston, a rectangular hole cut through the dressing room wall accommodated one operator, standing on a ladder and supported by a telephone lineman's sling. The same dressing room doubled as the office during the day!

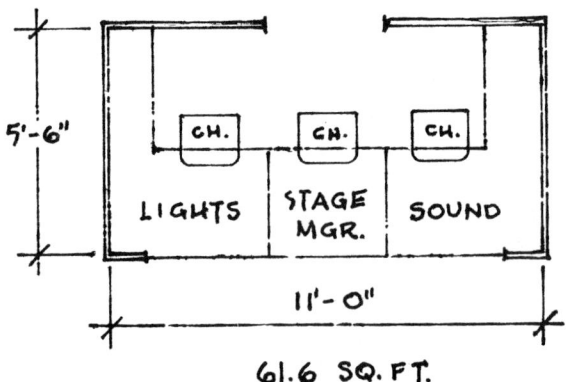

A technical control booth allowing sound technician, stage manager, and lighting technician to share space.

Lobby

The minimum amount of space needed for one standing person is 1 sq. ft. This minimum figure assumes that not all members of an audience will use the lobby at the same time; 2 sq. ft. per person creates a lobby of a somewhat more realistic size, but it is still far from generous.

If a *safe area* is required (see chapter 16), its minimum is also 2 sq. ft. per person. It is possible for the lobby to double as the safe area if it satisfies the appropriate fire code requirements.

Bear in mind that these square footage estimates are based upon free floor space; if you add furnishings within this area—chairs, tables, lamps, plants—you will need to increase the total square footage proportionately. (See chapter 10 for more about planning lobby space.)

Box Office

There are two basic approaches to creating a box office space: open and enclosed. If the box office is open—a table or counter set up within the lobby area—you will need to add at least 25 sq. ft. to the total lobby square footage to accommodate one box office person comfortably; if it is enclosed, allow a minimum of 30 sq. ft. (See chapter 10 for box office planning.)

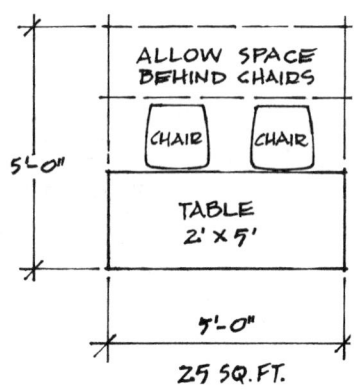

Open box office allows for a table and 1 or 2 chairs.

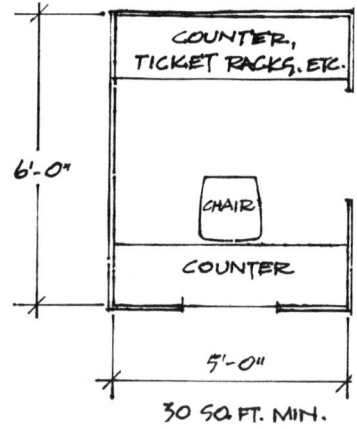

Enclosed box office allows for 1 person seated or 2 persons standing with 1'3" counter space on 2 sides, but does not include recommended allowance of space for a computer.

OPTIONAL AREAS

The functions of these so-called optional spaces must be accommodated. In a very small theatre, however, any given space may have multiple uses.

Shape and Size

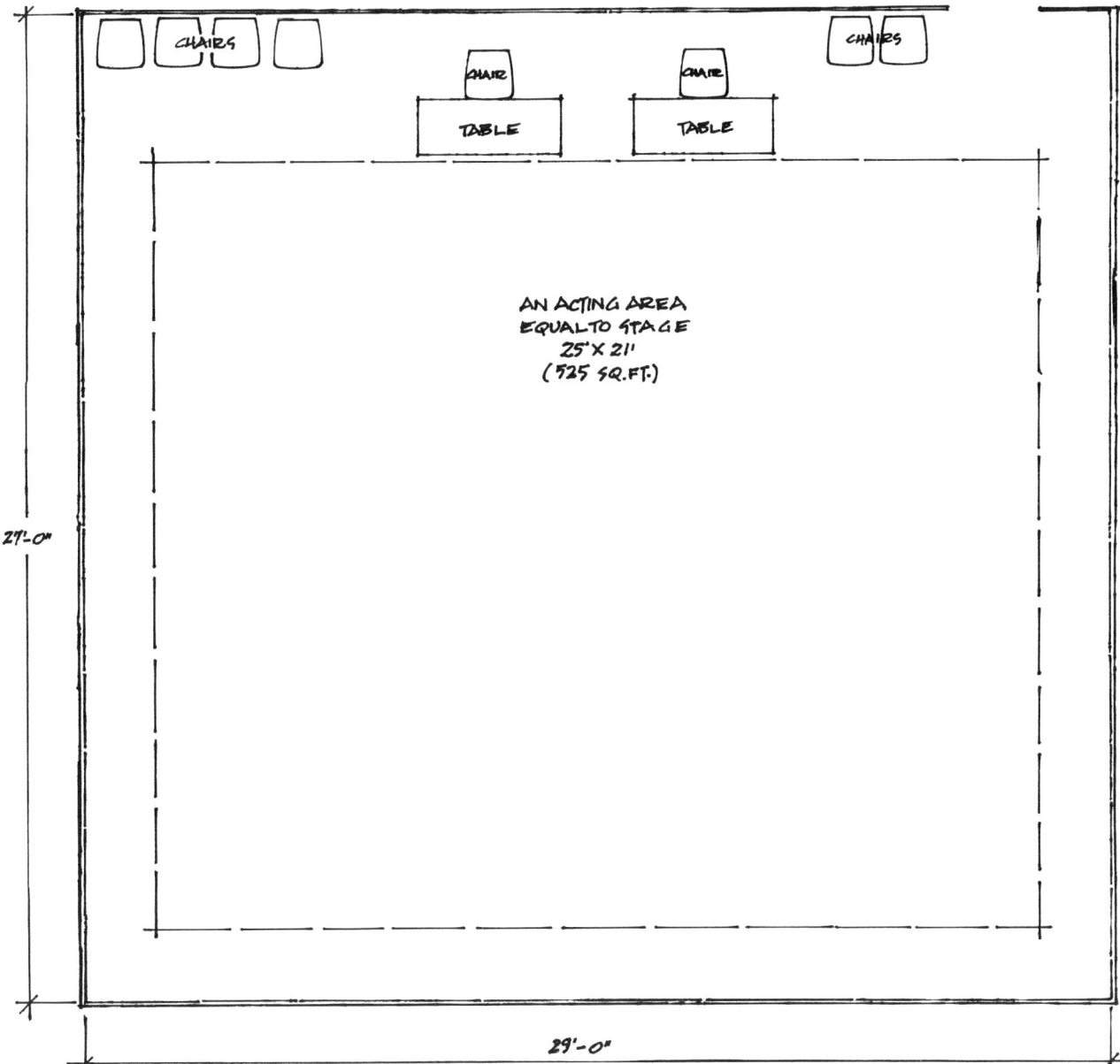

Rehearsal space: acting area surrounded by minimum off-stage area.

Lounge/Bar

A lounge or bar area adds a desirable public amenity: 4 sq. ft. per person allows for a minimum amount of comfort, assuming that the majority of the audience uses the space at one time. If you add a bar or concession counter, it will require a minimum of 25 sq. ft. added to the total. For example:

99 seats x 4 sq. ft. = 396 sq. ft. + 25 sq. ft. = 421 sq. ft. (total lounge)

Consider designing this area to comply with the "safe area" requirement mentioned above.

Rehearsal Space

When planning a rehearsal space, the basic square footage requirements should be at least equal to those of the acting area, ideally in the same configuration. If possible, include an additional area for a table and seating for the director and stage manager, and an off-stage waiting area for the actors and their rehearsal props.

Office Space

For an office, allow a minimum of 36 sq. ft. per person. If you plan to install filing cabinets and office machinery, additional square footage will be required.

Since the amount of space required for an office area should be directly proportional to the number of people who work within it, consider the total number who use the area at one time—administrators, managers, bookkeepers, secretaries, publicists, fundraisers, volunteers—and multiply that number by 36 sq. ft. (See chapter 10 for more about planning office spaces.)

Workshop Spaces

SCENERY AND CONSTRUCTION SHOP. There are two approaches to calculating square footage requirements for scenic construction space.

If you plan to build and paint scenery in one of the other spaces already mentioned—stage, lobby, lounge area—or in another space entirely, then you will need only an area in which to store tools, hardware, and painting supplies: 36 sq. ft. should be considered a bare minimum.

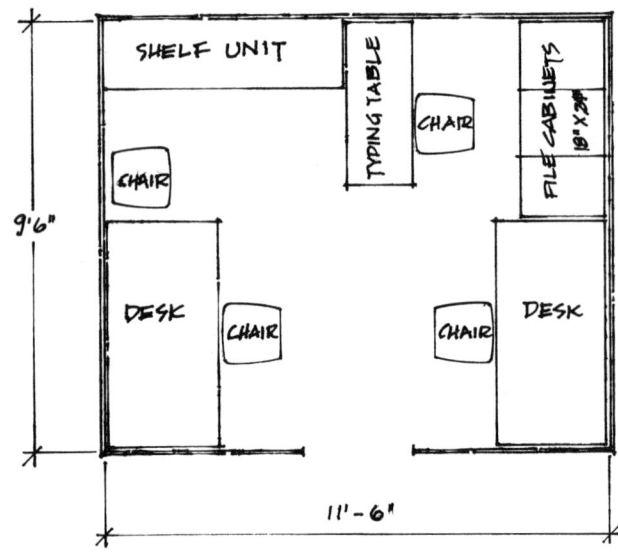

3-person office with files allows for 2 60" x 30" desks, a typing table, 4 chairs, 3 standard file cabinets, and a 1'6" x 5'6" shelf unit.

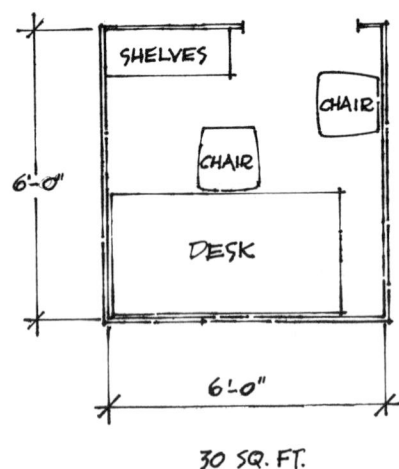

Office for 1 person allows a 60" x 30" desk, 2 chairs, and a shelf unit.

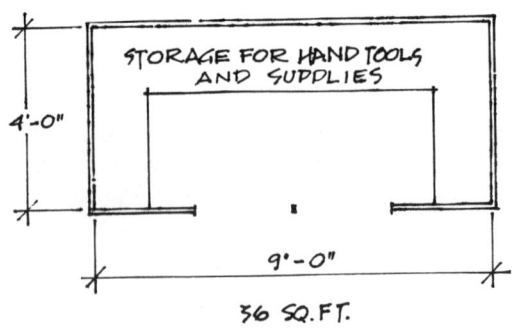

Minimum storage space, if there is no shop and scenery is built and painted in another space.

Shape and Size

If you plan to build and paint scenery in a separate scene shop area, you will need additional space: 196 sq. ft. gives a minimal shop area.

Two necessary items for this space are a slop sink and a fireproof paint locker or vault. Allow another 12 sq. ft. for each item, bringing your total estimate to 220 sq. ft.

COSTUME SHOP. The same two approaches hold for the costume shop as for the scene shop. If you plan to construct costumes in another building, your only requirement will be a storage area for supplies: 60 sq. ft. should be considered the minimum space needed.

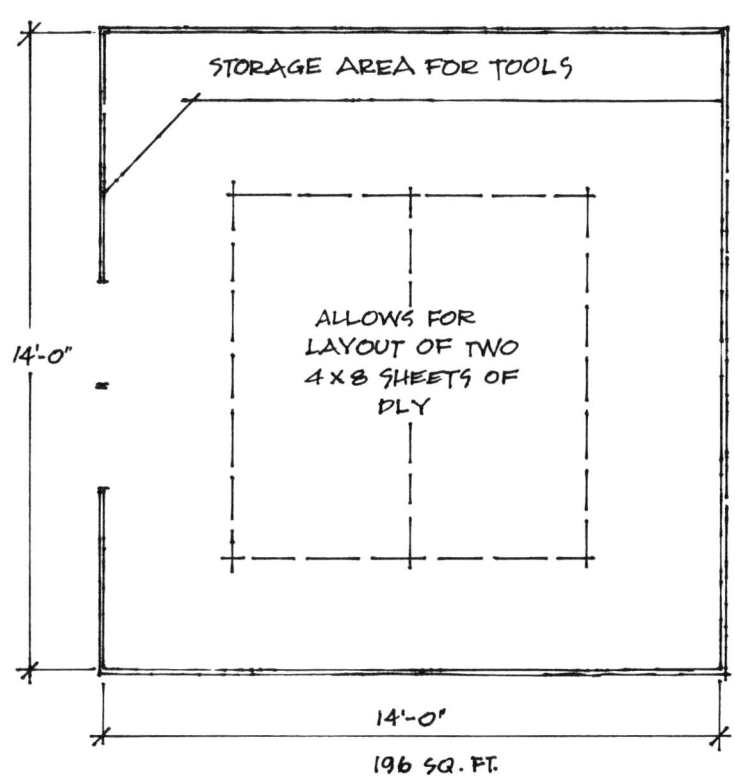

Minimum construction space assumes additional storage shelves and cabinets above head height.

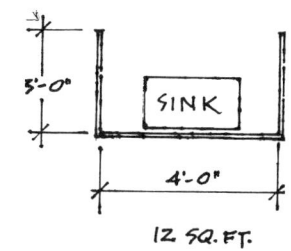
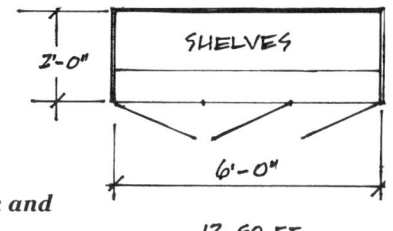

Minimum slop sink and paint locker.

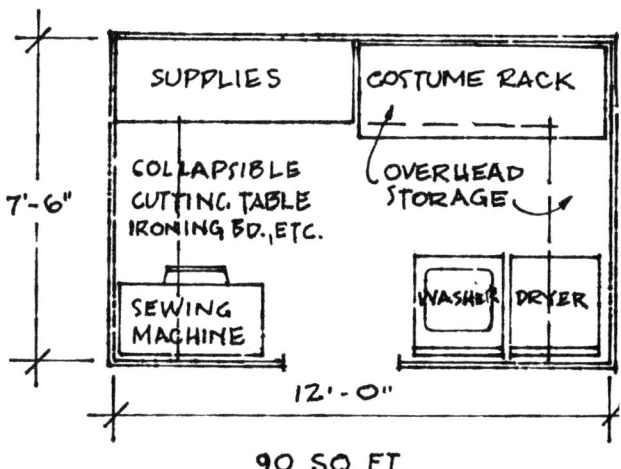

Minimum storage space for supplies assumes that costumes are built in another space, that costume maintenance will be done in the dressing room, and that costume storage will be elsewhere.

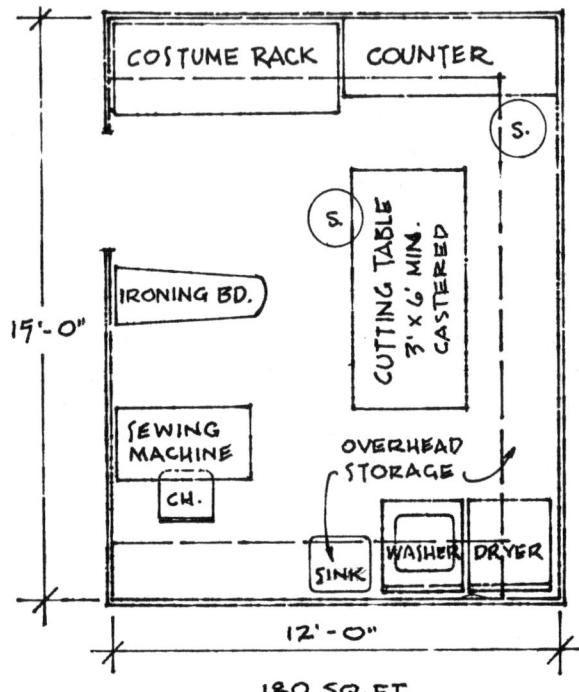

Minimum costume construction shop assumes costume storage will be elsewhere.

If you wish to construct costumes, you will need to plan on at least 144 sq. ft., 12' x 12', for a minimal costume shop.

Storage

Storage spaces are always at a premium. It is hard to determine a minimum square footage estimate, since it will depend on the number and size of the items that require storage. Take into consideration all possible storage needs: *costumes* (including hats, shoes, accessories, pocketbooks, costume props, supplies); *scenery* (platforms, step units, flats, draperies, screens, construction supplies); *properties* (hand props, furniture props, set dressing); *paint supplies* (brushes, buckets, cans, ladders); *lighting* (instruments, cables, spare lamps, replacement parts, tools); also, office supplies, janitorial supplies, scripts, programs, flyers, and those wonderful finds on the street that you know will come in handy "one of these days."

This seemingly endless list will vary from theatre to theatre. For example, rotating repertory companies need space to store full sets of scenery, costumes, and props, whereas companies doing only one show at a time may not need to store as much, since at the end of the run scenery is dismantled and most costumes and props are returned. "Flexible" spaces also need storage space for performing and seating as different configurations use different elements. One final point, to which all small companies readily attest: there is never enough storage space. Get as much as your budget will allow. (See chapter 10 for additional storage options.)

Estimating Total Square Footage

A rough square footage total can be obtained by adding all the individual areas together.

Theatre A and Theatre B in the chart that follows are representative of two small theatres with different space requirements based on the square footage estimates used in this chapter. Theatre A is a 99-seat theatre with only the very basic minimums. Theatre B is a 199-seat theatre with more ample facilities, but is still far from luxurious.

A comparison of these two examples quickly reveals that Theatre A is very small and not equipped for much scenery building and painting or costume construction. The square footage of Theatre A is comparable to a very small Off-Off-Broadway house used for readings and simple productions; therefore it includes no storage spaces. As there is no additional rehearsal space, the scheduling of production work, rehearsals, and performances cannot overlap unless extra space is rented elsewhere for rehearsal and production work.

Theatre B is somewhat better equipped to do full-scale productions, since there are small scenic and costume shops, a larger stage, and rehearsal space.

Note: Both examples are used only for illustration purposes; actual square footage allotments will vary greatly from theatre to theatre.

	Theatre A	*Theatre B*
	99 seats	199 seats
stage (acting area)	525 sq. ft. (25' x 21')	1,000 sq. ft (40' x 25')
off-stage	263 (50% of stage)	600 (generous)
seating	495 (99 x 5' minimum)	1,094.5 (199 x 5.5')
aisles (23% seating)	113.9	251.7
public restrooms	48 (men and women)	96 (men and women)
handicapped toilet	13.5	13.5
dressing rooms	96 (6-person)	160 (10-person)
actors' restrooms	24	66 (48 + 18 for 1 shower)
technical control	66 (3-person)*	66 (3-person)*
lobby	198 (2 sq. ft. per 398 person)	(also a "safe area")
box office	25 (open box office)	30 (enclosed box office)
lounge	—	821 (w/counter)
rehearsal space	—	1,500 (acting area + dir./ stage manager)
office	108 (3-person)	216 (6-person)
scene shop	36 (supply storage only; build on stage)	220 (a scenery building space, slop sink and paint locker)
costume shop	60 (supplies storage only; sew in lobby)	169 (144 + 25 for washer/ dryer and sink)
storage	—	200 (small storage area)
totals	2,071.4**	6,901.7**

* Does not include a space for dimmer racks: 5 ft. x 6 ft. (30 sq. ft.) minimum.

** Note: Square footage figures used above are net and do not include an allowance for corridor or mechanical spaces (such as boiler room or air conditioning equipment space). It is very difficult to estimate these spaces accurately, as their sizes will depend largely on the actual layout of the building. However, a minimum of 12% (a maximum of 30%) of the total net square footage should be added to your total square footage. The larger number will approximate the gross square footage of the space needed.

3 What to Look For

Not all spaces will make a theatre. The guidelines provided below are not intended to hamper an imaginative and flexible approach to the search for a space, but rather to provide direction about what to look for and what to avoid. The guidelines will aid greatly in the narrowing-down and weeding-out process and could, in the long run, save a great deal of time and expense.

It may be difficult to imagine the proportions of your theatre while standing in a raw space. Remember, when looking at a space, that it will be subdivided. So, before making a commitment, carefully plot on paper the dimensions of the theatre and all the necessary and optional spaces you plan to include. You may want to enlist professional help at this point.

GENERAL CHARACTERISTICS OF THE POTENTIAL SPACE

Height

Height is essential. Not only does a high ceiling enable you to rake seating for adequate sightlines, it also permits greater flexibility in handling scenic pieces and lighting. Height above the stage allows flying scenery. Height over the auditorium provides the chance to create a small balcony or install the control booth above the seating. Also, height creates an *illusion* of space that can help compensate for a small or narrow space.

Height can help solve the problem of not being able to afford all the square footage that you really need. With sufficient headroom, spaces can be double-decked: put an office space over the box office, stack costume storage over the dressing rooms and toilets.

If you have a space that is 25' x 100'—a total of 2,500 sq. ft.—you might gain an extra 1,000 sq. ft. by double-decking everything except the stage and auditorium. That's a lot of extra space for no extra rent. This approach requires materials and labor, so it is not entirely without cost. However, if you amortize the expense over the life of the lease, the cost will be negligible compared to rent for an equal amount of additional square footage. Creative lofting at San Francisco's Magic Theatre yielded extra costume storage and office space at no extra rent.

Chicago's ETA Creative Arts Foundation, which moved into a former window sash factory in 1979, found a unique solution to the problem of low

What to Look For

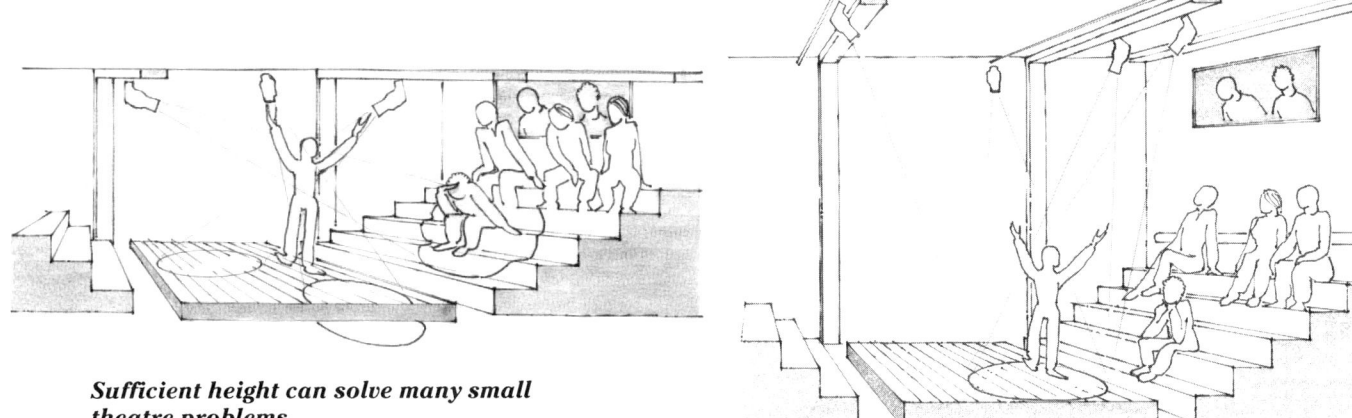

Sufficient height can solve many small theatre problems.

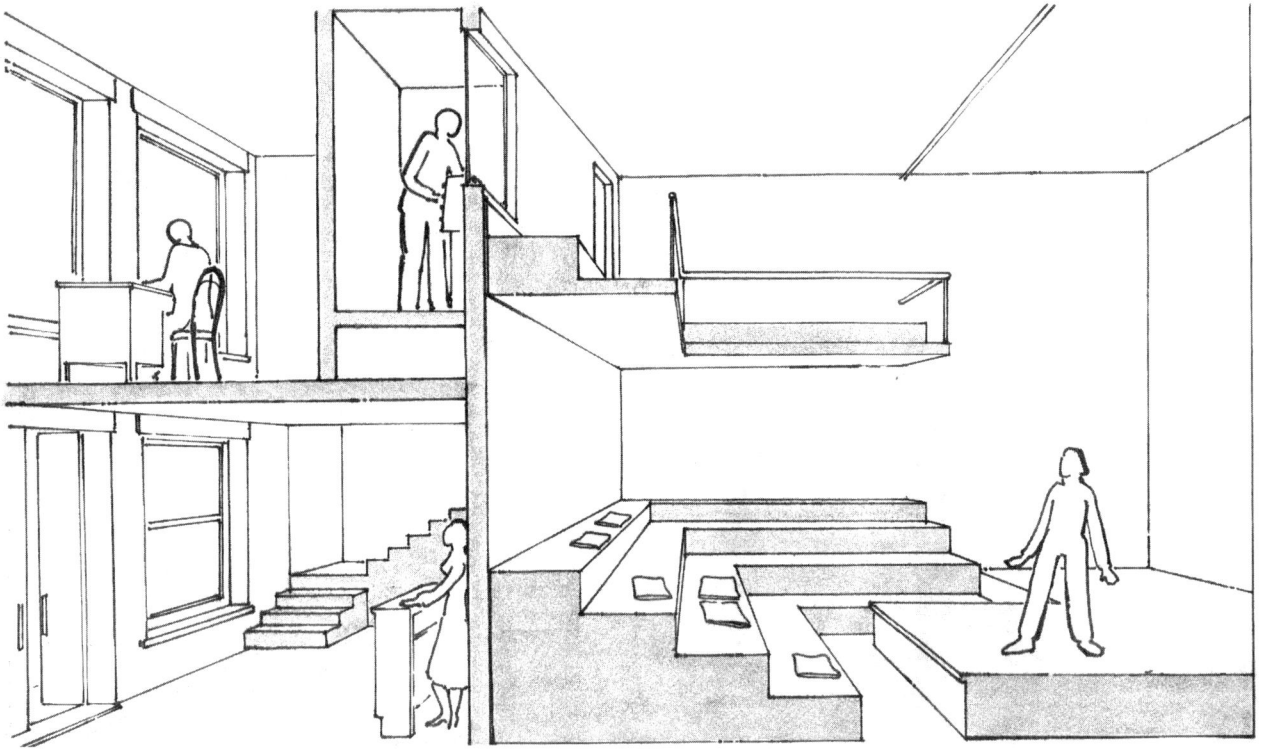

Double decking with office and control booth above lobby, and a small balcony.

Double decking with offices above lobby.

ceilings. Height was gained at the rear of the auditorium by tilting up the roof; at the front, by excavating 5' below grade. The stage is separated from rehearsal/classroom space at the back by folding walls that can be opened to enlarge the stage if needed. A raised platform at rear center of the auditorium straddling the cross aisle serves for the technical operation of the show, including sound and light boards and follow spots, when used. With its thrust stage and semi-circular seating, ETA Square has the look of an intimate Greek amphitheatre.

Free-Span Without Columns

Clear space without columns is very important. If columns do exist in a space under consideration, don't assume they can be removed. Measure the distance between the columns as well as the width of the room to determine how these columns will limit seating and staging configurations.

If a "flexible theatre" is a priority, search for a space without columns. Columns severely limit the possibility of using the space in more than one configuration. Although columns can sometimes be removed and replaced with a structural beam running across the ceiling, you'll need an engineer to let you know if it's possible. Costs begin at about $15,000 per column, but each case is so different that it is dangerous to estimate any costs without a professional.

Width and Depth

A narrow room, like those frequently found in small storefronts or brownstones, will force you to place all the seats very close to the acting space if you position them along the length. Placing seats in short rows across the width could put some members of the audience too far away.

What to Look For

ETA Creative Arts theatre.

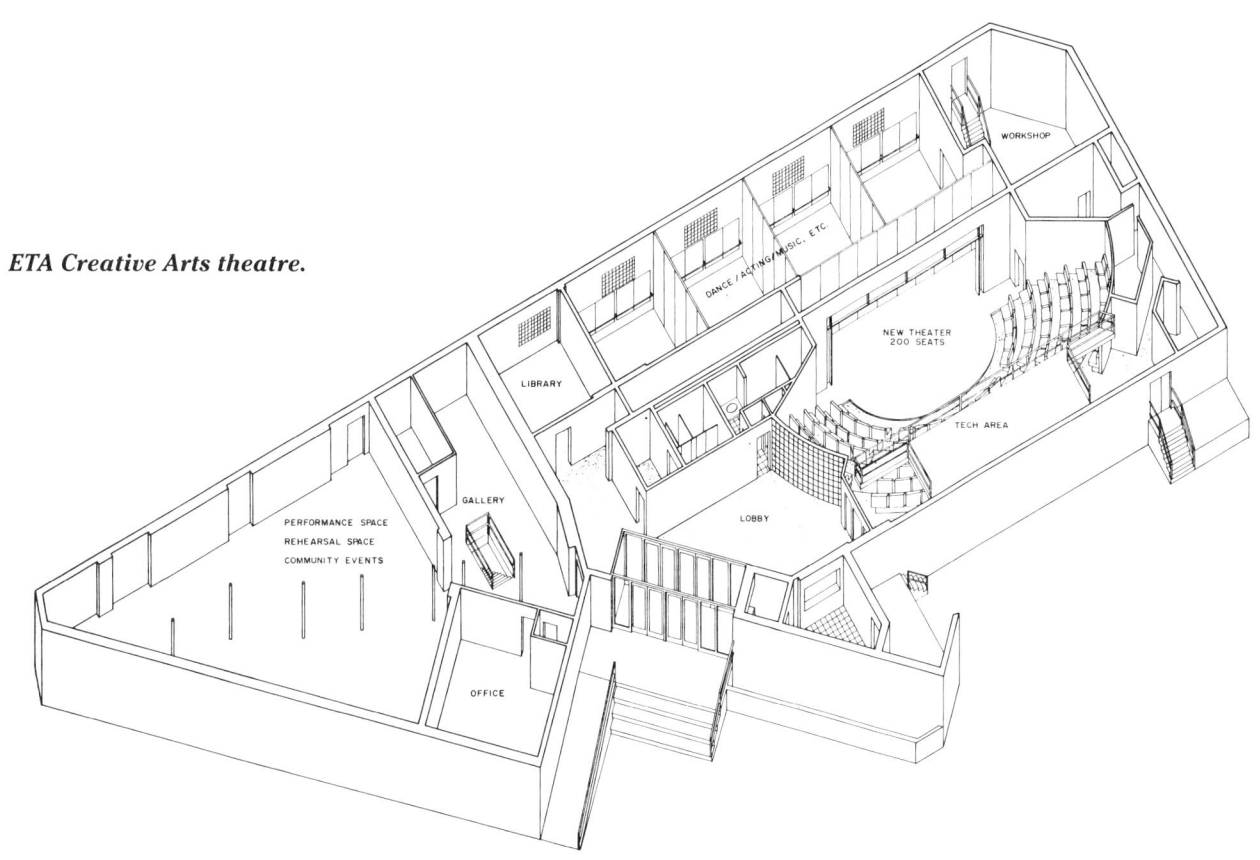

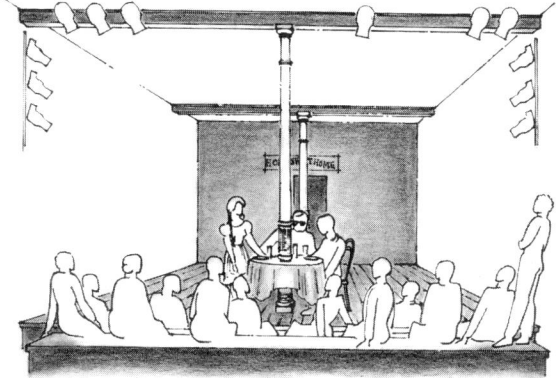

A row of load-bearing columns down the center of a loft or store space is very common. If the span between columns is 25' or more, it may be possible to design the theatre around them without too much compromise; if the span is much less, they can impose almost insurmountable problems.

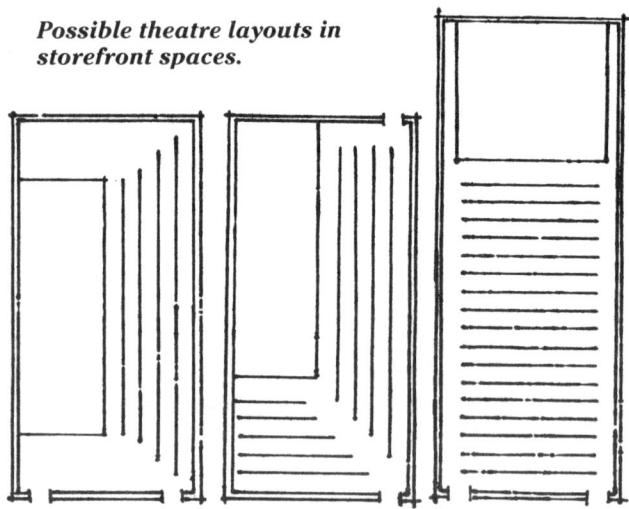

Possible theatre layouts in storefront spaces.

Location Within the Building

ADVANTAGES OF GROUND-FLOOR SPACE.
Renting ground-floor space is a wise strategy. You gain visibility on the street, and that can be a marketing bonus. Ground floor space almost certainly will be easier to bring up to code. It also provides easier access for loading in building materials, as well as sets, costumes, props, and furniture.

For a theatre of small capacity—74 people in New York City or 100 in Chicago—there is another clear advantage to being on the ground floor: such small theatres are required to have only one means of egress. This one egress must open directly onto the street, however, and not onto a public hallway—a condition difficult, if not impossible, to satisfy above the ground floor. (See chapter 15.) Upper floors may also present access problems for physically disabled patrons.

Often the basement will be included with ground-floor rentals; it is of little benefit to anyone else in the building, especially if access is through the ground-floor space. This adds substantial square footage, usually at a nominal increase in rent.

RENTING ON TWO ADJACENT FLOORS.
Renting on two adjacent floors instead of all on one floor provides a more compact arrangement and may be less expensive. With access stairs, a second floor can provide a ready-made cross-over for actors and crew. Basement and second-floor spaces are usable for most support functions.

INTAR, on 42nd Street's Theatre Row in Manhattan, broke through the ground floor to the basement to achieve an unusually steep rake in the seating and to create a two-story height over the stage space. The Judith Anderson Theatre (formerly the Lion), in another building on Theatre Row, chose to break through to the second floor to achieve height over the playing area and create a small balcony.

Chicago Dramatists Workshop has developed the basement area under the theatre as office, rehearsal, and play reading space. The area also provides limited storage space.

TYPES OF BUILDINGS

Cities across the country are likely to have the building types described in this section. Some have been built for or used as places of assembly and are therefore easier to bring up to code for theatre use.

Loft Buildings, Warehouses, and Manufacturing Buildings

Loft buildings, warehouses, or manufacturing buildings offer some good bets for conversion to theatre space. These vary in size from small, dumpy three-story buildings with brick facades, to cast iron structures, to large, heavy masonry buildings such as Theatre Artaud, a former metal-working factory with 11,250 sq. ft. of audience/performance space in San Francisco's Mission District. These manufacturing-type buildings are solidly built, constructed to house manufacturing companies using heavy machinery; they can withstand and have taken a lot of abuse. However, such

What to Look For

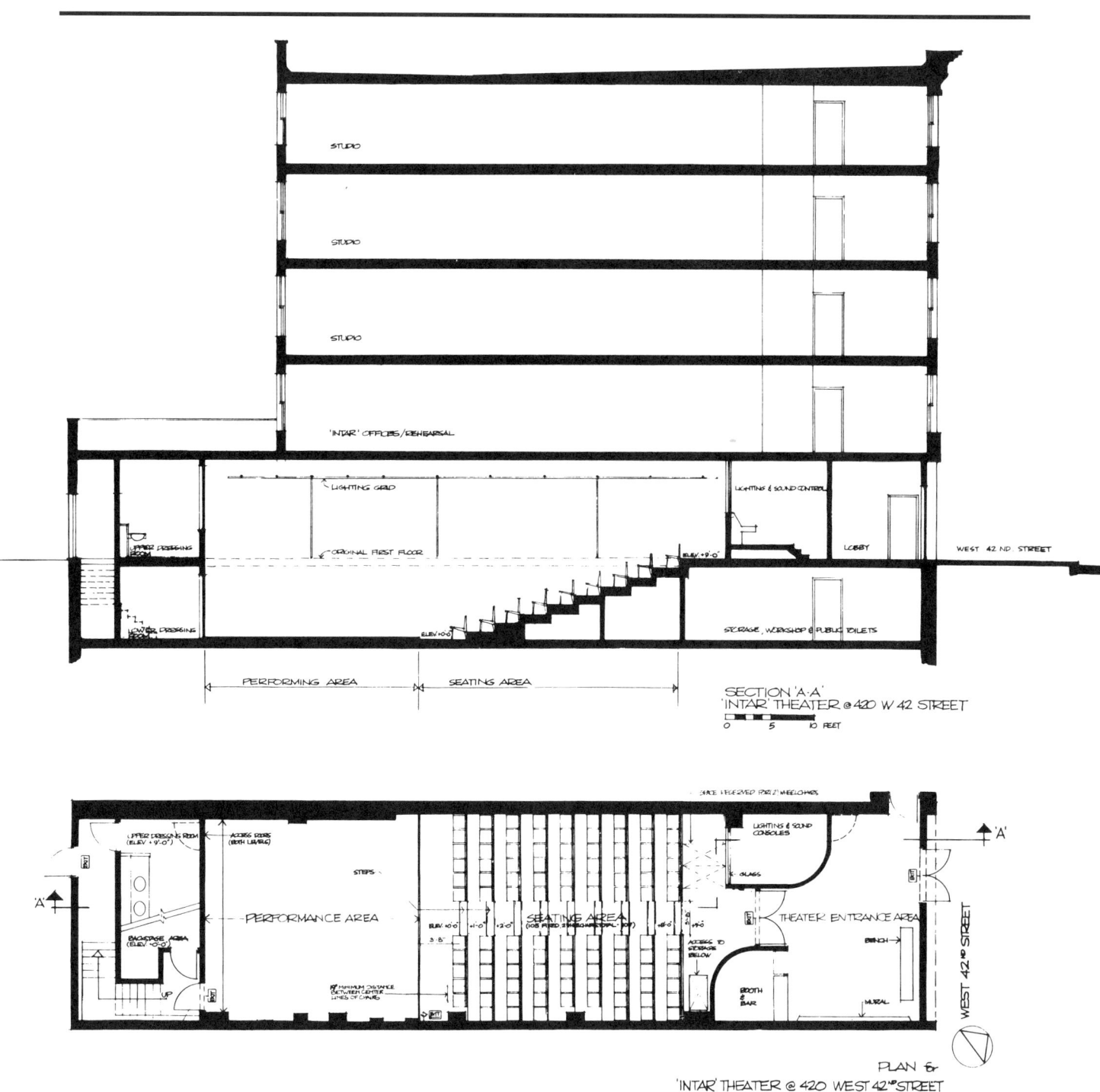

INTAR Theatre plan and section.

WILL IT MAKE A THEATRE?

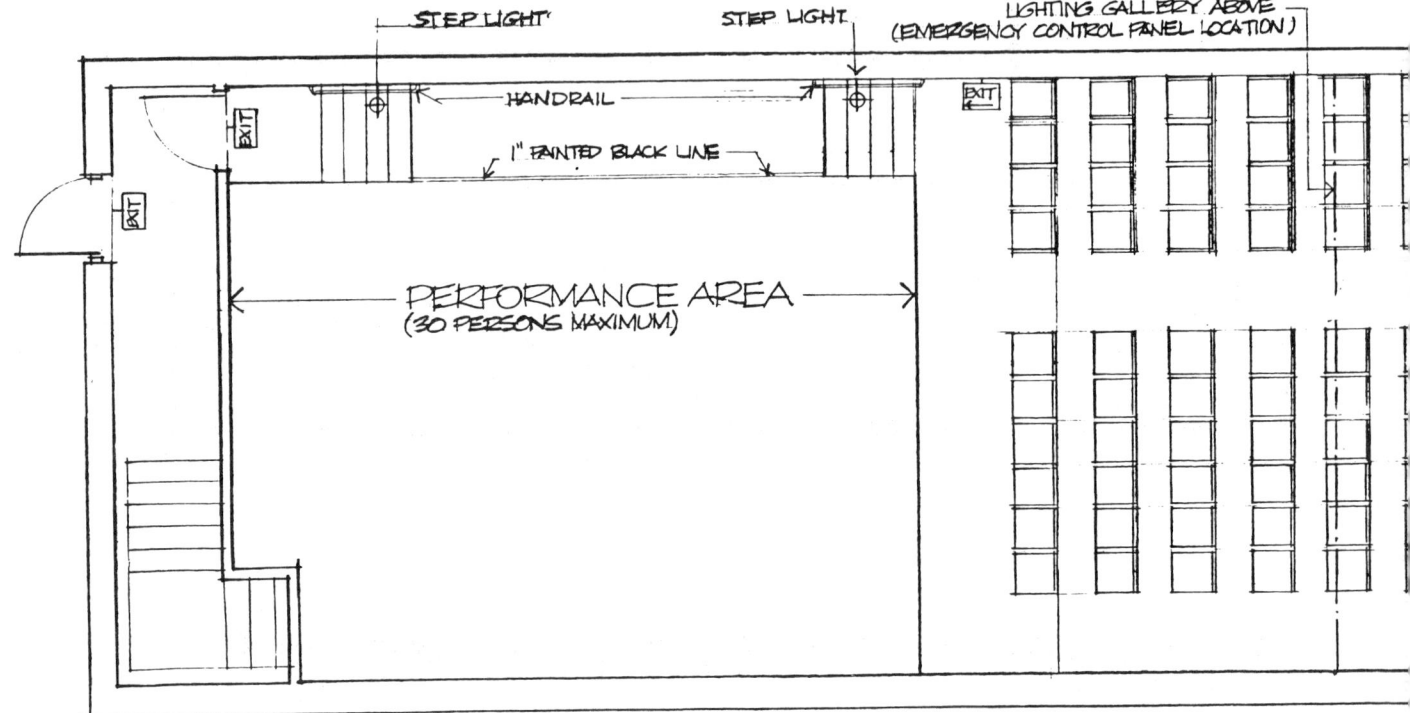

The Lion Theatre, renamed the Judith Anderson Theatre, is a 22'-wide brick building converted from residential and business space.

What to Look For

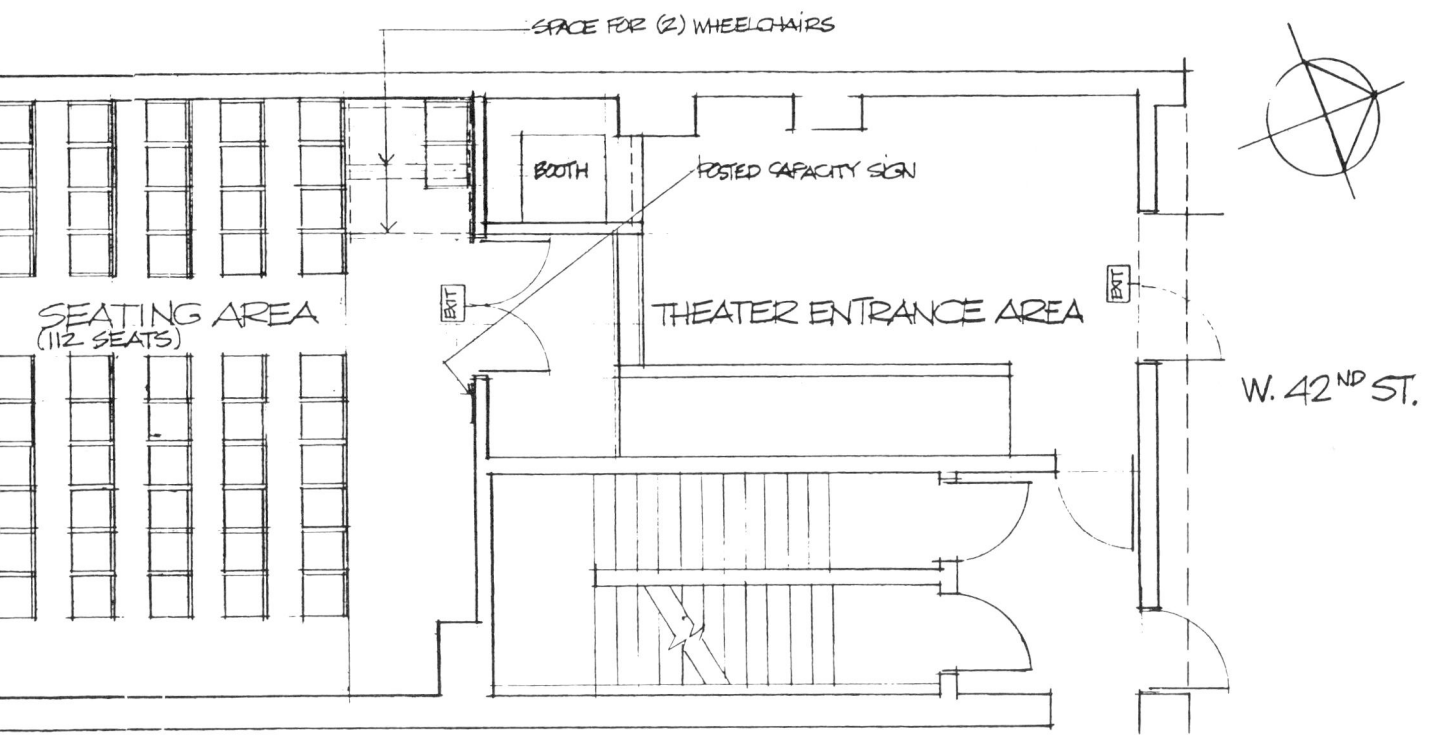

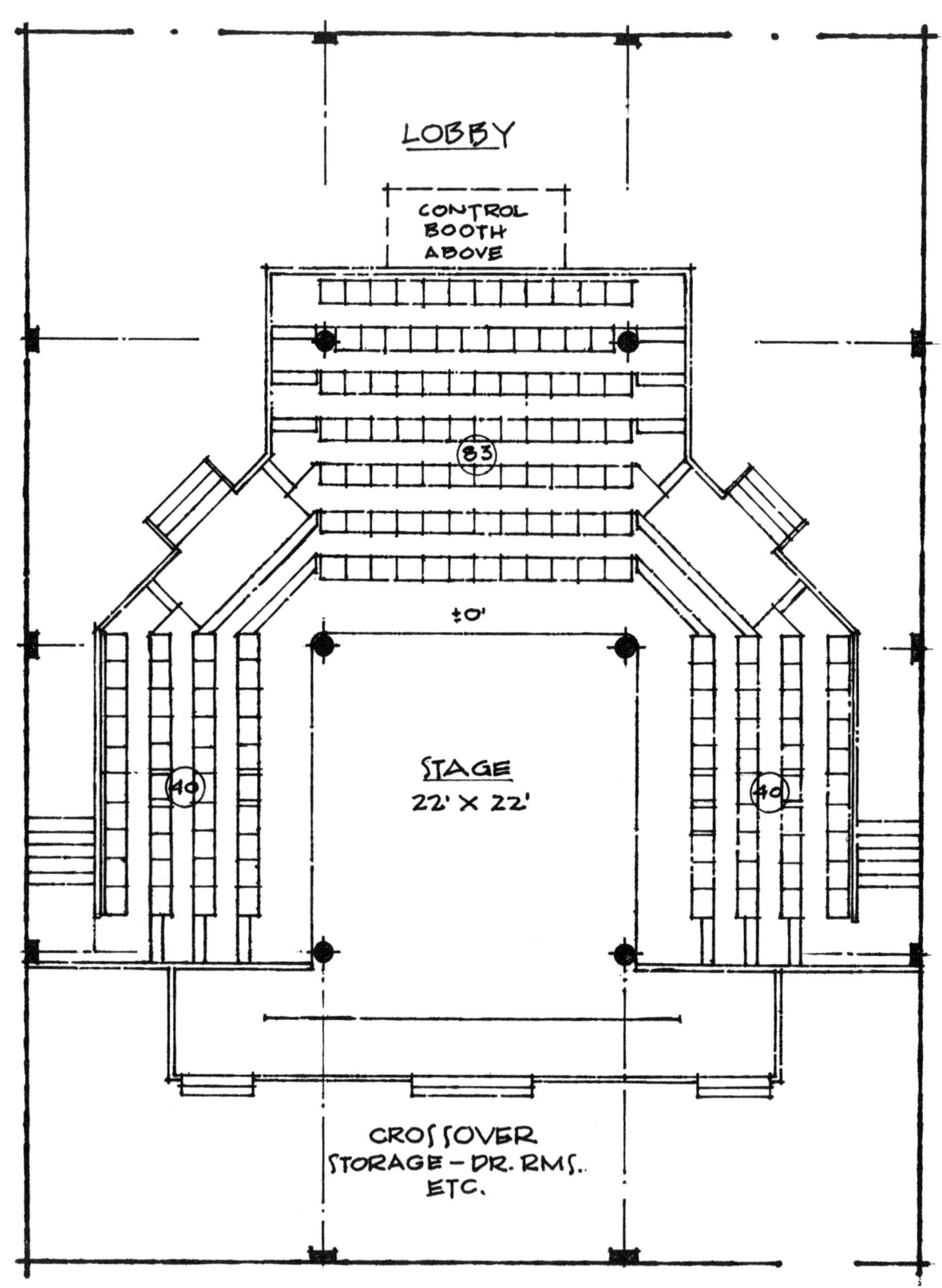

Lofts, warehouses, manufacturing buildings with columns. Possible plan solutions, not ideal.

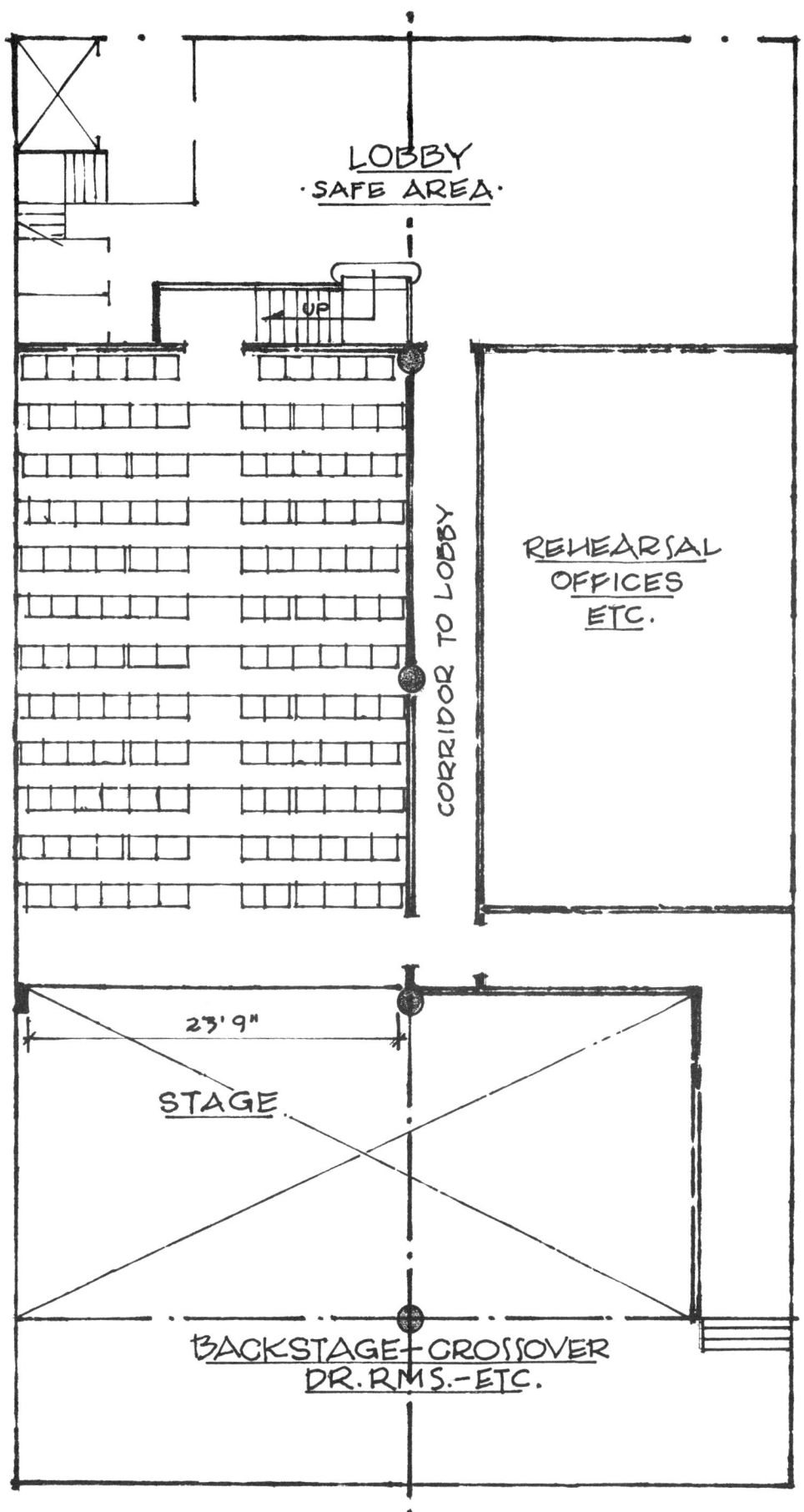

buildings often contain columns close together, limiting their potential for theatre use. When looking at these buildings check carefully for the span between columns: 25' between columns presents some problems; a span of less than 25' is almost impossible to work around because of lack of column-free acting space, adequate clear space for seating, and sightline problems.

Storefronts

Storefront theatres are especially popular in Chicago and Los Angeles. Many such commercial spaces were built without columns, which makes them very suitable for theatre conversion. In older cities, ground-floor commercial spaces were built with high ceilings. Unfortunately, this is not true in Los Angeles, where storefront ceilings tend to be very low.

Spaces used as stores usually have direct access from the sidewalk and generally include the basement—two more reasons to consider this type of space.

One potential drawback: storefronts usually have large glass windows for display. You may find an imaginative use for them; if not, be prepared to spend some money to replace the glass with a masonry wall. There should be no structural problem in doing this.

New York City's Pearl Theatre Company is an excellent example of a storefront conversion. A one-story, 20'-wide building, its high 20' ceiling allows for lofting. The plate glass windows have been replaced with masonry walls.

In Burbank, California, the Victory Theatre created performance spaces in two adjacent 11'-high storefront buildings. The smaller, 19'-wide, houses a 48-seat theatre and shop; the larger, 24'-wide, holds a 99-seat theatre with shop access. There are two independent lobbies and three dressing rooms. Plate glass windows in both buildings have been retained for display.

Banks

Some small theatres are housed in former banks. The famous Bouwerie Lane Theatre in New York, built as the German Exchange Bank in 1874 and converted to a theatre in the early 1960s, houses the Jean Cocteau Repertory Theatre. Other groups have used old banks as impressive lobby space for their theatres: Actors Theatre of Louisville and the Los Angeles Theatre Center are good examples of this strategy. Banks are traditionally built to last. They will handle live loads (see building code requirements, chapter 15), and most are fireproof construction. Banks usually have good ceiling height, plus a wider-than-usual free span between columns.

If you are fortunate enough to locate a bank space still intact, you will have quite a find. However, budget for the cost of dismantling heavy marble counters and removing vaults. The cost could be substantial, and the work cannot be handled without professional assistance.

Movie Theatres

Old movie theatres are an obvious building type to consider. The space will already have a box office, lobby, lounge, rest rooms, and a control booth—in short, almost all the optional spaces for a theatre, as well as the necessary ones. It might even have seats. Don't count on an adequate ready-made stage, however. This will probably have to be carved out of audience space; but since there doubtless will be more seats than you want, turning seating space into stage space will serve a dual purpose. There will not be dressing rooms or backstage support spaces either, although former movie/vaudeville houses that are converted into theatres often have minimal stage and support space. Another benefit of movie houses is that they are already classified as places of assembly.

Unfortunately, there are few small movie houses on the market in most cities, and the grand ones from the 1920s are white elephants, too big and too costly to renovate for a single non-profit tenant. However, a group of theatres might form a joint venture, perhaps with assistance from a developer, to remodel a large movie palace into several smaller theatre spaces. Chicago's Organic Theater Company successfully converted a neighborhood movie house into a 400-seat theatre, utilizing the entire space, while Minneapolis's Cricket Theatre reduced a 1,100-seat silent movie house to a 216-seat end stage with extended apron. And on a mini-scale, Paramount Pictures's Boston screening room is now a 60-seat legitimate house, home of the Boston Triangle Theatre Company.

Seven Stages, in Atlanta's Little Five Points District, converted a 600-seat, 1920s movie house into a 250-seat end stage and a flexible black box. The building's single story, including mezzanine, measures 6,500 sq. ft.

The company's first phase renovation included transforming former dressing rooms into the black box; installing a new HVAC system, noise isolation wall, and mainstage platforms; and generally upgrading and refurbishing performer, audience, and administrative areas. The auditorium's 20' floor-to-ceiling height enabled Seven Stages to double-deck new dressing rooms between the two performance spaces. Seating in both theatres is on risers, and the former projection booth has been extended to create a mainstage lighting booth and two staff offices.

Using 50% volunteer labor, phase one—completed in 1988—cost $51,000. Phase two's additional internal improvements, budgeted at $20,000, were completed in 1990.

Churches

Most churches were built with large halls for suppers or Sunday School meetings. While you may not be able to rent out a whole church property, some congregations, feeling the economic pinch of dwindling membership, lease out the parish hall in a variety of temporary or permanent arrangements.

Churches are traditionally conservative, so you'll need to convince them that you're responsible and that your productions won't conflict with or disrupt church activities. For insurance reasons, most churches will consider renting only to incorporated theatre companies—and, for tax reasons, only to nonprofits.

Former and existing church buildings convert easily to theatres because they are usually column free, high ceilinged, classified as places of assembly, and fireproof. In New York City, St. Clements, the Apple Corps, and the West Side Arts Theatre—which installed a floor to create two theatres—have put church space to theatrical use. In Charlotte, North Carolina, the Afro-American Cultural Center created a 180-seat, 3/4-round theatre in a two-story church.

Schools

School buildings offer many of the same advantages as churches, especially if they already have a small auditorium or gymnasium. In Atlanta, the Center for Puppetry Arts, Horizon Theatre, Nexus, and Arts Exchange all adapted existing spaces in former public schools to their own special needs.

Housing Developments and Community Centers

Many housing developments constructed, owned, and operated by city governments include community rooms. In Chicago, two Jane Addams Hull House Centers lease performance and support space to the Bailiwick Repertory and Chicago Theatre Company. The Leventhal-Sidman Jewish Community Center, in Newton, MA, boasts its own resident company, the Jewish Theatre of New England.

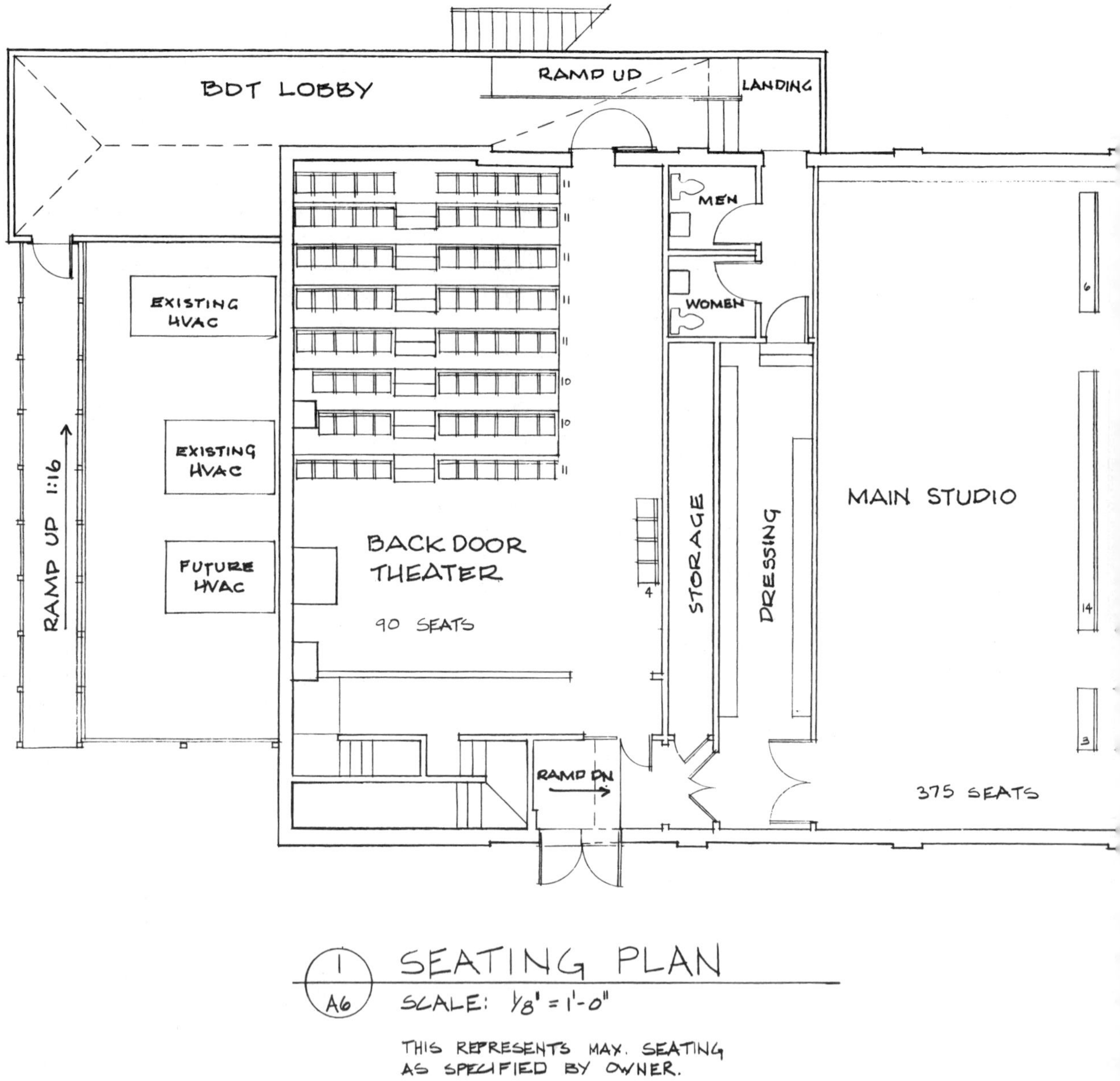

WILL IT MAKE A THEATRE?

[Floor plan: Seven Stages seating plan showing BDT Lobby, Ramp Up, Landing, Back Door Theater (90 seats) with Existing HVAC and Future HVAC, Men/Women restrooms, Storage, Dressing, Main Studio (375 seats), Ramp Up 1:16, Ramp Dn]

SEATING PLAN
1/A6   SCALE: 1/8" = 1'-0"

THIS REPRESENTS MAX. SEATING AS SPECIFIED BY OWNER.

Seven Stages, Atlanta, a converted movie theatre.
Architect: Gardner Spencer Smith & Associates. Joe Gardner, Principal-in-Charge;
Tanya Richard, Project Designer
Consulting Architect: (Schematic Programming & Design) Hoss Viscardi and Company
Structural Engineer: Case Engineering

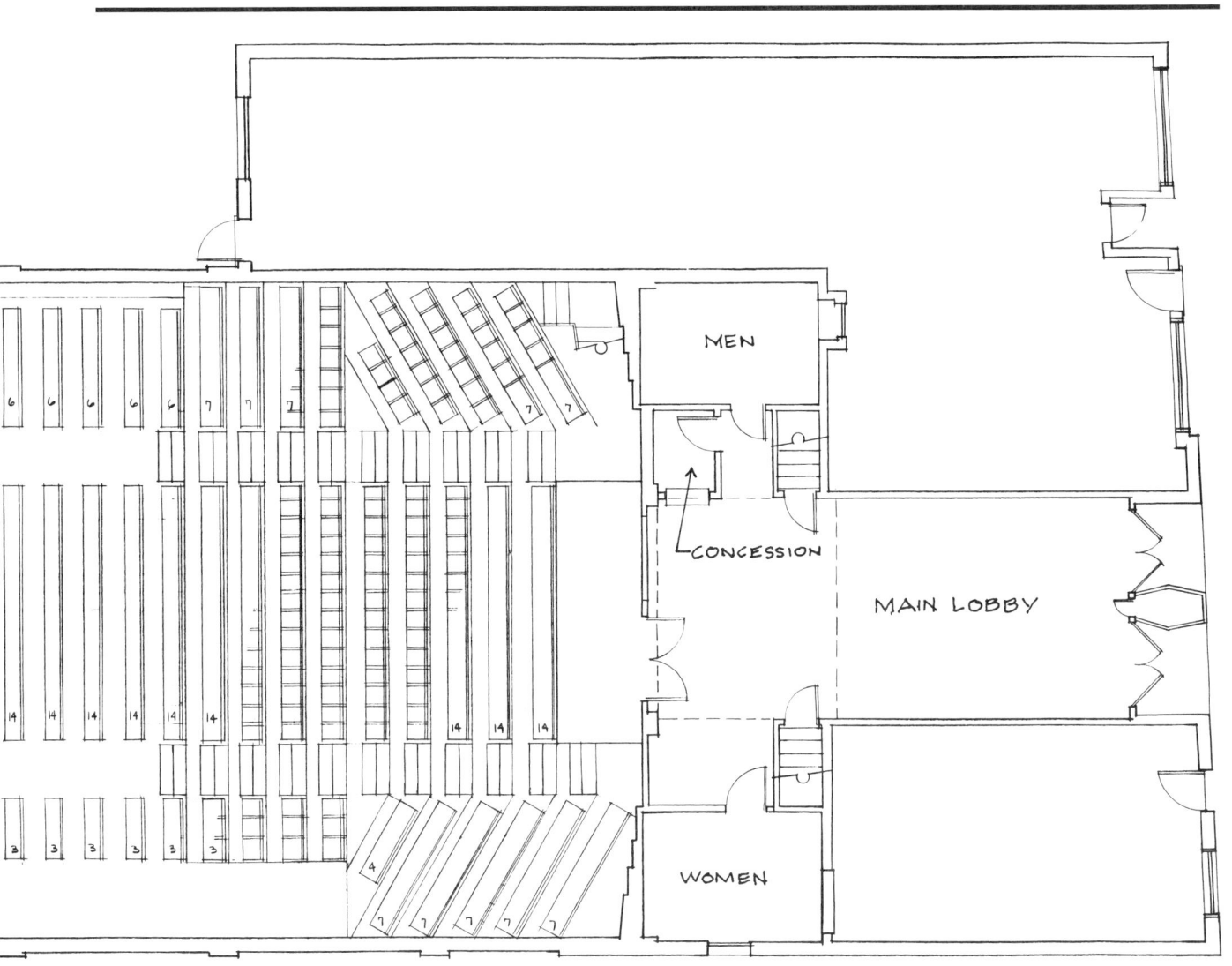

SEVEN STAGES
ATLANTA, GEORGIA

WILL IT MAKE A THEATRE?

North Elevation
Scale: 1/8"=1'-0"

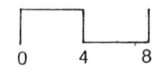
0 4 8

Charlestown Working Theatre, facade and plan.

OFFBEAT PLACES TO CONSIDER

All of the following spaces and building types have been converted by small theatre groups and should not be overlooked in your search.

Supermarkets and Department Stores

Former supermarkets offer large, open spaces with better-than-average ceiling height. They are usually in or near residential areas. Like other stores, they usually include basement space. Boston Baked Theatre renovated raw space in a department store basement to create a 185-seat cabaret. In New Jersey, New Brunswick's George Street Playhouse got its start in a converted A&P.

Mortuaries

Despite constant assertions that theatre is dead or dying, it is very much alive in San Francisco in two former mortuaries. There, on a single block in the Mission District, Intersection for the Arts and the Julian Theatre have turned former mortuary chapels into small performance spaces.

Pubs, Bars, Nightclubs, Restaurants, Ballrooms, and Art Galleries

Pubs, ballrooms, and galleries are particularly adaptable to cabaret theatre. These venues are already classified as places of assembly. Consequently, they are often fireproof and already have the secondary exits required by code. They usually

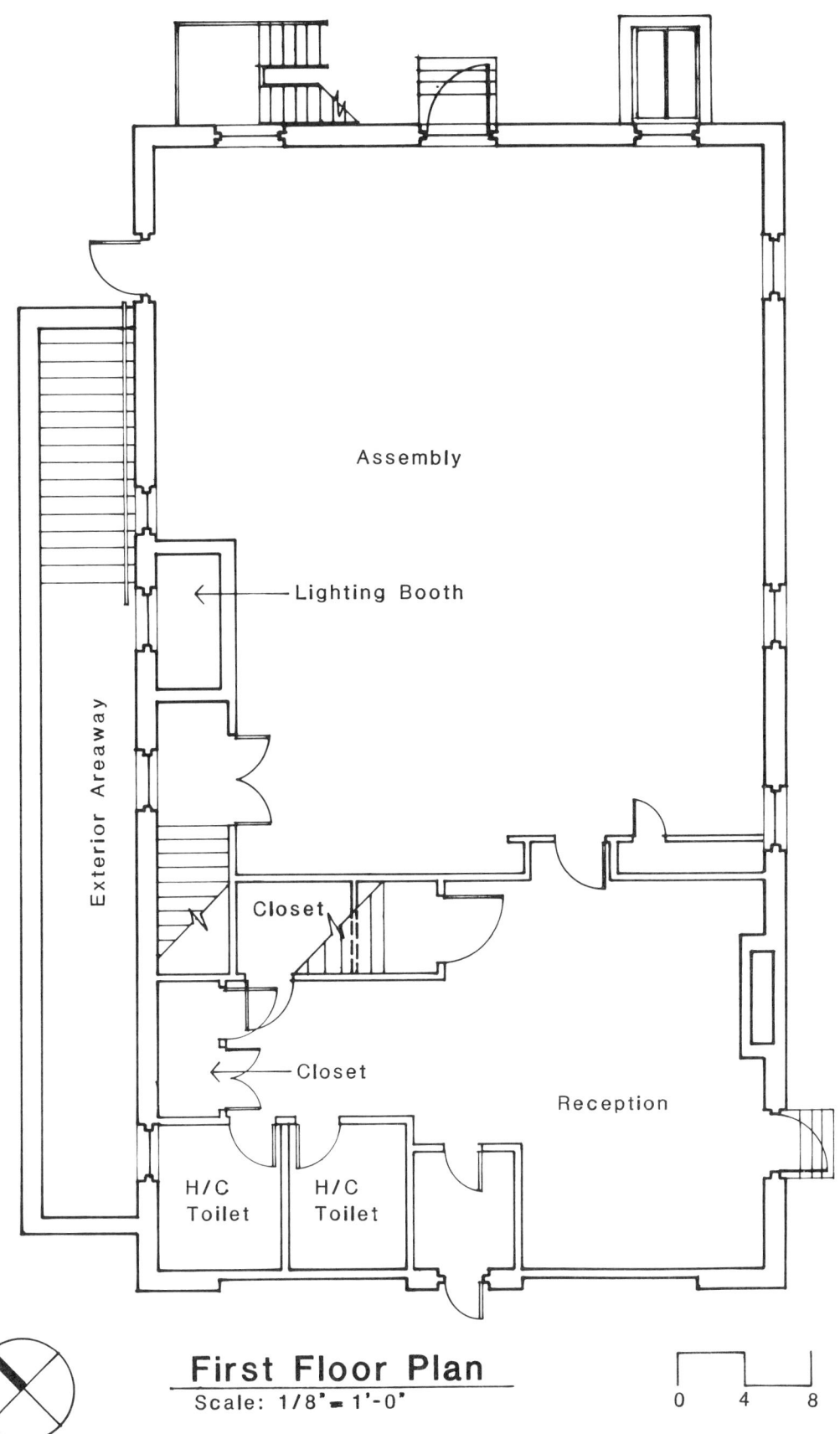

First Floor Plan
Scale: 1/8" = 1'-0"

include lobby, lounge, and bar areas, as well as public rest rooms and ample air conditioning.

Garages and Stables

Garages are usually sturdy, high ceilinged, column free, and wired for heavy electrical use. An excellent conversion is the Studio Theatre in Washington, DC. (See Profile, p. 144.) In Chicago, the Briar Street Theatre turned a 1910 stable into a 398-seat flexible space. (See Profile, p. 119.) Norfolk, Virginia's Old Dominion University converted a 1914 cavalry stable into a 100-seat experimental theatre.

City and Federal Surplus Properties

Some cities have surplus property for sale or rent. While usually found in marginal neighborhoods, suitable surplus property may sometimes be found in interesting areas ripe for theatre development. Here are just a few of the available building types from which to choose:

Firehouses

The Puerto Rican Traveling Theatre transformed an old West Side firehouse into one of New York City's most handsome medium-sized Off-Broadway theatres. The Latino Chicago Theatre Company and Boston's Charlestown Working Theatre successfully converted Victorian firehouses into flexible theatre spaces.

The Charlestown Working Theatre (CWT) has been created in a red brick, 1882 Victorian firehouse with a landmarked exterior. It has the distinction of being the only small theatre company in Boston that actually owns its building. The company rescued the firehouse from the wrecker's ball and finally cajoled the city into selling it to the company for one dollar. On a $200,000 operating budget, the programming has served the blue-collar Irish community very well, and now draws an audience from all parts of Boston.

Using chairs on movable risers that are normally set in a three-sided thrust configuration, the auditorium can accommodate up to 150. There is a handsome lobby complete with original pressed tin ceiling but, alas, no longer a brass pole for that very special "entrance." Work on the theatre has been phased. (See chapter 5.) Small grants and a lot of sweat equity have brought restoration and conversion to this level. However, with a total waiver on real estate tax due to not-for-profit status, no rent and no mortgage, CWT has a lot of financial plusses. There are even gardens surrounding the firehouse theatre for intermission strolling, tended by local volunteers.

Wharves and Warehouses

In San Francisco, the old Fort Mason complex of warehouses and piers has been turned into a cultural center that includes six theatres with support spaces. (See Profile, p. 60.)

Military/National Guard Armories

Black Spectrum Theatre converted an abandoned Naval Officers Club in Queens, New York, into a 425-seat performance space with a modular stage and movable seats, a cabaret lounge, office, and technical support areas. The surrounding 50,000 acres—all former Naval property—are now the Roy Wilkins Park, a well-chosen site for the community-minded Black Spectrum.

Courthouses, Police Stations, and Jails

In Los Angeles, the Bilingual Foundation of the Arts converted a 1930s cement-walled jail into a 99-seat thrust theatre. The 17'-high performance area was once the judge's chamber; the sound booth, formerly the prison line-up area.

City surplus buildings usually have major flaws: they have been neglected for years, so the roof leaks, a wall is cracked, the heating plant is deficient, or a section of the floor is collapsing. Still, if you find the right building at the right price, and have the resources and muscle power to put it into shape, it could be worth the investment.

Landmark Buildings

Landmark-designated buildings are another, if rare, source of potential theatre space.

While there are restrictions placed on what can be done to a building once it has been designated as a landmark, there are often benefits in the form of tax relief or funding for rehabilitation. The New York Shakespeare Festival, for example, received $125,000 from the New York State Preservation Trust when it initially converted the former Astor Library into a seven-theatre complex.

It is important that any landmark building under consideration possess a designation that allows for "adaptive reuse," a kind of preservation that permits alterations to the interior as long as the exterior of the building is not changed. Many cities have advocacy organizations concerned with protecting and preserving such buildings. Suggestions from an organization like The New York Landmarks Conservancy, for example, could lead to a suitable space.

Commercial Developments

Enlightened—and pragmatic—urban developers include entertainment components in their buildings, their goal being to keep the neighborhood active around the clock, or sometimes to obtain zoning concessions. Several theatre companies have used this to their own advantage.

StageWest in Springfield, Massachusetts, talked itself into 39,468 sq. ft. of the downtown Columbus Center. In the early 1980s, when city planners couldn't find a tenant for the complex's proposed cinema, a real estate developer—and StageWest board member—suggested substituting StageWest. Reconfigured, the theatre facilities cost $3 million (paid for by the city) and include a 450-seat proscenium/modified thrust and a 99-seat black box. The theatre now occupies the space rent-free, and the city charges patrons a modest parking fee to help defray costs.

In California, the San Diego Repertory Theatre applied to become prime tenant of the Horton Plaza Lyceum Theatre when it opened in 1986. A detailed agreement was worked out with the city, which made the 560-seat Lyceum and the 220-seat Lyceum Space available to a variety of local performing arts groups under the Rep's management. The city awarded the Rep a free seven-year lease and a four-year managerial contract requiring that the building present a minimum of 250 performances yearly.

Underground space, because it does not attract prime rental rates, is the one developers often choose to offer to theatre tenants. Below-grade facilities, though, carry special problems and hidden costs: poor visibility from the street, insufficient natural light, lack of height in the theatre, and high HVAC expenses are some possible drawbacks. For example, the Vineyard Theatre, located in the basement of a new multi-use commercial building in New York City had to pay the developer an unexpected $25,000 (and that at bargain prices) to excavate an additional 2', in order to obtain an 18' height from deck to grid.

The Huntington Theatre Company, resident at Boston University and housed in the old Boston Repertory Theatre, exemplifies the spacious facilities some companies have obtained by becoming affiliated with universities. This handsome theatre, which opened in 1925, is a traditional proscenium house with orchestra pit, traps, an elevator stage, and 855 comfortable seats in the orchestra, mezzanine, and balcony. The large stage has an excellent fly loft. But, like most theatres of its vintage, it was built with very limited support space —certainly inadequate for a modern repertory company and theatre school. Boston University bought the theatre in 1953 and systematically acquired the adjacent buildings, making space for two large rehearsal rooms—one fitted with stage lighting and sound equipment, plus removable seating/risers to create a black box performance space—a large scene shop (basketball hoops at

WILL IT MAKE A THEATRE?

Horton Plaza Lyceum plan.

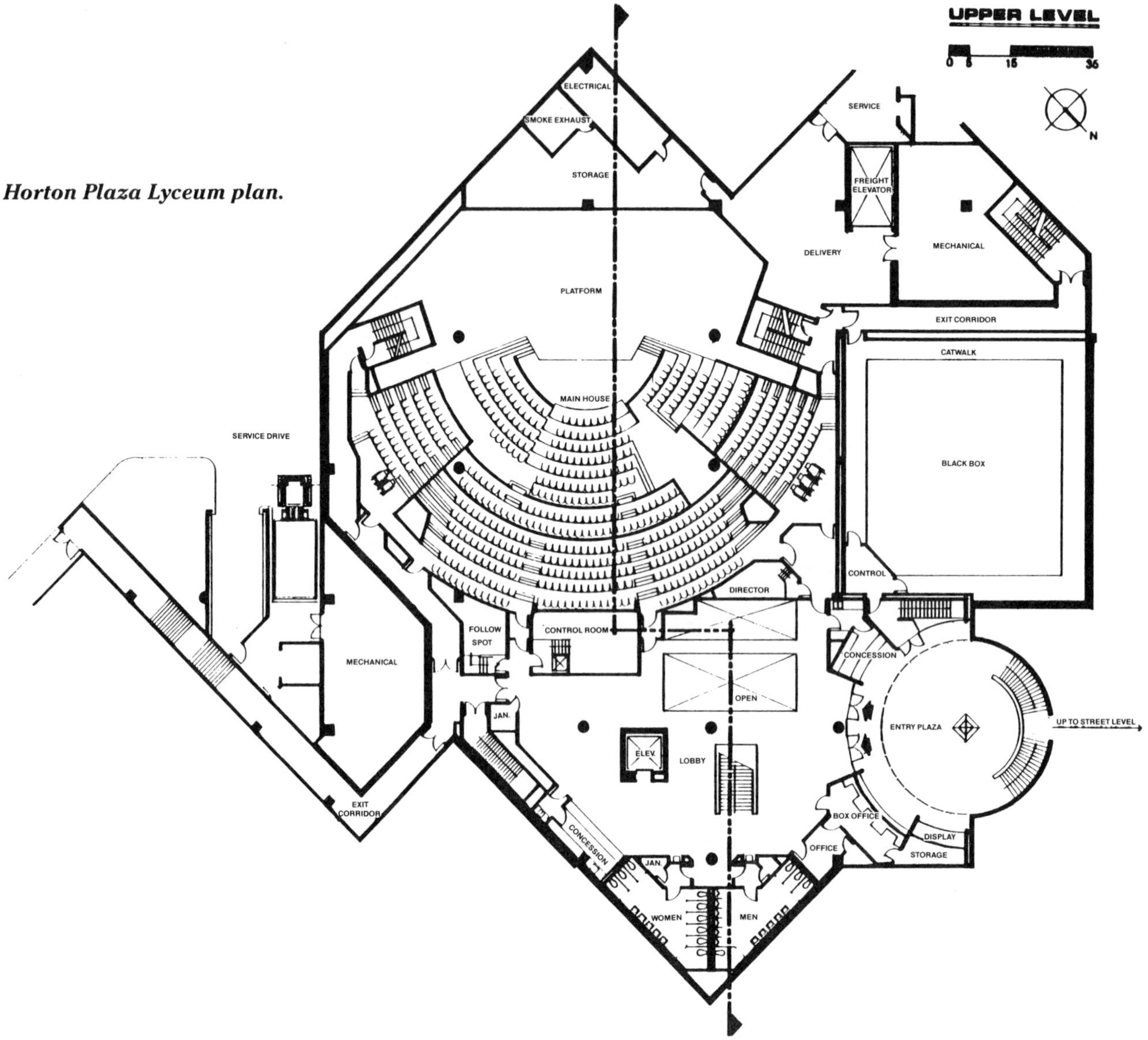

Horton Plaza Lyceum section.

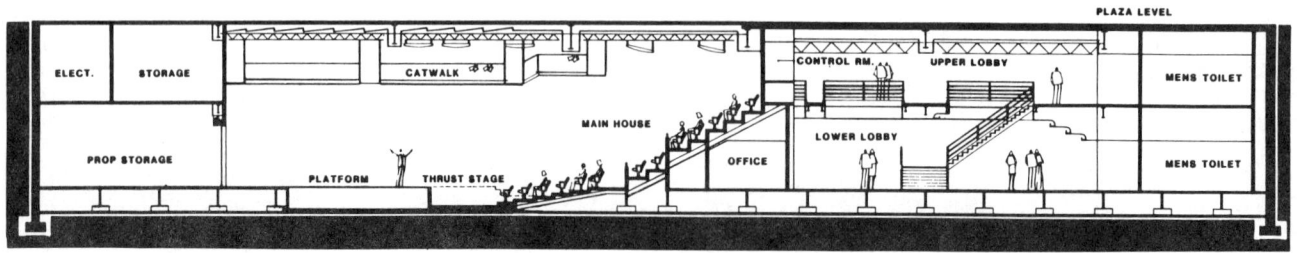

each end), an ample paint shop, a costume shop, dye room, wig room, costume maintenance space, green room, masses of dressing rooms, and spacious administrative offices. In short, the company is blessed with space!

As per the lease agreement, no money changes hands—not even on paper. Rent is basically in-kind: the company gets the facilties in exchange for its professional training services (some staff members are also on the Boston University faculty). The company's use is limited to some extent by the school's own production schedule. With a five-play season of new scripts and conservative standards, Huntington is programming to meet the taste of Boston audiences, who they say have "an intellectual curiousity and a concern for language." Huntington also believes the visual production is very important in Boston and mounts its plays well on an annual operating budget approaching $4 million. The well-equipped plant helps make this happen.

4
HOW TO FIND IT

The search for the right space is a tough task, requiring time, patience, and perseverance. Channels of communication are not centralized, so a variety of methods must be tapped. As the hunt begins, there are some general strategies you should pursue and a lot of information you should have on hand. Theatre service organizations in major cities throughout the country can provide leads to spaces and guidelines for their assessment.

Factors such as zoning, urban renewal efforts, property values, rent levels, and Equity requirements can make some areas of a city more suitable or less expensive for theatre use than others. This chapter highlights these factors and then reviews strategies for finding appropriate space, including use of classified ads, real estate agents, and organizations that handle specific types of spaces.

WHERE TO LOOK

When seeking nontraditional theatre space, keep an open mind about neighborhoods. At the same time, be aware of the problems that could arise from locating in an area with complications: one that is not zoned for theatre use, for instance, or one that is slated for redevelopment.

Zoning Districts

Zoning shapes a city. Developed to encourage certain activities in specified areas and to prevent incompatible activities, or uses, from intruding on one another, zoning is a basic and very important fact of life in any city. However compatible or unobtrusive you feel your theatre will be, the person next door may not share your enthusiasm. For this reason, zoning laws were adopted as a dispassionate document for determining what activities can locate where.

Under New York City's zoning laws, for example, certain activities are grouped into categories called "use groups." Theatre is a Use Group 8 activity and, as such, is permitted by right only in certain zoning districts. Whenever possible, locate in an allowed zoning district. Should you wish to locate in a district not zoned for theatre use, a variance will be required. (See chapter 14.)

Boston has made plans to transform its historic theatre district into the Midtown/Cultural District. By the early 1980s the district had become so run

Map of the Boston Midtown/Cultural District.

Vacant Buildings to be Renovated
- A. Saxon (Majestic) — for 799 seat proscenium theater
- B. Publix (Gaiety) — for visual arts center's international film cinema
- C. Pilgrim Theater — for Asian arts center (now adult films)
- D. Essex Theater — for 199 seat dance theater and for 199 seat experimental theater
- E. Paramount Theater — for dance club/cabaret
- F. Modem Theater — for 400 seat concert hall
- G. Liberty Tree Halls — for studio/rehearsal space
- H. Former Chauncy St. Power Station — for studio/rehearsal space
- I. Steinert Hall — reuse potential unknown

Existing Active Theaters
1. Charles Playhouse — 400 seats, 200 seats, 150 seats
2. Shubert Theater — 1,600 seats
3. Wang Center — 4,000 seats
4. Wilbur Theater — 1,200 seats
5. Colonial Theater — 1,650 seats
6. Opera House — 2,300 seats
7. Cinema — Chinese movie

New Facilities to be Constructed as part of Mixed-use Developments
- a. Parcel C-4 — for 199 seat experimental theater
- b. Hinge Block parcels — for several visual arts exhibits spaces and one 199 seat experimental theater new Y.M.C.U. facilities
- c. Parcel 30 — for 499 seat dance theater and for 399 seat flexible space theater
- d. Hayward Place Site — for 200 seat concert hall
- e. Former Gary Theater Site — for shop/storage space

Legend:
- Active Theaters
- Inactive Theaters
- "Theater Alleys"
- "Theater Boulevards"

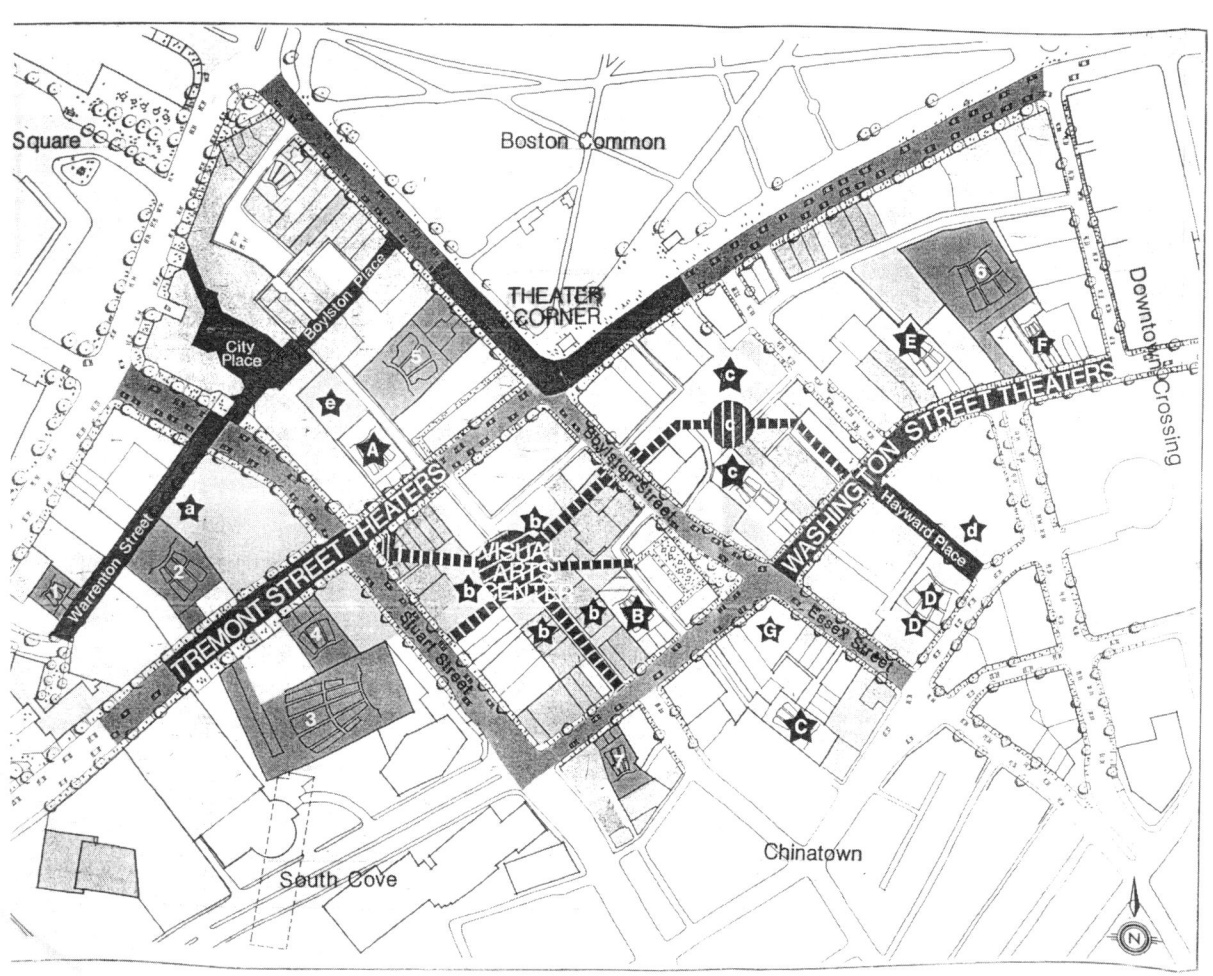

down that it was known locally as the "Combat Zone," a haven for crime, drugs, and porn shows. If restoration is carried out as planned, there will be nine new nonprofit theatres in the Midtown/Cultural District, plus one small commercial theatre. Also included are the restored Majestic Theatre and other privately financed venues. Nonperformance spaces, like rehearsal studios and offices for arts groups, will be complemented by other types of private development. Tradition and the stock of existing old theatres made it logical to place these proposed new venues in the old, though run-down, theatre district now relabeled the Midtown/Cultural District.

So, before setting out to look for a space, familiarize yourself with the zoning regulations outlined in this book and consult zoning maps available at the maps and publications office of your local city government. (See Agency Chart.) Double-check this information before signing a lease. Don't rely on the word of landlords or rental agents. Their primary interest is in renting the space; it is the tenant's responsibility to see that "use" conforms with zoning laws.

Urban Renewal Areas

Locating in an area slated for heavy redevelopment could affect your theatre in several ways. First, urban renewal projects invariably cause rents in the area to skyrocket. Try to protect yourself with a long-term lease. Second, redevelopment plans may call for the demolition of your building in two or three years' time—information that the landlord may be reluctant to disclose during lease negotiations. A demolition clause allows your lease to be terminated regardless of the term left if the building is to be razed.

On a more positive note, urban renewal projects may provide special opportunities for groups seeking theatre space because they often include components designated for nonprofit entertainment use. (See chapter 3.) If possible, get into a project in its early design stages, when overall plans can be more easily drawn or redrawn to suit your needs.

To determine whether a space is in an urban renewal area, or the likelihood of its demolition or redevelopment, consult the community board or neighborhood organization for the district. (See chapter 6.)

Property Values and Rents

Central locations are expensive and much in demand. Recently gentrified neighborhoods—such as SoHo in New York, Chicago's North Side, and Midtown Atlanta—likewise are expensive.

Neighborhoods adjacent to recently gentrified locales are likely to offer the most affordable options. However, the accessibility of these locations to audiences and critics must be weighed against the rental rates they offer.

Areas with Equity Contract Restrictions

In New York City, the area bounded by Fifth and Ninth Avenues between 34th and 56th Streets, as well as the area between Fifth Avenue and the Hudson River from 56th Street to 72nd Street, is restricted by the Actors' Equity Association. Without its explicit permission, Equity prohibits use of contracts other than the Broadway Production contract within this area.

GATHERING INFORMATION

To find a space, you'll need to be persistent and resourceful—and have good feet. There are several ways to discover leads.

Newspapers

A review of the classified ads (lofts, offices, stores, commercial space, miscellaneous) will orient you toward the prevailing rental rates in various neighborhoods and will put you on the trail of brokers who handle the kinds of properties that interest you.

Newspapers contain only a partial listing of what's really available. The majority of spaces are rented by managing agents who may advertise just one space that's representative of the properties they handle.

Real Estate Agents

Although very large management companies handle properties all over a city, smaller agents or brokers usually deal with a certain geographic locale or with a specific type of commercial space. To discover which rental agents handle specific areas, respond to classified ads. If you answer an ad and the space has already been rented, ask the agent if similar spaces are available. Be as precise as possible about your requirements—desired neighborhood, square footage, price, and special features, such as ground floor, a separate entrance, high ceilings. Take the time to look at spaces that may not exactly fit your requirements. Actually standing in the space may stimulate you to visualize how it could be altered to fit your needs. A real estate professional might be a sensible addition to your board of directors.

COMMISSIONS AND FEES. A commission may be charged when a space is leased. If you are dealing directly with a landlord, or with a management company hired by a landlord, there should not be a fee. If, however, you are dealing with a real estate agent hired by the management company, there may be a fee. Usually, for commercial space, this is paid by the landlord.

Before using an agent's services, be sure to check on whether or not a fee will be charged. Fees are sometimes as high as 10% of a year's rent. The amount is often a function of the strength or weakness of the real estate market.

If you are negotiating a sublease, or have answered an ad placed by the tenant, be aware that the previous tenant may want a "fixture fee" for improvements made to the space, alterations which may be of no use to you. While it is illegal for a tenant to demand a fixture fee, the practice is common. It may be possible to circumvent this payment by working directly with the managing agent, whose name usually appears on the building facade or in the lobby.

Walk the Streets

Another way to find space is simply to walk the streets where you want to locate. Often spaces for rent are not listed in any paper or with any agent. Instead, signs are hung out or placed in windows with a number to call. When asked how they went about looking for a space, most theatre groups say that at one point or another in their space search, they simply got out and walked or bicycled the streets.

If you see a vacant space that interests you, there is no harm in inquiring about its availability even if there's no "for rent" sign. The agent's name should be on the building.

When Boston's Lyric Stage Company found itself desperately needing more space, and with just two years to go on its lease, its founders acquired topographical maps showing every building and lot number in every city district they were considering. Slowly the list was narrowed, and finally they found their new home in the Young Women's Christian Association, a 1920s Deco building on Copley Square (See Profile, p. 105.)

Talk to Everyone You Know

Theatre people seem perpetually on the lookout for space. Even the groups that already have spaces keep searching. What they have seen that is not right for them may be right for you. So ask around.

Space Referral Banks

In response to the increasing difficulty arts groups and small businesses have faced in trying to locate space, many government agencies, as well as some service organizations, have created centralized space information banks. One example is New York City's Office of Economic Development, which

46
WILL IT MAKE A THEATRE?

Walk the streets.

maintains a computerized listing called The Space Bank. Another is A.R.T./New York's real estate project, which maintains up-to-date information on potential theatre spaces in the metropolitan area, as well as data on real estate trends. (See Resource Directory.)

Surplus Buildings

Federal surplus property can be located through the regional offices of the General Services Administration. Call or write the regional office for your state—listed in the "United States Government Offices" section of the telephone directory. Cities periodically publish surplus property auction lists. In New York City, for example, information can be obtained from the Department of General Services and the Division of Real Property. For information on local government agencies that handle the dispersement of surplus property in various cities, see the Agency Chart.

Landmark Buildings

City agencies charged with protecting landmark buildings (like the New York Landmarks Commission and the Commission on Chicago Landmarks) and nonprofit advocacy organizations (like the New York Landmarks Conservancy and the Los Angeles Historic Theatre Foundation) may provide leads on landmark buildings, as well as funds to help renovate them.

On the national level, contact the National Trust for Historic Preservation in Washington to obtain addresses and telephone numbers for its regional offices:

National Trust for Historic Preservation
1785 Massachusetts Avenue, NW
Washington, DC 20030
(202) 673-4000

5 Evaluating a Space

Leasing or buying a space is a major commitment. Take all the time necessary to make certain this is the right space, carefully inspecting the building's exterior, interior, and surrounding neighborhood. Take everything into account.

Cost will play a major role in your decision—not only the initial expense of leasing or buying the space, but also the cost of conversion, renovation, and repairs, plus the expenses involved in bringing the space up to code.

Be aware of potential problems that might not be readily apparent—heat in the winter (if you happen to be looking at the space in the summer), intrusive noises in the evening (if you are checking the space in the daytime). Find out who the other tenants are and if their use of the building would interfere with your activities in any way. Who would share entrances and exits and for what purposes? Spend time in the space during the day and at night.

The guidelines below, and the checklist at the end of the chapter, should lead you through a knowledgeable evaluation to the right choice.

THE NEIGHBORHOOD

Make notes of your first impression of a building and the surrounding area. Your initial impressions of the neighborhood are likely to be shared by your audience. Since you are looking for low-cost real estate, you doubtless will be looking at buildings in marginal neighborhoods. Take a look at other buildings on the street. What shape are they in? If some are being renovated, it's a good indication that the neighborhood is on the upswing. If, on the other hand, there are deserted or burned-out buildings, or signs of neglect, be wary.

Take a moment to imagine your audience and actors walking through the same streets, from a parking lot, bus stop, or train station. Are there restaurants or pubs nearby? Galleries or shops in which to browse? Any trees along the way? Visit at night. Do you feel safe? Is there some street life? Are there adequate streetlights?

What else about the street is of note? Is the garbage collected regularly? Are there businesses that might cause disturbances, such as clubs or discos?

Evaluating a Space

TRANSPORTATION AND ACCESSIBILITY

How easy will it be for the audience to reach the theatre? Is the area well serviced by buses and a subway or metro system?

Check the parking situation. Is there a parking lot nearby? Is on-street parking permitted during performance hours? Check posted signs to determine parking limitations. Even though, in some densely populated cities, only a small proportion of the audience comes by car, parking remains an important consideration. Most cities now mandate parking space for patrons as part of a "theatre complex." Chicago and Los Angeles, for example, require one parking space for every ten seats. Remember, too, that company members will have vehicles to park.

NOISE

A critical problem to evaluate is noise: either from adjacent tenants or from ambient exterior sources.

INTERNAL. Noise transmission most often occurs between floors. Find out who lives or works upstairs. Are they likely to make intrusive noise during performance hours?

Chicago's Baliwick Repertory, in a Hull House Community Center, coordinates its performances with the center's recreational program to avoid competing with shouts from the second-floor gym.

If there are other tenants sharing the floor you hope to occupy, check the partitions that separate the spaces. Send someone into the neighboring space with a radio or a set of drums while you listen on your side of the wall. If your neighbor has a loud stereo, you may have a problem. Remember also that while you may not hear adjacent tenants who make very little noise, they may very well hear you. Can you build, hammer, and saw during all-night tech sessions, or rehearse with shouts, loud music, or sound effects?

EXTERNAL. Noise factors from outside are harder to judge; at the same time they are usually not quite so troublesome. If there is a subway line nearby, there may be rumblings and vibrations created by the trains, as at the Public Theater in New York City. Often, heavy truck traffic will transmit vibrations as well as a low level of noise. These intrusions are a nuisance but probably acceptable. However, a bar or a disco next door or across the street can create havoc with a performance.

One Off-Off-Broadway producer recommends taking a sleeping bag and "living" in a space around the clock for a couple of days to check out the noise before signing a lease.

One final cautionary word: don't locate next door to a firehouse!

INSPECTION OF THE BUILDING

Initial impressions can be notoriously deceptive: nowhere is this truer than when looking at old buildings. They appear romantic, intriguing, full of "possibilities." While your emotional response on first encounter with a building is important, ultimately the condition behind the facade should carry more weight. So take a closer look at the condition of any building, applying common sense and the guidelines that follow. Before you reach a final decision, consult an architect or engineer.

The building conditions discussed below assume even greater importance if you plan to buy the space, but they should not be overlooked if you plan to rent.

What to Look for in the Building Exterior

SETTLING. See if the building is *plumb* horizontally and vertically. Old buildings tend to settle and get out of line—it is the degree to which they have settled that you should check. Look at the rows of windows and the lintels above the doors and windows; they will give a good indication of just how much the building is out of plumb.

MASONRY. Examine the masonry for signs of cracking and opening up. Also look for loose stones and sagging corners. If the building is brick, check to see if it needs repointing.

CORNICES. The condition of cornices is best ascertained from the roof. Note any cracks, crumbling, or missing pieces.

ROOF. It is very important to check the roof itself for damage. Walk around. Take note of the condition of any skylights, vents, chimneys, or water tower. Look for signs of leakage. Examine the ceiling directly under the roof for any signs of *spawling* (crumbling, rotten plaster) due to leakage, especially around electrical fixtures, molding, or chimneys.

FIRE ESCAPES. If there are fire escapes, check their condition by walking on them and taking note of any corrosion and any weak or missing sections.

STOOPS, ENTRANCES, AND DOORS. Exterior doors must conform to the building code, and they must open out. Check the alignment of the doors with the door frame for sagging. Test the condition of any steps leading to the doors, and the stoop, for signs of crumbling or missing sections. Consider if it will be possible to load scenery and props in and out through existing doors in their present size and location, and if they will accommodate the disabled.

BACK OF BUILDING. Examining the back of a building may be difficult in some cities. But it is important to check for the same problems or flaws listed above.

What to Look for in the Building Interior

The basement is a good place to identify the construction, since basements are often unfinished. Even in a finished basement, the owner will probably allow you to pull down a small piece of plaster for a good look at the construction. Wood construction is the least fireproof, exposed steel is better, and steel enclosed in masonry is the best.

The basement is a good place to check for the presence of asbestos. It is now illegal and must be removed, which will be costly since removal must be handled by certified professionals.

FLOORS. Check for any slanting, sagging, or warping of wooden floors; look for unevenness and cracks in concrete ones. Find out what materials are used in the construction of the floor, and if possible, get a look at the beam supports underneath to check for sagging or for dry rot if they are wooden.

Building codes specify *live load* requirements for theatres. Take note of the live load (see chapter 19) of the floor. In a commercial building this information should be posted; if it is not, ask the owner for the previous certificate of occupancy, or if all else fails, check at the plan room in the department of buildings. (See Agency Chart.)

STAIRS AND CORRIDORS. If the space you are considering is above the ground floor, take a good look at the stairs and corridors. Are they open or enclosed? What materials are used in their construction, wood or steel? Check for loose or broken steps, for sagging sections. Are the handrails intact? Any "winders" (stairs that make turns)? They're usually illegal. Check the width of the stairs and corridors—3'8" is the minimum New York City code requirement for *means of egress*. Also, if the stairs will be used as a means of egress, there are *fire rating* requirements (see chapter 15 for definitions), so check the construction of the walls surrounding the stairs and corridors. How difficult will it be to load in scenery and props on the stairs and through the corridors?

ELEVATORS. If there is an elevator, ride in it. If it is a loft building freight elevator, try operating it yourself. Check the load capacity, usually posted inside the elevator. Will its size accommodate scenery and materials as well as people? If shared, are there any restrictions on its use or a limit on

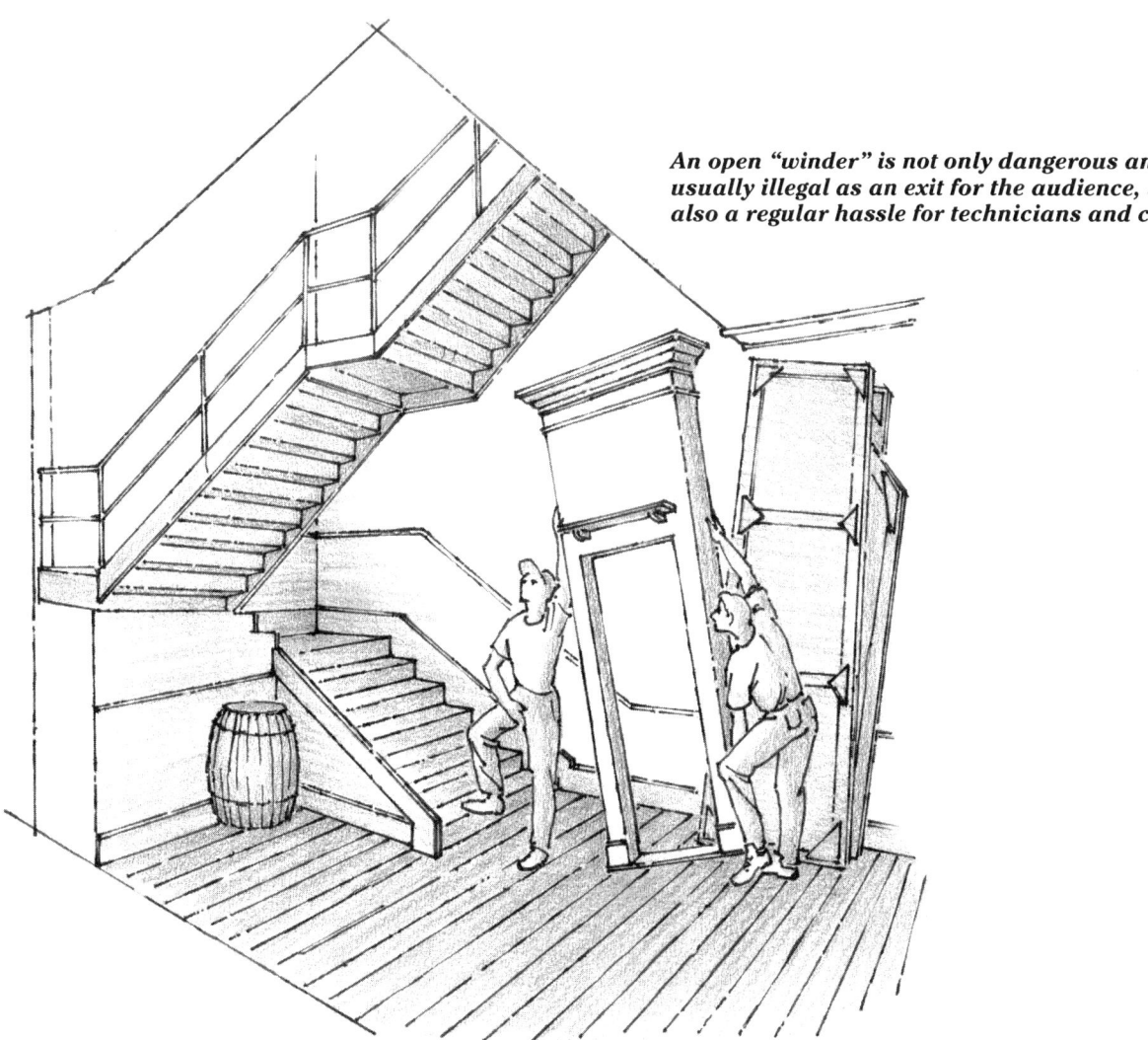

An open "winder" is not only dangerous and usually illegal as an exit for the audience, but also a regular hassle for technicians and crews.

hours of operation? Ask the other tenants if it breaks down frequently.

At New York City's Interart Theatre, in a building where the passenger elevator holds only four, audience members must use the freight elevator to reach the auditorium.

WALLS AND CEILINGS. Take note of the materials used in wall and ceiling construction. Are the walls fire-retardant? If Sheetrock, how many layers? Are studs of steel or wood? Check for signs of dampness and leakage. If there are indications of leaking, try to determine the origin: is it through the roof or through exterior masonry, or is it localized around plumbing, windows, or vents?

COLUMNS AND LOAD-BEARING WALLS. Determine which walls and columns are load bearing and essential to the structural support. Load-bearing walls and columns cannot be removed without the substitution of costly support beams.

WINDOWS AND SASHES. Check for alignment. Look for rotten frames and broken windowpanes that must be replaced. Try opening and closing all the windows.

BASEMENT. Look for a water level line; a "ring around the bathtub" could indicate basement flooding. Check the condition of the boiler.

HEATING, VENTILATION, AIR CONDITIONING. If possible, ask for each of these systems to be "fired up" so that you can check the operational efficiency and the noise level. If the building is occupied, check with the current tenants regarding the efficiency of these systems. Remember, HVAC systems must be available for use on a 24-hour basis, seven days a week.

ELECTRICAL POWER. Make note of the type (AC or DC), the amount of current (amperage), and the voltage supplied to the space. Usually each floor will have a fuse box or circuit breaker panel with the amperage marked. If not, take a look in the basement near the main service box for the building: 4-wire, 3- phase, 300-400 amp, 120-volt AC service should be considered the minimum a small theatre will need for stage lighting. Anything less will severely limit your stage lighting options and your creativity. Additional power will be necessary to service the support spaces.

If the amount of current available is inadequate, the local power company will run any additional amount of current needed in from the street free of charge, but a licensed electrician will have to install the proper circuit breakers and cable necessary to handle and distribute this additional load.

While you are at the box or panel, note the age and condition of the wiring: Old cloth-covered? Cracking rubber-covered? Or, with luck, new? Check the general condition of outlets and sockets, and note any exposed wires. Also check to see if the space has its own meter or if the meter is shared with another space. Ask if the building is grounded (now an electrical code requirement).

PLUMBING. To find out how well the plumbing works, turn on all the faucets and flush all the toilets. Check for plumbing leaks by examining the surrounding plaster. Make a note of the number and location of sinks, hot and cold taps, toilets, and drains. Compare these with your basic requirements. Relocating or adding plumbing and fixtures can be very expensive.

FIRE PREVENTION AND EMERGENCY SYSTEMS. Check the means employed for fire prevention within the space, such as a sprinkler system and fire extinguishers. Make a note of the location and condition of the system, and determine when it was last inspected. Ask to have the system tested. Note the date on the tags of any fire extinguishers. This provides a good indication of the last time the space was inspected. Inquire about smoke detectors and about the fire alarm system and how it works.

Check for an emergency light system. Ask to see it tested. Note the location of the lights. Do they illuminate all of the necessary spaces?

SECURITY. Check all the possible means of entry that could be used by unauthorized persons. While on the roof, note any doors, skylights, or trapdoors and the means of locking them. If there are fire escapes, note their accessibility to the windows.

How many exits are there in the space, and where do they lead? Are there any shared corridors? If the theatre will occupy the ground floor, note the location of the windows with relation to the sidewalks, passageways, and courtyards. Are they lockable? Any exterior entrances to the basement? If the theatre is on the ground floor, make sure that access to the floors above is not through the theatre space. In general, how easy will it be to secure this space from unauthorized entry?

ENERGY EFFICIENCY. Check doors, windows, HVAC systems, boiler and other equipment for energy efficiency. (See chapter 13.)

Depending on the locale, additional factors may require scrutiny. In Los Angeles and San Francisco, the building's ability to withstand seismic disturbances will require special investigation. In Los Angeles, the condition of the cooling system is important. In Chicago, the "windy city," tight construction and an efficient heating system are major concerns.

CAN IT BE BROUGHT UP TO CODE?

Usually, a potential space will not meet all building code requirements for theatres. It is quite possible to convert, renovate, and open a theatre in a space that is not up to code. But sooner or later as your visibility rises, you will be required by fire and building inspectors to eliminate the violations or face being shut down. Therefore, be sure the space you choose can be brought up to code, and if it is necessary to "phase" the repairs, do the ones that insure public safety first. Given the potential expenses and legal problems involved, it's wise to consult with an architect, contractor, or theatre designer on what will be required to bring a space up to code and how much it will cost.

Do not settle for a space that cannot be brought up to code—a space with an egress violation that is structurally impossible to correct; a space on a high floor of a nonfireproof loft building; or a space which, because of the industry above it, requires installation of an expensive 2-hour fire-rated ceiling. All of these are real problems currently existing in Off-Off-Broadway theatres.

Any space that needs major structural, electrical, or plumbing repairs; egress construction; or major exterior repair work should be avoided, no matter how cheap the rent.

The Charlestown Working Theatre of Boston has judiciously phased its renovations of a landmarked Victorian firehouse. First, with a small Community Development Block Grant, the exterior was stabilized. Next came the lobby work, repairs to the second-floor rehearsal room and administration office, plus installation of replacement windows that replicate the originals and conform to landmark specifications. Phase three, still ongoing, includes development of adequate dressing rooms with showers, a costume and prop shop, a scene shop and storage area in the basement, and the installation of a second staircase.

IS IT WORTH THE RENT?

To assess how much you will get for the rent being charged, compute the dollar-per-square-foot cost.

Dollar-per-Square-Foot Value

Measure the length and width of the space, and multiply them to determine the square footage. Then divide the total yearly rent by the total number of square feet to obtain a dollar-per-square-foot figure.

L. x W. = total sq. ft.

Annual rent ÷ total sq. ft. = $/sq. ft.

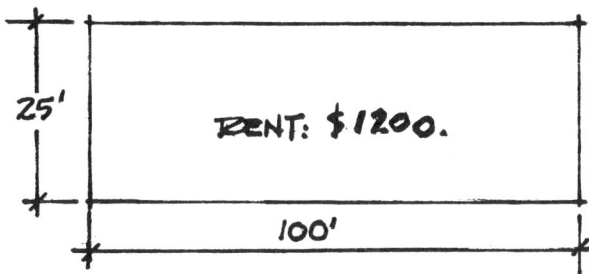

This will give you the net square footage or usable footage of the space. Landlords, however, charge rent on a gross square footage basis wherein they use external measuremnts from exterior wall to exterior wall. Gross square footage charges the tenant for corridors, stairways, restrooms, and other common spaces.

For example, an average storefront in most cities is approximately 25' x 100', giving a total of 2,500 gross sq. ft. per floor. If the monthly rent per floor is $1,200, then the annual rent is $14,400, so:

12 months x $1,200 = $14,400

14,400 ÷ 2,500 = $5.76/sq. ft.

This would be a good price in New York City, where, in 1991, $15 was an average high rent, $12 an average medium rent, and $10 an average low rent for unfinished space, in other than the midtown and downtown financial office areas.

Trade-Offs

By using the dollar-per-square-foot formula, it is easy to compare the value of several spaces to see which one offers the best deal—all things being equal. But nothing ever is equal. Finding a space will be a matter of "trade-offs": a good location and a high rent versus a not-quite-so-good location and a cheaper rent, for example. The trade-offs you make in selecting a space could affect your original goals, and to some extent dictate the kinds of productions you present. Some trade-offs made by existing companies are detailed below.

AMERICAN REPERTORY THEATRE. Since 1979, American Repertory Theatre (ART) has been housed in Harvard's Loeb Drama Center, Cambridge, Massachusetts. ART performs in the 566-seat theatre 40 weeks each year, getting it and its support spaces free in return for in-kind services such as teaching and producing student shows. ART has invested over $350,000 for capital improvements, most for lighting equipment and office space. Originally built for student use in 1960, the theatre is multiform: proscenium, three-sided thrust, and arena.

INTERART THEATRE AND ENSEMBLE STUDIO THEATRE. Both theatres are housed in a city-owned building in New York City's Clinton Urban Renewal area. The rent is low: less than $1.50 per square foot for Interart. But the companies are on a month-to-month, 30-day notice basis—as they have been for the past 17 years! An uneasy status and a gamble, since they are responsible for all improvements to their spaces. The city is obligated to maintain the public spaces—to take care of electrical repairs and elevator breakdowns—but it is very slow to act. The boiler keeps breaking down, so the theatres and staff offices are often cold.

Interart hopes to buy the building in partnership with the Clinton Preservation Local Development Corporation, which would then sell the building back to Interart outright. Interart would be required to, in turn, lease to all other current nonprofit tenants, including the Ensemble Studio Theatre.

COSTS OF RENOVATION AND CONVERSION

The realities of renovation or conversion cost must be faced early, before a final decision on space is made. Precise figures are difficult to determine in advance. Nonetheless, an estimate must be made before commencing work, and a capital budget must be developed. Here are three methods for figuring costs and arriving at a budget.

"Ballpark" per Square Foot Estimate

Commercial renovation costs are traditionally determined on a square foot basis. This shorthand method, most frequently employed by architects and engineers, is used for estimating a complete job—new plumbing, electrical wiring, heating, ventilating, and new exterior and interior finishes. Estimates could range from a low of $30 per sq. ft. to a high of $125 per sq. ft. for an adequate job. A 2,500-sq. ft. space could cost as little as $75,000 (primarily cosmetic) or as much as $312,000, depending on the design and the quality of the materials and labor involved.

When using this method to estimate the cost of a theatre renovation, make a separate budget for stage equipment. These budget figures should be developed with the help of a theatre consultant.

Master Plan Renovation or Conversion Study

A more accurate method for arriving at a cost estimate would be to engage a theatre consultant and an architect to develop a schematic design proposal. This study would include schematic drawings; description of the spaces, including square footage; and a capital budget developed by a professional estimator. Specialist theatre equipment would be listed and described as a separate budget item. This method is clearly the "Cadillac" approach to determining the cost estimate. It is probably also the most accurate, and for larger theatres, the right way to go. Sometimes it's possible to tap arts agencies to partially underwrite the costs of such feasibility studies.

Do-It-Yourself Estimate

Your capital budget will break down into three major items: 1) materials, 2) equipment, and 3) paid labor and fees. In all probability, a great deal in labor costs can be saved by doing much of the work yourself. Labor can amount to 50% or more of the estimated costs. Make a complete list of everything that will have to be done. Next make a list of all the required materials and equipment. Determine what labor you can do yourself or with the help of friends; then make a list of all the labor that must be paid for.

THE BUDGET. It is important to make a complete budget—even if some equipment will not be purchased immediately, if the work will be done in phases, or if some services will be rendered by your own staff or by volunteer labor. This budget will provide the complete picture.

MATERIALS. Start getting comparative prices over the phone for materials. Lumberyard prices can vary as much as 50%. Do some of the groundwork in estimating the cost of materials even before you find a space. If, for instance, you want risers for seating, figure out how much lumber it will take to build them based on the number of seats.

Also, estimate the cost of a running wall. Walls are normally made up of 4' x 8' Sheetrock and 2" x 4" lumber or metal framing. Estimate the cost of a wall 8' high and 16' long; use this figure as a measuring stick for walls.

Paint is another item that can be estimated once you know the approximate square footage you intend to buy or lease.

EQUIPMENT. Make a budget for stage and auditorium equipment: stage and house lighting systems; sound and communication systems; projection equipment, if any; stage masking and rigging systems; special dressing room and shop equipment; seating. Repeat the process of comparative pricing.

For example, if you plan to use traditional fixed seating or a type of movable seats, begin investigating what they cost. Also look for sources of used seating—a movie theatre going out of business or commercial theatre undergoing renovation.

Now make a list of other equipment that will be necessary in the other areas of the theatre such as the offices, rehearsal room, lobby, and box office. Start pricing this equipment.

PROFESSIONAL ASSISTANCE AND LABOR. Make a budget for anticipated professional fees and paid labor. For instance, architects', consultants', and general contractors' fees may vary widely. Comparative pricing can be done prior to finding your space.

Heeding the advice of those who have been through the budgeting process, you can count on the truth of one unhappy axiom—everything *always* costs more than anticipated.

EVALUATION

Once you have examined several buildings with a critical eye for structural defects and shortcomings, sit down with the on-site notes you have made and compare the structures, listing them in order of desirability.

Be aware of all the problems of a space before making a commitment. Walk into a potential space with your eyes wide open.

The evaluation checklist on page 235 can be reproduced on standard 8 1/2" x 11" sheets for use on each site. Fill it out, and keep a checklist for each space under consideration. Take along a clipboard, some graph paper to make rough floor plans, and a tape measure.

Profile: Victory Gardens / Body Politic

IN 1981 the Victory Gardens Theater (VG) and the Body Politic Theatre (BP) agreed to a joint ownership/shared-space plan that not only succeeded economically, but created an artistic bond that, according to VG and BP managers, keeps getting better and better. In a two-story, 20,000-sq. ft. building on North Lincoln Avenue in Chicago, these very different theatre companies coexist in a partnership that works. Theatre people being the individualists that they are, successful joint ventures like this are rare.

When asked how they had made the joint ownership work, VG and BP managing directors pointed to several reasons: 1) non-competitiveness—the two companies have very different goals and artistic agendas; 2) prior working relationships—before negotiations, VG had rented the ground-floor theatre for a season from BP; and 3) necessity—each company badly needed something the other had to offer. "We reached a certain point in our negotiations when we realized that the partnership was possible," said Sharon Phillips, who was BP's managing director during the negotiations. "Then we simply agreed that whatever problems arose, we would work through them together until we found a solution acceptable to both theatres." And so they did. Negotiations were extensive and detailed, even to the inclusion of a plan for arbitration proceedings, should they ever become necessary. They haven't.

> Negotiations were extensive and detailed, even to the inclusion of a plan for arbitration proceedings, should they ever become necessary. They haven't.

BODY POLITIC STORY

BODY POLITIC is Chicago's oldest Off-Loop theatre. Founded in 1966 as the Community Arts Foundation, its mandate, according to Albert Pertalion, artistic director, was to be a neighborhood improvement resource in a depressed area. In the mid-60s the entire block was scheduled for demolition. The area was so depressed that the foundation was able to buy the building for about $65,000. The theatre quickly became a haven for poets, artists, dancers, performers, and performances of all kinds—a hotbed of creative ferment. Its persistence helped turn the neighborhood around and set the gentrification process in motion.

Prior to the foundation's purchase, the Monte Carlo Bowling Alley occupied the second story and the U.S. Slicing Machine Company shared the first story with a pub. The pub remained, but the other spaces were converted into two theatres.

The newly renovated building was the venue for all kinds of experimental performances. The Organic Theater and the Dinglefest Theatre started there. In fact it was Paul Sills, creator of Story Theatre, who gave the Body Politic its name, taken from a quote by Harley Granville-Barker: "The theatre is a body politic and the art of it is a single art, though the contributors to it must be many." Another first in this creative environment was the premiere of David Mamet's first produced play, *Sexual Perversity in Chicago*.

In 1980, following a major restructuring, Body Politic became a single producing company, performing a season of plays in the upstairs theatre. BP's goal was to present plays with "a respect for the richness of language." It stands out, in Chicago, as a producer of Irish plays. Continuing the foundation's mandate to serve the community, BP developed an extensive outreach program, including Bible Story Theatre in schools, clubs and churches. It remains especially concerned with presenting theatre for the underprivileged, the disabled, and the hearing-impaired.

VICTORY GARDENS STORY

VICTORY GARDENS was created in 1974 by eight Chicago theatre artists. Its mission has always been to nurture Chicago playwrights and to present their new plays. The company holds the record for having

Profile: Victory Gardens/Body Politic

> Victory Gardens's first theatre was a highly unsatisfactory rental space. It was noisy, the ceiling leaked, the owner wanted to sell and refused to sign a long-term lease. In short, VG had no control over its destiny.

produced more new plays by Chicago playwrights than any other theatre in the city.

Victory Gardens's first theatre was a highly unsatisfactory rental space. It was noisy, the ceiling leaked, the owner wanted to sell and refused to sign a long-term lease. In short, VG had no control over its destiny. In 1981, after a two-year search for space, VG concluded that the downstairs theatre at Body Politic best suited its needs.

At the same time, Body Politic was in serious financial straits. Saddled with enormous debt, it had to retrench. VG, on the other hand, was in sound financial shape. When BP offered the theatre as a rental, VG countered with a proposal for joint ownership.

Victory Gardens bought 53% of the building in a deal that involved payment of $115,000 and the assumption of 53% of a long-term, $165,000 mortgage at 9.5% interest, due to expire in 2002. In return for this VG uses 6,000 sq. ft. while BP retains the use of 10,000 sq. ft. Both share the first-floor common lobby, box office, and public rest rooms.

Both companies retain joint ownership of the 3,500-sq. ft. pub space. Its current annual rental to a restaurant reaps $43,659, which very handily covers the debt service on the mortgage and the real estate tax. Not a bad deal.

THE SPACES

VICTORY GARDENS. VG's 6,000 sq. ft. include a 195-seat Main Theatre and a 60-seat Studio Theatre but no rehearsal space.

Victory Theatre/Body Politic. Restored and renovated facade.

LINCOLN AVENUE FACADE

WILL IT MAKE A THEATRE?

The company maintains administrative offices a few doors down the block to create a small storage space for costumes and props. A nearby storefront theatre provides space for building some scenery; some construction and painting is done on stage. Dressing rooms are cramped. The control booth, reached by a ladder, accommodates two, so the stage manager handles sound. There is no costume or prop shop; however, since VG does new plays with small casts and modern dress, wardrobe can usually be shopped, and props can be rented or borrowed.

Upon assuming joint ownership, VG did a $50,000 renovation of the first-floor theatre. The seating configuration is wide: three sections wrap around a modified thrust stage. Fixed seats are the comfortable, upholstered, flip-up type. The audience enters through doors located just to the side of the stage; unfortunately, this makes latecomers or early leavers a decidedly disturbing element. The ceiling is too low for good lighting positions, forcing the designer to rely on wide-angle and Fresnel-type equipment plus lots of shutters and high-hats.

The season includes five mainstage and three studio productions. Subscriptions have reached approximately 4,500 in recent seasons. The typical subscriber is well educated, upper middle class, and white. Annual operating budget figures have been at the $1,000,000 level. Earned income accounts for a healthy 60% of the budget. VG offers classes in ensemble acting and Shakespearean acting, which net the company approximately $45,000 annually.

BODY POLITIC. BP has a well-defined, well-proportioned thrust stage surrounded by three blocks of risers with comfortable fixed seats and a black back wall for scenery. Again, the ceiling is much too low; trying to light the actor without lighting the audience is a battle—lots of high-hats and barn doors! But the general ambience of the space is pleasant, and its sightlines are excellent. One of BP's capital improvement priority items is to raise the ceiling over the stage area.

> The theatre quickly became a haven for poets, artists, dancers, performers, and performances of all kinds—a hotbed of creative ferment.

The lobby is inviting—a shiny, bright blue floor, white walls, and large windows and a skylight that flood the space with light in the daytime. Benches, plants, and a soft drinks/coffee bar complete the furnishings. During productions the lobby also serves as a gallery for local artists. The rest rooms are located downstairs and are shared with Victory Gardens.

Other support spaces are cramped. Like Victory Gardens', the control booth is a very tight space reached by ladder from the lobby and accommodates only three people. There is virtually no offstage space. Props are borrowed, rented, pulled from stock, or built. There is no prop shop. Some costumes are built in a shop owned by the resident designer; some are rented from sources like the Goodman Theatre and Northwestern University. The majority of the scenery is built and painted in place on the stage. A two- to three- week turnaround time makes this possible. The BP rehearsal room approximates the size of the stage.

When BP switched from a February through October season to the more standard September to June run, subscriptions leapt from 1,500 to well over 2,000 for 1988-89. In FY 1990-91, BP's annual operating budget was $620,000. That same year, a fifth production was permanently added to the season.

SHARED OPERATIONS

BOX OFFICE. The great triumph of shared ownership has been the shared box office. One phone number handles both theatres' calls. Box office does a color coding: red for VG and blue for BP. The 8' x 15' space is open six days a week. Here, the box office manager supervises one assistant manager plus several part-timers who collectively put in 45 hours per week.

Both theatres shared a uniform price scale until 1988. The theatres use Hot Tix—Chicago's half-price ticket booth—and Ticketron. Victory Gardens recently obtained a computer system with an Art Soft package. BP hopes to buy into it soon.

ARTISTIC PROGRAMS. A joint effort, "Play Expo," has focused attention on the two theatres and has brought them closer together in their working relationships. Play Expo—more precisely, The Great Chicago Playwrights Exposition—premiered in the spring of 1987. Its goal was to "join artistic forces to bring national attention to talented new voices in Chicago theatre." The two companies intend to repeat Play Expo in the future. This collaboration has truly brought the two companies into closer cooperation than ever before and has served to strengthen the shared space, shared resources, and shared goals.

RENOVATION PLANS

In 1988, VG and BP began developing with their architect a Master Plan for renovation involving both spaces at an estimated cost of $625,000. Phase one of the plan calls for restoration and renovation of the building's facade, and providing separate entrances, canopies, and display boards for each theatre. The two theatres will continue to share one box office, however. Work on the facade is estimated at $75,000, and they will receive a facade rebate from the city for this improvement to the neighborhood. In addition, phase one will include upgrading the rest rooms at an estimated $45,000.

Future plans for improvements include installation of an elevator to serve wheelchair patrons and additional rest rooms for the disabled. These improvements are high on Body Politic's list.

Victory Gardens would like to correct the problem of low ceilings by turning the theatre 180 degrees and excavating to increase ceiling height. The master plan also includes excavation for new dressing rooms under the stage. These improvements require removing a column and adding steel beam reinforcements in addition to the expensive excavation. VG is uncertain if the gains justify the cost, estimated between $350,000 and $500,000. It is still evaluating whether it will implement this part of the plan.

From a partnership that began as a pragmatic solution to real estate and financial woes, both theatres have reaped tremendous artistic benefits as well.

> This collaboration has truly brought the two companies into closer cooperation than ever before and has served to strengthen the shared space, shared resources, and shared goals.

WILL IT MAKE A THEATRE?

Profile: FORT MASON CENTER

IN 1976, Fort Mason (southeast of the Golden Gate and a 15-minute car ride north from San Francisco's Mission District) was a run-down, unused white elephant: a military base ignored by the military. Today, it is a thriving cultural complex boasting theatre tenants ranging from the very contemporary Magic Theatre to Young Performers Theatre, a children's company; its performance venues range from the informal 50-seat Marina Music Hall to the spacious 440-seat Cowell Theater. All in all, the center is a home to over 50 arts, educational, and environmental organizations, a magnet for 1.7

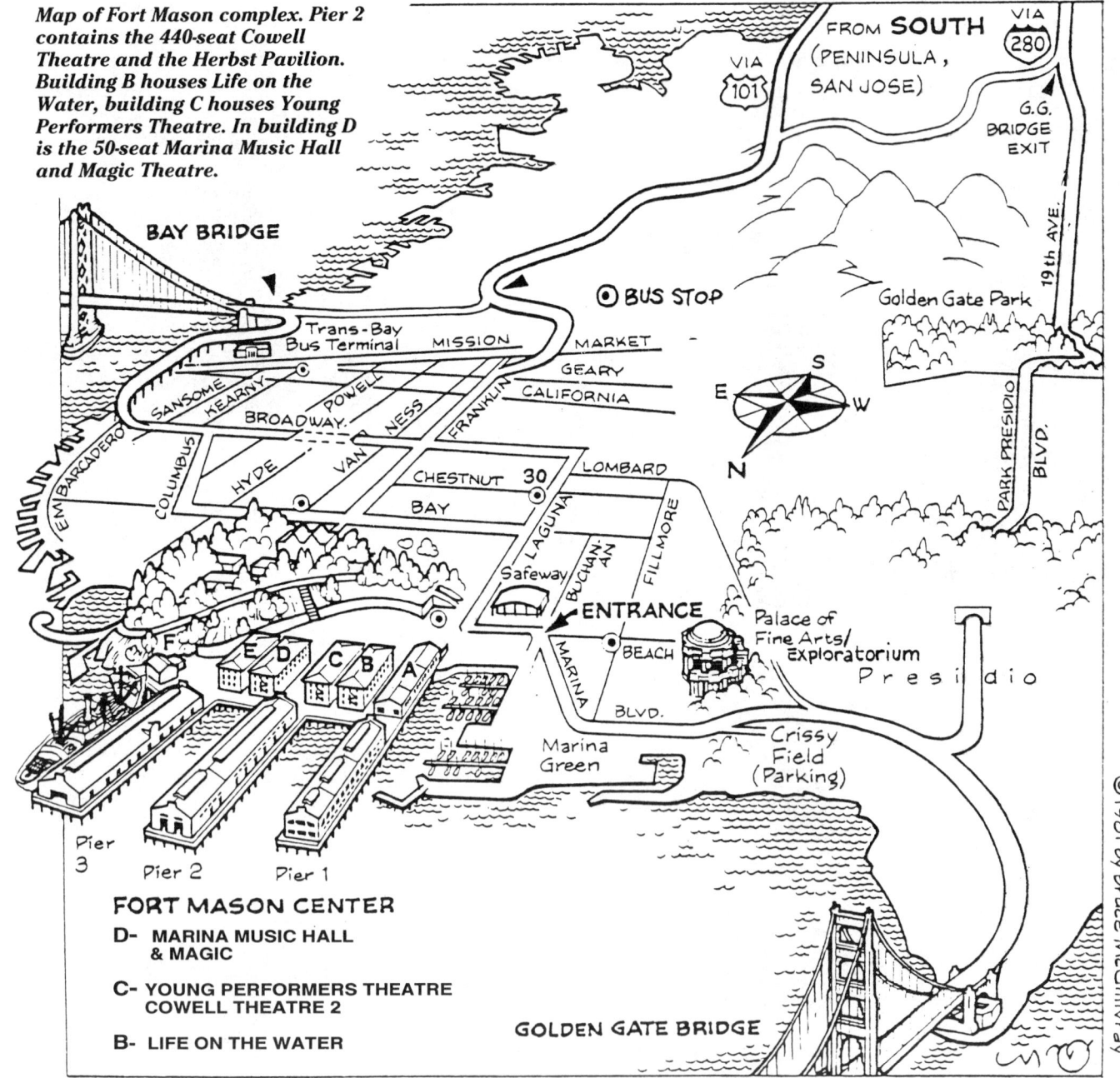

Map of Fort Mason complex. Pier 2 contains the 440-seat Cowell Theatre and the Herbst Pavilion. Building B houses Life on the Water, building C houses Young Performers Theatre. In building D is the 50-seat Marina Music Hall and Magic Theatre.

FORT MASON CENTER
D- MARINA MUSIC HALL & MAGIC
C- YOUNG PERFORMERS THEATRE COWELL THEATRE 2
B- LIFE ON THE WATER

Profile: Fort Mason Center

> Having rescued the buildings, the challenge was to figure out what, exactly, they were good for.

million annual visitors, and a model for recycling surplus buildings.

A U.S. military property since 1850, Fort Mason became an active Union defense post during the Civil War. Increased activity and additions over the next century created 300,000 sq. ft. of warehouses, piers, and offices. But by the early 1960s, the movement of troops by air rather than sea had made Fort Mason obsolete. In 1972, the U.S. Congress turned Fort Mason and several thousand acres of California shoreline over to the National Park Service (NPS), creating the Golden Gate National Recreation Area.

Having rescued the buildings, the challenge was to figure out what, exactly, they were good for. Four three-story warehouses of 36,000 sq. ft. each, a marine repair shop and a small service building totalling 27,000 sq. ft., and two enclosed piers totalling 125,000 sq. ft. were available for conversion. A nonprofit corporation was proposed as manager of the center, to be a liaison between the NPS and the tenants to come. In 1976, that corporation—the Fort Mason Foundation—began to create and administer a center that would "reflect and preserve the cultural diversity of the Bay Area, for all ages, cultural groups, and disciplines."

A unique partnership between community and federal government makes the National Park Service responsible for the buildings' grounds and exteriors, leaving their programming and interiors to the foundation's care. Fort Mason's 20-year lease from the NPS (through 2004) enables it to offer stable, long-term leases to resident groups. And though real estate is expensive elsewhere in San Francisco, Fort Mason rents monthly at $.52 per sq. ft.—less an $.08 per sq. ft. capital improvement credit for some groups. For their part, renters must provide low-cost or free activities. Admission to the complex is free, as are many museum and theatre events. Top ticket prices for performances and special exhibits are lower than average for San Francisco.

Low as they are, rents alone have been able to subsidize Fort Mason's annual operating expenses ($1,500,000 for FY 1991-92) since 1980. The center's financial stability makes it an attractive investment for potential capital funders. The foundation's first major capital campaign, launched in 1986, brought contributions from the Cowell, Fleishhacker, Irvine, and Zellerbach foundations, among others. By September 1991, $5.8 million of the $6 million goal was secured.

THE BUILDINGS

THE $2 MILLION Cowell Theater brought a much-needed mid-size rental house to San Francisco when it opened in April 1989. Its 13,500 sq. ft. at the north end of Pier 2 boast spectacular lobby views of San Francisco Bay, the Golden Gate Bridge and the Marin Headlands. The Cowell features a raised sprung-floor stage, 40' wide x 31' deep, with 20' wings, raked seating, and two stories of backstage space, including five dressing rooms, one of them accessible to disabled. Conversion retained the pier's original trussing and peaked roof, which soars to 40' at its highest. Three catwalks

> Intermission strollers share the pier aprons with fishermen, who can literally drop their hooks in the water 20' from the enclosed auditorium seats.

were added, along with a full component of equipment, including computerized lighting board and instruments, sound system, portable orchestra shell, cyc and HVAC. A spacious indoor corridor along the west side of the pier connects the Cowell with the Herbst Pavilion, which occupies the rest of the pier structure, and opens on the bay. The corridor is also a gallery for traveling exhibits. Intermission strollers share the pier aprons with fishermen, who can literally drop their hooks in the water 20' from the enclosed auditorium seats.

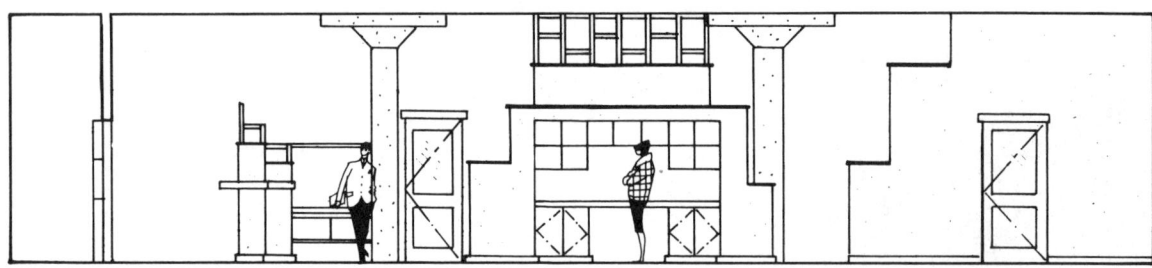

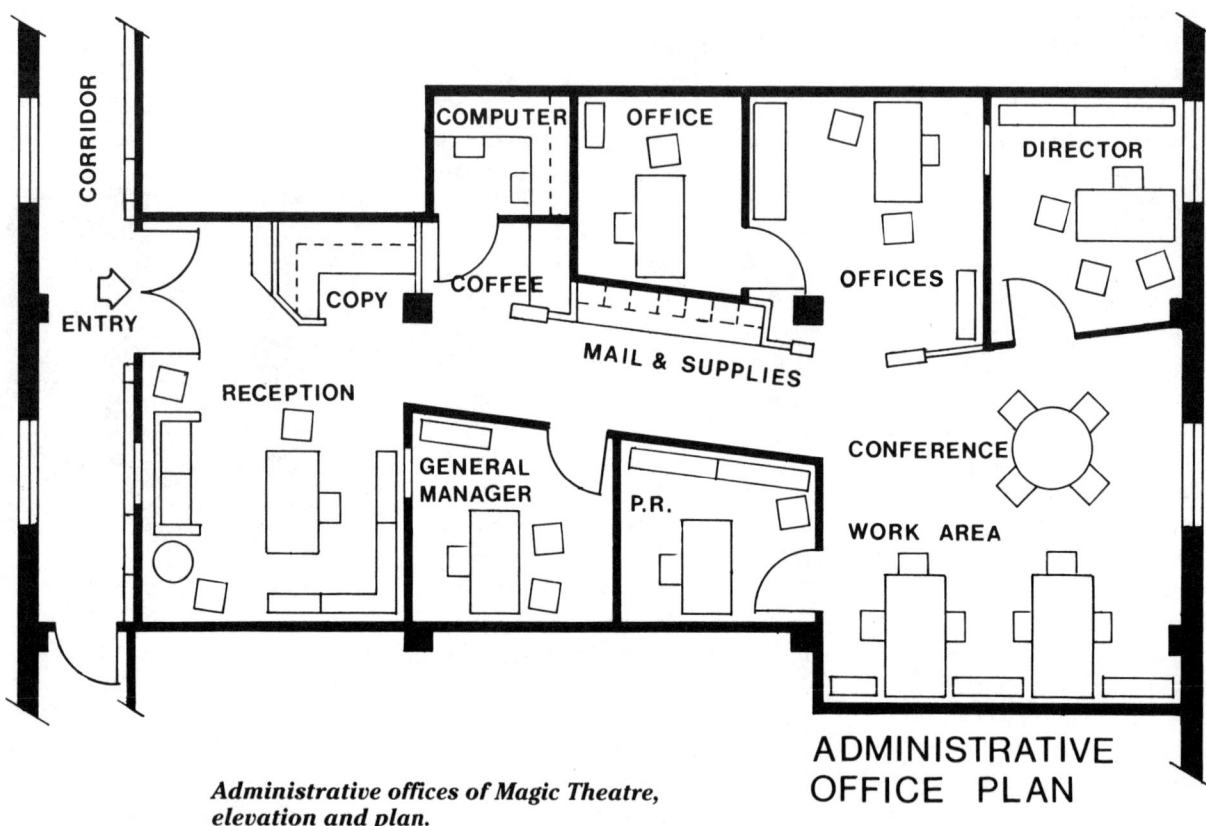

Administrative offices of Magic Theatre, elevation and plan.

Profile: Fort Mason Center

Fort Mason's imaginative adaptive reuse has installed the Modern Art Museum Rental Gallery in a former garage, the Mexican Museum in an abandoned sail shop, a popular restaurant/bakery in a storage area, and three resident theatre companies in a quartet of warehouses. Each third-floor performance space began as a 60' x 200' concrete structure, with a pitched-roof ceiling peaking at 25' and supported by five pairs of 19' on-center columns. The similarity ends here. Each of the three companies—Magic Theatre, Life on the Water, and Young Performers Theatre—has transformed its space to suit its own special needs. The Magic Theatre, whose tenancy dates back to 1977, appropriated two warehouse spaces for performance, plus additional footage on the second floor for offices. Magic's creative double-decking added another 1,440 sq. ft. to its original 11,440. Magic's Southside Theatre, a raised end stage, uses four columns to define its 290 sq. ft. acting area. Four other columns mark the aisles in the 150-seat auditorium with risers. In the Northside Theatre, a thrust stage, 153 seats are also on risers; columns and aisles divide the seating into three sections.

Life on the Water's modular flexible theatre accommodates a maximum of 270. Half the seats are on a cantilevered rake; beneath the rake, at the back of the house, a concessions counter faces the open lobby. Young Performers Theatre's audience sits on bleachers (capacity: 80 to 150) facing a 6' high end stage—which is convertible to thrust. Each company uses backstage space for its crossover.

Fort Mason Center's heterogeneous mix of cultural, educational, and environmental organizations makes for a stimulating resident community. It also makes the theatres accessible to diverse audiences, thereby expanding their clientele. An environmentalist at-

> The center's "we're open 365 days a year, 16 hours a day" policy further increases attendance and the odds for walk-ins.

tending a meeting at Oceanic Society may stick around for a show at Magic; a filmmaker may bring her child to Young Performers while she visits the Poetry Film Workshop. The center's "we're open 365 days a year, 16 hours a day" policy further increases attendance and the odds for walk-ins. Free and easy parking doesn't hurt either: there are 445 secured spaces on-site and 800 more in a 3/4-mile radius. Planning and scheduling, publicity and programming, transportation and parking, are coordinated by the foundation to every resident company's advantage.

Admittedly, Fort Mason Center is too idyllic for some. Given a choice, the Eureka Theatre Company opted to locate in the higher rent, less pretty Mission District: "Our audiences are ethnically and racially diverse; they're not comfortable at Fort Mason," explained Oscar Eustis, who was Eureka's artistic director at the time. In 1988, after ten years at the center, the San Francisco Bay Area Dance Coalition returned to the Mission District to be closer to its constituents. It is ironic that predominately white, upper-middle-class suburbs separate Fort Mason from the ethnic audiences many San Francisco theatres—like Eureka—say they want to attract.

What makes the Fort Mason Center work? Marc Kasky, executive director since 1980, offers several reasons:

SITE. Fort Mason is easy to find. It has a "strong, physical, positive identity." Parking (hard to find elsewhere in San Francisco) is safe and close by.

MANAGEMENT. Fort Mason is a cooperative effort of the non-profit community, the National Park Service, and the Foundation. Individually, none of these entities could have pulled off and sustained the project.

PROGRAMMING. "The center's artistic program is what the groups bring to it," says Kasky. The foundation does not impose an agenda upon its resident companies; they are not predetermined components of a festival complex. Programming grows from the inside out.

WILL IT MAKE A THEATRE?

INTERIOR ELEVATION

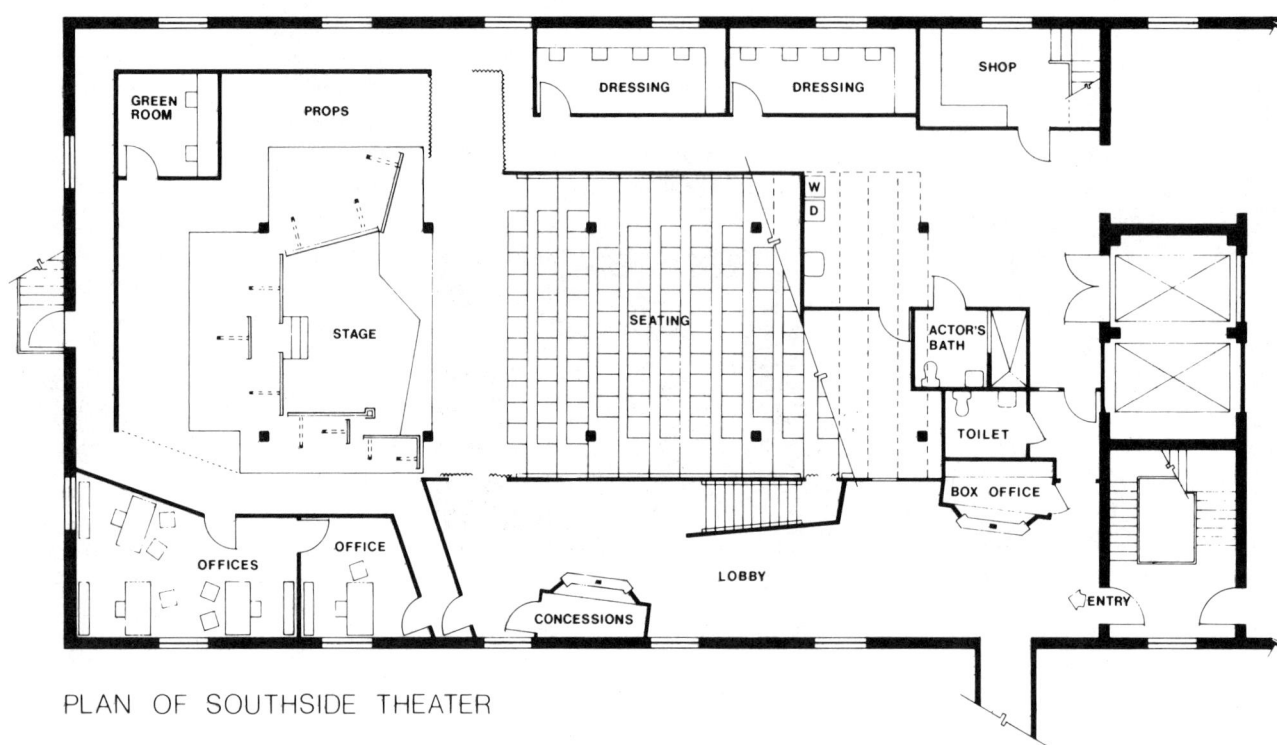

PLAN OF SOUTHSIDE THEATER

Magic Theatre's Southside theatre, elevation and plan. The control booth is double-decked above the box office.

More than 500 off-site organizations use the complex, adding even more diversity to the mix. The Herbst, Festival, and Cowell venues offer attractive performance space to homeless and/or non- resident performing troupes.

Fort Mason's concentration of companies and venues generates more publicity for "the whole phenomenon" than any single group could.

REAL ESTATE. For nonprofits, so often housed in low-rent, unpleasant spaces, so often evicted by gentrification, the attractive buildings and security offered by the Fort Mason Center are invaluable. Resident companies can safely invest their time and money in their facilities, knowing they'll be tenants for a long time. This stability also attracts board members and funders.

With factories, schools, warehouses, and military bases being closed around the country, the Fort Mason Center Foundation is continually visited by representatives of communities from Spain to Japan wanting to emulate its success. "The model is fairly simple," says Kasky. "Just partnership with public agency once the interest is there. It's no mystery."

PART TWO

HOW TO GET IT

6 Negotiating for a Space

BUYING OR RENTING

Most small theatre companies rent space when they start out. They can neither assume the expense nor the responsibility that comes with space ownership. With a rental, the landlord assumes many of the responsibilities for the facility, although the specifics are a matter to be negotiated in the lease.

However, an increasing number of small theatre companies are now seriously considering the option of buying space. They find it's the only way to control their artistic and financial future. In owning a building, a theatre group must be prepared to deal with the very real financial responsibilities that come with ownership: paying for operational and architectural expenses for both the interior and exterior; meeting the cost of fuel, gas, water, electricity; collecting rent from other tenants; and making mortgage payments. Some producers feel that the time consumed in owning and maintaining a building impedes the creative work.

The real estate market fluctuates greatly, dependent upon a large variety of factors; however, finding the right space at the right price is never easy.

Real Estate Taxes

Although a nonprofit theatre has tax-exempt status under federal law, it may not be exempt from paying local real estate taxes. If a theatre rents a portion of a building from a commercial landlord, its share of real estate taxes will be passed on to it by the landlord as part of the rent.

Even if a landlord has tax-exempt status (usually limited to religious, charitable, or educational organizations), a theatre tenant is not necessarily exempt from real estate taxes. A church, for example, may be required to pay real estate taxes on that part of the building it rents to a theatre since the theatre is not part of the religious mission. In New York City, tax advantages to a theatre company that owns its space are possible, but they are by no means automatic or easy to obtain. Theatres may find that their schools are not exempt from real estate taxes. For example, in Los Angeles and San Francisco, although nonprofits are generally exempt from paying real estate taxes, a theatre that teaches for a fee will find its classrooms are not exempt. In Chicago, buildings owned by nonprofits are not exempt from real estate taxes, but they are taxed at a lower rate than commercial businesses.

In Boston, 100% exemption for nonprofits is possible. Check with a local accountant, lawyer, or tax authority.

COMMERCIAL LEASES

Commercial leases are less stringently regulated than residential leases. As in any bartering situation, each party will try to get the best possible deal.

Any lease should clearly spell out the responsibilities of all parties. If either the tenant or the landlord makes concessions, promises of repairs, or changes in the standard lease, put them in writing. Avoid verbal agreements or "gentlemen's handshakes," since they are not enforceable contracts.

Background Research

Before entering into lease negotiations, both parties need to do some background checking. As a prospective tenant, you may be asked to provide the landlord with financial statements and character references.

Unfortunately, landlords perceive small theatres to be poor tenant risks. You may need to "prove yourself." Bring a board member, lawyer, or theatre consultant to meet with your landlord prior to lease negotiations. Assemble a packet of financial audits, annual reports, press materials, and past rent history. Impressing the landlord favorably makes lease negotiations go a lot more smoothly.

Just as a landlord checks potential tenants, you should investigate your prospective landlord and the representations made about the space. The information you glean may help at the bargaining table. The following is a list of items to check:

ZONING. Check with the buildings department to be sure that the space is in an area zoned for a theatre use. If not, a zoning variance must be obtained; most landlords are unwilling to go through this costly and lengthy procedure.

SQUARE FOOTAGE. Accurately measure the space to compute the dollar-per-square-foot value. (See chapter 5.) Often the square footage figures quoted by agents or brokers are only estimates. Remember, when a broker states the number of square feet, this calculation is from outside the walls (gross square footage). This estimate makes no deduction for columns, staircases, corridors, lavatories, mechanical or other space. These usually amount to a loss factor of about 20-25% of the space. The space remaining is the net square footage. Rent is paid on gross square footage, not net or usable square footage.

UNPAID TAXES. If the building's taxes are in arrears, the city may take over a building for tax default. Although the city will not evict you, if the building is subsequently sold at a public auction, the new owner has no obligation to retain the theatre as a tenant. Ask the owner to give you proof—specifically, the receipted bill for the payment of real estate taxes—or consult the "in rem" listing at the tax collection department to see if a court notice has been issued for nonpayment of taxes. You will need the block and lot number of the property to look up this information.

OUTSTANDING VIOLATIONS. Check with the buildings department to determine if there are any violations on the building. If there are, this will hold up your certificate of occupancy application. (See chapter 15.) Violations should be discussed during lease negotiations. The theatre should make it the owner's obligation to correct existing violations at the owner's expense. Also, add a clause covering any nontenant-created violations that occur during the term of the lease.

REPAIRS AND IMPROVEMENTS. Bring your notes listing all necessary repairs and improvements and your estimates of their cost to the bargaining table. It will be easier to negotiate for repairs and improvements if all parties have a clear idea of the dollar costs. Renovations and improvements needed to convert the space into a theatre are a point of negotiation. A landlord will occasionally pay for structural changes—strengthening the floor or ceiling, repairing the stairways, adding toilets or sinks, or running additional power to the space. More often, the theatre must pay for all improvements. Try to get a concession in the rent for the first 6 to 12 months, to offset part of these "front-end" expenditures.

PREVIOUS UTILITY BILLS. Find out how much the previous tenant paid in the past 12 months for heat, electricity, and any other utilities. This will give you a rough estimate of the minimum utility costs.

EXTENDED VACANCY. If the space has been empty for a long time, the landlord probably will be anxious to rent and may be receptive to concessions in the lease.

THE LANDLORD. Talk with other tenants in the building or to the previous occupant to find out if the landlord is responsive, trustworthy, and accessible.

Once you and the landlord have researched all these potential hazards, you are ready to enter formal lease negotiations.

Lease Negotiations

There are points of negotiation that are common to all commercial leases; in addition, there are special clauses that must be negotiated by theatres because of the special nature of the business. An attorney with real estate experience is of invaluable help.

The following apply to standard commercial lease negotiations:

LENGTH OF LEASE. A long lease will allow time to recoup any investments made on improvements or conversion. It also allows the theatre company to accurately budget its rent obligations. Do not consider less than a five-year lease. Each time the lease expires, the landlord has the right to raise the rent; usually there are no legal restrictions on the percentage of the increase, as in some residential leases.

RENEWAL OPTIONS. The right to renew the lease, after the initial lease term, should be negotiated at the outset. Establish the amount of rent for each renewal period if the option is exercised.

PASS-ALONG AND ESCALATION CHARGES. The landlord may request a clause to cover any increase in operating costs that occur during the lease term. This is in addition to the base rent. A *pass-along* (your portion of actual cost increase in operating expenses and real estate taxes) over the base year is very common. Make sure you do not pay more than your share. Escalations may be tied to the consumer price index or the Porter's Wage Index, or may be a set percentage increase.

OPERATIONAL COSTS. Heating, electricity, air conditioning, and any other costs involved with the actual operation of the building will need to be negotiated. Consider the times of day and night that the theatre will need heat and air conditioning. Many commercial buildings shut down operations at the end of a working day, so there may be extra costs to receive these services at night and on weekends.

NET LEASES. One way to possibly lower the rent is to negotiate a *net* lease. In such leases the tenant is responsible for the facility and its maintenance, as well as the real estate taxes. This gives the theatre freedom to make any necessary interior alterations and improvements. You will need to negotiate the responsibility for the structural systems: internal wiring, heating and air conditioning, plumbing, and the boiler.

If you are negotiating a net lease, insist that the landlord obtain a *nondisturbance agreement* from the mortgager. This is a written guarantee that, in the event of a foreclosure on the property, the theatre will be permitted to remain in the space for the duration of the lease.

Many lease arrangements are possible. For example, the Eureka Theatre in San Francisco negotiated a ten-year net lease making the landlord responsible only for the roof and exterior of the building. The Triangle Theatre of Boston signed a lease with an innovative rent scale: $100/month when dark, $300/week during rehearsals, $350/week during performances. When the theatre is dark, Triangle acts as rental agent for the space.

ASSIGNMENT AND SUBLEASING. *Assignment* gives the tenant the right to turn over the entire lease and premises to another party in the event that the tenant is unable to finish out the lease. *Subleasing* is a short-term renting of the space by the tenant, who remains responsible for the space.

Landlords sometimes resist such clauses and the best you may get is an agreement that "consent will not be unreasonably denied." The landlord may also ask for the right to examine all sublet agreements prior to approval. Try to arrange a subleasing agreement without approval. This will give you the flexibility to handle the unexpected opportunity, such as another company needing rehearsal space or a hit show in search of a home.

Note: If there is a sublease, the landlord may request a portion of the income. Avoid such a clause.

INSURANCE. Most landlords require that their tenants carry a specific quantity of liability insurance and name the landlord as additionally insured. This can be expensive. Ask about the fire insurance on the building to determine if the contents are insured. Most landlords only carry structural fire insurance and each tenant is responsible for insuring personal property and fixtures.

OPTION TO BUY. Try to include an option to meet any purchase offer on the building.

The following points apply specifically to theatrical leases:

DEFINITION OF USES. Theatrical *use* implies use of a space for shows, rehearsals, and all that goes into mounting a show; if the space is to accommodate other uses—offices for instance—specify this in the lease. Negotiate for the unexpected classes, lectures, and film showings—anything that may expand your theatre artistically or financially.

The right to advertise. An agreement must be made concerning use of exterior signs and banners: their location on the building or the street.

Other tenants. Negotiate a clause stating that adjacent spaces—above, below, or on either side of the theatre—may not be rented to any tenant whose activities interfere with the operation of the theatre (noise from machinery, for example). Also, negotiate a clause to exclude future tenants whose use of a space within the building would cause the operation of the theatre to become illegal, such as a high-hazard occupancy group like a fireworks factory.

Warranty of production content. The landlord may request protection or indemnification against productions that violate the law in any way.

SPACE PURCHASE

Purchasing a space is a *major* financial and psychological commitment. Because this decision will have long-term effects on almost every aspect of your operation, it should not be made lightly. Keep in mind that it's almost impossible for a small theatre company to buy a space without a strong and committed board of directors to raise the down payment and closing costs, and possibly guarantee the mortgage.

DOWN PAYMENT. Typically, the down payment will be 10% of the purchase price, but it can be as high as 20%. You'll need this money at the closing.

MORTGAGE. Obtaining a mortgage will not be easy. Most commercial banks are reluctant to make loans to small theatre companies. They see them as bad credit risks, and know it will make for poor public relations if they are forced to foreclose on a small theatre.

The bank will require you to submit a wide range of financial data, from budgets to grant letters to financial statements. The bank is concerned with your ability to repay the loan (debt service) and will, most likely, want one of your board members to personally guarantee the loan.

APPLICATION FEE. Every time you apply for a mortgage, there is an application fee. So shop around and talk to an officer, but don't submit an application until you're sure it's likely to be accepted.

POINTS. At the closing you will be required to give *points* to the bank. A point is 1% of the total mortgage. The number of points required depends on the bank and the interest rate of the loan. For example, one bank may offer a mortgage at 10% with 2 points, another a rate of 9.5% with 3 points. Basically, you're making a trade-off between more cash up front versus a higher debt.

RATE. You will have to chose between a *fixed rate* that stays the same over the term or an *adjustable* or *variable rate* mortgage. You will probably need someone with financial savvy to help you decide which type is more advantageous in the prevailing fiscal climate.

TERM. The term of the mortgage involves a simple trade-off: the longer the term, the more money you'll ultimately pay; the shorter the term, the higher your monthly payments.

BROKER'S FEE. Generally the seller is responsible for this fee. However, it is not unusual for the buyer to chip in to close the deal.

LAWYER'S FEE. Any theatre group about to obtain a space, whether buying or renting, should consult a real estate lawyer. You'll need a lawyer to check the deed, draw up the contract of sale, and confirm that all documents are in order.

TITLE SEARCH. Usually the bank does the title search, but you'll have to pick up the cost of verifying that the property has no encumbrances. Sometimes the buyer hires a title search company to do this work.

LEGAL ASSISTANCE

A lawyer on your board of directors may be able to give aid and advice. Or check with local theatre service organizations (see Resource Directory), or with Volunteer Lawyers for the Arts, Volunteer Consulting Group, or Business Volunteers for the Arts (see chapter 7). It's really important to have a real estate lawyer, not just any lawyer.

NEIGHBORHOOD ASSISTANCE

Every city has a network of neighborhood advocates whose mandate is to serve the best interests of their local districts. These advocates may be elected legislators, like Chicago's aldermen or the members of the city council in Boston, Los Angeles, and San Francisco. Or they may be advisory bodies like New York City's community boards or Atlanta's neighborhood planning units. In some cities—Chicago, for example—there are influential community groups (merchant and block associations) with no official government status. In varying degrees, these advocates all carry clout at City Hall, and it's worth the effort to get them on your side. (See Resource Directory for more detailed information.) Contact the group representing the district in which you have found a space as soon as possible, especially if a zoning variance is required. (See chapter 14.)

Even if you do not need a zoning change, community groups can help you negotiate the red tape of city agencies and can provide sound advice about procedure. Frequently, they can help leverage community development (CD) funds and in some cases may actually control disbursement of such money. Your council member or community board member may even be able to help you find a space—as happened in New York City with the Interart Theatre.

Neighborhood advocates will want to be convinced that your proposed theatre is in the best interests of the whole community before they endorse your project. They are likely to ask the following questions:

- Is theatre use viable? Is the theatre financially stable?
- What would a theatre mean for the existing neighborhood? How would it fit in with or complement existing uses? Would it enhance the community?
- What additional demands would a theatre make on the existing services in the community (e.g., sanitation, police)? Would it generate excessive noise, traffic, and parking problems? What are its hours of use? Are they compatible with neighbors' uses?

Think through these questions prior to appearing before your community board or alderperson. Bring as much evidence as you can to prove your theatre will benefit the community. (For information about community boards and zoning, see chapter 14.)

7
RESOURCES FOR MAKING IT HAPPEN

It is difficult for theatre companies, with or without a track record, to obtain capital funding. Funders more readily contribute to artistic programs than to bricks and mortar. In searching for funds, you'll want to tap all potential sources, but it's worth remembering that individuals are the single largest contributors to capital campaigns.

This chapter reviews the major sources of capital funding—government (federal, state, local), corporations, foundations, individuals, and loans. It also provides representative examples of the ways theatres have creatively assembled financing packages.

GOVERNMENT FUNDING

Government funding can be pursued at the federal, state, and local levels.

Federal Funding

At the federal level there are two major sources of funds: the National Endowment for the Arts (NEA) and Urban Development Action grants. A more specialized granter is the National Trust for Historic Preservation.

NATIONAL ENDOWMENT FOR THE ARTS (NEA). Three NEA programs accept applications for theatre design projects:

The Advancement Program— operates on a two-year cycle of eligibility and consists of two separate phases. The program's main thrust is phase 1, "Planning/Technical Assistance."

Phase 1 provides a field consultant who gives technical assistance. Additionally, with the field consultant's advance approval, organizations are reimbursed for expenses up to $5,000 for engaging additional specialists.

Phase 2 funds are only sporadically available. Following completion of the 15-month first phase, organizations are eligible for a phase 2 Advancement Grant. Generally, amounts range from $25,000 to $75,000, and must be matched at least 3-to-1 during the 30-month maximum grant period. Advancement Grant funds may be applied to facilities planning and design, purchase, or renovation. They may not be used for new construction.

Resources for Making it Happen

Challenge Grants— are intended to provide a special opportunity for arts institutions to strengthen long-term institutional capacity and to enhance artistic quality and diversity.

A key factor in awarding a Challenge Grant is whether the Challenge effort can be expected to have a significant, long-range impact.

The Challenge Program has two forms of support: Institutional Stabilization and Project Implementation. Organizations may apply for only one form of support. Grants range from $75,000 to $1 million, and must be matched 3-to-1 (4-to-1 for construction, renovation, purchase of a facility, or purchase of equipment). Grant periods may run up to the end of the grantee's third full fiscal year. Applicants seeking support for construction or renovation are required to submit extensive designs.

For more information, contact:

Challenge and Advancement Grant Programs
National Endowment for the Arts
Room 617, Nancy Hanks Center
1100 Pennsylvania Avenue, NW
Washington, DC 20506
(202) 682-5436

The Design Arts Program— promotes excellence in the disciplines of architecture, landscape architecture, urban design and planning, historic preservation, interior design, industrial and product design, and graphic design. The program supports work of exceptional merit that advances the design arts and benefits the public on a local, state, or national level by funding projects such as conceptual and schematic designs; feasibility studies; competitions; collaborations; research and theory; demonstrations; exhibitions; and communication tools including publications, audio-visual programs, films, and conferences.

Project Grants for Organizations support projects that advance design practice, research, theory, and communication.

Generally, Design Project Grants for Organizations are awarded for up to a two-year period with a $50,000 cap. The minimum grant is usually no less than $10,000. The program's funds must be matched at least 1-to-1. There are two deadlines per year. Design Arts will not fund projects that are eligible for Challenge III grants.

Project Grants for Arts Facilities Design support organizations seeking to research, devise, and/or implement projects that will contribute to the advancement of the design process in the renovation, rehabilitation, or creation of facilities that are intended to accommodate the specific artistic needs of a community. Arts organizations that are considering applying to the endowment's Challenge Program for funding that will support facility development are a priority. Grant monies are not available to fund market feasibility studies to determine whether a particular community can support such an arts facility.

Grants range from $5,000 to $25,000 and must be matched on at least a 1-to-1 basis. There are two application deadlines a year.

Design Arts Program
National Endowment for the Arts
Room 625, Nancy Hanks Center
1100 Pennsylvania Avenue, NW
Washington, DC 20506
(202) 682-5437

Other Federal Programs

THE NATIONAL TRUST FOR HISTORIC PRESERVATION. The National Trust makes grants and loans to those renovating historic buildings. Two of its programs are of special interest to theatres:

Preservation Services Fund Grants— usually from $500 to $5,000, must be matched at least one-to-one. Both nonprofits and public agencies are eligible for these monies, which are earmarked for consultant services and studies.

The National Preservation Loan Fund (NPLF)— makes over $1 million available to preservers of historic properties. The flexible financing program offers low-interest loans of $25,000-$150,000 for periods of three to five years.

Contact the Trust's Office of Financial Services in Washington, DC, at (202) 673-4054 for detailed information about the grants and loan fund, and about additional special programs.

State Funding

At the state level, there are several places to turn for funding: the state arts council, line items in the state budget, industrial revenue bonds, and state urban development corporations.

STATE ARTS COUNCILS. Although many state arts councils view their principal mandate as supporting artistic programming, an increasing number have developed special programs to target the space needs of arts groups. The New York State Council on the Arts, for example, launched a Capital Funding Initiative as part of its Architecture Planning and Design Program in 1987. It also offers project support for design studies and technical assistance grants. Other councils are developing programs in response to their constituencies' needs. (See Resource Directory.)

LINE ITEMS. Some theatres—for example, New York's Bond Street Theatre Coalition—have successfully gotten line items in state budgets for their theatres. Such efforts usually require extensive lobbying efforts with state representatives.

INDUSTRIAL REVENUE BONDS. In recent years, legislation by several states (including Massachusetts and New York) has made industrial revenue bonds available to creditworthy nonprofits. Once a state government issues the bonds, they are sold to organizations like banks or investment houses, who in turn may make them available to other investors. Usually the nonprofit is responsible for placing the bonds or obtaining guarantees. In New York City, the Economic Development Corporation issues Industrial Development Bonds.

STATE URBAN DEVELOPMENT CORPORATIONS (UDCs). An urban development corporation's goal is to create and retain jobs, particularly in economically distressed areas. It undertakes projects that would not be financially or organizationally feasible for the private sector alone and can provide low-interest financing to industrial and manufacturing businesses for the purpose of creating and retaining jobs. The New York State Urban Development Corporation was instrumental in the 1979 Theatre Row Project. The UDC is continuing to work on the revitalization of the block of West 42 Street between 7th and 8th Avenues, and is involved with Women's Interart Center in creating a rehearsal center in the Clinton district on Manhattan's West Side.

Local Funding

Local arts councils, local development corporations, and community development funds are among the organizations where funding can be obtained on the local level.

LOCAL ARTS COUNCILS. Although local arts councils do not make large grants to renovation projects, they often can be extremely responsive in providing low-interest loans, money for feasibility studies, and support services like space banks. New York City's Department of Cultural Affairs, for example, runs a Real Estate Assistance Program for consultants to help arts organizations relocate or renovate space with grants up to $9,500, and a Capital Assistance Program to help bring arts facilities in city-owned buildings up to code. The Boston Arts Lottery Council offers Pre-development Grants (technical assistance) of up to $5,000. In San Francisco, the hotel tax generates money that finances low-interest loans to arts groups. (See Resource Directory.)

COMMUNITY DEVELOPMENT (CD) FUNDS.
CD funds are available to private, nonprofit organizations for neighborhood facility improvements. ("Neighborhood" is defined here as meaning low- to moderate-income areas of New York City.) Tapping CD funds for small theatres is difficult, but not impossible. A theatre group with a landmark-designated building in need of renovation or a project to attain accessibility for the disabled might be eligible for CD funding.

A project requesting CD funds must be sponsored by a city agency and could be routed through the Mayor's Office of Economic Development—or in New York City through the Department of Cultural Affairs Community Arts Development Program (for nonprofit arts organizations only). Projects approved for CD funds must satisfy federal guidelines as well as city criteria.

LOCAL DEVELOPMENT CORPORATIONS (LDCs).
A nonprofit developer representing an aggregate of theatres can file to incorporate as a nonprofit local development corporation. New York City's 42nd Street Redevelopment Corporation—Theatre Row—for instance, is a local development corporation (see Profile, p. 76), as is the Brooklyn Academy of Music LDC.

Not a source of funds, a local development corporation is a means for steering groups towards sources of public monies or benefits, such as CD funds, tax abatements, or mortgage money. The city can lease or sell land and/or a building to an LDC without taking bids. This eliminates the financial risk to the theatre of extensive preparation of feasibility studies, only to lose the property to a higher bidder at public auction.

PUBLIC DEVELOPMENT CORPORATIONS (PDCs). A public development corporation can be involved in negotiation, design, construction, financing and project management. A PDC can sell city-owned commercial and industrial property, conduct feasibility studies, renovate old buildings in preparation for sale or lease, and prepare sites for development.

INDUSTRIAL AND COMMERCIAL INCENTIVE PROGRAMS. It may be possible for theatres to receive tax abatements if they renovate underutilized property. New York City also has a program that reimburses eligible firms for their moving expenses if they locate in specified areas of the city or are displaced because of conversion of their manufacturing space into residential use. (See Retention and Relocation Program, below.)

CORPORATIONS

Corporations generally do not support capital efforts. However, "special help" grants or "seed money" may sometimes be obtained for a specific stage in the building process if the corporation already has an established relationship with the theatre.

A case in point is Bankers Trust Company's contribution of $40,000 to Manhattan Theatre Club (MTC) toward the construction of a new lobby space at the theatre's headquarters on 55th Street. In this instance, a corporation that does not normally make capital grants was able to respond to an immediate need—MTC's displacement from its home on the East Side—because of its long-term relationship and commitment to MTC. Corporations that have a vested interest in a particular neighborhood may also be responsive to requests for capital funds, as was Guardian Life when the Vineyard Theatre constructed a theatre near Union Square.

FOUNDATIONS

Although corporate support of capital campaigns is limited, and sometimes capricious, selected foundations do provide such assistance.

Before approaching any foundation, a nonprofit should meticulously research both the

WILL IT MAKE A THEATRE?

Profile: Theatre Row

THEATRE ROW HISTORY

TWO decades ago, few would dare to tread the far reaches of West 42nd Street. But thanks to the pioneering spirit of a few intrepid theatre artists and some savvy financial packaging, a thriving theatre district graces a once derelict neighborhood.

In 1975, Robert Moss, then artistic director of Playwrights Horizons, was unexpectedly without a theatre for the coming season. Desperate, he temporarily rented a space on West 42nd Street, surrounded by porno palaces, peep shows, and massage parlors. To his surprise, Moss found that neither theatre people nor audiences objected to the neighborhood. He stayed, and Playwrights Horizon's success attracted the Lion and Nat Horne theatre companies. With three theatres on the street, Moss convinced Fred Papert, president of the 42nd Street Local Development Corporation, that a Theatre Row should be created from the remaining tenements on the block.

PROJECT DESCRIPTION.

In phase 1 of the project, five derelict tenements were redeveloped into five 99-seat Off-Off-Broadway theatres and ten floors of rehearsal and office space, totaling approximately 46,000 sq. ft. Located between Ninth and Dyer Avenues, the original tenants of Theatre Row (Black Theatre Alliance, Actors and Directors Lab, Lion Theatre Company, Intar, Harlem Children's Theatre, and South Street Theatre) joined the pioneering theatres on the block, Playwrights Horizons and the Nat Horne Theatre Company. Renovation began in November 1977. Four-wall construction on all spaces was completed and some of the theatres were opened in mid-May 1978.

Phase 2 of the project was to complete the upgrading of the Ninth to Tenth Avenue block. This phase included both redevelopment of all the properties on West 42nd Street between Dyer and Tenth Avenues into a restaurant

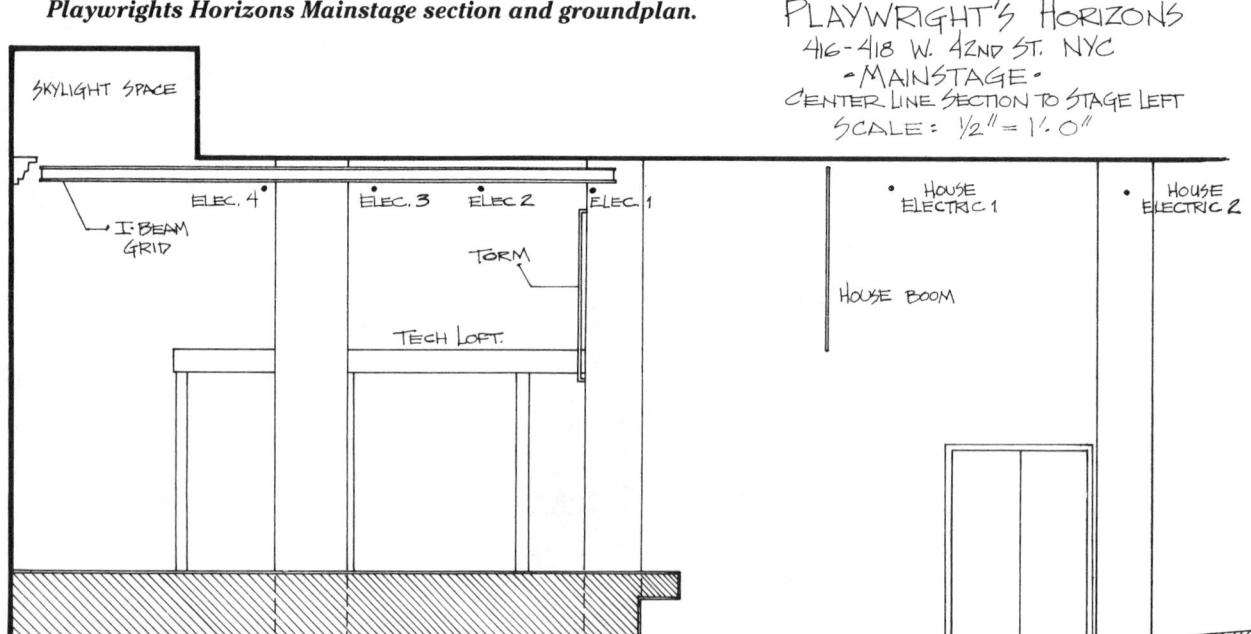

Playwrights Horizons Mainstage section and groundplan.

Profile: Theatre Row

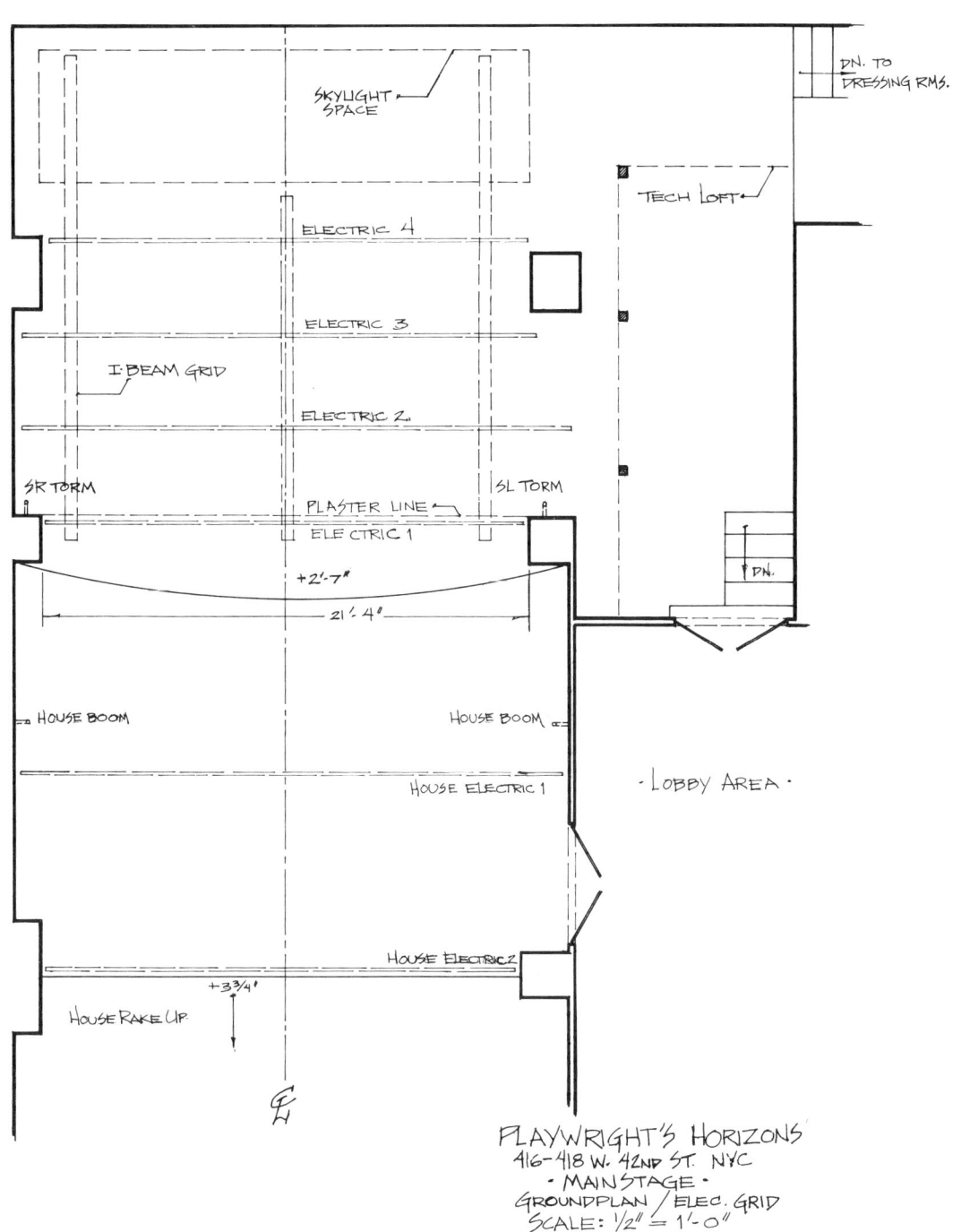

and market complex, theatres, and arts-related uses; as well as the redevelopment of the properties at the corner of Ninth Avenue and West 42nd Street into a restaurant, retail space, and mini-Shubert Alley. In conjunction with the Clinton community residents and performing artists, Theatre Row phases 1 and 2 would create a critical mass to provide an anchor for future redevelopment.

PROJECT SPONSOR. The 42nd Street Development Corporation, an LDC organized under section 1411 of the New York State Not-for-Profit Corporation Law, was created in April 1976 for the purpose of revitalizing 42nd Street west of Seventh Avenue.

According to state law, an LDC has broad economic development purposes—i.e., the creation of jobs. The statute specifies that an LDC is to act "in the public interest" and to "lessen . . . the burdens of government." The 42nd Street Development Corporation, while a private entity, is thus viewed as the project-implementing arm of the local government and as such receives support from the city of New York.

PROPERTY ACQUISITION. The 42nd Street Development Corporation began acquiring the Theatre Row properties in 1976 from two landlords. The corporation's tactic in acquisition was to forge a partnership with the mortgagees, taking title to the properties for no cash, subject to all the mortgages and tax arrearages. These mortgages, all of which were in default, had substantial balances. The properties' value was minimal, given tax arrearages and the buildings' derelict physical condition.

PROJECT PACKAGING. The critical element for the success of the project in the planning stage was tax abatement. Based on the expected rents and operating expenses, it was clear that the project could not support full real estate taxes. The project had to be removed from the tax rolls and a tax equivalency rental charged in lieu of full taxes.

This was accomplished through ownership of the properties by the New York State Urban Development Corporation (a public benefit corporation authorized by Chapter 252 of the Unconsolidated Laws of New York State). It was pursuant to the mayor's Business Investment Incentive Program (BIIP), which assists economic development projects to attain economic feasibility through tax relief.

City agencies and the board of estimate determined that the project met the criteria of the BIIP: (a) substantial new private investment; (b) job development; (c) substantial impact on an industry or an area; (d) no windfall profits (i.e., the tax relief was no more than required for feasibility); (e) participation by the city in the success of the project; and (f) payment of full taxes within a reasonable period of time.

In the case of Theatre Row, extensive negotiations with the City's Office of Economic Development; Office of Management and Budget, Corporation and Counsel; and Comptroller's Office began in late 1976 and continued until closing, on November 10, 1977, on the terms and conditions of the project.

The board of estimate approved the project by two separate resolutions, dated April 21 and June 23, 1977.

The basic structure of the deal follows:

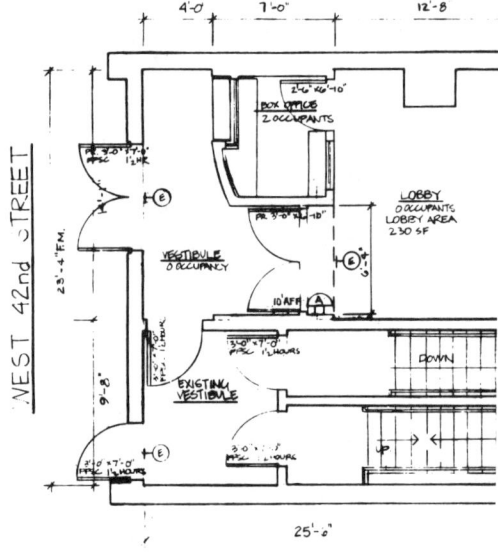

Profile: Theatre Row

- 42nd Street Development Corporation donated all the Theatre Row properties to UDC.

- Ownership by UDC removed the properties from the tax rolls.

- UDC leased the properties to 42nd Street Development Corporation for 30 years for a tax equivalency rental equal to 50% of the profits.

- The 42nd Street Development Corporation, in turn, sublet the properties to the theatre companies.

- The city takes title to the properties if there is a default under the lease or if the square footage used for nontheatre purposes exceeds specified limits. This insures that tax relief is given only to theatre users.

THE TENANTS. The 42nd Street Development Corporation solicited theatre companies as tenants, sending letters to approximately 300 companies.

It then held meetings, in late summer 1976 and November 1976, with many of these companies to discuss the kind of space that would be provided and general lease terms. The project provided the raw, up-to-code space in which

Theatre Row Theatre plan.

WILL IT MAKE A THEATRE?

the theatre companies would make their own improvements, creating their own performance and support spaces, providing and installing every component from dividing walls to makeup counters.

Through interviews, both by 42nd Street Development Corporation and theatre people, this group was narrowed down to 20. Selection of the final five theatres in spring of 1978 was based on their financial capability and artistic credibility.

PROJECT COSTS. The development costs as of the closing date in November of 1977 totaled $948,120 —a steep investment given the real estate climate in the late 1970s. By May 13, 1978, the opening date, this sum had increased to $1,045,730— due to construction extras required by a more complete engineering analysis, by UDC, by the tenants and by the 42nd Street Development Corporation. Many of these extras improved the overall project quality.

The construction contract for the project, originally bid at $700,000, rose to approximately $850,000 by the end of construction.

In addition to expenses such as professional fees and title insurance, which are included in the soft costs of the development budget, the Theatre Row budget included two other items: payment of back taxes and settlement of existing mortgages.

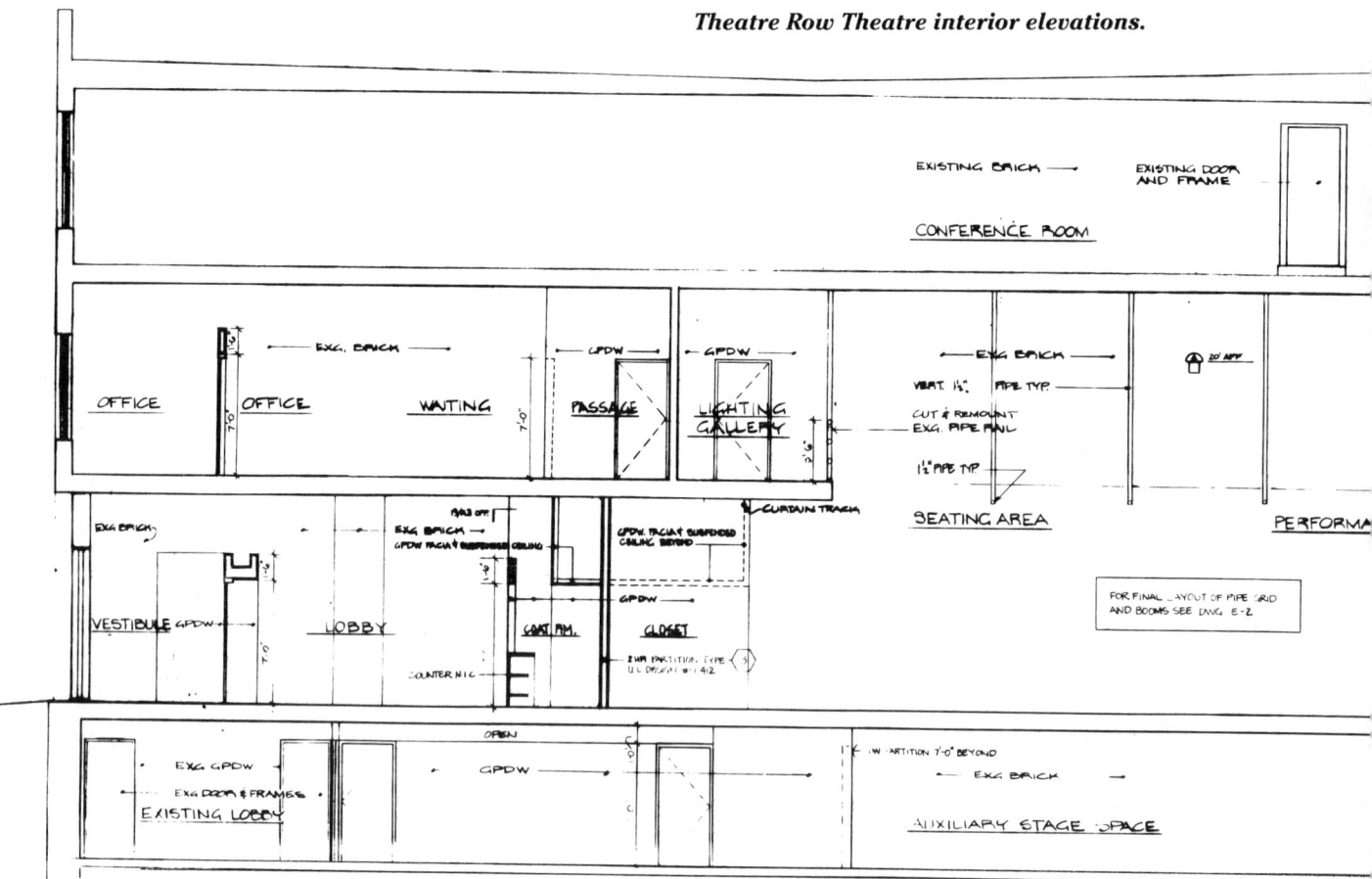

Theatre Row Theatre interior elevations.

Profile: Theatre Row

Because the properties were in substantial tax arrears, the city required payment of all back taxes as of the date of closing. Back taxes plus interest and penalties totaled $117,800.

When 42nd Street Development Corporation took title to the properties, it assumed all of the existing mortgages. However, these mortgages had to be paid or converted to second mortgages in order to allow a bank to grant a new mortgage for construction (construction mortgages must, by law, be *first* mortgages).

Tenants of the Row had to finance the building of stages, seating, lighting grids and equipment, dressing rooms, lobbies, box offices, and all other support spaces. They also were required to install their own internal theatrical wiring, sound systems, and partitions, and were even responsible for sealing interior walls that had been stripped to the brick when the buildings were gutted. Along the Row, on average, renovation cost $35/sq. ft.: approximately $87,500 per floor, or almost a quarter million per three-floor theatre.

PROJECT FINANCING. The renovation work, *excluding tenants' improvements*, was financed as follows:

A $485,000 mortgage, at 8.75% interest for a term of 24 years, provided by the Bowery, Emigrant, and Franklin Savings Banks.

A $250,000 grant from the Port Authority of New York and New Jersey. The Port Authority is prohibited by its charter from giving an outright grant. Therefore, in consideration of the city's relinquishing its right to the vacant property behind Theatre Row, the Port Authority gave the 42nd Street Development Corporation $250,000 and secured the land. The Port Authority also granted an easement on this property, to the 42nd Street Development Corporation, to be used as the secondary means of egress from the theatres as required by fire regulations.

A $250,000 bridge loan from the Ford Foundation until the Port Authority grant came through.

A $55,000 grant from the Robert Sterling Clark Foundation.

A $25,000 grant from the Rockefeller Brothers Fund.

A $25,000 grant from Jacqueline Onassis.

A $25,000 loan from United Broadway Church of Christ.

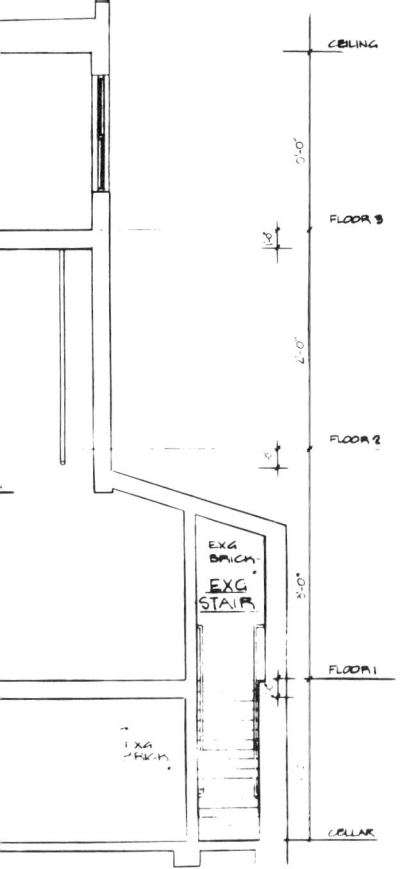
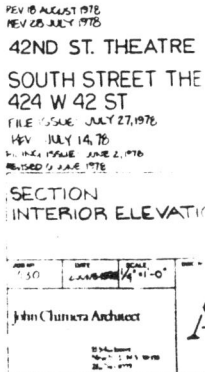

WILL IT MAKE A THEATRE?

A $22,500 loan from Frederic Papert, president of the 42nd Street Development Corporation.

The tenants' own renovations were financed largely through sweat equity. Work that required paid professional labor was scheduled as money became available. Some theatre companies performed for several years in unfinished spaces. Fundraising to meet capital costs took its toll on artistic programming, as well.

OPERATION OF PROJECT.
Temporary certificates of occupancy were granted on May 19, 1978. The theatre companies were in possession as of that date.

In addition to rent, the tenants pay an allocable share of the cost of heat, hot water, water charges, and insurance to the landlord, 42nd Street Development Corporation, which manages the project. The corporation provides boiler and structural maintenance. The tenants, however, arrange for their own superintendents.

The initial lease term for all tenants was five years with an option to renew for three years, followed by two additional renewal periods of six years each.

Rent for the initial five years was $1,000 per month for the theatre space and $500 per month for each rehearsal office floor. A rental increase for the three-year renewal period was tied to the amount needed to pay the FDIC mortgage. However, a maximum increase of 15% was allowable. Increases for each of the remaining six-year renewal periods are equal to 10% over the preceding year's rental. By 1989, theatres were paying approximately $3-$4 per sq. ft. per year.

Unfortunately, the first five-year renewal brought a rent hike higher than some theatres could afford. And renovation costs drained all programming funds from some companies. To meet payments, a few companies subleased their theatres on a show-by-show basis to generate income

> What was formerly a wasteland is now a thriving neighborhood. The theatres are lit nightly and hundreds of people flock to this well-known block.

when their own seasons were slack, seriously distorting the original Theatre Row concept.

By the early 1980s, Harlem Children's Theatre had left the Row and the Acting Company had taken over its space for offices. Black Theatre Alliance vacated as well; its neighbor, the Actors and Directors Lab, expanded into the space, using the upper floors for its school and running the Samuel Beckett Theatre below. Much later, the Lion Theatre Company disappeared, and its space was renamed the Judith Anderson Theatre.

Subsequent development—notably the Westside Airlines Terminal, a half-block-long video and recording studio—provides a commercial anchor to the block, as do restaurants and luxury housing units. Construction of additional theatres, including the Douglas Fairbanks and John Houseman, strengthens the Theatre Row concept. What was formerly a wasteland is now a thriving neighborhood. The theatres are lit nightly and hundreds of people flock to this well-known block.

In the late 1980s, the Actors and Directors Lab vacated both 410 and 412 West 42nd Street. In 1991, South Street Theatre was forced to give up its space due to the high costs of building improvements. In 1991, Playwrights Horizons leased 410, 412, 422 and 424 from the 42nd Street Development Corporation. It now houses its school in some of the upper floors, along with rehearsal studios and offices. The theatres are leased to non-profit Off- and Off-Off-Broadway theatre companies at favorable rates, again making Theatre Row a lively place where many small theatre companies can produce and create, renewing the original concept of Theatre Row.

But success threatens to alter the makeup of Theatre Row. Several private developers have advocated leveling the theatres and building high-rises. Although the new construction would include performance spaces, plans do not call for a 1-to-1 theatre replacement and those theatres built would be relegated to below-grade, less-desirable space.

The pressures of commercial development motivated Playwrights Horizons to activate a clause in its lease allowing it to meet any purchase offer on the property. (Playwrights Horizons, in 1975, unlike the other Theatre Row tenants, leased from Washington Beef Company, not the 42nd Street Development Corporation.)

In the fall of 1987, a committed board of directors energetically raised $1.4 million and Playwrights Horizons secured a $600,000 loan from Chemical Bank to meet the balance of the $2 million purchase price. With ownership, Playwrights need not be a passive player if additional development comes to the Row.

Two key lessons emerge from the Theatre Row story.

- The first is that a cooperative venture between theatres and government can revitalize neighborhoods and lead to a thriving theatre district.

- The second is more cautionary. If theatres are to continue to pioneer and rehabilitate undesirable neighborhoods, they must also find ways to insure their own survival in those upgraded gentrified neighborhoods—a problem that needs to be addressed *before* development begins.

The tenants of Theatre Row and the spaces they occupy are as follows:

Address	Space	*Original Tenants (fall, 1978)*	*Current Tenants*
410	5 floors, including theatre	Black Theatre Alliance, Inc.	Samuel Beckett Theatre and Playwrights Horizons Theatre School
412	5 floors, including theatre	Actors and Directors Lab and Harold Clurman Theatre	Playwrights Horizons Theatre School and Harold Clurman Theatre
414	ground floor	La Rousse (restaurant) and residential units	Josephine's (restaurant)
420	basement, 1st & 2nd floors, including theatre	INTAR	INTAR
420	3rd floor	The Acting Company	The Acting Company
420	4th & 5th floors	Harlem Children's Theatre	The Acting Company
422	2 floors, including theatre	Lion Theatre Company	Judith Anderson Theatre
424	3 floors, including theatre	South Street Theatre (Theatre Research, Inc.)	Theatre Row Theatre

foundation's guidelines and previous grants. While some may list capital funding as a top priority, their actual gifts to theatres may be minimal. Others, which appear in print to be uninterested in funding arts or buildings, have proven surprise contributors to both. The Kresge Foundation is notable for being consistently identified with capital funding. It supports well-established, accredited institutions and requires matching funds to honor its grants. Kresge generally wants to be the "last dollar," providing completion funds for projects that are well on their way. Recipients of Kresge grants for renovation include New York City's Joyce Theatre; Atlanta's Center for Puppetry Arts; San Francisco's Fort Mason Center; Fort Wayne, Indiana's Performing Arts Center; and the Milwaukee Repertory Theater.

Two books that might be useful in locating other foundation funding are: *The Directory of Building and Equipment Grants* and *The Capital Campaign Resource Guide*. (See Publications of Interest.)

For more thorough research, The Foundation Center—headquartered in New York and Washington, DC, with affiliated libraries around the country—offers the use of hundreds of books and periodicals about foundations. For more information about The Foundation Center, see the Resource Directory.

LOANS

Theatres may have difficulty proving to banks that they are creditworthy, although a theatre that owns its space may have more success in securing a loan because the space can serve as collateral. It's generally unwise to rely heavily on financing a project through loans: it's difficult to stir up enthusiasm for financial support to retire long-term debt.

INDIVIDUALS

Individuals represent the greatest potential for capital support. Special "naming" opportunities—

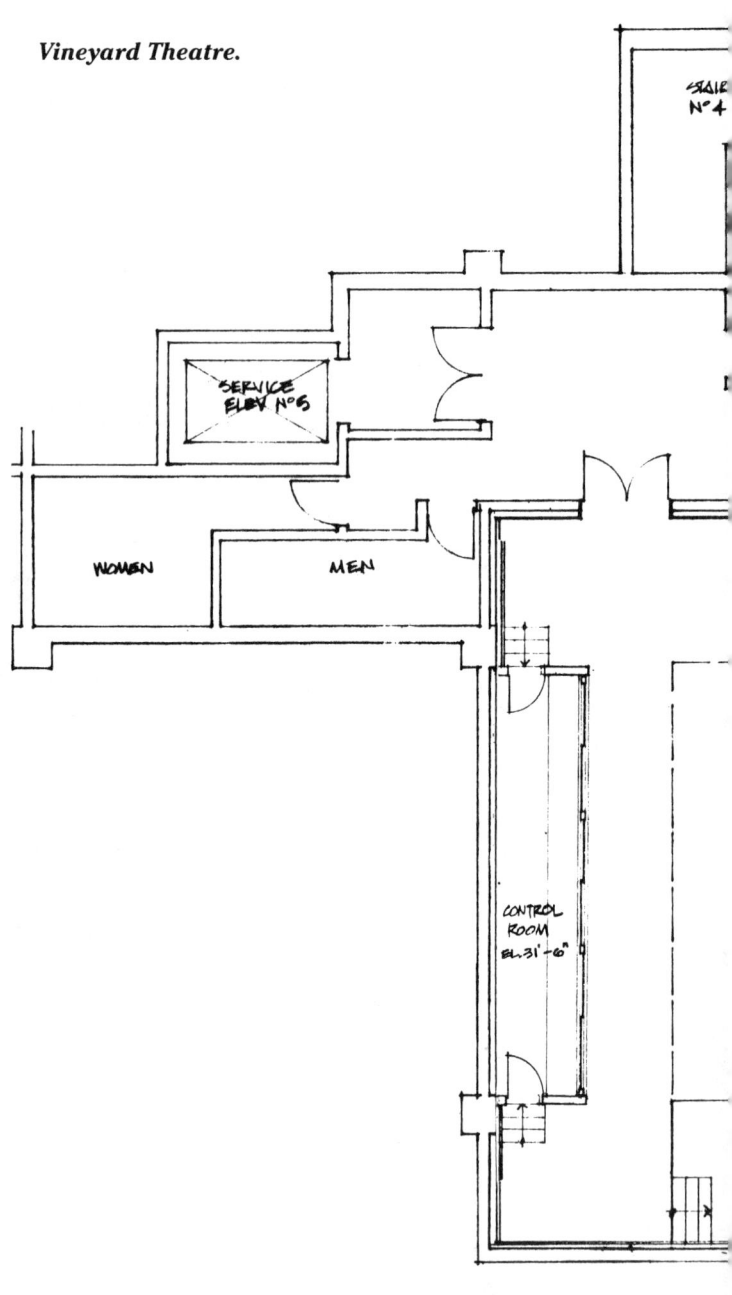

Vineyard Theatre.

Resources for Making it Happen

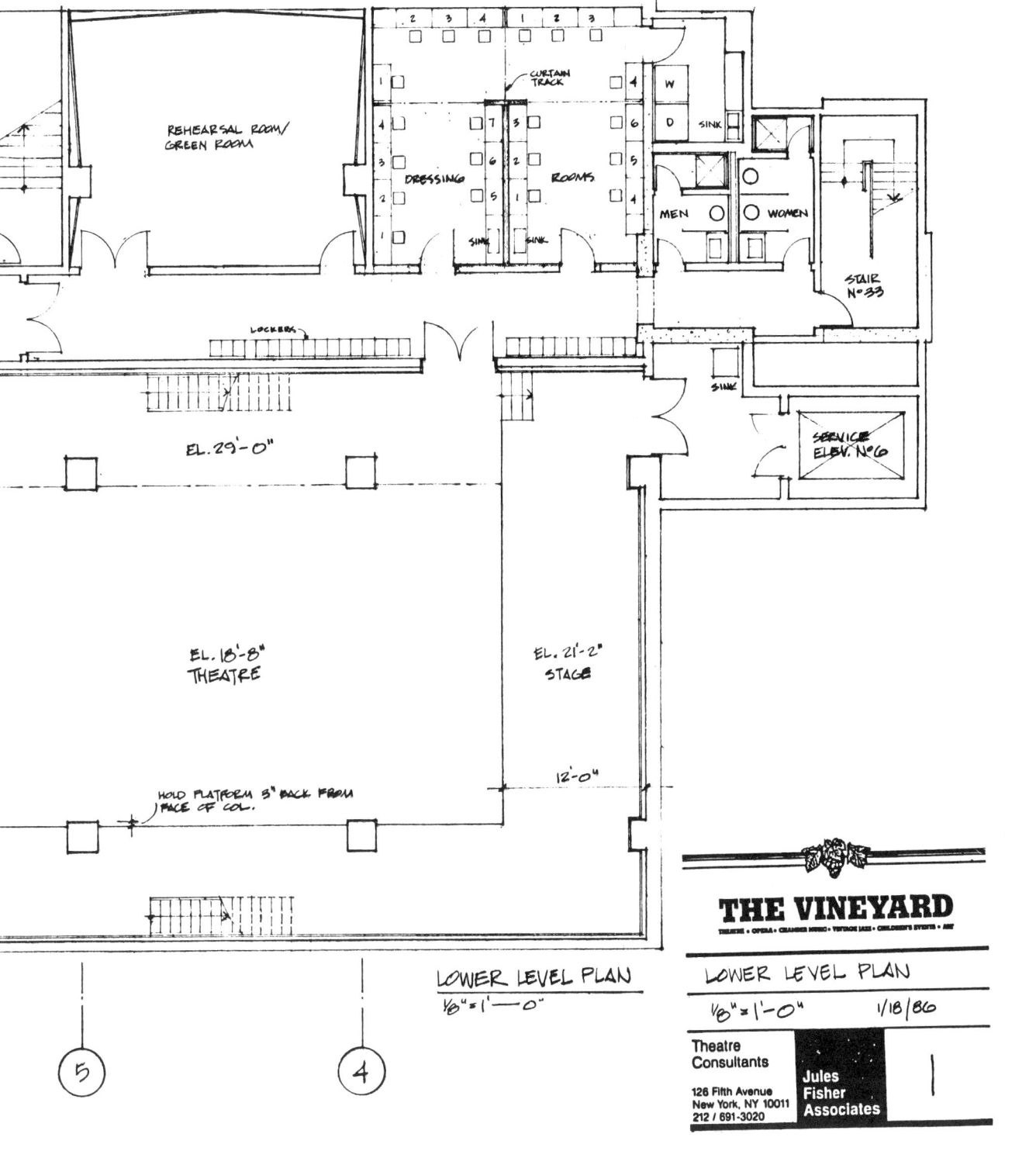

seats, bricks, lobby, the entire theatre—can often help leverage additional support from donors already committed to a company. Gifts "in memory of" also help attract contributors. Smaller gifts can be solicited from single-ticket buyers—through playbills, direct mail, and telephone solicitations.

ORGANIZING THE CAMPAIGN

The initial commitment for a capital campaign *must* come from the board of directors. A traditional campaign requires a two-to-five-year period. For major campaigns, consider retaining a consultant who can conduct a feasibility study and help organize an overall marketing plan.

A capital campaign committee, selected members of your board, or a targeted group of people with good business connections should be formed in the initial stages of the campaign. Some consultants recommend you have at least one-fourth of the money in place before making a public announcement about your efforts. Then you won't seem like just another company with a pipe dream but, rather, like a theatre well on its way to reaching its goal.

Every campaign is different—in terms of the mix of public and private support and in terms of how the effort is organized. The following examples suggest ways financing can be put together and point to some of the problems you may encounter.

SECOND STAGE. This New York City company launched a traditional campaign, raising $500,000 over two years to build its 108-seat theatre. The capital campaign committee formed within the board was pivotal. Six star-studded benefits raised about one-third of the money. Seat-naming and recognition plaques were part of the campaign, and a special appeal was made to Upper West Side residents—the theatre's major audience. Members of the board loaned the remaining funds, then forgave the loan at the end of the year.

THE VINEYARD THEATRE. The Vineyard got wind of a new development being planned by developer William Zeckendorf and persuaded him to include a theatre in this residential/commercial complex at Union Square. The theatre company, in turn, testified at community board meetings on behalf of the project—testimony that may have helped reduce the neighborhood resistance to the addition of a new high-rise.

The Vineyard persuaded Zeckendorf to deed, rather than lease, the space so the company could use it as collateral to mount an effective capital campaign. By April 1988, nearly eight years after the initial idea was born, the Vineyard had raised approximately $1.5 million towards its $2.5 million campaign. $919,550 of this was represented by in-kind support, including the space itself—valued at $850,000—and donated construction services. Over $500,000 came from individuals and $81,500 from corporations—mostly companies in the neighborhood. In 1989 the company received a $100,000 Challenge Grant from the NEA, half of it earmarked toward creating a capital reserve. Executive director Barbara Zinn Krieger's astuteness and family background in the construction business was a plus in pulling the whole deal off.

SERVICE ORGANIZATIONS

There are a number of national service organizations that may be particularly helpful in solving a small, nonprofit theatre group's space and renovation problems. For a listing of these groups, see the Resource Directory.

PART THREE

DESIGN AND PLANNING STRATEGIES

Introduction

This section surveys design possibilities, suggesting strategies for stage space, audience spaces, and support spaces, along with ways to save money and get the most for the least in services and materials. It shows how to "stretch" space when square footage is at a premium. Design ideas included here have little relevance to planning large, conventional theatres; they are targeted to small, nontraditional theatre spaces.

Uniqueness of design is one of the most attractive qualities of a small theatre. The nontraditional environment and ambiance draw an audience; the uniqueness of the space becomes a vivid and graphic expression of the company's esthetic.

Design of the space components of any theatre should follow a coherent program. Commence by considering the stage space, proceed to the design of the audience space in its relationship to the stage, then move to planning the necessary support spaces.

A successful theatre design must give equal attention to these three basic areas. No theatre that shortchanges stage, audience or support spaces can function with maximum efficiency. Special emphasis in this section is placed on rehearsal rooms and shops—the unseen work areas where theatre magic is fabricated. These are too often considered unimportant by managers, boards, and architects, especially when capital funding falls short of projected goals.

THE THEATRE CONSULTANT AND THE ARCHITECT

The right architect and theatre consultant will make design, planning, and renovation a much easier, less painful process. Their knowledge, experience, and imagination should add a substantial creative contribution. However, some small groups feel they can't afford specialists or are uncertain how to make the best use of such expertise. Learning what to expect from an architect or theatre consultant will help you make informed decisions about how to work with these professionals.

Design and Planning Strategies: Introduction

An architect together with the theatre consultant will design the space; he or she will coordinate all the work of consultants and contractors, and be responsible for getting bids and for holding to estimated costs, as well as for quality of construction. An architect's expertise also will be needed to handle zoning variance procedures and to present drawings to the community board. A licensed architect's or contractor's stamp and signature will be necessary when filing plans with the buildings department.

Only a handful of architects have had extensive experience in designing theatres; most have not. Therefore, a theatre consultant can be invaluable in interpreting your wish list for the architect. The theatre consultant can provide expertise in planning the stage and seating layout, stage sound and lighting systems, backstage and support spaces like shops, rehearsal spaces, and dressing rooms. The theatre consultant can also advise on specialized theatre equipment and obtain cost estimates.

The working dynamics of the architect/consultant/client collaboration will be unique since creating a theatre is a very personal exercise. In the past, it was general practice for the consultant to be a subcontractor to the architect. Today, the consultant is under contract directly to the client and hired in the initial stage of the project. In the theatre, form must follow function; therefore, it is advisable for the theatre consultant working in tandem with the architect to have first crack at schematically laying out the stage, seating, and ancillary spaces.

The following are some suggestions for making the best use of outside expertise in planning and carrying out your renovation:

- Make certain consultants' ideas are compatible with your concept.
- Check references of architects and consultants with other theatres that have used their services.
- Get these specialists in on the ground floor of the planning process.
- Seek their expert evaluation of any building you are seriously considering, with the architect paying particular attention to the

problem areas outlined in chapter 5. Have the theatre consultant focus on the space's potential as a theatre and the suitability to the type of productions you plan to mount.

- Enlist the help of the architect and consultant in preparing the cost estimate for the renovation.
- Let the architect advise on details of the lease, but be sure to have a real estate lawyer handle all of the lease negotiations. An architect should draw up preliminary drawings for submission to the buildings department. Try to get feedback from the buildings department before drafting final plans.
- Review energy efficiency requirements with the theatre consultant and architect. Consider engaging the services of an energy auditor.
- A theatre generalist sympathetic to your goals is your best consultant. If specialists are needed, the consultant can provide referrals.
- Recruit an architect and a consultant for your board of directors, and hope they will offer pro bono services.
- Try to obtain inexpensive architectural advice and assistance if you can't secure pro bono services; nonprofit architecture firms may offer reduced rates. Even less expensive are students and apprentice architects. But be wary; you often get what you pay (or don't pay) for.
- When hiring consultants, arrange for a flat fee without regard to hours. If consultants are engaged before the space has been selected and work commences, contract these services on an hourly rate, and arrange to make these payments applicable to the overall project fee, if possible.

A final note: one person should be given the authority and responsibility to deal with the architect and consultant. It should not be done by committee.

Whether you plan your theatre with or without the assistance of a consultant or architect, the ideas presented here are meant to trigger your imagination. This section does not present a blueprint for your space, instead, it attempts to present a wide range of possibilities.

8
THE STAGE SPACE

The first line to establish in any theatre is a "magic line"—a real or imaginary demarcation that joins the actors to the audience or, in some productions or theatres, intentionally separates and alienates them. All other lines will follow naturally, radiating from this first line. If this is the right line, it will be the start of a successful building. All the other lines separating and joining the stage and audience spaces and the support spaces, down to the location of the last dressing room mirror, are probably going to be right.

In small theatres, flexibility in stage size can be obtained cheaply because muscle power rather than machine power makes the space changes. This is the reverse of conventional thinking about flexibility in larger theatres where sophisticated equipment is employed to change configurations. As the small theatre company grows in size, operating budget, and scope of artistic programming, there will come a time when this concept of cheap flexibility may no longer be feasible.

The stage space, regardless of size or shape, has these basic components to consider: the floor, the walls, the means of access, and the overhead and rigging.

STAGE FLOOR

Performing directly on the existing floor of the building would seem an inexpensive and flexible way to create a stage, but it is seldom, if ever, feasible. In most old buildings, even if the floor is

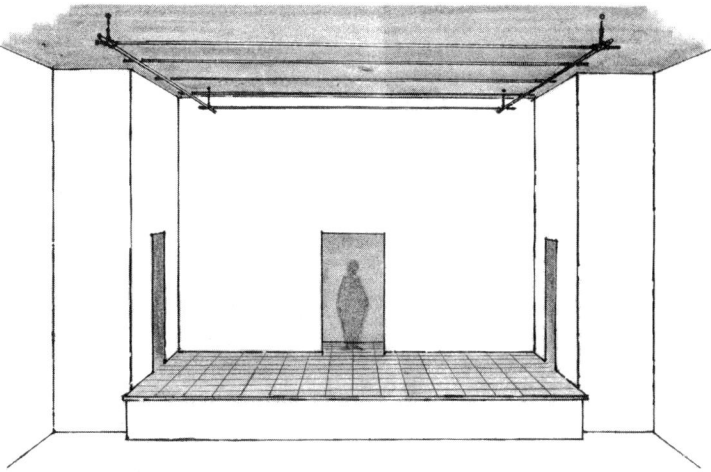

The Stage Space. Floor, overhead and rigging, walls and access.

WILL IT MAKE A THEATRE?

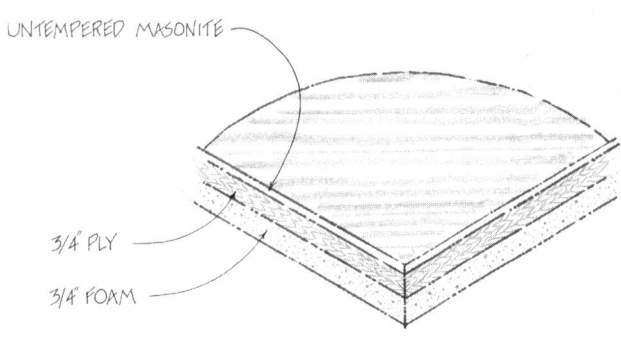

AMAS portable floor.

made of wood, it will be too rough, uneven, and/or inflexible. Floors of concrete, marble, or steel are too hard, too dangerous and unacceptable to Actors' Equity. So it is both desirable and necessary to lay an acceptable stage deck over the existing floor of the building.

Temporary and Portable Solutions

The AMAS Repertory Theatre in New York developed an inexpensive portable floor: a 3/4" foam base with 3/4" plywood on top, finished with an untempered Masonite surface. It is constructed

Temporary outdoor floor.

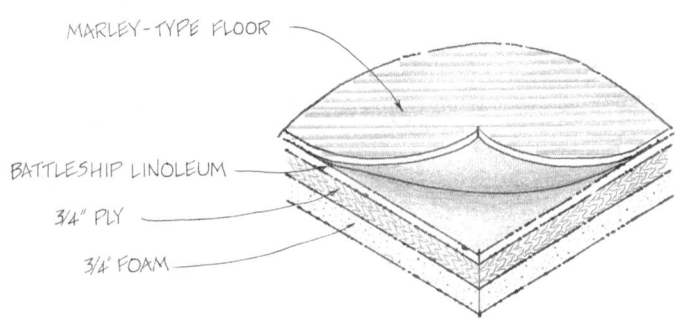

in 4' x 8" sections with the Masonite overlapping each plywood section by half to prevent seams from rising in the event the wood warps.

A variant on this floor was developed as a temporary outdoor dance floor: the base of 3/4" foam was covered, first with used battleship linoleum, and then with a top layer of Marley-type floor.

Both of these decks were laid directly over existing concrete floors. They were inexpensive, easy to make, resilient, and portable, but neither would be acceptable as a permanent floor.

TEMPORARY RAISED STAGE FLOORS. A raised stage clearly provides improved sightlines. If a simple modular platform system is devised, almost total flexibility in size, configuration and placement within the space can be achieved. Start with a simple system of 4' x 8' sections of 3/4"

Temporary raised platform.

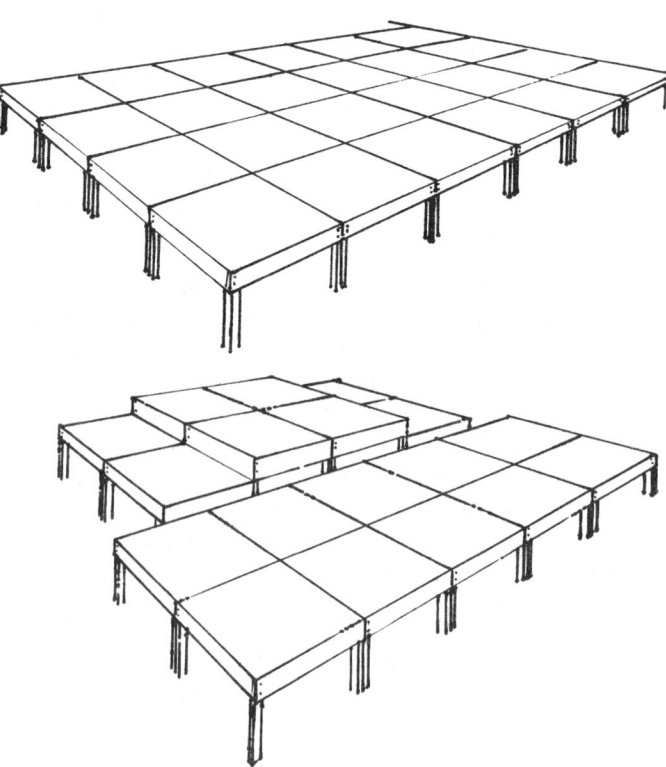

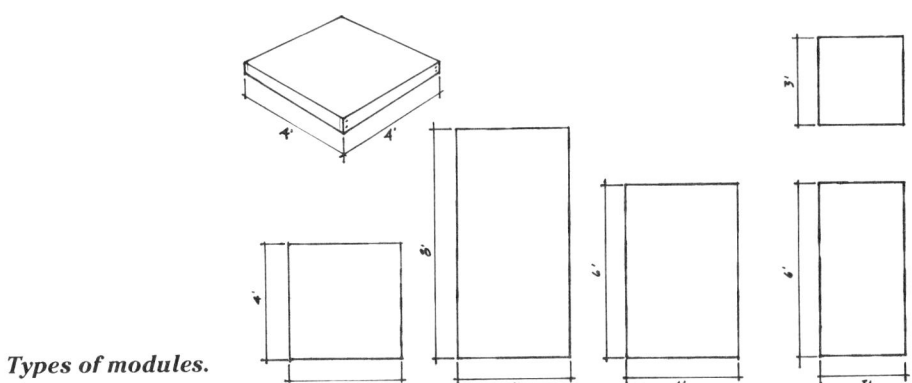

Types of modules.

Stages with hexagonal modules.

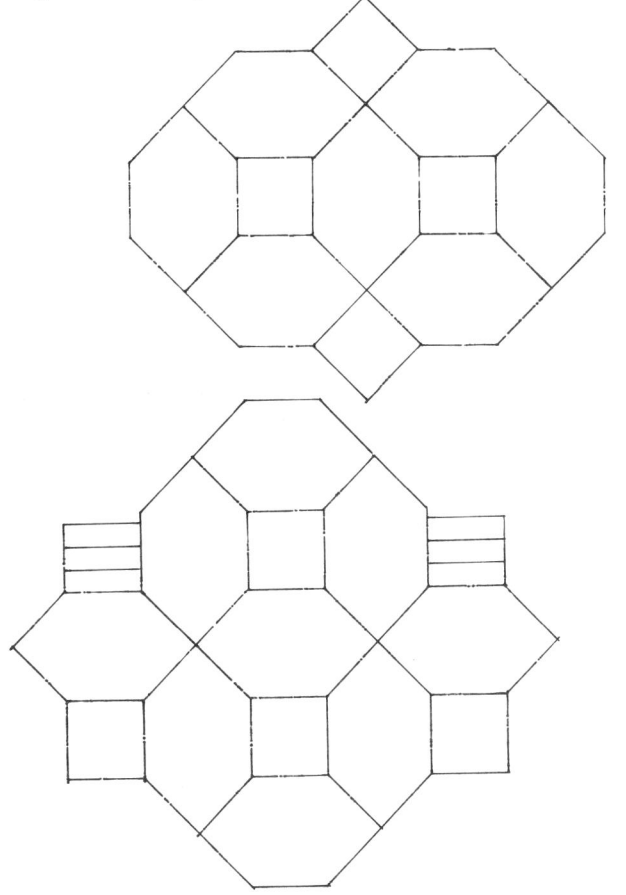

plywood platform tops "legged up" on 1" x 6" stock, and clamped or bolted together. A linoleum or Marley-type floor (particle board or Homosote are cheap, but not durable) can be laid over the platform for a better surface. Fire-retardant wood and other materials should be used throughout.

Vary the module to suit your space and design needs: 4' x 4', 3' x 6', 4' x 6'.

Special hexagonal and triangular units, in addition to squares and rectangles, can create even more varied, flexible, and dynamic playing areas.

Permanent Floors

A permanent stage deck should never be laid directly on concrete; instead, it should be laid on wooden sleepers. These sleepers should be 1" x 3" or heavier timbers crisscrossed on 16" centers and attached to the wood floor or concrete slab. Crisscrossing two layers of 3/4" plywood creates the least expensive and best floor. Hardply is preferable for the top layer. Marley-type floor, 1/4" Masonite, or rolled linoleum laid over the plywood also can make a good surface. Clean (sterilized) sand, fiberglass insulation, carpet padding, or Homosote between sleepers will help deaden noise.

Floor section.

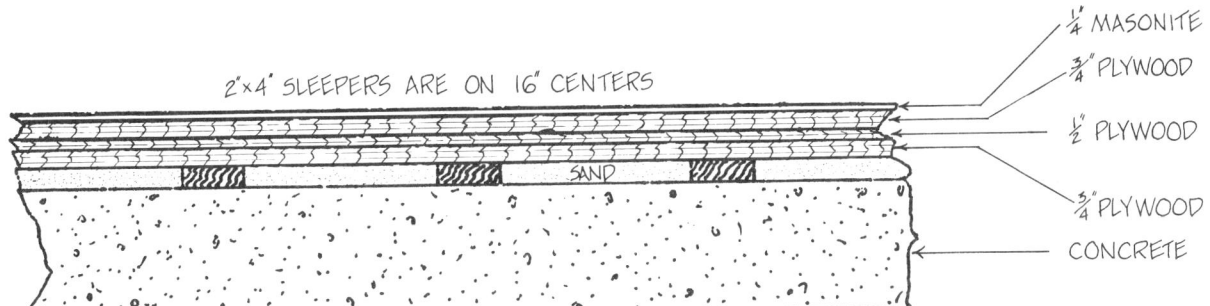

Stage floors must withstand heavy abuse and frequent repainting. They should be thought of as expendable, not sacred, and should be replaced whenever wear and tear require.

Resilience is an important factor, especially if the stage floor is used for dancing. Equity rules—which prohibit any dancing on marble or concrete floors in either rehearsal or performance, or on wood or any other substance laid directly over concrete—state: "An air space of at least 1-5/8 inches shall be provided between concrete, marble or similar surface." Equity also issues guidelines for constructing an approved dance or "sprung" floor. This very resilient floor is not practical, however, for theatre production. It has too much spring for the actor and could crack or give way under the weight of heavy stage scenery. Peter Brook made sand and earth floors fashionable. It is not known how actors feel about such "floors."

PERMANENT RAISED STAGES. Permanent stage floors, such as an end stage or a proscenium

Permanent raised stage.

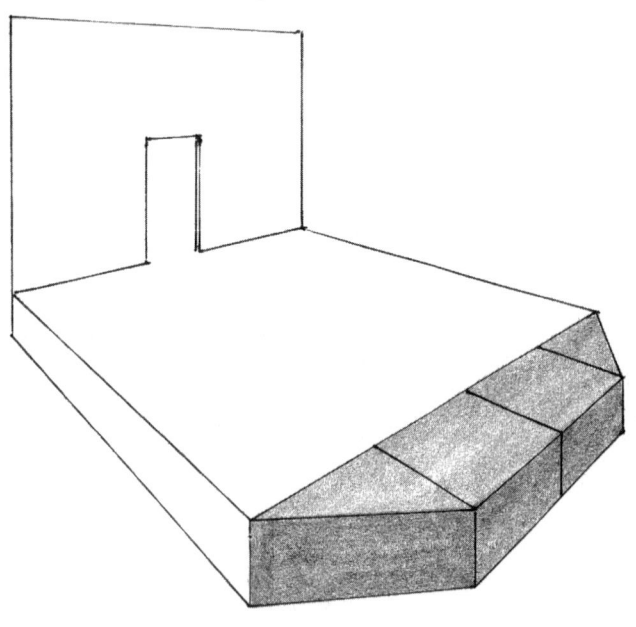

Floor padding.

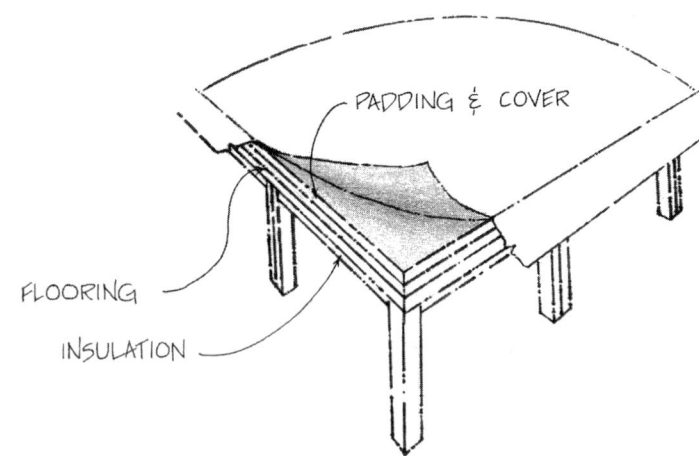

stage, require stronger structural support—steel rather than wood might be considered.

With a permanent stage, flexibility of shape can be achieved by removing modular sections and/or adding specially shaped pieces at the leading edge.

Reverberation—that exasperating, hollow thud from beneath the platform—can be reduced by lining the underside of platforms with ozite underpad, fiberglass insulation, or Homosote. Glue this insulation directly to the underside of the platform top before assembly—prior to attaching the top to the frame. In addition, the frame itself can be wrapped in foam rubber, fiberglass, or even covered in Homosote. For further noise suppression, Ozite, rubber, or neoprene padding cut to size can be applied to the bottom of each platform leg.

Once the permanent stage frame is in place, cover two crisscrossed layers of 3/4" plywood with Masonite, Marley-type floor, or rolled linoleum. Homosote or rug padding covered with painted canvas or carpet can, of course, be used on top of platforms to reduce surface noise. To face the sides of the platform, use Masonite, 1/4" plywood, velour, duvetyne, or a material that enhances the current stage setting.

New York City's old code requires all stage floors to have a live load value of 100 pounds per

Side masking running up and down stage is the most space efficient.
However, side masking running on and off stage, though it requires greater wing space, provides better access and better lighting positions. Cross-over space behind the setting should be approximately 3' minimum. Admittedly, it is often less. Some theatres solve the cross-over problem by placing cross-overs behind the stage house, through the basement, or above the stage.

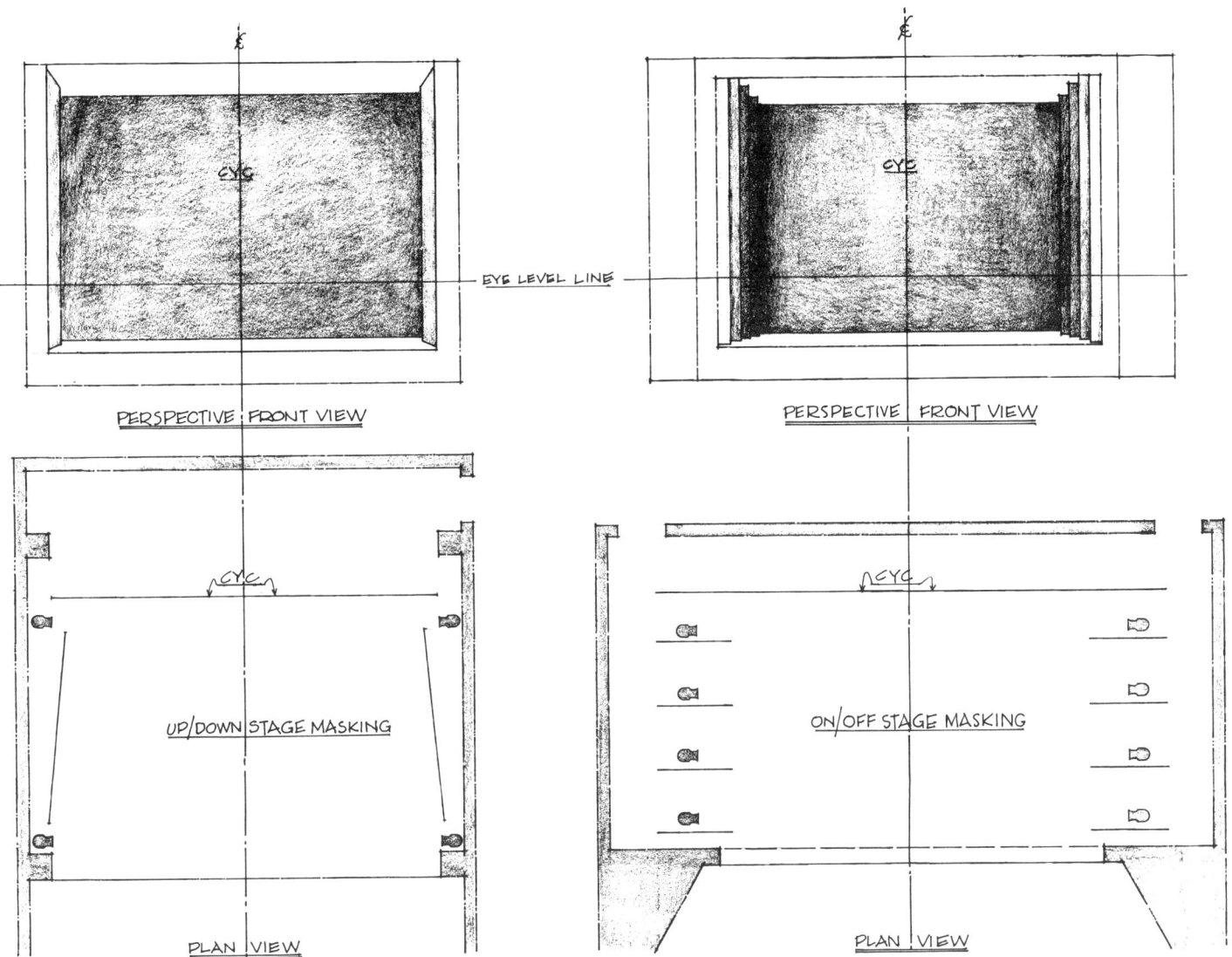

square foot; the new code requires 150 pounds per square foot. (See chapter 19 for live load requirements in other city codes.)

Although a technical director or stage carpenter can build this, it's probably worth the expense to have a general contractor construct the permanent deck. Have the work bid as part of the overall contract.

STAGE WALLS

It is usually preferable for stage walls to be "negative space." They should remain neutral and "unseen" until there is an artistic reason for using them. For this reason, stage walls are often painted matte black. However, gray or even white can create a neutral or negative background, if properly handled. Bare brick walls also provide neutrality, a design strategy adopted by many small theatre companies that feel exposed structural brick walls provide the right informal environment for their productions.

Often, the stage walls will be the exterior walls of the building. If not, the wall between stage and backstage support areas must form a sound barrier. Brick, cinderblock, or soundproof materials should be used. If the wall is of Sheetrock, put two layers of 5/8" Sheetrock on each side and fill the space between studs with fiberglass insulation to achieve better soundproofing. Most codes will require this wall to have a 2-hour fire rating.

WILL IT MAKE A THEATRE?

Establish a corridor or sound and light barrier between the stage and the backstage and support spaces. Actual doors are often not practical for small stages; open exits are frequently best. Though hanging curtains or backdrops can reduce light and noise transmission from off-stage, it may be necessary to create a sound/light lock behind these exits

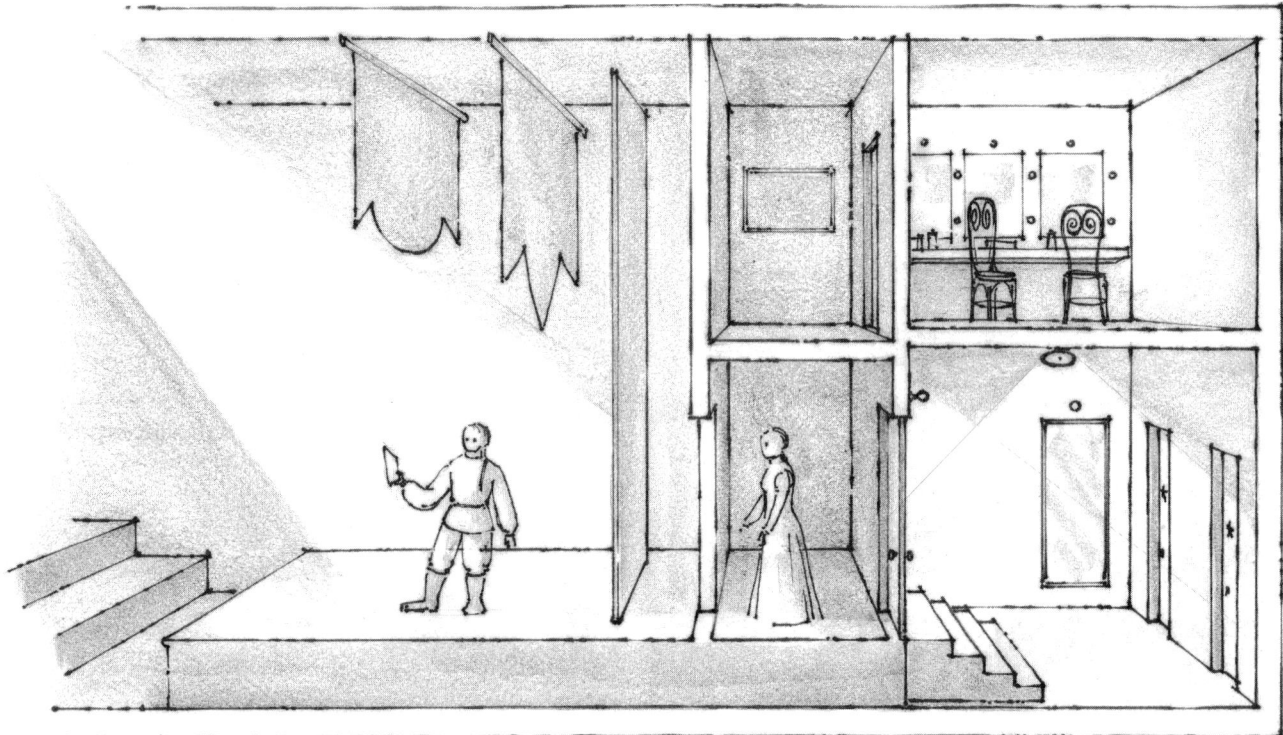

STAGE SIZE

The minimum stage sizes listed in chapter 2 are just that—absolute, bare-bones minimums. It is difficult to conceive of a stage that is too large—except, perhaps, the Lincoln Center's Vivian Beaumont Theater, which was initially planned to accommodate rotating repertory but became a very expensive staff parking lot for a while, until new management found ways to use the space more creatively.

Except in arena configurations, stage space must be provided for scenery, stage masking, machinery, lighting positions, and cross-overs, in addition to storage for show props and live scenery.

If either side wall of the stage must accommodate a counterweight or hemp and sandbag system to handle flown scenery, it will require approximately 2'6" of depth plus space for the operator—a minimum of 5' to 6' of additional wing space.

Substituting a motor-driven winch system above or behind the stage can solve this space problem, but it is expensive.

ACCESS TO THE STAGE

Building codes stipulate the number of exits required from the stage. In New York City, for example, the code requires at least two means of egress from the stage that are "remote from each other." This safety regulation applies to actors' access to the stage and it has nothing to do with the number of exits a set may require; nor does it have much relationship to the number of exits necessary to make the stage functional. It should be noted, however, that many small end stages without proscenium or curtain have satisfied the building department with one exit from the stage.

In the thrust or arena configuration, where audience and stage share the same volume of space

The Stage Space

A rolling scaffold, genie tower, or A-frame ladder is useful for grids of 30' or less.

and the stage is not enclosed, access to stage is usually not a problem.

To function well, both proscenium and end-stage theatres need a passage giving access to the stage from front-of-house without going through the auditorium. (This could be through the basement.) In a proscenium theatre, there also should be a door leading directly from the auditorium to the stage. A second door at this location will provide a better sound and light lock. In fact all doors leading to the stage should operate without noise and function as light and sound barriers. Easy access to the stage from catwalks and other front-of-house lighting positions as well as from the control booth is also desirable.

In addition to the doors for personnel, there should be an access door to the stage large enough to handle scenic pieces. Its size will vary greatly with the size and type of stage and scenery used.

OVERHEAD AND RIGGING

A good rule of thumb for any stage house over 30' in height is to install a counterweight or motorized winch rigging system, no matter how simple it may be. If your stage house is less than 30' high (usually the case in converted spaces), hanging scenery and lighting equipment can be handled from the floor with reasonable efficiency and safety. (A 20' A-frame ladder with full extension reaches 33' high. Large pneumatic "genie towers" rise to great heights; but the most practical for small stage use is the model that extends to 29', allowing a maximum working height of 36'. Scaffolds can go to great heights, but their size and instability on the floor make them impractical for small stage use.) Remember, too, that A-frame ladders, genie towers, and scaffolds require a level floor—no steeply raked stages, steps, or narrow platforms, please. This means you should do rigging and hang electrics before scenery load-in whenever possible.

FIXED GRID SYSTEM. When using a fixed pipe grid system, plan it to cover a large enough area of the ceiling for all overhead lighting positions. It may be advantageous to design a grid for the entire ceiling if the space is planned as a two-, three-, or four-sided arena, or as a flexible theatre space. In any configuration, the grid size should be larger than the playing area to provide both good overhead lighting angles and positions for front lighting the actor's face.

Front-lighting an actor or area is generally accomplished by using a minimum of two instruments, one from either side at approximately 45 degrees; four instruments, however, will allow two different set-ups of color to light each area.

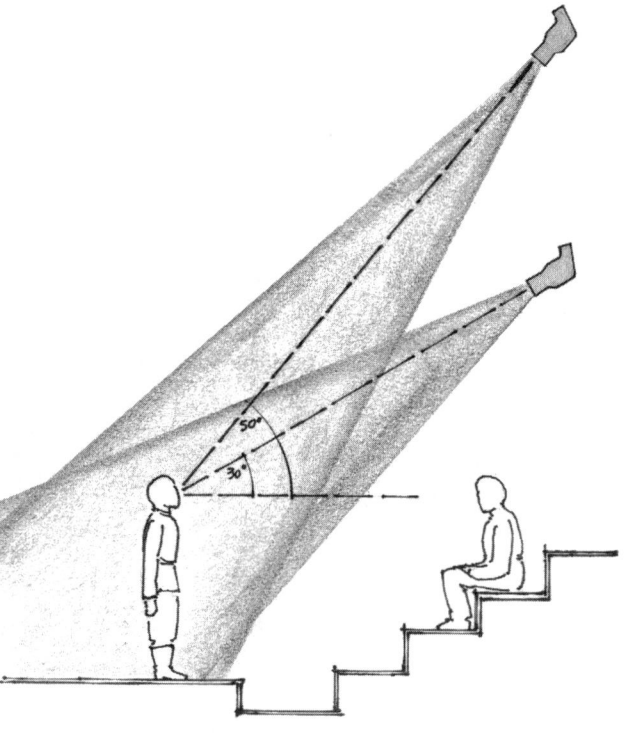

A vertical angle of 45 degrees is the universally accepted ideal angle for front light on the actor. Often this is not possible to achieve in the converted, nontraditional space; however, try to maintain angles between 30 degrees and 50 degrees.

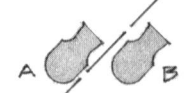
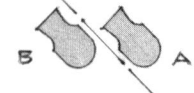

Design the grid so that side, back, and down lighting positions are provided. When planning the grid, keep in mind its relationship to the seats. For example, in an open stage configuration, lighting instruments must be hung so as not to shine into the eyes of the audience or to illuminate their bodies.

A combination of a steeper angle lighting position (instrument A) with raised seating minimizes spill in front rows. Note: Instrument B lights up entire front row, putting light directly in the audience's eyes.

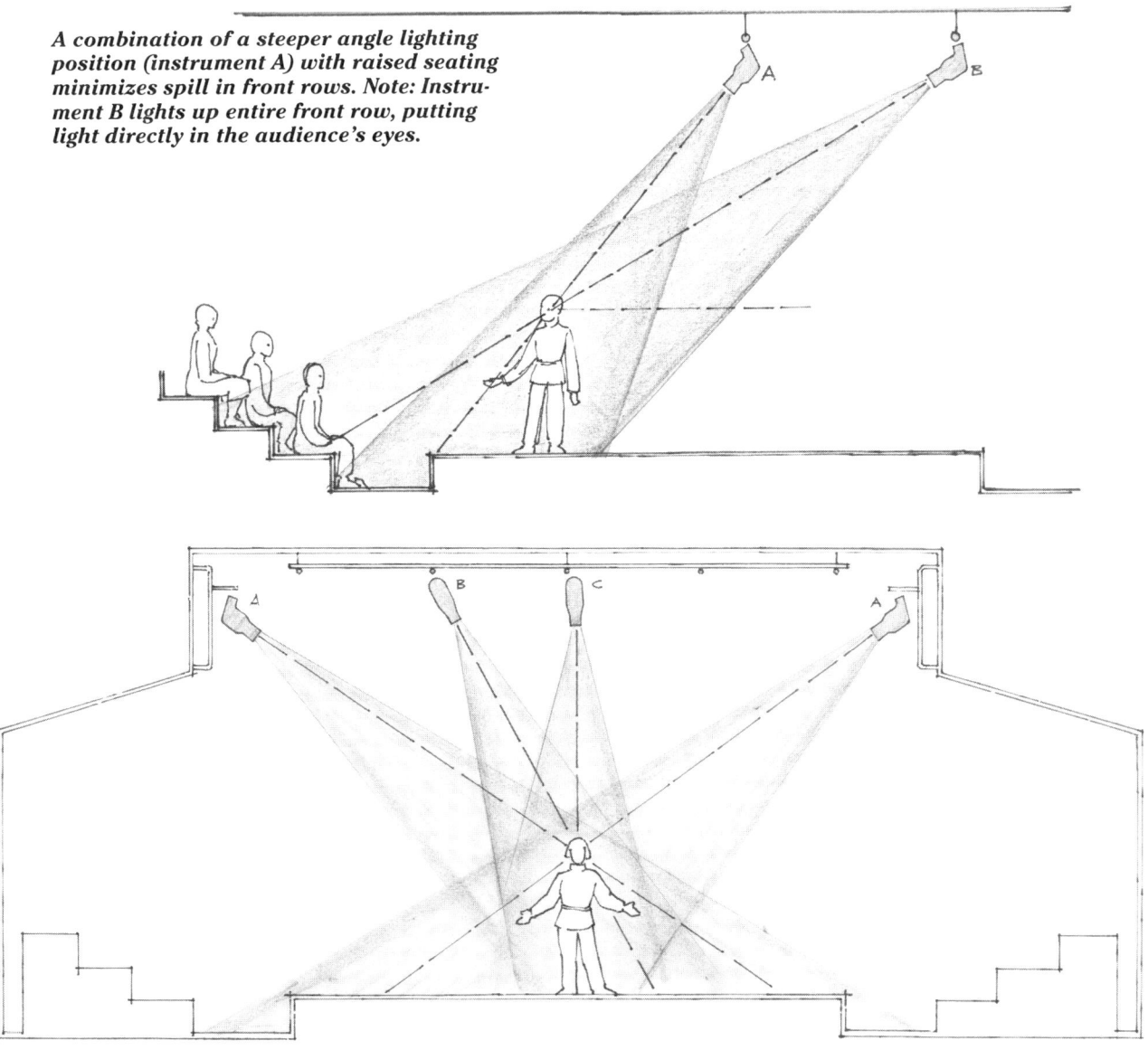

(A) Side, (B) Back, (C) Down lighting positions.

The layout of the grid may form a regular pattern using a uniform module, or it may vary according to the specific requirements of the space. A cross pattern of pipe, spaced approximately 4' x 4', is standard for a normal ceiling height and an average stage size; 3' x 3' will work for a small, low-ceilinged space.

Use standard 1-1/2" schedule 40 pipe for easy mounting of instruments. Distribute cable and outlets in raceways or in neatly tied bundles of cable with outlets.

If the ceiling height allows, suspend the grid 18" or more below the ceiling to permit easy mounting as well as overhanging for lighting instruments. Suspend the pipes from the ceiling on steel cable or pipe. If using cable, pipe stiffeners can be added to prevent pipes from twisting.

Clamping the pipe intersections together with Rotolok clamps or Cheeseboro adjustable swivel clamps will also provide stability and prevent twisting. Rotoloks, U-bolts, or C-clamps also can be used to secure additional, temporary lengths of pipe to

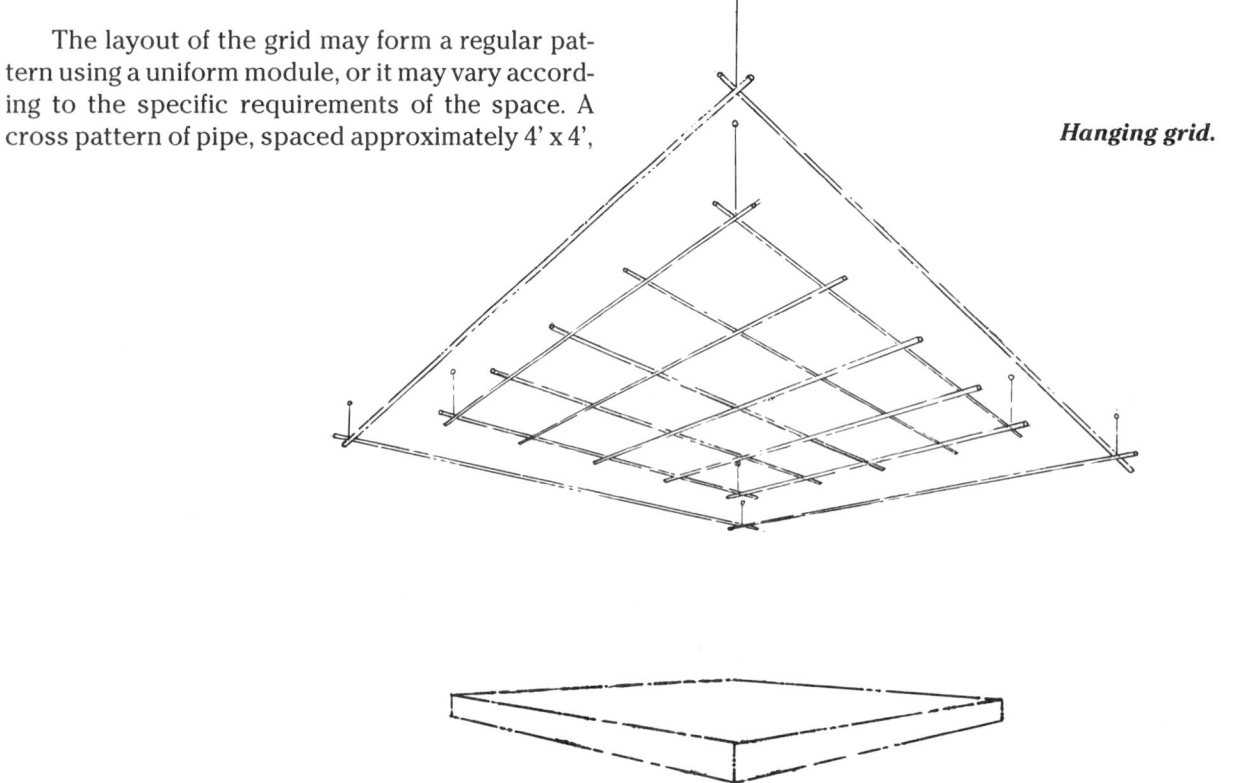

Hanging grid.

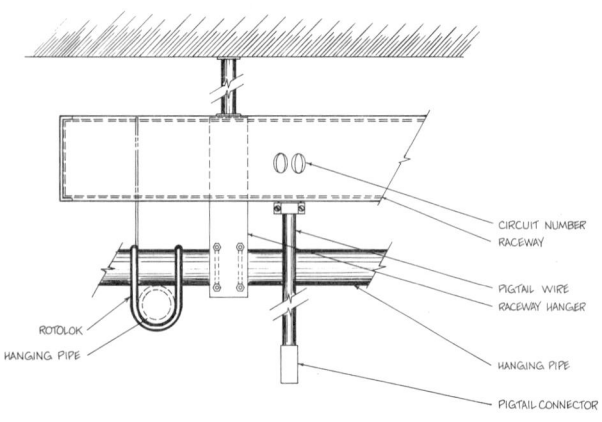

Detail for a permanent raceway system.

the grid system to handle special equipment for a specific production.

Remember, the weight of the grid will put additional stress on the ceiling; lighting instruments, cable, and scenery pieces will add more weight. A structural engineer can ascertain whether the ceiling will support this additional weight, and, if necessary, advise an alternate method of suspension or reinforcing the roof.

PARALLEL SYSTEM OF PIPES. If the theatre configuration is permanent and one directional, like an end stage, use a permanent system of individual pipes hung parallel to the leading edge of the playing area. Clamp on shorter intersecting pipes for special hanging positions. Vary spacing between pipes to provide for more pipes over the stage or playing area. (See Studio Theatre Profile, p. 144.)

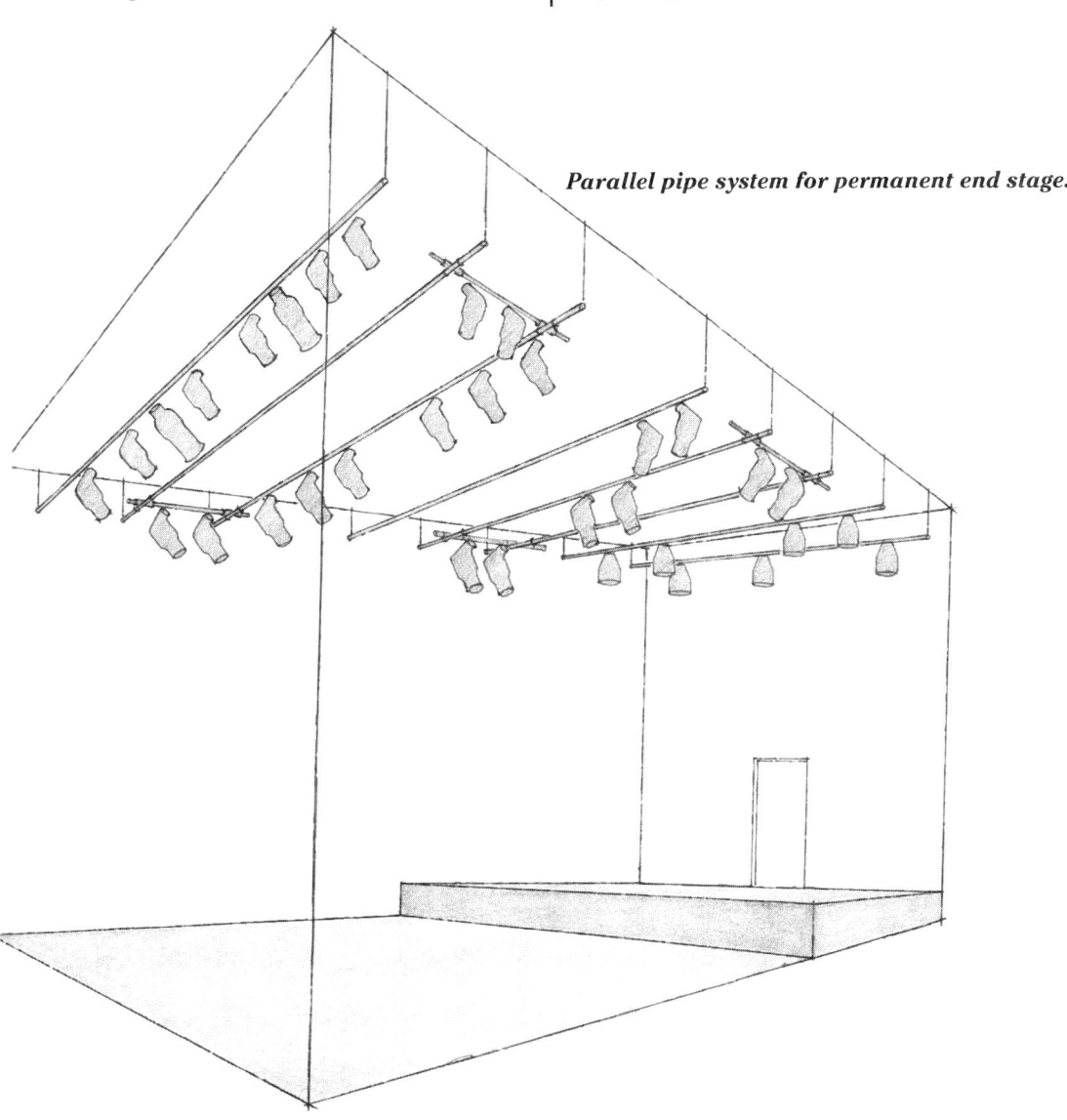

Parallel pipe system for permanent end stage.

WILL IT MAKE A THEATRE?

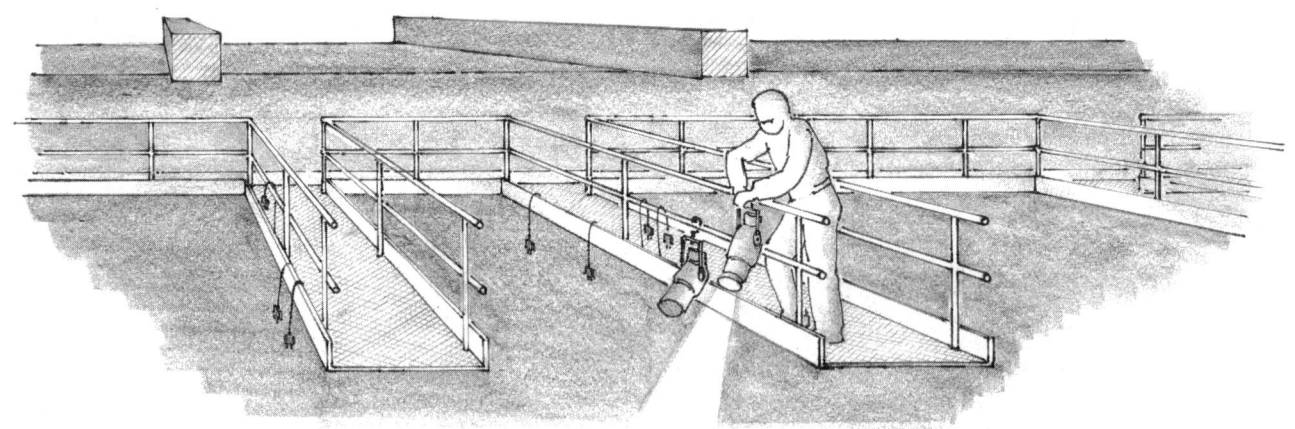

A system of catwalks.

A proscenium stage without a gridiron or fly loft can utilize the same type of parallel pipe system over the stage and auditorium.

TENSION-WIRE GRID. The tension-wire grid consists of a substructure grid of steel members supporting a walkable floor surface composed of woven aircraft cable arranged on approximately 2" centers. This mesh becomes a work surface for technicians. Stage lighting instruments can be positioned anywhere above the mesh and focused through it without appreciable light loss or distortion. Most often the tension-wire grid is located directly above the stage, although it could extend over the audience, as well. This system is expensive, but it could pay for itself through time and labor savings during production change-over periods. Obviously, this system requires sufficient height to allow headroom clearance for the technicians working on the grid. The tension grid would usually be 20' to 30' above the stage floor.

CATWALKS. Catwalks provide another system for easy mounting and focusing of stage lights and are preferable to a pipe grid accessed from the stage floor. In designing catwalks, allow sufficient headroom above the catwalk for a person to stand upright—7' is desirable. Also provide catwalks with nonskid floors. The catwalks must have rails; plan to make them of standard 1-1/2" schedule 40 pipe so they can serve as hanging positions for lights. Raceways mounted overhead, with outlets distributed as needed along the catwalks, are safe and easy to use. Neatly bundled cables afford a cheaper, portable solution. Consider the catwalk as a possible followspot or projector position.

Easy access from catwalks to the control booth, as well as to the stage, can save time and labor when focusing and lighting a production.

To make them as unobtrusive as possible, paint the catwalks a flat, dark color—preferably black. Or, if you prefer, make the catwalks a design feature of your theatre, painting them a bold color to contrast with the theatre ceiling.

Rigging Systems for Flown Scenery

For a proscenium stage with a loft high enough to fly scenery and lighting, a rigging system must be part of the design. An increasing number of companies are building or converting spaces that allow for traditional fly lofts, although they remain the exception for most small theatres. The rigging

The Stage Space

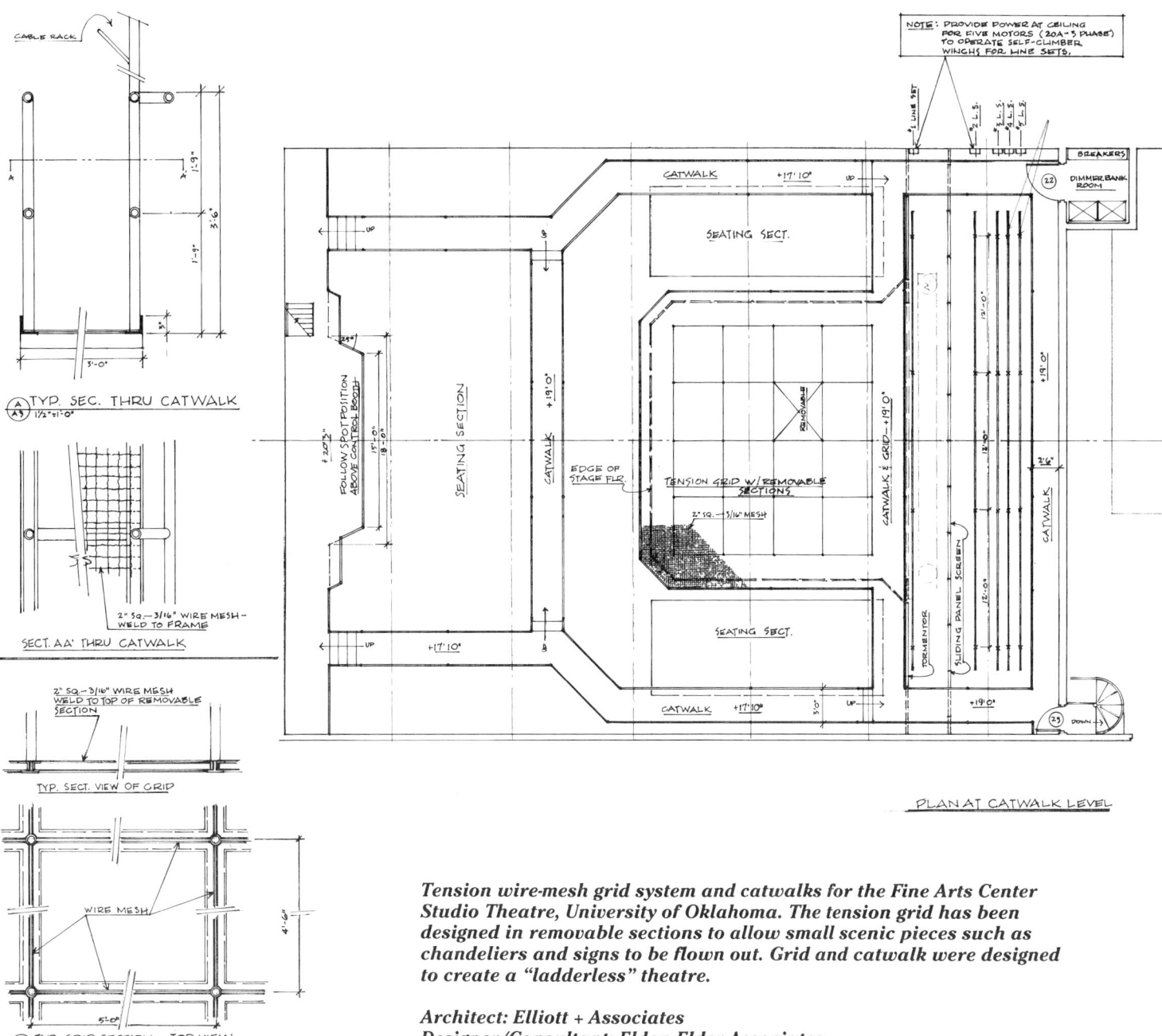

Tension wire-mesh grid system and catwalks for the Fine Arts Center Studio Theatre, University of Oklahoma. The tension grid has been designed in removable sections to allow small scenic pieces such as chandeliers and signs to be flown out. Grid and catwalk were designed to create a "ladderless" theatre.

Architect: Elliott + Associates
Designer/Consultant: Eldon Elder Associates

can be a simple, manually operated hemp line set; a counterweight system of steel cable line sets; a single spot line system either manually or winch operated; or a combination of the above.

COUNTERWEIGHT SYSTEMS. There are two standard counterweight systems: 1) the upright rigging system, and 2) the underhung system.

Upright counterweight rigging places the loft blocks and headblocks above the steel beams and gridiron. The system is serviced from above. Enough headroom is needed for technicians to stand, work, and move about on the grid—approximately 7' clearance. Obviously, this system can be as high as your stage house allows. The accepted minimum ratio of grid height to proscenium opening is 2-1/2 to 1 (50' high gridiron for a 20' high proscenium arch.) But the San Francisco Opera House gridiron is 120' high with a 28'-high proscenium, so there is no iron-clad ratio.

WILL IT MAKE A THEATRE?

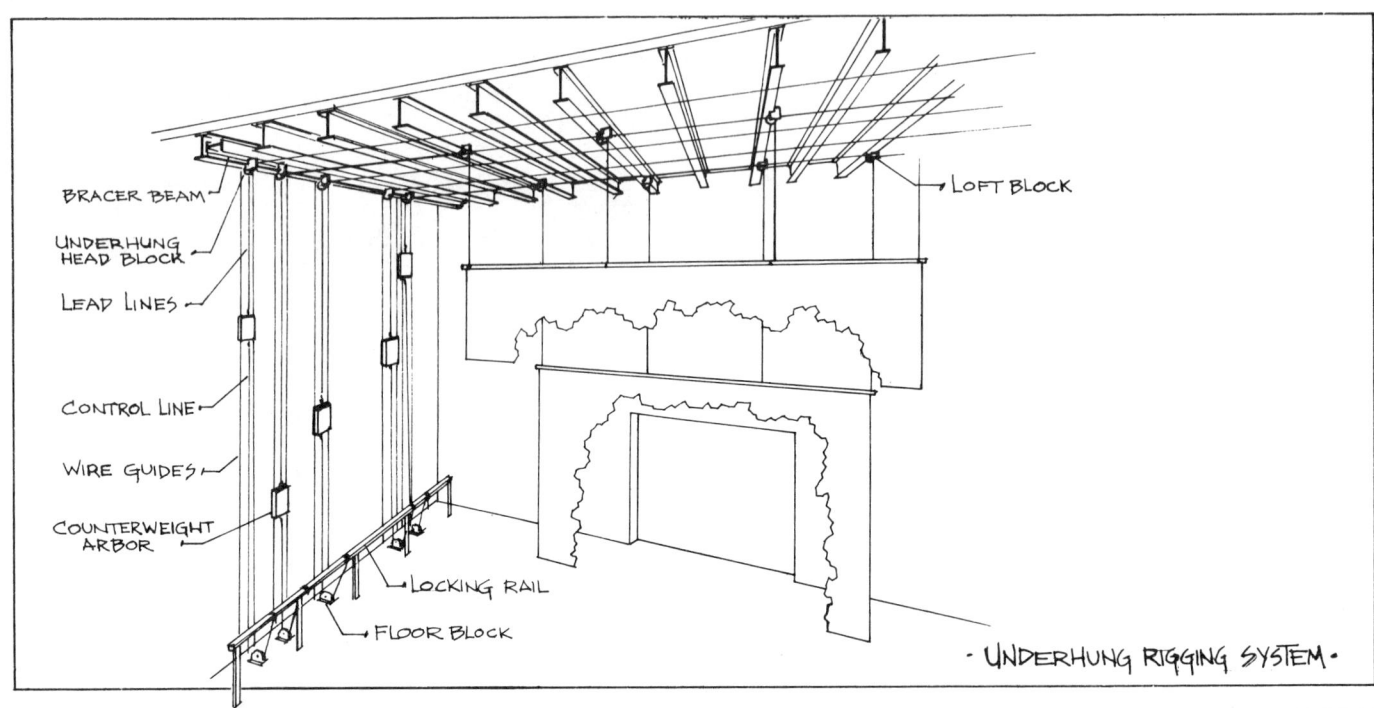

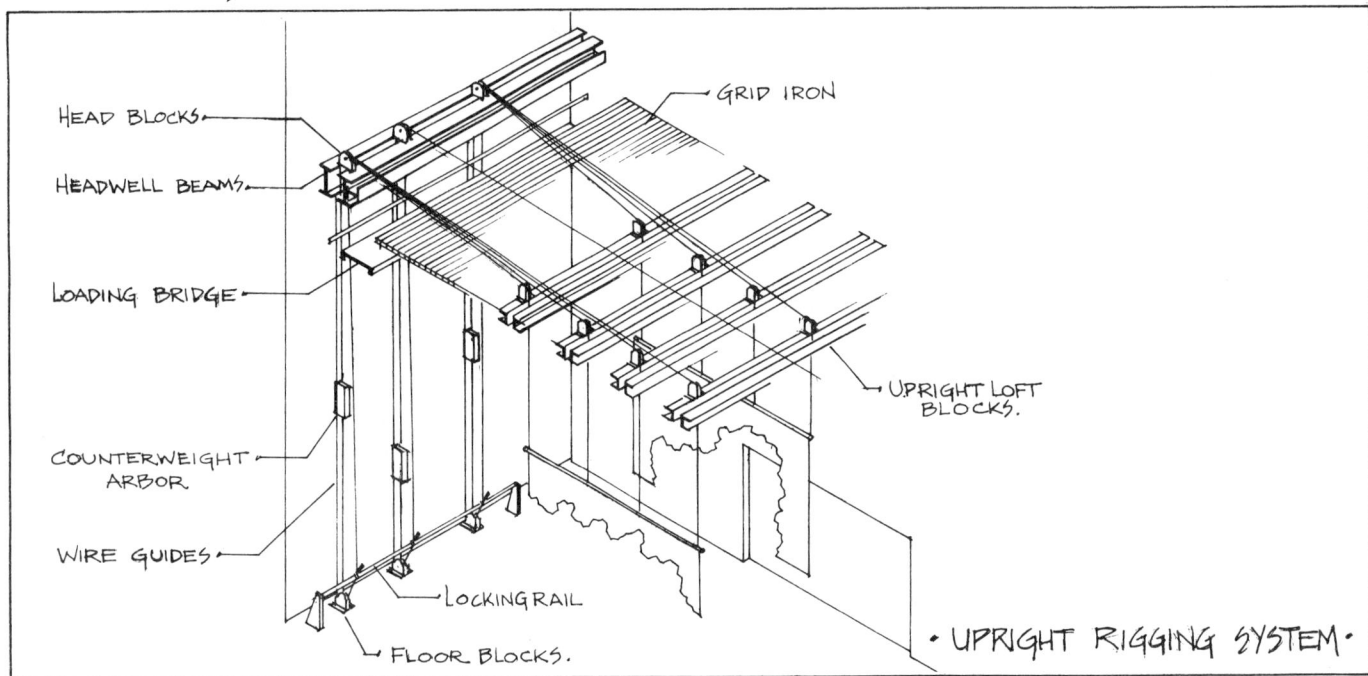

Very few nonprofit theatres have stages with enough height to install the upright system with gridiron, overhead rigging, and counterweights capable of flying full-height drops and scenic pieces. Boston's Huntington Theatre Company and Brandeis Repertory Theatre, both using large university facilities, are the exception, not the rule. The new Goodman Theatre in Chicago also will have a full loft in the renovated Harris/Selwyn theatre complex.

Underhung counterweight systems can conserve headroom. Underhung rigging places the loft blocks and head blocks on the underside of the steel beams. No space is required above the beams, so sheaves are often fastened directly to the structural steel I-beams above the stage house. This means that servicing or repairing the underhung system must be done from below, and this limits the system to the 30'-high rule of thumb. However, pipes can be lowered for easier loading. And pipes with lights and small scenic pieces may be flown out; full-height scenery and drops cannot.

Profile: Lyric Stage Company

FROM its founding in 1974 until 1987, the Lyric Stage Company developed a highly successful 103-seat theatre in a cramped second-floor space on Charles Street in Boston. A model small theatre operation, the company eventually outgrew its facility, often achieving audience capacities of 99-103%. In 1987, desperately in need of more space and with two years to go on their lease, Lyric Stage founders Polly Hogan and

> The architectural style could best be described as Art Deco with Classical references.

Ron Ritchell launched a systematic search for a larger, affordable space. They hoped that the new space would accommodate 275 to 300, and that it would retain the intimacy of their 103-seat, 3-sided thrust configuration.

As they searched block by block, the list of potential spaces slowly narrowed. Then, finally, they found it—their new home would be Ainsley Hall, on the third floor of the Young Men's Christian Union (YMCU). The landmarked Victorian building, built on Boylston Street in 1876, was right in the heart of the projected Midtown Cultural District. The perfect new home—or so they thought.

After the lease was signed, designs approved, drawings completed and demolition set to begin, it became evident that a more detailed engineering study of the 19th-century building would be necessary. Lyric Stage was committed to bringing its part of the building up to code, including installing a much larger, modern elevator. There was no assurance, however, that the rest of the building would pass inspection. Lyric Stage's question to the YMCU was, "If we invest all this money, will you bring the rest of the building up to code?" The disappointing answer from YMCU was "No." Further planning halted and negotiations were terminated.

Lyric Stage had to come up with a new plan of action. The 1928 auditorium in the Young Women's Christian Association (YWCA) at 140 Clarendon Street was a space the company had already seen during the search; it had been the second choice. It quickly became the first. It was a typical small auditorium—50' x 60'—with a balcony running around three sides. The floor was flat, with a raised proscenium arch stage at one end. The architectural style could best be described as Art Deco with Classical references.

The lease negotiations and plans for conversion of this space moved ahead quickly. The company employed the talents of the same architect, Stahl Associates, and the same theatre consultant, Richard Jeter, as for the space at the YMCU. Construction was underway during the summer of 1991 and completed by that fall.

Not only was the need to shift gears and start all over again a wrenching, painful, and expensive set-back, there were to be other crises and horror stories along the road. For example, the same morning that Lyric Stage was holding its backers' consortium breakfast, its bank was seized by the Feds. Then one of the principal donors, a prominent Boston department store, went into Chapter 11. But the Lyric Stage Company persevered, and the 244-seat theatre opened on November 6, 1991, in time to present a full 1991-92 season of seven productions in the New Lyric Stage Theatre.

In renovating the space, the Lyric's first goal was to create a thrust stage similar to the one in its original space. The performance area floor was raised 3'0" above the existing flat floor to create a 20' x 20' thrust stage. Seating starts level with the stage, and risers and

> The same morning that Lyric Stage was holding its backers' consortium breakfast, its bank was seized by the Feds.

platforms surrounded the performance space on three sides. Included in the design were enough removable, pop-out seats to create space for six wheelchairs. The proscenium arch (not shown in the perspective view) was retained, and the original stage became backstage for the new thrust.

WILL IT MAKE A THEATRE?

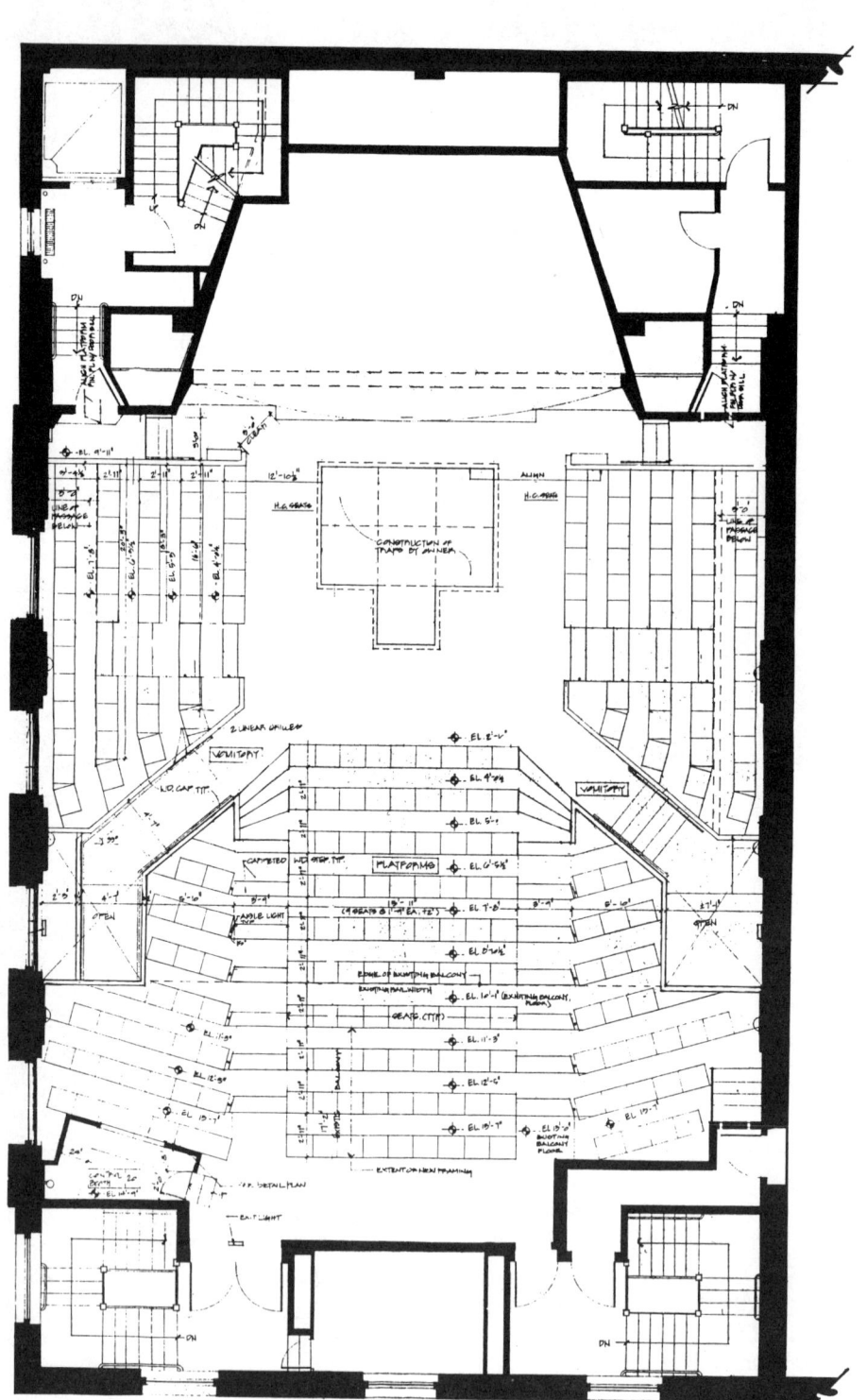

Lyric Stage upper level plan view.

Profile: Lyric Stage Company

A series of arched windows was blocked with infill walls. The original window recesses and trims and the proscenium arch frame were retained, however, as architectural features that define the space and help retain the period aura of the auditorium. The resulting space preserves the charm of the original structure, yet also serves the needs of the new inhabitants.

The theatre is essentially a "black box" theatre, except that it is not black. The walls are painted a dark green with a flat finish; the trim around the windows and the proscenium is a very similar dark green, but the finish is gloss. These colors create an afterglow of the skeletal framework, a continuing presence of the whole space, even when house lights are out. The risers and platforms are very dark blue with carpet only on the steps. The flip-up seats are upholstered in dark maroon. "The colors are very restful; the whole space is both physically and psychically comfortable," according to Polly Hogan.

> The resulting space preserves the charm of the original structure, yet also serves the needs of the new inhabitants.

The upper level plan view shows how the original stage became backstage space. The proscenium opening became a space for curtains, scenery or other scenic effects. The floor of the backstage is 6" higher than the new thrust stage.

The floor of the new thrust stage consists of two layers of 3/4" ply covered with 1/4" masonite. Fifteen-pound felt paper has been sandwiched between each layer to deaden sound.

The stage floor has seven 4' x 4' traps, accessed via a crawl space between the old and the new floors. The traps provide interesting possibilities for below-stage acting levels, for graves, and for pop-up effects. Additional acting levels are also provided at the original balcony level: Above the actors' passageways stage right and left of the proscenium are small removable platforms, which provide alternate performance areas for balcony scenes, for example.

Stage management stations are located on either side of the old proscenium in the passages that have been dubbed "actors' alley." The control booth, in the

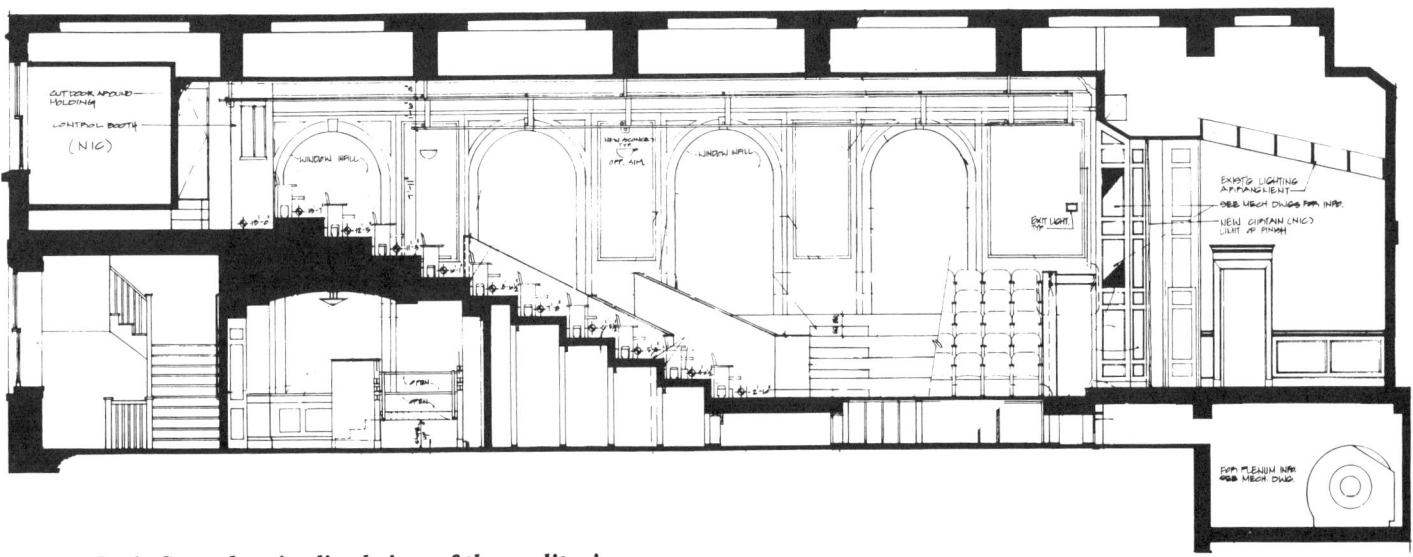

Lyric Stage longitudinal view of the auditorium.

house left corner of the auditorium on the upper level, is accessed through the auditorium. The booth accommodates two technicians.

The original auditorium had balconies on three sides. These were blasted out and replaced by seating risers. Two vomitories at the rear of the auditorium lead to the vestibule, upper lobby, and stairs. The two "actors' alleys" are linked to the voms, providing emergency exits. All four exits also lead to the fire stairs backstage right and left.

A small freight elevator in the upstage right corner is useful for bringing up props and taking down paint buckets. Next to the elevator, double doors open directly to the outside. A crane or a block and tackle can hoist large furniture pieces, pianos and scenery from street level.

Sprinklers have been installed in the new backstage area, in dressing rooms and actors' passageways, in public passages and vestibule, as well as under all the seating risers and platforms.

Advantages of the YWCA auditorium:

- The space was less costly to convert than the auditorium at the YMCU. One major saving was the cost of a new elevator. The YWCA building has two large, safe elevators. However, Lyric Stage did contribute $5,000 to help defray the cost of installing a lift for the handicapped. This new lift provides access from grade level up to the main floor level, making the entire building wheelchair accessible.
- Copley Square turned out to be an excellent location, better even than the YMCU. The Midtown Cultural District that was to become the revitalized theatre district for Boston is now completely stalled.
- The YWCA space package included good storage space in the basement.

Disadvantages of the YWCA auditorium:

- The 244-seat capacity is less than the 275-300 seats the company had hoped for.
- Offices are not centralized; they are scattered throughout the YWCA building and, therefore, less convenient.
- There is no shop space on the premises.

Terms of the lease at the YWCA:

- The new space has been leased for ten years, with two five-year options.

- Rent for the new space was pegged to the company's debt load, as follows:

    1992: $1,667 per month
    1993: $2,000 per month
    1994: $2,667 per month

    By 1994, the theatre company expects to have the paid the debt in full. The rent will increase substantially after 1994.

Special features of the lease at the YWCA:

- YWCA gave Lyric Stage six months' free rent during the construction period and the first two months of performance. Rent commenced in January 1992.
- The Lyric Stage Company will give one performance per year as a benefit fundraiser for the YWCA. Lyric Stage will take only costs for that performance.
- Lyric Stage wanted a beer and wine license and approached the YWCA with some trepidation. But the Y thought it was just fine and made only one stipulation: if the theatre were ever to leave, Lyric Stage would give the license to the Y.

Cost of renovation at the YWCA:

- Approximately $700,000, including demolition, construction, lighting and all fees to the architect and consultants.

Profile: Lyric Stage Company

Two dressing rooms and two toilets exist as before. The toilets were made wheelchair accessible and are shared by actors and audience, although this is far from ideal. An additional wash basin has been added in each dressing room, however, and a small toilet has been carved out of the corner dressing room. There are additional audience toilets two floors below.

During the renovations, the Lyric faced a crisis over theatre seats. Donated seats from a suburban movie theatre did not pass the stiff Boston Fire Department inspection. Ultimately, the Boston Redevelopment Association, out of the mayor's office, made a gift of seats taken from the Wang Center for the Performing Arts.

The longitudinal section drawing shows the seating platforms that rise from the new stage level on a 14 1/2" module, providing good sightlines from all seats. There are five rows of seats along each side and ten rows at the end.

The ceiling height of 22', now reduced to 19' by the raised stage, is still adequate to provide positions for instruments at good lighting angles. Lights are mounted on an underhung pipe grid spanning the entire ceiling. The room has a hung ceiling with open coffers above.

For the first season, fresh air was provided by the ventilation system that serviced the original auditorium. In 1992, the second phase of renovation, air conditioning for the entire space was added.

9
THE AUDIENCE SPACE

Seeing, hearing, comfort and safety are the primary considerations in designing the audience space. These are achieved through the successful combination of good sightlines, seating, acoustics and lighting.

SIGHTLINES

Uninterrupted viewing is usually achieved by a combination of horizontal and vertical sightlines. The rake of the floor, the staggering of the seats, and the height of the stage all affect the ability of the audience to see. The design of these elements should combine to create an uninterrupted view of the entire performance area.

VERTICAL SIGHTLINES. Elevating the rows of seats by sloping the auditorium floor or by using stepped risers will establish vertical sightlines. Theoretically, one-row vision requires sufficient elevation of each row for every member of the audience to see over the heads of the row directly in front. This is frequently impractical and other means, such as staggering the seating, must also be employed.

HORIZONTAL SIGHTLINES. Good horizontal viewing is usually accomplished by staggering the seating so that each member of the audience is looking directly at the stage area between the heads of the two persons in the row in front, and over the head of the person two rows in front. This plan is especially applicable to conventional proscenium or permanent end stage configurations.

SMALL THEATRE SIGHTLINE PROBLEMS. There are special problems in achieving good viewing for small spaces, especially for arena or thrust stage configurations. Many small theatres in converted spaces lay the stage floor directly on the floor of the building, rather than using a raised platform. To solve sightline problems in this setting, use a steeply raked system of risers. The lower the stage floor, the steeper the rake of the seating.

Creating good sightlines for three-sided, thrust, or four-sided arena stages is more complex than in a proscenium or end-stage theatre. These configurations rely more on vertical sightline solutions; staggering the seats with two-row vision is less effective. Actors may block one another from different parts of the audience, and the line of vision is no longer directly to the front, as in proscenium,

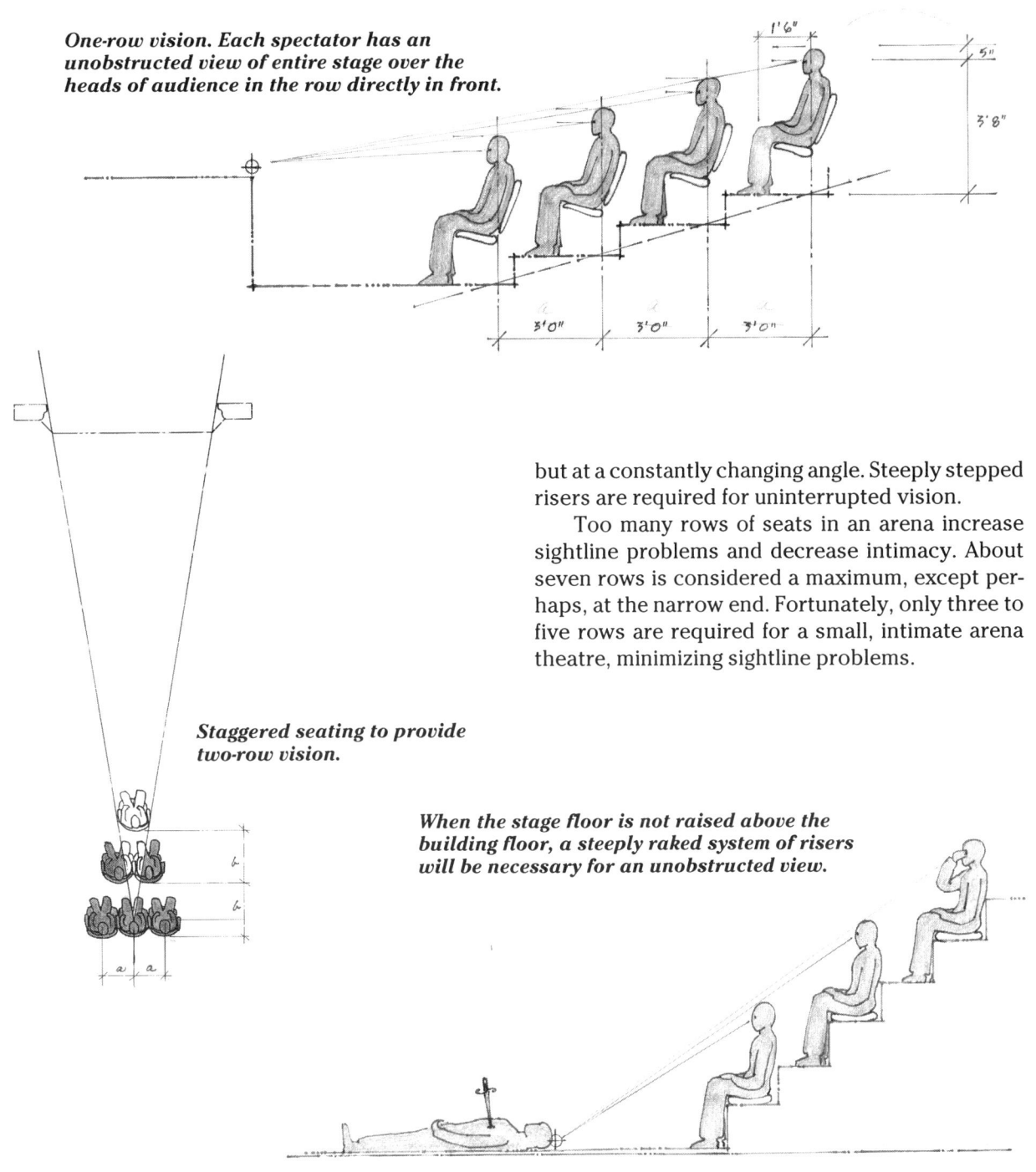

One-row vision. Each spectator has an unobstructed view of entire stage over the heads of audience in the row directly in front.

Staggered seating to provide two-row vision.

but at a constantly changing angle. Steeply stepped risers are required for uninterrupted vision.

Too many rows of seats in an arena increase sightline problems and decrease intimacy. About seven rows is considered a maximum, except perhaps, at the narrow end. Fortunately, only three to five rows are required for a small, intimate arena theatre, minimizing sightline problems.

When the stage floor is not raised above the building floor, a steeply raked system of risers will be necessary for an unobstructed view.

WILL IT MAKE A THEATRE?

CURVED ROWS AND STAGGERED SEATING.
In a narrow auditorium such as a storefront, end-stage theatre, the seats can be in straight rows. If the auditorium is wide, it will be necessary to curve the rows to orient all spectators to the stage. Curving the rows makes staggering the seats easier, however. Conventional theatre seats are manufactured in varying widths to assist in achieving staggered seating while maintaining straight aisles.

CONTINENTAL SEATING. Occasionally, continental seating may be desirable. It is useful only in a wide auditorium. The standard number of seats allowed in a row between two aisles is 14. Continental seating—based on the concept that every row is a cross-aisle—allows an increase in the number of seats in a row. But it also requires an increase in the back-to-back space between rows. In most codes, 36" is the minimum back-to-back allowance for continental seating, with an increase in this measurement proportionate to the number of additional seats over 14 in the row.

SEATS AND SEATING LAYOUT

In addition to solving sightline problems, there are esthetic and stylistic decisions to be made with regard to seating. Give serious thought to the seating layout in the earliest stages of planning: Will a permanent layout serve, or will flexible seating best suit your type of theatre and production style? If you chose flexibility in seating, do you want to achieve this with fixed seats on movable risers, or with seats that are themselves movable? Will a middle-of-the-road plan with some fixed seating sections and some movable sections give the right amount of flexibility? (See Studio Theatre Profile for an example of modified flexibility, p. 144) Make a firm, if somewhat arbitrary, decision about these options. (See seat and row spacing, pp 164 and 175)

MOVABLE PLATFORM MODULES FOR SEATING.
For greater flexibility in a space with a level floor, consider stepped seating risers in modules. The risers should be constructed of flame-retardant

If sightlines providing two-row vision are used for an arena or thrust stage, A may see X between C and D and over I, but will have difficulty seeing Y past D and J. B can see Y, but will have great difficulty seeing X!

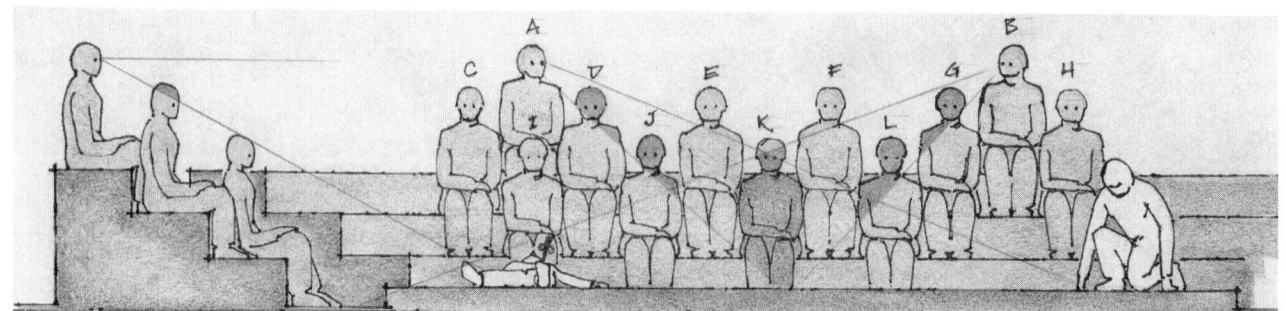

wood or of steel. Clamp or bolt riser units together. For greatest mobility and flexibility, mount small units on castered bases.

A practical width for the riser top is 3'. This will create a platform wide enough for flip-up seats, as well as for the non-flip, stack-type seat. Tops may be fire-retardant plywood or metal, which can be carpeted for greater sound absorption and a classier look.

Guardrails for audience safety are necessary but must not obstruct audience view. In most codes, the seating risers must have a live load rating of 60 lbs. per sq. ft.

TEMPORARY SEATING. Temporary scaffolding of the type used on construction sites has also been rigged to create flexible and unique seating. Padded and carpeted risers without seats can also provide an inexpensive solution to seating. This might be a scheme best suited for a young audience. The lack of a backrest can be tiring, and the audience's attention span can become limited.

COMMERCIAL MODULAR PLATFORMS.

There are many commercially fabricated platform modules on the market. However, they are predictably more expensive than homemade platforms. Audience safety as well as audience comfort is of utmost concern—one reason you may want to investigate commercially made risers. There are at least a half-dozen major manufacturers. Their products vary widely in weight, mobility, and price. An architect, theatre consultant, or technical director can help you make a comparative analysis. Guardrails and other safety features should be part of a commercially planned platform package.

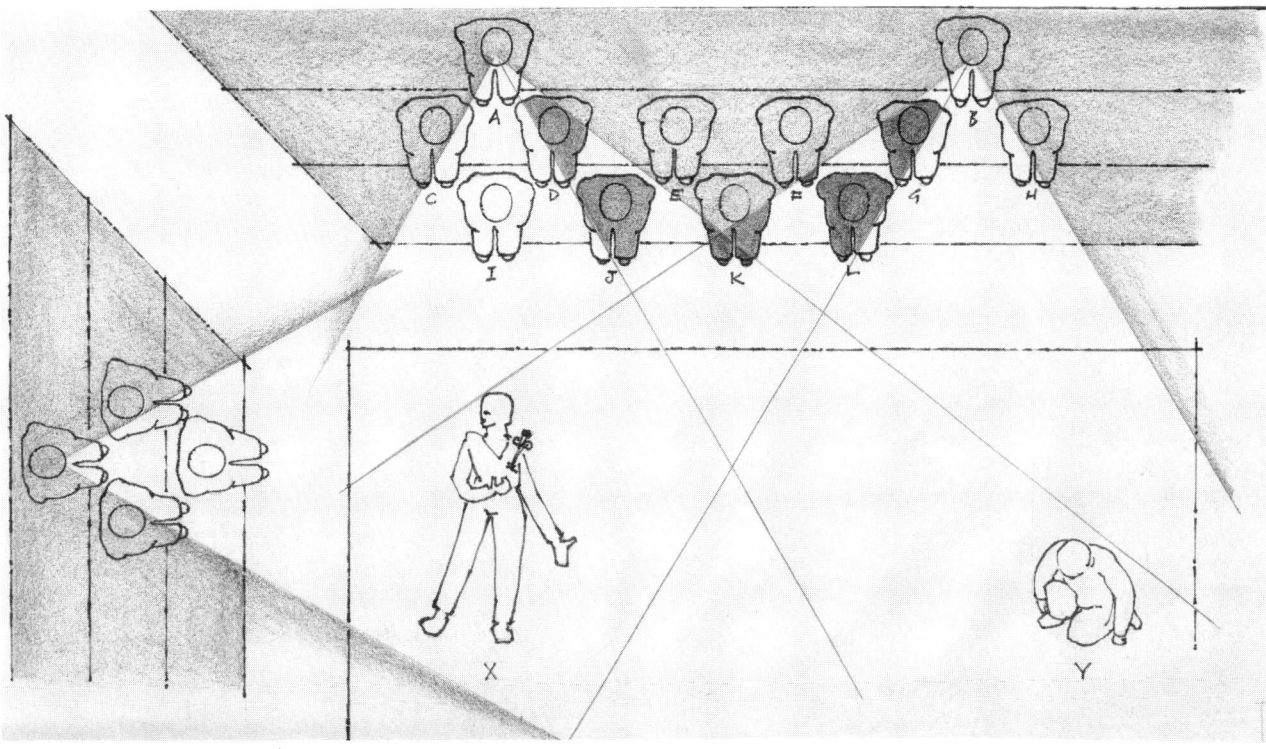

WILL IT MAKE A THEATRE?

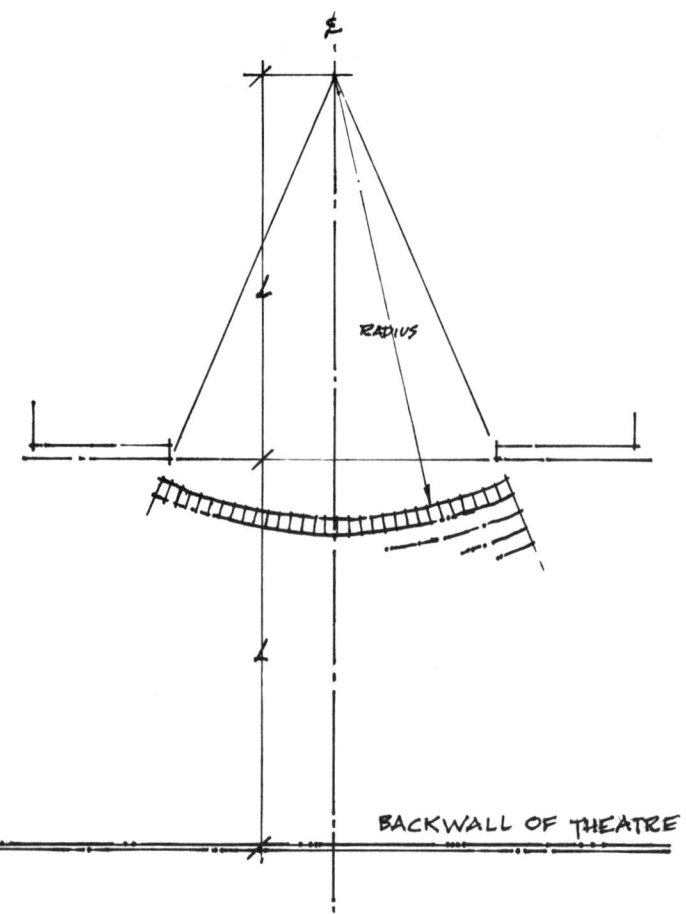

One system for determining the curve for rows of seats.

Note: Open voids under wooden risers won't pass muster with fire inspectors—they usually will require that the spaces be enclosed in Sheetrock. Nor, alas, is it legal to use this space for storage.

FIXED VS. MOVABLE SEATS. There are two approaches to seating your audience with chairs: *fixed* and *movable*.

Fixed seats—attached to the floor or risers—keep orderly rows, do not require continual straightening before each performance, and keep aisles and exits open in compliance with the codes. Fixed seats eliminate any noise of chairs scraping on uncovered surfaces and insure that sightlines are fixed. Fixed seats also keep the seat count constant and subscribers happily in the same location for the entire season. Most companies opt for fixed seating.

Movable seats, however, make it possible to reconfigure the basic shape and location of seating blocks and their relationship to the acting areas. They enable the space to be cleared quickly for other uses during nonperformance time. If movable seats are used, keep in mind that the New York City building code bases exit requirements on square footage rather than on actual number of seats. (See chapter 15.)

Whether fixed or movable seats are used, consider the following features when choosing seats:

- Seat width—discussed in detail in chapter 2.
- Seat backs—audience is able to sit for longer periods of time if backs are supported.
- Arm rests—an extra perhaps, but a plus in audience comfort.
- Padding—for seats and/or backs.
- Material—should be easy to clean, durable and stain repellent.
- Plastic and metal seats—may be easy to clean but are very uncomfortable.
- Acoustics—should be considered in decisions on padding and fabric selection.
- Color—should help create an appealing but unobtrusive environment. Should not distract the eye from the stage. Darker colors will absorb light when seats are empty and will not show dirt as quickly.

TYPES OF SEATS. Good seats are not necessarily expensive seats. Frequently, used theatre seats are available, or there are innovative do-it-yourself alternatives.

Brief descriptions of seats appropriate for a small theatre follow:

Theatre seats. Permanently installed rows of seats, the traditional seating approach. If ordered new, there are many design options:

arms, seat width, color, fabric, back slope, spring seats. Reconditioned theatre seats also may be purchased from seating companies. Allow ample lead time, especially for reconditioned seats, which can sometimes take months for delivery. Seats also may be retrieved from renovations of old theatres or television studios. The Shubert Organization's Property Maintenance Department frequently has used seats to give away. And in New York, the Department of Cultural Affairs's "Materials for the Arts" sometimes has used seats available free of charge. (See Resource Directory.)

Stackable and/or folding chairs. Plastic, wood, or metal, with or without upholstery. Can be placed on risers. For storage, they can be placed on rolling frames. Office furniture manufacturers make comfortable stacking or folding chairs that are inexpensive and work as theatre seats. Check out Playwrights Horizons in New York City.

Stadium seats. Molded plastic, with or without backs. Must be assembled in rows and attached to metal frames or boards. Can be dismantled by the row.

Pull-out seating sections. Available in folding chair or bleacher seat design. Self-contained unit of risers and chairs permanently mounted on metal frames. Whole unit can either collapse into a wall or create storage on wheels. Useful when audience seating space must serve more than one function.

Cushions placed on seating platforms. A cheap and simple solution to nonpermanent seating. Cushions can be cut from foam rubber and covered in durable, washable fabric such as heavy canvas.

Park benches and church pews. A nontraditional seating solution. Can be bolted directly to platforms to meet the requirements of fixed seating. Lines can be painted and numbers added to backs to indicate individual seating designations; cushions can be added for comfort.

Rented seats. As needed per show or for a season. An expensive approach, but one that solves maintenance problems. Most types of commercial seating listed above are available from chair rental companies.

Seating the Disabled

Provisions for seating the handicapped should be part of your plan. The Federal Rehabilitation Act of 1973 includes a provision, Section 504, to prevent discrimination against the disabled. This has led to state and local laws regarding handicapped accessibility. For example, in New York, local law 58, passed in 1987, amended the New York City building code to require that both new construction and rehab buildings be made accessible to all people, regardless of disabilities; and in 1988 the state of Illinois published an accessibility code that overrides local guidelines.

Seating positions for wheelchair patrons must be accessible by either ramps or elevators. Ramps cannot have a slope greater than 1 to 12. Steps are not allowed in this line of travel from the main entry to the handicapped seating. There should be at least one primary entrance accessible to wheelchairs. The minimum width for this entrance door and corridor is usually 36". These rules will vary slightly from code to code. Between 1 percent and 2 percent of total seating capacity is the usual required allocation for the disabled.

The Americans with Disabilities Act (ADA), passed in July 1990, concerns physical and programmatic accessibility, as well as employment practices. The aspects of physical access are less stringent than those of New York City's local law 58—in New York, the more stringent requirements prevail. If there are more lenient regulations in other cities, then the requirements of the ADA should be followed.

The following table, giving the ratio of required handicapped viewing positions to the capacity of the house in New York City will vary slightly in other locales, but this provides a reasonable standard:

Capacity of Assembly Place	Number of Viewing Positions
51 to 74	Minimum of 3
75 to 100	Minimum of 4
101 to 150	Minimum of 5
151 to 200	Minimum of 6
201 to 300	Minimum of 7
301 to 400	Minimum of 8
401 to 500	Minimum of 9
501 to 1000	2% total number of seats

Remember, a wheelchair requires the space of one-and-one-half seats. When not being occupied by wheelchair patrons, these spaces need not be left empty; plan removable seats to fill them. (Details on access for the disabled are included in the "New Code" section, p. 164 and in chapters 15 and 19.)

For additional information on architectural specifications, consult the American National Standards Institute (ANSI) standard A117.1-1986 and section 504 of the Federal Rehabilitation Act of 1973.

For local information on making your theatre accessible, contact your mayor's office for the handicapped or a comparable authority.

ACOUSTICS

Acoustical problems are usually minimal in small theatres. They often can be solved simply by adding sound absorptive materials on those surfaces that are reverberant, such as walls, ceilings, floors, seats, and platforms.

Sit in the space during performance time and listen. Is it noisy? If there is too much ambient noise, it may pay to hire an acoustician. The noise rating number (NR number) should be 25. Also, turn on the HVAC systems to see if they are quiet enough to run during a performance. Twenty decibels is the hearing threshold.

An occupied theatre seat is more absorbent

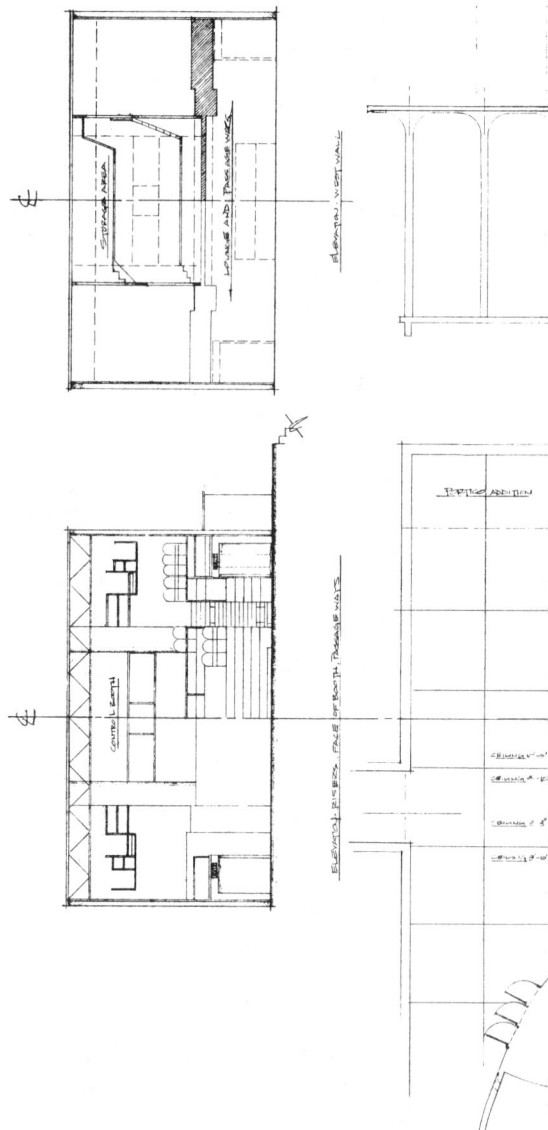

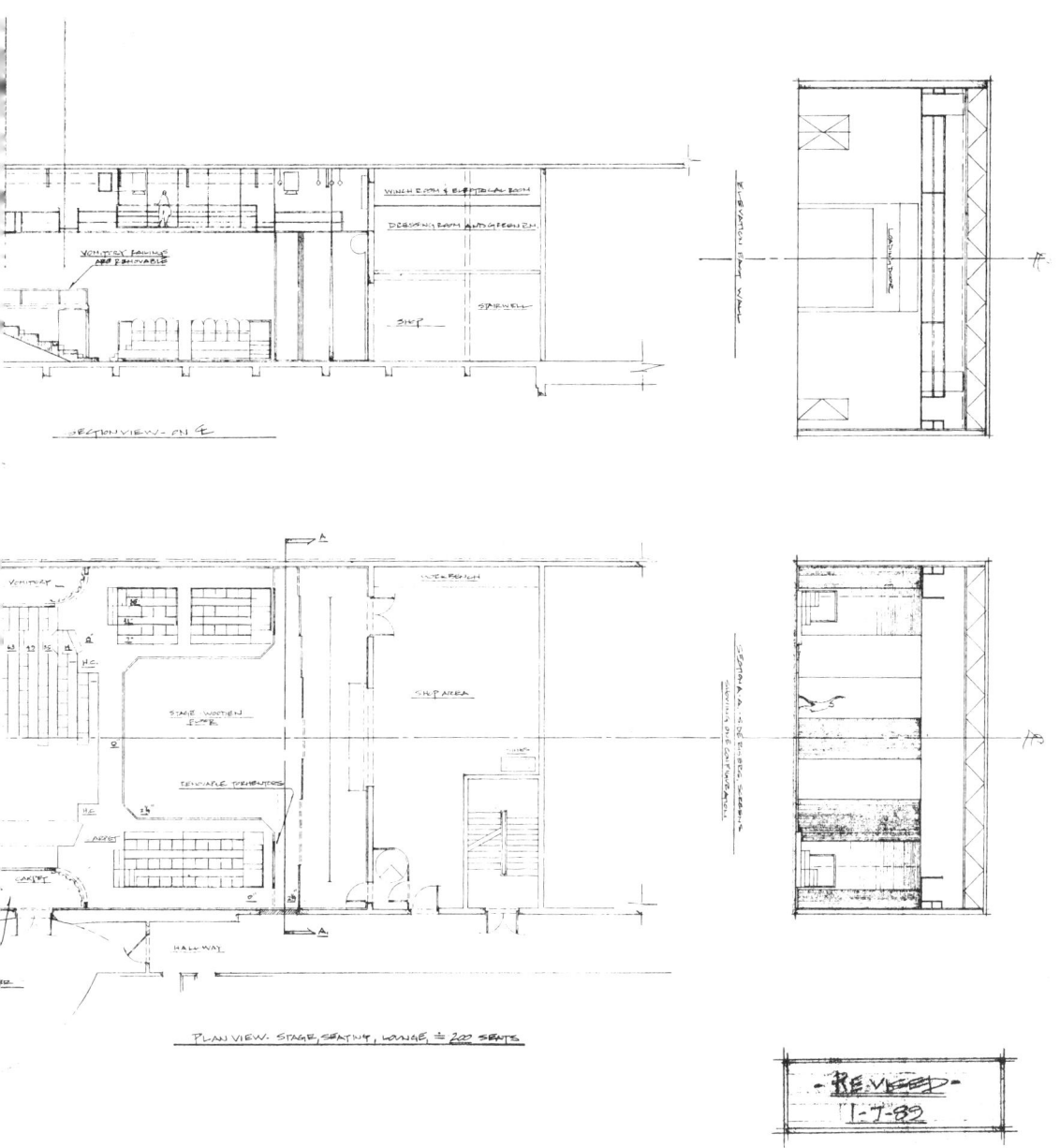

Studio Theatre, University of Oklahoma. The thrust stage interfaces with a steeply raked bank of risers with fixed seating. On either side of the thrust, the seating consists of two removable sections designed to expand the stage size for dance or classical drama or to provide a space for musicians.

than an empty one, so consider the best type of padding and covering on the chair to minimize this difference when the theatre is not filled to capacity.

Carpeting of aisles and seating platforms will reduce reverberation. In addition to tiles or other acoustic materials for walls and ceiling, consider covering the wall with carpet, draperies, or wall hangings to add absorbency to these surfaces. Carpeted panels can also be constructed and hung to allow tuning of acoustics.

Make sure all doors near or within the seating area close silently, fit well, and are constructed of soundproof materials.

It is possible to overdo sound insulation, and in a small space there is danger of deadening the sound *too* much. If there is no reverberation at all, the sound quality becomes unrealistic, and it becomes difficult to hear the actors.

For a space with acoustical problems, consult an acoustical specialist. Usually it is money well spent to have an acoustician check out the space and make recommendations.

The Double Image Theatre in New York City wanted to locate in basement space under the Promenade Theatre on upper Broadway. But the noise from the Promenade carried through the floor and even through structural steel columns, making the space impossible to use. The cost of soundproofing was estimated at approximately $400,000!

One general note: Any materials used within the seating area must be noncombustible or flame-retardant and comply with the local building code and fire prevention code requirements. (See chapters 16, 17 and 18.)

LIGHTING

Within the seating space there are three types of lighting: house lights, work lights, and emergency lights.

HOUSE LIGHTS. Sufficient visibility should be provided to allow audience members to gain safe and easy access to seats and to read the program. Incandescent light is preferable. Although fluorescent is more energy efficient, it is unattractive, unflattering, and difficult to dim. Place house lights on a dimmer-controlled circuit separate from stage lighting controls. Place aisle and exit lights on a separate non-dim circuit.

If the seating sections are flexible, the house lights and aisle lights must have the flexibility to be repositioned, too.

WORK LIGHTS. These lights will be necessary during nonperformance times to illuminate the house and stage for rehearsals, maintenance, and show preparation. Work lights should provide maximum visibility, but not require a great deal of electricity and should be controlled by on/off switches. Fluorescents can be used here. Put house work lights and stage work lights on separate circuits since there are times when they will not be used simultaneously.

EMERGENCY LIGHTS. The codes require places of public assembly to have emergency lights. These requirements are covered in detail by the electrical code and are discussed in chapters 16 and 19.

Profile:
Briar Street Theatre

THE 400-seat Briar Street Theatre is one of many in the theatre district on North Halsted Street. The 72' x 125' building, circa 1901, was once a horse and wagon barn for Marshall Field's delivery service, and, remarkably, has no columns supporting the upper floor. Its second story, where the dray horses were stabled, is suspended from heavy-duty trusses on large steel rods with adjustable turnbuckles. The ground floor where the vans were housed was therefore free of any

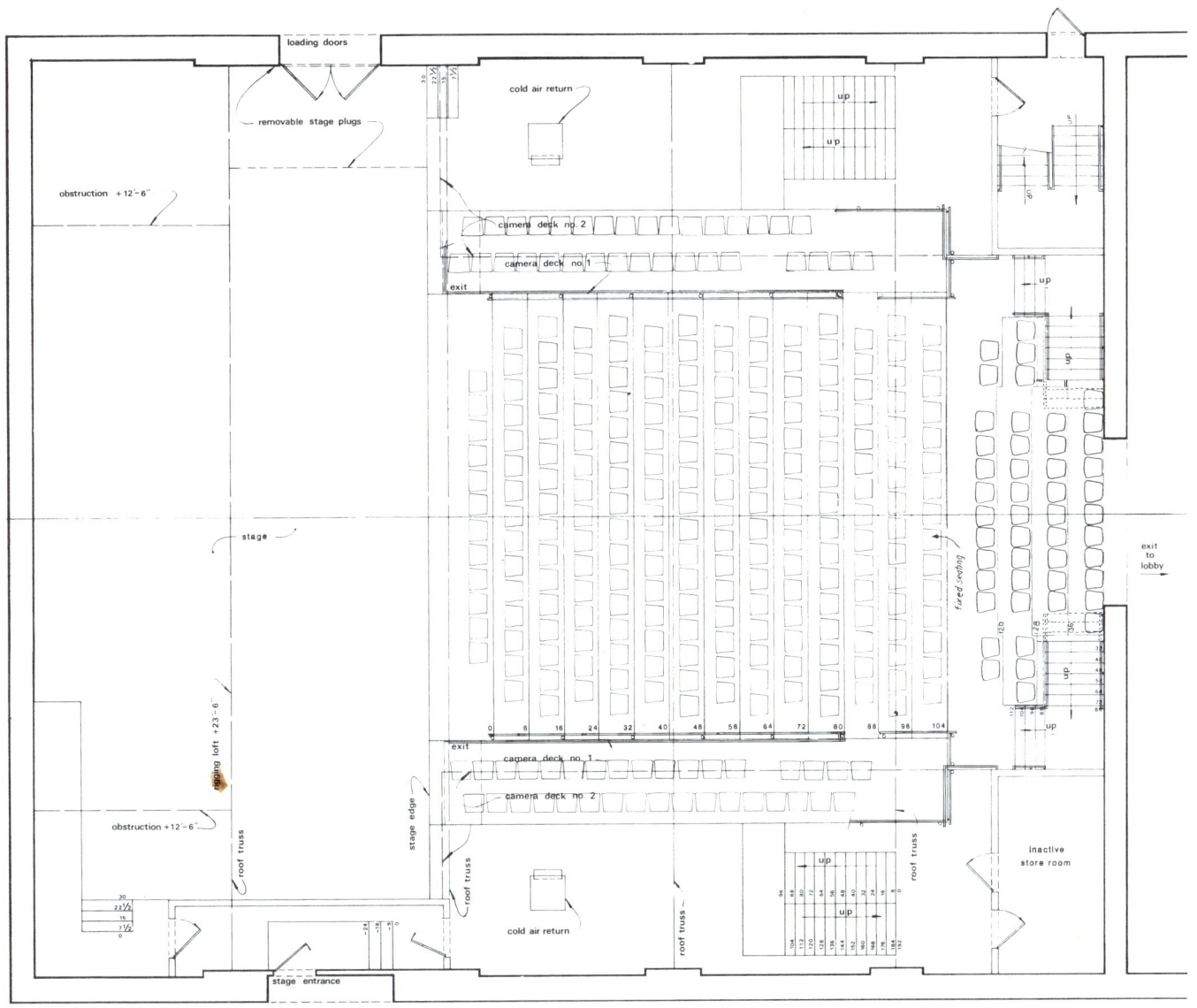

Plan view of Briar Street Theatre. The flexible seating arrangement allows the removal of the front rows of seats to create space for a thrust stage. The back and side sections of the second floor, left intact to stabilize the building, provide a place for stairs giving access from the rear to the main floor seats. These sections also provide side seating in a courtyard theatre style.

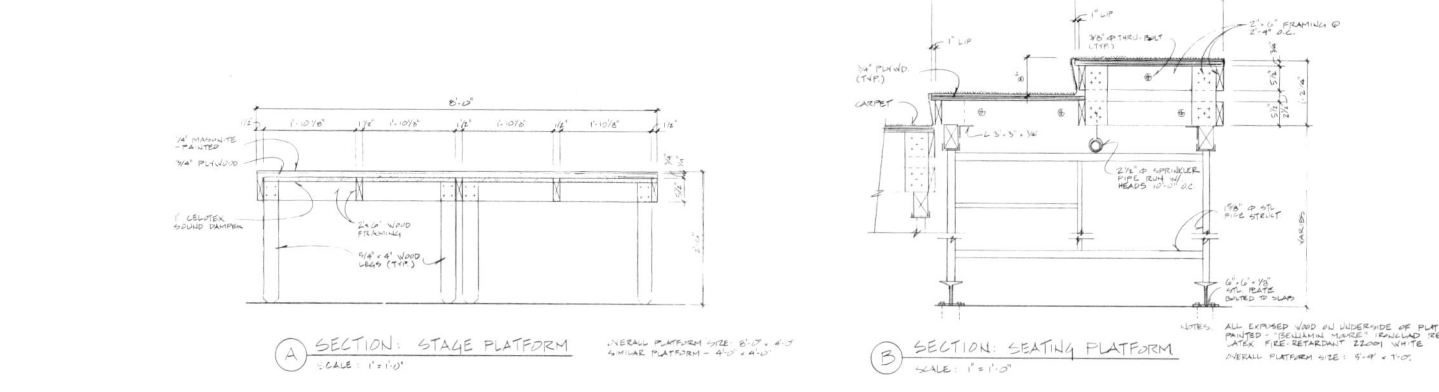

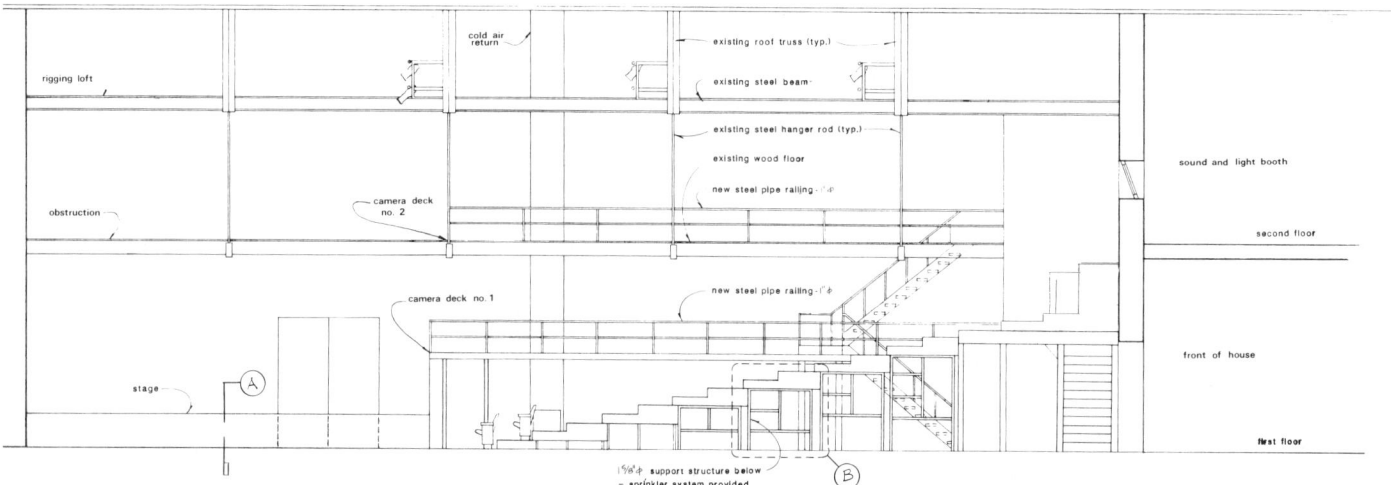

Section view of Briar Street Theatre showing moveable seating.

obstructions that might have impeded their maneuverability. This unusual construction made the building ideal for conversion into a multi-form theatre.

The 72'-wide end stage was deliberately left open. One drawback to this is that each production must create its own proscenium or portal to frame the space.

There were no special problems with the building or fire departments, except the need for sprinklers under the seats. Because the seats are in movable sections, Briar Street worked out a creative solution: a system of compression couplings—joints in the sprinkler pipes that can be easily and quickly uncoupled.

Dressing rooms are at the front of the theatre above the lobby and administration offices. This distance from the stage sometimes creates problems, so temporary onstage changing rooms are frequently required. The theatre has no scene or costume shop, but these are not too important in a rental house.

10 THE SUPPORT SPACES

Well-planned, efficient support spaces will save time, money and tempers. And it goes without saying they will contribute to a better product: the show.

TECHNICAL CONTROL BOOTH

In small theatres the technical control booth has often been an afterthought, consuming "valuable" space in the seating, lobby, or backstage area. Plan the control area as an integral part of the front-of-house, stage, and seating configuration. When planning the technical control booth, keep in mind the following:

- Provide a good view of the acting area. Install a window of double-thick, sound-insulating glass.
- Plan sections of the window to slide open and/or lift out to give technicians direct contact with stage and seating areas.
- Provide for the installation of a monitor speaker to enable technicians to hear as well as see the show when the window needs to be closed.
- Consider supplying an intercom system with outlets located at the stage manager's desk and stations located backstage, in the lobby, and, for technical and lighting rehearsals, in the center of the seating area.
- Soundproofing the booth will allow the stage manager and technicians to communicate without disturbing the audience.
- If possible, isolate the sound technician completely from other control booth noise —stage manager cueing and the like. The sound technician should not only be able to hear amplified sound from the stage, but also, through the operable window, live sound from the stage and auditorium: exactly what the audience hears.
- Consider providing an additional open space, centrally located within the audience space, with outlets for the sound control equipment.
- Run separate power supplies for sound and lighting control systems, especially if solid state dimmers will be used. The simplest way to do this is to provide separate breaker boxes for sound and lighting.

- If cable runs for lighting are in a direct line to the booth, their installation will be easier and less expensive.
- Provide adequate outlets and disconnect boxes to service all equipment. Allow for additional equipment needs.
- Consider the amount of equipment that will be used both now and in the future—allow for expansion.
- Consider the location and size of the booth for use as a possible front projection and/or followspot position.
- A direct access route from the booth to backstage, other than through the seating area, is useful during performances.

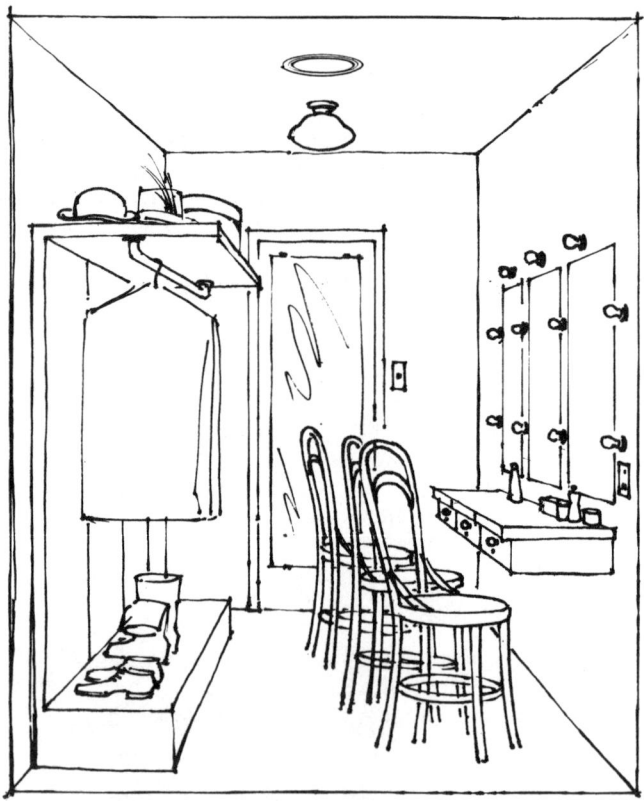

Dressing room. Use the checklist at right to determine that at least minimum space, efficiency, and comfort requirements are achieved.

- Doors to the booth should close quietly. They should be large enough to move control equipment in and out of the space.
- Provide adequate counter or tabletop space for stage manager, sound mixer, and lighting console. Provide comfortable chairs or stools for the staff, who will spend many hours in the booth.
- Provide both general overhead lights and lights for running the show in the booth. They should be on separate circuits, and all should be dimmable.
- Provide ventilation, heating, cooling and humidity control *separate* from the audience HVAC system.
- In a flexible theatre, position the booth in an elevated location so that the stage areas can be seen when using any theatre configuration. Provide a space for dimmer racks and a patch panel, if required. If possible, locate near the main power supply.

DRESSING ROOMS

Minimum dressing room sizes are discussed in chapter 2, but don't settle for minimums, if possible. The dressing room becomes the actors' second home. When planning the dressing room areas, take the following into account:

- If possible, locate dressing rooms on the same level as the stage, avoiding stairs.
- Provide good, shadowless light for each makeup mirror— incandescent light only— with separate on/off switch for each mirror. In addition, provide general illumination for the dressing room area. This light may be fluorescent to reduce heat and conserve energy, although it distorts colors.
- Provide convenient wall outlets beside mirrors for hair dryers and electric shavers. Allow one per actor.
- Provide at least one full-length mirror for each dressing area.

- Allow adequate hanging space for both costumes and street clothes. Equity recommends a minimum of 3' per actor for costumes, plus additional hanging space for street clothes.
- Although stage managers usually collect and lock up valuables, provide lockable drawers and/or small lockers for actors' makeup and personal items.
- Provide ventilation, heating, and cooling that is zoned with separate controls from the main HVAC system. An independent water heater could also save energy.
- Locate toilets within easy access of dressing rooms. (Toilet, wash basin and shower requirements are outlined in chapter 2.)
- Dressing rooms should be sprinklered.

To stretch space, consider portable dressing table/rack units that can either fold up into compact storage or roll out of the way.

The units could be complete with makeup counter, drawer, mirror, lights, and costume rack that rolls on casters; or they could be designed to collapse. If cleverly designed, the units, when spread out backstage, could form self-contained dressing areas by the addition of folding or stacking chairs. By stacking these dressing room units away when the theatre is dark, the space can be freed for scenery construction, costume construction, or other non-performance-related activities.

The Wisdom Bridge Theatre in Chicago, unable to carve out space for permanent dressing rooms, made good use of this scheme by moving two portable dressing rooms to different on-stage positions to accommodate the set for each production.

Any portable dressing room should be made of noncombustible material. The electrical code makes no provision for wiring a portable dressing room, but the same cables and connectors used for portable lighting equipment should provide adequate electrical power and safety to these units.

Flexible dressing rooms that can change to accommodate the casts of various shows are important since the male/female ratio of each production is likely to be different.

A green room or actors' lounge also should be included in your plans, if space is available. Don't

Portable dressing rooms set up.

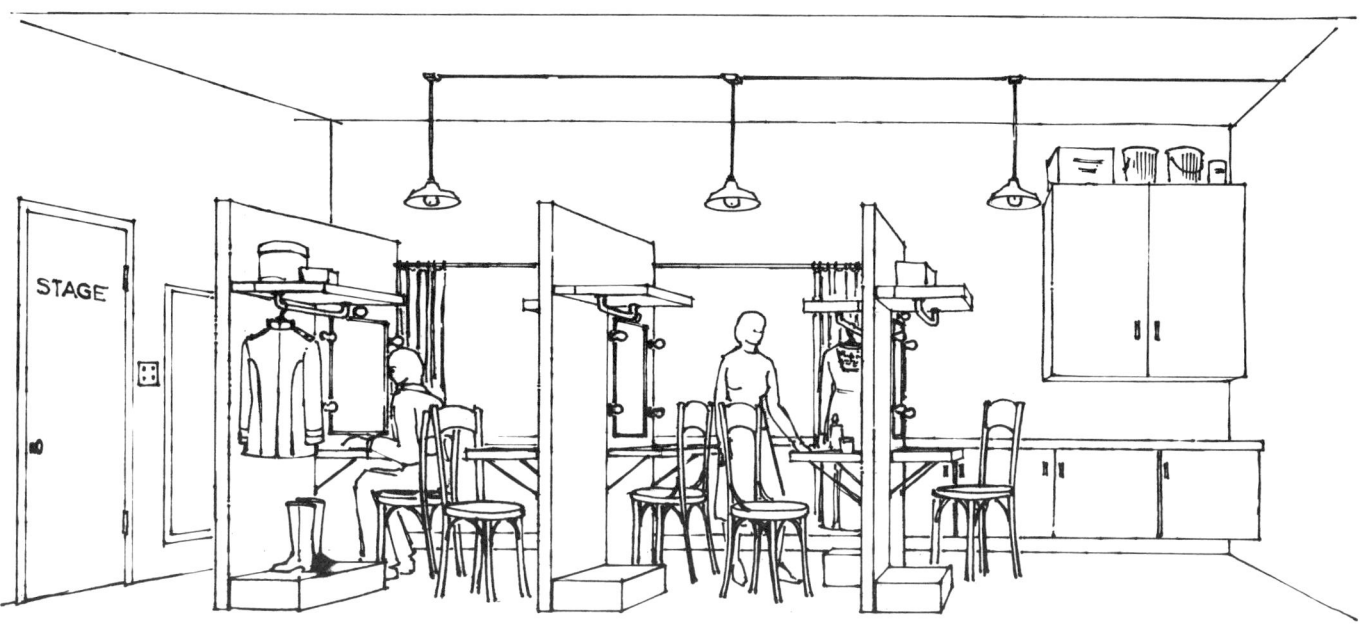

WILL IT MAKE A THEATRE?

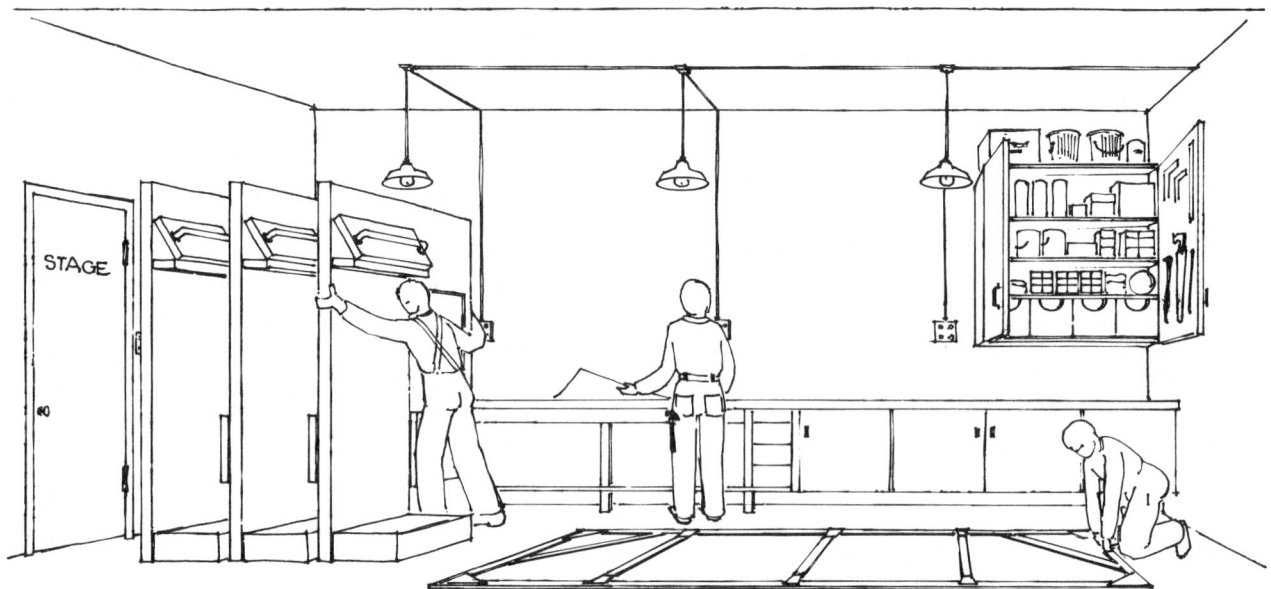

With dressing room units stacked, the multi-use space can become a shop or rehearsal space, or be used for other activities that do not conflict with the performance schedule.

forget to consult your Actors' Equity contract for "safe and sanitary" codes, as well as provisions for including an "Equity cot."

SHOP

Most small theatre companies are forced to build and paint scenery, make props, and construct costumes in spaces that must serve other functions. In such situations, provide adequate cabinets or lock-up storage rooms for tools, equipment, and supplies. (Minimum sizes are discussed in chapter 2.)

Plan your renovation so that these storage units are near the appropriate work areas. If this is not practical, use rolling storage cabinets, power tools, and worktables.

Sharing is another possible solution to the shop space problem. In New York City, for example, Playwrights Horizons set up Scenic Central, a non-profit scene painting and construction shop with rental storage space. (See Resource Directory, p.224)

Scenic and Paint Shop Checklist

If you are fortunate enough to have shop spaces, consider the following for the scene construction and paint areas:

- Highest possible ceilings with a minimum of 16' between any columns.
- Adequate, glareless light, with protected lamps. These can be fluorescent in the scene shop; incandescent lights are preferable for the paint area.
- Separate HVAC controls for energy conservation. If HVAC ducts and vents can follow the perimeter of the shop, the center space, where scenic units are assembled, will be free of obstructions.
- Workbenches and worktables. If

workbenches line the perimeter of the shop, have at least one free-standing worktable on casters. A framing table is recommended if space permits.

- Slop sink with hot and cold water and a large drain. A deep janitor-type sink is best.
- Hot plate or gas burners. Locate these in the paint area.
- Adequate electrical outlets. Plan for both present and future equipment needs. Plan distribution to accommodate placement of equipment.
- Compressed air for pneumatic tools and paint sprayers. The savings in labor will quickly pay for the initial installation cost.
- Sprinklers and a good ventilation and exhaust system.
- A fireproof vault or metal locker for paints, dyes, and chemicals to satisfy fire department regulations. It should be well ventilated and lockable.
- A good, level work deck. Wood is preferable to concrete.
- Access. Loading doors from street to shop should be sufficient to handle materials; doors from shop to stage must accommodate completed scenic pieces. In addition to loading doors, there should be regular-sized "people" doors to conserve energy.
- Space to store finished scenic pieces waiting to be painted or moved on stage.
- Wall telephones. They are out of the way and easier to handle than desk phones. Also a cordless phone and, possibly, a pager for the technical director.
- Lockers for work clothes and personal gear.
- Provisions for shop safety: medical cabinets—kept stocked—and equipment for personnel safety such as glasses, goggles, gloves, masks and aprons. For shop safety guidelines, check with OSHA or the life safety code.

Prop Shop

The prop shop requires all the above and can function in the same space if necessary. However, a separate space for fabricating props will keep them clear of sawdust and scene paint. Prop shops require less ceiling height and fewer power tools than scenic and paint shops.

Electric Shop

This space is needed for storing parts and supplies and for making repairs to sound and lighting equipment. It may be small but needs to be kept dust free; locate this space away from the scene shop. Provide good locks!

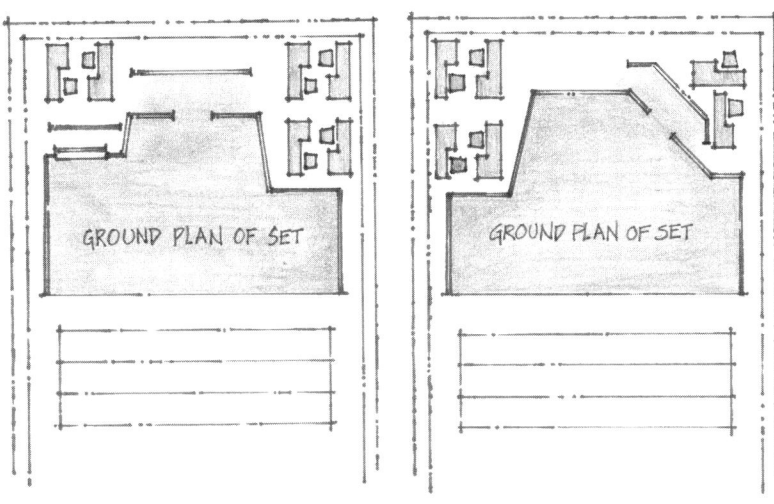

Costume Shop Checklist

Consider the following requirements for the costume shop if you are lucky enough to have adequate costume shop space. (Minimal sizes are discussed in chapter 2.)

- Even, glareless light plus localized work area lights and outlets for power equipment. Plan electrical outlets for present and future needs.
- Cutting tables. Allow space for 3' x 6', or 4' x 8' tables with cork tops—either the collapsible kind or the type equipped with casters that lock.
- A deep sink with hot and cold water.
- Washer/dryer space, electrical outlets and plumbing. Locate adjacent to the sink.
- Hot plate. Place it near the sink and dye vats.
- Fabric and supplies storage. This should be a clean, lockable space adjacent to the work area.
- Curtained area with full-length mirror for fittings.
- Racks for costumes in progress. These could collapse to save space or be castered to roll to dressing rooms.
- Adequate space for sewing machines and ironing boards. Folding boards would save space.
- Dress forms and space to store them.
- Wall telephones.
- Good heating, cooling, and ventilation with zone controls. The dye room and costume painting area should be separate from the costume construction area; they absolutely must have their own ventilation and exhaust systems.

STORAGE

There is never enough storage space, especially when building materials, costumes and props are scavenged and recycled, when plays are brought back into the repertory, and when labor comes cheaper than the cost of materials.

"Lofting," or creating storage lofts above other facilities and spaces, is a common way to stretch backstage support spaces. Often lofts can be created above dressing rooms, since they only require regular 8' ceilings.

Look for other wasted spaces or underutilized areas in your plan—over offices, under the control booth, in lobby benches—and devise storage systems to maximize their usefulness. Atlanta's Horizon Theatre built two levels of decking, complete with stairs, backstage for prop and scenery storage.

Several Off-Broadway and regional theatres with inadequate costume and storage space have given their theatrical costumes and period clothing to the TDF Costume Collection in New York City as a credit against future rentals. The Costume Collection also has a workroom available to theatres that do not have space or facilities to work on costumes. Two other organizations that might be approached for similar trade-offs are Atlanta's Production Values Inc. and San Francisco's Costume Bank. (See Resource Directory.)

REHEARSAL SPACE

Basic Requirements

Some basic requirements to consider in planning a rehearsal space:

- Wooden floor. Consider AEA recommendations. (See chapter 8.)
- Even, glareless light. This could be fluorescent to save energy.
- Good heat, ventilation and cooling with zoned controls. Good acoustics.
- Sound isolation from shops, stage and front-of-house.
- Easy access to toilets, drinking water and public telephones.

The Support Spaces

- Rehearsal room equipment: table with lights for director and stage manager; telephone (should be equipped with a light signal instead of a bell); chairs for actors; lockers, mirrors, and notice board.

For shape and size requirements, see chapter 2.

Multiple Usage

If you are fortunate enough to have a separate rehearsal space, consider designing it for multiple usage:

- As a second stage.
- For readings.
- For classes.
- For public receptions and parties.
- As a rental space for any of the above.
- As a lounge or lobby.
- As a costume shop, prop shop, or scene shop.

Full utilization of this space is largely a matter of good scheduling plus speed and efficiency of conversion once the theatre is in operation. If you list the projected multiple uses of the space before making the renovation, the following can be incorporated:

- Type and number of electrical outlets needed for shop, lounge, performance lighting equipment, or other uses.

Double-decking with costume storage above dressing room and control booth over aisle.

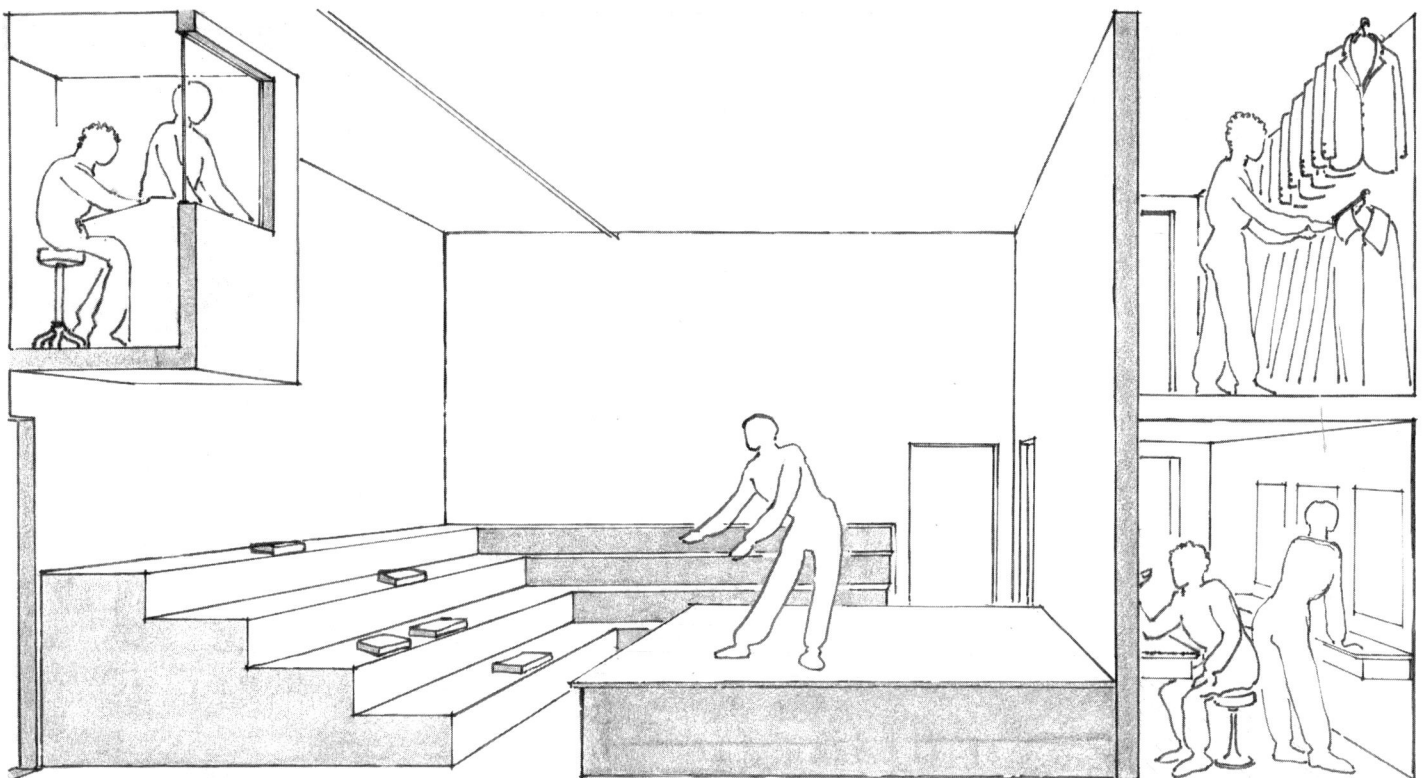

- Lighting for rehearsal and workspace, lighting equipment for readings or second stage usage, and lighting control to accommodate multiple uses.
- Necessary storage space.
- The best floor to serve all functions.
- Attractive but durable decor to make it a pleasant place for work and for public events.

Shared Rehearsal Space

Consider the possibility of shared rehearsal space with a theatre or theatres nearby. New York's Interart and Ensemble Studio theatres, located in the same building, share rehearsal space, as do Chicago's Victory Gardens and Body Politic (see Profile, p. 56). The number of spaces needed will depend on the production schedule. A theatre with multiple performance spaces and a heavy production schedule cannot make the best use of its stages without designated rehearsal spaces; and a repertory theatre cannot continue repertory programming if it has only one rehearsal space.

BOX OFFICE

Since ticket pick-ups and voucher redemptions are made right before curtain time, the box office or ticket counter must be designed for easy, rapid handling of this crowd.

Much of the rest of the time, the box office is little more than a telephone extension, monitored by an answering machine or a staff person with other duties who provides play information and telephone seat reservation services. A counter/table set-up in the lobby prior to performances may be preferable to a conventional box office for small theatres.

Traditional Box Office

If a traditional box office seems best, here are some design considerations to ponder:

- Be sure to provide adequate space for box office personnel, ticket racks, telephone, and either a safe, a locked cabinet, or a money drawer. If the box office will serve more than one performance space, allow for extra personnel, additional telephones, and ticket racks. If an expansion to include multiple performance spaces is contemplated in the future, provide box office space for this expansion during the planning period. (See chapter 2 for minimum sizes.)
- Provide space for eventual computerization, even if it's not part of your initial plan. This necessitates not only counter space for terminals and printer, but also dedicated outlets and shelf space for floppy disks and computer manuals.
- Consider locating the manager's office or another office adjacent to the lobby so that, with a connecting window or a Dutch door, it can double as a box office during daytime hours.
- Try to place the ticket window or counter adjacent to, but out of, the main traffic flow from street entrance to auditorium entrance.
- Make sure the box office is heated, ventilated, and adequately lighted. Ventilation and humidity control will become extremely important with computer-generated heat. The box office HVAC should have its own controls, zoned separately from the rest of the space. (See chapter 13.) Light the ticket counter well.
- Provide a conspicuous place to post a calendar of performance times and dates, as well as a seating chart positioned so box office personnel can point to seat locations.
- Plan the telephones with both bell and light signals if there is any chance that the sound from a bell signal will penetrate the performance space.
- Provide a security system. Consider a bulletproof window.

Ticket Counter/Table

An open counter removes the impersonal separation provided by a traditional box office, which could be desirable. But it also allows the possibility of flooding or crowding, making it difficult for box office personnel to function efficiently. An open counter increases the chances of theft, as well.

However, if an open-style ticket counter will serve best, consider these design solutions:

- A portable ticket rack that can be relocated for use during the nonperformance hours and/or locked up when not in use.
- A lockable telephone on a jack located behind the counter.
- A portable strong box.
- An alarm system to summon help in an emergency.
- Storage space for this portable counter. Consider a collapsible unit: some theatres just use a simple folding table.

Some theatres with limited space turn the ticket counter into a food service counter at intermission time. A sink will be needed if this is done. A portable ticket counter also might serve double duty as a concessions/drink counter. When the performance starts, the booth or counter is converted.

Shared Box Office Facilities

Most theatre companies that share a building also share a box office. Two Chicago examples include Victory Gardens/Body Politic (see Profile, p. 56) and the Theatre Building, which houses three theatres under one roof.

New York City's Ticket Central serves the 42nd Street Theatre Row and other subscribing companies. The shared box office service is available from 1 to 6 pm at Ticket Central. From 6 pm to show time, each theatre's box office is staffed with its own personnel and handles its own ticket transactions. Ticket Central provides these services:

- Phone reservations: Ticket Central takes all advance phone reservations up to a limit set by each subscribing theatre.
- Advance sale and credit card transactions.
- Mailing list development: Ticket Central gets addresses from persons making reservations.
- Information about ticket prices, productions, and theatre locations.
- Ticket stock: Ticket Central purchases the tickets for subscribing theatres.

LOBBY AND LOUNGE

Multiple uses for the lobby and lounge have been discussed elsewhere. (Minimum sizes are listed in chapter 2). Keep the following in mind when planning this area:

- Plan the lobby to be accessible to all front-of-house spaces: rest rooms, public telephones, lounge, offices, and of course, box office.
- The lobby must have easy access to the auditorium that not only meets code requirements, but is designed in such a way that noise and light cannot leak in to disturb or disrupt a performance or rehearsal. Light and sound lock doors are desirable.
- Consider use of the lobby as a "safe area" if required by the building code. (See chapter 15.)
- Adequate general illumination is necessary for safety and for reading programs. Additional specific lighting sources can add interest and accent.
- If there is a bar or counter for concessions and drinks in the lobby or lounge, plan to make it lockable.
- If the concession stand is a temporary booth/counter/table, set up for intermission only and plan a lockable storage space.
- If possible, plan a sink and refrigeration accessible to concession counter or bar.
- Plan for an ample number of electrical outlets in the lobby/lounge for concessions and other multiple uses.
- Plan lobby space for energy efficiency. (See chapter 13.)

OFFICE SPACE

Plan for future expansion of office staff, for the inevitable accumulation of paper, and for increased computerization. It is better to design too much than too little office space. Like storage space, there is never enough.

During the planning period, consider these design issues:

- If the front entrance of the theatre must serve as a general entrance during the day when the box office is not in use, the administration offices should be close to front-of-house for security. (For minimum space requirements, see chapter 2.)
- Place like functions near each other: press/subscription, casting/production, and business/audience development.
- Consider accessibility to rest rooms and drinking fountain.
- Plan office placement and design so that telephone, computer, and conversation noise will not penetrate the rehearsal areas or the performance space.
- Provide heat and ventilation with zoned control for maximum energy efficiency.
- Provide adequate general light and outlets for localized light at specific work areas and for office machines.
- Make offices attractive and comfortable; staffers spend long hours in their workspaces.

Profile: Latino Chicago Theatre Company

Juan Ramirez, Artistic Director
Gregorio Gomez, Managing Director

THE COMPANY. The Latino Chicago Theatre Company (LCTC) was founded in 1979 to bring a variety of bilingual productions to Latino and non-Latino audiences. The company is committed to creating opportunities for Latino theatre artists to enter the mainstream of the Chicago theatre movement and to act as a catalyst for the creation and support of new theatre companies.

THE SPACE. After moving through several temporary venues—a residency at Wright College, a WWII fallout shelter, a loft, and a storefront—the Latino Chicago Theatre Company finally settled in a permanent theatre. LCTC owns the building, an 1892 red brick firehouse (now designated a landmark) located in the Wicker Park/West Town section of the city. This places the theatre, where LCTC's two companies perform in Spanish and English, squarely in the center of the city's largest Latino population.

LCTC purchased the firehouse from the city for $1.00, and pays no property tax. How this came about is worthy of a Raymond Chandler thriller, including small-time city pols, an exposé, a confrontation with the mayor at an open forum, and a lot of guts and "street smarts" on the part of the Latino company members.

> The restoration and subsequent conversion of the firehouse to a theatre has been a hands-on, do-it-yourself project.

Juan Ramirez characterizes the company of 13 as "blue collar:" self-sufficient, trained to do building, wiring, and plumbing. The restoration and subsequent conversion of the firehouse to a theatre has been a hands-on, do-it-yourself project. The temporary theatre on the ground floor has bleacher seating for 75 on three sides of a temporary stage. Cushions are provided for audience comfort.

The conversion work has been planned in four phases. In the final development, phase four, the temporary theatre will be replaced by a 120-seat, permanent proscenium stage theatre with improved lighting, air conditioning, fly area, lobby and refreshment area, box office, and enclosed patio area.

The basement has space for a future cabaret. The second floor has the public washrooms, rehearsal space, costume shop, PR and managing director's offices, space to house visiting companies, and the artistic director's quarters. The present non-Equity company (five Mexican, five Puerto Rican, one Cuban, one Irish Catholic, one German Protestant) has been together since 1986, giving LCTC the feel of a real commune.

Profile: Steppenwolf Theatre

STEPPENWOLF Theatre, which has played a major role in shaping the national perception of Chicago as a vigorous nonprofit theatre town, has a new performance complex on North Halsted Street. The company purchased the site and owns the $8.28 million building. A 510-seat mainstage theatre with a 25' x 90' stage and a deep curved apron boasts no seat more than 36' from the stage. The proscenium width is adjustable. The building also includes a 120-seat studio theatre, rehearsal and administrative spaces, a library, and all necessary support spaces except a scene shop. The stage has a deluge system instead of a fire curtain; dressing rooms are sprinklered as well. There is a four-row-deep balcony and three small boxes on each side designed to "paper the walls with people."

The performance spaces are structurally and acoustically isolated from external sounds, mechanical systems noise, and from each other. The structure is, in effect, *two* buildings butted up against each other to block traffic-generated vibration and noise.

Although the scene shop is at an off-site location, the support spaces within the theatre complex are generous in size, well planned for their specific functions, and well laid-out in relation to stage, auditorium, and each other. In addition to a wide flight of stairs, two passenger elevators and a freight elevator link all floors.

Dressing rooms are in the basement with access to the stage by stairs or through the vomitories.

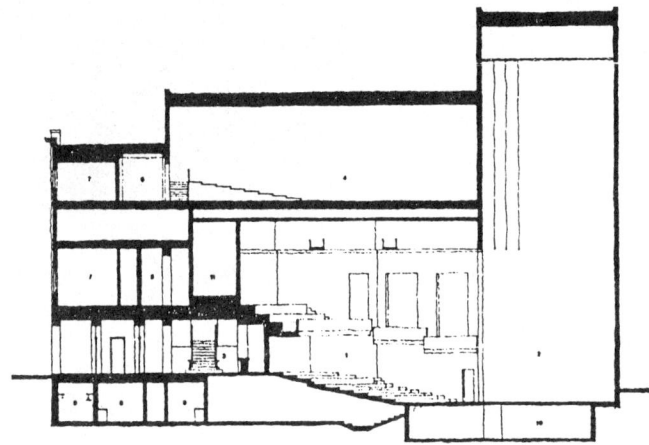

Steppenwolf Theatre east-west section. The most important space on the third floor is the rehearsal room that can be transformed into a 120-seat performance space for studio productions. This level has public toilets and is served by the elevators and main stairs.

Profile: Steppenwolf Theatre

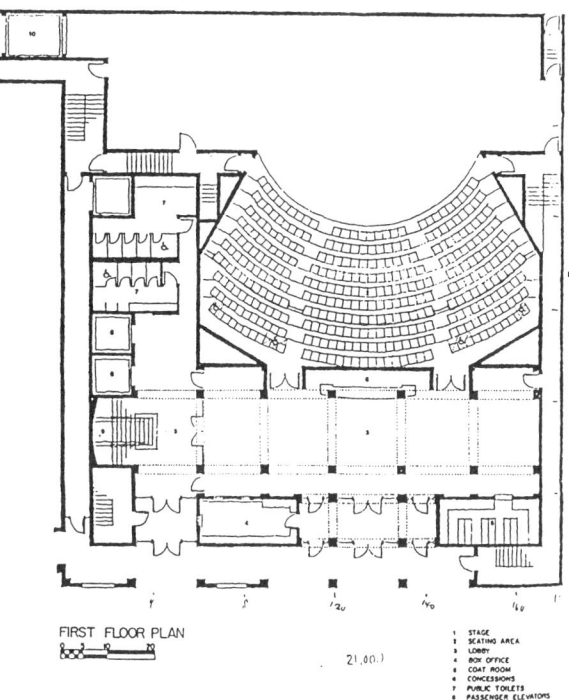

Steppenwolf Theatre first floor plan. In addition to the mainstage theatre, the first floor has a large lobby, with the box office on one side of the entrance doors and a coat room on the other, and a bar between the two auditorium entrances. Off the main lobby is a foyer linked to the balcony and upper-floor administrative offices by stairs and elevators. Public toilets are off this foyer, which has its own entrance from the street, providing access to the complex during non-performance times when the main doors are closed.

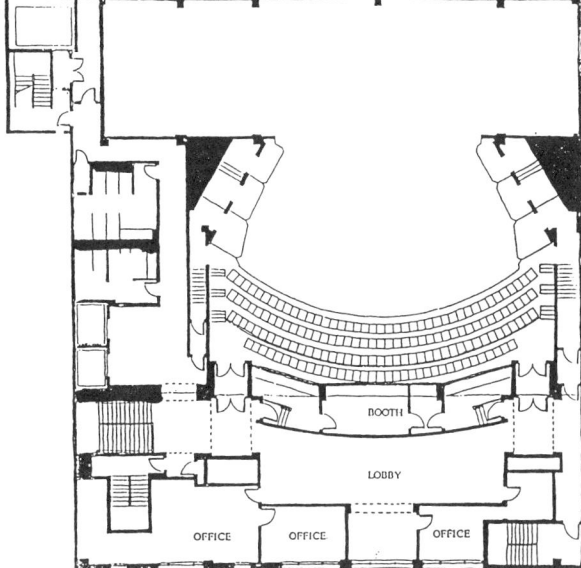

Steppenwolf Theatre second floor plan. A large lobby gives access to the balcony, the six side boxes, and the light and sound booth. There are additional public toilets on this level, and five large administrative offices, linked by internal staircase to more offices on the third floor.

There is also easy access to the trap room from this level. There are eight small and two large dressing rooms, reflecting Steppenwolf's frequent large-cast productions. Staff bathrooms with showers are directly across a corridor from the dressing rooms; the costume shop, adjacent to them. The costume

> Steppenwolf's image ... is reflected in the simple, rough texture of materials used for both exterior and interior surfaces.

shop's location in the basement means no natural light for the shop staff, which may be a less than ideal trade-off for proximity to the dressing rooms and actors. The production office, also in the basement, is fairly large and has ready access by stairs to the stage and loading dock.

Steppenwolf was formed in 1976 by a group of recent college graduates, and, like Chicago's Second City, has many loyal alumni who come back periodically to work there—which, of course, adds luster to the already international reputation the company enjoys. The new Steppenwolf Theatre complex, which opened in 1991, is visible proof of the company's healthy financial and artistic status. Steppenwolf's image—"uncompromising, aggressive, and quintessentially urban"—is reflected in the simple, rough texture of materials used for both exterior and interior surfaces.

11 Sources of Materials and Equipment

There are many inexpensive ways to get materials and equipment for renovating, equipping, and operating the nonprofit theatre.

DONATIONS

Like donations of cash, those of equipment and materials can be tax deductible. Theatres can approach businesses directly for this in-kind funding, often through their corporate community relations or public affairs officers.

In many cities, nonprofit organizations have been set up specifically to act as depositories for contributed materials, which they distribute to social service and arts organizations.

For example, New York City's Department of Cultural Affairs has run a recycling program called Materials for the Arts (MFA) since 1979. Businesses, individuals, and government agencies receive tax deductions for contributing a vast array of supplies, which are then distributed to registered nonprofits. Non-New Yorkers wishing to establish their own MFAs can consult *Materials for the Arts: A Handbook,* a booklet available from Materials for the Arts.

A sampling of organizations in New York City that make donated materials available to nonprofits suggests the range of places that the industrious theatre company can turn to for free materials. For contact information and similar organizations located in other cities, consult the Resource Directory.

Materials for the Arts. Office equipment, furniture, supplies, scenic and renovation construction materials, paints and fabric, tools, audio-visual equipment, musical instruments, trucks and vans.

Architectural Salvage Warehouse. Architectural components and detailing (doors, windows, even cupids).

Mayor's Business to Neighborhood Resources Bank. Used supplies, especially office furnishings.

SCAVENGING

Picking up discarded items can be lucrative. Check out areas with new construction or urban redevelopment projects where streets are lined with dumpsters.

AUCTIONS

In addition to auctions used to liquidate companies going out of business—like hotels or old theatres—many are held regularly by a number of government agencies. The following list of New York City auctions suggests the kinds that take place throughout the country.

POST OFFICE. The Post Office periodically auctions undeliverable, unreturnable, or damaged items in five U.S. cities. Just about anything that can be sent through the postal system may end up on the block. In New York City, notices of auction dates are displayed in local post offices.

Dead Parcel Branch
New York Division
JAF Building
380 West 33 Street, basement
New York, NY 10199-9543
(212) 330-2933

Similar auctions are held in Atlanta, Philadelphia, St. Paul and San Francisco.

In New York City, the Post Office also periodically sells its used vehicles. For information, call (212) 330-4912.

POLICE DEPARTMENT. In New York City, miscellaneous unclaimed properties, including office equipment and vehicles ranging from bicycles to trucks, are auctioned by the Police Department. For recorded information, call (718) 939-2300.

SURPLUS PROPERTY. Biweekly, the city of New York auctions off used equipment from its institutions and offices. For information call (212) 669-8546.

Consult the Agency Chart for addresses of agencies likely to hold auctions in other cities.

FEDERAL SURPLUS PROPERTY

By competitive bid, the General Services Administration sells surplus property from civilian agencies. Items include vehicles, plumbing and heating equipment, office machines and furniture, and paper products. Their condition varies. There are ten regional offices. Look in the telephone book's "United States Government Offices" section for your regional office number.

For military surplus property, contact:

Department of Defense
Surplus Sales Federal Center
P.O. Box 1370
Battle Creek, MI 49106-1370

WHOLESALE BUYING AND OTHER SOURCES

JOINT PURCHASING. A group of theatres needing the same supplies and equipment—lumber supplies, stage lighting equipment, lamps and replacement parts, plumbing and electrical supplies, theatre seats—can, by ordering in bulk, purchase these items at below-retail prices.

The Joint Purchasing Corporation (JPC), a nonprofit group purchasing organization, provides a contractual agreement between its members and a selected group of vendors who provide goods and services. Nonprofits pay a $100 annual fee, waived after purchases reach $5,000. JPC contractors include vendors of paint, lumber, office furniture, machines and supplies, and vehicle-leasing companies. Based in New York City, JPC maintains branch offices on Long Island; in Bergenfield, New Jersey; in Philadelphia and in St. Louis.

Joint Purchasing Corporation
130 East 59th Street
New York, NY 10022-1302
(212) 759-3456

THRIFT SHOPS. Thrift shops, run by the Salvation Army and other charitable organizations, are an excellent source for used office furniture, props, and costumes.

SALVAGE YARDS. Salvage yards handle materials from demolished buildings, such as plumbing fixtures, industrial lighting fixtures, and used building materials.

COOPERATIVE COSTUME SHOPS. Nonprofit organizations—such as the Costume Collection in New York City and Production Values in Atlanta—provide low-cost costume rentals and related services to theatres. (See Resource Directory.)

RENTING VS. BUYING

There are two schools of thought on renting versus buying. One line of thinking goes as follows: the newly established theatre should rent everything during the first phase. This keeps initial investment to a minimum, thus keeping the company flexible, unfettered by property if it should want to move or expand after two or three seasons. The extreme of this point of view is summed up by one theatre consultant, who advises, "A new nonprofit theatre should start by renting everything—including the toilets."

The argument for purchase runs as follows: "Why pay huge sums for rentals and have nothing to show for it several seasons later?" This, too, has its logic.

In the case of lighting and sound equipment—one of the largest equipment costs for a small theatre—arguments for renting include:

- Equipment provided should satisfy electrical code requirements.
- Certain types of maintenance and repair services are covered during the rental period.
- In the case of lighting instruments and projection equipment, new lamps should be provided with each rental.

Consider renting for the first season or two, testing out various dimmer boards, lighting instruments, and sound systems, and possibly working out a rental/purchase plan with a rental company.

A compromise worth considering is to purchase all permanent sound and lighting equipment—such as control equipment, speakers, work lights, house lights, lighting equipment for permanent concert or reading set-ups—and to rent all the special equipment used for each production. The payback period on this kind of equipment is relatively short (one to three years).

BUYING STAGE LIGHTING EQUIPMENT

When buying stage lighting equipment, there are a number of precautions and strategies that can save you money.

COMPARISON SHOPPING. Collect information and price lists from different manufacturers and dealers. See as much equipment as possible in operation. Check out types of equipment being used in theatres with similar sound and lighting equipment requirements and comparable grid height and stage size.

EXPERT ADVICE. A lighting designer or theatre consultant will be able to point out the advantages and/or disadvantages of various equipment, and to help you get the best equipment for your money.

USED EQUIPMENT. It is possible to save money by buying used equipment. But before buying, have a lighting technician test all the instruments, put a full load on all the dimmers, and get an estimate if any repairs are necessary. Make sure that replacement parts will be available.

MANUFACTURERS. When buying new equipment, carefully research the manufacturer:

reputable manufacturers will offer warranties and will guarantee their equipment.

PACKAGED LIGHTING SYSTEMS. There are packaged systems on the market that include a dimmer board, instruments, and cable, for what seem to be bargain prices. However, the instruments are sometimes second-rate, or the boards are of poor quality, limited capacity, or outdated. Get a professional opinion before buying.

LAMPS. When purchasing lighting instruments, it is cheaper to order the lamps separately from a wholesale lamp distributor. You will probably have to order by the case, but the discount off the list price makes it a worthwhile investment.

CONNECTORS AND CABLES. It is cheaper to buy new instruments without the connectors. Instrument manufacturers put on the connectors only after receiving an order. Their labor costs, usually at union scale, are added to the price. By ordering the connectors separately and doing the wiring yourself, you can save money. Connectors can be ordered from a theatrical supply house or directly from a manufacturer.

Consider making up cable yourself. As with connectors on instruments, supply houses have cable made up as orders come in. Someone will have to do the measuring, cutting, and wiring—so you will be paying for the labor as well as the materials. The cable needed can be purchased directly from an electrical supply house.

12
General Equipment Installations

This chapter reviews creating permanent versus portable installations, and provides guidelines on installing sound, electric and security systems.

PORTABLE VS. PERMANENT INSTALLATIONS

For small theatres planning stage lighting and sound systems, portable installations have decided advantages over permanent systems.

The electrical code's requirements for permanent installations necessitate engaging an electrical contractor and purchasing additional materials not required for portable systems. Therefore, it is to your benefit to describe the stage lighting circuitry as "portable" on all schematic drawings and to explain this to all electrical inspectors. Emphasize that each production is a separate entity requiring all stage lighting instruments to be repositioned and recircuited.

With the possible exception of making the board hook-up, portable systems can be installed without hiring a licensed electrician. If the system is portable, you can take it all with you if you move or go on tour. A portable system is readily adaptable to flexible space. Instruments, circuits, and even control consoles can all be moved to new positions to accommodate new configurations.

With a portable system, it is possible to begin small and to add later as your lighting needs increase and your budget permits. In a permanent system, it is wiser to make the complete installation initially. Permanent systems are designed for specific spaces, therefore it is difficult to adapt a permanent system to a new space.

On the other hand, if you own a space that has been designed with a fixed configuration, a permanent, hard-wired installation would be a sound capital expenditure.

SOUND SYSTEMS

Although the majority of small theatres may not need a sound system to reinforce or amplify actors' voices, a system including microphone outlets is necessary for special sound effects. Concerts or parties might also need sound systems. Consider the following when planning sound systems for a small theatre.

Speaker Locations

Plan the number of speakers with relation to the size and configuration of the space. For example, in a small end-stage or proscenium configuration two speakers would be barely adequate, whereas in an arena four speakers would provide a bare-bones minimum. While starting with these minimums, plan for growth. Provisions should also be made for two movable on-stage speakers for on-stage sound effects.

Speaker locations should be planned along with the seating and the layout of the space to avoid interference with audience sightlines and stage lighting positions.

If speakers are hung over the seating area, their minimum clearance must comply with the local fire code (7' in New York). In addition, they must not block any exits or aisles. If microphones are used, speakers and mikes must be placed to avoid feedback.

A monitor system with a microphone hanging over the stage with speakers in the dressing rooms should be provided so performers can hear the performance and their cues. There should also be an announcement microphone so the stage manager can address the actors in the dressing rooms, when necessary.

An intercom system should also be provided that will enable the stage manager to speak with the lighting technician, sound technician, assistant stage manager, or stage crew member to call cues during the performance. There should be provisions for an off-stage microphone and one in the booth for announcements.

Equipment

Rent or purchase professional sound equipment rather than equipment designed for home use. Professional systems are designed for longevity and can withstand the abuse of continual use.

Sound technology is evolving so quickly it is difficult to suggest specific necessary equipment. Today's sophisticated luxury items will be tomorrow's necessities. Here are a few basics, however.

REEL-TO-REEL TAPE DECKS. For theatrical use, reel-to-reel tape decks are preferable to cassette decks. Reel-to-reel machines are easier to edit. To facilitate running, all the cues for a show can be stored on one or two reels with leader separating each cue.

CASSETTE TAPE DECKS. Cassette decks are an inexpensive alternative to a second reel-to-reel for handling continuous background sound such as surf, crickets, birds, rain, and city ambience. Cassette decks, while good for continuous playing of a single cue, are impractical in a heavily cued show.

MIXERS. A mixer should be included as one of the basic components of a sound system—tape deck, amplifier, and speakers. A mixer with four individually assignable outputs is preferable so that sounds can be sent to individual speakers. Mixers allow auxiliary tape decks and microphones to be centrally controlled or mixed.

AMPLIFIERS. Amplifiers are essential to amplify the signal coming out of the mixer to power the speakers. Ideally, you should provide one amplifier for each speaker.

MIDI. MIDI (musical instrument digital interface) is a new form of sound technology. MIDI, which includes equipment such as samplers and synthesizers, is sometimes preferable to using cassettes and reel-to-reels. This technology is, however, additional to the basic sound system.

ELECTRICAL INSTALLATIONS

Electrical work requires careful planning to avoid future problems. Have a theatrical electrician help plan the installation. There are wiring problems peculiar to the circuitry used for theatrical lighting and sound equipment that the non-theatre electrician knows nothing about.

ADDITIONAL POWER. When bringing in additional power to your space, allow for future expansion by bringing in more than your present needs require.

HVAC. Isolate the heating, ventilation and air conditioning of different and separate areas of the theatre facility. In this way, cooling the theatre can happen during performance without having to cool all the offices and other support spaces not in use. This will lower your utility costs and be more efficient. (See chapter 13.)

REWIRING. If any rewiring or additional wiring needs to be done, bring it up to code specifications initially to avoid possible violations later. While it may seem costly, correcting violations later on can be even more costly and will necessitate hiring a licensed electrician. (See chapter 15.)

COST ESTIMATES. If an electrical contractor is hired, get the estimate broken down into labor and equipment. Some contractors make their money on resale of the equipment at a heavy mark-up. It may be cheaper for you to supply all the materials and pay the contractor only for labor.

SECURITY SYSTEMS

When planning security systems, think like a thief.

PANIC BARS. Panic bars allow free access to the exterior—by simply pushing on the bar—and at the same time prevent entry from outside the building. Install them on all exterior doors, except primary entrance, as a security measure. The fire department may require removal of all other hasps or locks on fire exits other than primary entrance.

POLICE LOCKS. Installing Fox brand or other police locks will give additional security when the theatre is closed.

WINDOW GATES AND SHUTTERS. If the theatre is on the ground floor or upper level windows are accessible, consider installing window gates or lockable metal shutters.

ALARMS. Burglar alarm systems provide additional security. If the space is broken into, an alarm is sounded both within the space and at the local police precinct. Alarm companies will do the installation, which averages about $100 per opening. Monitoring of all openings ranges between $20 and $40 per month.

Consider having a sleep-in technician function as a watchman, making a nightly check and opening up in the morning. In some cities, this may require a certificate of occupancy that includes residence.

Some insurance companies provide security evaluation services free of charge. Remember, the more secure the theatre, the cheaper the insurance.

13 ENERGY EFFICIENCY

Whether you buy or rent your space, are designing a theatre from scratch or are upgrading an existing facility, it's important to keep energy cost reduction measures in mind. Simple design changes and operational procedures can result in significant cost savings. Energy costs can be as high as $4.50 per sq. ft. in New York City. Energy-efficient design should be addressed in the early stages of the design process and be part of your capital budget. Once the theatre is open and running, it will be much more difficult to get funding for such improvements.

EVALUATING A SPACE FOR ENERGY EFFICIENCY

The first step toward creating an energy-efficient theatre is to conduct an energy audit. If funds allow, retain a professional energy auditor. The audit will help you plan energy-saving elements for your theatre.

- Incorporate design elements into the theatre space that will reduce energy costs.
- Purchase energy-efficient equipment.
- Develop operational plans that will help save money.
- Obtain information about systems in the building you are converting, such as HVAC, that will be useful in lease negotiations.

The basic energy audit consists of three parts:

EVALUATION. The auditor collects information about your organization and building. Be prepared to provide the following:

- Plans of existing building and proposed changes.
- Energy bills for the building (utilities will release these with the owner's approval).
- Schedules of when and how you use the building—performance, rehearsal, and office hours; summer and winter hours; day and evening hours; changing occupancies; relevant Equity safe and sanitary requirements.

The auditor will then perform an on-site inspection of the facility. Access to the entire building, including roof and basement, will be necessary.

ANALYSIS. The auditor prepares a detailed report, delineating how much is being spent on heat, electricity and cooling, and describing the present condition of every building system as it relates to energy consumption. Recommendations, estimated costs, and potential savings will be listed, along with the payback period (the number of years it will take for the energy cost savings to equal the cost of investing in the improvement). Payback periods are usually grouped as follows: little or no cost to implement with payback in less than 3 years; payback in 3 1/2 years; payback in more than 3 1/2 years. Theatres renting their space probably will be interested in recommendations that pay back in three years or less.

FOLLOW-UP. The auditor comes to your space and explains each of the suggestions and helps determine what changes can best reduce your consumption. Assistance on finding and purchasing materials and equipment is often available as part of the survey.

DESIGNING SPACE FOR ENERGY EFFICIENCY

Almost all energy conservation and cost reduction measures fall within the following categories.

Ventilation

Outside air brought into the ventilation system almost always needs to be either heated or cooled. The intake of outdoor air should be reduced to a minimum when the building is not fully occupied; open dampers only when the space is full. Use cooler outdoor air as a natural air conditioner by adjusting the damper. This can be done automatically with an economizer control, which brings in additional cooler outside air, thus reducing the need for air conditioning.

Infiltration

Outside air enters the building through inadvertent openings such as cracked windowpanes and open doors. Replace broken or cracked windowpanes, replace or install weather stripping, caulk around windows and doors.

Reduce infiltration of air near the box office entrance, for example, by adding a second door, revolving door, or air curtain. If you are conducting your own audit, use incense or some other form of smoke to determine where energy is leaving the building.

Heating and Cooling

Heating and cooling use the greatest amount of energy in any given year. All systems should be designed with zoned controls. For example, it is extremely wasteful to heat or cool the entire space during the day when only the offices and shops are in use.

Exposed heating pipes can create additional heating or cooling demands, and should be insulated. Make sure either the theatre or the landlord has a maintenance contract for the heating and cooling equipment.

Transmission

Energy is lost through the building's walls, roof, and windows. If a building is being renovated or converted, consider adding insulation to all exterior walls. Get assistance from an energy conservation specialist on the type of insulation most effective for your building.

Lighting

While little can be done to increase the efficiency of stage lighting, significant savings are possible in the purchase and use of nontheatrical lights. Energy-saving fluorescent lights should be used whenever possible. Exit lights, for instance, can almost always be converted to fluorescent. Energy-efficient lighting gives off less heat, reducing the need for air conditioning, and fluorescent lamps last longer, too.

Develop a plan detailing which lights should be used during office hours, rehearsal and performance. For example, don't use the stage lighting system for general illumination during nonperformance hours. Ornamental lighting fixtures in the lobby, while esthetically pleasing, rarely are energy efficient. Either change the way such lights are switched on and off, by connecting only every other lamp to one switch, or add fluorescent work lights.

Three-hour timing switches can be installed in dressing rooms to assure that electric heaters and lights are not left on after performances.

Electric

Become familiar with how you are being billed for electricity. Meet with service representatives of your utility company to review your billing structure. Find out if there are any discount rates available for nonprofits or for your specific section of the city.

Most electrical bills will include charges for the following.

Energy. Straightforward charge of energy usage (or consumption) in kilowatt-hours (kWh) for the given billing period.

Fuel Adjustment. Additional charge to make up for fluctuations in the price of fuel.

Customer-Related. The utility's cost for operation, maintenance, and collection; often listed under energy cost.

Demand. The customer's fair share of the utility's investment required to meet maximum requirements. A demand charge measured in kWh is based upon a measure of the peak usage of any 30-minute interval within the billing period.

A major concern for theatres is *demand charges*. In general, the cost of electricity is based not only on the total amount of electricity used each month, but also on peak demand during specified intervals. Theatres pay very high demand charges because they use so much energy during a production: interior and exterior lights, stage lights, heat, air conditioning. In other words, theatres often pay at all times for their high energy demands during a few hours of performance. One of the major ways to reduce energy costs is to figure out how to reduce demand. For example, an energy audit of the Second Stage Theatre in New York City found that 70% of its total electrical cost was made up of demand charges. The audit showed that by reducing demand by 10 kWh per month, the company could save $2,000 per year. One way to do this was pre-cooling the space and turning off air conditioning units during performances.

CREATING AN ENERGY MANAGEMENT PLAN

An energy management plan for your building can also substantially reduce costs. The staff should be trained to operate the building efficiently—not to flip on all the lights when someone is mopping the floor or turn up the entire heating system when one person is cold. Building maintenance people should be treated as professionals; they can save you a great deal of money. In short, you should develop a comprehensive building plan—how lights and HVAC are used during rehearsal, performance and office hours—and train all staff members to implement the plan.

Energy bills may also be reduced by taking advantage of tax breaks available to nonprofits. In New York State, for example, nonprofit organizations should not pay taxes on fuel.

For information on energy programs in your area, contact local utilities, the chamber of commerce, construction industry organizations, and the following federal agencies: Department of Commerce, General Services Administration, Public Building Service, National Bureau of Standards, Office of Energy Conservation.

Profile: THE OPEN EYE: NEW STAGINGS

THE Open Eye and the Studio Theatre both searched for many months before finding their current spaces. Both companies continued full performance schedules while fund-raising and renovating. The Eye took to the road; the Studio continued to play in—and pay rent on—its old space. Yet when it came to "making a theatre," the two companies' approaches could not have differed more in philosophy, style, and process.

Neither company had all its funding in place when it commenced conversion. The Open Eye began fundraising upon finding its space and started construction fifteen months later; the Studio Theatre plunged into fundraising before it had a building. Midway through construction, both companies had large deficits. Both negotiated low-interest loans and stepped up their campaigns.

Comfortable, homey, compact, the Open Eye's space cleverly and efficiently solves a range of practical design problems. At the Studio Theatre, where design concerns were motivated by both theatrical flair and practical considerations, the expansive space provides a dramatic complement to the drama on stage.

The Eye's production/business manager, Adrienne Brockway, commandeered lots of sweat equity and in-kind contributions to create the theatre. The Studio's artistic/managing director, Joy Zinoman, having been through a renovation before, vowed the company would not do the physical work itself.

In New York City, the Eye is putting down firm roots in its new community, and appears to have settled in for life. In D.C., Zinoman says she could easily move on in ten years' time with no regrets despite the capital investment of more than $800,000.

Opening within three months of each other, both theatres found design solutions that served their artistic agenda.

THE OPEN EYE: NEW STAGINGS, NEW YORK CITY

Company founded: 1972
Theatre opened: January 24, 1988
Site: Basement, Henry Lindenbaum Community Center, 270 West 89th Street
Size: 7,000 sq. ft.
Performance space: 115-seat end stage
Capital cost: $406,000
1991-92 operating budget: $380,000

THE STUDIO THEATRE, WASHINGTON, D.C.

Company founded: 1977
Theatre opened: October 25, 1987
Site: First and third floors, former auto body repair shop, 14th and P Streets
Size: 11,170 sq. ft.
Performance space: 200-seat modified thrust
Capital cost: $800,000
1991-92 operating budget: $1,000,000

Profile: The Open Eye: New Stagings

Amie Brockway, Artistic Director
Adrienne J. Brockway, Production/Business Manager

IN January 24, 1988, Open Eye: New Stagings officially opened its newly converted theatre: a 115-seat end stage on Manhattan's Upper West Side. The saga of the company's efforts to find and procure space—the ups and downs—typifies the twists and turns and sheer tenacity involved in so many Off-Broadway stories. Two and a half years of fundraising, conversion, and nomadic producing passed before the Open Eye had its new home.

> ... the theatre went through a down-to-the-wire guessing game of whether or not its lease would be renewed. January's "yes" became June's "no": with 30 days' notice, the Open Eye was out on the street.

THE LOCATION. The Open Eye's new headquarters, 7,000 sq. ft. in the basement of the Henry Lindenbaum Community Center, is just west of Broadway on 89th Street, in Manhattan's Upper West Side. In the early 1980s, the neighborhood was considered dangerous and the property expendable. But no longer: fifteen condominiums went up in 1987, while several small businesses closed down. Young executives have replaced elderly emigrés, while actors, artists, and musicians still cling to their rent-controlled apartments.

THE STORY. Choreographer/director Jean Erdman and her husband, mythologist Joseph Campbell, founded the Theatre of the Open Eye in their 14th Street loft in 1972. A year later, they moved to a second loft at Fifth Avenue near 16th Street, then to the Upper East Side's Church of the Holy Trinity in 1976.

But as the Church gave, it took away: first improving on, then adding to, then declaring off-limits sizable chunks of theatre space. In

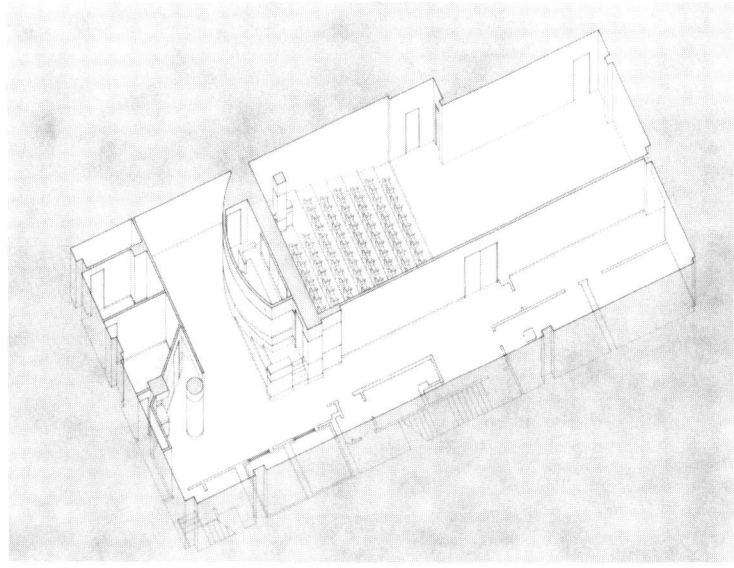

The Open Eye: New Stagings plan. The 365 sq. ft. lobby is low-ceilinged and irregularly shaped. On the other side of the curved wall to the right is the lighting booth. Measuring 8' at its widest, the 23' long booth overlooks the raked house from the back. It's a scant 25' from the farthest seats to the lip of the slightly raised stage, and 35' from the lip to the stage's back wall. Set depths usually range from 24' to 30', which allows for a cross-over. The lighting booth overlooks the raked house from the back. Off right, a 500-sq. ft. secured room serves as storage, scene shop, and auxiliary dressing room. Off left, a hallway running the length of the auditorium is also the green room; opening on to it are the makeup area/bathroom and a marketing/development office for two. A second door from the office leads into a lobby; a small buffer zone between provides both file storage and conference space.

> While the Open Eye has no religious affiliation with the Lindenbaum Center, it does schedule its performances around the Jewish sabbath and holidays, when money must not change hands.

1985, the Open Eye's final year of tenancy, the theatre went through a down-to-the-wire guessing game of whether or not its lease would be renewed. January's "yes" became June's "no": with 30 days' notice, the Open Eye was out on the street.

The company looked at several problematic spaces before a playwright friend told artistic director Amie Brockway (who assumed leadership of the theatre in 1986) about the Lindenbaum Center. Amie Brockway looked over the center's fourth-floor auditorium: "It wasn't quite right for us," recalls Adrienne Brockway, "but it was a space. And they wanted somebody here."

Then—almost as an afterthought —came a trip to the unused basement. Looking through the mess, Amie Brockway envisioned a theatre, and her vision has become a reality. By stairway or by one of two elevators, the audience enters a Wedgewood-inspired lobby. Its walls, horizontally banded in blue and white Homosote, are handy for mounting displays. To the left are the box office and two small administrative offices. The theatre space is intimate.

BELOW GRADE SPACE. Locating in the basement has its drawbacks. It added to the renovation costs: building codes required a $45,000 ventilation system, for example. System problems seem to originate from, or trickle down to, that floor. But there are plusses: in the winter, because the main feed from the steam lines adjoins the Open Eye space, there is little need for heat; in the summer, it's the coolest place in the building. All the same, the Eye does have four HVAC units and sometimes uses air conditioning during the cold season to dry out the air. The air conditioning also provides "white noise" to cover up the patter of little feet on the terrazzo floor just above the theatre lobby.

CONVERSION COSTS. The cost of the Open Eye's renovation, designed by theatre architect Mitchell Kurtz, totaled $406,000. The initial $150,000 estimate quickly escalated to $400,000 with the discovery of additional city building requirements. Adrienne Brockway made some creative cutbacks and trade-offs. She estimates that Eye staffers saved $8,000 by installing their own floor and carpeting (Community Board 7 contributed the carpet), $12,000 by doing their own painting, $135,000 by subcontracting plumbing and sprinklers to a nonunion firm. (See Trade Breakdown of Contract Sum, Box, next page.) Seats came gratis from the Shubert Organization's Property Maintenance Department. Non-traditional construction of the light grid, which was jobbed out, saved about $4,500: short lengths of pipe run perpendicular to the stage between support beams, and more can be added as needed. One trade-off, in order to get a certificate of occupancy, was an agreement with the city's department of buildings never to use several kinds of flammable materials on stage. This reduced the number of sprinkler vents required, so that the final cost of the system—$52,000—was slashed by several thousands of dollars.

> ... we have had a lot of parents from the school forget that this is a separate organization: they come down and say, 'See the school's theatre,' when they're showing things off.

Other kinds of trade-offs have been made with the landlord. While the Open Eye has no religious affiliation with the Lindenbaum Center, it does schedule its performances around the Jewish sabbath and holidays, when money must not change hands. With the exception of three or four holidays, the theatre has all-day, every-day access to the building. While only

Profile: The Open Eye: New Stagings

THE OPEN EYE: NEW STAGINGS

Owner Contract Agreement AIA Document A-101:
Trade Breakdown of Contract Sum

A. General Conditions	$14,500.00
B. Demolition	$9,500.00
C. Concrete	$1,700.00
D. Masonry	$4,880.00
E. Metals	$1,950.00
F. Rough Carpentry	$19,810.00
G. Finish Carpentry	$13,200.00
H. Doors, Windows, Glass	$7,807.00
I. Finish Hardware	$5,700.00
J. Gypsum Drywall and Plaster	$12,632.00
K. Painting and Finishing	*omitted*
L. Resilient Flooring and Carpet	*omitted*
M. Specialties	*omitted*
N. Heating and Ventilating	$41,000.00
O. Plumbing and Sprinkler	$55,500.00
P. Electrical	$68,400.00
Q. Miscellaneous Labor and Materials	$6,500.00
R. Fire Stops	$7,776.00
SUBTOTAL	$270,855.00
OVERHEAD (10%)	$27,086.00
SUBTOTAL	$297,940.50
PROFIT 8%	$23,835.24
CONTRACT SUM*	$321,775.74

*Subsequently subcontracted at savings of $135,000.00.

kosher food can be served at receptions, brown-baggers on the theatre's staff are free to eat what they please. "We're conscious of their wishes and try to strengthen the relationship," Adrienne Brockway says. "It's a fairly happy and healthy community here in the building," she adds. "And we have had a lot of parents from the school forget that this is a separate organization: they come down and say, 'See the school's theatre,' when they're showing things off."

The Eye has developed educational programs for the center and loans equipment and expertise to its landlord and other tenants, in return frequently enjoying free rehearsal space, photocopying, and computer privileges. Perhaps the most complimentary and unforeseen sign of community was an invitation to Adrienne Brockway to hire on as part-time facilities manager, because she knows the systems inside and out.

Rent per square foot on the first five-year lease worked out to $9.50. To help fund the theatre's renovation, the center credited the Eye $140,000 towards the rent. On the second five-year lease, cost increases on a sliding scale.

"Time and money," cautions Adrienne Brockway, "are the two things: renovation is always going to take longer and cost more than your original estimate. Don't believe the initial feasibility study; there will be expensive, hidden things."

Fundraising stretched out for 15 months before the basement conversion finally began in January 1987. At that point, $235,000 had been raised by four staff members while they simultaneously maintained a full production schedule. Ultimately, 225 individuals and corporations contributed. The Goldome Foundation and the Mary Livingston Griggs and Mary Griggs Burke Foundation gave capital funds. The New York State Council for the Arts Capital Funding Initiative also provided support.

The Open Eye used the fourth floor auditorium for its 1986-1987 season. But in the fall of 1987, when rising cost estimates postponed work on the basement, the auditorium was no longer available; the center had converted it to classrooms. So the Eye kept its head above water by taking its shows on the road.

THE PROGRAM. The Open Eye produces plays with universal themes—usually new works, but often classics approached in a new way. Music and movement often figure in the productions. The company also produces a special series for young audiences.

Very few of the Eye's former Upper East Side patrons visit the new space. Half of its current audience comes from the Upper West Side—most from between 79th and 105th Streets. The usual ticket holder is 35 to 55, although the Eye is aiming now for the college-to-under-30 crowd. "I think there is a big audience potential here," says Adrienne Brockway. "Every day we get calls: 'Please put me on your mailing list.' They are seeking us out—that, I like."

For its first full season in the finished space, 1988-1989, the company mounted two mainstage productions, two workshops, two director's projects, and three New Stagings for Youth. Operating on an Equity letter of agreement, the Open Eye budgeted its 1988-1989 season at just over $300,000.

Profile: THE STUDIO THEATRE

Joy Zinoman, Artistic and Managing Director
Keith Alan Baker, Associate Managing Director/Artistic Director, Secondstage

THE SPACE. Intimate, stylish, and slightly jazzy, the 200-seat Studio Theatre, at the corner of P Street and 14th Street NW in Washington, opened in October 1987.

The Studio Theatre occupies all of the first and most of the third floors of a factory/warehouse building, formerly the Petrovich Auto Repair Shop. It leases a total of 11,170 sq. ft. of space—almost double the 6,525 sq. ft. of space in the warehouse it formerly occupied. Classrooms for the Acting Conservatory, a vital part of the theatre concept and operation, occupy 1,500 sq. ft. on the third floor. The administrative offices are also on the third floor, as is a 1,200-sq. ft. scene shop, which is linked with the first floor and stage by a very large industrial-height elevator designed to move cars.

THE LOCATION. Situated at the edge of an upscale residential neighborhood a few blocks from Dupont Circle, the Studio Theatre put down roots in an area of warehouses and shops, several of which are being converted to performance spaces.

THE STORY. Even before there was a Studio Theatre, there was the successful and very profitable Acting Conservatory established by Joy Zinoman in 1975. The professional company, founded in 1978, grew organically from the school. Nomadic at first, the Studio Theatre first set up shop in permanent quarters at 1401 Church Street NW but soon outgrew its space. Luckily, it found its new home just a few blocks away.

The Studio Theatre gives off an aura of everything having been done just right. But artistic director Zinoman would be the first to say otherwise. Hindsight being 20/20, there are many things she and the designer, Russell Metheny, would have done differently—not in matters of design intent, but in terms of the construction process.

Zinoman and Metheny are perfectionists. The theatre had more than its share of Kafkaesque encounters with the building department: daily confrontations over changes and delayed permits, resulting in a total work stoppage of several weeks at one point. Zinoman says she never would have allowed work to commence on the third floor offices and classrooms before the first-floor plans were approved, had she known the great confusion this would create at the department of buildings: was this a school or was it a theatre? Compounding this chaos, the city was in the process of switch-

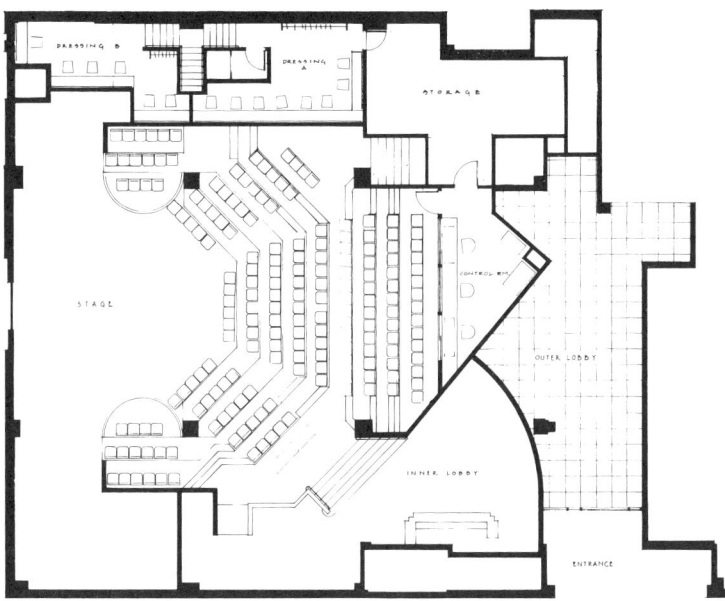

Studio Theatre seating diagram. The farthest seat is only 28' from the leading edge of the stage. In addition to the four main sections of seating, there are two loges, each seating 15, on either side of the modified thrust stage. These are removable. Taking away one loge could provide space for a small orchestra; removing both could allow for producing a major Greek tragedy.

Studio Theatre facade.

ing over from its old building code to the Building Officials and Code Administrators (BOCA) code with D.C. supplements. Despite these nightmares, the theatre opened on time. And while Metheny and Zinoman continue to fine-tune it, audiences are enthusiastic.

THE DESIGN. In setting the plan of the auditorium into the existing footprint of the warehouse, Metheny and the architect planned around the 30'-wide by 20'-deep column spans with great skill. The columns in no way limit the playing space, nor do they seriously obstruct sightlines. In fact, the way they break up the auditorium space heightens the intimacy and sense of expectation.

The theatre's 200-seat capacity is almost twice that of the old space. Metheny cleverly laid out the seating in six separate but interrelated sections that create real—not just perceived—intimacy.

Audience comfort has been a primary consideration. The padded, flip-up seats are a comfortable 36" back-to-back and upholstered in deep blue fabric flecked with gray. The auditorium and inner lobby carpeting is dusty rose; the walls, "raven's brown."

Sharing the outer lobby with the other tenants in the building has created few problems. To the left is the box office, and multiple

> Russell Metheny cleverly laid out the seating in six separate but interrelated sections that create real—not just perceived—intimacy.

doors lead to an inner lobby with ample space for intermission mingling as well as a bar for food and drinks. Carpeted, curved stairs finished with mahogany nosing lead to the auditorium. Concealed lighting along each step completes the dramatic effect. A special lift in the inner lobby and restrooms on both first and third floors were designed to serve the handicapped.

The ceiling height in the theatre is just over 15': not ideal, but enough to allow for good vertical sightlines and to double-deck the control booth and the box office.

Lighting equipment is hung from a suspended pipe grid using a 4' square module over the audience and a 2' x 4' module above the stage. It is equipped with five raceways to minimize cable runs and the spaghetti of overhead cables often found in small theatres. The computer board in the control booth is a Strand Century Light Palette M with capacity for 120 dimmers and 120 circuits. Daniel McLean Wagner, lighting designer, put the system

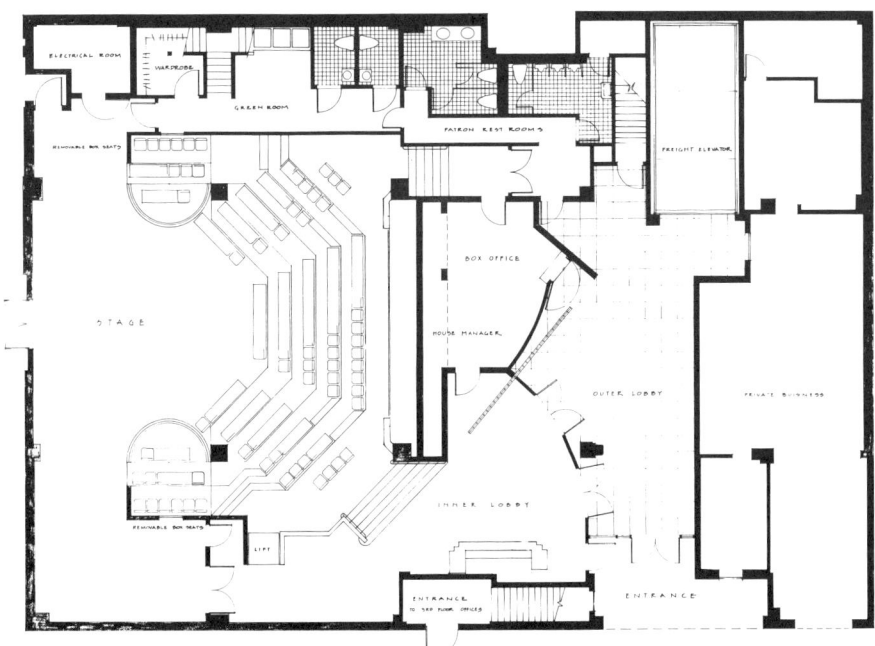

Studio Theatre intermediate level plan.

and installation outside the general contract, which gave him more financial and design control: the cost was $40,000 for the control board, dimmers, and grid.

The sound operator and stage manager are also located in the control booth. It stretches across the back of the auditorium above and behind the last row of seats, giving excellent sightlines to the stage.

Two dressing rooms, a green room, two restrooms, and a shower serve 20 actors. There is a wardrobe maintenance space but no in-house costume shop. This was one of the trade-offs Zinoman reluctantly made at the outset when deciding how much space the company could afford on its initial ten-year lease. With the building's other tenants on five-year leases, the Studio Theatre will

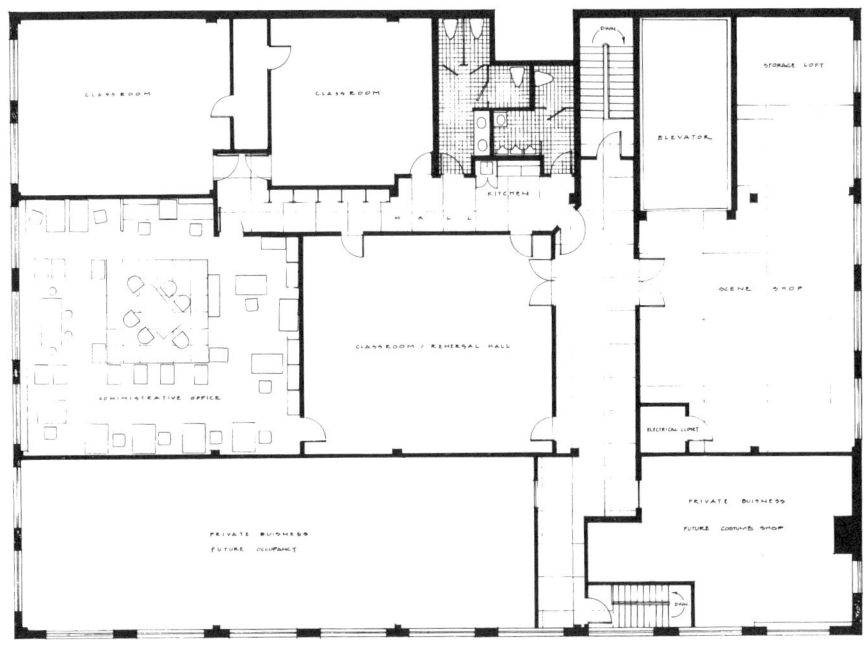

Studio Theatre third floor administrative offices, classrooms and support spaces.

have the opportunity to negotiate for future expansion. It plans to add a costume shop, along with much-needed storage space.

The offices are all in a single 1,500-sq. ft., open-plan room—a concept that gets "mixed reviews" from some staff. But Zinoman feels about the entire operation that "there are no secrets." A central atrium-like conference area with a large, oval table and chairs dominates the space; a ring of filing cabinets (painted stark white, but artfully splattered in black by Metheny) face outward toward the desks, which line the walls. One plus for this open plan is that everyone enjoys great natural light from the floor-to-ceiling, factory-style windows—as do the plants.

CONVERSION COST. The original estimate for the conversion of the warehouse into theatre came in at $500,000. It worsened with each revision, and the final bill was just under $800,000. By the end of capital funding phase 1, $575,000 had been raised for operating and some construction costs. In phase 2 at the beginning of 1988, the capital fund deficit stood at $390,000; $140,000 was retired that year, $100,000 the next, and $150,000 refinanced under a special long-term city loan at 6% interest. In order to make all this happen, there were regular Monday morning funding strategy sessions which were, for Zinoman, inviolate. During the initial capital funding campaign, the theatre hired a professional fund-raiser, but Zinoman soon took over the drive herself, realizing that donors want to see the theatre's "major players" when they give money.

THE PROGRAM. Since its creation in 1978, the Studio Theatre has become a major force in Washington's theatrical life. Zinoman clearly has her finger on the pulse of her audience. In one of the nation's most conservative cities, the Studio Theatre has created a family-oriented theatre with classics like *Ah, Wilderness!*, *A Raisin in the Sun*, *The Seagull*, and *Romeo and Juliet*. But it also has cultivated new and diverse audiences with D.C. premieres like *Ma Rainey's Black Bottom*, *As Is*, *The Slab Boys Trilogy*, *My Sister in This House*, and *North Shore Fish*, which opened the theatre.

The production budget for each play in the five-play season of 1986-1987 (the last year in the old 110-seat theatre) was $27,000. For the 1987-1988 season in the new space, it increased only to $31,000. By 1988-1989 the budget had jumped to $40,000 as the company moved away from volunteers and toward more paid staff.

A major component of the company's activities is the Acting Conservatory, which opened in 1975 with a single class and has grown to become the largest, most distinguished conservatory of its kind in Washington. The three-year curriculum offers 34 classes in a three-semester year. The work is based on Stanislavski Method realism. In 1986-87, the conservatory generated $90,000 in income; for 1987-1988, in the new space with better and expanded classrooms, the gross was $119,000; in fiscal year 1992 income was $130,000 and it continues to increase as full utilization of the new facilities becomes more efficient. There are places for 450 students in the 34 classes—one hundred more than in the old theatre. Plans call for a library in the future.

The Studio Theatre has a strong subscription base. It leapt from 900 in 1986-1987 to 1,500 in 1987-1988, and 2,000 in 1988-1989. Single ticket sales are also handled by a box office staff of three; the theatre also has a tie-in with the Ticket Place, the half-price office run by Washington's Cultural Alliance.

The audience profile changes noticeably in age, income, and ethnic composition with each play; the core subscribers are primarily white, middle income, and in their 40s and 50s.

The total operating budget for 1988-1989 was $900,000. Joy Zinoman reminisces, "It was $30,000, like, yesterday! . . . You know, I suppose I shouldn't admit this, but I thought it would be harder to do than it was."

PART FOUR

MAKING IT LEGAL:

AN INTERPRETATION OF REGULATIONS AND CODES

INTRODUCTION

The chapters that follow interpret New York City's zoning resolutions (chapter 14); its building, electrical, and fire prevention codes (chapters 15-17); and their application procedures (chapter 18). These chapters provide models for understanding codes in most cities. Chapter 19 outlines the similarities and differences among the codes in five other major theatre centers—Atlanta, Boston, Chicago, Los Angeles, and San Francisco—dealing exclusively with the sections of these codes that apply to small theatre spaces. While codes differ from place to place, the basic rules and principles are similar.

The Appendices at the end of this section list government agencies and contact information for the six cities. These organizations can provide additional information needed on zoning, codes, permits, and services.

IMPLICATIONS OF ZONING AND THE CODES

Code requirements are often onerous, but they should not be ignored in the hope that an inspector won't show up. Throughout the country there have been serious theatre and nightclub fires, primarily due to the owners' disregard for code requirements and the illegal use of spaces. As a result, building and fire departments in many cities have cracked down heavily on their requirements for places of public assembly, and they issue violations more frequently for illegal and nonconforming uses of space. Depending upon the seriousness of the violation, you may get a verbal warning, or you may receive written notification with a specified amount of time in which to comply. Or you could be threatened with an immediate shutdown of operations.

The main concern of an inspector is public safety. Correcting hazardous violations should, in any event, be your first concern too. If you can show that your theatre is safe and that you are attempting to keep it up to code, chances are good that you will not be overly bothered by inspectors.

ROUTINE ON-SITE INSPECTIONS

The fire department, department of buildings, and the bureau of gas and electricity all have the authority to make routine, on-site inspections. Past practice, however, indicates that small theatres are most likely to be visited routinely by the fire department, with only an occasional electrical inspection.

The fire department does routine inspections of all buildings within its geographical jurisdiction. Even such establishment places as Carnegie Hall and Avery Fisher Hall are visited regularly. It is conceivable that you could operate for a year without being visited, or you could receive a visit the day after you open, or—worse—the day *before* you open. Inspections usually occur in the evening while the space is operating.

The inspector will check to see that there are no violations of public assembly space or fire prevention regulations, such as using combustible materials where not permitted, having more seats than allowed or obstructing aisles or exits. Be prepared to present a complete set of all the records, drawings and permits as well as the fire inspection log. The importance of this cannot be stressed enough. (For an inspection checklist, see chapter 17.)

If temporary changes have been made for a particular production, explain that they are *temporary,* and the space will be changed back to what was originally approved. The inspector may let the matter pass. But if he returns six months later and finds these same "temporary changes," a lengthier explanation will be required.

It is best to handle inspectors in a friendly way, developing a relationship that lets the inspector know that every effort is being made to comply and that the safety of the public is of mutual concern. Keeping a fire inspection log (see chapter 17) and presenting it to the inspector along with all the records, requisite statements, and permits will prove your good intentions.

If you are visited by an inspector, *don't panic.* Nothing catastrophic is likely to happen. Walk the inspector through the space and answer questions, but don't volunteer information that's not requested. If a violation is found, ask what is wrong, why, and how it can be remedied. Depending on the inspector, you may get either some very good advice or just a quote from the applicable code book.

One Off-Off-Broadway theatre manager regularly receives an 8" x 10" glossy and bio of the fire inspector's nephew. The inspector is perennially distressed that the theatre does not call his nephew to audition, but there have been no written violations either.

14 ZONING

The zoning laws and codes affecting small theatres are complicated. Don't expect to grasp all the details at once. Most architects and other trained professionals refer to the law and codes again and again for specifics. Keep in mind that all requirements do not apply to every theatre situation.

USE GROUPS AND ZONING DISTRICTS

Zoning creates sets of regulations that separate different activities that go on in a city, so that they do not conflict with one another. Under the city of New York zoning resolution, which is primarily enforced by the department of buildings, these activities are divided into categories called *use groups*. Theatre falls into Use Group 8.

New York City is broken into zoning districts where the various use groups are permitted. There are three basic zoning districts: *residential (R)*, *commercial (C)*, and *manufacturing (M)*. These basic districts exist in most cities.

Numerical Designations

DENSITY. Each of these districts is further broken down by a numerical designation that generally indicates *density*, or how much of that activity can take place. For instance, a residential district may be designated R1—single family detached houses—or R8—high-rise apartment buildings; and a commercial district may be designated C1—small retail and service shops—or C8—heavy commercial services, like warehouses.

Use Group 8, which includes theatre activities, is permitted by right in zones designated C2, C4, C6, C8, M1 (excluding M1-5B), M2, and M3. Should a theatre company wish to locate in one of these zones, the use cannot be contested and no zoning variance is required. Generally, a zoning category can be upgraded—that is, a commercial use can go into a manufacturing zone—but it is more difficult to justify downgrading a category—putting a commercial use into a residential zone.

RESTRICTIONS AND REQUIREMENTS. To make matters even more complicated, each subcategory (C2, C4, etc.) also carries another numerical designation (C2-1, C4-5), which indicates other restrictions, such as maximum allowable floor area (the total floor area of a building permitted on a zoning lot) and building size, and requirements such as parking spaces and the amount of open area on a zoning lot. Parking requirements will vary with the district and the use. In some cases they may be waived by a modification granted by the board of standards and appeals, and reviewed by the department of buildings.

For information on restrictions and requirements for specific numerical designations, call the department of city planning. (See Agency Chart.)

Zoning Maps

When looking for a space, check the zoning maps of the areas in which you are interested to see where the C2, C4, C6, C8, M1, M2, and M3 districts are located. Once you have found a space, check the location again to make doubly certain that it is in one of these zoning districts. Zoning maps are available from the department of city planning. If the information on the map is not clear, call the department of city planning, zoning information. (See Agency Chart.)

GETTING A ZONING VARIANCE

If, despite all efforts, the space you finally choose is in a nontheatre zone, then by law, you

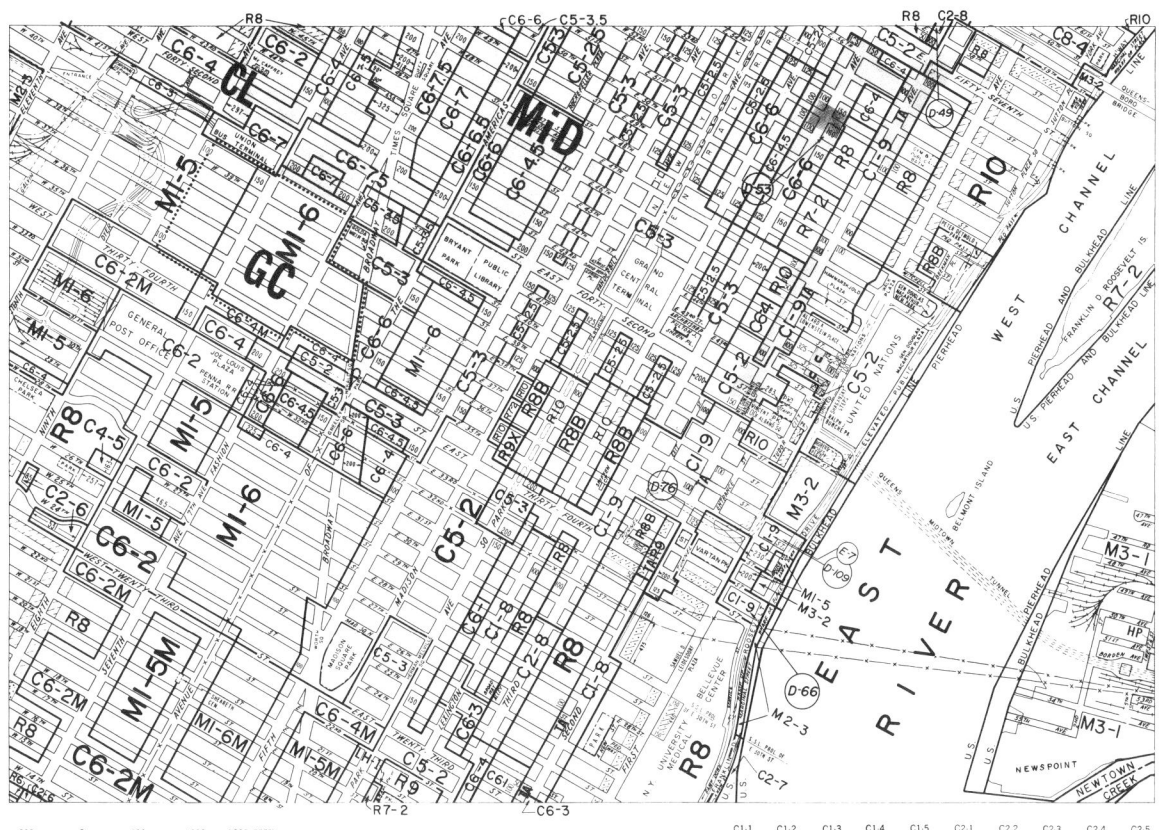

Zoning Map 8D, New York City. The Midtown Redevelopment (MiD) and Garment District (GC) theatre areas are marked.

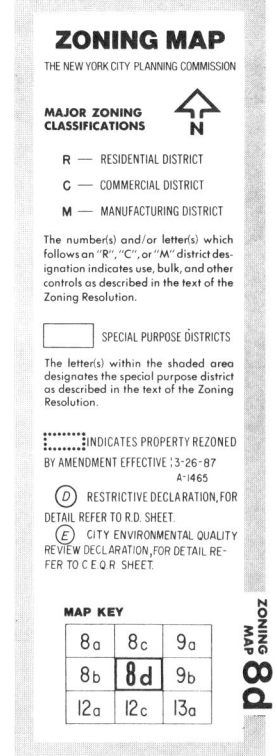

must file for a zoning variance. This can be a long process, and there are no guarantees that you will receive it. The following is the procedure for getting a variance in New York City. The procedure is similar in most cities.

Appearing Before the Community Board

The first step takes place at the local level. It requires contacting the community board in your district and explaining who you are, what you are doing, and that you would like to get on the agenda for the next meeting of the board. You will then be given the date and the place of the meeting and placed on the agenda under "new business."

When you appear at the meeting, you will be asked to explain who you are and to present your intentions, your artistic directions, your past experience in the theatre, and your financial viability. If you have drawings of what you plan to do to your space, present them at this time.

The matter will be disposed to committee for consideration and, no doubt, you will be asked to come to a committee meeting and to talk again in more detail.

Next, a public hearing will be scheduled and notice posted in the community that the issue will be open to public debate. Any interested community people can attend and voice objections to or support of your plan. The community board, taking public opinion into account, will move on the request by voting either favorably or unfavorably. (See chapter 6 for more information on community boards.)

Filing with the Department of Buildings

The next step is one of formality. You file plans with the department of buildings for the issuance of a new certificate of occupancy. Since your theatre is not a legal use you will be "officially rejected." You must be officially rejected in order to appeal for a zoning variance before the city's board of standards and appeals.

Board of Standards and Appeals Hearing

The appeals process is a legal hearing. You need to be represented by either the architect who submitted the plans, or a lawyer, or both. The board of standards and appeals will consider such things as the alteration of the character of the neighborhood, impaired use of adjacent property, and the effect of your use on public welfare.

If the community board has favorably advised the board of standards and appeals regarding your zoning variance, it is likely that it will pass.

You may further be required to appear before other city agencies before a variance is granted if your project involves city money—either through direct funding or tax abatement.

15
THE BUILDING CODE

Building codes are written to insure the safety of all structures and people who inhabit them. They establish requirements for such things as material, construction, number of exits, emergency lighting, ventilation, and plumbing.

The Building Code of the City of New York is one of the most comprehensive building codes in the country. Entirely rewritten in 1968, it has been amended regularly since then. It serves well in providing examples of the kinds of requirements that must be met in constructing or converting spaces for use as small theatres in urban communities.

Each of the other five cities highlighted in this book uses either an adaptation of a nationally approved code like the Building Officials and Code Administrators' (BOCA) code, or one of its own making. Each city adopts its own building code so you must inquire from the department of buildings in your city as to what code is in use. You should also recognize that the building, fire and electrical codes as discussed here present an overview of current code requirements in layperson's terms. As the codes are, for the most part, virtually unintelligible, it is advisable to consult with someone conversant with your current local codes.

The building code is law and, like most other laws, is subject to interpretation by those who administer it. Precisely how it will be interpreted cannot be known until plans are presented to the department of buildings for approval. The simpler the ideas for a space, the less difficulty there should be in obtaining approval.

DEFINITIONS

Familiarity with the following terms will be helpful in understanding building code requirements.

Access stairs. Stairs between two floors that do not meet requirements for an exit.

Assessed value. The value of the building as determined by the city for purposes of taxation. It does not necessarily reflect what the building may sell for on the open market.

Certificate of Occupancy (C of O). The document, issued by the department of buildings, which authorizes use of a certain space for specified activities by a certain number of people.

Corridor. An enclosed public passageway providing access from rooms or spaces to an exit.

Dead load. The weight of all permanent materials, equipment, and construction supported by a building, including its own weight.

Exit. A means of egress from the interior of a building to an open exterior space that is provided by the use of the following, either singly or in combination: exterior door openings, stairs or ramps, exit passageways, horizontal exits, interior or exterior stairs, or fire escapes. Does not include access stairs, aisles, corridors or corridor doors.

Exit passageway. A horizontal extension of stairs or ramps, a passage leading from a yard or court to an open exterior space.

Fire-resistance rating. A rating, given in hours, which indicates the amount of time a wall, floor, or ceiling must remain intact under conditions of fire. Following are ratings mentioned in this text, with definitions applied to wall construction.

1 hour	5/8" Sheetrock, both sides of wall on wooden studs
2 hour	Two 5/8" layers of Sheetrock, both sides of wall on steel or aluminum studs
3 hour	6" masonry wall with plaster both sides, or 8" masonry wall without plaster

(The principal concern a theatre has with fire ratings is to be certain that the means of egress from the space conform to the ratings required for theatre use.)

Fire-retardant. Materials that have been pressure-impregnated with chemicals so as to reduce combustibility.

First story. The first story above grade. However, if the building has a full basement, then the basement is considered the first story.

Flameproof. Materials that have been externally treated with chemicals in order to reduce combustibility.

Flame-spread rating. The degree of flame resistance of materials used for interior finish or decorative purposes; determined by the rate of flame spread in the standard tunnel test.

Grade. The finished surface of the ground, either paved or unpaved.

Live load. The weight of all occupants, materials, and equipment that are likely to be moved or relocated in a building, and that must be supported by the building in addition to the dead load. Live load is rated in pounds per sq. ft.

Load-bearing walls and columns. Walls and columns which support the wall and floor construction above.

Noncombustible material. A material that will not ignite when heated to a temperature of 1,200 degrees Fahrenheit.

Means of egress. The path of an exit. This can be a door; a door and a stairwell; or a door, a stairwell and a passageway.

Occupancy. The type of activity for which a building or space is used and/or the number of persons using a space. In a theatre space, this includes audience, actors and employees.

Place of Assembly permit. Permit required by and obtained from the department of buildings if you have more than the normally permitted number of persons using a space.

Safe area. An interior or exterior space that serves as a means of egress by providing a transitional area from an assembly place, and that also serves as a normal means of entry to the assembly place.

Unit width of egress. Usually 22": unit for stairs and enclosed passageways refers to how many people the stair or passage can accommodate at one time, single-file and moving.

OLD CODE OR NEW CODE

This section deals with the New York City codes. Study it even if you plan to locate outside New York; the codes developed by other cities do not vary greatly from New York's. Chapter 19 summarizes how several cities' codes differ from New York's.

The city of New York has two different codes in effect, referred to as the *old code* and the *new code.* The new code went into effect as of December 6, 1968. If an application for a building permit was filed with the department of buildings before December 6, 1968, or within 12 months after that date, the owner had the option of filing under either code.

The code that governs a specific space currently depends on the following circumstances:

- If a building was built under the new code, then any renovation in that building must conform to the *new code.*

- If a building was built under the old code, but the cost of renovation is 60% or more of the assessed value of the building, then the entire building must comply with the *new code,* even if only a part of it is being changed.

- If a building was built under the old code, but the cost of renovation is between 30% and 60% of the assessed value of the building, then only the part that is being changed must comply with the *new code.*

- If the building was built under the old code, and the cost of renovation is 30% or less than the assessed value of the building, the renovation can be filed under the *old code.*

Cost of renovation includes only the cost of materials and labor; it does not include professional fees, or money spent on furnishings or electrical work. Doing most of the work yourself will not exempt you from including the labor costs in the job, although they can be figured at a minimal number of hours at the minimum wage.

Although architects cite advantages to working under each of the codes, for small, nonprofit theatres there seem to be few, if any, advantages to filing under the new code. For example, wall, ceiling and floor fire ratings, which may meet the old code requirements for theatre use, may not be satisfactory to new code specifications. Their acceptability will depend on the building's classification, the theatre's occupancy group, and the occupancy groups located directly above, below and adjacent to your space.

Try by every means possible to renovate under the old code. This means keeping the renovation budget at 30% or less of the assessed value of the building. An experienced architect can be of enormous value in helping to convince the department of buildings that the renovation will not exceed the 30% mark.

The assessed value of a building can be checked at the bureau of real property assessment. (See Agency Chart.)

Occupancy

One of the main differences between the old code and the new code is that of the occupancy categories and their related requirements. The difference is significant for the small theatre in terms of bringing a space up to code.

Under the old code, there are two occupancy categories applicable to small theatre: *74 occupants or fewer* and *75 occupants or more.* The second of these categories actually covers occupancies between 75 and 298. For 299 occupants or more, the old code has a third category, designated *special occupancy.*

The new code has only two categories: *74 occupants or fewer* and *75 occupants or more.*

Under either code, the requirements for 74 occupants or fewer are the easiest to satisfy, and a place of assembly permit is not required.

When a theatre has an occupancy of more than 74 and fewer than 299, it is of great advantage to be under the old code since the building need not comply with the requirements for large theatres, but only those in the special occupancy category. In contrast, under the new code, any theatre in the second category, 75 occupants or more, must meet all the requirements laid out for large theatres. Whether the occupancy is 75, 300 or 1,000, the requirements are the same—the new code shows no mercy.

OLD CODE REQUIREMENTS

BUILDING CLASSIFICATION

The first concept with which the old code deals is *building classification*. It is important to be familiar with this when looking at spaces. A classification is assigned to a building depending on the type of materials used in its construction.

The building classifications followed by a brief description are given below:

Class 1—Fireproof. The exterior and interior are all masonry or concrete, including interior columns.

Class 2—Fire-protected. All masonry or concrete interior or exterior, very similar to Class 1. The difference between these two classes will be difficult to see. It has more to do with how much of a material was used and therefore how long the structure is protected against fire.

Class 3—Non-fireproofed. The exterior is masonry but the interior has wooden beams and floors with interior columns of wood or cast iron. Loft buildings with tin ceilings are likely to be class 3 buildings; the ceilings were put up to cover the wooden beams.

Class 4—Wood frame. All wooden exterior and interior.

Class 5—Metal or fireproofed wood structure. Walls are metal. Interior is fireproofed wood.

Class 6—Heavy timber. Exterior is usually masonry, interior is heavy timber construction with columns and beams not fewer than 10" to 12" in size.

These classifications cover every type of building built in New York City; the law permits theatre use in all of them. However, the location in the building where the theatre is allowed, and the amount of square footage it can occupy, differ according to the building classification.

Class 1. Theatre is permitted on any floor of the building without any limitation in size.

Class 2. Theatre is not permitted above 32' or the third story, and is limited to 7,500 sq. ft. in size.

Class 3. Theatre is permitted only on the first story of a multistory (three stories or more) building, but on either story of a two-story building, and is limited to 5,000 sq. ft. in size.

Class 4. Theatre is permitted in a one-story building and is limited to 600 sq. ft. in size.

Class 5. Theatre is permitted in a one-story building and is limited to 600 sq. ft. in size.

Class 6. Theatre is permitted only on the first story and is limited to 6,000 sq. ft. in size.

Obviously, class 4 and 5 buildings are out of the question for a theatre because of the size limitations. Fortunately, these two classes of buildings, along with class 6 buildings, are not very common in the city. Most likely you will be looking at class 1, 2 or 3 buildings.

It is important to know the location, square footage and floor restrictions among the various classes, but you cannot know the correct classification by just looking at the structure. The only way to be certain is to check the classification of the building, indicated on the current C of O for the space. If the C of O is not posted, the classification of the building may be found at the department of buildings. The square footage limitation for theatres includes all support spaces, even offices. It is possible, however, to locate offices or other support spaces on additional square footage within the same building if they are separate entities.

MEANS OF EGRESS

74 Occupants or Fewer (on first story)

Whether the theatre occupies the entire floor of a building or shares the floor with other tenants:

- Only one means of egress is required.
- Minimum door size is 3'8". It must swing in the direction of egress; if it opens inward, it will have to be rehung so that it opens outward.

74 Occupants or Fewer (above the first story)

If the theatre occupies an entire floor of the building:

- Two means of egress are required.
- Both exit stairs must have a 2-hour fire rating, be a minimum of 3'8" wide, and lead directly to the street. In some instances the door to the street will not be located at the foot of the stairs, but an exit passageway will lead from the stairs to the exterior door. This is fine as long as the passageway has the same fire rating as the stairs.

If a theatre shares a floor with other tenants:

- Only one means of egress from the space is required. However, it must lead from the theatre space into a public corridor leading to two exit stairs.
- This means of egress must be a minimum of 3'8" wide.

The following are the requirements for the corridor and the stairwell for tenants sharing a floor above the first story:

- The public corridor must have a 1-hour fire rating.

- Minimum width of the public corridor must be 3'8"; this will accommodate 50 persons. The width must be increased 6" for every additional 50 persons occupying the floor.
- Both exit stairs must have a 2-hour fire rating.
- Minimum width of each set of exit stairs is 3'8". This width will accommodate 120 persons per stairs or a total of 240 persons for both stairs. Be certain that the occupancy plus the number of other people on the floor does not exceed 240. This rule applies even if the other tenants use their space during the day and you use yours at night. Capacity is figured on the assumption that everyone is there at once.
- In a class 1 building above the third story or the 32' line, the capacity for 3'8" stairways drops to 60 persons per stair. Make sure that the total occupancy for the floor does not exceed 120, the limit permitted by the number of stairs.

Fulfilling these requirements is the responsibility of the landlord, but check to make certain they have been met.

75 Occupants or More (occupying entire floor)

If a theatre occupies an entire floor, on the first story or above the first story:

- Two means of egress are required.
- Minimum door size is 3'8", and it must swing in direction of egress.
- Exit stairs (for spaces above first story) must have a 2-hour fire rating and be a minimum of 3'8" in width.

75 Occupants or More (more than one tenant per floor)

If the tenant shares the floor with other tenants on the first story:

- Two means of egress are required.

- Minimum door size is 3'8" and must swing in the direction of egress.

If the theatre shares a floor with other tenants above the first story:

- Two means of egress are required, a minimum of 3'8" each; these must lead from the theatre space into a public corridor which leads to two exit stairs.

The requirements for the corridors and stairwells are the same as for 74 occupants or fewer, above the first story.

Other Requirements for Means of Egress

The following requirements apply to all means of egress regardless of occupancy categories.

DISTANCE BETWEEN EXITS. Where two means of egress are required, the second exit must be a minimum of one-third the depth of the building away from the first exit. In other words, if the building is 100' deep, the two exits must be at least 33' apart.

HANDRAILS. All stairs must have handrails on one side. If they are wider than 3'8", they must have handrails on both sides.

DOORS. All doors opening onto exit stairwells must have a 3/4-hour fire rating, be self-closing, and open in the direction of egress. A 3/4-hour fire-rated, self-closing door should have an underwriter's label or a label from the board of standards and appeals. If a new door is purchased, make sure you ask for a 3/4-hour fire-rated self-closing door that is labeled.

EXIT STAIRS. In order for stairs to be used as exit stairs, they must be enclosed in fire-rated construction and separated from any adjacent uses by a fire-rated door. Open stairs, of the type found in brownstones and in many class 3 loft buildings, and those that are not separated from the common hallway, are not acceptable as exit stairs.

Upper Floor Spaces

If you are considering a space on an upper floor of a class 3 loft building, be cautious. Many of these buildings do not have the required two means of egress from the upper floors. Usually there is no practical way to provide a second means of egress.

Also, many were built with wooden stairs that have winders, steps that are wedge-shaped and turn a corner. Wooden stairs are never legal, and winders are not permitted on stairs used as a legal means of egress. In these types of buildings, it is best to find a ground-floor space.

If a building does have two means of egress from the upper floors and the stairs are enclosed in concrete (usually class 1 and class 2 buildings), then, in all likelihood, they already will have the proper fire ratings and the correct door swings, and will lead to the right places in terms of egress requirements.

Note: Elevators are not permitted as means of egress.

SEAT AND ROW SPACING

No more than seven seats in a row are permitted if there is an aisle on only one side of the row. If there are aisles on both sides of the row, up to 14 seats are allowed in any one row.

There is no minimum front-to-back dimension required by the old code between rows of seats. Common sense should be followed here, or follow new code guidelines.

LIVE LOAD

Live load is the number of pounds per sq. ft. that a given floor can support. The code is concerned with live load as a safety factor. Each use or activity is assigned a minimum value, described in pounds per sq. ft.

The theatre auditorium is required to have a 60 pounds per sq. ft. live load value if there are fixed seats.

If there are movable seats, a 100 pounds per sq. ft. live load value is required.

The stage area is required to have a live load value of 100 pounds per sq. ft.

The floors must meet the live load requirements for theatre use. This is not something you have to calculate, as the building will have a previously assigned live load value. Check to make sure it is equal to, or more than, the live load required for theatre use. This information will appear on the certificate of occupancy for the previous use. If there's no C of O, the information will appear on the last alteration application. This can be found in the plan room at the department of buildings, filed under the building address. (See Agency Chart.)

Most manufacturing and loft buildings have a live load of 120 pounds per sq. ft., so space found in one of these buildings should present no problem. The first floors of most commercial structures were designed for 100 pounds per sq. ft. of live load; therefore, spaces that were originally stores, supermarkets and banks will have the necessary live load rating. Structures designed for residential or office use usually have live load values of 40 pounds and 50 pounds per sq. ft., respectively; these will not conform to theatre requirements.

EXIT LIGHTING

EXIT SIGNS. Illuminated exit signs must be placed over all exits. (See chapter 16.)

LIGHTING ON STAIRS. Lighting must be provided for all exit stairs. This should be the responsibility of the landlord, so make sure the landlord replaces bulbs when they burn out.

EMERGENCY LIGHTING

Emergency lighting, as required by the new code for public assembly spaces, is retroactive to old code buildings. The location of emergency lighting must be shown on architectural drawings, and electrical service must be run on a separate circuit. (See chapter 16.)

VENTILATION

Some means of providing fresh air and removing stale air must be provided in any building, be it a 74-seat theatre or an assembly hall occupied by several thousand people. The amount of ventilation required depends upon the size of the space and the number of people occupying it. There are formulas and tables in the code for calculating the amount of ventilation required.

Once you have calculated the ventilation index (measured in cubic feet per minute—cfm) for a space and figured the required amount of supply and exhaust, check the rating of any current ventilation system installed in the space to determine if it will meet the new cfm requirements for the theatre's occupancy.

If no ventilation system is present, light industrial or commercial fans can be installed to meet the code requirements. This will avoid the expense of installing a mechanical ventilation system. Light commercial or industrial fans are rated in cfm.

The code requirements for supply and exhaust present many problems to the small theatre. Obviously the simplest and cheapest way to comply is to install the properly rated fans in existing windows in a space, but fans are often noisy and distracting, and open windows will bring in street noise. Also, fans do not cool or warm the air as does a mechanical ventilation system.

PLUMBING AND SANITARY REQUIREMENTS

Under the old code, commercial establishments must supply at least one water closet for employees.

The old code is vague in its requirements for the audience. For places of public assembly, the old code states that a sufficient number of water closets and urinals must be supplied as directed by the borough superintendent. They must be in an accessible location and marked with signs clearly indicating their purpose. For a small theatre of either 74 or 100 seats, one facility for each sex will suffice.

SPRINKLERS

The old code does not require theatre spaces with 299 seats or fewer to be sprinklered. However, sprinklers sometimes are required in storage areas and dressing rooms by the fire department. The requirement will not come from the department of buildings when plans are initially submitted, but from the fire department, after routine on-site inspection.

Also, New York fire inspectors have frequently issued citations even to 74-seat workshop theatres, requiring them to install sprinklers over open or thrust stage areas, even though the theatres are in buildings coming under the old code.

FIRE-RETARDANT AND FLAMEPROOF

All materials used in the construction of a space must be fire-retardant or flameproof. If wood is used to construct platforms, stages, or walls, it must be fire-retardant wood that meets the standards of the Department of Buildings. Fire-retardant wood may not have a flame spread greater than 25 and must bear a label from the manufacturer stating this. Fire-retardant paint is not an acceptable means of fire treatment for ordinary wood.

All draperies and other fabrics must be flameproofed. Drapery materials for the theatre are usually purchased already flameproofed. However, if you use untreated materials, a standard flameproofing compound is available from any theatrical paint supply company. It is a dry chemical that is mixed with water and sprayed on.

To comply with the flameproofing requirement:

- Flameproofing treatment is good for one year, so each year flameproofing must be repeated. When this is done, write a statement, including the date and the calendar number on the can, and get this statement notarized. Keep it with your other records. (See flameproofing affidavit, chapter 18.)
- Save receipts showing the date of purchase and the quantity of purchase.

NEW CODE REQUIREMENTS

OCCUPANCY CLASSIFICATION

Under the new code, occupancy classifications have been established. (These should not be confused with use group classifications of the zoning resolution.) Two categories of occupancy classifications apply to the theatre:

F1-A. Includes buildings and spaces in which scenery or scenic elements are used.

F1-B. Includes buildings and spaces in which scenery or scenic elements are *not* used.

Scenery and scenic elements are defined as anything movable or temporary; they do not include movable seats or any permanent part of the theatre construction, such as stage walls.

Choosing the F1-A or F1-B category would be an important decision to make before drawing up plans and filing under the new code. Consider the limitations of F1-B carefully. Once a theatre is filed as an F1-B, the fire department can issue a violation if it inspects and finds any temporary scenic elements or props being used on stage. Even a chair placed on stage is defined as a temporary scenic element.

Requirements for Theatres with Scenery or Scenic Elements (F1-A)

If scenery is used, the following requirements apply to the stage areas and to the scenery:

- All scenery or scenic elements must be constructed of noncombustible materials and be rendered flameproof.
- Any scenery or scenic elements placed in the seating area must not obstruct exit signs, exit doors, or path of travel to exits.
- The stage floor construction must meet the same fire ratings as that of the building's floor. This also applies to any trapdoors set into the stage floor. In addition, the rooms or spaces beneath the trapdoors must also meet the same fire rating as that of the building's floor. These rooms or spaces cannot be used for workshops or storage areas—the only storage that is permitted is scenery that is used during a performance.
- The stage area must have two means of egress, remote from each other, which usually means on opposite sides of the stage.
- Emergency ventilation is a code requirement for the stage area. However, this code requirement was written with relation to the traditional proscenium theatre, so the specifications cannot be directly applied to other configurations such as arena and thrust stages. This does not mean that these types of stages are exempt from the emergency ventilation requirement, but rather that the department of buildings must interpret these specifications and their application on an individual basis.

Requirements for Theatres without Scenery (F1-B)

If you file under this category, your certificate of occupancy will designate F1-B use only, but the requirements are far less stringent than the ones for theatres with scenery.

- Raised platforms may be built as stages when they are supported on floors having the required fire-resistance ratings. In addition, the area below the platforms must be enclosed on all sides.
- The stage area must have two means of egress, remote from each other, which means on opposite sides of the stage.
- There are no requirements for emergency stage ventilation.

This category could be useful if you are doing only concerts or readings in the space.

BUILDING CLASSIFICATION

Buildings filed under the new code are classified according to construction groups: class I structures are noncombustible, and class II structures are combustible. The following are the classifications, with a run-down on where theatre can be located and how much space it can occupy. Be certain to check the classification before signing a lease.

Descriptions of building classifications have not been provided. These specifications are very detailed, and it is extremely difficult to distinguish visually between classifications. Any building classified under the new code, having been built since 1968, will have its classification listed on the certificate of occupancy.

Class IA. Theatre is permitted on any floor without any limit on square footage.

Class IB. Theatre is permitted on any floor without any limit on square footage.

Class IC. Theatre is permitted up to 85', or seven stories, without any limit on square footage.

Class ID. Theatre is permitted up to 75', or six stories, and is limited to 17,500 sq. ft.

Class IE. Theatre is permitted up to 40', or three stories, and limited to 10,500 sq. ft.

Class IIA. Theatre is permitted up to 75', or six stories, and is limited to 14,700 sq. ft.

Class IIB. Theatre is permitted up to 75', or six stories, and is limited to 14, 700 sq. ft.

Class IIC. Theatre is permitted only if building is sprinklered and then up to 50', or four stories, and limited to 12,600 sq. ft.

Class IID, Class IIE. Theatre is not permitted in either class.

MEANS OF EGRESS

74 Occupants or Fewer (on first story)

If the theatre has fixed seats:

- Only one means of egress is required.
- It must be a minimum of 3'8" in width, and open directly onto the street.

If the theatre has movable seats:

- For an audience area not exceeding 740 sq. ft. only one means of egress is required
- It must be a minimum of 3'8" in width, and open directly onto the street.

Egress requirement is figured on an occupancy based on 10 sq. ft. per person. If you intend to have 74 or fewer occupants in a space, be certain your audience area does not exceed 740 sq. ft. If you have 750 sq. ft. of audience area, your occupancy would be considered 75 (750 divided by 10), and two means of egress would be required, even if only 74 people were using the space.

74 Occupants or Fewer (above the first story)

Whether the theatre has fixed or movable seats, two means of egress are required.

If there are other tenants sharing the floor, only one means of egress is required from the theatre into a public corridor; but two means of egress are required from the public corridor.

75 Occupants or More

Under the new code, as under the old code, at least two means of egress are required when the occupancy is over 74, but unlike the old code, the means of figuring out *what kinds* of exits and *where* they are located is more complicated. Take your time in reading over this section and refer to the illustrations, as they will help to clarify the requirements.

PRIMARY AND SECONDARY EGRESS. Under the new code, if you have more than 74 persons, you may be required to have more than two means of egress, whether you are on the first story or above.

There are two types of egress defined under the new code: *primary* and *secondary*. These terms refer to the distance a member of the audience must travel to reach one or the other. These exit openings must be at least 25' apart.

- The maximum travel distance to a *primary* exit is 85'.
- The maximum travel distance to a *secondary* exit is 125'.
- In any theatre space, every member of the audience must be seated within 85' of one exit and 125' of another.

These travel distances are measured in *legs*. Each time a person is required to change direction along the path of egress (make a turn), this becomes another leg of travel. These legs are measured in the following way:

first leg	the actual distance
second leg	the actual distance
third leg	1.25 x the actual distance
fourth leg	1.40 x the actual distance
any leg with four or more stairs	1.25 x the actual distance

The first leg is always measured from the seat to the aisle, if the seat is not on the aisle. To compute the travel distance from any one seat, use the table above and add up the distances. Remem-

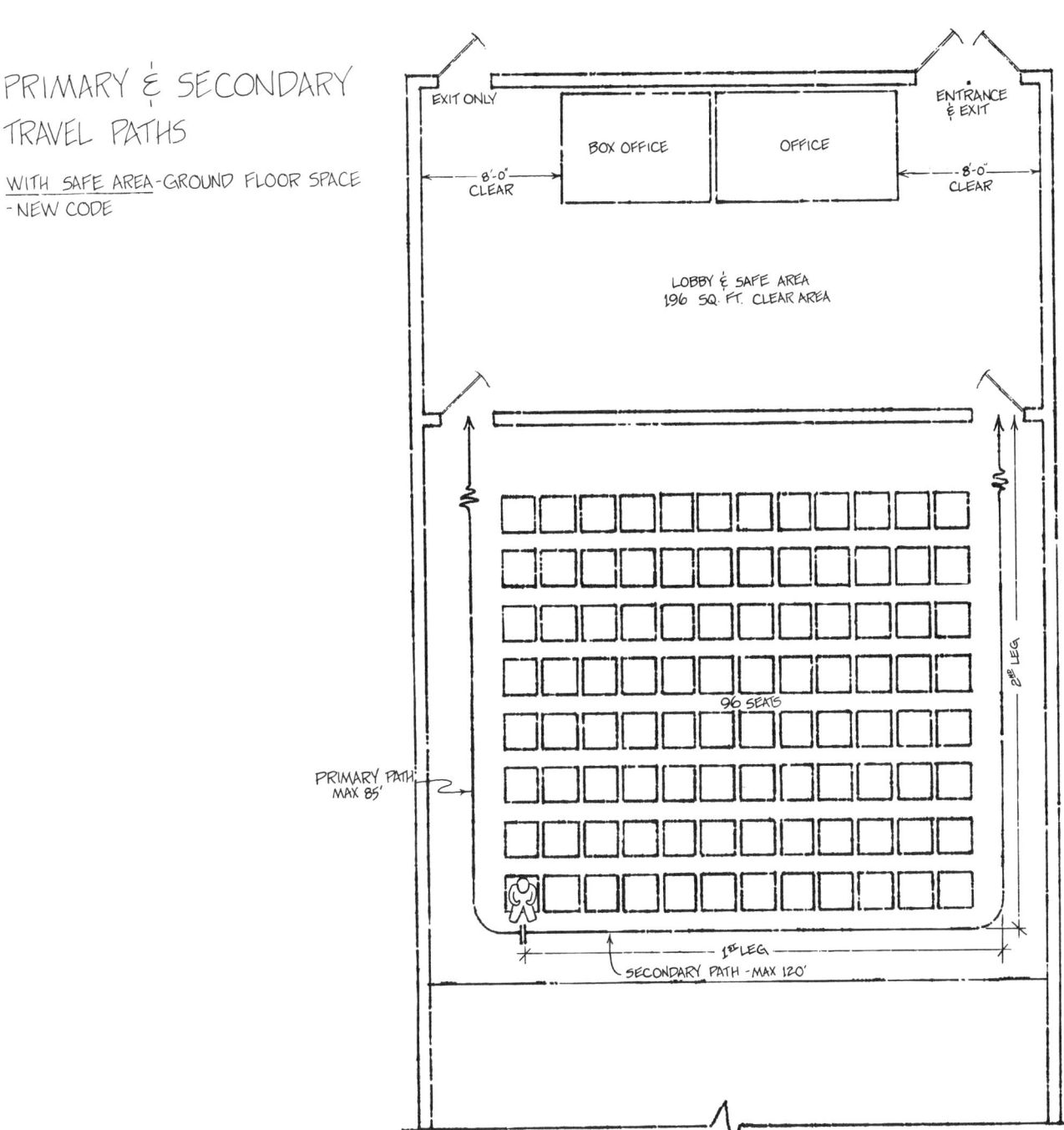

170
WILL IT MAKE A THEATRE?

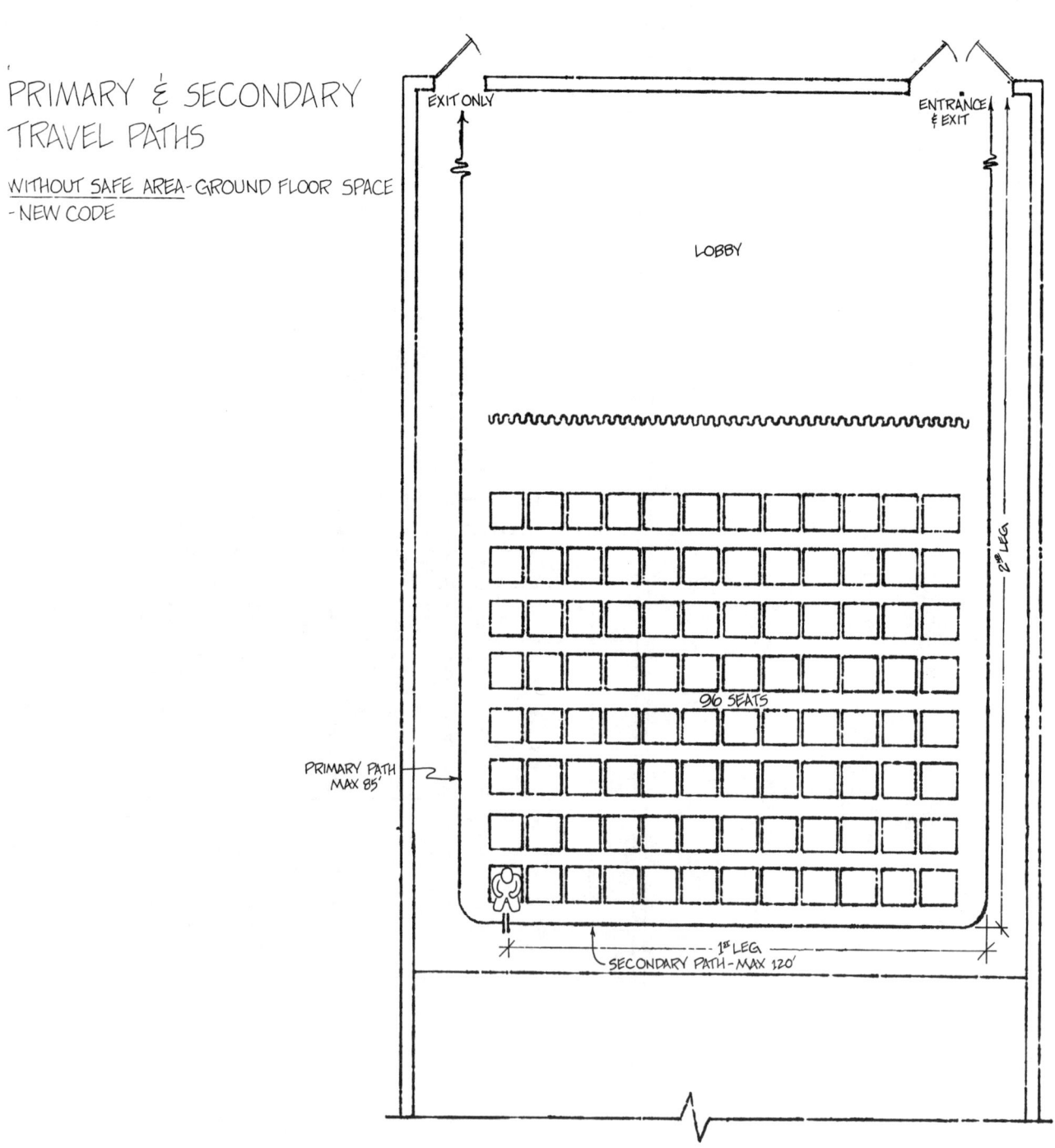

ber that from any one seat, the distance to one exit cannot be more than 85' and to the other exit not more than 125'. The simpler and straighter the path, the better. When there are too many turns or too many steps, the 1.25 and 1.40 factors force you to place exits closer to the seats. A 40' distance on a third leg becomes 50' on the formula, for example.

CLASSIFICATION OF EXITS. The new code also classifies exits according to where they lead people or how they lead people. There are three different types of exits under the new code, as follows:

Class 1. Exits that are normally used for entrance or exit. They must open directly to the outside or to a safe area.

Class 2. Exits that are used only for egress, not for entrance, and lead directly to the outside or to a safe area.

Class 3. Exits that open directly onto a corridor, a stairwell, or an exit passageway, leading to the outside.

NUMBER OF EXITS. The new code requires different numbers of the different classes of exits depending on varying circumstances. Listed below are only those requirements that will be needed by small theatres in typical situations:

- If the theatre has fixed seats and an audience area of more than 12 sq. ft. per person, both exits can be of any class.
- If the theatre has movable seats or fixed seats and an audience area of less than 12 sq. ft. per person, a theatre on the first story will be required to have one class 1 exit and one class 2 exit, or, if preferred, two class 1 exits. A theatre on the second or third story will be required to have one class 1 exit and one class 2 exit or, if preferred, two class 1 exits. A theatre above the third story must have all class 1 exits.

SAFE AREA. The concept of *safe area*, or *area of refuge*, as it is sometimes called, was introduced in the new code. It is a means of holding a number of people who are waiting to exit in an area that is separate from the main space of assembly and, theoretically, away from the fire or other disaster. A safe area is created by constructing a 2-hour fire-rated wall between the area and the assembly space. A lobby can function as a safe area if the wall between the two spaces has a 2-hour fire rating.

There are other requirements a safe area must meet:

- The area must provide at least 2 sq. ft. of clear space per person, not including furnishings, for the number of people using that exit. If 75 persons are using it, there will have to be at least 150 sq. ft. of clear floor area; if 100 persons are using it, there must be 200 sq. ft. of clear floor area.
- The minimum width of a safe area is 8'; this is measured at right angles to the direction of travel.
- No space containing hazardous uses— such as paint shop, scenery or costume shop, or storage space for mechanical, electrical, or A/C equipment—can open directly onto a safe area.

RELATIONSHIPS INVOLVING SAFE AREAS, TRAVEL DISTANCES AND EXITS. The easiest way to illustrate how these requirements relate to one another is through examples and drawings.

Above the ground floor you are required to have two exits. Since both Class 1 and Class 2 exits must open onto a safe area, or directly onto the street, you will have to make a safe area. The most expedient way to do this is to use your lobby space. In this situation, your primary and secondary travel distances are measured from the seat in the audience to the doors leading from the theatre space into the safe area.

On the ground floor you have a few options. Your exits can open directly onto the street, so you do not need a safe area. But in this case, you must measure your primary and secondary travel distances from the seat to these exterior doors. If you decide to use your lobby to create a safe area, then

WILL IT MAKE A THEATRE?

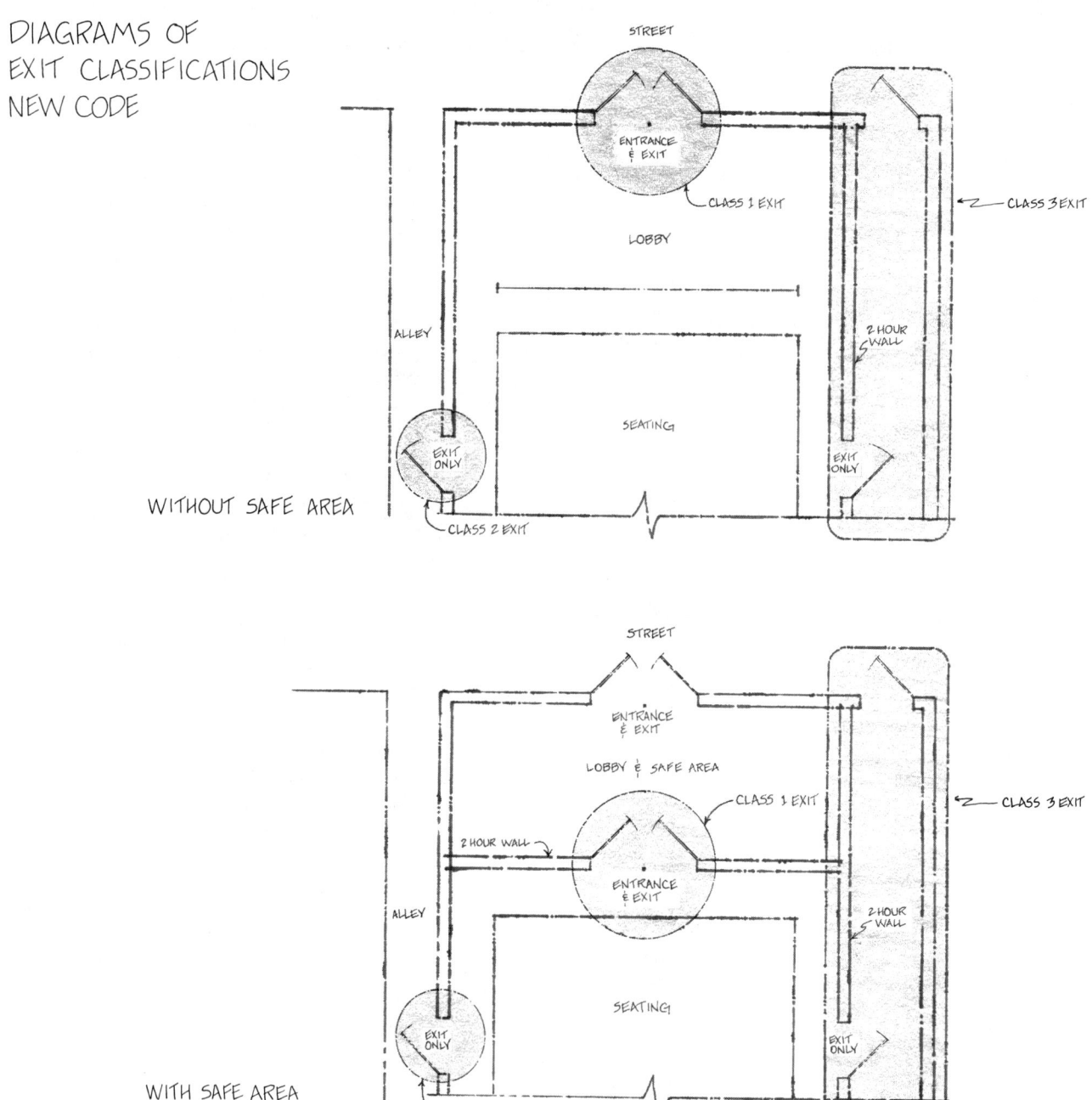

DIAGRAMS OF EXIT CLASSIFICATIONS NEW CODE

The Building Code

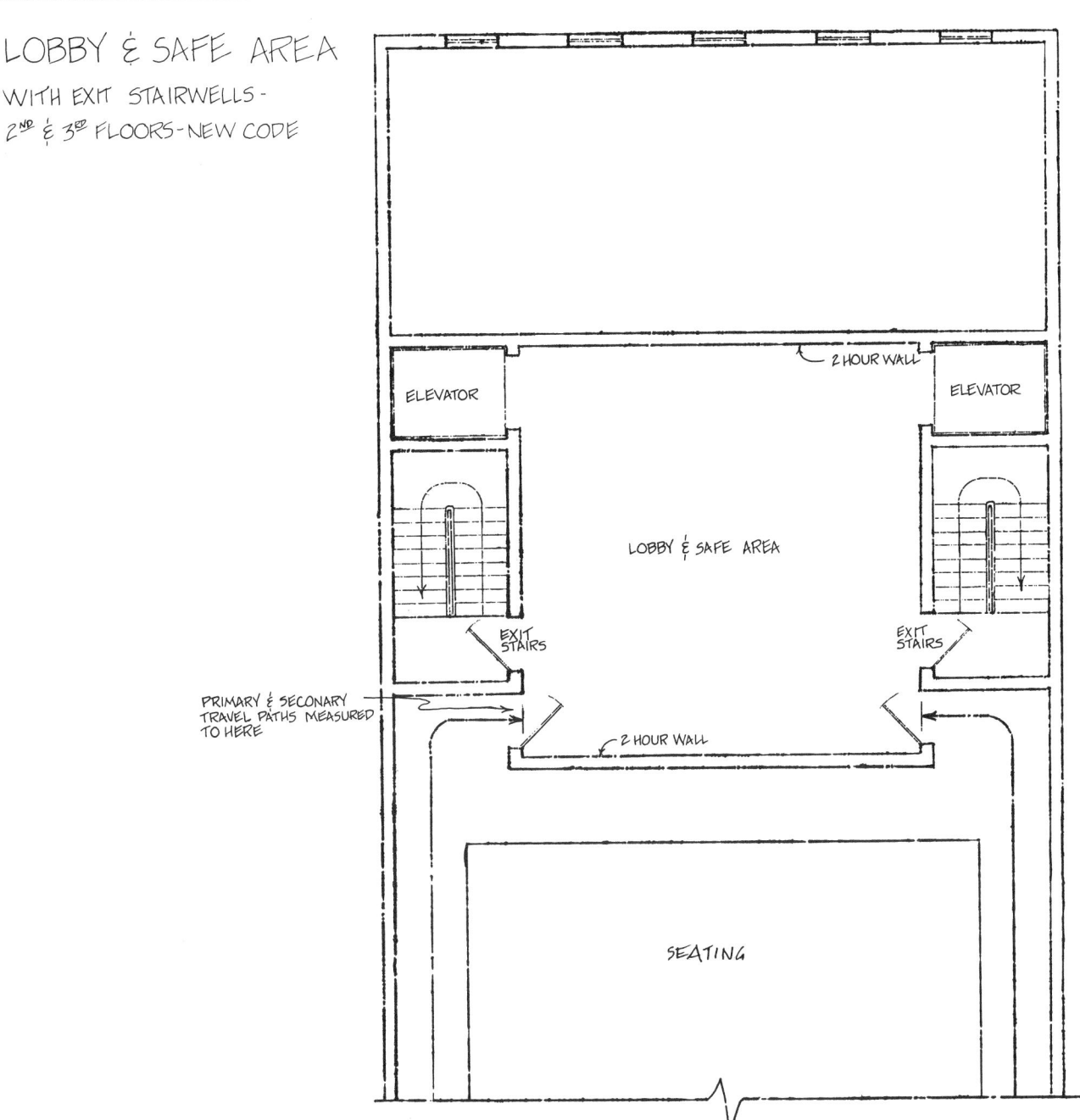

your primary and secondary travel distances are measured to the doors leading from the theatre space to the safe area.

Other Requirements for Means of Egress

The following requirements apply to all means of egress regardless of occupancy categories:

DISTANCE BETWEEN EXITS. When more than one exit is required from a floor of a building, each exit must be placed as remote from the other as is practicable.

DOORS. Exit doors and doors providing access to exits must be self-closing, swinging doors with a 1 1/2-hour fire rating, except that doors leading into stairs and exit passageways, and corridor doors, must have a 3/4-hour fire rating. The minimum door height shall be 6'8".

The minimum width for a single door is 35" except where occupancy is over 300; then it must be a minimum of 44". A double door must be at least 66", but not more than 88" wide.

EXIT STAIRS. The minimum allowable width is 3'8". The maximum vertical rise of a single flight of stairs between floors, landings, or between a floor and a landing may not exceed 8'. Stairs must have a clearance of 7' head height. The stairs must be constructed of noncombustible materials with solid, enclosed treads and risers. These stairs must be enclosed with construction materials that have a fire-resistance rating of not less than one hour, except as follows: class IA structures—4 hours, class IB structures—3 hours, and class IC structures—2 hours.

CORRIDORS. Internal corridors that are used as a part of the means of egress must be constructed of non-combustible materials that have a minimum fire-rating of 1 hour, except as follows: class IA structures—4 hours, class IB structures—3 hours, and class IC structures—2 hours.

The corridor height must be a minimum of 7'6" for at least 75% of the floor and at no point less than 7'.

DISTANCE FROM STAGE. All exit openings must be a minimum of 12' from any part of a stage using scenery or scenic elements (F1-A).

EXIT LIGHTING

EXIT SIGNS. Illuminated exit signs are required over all exit doors. All direction and exit signs must be placed to be visible from all locations in the assembly space. (See chapter 16.)

LIGHTING ON STAIRS. Lighting must be provided on all exit stairs.

EMERGENCY LIGHTING

Emergency lighting must be provided over the entire public assembly space.

The location of emergency lighting must be shown on architectural drawings and electrical service must be run on a separate circuit. (See chapter 16.)

VENTILATION

While the ventilation index formula and tables are the same as for the old code, the problems of meeting standards are more complicated. Many newer buildings do not have operable windows, as they were built with air-handling systems designed to heat, cool, and ventilate. If your theatre is in a building shared with other users and other uses, chances are the HVAC system was installed throughout the building and, no doubt, will already service your space. However, since the densities of the other occupancies in the building usually are lighter, the system probably was designed to handle a much smaller capacity than a theatre requires. For example, an office space is generally calculated as one person per 100 sq. ft., whereas a theatre's density is more likely to be one person per 10 sq. ft.

Obviously the best solution to this problem is to install your own mechanical ventilating system, even though this can be very costly.

The amount of ventilation required depends upon the size of the space and the number of people occupying it.

PLUMBING AND SANITARY REQUIREMENTS

The new code has minimum requirements for public toilets, determined by the number of people who occupy the space. They are as follows:

Toilets. 1 to 100 people, one water closet; 101 to 200 people, two water closets.

Urinals. 1 to 200 people, one urinal; 201 to 400 people, two urinals.

Sinks. For every 1 to 200 people, one sink.

Clearly, these numbers are absolute minimums, and more toilets, urinals, and sinks per person would be desirable.

DRINKING FOUNTAINS. For every 1,000, one drinking fountain; if more than one level or tier in the theatre, one drinking fountain per level.

SEAT AND ROW SPACING

The new code does not give a maximum number of seats permitted in any row, however it does require the following space between rows:

- A 12" minimum distance between the back of a seat and the front of the seat in the next row back.
- For every seat over seven that must be passed to reach an aisle, the 12" space between rows must be increased by 1/4".

PLATFORMS FOR FOLDING CHAIRS. If platforms for folding chairs are used instead of fixed seats, make sure that the size of the platform is large enough to permit the proper back-to-front row spacing (given above).

STEPPED PLATFORMS FOR SEATING. If stepped platforms, without chairs, are used for seating, the Code requires a minimum of 18" in width for each individual seat space, and at least 28" in depth, from front to back, for each platform. For every seat space over seven that must be passed to reach an aisle, the platform depth must be increased 1/4".

STEPS

If there are risers or steps in a space, the following requirements apply:

- Risers cannot be less than 4" or higher than 8".
- When more than one riser is used, none shall exceed 7 3/8".
- There can be no variation in riser height within a run of steps. In other words, if one riser is 4" high, all risers must be 4" high.
- Treads cannot be less than 9 1/2" in width.
- Intermediate steps between platforms must not exceed 10 1/2" in width.

LIVE LOAD

As under the old code, new code requirements for live load are a safety factor. Each use is assigned a live load value, described in pounds per sq. ft.

- If there are fixed seats, a 60 pounds per sq. ft. live load is required.
- If there are movable seats, a 100 pounds per sq. ft. live load is required.
- The stage area is required to have a live load of 150 pounds per sq. ft.

SPRINKLERS

Automatic sprinkler systems and fire alarm protection are required for stages within F-1A and F-1B places of assembly as well as F-4 occupancies used as cabarets. Dressing rooms and property storage rooms in F-1A, F-1B, and F-4 cabarets also require automatic sprinklers and fire alarm protection.

FIRE PROTECTION AND FINISH MATERIALS

The materials used for, or on, walls, floors, and ceilings of a theatre space must meet certain flame-spread ratings. Materials are rated with relation to the amount of time it takes them to burn.

The reference standards for flame-spread ratings are set by the National Board of Fire Underwriters and are used by the New York City building code. Most manufacturers of commercial building materials and interior-finish materials provide this data with the products they sell.

Any commercial goods purchased for use in a theatre should have a flame-spread rating between 26 and 75. Since most consumer goods are not required by law to furnish this information, materials purchased from a local hardware or fabric store may not show this rating. In this case, it would be advisable to flameproof them. (See p. 166.)

ZONING* & BUILDING CODE CHECKLIST

Notes

Zoning

zoning district: C2   C4   C6   C8   M1   M2   M3

Other: _____ (Variance required)

Subclassification: _____

Requirements and restrictions (check with Department of City Planning)

Building Code

classification

Old Code: 1   2   3   4   5   6

New Code: IA   IB   IC   ID   IE   IIA   IIB   IIC   IID*   II
(*theatre not permitted)

Floor location of space: _____ Is theatre permitted? _____

Sq. ft. available: _____   Sq. ft. allowed: _____

Assessed value of building: $_____

Renovation estimate: $_____

Building can be renovated under: Old Code   New Code

Live load rating of floor(s): _____ lbs. per sq. ft.
    Meets theatre requirements: yes   no

Ventilation requirements: Supply _____ cfm   Exhaust _____ cfm

Will present system (if any) meet requirements?   yes   no

Number of existing exits: _____   width: _____

Fire-rating _____

Will existing exits comply with means of egress requirements
    for theatre's proposed occupancy?   yes   no

Number of existing urinals: _____   watercloset: _____
                            sinks: _____   fountains: _____

Meet requirements: yes   no

* See Chapter 14 for zoning information.

16 THE ELECTRICAL CODE

The Electrical Code of New York City is one of the country's most stringent. At present, many cities use it as a model for their own electrical codes.

Licensed electricians and electrical engineers use this code as a reference for all electrical work, and it does cover everything from plug types to transmitting stations! Much of the code deals very technically with electrical installations and equipment, and will not be discussed here. This chapter discusses only the sections of the electrical code that deal directly with theatres, and describes briefly what is required to keep a system up to code standards.

Article 26 of the electrical code is the section that specifically addresses theatre. No matter how small a theatre may be, it will be required to meet the electrical code's specifications.

STAGE LIGHTING EQUIPMENT AND INSTALLATION

The Electrical Code divides all electrical equipment, wiring, and installations into two principal categories: *permanent* and *portable*.

Permanent, also called *stationary*, refers to anything attached to the wall and not intended for repositioning. In a theatre this would refer to all internal (in-house) wiring, including fuse boxes, outlets, disconnect boxes, and patch panels.

For permanent theatre installations, all wiring must be run in conduit, electrical metallic tubing or surface metal raceways, both on stage and in the house (over the seating area), as per article 26. In addition, all wiring must comply with many other specifications listed throughout the electrical code. If you are planning a permanent installation, it is necessary to hire a licensed electrician, since the code has many technical specifications for permanent wiring. Only a licensed electrician can file the specifications of changes and "sign off" when the job is done.

Portable is defined by the code as any electrical equipment that is capable of being readily moved due to its use. In a theatre this refers to lighting instruments, all rented equipment and cable, and any installations that must remain flexible. (All of the stage lighting equipment and boards used in Broadway houses are considered to be portable by code standards.)

Portable Switchboards

Portable control boards ("switchboards" in electrical code terminology) must plug into an outlet specifically designed for this purpose, with enclosed fuses capable of handling the total amount of power used by the board, and an externally operated switch. This outlet is commonly referred to as a "disconnect box" since it is capable of switching off or disconnecting all the power going to the board. This box should be mounted near, but not in, the dimmer room in order to provide easy access to it in case of an emergency.

Portable Cable

Portable cable or any nonpermanent wiring has many specifications for theatrical use. The cable must be flexible, which means that the outer covering should be rubber or thermoplastic, and the insulation for each conductor wire should be rubber or thermoplastic. The cable must be rated for hard usage and for use in damp places. The gauge (size) of the conductors cannot be smaller than #18, which means zip cord is not permitted (#14 and #12 cable are most commonly used in theatres).

The plug connectors used on portable cables cannot cause mechanical strain on the connections. (Pin plug or twist lock connectors are most commonly used in theatres and will meet this specification.) And, of course, the receiving half of the connection must be attached to the live end of the cable.

If cable is purchased or rented from a theatrical supply house, then all these specifications will be met. But if you plan to make up your own cables, read the code and double-check with an electrician before you purchase the supplies.

The code does not mention the running of cable, but theatrical electricians who have had experience with inspectors agree that neatness counts. This means tying or taping the cable every three to five feet along the pipe on which it runs. This will also relieve strain on the plug connections. If an inspector sees sloppily run cable, you may be required to redo it or install metallic tubing or raceways through which the cable must run.

Portable Strips, Plugging Boxes, and Arc Lamps

Portable strips, portable plugging boxes, and portable arc lamps are all mentioned in article 26 of the code. The requirements for all of these will be taken care of for you if you either rent or purchase this equipment.

DRESSING ROOMS

The code requires that conduit, electrical metallic tubing or surface metal raceways be used as the wiring method in dressing rooms, which is the same requirement applied to permanent installations.

The code further specifies that the lamps in a dressing room be protected by guards sealed or locked in place. These are usually metal or plastic baskets specially made to cover the light bulb and help to prevent contact with flammable materials.

HOUSE LIGHTS AND WORK LIGHTS

House lights and work lights are not specifically dealt with in the electrical code section on theatres. Depending upon the situation, they could be classified as portable or permanent, and should be wired accordingly.

EMERGENCY LIGHTING

Emergency lighting, which is also a building code requirement for public assembly spaces, is dealt with in more specific terms in the electrical code's article 31. Emergency lighting includes the exit lights and any additional lights necessary to properly illuminate, in an emergency situation, any portion of the theatre to which the public has access during the performance. Although not required by the code, it is a good idea to include the areas used by the actors and technicians.

Alternate Power Supply

Emergency lighting systems must have an alternate power supply in the event of an electrical power failure under such circumstances as a blackout or fire. There are two basic ways in which to provide this alternate power supply:

- Generator-powered system, supplied by a source other than the main electrical power supply.
- Battery-powered system. Many small theatres find this the most practical solution.

General Provisions

All emergency lighting systems must comply with the following:

- Wiring for emergency illumination must be entirely independent of all other wiring.
- The system must be capable of automatically switching to the alternate power supply (generator or batteries) in the event of electrical power failure.
- Emergency lights cannot be controlled by any stage lighting controls (including dimmer boards).
- The only switch or manual cut-off allowed in the emergency lighting system is at the main service. The switch must be accessible only to authorized persons and should be located in the lobby or another convenient place at the front of the building.
- The emergency lighting system must be tested frequently to assure it is in proper operating condition. Electrical and fire inspectors on routine inspection may ask that the system be tested.

There are many emergency lighting systems on the market. If purchasing or installing one, it is a good idea to seek expert advice to make certain that the system will comply with the code in your situation.

GROUNDING

The electrical code requires that all buildings—commercial and residential—have grounded wiring. The requirement is retroactive, so it applies to both old and new structures. As the old wiring of so many buildings is not grounded, this requirement is not being strictly enforced as yet. Grounding, in its simplest form, means the addition of a third wire (ground) where previously two wires were acceptable. Inspectors can, however, require that a two-wire system be grounded if they deem it necessary—usually where safety is involved.

Grounding is required if any rewiring is done or if new wiring is added to the old, ungrounded system. Fortunately, grounded cable and its corresponding electrical hardware are not appreciably more expensive than their two-wire counterparts.

17
THE FIRE PREVENTION CODE

The fire prevention code is probably the easiest with which to comply. Its requirements are based mainly on common sense and are designed for the safety of the public. Although there are variations from city to city, the New York code is representative, with the notable exception of Chicago's code, which is one of the most stringent in the country, due to the Great Chicago Fire of 1871 and the Iroquois Theatre fire in 1903.

The New York City fire prevention code has a number of regulations specifically designed for theatres and does enforce these regulations by means of routine inspections. It is only a matter of time before the fire department will make an inspection, as it does patrol its districts systematically and is aware of newcomers. You must pass an inspection by the fire department in order to receive your license.

There are some regulations in the fire prevention code that the New York building code also covers; these will not be mentioned again in this chapter.

INSPECTION CHECKLIST

Fire department inspectors have two different sets of checklists. The one they use depends upon the size of the theatre being inspected. The following items make up the checklist that applies to theatres with 299 or fewer seats. Each checklist item is followed here by a brief explanation and some suggestions from the fire department for meeting safety standards.

GOOD HOUSEKEEPING. All rubbish and debris should be disposed of, especially around the stage, backstage, and seating areas. Any storage areas should be maintained in an orderly fashion. It is strongly suggested that all paints and flammable liquids be kept in a closed, but ventilated, metal cabinet. Also, it is suggested that electrical cables be run overhead, and not on the floor, especially where there is heavy traffic and a chance that the cable may be worn through.

PORTABLE EXTINGUISHERS. Portable 2 1/2-gallon water-type extinguishers should be placed 75' apart for every 2,500 sq. ft. and should be mounted on hooks or shelves at least 2', but not more than 4 1/2', off the floor. The extinguishers must be tagged with the last date of inspection. It is also advisable to place a CO_2 extinguisher where the control boards are located, in case of electrical fire.

SPRINKLER HEADS IN EACH DRESSING ROOM. Theatres often wait until they are inspected by the fire department before going to the expense of installing sprinklers. If your space was built under the old code, which does not require sprinklers, it is possible that you may not have to install a sprinkler system, providing extinguishers are located within this area. However, the inspector may insist on the installation of sprinklers, nevertheless. If your conversion is under the new code, sprinklers will be required.

SMOKING. Smoking is prohibited inside of any theatre in New York City. Plainly visible "No Smoking" signs must be posted. No person may smoke in areas that are so posted.

(Exception: Smoking on stage may be permitted only when it is a necessary and rehearsed part of a performance and only by a regular performing member of the cast.)

LOCKED OR BLOCKED EXITS. Any exits to be used in an emergency must be left unlocked during all public performances and access to them must remain clear and unobstructed.

THEATRE LOG BOOK. Every theatre must keep an fire inspection log. This is the responsibility of the theatre "fireguard," a manager on hand at every performance to conduct an inspection and insure audience safety. Reproduced on the following pages are the instructions for keeping a log book as issued by the fire department, a blank log book form, and a page from a log book used by one small theatre.

FLAMEPROOFING AFFIDAVIT FOR SHOW SCENERY AND HOUSE DRAPERIES. For each new production, you are required to have a sworn affidavit stating that all the materials used in construction of the scenery are flameproofed. This affidavit should be filed with the fire commissioner, and a copy should be kept on file at the theatre so that you may show it to the inspectors. Reproduced below are the latest regulations from the fire department governing flameproofing, and examples of the standard affidavit used.

Flameproofing done by the fabric manufacturer should last the life of the fabric. Flameproofing sprayed on will last for one year and should be repeated annually; however, acceptance by the fire department may be renewed for up to three years. (See F.P. Directive 1-78 Rev.)

PERMITS

The fire department requires a number of special permits for the use of open flame, flash paper, flash pots and the like on stage. While the fees vary, several hundred dollars will be required to cover the cost of these permits and additional special inspection charges. All permits must be kept on file and shown to the fire inspector upon request.

> **DIVISION OF FIRE PREVENTION**
> **FIRE DEPARTMENT**
>
> F.P. Directive 10-62 (Revised)　　　　　　　　September 19, 1980
>
> The following is hereby promulgated for the information and guidance of members:
>
> ### THEATRE INSPECTION LOG BOOK
> **The following instructions are for the guidance of theatre managements for the purpose of standardizing Theatre Inspection Log Books and entries therein and it is recommended that:**
>
> In order to standardize the "Theatre Inspection Log Book" the following instructions were sent to all theatre agencies for distribution to the various theatres throughout the city;
>
> "In order to standardize the "Theatre Inspection Log Book" and entries therein, it is recommended that:
>
> 1. Each theatre provide and maintain a journal of the following specifications;
> a. Bound book with pen ruled lines and a red ruled margin;
> b. Pages to be 8½"x11", and consecutively numbered on the top at the corner;
> c. The face of the cover shall have the inscription "Theatre Inspection Log Book" and the name of the theatre;
> d. The inside front cover shall have a copy of the "Theatre Inspection Guide" affixed.
>
> 2. Daily entries in the journal are to be made by owners or managers as per the following samples, whichever applies;
> a. Date and Time. Mr. John Doe, Manager, inspected all parts of theatre in accordance with stipulatons of the Fire Department "Theatre Inspection Guide" and found all applicable items complied with and/or in good condition.
>
> Certified standpipe operator on duty:
> Mr. _____ Certificate No. _____
> Person designated to prevent any undue excitement or possible panic conditions:
> Mr. _____ (Not applicable to Motion Picture Theatres).
> Nearest street fire alarm box corner of _____ and _____
> 　　　　　　　　Signed: John Doe—Title
>
> b. Date and Time. Mr. John Doe, Manager, inspected all parts of theatre in accordance with stipulations of the Fire Department "Theatre Inspection Guide", and found all applicable items complied with, except the following: (Indicate conditions referred to and action taken, e.g. exit lights over north side door out-bulb replaced, etc.).
>
> Certified standpipe operator on duty:
> Mr. _____ Certificate No. _____
> Person designated to prevent any undue excitement or possible panic conditions:
> Mr. _____
> Nearest street fire alarm box corner of _____ and _____
> 　　　　　　　　Signed: John Doe—Title
>
> 3. The book shall be used for no other purpose and shall be kept in Manager's office for inspection by members of this Department. Failure to maintain this book as indicated above will result in the service of a violation order."
>
> Chief Officers, when making visits, investigating complaints, etc., shall examine subsequent entries made in the "Theatre Log Book", since the previous inspection was made by a chief officer, and shall record the results of such examinations therein; also conditions found and action taken if required.
>
> All other Department members inspecting theatres shall enter their name, purpose of visit and action taken if required.
>
> 　　　　　　　　　　　　　　　　AUGUSTUS A. BEEKMAN
> 　　　　　　　　　　　　　　　　Fire Commissioner.
>
> NOTE:　Theatre Inspection Guide reproduced on reverse side.

Theatre inspection log book.

WILL IT MAKE A THEATRE?

Theatre inspection guide. Both the instructions and this guide should be attached to the inside of the log book for easy reference. This guide can be used to help maintain a violation-free theatre. The references to standpipes and standpipe operators do not apply to theatres that have under 300 seats.

THEATRE INSPECTIONAL GUIDE

1. Note the location of street fire alarm box nearest to stage door for immediate transmission of alarms of fire.
2. Building alarm box on stage shall be *tested daily and prior to each performance* and maintained in proper working order at all times. This alarm may be transmitted in addition to street fire alarm box. Telephone on premises may also be used to transmit alarm.
3. Inspect all emergency exits, stairways, courts and passageways to determine condition, availability for use and compliance with law.
4. Cause asbestos curtain to be lowered at the close of each performance.
5. Examine all automatic fire doors to determine operative condition and availability for use.
6. Inspect all portions of standpipe and sprinkler systems, including pumps and tanks; also all fire appliances to determine condition and readiness for immediate use. Certified standpipe operator to be present at all times when theatre is open to the public.
7. Report unserviceable standpipe or sprinkler systems, to officer of company in whose district theatre is located.
8. Examine automatic skylight to determine operative condition and readiness for use.
9. Inspect all parts of theatre, particularly backstage and under the stage for accumulations of rubbish, and maintain free of same at all times.
10. Require all doors in proscenium wall to be kept closed during performances.
11. Prohibit smoking in all portions of backstage, under the stage, in dressing rooms and other rooms or space related to stage portion of theatre.
12. Require necessary extinguishers to be readily available when materials of a hazardous nature are used in performance.
13. Required Fire Department permits to be obtained and kept available for inspection.
14. Require necessary precautions to be taken when articles of a hazardous nature are used.
15. Designate responsible person to be prepared at all times to take a position in front of the audience to prevent any undue excitement or possible panic conditions in the event of an emergency.
16. During each performance inspect all portions of auditorium. Note any obstructions in aisles or passageways or violations of law relative to standees; and take immediate corrective action when violations are found.
17. At conclusion of stage performance, require stage trap doors closed and stage elevators made flush with stage floor.
18. Air conditioning system fresh air intakes to be kept clear of rubbish and/or combustible materials at all times.
19. Provide a log book and record daily the inspections made as indicated above; violations observed and action taken. This book to be kept available at all times for inspection by members of this department.

NOTE: The above items applicable to Motion Picture Theatres shall be observed and records kept as indicated above.

By Order of,

AUGUSTUS A. BEEKMAN
Fire Commissioner

13-131-0604

The Fire Prevention Code

DATE: _____
TIME: _____
_____, Manager, inspected all parts of theatre in accordance with stipulations of the Fire Department "Theatre Inspection Guide," and found all applicable items complied with and/or in good condition. The person designated to prevent any undue excitement or possible panic is _____.
The nearest fire alarm box is at the corner of _____ and _____.

Sample page from a log book.

```
STATE OF NEW YORK
COUNTY OF NEW YORK

Gentlemen:

We flameproofed the following:

Date: 2/14/72    Materials: All fabric on wings, velour
                            fireproof lumber, downstage
                            apron all lumber fireproofed.

Used for:  "Any Show" Production at
           Anybody's Theatre
           Any Street
           New York, New York

With approved flameproofing compound approved by the
Board of Standards and Appeals, for use in New York
City under Cal #539-53-SM.

This flameproofing compound is guaranteed for a period of
one year from the above date, in accordance with the rules
of the Board of Standards and Appeals providing fabric is
not impaired either by wetting or being subject to excessive
moisture.

                                          Anybody's Theatre Inc.

Sworn and subscribed to before me
This ___ day of _____ 19___
Mr. John Doe
Notary Public, State of New York
```

Sample standard flameproofing affidavit.

BUREAU OF FIRE PREVENTION
FIRE DEPARTMENT

F.P. Directive 1-78 (Revised)   December 28, 1982
(Revokes F.P. Directive 1-78 Dated February 3, 1978)

BY VIRTUE OF THE AUTHORITY VESTED IN ME UNDER SECTIONS 1105 and 489 of the City Charter, I hereby promulgate amendments to regulations concerning flameproofing of decorations, drapes, curtains and scenery. (Filed with the City Clerk on Feb. 8, 1982.)

REGULATIONS RELATIVE TO THE FLAMEPROOFING OF DECORATIONS, DRAPES, CURTAINS AND SCENERY.

(Filed with the City Clerk on November 1, 1977 and amended February 8, 1982)

The following is promulgated for the information and guidance of all personnel:

A. SCOPE:

These regulations shall be applicable to the testing, certification and approval of decorations, drapes, curtains and scenery used for artistic enhancement in any building of a public character, except those premises exempted in Section C19-161.1 of the Administrative Code.

B. AUTHORITY:

Vested in the Fire Commissioner by Section 489 of the City Charter and Section C19-161.0 of Chapter 19 of the Administrative Code of the City of New York and Rule 6.1 of the Rules of the Board of Standards and Appeals for Tests of Fire-Resistive Flameproofed Materials such as Textiles, Paper, Similar Materials and Adhesives Used for Decorative Purposes and Treated Acoustical Draperies, Carpets and Similar Material for Use in Places of Public Assembly and Special Occupancy Structures.

C. REGULATIONS:

1. *Affidavits Relative to Flameproofed Materials*

    a. Flameproofing of combustible materials required pursuant to C19-161.1, Administrative Code shall be done only by or under the supervision of a person holding a Certificate of Fitness for such purpose, issued by the Fire Department upon application and appropriate examination pursuant C19-13.0, C19-14.0, C19-19.0 and C19-23.0, Administrative Code.

    b. The owner, lessee or proprietor of any building or occupancy of a public character as defined in Section C19-161.1 of the Administrative Code shall arrange to have a person holding a Fire Department Certificate of Fitness for flameproofing attest to the flameproofing of combustible decorations, drapes, curtains and scenery used for artisitc enhancement in such building or occupancies by filing an affidavit with the Fire Commissioner.

    c. The required affidavit shall be sworn to by the person holding the Fire Department Certificate of Fitness that flameproofed the combustible materials and shall state in such affidavit that the fabric composition, and flameproofing method of application complies with the approval of the Board of Standards and Appeals and the Board of Standards and Appeals Cal. No. of the flameproofing compound, and that the materials flameproofed were personally tested after flameproofing by the person holding the Certificate of Fitness and found to be satisfactory. The affidavit shall include the date of treatment and the warranted period of flameproofing effectiveness.

F.P. Directive 1-78.

3. *Fire Department Acceptance:*

a. The acceptance, by the Fire Department, of decorations, drapes, curtains and scenery in buildings or occupancies of a public character, shall be contingent on the existence and filing of the required affidavit of flameproofing or non-combustibility and the satisfactory passage of a field flame test executed by a Fire Department Inspector.

b. The acceptance, by the Fire Department, of combustible decorations that have been flameproofed shall be limited to one (1) year periods.

c. The acceptance, by the Fire Department, may be renewed after the initial one year acceptance period, provided that the original affidavit is filed with the Fire Commissioner and a copy on the premises and the materials satisfactorily pass a field flame test executed by a Fire Department Inspector.

d. Each renewal of acceptance shall be limited to a one (1) year period or until the next dry cleaning or washing process. A record of each dry cleaning or washing shall be maintained on the premises for inspection by the Fire Department.

e. Renewal of acceptance shall not be extended more than two (2) years beyond the original one (1) year acceptance.

f. Flameproofed combustible decorations accepted for three (3) consecutive years shall not be field tested or acceptable. Such decorations shall be the subject of a violation order with a compliance time of sixteen (16) days, to remove or have same flameproofed and file a new affidavit of flameproofing.

4. *Fire Department Disapproval:*

a. No combustible or reported non-combustible decorative material shall be acceptable if required affidavits are not filed and on the premises, or does not pass the field flame test executed by a Fire Department Inspector.

b. Decorative materials disapproved due to failure of a field flame test shall be the subject of a violation order for forthwith removal, and may be cause for revocation and/or enforcement action against the Certificate of Fitness holder, if warranted.

c. Decorative materials disapproved due to the lack of required affidavits shall be the subject of a violation order to remove such decorative material or have same flameproofed and file a flameproofing affidavit. Compliance time shall be forthwith, except as provided in 3f above.

5. *Decorative Materials Approved by the Board of Standards and Appeals for Use in Occupancies of a Public Character:*

a. Decorative materials approved by the Board of Standards and Appeals shall be acceptable to the Fire Department provided that the owner, lessee or proprietor files an affidavit with the Fire Commissioner and maintains a copy thereof on the premises attesting to the fact that such decorations have been approved by the Board of Standards and Appeals and includes therein the Board of Standards and Appeals Cal. No. for the materials.

b. Acceptance, by the Fire Department of such material, shall also be dependent on the satisfactory passage of a field flame test executed by a Fire Department Inspector.

c. Enforcement procedures as described above for unacceptable decorative materials shall be executed for failure to provide affidavits or the failure of field flame testing.

6. *Modifications:*

Whenever circumstances, conditions, limitations, or surroundings are unusual, or are such as to render it impracticable to comply with all the foregoing requirements, the Fire Commissioner may waive or modify such provisions over which he has jurisdiction to such extent as he may deem necessary consistent with public safety.

7. *Saving Clause:*

If any clause, sentence, paragraph, section or part of this article shall be adjudged by any court of competent jurisdiction to be invalid, such judgment shall not affect, impair or invalidate the remainder thereof, but shall be confined in its operation to the clause, sentence, paragraph, section or part thereof directly involved in the controversy in which such judgment shall have been rendered.

JOSEPH E. SPINNATO
Fire Commissioner

Original Application for Permit.

18 Application Procedures

PRELIMINARY PROCEDURES

Before committing yourself to a space, complete the following steps. The procedures outlined here apply to New York City, but nearly identical procedures are in effect throughout the country.

Check Zoning Map

1. Go to the maps and publications room at the department of city planning and check the zoning map of the district in which the potential theatre is located. Double-check the zoning designation, making sure that theatre is permitted.

2. Check with the zoning information desk of the department of city planning regarding the sub-designations, to find out what restrictions or requirements are placed on this location.

Check Certificate of Occupancy (C of O)

1. Look on the existing C of O, which should be on file with the building's manager, to check the building's classification.

2. If the C of O is not available, take the exact address and go to the index room at the department of buildings where C of Os are on file.

3. If a C of O does not exist, you will be given a block and lot number on the building's folder, which will allow you to look up the building classification listed on the last altered building application for the building.

4. Even if a C of O exists, look up the building's last legal use, the live load rating of the floor, and whether any outstanding violations on the building exist.

5. Double-check all information, using the checklist provided at the end of chapter 15, to make sure that theatre is permitted in the building and that all the necessary requirements for theatre use are met.

Do not take an agent's, building manager's, or owner's word on any of these matters.

APPLICATION PROCEDURES FOR PERMITS AND LICENSES

The process of filing plans and applications for the various permits and licenses a theatre needs to operate legally can take anywhere from two months to half a year!

A lot of this time can be saved by hiring an architectural firm that does its own expediting with the department of buildings. It will organize the filing of applications, keep track of their progress, and insure that they do not become mired in departmental red tape.

Occasionally, architects don't do their own expediting; in such cases you may want to hire a professional expediter, recommended by the architect.

If you do your own expediting (not recommended), be prepared for a great deal of phone calling, paperwork and follow-through. The application procedures outlined in this section involve a considerable amount of red tape; patience and perseverance will be necessary.

Altered Building Application

This form, obtained from the department of buildings, must be filed even if no alterations or renovations are to be done, in order to indicate a change of use so that a new C of O may be issued.

The filing fee is a minimum of $55. If renovation work is planned, the fee will be based on the cost of the renovation but may not exceed 30% of the total.

Written permission from the building's owner must be obtained for renovation work, and plans must be filed showing the proposed alteration. Two sets of these plans must be filed by a licensed architect or engineer, who will stamp them to verify their accuracy.

The plans for renovation filed with this application will be reviewed by a plan examiner to see if all the building code requirements are met. The architect who has stamped and filed these plans will be notified if the examiner has any objections. If either you or the architect feel the examiner's interpretation of the code with regard to your plan is not accurate, a review may be requested. The chief engineer of the department of buildings will then evaluate the appeal and determine the validity of the interpretation. If a decision is made in the examiner's favor, then appropriate changes must be made and the plans refiled.

Once the plans are approved, a work permit will be issued. Construction work can be done only by a licensed general contractor, or by you—if you state that you will be acting as your own general contractor. You will be required to sign an affidavit stating this, as well as stating that you will obtain proper liability coverage for anyone working on the construction.

As the end of the construction approaches, arrangements must be made for final inspection by a construction inspector from the department of buildings. The inspector will check that the construction conforms to the plans submitted with the altered building application. If any changes have been made, they must be in compliance with the code, and a new set of plans indicating all these changes must be submitted before final approval is given by the inspector.

Once final approval is given, a new certificate of occupancy will be issued by the department of buildings.

Plans for the Department of Buildings

It is possible to save money by drawing up the required plans for the altered building application yourself. However, a licensed architect or engineer will be needed to review, stamp, and file the plans. The cost for this service will be considerably less than if professionals had done all the drawings. This can, however, be "penny wise and pound foolish." A licensed architect is always recommended.

The drawings must indicate the existing structure and any proposed changes being made, including the materials to be used in construction. They must be accurate and drawn to scale. The plans must include the following information: designated

Altered building application.

WILL IT MAKE A THEATRE?

B Form 14 (Back) (Rev. 8/82)

OWNER	ADDRESS	ZIP	TEL.
OFFICER OF CORPORATION	ADDRESS	ZIP	TEL.
OFFICER OF CORPORATION	ADDRESS	ZIP	TEL.
LESSEE	ADDRESS	ZIP	TEL.

OWNER'S STATEMENT REGARDING OCCUPIED HOUSING ACCOMODATIONS

To the Borough Superintendent: The undersigned owner herewith certifies: (Check one box)
☐ That the building to be altered contains no occupied housing accomodations subject to control under Title "Y" of Chapter 51 of the Administrative Code.
☐ That the owner has notified the city rent agency of his intention to file this application and has complied with all requirements imposed by the regulations of such agency as preconditions for such filing.

OWNER OR OFFICER OF CORPORATION (SIGNATURE)	DATE

☐ OWNER'S INSPECTION REQUEST (Check if applicable)

In lieu of inspections by inspectors of the Department of Buildings, the owner ☐ authorizes ☐ retains ☐ employs the following ☐ Registered Architect ☐ Professional Engineer to make all inspections during the progress and upon completion of all work.

AUTHORIZATION OF OWNER

The undersigned owner herewith authorizes the applicant to file this application for the work specified herein.

OWNER OR OFFICER OF CORPORATION (SIGNATURE)	DATE

ARCHITECT/ENGINEER'S STATEMENT: I will make inspections during the progress and upon completion of work. Controlled inspection reports and other reports relating to quality of concrete, ventilation, fire dampers and other requirements shall be filed by me before the work is reported completed.

Upon completion of the work and after my final inspection, I shall file a certification (B Form 23A) attesting to the fact that all work was performed and completed in accordance with the accepted plans and with the provisions of the Building Code and other applicable laws and regulations. Any exceptions shall be reported promptly in writing.

Should my retention be terminated for any reason prior to the completion of the work, I shall immediatley inform the Department of Buildings in writing. This notice of termination will be accompanied by a Certification (B Form 23A) and appropriate controlled inspection reports to the date of termination.

INSPECTING ARCHITECT OR ENGINEER	ADDRESS	ZIP	TEL.
RA or PE No.	AFFIX SEAL:		
INSPECTING ARCHITECT OR ENGINEER (SIGNATURE)		DATE	

APPLICANT'S STATEMENT:

I hereby state: That I prepared or supervised the preparation of the following type(s) of plans and specifications herewith submitted:
☐ Zoning ☐ Architectural ☐ Structural ☐ Mechanical ☐ Plumbing & Drainage

That to the best of my knowledge and belief, the plans and work shown thereon comply with the provisions of the Building Code and other applicable laws and regulations, (Check if applicable) ☐ except for practical difficulties set forth in the accompanying signed statement.

That I am authorized by the owner of all that certain lot, piece or parcel of land, shown on the diagram above to make application for the approval of such detailed statements of specifications and plans, other work (if any) and amendments thereto, in the said owner's behalf.

APPLICANT	ADDRESS	ZIP	TEL.
If Applicant is a Licensed Architect or Professional Engineer, enter RA or PE No. below.	AFFIX SEAL:		
RA or PE No.			
APPLICANT (SIGNATURE)		DATE	

FALSIFICATION OF ANY STATEMENT IS A MISDEMEANOR UNDER SECTION 643a-10.0 OF THE ADMINISTRATIVE CODE AND IS PUNISHABLE BY A FINE OF NOT MORE THAN FIVE HUNDRED DOLLARS OR IMPRISONMENT OF NOT MORE THAN SIX MONTHS OR BOTH.
BRIBERY IS A CRIME: A PERSON WHO GIVES OR OFFERS A BRIBE TO ANY EMPLOYEE OF THE CITY OF NEW YORK, OR AN EMPLOYEE WHO TAKES OR SOLICITS A BRIBE IS GUILTY OF A FELONY PUNISHABLE BY IMPRISONMENT FOR UP TO SEVEN YEARS OR A FINE, OR BOTH. PENAL LAW SECTION 200.00 AND 200.10.

☐ EXEMPTION FROM PAYMENT OF FEE STATE BASIS IN ACCORDANCE WITH C26-30.0		ESTIMATED COST	
PAYMENTS	INITIAL FEE PAYMENT:		
	2nd FEE PAYMENT:	VERIFIED BY:	DATE
	CASHIER STAMP:		
	ADDITIONAL FEES REQUIRED:	VERIFIED BY:	DATE
	CASHIER STAMP:		DATE
APPROVAL	EXAMINED AND RECOMMENDED FOR ☐ APPROVAL ☐ ACCEPTANCE UNDER DIR. 14/75. EXAMINER:		DATE
	BOUGH SUPERINTENDENT:		

BUILDING DEPARTMENT FEES
Effective July 13, 1987

ESTIMATED COST	FILING FEE	TOTAL FEE	ESTIMATED COST	FILING FEE	TOTAL FEE
1,000	55.00	55.00	31,000	197.50	395.00
2,000	55.00	75.00	32,000	202.50	405.00
3,000	55.00	95.00	33,000	207.50	415.00
4,000	57.50	115.00	34,000	212.50	425.00
5,000	67.50	135.00	35,000	217.50	435.00
6,000	72.50	145.00	36,000	222.50	445.00
7,000	77.50	155.00	37,000	227.50	455.00
8,000	82.50	165.00	38,000	232.50	465.00
9,000	87.50	175.00	39,000	237.50	475.00
10,000	92.50	185.00	40,000	242.50	485.00
11,000	97.50	195.00	41,000	247.50	495.00
12,000	102.50	205.00	42,000	252.50	505.00
13,000	107.50	215.00	43,000	257.50	515.00
14,000	112.50	225.00	44,000	262.50	525.00
15,000	117.50	235.00	45,000	267.50	535.00
16,000	122.50	245.00	46,000	272.50	545.00
17,000	127.50	255.00	47,000	277.50	555.00
18,000	132.50	265.00	48,000	282.50	565.00
19,000	137.50	275.00	49,000	287.50	575.00
20,000	142.50	285.00	50,000	292.50	585.00
21,000	147.50	295.00	51,000	297.50	595.00
22,000	152.50	305.00	52,000	302.50	605.00
23,000	157.50	315.00	53,000	307.50	615.00
24,000	162.50	325.00	54,000	312.50	625.00
25,000	167.50	335.00	55,000	317.50	635.00
26,000	172.50	345.00	56,000	322.50	645.00
27,000	177.50	355.00	57,000	327.50	655.00
28,000	182.50	365.00	58,000	332.50	665.00
29,000	187.50	375.00	59,000	337.50	675.00
30,000	192.50	385.00	60,000	342.50	685.00

CONSTRUCTION FEE ABOVE $5,000, add $10 per $1,000

FILING FEE IS 50% OF TOTAL FEE

Table of filing fees for altered building application.

WILL IT MAKE A THEATRE?

B Form 17 (Rev. 8/85)

THE CITY OF NEW YORK
DEPARTMENT OF BUILDINGS

MANHATTAN ☐
Municipal Building
New York, N.Y. 10007
(212) 566-2392

BROOKLYN ☐
Municipal Building
Brooklyn, N.Y. 11201
(718) 643-7943

BRONX ☐
1932 Arthur Avenue
Bronx, N.Y. 10457
(212) 579-6939-6940

QUEENS ☐
12-06 Queens Blvd.
Kew Gardens, N.Y. 11415
(718) 520-3268

STATEN ISLAND ☐
Boro Hall
St. George, N.Y. 10301
(718) 390-5202

STATEMENT "A"

BLOCK .... LOT ....

LOCATION ....
House Number   Street   Distance from Nearest Corner   Borough

TO THE COMMISSIONER:

APPLICATION IS HEREBY MADE FOR APPROVAL OF THE PLANS AND SPECIFICATIONS HEREWITH SUBMITTED FOR THE ERECTION OR ALTERATION OF THE STRUCTURE HEREIN DESCRIBED SUBJECT TO THE FOLLOWING CONDITIONS:

THIS APPLICATION SHALL BE DEEMED TO HAVE BEEN ABANDONED 12 MONTHS AFTER DATE OF SUBMISSION UNLESS IT HAS BEEN DILIGENTLY PROSECUTED AFTER REJECTION IN WHOLE OR IN PART (ADMINISTRATIVE CODE, C26-109.9).

WORK WILL NOT BE COMMENCED UNTIL THE WORK PERMIT IS OBTAINED (ADMINISTRATIVE CODE, C26-109.1).

APPROVAL OF PLANS SHALL BE VOIDED IF A WORK PERMIT APPLICATION IS NOT SUBMITTED WITHIN 12 MONTHS OF THE DATE OF PLAN APPROVAL (ADMINISTRATIVE CODE, C26-108.8)

AN APPLICATION FOR A WORK PERMIT SHALL BE ACCOMPANIED BY SATISFACTORY EVIDENCE OF COMPLIANCE WITH THE PROVISIONS OF THE STATE WORKMEN'S COMPENSATION LAW (ADMINISTRATIVE CODE, C26-110.1, C26-111.1, C26-112.1).

A WORK PERMIT SHALL EXPIRE BY LIMITATION IF THE PERMITTED WORK IS NOT COMMENCED WITHIN 12 MONTHS OF THE DATE OF ISSUANCE (ADMINISTRATIVE CODE, C26-118.6).

WORK WILL BE INSPECTED BY ARCHITECTS, ENGINEERS AND DESIGNATED PERSONS IN ACCORDANCE WITH ADMINISTRATIVE CODE C26-106.3.

....
(Typewrite Name)

states that he resides at ....

in the Borough of .... ; in the City of .... ;

in the State of .... ; that he is making this application for the approval of ....

.... plans and
(Architectural, Structural, Mechanical, Etc.)

specifications herewith submitted and made part hereof.

Applicant further states that he has prepared or supervised the preparation of such

.... plans and that to
(Architectural, Structural, Mechanical, Etc.)

the best of his knowledge and belief, the plans and work shown thereon comply with the provisions of the building code and other applicable laws and regulations, except for the following where there are practical difficulties, as set forth in accompanying documents: ....

Applicant further states that he is duly authorized by ....
(Name of Owner)

who is the owner in fee of all that certain lot, piece or parcel of land, shown on the diagram annexed hereto and made a part hereof, to make application for the approval of such detailed statements of specifications and plans, elevator or plumbing work (if any) and amendments thereto, in the said owner's behalf.

Applicant further states that the full names and residences, street and number, of the owner or owners of the said land, and also of every person interested in said building or proposed structure, are as follows:

Owner's name .... Address ....
(If a corporation, give full name and address of at least two officers.)

....
....
....

Lessee .... Address ....
.... Address ....
Architect .... Address ....
Engineer .... Address ....
Superintendent .... Address ....

EXAMINED AND RECOMMENDED
FOR APPROVAL ON ...., 19 ......
                                                                    Examiner
APPROVED ...., 19 ......
                                                        Borough Superintendent

NOTICE—This statement must be TYPEWRITTEN and filed in QUADRUPLICATE

Department of Buildings Statement "A".

Application Procedures

B Form 17 (back) (Rev. 8/82)

That the said land and premises above referred to are situated, bounded and described as follows:
(NOTE—See diagram below)

BEGINNING at a point on the .... side of ....
distant .... feet from the corner formed by the intersection of ....
and ....

running thence .... feet; thence .... feet;
    (Direction)   (Direction)

thence .... feet; thence .... feet;
  (Direction)   (Direction)

to the point or place of beginning, being designated on the map as

Block No. .... **Lot No.** ....

(SIGN HERE) .... Applicant

                      Affix Seal of Registered
                      Architect or Professional
                      Engineer Here.

AUTHORIZATION OF OWNER: I hereby state that I have authorized the applicant to file this application for the work specified herein.

....
(Signature of Owner or Officer of Corp.)

FALSIFICATION OF ANY STATEMENT IS A MISDEMEANOR UNDER SECTION 643a-10.0 OF THE ADMINISTRATIVE CODE AND IS PUNISHABLE BY A FINE OF NOT MORE THAN FIVE HUNDRED DOLLARS OR IMPRISONMENT OF NOT MORE THAN SIX MONTHS OR BOTH.

BRIBERY IS A CRIME: A PERSON WHO GIVES OR OFFERS A BRIBE TO ANY EMPLOYEE OF THE CITY OF NEW YORK, OR AN EMPLOYEE WHO TAKES OR SOLICITS A BRIBE IS GUILTY OF A FELONY PUNISHABLE BY IMPRISONMENT FOR UP TO SEVEN YEARS OR A FINE, OR BOTH. PENAL LAW SECTION 200.00 AND 200.10.

Above Block and Lot Verified .... 19.......

....
Department of

House Number .... Dated .... 19 ....
                            Bureau of

PLOT DIAGRAM must be drawn to indicated scale, showing the correct street lines from the city plan; the plot to be built upon in relation to the street lines and the portion of the lot to be occupied by the building; the legal grades and the existing grades, properly identified, of streets at nearest points from the proposed buildings in each direction; the House numbers and the block and lot numbers. Obtain this data in each borough office. Show dimensions of lot, building, courts and yards.

Status of Street: private— ....; public highway— ....; other ....
The legal width of .... is .... ft.; sidewalk width should be .... ft.
The legal width of .... is .... ft.; sidewalk width should be .... ft.
The street lines as shown in the diagram are substantially correct. Proposed changes in street lines and grades, if any, are indicated in red. The legal grades and the existing grades are indicated on the diagram thus: Legal Grade, 25.00. Existing, 24.00.
Above house numbers, street status, street lines and grades shown below verified.

Dated .... 19 ....
                  Bureau of

DIAGRAM

N.
↑

The north point of
the diagram must
agree with the arrow

(For New Buildings give information below:)

SIZE OF BUILDINGS: At street level........................... feet front .... feet deep........................... feet rear

At typical floor level........................... feet front .... feet deep........................... feet rear

stage area, designated audience area with a seating arrangement, designated exits and aisles, and location of exit lights and emergency lights. Also include plans for the rest of the space, including the location and size of the dressing rooms, lobby, offices, rest rooms, shops, and storage areas. It is important that the drawings be accurate.

For further information, consult sections 27-157, 27-158, and 27-159 of the New York City building code.

Certificate of Occupancy Application

Although a C of O will not be issued by the department of buildings until all renovations, plumbing, and electrical work have been inspected and approved, you should file for a new C of O immediately upon filing plans, to set the procedure in motion. You will need the building owner's authorization to file.

If your space is located in a building of three stories or fewer, a new C of O will need to be obtained for the entire building. If your space is located in a building of four or more stories and the amount of space occupied is less than 20% of the entire building, then you will need a C of O for the space you actually occupy; however, if you occupy 20% or more of the building, then you will need a new C of O for the entire building.

Application for Permit for a Place of Assembly

Although this permit, commonly known as a "PA license," will not be issued until after the new C of O is issued, you should initiate the filing procedure with the department of buildings at the same time the altered building application is filed. You will need to file this permit only if your proposed occupancy exceeds 74.

A separate set of plans must be filed with this application, indicating seating plans, any alternate seating plans, and the location of the exit signs.

The fire department receives notification when this application is submitted and then schedules an inspection. This must be made before the permit is approved. If you apply for a cabaret license as well, you must also pass a more stringent fire department inspection before receiving that license.

The place of assembly permit must be renewed annually. The filing fee is $55.

Applications for Sign Permits

This application, obtained from the department of buildings, covers any exterior signs. A licensed rigger files this application, stating that the rigger is either doing the work or supervising it. Plans must be submitted showing the size and location of the sign, the materials used in its construction, and the means of supporting and anchoring the sign.

If the sign is to be illuminated, an additional application from a licensed electrician will have to be filed with the department of gas and electricity, stating that the electrician is either doing the wiring or is supervising the work. A schematic plan of the wiring must also be filed.

The fees for sign permits are based on the installation costs and on the square footage of the sign.

Permits for Awnings and Canopies

Applications for awning or cloth canopy permits must be filed with the bureau of highways, department of transportation, because they extend over the sidewalk.

Marquees and solid canopies are considered permanent construction and therefore part of the building. The building code is very restrictive about their construction and erection.

The stringent requirements regarding the construction and materials used in the manufacture of awnings necessitate the filing of a notarized letter from the manufacturer stating that the awning conforms to these requirements. Make sure the application for this permit has been approved prior to purchasing or setting up the awning. This way you will be guaranteed that the manufacturer complies with the requirements.

This application also will apply to any signs, banners, or pennants that project from the wall.

Application for C of O.

WILL IT MAKE A THEATRE?

B Form 97 (Rev. 8/77)

THE CITY OF NEW YORK
DEPARTMENT OF BUILDINGS

☐ MANHATTAN ☐ BROOKLYN ☐ BRONX ☐ QUEENS ☐ STATEN ISLAND
Municipal Bldg., Municipal Bldg., 1932 Arthur Avenue, 126-06 Queens Blvd., Boro Hall,
New York, N. Y. 10007 Brooklyn, N. Y. 11201 Bronx, N. Y. 10457 Kew Gardens, N. Y. 11415 St. George, N. Y. 10301

APPLICATION FOR PERMIT FOR A PLACE OF ASSEMBLY

BLOCK _____ LOT _____

ZONING DISTRICT _____

LOCATION _____
          House Number   Street

_____
Distance from Nearest Corner   Borough

DO NOT WRITE IN THIS SPACE

1. Location of space or room _____ on _____ story

2. Type of occupancy _____

3. When was above occupancy established? _____ C.O. # _____

4. Max. No. of persons to be accommodated: PATRONS _____ EMPLOYEES _____ TOTAL NO. _____

5. State number of different seating arrangements to be used _____

6. Classification of building: (Construction) _____ (Use) _____

7. Application No. under which work (if any) is to be performed _____

VERIFIED BY _____ DATE _____

Fee payment — (see C26-34-0) _____

STATE AND CITY OF NEW YORK)
COUNTY OF _____) SS.: _____ being duly
                                     (Typewrite Name of Applicant)

Sworn, deposes and says: That he resides at _____ Borough of _____,
City of New York; that he is the agent for the (owner-lessee) of the premises above described, and is duly authorized to make this application for the approval of the plan and specifications herewith submitted, and made a part hereof, for the work to be done in the building therein described, with the understanding that this application shall be deemed to have been abandoned 12 months after date of submission, if after it has been rejected in whole or in part, he takes no further action; and the applicant agrees to comply with all provisions of the Administrative Code and all laws and regulations applicable to the use and maintenance of such space in effect at this date; that any work to be done is duly authorized by the owner.

Deponent, further says that the full names and residence of the owners or lessees of said premises are:

OWNER _____ ADDRESS: _____

LESSEE: _____ ADDRESS: _____

Sworn to before me this _____

day of _____ 19 ___ (Sign here) _____
                                              Applicant

_____
Notary Public or Comm. of Deeds

If Licensed Architect or Professional
Engineer, affix seal.

EXAMINED AND RECOMMENDED
FOR APPROVAL ON _____, 19 ___ _____, Examiner

APPROVED _____, 19 ___ _____, BOROUGH SUPT.

NOTICE—This Application must be TYPEWRITTEN and filed in QUADRUPLICATE
For instructions as to the requirements and filing of this application,
see the other side of this sheet.

Application for permit for a place of assembly.

Once obtained, permits must be renewed annually.

Application for Inspection and Certification of Electrical Work

To be in strict compliance with the electrical code, a licensed electrician must file an application for a certificate of electrical inspection with the bureau of gas and electricity for any electrical work —installation, alteration, or repairs. The licensed electrician will describe in detail the work to be done and submit wiring diagrams in duplicate. The application must be filed before work begins.

If the electrician is filing an application for work that is to be done by an unlicensed contractor, this must be stated on the application.

There are filing fees involved: an initial filing fee of $5, payable upon application, and an additional fee based upon the type and amount of work. (See rates listed on the application.) This additional filing fee must be paid before a certificate of electrical inspection is validated by an inspector. After the work is completed, an inspector will come by, check the work, and issue an inspection certificate, which you will be required to keep on file.

If the electrical work being done is to correct a written violation, the procedure is the same, but the filing fees are doubled.

Permits to Install or Alter Plumbing

If any plumbing work needs to be done, a licensed plumber must apply for a permit and file schematic plans. The application must state that the plumber is either executing or supervising the work. This application should be filed at the department of buildings before work begins. A plumbing inspector must approve the work before the department of buildings issues a final approval.

Fees will be based upon the same schedule that applies to the altered building application, except where the alterations are under $1,000 and involve neither structural changes nor a change in occupancy. In the latter case the fee is $11 for the first $500 and $22 for costs over $500 but under $1,000.

Requirements for the Handicapped

When the cost of any alterations made within a 12-month period immediately following the filing of a building application exceeds 50% of the replacement cost of the building, then the entire building must provide for those with physical disabilities. Also, if there is a change in the occupancy classification of the building, then the entire building must be made to comply. If there is a change in the use of a space in the building, only this space must be brought into compliance. However, if the cost of any alteration is less than 50% of the replacement cost, the handicapped accessibility need only be in the areas altered.

VIOLATIONS

If you are inspected by any of the departments and violations are found, they must be presented to you in writing. Generally, you are given anywhere from 24 hours to 30 days in which to comply; only if a gross violation has occurred will you be threatened with immediate shutdown. To comply, you must hire the appropriate licensed professional to remove the violation within the specified period of time. If the inspector returns to check on the violation, you must have proof in writing that you have hired a licensed professional to do the work. It is possible to hire the licensed professional only to file and sign the proper applications for inspection and to supervise the work, with your theatre providing the actual labor.

If the inspector identifies a violation verbally, then you are not required by law to correct it; but it is wise to do so, since you may be issued a written violation the next time around.

If you need help or advice in correcting a violation, or dealing with an agency, contact your local theatre service organization for assistance.

THE CITY OF NEW YORK
BUREAU OF HIGHWAYS
BOROUGH OF _____

Permit Fee $50.00 $110.00   Permit No. _____
*Street Opening Permit, if required $~~105.00~~   (Do Not Fill in)

Make Checks Payable to Commissioner of Highways   _____ 19 _____

    Application is hereby made for a permit to maintain a CANOPY over the sidewalk at the entrance to the building or premises located at:

_____ Street or Avenue

Between _____ and _____

Sixe of Canopy _____ wide x _____ long x _____ Clear Heights.

Check one of the following:

Hotel _____ Residence _____ Restaurant _____ Other _____
                                          (Other than Sidewalk Cafe) (Specify)

*A street opening permit is required if the street area is to be disturbed for erection or alteration of a canopy.

IMPORTANT: If this application is made in connection with a Sidewalk Cafe, the request for a Canopy permit must be made to the Department of Consumer Affairs.

    Applicants for Canopy Permits shall submit to the Borough Permit Office of the Bureau of Highways:

1. Written consent of the owner of the building.

2. A statement of the basic construction details, such as the type, description and color of the canopy covering; the type, diameter and guage of all supporting members; description of the frame, wind bracing assembly and fastenings to the sidewalk and building.

3. A statement that the design and construction of the canopy is in conformance with the established Design Criteria, the Standard Drawing of Design Criteria No. H-1029 on file in the department, and the rules and regulations of the department.

4. A sketch showing the canopy dimensions and location and all street obstructions within 15 feet on both sides of the canopy.

5. A certificate that the covering is flameproof.

6. Consent of the Fire Department for the erection of a canopy within 15 feet of a hydrant.

7. Consent of Bureau of Traffic where existing parking meters are located within the proposed canopy area.

8. A Street Obstruction Bond.

9. A Public Liability Insurance Policy.

    The PERMIT to be granted subject to the following conditions:

    The applicant agrees to comply with all the rules and regulations of the Bureau of Highways as well as all other laws and regulations relating to such work; and the acceptance of the permit shall be deemed an agreement to abide by all of its terms and conditions.

APPROVED: Deputy Commissioner of Highways   Signed: _____

By _____   Printed: _____
           _____ 19 _____   Authorized Representative of
                                                                            Applicant

Permit for awning and canopy.

Application Procedures

NEW YORK CITY
DEPARTMENT OF TRANSPORTATION
BUREAU OF HIGHWAY OPERATIONS

M11 (REV. 3-83) FRONT

APPLICATION FOR PERMIT

NOTICE: MAKE CHECKS PAYABLE TO THE BUREAU OF HIGHWAY OPERATIONS, CITY OF NEW YORK. CHECKS IN EXCESS OF $500.00 MUST BE CERTIFIED.

BOROUGH OF _____

COMMUNITY BOARD NUMBER _____

PERMIT NO. _____ REISSUE _____ (PERMIT NO.)

FEES, ETC. PERMIT FEE _____
　　　　　　INSPECTION _____
　　　　　　TUNNELING _____
　　　　　　DEPOSIT _____
　　　　　　TOTAL _____

DATE _____ 19 ____

KIND OF PAVEMENT _____

_____ SQ. YDS. RATE/ SQ. YD. $ _____

APPLICATION IS MADE BY _____ (NAME OF PERMITTEE)

BUSINESS ADDRESS _____ (ZIP CODE) (TELEPHONE NO.)

FOR PERMISSION TO CLOSE / USE / OPEN THE SIDEWALK / ROADWAY IN FRONT OF BUILDING NO. _____ STREET OR AVENUE

BETWEEN _____ AND _____

FOR THE PURPOSE OF _____

_____ (NO. OPENINGS)   _____ (AREA SIZE)   _____ (FRONTAGE LENGTH, FT.)

ROADWAY _____ (TYPE OF PAVEMENT)   _____ (TOTAL AREA)   _____ (SQ. YDS.)

WORK TO START _____ (DATE)   WORK TO BE COMPLETED _____ (DATE)

THE PERMIT TO BE GRANTED SUBJECT TO THE FOLLOWING CONDITIONS:

THE APPLICANT AGREES TO COMPLY WITH ALL THE RULES AND REGULATIONS OF THE BUREAU OF HIGHWAY OPERATIONS, AS WELL AS OTHER LAWS AND REGULATIONS RELATING TO SUCH WORK; AND THE ACCEPTANCE OF THE PERMIT SHALL BE DEEMED AN AGREEMENT TO ABIDE BY ALL OF ITS TERMS AND CONDITIONS. NO PERMIT WILL BE ISSUED UNLESS THE APPLICANT HAS ON FILE ALL INSURANCE AS REQUIRED IN ACCORDANCE WITH THE RULES AND REGULATIONS OF THE BUREAU OF HIGHWAY OPERATIONS.

SHOW NORTH

BUILDING LINE
CURB LINE

CURB LINE
BUILDING LINE

SPECIAL CONDITIONS: _____

APPROVED FOR THE COMMISSIONER

BY: _____

SIGNED: _____

PRINTED: _____ AUTHORIZED REPRESENTATIVE OF APPLICANT

OVER

19
Other Cities, Other Codes

More than 3,900 different building codes are estimated to be in use in the United States. However, several national organizations publish standard codes, which are often adapted or adopted. Of these, the most frequently used are: the Uniform Building Code (UBC), the Building Officials and Code Administrators (BOCA), and the Standard Building Code (SBC) published by the Southern Building Code International. Each city has the right to adopt its own building code; check with your local building or inspectional services department to determine which codes your city uses.

New York City enacted the first building code; it has served as the model and has set guidelines for many subsequent building codes and building laws throughout the country.

This chapter highlights the differences between New York's codes and those of Atlanta (SBC, 1982 edition), Boston (BOCA, 1978 edition), Chicago (City of Chicago Building Code, 1987), Los Angeles (UBC, 1985 edition), and San Francisco (UBC, 1979 edition).

Though these codes originated in different parts of the country, many of their sections are similar. Therefore, to avoid repetition, some sections on Atlanta, Boston, Chicago, Los Angeles, and San Francisco refer back to the New York codes (chapters 15, 16, and 17).

Most cities have copies of their building codes on record in a library or municipal research center; specific locations are included in the Agency Chart.

ATLANTA

Atlanta uses the 1982 edition of the Standard Building Code (SBC)—commonly known as the Southern Building Code—with amendments of its own.

Photocopies of this 1982 edition, no longer published, are available from the Engineering Department of the Southern Building Code Congress International (205) 591-1853. Cost of the photocopy is $75 for the first hour of labor plus 20 cents per page. However, a copy may be studied at the Fulton County Reference Library, 1 Margaret Mitchell Square, Atlanta, GA 30303.

Because Atlanta zoning allows theatres to locate in commercial, industrial, and "special interest" zones (where pedestrian traffic is encouraged), theatres may be found in all kinds of neighborhoods throughout the metro area. However, parking is tight, so the city requires that space be provided in commercial and industrial zones for one car per every 100 sq. ft. of a building's external envelope.

Definitions

Place of assembly occupancies, defined as group A, are divided into two categories:

Group A-1—Large Assembly. Theatre spaces of 700 or more persons and a working stage.

Group A-2—Small Assembly. Theatres of fewer than 700 persons that do or do not have a working stage.

The stage itself is divided into two categories:

- The working stage—the traditional proscenium stage separated from the audience by a proscenium wall.
- The stage platform—a raised, but unenclosed, section of the floor within the assembly hall that may be permanent, temporary or portable.

Aisles and Seating

According to the SBC, the minimum width for the aisles shall not be less than 42" at the farthest point from the exit, increasing 1 1/2" for every 5' to the exit. However, when the aisle has seats on only one side, it may have a minimum width of 36"; when an aisle serves 60 seats or fewer, it can be 30" wide. Cross aisles must not be less than 42" wide. Aisles that border on an exit must not be less than 4'8".

The number of seats per row in *standard seating* (14) conforms to the New York code. Seats must be securely fastened to the floor except in boxes with no more than 14 seats.

For *continental seating* (see chapter 9), the minimum width of a seat shall be 20"; the back-to-front seat dimension in row spacing should be measured as follows:

- 18" between rows of 18 seats or fewer
- 20" between rows of 19 to 35 seats
- 21" between rows of 36 to 45 seats
- 22" between rows of 46 to 59 seats
- 24" between rows of 60 seats or more

The travel distance to an exit from any seat should not be more than 150'. This distance can increase to 200' when the building is equipped with sprinklers.

Exits

When the occupancy of a place of assembly is from 1 to 500 persons, the minimum number of exits should be two; 501 to 1,000 occupancy requires three.

In continental seating, one pair of exit doors should be provided every 5' along each side aisle. All exit enclosures should have a 2-hour fire-resistance rating, and their width should not be less than 32".

The stage should have exits from both sides that are at least 3' in width.

Emergency Lighting

In all occupancies of 50 or more, the exits should be equipped with exit signs. If the occupancy is more than 300, the main source of power must be augmented by an independent source with a 1 1/2-hour duration for emergencies. This standby power system should provide a generator that starts automatically within 60 seconds of a power failure. The fire alarm system, fire detection system, emergency lighting, and communications system should all be controlled by the emergency power system.

Flameproofing

The proscenium curtain should be designed and constructed to resist passage of flame for five minutes.

Foyer/Lobby

The width of the foyer or lobby at any point must be at least the combined width of the aisles, stairways, and tributary passageways. It must also be level with the back of the auditorium.

Handicapped Access

For handicapped access, corridors should have a minimum width of 44", doorways of 32". An auditorium with fixed seating arrangements requires at least two wheelchair viewing positions, which cannot interfere with normal egress patterns.

Means of Egress

The maximum number of persons per unit of an exit width (22") through doors and corridors from an assembly space is 100, while the maximum number of persons for a stairway is 75. The minimum aggregate width of the main entrance doorway must accommodate 50% of the occupancy, and should not be less than 36". The minimum width of exit corridors should be 44"; the minimum height, 8'.

For balconies with a seating capacity of more than 50, at least two means of egress should be provided—one from each side of the balcony. All exit courts and passageways, when 10' or less in width, must have a minimum fire-resistance rating of 3/4 hour.

Minimum Live Loads

Minimum live loads for group A-1 and A-2 theatres vary slightly from the New York code:

Occupancy or Use	Minimum Live Load (lbs./sq. ft.)
Aisles, corridors and lobbies	100
Orchestra floor	50
Balcony floor	50
Stage floor	150

Ramps

Generally, the slope of a ramp should not be greater than 1 in 8. However, ramps for the disabled must not have a slope greater than 1 in 12. Their minimum width should be 44", and they must be constructed of noncombustible material with a non-slip surface.

Stage Construction

Requirements parallel those in the New York code.

Stairs

Stair dimensions follow the New York code.

Filing Procedures

If, within a 12-month period, a building is altered or repaired to more than 50% of its "then physical value," the structure, even if built before passage of the SBC (1982), must conform to the SBC's requirements for new buildings. Physical value is determined by the director of the bureau of buildings. However, if the cost of repairs or alterations is between 25% and 50% of the unaltered value of the building, only the altered areas must conform to the SBC.

If the occupancy of a building is entirely changed, then the entire building must conform to the SBC. When only a portion is changed, it alone must conform. In this case, you will need to check the requirements of mixed occupancies.

Structures classified by local jurisdiction as historical buildings are not necessarily subject to the Atlanta code. The director of the bureau of buildings judges the safety of historic buildings.

Fees for permits are based on the construction cost of the proposed work: $3 per $1,000 of construction cost, or $10 minimum, whichever is greater. The certificate of occupancy, according to the SBC, will be issued five days after the application has been submitted. The fee for a C of O is $25.

Inspections

Atlanta follows New York's procedure except for the inspection of signs.

Basic Permits

The SBC resembles the New York code in basic permits requirements, except for time limitations. The SBC allows only a six-month period until the permit expires. However, a building official can grant up to a 90-day extension for a permit.

For information on permits, contact:

Permit Information Department
Bureau of Buildings
55 Trinity Avenue
Atlanta, GA 30335

BOSTON

Boston has adopted the Commonwealth of Massachusetts State Building Code, which is based substantially on the 1978 edition of the BOCA code. A copy of the code is available for study in the Government Document Section of the Boston Public Library, 6066 Boylston Street, Boston, MA 02117. The building code book may be purchased at the State Book Store, Room 116, State House, Boston, MA, 02133 for $34.00. It may also be purchased by mail for $37.65. Call (617) 727-2834 for hours and procedure.

Definitions

The Boston code categorizes assembly buildings in group A. Theatres are in A-1; theatres with stages are in A-1-A.

This code also makes a distinction between a stage and a platform. A stage refers to the traditional proscenium configuration, defined in this code as a partially enclosed portion of a building where scenery or other effects may be installed.

Thrust and arena stages fall into the category of a raised platform. By definition, the raised platform limits the raised area to 17 1/2% of the assembly room floor or 1,550 sq. ft., whichever is less. Also included in this classification is the enclosed raised platform, which is similar to a proscenium stage but has no fly gallery and does not extend more than 8' behind the curtain line.

Aisles and Seating

The minimum width of aisles with seats on both sides should be 42", with increases of 1/4" for every foot of aisle length from the beginning of the aisle to an exit door or cross aisle. However, when there are seats on one side only, the aisles can be as narrow as 30".

Cross aisles should also be at least 42" wide, though when bordering on an entrance, they must be at least 48" wide. The cross aisles should be placed every 22 rows when on the main floor area, but in the balconies and galleries, one or more should be provided when there are more than 10 rows of seats.

The number of seats between aisles in a standard row (14) is the same as in the New York code; however, a 32" back-to-back measurement is required. The average width for seats should be 20". Orchestra and balcony seats need to be fastened to the floor.

Exits

The number of exits is calculated in the same manner as in the New York code. Exit doors must have a minimum width of 42".

Emergency Lighting

In case of a power failure, an independent source of power should provide illumination to all means of egress for one hour.

Flameproofing

All draperies and hangings suspended from the ceiling should be noncombustible. The proscenium fire curtain should withstand a 1/2-hour fire test.

Foyer/Lobby

The foyer should have a minimum floor area of 1 1/2 sq. ft. per occupant and should be at the same level as the back of the auditorium. The wall separating the foyer from the auditorium should be constructed of materials with no less than a 2-hour fire resistance rating.

Handicapped Access

For grades and widths of ramps, Boston's code dimensions are the same as for New York. However, no required number of spaces for wheelchairs is designated by the Boston code.

Means of Egress

The Boston and New York codes are the same concerning the number of stairways required from every floor of the building. In the Boston code, however, the capacity of a stairway is measured in *unit width for egress*. Unit width for egress means the width of the stairs themselves (22") and how many people, single-file and moving, that stairway can accommodate at one time. Stairways without a fire suppression system have a capacity of 75 persons per 22". Stairways with a fire suppression system have a capacity of 113 persons per 22".

Doors, ramps, and corridors without a fire suppression system must have a capacity of 100 persons per 22". For those with a fire suppression system, capacity is 150 persons. In all cases, doors and corridors serving as exit ways are required to have a fire-resistance rating of one hour.

Minimum Live Loads

Minimum live loads for theatres in groups A-1 and A-1-A are as follows:

Occupancy or Use	*Minimum Live Load (lbs./sq. ft.)*
Aisles, corridors, and lobbies	100
Orchestra floor	60
Balcony	60
Stage floor	150

Ramps

Boston and New York codes follow the same guidelines for ramp dimensions.

Sprinklers

See New York code.

Stage Construction

Walls on all sides should have a fire-resistance rating of not less than 4 hours. The floor should have a rating of 3 hours. The dressing rooms and support areas should have walls with 3-hour ratings.

Stairs

See New York code.

Filing Procedure

While Boston's Inspectional Services Department (ISD) has the same responsibility as New York's Department of Buildings, it has the added responsibility of zoning regulation and enforcement. The ISD handles four types of permits: electrical and fire systems, gas, plumbing and sprinkler, and building. All but the building permit must be filed by a licensed contractor; the owner of a building applies for the building permit. Processing a permit for alterations can take six to eight weeks.

There are two applications for building permits: the long form, which is used for additions and structural changes, and the short form, used for minor repairs. Fees for the long form application are $7 per $1,000 of estimated cost of the project for the first $100,000 and $10 per $1,000 of estimated cost in excess of $100,000. The base fee for the short form application is $7 plus $10 for each $1,000. When filing for an amendment to the original plan, the fee is $30, plus $10 for each $1,000 of estimated cost. If no work is done on the permit within six months of filing, the permit will be deemed abandoned—although building officials may grant extensions of 90 days. When all work has been completed, a certificate of occupancy will be issued. About three weeks will elapse between submission of the application and issuance of the C of O. The fee for a C of O is $50 for places of assembly.

With regard to zoning, special rules govern an application for a theatre in the area that is to be the Midtown Theatre District. It is necessary to see the zoning administrator for special rules governing such applications. A zoning review can take from two days to two weeks. The fire department must also be contacted when any renovating or remodeling is to be done. If a theatre is in a historical district, the Landmarks Commission will have to review the application.

For information on permits, contact:

Plans and Permits Division
Inspection Services Department
1010 Massachusetts Avenue
Boston, MA 02118

CHICAGO

Chicago is well known for its tough building and fire codes and for their strict enforcement; however, the Chicago Building Code is one of the best organized and most readable—if any codes are—in the country.

Chicago uses the City of Chicago Building Code, 1987 edition. Developed by the city, it is not based on any one national code, but represents a compilation of several. The Chicago City Council has power to amend and change these regulations. The City of Chicago Building Code is published by: Index Publishing Corporation, 323 West Randolph Street, Chicago, IL 60606.

Definitions

The Chicago code classifies assembly spaces as class C. Large assembly spaces with a capacity of 300 persons or more are classified as class C-1. Small assembly spaces of fewer than 300 persons are classified as class C-2. All theatres come under the classification of assembly spaces. The permit under which theatres operate is the Place of Public Amusement (PPA).

Small theatres are likely to fall into one of the following categories:

Theatrical Community Center. Assembly spaces of under 300 seats (Class C-2) in buildings operated by nonprofit organizations. This category gives theatres of 300 seats or fewer seats special perks, specifically in regard to zoning.

Playhouse-in-the-Round. A theatre building with a platform stage fully opened to the audience from at least three sides. These theatres cannot have fly galleries.

Mercantile Unit. A unique classification, mercantile units (class F), allows small theatres with not more than 100 seats located in a building of another occupancy or use to be classified according to that use. For theatres like Stage Left and Chicago Dramatists Workshop (office buildings), and Live Bait (a residential building), this can mean enormous breaks in the number of required exits, public toilets and parking spaces, and in other areas of code compliance.

Aisles and Seating

The back-to-back measurement for standard rows of seats is not less than 34". If the back-to-back distance is increased to 42", then rows of 48 seats (continental seating) are permitted.

Aisles must not be less than 36" in width. However, aisles with seats on only one side and aisles serving not more than a total of 60 seats can be a minimum width of 30". Transverse aisles should be at least 44". A transverse aisle must be provided at any level change of 12'.

Generally, when there are 200 or more seats in the assembly space, the seats must be securely fastened to the floor. The exceptions are box seats having not more than 14 seats, and temporary seating secured together in units of no fewer than 5 seats.

Exits

The minimum number of exits from each seating level (i.e., orchestra or balcony) should be as follows:

Capacity	Minimum Number of Exits
50 or less	1
51 to 300	2
301 to 1,000	3
More than 1,000	4

The capacity of stairs and other vertical exits is 60 persons per 22" of exit width. Doorways, corridors, and horizontal exits should accommodate 90 persons per 22" of exit width. These exits should be as remote from each other as possible. The foyer of the theatre at the main floor level should connect to a public street or streets through a corridor equal in width to the combined width of the required exits.

Emergency Lighting

Where the seating capacity of a theatre is 100 persons or more, an emergency lighting system should be provided. Theatres must have a system that consists of three sources of supply of electrical power: the normal source of power, an auxiliary source, and a final reserve source supplied by batteries or an on-site generator. The power must switch automatically among sources. In addition, lighted signs must be installed to mark ways of egress.

Foyer/Lobby

The capacity of a foyer or waiting space is calculated at 3 sq. ft. per person.

Handicapped Access

Capacity	Number of Viewing Spaces
Up to 50 seats	2
51 to 400 seats	4
401 or more seats	An even number of spaces not less than 1% of total seats.

Means of Egress

The maximum travel distance from a seat to an exit is 150'. The travel distance may be increased 100% if a sprinkler system is provided with a 2-source water supply. One source should be provided with an emergency power supply.

All exit courts and passageways should have a 3-hour fire-resistance rating. The width of exit courts and exit passageways should not be less than 66" and should increase 22" for every 90 persons served over 300 persons.

Minimum Live Loads

See New York requirements.

Sprinklers

The Chicago and New York codes are the same regarding the location of sprinklers. A fire marshall will inspect annually.

Stage Construction

Stages are divided into two types. Type 2 stages are usually located in schools, community, or multipurpose buildings in which the use of a stage for theatrical performances is only occasional. Type 1 stages are "every other type of stage besides Type 2."

Another category applies to platforms erected for temporary use. If these platforms are under 24" in height, plans do not need to be submitted to and approved by the department of inspections, nor need a permit be issued by the commissioner. A temporary platform of over 24" in height or larger than 1,500 sq. ft. requires a permit. No permit can be issued for longer than 15 days, though after an inspection by the department of inspections, an extension to the permit can be issued. The permit fee is $60.

Stairs

Chicago and New York have the same required dimensions for height and width of stairs.

Filing Procedures

The permit fee for alterations and repairs to any structure is $10 for the first $1,000 of estimated cost and $5 for each additional $1,000 of estimated cost. The minimum charge is $50. The permit fee for a theatre fire curtain is $104. The fee for stages and orchestra platforms is $100. The inspections department maintains a public information service, which answers questions about building code violations. (See Agency Chart.)

Inspections

The inspections process is the same as New York's. For information on permits, contact:

Application Review
Department of Inspectional Services
121 North LaSalle
Chicago, IL 60602

LOS ANGELES

In 1987, Los Angeles adopted the 1985 edition of the Uniform Building Code. There have been subsequent changes to that code, plus amendments made by the city. Building News, Inc. publishes the City of Los Angeles Building Code and the Uniform Building Code in a single book that clarifies how the two codes differ.

Earthquake Regulations

In 1934, after 1933's disastrous Long Beach Earthquake, the City of Los Angeles Building Code was greatly revised and rules regarding theatres tightened. Principal code changes outlawed the use of unreinforced masonry in bearing walls. Steel reinforcment and no brick are two basic structural features required for any theatre building. Anyone considering conversion of a pre-1934 space into a theatre should check carefully that the building can be brought up to code.

Because of earthquakes, the Los Angeles code pays particular attention to buildings with unreinforced masonry bearing walls constructed or approved for construction before 1933. Every building in Los Angeles must have a structural analysis made by a state-licensed engineer or architect to determine whether it meets the minimum earthquake standards.

Definitions

An assembly building is defined as a building or portion used for the gathering of 50 or more persons.

Theatres and places of public assembly are further classified as *high-risk, medium-risk,* or *historical* buildings. High-risk buildings have an occupancy of 100 or more. Medium-risk buildings have an occupancy load of 20 to 100. Historical buildings, so designated by an appropriate federal, state, or city agency, must comply with the State Historical Building Code requirements.

The Los Angeles code classifies stages as *legitimate, regular,* and *thrust.* A legitimate stage is a proscenium with a fly gallery. A regular stage is a platform within an assembly room without a fly gallery, such as a theatre-in-the-round. A thrust stage is a platform extending beyond the proscenium into the audience.

Aisles and Seating

In standard seating (14 seats per row) where there are aisles on both sides, the aisles should be 42" wide. The aisle width should increase by 1 1/2" for every 5' of its length. When there is an aisle on only one side of the seats, that aisle must be no less than 36" wide.

For seat spacing in standard seating, there should not be less than 12" from the back of one seat to the front of the seat behind it. In continental seating, the number of seats per row increases under the following formulae:

1. The distance between a seat and the one immediately behind it should be as follows:

- 18" distance between seats in rows of 1 to 18 seats

- 20" distance between seats in rows of 19 to 35 seats
- 21" distance between seats in rows of 36 to 45 seats

2. Exit doors should be provided along each side aisle at the rate of one pair of doors for each five rows of seats.

3. Each pair of exit doors must provide a minimum width of 66" and discharge into a foyer or exterior of a building.

The dimensions for cross aisles and for the slope of aisles follow the New York code.

Exits

Every story or portion used as a place of assembly with an occupancy load of ten or more persons must have at least two exits. Every story or portion having an occupancy load of 501 to 1,000 must have no fewer than three exits. The exits must be an equal distance from the area served, and that distance must be not less than one half of the diagonal dimension of the area served by the exits. Doors must be at least 36" wide.

Exit Lighting

When an occupancy of 50 or more is served, exit signs should be placed to indicate clearly the direction of egress.

Handicapped Access

Handicapped access is required by the California Administrative Code. Under this code, all primary entrances to a building are required to be accessible to the physically disabled. The code requires accessibility to elevators. The slope of ramps should not be steeper than 1 to 12.

Means of Egress

All interior stairways must be enclosed and have a 2-hour fire resistance construction. An exit courtyard must have a minimum width of 44".

Minimum Live Load

Assembly areas with fixed seating should have a minimum uniform live load of 50 pounds per sq. ft. Movable seating and other areas should have a uniform live load of 125.

Ramps

When the auditorium space has fixed seating, the room floor cannot have a slope of greater than 1 to 5. The slope of general ramps should not exceed 1 to 8, and should have a landing at the top and bottom.

Sprinklers

Los Angeles's code follows New York's new code in that spaces, stairs, stage, dressing rooms, workshops, and any room in which the total area exceeds 500 sq. ft. must have automatic sprinklers. The exceptions to this are stages and platforms open to the auditorium room on three or more sides.

Stage Construction

Legitimate stages must be completely separated from the audience by a wall of not less than 2-hour fire-resistant noncombustible construction. Backstage, there should be at least one well-marked exit providing not less than 32" clear width and opening directly to the street.

Stairs

Stairways serving an occupancy of 50 or more must be not less than 44" in width.

Filing Procedure

As long as an existing building "remains safe and not a hazard," and as long as there are no adopted regulations that specifically apply to the building, it may conform to the codes under which it was built. When alterations or repairs are made to an existing building, when this work does not exceed 10% of the replacement cost of the building, and when no further hazards exist, then these repairs may be of the same types as the existing structure.

However, when these repairs exceed 10% of the replacement cost of the building, then all the work must conform to the 1987 code requirements for new buildings of like construction. Unreinforced masonry bearing walls that were constructed or under construction prior to October 6, 1933, need to conform with this code's provisions on earthquake hazard. The city of Los Angeles is in seismic zone 4, in which no new buildings with unreinforced masonry bearing walls are allowed.

The permit fee for a building is based on the total valuation.

For information on permits, contact:

*Public Counter of Permits
and Permit Information Building Bureau
200 N. Spring Street, Room 460, Counter B
Los Angeles, CA 90012*

SAN FRANCISCO

The San Francisco building code is based primarily on the 1979 edition of the Uniform Building Code and also includes several appendices and amendments dealing with specific conditions for San Francisco, such as high-density development and small lot sizes. Copies of the code can be purchased at Civic Center Books, 360 Golden Gate Avenue, San Francisco, CA 94102.

San Francisco categorizes theatres as retail establishments, and allows them in any of its three basic zones: residential, commercial, and high-rise commercial. Federal requirements for handicapped accessibility are among those most strictly enforced.

Fort Mason Center, owned by the National Park Service, uses the unembellished UBC. Although the San Francisco fire department cannot legally enforce its recommendations on Fort Mason and its tenants, they are carefully honored by the center.

At Fort Mason Center, the National Park Service is responsible for the structural (i.e., seismic) integrity of the buildings. As to San Francisco's seismic requirements for theatres, they are often described as "unclear," and problems often arise when creating a new use for a building. Therefore, before entering into a lease, it is worth the expense of hiring an engineer to make sure the building in question is seismically sound.

Parking requirements in San Francisco are based on a theatre building's square footage.

Other Bay Area cities, of course, have their own codes and regulations.

Definitions

The San Francisco code defines assembly spaces as buildings used for the gathering of 50 or more persons. Group A categorizes assembly spaces: the occupancy designations are A-1 and A-2. A-1 is any assembly building with a stage and occupancy of 1,000 or more; A-2 is any building or portion of a building having an assembly room with a stage and an occupancy of less than 1,000.

Aisle and Seating

Standard width for an aisle should be 42" when seats are on both sides and not less than 36" when there are seats on one side only. These aisles must increase 1 1/2" in width for each 5' in length in the direction of the exit. With continental seating, aisles cannot be less than 44" in width. In places with standard seating, aisles should be located so that there will not be more than six intervening seats between any seat and the nearest aisle. In places with continental seating, the number of intervening seats may increase to 29 seats when exit doors are provided along each side aisle at the rate of one pair of doors, 66" wide, for every five rows of seats.

The spacing of rows with standard seating is the same as in the New York code. However, with continental seating, the spacing of rows is as follows:

- 18" clear for rows of 18 seats or fewer.
- 20" clear for rows of 19 to 35 seats.
- 21" clear for rows of 36 to 45 seats.
- 22" clear for rows of 46 or more seats.

These distances are measured from the seat back to the front-most projection of the seat directly behind it.

Exits

Every floor having an occupancy load of 501 to 1,000 persons should have no fewer than three exits. Every floor or portion used as a place of assembly with an occupancy load of 10 or more persons must have at least two exits. Single doors cannot be less than 36" wide or more than 48" wide.

Handicapped Access

San Francisco bases its code for handicapped access on the Federal Rehabilitation Act passed in 1973.

Means of Egress

The width of corridors shall be at least 44" when allowing for an occupancy load of 10 or more. The construction shall be of a 1-hour fire-resistance rating when serving an occupancy load of 30 or more.

Stairways serving an occupancy load of 50 or more should not be less than 44" in width. If the occupancy load is under 50, the stairway can be 36".

Exit courtyards also must have a minimum width of not less than 44".

Minimum Live Load

Occupancy or Use	Uniform Live Load (lbs./sq. ft.)
Fixed seating area	75
Stage area and enclosed platform	150

Ramps

The San Francisco code and the New York code have the same requirements for ramp dimensions.

Sprinklers

The requirements for sprinklers are the same as New York's.

Stage Construction

The proscenium wall must be of not less than 2-hour fire-resistant noncombustible construction. The construction of the stage floor has the same requirements as the New York code.

Stairs

The dimensions for the treads and risers follow the same basic standards as New York's.

Filing Procedures

Filing procedures are similar to New York's. However, the plans should include calculations for the structural and seismic design of the building.

Inspections

The requirements for inspections are similar to those of New York.

For information on permits, contact:

Central Permit Bureau
450 McAllister
San Francisco, CA 94102

Appendix: Resource Directory

NATIONAL SERVICE ORGANIZATIONS

This survey of service organizations is limited to those which might be of help in solving a small, not-for-profit theatre group's space and renovation problems. The services available range from help with loans, to advice and technical assistance, to programs that increase box office sales. There are also organizations that provide information about or publish handbooks, directories, or journals on relevant topics, such as funding, consultation resources and city codes.

American Society of Theatre Consultants (ASTC)

Founded in 1984, ASTC is a professional organization of theatre consultants who work throughout the U.S. Its approximately 20 members represent many of the country's full-time theatre consulting firms.

American Society of Theatre Consultants
c/o Edgar L. Lustig
12226 Mentz Hill Road
St. Louis, MO 63128
(314) 843-9218

Business Volunteers for the Arts (BVA)

BVA "recruits and trains corporate executives as arts management consultants, then places them on a pro bono basis with nonprofit arts organizations." Areas covered include property management, tenancy rights/leases, capital improvement planning, space planning and historic preservation. Headquartered in New York, the organization has 30 affiliates around the country.

BVA/Atlanta
Atlanta Chamber of Commerce
235 International Boulevard N.W.
P.O. Box 1740
Atlanta, GA 30301-1740
(404) 586-8536

BVA/Chicago
55 East Monroe, Suite 1640
Chicago, IL 60603
(312) 372-1876

BVA/Los Angeles
ARTS, Inc.
315 West 9th Street, Suite 201
Los Angeles, CA 90015
(213) 627-9276

BVA/New York
Arts and Business Council
25 West 45 Street, Suite 707
New York, NY 10036
(212) 819-9287

BVA/San Francisco
San Francisco Chamber of Commerce
465 California Street
San Francisco, CA 94104
(415) 392-4511

The Foundation Center

The Foundation Center's libraries offer the use of hundreds of books and periodicals about foundations: who they are, what they fund and how to find them. Among the center's most useful resources for capital funding research are the *Capital Campaign Resource Guide* (published by San Francisco's Public Management Institute) and the center's COMSEARCH printouts, which categorize the gifts of the nation's top 500 granters. Equally informative are the Center's own books, including *The Foundation Directory, The Foundation Grants Index,* and *Source Book Profiles.* For information on these publications, and for a complete list of the center's cooperating collections, call (800) 424-9836.

The Foundation Center
79 Fifth Avenue
New York, NY 10003
(212) 620-4230

National Collections
79 Fifth Avenue
New York, NY 10003
(212) 620-4230

1001 Connecticut Avenue, N.W.
Suite 938
Washington, DC 20036
(202) 331-1400

Field Offices
312 Sutter Street
San Francisco, CA 94108
(415) 397-0902/0903

Hanna Building
1422 Euclid Avenue, Suite 1356
Cleveland, OH 44115
(216) 861-1933/1934

Affiliates
Associated Grantmakers of Massachusetts
294 Washington Street
Boston, MA 02108
(617) 426-2608

The Donors Forum
53 West Jackson Boulevard, Room 430
Chicago, IL 60604
(312) 431-0265

Foundation Funding Information Center
606 South Olive Street
Los Angeles, CA 90014-1526
(213) 413-4042

Theatre Development Fund (TDF)

Originally a New York City service organization, TDF has broadened its base through its National Services department. The most visible of TDF's New York public service activities is the Times Square Theatre Center (TKTS), a discount ticket booth. TKTS offers half-price tickets on the day of performance to Broadway, Off-Broadway, music, and dance audiences in four locations. Its National Services department has also helped to establish half-price booths in many cities including Boston, Chicago, and San Francisco. Other TDF services include the Theatre Access Project (TAP) for the disabled and the Costume Collection.

Theatre Development Fund
1501 Broadway
New York, NY 10036
(212) 221-0885

The United States Institute for Theatre Technology (USITT)

USITT is a national organization of, and resource center for, professional theatre designers and technicians. It provides an informal referral service for theatre planing and technical operating professionals, and maintains files on consultants and their work. Major concerns are the "promotion of safe practices and procedures, and promulgation of standards for the design and operation of theatrical equipment."

USITT, Inc.
10 West 19th Street, Suite 5A
New York, NY 10011-4206
(212) 924-9088

Volunteer Lawyers for the Arts (VLA)

Legal assistance is provided free after payment of an initial administrative fee ranging from $30 to $300. This includes help with certain types of real estate problems relating to performing arts organizations.

Services are limited to nonprofit arts organizations with annual operating budgets of under $500,000. Assistance is by appointment only; written requests can be made for information. If a group is eligible, VLA assigns a volunteer lawyer who will aid in the resolution of the legal problem. Each VLA office is a separate entity and therefore fees and services vary. Most legal problems are time-consuming, and you can expect the entire procedure to be lengthy.

Atlanta
Georgia Volunteer Lawyers for the Arts
Suite 2330, 34 Peachtree Street, N.W.
Atlanta, GA 30303
(404) 525-6046

Boston
Volunteer Lawyers for the Arts
The Artists Foundation, Inc.
8 Park Plaza
Boston, MA 02116
(617) 523-1764

Chicago
Lawyers for the Creative Arts
213 West Institute Place, Suite 411
Chicago, IL 60610
(312) 944-2787

Los Angeles
California Lawyers for the Arts
315 West 9 Street, 11th Floor
Los Angeles, CA 90015
(213) 623-8311

New York
Volunteer Lawyers for the Arts
1 East 53rd Street
New York, NY 10022
(212) 319-2787

San Francisco
California Lawyers for the Arts
Fort Mason Center
Building C, Room 225
San Francisco, CA 94123
(415) 775-7200

SIX CITIES RESOURCE DIRECTORY

ATLANTA

City Hall

Atlanta's 24 neighborhood planning units (NPUs) are advisory bodies that act as liaisons between the city government and its citizens. Although not official decision makers, they can be helpful to a company applying for rezoning, a special permit or a variance. The NPUs forward their comments to Atlanta's zoning review board which, in turn, sends the information to the city council.

Neighborhood Planning Coordinator
Office of Planning and Development
City Hall
55 Trinity Avenue
Atlanta, GA 30335
(404) 330-6070

Atlanta Economic Development Corporation (AEDC)

Through the AEDC, the Small Business Loan Administration provides direct loans and loan guarantees (limited to $750,000) to eligible small businesses for the financing of fixed assets. The AEDC also co-sponsors the Business Improvement Loan Fund (BILF) "designed to encourage the revitalization of targeted Atlanta business districts." Financial assistance is available through BILF in the form of interest subsidies, direct loans, or loan participations.

Atlanta Economic Development Corporation
230 Peachtree Street N.W., Suite 1650
Atlanta, GA 30303
(404) 658-7000

Atlanta Theatre Coalition (ATC)

ATC is a support and advocacy group. Full membership is open to any producing or presenting theatre organization in the Metro Atlanta area. Associate members—interested non-theatre groups or individuals—may serve on committees, but do not vote. Full dues are computed on the basis of annual income.

Atlanta Theatre Coalition
P.O. Box 7270
Atlanta, GA 30357
(404) 873-1185

Community Design Center

The nonprofit center provides technical assistance, urban planning, and architectural advice to groups and communities that cannot afford to purchase these services from the private sector. Fees, although low, vary from project to project.

Community Design Center
1083 Austin Avenue
Atlanta, GA 30307
(404) 523-6966

Fulton County Arts Council

The arts council gives grants to artists and arts organizations in Fulton County. Funds are available for nonprofit groups to develop artistic and managerial skill; promote accessibility to, and a wide spectrum of arts programming; and introduce the arts to new audiences.

Fulton County Arts Council
34 Peachtree Street N.W.
Suite 2330
Atlanta, GA 30303
(404) 730-5780

Metropolitan Atlanta Community Foundation, Inc. (Metro Atlanta)

Metro Atlanta is a public foundation whose permanent endowment fund is used "for the enhancement of the community." Theatre groups may be able to obtain grants from unrestricted and field-of-interest funds.

Metropolitan Atlanta Community Foundation, Inc.
50 Hurt Plaza, Suite 449
Atlanta, GA 30303
(404) 688-5525

Production Values, Inc. (PVI)

Modeled after the Costume Collection in New York, PVI provides low-cost costume rental on a sliding scale linked to seating capacity and number of performances. Barter arrangements are possible, as well. PVI also designs and builds costumes, and has been known to store sets.

Production Values, Inc.
331 Elizabeth Street N.E.
Atlanta, GA 30307
(404) 584-5529

BOSTON

City Hall

Boston's 13-member city council consists of 9 district councilmembers and 4 members-at-large.

The city publishes a handbook, "Organization of the City Government of Boston," which gives specific contact information.

City Council
Boston City Hall, 5th Floor
Boston, MA 02201
(617) 725-3040

ARTS/Boston

Founded in 1975, ARTS/Boston is a nonprofit audience development organization serving Boston's cultural community. A number of programs are available to participating theatres.

BOSTIX. A half-price ticket outlet modeled on Theatre Development Fund's TKTS in New York, and linked with Ticketron.

ARTS/MAIL. A monthly guide to arts events, created to move hard-to-sell tickets. Via the guide, clip-out coupons for ordering half-price tickets reach 2,200 theatregoers in the greater Boston area.

ARTS/Boston
100 Boylston Street, Suite 735
Boston, MA 02116
(617) 423-4454

Boston Arts Lottery Council

Funded by state monies and administered by Boston's office of the arts and humanities, this program's purpose is to support activities within the city which are available to, or benefit, the general public. Technical assistance grants of up to $5,000 are awarded to theatres yearly. Typically, grants range from $1,500 to $2,000.

Boston Arts Lottery Council
Office of the Arts and Humanities
Boston City Hall, Room 608
Boston, MA 02201
(617) 725-3245

Massachusetts Cultural Council Space Program

Short-term, free technical assistance provided by on-staff consultants skilled in real estate development.

CULTURAL FACILITIES TECHNICAL ASSISTANCE. Up to $10,000 is given for predevelopment costs associated with the rehabilitation or construction of a cultural facility. Money may be used for architectural, financial, engineering, legal or other technical services.

RESOURCE AWARDS. Created to encourage the exchange of ideas and strategies among artists, lenders, and developers about securing, renovating or building performance, live/work or studio space. Maximum grant is $10,000.

Massachusetts Cultural Council
80 Boylston Street, 10th Floor
Boston, MA 02116
(617) 727-3668

Massachusetts Cultural Alliance

The nonprofit Alliance provides management, referral, communication, and advocacy services to almost 300 cultural organizations throughout the state. Membership benefits include a quarterly newsletter and networking forum.

Massachusetts Cultural Alliance
33 Harrison Avenue
Boston, MA 02111
(617) 423-0260

Massachusetts Health and Educational Facilities Authority

The Authority's mandate is to provide "access to the capital market for 501(c)(3) organizations," including cultural institutions. Low-interest loans "in excess of $100,000 best fit the Authority."

Massachusetts Health and
Educational Facilities Authority
99 Summer Street
Boston, MA 02110-1240
(617) 737-8377

Massachusetts Industrial Finance Agency

Qualified nonprofits can make use of the Agency's tax-exempt 501(c)(3) bonds program for construction of new facilities, expansion or renovation of existing buildings, or purchase of new equipment.

Massachusetts Industrial Finance Agency
75 Federal Street
Boston, MA 02110
(617) 451-2477

StageSource: The Alliance of Theatre Artists and Producers

StageSource is a nonprofit theatre resource center founded in 1984. Member services include: a talent bank, professional seminars, hotline (for discounted tickets, announcements of classes, auditions, and staff openings), a bimonthly newsletter, and yearly guide to theatres in the greater Boston area. StageSource serves 600 individual and 75 producer members throughout New England.

StageSource:
The Alliance of Theatre Artists and Producers
1 Boyleston Place
Boston, MA 02116
(617) 423-2475

CHICAGO

City Hall

Chicago is divided into 50 political units called wards. An elected alderperson represents each of these in the city council. If you get in trouble at city hall, your alderperson can turn down the heat. Additionally, there are neighborhood organizations of several types—homeowner, tenant, merchant. To find out about these recources, contact the board of elections.

Board of Elections
121 North LaSalle Street
Chicago, IL 60602
(312) 269-7900

The African American Arts Alliance of Chicago

The alliance's 30-plus members represent all arts areas, including theatre. It provides technical assistance, training programs, and advocacy for African-American Artists. It also administers selection and presentation of the annual Paul Robeson Award.

The African American Arts Alliance of Chicago
1809 East 71 Street
Chicago, IL 60649
(312) 288-5100

The Chicago Community Trust

The trust makes grants and, where appropriate, loans to tax-exempt, nonprofit organizations serving residents of Chicago and Cook County in areas including the arts and humanities. Grants are given four times yearly; there is no maximum grant awarded.

The Chicago Community Trust
222 North La Salle Street, Suite 1400
Chicago, IL 60601
(312) 372-3356

Community Development Block Grants

Grants are available yearly through the Not-for-Profit Facility Rehabilitation Program, including bricks and mortar funding. The average grant is $46,000.

Community Development Block Grants
121 North La Salle Street, Room 1006
Chicago, IL 60602
(312) 744-7223

Department of Cultural Affairs— Cultural Develpoment Division

This office provides information about zoning codes and can help with locating spaces, including city-owned properties.

Department of Cultural Affairs
78 East Washington Street
Chicago, IL 60602
(312) 744-6254

Executive Service Corps

The corps's roster of volunteer executive retirees includes architects and engineers available to consult with nonprofits on facilities design and maintenance.

Executive Service Corps
25 East Washington Street, Suite 801
Chicago, IL 60602
(312) 580-1840

Illinois Arts Council (IAC)

IAC encourages arts development throughout Illinois, providing financial assistance, information, and advocacy to individuals and organizations. Its "Building by Design" program, initiated in 1987, offers funding in four categories. Available to eligible nonprofits are: Initial Planning ($5,000 maximum), Needs Assessment ($20,000 maximum), Feasibility ($30,000 maximum), and Design ($50,000 maximum) grants. Matching funds are required on at least a 1 to 1 basis, and grants are made annually.

Illinois Arts Council
State of Illinois Center
100 West Randolph, Suite 10-500
Chicago, IL 60601
(312) 814-6750
(800) 237-6994

League of Chicago Theatres

A coalition of 125 theatres and theatre companies, the League of Chicago Theatres handles a variety of programs, including: three Hot Tix centers, a 24-hour performance and ticket information hotline, cooperative advertising and promotion, and advocacy. It funds the Chicago Theatre Foundation, which publishes several periodicals, sponsors twice-yearly professional retreats and offers health insurance, credit union and other services.

League of Chicago Theatres
67 East Madison, Suite 2116
Chicago, IL 60603
(312) 977-1730

LOS ANGELES

City Hall

Each of Los Angeles's city council districts is presided over by a nonpartisan elected councilmember. Those portions of Los Angeles County that are unincorporated, as well as some that are incorporated but have small operating budgets, fall instead under the jurisdiction of members of the county board of supervisors. To find out about your city or county representative, contact the city clerk.

Los Angeles City Clerk's Office
200 North Spring Street, Room 395
Los Angeles, CA 90012
(213) 485-5705

Actors' Equity Association

The regional office has information on Equity's safe and sanitary requirements, the 99-Seat Plan, contracts, etc.

Actors' Equity Association
6430 Sunset Boulevard, Suite 700
Los Angeles, CA 90028
(213) 462-2334

Arts Resources and Technical Services, Inc. (ARTS Inc.)

ARTS Inc. provides inexpensive technical assistance, primarily managerial, to nonprofit arts organizations. An affiliate of Business Volunteers for the Arts, it sponsors planning and grant-writing workshops, and publishes mailing lists and a Directory. Short-term, low- or no-interest loans up to $15,000 are available from ARTS Inc. to alleviate cash-flow problems. These must be secured by a government grant or other secure receivables.

Arts Resources and Technical Services, Inc.
315 West Ninth Street, Suite 201
Los Angeles, CA 90015
(213) 627-9276

California Community Foundation

The foundation administers a pool of many funds, some restricted, some not. Included in its six funding categories are: the arts and humanities, education, and community development.

California Community Foundation
606 South Olive Street, Suite 2400
Los Angeles, CA 90014-1526
(213) 413-4042

Community Redevelopment Agency of the City of Los Angeles (CRA L.A.)

CRA L.A. is charged with revitalizing nineteen designated "blighted" areas of the city. For renovations within some of these, low-interest loans and technical assistance in planning, engineering, and grant-writing may be available.

Community Redevelopment Agency
of the City of Los Angeles
345 South Spring Street
Los Angeles, CA 90013
(213) 977-1951

Los Angeles Cultural Affairs Department

The department is responsible for several programs and services. These include Special Projects, a program to help theatre companies locate performance and administrative space; and Technical Services, which offers a variety of consultants. Department staffers consult for free; when the department refers groups to outside consultants, fees are negotiated on an individual basis. The department also administers five arts centers in L.A. County; provides cultural affairs grants, as available, to assist companies with productions; and advocates for the arts.

Los Angeles Cultural Affairs Department
City Hall
200 North Spring Street, Room 2403
Los Angeles, CA 90012
(213) 485-2437

The National/State/County Partnership

The partnership was created to "address the needs of low-budget, developing arts organizations in their formative years." It does not give bricks and mortar funding. However, an L.A.-based company with a track record would be eligible for technical assistance monies via an administrative grant. Administered by the L.A. County Music and Performing Arts Commission, the grants are on a five-year track, with matching fund requirements beginning at 1 to 1 and increasing to 3 to 1 by the final year. Typical first- and second-year grants range from $1,000 to $10,000.

The National/State/County Partnership
135 North Grand Avenue
Los Angeles, CA 90012
(213) 974-1317

Theatre League Alliance (Theatre L.A.)

Theatre L.A.'s countywide network of over 70 commercial, nonprofit, educational, and community theatres, plus independent producers, offers a variety of member services. These include cooperative advertising, lists of rentable rehearsal and performance spaces, a monthly newsletter, workshops, seminars and a job bank. Dues are .1%

of the member company's annual budget, with set minimum and maximum amounts.

Theatre League Alliance
644 South Figueroa Street
Los Angeles, CA 90017
(213) 614-0556

NEW YORK

City Hall

New York's community boards were established to advise the city planning commission on matters of land use. Their responsibilities include establishing land use policy, passing on proposed new construction, and reviewing zoning variances for change of use. The borough of Manhattan has 12 community boards whose chairs are included on the borough board which, in turn, is directly responsible to the borough president. Local community boards are comprised of approximately 50 political appointees, all of whom reside or do business in the district. Each community board has a district office and a full-time district manager. Contact the community assistance office at the mayor's office to find out about these resources.

Community Assistance Unit
Office of the Mayor
51 Chambers Street, 6th Floor
New York, NY 10007
(212) 566-1272

Actors' Equity Association

Equity's main office can provide information about the union's safe and sanitary requirements, contracts, etc.

Actors' Equity Association
165 West 46th Street
New York, NY 10036
(212) 869-8530

Alliance of Resident Theatres/New York (A.R.T./New York)

A.R.T./New York is the service organization for New York's nonprofit Off- and Off-Off-Broadway theatre companies. Founded in 1972, it acts as advocate for the theatre community, and provides a variety of services in the areas of theatre management and production. Services include real estate assistance, low-cost liability insurance, a discounted payroll service, a collaborative marketing campaign, consultancies and a loan fund.

Alliance of Resident Theatres/New York
131 Varick Street, Suite 904
New York City, NY 10013
(212) 989-5257

The Costume Collection

Administered by the Theatre Development Fund, the Costume Collection provides low-cost costumes and costume-related services to nonprofit performing arts organizations nationwide.

The collection also rents a workroom to nonprofit costume designers in exchange for cash or barter of costumes constructed there. Additional services include a research library and a work-study program for costume design students.

The Costume Collection
1501 Broadway, Suite 2110
New York, NY 10036
(212) 221-0885

Department of Business Services Retention and Relocation Program (RR)

RR reimburses eligible firms in New York for their moving expenses if these commercial firms are relocating within specified areas of the city and they are displaced because of conversion of their manufacturing space for residential use. For more information, call New York City's Department of Business Services at (212) 696-2442.

Department of Cultural Affairs, City of New York (DCA)

REAL ESTATE ASSISTANCE PROGRAM. The DCA, in cooperation with the New York City Community Trust, established the Real Estate Assistance Program to help nonprofit arts organizations implement relocation projects. Grants up to $9,500 are available to groups "that have located suitable space and need financial assistance for legal, accounting, architectural, design, or other consulting costs in connection with the acquisition or renovation of such space." Applicants must demonstrate that the space in question will enable them "to continue or expand the programming services" currently being offered; that, indeed, the space can be acquired, renovated, and maintained for at least three years after that grant date; and that the amount of the grant requested will not exceed 20% of the project's total cost (excluding rental, maintenance, or financing charges).

THE ARTS PRESERVATION CORPORATION'S REVOLVING LOAN FUND. The fund was created in 1988 to help arts institutions obtain affordable and long-term space in New York. It offers loans of up to $50,000 at two or three points below the prime lending rate. As private, corporate and city donations are added to the fund's initial $230,000, loan maximums are likely to increase. Repayment schedules vary with each project—in most cases, running from three to ten years. There are two steps to applying. First, a company's two-page "pre-application" is assessed by the fund for its feasibility. Then, upon invitation, a detailed formal application is submitted by the company and reviewed by the fund's board of directors. The fund is likely to favor loans for hard renovation costs (bricks and mortar) over those for soft (e.g. design).

CAPITAL ASSISTANCE PROGRAM (CAP). Also created in 1988, CAP's interest is in bringing New York arts facilities up to code. By providing funds for code compliance and renovation, it seeks to put additional arts spaces on the market. These funds are available only to groups in city-owned buildings.

Department of Cultural Affairs
City of New York
2 Columbus Circle
New York, NY 10019
(212) 841-4100

Economic Development Corporation (EDC)

The New York City Economic Development Corporation is the financing vehicle for New York City's economic development efforts. EDC administers various financial assistance programs to encourage industrial, manufacturing and not-for-profit business expansion and relocation throughout New York's five boroughs. These programs include direct loans and benefit programs.

To be eligible for the EDC programs, the project must foster a substantial number of permanent jobs available to low- and moderate-income workers, demonstrate a healthy financial condition and an ability to repay the loan, and show that the project would not proceed in New York without assistance.

THE INDUSTRIAL DEVELOPMENT AGENCY (IDA). EDC is the city's administrator for the Industrial Development Agency, which issues tax-exempt bonds on behalf of eligible not-for-profit organizations. IDA issues triple and double tax-exempt Industrial Development Bonds (IDBs) on behalf of eligible industrial and commercial companies and not-for-profit organizations. Bonds are purchased by financial institutions and individual investors. Bonds are available for eligible businesses whose financial needs are greater than $1 million.

Eligibility for IDA loans include undertaking one or more of the following:

- acquiring land and/or a building;
- renovating an existing facility;
- purchasing machinery and/or equipment;
- constructing a new facility.

REVOLVING LOAN FUND (RLF). Financing is available for 501(c)(3) nonprofits who need between $5,000 and $300,000 and who have working capital needs or are undertaking one of the following:

- acquiring land and/or building;
- renovating an existing facility;
- purchasing machinery and/or equipment;
- constructing a new facility;

The interest rate is fixed, averaging about 7%. All loans must be fully collateralized by real estate or machinery and equipment.

For further information on the IDA or the RLF in New York City, contact:

Economic Development Corporation
110 Williams Street
New York, NY 10038
(212) 619-5000

The Fund for the City of New York

This fund is not actually arts-oriented, and it has no funds for bricks or mortar. There are, however, two areas in which it might be able to help. The first is in providing technical assistance. The second, and where the fund can probably be most helpful, is in giving short-term loans for cash flow problems, in the case, for instance, of the theatre that has an NEA- or NYSCA-type grant and is waiting for the actual cash. No interest is charged, just a 1.5% service charge.

The Fund for the City of New York
121 Sixth Avenue, 6th Floor
New York, NY 10013
(212) 925-6675

The New York Landmarks Conservancy

The nonprofit conservancy protects, preserves, and promotes continued use of architecturally and historically significant buildings. Monies for their exterior renovation are available through the Conservancy's NYC Historic Properties Loans, Inc. (below-market loans ranging from $3,500-$200,000) and the City Venture Fund (grant/loan combinations for community revitalization projects). The Conservancy's Technical Preservation Services Center offers technical assistance and publishes several restoration manuals.

The New York Landmarks Conservancy
141 Fifth Avenue
New York, NY 10010
(212) 995-5260

New York State Council on the Arts (NYSCA)

NYSCA's Architecture Planning and Design Program features several areas of funding:

PROJECTS SUPPORT. These funds are available for design studies, architectural and design competitions, feasibility studies, adaptive reuse studies, and historic structures reports, among others. Innovative solutions to design problems are of particular interest, and jointly sponsored projects are encouraged.

CAPITAL FUNDING INITIATIVE (CFI). Funds are for "the improvement, expansion, or rehabilitation of existing buildings owned or leased by nonprofit institutions." When monies are available, CFI offers both grants and loans, with NYSCA funding up to 50% of the cost of a capital project. Grant ceilings vary yearly with the state's budget. In 1988/89 maximums were: $5,000 for a technical assistance grant (for hiring consultants to assist in capital project planning), $25,000 for a capital grant, and $100,000 for a low-interest capital loan.

TECHNICAL ASSISTANCE These grants help "provide professional design or managerial advisory services by expert consultants" to New York State nonprofit organizations. Grantees receive consultants' fees up to $200 a day for three days, plus travel expenses.

NYSCA is also interested in innovative design, and has given up to $30,000/year for "seminal or experimental" projects.

New York State Council on the Arts
915 Broadway, 8th Floor
New York, NY 10010
(212) 387-7068

Scenic Central

Created by Playwrights Horizons, Scenic Central is a nonprofit shop for New York theatre companies. In addition to building sets for Playwrights Horizons productions, Scenic Central contracts to build and paint scenery for other nonprofits at discounted rates. Its contracts with commercial (but non-union) TV and fashion shows, help subsidize production costs for nonprofit clients. The shop is also available for rental, as are 10,000 sq. ft. of storage space.

Scenic Central
196 Van Dyke Street
Brooklyn, NY 11231
(718) 797-1196

The Volunteer Consulting Group (VCG)

VCG "provides professional management assistance to nonprofit organizations" in the tri-state area by teaming up volunteer business professionals with nonprofit organizations. Its assistance covers finance, budgeting, accounting, insurance advice, internal operations, marketing, organizational structure and policies, and real estate. Charges are based on ability to pay.

The Volunteer Consulting Group, Inc.
9 East 41 Street, 8th Floor
New York, NY 10017
(212) 687-8530

SAN FRANCISCO

City Hall

In San Francisco, where city and county boundaries are contiguous, the county board of supervisors is the sole legislative body. Its 11 members, elected at large, are the ultimate appeal in the matter of a building's use.

Board of Supervisors
400 Van Ness Avenue, Room 235
San Francisco, CA 94102
(415) 554-5184

Arts Spaces Initiative Program, Grants for the Arts

Grants are available to nonprofits for: feasibility studies exploring purchase and development of a permanent home ($35,000 maximum); relocation to a permanent or a temporary space ($10,000 maximum); general renovation and code improvement ($50,000 maximum).

Arts Spaces Initiative Program, Grants for the Arts
289 City Hall
San Francisco, CA 94102
(415) 554-6710

Non-Profit Performing Arts Loan Program

Low-interest (3%) loans are available to performing arts groups with budgets under $1 million intending to acquire or improve 50- 499-seat facilities within San Francisco. Loans of up to $100,000 may be used to correct code violations, for "reasonable" architect and engineering fees, and for most acquisition costs. Recipients must maintain $1 million liability insurance for the life of the loan.

Non-Profit Performing Arts Loan Program
10 U.N. Plaza, Suite 1600
San Francisco, CA 94102
(415) 554-8788

Performing Arts Services (PASS)

PASS assists arts organizations in marketing and audience development through: the STBS Ticket Booth (which sells advance full-price and half-price tickets), Special Audiences (which distributes tickets to member social service organizations), PASS

Extras (which offers discounted tickets through the mail), and PATS (a mailing and phone room service).

Performing Arts Services
1182B Market Street, Suite 216
San Francisco, CA 94102
(415) 433-7828

San Francisco Arts Commission

For arts organizations within the city and county of San Francisco, the commission provides general advocacy and information on city arts resources, municipal regulations and policies (codes, permits, etc.). Publications include *The Inspector Cometh: A Guidebook for Arts Presenters in San Francisco,* by Richard Reineccius. It also maintains four cultural centers under the Neighborhood Arts program.

San Francisco Arts Commission
25 Van Ness Avenue, Suite 240
San Francisco, CA 94102
(415) 554-9671

Support Services for the Arts (SSA)

SSA offers low-cost publicity, lighting and sound equipment, and technical assistance for arts groups, as well as the San Francisco Costume Bank.

SAN FRANCISCO COSTUME BANK. The Costume Bank provides low-cost, sliding-scale costume rentals, consultation, construction services and facilities, workshops and job referrals.

Support Services for the Arts
934 Brannan Street
San Francisco, CA 94103
(415) 552-2131
(415) 921-8722

Theatre Bay Area

TBA is a coalition of 45 theatre companies and over 2,500 individual members throughout the Bay Area. It provides publications including *Callboard* (a monthly trade magazine), conferences, forums, biannual Bay Area general auditions, talent bank, job board, library referrals and student internship program.

Theatre Bay Area
657 Mission, Suite 402
San Francisco, CA 94105
(415) 957-1557

The Voluntary Arts Contribution Fund Grants for the Arts

The fund's first priority is modest capital improvement; its maximum grant is $5,000. Recently, the fund distributed $70,000 to 29 organizations.

The Voluntary Arts Contribution Fund Grants for the Arts
289 City Hall
San Francisco, CA 94102
(415) 554-6710

Appendix: Six Cities Agency Chart

NEW YORK CITY AGENCIES (Area code 212 unless noted.)

Name and Address	Phone	Service
General Information on City Agencies	N/A	
Department of Buildings 60 Hudson Street 5th Floor New York, NY 10013	312-8500	Location of all offices listed under department of buildings
Manhattan Borough Superintendent 5th Floor	312-8501	Questions for Manhattan only. Call executive office for other boroughs.
Plan Examiner's Office 5th Floor	312-8900	To check eligibility for place of assembly permits. Will help with questions about public assembly space requirements.
Building Permits 5th Floor	312-8972	
Certificate of Occupancy 5th Floor	312-8550	Will help with location of C of O. Will give information to be used at plan desk.
Executive Office 14th Floor	312-8000	General information; will channel calls to appropriate office.
Plumbing Division Room 503	312-8600	

Appendix: Six Cities Agency Chart

Bureau of Electrical Control Municipal Building, Room 2337 New York, NY 10007	669-8353	
Department of Planning 22 Reade Street New York, NY 10007	720-3276	
General Information	720-3276	
Public Affairs	720-3503	
Zoning Information and Technical Review	720-3291	
Maps and Publications 22 Reade Street, 1st Floor New York, NY 10007-1216	720-3667	Questions about zoning classifications. Zoning area maps for all boroughs. Zoning handbook, community district maps and fact books.
Department of Finance 1 Centre Street, Room 500 New York, NY 10007	669-4855	Location of all offices listed under department of finance.
Real Property Assessment Bureau Room 910	669-4896	Assessment information for all boroughs.
Tax Collection Division 25 Elm Place, 4th Floor Brooklyn, NY 11201	718-935-6394	
Department of Transportation Highway Inspection and Quality Assurance 295 Lafayette Street, Room 402 New York, NY 10012	323-8501	Information, applications for permits for awnings, signs, canopies.
General Services	N/A	
Division of Facilities and Technical Services Municipal Building 1 Centre Street, 20th Floor New York, NY 10007	669-7221	
Board of Standards and Appeals 161 Sixth Avenue New York, 10013	807-3700	
Fire Department Bureau of Fire Prevention 250 Livingston Street Brooklyn, NY 11201	718-403-1416	
Public Assembly Room 504	718-403-1380	
Certificate of Fitness Room 436	718-403-1319	
Municipal Reference and Research Center 31 Chambers Street, Room 112 New York, NY 10007	566-4284	
Citybooks (Mail orders only) 2223 Municipal Bldg. New York, NY 10007	669-8245	(pick up at 61 Chambers Street)

WILL IT MAKE A THEATRE?

Name and Address	Phone	Service
The Mayor's Office for People with Disabilities 52 Chambers Street, Room 206 New York, NY 10007	788-2830	
Department of General Services Bureau of Sales Division of Real Property Sales Lafayette Street, Room 2200 New York, NY 10007	374-3135	Information on auctions of buildings in all boroughs.
Landmarks Preservation Commission 275 Broadway, 23rd Floor New York, NY 10007		Designates city landmarks and approves their alteration.

ATLANTA CITY AGENCIES (Area code 404)

Name and Address	Phone	Service
General Information on City Agencies	658-6000	
Bureau of Buildings 55 Trinity Ave. SW Atlanta, GA 30335	330-6150	
Director	330-6152	
Plan Coordinator	330-6153	
Zoning Enforcement	330-6175	
Permit Information	330-6150	
Certificate of Occupancy Room 800	330-6160	
Plumbing Inspection Division	330-6170	
Division of Electrical Inspection 55 Trinity Ave. SW Atlanta, GA 30335	404-330-6180	
Bureau of Planning 55 Trinity Ave. SW, Suite 3350 Atlanta, GA 30335	330-6145	
Zoning 55 Trinity Ave. SW Atlanta, GA 30335	330-6145	
Business License 55 Trinity Ave. SW Atlanta, GA 30335	330-6213	
Department of Finance 68 Mitchell St. SW Atlanta, GA 30335	330-6430	

Bureau of Purchasing and Real Estate 55 Trinity Ave. SW Atlanta, GA 30335	330-6204
Bureau of General Services 55 Trinity Ave. SW, Room 4500 Atlanta, GA 30335	330-6225
Zoning Enforcements	N/A
Fire Safety Department 46 Courtland Street Atlanta, GA 30335	659-5600
Fire Inspections	658-6904
Deputy Chief	659-5600
Fire Headquarters	659-5600
Assistant Chief of Fire Prevention and Suppression	658-6902
Fulton County Reference Library 1 Margaret Mitchell Square Atlanta, GA 30303-1089	730-4636
Bureau of Cultural Affairs 236 Forsyth St. SW, Suite 402 Atlanta, GA 30303	653-7160

BOSTON CITY AGENCIES (Area Code 617)

Name and Address	Phone	Service
General Information on City Agencies	725-4000	
Inspection Services Department 1010 Massachusetts Ave. Boston, MA 02118	442-0046	
Plans and Permits Division	442-1345	
Examiner's Board	725-4777	
Zoning	442-1345	
Appeal Board	725-4775	
Applications	442-0046	
Certificate of Occupancy	442-0046 or 442-0783	
Construction and Safety	442-0046	
Electrical	442-0046	
Plumbing	442-0046	
Sprinkler	442-0046	

Boston Redevelopment Authority 1 City Hall Square Boston, MA 02201	722-4300	
Mayor's Office of Consumer Affairs and Licensing Boston City Hall, Room 613 Boston, MA 02201	725-4165	Entertainment license.
Real Property Department Boston City Hall, Room 811 Boston, MA 02201	725-4105	
Tax Collection Room M16	725-4120	
Fire Department 115 Southampton St. Boston, MA 02118	725-3550	
Public Information	725-3415	
Fire Prevention	725-3336	
Government Documents Boston Public Library 666 Boylston Street Boston, MA 02117	536-5400, ext. 226	
State Bookstore State House Boston, MA 02133	727-2834	

CHICAGO CITY AGENCIES (Area Code 312)

Name and Address	Phone	Service
Mayor's Office of Inquiry and Information	744-5000	
Department of Buildings 121 N. LaSalle, 8th and 9th Floors Chicago, IL 60602	744-3400	
Application Review	744-3497	
Architectural Examiners	744-3450 or 744-3489	
Fee Estimators	744-3450 or 744-3489	
Permits	744-3490	
Certificate of Occupancy Room 800	744-3507	
Electrical Inspector	744-3464	
Plumbing Inspector	744-3502	
Electrical Section Room 805	744-3458	

Department of Planning 121 N. LaSalle Chicago, IL 60602	744-4190	
Department of Zoning 121 N. LaSalle Chicago, IL 60602	744-3455	
Zoning Board of Appeals	744-3887	
Zoning Violations	744-3508	
Department of Revenue 121 N. LaSalle, Room 107 Chicago, IL 60602	744-3947	Business licenses.
Department of Finance 121 N. LaSalle Chicago, IL 60602	744-7100	
County Assessors 118 N. Clark, 3rd Floor Chicago, IL 60602	443-5500	
Tax Collection Room 112	443-6200	
Department of General Services 510 Peshtigo Court Chicago, IL 60611	744-7711	
Building Board of Appeals 320 N. Clark, Room 800 Chicago, IL 60602	744-4466	
Zoning Board of Appeals 121 N. LaSalle, Room 806 Chicago, IL 60602	744-3889	
Department of Fire 121 N. LaSalle Chicago, IL 60602	744-4756	
Fire Prevention Chief	744-8955	

Fire Prevention Offices:
    Central, 444 N. Dearborn
    North, 211 W. Eastwood Ave.
    South, 7974 S. Chicago Ave.
    West, 1101 S. California Ave.
	744-4716
	744-1089
	747-7555
	746-5336	

Municipal Reference Library 121 N. LaSalle, Room 1004 Chicago, IL 60602	744-4992	
Index Publishing Corp. 415 N. State St. Chicago, IL 60610	644-7800	

LOS ANGELES CITY AGENCIES (Area Code 213)

Name and Address	Phone	Service
Government Information	485-2121	
Building and Safety Department Building Bureau 200 N. Spring Street, Room 460 Los Angeles, CA 90012		
Building Inspection: Information	485-7901	
Inspection Requests Commercial	485-7901	
Structural Plan Checking	485-3431	
Public Counter and Building Permit Information Room 460, Counter B	485-3431	
Zoning Counter and Zoning Information	485-2327	
Earthquake Safety	485-6177	
Certificate of Occupancy Room 975	485-7094	
Plumbing Information	485-7865	
Plumbing Inspection Request	485-7865	
Mechanical Bureau 200 N. Spring St. Los Angeles, CA 90012		
Electrical Information	485-2333	
Electrical Plan Checking	485-5325	
Inspection Requests	485-2071	
Construction Licenses and Permits	485-3787	
Electrical Permits Room 460, Counter P	485-2333	
Planning Department 200 N. Spring St. Los Angeles, CA 90012		
Planning Information Public Counters	485-7826	
Executive Offices	237-1986	
Board of Zoning Appeals	485-2470	
Zoning Administration	485-3851	
City Clerk Office Room 101, 201 N. Main St. Los Angeles, CA 90012	626-9271	Business licenses.

Tax Assessor's Office Room 225, 500 Temple Street Los Angeles, CA 90012	974-3211	
Tax Collection 1st Floor, 500 Temple Street Los Angeles, CA 90012	974-2111	
General Services 200 N. Main Street City Hall East, Room 800 Los Angeles, CA 90012		
Finance Room 800	485-2666	
Building Services Room 800	485-5805	
Standards 2319 Dorris Place Los Angeles, CA 90012	485-2242	
Fire Prevention Bureau 200 N. Main Street City Hall East Los Angeles, CA 90012	485-5982	
Information	485-5971	
Public Information and Press News	485-6054	
Public Safety	485-5976	
Municipal Reference Library 200 N. Main Street City Hall East, Room 530 Los Angeles, CA 90012	485-3792	
Building News, Inc. 3055 Overland Avenue Los Angeles, CA 90034	202-7775	
Department of General Services Salvage Section 555 Ramirez Street Piper Technical Ctr., Room B10 Los Angeles, CA 90012	485-2245	

SAN FRANCISCO CITY AGENCIES (Area Code 415)

Name and Address	Phone	Service
General Information	554-4000	
Bureau of Buildings Information	558-6087	
Bureau of Building Inspection 450 McAllister San Francisco, CA 94102	558-6096	
Building Inspectors Division	558-6096	

Superintendent 1390 Market St. San Francisco, CA 94102	554-8742
Public Counter	558-6002
Central Permit Bureau	558-6070
Plans Approval Division	558-6133
Fire Inspectors	558-6177
Certificate of Occupancy Room 302	558-6220
Electrical Inspections Division	558-6030
Plumbing Inspections Division	558-6054
Planning Department 450 McAllister San Francisco, CA 94102	
Zoning Information	558-6377
Zoning Violations	558-6260
Landmarks Board	558-6345
Recorded Information	558-6320
Planning Information	558-6264
Administration	558-6414
Assessor's Office 400 Van Ness Ave. City Hall, Room 101 San Francisco, CA 94102	554-5524
Real Property Valuation	554-5609
Mapping	554-5830
Business Tax Room 107	554-4426
Real Estate Tax Room 101	554-3660
Board of Supervisors 400 Van Ness Ave., Room 235 San Francisco, CA 94102	554-5184
Department of the Tax Collector Real Estate Division 400 Van Ness Ave., Room. 107 San Francisco, CA 94102	554-4470

Appendix: Evaluation Checklist

SPECIFICS

Date of visit: _____
Weather: sunny rainy hot cold damp dry snowy
Building address: _____
Building orientation: N S E W NE NW SE SW
Contact: _____
  owner agent other _____ **Phone:** _____
Rent per month: _____ **Annual rent:** _____
Total square footage: _____ **Cost per sq. ft.:** _____
Dimensions: height   width   depth   total sq. ft.

1st fl.				
2nd fl.				
3rd fl.				

Neighborhood: residential commercial manufacturing
Building type: brownstone storefront loft
              other _____
Building age: _____
Previous use: _____
Neighbors: business residence occupied vacant
  right _____
  left _____
  above _____
  below _____
Building's zoning designation: _____

NEIGHBORHOOD

Nearest subway stops: _____
Nearest bus stops: _____
On-the-street parking: _____
  restrictions: _____
Nearest parking lot: _____
  hours: _____ fee: _____
Street and sidewalks: potholes cracks crumbling irregular
              good
Street lights: well-lit adequate poor
Garbage collection: regular irregular none

Nearest restaurants and pubs: _____
_____
  hours: _____
Nearby shops, hardware stores, etc. : _____

Special factors: Urban Renewal   landmark building
  Equity contract restrictions _____
  city-owned federal-owned other: _____
General impression: _____
_____
_____
_____

EXTERIOR CONDITIONS

Facing: board brick brownstone clapboard other _____
   general condition: _____
Steps: stone wood concrete other _____
   general condition: _____
Doors: wood steel metal glass other _____
   frames: wood steel   dimensions: _____
   general condition: _____
Backyard: dirt concrete other _____
   dimensions: _____
   general condition: _____

Roof access: ladder stairs trap door
Roof: new old holes leaks cracks bubbles
   general condition: _____
Roof parapet: wood molding gutter drainpipe other _____
   general condition: _____
Fire escapes: yes no
   general condition: _____
Repairs needed: _____
General impression: _____
_____

INTERIOR CONDITIONS

Floors: wood concrete linoleum tile other _____
   live weight load: _____ lbs. per sq. ft.
   general condition: _____
Stairs: wood marble concrete metal stone
   open enclosed width: _____
   general condition: _____
Corridors: wall construction: _____
   width: _____ general condition: _____
Elevators: yes no passenger freight   manual automatic
   dimensions: _____ capacity ____ lbs.
Walls and ceilings: brick plaster sheet rock concrete block
   drywall other _____
   general condition: _____
Columns: yes no measurements between: _____

Windows: number: ____ dimensions: _____
   frames: wood steel aluminum
   glass: broken cracked missing panes
   general condition: _____
Basement: finished unfinished material: _____
   beams: wood steel concrete & steel
   floor: dirt wood tile lineoleum other _____
   general condition: dry damp water marked
repairs needed: _____
general impression: _____
_____
_____
_____
_____

MECHANICAL SYSTEMS

Heating: steam hot water forced air unit ventilating
   oil electricity
   age: _____ general condition: _____
Air conditioning: throughout roof units none
   general condition: _____
Electrical: A/C D/C
   service: to floor: ___ phase ___ wire ___ amps ___ volts
         to buildings: ___ phase ___ wire ___ amps ___ volts
   circuit breaker panel fuse box   location: _____
   number and location of outlets: _____

   additional service required: yes no
   general condition of wiring: _____

Plumbing: clear patched broken
   number and location of bathrooms: _____
   number and location of sinks: _____
   hot water heater: adequate inadequate inoperable
                      capacity: _____ gallons
   general condition: _____
Security: doors: locks gates bars
        windows: locks gates bars
   number of exits: _____ alarm system: yes no
Emergency systems: sprinklered extinguishers fire alarm
                  emergency lighting
Repairs needed: _____
General impression: _____
_____
_____

Publications of Interest

GENERAL

The American Theatre Planning Board, Inc. *Theatre Check List*. Middletown, CT: Wesleyan University Press, 1969 (out of print).

Association of British Theatre Technicians. *Theatre Planning*. Edited by Roderick Ham. Toronto: University of Toronto Press, 1972.

Burris-Meyer, Harold, Vincent Mallory and Lewis S. Goodfriend. *Sound in the Theatre*. New York: Radio Magazines, Inc., 1979. Distributed by Theatre Arts Books.

Farber, Donald C. *From Option to Opening*, Rev. ed. New York: Drama Book Specialists, 1989.

Foundation for the Extension and Development of American Professional Theatre. *Investigation Guidelines for Setting Up a Not-for-Profit Tax-Exempt Theatre*. New York: FEDAPT, 1985.

Joseph, Stephen. *New Theatre Forms*. New York: Theatre Arts Books, 1968 (out of print).

Langely, Stephen. *Theatre Management in America: Principle and Practice*. New York: Drama Book Specialists, 1980.

McNamara, Brooks, Jerry Rojo and Richard Schechner. *Theatres, Spaces, and Environments: 18 Projects*. New York: Drama Book Specialists, 1975 (out of print).

Mielziner, Jo. *The Shapes of Our Theatre*. New York: Clarkson N. Potter, Inc., 1970 (out of print).

Architectural Graphic Standards. 7th ed. Edited by Robert Packard. New York: John Wiley and Sons, 1981.

THEATRE AND STAGE MANAGEMENT AND PRODUCTION

Baker, Hendrik. *Stage Management and Theatre Crafts*. Rev. ed. New York: Theatre Art Books, 1981.

Beck, Kirsten. *How to Run a Small Box Office*. New York: Off Off Broadway Alliance (now A.R.T./NY), 1981.

Langley, Stephen. *Theatre Management in America: Principle and Practice: Producing for the Commercial, Stock, Resident, College, and Community Theatre*. Rev. ed. New York: Drama Book Publishers, 1980.

Lounsbury, Warren C. *Theatre Backstage from A to Z.* Rev. ed. Seattle: University of Washington Press, 1989.

PLANNING AND BUILDING FOR RELATED ARTS

Armstrong, Leslie and Roger Morgan. *Space for Dance: An Architectural Guide for Dance and Performing Arts Facilities.* Commissioned by the Design Arts Program and the Dance Program of the National Endowment for the Arts. Washington, DC: Publishing Center for Cultural Resources, 1984.

Brown, Catherine R., William B. Fleissig and William R. Morrish. *Building for the Arts: A Guidebook for the Planning and Design of Cultural Facilities.* Santa Fe: Western States Arts Federation, 1989.

Golden, Joseph. *Help! A Guide to Seeking, Selecting, and Surviving an Arts Consultant.* Syracuse: Cultural Resources Council, 1983.

THEATRE DESIGN AND PLANNING

Burris-Meyer, Harold and Edward C. Cole. *Theatres and Auditoriums.* 2nd ed. Huntingdon, NY: Robert E. Krieger Publishing Co., Inc., 1975 (out of print).

Mielziner, Jo. *The Shape of Our Theatre.* Edited by C. Ray Smith. New York: Clarkson N. Potter, Inc., 1970.

SOUND SYSTEMS AND ACOUSTICS

Burris-Meyer, Harold, Vincent Mallory and Lewis S. Goodfriend. *Sound in the Theatre.* New York: Radio Magazines, Inc., 1979. Distributed by Theatre Arts Books.

Collison, Davis. *Stage Sound.* New York: Applause Theatre Books Publishers, 1990.

SCENIC DESIGN AND STAGE TECHNOLOGY

Pecktal, Lynn. *Designing and Painting for the Theatre.* New York: Holt, Rinehart and Winston, Inc., 1975.

STAGE LIGHTING

McCandless, Stanley. *A Syllabus of Stage Lighting.* New York: Drama Book Publishers, 1964 (out of print).

Pilbrow, Richard. *Stage Lighting.* New York: Applause Theatre Books Publishers, 1990.

Rosenthal, Jean and Lael Wertenbaker. *Magic of Light: The Craft and Career of Jean Rosenthal.* Waltham, MA: Little, Brown & Co., 1972.

ENERGY EFFICIENCY

Energy Conservation for Performing Arts Facilities. Available from the Alliance of Resident Theatres/New York, 131 Varick Street, Room 904, New York, NY 10013.

How to Reduce Energy Costs in Your Building. Boston: Center for Information Sharing, 1983. Available from The Philadelphia Electric Company, 2301 Market Street, Philadelphia, PA 19101.

A Guide to Saving Lighting Energy Dollars. 1980. Available from The New York State Energy Office, Two Rockefeller Plaza, Albany, NY 12223 (800-342-3722).

Resource Directory of Energy Services Available to Not-for-Profit Organizations in New York State. 1987. Available from The New York State Energy Office, Two Rockefeller Plaza, Albany, NY 12223 (800-342-3722).

PARTNERSHIPS

Agard, Mary Berryman, and June Spencer. *50 Cities: Local Government and the Arts.* Commissioned by the Fulton County Arts Commission, Atlanta, GA. Madison, WI: Opinion Research Associates, Inc., 1987.

Snedcof, Harold R. *Cultural Facilities in Mixed-Use Development.* Washington, DC: The Urban Land Institute, 1985.

MATERIALS, SUPPLIES AND RESOURCES

The Association of Theatrical Artists and Craftspeople, ed. *The New York Theatrical Sourcebook.* New York: Broadway Press, published annually.

Theatre Crafts Directory. New York: Theatre Crafts Associates, published annually.

FUNDRAISING

Capital Campaign Resource Guide. San Francisco: Public Management Institute, 1990.

Eckstein, Richard M., researcher. *Directory of Building Equipment Grants.* Margate, FL: Research Grant Guides, 1988.

The Foundation Directory. New York: The Foundation Center, published biannually, plus yearly supplement.

The Foundation Grants Index. New York: The Foundation Center, published annually.

PERIODICALS

Lighting Dimensions. Lighting Dimensions Associates, 135 Fifth Avenue, New York, NY 10010. Published 9 times a year.

Theatre Crafts. Theatre Crafts Associates, 135 Fifth Avenue, New York, NY 10010. Published 10 times a year.

Theatre Crafts and Technology. United States Institute for Theatre Technology, 330 West 42nd Street, New York, NY 10036. Published quarterly.

INDEX

A

Accessibility, 49
Access stairs, 159
Acoustics, 116
Acting area. *See* Stage space
Acting Company (NYC), 82
Actors and Directors Lab (NYC), 76, 82
Actors Equity Association (AEA), 14, 44, 92, 124, 219, 221
Actors Theatre (Louisville), 32
Administrative needs. *See* Office space
Administrative offices. *See* Office space
African American Arts Alliance of Chicago, 218
Afro-American Cultural Center (Charlotte, North Carolina), 33
Air conditioning, 51, 140, 146
Aisles
  building codes and, 203, 205, 207, 209–212
  size requirements, 14
Alarms, 140
Alliance of Resident Theatres/New York (A.R.T./New York), 47, 221
AMAS Repertory Theatre (NYC), 92
American Repertory Theatre (ART; Boston), 54
American Society of Theatre Consultants (ASTC), 213
Americans with Disabilities Act (ADA), 14, 115
Amplifiers, 139
Apple Corps (NYC), 33
Application fee for mortgage, 70
Application procedures, New York City, 189–201
  for permits and licenses, 190–199
    altered building application, 190
    awnings and canopies, 196, 199
    Certificate of Occupancy, 196
    Department of Buildings, 190, 196
    inspection and certification of electrical work, 199
    to install or alter plumbing, 199
    place of assembly, 196
    signs, 196
    violations, 199
  preliminary, 189
Architects, 88–90, 105
Arena
  four-sided (theatre-in-the-round), 10
    overhead and rigging for, 98
  three-sided (open or thrust stage), 10, 58, 105, 107
    access to, 96–97
    overhead and rigging for, 98–99
  two-sided (center stage), 10
    overhead and rigging for, 98
Armories, 38
Art galleries, 36, 38
Arts/Boston, 217
Arts councils
  local, 74–75
  state, 74
Arts Resources and Technical Services, Inc. (ARTS Inc.), 220
Arts Spaces Initiative Program Grants for the Arts, 224
Assessed value, 159
Assessor's Office (San Francisco), 234
Assignment of lease, 69
Atlanta, Georgia
  agencies, 228–229
  building code, 202–205
  service organizations, 213, 215–216
Atlanta Economic Development Corporation (AEDC), 216
Atlanta Theatre Coalition (ATC), 216
Auctions, 135
Audience, 6, 58
Audience space, 110–118
  acoustics, 116, 118
  lighting and, 118
  seats and seating layout and, 112–116, 150
  sightlines and, 110–112
Awnings, 196, 199

Index

B

Back of building, 50
Bailiwick Repertory (Chicago), 33, 49
Ballrooms, 36, 38
Banks, 32
Bar/lounge, 17, 36, 38, 129
Basement, 51
Bilingual Foundation of the Arts (Los Angeles), 38
Black Spectrum Theatre (NYC), 38
Black Theatre Alliance, Inc. (NYC), 76, 83
Board of Standards and Appeals (NYC), 158, 227
Board of Supervisors (San Francisco), 234
Body Politic Theatre (BP; Chicago), 56–59, 128–129
Bond Street Theatre Coalition (NYC), 74
Boston
 agencies, 229–230
 building code, 205–207
 service organizations, 214–218
Boston Arts Lottery Council, 217
Boston Baked Theatre, 36
Boston Redevelopment Association, 109
Boston Redevelopment Authority, 230
Bouwerie Lane (NYC), 32
Box office, 58–59, 128–129
 size requirements, 16
Brandeis Repertory Theatre (Boston), 104
Briar Street Theatre (Chicago), 38, 119
Brockway, Adrienne, 144, 146
Brockway, Amie, 146
Broker's fees, 70
Brook, Peter, 94
Budget, 55, 152
 operating, 58
Building
 inspection of, 49–52
 landmark, 39, 47
 location within, 26
 types of, 26–41
Building and Safety Department (Los Angeles), 232
Building Board of Appeals (Chicago), 231
Building classification
  in new code, 167–168
  in old code, 162
Building Code, New York City, 159–177. *See also* New code requirements; Old code requirements
 definitions, 159–160
 inspections and, 50
 old code vs. new code in, 161–162
 seating and, 114
 size requirements and, 11, 14
 stage and, 94–96
Building codes, 202–212. *See also* Building Code, New York City
 Atlanta, 202–205
 Boston, 205–207
 bringing building up to, 52–53
 checklist for, 177
 Chicago, 207–209
 inspections and, 49–52
 Los Angeles, 209–211
 San Francisco, 211–212
 Washington, D.C., 150
Building News, Inc. (Los Angeles), 233
Building Officials and Code Administrators (BOCA), 150, 159, 202
Bureau of Building Inspection (San Francisco), 233
Bureau of Buildings (Atlanta), 228
Bureau of Cultural Affairs (Atlanta), 229
Bureau of Electrical Control (NYC), 227
Bureau of General Service (Atlanta), 229
Bureau of Planning (Atlanta), 228
Bureau of Purchasing and Real Estate (Atlanta), 229
Business Investment Incentive Program (BIIP), 78
Business License (Atlanta), 228
Business Volunteers for the Arts (BVA), 70, 213
Buying materials and equipment
 for lighting, 136
 renting vs., 136
 wholesale, 135
Buying space, 56–57, 66, 69–70, 131–132

C

Cables, 137
California Community Foundation, 220
Campbell, Joseph, 145
Canopies, 196, 199
Carpeting, 118
Cassette tape decks, 139
Cast requirements, 6
Catwalks, 61, 102–103
Ceilings, 51, 58–59, 124, 150
Center stage (two-sided arena), 10
 overhead and rigging for, 98
Certificate of Occupancy (C of O), 159, 189
 application for, 196
Charlestown Working Theatre (CWT; Boston), 38, 53
Checklist
 fire inspection, 181
 scenery and construction shop, 124–125
 shop, 124–126
Chicago
 agencies, 230–231
 building code, 207–209
 energy efficiency in, 52
 service organizations, 213–215, 218–219
Chicago Community Trust, 218
Chicago Dramatists Workshop, 26
Chicago Theatre Company, 33
Churches, 33
Citybooks (NYC), 227
City Clerk Office (Los Angeles), 232
City Hall, as resource, 215–219, 221, 224
Codes. *See* Application procedures, New York City; Building Code, New York City; Building codes
Columns, 24–25, 51
 load-bearing, 160
Commercial developments, 39, 41
Commercial leases, 61, 67–69, 108
 negotiations for, 68–69
Commission on Chicago Landmarks, 47
Commissions of real estate agents, 45
Community boards, zoning variance and, 158
Community centers, 33
Community Design Center, 216
Community Development Block Grants, 218
Community development (CD) funds, 71, 75

Administração
da Produção e Operações

Administração da Produção e Operações

8ª Edição

Norman Gaither
Universidade do Texas A&M

Greg Frazier
Universidade do Texas – Arlington

Tradução
José Carlos Barbosa dos Santos

Revisão Técnica

Petrônio Garcia Martins
Professor da Faculdade de Engenharia Industrial – FEI,
da UNIFMU e da Universidade Paulista – UNIP

Austrália • Brasil • Japão • Coréia • México • Cingapura • Espanha • Reino Unido • Estados Unidos

**Administração da Produção e Operações –
8ª edição**

**Norman Gaither
Greg Frazier**

Diretor Editorial: José Martins Braga

Título do Original em Inglês: Production and Operations Management, 8th ed.

Tradução: José Carlos Barbosa dos Santos

Revisão Técnica: Petrônio Garcia Martins

Gerente de Produção: Maria Celina J. Moriya

Preparação de Texto: Barbara E. Benevides

Revisão: Arnaldo Rocha de Arruda
Ursula Augusta

Composição: Marco Zero

Capa: Marco Zero
Fábio R. Andrade

© 1999 by South-Western College Publishing.
© 2002 Cengage Learning Edições Ltda.

Todos os direitos reservados. Nenhuma parte deste livro poderá ser reproduzida, sejam quais forem os meios empregados, sem a permissão, por escrito, da Editora.
Aos infratores aplicam-se as sanções previstas nos artigos 102, 104, 106 e 107 da Lei nº 9610, de 19 de fevereiro de 1998.

> Para informações sobre nossos produtos, entre em contato pelo telefone **0800 11 19 39**
>
> Para permissão de uso de material desta obra, envie seu pedido para **direitosautorais@cengage.com**

© 2002 Cengage Learning. Todos os direitos reservados.

ISBN-10: 85-221-0237-6

Cengage Learning
Condomínio E-Business Park
Rua Werner Siemens, 111 – Prédio 20 – Espaço 04
Lapa de Baixo – CEP 05069-900 – São Paulo – SP
Tel.: (11) 3665-9900 – Fax: (11) 3665-9901
SAC: 0800 11 19 39

Para suas soluções de curso e aprendizado, visite
www.cengage.com.br

Impresso no Brasil.
Printed in Brazil.
8 9 10 11 12   06 05 14 03 02

Sumário

Parte I
Administração da Produção e Operações
Introdução e Visão Geral

Capítulo 1 Administração da Produção e Operações: Uma Apresentação 4

Marcos Históricos na APO 7
Fatores Que Afetam a APO Hoje 14
Diferentes Maneiras de Estudar a APO 14

Capítulo 2 Estratégias de Operações: Usando a Qualidade, o Custo e o Serviço Como Armas Competitivas 22

Condições dos Negócios Globais de Hoje 24
Estratégias de Operações 38
Formando Estratégias de Operações 45
Competitividade das Empresas Manufatureiras Americanas 49

Capítulo 3 Previsões na APO: O Ponto de Partida para Todo o Planejamento 53

Métodos Qualitativos de Previsão 55
Modelos Quantitativos de Previsão 57
Como Ter um Sistema de Previsão Bem-Sucedido 81
Softwares para Previsões 85
Previsão em Pequenos Negócios e Novos Empreendimentos 85

Parte II
Decisões Estratégicas
Planejando Produtos, Processos, Tecnologias e Instalações

Capítulo 4 Projetando e Desenvolvendo Produtos e Processos de Produção: Operações de Manufatura e Serviços 96

Projetando e Desenvolvendo Produtos e Serviços 97
Planejamento e Projeto de Processos 103
Fatores Importantes Que Afetam as Decisões sobre o Projeto de Processos 104
Tipos de Projeto de Processos 107
Inter-Relações entre Projeto de Produtos, Projeto de Processos e Política de Estoques 113
Projeto de Processos nos Serviços 114
Decidindo entre Alternativas de Processamento 117
Um Passeio pelas Instalações 124

Capítulo 5 Tecnologia de Produção: Escolha e Administração 143

Proliferação da Automação 143
Tipos de Automação 144
Sistemas Automatizados de Produção 147
Fábricas do Futuro 151
Automação nos Serviços 153
Questões de Automação 155
Decidindo entre Alternativas de Automação 160

Capítulo 6 Planejamento da Capacidade de Longo Prazo e Localização de Instalações 168

Planejamento da Capacidade de Longo Prazo 170
Localização de Instalações 179

Capítulo 7 Layout das Instalações: Manufatura e Serviços 196

Layouts de Instalações de Manufatura 197
Analisando Layouts de Instalações de Manufatura 203
Layouts de Instalações de Serviço 221

Parte III
Decisões Operacionais
Planejando a Produção para Atender a Demanda

Capítulo 8 Sistemas de Planejamento da Produção 234

Hierarquia do Planejamento da Produção 235
Planejamento Agregado 235
Programa Mestre de Produção 249
Tipos de Sistemas de Planejamento e Controle da Produção 257

Capítulo 9 Sistemas de Estoques com Demanda Independente 268

Pontos de Vista Opostos sobre Estoques 269
Natureza dos Estoques 272
Sistemas do Lote Padrão 272
Sistemas do Intervalo Padrão 292
Outros Modelos de Estoques 294
Algumas Realidades do Planejamento de Estoques 298

CAPÍTULO 10 Sistemas de Planejamento das Necessidades de Recursos 308

Planejamento das Necessidades de Materiais 310
Planejamento das Necessidades de Capacidade 330

CAPÍTULO 11 Planejamento e Controle do Chão de Fábrica na Manufatura 340

Programando a Manufatura Focalizada no Processo 341
Programando a Manufatura Focalizada no Produto 354
Sistemas Computadorizados de Programação 361

CAPÍTULO 12 Planejamento e Programação de Operações de Serviço 368

Programação de Operações de Serviço de Quase-Manufatura 373
Programação de Operações de Serviço Tendo o Cliente Como Participante 379
Programação de Operações de Serviço Tendo o Cliente Como Produto 388

CAPÍTULO 13 Manufatura Just-in-Time 404

A Filosofia da Manufatura Just-in-Time 406
Pré-Requisitos da Manufatura JIT 409
Elementos da Manufatura JIT 410
Benefícios da Manufatura JIT 420
Sucesso e Manufatura JIT 422

CAPÍTULO 14 Administração da Cadeia de Suprimentos 426

Administração da Cadeia de Suprimentos 427
Atividade de Compras 430
Atividade de Compras Just-in-Time 439
Logística 439
Armazenamento 442
Agilização 446
Benchmarking do Desempenho de Gerentes de Materiais 447
Terceirização de Provedores de Administração da Logística 447

PARTE IV

DECISÕES QUANTO AO CONTROLE
PLANEJANDO E CONTROLANDO OPERAÇÕES PARA OBTER PRODUTIVIDADE, QUALIDADE E CONFIABILIDADE

CAPÍTULO 15 Produtividade, Trabalho em Equipe e Empowerment: Comportamento, Métodos de Trabalho e Medida do Trabalho 456

Produtividade e Comportamento Humano 458
Projetando Funções dos Trabalhadores 464
Empowerment dos Trabalhadores 467
Análise dos Métodos de Trabalho 467
Medida do Trabalho 469
Saúde e Segurança dos Empregados 480

CAPÍTULO 16 Gerência da Qualidade 488

Natureza da Qualidade 489
Gerência da Qualidade Tradicional 491
Gerência da Qualidade Moderna 492
Padrões Emergentes da Qualidade 495
Programas de Gestão da Qualidade Total 498
Gerência da Qualidade no Setor de Serviços 508

CAPÍTULO 17 Controle da Qualidade 513

Conceitos Estatísticos no Controle da Qualidade 514
Gráficos de Controle 517
Computadores no Controle da Qualidade 523
O Controle da Qualidade no Setor de Serviços 524

CAPÍTULO 18 Planejando e Controlando Projetos 528

Gerência de Projeto 529
Técnicas de Planejamento e Controle de Projeto 532
Software para Gerência de Projetos 554
Uma Avaliação do PERT/CPM 554

APÊNDICES 563

RESPOSTAS DE ALGUNS DOS PROBLEMAS PROPOSTOS 565
GLOSSÁRIO 569

ÍNDICE ANALÍTICO 583
TABELAS 595

Prefácio

À medida que as organizações ocupam posições de liderança, elas se tornam mais enxutas e ágeis, e esperam muito que suas operações modernizadas sejam confiáveis e eficientes. Nesse ambiente dinâmico, a administração da produção e operações (APO) se torna mais importante do que nunca. As operações são a peça de integração crítica que permite o funcionamento conjunto de todas as áreas funcionais de uma organização. A organização integrada de maneira bem-sucedida enfrentará a competição global com produtos de qualidade, notável serviço ao cliente e controle de custos eficiente.

Esta 8ª edição de *Administração da produção e operações* apresentará aos estudantes os diversos tópicos e questões relacionados à APO com que se defrontam os principais fabricantes e organizações de serviço. Discorremos aqui sobre novos desenvolvimentos no campo da APO e novos recursos de informação disponíveis, como por exemplo a Internet, sem perder o foco nos conceitos fundamentais da APO. A meta deste texto é ajudar os estudantes a obter um entendimento daquilo que envolve a APO, de como a APO se relaciona com outras áreas funcionais numa organização, dos tipos de decisões que surgem na APO e das abordagens comuns à tomada de decisões.

Os estudantes devem ter concluído cursos de álgebra e introdução à estatística em níveis secundários como requisitos prévios para os cursos que usam este livro didático. Não obstante os conceitos matemáticos e estatísticos deste livro não serem complexos, os estudantes que possuem um preparo nesses tópicos tendem a ter um desempenho melhor.

O Que Há nesta Oitava Edição?

Norman Gaither apresenta seu novo co-autor, Greg Frazier, da Universidade do Texas, em Arlington. O professor Frazier traz uma bagagem de conhecimentos muito grande, sólido background de pesquisa e experiência prática. Temos o prazer de oferecer seus conhecimentos e novas perspectivas deste livro.

Embora a premissa básica de *Administração da produção e operações* não se tenha modificado, a nova edição contém uma série de importantes mudanças e opiniões. Quase todos os recursos de Instantâneos da Indústria contidos no livro são novos ou atualizados. Os exemplos e tabelas ao longo do livro foram atualizados. Os novos recursos e a cobertura de tópicos incluem:

- **Novos problemas e casos.** Dezenas de novos problemas e casos foram incluídos. Quando pertinente, esses materiais estimulam o uso de aplicativos de planilha eletrônica.
- **Tarefas na Internet.** Ao final de cada capítulo o estudante encontrará atribuições de tarefas na Internet, que lhe darão a oportunidade de pesquisar os vários recursos da Internet para obter informações pertinentes aos tópicos abordados. Algumas das atribuições de tarefas exigem respostas por escrito, que estimulam o raciocínio crítico e habilidades de comunicação.
- **Sites da Web.** Quando pertinente são fornecidos os sites das empresas e organizações analisadas. Isso permitirá que os estudantes façam pesquisas adicionais sobre tópicos referentes à APO em organizações particulares.
- **Estratégia de operações.** O papel cada vez mais importante desempenhado pela competição global e pelas forças ambientais na estratégia de operações é destacado no Capítulo 2.
- **Administração da cadeia de suprimentos.** O Capítulo 14 apresenta aos estudantes o conceito de administração da cadeia de abastecimento. Tópicos como atividade de compras, logística e armazenamento são apresentados a partir da perspectiva de administrar o fluxo de materiais dos fornecedores de matéria-prima até os consumidores finais de bens acabados.
- **A APO nos serviços.** As operações de serviços são enfatizadas nesta edição. A aplicação de estratégia de operações, planejamento, automação e qualidade nas operações de serviços é discutida de maneira especial. Exemplos, problemas e casos são incluídos no cenário dos transportes, venda a varejo e armazenamento, atividades bancárias e outras indústrias de serviços. O Capítulo 12 trata de muitas das decisões operacionais nos serviços.

Auxílios de Ensino e Aprendizagem

Os recursos distintivos da oitava edição incluem:

- **Uma abrangente, prática, equilibrada e não teórica abordagem à APO.** O livro coloca o estudante diretamente na função de produção/operações numa variedade de situações: manufatura e serviços, pequenos negócios e grandes corporações, abordagens quantitativas e gerenciais, novos negócios e negócios de alta tecnologia e tradicionais. Muitos dos problemas e exemplos do livro foram tirados de situações reais na indústria.

- **Uma abordagem de solução de problemas e tomada de decisões.** Cada capítulo inclui exemplos de problemas de APO com soluções completas. Esses exemplos são resolvidos passo a passo a fim de que os leitores possam seguir cada detalhe das soluções. Um ponto forte do livro são seus numerosos problemas e casos, que podem ser trabalhados diretamente a partir das informações contidas nos capítulos. Os problemas apresentam dificuldade crescente à medida que se avança por um conjunto de problemas.

  Os capítulos foram estruturados especialmente para a aprendizagem dos estudantes, que poderão se movimentar entre conceitos, exemplos resolvidos, atribuições de problemas com a ajuda de respostas para alguns deles. Esse processo visa construir o entendimento e a confiança dos estudantes.

- **Uma ênfase contínua em tópicos contemporâneos.** Isto inclui:

  Competição global, administração da qualidade e serviço ao cliente. Esses itens são apresentados no Capítulo 2. Uma vez que a competição global, a administração da qualidade e o serviço ao cliente afetam todas as facetas da APO, sua influência será discutida em todo o livro. Os Capítulos 16 e 17 apresentam a filosofia global e métodos de administrar a qualidade.

  Manufatura just-in-time (JIT). O Capítulo 13 discute a filosofia e os métodos de planejar e controlar operações de manufatura. As maneiras pelas quais o JIT afeta coisas como atividade de compras e administração de materiais, relações e práticas de pessoal, controle da qualidade, serviço ao cliente e outros conceitos são integradas em todo o livro.

  Tecnologia avançada de produção. O Capítulo 1 apresenta aos estudantes a automação e tópicos relacionados. O Capítulo 2 discute as implicações estratégicas da manufatura high-tech. O Capítulo 5 discute os tipos de máquinas automatizadas, sistemas de produção automatizados e conceitos e questões relacionados. Esses tópicos são descritos e ilustrados a partir da perspectiva do gerente de operações e como eles afetam o desempenho estratégico das operações.

- **Instantâneos da Indústria.** Relatos especiais de aplicações na indústria são apresentados em cada capítulo. Esses Instantâneos da Indústria estão destacados para salientar sua importância em relação ao tópico em discussão. Quando possível, os nomes reais de empresas e pessoas são usados para demonstrar aos estudantes a pertinência daquilo que ensinamos nos cursos sobre a APO.

- **Resumo Final: O Que os Fabricantes de Classe Mundial Estão Fazendo.** Esse recurso único ao final da maioria dos capítulos substitui os resumos convencionais. As discussões aplicam conceitos contidos no capítulo às explanações daquilo que as empresas internacionais mais bem administradas estão fazendo nos mercados globalmente competitivos. Em função disso, as mais novas e avançadas idéias a respeito de como estruturar, analisar e gerenciar sistemas de produção são integradas ao longo do texto.

Agradecimentos

Numerosas pessoas merecem especial reconhecimento por suas contribuições a este projeto. Em particular, Pat McMullen, da Universidade do Maine, forneceu feedback e idéias valiosos. Outros que contribuíram tanto para as revisões formais como informais do texto manuscrito merecem reconhecimento especial:

F. J. Brewerton, *University of Texas-Pan American*
George D. Brower, *Moravian College*
Russel A. Chambers, *Urbana University*
Dinesh S. Dave, *Appalachian State University*
Abe Feinberg, *California State University, Northridge*
Jorge Haddock, *Rensselaer Institute of Technology*
Steve Hora, *University of Hawaii*
Jeffrey B. Kaufmann, *Saint Mary's University*
Jeffrey F. Sherlock, *Huntington College*
Arijit K. Sengupta, *New Jersey Institute of Technology*
K. Paul Yoon, *Fairleigh Dickinson University*

Por último, mas não menos importante, também agradecemos os esforços da Equipe Editorial de Administração e Marketing da South-Western College Publishing, que trabalhou conosco na revisão. Nosso editor, Charles McCormick Jr., a editora de desenvolvimento, Alice Denny, a editora de produção, Kara Zum-Bahlen, e o gerente de marketing, Joe Sabatino, devem ser mencionados de forma especial.

Norman Gaither
Greg Frazier

Este livro é dedicado a:
Charles e Lavonne Frazier
Amanda Lynn Frazier

Sobre os Autores

Depois de muitos anos de colaboração profissional e amizade, Norman Gaither e Greg Frazier reuniram-se para a 8ª. edição deste livro.

Norman Gaither

Norman Gaither é professor emérito de Análise e Pesquisa Comercial na Texas A&M University. Ele recebeu seu PhD e seu MBA da Universidade de Oklahoma e seu BSIE da Oklahoma State University. Antes de lecionar, o professor Gaither trabalhou na Olin Corporation, onde ocupou os cargos de engenheiro industrial chefe, gerente de fábrica e diretor de operações, e na BF Goodrich Company, como engenheiro industrial sênior.

Os escritos do professor Gaither sobre uma ampla variedade de tópicos da APO foram publicados em *Management Science, Decision Sciences, International Journal of Production Research, Journal of Production and Inventory Management, Academy of Management Journal, Academy of Management Review, Simulation, Journal of Purchasing and Materials Management, Journal of Operations Management, IIE Transactions, Journal of Cost Analysis* e *International Journal of Operations and Productions Management*.

O professor Gaither participa do conselho editorial do *Journal of Production and Inventory Management*, da American Production and Inventory Control Society (APICS), do *International Journal of Production Research, Production and Operations Management*, da Production and Operations Management Society (POMS) e do *Journal of Operations Management*, da Operations Management Association (OMS). Ele é um AACSB Federal Faculty Fellow.

O professor Gaither permanece ativo nos assuntos de administração de produção e operações no governo americano, na indústria e em diversas sociedades profissionais.

Greg Frazier

Greg Frazier é professor-assistente de Administração da Produção e Operações no Departamento de Sistemas de Informação e Ciências da Administração na Universidade do Texas, em Arlington. Ele é um APICS Certified Fellow in Production and Inventory Management (CFPIM) e tem participado como Faculty Fellow na Boeing Company.

O dr. Frazier recebeu um BS em engenharia mecânica e um MBA da Texas A&M University. Seu PhD em administração da produção e operações também é da Texas A&M, onde Norman Gaither presidiu sua comissão de dissertação.

A longa associação do dr. Frazier com Norman Gaither resultou na co-autoria de várias publicações, em diversos jornais, inclusive no *Journal of Operations Management, International Journal of Production Research* e no *Production and Inventory Management Journal*. Ele também teve publicações suas em veículos como o *International Journal of Production Economics*, o *Journal of Productivity Analysis* e o *Business Horizons*.

PARTE I

ADMINISTRAÇÃO DA PRODUÇÃO E OPERAÇÕES
Introdução e Visão Geral

CAPÍTULO 1
Administração da Produção e Operações: Uma Apresentação

CAPÍTULO 2
Estratégias de Operações: Usando a Qualidade, o Custo e o Serviço Como Armas Competitivas

CAPÍTULO 3
Previsões na APO: O Ponto de Partida para Todo o Planejamento

A administração de operações continua sendo uma área excitante de estudo neste limiar do século XXI. Muitas indústrias estão atravessando um período de rápidas mudanças, acarretadas pelos avanços tecnológicos. As melhorias nas tecnologias de comunicações permitiram que dezenas de milhares de empresas estendessem suas operações globalmente. Os avanços nas tecnologias de computadores estão mudando a maneira pela qual as organizações administram suas operações e como elas interagem com outras organizações. O explosivo crescimento da Internet e da World Wide Web está criando novas indústrias e está apresentando novos desafios de administração de operações. Além disso, o contínuo crescimento das indústrias de serviços nos Estados Unidos desviou o estudo da administração da produção e operações de seu foco anterior, voltado principalmente para a manufatura, para seu foco atual, mais equilibrado, nos serviços e manufatura.

Os clientes esperam cada vez mais produtos de mais alta qualidade a preços mais baixos e com entrega mais rápida. Por esse motivo, o estudo da administração de operações é mais importante do que nunca. Se você optar por uma carreira na administração de operações, este curso lhe proporcionará uma importante introdução ao campo. Se ingressar em outra profissão, como, por exemplo, contabilidade, marketing, finanças, sistemas de informação, pessoal ou engenharia, este livro será importante porque você interagirá com a administração de operações e seus problemas, oportunidades e desafios.

A Parte I deste livro apresenta:

1. Uma visão geral do campo da administração de operações — sua história, desafios atuais e futuros, e os fatores que provavelmente modelarão a estrutura dos sistemas de produção.
2. Diferentes estruturas para estudar a administração de operações — a produção como um sistema, a produção como uma função organizacional e a tomada de decisões na administração da produção e operações (APO) são maneiras úteis de ver a APO. Cada capítulo do livro se enquadra nesta estrutura: decisões estratégicas (Parte II), decisões operacionais (Parte III) e decisões de controle (Parte IV).
3. Um estudo da estratégia de negócios e da estratégia de operações necessárias para competir em mercados internacionais — uma avaliação do clima dos negócios, um estudo do processo de desenvolvimento de estratégias de operações e uma exploração das estratégias disponíveis para permitir que os negócios possam competir no ambiente empresarial global de amanhã.
4. Uma pesquisa dos métodos e sistemas de previsão como um ponto de partida para desenvolver estratégias de negócios e de operações bem-sucedidas.

capítulo 1

ADMINISTRAÇÃO DA PRODUÇÃO E OPERAÇÕES
UMA APRESENTAÇÃO

Introdução

Marcos Históricos na APO
*A Revolução Industrial
Período Pós-Guerra Civil
Administração Científica
Relações Humanas e Behaviorismo
Pesquisa Operacional
A Revolução dos Serviços*

Fatores Que Afetam a APO Hoje

Diferentes Maneiras de Estudar a APO
*A Produção Como um Sistema
    Um Modelo de Sistema de Produção • Diversidade de
    Sistemas de Produção
A Produção Como uma Função Organizacional
Tomada de Decisões na APO
    Decisões Estratégicas, Operacionais e de Controle •
    Estrutura Baseada na Decisão*

Resumo Final: O Que os Fabricantes de Classe Mundial Estão Fazendo

Questões de Revisão e Discussão

Tarefas na Internet

AGREGANDO VALOR ATRAVÉS DE UMA MELHOR ADMINISTRAÇÃO DAS OPERAÇÕES DE PRODUÇÃO E SERVIÇO

Uma melhor administração das operações de uma empresa pode agregar valor à empresa ao melhorar sua competitividade e lucratividade a longo prazo. Considere os exemplos que se seguem de importantes decisões sobre operações em algumas empresas: a Intel precisa construir uma fábrica de muitos bilhões de dólares para produzir sua próxima geração de chips de computador. Onde ela deve construí-la? A American Airlines precisa alocar recursos para atender toda sua demanda de clientes por viagens aéreas no próximo mês. Como ela deve designar aeronaves de diferentes tamanhos para as rotas de vôo, pilotos para as aeronaves e comissários de bordo para os vôos? A Hewlett-Packard precisa aumentar a produção de um novo modelo de cartuchos de tinta de impressora numa linha de produção que já está rodando com capacidade total. Qual é a maneira mais eficiente quanto ao custo de redesenhar a linha de produção para aumentar o volume produzido? O gerente do centro de chamadas de emergência 911 de Chicago quer utilizar melhor o quadro de funcionários que atende às chamadas e evitar longas esperas por parte dos usuários do 911, melhorando a precisão das previsões. Qual método deve ser usado para prever o número de chamadas ao 911 recebidas durante cada turno de trabalho?

Esses exemplos são uma amostra dos problemas enfrentados pelos gerentes de operações. Decisões de operações ruins podem prejudicar a posição competitiva de uma empresa e aumentar seus custos. Boas decisões podem melhorar o valor da empresa, aumentando sua lucratividade e crescimento. Entender os conceitos fundamentais da administração de operações e ser capaz de usar uma variedade de ferramentas comuns de tomada de decisões e abordagens de resolução de problemas é fundamental para tomar melhores decisões de operações.

Conforme o parágrafo precedente sugere, a administração da produção e operações é uma disciplina importante na luta para se permanecer competitivo num mercado global sempre mutante.

Entre as muitas funções nos negócios, três merecem destaque: produção, marketing e finanças. Este livro é sobre a administração da produção e operações.

***Administração da produção e operações (APO)** é a administração do sistema de produção de uma organização, que transforma os insumos[1] nos produtos e serviços da organização.*

Um sistema de produção transforma insumos — matérias-primas, pessoal, máquinas, prédios, tecnologia, dinheiro, informação e outros recursos — em saídas — produtos e serviços. Esse processo de transformação é o coração daquilo que chamamos **produção**, e é a atividade predominante de um sistema de produção. Uma vez que os gerentes na APO, aos quais chamaremos simplesmente **gerentes de operações**, administram o sistema de produção, sua principal preocupação reside nas atividades do processo de transformação ou produção.

Gerentes na função de marketing são responsáveis por criar demanda para os produtos e serviços de uma organização. Gerentes na função de finanças são responsáveis por atingir os objetivos financeiros da firma. Os negócios não podem obter sucesso sem produção, marketing ou finanças. Sem produção, nenhum produto ou serviço poderia ser produzido; sem marketing, nenhum produto ou serviço poderia ser vendido; e sem finanças o resultado certamente seria fracasso financeiro. Embora produção, marketing e finanças atuem independentemente para atingir suas metas funcionais individuais, eles trabalham em conjunto para realizar as metas da organização. A realização das metas organizacionais de lucratividade, sobrevivência e crescimento num clima empresarial dinâmico exige um trabalho em equipe cooperativo entre essas funções comerciais primárias. Embora os gerentes de produção, marketing e finanças tenham muito em comum, suas decisões podem ser diferentes. Neste estudo da APO, prestaremos atenção especial nas decisões que os gerentes de operações tomam e em como eles as tomam.

São muitas as oportunidades de carreira no campo da administração da produção e operações. A Tabela 1.1 ilustra alguns dos empregos disponíveis atualmente. Esses postos podem levar a empregos de

---

[1] *Insumo* (do inglês *in*(*put*) + (*con*)*sumo*): neologismo com que se traduz a expressão inglesa *input*, que designa todas as despesas e investimentos que contribuem para a obtenção de determinado resultado, mercadoria ou produto até o acabamento ou consumo final. Insumo (*input*) é tudo aquilo *que entra*; produto (*output*) é tudo aquilo *que sai*. (N. do T.)

Tabela 1.1 — Algumas Ocupações na Administração da Produção e Operações

Indústria Manufatureira: Título da Função	Setor de Produção/Staff	Descrição da Função/Obrigações	Indústria de Serviços: Título da Função
Supervisor de produção	Setor de produção	Supervisiona os empregados à medida que os produtos ou serviços são produzidos. É responsável pelo desempenho de custo, qualidade e programação.	Supervisor de departamento
Planejador de compras/ comprador	Staff	Compra produtos ou serviços para manter a produção. É responsável pelo desempenho do fornecedor.	Agente de compras
Analista de estoques	Staff	Supervisiona todos os aspectos dos estoques. É responsável pelos níveis de estoques, auditorias, precisão de registros, pedidos e expedição.	Analista de estoques
Controlador da produção	Staff	Autoriza a produção de pedidos, desenvolve programas e planos de produção e faz a expedição de pedidos. Responsável por cumprir datas de vencimento dos clientes e abastecimento eficiente da linha de produção.	Programador de staff Programador de entrega
Analista de produção	Staff	Analisa problemas de produção, desenvolve previsões, planeja para novos produtos e executa outros projetos especiais.	Analista de operações
Especialista em qualidade	Staff	Supervisiona a aceitação por amostragem, controle de processo e administração da qualidade. Responsável pela qualidade do produto dos fornecedores e da produção.	Especialista em qualidade

nível médio na carreira, como, por exemplo, gerente de manufatura, gerente de operações, gerente de instalações, gerente de fábrica, gerente de controle da produção, gerente de estoques, gerente de análise da produção e gerente de controle da qualidade, ou a postos executivos, como, por exemplo, vice-presidente de manufatura, vice-presidente de administração de materiais, vice-presidente de operações e até mesmo presidente ou diretor de operações. Grandes corporações como Wal-Mart, Motorola, Eastman Kodak, General Foods, NationsBank, Johnson & Johnson, Texaco, Trane, Ford, General Electric e Procter & Gamble, e muitas empresas menores estão batendo à porta de faculdades e universidades para contratar pessoas criativas para abrirem caminho na carreira em operações de manufatura e serviços.

Por que você seguiria uma carreira na administração de operações? Tenho perguntado a muitos gerentes de operações o que eles apreciam em seus trabalhos, e suas respostas são interessantes. A resposta de um gerente de operações da Motorola foi especialmente ilustrativa:

> *Em meu emprego, estou fazendo o trabalho principal dos negócios — fabricar produtos para os clientes. Estar envolvido no processo de produzir produtos e serviços é algo palpável que eu posso agarrar e entender. Todo dia é interessante porque há essa variedade de coisas para eu fazer, desde resolver problemas relacionados à qualidade até instalar uma nova máquina robótica. E há muitas oportunidades para lidar com pessoas, desde fornecedores até nosso pessoal e clientes. Depois de estar aqui, acho que eu não conseguiria enfrentar um trabalho que lidasse somente com coisas intangíveis, como débitos e créditos.*

Um trabalho interessante e desafiador, oportunidades de progresso na empresa e altos salários são as principais razões apresentadas pelos gerentes de operações para gostarem de seus trabalhos.

Como uma pessoa se qualifica para uma carreira na administração da produção e operações? Entender os conceitos estudados neste curso é um primeiro passo. Um diploma em administração da produção e operações ou outra disciplina comercial pode qualificá-lo para programas de treinamento, e então você está encaminhado.

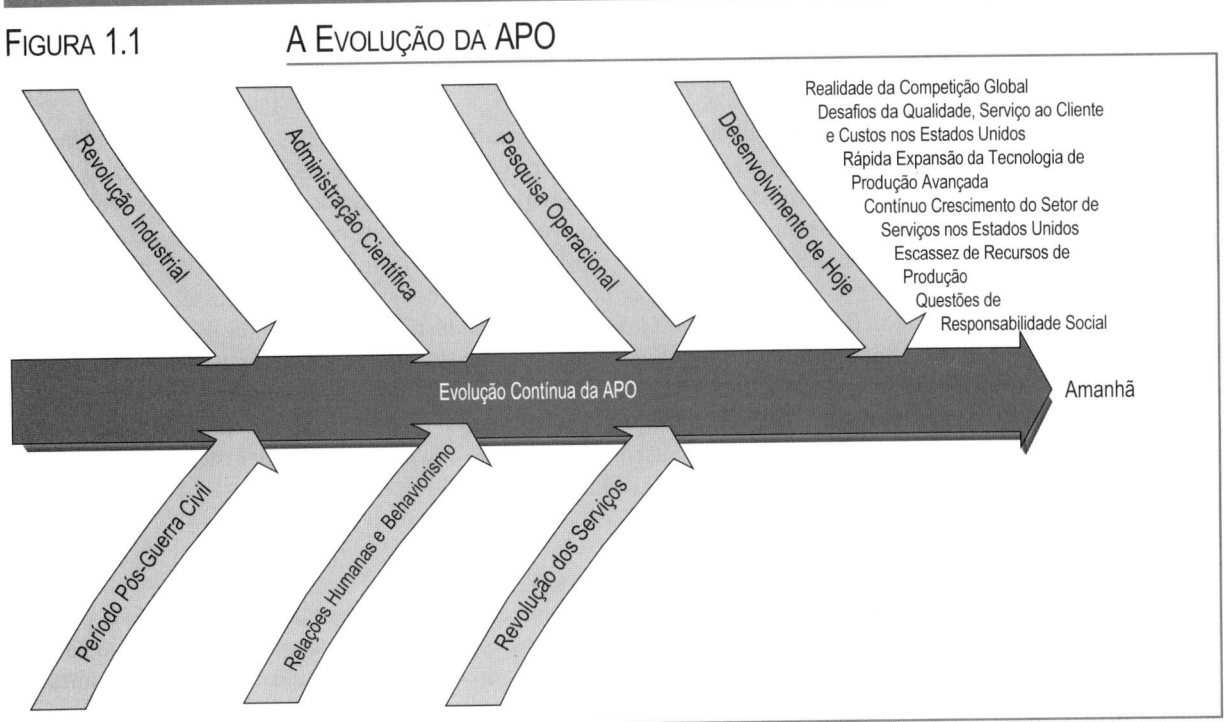

FIGURA 1.1 — A EVOLUÇÃO DA APO

A APO evoluiu até sua forma presente adaptando-se aos desafios de cada nova era. A Figura 1.1 ilustra que a APO atualmente é uma interessante combinação de práticas consagradas do passado e de uma busca de novas maneiras de gerenciar sistemas de produção. Este estudo introdutório sobre a APO ilustrará tanto os desenvolvimentos históricos como os desafios atuais na APO.

MARCOS HISTÓRICOS NA APO

Para um exame de seu impacto sobre a APO, estudaremos seis desenvolvimentos históricos: a Revolução Industrial, o período pós-Guerra Civil, a administração científica, as relações humanas e o behaviorismo, a pesquisa operacional e a revolução dos serviços.

A REVOLUÇÃO INDUSTRIAL

Sempre existiram sistemas de produção. As pirâmides egípcias, o Partenon grego, a Grande Muralha da China e os aquedutos e estradas do Império Romano atestam a indústria dos povos da Antigüidade. Mas as maneiras pelas quais esses povos antigos produziam produtos eram bem diferentes dos métodos de produção atuais. Os sistemas de produção anteriores a 1700 muitas vezes são chamados de **sistemas caseiros**, porque a produção dava-se nas casas ou cabanas, onde os artesãos orientavam aprendizes a executarem trabalho manual nos produtos.

Na Inglaterra de 1700 ocorreu um desenvolvimento ao qual nos referimos como **Revolução Industrial***. Esse avanço envolveu dois elementos principais: a difundida substituição da força humana e da água pela* **força mecanizada** *e o estabelecimento do* **sistema fabril***.* O motor a vapor, inventado por James Watt em 1764, forneceu a força motriz para as fábricas e estimulou outras invenções da época. A disponibilidade do motor a vapor e de máquinas de produção tornou possível reunir trabalhadores em fábricas distantes dos rios. E o grande número de trabalhadores congregados em fábricas criou a necessidade de organizá-los de uma maneira lógica para produzirem produtos. A publicação de *A riqueza das nações*, de Adam Smith, em 1776, avaliava os benefícios econômicos da **divisão do trabalho**, também chamada **es-**

pecialização de mão-de-obra, que dividia a produção em tarefas menores, especializadas, que eram atribuídas aos trabalhadores ao longo de linhas de produção. Dessa forma, as fábricas do final dos anos 1700 desenvolveram não somente maquinaria de produção, mas também maneiras de planejar e controlar o trabalho.

A Revolução Industrial se espalhou da Inglaterra para outros países europeus e para os Estados Unidos. Em 1790, Eli Whitney, inventor americano, desenvolveu o conceito de **peças intercambiáveis**. Whitney projetou rifles para serem fabricados pelo governo americano numa linha de montagem de tal forma que as peças fossem produzidas com uma tolerância que permitisse que cada peça se encaixasse corretamente desde a primeira vez. Esse método de produção substituiu o antigo método de ou classificar as peças para encontrar uma que se encaixasse, ou modificar uma peça a fim de que ela se encaixasse.

A primeira grande indústria nos Estados Unidos foi a indústria têxtil. Quando da Guerra de 1812, havia quase 200 fábricas têxteis na Nova Inglaterra. A Revolução Industrial avançou ainda mais com o desenvolvimento do motor a gasolina e da eletricidade nos anos 1800. Outras indústrias emergiram, e a necessidade de produtos para sustentar a Guerra Civil estimulou o estabelecimento de mais fábricas. Em meados dos anos 1800, o antigo sistema caseiro de produção foi substituído pelo sistema fabril, mas as enormes melhorias para as fábricas ainda estavam por acontecer.

PERÍODO PÓS-GUERRA CIVIL

Uma nova era industrial para os Estados Unidos foi conduzida com a chegada do século XX. O período pós-Guerra Civil montou o cenário para a grande expansão da capacidade de produção no novo século. A abolição do trabalho escravo, o êxodo de trabalhadores do campo para as cidades e a maciça influência de imigrantes no período de 1865-1900 forneceram uma grande força de trabalho para os centros urbanos industriais em franco desenvolvimento.

O final da Guerra Civil testemunhou o início de modernas formas de capital através do estabelecimento de companhias com ações em comum. Esse desenvolvimento levou à separação entre o capitalista e o empregador, com os administradores se tornando empregados assalariados dos financistas que possuíam o capital. Durante o período pós-Guerra Civil, J. P. Morgan, Jay Gould, Cornelius Vanderbilt e outros construíram impérios industriais. Esses empresários e a enorme acumulação de capital nesse período criaram uma grande capacidade de produção nos Estados Unidos, que se espalhou rapidamente na virada do século.

A rápida exploração e colonização do Oeste criou a necessidade de numerosos produtos e de um meio de levá-los aos colonos, ávidos por esses produtos. O período pós-Guerra Civil produziu grandes ferrovias, a segunda grande indústria dos Estados Unidos. Linhas férreas foram estendidas; novos territórios foram desenvolvidos; e já no início do século XX um sistema de transporte eficiente e econômico, de alcance nacional, estava em operação.

Em 1900, todos esses desenvolvimentos — expansão do capital e capacidade de produção, ampliada força de trabalho urbana, novos mercados ocidentais e um eficiente sistema de transporte nacional — prepararam o cenário para a grande explosão de produção do início do século XX.

ADMINISTRAÇÃO CIENTÍFICA

O ambiente socioeconômico do novo século formou o caldeirão no qual a administração científica foi formulada. O elo perdido era a administração — a capacidade de desenvolver essa grande máquina de produção para satisfazer os maciços mercados de então. Um núcleo de engenheiros, executivos comerciais, consultores, educadores e pesquisadores desenvolveu os métodos e a filosofia denominados **administração científica**. A Tabela 1.2 apresenta as principais personagens da era da administração científica.

Frederick Winslow Taylor é conhecido como o pai da administração científica. Ele estudou os problemas fabris de sua época cientificamente e popularizou a noção de eficiência — obter o resultado desejado com o menor desperdício de tempo, esforço e materiais.

No final dos anos 1800, após freqüentar a escola preparatória e depois de um programa de aprendizagem para mecânicos, Taylor trabalhou durante seis anos na Midvale Steel Company, na Pensilvânia. Durante esses anos, ele progrediu rapidamente de operário a mecânico, a encarregado, a mecânico de manutenção, chefe e, finalmente, a engenheiro chefe, enquanto, ao mesmo tempo, freqüentava a escola

TABELA 1.2 — ADMINISTRAÇÃO CIENTÍFICA: OS ATORES E SEUS PAPÉIS

Contribuinte	Tempo de Duração	Contribuições
Frederick Winslow Taylor	1856–1915	Princípios de administração científica, princípio da exceção, estudo do tempo, análise de métodos, padrões, planejamento, controle
Frank B. Gilbreth	1868–1934	Estudo dos movimentos, métodos, *therbligs*, contratos de construção, consultoria
Lillian M. Gilbreth	1878–1973	Estudos da fadiga, ergonomia, seleção e treinamento de empregados
Henry L. Gantt	1861–1919	Gráficos de Gantt, sistemas de pagamento por incentivo, abordagem humanística ao trabalho, treinamento
Carl G. Barth	1860–1939	Análise matemática, régua de cálculo, estudos de suprimentos e velocidade, consultoria para a indústria automobilística
Harrington Emerson	1885–1931	Princípios da eficiência, economia de milhões de dólares em ferrovias, métodos de controle
Morris L. Cooke	1872–1960	Aplicação da administração científica à educação e ao governo

para receber um diploma em engenharia mecânica. Foi durante essa época que Taylor descobriu seu interesse em usar a investigação e a experimentação científicas para melhorar as operações de manufatura. Na Midvale Steel, suas investigações científicas levaram a melhorias na eficiência dos trabalhadores que resultaram em grandes economias em custos de mão-de-obra.

O **sistema de produção** de Taylor, uma abordagem sistemática para melhorar a eficiência do trabalhador, empregava os seguintes passos:

1. A habilidade, a força e a capacidade de aprendizagem eram determinadas para cada trabalhador, de forma a colocar as pessoas em funções nas quais pudessem se adaptar melhor.
2. Cronometragens eram usadas para definir com precisão a produção padrão por trabalhador em cada tarefa. O produto esperado em cada tarefa era usado para planejar e programar o trabalho e para comparar diferentes métodos de executar as tarefas.
3. Cartões de instrução, roteiros e especificações de materiais eram usados para coordenar e organizar a fábrica, a fim de que os métodos e o fluxo de trabalho pudessem ser padronizados, e os padrões de produção da mão-de-obra pudessem ser satisfeitos.
4. A supervisão foi melhorada através de cuidadosa seleção e treinamento. Taylor apontava freqüentemente que a administração era negligente em executar suas funções. Ele acreditava que a administração tinha de aceitar as responsabilidades de planejamento, organização, controle e determinação de métodos, e não deixar essas importantes funções para os trabalhadores.
5. Sistemas de pagamento por incentivo foram iniciados para aumentar a eficiência e aliviar dos encarregados sua responsabilidade tradicional de impulsionar os trabalhadores.

Em 1893 Taylor deixou a Midvale e fundou sua própria empresa de consultoria, para que pudesse aplicar seu sistema a uma faixa mais ampla de situações. Os analistas que seguiram Taylor ficaram conhecidos como **especialistas em eficiência**, **engenheiros de eficiência** e, finalmente, **engenheiros de produção**. Além do título de pai da administração científica, Taylor é conhecido como pai da engenharia de produção.

Os outros pioneiros da administração científica relacionados na Tabela 1.2 se reuniram para difundir o evangelho da eficiência. Cada um deles contribuiu com técnicas e abordagens valiosas, que por fim modelaram a administração científica numa poderosa força para facilitar a produção em massa.

O grande marco da administração científica ocorreu na Ford Motor Company no início do século XX. Henry Ford (1863-1947) projetou o Ford Modelo T para ser construído em linhas de montagem. As

> ## INSTANTÂNEO DA INDÚSTRIA 1.1
>
> ### ADMINISTRAÇÃO CIENTÍFICA NA FÁBRICA DE ROUGE DA FORD
>
> Em 1908 Ford contratou Walter Flanders, especialista em eficiência industrial, para reorganizar sua fábrica para produzir carros Modelo T. A fábrica foi montada para operar como "um rio e seus afluentes". Cada seção da fábrica foi mecanizada e acelerada. As peças do Modelo T fluíam numa produção em linha reta, com peças pequenas que se tornavam continuamente maiores. Iniciando pelo departamento de montagem de bobinas de indução e espalhando-se pela fábrica inteira, até o departamento de montagem final, as peças e as montagens eram transportadas por correias transportadoras automáticas, e toda tarefa de trabalho era dividida em partes menores e agilizadas.
>
> Os resultados foram surpreendentes. Onde anteriormente eram necessárias 728 horas de um trabalhador para montar um Modelo T, agora eram necessários somente 93 minutos. Isso aumentou a velocidade de produção, reduziu enormemente o custo de cada Modelo T, aumentou o saldo de caixa da Ford de 2 milhões para 673 milhões de dólares e permitiu a redução do preço do Modelo T de 780 para 360 dólares. O mundo jamais vira algo igual. Os carros simplesmente pululavam das linhas de montagem.
>
> Em sua maturidade em meados de 1920, a Rouge, localizada na periferia de Detroit, transformava em anões todos os outros complexos industriais. Seus mais de 4 milhões de metros quadrados abrigavam 93 prédios, sendo 23 deles de grande porte. Havia 159,6 quilômetros de ferrovia e 43,5 quilômetros de correias transportadoras. Cerca de 75 mil homens trabalhavam lá, sendo que 5 mil deles estavam encarregados tão-somente da limpeza: usavam 86 toneladas de sabão e 5 mil esfregões por mês! A Rouge tinha sua própria usina siderúrgica e uma fábrica de vidro no local.
>
> *Fonte:* Halberstam, David. *The Reckoning*, Nova Iorque, Morrow, 1986, p. 79-82 e 87.

linhas de montagem da Ford incorporavam os elementos principais da administração científica — desenhos de produto padronizados, produção em massa, baixos custos de manufatura, linhas de montagem mecanizadas, especialização de mão-de-obra e peças intercambiáveis. O Instantâneo da Indústria 1.1 descreve a instalação de Rouge da Ford na década de 1920. Em Rouge, a tecnologia das linhas de montagem, que tinham o refinamento de uma obra de arte, ampliou-se e desenvolveu-se com o crescimento da capacidade de produção durante a Segunda Guerra Mundial.

Não obstante Ford não ter inventado muitos dos métodos de produção que usava, talvez ele, mais do que qualquer outro líder industrial de seu tempo, tenha incorporado em suas fábricas o melhor em termos de métodos eficientes de produção daquele período. De fato, ele foi responsável em grande parte por popularizar as linhas de montagem como *a* maneira de produzir grandes volumes de produtos a baixo custo. Ford não somente estava preocupado com a produção em massa; ele também se preocupava com seus trabalhadores. Ele pagava a seus trabalhadores mais do que o salário vigente na época, de forma que eles podiam dar-se ao luxo de comprar seus carros, e estabeleceu os "departamentos sociológicos", precursores dos atuais departamentos de pessoal. O excerto que se segue, do livro *Today and Tomorrow*[2], escrito em 1926 por Henry Ford, descreve a opinião de Ford a respeito de como sua abordagem à produção em massa teve impacto sobre a sociedade.

> *Peguemos apenas uma idéia, uma idéia — pequena em si mesma — a idéia que qualquer um poderia ter tido, mas que ocorreu a mim desenvolver: a de fazer um automóvel pequeno, forte, simples, fazê-lo barato e pagar altos salários em sua fabricação. Em 1º de outubro de 1908 fiz o 1º de nossos pequenos carros. Em 4 de junho de 1924, fizemos o 10.000.000º. Agora, em 1926, estamos em nosso 13.000.000º.*
>
> *Isso é interessante, mas talvez não seja o mais importante. O importante é que, a partir de um simples punhado de homens empregados numa fábrica, desenvolvemo-nos para uma grande indús-*

---

[2] Henry Ford, *Today and Tomorrow*, Londres, William Heinemann, 1926, p. 1-2.

tria que emprega diretamente mais de 200 mil homens, sendo que nenhum deles recebe menos de seis dólares por dia. Nossos distribuidores e postos de serviço empregam outros 200 mil homens. Mas de forma alguma manufaturamos tudo o que usamos. Compramos aproximadamente o dobro do que manufaturamos, e afirmamos com segurança que 200 mil homens estão empregados em nosso trabalho em fábricas no exterior. Isso dá um total aproximado de 600 mil empregados, direta e indiretamente, o que significa que cerca de 3 milhões de homens, mulheres e crianças ganham a vida em função de uma idéia simples posta em prática somente 18 anos atrás. E isso sem levarmos em conta o grande número de pessoas que, de uma forma ou de outra, ajudam na distribuição ou manutenção desses carros. E esta é uma idéia que está apenas no início.

O impulso da administração científica estava no nível mais baixo da hierarquia da organização — o setor de produção, trabalhadores, encarregados, superintendentes e administração média inferior. Os pioneiros da administração científica concentravam-se no nível de fábrica, porque era ali que a maioria dos problemas administrativos da época estava. Era necessário **produção em massa** e **eficiência**, ao mesmo tempo que se concentravam nos detalhes das operações. Os métodos de administração científica cumpriam esse desafio.

Relações Humanas e Behaviorismo

Os trabalhadores das fábricas da Revolução Industrial, recém-saídos do campo, eram despreparados, inábeis e indisciplinados. Não obstante eles não gostarem do trabalho na fábrica, esses empregos os separavam da fome. Os gerentes de fábrica desenvolviam rígidos controles para forçá-los a trabalhar arduamente. Esse legado de controles rígidos vigorou nos anos 1800 e início dos anos 1900. Fundamental nesse método de administração era a pressuposição de que os trabalhadores tinham de ser colocados em empregos projetados para assegurar que eles trabalhassem árdua e eficientemente.

Entre as duas grandes guerras, entretanto, começou a surgir nos Estados Unidos uma filosofia entre os gerentes segundo a qual os trabalhadores eram seres humanos e deviam ser tratados com dignidade no trabalho. O **movimento das relações humanas** iniciou-se em Illinois com o trabalho de Elton Mayo, F. J. Roethlisberger, T. N. Whitehead e W. J. Dickson na instalação da Western Electric Company, em Hawthorne, Illinois, no período de 1927-1932. Os **Estudos de Hawthorne** foram iniciados a princípio por engenheiros de produção e tinham como meta determinar o nível ótimo de iluminação para obter o máximo de produção dos trabalhadores. Quando esses estudos produziram resultados confusos sobre a relação entre o ambiente físico e a eficiência dos trabalhadores, os pesquisadores deram-se conta de que fatores humanos deviam estar afetando a produção. Essa foi talvez a primeira vez que tanto pesquisadores como administradores reconheceram que fatores humanos afetavam não somente a motivação e a atitude das pessoas como também a produção.

Esses primeiros estudos das relações humanas logo abriram caminho para uma ampla variedade de pesquisas sobre o comportamento dos trabalhadores em seus ambientes de trabalho. *A obra e os escritos de Chester Barnard, Abraham Maslow, Frederick Herzberg, Douglas McGregor, Peter Drucker e outros disseminaram entre os gerentes industriais um entendimento básico dos trabalhadores e suas atitudes em relação a seu trabalho. A partir do trabalho desses* **behavioristas**, *como logo passaram a ser conhecidos, ocorreu uma gradual mudança na maneira pela qual os administradores pensavam e tratavam os trabalhadores.* Ainda estamos aprendendo como utilizar o grande potencial presente nos trabalhadores industriais. Obter sucesso no ambiente comercial global de hoje depende mais do que nunca de dar vazão às capacidades subutilizadas dos empregados. Os gerentes de operações devem, portanto, tentar criar um clima organizacional que encoraje os empregados a dedicar sua energia, engenho e habilidade à consecução dos objetivos organizacionais.

Pesquisa Operacional

A campanha européia da Segunda Guerra Mundial usou enormes quantidades de força de trabalho, suprimentos, aviões, navios, materiais e outros recursos que tiveram de ser desdobrados num ambiente extremamente agitado. Nunca antes as organizações enfrentaram decisões administrativas tão complexas. Por causa dessa complexidade, equipes de **pesquisa operacional** eram formadas em todos os ramos dos

TABELA 1.3	CARACTERÍSTICAS DA PESQUISA OPERACIONAL (PO)
	1. A PO aborda a solução de problemas e a tomada de decisões a partir da perspectiva do sistema total.
	2. A PO não usa necessariamente equipes interdisciplinares, mas é interdisciplinar; ela recorre a técnicas de ciências como a biologia, física, química, matemática e economia e aplica as técnicas apropriadas de cada campo ao sistema estudado.
	3. A PO não faz experiências com o próprio sistema, mas constrói um modelo do sistema sobre o qual realiza experiências.
	4. A construção de modelos e a manipulação matemática constituem a metodologia que tem sido, talvez, a contribuição-chave da PO.
	5. O foco principal está na tomada de decisões.
	6. Computadores são usados extensivamente.

serviços militares. Estas equipes utilizavam muitas das disciplinas acadêmicas da época. Os conceitos de **abordagem por sistemas totais** e de **equipes interdisciplinares** e a utilização de **técnicas matemáticas complexas** evoluíram em conseqüência das condições caóticas existentes nas imensas organizações militares envolvidas na Segunda Guerra Mundial.

Depois da Segunda Guerra Mundial os pesquisadores das operações militares e suas abordagens encontraram seu caminho de volta para as universidades, indústrias, agências governamentais e firmas de consultoria. Esses pesquisadores introduziram a pesquisa operacional nos currículos de faculdades e universidades, desenvolveram firmas de consultoria que se especializaram em pesquisa operacional e formaram sociedades de pesquisa operacional. E as características da pesquisa operacional (mostradas na Tabela 1.3) tornaram-se aquelas que conhecemos hoje.

Durante o período pós-Guerra, a pesquisa operacional tornou-se, e talvez ainda o seja hoje, conhecida principalmente por suas técnicas quantitativas, como por exemplo a programação linear, a PERT/CPM e os modelos de previsão. Uma vez que as firmas se tornam maiores e usam níveis mais elevados de tecnologia, a adoção das técnicas é mais intensa. A pesquisa operacional ajuda os gerentes de operações a tomarem decisões quando os problemas são complexos e quando o custo de uma decisão errada é elevado e duradouro. Problemas como os que se seguem comumente são analisados usando-se técnicas de pesquisa operacional:

1. Uma companhia tem 12 fábricas que embarcam produtos para 48 armazéns no país inteiro. Para maximizar os lucros, quantas unidades de cada produto devem ser embarcadas de cada instalação para cada armazém por mês?
2. Uma firma pretende construir uma unidade de produção de $ 157 milhões. O projeto envolve recursos da companhia, 2 contratados principais e 75 subcontratados ao longo de um período de quatro anos. Como a empresa pode planejar a conclusão de cada atividade do projeto e a utilização de trabalhadores, materiais e contratados a fim de que o custo e a duração do projeto sejam minimizados?

A pesquisa operacional, à semelhança da administração científica, procura substituir a tomada de decisões intuitiva para grandes e complexos problemas por uma abordagem que identifique a alternativa ótima, ou a melhor, por meio de análise. Os gerentes de operações, à semelhança dos gerentes da área de marketing, finanças e outras especialidades da administração, têm adotado as abordagens e técnicas da pesquisa operacional para melhorar suas tomadas de decisão.

A REVOLUÇÃO DOS SERVIÇOS

Um dos importantes desenvolvimentos de nosso tempo é a disseminação dos serviços nas economias. A criação de organizações de serviços acelerou-se de maneira abrupta depois da Segunda Guerra Mundial e ainda está se expandindo. *Mais de 2/3 da força de trabalho americana está empregada em serviços, e*

TABELA 1.4 — ALGUMAS INDÚSTRIAS DE SERVIÇOS E EMPRESAS DE SERVIÇOS

Indústrias de Serviços	Empresas Representantes
Empresas aéreas	AMR, UAL, Delta Air Lines, Northwest Airlines
Bancos comerciais	Citicorp, BankAmerica, J. P. Morgan & Co.
Serviços de computador e de bancos de dados	Dun & Bradstreet, ACNielsen, America Online
Serviços financeiros diversificados	Fannie Mae, American Express, American General
Entretenimento	Walt Disney, Viacom, Time Warner
Alimentos e drogarias	Kroger, Safeway, Albertson's, Walgreen, Eckerd
Serviços de alimentos	PepsiCo, McDonald's, ARAMARK, Wendy's
Comerciantes gerais	Wal-Mart Stores, Sears, Roebuck & Co., Kmart
Atendimento à saúde	Columbia/HCA, United HealthCare, Humana
Hotéis, cassinos, estações de férias	Marriott, ITT, Hilton Hotels, Harrah's Entertainment
Seguros	Prudential, New York Life, CIGNA, Aetna, State Farm
Entrega de correspondência, pacotes e fretes	United Parcel Service, Federal Express, Airborne Freight
Serviços marítimos	APL Limited, Alexander & Baldwin
Publicações, impressão	Gannett, Times Mirror, McGraw-Hill, Knight-Ridder
Ferrovias	CSX, Union Pacific, Norfolk Southern, Conrail
Instituições de poupança	Great Western Financial, Washington Mutual
Varejistas especialistas	Costco, Home Depot, Toys-R-Us, The Limited
Telecomunicações	AT&T, GTE, BellSouth, MCI, Sprint
Ajuda temporária	Manpower, Olsten, Kelly Services
Leasing de caminhões	Ryder Systems, Amerco
Transporte em caminhões	CNF, Caliber Systems, Roadway Express, J.B. Hunt
Serviço público, gás e eletricidade	Southern Co., PG&E, Edison, Entergy
Gerenciamento do lixo[3]	WMX Technologies, Ogden, USA Waste Services
Atacadistas	Fleming, Supervalu, McKesson, SYSCO

Fonte: Da lista da Fortune 500 das 1.000 maiores empresas de 1997, com acesso através de **www.fortune.com**.

mais da metade desses trabalhadores está em empregos de escritório; aproximadamente 2/3 do produto interno bruto (PIB) são produzidos pelos serviços; há um enorme superávit comercial nos serviços; e o investimento por trabalhador de escritório agora ultrapassa o investimento por trabalhador de fábrica. Considere a diversidade das indústrias de serviço e suas empresas, relacionadas na Tabela 1.4, que não inclui as agências de governos municipais, estaduais e federal que oferecem serviços públicos.

O impacto dessa explosão das organizações de serviços sobre a administração de operações tem sido enorme. Freqüentemente, ao longo do livro, exploraremos algumas das dificuldades e oportunidades na administração desses muitos serviços, privados e públicos.

Um suplemento de 1997 da *Harvard Business Review* relacionou os avanços que exerceram impacto sobre a APO nos anos 1980 e 1990:

- Robótica e controle numérico
- Projeto auxiliado por computador
- Controle estatístico do processo para obter qualidade (administração da qualidade total)
- Manufatura enxuta (*just-in-time*)
- *Benchmarking*
- Padrões ISO
- Competição baseada no tempo
- Reengenharia do processo
- *Outsourcing*
- Administração da cadeia de suprimentos
- Organização "virtual"

---

[3] Gerenciamento do lixo: tradução literal de *waste management* (empresas que trabalham com processamento e reaproveitamento do lixo). A Ogden Corporation, por exemplo, reaproveita o lixo, transformando-o em energia elétrica. (N. do T.)

Estes e outros fatores continuam a combinar-se com desenvolvimentos históricos para modelar as maneiras pelas quais administramos os sistemas de produção.

FATORES QUE AFETAM A APO HOJE

Dos muitos fatores que afetam a APO atualmente, seis tiveram um impacto maior:

1. Realidade da competição global
2. Qualidade, serviço ao cliente e desafios de custo nos Estados Unidos
3. Rápida expansão da tecnologia de produção avançada
4. Contínuo crescimento do setor de serviços nos Estados Unidos
5. Escassez de recursos de produção
6. Questões de responsabilidade social

Um impacto-chave desses fatores sobre os gerentes de operações é que as fronteiras de um país não mais oferecem proteção contra importações estrangeiras. A competição tornou-se intensa e está crescendo. *Para obter sucesso na competição global, as empresas devem ter um compromisso com a receptividade do cliente e com a melhoria contínua rumo à meta de desenvolver rapidamente produtos inovadores que tenham a melhor combinação de excepcional qualidade, entrega rápida e no tempo certo, e preços e custos baixos.* E essa competição determina que os gerentes de operações usem métodos de produção mais sofisticados, que se tornaram possíveis graças à crescente tecnologia de produção avançada.

Como se os desafios da competição global para a APO não bastassem, o trabalho dos gerentes de operações é complicado pela necessidade de uma administração mais eficiente do crescente setor de serviços; escassez de capital, materiais e outros recursos para a produção; e a necessidade de os gerentes de operações exercerem mais responsabilidade social. Dados esses fatores, como os gerentes de operações podem superar-se e obter sucesso? Como podem desenvolver planos de ação de longo prazo para obter sucesso numa atmosfera caracterizada por esses fatores é o tema central do Capítulo 2.

Esses fatores criam, de fato, uma interessante e desafiadora oportunidade para os gerentes de operações ou outros que estudam a APO.

DIFERENTES MANEIRAS DE ESTUDAR A APO

Ao longo dos anos surgiram muitas maneiras de abordar o estudo da APO. Entre as abordagens tradicionais, três tendem a predominar: a produção como um sistema, a produção como uma função organizacional e a tomada de decisões na APO.

A PRODUÇÃO COMO UM SISTEMA

Nas palavras de Russell Ackoff, pioneiro na teoria dos sistemas: "*Um **sistema** é um todo que não pode ser separado sem que ocorra a perda de suas características essenciais e, por isso, deve ser estudado como um todo. Agora, em vez de explicarmos um todo em termos de suas partes, as partes começaram a ser estudadas em termos do todo*". Os conceitos do campo da teoria dos sistemas são úteis para entendermos a produção como um sistema.

Um **sistema de produção** recebe **insumos** na forma de materiais, pessoal, capital, serviços públicos e informação. Esses insumos são modificados num **subsistema de transformação** para os produtos e serviços desejados, denominados **produtos**. Uma parcela do produto é monitorada no **subsistema de controle** para determinar se ele é aceitável em termos de quantidade, custo e qualidade. Se o produto for aceitável, nenhuma mudança será necessária no sistema; caso contrário, será necessária uma ação corretiva por parte da administração. O subsistema de controle assegura o desempenho do sistema ao fornecer *feedback* aos gerentes para que possam tomar ações corretivas.

Um Modelo de Sistema de Produção A Figura 1.2 ilustra um modelo de sistema de produção. Os insumos são classificados em três categorias gerais — insumos externos, insumos de mercado e recursos primários. Os **insumos externos** geralmente têm caráter de informação e tendem a fornecer aos gerentes de operações dados sobre as condições externas ao sistema de produção. Entradas legais ou políticas po-

FIGURA 1.2 — UM MODELO DE SISTEMA DE PRODUÇÃO

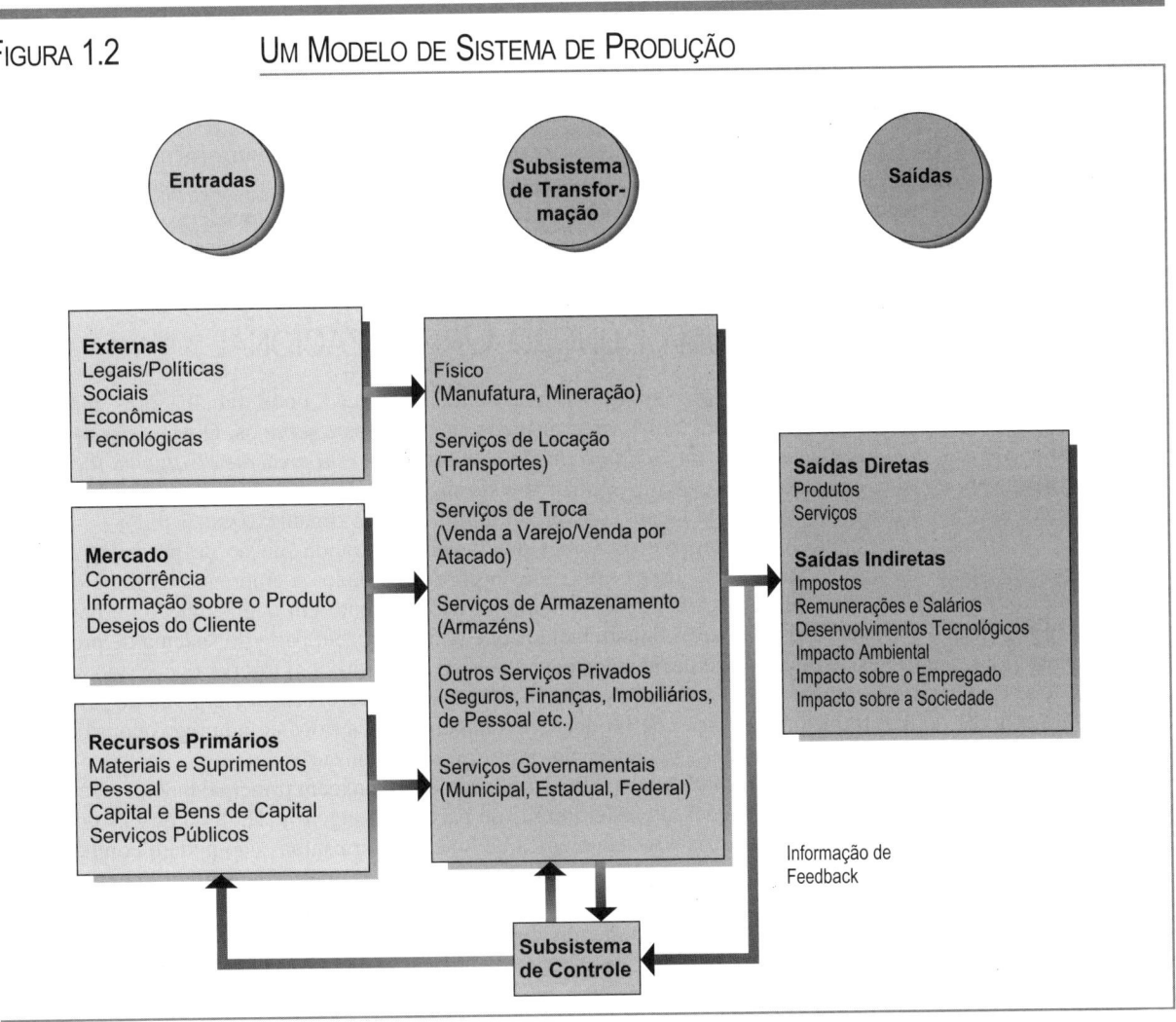

dem estabelecer restrições dentro das quais o sistema deve operar. Entradas sociais e econômicas permitem que os gerentes de operações tomem conhecimento das tendências que podem afetar o sistema de produção. Entradas tecnológicas podem vir, entre outros, de jornais comerciais, boletins do governo, informativos de associações comerciais e fornecedores. Essas informações fornecem aos gerentes novidades sobre importantes avanços em tecnologia que afetariam a maquinaria, ferramentas ou processos.

À semelhança dos insumos externos, os **insumos de mercado** tendem a ter um caráter informativo. Informações referentes à concorrência, design do produto, desejos do cliente e outros aspectos do mercado são essenciais se o sistema de produção quiser reagir às necessidades do mercado. Insumos que sustentam diretamente a produção e entrega de bens e serviços são chamados **recursos primários**. São recursos primários: matérias-primas e suprimentos, pessoal, capital e bens de capital e serviços públicos (água, gás, petróleo, carvão, eletricidade).

Os **produtos diretos** dos sistemas de produção comumente são de duas formas: tangíveis e intangíveis. Um conjunto enorme de **bens tangíveis**, ou produtos, é produzido a cada dia — automóveis, secadores de cabelo, palitos de dente, calculadoras, roupas, tratores, bolos, máquinas de escrever e sabão. Similarmente, os serviços — **produtos intangíveis** dos sistemas de produção — parecem inexauríveis: educação, coleta de lixo, cortes de cabelo, contabilidade de impostos, assistência médica, serviços bancários, seguros, hospedagem e transportes.

Curiosamente, muitas vezes negligenciamos os **produtos indiretos** dos sistemas de produção. Impostos, lixo e poluição, avanços tecnológicos, remunerações e salários e atividades de alcance comunitário são exemplos de **produtos indiretos**. Não obstante eles não receberem a mesma atenção que as saídas de bens e serviços que geram as receitas que perpetuam os sistemas, os produtos indiretos são tanto causa de preocupação como de orgulho. A consciência de que esses fatores são de fato produtos de nossos sistemas de produção faz com que os gerentes de produção realizem seus trabalhos mais eficientemente.

Diversidade de Sistemas de Produção Todas as organizações têm pelo menos um sistema de produção. Existe uma ampla variedade desses sistemas, diversos deles mostrados na Tabela 1.5. A maneira pela qual um sistema de produção se manifesta como parte de uma organização difere consideravelmente de empresa para empresa. Vamos examinar alguns esquemas organizacionais diversos quanto a essas funções de produção.

A Produção Como uma Função Organizacional

O coração de um sistema de produção é seu subsistema de transformação, onde trabalhadores, matérias-primas e máquinas são utilizados para transformar insumos em produtos e serviços. *O processo de transformação está no âmago da administração da produção e operações e está presente de alguma forma em todas as organizações.* O lugar onde esse processo de transformação é executado e aquilo a que chamamos departamento ou função onde ele está localizado variam muito entre as organizações.

A Tabela 1.6 compara os empregos e os nomes dos departamentos da função de produção de três tipos diferentes de firmas. São mostrados os títulos de cargo típicos dados a empregos da linha de produção e do *staff* dentro da função de produção, o nome do departamento em que a função de produção está localizada, e os empregos em outros departamentos que também fazem parte do sistema de produção maior, mas que não estão diretamente designados para a função de produção. Observe que serviços como a venda a varejo e o transporte em caminhões tendem a usar a palavra *operações* em vez de *produção* para o nome do departamento da função de produção, e também que os tipos de empregos considerados funções da linha de produção tendem a depender do propósito da organização.

Foi afirmado no início deste capítulo que a APO surgiu como personagem principal na luta para tornar as empresas americanas competitivas frente às empresas de países estrangeiros. Há um consenso de que, no mundo da competição global e expansão tecnológica de hoje, as companhias não podem competir somente com marketing, finanças, contabilidade e engenharia. Cada vez mais concentramo-nos na APO quando pensamos na competitividade global, porque é aqui que a imensa maioria dos trabalhadores de uma empresa, os ativos de capital e as despesas residem. E é na APO que reside a capacidade de produzirmos produtos e serviços de baixo custo, de superior qualidade, na hora certa. Necessitamos de novos produtos, marketing competente e finanças astutas, mas também devemos ter um forte entrosamento da função de operações com as outras funções da organização — se é que pretendemos ter sucesso na competição internacional.

Voltemo-nos agora para outra maneira de estudar a APO — a tomada de decisões dos gerentes de operações.

Tomada de Decisões na APO

Definimos anteriormente a APO em termos daquilo que os gerentes de operações fazem. Eles administram todas as atividades dos sistemas de produção, que transformam insumos em produtos e serviços da organização. Essa definição afirma em termos muito gerais *o que* a APO faz, embora o *como* os gerentes de operações administram pode ser mais importante para entendermos a APO. *É possível que nenhuma outra abordagem nos ajude a entender melhor como os gerentes de operações administram do que o exame das decisões na APO, porque, em geral, os gerentes de operações administram tomando decisões a respeito de todas as atividades dos sistemas de produção.*

Decisões Estratégicas, Operacionais e de Controle Classificar as decisões na APO é difícil, mas, segundo minha experiência como gerente de operações, elas tendem a cair em três categorias gerais:

- **Decisões estratégicas:** Decisões sobre produtos, processos e instalações. Essas decisões são de fundamental importância e têm impacto de longo prazo sobre a organização.
- **Decisões operacionais:** Decisões a respeito de como planejar a produção para atender a demanda. Essas decisões são necessárias se a produção contínua de bens e serviços pretende satisfazer as exigências do mercado e garantir lucros para a companhia.

TABELA 1.5 — ALGUNS SISTEMAS DE PRODUÇÃO TÍPICOS

Sistema de Produção	Insumos Primários	Subsistemas de Transformação	Saídas (Produtos)
Fábrica de alimentos para animais de estimação	Grãos, água, carnes, pessoal, ferramentas, máquinas, sacos de papel, latas, prédios, serviços públicos	Transforma matéria-prima em bens (físicos) acabados	Produtos para animais de estimação
Lanchonete	Carne, pão, verduras, temperos, suprimentos, pessoal, serviços públicos, máquinas, caixas de papelão, guardanapos, prédios, clientes famintos	Transforma matérias-primas em produtos e pacotes (físicos) de *fast-food*	Clientes satisfeitos e produtos de fast-food
Fábrica de automóveis	Peças compradas, matéria-prima, suprimentos, pinturas, ferramentas, equipamentos, pessoal, prédios, serviços públicos	Transforma matéria-prima em automóveis acabados através de operações (físicas) de fabricação e montagem	Automóveis
Firma de transporte em caminhões	Caminhões, pessoal, prédios, combustível, bens a serem embarcados, suprimentos de embalagem, peças de caminhão, serviços públicos	Empacota e transporta produtos da origem até o destino	Produtos entregues
Loja de departamentos	Prédios, vitrinas, cartões de compra, máquinas, produtos em estoque, pessoal, suprimentos, serviços públicos, clientes	Atrai clientes, armazena bens, vende produtos	Bens comercializados
Escritório de contabilidade	Suprimentos, pessoal, informação, computadores, prédios, mobiliário de escritório, máquinas, serviços públicos	Atrai clientes, compila dados, fornece informações administrativas, computa impostos	Informação administrativa, serviços tributários e declarações financeiras auditadas
Funilaria	Carros danificados, pinturas, suprimentos, máquinas, ferramentas, prédios, pessoal, serviços públicos	Transforma latarias de automóveis em cópias fiéis dos originais	Latarias de automóveis consertadas
Colégio ou universidade	Estudantes, livros, suprimentos, pessoal, prédios, serviços públicos	Transmite informações e desenvolve habilidades e conhecimento	Pessoas instruídas
Departamento de polícia	Suprimentos, pessoal, equipamentos, automóveis, mobiliário de escritório, prédios, serviços públicos	Detecta crimes, leva criminosos à Justiça, mantém a ordem	Níveis de violência aceitáveis e comunidades pacíficas
Serviço Nacional de Controle da Pesca	Suprimentos, pessoal, navios, computadores, aeronaves, serviços públicos, mobiliário de escritório, equipamentos	Detecta infratores da lei federal de pesca, leva-os à Justiça, preserva os recursos de pesca	Estoque de peixes

TABELA 1.6   FUNÇÕES DE PRODUÇÃO E OPERAÇÕES E EMPREGOS EM ORGANIZAÇÕES DIVERSAS

Tipo de Firma	Departamentos e Empregos da Função de Produção		Nome do Departamento da Função de Produção	Algumas Atividades do Sistema de Produção em Outros Departamentos (Empregos — Departamento)
	Alguns Empregos do Setor de Produção	Alguns Empregos do Staff		
Manufatura	Vice-presidente de manufatura Gerente de fábrica Gerente de produção Superintendente Encarregado Líder de equipe Chefe de seção	Engenheiro de manufatura Engenheiro de produção Gerente de controle da qualidade Engenheiro de controle da qualidade Gerente de materiais Analista de estoques Programador de produção	Manufatura	Agente de compras — compras Comprador — compras Especialita em pesoal — depto. de pessoal Projetista de produtos — marketing e engenharia Analista de orçamento — contabilidade Especialista em expedição — departamento de expedição
Venda a varejo	Vice-presidente de operações Gerente de loja Gerente de operações Supervisor de departamento Equipe de vendas Almoxarife	Gerente de atendimento ao cliente Gerente de segurança Gerente de manutenção Especialista em suprimentos Gerente de armazém	Operações	Agente de compras — merchandising Comprador — merchandising Analista de controle de comercialização — merchandising Analista de orçamento — contabilidade Inspetor — merchandising
Transporte em caminhões	Proprietário Vice-presidente de operações Gerente de filial Supervisor de embarque/desembarque Gerente de operações com caminhões Motorista Trabalhador da área de embarque/desembarque	Especialista em tarifas Diretor de manutenção Programador de escalas de caminhões Mecânico de reparos Despachante	Operações	Gerente de pessoal — depto. de pessoal Gerente de lojas — serviços administrativos Analista de orçamento — contabilidade Analista de sistemas — contabilidade Gerente de compras — serviços administrativos

- **Decisões de controle:** Decisões a respeito de como planejar e controlar as operações. Essas decisões privilegiam as atividades diárias dos trabalhadores, a qualidade dos produtos e serviços, os custos de produção e gastos gerais e a manutenção de máquinas.

As **decisões estratégicas** dizem respeito às estratégias de operações e ao plano de ação de longo prazo para a firma. Essas decisões são tão importantes que em geral o pessoal da produção, do departamento de pessoal, engenharia e finanças se reúne para estudar cuidadosamente as oportunidades comerciais e chegar a uma decisão que coloque a organização na melhor posição para alcançar suas metas de longo prazo. Exemplos desse tipo de decisão de planejamento são:

- Decidir se convém lançar um projeto de desenvolvimento de novo produto.
- Decidir sobre o desenho de um processo de produção para um novo produto.
- Decidir como alocar matérias-primas escassas, serviços públicos, capacidade de produção e pessoal entre oportunidades comerciais novas e existentes.
- Decidir quais novas fábricas são necessárias e onde localizá-las.

As **decisões operacionais** devem resolver todas as questões referentes ao planejamento da produção para atender as exigências de produtos e serviços dos clientes. A principal responsabilidade das operações é pegar os pedidos de produtos e serviços dos clientes, gerados pela função de marketing, e entregá-los de maneira que haja *clientes satisfeitos* a custos razoáveis. Para pôr em prática essa responsabilidade, diversas decisões são tomadas. Exemplos desse tipo de decisão são:

TABELA 1.7	ESTRUTURA DESTE LIVRO EM TERMOS DE DECISÕES APO	
Tipo de Decisão	**Capítulo**	**Natureza do Conteúdo do Capítulo**
Parte II Decisões Estratégicas: Planejando produtos, processos, tecnologias e instalações	4. Produtos e Processos de Produção	Desenvolver planos de longo prazo incluindo planos de produto e design do processo
	5. Tecnologia de Produção	Escolher e administrar tecnologia de produção
	6. Planejamento da Capacidade de Longo Prazo e Localização de Instalações	Responder perguntas relativas a *quanto* e *onde* acerca da capacidade de de produção a longo prazo
	7. Layout das Instalações	Planejamento e organização de instalações
Parte III Decisões Operacionais: Planejamento da produção para atender a demanda	8. Sistemas de Planejamento da Produção	Planejamento agregado e programa mestre da produção
	9. Sistemas de Estoques com Demanda Independente	Planejar e controlar estoques de produtos acabados
	10. Sistemas de Planejamento das Necessidades de Recursos	Planejar materiais e necessidades de capacidade
	11. Planejamento e Controle do Chão de Fábrica	Decisões de curto prazo a respeito de o que produzir em cada centro de trabalho
	12. Planejamento e Programação de Operações de Serviços	Decisões sobre o planejamento e controle da produção de serviços
	13. Manufatura Just-in-Time (JIT)	Decisões sobre como planejar e operar sistemas de manufatura JIT
	14. Administração da Cadeia de Suprimentos	Administrar todas as facetas do sistema de materiais
Parte IV Decisões de Controle: Planejamento e controle de operações	15. Produtividade e Empregados	Planejar para a utilização eficaz e eficiente de recursos humanos nas operações
	16. Administração da Qualidade	Planejamento do sistema para obter a qualidade dos produtos e serviços
	17. Controle da Qualidade	Controle estatístico da qualidade
	18. Planejamento e Controle de Projetos	Planejamento e controle de projetos

- Decidir quanto estoque de produtos acabados manter para cada produto.
- Decidir quais produtos e quanto de cada um incluir no programa de produção do mês seguinte.
- Decidir se convém aumentar a capacidade de produção no próximo mês fazendo com que o departamento de fundição trabalhe horas extras ou subcontratar parte da produção com os fornecedores.
- Decidir os detalhes de um plano para comprar matéria-prima para sustentar o programa de produção do próximo mês.

Essas decisões são fundamentais para o sucesso da função de produção e para a organização inteira.

As **decisões de controle** concentram-se em uma variedade de problemas nas operações. Os gerentes de operações sabem que, no dia-a-dia, seus trabalhadores nem sempre têm o desempenho esperado, a qualidade do produto pode variar, e a maquinaria de produção pode apresentar defeitos, e isso normalmente acontece quando menos se espera. Os gerentes de operações se envolvem em planejar, analisar e controlar atividades a fim de que um mau desempenho dos trabalhadores, qualidade inferior do produto e excessivas quebras de máquinas não interfiram na operação rentável do sistema de produção.

Exemplos desse tipo de decisão são:

- Decidir o que fazer se um departamento falhar em atingir sua meta de custo de mão-de-obra.
- Desenvolver padrões de custo de mão-de-obra para um design de produto revisado que está prestes a entrar em produção.
- Decidir quais devem ser os novos critérios de controle da qualidade para aceitação de um produto que sofreu uma mudança de design.
- Decidir com que freqüência deve ser feita a manutenção preventiva numa peça-chave da maquinaria de produção.

As decisões a respeito de trabalhadores, qualidade do produto e maquinaria de produção, quando tomadas em conjunto, podem ser o aspecto de maior relevo do trabalho de um gerente de operações.

Estrutura Baseada na Decisão Este livro está organizado em função da seguinte estrutura geral: **decisões estratégicas** — planejar produtos, processos e instalações; **decisões operacionais** — planejar a produção para atender a demanda; e **decisões de controle** — planejar e controlar operações. A Tabela 1.7 esboça o restante do livro em termos dessa estrutura.

Resumo Final

O Que os Fabricantes de Classe Mundial Estão Fazendo

Neste capítulo discutimos o surgimento da APO, definimos APO, falamos a respeito de desenvolvimentos históricos e contemporâneos na APO e apresentamos três maneiras de estudá-la. A Revolução Industrial, o período pós-Guerra Civil, a administração científica, as relações humanas e o behaviorismo, a pesquisa operacional e a revolução dos serviços representam importantes desenvolvimentos históricos na APO. Hoje, a competição global, os computadores, a tecnologia avançada de produção e as questões de responsabilidade social estão apresentando desafios para a APO e modelando a natureza dos sistemas de produção para o futuro.

A APO é em geral estudada de três maneiras: a produção como um sistema, a produção como uma função organizacional e a tomada de decisões na APO. Os sistemas de produção transformam insumos, como materiais, mão-de-obra, capital e serviços públicos, em saídas, que são os produtos e serviços da organização. Entender os conceitos de sistemas (insumos, produtos e subsistemas de transformação) leva a uma melhor administração desses sistemas. Estudar a produção como uma função organizacional ajuda a identificar a atividade de transformação numa variedade de organizações. Todas as organizações, independentemente de seus propósitos, têm funções de produção — departamentos onde o processo de transformação realmente ocorre. Estudar a tomada de decisões na APO demonstra como os gerentes de operações realizam seu trabalho. A análise das decisões estratégicas (planejamento de produtos, processos e instalações), as decisões operacionais (planejamento da produção para atender a demanda) e as decisões de controle (planejamento e controle de operações) foram descritas como uma maneira útil de visualizar a tomada de decisões na APO.

*Durante o curso deste livro, será importante entendermos o que as companhias internacionais mais bem administradas estão fazendo em relação a seus concorrentes. Chamaremos essas empresas de **fabricantes de classe mundial**. Focalizar esses fabricantes nos dará um insight sobre as abordagens mais avançadas para a estruturação, análise e administração de sistemas de produção. Para ajudar nesta tarefa, ao término de cada capítulo apresentaremos as idéias mais avançadas sobre os tópicos discutidos numa seção chamada **Resumo Final: O Que os Fabricantes de Classe Mundial Estão Fazendo**, que permitirá uma completa integração das idéias mais recentes sobre as questões importantes que os gerentes de operações enfrentam hoje.*

Questões de Revisão e Discussão

1. Defina *APO*.
2. Cite e descreva três cargos na APO. Quais são os prós e contras de uma carreira na APO?
3. O que foi a Revolução Industrial?
4. Que papel a colonização do Oeste americano desempenhou no desenvolvimento de fábricas no período pós-Guerra Civil?
5. Descreva a abordagem à administração do setor de produção de Frederick Winslow Taylor.
6. Quais os principais pioneiros na administração científica e quais foram suas contribuições?
7. Qual foi a abordagem de Henry Ford à produção em massa?
8. Quem eram os pesquisadores dos *estudos de Hawthorne*? Explique o impacto das relações humanas e do behaviorismo nos sistemas de produção atuais.
9. Quais as características da pesquisa operacional?

10. Em que medida as técnicas de pesquisa operacional são usadas nas organizações de negócios?
11. Qual o significado da expressão *revolução dos serviços*? Cite cinco indústrias de serviços. No Brasil, qual porcentagem aproximada do emprego e do PIB se origina no setor de serviços?
12. Quais os fatores que mais afetam a APO hoje?
13. Defina *sistema de produção*. Como o conceito de sistema de produção auxilia no entendimento da APO?
14. Quais são os insumos para os sistemas de produção? Como eles podem ser classificados?
15. Defina *subsistemas de transformação*. Como eles podem ser classificados?
16. Quais são as saídas (produtos) dos sistemas de produção?
17. Defina *subsistemas de controle*. Todas as organizações os têm? Descreva alguns deles. O que eles controlam?
18. Descreva os principais insumos, produtos e subsistemas de transformação das seguintes organizações: (a) negócio de lavagem a seco, (b) fábrica de computadores, (c) clínica médica, (d) corpo de bombeiros e (e) repartição pública.
19. Cite duas organizações que não têm funções de produção. Justifique sua resposta.
20. Quais os prováveis cargos dos altos gerentes de operações numa firma de venda a varejo e numa firma manufatureira? Compare e contraponha a natureza desses empregos.
21. Defina *decisão estratégica*. Dê um exemplo de decisão estratégica para: (a) um varejista, (b) um fabricante e (c) uma agência governamental.
22. Defina *decisão operacional*. Dê um exemplo de decisão operacional para: (a) um centro de computação, (b) uma universidade e (c) uma indústria.
23. Defina *decisão de controle*. Dê um exemplo de decisão de controle para: (a) um museu, (b) um návio e (c) um carrinho de cachorro-quente.
24. Defina *fabricante de classe mundial*.

TAREFAS NA INTERNET

1. Cada dia mais empresas estão oferecendo emprego em suas páginas da World Wide Web. Encontre na Internet duas empresas com lista de oferta de empregos com a função de administração da produção e operações. Imprima a página da Web que mostra listagens de emprego relevantes e inclua o site da empresa.
2. Na Internet, visite o site da revista *Fortune* (**www.fortune.com**) e localize as páginas da Web de Fortune 500. Encontre três empresas de serviços que não estão listadas na Tabela 1.4. Em qual categoria de indústria está cada companhia? Qual a classificação da revista *Fortune* para cada companhia?
3. O Institute for Operations Research and Management Sciences (INFORMS) é uma organização profissional para pessoas da indústria e dos meios acadêmicos que estão interessadas em pesquisa operacional. Visite o site do grupo (**www.informs.org**) e localize as páginas da Web correspondentes a sua publicação *OR/MS Today*. Encontre e resuma brevemente um dos artigos on-line dessa publicação.

ESTRATÉGIAS DE OPERAÇÕES
Usando a Qualidade, o Custo e o Serviço Como Armas Competitivas

Introdução

Condições dos Negócios Globais de Hoje
   Realidade da Competição Global
      Natureza Mutável dos Negócios Mundiais • Empresas Internacionais • Alianças Estratégicas e Compartilhamento da Produção • Flutuação das Condições Financeiras Internacionais
   Desafios da Qualidade, Serviço ao Cliente e Custos
   Tecnologia Avançada da Produção
   Crescimento Contínuo do Setor de Serviços
   Escassez de Recursos de Produção
   Questões de Responsabilidade Social
      Impacto Ambiental • Impacto sobre os Empregados

Estratégias de Operações
   Prioridades Competitivas da Produção
   Elementos de Estratégia de Operações
      Posicionando o Sistema de Produção • Foco da Produção • Planos de Produto/Serviço • Planos de Processo e Tecnologia de Produção • Alocação de Recursos para Alternativas Estratégicas • Planos de Instalações: Capacidade, Localização e Layout
   Estratégia de Operações nos Serviços
      Características dos Serviços e Produtos Manufaturados • Prioridades Competitivas para os Serviços • Posicionando Estratégias para os Serviços

Formando Estratégias de Operações
   Evolução das Estratégias de Posicionamento
   Vinculação de Estratégias de Operações e de Marketing
   Variedade de Estratégias Pode Ser Algo Bem-Sucedido

Competitividade das Empresas Manufatureiras Americanas

Resumo Final: O Que os Fabricantes de Classe Mundial Estão Fazendo

Questões de Revisão e Discussão

Tarefas na Internet

Estudo de Caso
   Estratégia de Operações para a CSI na Europa

Estratégias na Dell e no Correio Americano

Toda organização precisa de um plano que descreva como ela atingirá suas metas e competirá de maneira bem-sucedida por clientes. Não obstante a Dell Computer e o Correio dos Estados Unidos serem organizações muito diferentes, observe nos excertos seguintes, extraídos de seus sites, como ambos têm como prioridade a satisfação do cliente.

A Dell Computer Corporation foi fundada em 1984 com um plano arrojado: levar os computadores certos diretamente a nossos clientes com o mais baixo preço possível. Fazer negócios diretamente faz mais do que diminuir preços ao eliminar a figura do revendedor — garante uma relação sem precedentes entre o cliente e o fabricante, relação essa que se estende ao longo do ciclo de vida do produto.

Quer você esteja comprando um sistema de computador para uso próprio ou para sua empresa, a Dell oferece uma solução personalizada para atender suas necessidades. Cada computador é construído de acordo com suas especificações e recebe o suporte de um serviço de qualidade superior ao longo de sua vida.

A Dell enfatiza a satisfação do cliente ao integrar efetivamente todas as operações. Por meio de Pesquisa e Desenvolvimento (P&D) cooperativos, a empresa se beneficia do conhecimento de seus destacados parceiros em tecnologia. Os parceiros da Dell se beneficiam do retorno recebido das vendas e dos grupos de suporte de tecnologia, bem como das dezenas de milhares de chamadas telefônicas que a Dell recebe diariamente.

Uma filosofia de negócios de construir sob encomenda (build-to-order) combina o conhecimento em profundidade das exigências dos clientes com as mais recentes ofertas de tecnologia. A estrutura de manufatura infinitamente flexível e a superior administração de estoques da Dell possibilitam que a empresa atenda rapidamente pedidos únicos de clientes, de qualquer tamanho e complexidade.

A Dell acredita que nenhuma abordagem é mais adequada para entender e atender as necessidades de diferentes segmentos de clientes do que seu modelo de negócios de relação direta. A empresa continuará a trabalhar para garantir sua posição entre os líderes da indústria através de suas relações diretas com seus clientes, sua comprovada estratégia de distribuição e sua focalização em operar eficientemente.

****

As metas fundamentais do Correio dos Estados Unidos são satisfazer o cliente, melhorar a eficiência dos empregados e da organização, e melhorar o desempenho financeiro. O Correio terá como função básica a obrigação de oferecer serviços postais para unir a nação por meio da correspondência pessoal, educacional, literária e comercial das pessoas. Ele deve oferecer serviços rápidos, confiáveis e eficientes em todas as regiões, e prestar serviços postais a todas as comunidades.

Somos o Correio. Nossa meta é evoluirmos para o primeiro lugar como provedor de comunicações postais no século XXI, oferecendo produtos e serviços de tal qualidade que sejam reconhecidos como os melhores da América. Crescer através da criação de um valor único representa uma opção clara. Requer disciplina, prioridades e focalização nas exigências dos clientes.

Quatro estratégias principais motivam o princípio de crescimento: comprometer-se com a excelência do serviço ao cliente, praticar uma administração de custos agressiva, tornar-se uma empresa em crescimento no século XXI e criar valor único para o cliente.

O plano estratégico de cinco anos do Correio, iniciado em 1998, reflete um processo de coleta de dados, análise e tomada de decisões que se desenvolveu dentro do ambiente mais desafiador que o Correio já enfrentou. A competição sofisticada, novas tecnologias, globalização e elevadas expectativas do cliente levaram-nos a dirigir o Correio para um caminho transformador de melhoria do processo, maior produtividade e compromisso com a inovação de produtos e serviços. Somente percorrendo esse caminho — que nos levará tanto ao aumento de receita como à contenção de custos — será garantida a capacidade do Correio para realizar sua missão histórica de oferecer um serviço confiável e eficiente.

Desde o início do século XX até a década de 1970 a manufatura americana enfatizou os mercados de massa, os designs de produtos padrões e a produção de volumes elevados. No final da década de 1970 e nos anos 1980, as companhias japonesas começaram a oferecer produtos de consumo de qualidade superior, confiabilidade e durabilidade a um custo menor do que aquele que os fabricantes americanos podiam oferecer. A capacidade de as empresas japonesas evitarem o *trade-off*[1] percebido há muito tempo entre custo e qualidade do produto foi atribuída a suas estratégias de manufatura.

Quando empresas americanas começaram a perder fatias de mercado para empresas japonesas em muitas indústrias durante a década de 1980, deu-se um frenético esforço nos Estados Unidos para imitar as práticas manufatureiras japonesas. Inúmeras empresas americanas enviaram gerentes e executivos para visitar fábricas japonesas e observar suas práticas de manufatura. Controle estatístico do processo, just-in-time, qualidade da fonte, *Kanbans*, círculos da qualidade, empregados flexíveis e reduções de configuração são algumas das práticas japonesas adotadas nos Estados Unidos durante a década de 1980 como parte de um esforço nacional posto em prática pelas companhias americanas para "colocar-se em dia" com os novos padrões de desempenho manufatureiro estabelecidos pelos japoneses.

Conforme algumas empresas descobriram mais tarde, simplesmente copiar as táticas operacionais de outras companhias não basta para obter sucesso numa indústria competitiva. Não obstante muitos desses esforços de melhoria nos Estados Unidos terem sido implementados com sucesso, inúmeros outros não o foram. E mesmo quando as práticas japonesas foram implementadas de maneira bem-sucedida por empresas americanas, nem sempre ocorreu aumento da lucratividade. De acordo com Michael Porter, conhecido autor da Harvard Business School, "O problema fundamental é falta de distinção entre eficácia operacional e estratégia". **Eficácia operacional** é a capacidade de executarmos atividades de operações similares melhor do que nossos concorrentes. Na década de 1980, as empresas japonesas estavam bem adiante das americanas em termos de eficácia operacional.

Para se obter superior desempenho nos negócios, tanto eficácia operacional quanto boa estratégia são fundamentais. Não obstante Porter destacar que as empresas devam melhorar continuamente sua eficácia operacional para obter maior lucratividade, ele também salienta que é muito difícil para as empresas competirem de maneira bem-sucedida a longo prazo baseando-se *apenas* na eficácia operacional: "Os concorrentes podem imitar rapidamente técnicas administrativas, novas tecnologias, melhorias em insumos e maneiras superiores de satisfazer as necessidades dos clientes". Quando as empresas americanas e de outros países adotaram as práticas de administração japonesas, a vantagem competitiva de superior eficácia operacional nas empresas japonesas simplesmente desapareceu na década de 1990 para muitos produtos.

Colocando de maneira simples, a estratégia competitiva de uma empresa é seu plano a respeito de como a empresa competirá no mercado. Uma estratégia eficaz é crucial em mercados competitivos. Para sustentar uma vantagem competitiva, as empresas devem decidir como se diferenciar dos concorrentes, o que Porter descreve como a "essência da estratégia": *O desafio para os gerentes de operações não é apenas melhorar as operações de suas empresas para conseguir eficácia operacional, mas também determinar como a eficácia operacional pode ser usada para obter uma vantagem competitiva sustentável.*

O competitivo ambiente empresarial de hoje se modifica muito mais rápido do que há 20 anos, principalmente em virtude dos avanços tecnológicos. Para permanecer competitivas, as empresas de hoje devem ser flexíveis e ser capazes de reagir rapidamente às mudanças em seu ambiente e às mudanças nas exigências do cliente. Em nosso ambiente global rapidamente mutável, administrar operações eficazmente é mais importante do que nunca para o sucesso competitivo. Desenvolver uma estratégia competitiva que explore as potencialidades das operações de uma empresa pode criar uma poderosa vantagem competitiva. Mas, antes de desenvolver uma estratégia competitiva que seja eficaz, vamos examinar alguns dos fatores que estão exercendo impacto sobre a formulação de estratégias de negócios atualmente.

CONDIÇÕES DOS NEGÓCIOS GLOBAIS DE HOJE

O ponto de partida para desenvolver uma estratégia de negócios — um plano de ação de longo prazo para realizar a missão corporativa — é estudar as condições dos negócios de hoje como base para prever as de amanhã. A Tabela 2.1 relaciona alguns dos desenvolvimentos que afetam as condições dos negócios atuais.

---

[1] *Trade-off* (ou *tradeoff*): troca ocasional ou transigência em face de duas alternativas, geralmente de igual valor; acordo, acerto; concessão; compensação (a Curva de Phillips mostra o tradeoff entre inflação e desemprego). (N. do T.)

TABELA 2.1	FATORES QUE AFETAM AS CONDIÇÕES DOS NEGÓCIOS GLOBAIS DE HOJE
	1. Realidade da competição global
	2. Desafios da qualidade, serviço ao cliente e custos
	3. Tecnologia avançada da produção
	4. Crescimento contínuo do setor de serviços
	5. Escassez de recursos de produção
	6. Questões de responsabilidade social

REALIDADE DA COMPETIÇÃO GLOBAL

Apresentamos a seguir uma discussão a respeito da natureza mutável dos negócios mundiais empresas internacionais, alianças estratégicas e compartilhamento de produção, e flutuação das condições financeiras internacionais.

Natureza Mutável dos Negócios Mundiais O produto interno bruto (PIB) dos Estados Unidos, a quantia gasta a cada ano em bens e serviços, é superior a US$ 8 trilhões. É o maior PIB do mundo, o que torna o mercado americano um grande alvo para produtos/serviços estrangeiros. *As empresas do mundo inteiro estão exportando agressivamente seus produtos/serviços para os Estados Unidos. Em parte devido a essa aumentada concorrência interna, muitas empresas americanas estão se voltando para mercados estrangeiros para angariar lucros.*

Comunicações, transportes e políticas de comércio global relativamente amigáveis tornaram mais fáceis as exportações para as empresas americanas. E os recentes desenvolvimentos políticos e econômicos têm tornado os mercados estrangeiros atraentes. Representantes de 108 nações trabalharam para desenvolver o Acordo Geral de Tarifas e Comércio (GATT), voltado a facilitar o comércio internacional entre fronteiras nacionais. Países da Europa Oriental e a antiga União Soviética estão tentando migrar para economias baseadas no mercado, e isso está criando mercados atraentes. O crescimento do PIB de países como o Brasil, o México, a Malásia, a Coréia do Sul, a China e Taiwan é maior do que o do PIB dos Estados Unidos, e seus crescentes mercados são alvos para produtos e serviços americanos. A Tabela 2.2 ilustra a extensão desse aumento nas exportações feitas por empresas americanas.

*Todo esse comércio internacional resultou numa economia global que interliga as economias de todas as nações naquilo que foi denominado **aldeia global**. Os eventos econômicos de um país afetam as economias de todos os países. Por exemplo, uma recessão num país afeta todos os outros países, e a recessão de um país pode tornar-se uma recessão global.*

A formação de blocos comerciais certamente afeta o comércio internacional. A União Européia (UE) da Europa Ocidental permite que quase todos os bens fluam sem restrições através das fronteiras da UE; além disso, padrões de produto válidos em toda a UE têm sido adotados, e impostos de valor agregado foram padronizados. O Acordo de Livre Comércio da América do Norte (NAFTA) une o Canadá, os Estados Unidos e o México num grande bloco de negócios que aumentou o comércio entre as fronteiras desses países. O comércio dentro e através desses blocos jamais será o mesmo. As empresas serão obrigadas a se reestruturar e modernizar para competir num bloco em vez de fazê-lo em escala nacional para sobreviver. Embora muitos detalhes ainda estejam sendo trabalhados nesses acordos, eles são a onda do futuro e certamente vão aumentar as oportunidades de comércio internacional.

Um dos mais importantes novos mercados para os fabricantes de classe mundial e fornecedores de serviços é a China. Tendo a maior população mundial, de 1,2 bilhão de pessoas, o potencial da China como importadora de bens e serviços estrangeiros é imenso. Por exemplo, considere esta afirmação: "A China representa o maior mercado de aviões comerciais do mundo e se espera que ela encomende 1.900 aviões no valor de US$ 140 bilhões ao longo dos próximos 20 anos". A General Motors Corporation prevê que em 25 anos o mercado da China se rivalizará com os 15 milhões de novos veículos vendidos a cada ano nos Estados Unidos.

TABELA 2.2 — CRESCIMENTO DAS EXPORTAÇÕES AMERICANAS

País	Exportações em 1996 (bilhões de dólares)	Aumento Percentual desde 1992	País	Exportações em 1996 (bilhões de dólares)	Aumento Percentual desde 1992
Canadá	134,2	48	Bélgica	12,5	28
Japão	67,6	41	China	12,0	62
México	56,8	40	Austrália	12,0	35
Inglaterra	31,0	36	Itália	8,8	1
Coréia do Sul	26,6	82	Malásia	8,5	96
Alemanha	23,5	11	Suíça	8,4	84
Taiwan	18,5	21	Arábia Saudita	7,3	2
Cingapura	16,7	74	Tailândia	7,2	80
Holanda	16,7	21	Filipinas	6,1	122
França	14,5	−1	Israel	6,0	47
Hong Kong	14,0	54	Espanha	5,5	−1
Brasil	12,7	121	Cuba	5,5	348

Fonte: Government Information Sharing Project, Oregon State University.

Lenta, mas seguramente, a China está permitindo que mais empresas estrangeiras compitam em seus mercados, antes fechados. O impacto futuro da China sobre o comércio global não pode ser ignorado. Nas palavras de Randy Yeh, diretor da Lucent Technologies: "A China é simplesmente irresistível. Se você quiser ser um jogador global, tem de estar aqui".

O Instantâneo da Indústria 2.1 discute os prováveis impactos sobre as empresas americanas para o caso de a China abrir seus mercados a estrangeiros.

Empresas Internacionais *Essa dinâmica de mercado cria a necessidade de **empresas internacionais**, aquelas cujo escopo de operações se espalha pelo globo enquanto compram, produzem e vendem em mer-*

INSTANTÂNEO DA INDÚSTRIA 2.1

ABERTURA DE MERCADOS DA CHINA A EMPRESAS ESTRANGEIRAS

Empresas do mundo inteiro estão considerando os possíveis impactos que resultariam se a China se unisse à Organização Mundial do Comércio (OMC) e passasse a se comportar conforme as regras que regem o comércio no resto do mundo.

A entrada da China na OMC, composta de 132 países, algo que provavelmente ainda demorará alguns anos, poderia fazer aquilo que duas décadas de reforma econômica não fizeram: abrir o maior mercado mundial. Eis aqui alguns dos impactos previstos para as empresas dos Estados Unidos.

- Os produtos americanos se tornariam mais baratos, alguns da noite para o dia, e outros gradualmente, ao longo de períodos de até 15 anos.
- Muitos produtos, especialmente carne e outros produtos agrícolas, poderiam ser vendidos na China pela primeira vez.
- Indústrias inteiras, atualmente fechadas a estrangeiros ou restritas a poucas companhias escolhidas a dedo, poderiam ser abertas quando cotas de importação, exigências para licenciamento e outras barreiras caíssem. Entre os setores que mais provavelmente se beneficiariam podemos incluir as empresas de telecomunicações, de seguros, de filmes e TV, atividades bancárias, venda a varejo e títulos mobiliários.
- As incômodas restrições que defendem os produtores chineses da concorrência e enchem os cofres do governo com o recolhimento de impostos começariam a cair.
- As companhias americanas estariam livres para fixar preços para seus próprios produtos e para vender diretamente aos consumidores. Atualmente elas precisam passar por distribuidores chineses e outros intermediários.

Fonte: James Cox, "The Push to Open China: World Trade Status Would Benefit Foreign Firms". *USA Today*, 27 de outubro de 1997.

TABELA 2.3 — AS 20 MAIORES EMPRESAS PRIVADAS MUNDIAIS

Companhia (país de origem)	Valor de Mercado (bilhões de dólares)
General Electric (Estados Unidos)	214
Royal Dutch/Shell (Holanda/Inglaterra)	178
Coca-Cola (Estados Unidos)	167
Nippon Telegraph & Telephone (Japão)	153
Exxon (Estados Unidos)	153
Microsoft (Estados Unidos)	151
Merck (Estados Unidos)	125
Intel (Estados Unidos)	116
Toyota Motor (Japão)	112
Philip Morris (Estados Unidos)	108
Novartis (Suíça)	99
Procter & Gamble (Estados Unidos)	96
Bank of Tokyo–Mitsubishi (Japão)	94
International Business Machines (Estados Unidos)	90
Johnson & Johnson (Estados Unidos)	86
Roche Holding (Suíça)	85
Bristol-Myers Squibb (Estados Unidos)	81
Pfizer (Estados Unidos)	77
Wal-Mart Stores (Estados Unidos)	77
Glaxo Wellcome (Inglaterra)	74

Fonte: "The Global Giants". *Wall Street Journal*, 18 de setembro de 1997. Reimpresso com permissão de *Wall Street Journal* © 1997, Dow Jones & Company, Inc. Todos os direitos internacionais reservados.

cados internacionais. A Tabela 2.3 relaciona as 20 maiores empresas públicas mundiais. Aqui estão três exemplos de empresas que mudaram o quartel-general de unidades comerciais inteiras para países estrangeiros:

- A AT&T, empresa americana, mudou sua sede de operações com telefone com fio para a França.
- A DuPont, empresa americana, mudou sua sede de operações com produtos eletrônicos para o Japão.
- A Hyundai Electronics Industries, empresa sul-coreana, mudou sua sede de operações com computadores pessoais para os Estados Unidos.

Na mutante natureza da competição global, empresas internacionais do mundo inteiro procuram oportunidades de lucros relativamente desobrigados dos encargos impostos por fronteiras nacionais.

Nem sempre temos conhecimento dos países de origem dos produtos que compramos diariamente. Para ilustrarmos esse ponto, faça o teste da Tabela 2.4. Alguns futuristas, como Alvin Toffler, acham que as empresas internacionais estão evoluindo na direção de **corporações sem pátria**; não mais americanas, japonesas ou alemãs, mas, ao contrário, empresas não nacionais. Elas são "corporações sem pátria, globalizadas, com operações, acionistas e gerentes de todas as partes do mundo, amplamente indiferentes à localização, exceto em função da eficiência econômica". Qual é mais americano: um Chrysler Eagle Summit feito na Diamond-Star Motors da Mitsubishi, em Illinois, que contém 52% de peças americanas, ou um Toyota Camry feito em Georgetown, Kentucky, com 74% de peças americanas? A operação da Honda em Ohio é japonesa? A IBM no Japão é uma empresa americana? Aqueles que não concordam, como Robert Kuttner, acreditam que esse ponto de vista é "em certo sentido emergente — mas prematuro, pois a maioria das companhias estrangeiras ainda pensa em termos do que é bom para seus países de origem".

Alianças Estratégicas e Compartilhamento da Produção Diante dos acordos internacionais de livre comércio e da formação de blocos comerciais regionais, o escopo de operações de uma empresa tende a deslocar-se do nacional para o global. *Esses deslocamentos criam a necessidade de formação de **alianças estratégicas** (joint ventures[2]) entre companhias internacionais, para explorarem oportunidades comerciais globais.* Embora as razões para as alianças estratégicas possam diferir, muitas vezes elas são moti-

---

[2]*Joint venture:* associação de capital; participação acionária; empreendimento conjunto. (N. do T.)

TABELA 2.4	TESTE: QUAL É O PAÍS DE ORIGEM DA EMPRESA-MÃE DESTES PRODUTOS?

1. Eletrodomésticos Braun: (a) Suíça (b) Alemanha (c) Estados Unidos (d) Japão
2. Canetas Bic: (a) Japão (b) Alemanha (c) Estados Unidos (d) França
3. Sorvete Haägen-Dazs: (a) França (b) Suécia (c) Inglaterra (d) Estados Unidos
4. Televisores RCA: (a) Japão (b) Estados Unidos (c) França (d) Coréia
5. Camisas Arrow: (a) Tailândia (b) Itália (c) Estados Unidos (d) França
6. Chocolate Godiva: (a) França (b) Bélgica (c) Suíça (d) Estados Unidos
7. Vaselina: (a) Estados Unidos (b) França (c) Inglaterra/Holanda (d) Alemanha
8. Pneus Firestone: (a) Japão (b) Estados Unidos (c) Alemanha (d) França
Respostas: **1**. c (Gillette Company), **2**. d (Bic SA), **3**. c (Grand Metropolitan PLC), **4**. c (Thomson SA), **5**. d (Bidermann International), **6**. d (Campbell Soup Company), **7**. c (Unilever PLC), **8**. a (Bridgestone).

Fonte: "Buying American an Elusive Goal". *Houston Chronicle*, 2 de fevereiro de 1992.

vadas pelo produto ou tecnologia de produção, acesso ao mercado, capacidade de produção ou associação de capital e a convicção de que uma joint venture será mais bem-sucedida do que se empresas individuais seguirem por conta própria. O Instantâneo da Indústria 2.2 descreve alianças estratégicas entre algumas das maiores empresas internacionais. Espera-se que esses empreendimentos cresçam no futuro.

Há outros exemplos de alianças dentro dos Estados Unidos. Assim, metade da Sematech, corporação sem fins lucrativos baseada em Austin, Texas, formada em 1987, é financiada por 12 companhias americanas, e a outra metade é financiada pelo governo americano. O objetivo da Sematech era desenvolver uma tecnologia e métodos que tornassem os fabricantes americanos de chips de computador competitivos no mercado global. O Lawrence Livermore National Laboratory, de Livermore, Califórnia, contratou negócios com a GM, Boeing, Caterpillar e outras para disseminar e implementar suas tecnologias.

Parece que as leis antitruste nos Estados Unidos estão sendo interpretadas de maneira mais liberal para permitir maior cooperação entre as empresas americanas em face da competição global. Há muito tempo as empresas japonesas praticam o keiretsu, que é a ligação de empresas em grupos industriais. Um **keiretsu** financeiro reúne empresas com posse cruzada (*cross-holding*) de ações, vendas e compras dentro do grupo, e consultas. Um keiretsu de produção, exemplificado pela Toyota Motor Corporation, é uma cadeia de relações de longo prazo que se integram entre um grande fabricante e seus fornecedores.

Compartilhamento de produção, *termo cunhado por Peter Drucker, significa que um produto pode ser projetado e financiado por um país, a matéria-prima pode ser produzida em muitos países e embarcada para outros para processamento adicional, as peças podem ser embarcadas para um outro país ainda, e o produto pode ser vendido através de mercados internacionais.* O país que tivesse qualidade mais elevada e menor custo para uma atividade executaria essa parte da produção do produto. Como um exemplo de compartilhamento de produção, o automóvel Festiva, da Ford, foi desenhado nos Estados Unidos, projetado pela Mazda no Japão e construído pela Kia na Coréia do Sul principalmente para o mercado americano. Também, o automóvel Mercury Capri foi desenhado pela Ghia and Italdesign na Itália e montado na Broadmeadows, Austrália, principalmente com componentes japoneses, para o mercado americano.

Flutuação das Condições Financeiras Internacionais   Inflação, taxas de câmbio flutuantes, taxas de juros flutuantes, volatilidade dos mercados financeiros internacionais, dívidas nacionais imensas de muitos países e enormes desequilíbrios comerciais entre parceiros comerciais internacionais criaram condições financeiras complexas para os negócios globais.

TABELA 2.5 — DÓLAR *VERSUS* IENE E MARCO ALEMÃO

Ano	Iene por Dólar	Marco por Dólar
1975	305	2,7
1980	215	2,0
1985	210	2,4
1990	135	1,6
1995	85	1,4

Consideremos o efeito das mudanças nas taxas de câmbio da moeda. Os Estados Unidos, a Alemanha e o Japão são os três maiores exportadores mundiais. A Tabela 2.5 ilustra a grande variação nas taxas de câmbio da moeda entre esses três parceiros comerciais. A importância da queda no valor do dólar americano no período de 1975-1995 é impressionante. Por exemplo, *se levarmos em conta somente os efeitos das mudanças nas taxas de câmbio,* um produto produzido e vendido nos Estados Unidos por US$ 1 seria vendido no Japão por 210 ienes em 1985 e por 135 ienes em 1990 — uma queda de preço de 36%:

INSTANTÂNEO DA INDÚSTRIA 2.2

ALIANÇAS ESTRATÉGICAS

- A National Semiconductor Corporation dos Estados Unidos uniu-se à Toshiba Corporation do Japão. A Toshiba uniu-se à Samsung Electronics Company da Coréia, e a IBM uniu-se à Toshiba para entrar nos negócios de chips de memória *flash*[a].
- A Texas Instruments está unindo-se à Acer Inc. num investimento de US$ 400 milhões na fábrica de *wafers*[3] em Taipé[b].
- Em contratos que totalizam mais de US$ 750 milhões, a IBM constrói computadores para a Hitachi e para a CompuAdd, placas de PC para fabricantes de computador e sistemas de diagnóstico para a Chrysler; a TI constrói computadores para a Sun Microsystems e Gateway 2000 e conexões de rede para a Wellfleet Communications e Cisco Systems; e a DEC faz placas de computador para a Apple Computer e sistemas de entretenimento em vôo para a Hughes Aircraft[c].
- A General Motors Corp., incapaz de romper o difícil mercado sul-coreano sozinha, está em conversações com os fabricantes de automóveis da Coréia do Sul para encontrar um parceiro local para ajudá-la a vender e comercializar seus carros nesse mercado sem que para isso seja necessário criar um sistema de distribuição inteiramente novo. Rumores apontam a Kia Motor Corp. como um provável sócio[d]. A GM também está planejando uma *joint venture* em Shenyang, no nordeste da China, com um sócio local, a First Auto Works, para desenvolver um veículo tipo cavalo mecânico[e].
- A Renault SA da França assinou uma carta de intenções com a cidade de Moscou para fabricar até 120 mil veículos anualmente na fábrica de automóveis AO Moskvich na periferia da capital russa. Os franceses pretendem assumir 50% da joint venture e investir US$ 350 milhões[f].

Fontes:
[a] "Toshiba, Samsung to Jointly Develop Memory Chip". *Wall Street Journal*, 22 de dezembro de 1992. "Chip Makers Sign 'Flash Agreement'". *New York Times*, 15 de dezembro de 1992. "IBM, Toshiba to Build Memory Chips". *Houston Chronicle*, 22 de junho de 1992.
[b] "TI to Spend $500 Million to Expand Italian Plant". *Dallas Morning News*, 1º de dezembro de 1994.
[c] "Farming Out Work". *Business Week*, 17 de maio de 1993.
[d] "GM Seeks Partnership with a South Korean Auto Maker". *Wall Street Journal*, 2 de outubro de 1997.
[e] "Auto Giants Build a Glut of Asian Plants, Just as Demand Falls". *New York Times*, 5 de novembro de 1997.
[f] "Renault Plans Auto-Manufacturing Venture in Moscow". *Wall Street Journal*, 3 de novembro de 1997.

---

[3]*Wafer:* lâmina. (1) Material básico da fabricação de circuitos integrados. É uma fatia de aproximadamente 0,85 mm de espessura, retirada de um cilindro de cristal de silício com 7,5 a 15 cm de diâmetro. A lâmina passa por uma série de passos de fotomáscara, gravação e implantação. (2) Pequeno cartucho de fita magnética com elo contínuo, usado para armazenamento de dados. (N. do T.)

$$\text{Preço de 1990} = \text{preço de 1985} \times \frac{\text{taxa de câmbio de 1990}}{\text{taxa de câmbio de 1985}}$$

$$= \text{preço de 1985} \times \frac{135}{210} = \text{preço de 1985} \times 0{,}643$$

Por outro lado, um produto que foi produzido e vendido no Japão por 210 ienes em 1985 foi vendido nos Estados Unidos nesse mesmo ano por US$ 1, e em 1990 por US$ 1,56 — um aumento de preço de 56%:

$$\text{Preço de 1990} = \text{preço de 1985} \times \frac{\text{taxa de câmbio de 1985}}{\text{taxa de câmbio de 1990}}$$

$$= \text{preço de 1985} \times \frac{210}{135} = \text{preço de 1985} \times 1{,}56$$

E a variação entre o dólar e o marco alemão, nesse mesmo período, foi quase tão grande quanto a variação entre o dólar e o iene.

A queda no valor do dólar nas duas últimas décadas teve efeitos de longo e de curto prazo tanto para produtores americanos como para estrangeiros. Em curto prazo, os preços de produtos e serviços americanos no exterior caíram e a demanda aumentou. Por outro lado, os preços dos produtos japoneses nos Estados Unidos se elevaram, mas não tanto quanto o esperado, porque margens de lucro menores foram aceitas numa tentativa de manter a fatia de mercado. Dois efeitos notáveis resultaram:

1. Em combinação com o *crescente temor do aumento das cotas de importação americanas,* as companhias estrangeiras, especialmente as japonesas, compraram ou adquiriram fábricas nos Estados Unidos para sustentar sua produção/serviços para os mercados americanos. A indústria automobilística foi agudamente afetada por esse desenvolvimento. Na década de 1990, os fabricantes japoneses forneceram cerca de 40% a 50% dos automóveis americanos, incluindo importações, transplantes, joint ventures e peças.
2. Muitos dos fabricantes japoneses passaram a fabricar produtos de preços mais elevados. Com isso, empresas da Coréia do Sul e de outros países começaram a preencher o espaço deixado pelos japoneses no mercado americano de bens de consumo duráveis de preços baixos.

Uma lição importante foi aprendida: *os fabricantes americanos devem desenvolver estratégias de negócios com flexibilidade incorporada, mantendo um olhar atento nos mercados financeiros internacionais. Eles devem estar preparados para adotar rapidamente estratégias de mudança quando as condições financeiras mundiais se modificarem.* Algumas decisões estratégicas, como construir uma fábrica em solo estrangeiro, são difíceis, mas normalmente os riscos podem ser reduzidos. Fábricas menores e mais flexíveis podem ser construídas, ou fornecedores estrangeiros podem ser usados para fornecer matérias-primas, peças ou produtos. Além disso, planejamento e previsão cuidadosos devem ser partes integrantes do planejamento estratégico, a fim de que o maior número de mudanças possível possa ser antecipado e considerado em planos de longo prazo.

DESAFIOS DA QUALIDADE, SERVIÇO AO CLIENTE E CUSTOS

Algumas companhias americanas são especialmente vulneráveis à competição global atual, em virtude da qualidade de produção, serviço ao cliente e custos de produção.

Na década de 1980, quando a qualidade de bens e serviços americanos era considerada inferior, muitas empresas americanas deram uma olhada séria em si mesmas. Elas determinaram que a competição na década de 1990 e além seria baseada principalmente na qualidade dos produtos e serviços. Concluíram que a propaganda verbal e os slogans do passado não mais bastariam para sobreviver. A meta de **qualidade adequada** teve de ser substituída pelo objetivo de **qualidade de produto e serviço perfeito.**

Hoje muitas empresas americanas, tanto pequenas como grandes, adotaram a *administração da qualidade total (TQM)* como um modo de vida, e suas organizações jamais serão as mesmas. A TQM faz com que uma empresa se concentre nas necessidades do cliente e estruture a organização de acordo com essas necessidades. Foram necessárias mudanças fundamentais na maneira pela qual os negócios operavam antes que a TQM pudesse ser efetiva. A cultura organizacional inteira teve de se modificar a fim de que todas as atividades da organização pudessem ser reorientadas e comprometidas com o ideal de qualidade perfeita. As pessoas que faziam os produtos e entregavam os serviços tiveram de receber poder, para que pudessem atingir o objetivo de qualidade perfeita. E o objetivo de qualidade perfeita teve de assumir precedência sobre todos os outros objetivos. A organização como um todo precisou abraçar o compromisso com a melhoria contínua da qualidade de produtos e serviços. Como resultado, atualmente a qualidade de muitos produtos e serviços americanos se iguala ou excede a de seus concorrentes estrangeiros.

Para obter sucesso na competição global no século XXI, as empresas devem desenvolver produtos inovadores e reagir rapidamente às necessidades do cliente. As antigas formas de organização burocrática idealizadas para fornecer estabilidade são incompatíveis com a natureza sempre mutante dos negócios globais de hoje. Na década de 1990, grandes empresas americanas descobriram que, em suas próprias formas organizacionais burocráticas, a inovação de produto e a receptividade ao cliente eram inadequadas. Empresas como a General Motors e a International Business Machines desmontaram unidades empresariais inteiras, tornando-as negócios empreendedores (entrepreneurial) autônomos, a fim de que pudessem competir com concorrentes menores, mais agressivos. Em outras empresas, como a Xerox, a Motorola, a Chrysler, a General Electric e a AT&T, as estruturas organizacionais foram modificadas para acomodar as mudanças. Antigas estruturas organizacionais verticais foram transformadas em estruturas mais horizontais ao eliminar camadas inteiras de administração. Equipes interdisciplinares receberam autoridade para tomar decisões para projetar, desenvolver e introduzir novos produtos, poupando tempo e dinheiro e reagindo melhor ao mercado. Mais progresso é necessário, e as empresas americanas pretendem sobreviver no futuro. Discutiremos o serviço ao cliente mais tarde, ainda neste capítulo.

Na década de 1980, diversos fatores combinados começaram a exercer grande pressão sobre os fabricantes americanos para reduzirem os custos e os preços de seus produtos. Um impacto importante era que os fabricantes asiáticos comercializavam produtos com preços mais baixos em mercados americanos. Por exemplo, na década de 1980 o custo com mão-de-obra dos três maiores fabricantes de automóveis americanos era US$ 1.500 a mais por automóvel se comparado com o custo dos fabricantes japoneses. Na década de 1990, os fabricantes de automóveis americanos tinham eliminado completamente a vantagem de custo desfrutada pelos fabricantes de automóveis japoneses, como a Toyota e a Honda. Outro desenvolvimento nas décadas de 1980 e 1990 teria efeitos dramáticos sobre os preços e os custos de produtos americanos. Varejistas gigantes, como a Wal-Mart, Kmart, Home Depot, Target, Circuit City, Costco, Toys 'R' Us e outros empurraram os concorrentes mais fracos para fora do mercado. Esses varejistas representam um mercado tão imenso que exercem uma grande influência sobre os fornecedores fabricantes para que modernizem suas operações e reduzam os custos e os preços. Perder um contrato de abastecimento para a Wal-Mart porque um competidor tem um preço mais baixo é um enorme incentivo para reduzir os preços continuamente. Muitas empresas americanas reagiram a esses desafios tentando reduzir os custos de gastos gerais e de mão-de-obra.

Custos de gastos gerais são todos os não diretamente relacionados à produção e à venda de produtos e serviços. Empresas americanas mais antigas tendem a tornar-se inchadas com grandes staffs, fábricas supérfluas, programas de atendimento à saúde e de aposentadoria caros, e folhas de pagamento excessivas. Para reduzir os custos de gastos gerais, muitas delas anunciaram mudanças nos programas de atendimento à saúde e de aposentadoria, dispensas de pessoal e fechamento de instalações na década de 1990.

Alguns analistas acreditam que o elevado custo de oferecer atendimento à saúde para trabalhadores idosos e aposentados seja o fator que mais encarece a produção de automóveis nas fábricas americanas em relação às japonesas. Relata-se que a GM e a Ford gastam mais em atendimento à saúde do que com aço. A DuPont assumiu encargos de US$ 5 bilhões para oferecer atendimento à saúde a seus aposentados.

Durante a década de 1990, muitas empresas americanas eliminaram empregos num esforço para serem mais eficientes e competitivas. Entre 1990 e 1997, a General Motors cortou 107 mil empregos, e a GM planeja dispensar mais 42 mil empregados em 2002, à medida que modernizar suas fábricas-chaves e fechar instalações mais antigas. Outras empresas, como a Eastman Kodak, Raytheon, Levi Strauss, Boeing, Citicorp, Xerox, AT&T, IBM, Johnson & Johnson e Westinghouse, anunciaram dispensas de empregados e fechamentos de instalações na década de 1990. Esse *downsizing* de grandes corporações visava

---

[4]*Bottom line:* (1) Última linha num relatório financeiro, que mostra o lucro e o prejuízo. (2) O ponto decisivo; o ponto essencial ou de destaque: (2a) consideração principal ou a mais importante; (2b) considerações financeiras (como custo ou prejuízo); (2c) o resultado final. (N. do T.)

não só reduzir os custos de gastos gerais e melhorar a *bottom line*[4], mas também fazer uma sangria em unidades comerciais inteiras, a fim de que elas se tornassem mais flexíveis, empreendedoras (entrepreneurial) e receptivas às necessidades do cliente em seus negócios centrais. Embora o downsizing corporativo pareça haver se desacelerado no final da década de 1990, muitas empresas continuam a anunciar cortes de emprego enquanto tentam competir mais eficientemente na economia global.

Muitas empresas americanas implementaram durante as décadas de 1980 e 1990 a **manufatura just-in-time (JIT)** para reduzir os custos de estoque e tornar suas operações mais flexíveis. No JIT, as matérias-primas chegam exatamente quando são necessárias em cada passo do processo de produção, reduzindo assim os níveis de estoque, tempo de produção e desperdício.

Para reduzir os custos de mão-de-obra, a maioria das empresas se concentra nos preços da mão-de-obra, produtividade da mão-de-obra e automação de fábrica. Empresas da Alemanha, Canadá, Estados Unidos e Japão têm preços de mão-de-obra substancialmente mais elevados do que a Coréia do Sul, Taiwan e o México. *Como os países que têm custo de mão-de-obra elevado competem? Três abordagens são comuns: mudar a produção para países que possuem um custo de mão-de-obra mais baixo, negociar preços de mão-de-obra mais baixos com os sindicatos e trabalhadores e automatizar operações para reduzir o número de trabalhadores.* Nas décadas de 1970 e 1980, empresas do Japão e dos Estados Unidos mudaram grande parte da produção para Taiwan, Coréia do Sul, México e outros países em que o custo da mão-de-obra é mais baixo. Isso era especialmente verdadeiro em relação a operações do tipo **mão-de-obra intensiva**, que tinham um custo de mão-de-obra elevado em relação a outros custos. E, nos Estados Unidos, temos visto concessões sem precedentes no valor dos salários por parte dos sindicatos de trabalhadores. As empresas japonesas têm investido fortemente em sistemas de produção automatizados, assim como muitas empresas americanas estão investindo em projetos de automação. Conforme discutiremos posteriormente, a automação não somente reduz o custo da mão-de-obra e aumenta a produtividade como também pode melhorar a qualidade do produto e agilizar a introdução de novos produtos.

Mas empresas de países que têm custo de mão-de-obra baixo também têm investido em métodos de produção de alta tecnologia (*high-tech*) mais novos. A Hyundai, a Gold Star e a Samsung da Coréia do Sul exemplificam aquilo que acontece quando empresas de um país que tem baixo custo de mão-de-obra usam os métodos de produção de alta tecnologia mais recentes. Elas podem tornar-se fornecedoras internacionais de tudo, desde carros pequenos a DVDs, a preços baixos.

Qualidade, flexibilidade e desempenho de custo ruins têm resultado direta ou indiretamente em perda de empregos nos Estados Unidos. Os americanos têm perdido seus empregados por duas razões principais: primeiro, alguns produtos anteriormente produzidos nos Estados Unidos agora o são em países estrangeiros — esta é uma perda de empregos direta; segundo, equipamentos de produção com tecnologia avançada têm sido instalados para superar os problemas de qualidade e custo em empresas americanas. Isso eliminou alguns empregos da produção e criou outros, que exigem novas habilidades que faltam à força de trabalho existente. Esses eventos criaram a necessidade de estratégias de negócios das empresas americanas para lidar com a **demissão de trabalhadores, reestruturação de empregos** e **retreinamento de trabalhadores.**

Tudo isso acontece quando os gerentes tentam administrar uma força de trabalho sempre mutável e cada dia mais diversa. Diversidade no tocante a raça, origem étnica e sexo, mas também no que se refere a idade, orientação sexual, deficiências físicas e mentais, origem socioeconômica e até modo de vida. Nos Estados Unidos, por exemplo, os aspectos demográficos estão caminhando para uma diversidade cada dia maior: de uma população de 150 milhões em 1950, composta de 90% de brancos, para uma de 250 milhões em 1990, com 80% de brancos e um número crescente de idosos hispânicos e asiático-americanos. O desafio não é somente lidar com a diversidade, mas também usá-la como uma força para tornar as empresas mais competitivas. Discutiremos isso mais detalhadamente no Capítulo 15.

Muitas empresas americanas aceitaram o desafio de melhorar a qualidade de produtos e serviços, serviço ao cliente e custo; muitas mais devem fazê-lo se quiserem sobreviver. Um caminho para responder a esse desafio passa pela automação.

TECNOLOGIA AVANÇADA DA PRODUÇÃO

O uso da automação na produção é um dos desenvolvimentos que mais afetaram a manufatura e os serviços no século XX. A Tabela 2.6 descreve alguns dos sistemas avançados de produção.

Tabela 2.6 — Alguns Sistemas de Produção de Alta Tecnologia (High-Tech)

Termo	Definição e Descrição
Projeto auxiliado por computador (CAD)	Software e hardware especializados para permitir que engenheiros projetem produtos diretamente em terminais de computador. Podem estar vinculados a sistemas de computador maiores, a fim de que os projetos possam ser comunicados a outros. Empresas como a General Electric, Texas Instruments, Exxon, Eastman Kodak, Xerox, General Motors, Boeing, DuPont e Caterpillar têm esses sistemas.
Manufatura auxiliada por computador (CAM)	Sistemas de computador especializados que convertem as informações CAD em instruções para a maquinaria de produção automatizada. A CAM não está tão bem desenvolvida como o CAD. O hardware, como por exemplo os microprocessadores, que são o cérebro da maquinaria automatizada, está disponível, mas o software necessário para converter os projetos em instruções de manufatura completas não está tão amplamente disponível.
Sistemas flexíveis de manufatura (FMS)	Grupos de máquinas automatizadas que são controladas por computadores. Esses grupos produzem uma variedade de produtos na mesma maquinaria. Os computadores dão as instruções, os robôs manipulam as peças e materiais, e as configurações de máquina são modificadas automaticamente para produzir diferentes produtos. A instalação de medidores de eletricidade da General Electric de New Hampshire produz 2 mil diferentes medidores no mesmo equipamento flexível e é um exemplo dessa abordagem.
Sistemas de armazenamento e recuperação automatizados (ASRS)	Armazéns controlados por computador que incluem substituição automática de peças, remoção automática de peças quando necessário na produção ou embarque e transporte automático de peças para dentro e para fora do armazém.
Sistemas de identificação automáticos (AIS)	Códigos de barras, freqüências de rádio ou caracteres óticos que são desenhados para representar dados são lidos por *scanners* que transmitem dados para os computadores. Um exemplo desses sistemas pode ser visto em muitas caixas de supermercados. Os códigos de barras constantes nos itens são passados pelo scanner, e o preço, a descrição do item, o número de estoque e outros dados são lidos e armazenados num computador para ser processados.

Tanto para pequenas como para grandes organizações, esses sistemas de máquinas estão revolucionando muitas fábricas e operações de serviços nos Estados Unidos e em outros países pelo mundo afora. *Não obstante o custo inicial desses ativos ser elevado, os benefícios vão além de uma redução nos custos da mão-de-obra. Alguns de seus benefícios incluem o aumento da qualidade de produtos/serviços, a redução da sucata e de custos de materiais, respostas mais rápidas às necessidades do cliente e introdução mais rápida de novos produtos e serviços.*

O Japão produz e usa cerca de 2/3 da maquinaria de produção automatizada mundial. Sistemas de produção automatizados estão disponíveis a qualquer empresa do mundo atualmente. Isso significa que as fábricas e operações de serviço nos Estados Unidos não podem usar a tecnologia de produção automatizada como uma vantagem competitiva de *longo prazo*, porque a competição estrangeira também tem acesso a essa tecnologia. Mas não investir nessa tecnologia pode colocar as fábricas e operações de serviços americanas numa desvantagem competitiva a longo prazo, e retardar seria desastroso.

Para alguns fabricantes americanos, esses sistemas de alta tecnologia podem formar uma parte importante de suas estratégias de negócios para permanecerem competitivos na competição global. Para outros, o custo da admissão ao jogo pode tornar-se proibitivo. Estudaremos mais sobre esses sistemas avançados de produção no Capítulo 5.

CRESCIMENTO CONTÍNUO DO SETOR DE SERVIÇOS

O surgimento de uma variedade de organizações privadas e públicas para oferecer serviços a nossa crescente população é um dos fatos mais instigantes a respeito da economia de hoje. Um setor de serviços crescente, entretanto, não significa necessariamente um setor de manufatura decadente. E é importante reconhecer as inter-relações entre os setores de manufatura e serviço.

O setor manufatureiro nos Estados Unidos permaneceu constante em aproximadamente 20% a 21% do PIB americano ao longo das três últimas décadas, enquanto a porcentagem de emprego total na manufatura caiu cerca de 20% e está rumando para os 15%. Alguns especulam que o setor manufatureiro nos Estados Unidos caminha para parecer bastante com o setor de agricultura, que emprega somente 3% da mão-de-obra total americana, mas produz tanto alimento que o governo paga para alguns produtores não produzirem. *Embora o número de empregos na manufatura esteja caindo, isso resulta de uma maior produtividade ao fazer as coisas melhor, sem diminuir a produção. Isso é exatamente o que o setor de manufatura nos Estados Unidos tem feito para sobreviver em guerras competitivas — e o setor de serviços nos Estados Unidos também terá de se modernizar e melhorar suas operações se quiser sobreviver.*

Muitas empresas de serviços existem somente porque o setor de manufatura compra seus serviços; desse modo, um setor de manufatura forte e vigoroso é necessário para sustentar o setor de serviços. As empresas de serviços em indústrias como as da construção, controle de poluição, publicidade, publicações, serviços comerciais, serviços financeiros, seguros, hotelaria, atendimento à saúde, atividades bancárias, telecomunicações, serviços públicos, ferrovias e transporte em caminhões não poderiam sobreviver sem um setor manufatureiro saudável. Em seu livro *Manufacturing Matters: The Myth of the Post-Industrial Economy,* Cohen e Zysman afirmam que os empregos em serviços vinculados à manufatura elevaram a porcentagem de empregos que dependem da manufatura de aproximadamente 20% para algo entre 40% e 60% nos Estados Unidos.

Similarmente, muitas companhias manufatureiras vendem alguns de seus produtos para empresas de serviços; dessa forma, um setor de serviços robusto sustenta o setor de manufatura. Além disso, muitas inovações tecnológicas foram desenvolvidas primeiro na manufatura e se demonstraram cruciais para manter competitivos os serviços. *Essa rede de inter-relações entre serviços e manufatura invoca a expressão* **economia de serviços**, *porque muitos serviços evidentemente não poderiam existir sem um forte setor manufatureiro, e o inverso, indubitavelmente, é verdadeiro.* Devemos reconhecer o setor de serviços como uma grande e crescente presença na economia americana. Se o setor de serviços nos Estados Unidos quiser prosperar, entretanto, à semelhança do setor manufatureiro, ele deve continuar a melhorar a qualidade, a flexibilidade e o custo. As empresas de serviços americanas não estão imunes à concorrência estrangeira. Entre os dez maiores bancos no mundo, um deles é americano e oito são japoneses, e a maior empresa de propaganda no mundo é japonesa. Há um número enorme de exemplos de má qualidade de serviços: sua camisa volta da lavanderia com um botão quebrado; uma semana depois do pagamento de uma exorbitante conta na oficina, aquele sinistro ruído reaparece no motor de seu carro; o representante do serviço de atendimento ao cliente diz que dará um retorno a você, e não o faz; um caixa automático engole seu cartão. Esses lembretes de que nem tudo é perfeito nas operações de serviços motivam-nos a desenvolver maneiras mais eficazes de administrar as operações de serviços.

Muitos gerentes de operações estão empregados no setor de serviços, e por certo esse número crescerá ainda mais. Esses gerentes estão adaptando algumas das abordagens de planejamento, análise e controle dos sistemas de manufatura para os serviços, e, em consequência, os sistemas de serviços melhoraram. Por exemplo, o Methodist Hospital, em Houston, desenvolveu um sistema de controle de estoques muito eficiente. O gerente que o desenvolveu, no entanto, teve seu primeiro contato com um sistema nesses moldes na Armco Steel Corporation. Muitas das abordagens desenvolvidas na manufatura, porém, não são facilmente aplicadas nos serviços, e novas abordagens devem ser desenvolvidas e testadas.

O que é necessário nos serviços, talvez mais do que em qualquer outro lugar, é uma maneira mais eficiente de desenvolver estratégias de operações. Isso será discutido mais tarde, ainda neste capítulo.

ESCASSEZ DE RECURSOS DE PRODUÇÃO

A escassez de recursos de produção sempre trará dores de cabeça aos gerentes de operações. Certas matérias-primas, como o titânio e níquel, carvão, gás natural, água, produtos derivados do petróleo e outros recursos, ficam periodicamente indisponíveis, e provavelmente se tornarão mais escassas no futuro.

INSTANTÂNEO DA INDÚSTRIA 2.3

LIMPAR COMPENSA

Companhia	Mudança de Manufatura	Benefício
AT&T	Processo de limpeza de placa de circuitos.	Eliminou a utilização de produtos químicos destruidores da camada de ozônio, reduziu os custos de limpeza em US$ 3 milhões ao ano.
Carrier	Reforçou o corte de metal e redesenhou peças de condicionadores de ar.	Eliminou solventes tóxicos, reduziu os custos de manufatura em US$ 1,2 milhão ao ano.
Clairol	Em vez de água, passou a usar bolhas de espuma para a lavagem de tubos na manufatura de produtos para tratamento dos cabelos.	Reduziu em 70% o desperdício de água, economizando US$ 240 mil anualmente em custos de remoção.
W. R. Grace	Reformulou solventes e mudou o processo na operação de selagem e vedação.	Reduziu o lixo tóxico em 50%.
3M	Desenvolveu um adesivo para fitas de fechamento de caixas que não exige solventes.	Eliminou a necessidade de adquirir US$ 2 milhões em equipamentos de controle da poluição.
Polaroid	Eliminou o mercúrio das baterias. Modernizou as instalações de produtos químicos fotográficos.	As baterias agora são recicláveis. Reduziu a geração de refugo em 31% e os custos de remoção em US$ 250 mil por ano.
Reynolds Metals	Substituiu as tintas à base de solventes por tintas à base de água nas instalações de embalagem.	Reduziu as emissões em 65% e economizou US$ 30 milhões em equipamentos de produção.
Union Carbide	Desenvolveu um sistema que substitui os solventes por dióxido de carbono como meio para pulverizar tinta.	Reduziu as emissões orgânicas voláteis em 72%.
Whyco Chromium	Mudou o processo que torna porcas, parafusos e outros prendedores resistentes à corrosão.	Reduziu o custo do processo em 25%.
Compaq	Instalou um novo processo para usar um fluxo não corrosivo para unir componente a placas de circuitos de computador.	Eliminou a emissão de produtos químicos destruidores da camada de ozônio em suas fábricas.

Fontes: "Some Companies Cut Pollution by Altering Production Methods". *Wall Street Journal*, 24 de dezembro de 1990. "Compaq Plans to End Its Use of Ozone-Eater". *Houston Chronicle*, 13 de junho de 1991.

Dada a oferta finita desses recursos escassos para as empresas e dada uma demanda sempre crescente, uma questão importante na formação da estratégia de negócios é como alocar esses recursos entre oportunidades de negócios.

QUESTÕES DE RESPONSABILIDADE SOCIAL

As atitudes nas salas de diretoria nos Estados Unidos em relação à responsabilidade social estão evoluindo do fazer aquilo que é um direito legal das empresas para fazer aquilo que é certo. Embora as razões para essa evolução sejam variadas e complexas, estes fatores são considerados importantes:

1. **Atitudes do consumidor.** Há uma crescente evidência de que consumidores e grupos de consumidores estão influenciando as empresas para agirem com responsabilidade. Essa influência é sentida, por exemplo, em resoluções apresentadas em reuniões de acionistas, preferências do con-

INSTANTÂNEO DA INDÚSTRIA 2.4

RECICLAGEM E CONSERVAÇÃO NA INDÚSTRIA

- O McDonald's está construindo uma nova lanchonete em Westland, Michigan, que incorporará um sistema de aquecimento e resfriamento geotérmico que usa as temperaturas naturais constantes da Terra presentes no subsolo[a].
- Em virtude do fato de muitos adesivos causarem problemas em usinas de reciclagem de papel, a 3M projetou um adesivo único em seus blocos de anotações Post-It que se dissolve em água e é lavado nas primeiras etapas do processo de reciclagem[b].
- Inúmeras empresas encontraram maneiras interessantes de reciclar o segundo material plástico mais usado no mundo, o cloreto de polivinil (PVC). A Collins & Aikman Floorcoverings, sediada na Geórgia, o transforma em revestimento para carpetes, pisos industriais, barreiras sonoras para auto-estradas e tabiques náuticos[c].
- A DuPont desenvolveu conjuntamente o 3GT, um tecido de poliéster bioprojetado (*bioengineered*) feito de amido de milho que tem um custo menor do que o poliéster à base de petróleo e que pode ser reciclado indefinidamente.
- A Sonoco criou uma "lata de papel" retangular para a Lipton Iced Tea que é 70% reciclável.
- A 3M desenvolveu um revestimento plástico para a Marinha para substituir a pintura em caminhões, navios e trens. Ele é mais leve do que a tinta — o que leva a uma eficiência de combustível maior.
- A S. C. Johnson reformulou o inseticida Raid, transformando-o de uma fórmula à base de solvente para uma fórmula à base de água.
- A Toyota está introduzindo um carro híbrido que atinge 106 km/h numa combinação de gasolina e eletricidade.
- A Finkl & Sons, forjadora de aço de Chicago, recicla mais de 95% de seu refugo sólido e reduziu o uso de energia em 36,4% no decorrer de 10 anos, o que a torna uma das forjadoras mais eficientes do mundo.
- A British Petroleum investiu US$ 160 milhões no desenvolvimento de energia solar e construiu uma vila olímpica completamente movida a energia solar para os Jogos de Verão de 1998 na Austrália[d].
- A Xerox Corp. deu vários passos para reduzir o refugo de fábrica e reusar ou reciclar mais peças. Os projetistas reduziram o número de produtos químicos usados em cartuchos de impressora de 500 para 50, para facilitar a reciclagem. Os cartuchos de impressão e *toners* agora vêm com rótulos de reembolsos previamente pagos, aumentando os índices de reutilização em até 60%. Os esforços pouparam à Xerox um valor estimado de US$ 200 milhões ou mais por ano[e].

Fontes:
[a] "Michigan McDonald's Will Have Geothermal Power". *Houston Chronicle*, 19 de outubro de 1997.
[b] "Paper Recyclers Unable to Lick Sticky Problem". *USA Today*, 7 de outubro de 1997. "Post-Its Don't Cause Problems for Recycling Mills". *USA Today*, 22 de outubro de 1997.
[c] "Demand Increases: Reprocessed PVC Products Create a New Market". *Dallas Morning News*, 10 de outubro de 1997.
[d] "Leading the Way to Eco-Friendly Profits". *Business Week*, 10 de novembro de 1997.
[e] "A Society That Reuses Almost Everything". *Business Week*, 10 de novembro de 1997.

sumidor por produtos/serviços socialmente responsáveis, ações legais por responsabilidade pelo produto, e atividades políticas e de formação de *lobbies*.

2. **Regulamentos do governo.** Agências e leis municipais, estaduais e federais são uma força crescente de controle do comportamento dos negócios nos Estados Unidos. A EPA (Environmental Protection Agency), a OSHA (Occupational Safety & Health Act), a Clean Air Act de 1990, regulamentos estaduais e federais de segurança do produto, e a Family Leave Act de 1993 são apenas algumas das muitas restrições sociais impostas aos negócios.

3. **Interesse próprio.** As empresas estão mudando seu comportamento em relação às questões sociais porque perceberam que os lucros a longo prazo serão maiores se agirem com responsabilidade.

Serão discutidas a seguir estas categorias de questões de responsabilidade social: impactos ambientais e impactos sobre os empregados.

INSTANTÂNEO DA INDÚSTRIA 2.5

ESFORÇOS AMBIENTAIS NA COMPAQ

A Compaq tem o compromisso de conduzir os negócios de uma maneira que seja compatível com o meio ambiente e proteger a qualidade das comunidades nas quais a empresa opera. A Compaq assumiu um papel de liderança ao desenvolver programas focalizados na eficiência de energia em produtos e prédios, reciclagem, projeto voltado ao meio ambiente, redução de refugo e controle ambiental. As operações da Compaq minimizam os subprodutos de manufatura, e a empresa tem implementado programas de reciclagem para vários materiais, incluindo papel de escritório, latas de alumínio e sucata eletrônica.

Em junho de 1997, a Compaq recebeu o prêmio 1997 World Environment Center´s Gold Medal for International Achievement em reconhecimento por seu desempenho e compromisso com o meio ambiente, saúde, liderança em segurança. Em março de 1997, pelo segundo ano consecutivo, a U.S. Environmental Protection Agency nomeou a Compaq "PC Partner of the Year". O prêmio reconhece os destacados esforços da Compaq para promover o Energy Star, programa que visa desenvolver computadores eficientes que reduzam o consumo de energia, e oferecer produtos cumpridores desse programa. A empresa também participa de outros programas, inclusive o Green Lights, para iluminação eficiente.

Eficiência de Energia
Como parte do Energy Star Computer Program da EPA, a Compaq participa ainda de um esforço voluntário para educar clientes e empregados em métodos que podem ser usados para reduzir o consumo de energia. Em 1995, 100% dos monitores de computadores portáteis e de mesa cumpriam o programa Energy Star, e a empresa incorporou recursos de economia de energia em 100% de seus PCs de mesa.

Reciclagem
As equipes de engenharia da Compaq estão avaliando ativamente alternativas para projetos de produto que facilitem o processo de desmontagem e reciclagem no final do ciclo de vida de um produto. A empresa chama esse esforço de Design for Environment (DFE) e está ampliando o programa para abranger todos os projetos de novos produtos. O programa DFE inclui elementos como utilização de energia, capacidade de reciclagem de materiais, uso de materiais reciclados, facilidade de desmontagem e facilidade de reciclagem para reduzir o impacto ambiental em cada etapa da vida do produto.

Tratamento de Lixo
A Compaq também desenvolveu e implementou um abrangente processo de revisão dos fornecedores quanto ao tratamento e reciclagem do lixo, o que inclui uma revisão *in loco* e controle do tratamento de lixo comercial, armazenagem, remoção e facilidades de reciclagem antes do uso. A meta desse programa é garantir que a Compaq identifique e use instalações de tratamento de lixo que operem de maneira correta.

Auditoria
A Compaq monitora continuamente as melhorias de seus programas ambientais através de auditorias formais, bem como de suas exigências da certificação International Standards Organization (ISO 14000).

Fonte: **www.compaq.com/inside/background/index.html**.

Impacto ambiental São muitas as preocupações com o ambiente global: camada de ozônio, florestas tropicais, aquecimento global, chuva ácida, derramamento de petróleo e produtos químicos, tratamento de lixo tóxico e radiativo, poluição do ar, do solo e da água, poluição visual e sonora, conservação da energia, redução de lixo em aterros sanitários, reciclagem de papel, vidro, alumínio e aço.

Os Instantâneos da Indústria 2.3, 2.4 e 2.5 descrevem o que algumas empresas americanas estão fazendo para proteger o ambiente global e preservar recursos naturais. Algumas empresas têm visto esses desenvolvimentos como oportunidades comerciais. Indústrias inteiramente novas foram criadas nos Estados Unidos para sustentar produtos e serviços relacionados ao meio ambiente. Essas indústrias fornecem produtos que variam de escovões para chaminés e equipamentos para limpar derramamentos de óleo a serviços de consultoria que oferecem orientação sobre o meio ambiente.

Com a tendência rumo a empresas internacionais e compartilhamento da produção, a necessidade de padronizar os regulamentos governamentais sobre o meio ambiente parece evidente; caso contrário, as empresas procurarão se instalar em países onde há menos regulamentação. É o que acontece, por exemplo, ao longo da fronteira entre os Estados Unidos e o México. A menos que as regulamentações ambientais entre esses dois países sejam padronizadas através do acordo do NAFTA, certamente o meio ambiente sofrerá nessa região. Algum progresso já foi obtido nos acordos internacionais, evidenciado por conferências em todo o mundo sobre proteção do meio ambiente e acordos internacionais regulamentando a liberação de clorofluorcarbonos industriais (CFCs) e sobre a redução da caça a baleias e golfinhos.

A International Organization for Standardization desenvolveu recentemente um conjunto de diretrizes ambientais chamada ISO 14000. Essas diretrizes ajudam uma empresa a desenvolver maneiras de administrar e controlar melhor o impacto de suas atividades, produtos ou serviços sobre o meio ambiente, com um foco na prevenção e melhoria contínua. Se uma empresa seguir as diretrizes e critérios da ISO 14000, ela poderá candidatar-se ao certificado ISO 14000.

Impacto sobre os Empregados A escassez de mão-de-obra, a pressão social e dos consumidores, a ética e as leis municipais, estaduais e federais trabalham em conjunto, nos Estados Unidos, para fazer com que as empresas desenvolvam programas de segurança e saúde dos empregados; práticas de contratação e promoção justas com respeito a idade, raça, cor, sexo, preferência religiosa e deficiências; programas de benefício que incluem atendimento à saúde para as famílias dos empregados; programas de creches para filhos de pais que trabalham; licenças do trabalho para grávidas; programas de atendimento aos idosos dependentes de empregados; planos de aposentadoria e outras políticas. Alguns programas são obrigatórios por lei e são supervisionados por agências governamentais; outros são assumidos voluntariamente. Grupos de interesse especial têm realizado boicotes contra os produtos/serviços de empresas consideradas não engajadas em tratamento justo dos empregados.

Esses programas são caros. *Os programas de benefício aos empregados são tidos como um dos principais fatores na vantagem de custo que as fábricas de automóveis japonesas desfrutam nos Estados Unidos e em outros países quando comparadas com as fábricas americanas.* Mas o moral, a produtividade, o recrutamento e a manutenção de empregados, a rotatividade de pessoal, a demanda de consumo de produtos de uma empresa e o custo da defesa contra ações legais e boicotes são todos afetados pelas políticas voltadas aos empregados. E a ética, o código de comportamento da empresa quanto àquilo que é considerado certo ou errado, também tem seu papel. Os benefícios ao empregado e os programas da empresa voltados ao empregado são todos de importância estratégica, porque a lucratividade a longo prazo é muito afetada.

À medida que nossa sociedade e o mercado global evoluem, mais e mais empresas têm declarado formalmente sua intenção de ser socialmente corretas. Consideremos o compromisso da Boeing com a boa cidadania corporativa: "Ofereceremos um ambiente de trabalho seguro e protegeremos o meio ambiente. Promoveremos a saúde e o bem-estar das pessoas da Boeing e de suas famílias. Trabalharemos com nossas comunidades fazendo trabalho voluntário, dando suporte financeiro à educação e a outras causas dignas".

ESTRATÉGIAS DE OPERAÇÕES

A Figura 2.1 mostra que as estratégias de operações derivam diretamente da missão corporativa e da estratégia de negócios.

Uma missão corporativa é um conjunto de metas de longo prazo únicas para cada organização e que inclui declarações sobre o tipo de negócio em que a empresa quer estar, quem são seus clientes, suas convicções básicas a respeito dos negócios e suas metas de sobrevivência, crescimento e lucratividade. ***Estratégia de negócios** é um plano de ação de longo prazo de uma organização e constitui um mapa de como realizar a missão corporativa.* Essas estratégias são incorporadas ao plano de negócios da empresa, que inclui um plano para cada área funcional dos negócios, inclusive produção, marketing e finanças. A estratégia de negócios é desenvolvida enquanto se considera uma avaliação das condições comerciais globais e as competências essenciais ou as fraquezas das unidades de negócios da empresa. As condições comerciais globais incluem fatores como análise dos mercados, análise da concorrência nesses mercados e desenvolvimentos econômicos, políticos, tecnológicos e sociais.

FIGURA 2.1 — DESENVOLVENDO UMA ESTRATÉGIA DE OPERAÇÕES

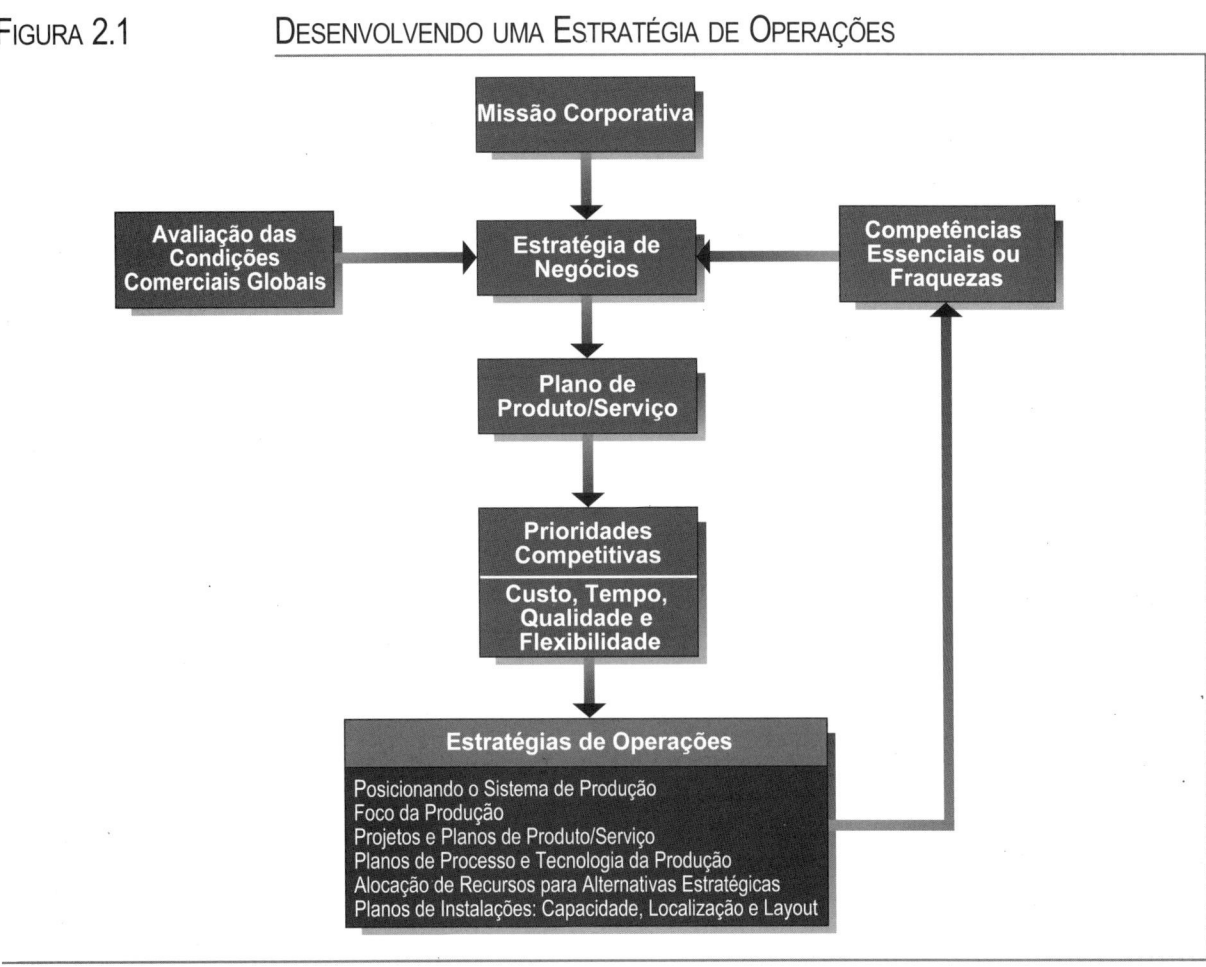

As **competências essenciais** ou fraquezas representam as grandes vantagens ou desvantagens para captar mercado. Elas incluem coisas como tecnologia avançada de produção, força de trabalho habilitada e dedicada, capacidade de pôr rapidamente novos produtos em produção, equipe de vendas talentosa ou equipamento de produção desgastado. O foco central na formação da estratégia de negócios é encontrar maneiras de capitalizar as competências essenciais de uma empresa e desenvolver novas competências, a fim de que fatias de mercado possam ser desenvolvidas ou aumentadas.

Estratégia de operações é um plano de ação de longo prazo para a produção de produtos e serviços de uma empresa e constitui um mapa daquilo que a função de produção deve fazer se quiser que suas estratégias de negócios sejam realizadas. As estratégias de operações incluem decisões sobre questões como quais novos produtos devem ser desenvolvidos e quando eles devem ser introduzidos na produção, quais novas instalações são necessárias e quando, quais novas tecnologias e processos de produção devem ser desenvolvidos e quando, e quais esquemas de produção serão seguidos para produzir os produtos e serviços.

Um melhor entendimento das prioridades competitivas nos ajudará a captar o escopo da estratégia de operações.

PRIORIDADES COMPETITIVAS DA PRODUÇÃO

A Tabela 2.7 relaciona as prioridades competitivas, que podem ser imaginadas como as coisas que os clientes querem dos produtos e serviços e, desse modo, podem ser usadas como ferramentas para captar fatias de mercado. Mas todas essas prioridades competitivas comumente não podem ser usadas para um único produto. Por exemplo, uma companhia pode não ser capaz de oferecer grande flexibilidade e, ao mesmo tempo, oferecer uma produção a um custo muito baixo. A estratégia de negócios determina a com-

TABELA 2.7   PRIORIDADES COMPETITIVAS

Prioridade Competitiva	Definição	Algumas Maneiras de Criar
Baixos custos de produção	Custo unitário de cada produto/serviço, inclusive custos de mão-de-obra, materiais e gastos gerais	Redesenho de produto Nova tecnologia de produção Aumento nos índices de produção Redução de sucata Redução de estoques
Desempenho de entrega	Entrega rápida	Maior estoque de produtos acabados Maiores índices de produção Métodos de entrega rápida
	Entrega no tempo certo	Promessas mais realísticas Melhor controle de produção de encomendas Melhores sistemas de informação

Produtos e serviços de alta qualidade	Percepções dos clientes quanto ao grau de excelência exibido pelos produtos e serviços	Quanto aos produtos e serviços, melhorar:
		  Aparência
		  Índices de mau funcionamento ou defeito
		  Desempenho e função
		  Capacidade de duração (reduzir desgaste)
		  Serviço pós-venda

Serviço ao cliente e flexibilidade	Capacidade de mudar rapidamente a produção conforme os produtos e serviços da encomenda e outros volumes de produção; receptividade ao cliente	Mudança no tipo de processo de produção usado Uso de CAD/CAM Redução da quantidade de trabalho em andamento através do JIT Aumento da capacidade de produção

binação dessas prioridades apropriada para cada produto ou serviço. *Assim que as prioridades competitivas são definidas para um produto ou serviço, a estratégia de operações deve determinar então o sistema de produção necessário para fornecer as prioridades para o produto ou serviço.*

ELEMENTOS DE ESTRATÉGIA DE OPERAÇÕES

A estratégia de operações será discutida nas seções que se seguem: (1) posicionando o sistema de produção, (2) foco da produção, (3) planos de produto/serviço, (4) planos de processo e tecnologia de produção, (5) alocação de recursos para alternativas estratégicas e (6) planos de instalações: capacidade, localização e *layout*.

Posicionando o Sistema de Produção *Posicionar o sistema de produção da atividade manufatureira significa escolher o tipo de design de produto, o tipo de sistema de processamento de produção e o tipo de política de estoques de produtos acabados para cada grupo de produtos na estratégia de negócios.*

Há dois tipos básicos de design de produto: personalizado e padrão. **Produtos personalizados** são projetados de acordo com as necessidades de determinados clientes. A escolha desse tipo de produto resulta em muitos produtos, produzidos em pequenos lotes e que normalmente requerem flexibilidade e entrega no tempo certo. Um sistema de tratamento de imagens de ressonância magnética para um grande hospital é um exemplo desse tipo de produto. A escolha de **produtos padrões** resulta somente em alguns modelos de produtos, produzidos continuamente ou em lotes muito grandes e que normalmente requerem entrega rápida e baixo custo de produção. Um televisor é um exemplo de produto padrão.

Há dois tipos clássicos de processos de produção: o focalizado no produto e o focalizado no processo. A **produção focalizada no produto** também é chamada produção de fluxo de linha, linha de produção e linha de montagem. Nessa abordagem, as máquinas e trabalhadores necessários para produzir um produto são agrupados num conjunto. Esse tipo de produção normalmente é melhor se houver somente alguns produtos padrões, cada um com um volume elevado. Linhas de montagem para a fabricação de automóveis são um bom exemplo desse sistema. Na produção focalizada no produto é difícil e caro mudar para outros produtos e volumes de produção, ou seja, esse sistema não é muito flexível. A **produção focalizada no processo** normalmente é melhor quando se produz muitos produtos únicos, cada um com um volume relativamente baixo. Cada departamento de produção costumeiramente executa somente um tipo de processo, como, por exemplo, pintura. Todos os produtos que necessitam ser pintados são transportados para o departamento de pintura. Os produtos personalizados normalmente exigem essa forma de produção. Nos sistemas focalizados no processo é relativamente fácil e barato mudar para outros produtos e volumes de produção, ou seja, esse sistema apresenta grande flexibilidade. Se uma estratégia de negócios exigir produtos personalizados cuja estratégia de marketing requer as prioridades competitivas de flexibilidade e entrega no tempo certo, então a produção focalizada no processo normalmente será a preferida.

Há dois tipos de políticas de estoque de produtos acabados: produzir para estoque e produzir sob encomenda. Na política de **produzir para estoque**, os produtos são produzidos antecipadamente e colocados em estoque. Então, quando são recebidas as encomendas dos produtos, eles são embarcados imediatamente do estoque. Na política de **produzir sob encomenda**, os gerentes de operações esperam até que tenham em mãos os pedidos dos clientes antes de produzir os produtos. Se a entrega rápida de produtos for importante, então a política de produzir para estoque normalmente é preferida, porque os produtos podem ser embarcados diretamente do estoque de produtos acabados. O McDonald's usa a política de produzir para estoque, e a Burger King usa a política de produzir sob encomenda ("Have it your way" — "Faça-o do seu jeito").

Escolhidos o tipo de design de produto, o processo de produção e a política de estoque de produtos acabados, grande parte da estrutura necessária de uma fábrica terá sido estabelecida. Para explorarmos ainda mais a estrutura de uma fábrica, consideremos seu escopo de operações.

Foco da Produção Um elemento importante da estratégia de operações é um plano para que cada instalação de produção seja especializada de alguma maneira. Wickham Skinner chama essa idéia de fábrica especializada de **fábrica focalizada**: "Uma fábrica que se concentra numa combinação (*mix*) de produtos estreita para um nicho de mercado particular terá um desempenho superior à planta convencional que tenta uma missão mais ampla. Uma vez que seus equipamentos, sistemas de suporte e procedimentos podem concentrar-se numa tarefa limitada para um conjunto de clientes, seus custos e, especialmente, seus gastos gerais provavelmente serão inferiores aos da planta convencional. Mas, o mais importante é que essa planta pode tornar-se uma arma competitiva, porque todo seu aparato está concentrado em realizar a tarefa de manufatura particular exigida pela estratégia e objetivo de marketing globais da empresa".

Nas décadas de 1970 e 1980 as fusões corporativas ocorreram num ritmo sem precedentes. Em muitas dessas fusões, as operações eram consolidadas em grandes, diversas e não focalizadas instalações de produção, e, muito freqüentemente, o resultado era que elas não faziam nada especialmente bem-feito. Hoje, muitas instalações de produção americanas tornaram-se menores e mais focalizadas. Um exemplo dessas instalações menores e mais especializadas são as miniusinas na indústria siderúrgica nos Estados Unidos. Essas usinas fazem uma reduzida variedade de produtos de aço, estão localizadas próximo a seus mercados, usam quantidades significativas de sucata de metal como estoque básico e comumente têm planos de incentivo para seus empregados. Menores e muito lucrativas, essas usinas estão captando uma fatia cada vez maior do mercado americano.

As fábricas e as instalações de serviços normalmente tornaram-se mais focalizadas de duas maneiras: especializando-se somente em alguns modelos de produto ou em alguns processos de produção. *É desejável que as fábricas e instalações de serviços sejam especializadas de alguma maneira, a fim de que não sejam vulneráveis a concorrentes menores e mais especializados que podem oferecer a um grupo particular de clientes um conjunto melhor de custo, entrega, qualidade e desempenho no atendimento.* Evidentemente, não podemos concluir que instalações menores são sempre melhores. As economias de escala têm de levar em consideração o tamanho das instalações de produção, como discutiremos no Capítulo 6. Todavia, a tendência para que as facilidades de produção nos Estados Unidos sejam grandes e pesadas é reconhecida.

| FIGURA 2.2 | ETAPAS NO CICLO DE VIDA DE UM PRODUTO |

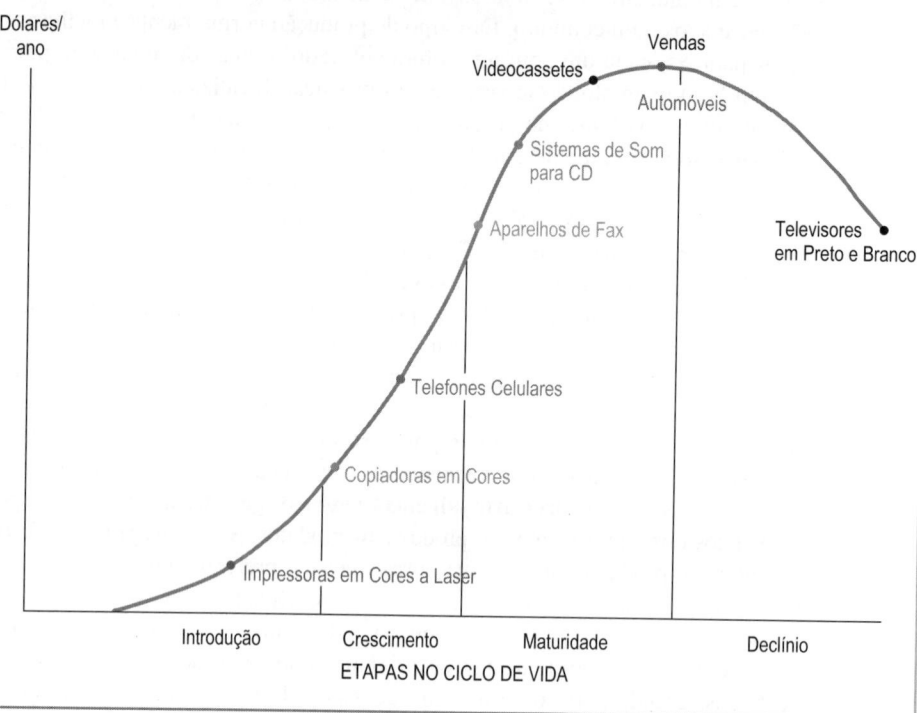

Planos de Produto/Serviço Uma parte importante da estratégia de negócios são planos para que novos produtos e serviços sejam projetados, desenvolvidos e introduzidos. A estratégia de operações é diretamente influenciada pelos planos de produto/serviço por estes motivos:

1. Quando os produtos são projetados, todas as características detalhadas de cada produto são estabelecidas.
2. Cada característica de produto afeta diretamente como o produto deve ser feito ou produzido.
3. A maneira como o produto é feito determina o design do sistema de produção, e o design do sistema de produção é o coração da estratégia de operações.

A Figura 2.2 ilustra o conceito de ciclo de vida de um produto. Quando o produto é projetado e desenvolvido, ele entra na etapa de **introdução** de seu ciclo de vida. Nessa etapa, as vendas se iniciam, a produção e o marketing estão se desenvolvendo, e os lucros são negativos. Os produtos bem-sucedidos deslocam-se para a etapa de **crescimento**, quando as vendas se elevam drasticamente, os esforços de marketing se intensificam, a produção se concentra em ampliar a capacidade de maneira suficientemente rápida para acompanhar a demanda e os lucros começam a aparecer. Em seguida vem a etapa de **maturidade**, quando a produção se concentra em altos volumes de produção, eficiência e baixos custos; o marketing se desloca para a promoção de vendas voltada a aumentar ou manter a fatia de mercado; e os lucros estão em seu pico. Finalmente, o produto entra na etapa de **declínio** de seu ciclo de vida, caracterizada por lucros e vendas decrescentes. Por fim, o produto pode ser retirado do mercado pela empresa ou substituído por novos produtos. Há uma tendência rumo ao encurtamento do ciclo de vida de produto, especialmente em indústrias como a de computadores e de bens de consumo. O encurtamento do ciclo de vida de produto apresenta três efeitos importantes:

1. A quantidade de dispêndios em projeto e desenvolvimento de produtos é aumentada.
2. Os sistemas de produção tendem a ser derrotados por modelos de produto continuamente mutantes. Isto cria a necessidade de sistemas de produção flexíveis que podem ser facilmente modificados para outros produtos.

3. As estratégias de operações enfatizam a capacidade de colocar rapidamente novos designs de produto no fluxo produtivo. O CAD/CAM, definido na Tabela 2.6, está permitindo que algumas empresas reajam com maior velocidade para projetar e redesenhar produtos e lançá-los em produção rapidamente.

Estudaremos mais sobre essas questões estratégicas no Capítulo 4.

Planos de Processo e Tecnologia de Produção Uma parte fundamental da estratégia de operações é a determinação de como os produtos serão produzidos. Isso envolve planejar cada detalhe dos processos e instalações de produção. A variedade de tecnologias de produção disponível para produzir tanto produtos como serviços é grande e está crescendo continuamente. Combinar equipamentos de produção de alta tecnologia com equipamentos convencionais e idealizar programas de produção globais eficientes é realmente desafiador. Uma tecnologia de produção automatizada é uma força importante a ser usada quando as empresas lutam para captar fatias de mercado globais. Os Capítulos 4 e 5 contêm os conceitos e questões importantes relacionados a esses tópicos.

Alocação de Recursos para Alternativas Estratégicas Todas as empresas de hoje têm limitados recursos disponíveis para produção. Moeda sonante e fundos de capital, capacidade, laboratórios de pesquisa, trabalhadores, engenheiros, máquinas, matérias-primas e outros recursos são escassos em graus variáveis para cada empresa. Uma vez que a grande maioria dos recursos é usada em produção, sua escassez exerce forte impacto sobre os sistemas de produção de grande parte das empresas. Esses recursos devem ser divididos, ou distribuídos, entre os produtos, unidades comerciais, projetos ou oportunidades de lucro, de uma maneira que maximize a realização dos objetivos das operações. As decisões referentes a alocações, restringidas pela disponibilidade de recursos, cons-tituem um tipo comum de decisão estratégica a ser tomada pelos gerentes de operações atualmente.

Planos de Instalações: Capacidade, Localização e Layout A capacidade de fornecimento de produção de longo prazo para produzir os produtos e serviços de uma empresa é uma parte crucial do estabelecimento da estratégia de operações. Os equipamentos de produção talvez precisem ser comprados, tecnologias de produção especializadas talvez devam ser desenvolvidas, novos equipamentos de produção talvez precisem ser feitos ou comprados e instalados, e novas fábricas talvez precisem ser construídas. As decisões envolvidas têm efeitos duradouros e estão sujeitas a grande risco. Se decisões ruins forem tomadas, ou se as circunstâncias mudarem depois que a empresa tiver se comprometido com certas alternativas, ela terá de arcar com os resultados dessas decisões durante muitos anos. O Capítulo 6 é dedicado a essas decisões. A organização interna dos trabalhadores, os processos de produção e os departamentos dentro das instalações são partes cruciais da estratégia de posicionamento que afetam a capacidade de fornecer o volume, a qualidade e o custo de produtos desejados. O Capítulo 7 é dedicado a essas decisões.

Se há algo que aprendemos com nossos concorrentes estrangeiros é que prestar atenção nos detalhes de produção pode ser de importância estratégica. Planejar eficientemente a força de trabalho, manter boas relações trabalhistas com os sindicatos de trabalhadores, administrar o pessoal, fazer entregas no tempo certo, manter-se no topo da administração da qualidade de produto e manter a maquinaria de produção em ótimas condições de trabalho podem, quando tomados em conjunto, ter igual importância para qualquer uma das decisões estratégicas discutidas nesta seção. Muitas dessas questões são tratadas nas Partes III e IV deste livro.

ESTRATÉGIA DE OPERAÇÕES NOS SERVIÇOS

A maior parte daquilo que foi discutido a respeito dos elementos da estratégia de operações nesta seção se aplica igualmente bem tanto à manufatura como aos serviços. Mas há algumas diferenças.

Características dos Serviços e Produtos Manufaturados A Tabela 2.8 descreve as características dos produtos manufaturados e serviços, mas ela realmente descreve os extremos máximos de um *continuum*, porque, enquanto algumas organizações de serviço são notavelmente diferentes de fabricantes, outras po-

| TABELA 2.8 | CARACTERÍSTICAS DE SERVIÇOS E PRODUTOS MANUFATURADOS |

Serviços	Produtos Manufaturados
Produtos intangíveis	Produtos tangíveis
Os produtos não podem ser mantidos em estoque	Os produtos podem ser mantidos em estoque
Contato extensivo com o cliente	Pouco contato com o cliente
Tempos de execução[5] breves	Tempos de execução longos
Uso intensivo de mão-de-obra	Uso intensivo de capital
Qualidade de serviços determinada subjetivamente	Qualidade de produtos determinada objetivamente

dem ser muito semelhantes. Além disso, tanto as empresas de manufatura como as de serviço podem fornecer tanto produtos tangíveis como serviços intangíveis. Assim, uma organização de serviços — por exemplo, um restaurante — fornece alimentos, um bem tangível, para os clientes. Um fabricante — por exemplo, uma fábrica de computadores — pode fornecer serviços aos clientes, como assistência técnica, crédito e consertos em campo — bens intangíveis.

Produtos manufaturados são **bens tangíveis** — eles têm forma física, podem ser vistos e tocados, e comumente devem ser remetidos aos clientes. Os serviços, entretanto, são **intangíveis** — normalmente eles não têm forma física. O consumo dos mesmos freqüentemente é simultâneo com a produção.

Uma vez que os produtos manufaturados são tangíveis, a demanda de clientes pode ser antecipada, e os produtos muitas vezes podem ser produzidos, transportados e mantidos em estoques até que os clientes precisem deles. Isso permite aos fabricantes optar por quando produzir os produtos. Estoques podem ser usados como um divisor entre uma capacidade de produção estável e uma demanda de clientes altamente variável. Isso significa que quando os níveis de produção são mantidos constantes, em períodos de baixa demanda os níveis de estoque de bens acabados se elevarão, e em períodos de pico de demanda os níveis de estoque de bens acabados cairão. Isso não quer dizer que todos os fabricantes têm estoques de bens acabados, porque alguns fabricantes preferem esperar até que haja uma demanda dos produtos para só então produzi-los e embarcá-los diretamente para os clientes. *Os serviços em geral não podem ser produzidos antecipadamente à demanda de clientes e devem ser entregues no tempo da demanda ou mais tarde. Isso significa que as operações de serviços devem planejar os níveis de produção para que sejam aproximadamente iguais à demanda de clientes.*

Normalmente os clientes não interferem no processo de manufatura. De fato, na maioria dos casos os clientes têm pouco contato com o sistema de manufatura. Nas operações de serviços, entretanto, os clientes rotineiramente se envolvem no processo de produção. Em hospitais, restaurantes e bancos, os clientes entram no processo de produção, são encaminhados para as operações de serviços necessárias e saem do sistema de serviços. Em quase todos os serviços, o pessoal de operações necessita de treinamento em habilidades pessoais, porque o elemento-chave do controle da qualidade é a maneira pela qual o pessoal do setor de operações realiza suas transações com os clientes.

Os clientes muitas vezes precisam encomendar com antecedência produtos manufaturados, porque os fabricantes podem demorar para embarcá-los desde o recebimento do pedido. Os serviços, por outro lado, muitas vezes precisam ser entregues imediatamente. Em serviços com padrões de demanda altamente irregulares, como, por exemplo, consultórios médicos, os clientes na maioria das vezes precisam marcar consultas antecipadamente, para nivelar a demanda, ou "pegar uma senha", para definir prioridades de processamento. Mas quando é exigido muito tempo para gerar o serviço, como, por exemplo, nas financeiras, os clientes devem fazer o pedido muito antes do serviço que é esperado.

Em geral imaginamos os fabricantes instalados a certa distância dos clientes, altamente automatizados e com uso intensivo de capital, como acontece nas montadoras de automóveis. Mas isso nem sempre é verdadeiro, como é o caso de uma pequena confecção de roupas. E normalmente imaginamos os serviços perto dos clientes e com uso intensivo de mão-de-obra. Mas o inverso também pode ser verdadeiro, como é o caso de uma companhia de serviços públicos de eletricidade.

Na manufatura, a determinação do nível de qualidade dos produtos normalmente se baseia em provas objetivas. Uma pesquisa do Gallup de compradores de automóveis indicou que os clientes estavam inte-

---

[5] Tempo de execução (*lead time*): o tempo transcorrido entre o início e o final da execução de uma atividade.

ressados em desempenho do produto, durabilidade, facilidade de conserto, serviço ao cliente e satisfação do cliente. Os três primeiros desses elementos da qualidade de produto podem ser medidos, uma vez que se pode apresentar uma prova objetiva para determinar o nível de qualidade dos produtos. Já os dois últimos fatores — serviço ao cliente e satisfação do cliente —, difíceis de medir, deveriam servir de base para as organizações de serviços na determinação da qualidade de seus serviços. Instalações agradáveis, pessoal amigável e cortês, rapidez e destreza para executar o serviço, habilidade do médico, solidez do conselho do planejador financeiro e outros fatores dificilmente podem ser mensurados, mas afetam a percepção da qualidade dos serviços.

Dadas essas diferenças entre produtos manufaturados e serviços, vamos discutir agora as prioridades competitivas disponíveis aos serviços.

Prioridades Competitivas para os Serviços   A Tabela 2.7 relacionou essas prioridades competitivas para as empresas: baixos custos de produção, entrega rápida e no tempo certo, produtos/serviços de alta qualidade e serviço ao cliente. Todas as prioridades contidas na Tabela 2.7 também estão disponíveis às empresas de serviços. As empresas de serviços raramente oferecem todas as prioridades para os clientes, e para cada serviço deve ser escolhido um conjunto de prioridades que forneça a maior vantagem de mercado. A compensação (*trade-off*) entre custo e qualidade de serviço é talvez a mais evidente. Um pequeno varejista que enfatiza um estreito contato pessoal com os clientes pode ter serviços de alta qualidade, mas seus custos provavelmente serão mais elevados do que os dos grandes varejistas.

Posicionando Estratégias para os Serviços   Uma estratégia de posicionamento na manufatura inclui o tipo de política de estoque de bens acabados (produzir para estoque ou produzir sob encomenda), tipo de design de produto (padrão ou personalizado) e tipo de processo de produção (focalizado no produto ou no processo). Essa estratégia de posicionamento não seria possível para os serviços em virtude das diferenças relacionadas na Tabela 2.8. Essas diferenças determinam que uma estratégia de posicionamento para os serviços inclui:

1. **Tipo de design de serviço**, com diversas dimensões interessantes — produtos padrões ou personalizados, quantidade de contato com o cliente e combinação de bens físicos e serviços intangíveis.
2. **Tipo de processo de produção** — quase-manufatura: o cliente como participante e o cliente como produto.

Como se pode ver, o tipo de design de serviço e o tipo de processo de produção são muito diferentes de seus concorrentes. O McDonald's tem uma estratégia de posicionamento muito bem-sucedida, como é evidenciado por sua lucratividade a longo prazo. Ele optou por oferecer aos clientes um design de serviço altamente padronizado, com uma pequena quantidade de bens físicos dominando os serviços intangíveis. Seu processo de produção de suporte (*back-room*) é uma abordagem de quase-manufatura. A Burger King tem diferenças somente sutis — a empresa do "Faça-o do seu jeito" fornece aos clientes produtos e serviços ligeiramente mais personalizados e um pouco mais de contato e envolvimento com o cliente.

Exatamente como na manufatura, a estratégia de posicionamento da empresa de serviços determina a estrutura do sistema de produção. Essa estrutura é crucial para o sucesso das organizações de serviços. Discutiremos mais detalhadamente o design do sistema de produção do setor de serviços no Capítulo 4.

Agora que examinamos os elementos da estratégia de operações, vamos considerar como realizar a integração desses elementos numa estratégia de operações abrangente.

FORMANDO ESTRATÉGIAS DE OPERAÇÕES

A formação de estratégias de operações segue o procedimento apresentado na Figura 2.1. O cerne da estratégia de operações é a formação de estratégias de posicionamento (produtos personalizados ou padronizados, produção focalizada no produto ou no processo, e estoques baseados na produção para estoque ou produção sob encomenda), porque isso define a estrutura fundamental e a capacidade do sistema de produção. *É crucial que a estrutura de operações determinada pela estratégia de posicionamento esteja vinculada a planos de produto e prioridades competitivas definidos na estratégia de negócios.* Essa vincu-

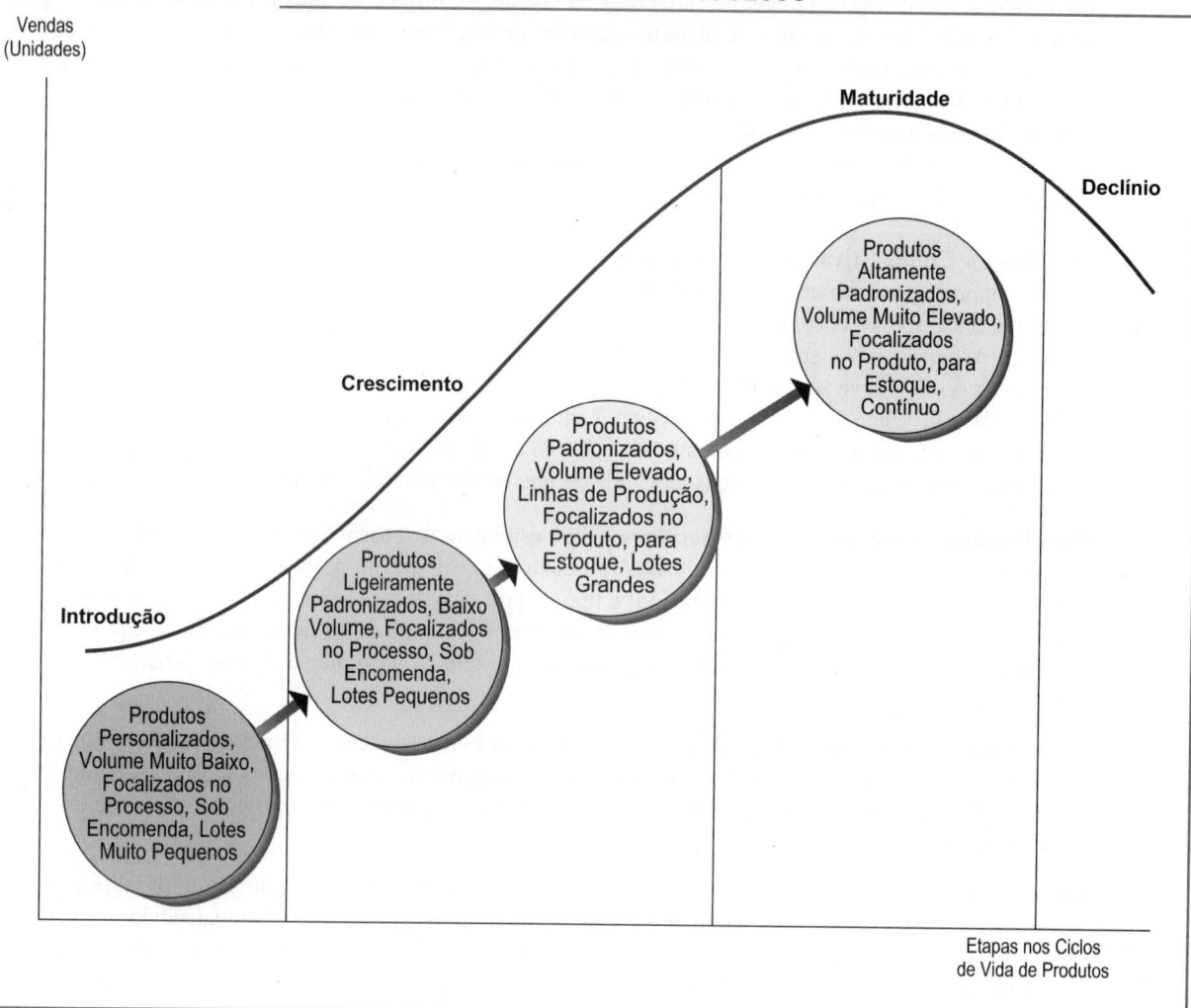

FIGURA 2.3 — EVOLUÇÕES DAS ESTRATÉGIAS DE POSICIONAMENTO DE UM PROJETO: CICLOS DE VIDA DO PROCESSO

lação assegura não somente que a estratégia de operações suporte a estratégia de negócios, mas também que a produção assuma um papel ativo e possa então ser usada como uma arma competitiva na luta para captar fatias de mercado em mercados globais.

Nesta seção discutiremos a evolução das estratégias de posicionamento para produtos, operações de vinculação e estratégias de marketing, e a diversidade de estratégias de operações.

EVOLUÇÃO DAS ESTRATÉGIAS DE POSICIONAMENTO

Hayes e Wheelwright sugeriram que as características dos sistemas de produção tendem a evoluir à medida que os produtos se movem ao longo de seus ciclos de vida de produto. A Figura 2.3 ilustra essa evolução. Nos primeiros estágios do ciclo de vida desses produtos, eles serão projetados de forma personalizada e produzidos em lotes muito pequenos numa fábrica focalizada no processo e de produção sob encomenda. À medida que a demanda de mercado do produto cresce, o tamanho e o volume de lote do produto se elevam, e observamos a estratégia de posicionamento deslocar-se para um design de produto padrão, produzido em fábricas focalizadas no produto e de produção para estoque. Finalmente, quando a demanda do produto atinge sua maturidade, o produto altamente padrão é produzido continuamente em fábricas dedicadas focalizadas no produto e de produção para estoque.

TABELA 2.9	ESTRATÉGIAS PURAS DE POSICIONAMENTO		
	Tipo de Produto	Tipo de Processo de Produção	Política de Estoques de Bens Acabados
	Padronizado	Focalizado no produto	Produzir para estoque
	Personalizado	Focalizado no processo	Produzir sob encomenda

O conceito ilustrado na Figura 2.3 se aplica a novos produtos tradicionais com longos ciclos de vida. Produtos redesenhados normalmente não iniciam seus ciclos de vida de produto na fase de introdução; ao contrário, eles reentram no ciclo aproximadamente na etapa do produto que está sendo substituído. Produtos com ciclos de vida especialmente curtos não seguem de maneira precisa a evolução ilustrada na Figura 2.3. Por exemplo, o telefone celular da Motorola atingiu a etapa de maturidade tão rápido que o sistema de produção teve de ser projetado para essa etapa logo depois de sua introdução no mercado.

O padrão de mudança ilustrado na Figura 2.3 tem importantes implicações para a estratégia de operações. *As estratégias de operações devem incluir planos para modificar os sistemas de produção para um conjunto mutável de prioridades competitivas quando os produtos amadurecerem, e o capital e a tecnologia de produção necessários para sustentar essas mudanças devem ser fornecidos.*

VINCULAÇÃO DE ESTRATÉGIAS DE OPERAÇÕES E DE MARKETING

A Tabela 2.9 apresenta duas estratégias de posicionamento que são combinações de tipo de produto, tipo de processo de produção e política de estoques de produtos acabados que comumente ocorrem juntos. Essas estratégias muitas vezes são chamadas **estratégias puras de posicionamento**. Outras combinações são chamadas **estratégias mistas de posicionamento.**

A Tabela 2.10 apresenta uma variedade de estratégias de posicionamento. Um importante princípio é sugerido nas Tabelas 2.9 e 2.10: *Todos os elementos da estratégia de operações (estratégias de posicionamento, foco das instalações de produção, projeto de produto, planejamento das instalações, e planos de tecnologia e processamento de produção) devem estar cuidadosamente vinculados. O mais importante é que a estratégia de posicionamento deve estar vinculada com a estratégia de mercado.* Nas décadas de 1980 e 1990, muitos fabricantes estrangeiros desenvolveram estratégias puras de posicionamento (produtos altamente padronizados, produção focalizada no produto e estoques baseados na produção sob encomenda) para produtos de consumo duráveis produzidos em massa. Essa estratégia de posicionamento combinou-se perfeitamente com suas estratégias de mercado, que se baseavam em preço baixo, rápida entrega de produto e elevada qualidade de produto. Ao mesmo tempo, algumas empresas americanas tinham estratégias de negócios que exigiam que suas funções de produção fossem do tipo "todas as coisas para todas as pessoas" e não levassem em conta a estrutura do sistema de produção e suas estratégias de posicionamento. Essas estratégias de negócios nos Estados Unidos podem não ter permitido que os sistemas de produção desenvolvessem estratégias de posicionamento que pudessem competir com suas concorrentes estrangeiras tanto em termos de custo como de qualidade de produto.

VARIEDADE DE ESTRATÉGIAS PODE SER ALGO BEM-SUCEDIDO

Como indica a Figura 2.1, a estratégia de operações deve ser derivada de uma avaliação das condições globais de negócios, das prioridades competitivas necessárias para captar segmentos de mercado e das competências essenciais ou fraquezas de uma empresa. A estratégia de operações apropriada pode depender das potencialidades e fraquezas de uma empresa. Duas empresas, cada uma com diferentes potencialidades e fraquezas, podem desenvolver diferentes estratégias de operações no mesmo mercado e, surpreendentemente, podem ser bem-sucedidas. Por exemplo, consideremos a Chrysler e a General Motors na década de 1970. Embora semelhantes em muitos aspectos, a Chrysler era menor, com uma boa comunicação entre seus distribuidores e suas fábricas, e um capital muito pequeno. A GM era imensa e rica em termos de capital. A Chrysler desenvolveu uma estratégia de posicionamento de produção sob en-

TABELA 2.10 — VINCULANDO ESTRATÉGIAS DE POSICIONAMENTO COM ESTRATÉGIAS DE MERCADO

Algumas Estratégias Comuns de Posicionamento	Produtos Personalizados		Produtos Padronizados	
	Volume Baixo	Volume Elevado	Volume Baixo	Volume Elevado
Focalizada no produto para estoque				*Estratégia de mercado:* Competição baseada amplamente no custo de produção, na entrega rápida de produtos e na qualidade. *Exemplo:* televisores
Focalizada no produto, sob encomenda			*Estratégia de mercado:* Competição baseada amplamente no custo de produção, em manter promessas de entrega e na qualidade. *Exemplo:* ônibus escolares	
Focalizada no processo, para estoque		*Estratégia de mercado:* Competição baseada amplamente na flexibilidade, na qualidade e na rápida entrega dos produtos. *Exemplo:* instrumentos médicos		
Focalizada no processo, sob encomenda	*Estratégia de mercado:* Competição baseada amplamente em manter as promessas de entrega, na qualidade e na flexibilidade. *Exemplo:* supercomputadores			

comenda que exigia níveis de estoques de bens acabados menores e menos capital, enquanto a GM permanecia com sua estratégia de posicionamento de produção para estoque. Ambas as estratégias de operações mostraram-se bem-sucedidas no decorrer da década seguinte, porque a GM manteve sua imensa fatia de mercado e a Chrysler saiu de sua crise financeira. Porém, outros desenvolvimentos mudariam drasticamente a sorte tanto da GM como da Chrysler na década de 1990.

Além das potencialidades e fraquezas de uma empresa, a estratégia de operações apropriada também pode depender da natureza dos produtos de uma empresa e de sua indústria. Já discutimos como as prioridades competitivas e as estratégias de posicionamento dos serviços tendem a diferir da manufatura em virtude das características dos serviços e de suas operações. De maneira semelhante, um pequeno negócio, um novo negócio e um negócio de alta tecnologia desenvolverão estratégias de operações diferentes das de seus concorrentes.

Em geral falta aos pequenos negócios quase tudo — desde capital a habilidades de empregados e capacidade de produção. Os pequenos e os novos fabricantes comumente preferem estratégias de posicionamento com produtos personalizados, produção focalizada no processo e políticas de produção sob encomenda, porque esses sistemas são mais flexíveis e requerem menos capital. À medida que seus produtos se movem ao longo de seus ciclos de vida, os sistemas de produção normalmente amadurecem rumo a políticas de produtos padronizados, produção focalizada no produto e produção para estoque — se querem competir com corporações maiores.

As pequenas empresas de serviços podem competir de maneira bem-sucedida com grandes corporações esculpindo um nicho de especialidades, com ênfase no contato com o cliente, para desenvolver uma relação de fidelidade. Por exemplo, quando um grande supermercado chega a uma cidade, os pequenos varejistas sobreviventes normalmente criam diferenciais em que o preço não é a principal prioridade competitiva, e onde o atendimento ao cliente feito de maneira próxima e pessoal é enfatizado.

TABELA 2.11 — Quão Competitivas São as Empresas Manufatureiras Americanas Frente a Seus Competidores Estrangeiros?

Capacidades Competitivas	Competitividade			
	Muito Fraca	Fraca	Forte	Muito Forte
Personalização de produtos		X		
Distribuição ampla de produtos			X	
Suporte ao produto			X	
Serviço pós-venda			X	
Entrega de produtos no tempo certo			X	
Entrega rápida de produtos			X	
Produtos confiáveis				X
Elevado desempenho de produtos			X	
Baixo número de defeitos			X	
Linha ampla de produtos			X	
Flexibilidade de combinação de produtos		X		
Flexibilidade de volume de produção		X		
Introdução rápida de novos produtos	X			
Capacidade de fazer rápidas mudanças no design	X			
Preços competitivos	X			

Fonte: Miller, Jeffrey G. e Jay S. Kim. "Beyond the Quality Revolution: U.S. Manufacturing Strategy in the 1990s". *A Research Report of the Boston University School of Management Manufacturing Roundtable,* 1990.

Para as empresas de serviços que usam tecnologia intensivamente, os ciclos de vida do produto tendem a ser breves, e os sistemas de produção tendem a usar capital intensivamente. Isso significa que os sistemas de produção devem ser capazes de produzir novos produtos e serviços em volumes elevados logo depois de sua introdução. Os sistemas de produção nesses negócios devem ser muito flexíveis e capazes de introduzir rapidamente novos produtos. Essas empresas devem ter duas potencialidades-chaves se quiserem ser bem-sucedidas: pessoal técnico altamente capaz e capital suficiente.

A formação de estratégias de operações envolve tomar decisões sobre a estrutura do sistema de produção, decisões sobre projetos de produto, processos de produção, tecnologias de produção e instalações de produção. A Parte II deste livro considera essas decisões estratégicas.

As empresas manufatureiras americanas devem continuar a olhar para o futuro. Quando operam num ambiente caracterizado por rápidas mudanças, elas devem definir estratégias de operações baseadas em suas potencialidades atuais, reduzir o impacto de suas fraquezas, criar novas potencialidades e perceber as mudanças nas condições globais de negócios.

COMPETITIVIDADE DAS EMPRESAS MANUFATUREIRAS AMERICANAS

Vimos na Tabela 2.7 que a função de produção dentro de uma empresa tem a sua disposição as prioridades competitivas de baixo custo de produção, entregas rápidas e no tempo certo, produtos e serviços de elevada qualidade, e serviço ao cliente. Qual combinação dessas prioridades deve ser usada para captar vendas de um produto particular em mercados internacionais? Essa é uma questão complexa, cuja resposta depende da análise da empresa quanto aos mercados globais futuros, de suas próprias potencialidades e fraquezas em comparação com a de seus concorrentes, e de sua visão da importância de cada prioridade para aumentar ou manter a fatia de mercado e a lucratividade.

A Tabela 2.11 mostra como os executivos americanos acham que estão se comportando em relação a seus concorrentes estrangeiros. Esses executivos classificam suas empresas segundo sua capacidade de competir com qualquer fabricante internacional em 15 fatores que são apenas uma divisão mais detalhada das prioridades competitivas da Tabela 2.7. Estudando a Tabela 2.11 podemos vislumbrar quais prioridades competitivas serão enfatizadas pelas empresas americanas em suas estratégias de negócios futuras. Os fabricantes americanos acreditam que têm certas vantagens competitivas sobre seus concorrentes estrangeiros. Entre essas vantagens estão produtos confiáveis, elevado desempenho de produto e baixo número de defeitos — todas, medidas da qualidade do produto. Outras potencialidades são distribuição de produto, suporte ao produto, serviço pós-venda e entrega dos produtos no tempo certo. As empresas americanas indubitavelmente tentarão aumentar suas fatias de mercado internacionais desenvolvendo estratégias de mercado que explorem essas potencialidades.

Mas tudo isso não é novidade. Existem diversas fraquezas evidentes em relação às empresas manufatureiras americanas. Entre elas, a rápida introdução de novos produtos, fazer mudanças rápidas de design de produto e flexibilidade de produto e volume — todas, medidas da flexibilidade de manufatura que levam o serviço ao cliente. Além disso, os custos e os preços dos produtos permanecem como uma importante fraqueza competitiva. As empresas americanas estão trabalhando arduamente para fortalecer suas funções de produção e torná-las mais flexíveis e mais competitivas em termos de custo e preço.

E devem fazê-lo, pois os concorrentes estrangeiros certamente desenvolverão estratégias de negócios para explorar as fraquezas das empresas manufatureiras americanas.

O que tudo isso significa é que a batalha por fatias de mercados globais no futuro terá a produção ou como uma arma competitiva, ou como uma fraqueza competitiva. Para as empresas que deram ou que derem os passos necessários para tornar seus sistemas flexíveis e competitivos quanto ao custo e ao preço, a produção será uma arma decisiva que poderá ser usada para captar grandes fatias de mercados internacionais. As empresas que não deram ou não derem esses passos entrarão na batalha competitiva por mercados internacionais com uma mão atada às costas.

Resumo Final

O Que os Fabricantes de Classe Mundial Estão Fazendo

Os fabricantes de classe mundial se distinguem ao desenvolver estratégias de negócios e de operações para captar crescentes fatias de mercados globais. Grande parte de seu pessoal contribui para o desenvolvimento desses planos de longo prazo. Nenhuma função organizacional em particular domina o planejamento dos negócios. O plano de negócios de longo prazo representa a melhor idéia e análise sobre o que deve ser feito para captar fatias de mercados globais. Em razão da solidez de seu processo de planejamento de longo prazo, os fabricantes de classe mundial investem com confiança em todas as áreas de seus negócios para o longo prazo: treinamento e educação do pessoal, desenvolvimento de mercado e de novos produtos/serviços, fábricas e processos de produção high-tech avançada, e pesquisa e desenvolvimento. Esses investimentos os posicionam para explorar as oportunidades em seus planos de negócios.

Em especial, os fabricantes de classe mundial:

- Colocam os clientes em primeiro lugar. São mais receptivos às necessidades dos clientes, estão dispostos a personalizar produtos e apressar ou mudar pedidos dos clientes.
- Colocam mais rapidamente novos produtos/serviços no mercado.
- São fabricantes com a administração da qualidade total (TQM). São conhecidos pela qualidade de seus produtos/serviços; a qualidade é enfatizada em todos os níveis da organização.
- Têm elevada produtividade de mão-de-obra e baixos custos de produção, igualando-se a ou superando seus concorrentes.
- Mantêm baixos estoques.
- Em geral, pensam, comercializam seus produtos e compram suprimentos mais globalmente.
- Adotam e desenvolvem rapidamente novas tecnologias de produção e implementam tecnologias comprovadas.
- Desenvolvem instalações de produção especializadas e mais focalizadas.
- Aparam as organizações para que sejam enxutas e flexíveis, a fim de se adaptarem a condições internacionais em constantes mudanças.
- São menos resistentes a alianças estratégicas e joint ventures para explorar oportunidades globais.
- Consideram questões sociais relevantes quando definem estratégias.

Questões de Revisão e Discussão

1. Explique o que significa *eficácia operacional*.
2. Em sua opinião, como devem ser organizados os desenvolvimentos relacionados na Tabela 2.1, em ordem de importância? Defenda seu ponto de vista.
3. Quais os três principais países para as exportações brasileiras?
4. Por que a China é tão importante para potenciais exportações dos Estados Unidos no futuro?
5. O que é ISO 14000?
6. Defina e exemplifique compartilhamento de produção.
7. Discuta os prós e os contras de as empresas americanas usarem tecnologia avançada de produção para combater a competição estrangeira.
8. Como as empresas estrangeiras mudaram suas estratégias de negócios nos últimos anos? Quais fatores motivaram essas mudanças?
9. Suponhamos que US$ 1 pudesse comprar 125 ienes e dois anos mais tarde US$ 1 pudesse comprar 150 ienes. Se o único fator considerado fosse a mudança das taxas de câmbio, o preço de um produto japonês vendido nos Estados Unidos se elevaria ou diminuiria nesse período? Em que porcentagem o preço mudaria?
10. Qual conselho você daria aos gerentes atuais sobre o desenvolvimento da estratégia de negócios, dado que as condições financeiras internacionais estão se modificando rapidamente? Apresente a defesa de seu conselho.
11. Apresente uma prova da importância dos sistemas de serviço na economia americana.
12. Cite cinco recursos escassos para os sistemas de produção atuais. O que os gerentes podem fazer para combater essa escassez?
13. Defina missão corporativa, estratégia de negócios e estratégia de operações.
14. Como a estratégia de operações está relacionada com a estratégia de negócios? Como a estratégia de operações impacta a estratégia de negócios?
15. Cite e descreva quatro prioridades competitivas. Discuta como elas são criadas.
16. Defina: (a) posicionamento do sistema de produção na manufatura e nos serviços, (b) foco das fábricas e instalações de serviços, (c) planos de processo e tecnologia de produção, d) alocação de recursos para alternativas estratégicas e (e) planejamento de instalações.
17. Defina o conceito de ciclo de vida de um produto. Apresente um exemplo de produto para cada uma das etapas do ciclo de vida de um produto.
18. O que significa "evolução das estratégias de posicionamento de produtos"? Qual a importância desse conceito para a estratégia de operações?
19. Quais as vantagens de uma estratégia de posicionamento "focalizado no produto, produto personalizado, produto para estoque"?
20. Defina e exemplifique estratégia pura de posicionamento e estratégia mista de posicionamento.
21. Explique estas afirmações: (a) "Todos os elementos da estratégia de posicionamento devem estar perfeitamente combinados com a estratégia de mercado". (b) "A estratégia de operações deve estar vinculada a planos de produto/serviço e prioridades competitivas."
22. Resuma o que os fabricantes de classe mundial fazem em relação à estratégia de negócios e de operações.

Tarefas na Internet

1. Procure na Internet um desenvolvimento recente no Mercosul ou um impacto causado por ele. Escreva um breve resumo do desenvolvimento ou impacto e indique o site.
2. Procure na Internet uma empresa americana com operações na China. Descreva o tipo de operação que a empresa tem na China e indique o site da empresa.
3. Procure na Internet uma descrição dos componentes da ISO 14000. Dê uma descrição desses componentes e indique o site.

4. Encontre um exemplo de empresa que está usando seu site da Internet para permitir que o público saiba sobre sua posição ou ações referentes a sua responsabilidade ambiental ou social. Imprima essa página e indique o site.
5. Pesquise o site do McDonald's (**www.mcdonalds.com**) para encontrar o número de países em que ele tem lanchonetes. Quantas lanchonetes o McDonald's tem?

Estudo de Caso

Estratégia de Operações para a CSI na Europa

A Computer Specialties Inc. (CSI) está desenvolvendo seu plano de negócios qüinqüenal. As rápidas mudanças na Europa têm levado a companhia a explorar maneiras de produzir e comercializar três modelos de seu computador *mainframe* de tamanho médio nesses novos mercados promissores. O plano para essa linha de produtos exige uma joint venture com a Sprecti Mache, uma companhia alemã especializada em comercializar produtos técnicos para governos e empresas tanto na Europa Ocidental como na Oriental. A CSI seria responsável pela manufatura dos computadores, e a Sprecti os venderia. O plano exige que os produtos sejam entregues diretamente das fábricas americanas da CSI durante dois anos, período em que serão construídas as instalações na Europa. As novas operações de manufatura na Europa estarão sob direção da CSI Europe, uma nova divisão internacional da CSI.

Tarefas

1. Escreva uma lista de elementos que teriam de ser incluídos numa estratégia de operações para a CSI Europe.
2. Relacione brevemente a informação que você precisaria ter antes que uma estratégia de operações pudesse ser desenvolvida para a CSI Europe.
3. Para cada um dos itens de informação incluídos em sua lista na questão 2, sugira maneiras pelas quais a informação poderia ser obtida.
4. Descreva brevemente uma estratégia de posicionamento para a CSI Europe. Declare quaisquer pressuposições que fizer sobre a empresa, seus produtos e seus clientes.
5. Discuta a importância de vincular os planos de produto, prioridades competitivas e estratégia de operações da CSI.
6. Discuta a importância de vincular os planos de mercado da Sprecti Mache com a estratégia de posicionamento da CSI Europe.

capítulo 3

PREVISÕES NA APO
O PONTO DE PARTIDA PARA TODO O PLANEJAMENTO

Introdução

Métodos Qualitativos de Previsão

Modelos Quantitativos de Previsão
   Precisão da Previsão
   Previsões de Longo Prazo
      Ciclos, Tendências e Sazonalidade • Regressão Linear e Correlação • Intervalos das Previsões • Sazonalidade em Previsões de Séries Temporais
   Previsões de Curto Prazo
      Avaliando o Desempenho do Modelo de Previsão • Previsões Ingênuas • Método da Média Móvel • Método da Média Ponderada Móvel • Método da Exponencial Móvel • Exponencial Móvel com Tendência

Como Ter um Sistema de Previsão Bem-Sucedido
   Como Escolher um Método de Previsão
      Custo e Precisão • Dados Disponíveis • Intervalo de Tempo • Natureza dos Produtos e Serviços • Resposta ao Impulso e Atenuação de Ruído
   Como Monitorar e Controlar um Modelo de Previsão

Softwares para Previsões

Previsão em Pequenos Negócios e Novos Empreendimentos

Resumo Final: O Que os Fabricantes de Classe Mundial Estão Fazendo

Questões de Revisão e Discussão

Tarefas na Internet

Problemas

Estudo de Caso
   XYZ Inc.

A COMPAQ PREVÊ O MERCADO DE COMPUTADORES PESSOAIS

Em meados da década de 1980 a Compaq Computer Corporation enfrentou uma decisão que afetaria profundamente seu futuro. Sabendo que a IBM introduziria logo sua versão do computador portátil e ameaçaria o predomínio da Compaq nesse lucrativo mercado, a empresa tinha duas opções: permanecer com seus computadores portáteis ou ampliar as ofertas de mercado para incluir computadores de mesa. Esta última iniciativa obrigaria a empresa de um ano de idade a defrontar-se com a IBM em seu próprio terreno. Além disso, a Compaq teria de fazer um investimento substancial em desenvolvimento de produto e capital de giro e expandir sua organização e capacidade de produção.

Alguns fatores dificultavam as previsões da Compaq quanto ao tamanho, direção e tendências de preço do mercado de computadores pessoais: a entrada de novos computadores portáteis da IBM, uma redução de preço de 23% pela IBM e sua potencial erosão de margens de lucro, a entrada dos computadores portáteis *laptop* introduzidos pela Hewlett-Packard e Data General, o lançamento do novo PC AT da IBM e a introdução de computadores de mesa pela Sperry, NCR, ITT e AT&T.

A Compaq decidiu entrar no segmento de computadores de mesa (*desktop*) do mercado e foi bem-sucedida, tanto do ponto de vista financeiro como competitivo. O crescimento de vendas da Compaq foi enorme: de US$ 111 milhões em 1983 para US$ 329 milhões em 1984, US$ 1,2 bilhão em 1988, US$ 3,6 bilhões em 1991, US$ 12,6 bilhões em 1994 e US$ 20 bilhões em 1996. Em setembro de 1997, a Compaq liderava a indústria de computadores em vendas de *notebooks*, com uma fatia de mercado de 28,8%, superando pela primeira vez a Toshiba. No terceiro trimestre de 1997 a Compaq era a maior produtora mundial de computadores pessoais, com uma fatia de mercado mundial de 13,7% e uma fatia de mercado americano de 19,1%, partindo de uma fatia de mercado mundial de 10,2% e de uma fatia de mercado americano de 14,4% no ano anterior.

A administração da Compaq atribui grande parte desse sucesso a sua capacidade de prever mercados futuros corretamente. Sua abordagem de previsão lhe permitiu implementar seus planos para desenvolver novos produtos, desenvolver nova tecnologia de produtos e ampliar sua capacidade de produção.

É imperativo que as empresas tenham abordagens eficazes para prever, e que a previsão seja parte integrante do planejamento dos negócios. Quando os gerentes planejam, eles determinam no presente quais cursos de ação serão tomados no futuro. *O primeiro passo no planejamento é, portanto,* **prever***, ou estimar a demanda futura por produtos e serviços e os recursos necessários para produzi-los.* As estimativas da demanda futura referente a produtos e serviços, comumente chamadas **previsões de vendas**, são o ponto de partida para todas as outras previsões na APO.

Os gerentes de operações necessitam de previsões de longo prazo para tomar decisões estratégicas a respeito de produtos, processos e instalações. Também necessitam de previsões de curto prazo para ajudá-los a tomar decisões a respeito de questões de produção mais imediatas. A Tabela 3.1 resume alguns motivos que ilustram por que os gerentes de operações devem desenvolver previsões. A Tabela 3.2 fornece exemplos de coisas comumente previstas na APO. As previsões de longo prazo normalmente abrangem um ano ou mais e estimam a demanda de linhas de produto inteiras, como, por exemplo, produtos para tratamento de jardins. As previsões de médio prazo em geral abrangem alguns meses e agrupam produtos em famílias de produtos, como, por exemplo, cortadores de grama. As previsões de curto prazo geralmente abrangem algumas semanas e se concentram em produtos específicos, como, por exemplo, o cortador de grama modelo Z.

A Figura 3.1 ilustra que a previsão é uma parte integrante do planejamento dos negócios. As entradas são processadas por meio de modelos ou métodos de previsão para desenvolver estimativas da demanda. *Essas estimativas da demanda não são as previsões de venda — elas são o ponto de partida para as equipes de administração desenvolverem previsões de vendas.* As previsões de vendas se tornam entradas tanto para a estratégia de negócios como para previsões dos recursos de produção.

Os métodos ou modelos de previsão podem ser qualitativos ou quantitativos, por natureza.

Tabela 3.1 — Alguns Motivos Que Ilustram Por Que Fazer Previsões É Fundamental na APO

1. **Planejamento de novas instalações.** Projetar e construir uma nova fábrica ou projetar e implementar um novo processo de produção pode demorar anos. Essas atividades estratégicas na APO exigem previsões de longo prazo da demanda por produtos existentes ou novos a fim de que os gerentes de operações possam ter o tempo de execução (*lead time*) necessário para construir fábricas e instalar processos para produzir os produtos e serviços necessários.
2. **Planejamento da produção.** Os índices de produção devem ser alterados para cima e para baixo para atender as demandas por produtos e serviços que variam de mês a mês. Muitas vezes são necessários meses para mudar a capacidade dos processos de produção. Os gerentes de operações necessitam de previsões de médio prazo a fim de que possam ter o tempo de execução necessário para produzir essas demandas.
3. **Programação da força de trabalho.** A força de trabalho deve ser alterada para cima ou para baixo para atender as demandas por produtos e serviços que variam de semana a semana. Os gerentes de operações necessitam de previsões de curto prazo a fim de que possam ter o tempo de execução necessário para efetuar mudanças na força de trabalho para produzir as demandas semanais.

Tabela 3.2 — Alguns Exemplos de Coisas Que Devem Ser Previstas na APO

Horizonte da Previsão	Intervalo de Tempo	Exemplos de Coisas Que Devem Ser Previstas	Algumas Unidades Típicas de Previsões
Longo prazo	Anos	Novas linhas de produtos	Dólares
		Linhas de produtos antigas	Dólares
		Capacidades de fábrica	Galões, horas, libras, unidades ou clientes por período de tempo
		Fundos de capital	Dólares
		Necessidades da instalação	Espaço, volume
Médio prazo	Meses	Grupos de produtos	Unidades
		Capacidades departamentais	Horas, libras, galões, unidades ou clientes por período de tempo
		Força de trabalho	Trabalhadores, horas
		Matérias-primas compradas	Unidades, libras, galões
		Estoques	Unidades, dólares
Curto prazo	Semanas	Produtos específicos	Unidades
		Classes de habilidade de mão-de-obra	Trabalhadores, horas
		Capacidades de máquina	Unidades, horas, galões, libras ou clientes por período de tempo
		Dinheiro vivo	Dólares
		Estoques	Unidades, dólares

Métodos Qualitativos de Previsão

A Tabela 3.3 descreve diversos métodos qualitativos de previsão usados para desenvolver previsões de vendas. Esses métodos, que normalmente se baseiam em julgamentos a respeito dos fatores causais que fundamentam as vendas de produtos ou serviços particulares e em opiniões sobre a probabilidade relativa de esses fatores causais estarem presentes no futuro, podem envolver diversos níveis de sofisticação — de pesquisas de opinião cientificamente conduzidas a suposições intuitivas sobre os eventos futuros.

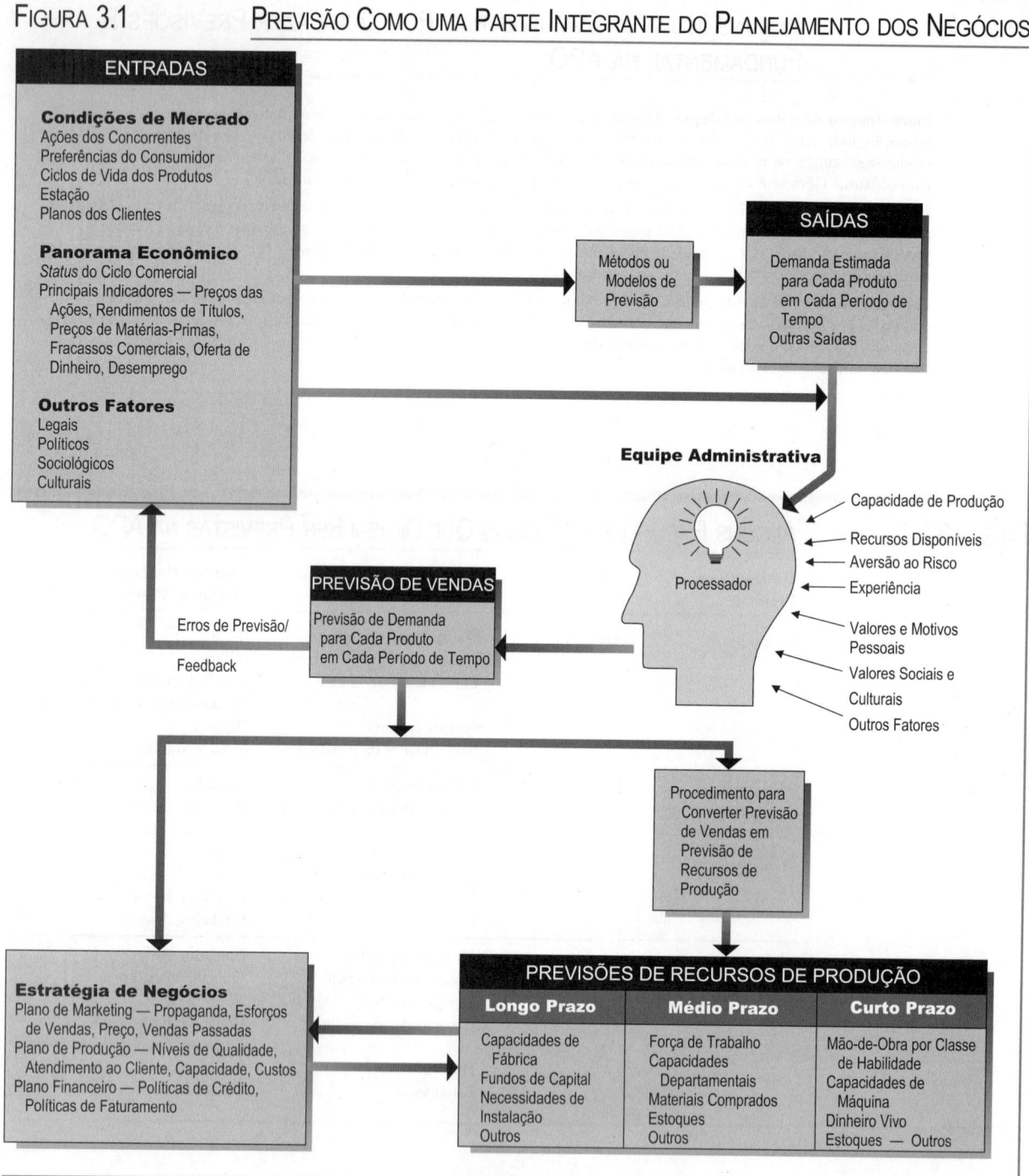

FIGURA 3.1 — Previsão Como uma Parte Integrante do Planejamento dos Negócios

O **consenso do comitê executivo** e o **método Delphi** descrevem procedimentos para assimilar informações dentro de um comitê executivo com o propósito de gerar uma previsão de vendas e são úteis tanto para produtos e serviços existentes como para novos. Por outro lado, a **pesquisa da equipe de vendas** e a **pesquisa de clientes** descrevem métodos que são usados principalmente para produtos e serviços existentes. A **analogia histórica** e os testes e as **pesquisas de mercado** descrevem procedimentos úteis para novos produtos e serviços. O método de previsão, portanto, depende da etapa do ciclo de vida de um produto.

TABELA 3.3 — MÉTODOS QUALITATIVOS DE PREVISÃO

1. **Consenso do comitê executivo.** Executivos com capacidade de discernimento, de vários departamentos da organização, formam um comitê que tem a responsabilidade de desenvolver uma previsão de vendas. O comitê pode usar muitas informações (inputs) de todas as partes da organização e fazer com que os analistas do staff forneçam análises quando necessário. Essas previsões tendem a ser previsões de compromisso, não refletindo as tendências que poderiam estar presentes caso tivessem sido preparadas por um único indivíduo. Esse método de previsão é o mais comum.

2. **Método Delphi.** Esse método é usado para se obter o consenso dentro de um comitê. Por esse método, os executivos respondem anonimamente a uma série de perguntas em turnos sucessivos. Cada resposta é repassada a todos os participantes em cada turno, e o processo é então repetido. Até seis turnos podem ser necessários antes que se atinja o consenso sobre a previsão. Esse método pode resultar em previsões com as quais a maioria dos participantes concordou apesar de ter ocorrido uma discordância inicial.

3. **Pesquisa da equipe de vendas.** Estimativas de vendas regionais futuras são obtidas de membros individuais da equipe de vendas. Essas estimativas são combinadas para formar uma estimativa de vendas única para todas as regiões, que deve então ser transformada pelos gerentes numa previsão de vendas para assegurar estimativas realísticas. Esse é um método de previsão popular para empresas que têm um bom sistema de comunicação em funcionamento e uma equipe de vendas que vende diretamente aos clientes.

4. **Pesquisa de clientes.** Estimativas de vendas futuras são obtidas diretamente dos clientes. Clientes individuais são pesquisados para determinar quais quantidades dos produtos da empresa eles pretendem comprar em cada período de tempo futuro. Uma previsão de vendas é determinada combinando-se as respostas de clientes individuais. Esse método é um dos preferidos das empresas que têm relativamente poucos clientes, como, por exemplo, concessionárias de veículos.

5. **Analogia histórica.** Esse método une a estimativa de vendas futuras de um produto ao conhecimento das vendas de um produto similar. O conhecimento das vendas de um produto durante várias etapas de seu ciclo de vida é aplicado à estimativa de vendas de um produto similar. Esse método pode ser especialmente útil na previsão de vendas de novos produtos.

6. **Pesquisa de mercado.** Nas **pesquisas de mercado**, questionários por correspondência, entrevistas telefônicas ou entrevistas de campo formam a base para testar hipóteses sobre mercados reais. Em **testes de mercado**, produtos comercializados em regiões ou centros de compras tipo *outlets* são estatisticamente extrapolados para mercados totais. Esses métodos comumente são preferidos para novos produtos ou para produtos existentes a serem introduzidos em novos segmentos de mercados.

MODELOS QUANTITATIVOS DE PREVISÃO

Os modelos quantitativos de previsão são modelos matemáticos baseados em dados históricos. Esses modelos supõem que dados passados são relevantes para o futuro. Alguns dados relevantes quase sempre podem ser encontrados. Aqui discutimos diversos modelos quantitativos, precisão da previsão, previsões de longo prazo e previsões de curto prazo.

A Tabela 3.4 exibe os modelos quantitativos de previsão que vamos estudar neste capítulo. Não obstante existirem muitos outros modelos quantitativos de previsão, os modelos da Tabela 3.4 fornecem uma introdução útil para se fazer previsões na APO. Todos esses modelos podem ser usados com séries temporais. Uma **série temporal** é um conjunto de valores observados medidos ao longo de períodos de tempo sucessivos.

PRECISÃO DA PREVISÃO

Precisão da previsão refere-se a quão perto as previsões chegam dos dados reais. Uma vez que as previsões são feitas *antes* que os dados reais se tornem conhecidos, a precisão das previsões pode ser determinada somente depois da passagem do tempo. Quando as previsões ficam muito próximas dos dados reais, dizemos que elas têm **alta precisão** e que o **erro de previsão** é baixo. Determinamos a precisão dos modelos de previsão mantendo uma contagem contínua do quanto as previsões deixaram de atingir os pontos de dados reais ao longo do tempo. Se a precisão de um modelo for baixa, modificamos o método ou escolhemos um novo. Discutiremos maneiras de medir e monitorar o desempenho do modelo de previsão posteriormente neste capítulo.

TABELA 3.4   ALGUNS MODELOS QUANTITATIVOS DE PREVISÃO

1. **Regressão linear.** Um modelo que usa o chamado método dos mínimos quadrados para identificar a relação entre uma variável dependente e uma ou mais variáveis independentes presentes em um conjunto de observações históricas. Na regressão simples existe somente uma variável independente; já na regressão múltipla há mais de uma variável desse tipo. Se o conjunto de dados históricos for uma série temporal, a variável independente será o período de tempo, e a variável dependente na previsão serão as vendas. Um modelo de regressão não tem de ser baseado numa série temporal; nesses casos, o conhecimento de valores futuros da variável independente (que também pode ser chamada de **variável causal**) é usado para prever valores futuros da variável dependente. A regressão linear comumente é usada em previsões de longo prazo; mas, se tivermos o cuidado de escolher o número de períodos incluídos nos dados históricos e se o conjunto de dados for projetado somente alguns períodos no futuro, a regressão também poderá ser apropriadamente usada na previsão de curto prazo. Regressão supõe equinormalidade, o que significa que os valores observados da variável dependente (y) são tidos como normalmente distribuídos nas proximidades de seu ponto médio $\bar{y}$ e que o desvio padrão da previsão (s_{yx}) é constante ao longo da linha de tendências.

2. **Média móvel.** Um tipo de modelo de previsão com série temporal de curto prazo que prevê vendas para o período seguinte. Nesse modelo, a média aritmética das vendas reais correspondente a um número específico de períodos de tempo mais recentes é a previsão para o período seguinte.

3. **Média ponderada móvel.** Este modelo é semelhante ao modelo da média móvel descrito acima, exceto que, ao invés de uma média aritmética de vendas passadas, a média ponderada das vendas passadas é a previsão para o período de tempo seguinte.

4. **Exponencial móvel.** Também um modelo de previsão com série temporal de curto prazo que prevê as vendas para o período de tempo seguinte. Neste método, as vendas previstas para o período passado são modificadas pela informação a respeito do erro previsto do último período. Esta modificação da previsão do período passado é a previsão para o período de tempo seguinte.

5. **Exponencial móvel com tendência.** O modelo de exponencial móvel descrito acima, mas modificado para acomodar dados com um padrão de tendências. Esses padrões podem estar presentes em dados de médio prazo. Chamado também **suavização exponencial dupla**[1], tanto a estimativa da média como a estimativa da tendência são suavizadas, sendo usadas duas constantes de amortecimento.

PREVISÕES DE LONGO PRAZO

Previsão de longo prazo significa estimar condições futuras ao longo de intervalos de tempo normalmente maiores do que um ano. Previsões de longo prazo são necessárias na APO para sustentar as decisões estratégicas a respeito do planejamento de produtos, processos, tecnologias e instalações — tópicos da Parte II deste livro. Essas decisões são tão importantes para o sucesso a longo prazo dos sistemas de produção que um esforço organizacional intenso é aplicado no desenvolvimento dessas previsões. Eis alguns exemplos dessas decisões:

1. **Projetar um novo produto.** Se o volume de vendas justificar uma maquinaria de produção automatizada, muito esforço de projeto de produto será necessário para assegurar a facilidade de processamento através de máquinas automatizadas.

2. **Determinar a capacidade de produção para um novo produto.** Quanta capacidade é necessária, quantas novas fábricas são necessárias e onde elas devem ser localizadas.

3. **Planejar para o abastecimento de materiais a longo prazo.** As previsões permitem que os gerentes de operações "prendam" fornecedores em contratos de abastecimento de matérias-primas a longo prazo.

Comprar e construir novas máquinas e prédios e desenvolver novas fontes de matérias-primas demanda tempo, e previsões de longo prazo dão aos gerentes o tempo necessário para desenvolver planos para essas atividades.

Ciclos, Tendências e Sazonalidade   Não obstante os dados de longo prazo poderem parecer irregulares, se olharmos além dessa aparência superficial poderemos identificar padrões de dados subjacentes bastante simples. A Figura 3.2 mostra como os dados históricos de vendas tendem a ser compostos de diversos componentes, entre eles tendências, ciclos, sazonalidade e flutuação aleatória ou ruído. As **tendências** de longo prazo são ilustradas por uma linha com inclinação para cima — ou para baixo. Um **ciclo** é um padrão de dados que pode cobrir diversos anos antes de se repetir. **Flutuação aleatória**, ou **ruído**, é um

---

[1] O termo *smoothing* do método *exponential smoothing* tem surgido na literatura de língua portuguesa com várias traduções, sendo as mais comuns *suavização* e *amortecimento*. (N. do R.T.)

FIGURA 3.2 — Padrões de Dados numa Previsão de Longo Prazo

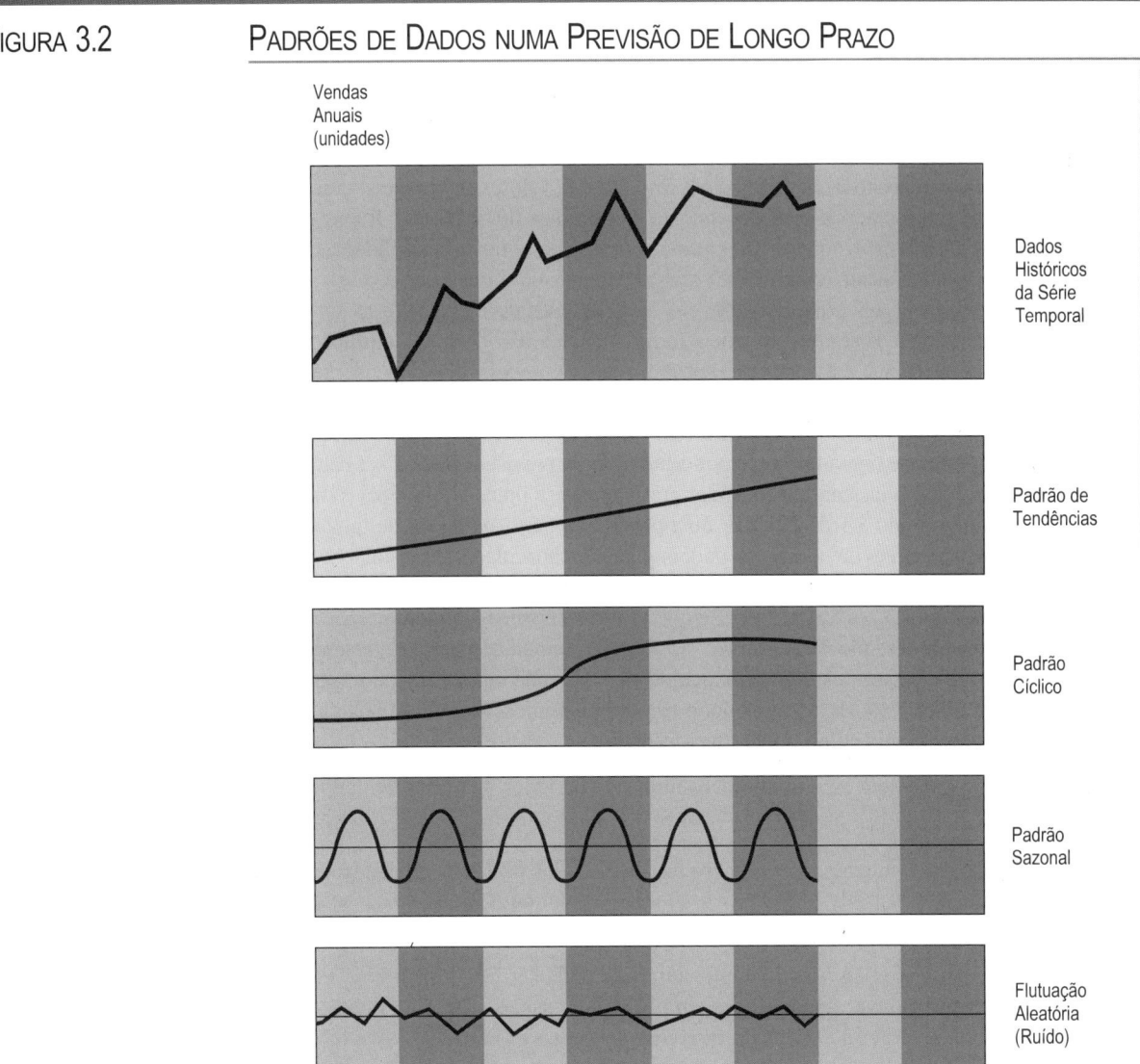

padrão resultante da variação aleatória ou causas inexplicáveis. A sazonalidade é um padrão de dados que se repete depois de um período de tempo, em geral um ano. As estações do ano (verão etc.) são bem conhecidas, mas padrões sazonais como os seguintes também podem ocorrer:

Intervalo de Tempo Antes Que o Padrão Seja Repetido	Extensão do Período	Número de Períodos no Padrão
Ano	Trimestre	4
Ano	Mês	12
Ano	Semana	52
Mês	Semana	4
Mês	Dia	29–31
Semana	Dia	7

Na Figura 3.2, seis anos de dados históricos de vendas estão plotados no gráfico superior. Previsões de longo prazo poderiam ser desenvolvidas encaixando-se graficamente uma linha através desses dados passados e estendendo-a para a frente no futuro. As previsões de vendas para os períodos 7 e 8 poderiam então ser lidas no gráfico. Essa abordagem gráfica para previsões de longo prazo é usada na prática, mas seu principal inconveniente é a incapacidade de encaixar acuradamente uma linha através dos dados passados. A análise de regressão constitui uma maneira mais acurada de desenvolver previsões com uma linha de tendências.

Regressão Linear e Correlação A **análise de regressão linear** é um modelo de previsão que estabelece uma relação entre uma variável dependente e uma ou mais variáveis independentes. Usamos nosso conhecimento a respeito dessa relação e a respeito dos valores futuros das variáveis independentes para prever os valores futuros da variável dependente. Na **análise de regressão linear simples** há somente uma variável independente. Se os dados forem uma série temporal, a variável independente será o período de tempo, e a variável dependente comumente serão as vendas, ou o que quer que seja que queiramos prever.

A Tabela 3.5 exibe as variáveis, as definições de variáveis e as fórmulas para a análise de regressão linear simples. Esse modelo tem a forma Y = a + bX, chamada **equação de regressão**, em que Y é a variável dependente e a variável a ser prevista, X é a variável independente, *a* é o intercepto de *y*, e *b* é a inclinação da linha de tendências. As fórmulas da Tabela 3.5 permitem-nos computar os valores *a* e *b*. Uma vez que esses valores constantes forem conhecidos, um valor futuro de X poderá ser introduzido na equação de regressão, e um valor correspondente de Y (a previsão) poderá ser calculado. Conceitualmente, esse procedimento é o mesmo que estender graficamente a linha de tendências da Figura 3.2.

O Exemplo 3.1 desenvolve uma previsão a partir de dados de uma série temporal. O exemplo mostra como os gerentes de operações podem planejar capacidades de instalações desenvolvendo previsões de vendas a longo prazo. Nesse exemplo, a variável independente *x* representa o período de tempo. A única exigência imposta aos valores de *x* é que eles devem ser igualmente espaçados; dessa forma, os valores de *x* poderiam ter sido 1990, 1991, · · ·, 1999 ou qualquer outra representação significativa de períodos de tempo. Se tivéssemos de fazer cálculos sem o uso de um computador, poderíamos manipular os valores de *x* para obter $\sum x = 0$; desse modo, o cálculo de *a* e *b* seria muito mais fácil, porque $\sum x$ sairia das equações de regressão. Eis como poderíamos fazer isso:

1. Se houvesse um número ímpar de períodos passados de dados (digamos 5), os valores de *x* seriam −2, −1, 0, +1, +2. $\sum x = 0$, e o valor de X usado na equação de regressão para o ano seguinte seria +3.
2. Se houvesse um número par de períodos passados de dados (digamos 6), os valores de *x* seriam −5, −3, −1, +1, +3, +5. $\sum x = 0$, e o valor de X usado na equação de regressão para o ano seguinte seria +7.

Uma regressão linear simples também pode ser usada quando a variável independente *x* representa uma outra variável que não seja tempo. Nesse caso, a regressão linear é representativa de uma classe de modelos de previsão chamada **modelos de previsão causais**. Esses modelos desenvolvem previsões depois de estabelecer e medir uma associação entre a variável dependente e uma ou mais variáveis independentes. Essa classe de modelos é excelente para prever **pontos viragem** nas vendas.

O Exemplo 3.2 usa o valor das construções regionais como a variável independente *x* para prever as vendas de uma companhia *y*, que é a variável dependente. Neste exemplo, uma previsão de vendas a longo prazo é necessária para auxiliar o gerente a planejar o número de engenheiros e instalações para o próximo ano. Esse exemplo também explica como o coeficiente de correlação e o coeficiente de determinação podem ser usados para avaliar o modelo de previsão desenvolvido através da análise de regressão linear.

*O coeficiente de correlação (*r*) explica a importância relativa da relação entre y e x; o sinal de* r *mostra a direção da relação, e o valor absoluto de* r *mostra a força da relação.* O *r* pode assumir qualquer valor entre −1 e +1. O sinal de *r* é sempre o mesmo que o de *b*. Um *r* negativo indica que os valores de *y* e *x* tendem a mover-se em direções opostas, e um *r* positivo indica que os valores de *y* e *x* movem-se na mesma direção. Eis os significados de diversos valores de *r*:

- −1 Uma relação negativa perfeita; à medida que *y* cresce, *x* desce unidade por unidade e vice-versa.
- +1 Uma relação positiva perfeita; à medida que *y* cresce, *x* cresce unidade por unidade e vice-versa.
- 0 Não existe nenhuma relação entre *y* e *x*.
- +0,3 Uma relação positiva fraca.
- −0,9 Uma relação negativa forte.

TABELA 3.5 — DEFINIÇÕES E FÓRMULAS DE VARIÁVEIS PARA ANÁLISE DE REGRESSÃO LINEAR SIMPLES

x = valores de variáveis independentes
y = valores de variáveis dependentes
n = número de observações
a = intercepto do eixo vertical
b = inclinação da linha de regressão
ȳ = valor médio da variável dependente

Y = valores de y que se situam na linha de tendências Y = a + bX
X = valores de x que se situam na linha de tendências
r = coeficiente de correlação
r² = coeficiente de determinação

$$a = \frac{\sum x^2 \sum y - \sum x \sum xy}{n \sum x^2 - (\sum x)^2}$$

$$b = \frac{n \sum xy - \sum x \sum y}{n \sum x^2 - (\sum x)^2}$$

$$Y = a + bX$$

$$r = \frac{n \sum xy - \sum x \sum y}{\sqrt{[n \sum x^2 - (\sum x)^2][n \sum y^2 - (\sum y)^2]}}$$

EXEMPLO 3.1

ANÁLISE DE REGRESSÃO LINEAR SIMPLES: UMA SÉRIE TEMPORAL

A Specific Motors produz motores eletrônicos. A fábrica da Specific opera em sua capacidade quase total há algum tempo. Jim White, o gerente de fábrica, acha que o crescimento de vendas prosseguirá, e ele quer desenvolver uma previsão a longo prazo a ser usada para planejar as exigências de instalações para os próximos três anos. Os registros de vendas dos últimos dez anos acumularam-se:

Ano	Vendas Anuais (milhares de unidades)	Ano	Vendas Anuais (milhares de unidades)
1	1.000	6	2.000
2	1.300	7	2.200
3	1.800	8	2.600
4	2.000	9	2.900
5	2.000	10	3.200

Estudamos as fórmulas e definições de variáveis na Tabela 3.5 e depois construímos a tabela a seguir para estabelecer os valores a serem usados nas fórmulas. (Uma planilha eletrônica nos será útil para efetuarmos muitos dos cálculos.)

Ano	Vendas Anuais (milhares de unidades) (y)	Período de tempo (x)	x²	xy
1	1.000	1	1	1.000
2	1.300	2	4	2.600
3	1.800	3	9	5.400
4	2.000	4	16	8.000
5	2.000	5	25	10.000
6	2.000	6	36	12.000
7	2.200	7	49	15.400
8	2.600	8	64	20.800
9	2.900	9	81	26.100
10	3.200	10	100	32.000
Totais	$\sum y = 21.000$	$\sum x = 55$	$\sum x^2 = 385$	$\sum xy = 133.300$

Solução

1. Vamos resolver agora os valores *a* e *b*:

$$a = \frac{\sum x^2 \sum y - \sum x \sum xy}{n \sum x^2 - (\sum x)^2} = \frac{(385)(21.000) - (55)(133.300)}{10(385) - (55)^2}$$

$$= \frac{8.085.000 - 7.331.500}{3.850 - 3.025} = \frac{753.500}{825} = 913.333$$

$$b = \frac{n \sum xy - \sum x \sum y}{n \sum x^2 - (\sum x)^2} = \frac{(10)(133.300) - (55)(21.000)}{825}$$

$$= \frac{1.333.000 - 1.155.000}{825} = \frac{178.000}{825} = 215,758$$

2. Agora que conhecemos os valores de *a* e *b*, a equação de regressão pode ser usada para prever as vendas de anos futuros:

$$Y = a + bX = 913.333 + 215.758X$$

3. Se desejássemos prever as vendas em milhares de unidades para os três anos seguintes, substituiríamos 11, 12 e 13, os três valores seguintes para *x*, na equação de regressão por X:

$Y_{11} = 913,333 + 215,758(11) = 3.286,7$, ou 3.290 milhares de unidades.
$Y_{12} = 913,333 + 215,758(12) = 3.502,4$, ou 3.500 milhares de unidades.
$Y_{13} = 913,333 + 215,758(13) = 3.718,2$, ou 3.720 milhares de unidades.

As previsões são arredondadas para um dígito significativo a mais do que os dados originais. Note que os dados de vendas contêm somente dois dígitos significativos; as previsões são arredondadas para três.

No Exemplo 3.2, r = +0,894. Isso significa que há uma relação positiva forte entre a demanda por serviços de engenharia e o valor dos contratos liberados.

Não obstante o coeficiente de correlação ser útil para medir a relação entre *x* e *y*, termos como *forte*, *moderado* e *fraco* não são medidas muito específicas de relação. O coeficiente de determinação (r^2) é o quadrado do coeficiente de correlação.

Exemplo 3.2

Análise de Regressão Linear Simples

Jack Weis, o gerente-geral da Precision Engineering Corporation, acha que os serviços de engenharia de sua empresa, prestados a empresas de construção de rodovias, estão diretamente relacionados com o valor dos contratos de construção de rodovias em sua região. Ele se questiona se isso é realmente assim e se essa informação poderá ajudá-lo a planejar melhor suas operações. Jack pediu a Bill Brandon, um de seus engenheiros, para realizar uma análise de regressão linear simples sobre dados históricos. Bill planeja fazer o seguinte: a) desenvolver uma equação de regressão para prever o nível de demanda por serviços da Precision; b) usar a equação de regressão para prever o nível de demanda para os próximos quatro anos; e c) determinar o quanto a demanda está relacionada com o valor dos contratos de construção liberados.

Capítulo 3 – Previsões na APO

SOLUÇÃO

a) Desenvolva uma equação de regressão:

1. Bill reexamina registros municipais, estaduais e federais para coligir o valor em dólares dos contratos liberados na região geográfica durante dois anos, por trimestres.
2. Ele examina a demanda por serviços para sua empresa ao longo do mesmo período.
3. São preparados os seguintes dados:

Ano	Trimestre	Vendas da Precision Engineering Services (milhares de dólares)	Valor Total dos Contratos Liberados (milhares de dólares)
1	Q_1	8	150
	Q_2	10	170
	Q_3	15	190
	Q_4	9	170
2	Q_1	12	180
	Q_2	13	190
	Q_3	12	200
	Q_4	16	220

4. Bill desenvolve agora os totais necessários para efetuar a análise de regressão. As fórmulas e definições de variáveis se encontram na Tabela 3.5. (Uma planilha eletrônica nos será útil para efetuarmos muitos dos cálculos.)

Período de tempo	Vendas (y)	Contratos (x)	x^2	xy	y^2
1	8	150	22.500	1.200	64
2	10	170	28.900	1.700	100
3	15	190	36.100	2.850	225
4	9	170	28.900	1.530	81
5	12	180	32.400	2.160	144
6	13	190	36.100	2.470	169
7	12	200	40.000	2.400	144
8	16	220	48.400	3.520	256
Totais	$\sum y = 95$	$\sum x = 1.470$	$\sum x^2 = 273.300$	$\sum xy = 17.830$	$\sum y^2 = 1.183$

5. Use estes valores nas fórmulas da Tabela 3.5 para computar a e b:

$$a = \frac{\sum x^2 \sum y - \sum x \sum xy}{n \sum x^2 - (\sum x)^2} = \frac{(273.300)(95) - (1.470)(17.830)}{8(273.300) - (1.470)^2}$$

$$= \frac{25.963.500 - 26.210.100}{2.186.400 - 2.160.000} = \frac{-246.600}{25.500} = -9,671$$

$$b = \frac{n \sum xy - \sum x \sum y}{n \sum x^2 - (\sum x)^2} = \frac{(8)(17.830) - (1.470)(95)}{25.500} = \frac{142.640 - 139.650}{25.500}$$

$$= \frac{2.990}{25.500} = 0,1173$$

6. A equação de regressão é, portanto, $Y = -9,671 + 0,1173X$.

b) Preveja o nível de demanda para os quatro trimestres seguintes:

1. Bill prepara estimativas dos contratos trimestrais para os quatro trimestres seguintes em milhares de dólares. São elas: 260, 290, 300 e 270.
2. Em seguida, Bill prevê a demanda por serviços de engenharia da Precision (em milhares de dólares) para os quatro trimestres seguintes usando a equação de regressão $Y = -9{,}671 + 0{,}1173X$:

$$Y_1 = -9{,}671 + 0{,}1173(260)$$
$$= -9{,}671 + 30{,}498$$
$$= 20{,}827$$

$$Y_2 = -9{,}671 + 0{,}1173(290)$$
$$= -9{,}671 + 34{,}017$$
$$= 24{,}346$$

$$Y_3 = -9{,}671 + 0{,}1173(300)$$
$$= -9{,}671 + 35{,}190$$
$$= 25{,}519$$

$$Y_4 = -9{,}671 + 0{,}1173(270)$$
$$= -9{,}671 + 31{,}671$$
$$= 22{,}000$$

A previsão total (em milhares de dólares) para o ano seguinte é o total das quatro previsões trimestrais:

$$20{,}827 + 24{,}346 + 25{,}519 + 22{,}000 = \$\,92{,}7$$

Note que a previsão é arredondada para um dígito significativo a mais do que os dados originais.

c) Avalie quão estreitamente a demanda está relacionada com o valor dos contratos de construção liberados:

$$r = \frac{n\sum xy - \sum x \sum y}{\sqrt{[n\sum x^2 - (\sum x)^2][n\sum y^2 - (\sum y)^2]}} = \frac{2.990}{\sqrt{[25.550][8(1.183) - (95)^2]}}$$

$$= \frac{2.990}{\sqrt{[25.500][9.464 - 9.025]}} = \frac{2.990}{\sqrt{(25.500)(439)}} = \frac{2.990}{\sqrt{11.194.500}}$$

$$= \frac{2.990}{3.345{,}8} = 0{,}894$$

$$r^2 = 0{,}799$$

O valor dos contratos liberados explica aproximadamente 80% ($r^2 = 0{,}799$) da variação observada na demanda trimestral de serviços da Precision.

A modificação aparentemente insignificante de *r* para *r²* permite-nos mudar de medidas subjetivas da relação para medidas mais específicas. Há três tipos de variação em *y*: total, explicada e não explicada:

Variação total	=	Variação explicada	+	Variação não explicada
$\sum(y - \bar{y})^2$		$\sum(Y - \bar{y})^2$		$\sum(y - Y)^2$

A Figura 3.3 ilustra essas variações. A **variação total** é a soma dos desvios quadráticos de cada valor de *y* a partir de sua média $\bar{y}$. A **variação explicada** é a soma dos desvios quadráticos dos valores de Y que se situam na linha de tendências a partir de $\bar{y}$. A **variação não explicada**, ou a variação a partir de fontes aleatórias ou não identificadas, é a soma dos desvios quadráticos de *y* a partir dos valores de Y na linha de tendências.

O **coeficiente de determinação** é estabelecido pela razão da variação explicada pela variação total:

$$r^2 = \frac{\sum(Y - \bar{y})^2}{\sum(y - \bar{y})^2}$$

O coeficiente de determinação, portanto, ilustra quanto da variação na variável dependente y *é explicada por* x *ou pela linha de tendências.* Se $r^2 = 80\%$, como no Exemplo 3.2, podemos dizer que o valor

FIGURA 3.3 — Variação da Variável Dependente (y)

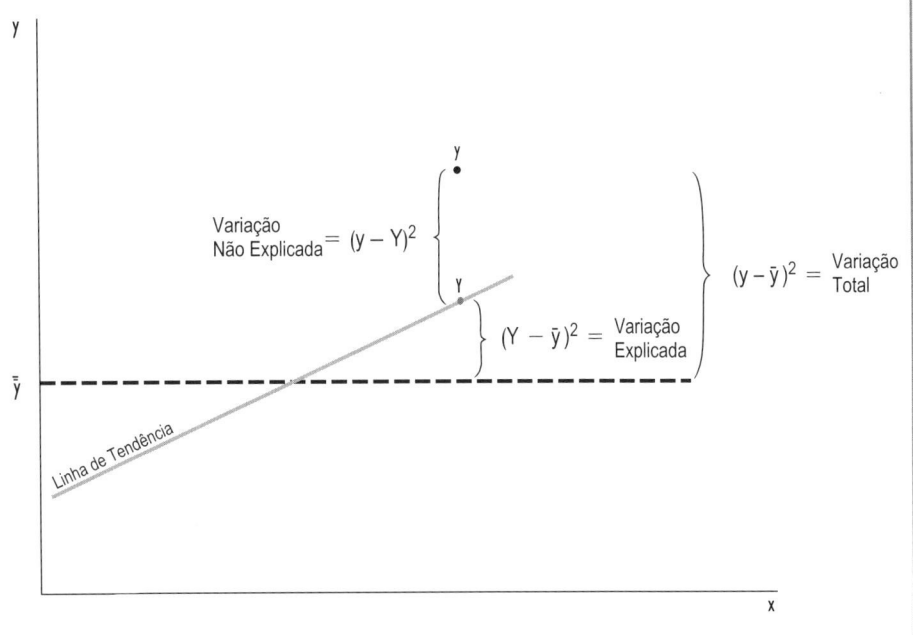

dos contratos liberados (x) explica 80% da variação nas vendas de serviços de engenharia (y). 20% da variação nas vendas de serviços de engenharia não são explicados pelo valor dos contratos, e, dessa forma, eles são atribuídos a outras variáveis ou a uma variação ocasional.

Tanto o coeficiente de correlação como o de determinação são medidas úteis da força da relação entre variáveis dependentes e independentes e, dessa forma, também do valor das equações de regressão como modelos de previsão. Quanto mais forte a relação, maior probabilidade de as previsões resultantes das equações de regressão serem precisas.

A análise de regressão linear simples tem suas limitações para desenvolver previsões com elevada precisão no mundo real do governo e dos negócios. Não obstante haver alguns casos em que uma variável independente explique o bastante a respeito da variação da variável dependente para fornecer suficiente precisão, modelos mais sofisticados podem ser necessários.

Embora as fórmulas mais complexas estejam além do escopo desta discussão, é usada **análise de regressão múltipla** quando há duas ou mais variáveis independentes. Um exemplo de equação de regressão multilinear é:

$$Y = 15,5 + 2,9X_1 + 12,8X_2 - 1,2X_3 + 8,5X_4$$

em que:

Y = vendas do próximo trimestre em milhares de unidades

X_1 = cargas de vagões (em milhões de toneladas) no trimestre anterior

X_2 = crescimento percentual do PIB

X_3 = índice de desemprego na região

X_4 = população da região (em milhões de habitantes)

Essa equação é usada exatamente como a equação de regressão linear simples ($Y = a + bX$): os valores estimados das variáveis independentes (X_1, X_2, X_3 e X_4) são substituídos na equação de regressão linear para calcularmos o valor da variável dependente (Y).

Note na equação de regressão múltipla acima que a variável X_1 indica cargas de vagões no trimestre *anterior*. Esses dados são usados para prever as vendas do trimestre *seguinte*. Nesse caso, os carregamentos de vagões de carga antecipam as vendas em um trimestre. Chamamos X_1 de **indicador de antecipação**, porque seu valor é *conhecido* antes que as vendas ocorram. *É sempre desejável encontrar indicadores de antecipação quando se faz previsões, porque isso evita a necessidade de estimar os valores das variáveis independentes,* como fizemos na etapa b.1 do Exemplo 3.2.

A **análise de regressão múltipla não linear, regressão passo a passo** e **coeficientes de correlação parciais** e **múltiplos** também fazem parte da família de técnicas conhecidas como análise de regressão e correlação, mas estão além do escopo deste livro.

Os conceitos apresentados aqui, porém, em geral se aplicam a essas técnicas mais sofisticadas, e Y, X, *a*, *b* e *r* têm todos suas contrapartes nos modelos mais complexos.

Intervalos das Previsões Quando a análise de regressão linear gera previsões para períodos futuros, estas são somente estimativas e estão sujeitas a erros. A presença de erros de previsão ou variações ocasionais é um fato real para quem faz previsões; previsão é um processo permeado de incertezas. Uma maneira de lidar com essas incertezas consiste em desenvolver intervalos de confiança para as previsões.

A Figura 3.4 mostra graficamente como intervalos de confiança poderiam ser definidos para as previsões. Dez períodos de dados são usados para desenvolver uma linha de tendências. Estendendo-se a linha de tendências para a frente até o Período 12, obtém-se uma previsão de 2.400 unidades. Ao traçarmos limites superiores e inferiores através dos dados paralelos à linha de tendências de tal forma que as vendas anuais reais somente raramente ultrapassem os limites, os limites superior e inferior podem ser estendidos até o Período 12 para obtermos um limite superior de 3.300 unidades e um limite inferior de 1.500 unidades. Se os limites estiverem bem próximos, os dados históricos estavam estreitamente agrupados nas proximidades da linha de tendências, e teremos mais confiança em nossas previsões.

Não obstante essa abordagem gráfica ser às vezes usada para definir limites superiores e inferiores ou intervalos de previsão, um método mais preciso está disponível. O Exemplo 3.3 usa a seguinte fórmula para estimar intervalos para uma previsão:

$$s_{yx} = \sqrt{\frac{\sum y^2 - a\sum y - b\sum xy}{n - 2}}$$

A expressão s_{yx} é denominada **erro padrão da previsão**, ou **desvio padrão da previsão**, e é uma medida de como os pontos dos dados históricos estavam dispersos nas proximidades da linha de tendências. Se s_{yx} for pequeno em relação à previsão, os pontos dos dados passados estavam estreitamente agrupados nas proximidades da linha de tendências, e os limites superior e inferior estão bem próximos.

O intervalo de previsão permite que os analistas lidem com a incerteza que cerca suas previsões desenvolvendo previsões da melhor estimativa e os intervalos dentro dos quais os dados reais têm probabilidade de cair.

Sazonalidade em Previsões de Séries Temporais Os **padrões sazonais** comumente são flutuações que se desenvolvem dentro de um ano e tendem a ser repetidos anualmente. Essas sazonalidades podem ser causadas ou determinadas pelo clima, feriados, dias de pagamento, eventos escolares ou outros fenômenos. O Instantâneo da Indústria 3.1 descreve a experiência da L. L. Bean para prever padrões sazonais.

O Exemplo 3.4 demonstra como desenvolver previsões com uma análise de regressão linear quando a sazonalidade estiver presente em dados da série temporal. O exemplo segue estes passos:

1. Escolha um conjunto de dados históricos representativo.
2. Desenvolva um índice de sazonalidade para cada estação (isto é, mês ou trimestre).
3. Use os índices de sazonalidade para dessazonalizar os dados; em outras palavras, remova os padrões sazonais.
4. Execute uma análise de regressão linear sobre os dados dessazonalizados. Isso resultará numa equação de regressão da forma Y = a + bX.
5. Use a equação de regressão para computar as previsões para o futuro.
6. Use os índices de sazonalidade para reaplicar os padrões sazonais às previsões.

Quando desenvolvemos previsões sazonalizadas usando análise de regressão linear, como no Exemplo 3.4, e desejamos variar essas previsões, o procedimento é direto. As previsões dessazonalizadas seriam variadas, e depois essas previsões, juntamente com seus limites superiores e inferiores, seriam sazonalizadas multiplicando-se as mesmas por seus índices de sazonalidade.

Figura 3.4   Erros de Previsão

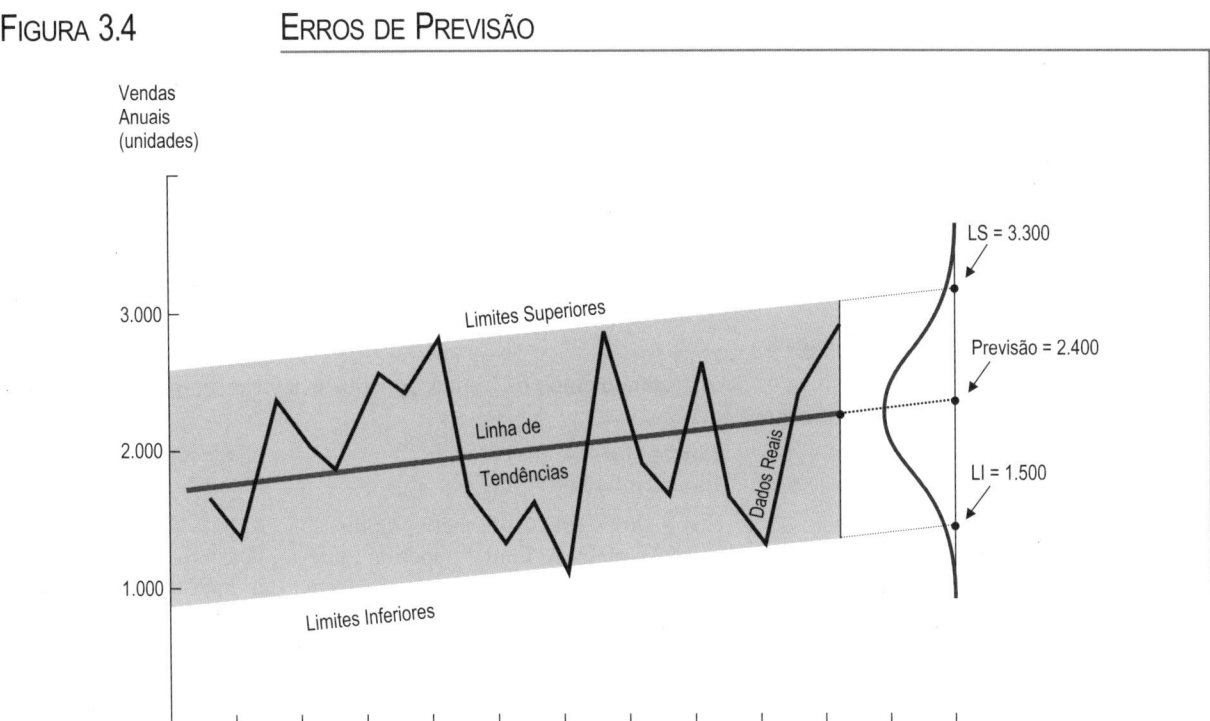

Exemplo 3.3

Intervalos das Previsões de Séries Temporais

Os dados de vendas anuais da Specific Motors do Exemplo 3.1 são usados aqui. A distribuição de valores de previsão correspondentes a um período de tempo futuro tem um desvio padrão (s_{yx}), que é uma medida relativa de como a distribuição está dispersa nas proximidades de seu valor esperado (Y). As distribuições de todos os valores de previsão de períodos de tempo futuros são assumidas como distribuições t de Student.

Solução

1. No Exemplo 3.1 computamos todos estes valores: $\sum y = 21.000$; $\sum x = 55$; $\sum x^2 = 385$; $\sum xy = 133.300$; n = 10; $\bar{x} = 5{,}5$; $\bar{y} = 2.100$. Computemos agora $\sum y^2$:

Ano	y (milhares de unidades)	y^2	Ano	y (milhares de unidades)	y^2
1	1.000	1.000.000	6	2.000	4.000.000
2	1.300	1.690.000	7	2.200	4.840.000
3	1.800	3.240.000	8	2.600	6.760.000
4	2.000	4.000.000	9	2.900	8.410.000
5	2.000	4.000.000	10	3.200	10.240.000
			Total		$\sum y^2 = 48.180.000$

2. Computemos agora o valor de s_{yx}:

$$s_{yx} = \sqrt{\frac{\sum y^2 - a\sum y - b\sum xy}{n - 2}}$$

$$\sqrt{\frac{48.180.000 - 913,333(21.000) - 215,758(133.300)}{10 - 2}}$$

$$= \sqrt{\frac{48.180.000 - 19.179.993 - 28.760.541,4}{8}} = \sqrt{\frac{239.465,6}{8}} = \sqrt{29.933,2}$$

$$= 173,0 \text{ mil unidades}$$

3. Agora que temos o valor de s_{yx}, computemos os limites superior e inferior da previsão para o Período de Tempo 11*:

$$\text{Limite superior} = Y_{11} + t\, s_{yx}$$
$$\text{Limite inferior} = Y_{11} - t\, s_{yx}$$

em que t é o número de desvios padrões tirados da média da distribuição para fornecer determinada probabilidade de ultrapassar esses limites superior e inferior ocasionalmente. Digamos, por exemplo, que você queira definir os limites de forma que haja somente uma probabilidade de 10% (5% em cada extremidade) de ultrapassar os limites ocasionalmente. (Veja a Tabela de Distribuição de Probabilidades t de Student, ao final deste livro.) Uma vez que os graus de liberdade (g.l.) = n − 2 para uma análise de regressão simples e o nível de significação é 0,10, o valor de t é igual a 1,860, e:

Limite superior = 3.286,7 + 1,86(173) = 3.608,5, ou 3.610 mil unidades
Limite inferior = 3.286,7 − 1,86(173) = 2.964,9, ou 2.960 mil unidades

Note que os limites são arredondados para um dígito significativo a mais do que os dados originais.

4. Agora podemos descrever o que temos: há uma probabilidade de 90% de que nossas vendas anuais para o próximo ano estejam entre 3.610 e 2.960 mil unidades. Há somente uma probabilidade de 10% de que nossas vendas se situem fora desses limites. Nossa melhor estimativa é 3.290 mil unidades.

*Outra expressão dos limites superior e inferior da previsão Y às vezes é usada quando o ponto da previsão está bem afastado dos dados originais: limites = $Y \pm t(s_f)$, em que $s_f = s_{yx}\sqrt{1 + 1/n + [(X_0 - \bar{X})^2/\sum(X - \bar{X})^2]}$, e X_0 é o valor de X para os quais um valor de Y está sendo previsto.

PREVISÕES DE CURTO PRAZO

Previsões de Curto Prazo comumente são estimativas das condições futuras no decorrer de intervalos de tempo que variam de alguns dias a diversas semanas. *Essas previsões podem abranger períodos de tempo curtos sobre os quais ciclos, sazonalidade e padrões de tendências têm pouco efeito.* O padrão de dados que mais afeta essas previsões é a flutuação aleatória.

As previsões de curto prazo fornecem aos gerentes de operações informações para tomarem decisões como estas:

- Quanto estoque de um produto particular deve ser mantido no próximo mês?
- Quanto de cada produto deve ser produzido na semana seguinte?
- Quanto de cada matéria-prima deve ser encomendado para ser entregue na próxima semana?
- Quantos trabalhadores devem trabalhar em tempo integral e horas extras na próxima semana?

Avaliando o Desempenho do Modelo de Previsão Os modelos de previsão de curto prazo são avaliados em função de três características: resposta ao impulso, capacidade de atenuação de ruído e precisão.

INSTANTÂNEO DA INDÚSTRIA 3.1

PREVENDO AS CHAMADAS TELEFÔNICAS NA L. L. BEAN

A L. L. Bean é uma varejista muito conhecida de roupas de alta qualidade. Aproximadamente 10% de suas vendas são derivadas de pontos-de-venda a varejo, 20% de encomendas feitas via correio e 70% de encomendas via ligação gratuita. Os agentes de atendimento aos clientes da empresa são especialmente treinados para cuidar de uma ampla variedade de dúvidas dos consumidores, ao passo que os agentes de vendas são treinados principalmente para tirar pedidos de venda.

Para planejar eficazmente o rodízio de funcionários, é importante para a L. L. Bean prever de maneira acurada o número de chamadas telefônicas diárias para vendas e atendimento ao cliente. Os programadores usam então as previsões para estabelecer os horários de trabalho dos empregados para um período de três semanas. Previsões imprecisas são muito dispendiosas para a L. L.Bean: previsões muito altas resultam em excessivo custo de mão-de-obra direta, e previsões muito baixas resultam em programar poucos empregados, o que gera insatisfação dos clientes, vendas perdidas e elevadas contas telefônicas, em decorrência de tempos de espera maiores. Um complicador adicional para o desafio de fazer previsões e programar funcionários é a natureza errática e a extrema sazonalidade dos negócios da L. L. Bean. A companhia recebe quase 20% de suas chamadas anuais nas três semanas que antecedem o Natal, período em que normalmente duplica o número de agentes e quadruplica a quantidade de linhas telefônicas.

Num esforço para melhorar a precisão da previsão, novos modelos de previsão foram desenvolvidos usando-se a metodologia da média móvel integrada auto-regressiva (ARIMA, ou de Box-Jenkins). As melhorias foram substanciais. Um gerente da L. L. Bean descreveu-as da seguinte maneira: "Estamos usando o novo modelo de previsão há quase cinco meses e nos beneficiamos muito de sua melhorada precisão. No passado prevíamos o volume de chamadas usando uma abordagem menos sofisticada do ponto de vista estatístico, a qual se baseava principalmente na previsão de encomendas fornecida pelo departamento de marketing.

As economias anuais decorrentes da mudança para o novo sistema de previsão são estimadas em US$ 300 mil. Isso não inclui as substanciais economias contínuas decorrentes de reduzirmos grandemente a mão-de-obra necessária para preparar as previsões a cada semana".

Fonte: Andrews, Bruce H. e Shawn M. Cunningham. "L. L. Bean Improves Call-Center Forecasting". *Interface* 25, n. 6 (novembro-dezembro de 1995).

EXEMPLO 3.4

PREVISÕES DE SÉRIES TEMPORAIS SAZONALIZADAS

Jim White, gerente de fábrica da Specific Motors, está tentando planejar as necessidades de caixa, pessoal, matérias-primas e suprimentos para cada trimestre do ano seguinte. Os dados de vendas trimestrais correspondentes aos três últimos anos parecem refletir de modo correto o padrão de saída sazonal que deve ser esperado no futuro. Se Jim pudesse estimar as vendas trimestrais para o ano seguinte, as necessidades de caixa, pessoal, matérias-primas e suprimentos poderiam ser determinadas. (É útil usarmos uma planilha eletrônica para efetuar muitos dos cálculos.)

SOLUÇÃO

1. Primeiro computamos os índices de sazonalidade:

	Vendas Trimestrais (milhares de unidades)				Total
Ano	Q_1	Q_2	Q_3	Q_4	Anual
8	520	730	820	530	2.600
9	590	810	900	600	2.900
10	650	900	1.000	650	3.200
Totais	1.760	2.440	2.720	1.780	8.700
Média trimestral	$586\frac{2}{3}$	$813\frac{2}{3}$	$906\frac{2}{3}$	$593\frac{1}{3}$	725*
Índice de sazonalidade (I.S.)**	0,809	1,122	1,251	0,818	

*Média trimestral total = 8700/12 = 725.
**I.S. = Média trimestral/Média trimestral global.

2. Em seguida, dessazonalizamos os dados dividindo cada valor trimestral por seu I.S. (índice de sazonalidade). Por exemplo, 520 ÷ 0,809 = 642,8; 730 ÷ 1,122 = 650,6; e assim por diante.

	Dados Trimestrais Ajustados Dessazonalizados			
Ano	Q_1	Q_2	Q_3	Q_4
8	642,8	650,6	655,5	647,9
9	729,3	721,9	719,4	733,5
10	803,5	802,1	799,4	794,6

3. Em seguida realizamos uma análise de regressão nos dados dessazonalizados (12 trimestres) e fazemos uma previsão para os quatro trimestres seguintes:

Período de tempo	x	y	y^2	x^2	xy
Ano 8, Q_1	1	642,8	413.191,84	1	642,8
Ano 8, Q_2	2	650,6	423.280,36	4	1.301,2
Ano 8, Q_3	3	655,5	429.680,25	9	1.966,5
Ano 8, Q_4	4	647,9	419.774,41	16	2.591,6
Ano 9, Q_1	5	729,3	531.878,49	25	3.646,5
Ano 9, Q_2	6	721,9	521.139,61	36	4.331,4
Ano 9, Q_3	7	719,4	517.536,36	49	5.035,8
Ano 9, Q_4	8	733,5	538.022,25	64	5.868,0
Ano 10, Q_1	9	803,5	645.612,25	81	7.231,5
Ano 10, Q_2	10	802,1	643.364,41	100	8.021,0
Ano 10, Q_3	11	799,4	639.040,36	121	8.793,4
Ano 10, Q_4	12	794,6	631.389,16	144	9.535,2
Totais	$\sum x = 78$	$\sum y = 8.700,5$	$\sum y^2 = 6.353.909,75$	$\sum x^2 = 650$	$\sum xy = 58.964,9$

4. Usamos então esses valores para substituir nas fórmulas encontradas na Tabela 3.5:

$$a = \frac{\sum x^2 \sum y - \sum x \sum xy}{n\sum x^2 - (\sum x)^2} = \frac{650(8.700,5) - 78(58.964,9)}{12(650) - (78)^2} = 615,421$$

$$b = \frac{n\sum xy - \sum x \sum y}{n\sum x^2 - (\sum x)^2} = \frac{12(58.964,9) - 78(8.700,5)}{12(650) - (78)^2} = 16,865$$

$$Y = a + bX = 615,421 + 16,865X$$

5. Substituímos então os valores 13, 14, 15 e 16 — os quatro trimestres seguintes para x — na equação de regressão. Estas são previsões dessazonalizadas, em milhares de unidades, para os quatro trimestres seguintes.

$$Y_{13} = 615{,}421 + 16{,}865(13) = 834{,}666 \quad Y_{15} = 615{,}421 + 16{,}865(15) = 868{,}396$$
$$Y_{14} = 615{,}421 + 16{,}865(14) = 851{,}531 \quad Y_{16} = 615{,}421 + 16{,}865(16) = 885{,}261$$

6. Usamos agora os índices de sazonalidade (I.S.) para sazonalizar as previsões:

Trimestre	I.S.	Previsões Dessazonalizadas	Previsões Sazonalizadas [I.S. × previsões dessazonalizadas] (milhares de unidades)
Q_1	0,809	834,666	675
Q_2	1,122	851,531	955
Q_3	1,251	868,396	1.086
Q_4	0,818	885,261	724

Note que as previsões são arredondadas para um dígito significativo a mais do que os dados originais.

Resposta ao Impulso Versus *Capacidade de Atenuação de Ruído* A previsão de curto prazo envolve pegar dados do passado e projetar os valores estimados para esses dados um ou mais períodos no futuro. Diz-se que as previsões que refletem cada pequena flutuação casual em dados passados incluem variação aleatória, ou **ruído**. Essas previsões são erráticas de período a período. Se, por outro lado, as previsões tiverem pouca flutuação de período a período, diz-se que elas têm **atenuação de ruído.**

Previsões que reagem muito rápido a mudanças nos dados históricos são descritas como tendo uma **elevada resposta ao impulso**. Por outro lado, quando as previsões refletem pouco das mudanças nos dados históricos, diz-se que elas têm **baixa resposta ao impulso**. Normalmente é desejável ter-se previsões que têm tanto elevada resposta ao impulso quanto capacidade de atenuação de ruído, mas isso não é possível. Um sistema de previsão que reage muito rápido a mudanças nos dados necessários capta uma grande quantidade de ruído. Aqueles que fazem previsões, portanto, costumeiramente devem escolher qual característica — elevada resposta ao impulso ou elevada capacidade de atenuação de ruído — tem mais valor quando selecionam modelos de previsão para aplicações particulares.

Médias da Precisão da Previsão Precisão do modelo de previsão refere-se a quão próximo os dados reais seguem as previsões. Três medidas da precisão da previsão são comumente usadas: (1) desvio padrão para a previsão (s_{yx}), já discutido, (2) erro quadrático médio (EQM), ou simplesmente $(s_{yx})^2$ e (3) desvio absoluto médio (DAM), que é computado com as fórmulas que se seguem:

$$DAM = \frac{\text{Soma do desvio absoluto para n períodos}}{n}$$

$$DAM = \frac{\sum_{i=1}^{n} |\text{Demanda real} - \text{Demanda prevista}|_i}{n}$$

Assim como s_{yx} e EQM, se o DAM for pequeno, os dados reais seguem estreitamente as previsões da variável dependente, e o modelo de previsão fornece previsões acuradas. Quando os erros de previsão estão normalmente distribuídos, os valores do DAM e s_{yx} estão relacionados à expressão:

$$S_{yx} = 1{,}25 DAM$$

DAM, s_{yx}, e EQM são usados para medir a precisão *após o fato* tanto do modelo de previsão de médio prazo como do de longo prazo. No caso de modelos de previsão de curto prazo, entretanto, o DAM também pode ser usado para determinar valores bons dos parâmetros dos modelos de previsão *antes* que os modelos sejam aplicados.

Previsões Ingênuas Modelos de previsão ingênuos são aqueles que são rápidos e fáceis de usar, não têm virtualmente nenhum custo e são fáceis de entender. Exemplos de previsões ingênuas são (1) usar as vendas de ontem como previsão de vendas de ámanhã e (2) usar as vendas correspondentes à mesma data do ano passado para a previsão de vendas de amanhã. A principal objeção relativa ao uso dessas abordagens ingênuas para previsão de curto prazo é que elas são tão simplistas que têm a probabilidade de resultar em substanciais erros de previsão. Há algumas aplicações, entretanto, nas quais as abordagens ingênuas são tão precisas quanto os modelos mais complexos, ou o erro de previsão não é custoso o bastante para justificar modelos de previsão mais caros.

Método da Média Móvel O método da média móvel tira a média dos dados de alguns períodos recentes, que se torna a previsão para o período seguinte. O Exemplo 3.5 demonstra como usar o método da média móvel. De especial importância é o número de períodos (períodos de recorrência — PR) de dados a serem incluídos na média.

EXEMPLO 3.5

PREVISÃO DE CURTO PRAZO COM MÉDIA MÓVEL

A gerente de estoques Shirley Johnson quer desenvolver um sistema de previsão de curto prazo para estimar a quantidade de estoque que flui de seus armazéns cada semana. Ela acha que a demanda por estoques, de maneira geral, tem permanecido constante, com leves flutuações aleatórias de semana a semana. Um analista do escritório central da companhia sugeriu que ela use uma média móvel de 3, 5 ou 7 semanas. Antes de escolher uma delas, Shirley decide comparar a precisão de cada uma quanto ao período de 10 semanas mais recente.

SOLUÇÃO

1. Compute as previsões com médias móveis de 3, 5 e 7 semanas:

Semana	Demanda Real por Estoque (milhares de dólares)	Previsões PR = 3 Semanas	PR = 5 Semanas	PR = 7 Semanas
1	100			
2	125			
3	90			
4	110			
5	105			
6	130			
7	85			
8	102	106,7	104,0	106,4
9	110	105,7	106,4	106,7
10	90	99,0	106,4	104,6
11	105	100,7	103,4	104,6
12	95	101,7	98,4	103,9
13	115	96,7	100,4	102,4
14	120	105,0	103,0	100,3
15	80	110,0	105,0	105,3
16	95	105,0	103,0	102,1
17	100	98,3	101,0	100,0

Note que as previsões são arredondadas para um dígito significativo a mais do que os dados originais.

Exemplo de computações — previsões para a 10ª semana:

$$F_3 = \frac{85 + 102 + 110}{3} = 99,0$$

$$F_5 = \frac{105 + 130 + 85 + 102 + 110}{5} = 106,4$$

$$F_7 = \frac{90 + 110 + 105 + 130 + 85 + 102 + 110}{7} = 104,6$$

Observação: Para prever para a 10ª semana, lembre-se de que os únicos dados históricos sobre a demanda por estoques reais semanais com os quais você poderá trabalhar são as semanas 1 a 9. Assim, você não poderá incluir os dados reais correspondentes à 10ª semana para computar as previsões da 10ª semana.

2. Em seguida, compute o desvio absoluto médio (DAM) para as três previsões:

Semana	Demanda Real por Estoque (milhares de dólares)	Previsão					
		PR = 3 Semanas		PR = 5 Semanas		PR = 7 Semanas	
		Previsões	Desvio Absoluto	Previsões	Desvio Absoluto	Previsões	Desvio Absoluto
8	102	106,7	4,7	104,0	2,0	106,4	4,4
9	110	105,7	4,3	106,4	3,6	106,7	3,3
10	90	99,0	9,0	106,4	16,4	104,6	14,6
11	105	100,7	4,3	103,4	1,6	104,6	0,4
12	95	101,7	6,7	98,4	3,4	103,9	8,9
13	115	96,7	18,3	100,4	14,6	102,4	12,6
14	120	105,0	15,0	103,0	17,0	100,3	19,7
15	80	110,0	30,0	105,0	25,0	105,3	25,3
16	95	105,0	10,0	103,0	8,0	102,1	7,1
17	100	98,3	1,7	101,0	1,0	100,0	0,0
Desvio absoluto total			104,0		92,6		96,3
Desvio absoluto médio (DAM)			10,40		9,26		9,63

3. A precisão da previsão PR = 5 é a melhor, porque seu DAM tende a ser menor do que com 3 ou 7 semanas. A precisão da previsão do período médio de 7 semanas está muito próxima da de 5 semanas; portanto, uma verificação futura é recomendada.
4. Agora ela usa um PR de 5 semanas para prever as necessidades de caixa para a semana seguinte, a 18ª:

$$\text{Previsão} = \frac{115 + 120 + 80 + 95 + 100}{5} = 102 \text{ ou } \$ 102.000$$

A Figura 3.5 plota as três previsões com média móvel em relação aos dados reais do Exemplo 3.5. Note que *quanto maior for o PR, maior será a capacidade de atenuação de ruído e menor será a resposta ao impulso da previsão, e vice-versa*: a previsão PR = 7 tem uma capacidade de atenuação de ruído ligeiramente maior e uma resposta ao impulso ligeiramente menor que as outras duas previsões, porque sua curva exibe menos variação de período a período. O PR mais acurado tende a variar conforme as características únicas de cada conjunto de dados; por conseguinte, o PR deve ser determinado por experimentação, como no Exemplo 3.5. A escolha de um PR dependerá dos critérios de precisão, resposta ao impulso e capacidade de atenuação de ruído. O que é mais desejável: elevada resposta ao impulso ou elevada capacidade de atenuação de ruído? Quanta precisão pode ser deixada de lado para se conseguir qualquer uma dessas duas características? Na análise final, o PR escolhido dependerá de um completo conhecimento do uso pretendido das previsões e da natureza da situação de previsão.

FIGURA 3.5 PREVISÕES COM MÉDIA MÓVEL *VERSUS* REAIS NECESSIDADES DE CAIXA DO EXEMPLO 3.5

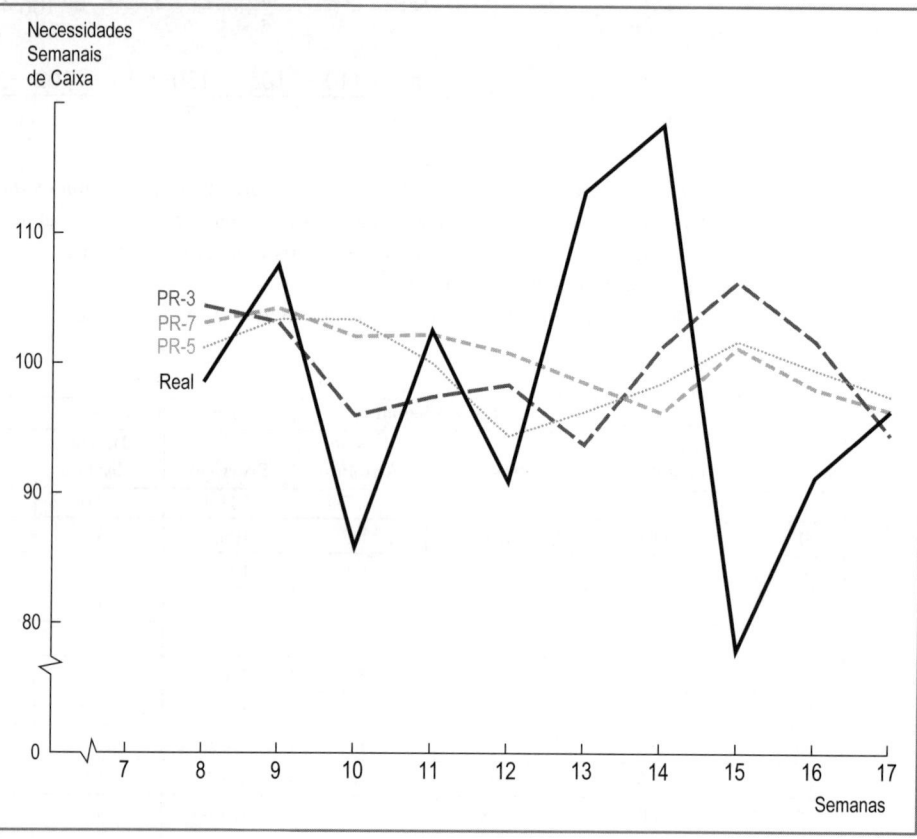

Método da Média Ponderada Móvel O método da média móvel já discutido pesa igualmente os dados históricos ao desenvolver uma previsão. Em algumas situações, pode ser desejável aplicar pesos desiguais aos dados históricos. Por exemplo, se dados mais recentes forem considerados mais relevantes para uma previsão, pesos maiores poderiam ser aplicados a esses dados da seguinte maneira:

Semana	Dados Reais	Peso
7	85	0,20
8	102	0,30
9	110	0,50

$$\text{Previsão}_{10} = 0{,}2(85) + 0{,}3(102) + 0{,}5(110) = 102{,}6, \text{ ou } \$ 102.600$$

Essa simples modificação no método da média móvel permite que aqueles que fazem previsões especifiquem a importância relativa de cada período de dados passado.

Método da Exponencial Móvel As variáveis, as definições de variáveis e as fórmulas para previsões com a exponencial móvel se encontram na Tabela 3.6. A **exponencial móvel** pega a previsão correspondente ao período anterior e faz um ajuste para obter a previsão para o período seguinte. Esse ajuste é uma proporção do erro de previsão no período anterior e é computado multiplicando-se o erro de previsão do período anterior por uma constante que está entre zero e um. Essa constante alfa (α) é chamada **constante de amortecimento**. O Exemplo 3.6 demonstra como usar a exponencial móvel para desenvolver previsões.

Capítulo 3 – Previsões na APO

TABELA 3.6	FÓRMULAS E DEFINIÇÕES DE VARIÁVEIS PARA PREVISÕES COM AMORTECIMENTO EXPONENCIAL

F_t = previsão para o período t, o período seguinte
F_{t-1} = previsão para o período $t - 1$, o período anterior
A_{t-1} = dados reais para o período $t - 1$, o período anterior
α = constante de amortecimento, de 0 a 1.

$F_t = F_{t-1} + \alpha(A_{t-1} - F_{t-1})$, a qual pode ser expressa como:
$F_t = \alpha A_{t-1} + (1 - \alpha)F_{t-1}$

As pessoas que fazem previsões escolhem valores para α baseando-se em critérios de precisão, resposta ao impulso e capacidade de atenuação de ruído. Como se pode ver no Exemplo 3.6, níveis mais elevados de α nem sempre resultam em previsões mais acuradas. Cada conjunto de dados tende a ter qualidades únicas, de forma que é aconselhável fazer experimentação com diferentes níveis α a fim de obter precisão na previsão.

A Figura 3.6 plota as previsões com exponencial móvel (α = 0,1, 0,2 e 0,3) em relação à real demanda semanal por estoques do Exemplo 3.6. Note que *quanto mais elevado for α, mais elevada será a resposta ao impulso, e menor será sua capacidade de atenuação de ruído, e vice-versa*. Quando $\alpha = 0,3$, a previsão exibe uma resposta ao impulso ligeiramente mais elevada e uma capacidade de atenuação de ruído ligeiramente mais baixa, porque sua curva exibe uma variação maior de período a período.

A exponencial móvel costumava ser chamada de **média móvel exponencialmente ponderada**, expressão que nos lembra que a *exponencial móvel, à semelhança dos modelos de média móvel e média ponderada móvel, desenvolve previsões que são efetivamente médias. A exponencial móvel pondera os dados de períodos recentes como se tivessem maior peso do que os dados de períodos mais distantes*.

A Figura 3.7 ilustra os pesos correspondentes a algumas constantes de amortecimento.

Exponencial Móvel com Tendência Geralmente consideramos o planejamento de curto prazo para cobrir intervalos de tempo tão breves que a sazonalidade e a tendência não são fatores importantes na previsão de curto prazo. À medida que nos movemos das previsões de curto prazo para as previsões de médio prazo, entretanto, a sazonalidade e a tendência tornam-se mais importantes.

A incorporação de um componente de tendência em previsões exponencialmente amortecidas é chamada **exponencial móvel dupla**, porque a estimativa da média e a estimativa da tendência são ambas amortecidas.

EXEMPLO 3.6

PREVISÃO DE CURTO PRAZO COM A EXPONENCIAL MÓVEL

Shirley Johnson, do Exemplo 3.5, conversa com um analista do escritório central da empresa sobre a previsão da demanda semanal por estoques que saem de seus armazéns. O analista sugere que Shirley considere usar a exponencial móvel com constantes de amortecimento de 0,1, 0,2 e 0,3. Shirley decide comparar a precisão das constantes de amortecimento correspondente ao período de 10 semanas mais recente.

SOLUÇÃO

1. Primeiro estudamos as fórmulas e as definições de variáveis da Tabela 3.6. Computamos as previsões semanais entre as semanas 8ª e 17ª:

Semana	Demanda Real por Estoque (milhares de dólares)	Previsões		
		$\alpha = 0,1$	$\alpha = 0,2$	$\alpha = 0,3$
7	85	85,0*	85,0	85,0
8	102	85,0	85,0	85,0
9	110	86,7	88,4	90,1
10	90	89,0	92,7	96,1
11	105	89,1	92,2	94,3
12	95	90,7	94,8	97,5
13	115	91,1	94,8	96,8
14	120	93,5	98,8	102,3
15	80	96,2	103,0	107,6
16	95	94,6	98,4	99,3
17	100	94,6	97,7	98,0

*Todas essas previsões para a 7ª semana foram escolhidas arbitrariamente. Previsões iniciais precisam usar exponencial móvel. Tradicionalmente definimos essas previsões como iguais aos dados reais do período.

Note que as previsões são arredondadas para um dígito significativo a mais do que os dados originais. Eis exemplos de cálculos para as previsões da 10ª semana:

$$F_{10} = F_9 + \alpha(A_9 - F_9)$$
$\alpha = 0,1$: $F_{10} = 86,7 + 0,1(110 - 86,7) = 89,0$
$\alpha = 0,2$: $F_{10} = 88,4 + 0,2(110 - 88,4) = 92,7$
$\alpha = 0,3$: $F_{10} = 90,1 + 0,3(110 - 90,1) = 96,1$

Observação: Quando as previsões da 10ª semana são feitas, os únicos dados históricos disponíveis são até a 9ª semana. Somente os dados reais da 9ª semana e as previsões da 9ª semana são usados para computar as previsões da 10ª semana.

2. Em seguida, computamos o desvio absoluto médio (DAM) para as três previsões:

Semana	Demanda Real por Estoque (milhares de dólares)	Previsões					
		$\alpha = 0,1$		$\alpha = 0,2$		$\alpha = 0,3$	
		Previsões	Desvio Absoluto	Previsões	Desvio Absoluto	Previsões	Desvio Absoluto
8	102	85,0	17,0	85,0	17,0	85,0	17,0
9	110	86,7	23,3	88,4	21,6	90,1	19,9
10	90	89,0	1,0	92,7	2,7	96,1	6,1
11	105	89,1	15,9	92,2	12,8	94,3	10,7
12	95	90,7	4,3	94,8	0,2	97,5	2,5
13	115	91,1	23,9	94,8	20,2	96,8	18,2
14	120	93,5	26,5	98,8	21,2	102,3	17,7
15	80	96,2	16,2	103,0	23,0	107,6	27,6
16	95	94,6	0,4	98,4	3,4	99,3	4,3
17	100	94,6	5,4	97,7	2,3	98,0	2,0
Desvio absoluto total			133,9		124,4		126,0
Desvio absoluto médio (DAM)			13,39		12,44		12,60

3. A constante de amortecimento $\alpha = 0,2$ apresenta uma precisão ligeiramente melhor quando comparada com $\alpha = 0,1$ e $\alpha = 0,3$.
4. Em seguida, usando $\alpha = 0,2$, computamos a previsão (em milhares de dólares) para a 18ª semana:

$F_{18} = F_{17} + 0,2(A_{17} - F_{17})$
$= 97,7 + 0,2(100 - 97,7) = 97,7 + 0,2(2,3) = 97,7 + 0,46 = 98,2$, ou $ 98.200

| FIGURA 3.6 | PREVISÕES COM EXPONENCIAL MÓVEL *VERSUS* REAIS NECESSIDADES DE CAIXA DO EXEMPLO 3.6 |

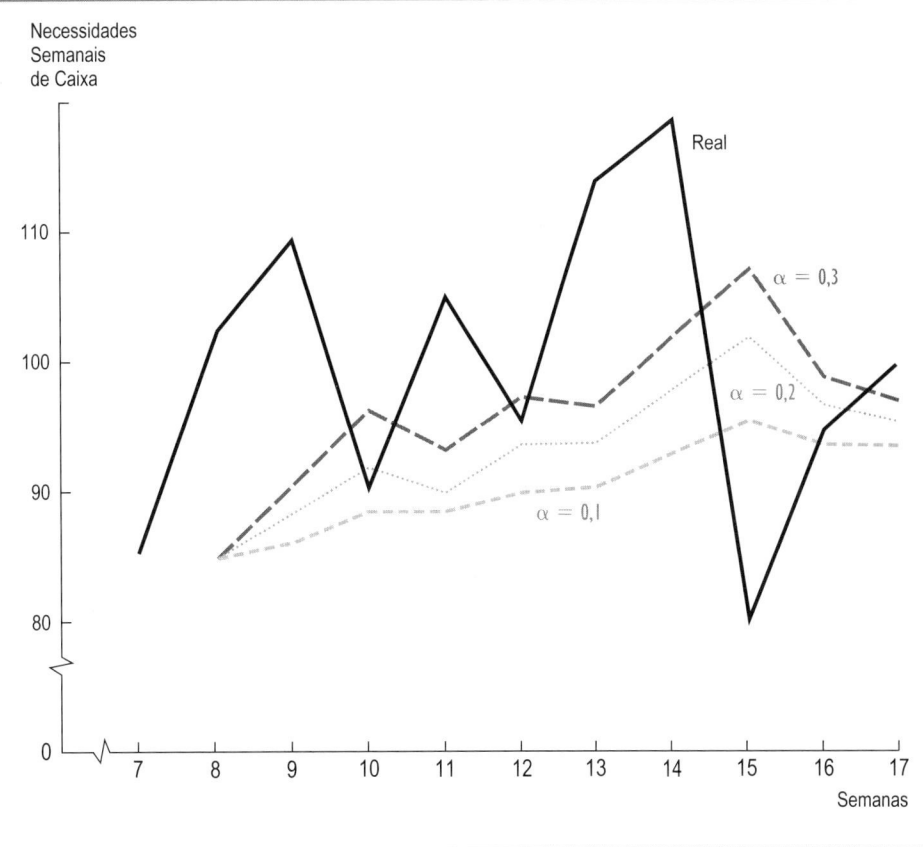

Tanto α, a constante de amortecimento para a média, como β, a constante de amortecimento para a tendência, são usadas nesse modelo.

A Tabela 3.7 exibe fórmulas para incorporar um componente de tendência nas previsões com exponencial móvel, e o Exemplo 3.7 ilustra o uso das fórmulas.

A previsão com tendência no mês 7 é computada desta maneira:

$$FT_t = S_{t-1} + T_{t-1}$$
$$FT_7 = S_6 + T_6$$
$$= 149,28 + 3,81 = 153,09, \text{ ou } \$ 153,1 \text{ mil}$$

EXEMPLO 3.7

PREVISÕES COM EXPONENCIAL MÓVEL COM TENDÊNCIA

Ann Hickman deve prever as vendas de sua empresa de transporte rodoviário a fim de poder planejar suas necessidades de caixa, pessoal e combustível no futuro. Ela acredita que as vendas durante o último período de seis meses devem ser representativas das vendas futuras. Desenvolva uma previsão com exponencial móvel com tendência para as vendas do mês 7 se $\alpha = 0,2$, $\beta = 0,3$, e as vendas passadas, em milhares de dólares, forem:

TABELA 3.7 — FÓRMULAS, DEFINIÇÕES DE VARIÁVEIS E PROCEDIMENTO PARA PREVISÕES COM EXPONENCIAL MÓVEL COM TENDÊNCIA

Definições de Variáveis

S_t = previsão amortecida no período t
T_t = estimativa da tendência no período t
A_t = dados reais no período t
t = o período de tempo seguinte
$t - 1$ = o período de tempo anterior
FT_t = previsão com tendência no período t
α = constante de amortecimento para a média, de 0 a 1
β = constante de amortecimento para a tendência, de 0 a 1

Fórmulas

$FT_t = S_{t-1} + T_{t-1}$
$S_t = FT_t + \alpha(A_t - FT_t)$
$T_t = T_{t-1} + \beta(FT_t - FT_{t-1} - T_{t-1})$

Procedimento

Se quiséssemos concluir a previsão com exponencial móvel com tendência para a semana 7, seguiríamos este procedimento:

1. Para começar, precisamos conhecer os valores de α e β. Os valores das constantes de amortecimento α e β estão entre 0 e 1 e devem ser estimados ou derivados experimentalmente.
2. S_6 e T_6 teriam sido computados anteriormente.
3. Compute: $FT_7 = S_6 + T_6$. Esta é a previsão com exponencial móvel com tendência para a semana 7.
4. Na preparação para computar a previsão para a semana seguinte, computamos S_7 e T_7. Conhecendo os valores de FT_7, FT_6, α, β e T_6, e depois o valor de A_7, computamos:
   $S_7 = FT_7 + \alpha(A_7 - FT_7)$
   $T_7 = T_6 + \beta(FT_7 - FT_6 - T_6)$

Mês (t)	Vendas (milhares de dólares) (A_t)
1	130
2	136
3	134
4	140
5	146
6	150

SOLUÇÃO

1. Estimamos uma previsão inicial para o mês 1: uma previsão ingênua para o mês 1 seriam as vendas reais no mês 1, ou 130.

$$FT_1 = A_1 = 130$$

2. Estimamos um componente de tendência inicial. Uma maneira de estimar o componente de tendência é subtrair as vendas reais no mês 1 das vendas reais no mês 6 e depois dividir por 5 o número de períodos entre 1 e 6:

$$T_1 = \frac{A_6 - A_1}{5} = \frac{150 - 130}{5} = 4$$

3. Em seguida, usando a previsão inicial e o componente de tendência inicial dos itens 1 e 2 acima, computamos uma previsão para as vendas em cada um dos meses que levam à previsão para o mês 7:

Mês (t)	Vendas (milhares de dólares) (A_t)	FT_t	+	$\alpha(A_t$	−	$FT_t)$	=	S_t
1	130	130	+	0,2 (130	−	130)	=	130,00
2	136	134	+	0,2 (136	−	134)	=	134,40
3	134	138,40	+	0,2 (134	−	138,40)	=	137,52
4	140	141,64	+	0,2 (140	−	141,64)	=	141,31
5	146	145,17	+	0,2 (146	−	145,17)	=	145,34
6	150	149,10	+	0,2 (150	−	149,10)	=	149,28

Mês (t)	Vendas (milhares de dólares) (A_t)	T_{t-1}	+	$\beta(FT_t$	−	FT_{t-1}	−	$T_{t-1})$	=	T_t
1	130							dado	=	4,00
2	136	4,00	+	0,3 (134	−	130	−	4,00)	=	4,00
3	134	4,00	+	0,3 (138,40	−	134	−	4,00)	=	4,12
4	140	4,12	+	0,3 (141,64	−	138,40	−	4,12)	=	3,86
5	146	3,86	+	0,3 (145,17	−	141,64	−	3,86)	=	3,76
6	150	3,76	+	0,3 (149,10	−	145,17	−	3,76)	=	3,81

Mês (t)	Vendas (milhares de dólares) (A_t)	S_{t-1}	+	T_{t-1}	=	FT_t
1	130			dado	=	130,00
2	136	130	+	4,00	=	134,00
3	134	134,40	+	4,00	=	138,40
4	140	137,52	+	4,12	=	141,64
5	146	141,31	+	3,86	=	145,17
6	150	145,34	+	3,76	=	149,10
7	—	149,28	+	3,81	=	153,09

O Exemplo 3.7 poderia ter incorporado um componente de sazonalidade nas previsões, exatamente como foi feito no Exemplo 3.4. Índices de sazonalidade teriam sido desenvolvidos para cada período, os índices teriam sido usados para dessazonalizar os dados, as fórmulas da Tabela 3.7 teriam sido usadas para dessazonalizar as previsões, e depois os índices teriam sido usados para colocar os padrões sazonais nas previsões.

A exponencial móvel é um caso especial do *modelo Box-Jenkins*, cujos métodos de autocorrelação examinam os pontos de dados históricos reais e encaixam uma função matemática nesses dados. A função matemática torna-se então o modelo de previsão para estimativas futuras. Disponível em muitos pacotes padrões de previsão computadorizada, esse método é relatado como o mais acurado de todos os métodos de previsão de curto prazo. Entretanto, aproximadamente 60 pontos de dados são necessários, certo tempo é necessário para se obter resultados de previsão, e o modelo é moderadamente dispendioso. Estes e outros desenvolvimentos na previsão com exponencial móvel tornam-na uma poderosa força nas previsões de curto prazo.

Agora que examinamos alguns métodos e questões de previsão, concluímos considerando como se pode ter um sistema de previsão bem-sucedido e discutindo os tipos de software de computador disponíveis para fazer previsões.

FIGURA 3.7   PONDERAÇÃO DE DADOS PASSADOS NA EXPONENCIAL MÓVEL

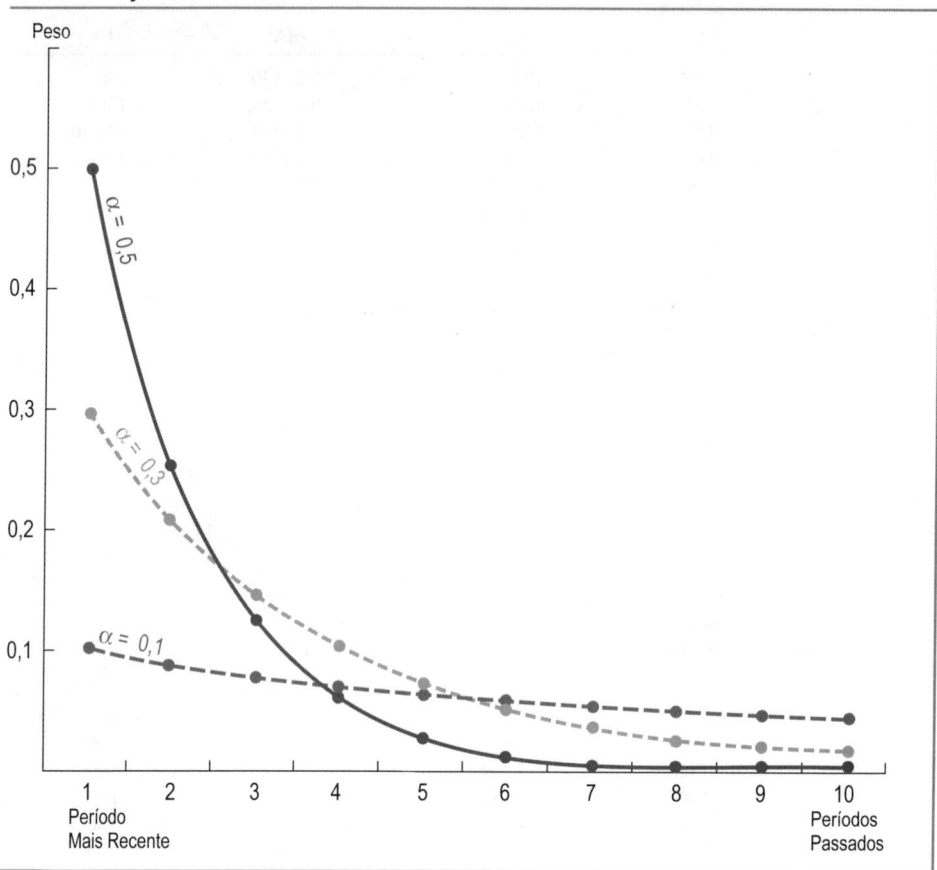

INSTANTÂNEO DA INDÚSTRIA 3.2

USANDO UM SISTEMA ESPECIALISTA DE PREVISÃO NA XEROX

Mudaram a maneira de fazer previsões na Xerox Corporation. Na maneira antiga de desenvolver previsões de vendas, sete analistas usavam uma colcha de retalhos de modelos e métodos de previsão. Numa ponta, eles traçavam graficamente os dados históricos e extrapolavam-nos na direção do futuro para os muitos tipos de máquinas copiadoras de sua linha de produtos. Esses gráficos eram então distribuídos a todos os interessados e partes envolvidas dentro da corporação. Na outra ponta, alguns analistas usavam planilhas eletrônicas. Esse conjunto de métodos e abordagem trabalhosa para desenvolver previsões se alongava tanto que a equipe de previsão começava a trabalhar nas previsões do ano seguinte em meados do ano atual, e somente tinha tempo suficiente de desenvolver previsões para 12 meses no futuro. Essa abordagem era tão trabalhosa e as previsões eram tão imprecisas que a Xerox organizou um esforço para desenvolver um sistema especialista para fazer grande parte da previsão.

Foram necessários dois anos para desenvolver o sistema especialista, mas agora os analistas podem esperar até outubro para começar a desenvolver as previsões de vendas para o ano seguinte. O novo sistema faz previsões de três anos no futuro, o que dá à companhia uma visão mais abrangente do futuro para seus negócios.

E isso não é tudo — o sistema monitora continuamente seu próprio desempenho e atualiza seus parâmetros a fim de que a precisão da previsão seja constantemente refinada. O tempo economizado usando o sistema especialista permite à equipe considerar os impactos de coisas como inflação e atividade dos concorrentes nas vendas futuras da Xerox.

Fonte: "Software Even a CFO Could Love". *Business Week,* 2 de novembro de 1992.

Como Ter um Sistema de Previsão Bem-Sucedido

A Figura 3.1 ilustrou o papel das previsões no planejamento dos negócios. Algumas das razões para uma previsão ineficaz são encontradas na Tabela 3.8. De especial importância é considerarmos como escolher o método de previsão e como controlar o modelo de previsão.

Como Escolher um Método de Previsão

Diversos fatores devem ser considerados na escolha de um método de previsão: (1) custo, (2) precisão, (3) dados disponíveis, (4) intervalo de tempo, (5) natureza dos produtos e serviços e (6) resposta ao impulso e atenuação de ruído.

Custo e Precisão Na escolha de um método de previsão pode haver uma compensação (trade-off) entre custo e precisão; em outras palavras, mais precisão na previsão pode ser obtida a um custo. Abordagens de alta precisão usam mais dados; os dados comumente são mais difíceis de se obter, e é mais dispendioso projetar, implementar e operar os modelos. Certos modelos, como, por exemplo, os modelos estatísticos, as analogias históricas e o consenso do comitê executivo, tendem a ter um custo moderado ou baixo, e levam mais tempo para ser usados. Cada organização deve assumir a compensação de custo e precisão apropriada a sua própria situação.

Os Instantâneos da Indústria 3.2, 3.3 e 3.4 comparam três diferentes abordagens à realização de previsões. O primeiro descreve um sistema de previsão caro e complexo; o segundo descreve um sistema de previsão barato e simples; e o terceiro descreve um sistema dinâmico para escolher modelos de previsão. O fato de todas as três organizações parecerem estar satisfeitas com a precisão e o custo de seu sistema de previsões demonstra que não existe uma abordagem de previsão que seja apropriada para todas as situações. Em muitas situações, métodos de previsão simples e de baixo custo tendem a fornecer previsões tão precisas quanto os métodos de previsão complexos e de alto custo.

Dados Disponíveis Os dados que estão disponíveis e são relevantes para as previsões são um fator importante na escolha de um método de previsão. Por exemplo, se as atitudes e intenções dos clientes forem um fator relevante nas previsões, e se puderem ser obtidos dados dos clientes com respeito a suas atitudes

TABELA 3.8 — Algumas Razões para Previsões Ineficazes

1. Falha da organização em envolver uma seção transversal ampla de pessoas na realização da previsão. O esforço individual é importante, mas envolver quem tem informações pertinentes e quem precisará implementar a previsão também é importante.

2. Deixar de reconhecer que a previsão é fundamental para o planejamento dos negócios (veja a Figura 3.1).

3. Deixar de reconhecer que as previsões sempre estarão erradas. As estimativas da demanda futura tendem a estar sujeitas a erro, e a magnitude do erro tende a ser maior para as previsões que cobrem intervalos de tempo muito longos ou extremamente curtos. Quando os gerentes de operações têm expectativas pouco realistas das previsões, o fato de as previsões não terem sido feitas a tempo muitas vezes é usado como uma desculpa para um mau desempenho nas operações.

4. Deixar de prever as coisas certas. As organizações podem prever a demanda por matéria-prima que entra nos produtos acabados. A demanda por matéria-prima não precisa ser prevista, porque essas demandas podem ser computadas das previsões para os produtos acabados. Prever um número demasiado de coisas pode sobrecarregar o sistema de previsão e fazer com que ele se torne dispendioso e consuma muito tempo.

5. Deixar de escolher o método de previsão apropriado.

6. Deixar de acompanhar o desempenho dos modelos de previsão de forma que a precisão da previsão possa ser melhorada. Os modelos de previsão podem ser modificados quando necessário para controlar o desempenho das previsões.

> ## INSTANTÂNEO DA INDÚSTRIA 3.3
>
> ### PREVISÃO DE VENDAS DE SINALIZADORES NA OLIN CORPORATION
>
> Na Morgan Hill Works, da Olin Corporation, localizada em Morgan Hill, Califórnia, o gerente de fábrica Perry Spangler está planejando o cronograma para a produção de sinalizadores ferroviários para o primeiro trimestre do próximo ano. Esses produtos são vendidos a todas as grandes ferrovias nos Estados Unidos. O sr. Spangler sabe que as previsões de vendas precisam estar bem próximas das vendas reais, mas, desde que os sinalizadores são um item de produção para estoque, um estoque amplo comumente está disponível para ser embarcado para os clientes no caso de pequenas imprecisões nas previsões.
>
> Há algum tempo, o sr. Spangler faz as previsões de vendas do sinalizador usando uma técnica de gráficos simples (Figura 3.8). Num lado do gráfico ele plota os milhões em cargas de vagões de carga em cada trimestre, que são as informações que ele encontra numa publicação do Departamento do Comércio americano. No outro lado ele plota as vendas de sinalizadores da Olin em milhares de grosas (uma grosa é igual a doze dúzias, ou 144 sinalizadores). Ele notou uma relação muito estreita entre as cargas de vagões de carga e as vendas de sinalizadores do trimestre atual: as cargas de vagões de carga em milhões no trimestre anterior vezes 0,3 eram quase iguais às vendas de sinalizadores em milhares de grosas no trimestre atual.
>
> Conseqüentemente, o sr. Spangler estima que as vendas de sinalizadores ferroviários no primeiro trimestre do próximo ano serão:
>
> Vendas = 0,3 x 55 milhões em cargas do quarto trimestre
> = 16,5, ou 16.500 grosas
>
> Ele acredita que essa relação é lógica, porque as vendas de sinalizadores ferroviários devem estar diretamente relacionadas com o número de vagões ferroviários colocados em serviço. Ele está satisfeito com a precisão das previsões e com a facilidade de prepará-las.

e intenções, então uma pesquisa dos clientes poderá ser um método apropriado para desenvolver estimativas de demanda. Por outro lado, se a exigência for prever as vendas de um novo produto, então uma pesquisa dos clientes talvez não seja uma maneira prática de desenvolver uma previsão. Analogia histórica, pesquisa de mercado, consenso do comitê executivo ou algum outro método talvez tenha de ser usado.

Intervalo de Tempo A escolha de um método de previsão apropriado é afetada pela natureza do recurso de produção que deve ser previsto. Programação de trabalhadores, dinheiro, estoques e máquinas são de curto prazo por natureza, e podem ser previstos com modelos de média móvel ou exponencial móvel. Necessidades de recursos de produção de longo prazo, como capacidades de fábrica e fundos de capital, podem ser estimadas por regressão, consenso do comitê executivo, pesquisa de mercado ou outros métodos apropriados para previsões de longo prazo.

Natureza dos Produtos e Serviços Os gerentes são aconselhados a usar diferentes métodos de previsão para diferentes produtos. Fatores como se o produto tem volume elevado e custo elevado, se o produto é um bem manufaturado ou um serviço, e onde o produto está em seu ciclo de vida, afetam, todos, a escolha de um método de previsão.

Resposta ao Impulso e Atenuação de Ruído Conforme apontamos em nossa discussão a respeito da previsão de curto prazo, deve haver um equilíbrio entre o quão receptivo queremos que o modelo de previsão seja a mudanças nos dados de demanda reais e nosso desejo de suprimir variações ocasionais indesejáveis ou ruído nos dados. Cada modelo de previsão difere em termos de sua resposta ao impulso e sua capacidade de atenuação de ruído, e o modelo escolhido deve enquadrar-se à situação de previsão.

Assim que os gerentes tiverem escolhido o modelo de previsão a ser usado, o desempenho do modelo deve ser acompanhado.

COMO MONITORAR E CONTROLAR UM MODELO DE PREVISÃO

É importante que o desempenho dos modelos de previsão seja monitorado e controlado. Uma maneira simples de ilustrar a monitoração das previsões consiste em usar um **gráfico de balanceamento**. A Figura 3.9 é um exemplo de gráfico de balanceamento usado na Intel Corporation. Para interpretar o gráfico, considere a linha correspondente a março. O número 10 na coluna de fevereiro representa as vendas reais para

FIGURA 3.8 — VENDAS DE SINALIZADORES FERROVIÁRIOS DA OLIN CORPORATION

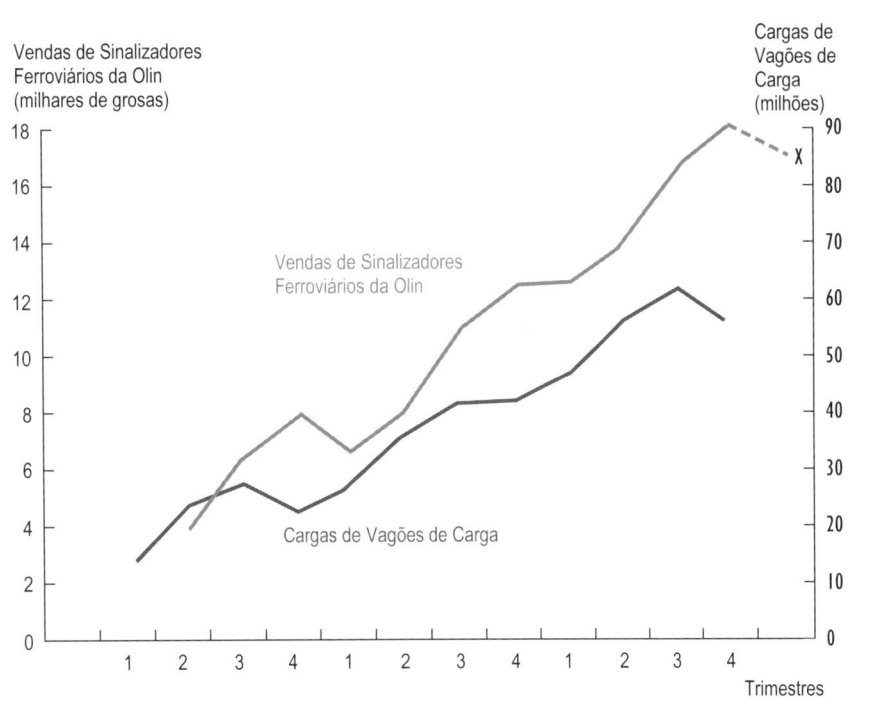

INSTANTÂNEO DA INDÚSTRIA 3.4

PREVISÃO DO FOCO NA AMERICAN HARDWARE SUPPLY

Bernard Smith, da American Hardware Supply, desenvolveu um sistema para escolher métodos de previsão. Sua abordagem, denominada **previsão do foco**, baseia-se em dois princípios: (1) métodos de previsão mais sofisticados e caros nem sempre fornecem as melhores previsões, e (2) não há uma técnica de previsão única que possa ser usada para todos os produtos e serviços.

O sistema de previsão da American Hardware Supply tinha de prever quantidades de compra de aproximadamente 100 mil itens. Os compradores tendiam a não usar o antigo modelo de previsão com exponencial móvel porque ou não o entendiam ou não confiavam nele. Em vez disso, valiam-se de abordagens de previsão muito simples, como usar os valores da demanda por um item do período anterior para o período seguinte. O sr. Smith selecionou sete métodos de previsão, inclusive os métodos simples que eram usados pelos compradores, o antigo modelo de exponencial móvel e alguns novos métodos de previsão estatísticos. A cada mês, todos os modelos eram usados para prever a demanda para cada item. O modelo que fornecia a melhor previsão para um item era usado para prever a demanda para esse item no mês seguinte.

Não obstante os compradores poderem ultrapassar as previsões estabelecidas para o período, dizem que a abordagem está fornecendo excelentes previsões para a American Hardware Supply.

Fonte: Bernard Smith. *Focus Forecasting: Computer Techniques for Inventory Control.* Essex Junction, VT: O. Wight Limited Publications, 1984.

fevereiro, que não eram conhecidas até o dia 1º de março. O número 15 na coluna de março representa a previsão de março feita no início de março, e o número 16 na coluna de junho representa a previsão de junho feita no início de março. Note que, examinando o número de colunas, podemos comparar as vendas reais com previsões antigas feitas para cada mês. Por exemplo, na coluna de junho, podemos ver que as previsões de junho feitas no período de março até primeiro de junho eram demasiadamente otimistas. Essas comparações permitem julgamentos subjetivos sobre os padrões e a magnitude dos erros de previsão a fim de que a precisão das previsões futuras possa ser melhorada.

Uma maneira mais precisa de monitorar e controlar previsões é definir limites superiores e inferiores para o quanto as características de desempenho de um modelo podem deteriorar-se antes que possamos mudar os parâmetros do modelo. Uma maneira comum de acompanhar o desempenho de modelos de previsão consiste em usar aquilo que é chamado **sinal de rastreamento (tracking signal):**

$$\text{Sinal de rastreamento} = \frac{\text{Soma algébrica dos erros ao longo de } n \text{ períodos}}{\text{Desvio absoluto médio ao longo de } n \text{ períodos}}$$

$$= \frac{\sum_{i=1}^{n} (\text{Demanda real} - \text{Demanda prevista})_i}{\text{DAM}}$$

$$= \frac{\sum_{i=1}^{n} (\text{Demanda real} - \text{Demanda prevista})_i}{\frac{\sum_{i=1}^{n} |\text{Demanda real} - \text{Demanda prevista}|_i}{n}}$$

O sinal de rastreamento mede o erro de previsão cumulativo ao longo de n períodos em termos do DAM. Por exemplo, se a soma algébrica dos erros correspondentes a 12 períodos tiver sido 1.000 unidades positivas e o DAM nesses mesmos 12 períodos for 250 unidades, então o sinal de rastreamento será +4, o que é muito alto. Isso indica que os dados reais eram maiores do que as previsões num total de +4 DAMs ao longo de 12 períodos, o que é aproximadamente $5s_{yx}$ devido à relação $s_{yx} = 1{,}25$ DAM. Se a soma algébrica dos erros para 12 períodos tiver sido 1.250 unidades negativas e o DAM nesses mesmos 12 perío-

FIGURA 3.9   GRÁFICO DE BALANCEAMENTO PARA PREVISÕES DE VENDAS NA INTEL CORPORATION

Previsões de Vendas Mensais											
Previsões Feitas em	JAN	FEV	MAR	ABR	MAIO	JUN	JUL	AGO	SET	OUT	NOV
JAN.	11	14	18	14							
FEV.	11	13	16	15	14						
MAR.		10	15	15	17	16					
ABR.			14	16	16	16	14				
MAIO				13	16	15	16				
JUN.					13	13	15	15	20		
JUL.						12	15	18	16	17	
AGO.											

Observação: Os números em destaque são as vendas mensais reais.

Capítulo 3 – Previsões na APO

TABELA 3.9   REGRAS DE UMA COMPANHIA PARA MUDAR A CONSTANTE DE AMORTECIMENTO (α)

Limites para Valor Absoluto do Sinal de Rastreamento	Não Mude	Leve: Aumente α em 0,1	Moderado: Aumente α em 0,3	Pânico: Aumente α em 0,5
0–2,4	✓			
2,5–2,9		✓		
3,0–3,9			✓	
Acima de 4,0				✓

dos for 250 unidades, então o sinal de rastreamento será –5, o que é muito baixo. Isso indica que os dados reais eram menores do que a previsão num total de –5 DAMs ao longo dos 12 períodos, o que também pode ser considerado como $6{,}25s_{yx}$. Se o modelo de previsão estiver se comportando bem, o sinal de rastreamento deve ser aproximadamente zero, o que indica que haveria tantos pontos de dados reais acima das previsões quanto abaixo. A capacidade do sinal de rastreamento para apontar a direção do erro de previsão é muito útil, porque indica se as previsões devem ser reduzidas ou aumentadas: se o sinal de rastreamento for positivo, aumentam-se as previsões; se for negativo, reduzem-se as previsões.

O valor do sinal de rastreamento pode ser usado para disparar automaticamente novos valores de parâmetro dos modelos, corrigindo assim o desempenho do modelo. Por exemplo, regras como as encontradas na Tabela 3.9 poderiam ser usadas para mudar os parâmetros do modelo de previsão. Mas não devemos supor que α seja sempre aumentado para reduzir o erro, porque isso depende dos dados. Não existem regras universais; ao contrário, as regras devem ser idealizadas de forma personalizada por cada empresa para enquadrar seus dados por meio de experimentação. Se forem impostos baixos limites para o sinal de rastreamento, então os parâmetros do modelo de previsão precisarão ser revisados com muita freqüência. Mas se forem impostos altos limites para o sinal de rastreamento, então os parâmetros do modelo de previsão não serão mudados com freqüência suficiente, e a precisão das previsões sofrerá.

SOFTWARES PARA PREVISÕES

Tanto o governo como a indústria usam computadores para fazer muitos de seus cálculos. Numerosos programas de computador baseados nos modelos de previsão apresentados neste capítulo estão disponíveis para efetuar esses cálculos.

Os pacotes de software listados em seguida são exemplos de programas que fornecem capacidade de previsão. Os três primeiros são usados principalmente para previsão, e os quatro últimos têm módulos de previsão incluídos.

- *Forecast Pro*
- *AFS*
- *tsMetrix*
- *SAS*
- *SPSS*
- *SAP*
- *POM Computer Library*

PREVISÃO EM PEQUENOS NEGÓCIOS E NOVOS EMPREENDIMENTOS

Uma característica dos pequenos negócios e dos novos empreendimentos é que eles tipicamente enfrentam escassez de quase tudo: de capital a espaço físico e habilidades especiais. Isso é especialmente verdadeiro em relação à capacidade de fazer previsões — o que não equivale a dizer que eles não fazem previsões; antes, indica que eles podem não ter a massa crítica de pessoas para participar da realização da previsão, pessoal suficiente que tenha tempo de fazer estudos de previsão ou, em alguns casos, as habilidades necessárias para desenvolver boas previsões.

A maioria dos métodos de previsão neste capítulo provavelmente estaria dentro de suas capacidades. Quase certamente eles poderiam usar alguns desses métodos — métodos de consenso do comitê executivo, pesquisa da equipe de vendas, pesquisa de clientes, regressão de série temporal simples e média móvel. Mas a realização de previsões nesses negócios é difícil por estas razões:

1. Esses negócios não são ambientes ricos em dados.
2. Pode não haver uma longa história de dados.
3. A previsão de novos negócios é sempre difícil, e essas empresas podem não ter muita experiência com novos produtos ou para prever sucessos e fracassos.

Mas nem tudo está perdido — há ajuda disponível para essas e outras empresas que têm necessidade de previsão particulares. Há muita informação e dados disponíveis em fontes fora das empresas. Em muitos países agências governamentais em níveis municipais, regionais, estaduais e federais podem ser uma fonte de dados de previsão. No Brasil são fontes de dados a ANFAVEA, a Revista Conjuntura Econômica, o IBGE, a SEAD etc. Em nível municipal, muitas câmaras do comércio armazenaram uma grande quantidade de dados referentes às atividades econômicas em suas regiões. Essas informações e dados podem fornecer a empresas pequenas e iniciantes dados econômicos que podem ser combinados com seus próprios dados para formar a base para suas previsões.

Uma enorme quantidade de informação e dados a respeito de atividades econômicas também estão disponíveis nas associações da indústria. A FIESP e outras associações sem fins lucrativos constituem um rico recurso de informações e dados, e constituem uma boa fonte para pequenas e novas empresas. Outra fonte de ajuda para fazer previsões são as empresas privadas de consultoria. Elas podem fazer estudos em profundidade de novos produtos e estimar seu potencial de vendas. Esses serviços são usados tanto por pequenas empresas e novos negócios como por grandes corporações. Isso é especialmente verdadeiro para novos produtos, em relação aos quais as empresas têm pouca ou nenhuma experiência. Consultores de grandes empresas de consultoria podem obter dados de fontes não disponíveis ao cliente. Por exemplo, graças a suas redes de clientes, esses consultores têm acesso a muitas empresas que possuem produtos concorrentes ou similares. As empresas de consultoria constituem uma boa fonte de serviços de previsão de vendas, não obstante eles serem caros para a maioria dos pequenos e novos negócios.

Resumo Final

O Que os Fabricantes de Classe Mundial Estão Fazendo

Fazer previsões na APO é estimar a demanda futura por produtos e serviços e os recursos necessários para produzi-los. Fazer previsões é fundamental para o planejamento dos negócios. A sobrevivência, o crescimento e a lucratividade a longo prazo, bem como a eficiência e a eficácia a curto prazo, dependem de previsões acuradas.

As previsões de longo prazo em geral abrangem um ano ou mais; as de médio prazo compreendem diversos meses; e as de curto prazo alcançam somente algumas semanas. Consenso do comitê executivo, Delphi, pesquisas da equipe de vendas e de clientes, analogia histórica e pesquisa de mercado são exemplos de métodos qualitativos de previsão. Modelos quantitativos de previsão, como regressão linear e análise de correlação, regressão linear sazonalizada, médias móveis, médias móveis ponderadas, exponencial móvel e exponencial móvel com tendência são analisados neste capítulo.

Fabricantes de classe mundial, grandes ou pequenos, estão predispostos a ter métodos eficazes de previsão porque têm excepcionais sistemas de planejamento de negócios a longo prazo. Planos de negócios de longo prazo permeiam a organização inteira e afetam todas as faces do negócio. Esses planos são atualizados freqüentemente, porque as empresas têm uma perspectiva incorporada, futura e de longo prazo que gera constantemente oportunidades de negócios e ações necessárias. O desenvolvimento desses planos envolve uma ampla seção transversal do pessoal de muitas funções organizacionais. Literalmente, é trabalho de todos fazer um planejamento de negócios de longo prazo, e todos são afetados pelas previsões.

Uma vez que a realização de previsões é fundamental para o planejamento a longo prazo, os fabricantes de classe mundial têm um esforço de previsão formal. Especialistas mantêm sofisticados softwares capazes de armazenar grandes quantidades de dados e ainda obtêm informações fora de suas empresas. Grupos de pesquisa do sistema bancário, centros de pesquisa de associações comerciais, pesquisas universitárias, publicações de agências governamentais e outras fontes são usados. Esse esforço visa oferecer as melhores estimativas de vendas a longo prazo de produtos e serviços novos e existentes em mercados globais, permitindo assim que os planos de negócios das empresas incluam ações para captar fatias de mercado.

Fabricantes de classe mundial desenvolvem métodos para monitorar o desempenho de seus modelos de previsão. Uma vez que os planos de negócios são atualizados freqüentemente, é crucial que eles reflitam quaisquer afastamentos dos dados reais a partir das previsões.

Esse esforço não somente resulta em planos de negócios que refletem o pensamento e informações mais recentes, mas os modelos de previsão evoluem para se tornar os mais acurados disponíveis para seu tipo de aplicação.

Embora os fabricantes de classe mundial tenham uma propensão para o longo prazo, isso não significa que eles negligenciam o curto prazo. O que eles têm realmente é uma propensão para o planejamento e o controle, o que os leva a desenvolver também excelentes previsões de curto prazo. Isso é especialmente verdadeiro na produção. A previsão eficaz da capacidade de produção, tamanho da força de trabalho, quantidade de matérias-primas compradas, níveis de estoque e caixa impulsiona um sistema de planejamento da produção bem gerenciado. Esse sistema garante a produção oportuna de produtos e serviços da mais alta qualidade, pelo menor custo, com pouco estoque, ao mesmo tempo que permanece receptivo às necessidades do cliente.

QUESTÕES DE REVISÃO E DISCUSSÃO

1. O que é previsão?
2. Cite três razões fundamentais para os gerentes de operações fazerem previsões.
3. Cite e descreva três métodos qualitativos de previsão usados atualmente nos negócios. Quais métodos qualitativos de previsão seriam apropriados para novos produtos?
4. Descreva como a realização de previsões é fundamental para o planejamento dos negócios.
5. Descreva brevemente os passos na análise de regressão linear.
6. A análise de regressão linear baseia-se na identificação de variáveis independentes e na coleta de dados históricos para essas variáveis. Cite algumas variáveis independentes para prever essas variáveis dependentes: (a) demanda por serviços hospitalares, (b) estudantes que ingressam em faculdades, (c) vendas em carrinhos de cachorro-quente, (d) serviços do departamento de polícia do município.
7. Cite os quatro componentes ou padrões de dados da demanda de longo prazo na realização de previsões.
8. O que quer dizer a expressão *intervalo de previsão*?
9. Defina e descreva o *coeficiente de correlação* e o *coeficiente de determinação.*
10. Quais os três tipos de variação da variável dependente *y* na análise de regressão linear? Como esses tipos estão relacionados? Como eles são calculados?
11. O que é análise de regressão? De que maneira a regressão múltipla é diferente da regressão linear simples?
12. O que é resposta ao impulso e atenuação de ruído? Como eles estão relacionados?
13. Quais entradas são necessárias na análise de regressão linear? Quais são as saídas dessa análise?
14. Quais as vantagens fundamentais e as desvantagens das médias móveis e da exponencial móvel?
15. Explique em que o método da média móvel é diferente do método das médias móveis ponderadas. Quem tem a maior resposta ao impulso: PR = 3 ou PR = 5? Explique.
16. As previsões com exponencial móvel são médias ponderadas? Explique.
17. Como a exponencial móvel é diferente da exponencial móvel com tendência? Por que a exponencial móvel com tendência é chamada exponencial móvel dupla?
18. O que é s_{yx}? Como ele é calculado? Quais são seus usos? O que é EQM (erro quadrático médio)? Como ele é calculado?
19. O que é desvio absoluto médio (DAM)? Como ele é calculado? Quais são seus usos?
20. Cite três razões comuns para os sistemas de realização de previsões falharem.
21. O que é sinal de rastreamento? Como ele é calculado? Como ele é usado?

Tarefas na Internet

1. Procure na Internet por sites de companhias que produzem software de previsão. Encontre uma empresa que liste os métodos de previsão usados em seu software. Imprima esta página e indique o site onde você encontrou a informação.
2. Procure na Internet por uma revista ou jornal recente que traga alguma notícia sobre a realização de previsões. Imprima ou resuma esse artigo e indique o endereço do site.
3. Visite o site do *Institute of Business Forecasting* (**www.ibforecast.com/**) e localize a página da Web para "Jobs in Forecasting". Faça uma lista de empresas e títulos de cargos de trabalho. Em qual emprego você estaria mais interessado? Por quê?

Problemas

Regressão Simples

1. Os dados a seguir mostram o número de nascimentos em cada um dos últimos oito anos em uma pequena maternidade.

Ano	Nascimentos	Ano	Nascimentos
1	565	5	615
2	590	6	611
3	583	7	610
4	597	8	623

   a) Use a regressão linear simples para prever o número anual de nascimentos para cada um dos três próximos anos.
   b) Determine o coeficiente de correlação para os dados e interprete seu significado.
   c) Encontre o coeficiente de determinação para os dados e interprete seu significado.

2. A Integrated Products Corporation (IPC) precisa estimar suas vendas para o próximo ano. Os seis últimos anos de dados de receita correspondentes à linha de computadores XT da empresa encontram-se na tabela a seguir:

Ano	Receitas das Vendas (milhões de dólares)	Ano	Receitas das Vendas (milhões de dólares)
1	2,4	4	27,8
2	5,9	5	35,9
3	15,5	6	38,1

   a) Supondo que os dados de vendas acima sejam representativos das vendas esperadas para o próximo ano, use a análise de regressão de série temporal para prever as receitas de vendas do próximo ano (ano 7).
   b) Determine o coeficiente de correlação para os dados e interprete seu significado.
   c) Encontre o coeficiente de determinação para os dados e interprete seu significado.

3. No Problema 2, a IPC pondera se a análise de regressão linear de série temporal é a melhor maneira de se prever as vendas do próximo ano. Eles estão examinando os seguintes dados da indústria:

Ano	Receitas de Vendas de PCs XT (milhões de dólares)	Receitas de Vendas de PCs de Toda a Indústria (bilhões de dólares)
1	2,4	4,6
2	5,9	8,6
3	15,5	10,7
4	27,8	14,8
5	35,9	18,5
6	38,1	19,4

a) Realize uma análise de regressão entre as receitas de vendas anuais de computadores pessoais XT e as receitas de vendas anuais de PCs de toda a indústria. Qual é a previsão das receitas de vendas de computadores pessoais XT para o próximo ano (ano 7) se a estimativa das receitas de vendas de PCs da indústria no próximo ano é de US$ 21,9 bilhões?

b) Qual a melhor previsão: a do Problema 2 ou a deste problema? Justifique sua resposta.

4. O Chasewood, um complexo de 300 apartamentos localizado perto da Universidade de Fairway, atrai principalmente estudantes universitários. A gerente, Joan Newman, suspeita que o número de apartamentos alugados em cada semestre sofre o impacto do número de estudantes matriculados na universidade. As matrículas na universidade e o número de apartamentos alugados durante os oito últimos semestres são:

Semestre	Matrículas na Universidade (milhares)	Número de Apartamentos Alugados
1	7,2	291
2	6,3	228
3	6,7	252
4	7,0	265
5	6,9	270
6	6,4	240
7	7,1	288
8	6,7	246

a) Use uma análise de regressão simples para desenvolver um modelo para prever o número de apartamentos alugados com base nas matrículas na universidade. Se forem esperadas 6.600 novas matrículas, quantos apartamentos serão alugados?

b) Qual porcentagem de apartamentos alugados é explicada pelas matrículas na universidade?

c) Qual a utilidade de se saber o número de novos alunos para se prever o número de apartamentos alugados?

Médias Móveis

5. O número de auditores fiscais no Texas necessários pelo serviço do Imposto de Renda muda de trimestre a trimestre. Os 12 últimos trimestres de dados são mostrados a seguir:

Ano	Trimestre	Auditores
1	1	132
	2	139
	3	136
	4	140
2	1	134
	2	142
	3	140
	4	139
3	1	135
	2	137
	3	139
	4	141

a) Use médias móveis para prever o número de auditores necessários para o próximo trimestre se PR = 2, PR = 4 e PR = 6.

b) Quais dessas previsões exibe a melhor precisão de previsão ao longo dos últimos seis trimestres de dados históricos com base no desvio absoluto médio?

Exponencial Móvel

6. A Sporting Charge Company compra grandes quantidades de cobre para usar em seus produtos manufaturados. Bill Bray está desenvolvendo um sistema de previsão para os preços do cobre. Ele acumulou estes dados históricos:

Mês	Preço do Cobre/Libra	Mês	Preço do Cobre/Libra
1	$ 0,99	9	$ 0,98
2	0,97	10	0,91
3	0,92	11	0,89
4	0,96	12	0,94
5	0,93	13	0,99
6	0,97	14	0,95
7	0,95	15	0,92
8	0,94	16	0,97

   a) Use a exponencial móvel para prever mensalmente os preços do cobre. Compute quais teriam sido as previsões para todos os meses de dados históricos para $\alpha = 0,1$, $\alpha = 0,3$ e $\alpha = 0,5$ se a previsão para todos os α no primeiro mês fosse US$ 0,99.
   b) Qual valor alfa (α) resulta no menor desvio absoluto médio ao longo do período do mês 16?
   c) Use o alfa (α) do item *b* para computar o preço previsto do cobre para o mês 17.

7. Bill Bray deseja comparar dois sistemas de previsão para prever os preços do cobre a partir dos dados do Problema 6: média móvel (PR = 3) e exponencial móvel ($\alpha = 0,3$).
   a) Compute os dois conjuntos de previsões mensais ao longo dos últimos 10 meses (7 a 16). A previsão com exponencial móvel no mês 6 foi US$ 0,954.
   b) Trace no gráfico as duas previsões para cada um dos últimos 10 meses em relação aos preços atuais do cobre. Quais conclusões se pode tirar a respeito do gráfico?
   c) Escolha o melhor sistema e preveja os preços do cobre para o mês 17.

8. Usando os dados do Problema 1, determine se uma constante de amortecimento $\alpha = 0,1$, $\alpha = 0,5$ ou $\alpha = 0,9$ deve ser usada para desenvolver previsões com exponencial móvel de forma que o DAM ao longo dos oito últimos períodos seja minimizado. Suponhamos que a previsão no primeiro período seja 565. Por que alguém preveria que esse valor para α resultaria na melhor precisão de previsão?

9. A partir dos dados do Problema 1, desenvolva uma previsão para o ano 9 usando o modelo da exponencial móvel com tendência. Inicie sua análise no ano 4: $FT_4 = 597$, $T_4 = 7$, $\alpha = 0,4$ e $\beta = 0,3$.

10. A partir dos dados do Problema 2, desenvolva uma previsão para o ano 7 usando o modelo da exponencial móvel com tendência. Inicie sua análise no ano 1 e suponha que $\alpha = 0,3$ e $\beta = 0,2$. Estime FT_1 e T_1, como no Exemplo 3.7.

Regressão Múltipla

11. A General Computer Services (GCS) presta serviços de computador em Washington. Os serviços comumente exigem dados rotineiros e processamento computadorizado para aumentar as funções de computador nas instalações dos clientes. Um analista de produção da GCS desenvolveu uma equação de regressão linear que estima o número de horas de faturamento de um pedido:

$$Y = 19,0 + 0,075X_1 + 5,95X_2 + 25,50X_3$$

   em que:

   Y = número de horas de faturamento por pedido
   X_1 = número de pedidos feitos pelos clientes durante os últimos cinco anos
   X_2 = número da semana no mês em que o pedido foi recebido (1, 2, 3 e 4)
   X_3 = inverso do número de empregados da empresa nas instalações dos clientes
   $R^2 = 0,89$

a) Estime o número de horas de faturamento necessárias no próximo pedido, em que $X_1 = 150$, $X_2 = 2$ e $X_3 = 5$.
b) Qual é o significado de $R^2 = 0{,}89$?

12. A Burling Company constatou que suas vendas mensais parecem estar relacionadas com o número de vendedores que ela contrata, o valor gasto em publicidade e o preço de seu produto. Um modelo de previsão de vendas com regressão múltipla foi desenvolvido:

$$Y = 12.348 + 657X_1 + 0{,}469X_2 - 240X_3$$

em que:

Y = número de unidades vendidas em um mês
X_1 = número de vendedores contratados
X_2 = valor em dólares gasto em propaganda em um mês
X_3 = preço cobrado por uma unidade do produto

O gerente de vendas da Burling gostaria de obter uma previsão de vendas para o próximo mês se 17 integrantes do departamento de vendas forem utilizados, US$ 21 mil forem gastos em propaganda, e o preço por unidade do produto for fixado em US$ 31,99.
a) Use o modelo de previsão com regressão múltipla para desenvolver uma previsão para o número de unidades do produto a serem vendidas no próximo mês.
b) Explique a pressuposição implícita em sua previsão.

Intervalos das Previsões

13. A partir dos dados do Problema 1:
    a) Compute o desvio padrão da previsão.
    b) Determine quais intervalos de confiança superiores e inferiores podem ser estimados para a previsão do ano 11 se um nível de significância de 0,01 for usado.

14. A partir dos dados do Problema 2, qual o intervalo da previsão para o próximo ano se for usado um intervalo de confiança de 95%?

15. A partir dos dados do Problema 3:
    a) Se ainda não o tiver feito, compute a previsão das receitas de vendas da IPC para o próxino ano.
    b) Qual o intervalo da previsão das receitas de vendas da IPC para o próximo ano se for usado um nível de significância de 0,01 (intervalo de confiança de 99%)?

Previsões Sazonalizadas

16. Um revendedor de tratores está no negócio há três anos e meio e precisa estimar as vendas para o próximo ano. As vendas nos anos passados tenderam a ser sazonais, como mostrado a seguir:

Ano	Vendas Trimestrais (número de produtos)			
	Q_1	Q_2	Q_3	Q_4
1				32
2	49	72	114	41
3	55	88	135	44
4	60	93	149	49
5	63			

a) Desenvolva previsões para os quatro próximos trimestres.
b) Desenvolva um intervalo de confiança de 90% para cada uma de suas previsões.

17. A Servco presta serviços de armazenamento de produtos farmacêuticos para seus clientes. A Servco armazena um máximo de 325 mil caixas de produtos em sua instalação atual. Uma vez que seus negócios estão crescendo, a administração da empresa pondera se devem adquirir outro armazém. Um analista coletou estes dados de demanda:

Ano	Trimestre	Estoques (milhares de caixas)	Ano	Trimestre	Estoques (milhares de caixas)	Ano	Trimestre	Estoques (milhares de caixas)
1	1	205	2	1	220	3	1	240
1	2	180	2	2	190	3	2	210
1	3	210	2	3	230	3	3	265
1	4	230	2	4	250	3	4	280

a) Use a análise de série temporal sazonalizada para prever os níveis de estoque para cada um dos quatro trimestres do próximo ano.
b) Encontre os limites superior e inferior da capacidade de estoques com um intervalo de confiança de 95%.
c) A Servco deve aumentar sua capacidade de armazenamento?

18. A partir dos dados do Problema 5:
a) Use médias móveis para prever o número de auditores necessários para o primeiro trimestre do próximo ano se PR = 4 e PR = 8.
b) Essas previsões refletem um padrão sazonal? Por quê?
c) Desenvolva índices de sazonalidade trimestrais a partir dos dados originais. Aplique o índice de sazonalidade apropriado a suas previsões a partir do item *a*.

Estudo de Caso

XYZ Inc.

Maria Cortez, analista de investimentos de um negócio de planejamento financeiro em Santa Rosa, Califórnia, foi solicitada a escolher uma abordagem de previsão para prever o preço de fechamento do dia seguinte das ações ordinárias da XYZ Inc. A sra. Cortez obteve os preços de fechamento de ações dos últimos 40 dias, que são mostrados a seguir:

Dia	Preço	Dia	Preço	Dia	Preço	Dia	Preço
1	43,50	11	41,25	21	44,50	31	45,00
2	42,75	12	42,00	22	44,50	32	44,00
3	42,75	13	42,00	23	43,75	33	43,75
4	42,00	14	42,75	24	44,75	34	44,00
5	42,25	15	43,00	25	45,25	35	43,25
6	42,50	16	43,50	26	45,25	36	43,75
7	41,50	17	42,75	27	45,00	37	43,00
8	41,25	18	43,00	28	45,50	38	42,00
9	41,75	19	44,25	29	45,75	39	42,25
10	41,25	20	44,00	30	44,75	40	41,75

Tarefas

Use uma planilha eletrônica, como a do Excel, para ajudá-lo na análise da previsão.
1. Plote os dados em um gráfico.
2. Preveja os dias 4 a 40 usando estas abordagens de previsão:

a) Média móvel com PR = 1.
   b) Média móvel com PR = 3.
   c) Exponencial móvel com $\alpha = 0{,}4$ ($F_1 = 43{,}00$).
   d) Exponencial móvel com $\alpha = 0{,}8$ ($F_1 = 43{,}00$).
3. Use valores de DAM baseados nos dias 4 a 40 para decidir-se a respeito de qual abordagem de previsão escolher. Preveja o dia 41 com essa abordagem.
4. Explique por que se poderia esperar que métodos de previsão com uma resposta ao impulso mais elevada sejam mais acurados do que os métodos que têm uma resposta ao impulso menor ao prever dados de estoque diários.

PARTE II

DECISÕES ESTRATÉGICAS
Planejando Produtos, Processos, Tecnologias e Instalações

Capítulo 4
Projetando e Desenvolvendo Produtos e Processos de Produção: Operações de Manufatura e Serviços

Capítulo 5
Tecnologia de Produção: Escolha e Administração

Capítulo 6
Planejamento da Capacidade de Longo Prazo e Localização de Instalações

Capítulo 7
Layout das Instalações: Manufatura e Serviços

O Capítulo 2 discutiu a estratégia de operações, que é incorporada no plano de produção de longo prazo. Esse plano especifica estratégias de posicionamento, o foco da produção, planos de processo e tecnologia de produto e produção, alocação de recursos para alternativas estratégicas e planejamento de instalações. Assim que essas questões são decididas e colocadas em prática, a estrutura fundamental da função de operações é estabelecida. O sucesso das empresas americanas para competir por fatias de mercado em mercados globais repousa em grande parte no uso de sistemas de produção como armas competitivas. Para que isso aconteça, as organizações de produção devem ser flexíveis, a fim de que sejam mais receptivas às necessidades do cliente e, ao mesmo tempo, capazes de produzir produtos e serviços competitivos tanto em termos de qualidade como de custo.

Com essa finalidade em vista, o primeiro passo é projetar e estruturar operações tendo em mente essas melhorias de desempenho. Muitas das decisões estratégicas das operações são cobertas na Parte II deste livro. Fundamentais entre elas são as decisões a respeito de como projetar produtos e processos de produção, escolher tecnologia de produção, alocar recursos escassos para alternativas estratégicas e planejamento de instalações. Ao tomar essas decisões estratégicas, os gerentes de operações devem resolver questões como estas: dadas nossas estratégias de operações, quais projetos de produto e tipos de processos de produção devem ser escolhidos? Qual nível de tecnologia de produção é apropriado para nossos produtos e serviços? Quais tecnologias e processos de produção específicos devemos usar para produzir nossos produtos e serviços nos volumes e nos níveis de qualidade, custos, flexibilidade e serviço necessários ao cliente? Como devemos alocar nosso capital, pessoal-chave e espaço de fábrica entre as principais linhas de produção para maximizar os lucros? Quanta capacidade de produção é necessária em cada período de tempo para cada uma de nossas principais linhas de produção? Quais instalações são necessárias e onde elas devem estar localizadas? Como as etapas e departamentos de produção devem ser organizados dentro das instalações de produção?

O Capítulo 4 considera as questões que envolvem a determinação de projetos de produto e processos de operações de manufatura e serviço. O Capítulo 5 discute a escolha e a administração da tecnologia de produção. O Capítulo 6 preocupa-se com o planejamento de longo prazo da capacidade e com a localização de instalações. O Capítulo 7 versa sobre o layout das instalações — a disposição de trabalhadores, departamentos e processos de produção dentro das instalações.

capítulo 4

PROJETANDO E DESENVOLVENDO PRODUTOS E PROCESSOS DE PRODUÇÃO
OPERAÇÕES DE MANUFATURA E SERVIÇOS

Introdução

Projetando e Desenvolvendo Produtos e Serviços
Fontes de Inovação de Produto
Desenvolvendo Novos Produtos
Colocando Mais Rapidamente Novos Produtos no Mercado
Melhorando os Produtos Existentes
Projetando para Obter Facilidade de Produção
Projetando para Obter Qualidade
Projetando e Desenvolvendo Novos Serviços

Planejamento e Projeto de Processos

Fatores Importantes Que Afetam as Decisões sobre o Projeto de Processos
Natureza da Demanda por Produtos/Serviços
Grau de Integração Vertical
Flexibilidade de Produção
Grau de Automação
Qualidade do Produto/Serviço

Tipos de Projeto de Processos
Focalizado no Produto
Focalizado no Processo
Tecnologia de Grupo/Manufatura Celular

Inter-Relações entre Projeto de Produtos, Projeto de Processos e Política de Estoques

Projeto de Processos nos Serviços

Decidindo-se entre Alternativas de Processamento
Tamanho de Lote e Variedade de Produto
Necessidades de Capital para Projetos de Processos
Análise Econômica
Gráficos de Montagem
Gráficos de Processo

Um Passeio pelas Instalações
Uma Fábrica Dedicada, Focalizada no Produto: Safety Products Corporation
Uma Fábrica Focalizada no Processo: R. R. Donnelley & Sons
Uma Operação de Serviço: Centro de Distribuição Regional da Wal-Mart

Resumo Final: O Que os Fabricantes de Classe Mundial Estão Fazendo

Questões de Revisão e Discussão

Tarefas na Internet

Problemas

Estudo de Caso
Computer Products Corporation (CPC)

Introdução

ESTRATÉGIAS VITORIOSAS DE OPERAÇÕES PARA O SÉCULO XXI

Para obter sucesso além do ano 2000, as empresas devem construir uma infra-estrutura que lhes permita:

1. Desenvolver e projetar rapidamente novos produtos inovadores de superior qualidade e comprometer-se com uma política de melhorar continuamente os projetos de produtos existentes.
2. Construir sistemas flexíveis de produção capazes de produzir rapidamente produtos de ótima qualidade e baixo custo que possam ser modificados para se acomodar às necessidades do cliente.

A obtenção dessas metas exige mudanças fundamentais na maneira de as empresas projetarem e desenvolverem produtos e processos de produção. Ainda que sejam caras e consumam tempo, essas ações prometem mudar drasticamente não somente a aparência das organizações industriais, mas também a maneira de elas agirem e se comportarem.

Cada vez mais as empresas têm reorganizado seus esforços de projeto e desenvolvimento de produtos. Equipes de trabalho autônomas compostas de engenheiros de pesquisa e desenvolvimento e pessoal de marketing, produção e da área financeira têm liberdade e responsabilidade por todo o esforço de projeto e desenvolvimento. Usando a mais recente tecnologia de projeto, essas equipes economizam enormes quantidades de tempo e dinheiro ao introduzir novos produtos no mercado.

Muitas empresas estão atualmente na dianteira em termos da instalação dos chamados sistemas de produção enxutos, menores e mais compactos. Os trabalhadores são organizados em equipes de trabalho, e peças e ferramentas são posicionadas próximo de onde são necessárias. As linhas de montagem usam robôs e outras máquinas automatizadas, baseadas em computador. A produção e os pedidos de materiais são tão estreitamente coordenados com a demanda por clientes que pouco estoque é necessário. Os resultados podem ser surpreendentes. Os pedidos dos clientes são rapidamente embarcados, com produtos de superior qualidade, com um número menor de trabalhadores e custos muito mais baixos.

Conforme o relato acima indica, projetar e desenvolver produtos e processos de produção são elementos-chaves em estratégias bem-sucedidas na economia global de hoje. Iniciemos nosso estudo desses importantes tópicos.

PROJETANDO E DESENVOLVENDO PRODUTOS E SERVIÇOS

No Capítulo 2 discutimos a importância do projeto de produtos na estratégia de operações. Foi destacado que quando os produtos são projetados:

1. As características detalhadas de cada produto são estabelecidas.
2. As características de um produto afetam diretamente a maneira pela qual um produto pode ser produzido.
3. A maneira pela qual o produto é produzido determina o design do sistema de produção.

Adicionalmente, *o projeto do produto afeta diretamente sua qualidade, os custos de produção e a satisfação do cliente. O projeto de produtos e serviços é, portanto, crucial para o sucesso na competição global.*

Na discussão a respeito do projeto de produtos, consideraremos as fontes de inovação de produto, o desenvolvimento de novos produtos, a introdução mais rápida de novos produtos no mercado, a melhora dos projetos de produtos existentes, o projeto de produtos para facilitar a produção, o projeto de produtos para obter qualidade, e o projeto e o desenvolvimento de novos serviços.

FONTES DE INOVAÇÃO DE PRODUTO

Novas idéias de produtos e serviços podem vir de muitas fontes: clientes, gerentes, marketing, produção e engenharia. As grandes corporações têm departamentos de pesquisa e desenvolvimento formais. Esses departamentos:

INSTANTÂNEO DA INDÚSTRIA 4.1

PESQUISA APLICADA EM ACÚSTICA

Em sentido figurado, podemos dizer que os compressores são as vísceras dos condicionadores de ar, refrigeradores e sistemas de resfriamento industrial. Uma vez que pistões, virabrequins e outras partes móveis são essenciais, os compressores consomem muita eletricidade enquanto bombeiam gases refrigerantes por meio de tubos de resfriamento. Mas não por muito tempo, se a MacroSonix Corp de Richmond conseguir seu intento. Seu presidente, Tim S. Lucas, inventou um compressor que consome pouca energia e que não exige partes móveis. Recentemente, ele mostrou um protótipo em um encontro de engenheiros acústicos em San Diego.

O segredo do compressor: ondas sonoras superpoderosas. A energia transmitida pelo som já é usada pela soldagem ultra-sônica. Além de certa amplitude, todavia, a energia sonora se dissipa como ondas de choque. Lucas descobriu que poderia contornar essa dissipação modelando de maneira precisa as ondas sonoras dentro de recipientes especiais, chamados ressonadores. Esses ressonadores podem gerar ondas sonoras que carregam 1.600 vezes mais energia do que jamais se conseguiu antes, além de criar pressões que atingem 500 libras por polegada quadrada. "É uma das coisas mais excitantes surgidas na acústica em diversos anos", afirma Gregory W. Swift, especialista em acústica do Los Alamos National Laboratory.

Fonte: Gross, Neil. "Cool Air: A Sound Approach". *Business Week*, 15 de dezembro de 1997. Reimpresso da edição da *Business Week* de 15 de dezembro de 1997, com autorização especial, copyright © 1997 by The McGraw-Hill Companies, Inc.

1. Pegam aquilo que pode ser aprendido da **pesquisa básica** (conhecimento científico geral sem nenhum uso comercial).
2. Envolvem-se em **pesquisa aplicada** (conhecimento específico que pode ter usos comerciais).
3. Trabalham rumo a projeto e desenvolvimento de novos produtos e serviços e processos de produção.

O Instantâneo da Indústria 4.1 ilustra os resultados da pesquisa aplicada. A idéia de produto resultante parece ter muitas aplicações comerciais potenciais. Vamos explorar mais de perto agora as atividades relacionadas ao desenvolvimento de novos produtos.

DESENVOLVENDO NOVOS PRODUTOS

A Figura 4.1 mostra alguns dos passos importantes no projeto e desenvolvimento de novos produtos. Assim que uma oportunidade de novo produto é reconhecida, **estudos da viabilidade técnica e econômica** iniciais determinam a conveniência de se estabelecer um projeto para desenvolvê-lo. Se os estudos da viabilidade iniciais forem favoráveis, os engenheiros prepararão um **projeto protótipo** inicial, que deverá exibir a forma, o ajuste e a função básicos do produto final, mas que não será necessariamente idêntico ao modelo de produção. Os testes de desempenho e redesenho do protótipo prosseguirão até que esse processo de projetar-testar-redesenhar produza um protótipo que tenha um desempenho satisfatório. Em seguida será realizada uma **percepção e avaliação de mercado** por meio de demonstrações a clientes potenciais, testes de mercado ou pesquisas de mercado. Se a resposta ao protótipo for favorável, será realizada uma **avaliação econômica do projeto protótipo** para avaliar o volume de produção, custo e lucros para o produto. Se forem satisfatórios, o projeto entrará na fase de projeto de produção.

O **projeto de produção** evoluirá através de testes de desempenho, exames e testes de produção, testes de marketing e estudos econômicos. Ele exibirá baixo custo, qualidade confiável, superior desempenho e a capacidade de ser produzido nas quantidades desejadas no equipamento de produção pretendido. Os projetos de produção são continuamente modificados para se adaptar a condições de mercado mutáveis e tecnologias de produção mutáveis, e para permitir melhorias de manufatura.

Cerca de 5% de todas as idéias de novos produtos sobrevivem à produção, e somente cerca de 10% dessas idéias é bem-sucedida. É melhor cancelar cedo projetos de desenvolvimento de novos produtos e serviços que não sejam promissores, a fim de que o esforço humano e o dinheiro de desenvolvimento pos-

FIGURA 4.1   DESENVOLVENDO NOVOS PRODUTOS

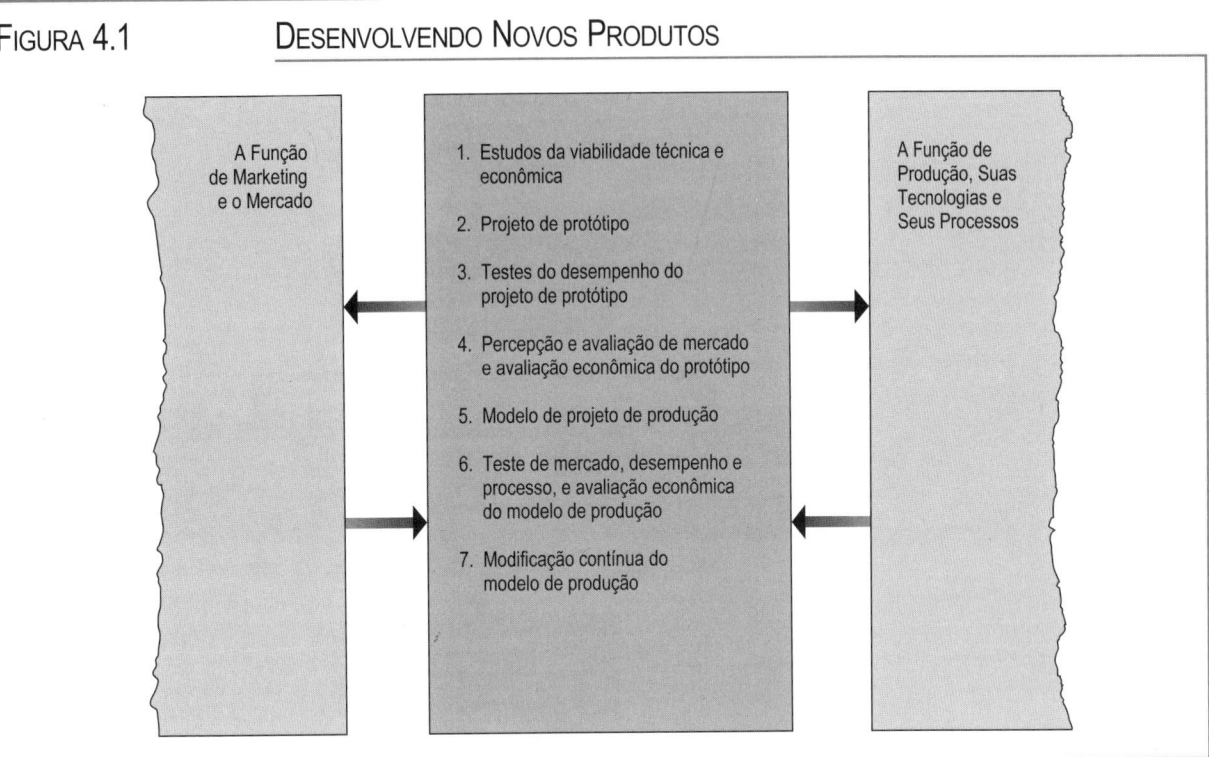

sam ser dirigidos para outros projetos. Isso é mais fácil de dizer do que fazer, porque gerentes, engenheiros e pessoal de marketing tornam-se emocionalmente envolvidos em seus projetos e relutam em abandoná-los. Esse fato justifica a necessidade de equipes de revisão administrativas imparciais fazerem revisões periódicas do progresso de projetos de novos produtos e serviços.

COLOCANDO MAIS RAPIDAMENTE NOVOS PRODUTOS NO MERCADO

Para ser bem-sucedidas na competição global, as empresas devem projetar, desenvolver e introduzir produtos mais rapidamente. Uma abordagem para agilizar o projeto e a introdução de novos produtos é através do uso de equipes de projeto e desenvolvimento autônomas. Em companhias como a General Motors, IBM, Xerox, Motorola, Chrysler, General Electric, Toyota, Nissan, Honda e AT&T, as equipes de projeto têm responsabilidade pela tomada de decisões e mais liberdade para projetar e introduzir novos produtos. Os resultados têm sido extraordinários. O tempo necessário para fazer com que novos produtos sejam projetados, desenvolvidos e introduzidos no mercado tem sido reduzido, e enormes somas de dinheiro têm sido economizadas. A fonte dessas economias é que essas equipes não têm de lidar com a rotina burocrática exigida para se obter as aprovações necessárias para tudo: dos detalhes de projeto ao estabelecimento de preços e aos gastos com publicidade.

Outra ferramenta para se atingir a meta de introdução mais rápida de novos produtos é o CAD/CAM (projeto auxiliado por computador/manufatura auxiliada por computador). Os engenheiros podem sentar-se em estações de trabalho computadorizadas, gerar muitas visualizações de peças e montagens, girar imagens, ampliar visualizações e verificar a interferência entre as partes. Os projetos podem ser armazenados num banco de dados, comparados com outros projetos e armazenados para ser usados em outros produtos. Chegado o momento da manufatura, as informações de projeto do produto contidas no banco de dados são convertidas para uma linguagem que a maquinaria de produção entende. O sistema de produção pode então ser automaticamente preparado para os novos produtos.

Tradicionalmente, projetar produtos e projetar processos de produção para produzir os produtos eram duas atividades distintas. As empresas percorriam todas as etapas para projetar produtos, e então esses pro-

FIGURA 4.2 — ENGENHARIA SIMULTÂNEA: PROJETO DE PROCESSO E PRODUTOS/SERVIÇOS

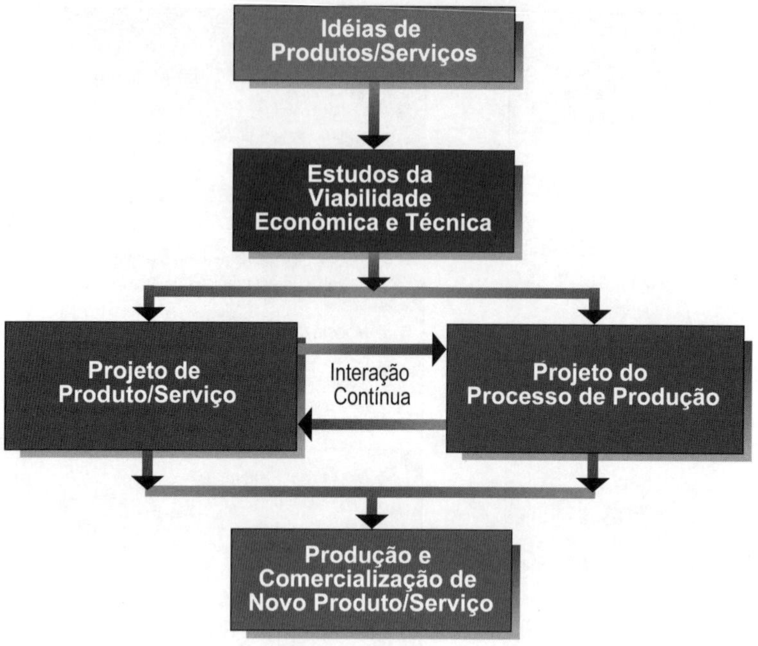

```
Idéias de Produtos/Serviços
        ↓
Estudos da Viabilidade Econômica e Técnica
        ↓
Projeto de Produto/Serviço  ←Interação Contínua→  Projeto do Processo de Produção
        ↓                                                    ↓
        → Produção e Comercialização de Novo Produto/Serviço ←
```

jetos eram *jogados sobre o muro* para o pessoal da produção projetar os processos de produção. Mas essa abordagem tomava muito tempo para colocar novos produtos no mercado.

A Figura 4.2 ilustra o conceito de **engenharia simultânea** ou **engenharia concorrente**, o que significa que o projeto de produto/serviço se desenvolve ao mesmo tempo que o projeto do processo, com interação contínua. *O conceito de engenharia simultânea compactou significativamente o ciclo de projeto, produção e introdução de novos produtos.*

O Instantâneo da Indústria 4.2 ilustra como a Boeing usa simulação de computador para agilizar o processo de desenvolvimento de produtos.

As atividades de produção, marketing, finanças e engenharia relacionadas com o projeto e desenvolvimento de produtos e serviços são intensas quando novos produtos/serviços são desenvolvidos. À medida que os produtos/serviços avançam pelas etapas mais avançadas de seus ciclos de vida, esses esforços se deslocam para preocupações a respeito de como melhorar os projetos de produtos existentes.

MELHORANDO OS PRODUTOS EXISTENTES

As empresas estão fazendo um esforço cada vez maior para modificar e melhorar produtos existentes. O foco desse esforço é melhorar o desempenho, a qualidade e o custo com o objetivo de manter ou melhorar a fatia de mercado de produtos que estão em fase de amadurecimento. E pequenas mudanças podem ser significativas. Por exemplo, na Toyota, um programa contínuo está a caminho para aprimorar projetos de produto para reduzir os custos de produção. Produtos foram redesenhados a fim de que as lanternas traseiras pudessem ser presas com um conector em vez de dois, economizando US$ 0,42; o grampo de plástico que ancora o quebra-vento foi diminuído, economizando US$ 1,05; e o lado de baixo do carro foi revestido somente onde era necessário, economizando US$ 2,00. Essas melhorias muitas vezes são chamadas **análise de valor**. Ao enfatizar melhorias de projeto de produto *contínuas*, essas pequenas melhorias constantes somaram-se a enormes melhorias de longo prazo nos custos da qualidade do produto e da produção.

> ### INSTANTÂNEO DA INDÚSTRIA 4.2
>
> SIMULAÇÕES DA REALIDADE VIRTUAL NO PROCESSO DE PROJETO DE PRODUTO NA BOEING
>
> Graças aos softwares cada vez mais avançados, simulações computadorizadas podem acelerar o processo de projeto, certificando-se de que muitas peças e sistemas se encaixam apropriadamente dentro de um produto. A Boeing usa uma simulação de computador que pode ser considerada uma forma de *realidade virtual* para auxiliar os engenheiros de projeto a integrar muitos dos sistemas componentes dentro de suas aeronaves. Por exemplo, diferentes grupos de engenheiros projetam a tubulação de água potável, sistemas elétricos e de circulação de ar independentemente, usando o software CAD. O software de simulação lê então todos os arquivos CAD correspondentes aos diferentes sistemas ou combina-os tridimensionalmente. Os engenheiros da Boeing podem usar a simulação computadorizada para executar um *fly-through virtual animado*, para visualizar os sistemas de tubulação, elétrico ou de circulação de ar do avião. O computador simula uma viagem com uma câmara de vídeo ao longo das tubulações e cabos dentro do avião. O usuário controla a velocidade e a direção da câmara virtual à medida que ela avança.
>
> A simulação permite que os projetistas de um sistema verifiquem se há interferência do projeto na estrutura do avião e em outros sistemas. O uso de flythroughs virtuais para verificar problemas de projeto resultou num número menor de mudanças de engenharia, o que por sua vez agiliza o processo de desenvolvimento de produtos e reduz os custos de projeto e desenvolvimento.

PROJETANDO PARA OBTER FACILIDADE DE PRODUÇÃO

Qualidade de produto, custo de produção, número de fornecedores e níveis de estoques podem ser afetados pelo projeto de produto. *Projetar produtos para obter facilidade de produção é fundamental para que os fabricantes nacionais sejam competitivos em relação aos fabricantes estrangeiros.*

Três conceitos estão estreitamente relacionados com o ato de projetar para obter facilidade de produção: especificações, padronização e simplificação.

Uma **especificação** é uma descrição detalhada de um material, peça ou produto, incluindo medidas como viscosidade, acabamento de superfície, classificação de pH e dimensões físicas. Essas especificações fornecem aos departamentos de produção informações precisas sobre as características do produto a ser produzido. O **sistema de partes intercambiáveis** de Eli Whitney exigia que cada peça de um rifle fosse manufaturada de acordo com **tolerâncias** específicas. As tolerâncias são estabelecidas como um mínimo e um máximo para cada dimensão de um produto. Por exemplo, um mínimo de 3,999 polegadas (10,15746 cm) e um máximo de 4,001 polegadas (10,16254 cm) poderia ser especificado como 4,000 ± 0,001 polegadas (10,16 cm ± 0,00254 cm). Especificações, incluindo tolerâncias, são necessárias para permitir tanto a facilidade de montagem como o eficaz funcionamento dos produtos acabados. De maneira geral, peças produzidas de acordo com tolerâncias mais estreitas (menores desvios da dimensão visada) se encaixarão melhor, mas produzi-las pode custar mais se um equipamento mais acurado e caro for exigido ou se um tempo de processamento extra for necessário para atingir a precisão desejada.

Padronização refere-se à atividade de projeto que reduz a variedade entre um grupo de produtos ou peças. Por exemplo, se um grupo de produtos com 20 modelos fosse redesenhado para ter somente 10 modelos, iríamos nos referir ao novo grupo como mais padronizado. A padronização de grupos de produtos ou peças normalmente resulta num volume mais elevado de cada modelo de produto ou peça, o que pode levar a custos de produção menores, qualidade de produto mais elevada, maior facilidade de automação e menor investimento em estoques.

Simplificação de um projeto é a eliminação dos recursos complexos de forma que a função pretendida seja executada, mas com custos reduzidos, qualidade mais elevada ou mais satisfação do cliente. A satisfação do cliente pode ser aumentada fazendo-se um produto mais fácil de reconhecer, comprar, instalar, manter ou usar. Os custos podem ser reduzidos por meio de uma montagem mais fácil, eliminação de operações, materiais substitutos menos dispendiosos e menos material desperdiçado como sucata.

Os conceitos de especificações, tolerâncias, padronização e simplificação são todos importantes no projeto de produtos para se obter facilidade de produção. De especial importância é que os produtos devem ser projetados para acomodar maquinaria automatizada. Esse tópico será discutido mais detalhadamente no Capítulo 5.

Projetando para Obter Qualidade

Um elemento crucial do projeto de produtos é seu impacto sobre a qualidade. Se os produtos recebidos pelos clientes serão ou não de superior qualidade é algo que em última análise é determinado em grande parte pela extensão em que os produtos são projetados para se obter qualidade. *Incorporar qualidade de produto nos projetos de produto é o primeiro passo para se produzir produtos de superior qualidade.* A qualidade é determinada pela *percepção* do cliente quanto ao grau de excelência das características dos produtos e serviços.

Estudaremos os princípios de se projetar produtos para obter qualidade no Capítulo 16.

Projetando e Desenvolvendo Novos Serviços

No Capítulo 2 discutimos estratégias de posicionamento para os serviços — o tipo de projeto de produto (personalizado ou padrão), o tipo de projeto de processo (focalizado no produto ou no processo) e a quantidade de contato com o cliente (elevada ou baixa). Agora deve estar claro que classificar projetos de serviço em classificações enxutas e simples não é fácil. Talvez a coisa mais evidente a respeito dos projetos de serviços seja sua diversidade, mas há três dimensões gerais do projeto de serviços:

1. **O grau de padronização de um serviço.** A natureza do serviço tem um aspecto personalizado para todos os clientes ou classes de clientes, ou a natureza do serviço é a mesma para todos os clientes?
2. **O grau de contato com o cliente ao prestar o serviço.** Há um nível elevado de contato com o cliente, como numa loja de roupas, ou um nível baixo de contato com o cliente, como num restaurante de fast-food?
3. **A combinação de bens físicos e serviços intangíveis.** A combinação é predominantemente de serviços intangíveis, como numa universidade, ou é composta de bens físicos, como num terno feito sob medida?

Há tanto vantagens como desvantagens na quantidade de cada uma dessas dimensões a ser incluída num projeto de serviço. Por exemplo, serviços que são padronizados com um baixo grau de contato com o cliente normalmente são menos dispendiosos e mais rápidos de entregar e podem ser mais apropriados para as estratégias de alguns serviços. Por outro lado, serviços personalizados com um grau elevado de contato com o cliente podem ser apropriados para as estratégias de outros serviços. Todas essas dimensões se reúnem quando projetos de serviços são estabelecidos, e a escolha final dos projetos deve se basear nas prioridades competitivas desejadas das estratégias de negócios empregadas, como ilustra a Figura 2.1 no Capítulo 2.

Considere as dimensões discutidas acima a respeito de projetos de serviço — grau de padronização, grau de contato com o cliente, e combinação de bens físicos e serviços intangíveis. Devido à natureza intangível de alguns serviços, é quase impossível separar a consideração da natureza do serviço e o processo de produção para gerar e entregar o serviço. Por exemplo, o grau de contato com o cliente diz tanto sobre o processo de produção do serviço como sobre sua natureza. Esta é uma coisa a respeito do projeto de serviços que é distintamente diferente do projeto de produtos. Discutiremos mais sobre como projetar processos de produção para serviços ainda neste capítulo.

A maneira pela qual cuidamos do desenvolvimento de novos serviços é similar ao desenvolvimento de novos produtos ilustrado na Figura 4.1. Mas há algumas diferenças importantes. A menos que os serviços sejam predominantemente de bens físicos, seu desenvolvimento normalmente não exige as atividades de engenharia, testes e construção de protótipos do projeto de produtos. E porque muitos negócios de serviços envolvem serviços intangíveis, a percepção de mercado tende a ser obtida mais por meio de pesquisas do que de testes e demonstrações de mercado.

Em seguida estudaremos como planejar e projetar os processos que devem *produzir* os produtos e serviços de operações.

Planejamento e Projeto de Processos

Ao projetar processos de produção, delineamos e descrevemos os processos específicos a serem usados na produção. A Tabela 4.1 relaciona alguns processos de produção comuns. O planejamento de processo é intenso para novos produtos e serviços, mas replanejamento também pode ocorrer quando a capacidade necessita de mudança, as condições dos negócios ou de mercado se modificam, ou máquinas tecnologicamente superiores se tornam disponíveis. *O tipo de processo de produção a ser escolhido deve necessariamente decorrer diretamente das estratégias de operações* discutidas no Capítulo 2. O projeto de produtos e o projeto de processos de produção são inter-relacionados. A Figura 4.2 ilustrou o conceito de **engenharia simultânea**, que significa que o projeto de produto/serviço se desenvolve ao mesmo tempo que o projeto de processo, com interação contínua.

A Figura 4.3 ilustra os elementos do planejamento e projeto do processo e suas entradas e saídas. O conhecimento sobre as estratégias de operação, projetos de produto/serviço, tecnologia do sistema de produção e mercados é usado para desenvolver um plano detalhado para produzir produtos e serviços. O resultado desses estudos é uma completa determinação das etapas do processo tecnológico individual a ser usado e as ligações entre as etapas; a escolha do equipamento, projeto de construções e facilidades de layout; e o número de pessoal necessário, suas habilidades e suas necessidades de supervisão.

Assim que um planejamento de processo é concluído, a estrutura e o caráter fundamental da função de operações são definidos. Essa importante atividade determina em grande parte os detalhes de como os produtos/serviços serão produzidos, e posiciona a produção a ser usada pelo negócio para captar mercados mundiais.

O que faz o planejamento do processo? Diversos departamentos, como por exemplo engenharia de manufatura, engenharia de fábrica, engenharia de ferramentas, compras, engenharia de produção, engenharia de projetos e, é claro, produção, podem ser envolvidos. Engenheiros são envolvidos porque a própria natureza do planejamento de processo é inseparável da tecnologia de produção. Por exemplo, na indústria eletrônica, termos como soldagem de fluxo, auto-inserção de componentes e banhos de ácido em circuito impresso (CI) fazem parte da linguagem diária do planejamento de processo.

TABELA 4.1 — Alguns Processos de Produção

Alguns Processos de Metalurgia

Montagem	Fundição e Moldagem	Corte	Formação	Acabamento
Soldar forte	Fundição:	Mandrilar	Desenhar	Polir com
Cimentar	matriz, areia,	Perfurar	Extrusar	jato de areia
Prender	investimento	com broca	Perfurar	Brunir
Ajustar por pressão	Molde:	Frezar	Rolar	Limpar
Ajustar por	injeção	Polir	Rebarbar	Rebarbar
retração	fundição a pó	Moer	Estampar	Tratar a calor
Soldar	molde	Modelar	Enrolar	Pintar
Caldear	permanente	Tornear	Polir	

Alguns Processos Não Metalúrgicos

Produtos Químicos	Alimentos	Mineração	Produtos Têxteis	Madeira
Quebrar	Enlatar	Secar	Trançar	Desembarcar
Cozer	Cozer	Triturar	Tricotar	Curar
Curar	Triturar	Escavar	Polir	Juntar
Destilar	Congelar	Extrair	Encolher	Queimar
Evaporar	Pasteurizar	Carregar	Enrolar	Aplainar
Moer	Comprimir	Peneirar	Lavar	Serrar
Peneirar	Esterilizar	Fundir	Tecer	Tornear

FIGURA 4.3 — O SISTEMA DE PLANEJAMENTO E PROJETO DE PROCESSO

Entradas (inputs)

1. **Informação sobre Produtos/Serviços**
   Demanda por Produto/Serviço
   Preços/Volumes
   Padrões
   Ambiente Competitivo
   Desejos/Necessidades do Consumidor
   Características do Produto Desejado

2. **Informação sobre o Sistema de Produção**
   Disponibilidade de Recursos
   Aspectos Econômicos da Produção
   Tecnologias Conhecidas
   Tecnologia Que Pode Ser Adquirida
   Potencialidades Predominantes
   Fragilidade

3. **Estratégia de Operações**
   Estratégias de Posicionamento
   Armas Competitivas Necessárias
   Foco das Fábricas e Instalações de Serviços
   Alocação de Recursos

Planejamento e Projeto de Processo

1. **Escolha o Tipo de Processo**
   Coordenado com Estratégias

2. **Estudos da Integração Vertical**
   Capacidades do Fornecedor
   Decisões de Aquisição
   Decisões de Fazer ou Comprar

3. **Estudos do Processo/Produto**
   Passos Tecnológicos Principais
   Passos Tecnológicos Menos Importantes
   Simplificação de Produto
   Padronização de Produto
   Projeto de Produto para Obter Produtividade

4. **Estudos do Equipamento**
   Nível de Automação
   Ligações de Máquinas
   Escolha do Equipamento
   Ferramentaria

5. **Estudos dos Procedimentos de Produção**
   Seqüência de Produção
   Especificações de Materiais
   Necessidades de Pessoal

6. **Estudos das Instalações**
   Projetos de Construção
   Layout das Instalações

Saídas (outputs)

1. **Processos Tecnológicos**
   Projeto de Processos Específicos
   Ligações entre Processos

2. **Facilidades**
   Projeto de Construções
   Layout das Instalações
   Escolha de Equipamentos

3. **Estimativas de Pessoal**
   Requisitos do Nível de Habilidades
   Número de Empregados
   Treinamento/Retreinamento
   Requisitos
   Requisitos de Supervisão

FATORES IMPORTANTES QUE AFETAM AS DECISÕES SOBRE O PROJETO DE PROCESSOS

A Tabela 4.2 mostra os principais fatores que afetam as decisões sobre o projeto de processos.

NATUREZA DA DEMANDA POR PRODUTOS/SERVIÇOS

Primeiramente, os processos de produção devem ter capacidade adequada para produzir o volume dos produtos e serviços que os clientes querem. E deve-se fazer provisão para expandir ou restringir a capacidade para acompanhar o ritmo das tendências de vendas. Alguns tipos de processos podem ser mais facilmente expandidos do que outros, e a escolha do tipo de processo de produção será afetada pela demanda por produtos/serviços prevista. Os planos de negócios definem os preços de produtos e serviços. Os preços afetam o volume de vendas, o projeto de produtos e a capacidade de produção necessária e os custos. Portanto, a escolha do preço e a escolha do projeto de processos de produção devem ser sincronizadas.

GRAU DE INTEGRAÇÃO VERTICAL

Uma das primeiras questões a serem resolvidas quando se desenvolve projetos de processamento de produção é determinar quanto da produção de produtos/serviços uma empresa deve manter sob seu próprio teto. **Integração vertical** é a quantidade da cadeia de produção e distribuição, de fornecedores de componentes à entrega de produtos/serviços aos clientes, que está sob responsabilidade de uma empresa. O grau segundo o qual uma empresa decide ser verticalmente integrada determina quantos processos de produção precisam ser planejados e projetados.

TABELA 4.2	FATORES IMPORTANTES QUE AFETAM A ESCOLHA DE PROJETOS DE PROCESSO
	1. Natureza da demanda por produto/serviço: padrões de demanda e relações de preço-volume
	2. Grau de integração vertical: integração progressiva e regressiva
	3. Flexibilidade de produção: flexibilidade de produto e volume
	4. Grau de automação
	5. Qualidade de produto

Devido à escassez tanto de capital como de capacidade de produção, os pequenos negócios e os novos empreendimentos normalmente têm um grau muito baixo de integração vertical. No início, em geral, quando novos produtos são introduzidos no mercado,
sua produção é terceirizada. Da mesma forma, a distribuição dos produtos é feita por empresas de transporte e distribuidoras. À medida que os negócios crescem e os produtos amadurecem, entretanto, cada vez mais a produção e a distribuição de produtos voltam a ser feitas internamente (in-house), quando as empresas procuram mais maneiras de reduzir os custos e consolidar seus negócios.

A decisão de fabricar componentes (ou executar serviços) ou comprá-los de fornecedores (outsourcing) não é simples. Uma questão é se o custo de fazer os componentes é menor ou não do que o de comprá-los de fornecedores. Outras questões também são importantes, como a disponibilidade de capital de investimento para ampliar a capacidade de produção, a capacidade tecnológica, e se os processos de produção necessários são de propriedade da empresa.

Estamos vivenciando uma tendência rumo ao **outsourcing estratégico**, que nada mais é que o outsourcing de processos com o propósito principal de ser capaz de reagir mais rapidamente a mudanças nas necessidades dos clientes, ações da concorrência e tecnologias.

O Instantâneo da Indústria 4.3 discute o conceito de outsourcing estratégico.

FLEXIBILIDADE DE PRODUÇÃO

A empresa com flexibilidade de produção é capaz de responder rapidamente às necessidades dos clientes. A flexibilidade tem duas formas: flexibilidade de produto e flexibilidade de volume, ambas determinadas em grande parte quando os processos de produção são projetados.

A **flexibilidade de produto** indica a capacidade do sistema de produção de mudar rapidamente da produção de um produto/serviço para a produção de outro. A flexibilidade de produto é necessária quando as estratégias de negócios exigem muitos produtos/serviços projetados de forma personalizada, em volumes bastante pequenos, ou quando novos produtos devem ser introduzidos rapidamente. Nesses casos, os processos de produção devem ser projetados para incluir equipamentos de uso geral e empregados com treinamento multifuncional, que podem facilmente mudar de um produto/serviço para outro. Além disso, novas formas de automação flexíveis permitem uma grande flexibilidade de produto.

A **flexibilidade de volume** indica a capacidade de aumentar ou reduzir rapidamente o volume de produtos/serviços produzido. A flexibilidade de volume é necessária quando a demanda está sujeita a picos e vales, e quando não é prático estocar produtos em antecipação à demanda por clientes. Nesses casos, os processos de produção devem ser projetados com capacidades de produção que possam ser rapidamente expandidas e contratadas, a um baixo custo.

As operações de manufatura costumeiramente são **capital-intensivas**, ou seja, o recurso predominante usado é o capital, e não a mão-de-obra. Dessa forma, na presença de uma demanda por produtos variável, o equipamento de capital nos processos de produção deve ser projetado com capacidades de produção que estejam próximas dos níveis de demanda de pico.

GRAU DE AUTOMAÇÃO

Uma questão-chave quando se projeta processos de produção é determinar quanta automação integrar no sistema de produção. Uma vez que equipamentos automatizados são muito caros e administrar a integração da automação em operações existentes ou novas é difícil, os projetos de automação não são executados de

> ## INSTANTÂNEO DA INDÚSTRIA 4.3
>
> ### Outsourcing[1] Estratégico — Da Integração Vertical para a Virtual
>
> O outsourcing estratégico está emergindo como uma das ferramentas administrativas de mais rápido crescimento. Tradicionalmente, o outsourcing ajudava as empresas a reduzir custos, melhorar o foco dos negócios e liberar a administração de algumas de suas operações diárias. E ainda faz isso. Mas hoje as empresas estão usando o outsourcing para ganhar flexibilidade de longo prazo, melhores práticas consistentes e novas habilidades.
>
> O outsourcing estratégico oferece aos negócios maneiras inovadoras de entrar ou de criar novos mercados rapidamente sem um significativo investimento inicial de recursos. Ele proporciona um ambiente modular no qual é possível programar para cima e para baixo, dependendo das forças sazonais e das necessidades de produção.
>
> À medida que o ritmo das mudanças se acelera, algumas empresas podem se destacar em todas as frentes. Elas não podem, porém, se dar ao luxo de se sobrecarregar com a responsabilidade de construir e manter uma infra-estrutura para certas partes essenciais — mas não centrais — de seus negócios, como, por exemplo, telefonemas, correspondências, cobranças de créditos, redes ou serviços de atendimento ao cliente. Fazer o outsourcing de processos não críticos permite que a empresa se concentre melhor naquilo que ela faz melhor: seus processos centrais de negócios.
>
> Na crista do outsourcing estratégico, empresas que ocupam posições de liderança estão cavalgando com sucesso as ondas da globalização, o advento de tecnologias de comunicações e de computadores avançadas, e aumentando a complexidade e a hipercompetição. Elas também estão usando tecnologias de comunicações e de rede para criar um elo vital com seus fornecedores e sócios, resultando naquilo que poderia ser chamado de integração vertical.
>
> *Fonte:* "Outsourcing: From Vertical to Virtual—The Race to Change". *Business Week*, 15 de dezembro de 1997.

forma negligente. A automação pode reduzir a mão-de-obra e os custos relacionados, mas em muitas aplicações a enorme quantidade de investimentos exigida pelos projetos de automação não pode ser justificada somente pela economia de mão-de-obra. Cada vez mais as metas relacionadas à melhoria da qualidade e da flexibilidade do produto motivam as empresas a fazerem enormes investimentos em projetos de automação. Como acontece com outros fatores que afetam o projeto de processos de produção, o grau de automação apropriado para a produção de um produto/serviço deve ser impulsionado pelas estratégias de operações da empresa. Se essas estratégias exigirem elevada qualidade de produto e flexibilidade de produto, a automação pode ser um elemento importante da estratégia de operações.

QUALIDADE DO PRODUTO/SERVIÇO

No ambiente competitivo atual, a qualidade do produto tornou-se uma arma importante na batalha por mercados internacionais. Antigamente achava-se que a única maneira de se obter produtos de alta qualidade era produzi-los em pequenas quantidades por artesãos especializados que executavam minuciosos trabalhos manuais. Os automóveis Mercedes e Rolls-Royce são exemplos de produtos que eram produzidos com essa abordagem. Hoje, muitos produtos de produção em larga escala, como os automóveis da Toyota, são considerados de qualidade muito elevada. A escolha do projeto de processo de produção certamente é afetada pela necessidade de superior qualidade de produto. Em cada etapa do projeto do processo, a qualidade do produto entra na maioria das decisões importantes. Para muitas empresas, a questão de quanta qualidade do produto é necessária está diretamente relacionada com o grau de automação integrado nos processos de produção, já que máquinas automatizadas podem produzir produtos de incrível uniformidade.

Discutimos o que é projeto de processo, como ele é conseguido e quais fatores o afetam. Vamos estudar agora os tipos principais de projetos de processo encontrados na prática.

---

[1]*Outsourcing:* fonte externa; o ato de dirigir-se a fontes externas; sistema usado por grandes empresas que consiste em contratar subempreiteiros para executar tarefas específicas em seu lugar.

Tipos de Projeto de Processos

Nas primeiras etapas do planejamento do processo devemos nos decidir sobre o tipo básico de organização do processamento da produção a ser usado para produzir cada produto. Os tipos comuns de organizações de processamento da produção são o focalizado no produto, o focalizado no processo e a tecnologia de grupo/manufatura celular.

Focalizado no Produto

*A expressão **focalizado no produto** é usada para descrever um tipo de organização de processamento da produção em que os departamentos de produção são organizados de acordo com o produto/serviço produzido.* Em outras palavras, em geral todas as operações de produção necessárias para produzir um produto/serviço são agrupadas num departamento de produção.

A produção focalizada no produto é às vezes chamada de **linha de produção**, ou **produção contínua**. Ambos esses termos descrevem a natureza dos roteiros que os produtos seguem ao longo da produção. Os produtos/serviços tendem a seguir caminhos lineares diretos, sem recuos ou desvios. Na produção contínua, os produtos/serviços tendem a avançar ao longo da produção sem sofrer interrupção. A Figura 4.4 ilustra os caminhos lineares e contínuos bastante diretos que as matérias-primas, componentes, submontagens, montagens e produtos acabados seguem na produção focalizada no produto.

A organização focalizada no produto é aplicada a duas formas gerais de produção: manufatura discreta e manufatura por processo. **Manufatura discreta** significa a manufatura de produtos distintos ou separados, como, por exemplo, automóveis ou lavadoras de louça. Esses produtos podem ser produzidos em lotes, o que exige que o sistema seja modificado para outros produtos entre os lotes. Ou o sistema pode ser dedicado somente a um produto, e nesse caso ele quase nunca é modificado para outros produtos. Na manufatura discreta, a expressão **focalizado no produto** às vezes também é usada como sinônimo da expressão **linha de produção**, ou **linha de montagem**, como no caso das áreas de montagem de automóveis.

Na **manufatura por processo**, os fluxos de materiais se movem entre operações de produção, como, por exemplo, peneiramento, moagem, cozimento, mistura, separação, mesclagem, quebra, fermentação, evaporação, redução e destilação. Essa forma de produção é comum nas indústrias de alimentos, produtos químicos, refino de petróleo, produtos petroquímicos, plásticos, papel e cimento, bem como nas cervejarias. Como na manufatura discreta, a produção focalizada no produto na manufatura por processo tam-

Figura 4.4	Produção Focalizada no Produto

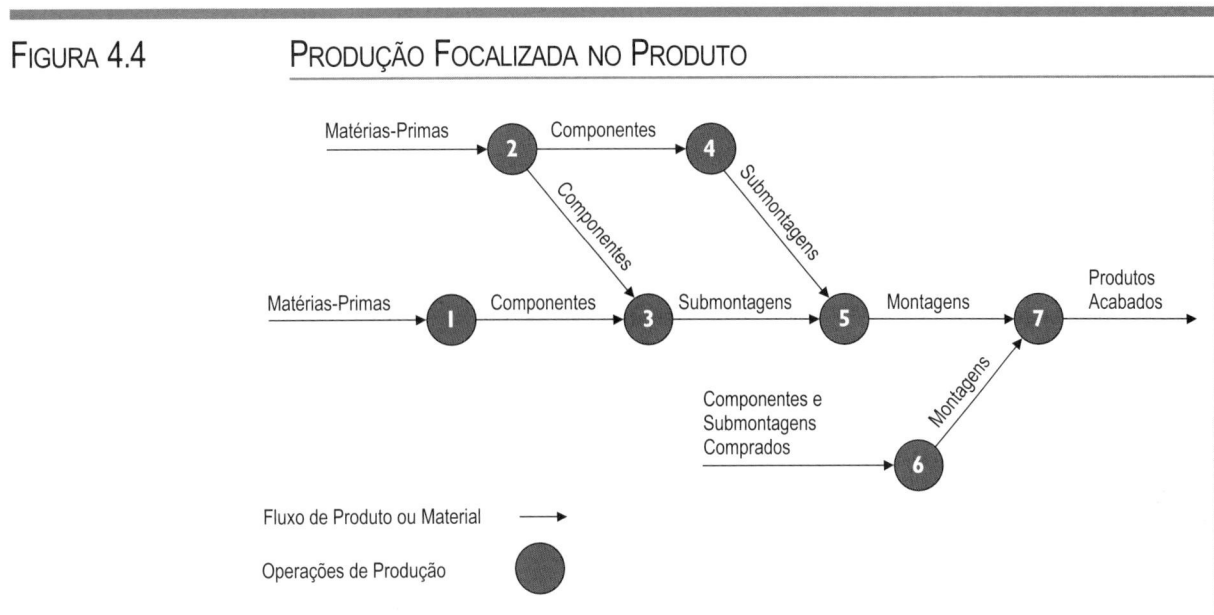

bém pode ser chamada **produção contínua**. Ela é chamada produção contínua porque os materiais tendem a se mover ao longo da produção de forma linear, sem muita interrupção.

Em comparação com outros tipos de produção, os sistemas focalizados no produto na manufatura normalmente exigem níveis de investimento mais elevados. Esse alto investimento provém (1) do uso de equipamentos de manipulação de materiais de posição fixa mais caros, como, por exemplo, esteiras transportadoras aéreas e (2) do uso de equipamentos especializados para um produto/serviço em particular, como máquinas de soldagem automáticas especialmente projetadas e modeladas para um único produto. Adicionalmente, a flexibilidade de produto desses sistemas tende a ser bastante baixa, porque normalmente é difícil adaptá-los para outros produtos/serviços. Para compensar esses inconvenientes, temos as vantagens de pouca exigência de habilidade de mão-de-obra, reduzido treinamento de trabalhadores, reduzida supervisão e facilidade de planejamento e controle da produção.

Essa disposição de equipamentos e pessoal era, até depois da Primeira Guerra Mundial, unicamente americana. Desde a Segunda Guerra Mundial, sistemas de produção focalizados no produto são usados em todos os países industrializados do mundo. A principal razão para o extensivo uso desse tipo de produção é simples: ele oferece aquilo que a maioria dos gerentes de operações mais aprecia — elevado volume de produção, baixos custos unitários e facilidade de planejamento e controle de produção.

FOCALIZADO NO PROCESSO

A expressão *focalizado no processo* é usada para descrever uma forma de produção na qual as operações de produção são agrupadas de acordo com o tipo de processo. Em outras palavras, todas as operações de produção que têm processos tecnológicos similares são agrupadas para formar um departamento de produção. Por exemplo, todas as operações de produção de uma fábrica que envolvem pintura são agrupadas num lugar para formar um departamento de pintura.

Os sistemas focalizados no processo são às vezes chamados de **sistemas de produção intermitente**, porque a produção é executada nos produtos de maneira intermitente, ou seja, em base *start-and-stop* (iniciar e parar). Os sistemas focalizados no processo são também chamados **job shops** (oficinas), porque os produtos se movem de departamento em departamento em lotes (tarefas) que comumente são determinados conforme os pedidos dos clientes. A Figura 4.5 ilustra os caminhos seguidos por dois produtos hipotéticos ao longo de uma job shop.

Como vemos na Figura 4.5, nas job shops os produtos seguem roteiros altamente irregulares, do tipo *stop-and-go* e ziguezague, com desvios e recuos. Nessa figura, Tarefa X e Tarefa Y representam dois projetos de produto distintos. Devido a seus diferentes projetos, eles requerem diferentes operações de produção e devem ser encaminhados através de departamentos de produção diversos e em diferentes seqüências. Note que, na Figura 4.5, às vezes tanto Tarefa X como Tarefa Y devem ser processados através do mesmo departamento; por exemplo, de montagem. Digamos que o departamento de montagem não tenha capacidade de produção suficiente para trabalhar em ambas as tarefas simultaneamente. Isso significa que uma das tarefas deve esperar sua vez. Essa é a natureza fundamental das job shops. As tarefas consomem a maior parte de seu tempo *esperando* para ser processadas nos departamentos de produção.

Os sistemas de produção focalizados no processo incluem hospitais, oficinas de automóveis e fábricas. A vantagem fundamental desses sistemas é sua flexibilidade de produto — a capacidade de produzirem pequenos lotes de uma ampla variedade de produto. Adicionalmente, é comum que eles exijam menos investimento inicial, uma vez que tipicamente usam equipamentos de uso geral e equipamentos móveis de manuseio de materiais, na maioria das vezes menos dispendiosos. Esses sistemas, entretanto, exigem maior habilidade e mais treinamento dos empregados, mais supervisão, mais supervisão tecnicamente treinada e planejamento e controle de produção mais complexos.

Os sistemas focalizados no produto e focalizados no processo representam duas abordagens para organizar a produção. Na prática, também encontramos combinações e tipos híbridos dessas duas abordagens.

TECNOLOGIA DE GRUPO/MANUFATURA CELULAR

Tecnologia de grupo/manufatura celular (group technology/cellular manufacturing — GT/CM) é uma forma de produção apenas recentemente adotada nos Estados Unidos. Relata-se que ela foi usada pela primeira vez na União Soviética no final da década de 1940 por Mitrofanov e Sokolovskii. Desde o final

FIGURA 4.5 — PRODUÇÃO FOCALIZADA NO PROCESSO

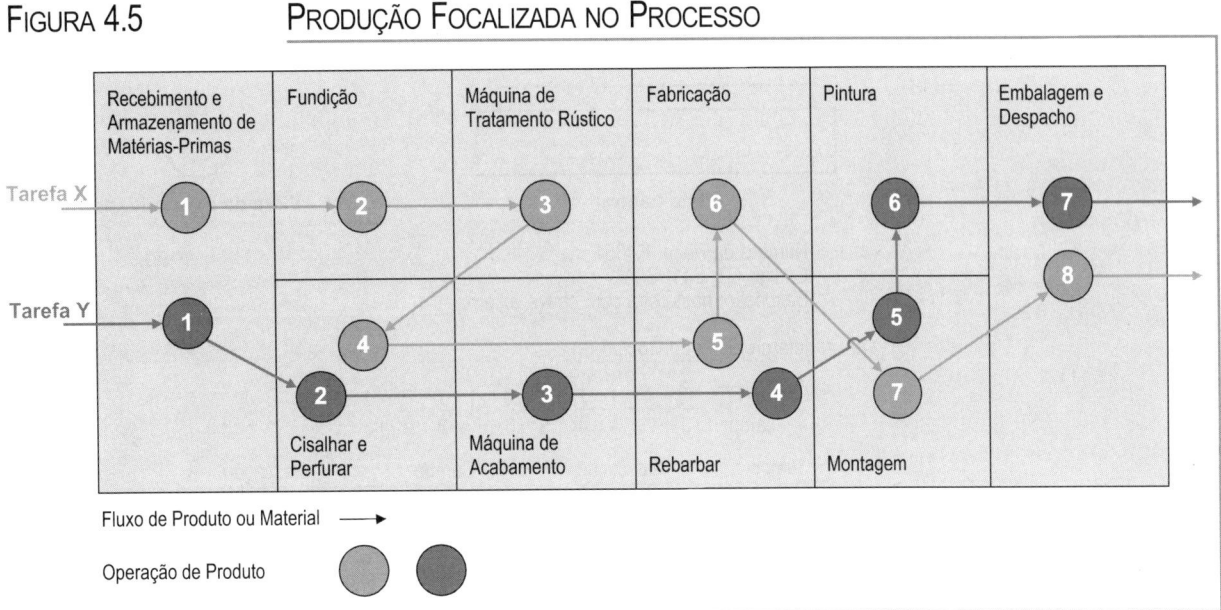

da Segunda Guerra ela tem sido estudada e aplicada na maior parte da Europa e na Índia, Hong Kong, Japão e Estados Unidos. A maioria das aplicações dessa forma de produção tem sido em metalurgia.

A manufatura celular é um subconjunto do conceito de tecnologia de grupo. Na **tecnologia de grupo**, um sistema de codificação é desenvolvido para as peças feitas numa fábrica. Cada peça recebe um código de múltiplos dígitos que descreve suas características físicas. Por exemplo, digamos que uma peça seja cilíndrica, de aço inoxidável, com 15,24 cm de comprimento e 2,54 cm de diâmetro. O código da peça indicaria essas características físicas. A Figura 4.6 mostra um exemplo de código GT para essa peça. Por meio do uso de um sistema de codificação de peças, as atividades de produção são simplificadas da seguinte maneira:

1. É mais fácil determinar como encaminhar as peças ao longo da produção porque as etapas de produção necessárias para fazer uma peça são evidentes a partir de seu código.
2. O número de projetos da peça pode ser reduzido devido à padronização da peça. Quando novas peças são produzidas, os códigos das peças existentes podem ser acessados num banco de dados de computador para identificar peças semelhantes. Novos projetos podem ser feitos como os existentes.
3. Peças com características similares podem ser agrupadas em **famílias de peças**. Uma vez que as peças com características similares são feitas de maneira semelhante, as peças de uma família de peças normalmente são feitas nas mesmas máquinas, com ferramentaria similar.
4. Algumas famílias de peças podem ser designadas a células de manufatura para serem fabricadas, normalmente uma família de peças para uma célula. A organização do chão de fábrica em células é chamada **manufatura celular.**

Em job shops de metalurgia, as peças são feitas em equipamentos como tornos mecânicos, furadeiras, brocas e esmerilhadeiras. As job shops fazem uma grande variedade de projetos de peças que são produzidas em pequenos lotes e sem freqüência. Por meio da tecnologia de grupo, alguns projetos de peças tornam-se mais padronizados, o que tende a aumentar o tamanho dos lotes e exige que eles sejam produzidos mais freqüentemente. Famílias de peças que precisam ser produzidas mais freqüentemente em tamanhos médios de lote tornam-se candidatas à manufatura celular.

A Figura 4.7 ilustra como uma célula de produção poderia ser criada dentro de uma job shop. Nesse exemplo, as peças de uma família de peças exigem as seguintes etapas de processamento, em ordem: cortar numa serra, tornear num torno mecânico, moer, perfurar e rebarbar. Uma máquina de cada tipo é retirada de cada departamento de processamento na job shop e deslocada para uma área dentro do chão de

FIGURA 4.6 — EXEMPLO DE CODIFICAÇÃO GT

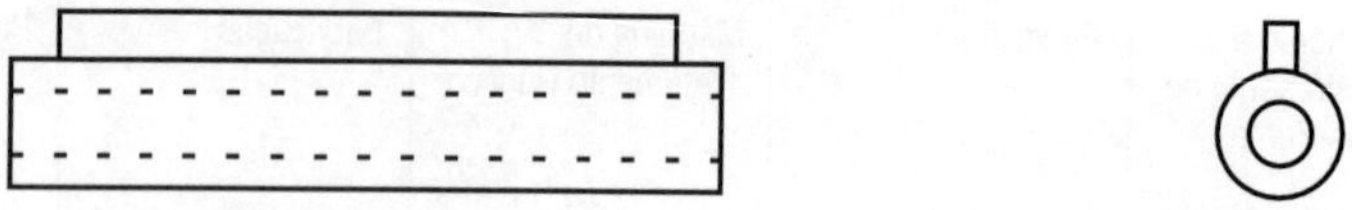

Vista Lateral

Vista da Extremidade

Número da Peça: R4851
Código GT: 341PS0117
Descrição: haste oca com chave externa

Interpretação do Código GT

Código GT: 3 4 1 P S 0 1 1 7
campo: 1 2 3 4 5 6 7 8 9

Campo	Descrição	Campo	Descrição
1	1—metal laminado 2—bloco de metal 3—estoque de barras	6	1—características da superfície interior 0—número de características da superfície interna
2	1—aço de alto-carbono 2—aço de baixo-carbono 3—liga de alumínio 4—aço inoxidável	7	1—características da superfície externa 0—número de características da superfície externa
3	1—cavidade interna 0—número de cavidades internas	8	tolerâncias internas (polegadas) 1—±0,001 3—±0,003 5—±0,005 7—±0,007 9—±0,009
4	R—acabamento interno rústico S—acabamento interno suave P—acabamento interno polido		
5	R—acabamento externo rústico S—acabamento externo suave P—acabamento externo polido	9	tolerâncias externas (polegadas) 1—±0,001 3—±0,003 5—±0,005 7—±0,007 9—±0,009

fábrica para criar uma célula. As máquinas com linhas tracejadas na Figura 4.7 (Serra 2, Torno 3, Esmerilhadeira 3, Furadeira 1, Moinho 1, Rebarbadora 3) são as levadas para criar a célula. As máquinas de uma célula, de maneira mais freqüente, são organizadas em forma de U, como é mostrado na parte inferior da figura, de forma que as peças de uma família de peças possam fluir através da célula de uma maneira eficiente. É fácil ver como o fluxo de peças foi simplificado. Na figura, a linha tracejada mostra o fluxo anterior dessas peças através da job shop. Já a linha sólida mostra o novo fluxo através da célula. A job shop restante mantém a flexibilidade para produzir uma ampla variedade de projetos de peças.

Duas características fundamentais diferenciam as ilhas de manufatura celular da job shop circunjacente mais ampla: há um grau maior de similaridade entre as peças dentro das células, e o fluxo das peças dentro das células tende a ser mais parecido com os sistemas focalizados no produto.

As vantagens da manufatura celular sobre as job shops são muitas. Uma vez que as peças dentro de uma família numa célula exigem as mesmas máquinas com ferramentaria similar e exigem operações de produção similares:

1. As mudanças de máquinas entre lotes de peças são simplificadas, reduzindo assim os custos das mudanças e aumentando a capacidade de produção.
2. A variabilidade de tarefas é reduzida, e os períodos de treinamento para trabalhadores são abreviados.

FIGURA 4.7 — MANUFATURA CELULAR

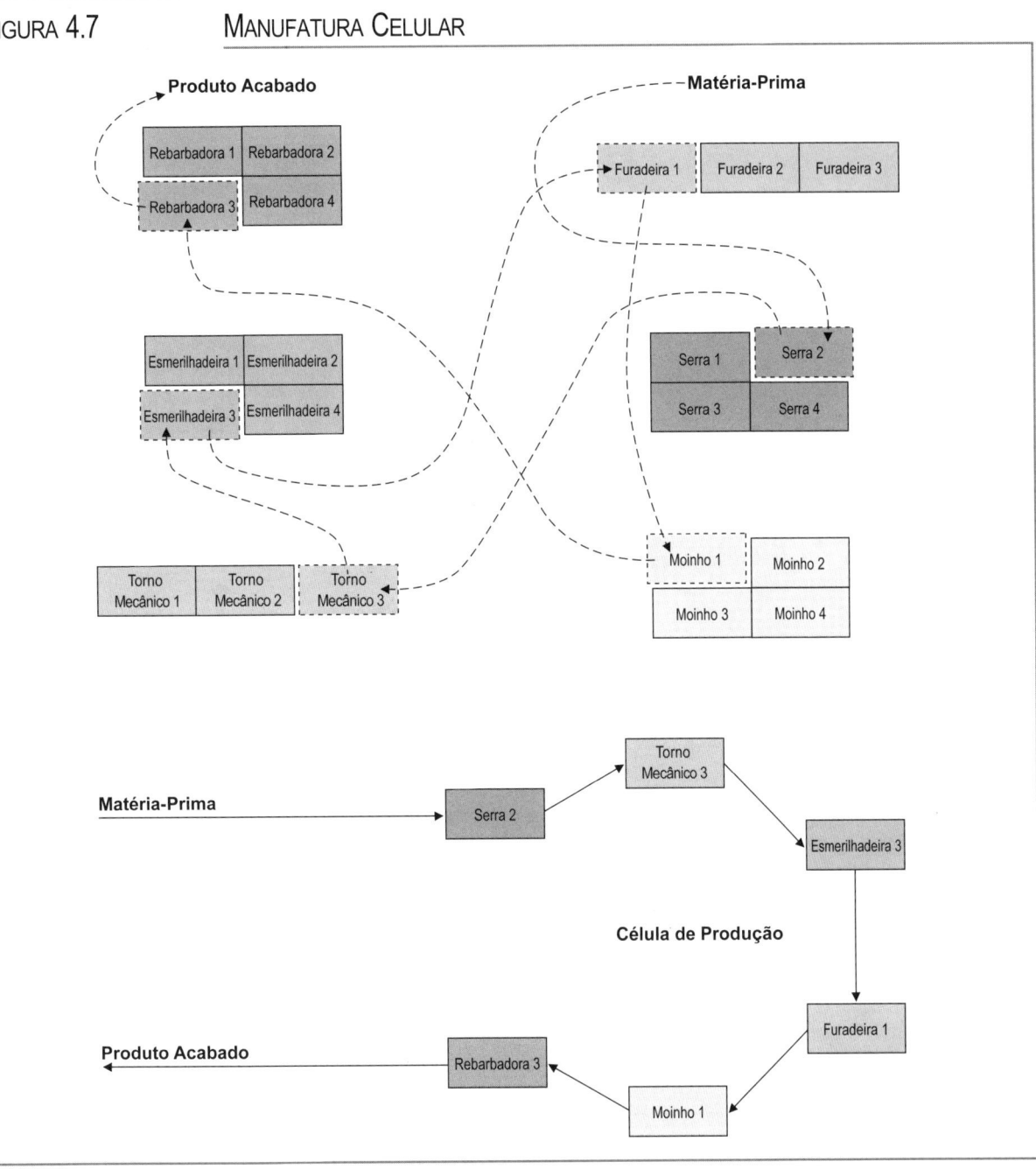

3. Há mais roteiros diretos ao longo da produção, permitindo que as peças sejam feitas mais rapidamente e embarcadas mais rápido.
4. As peças despendem menos tempo esperando, e os níveis de estoques em processo são reduzidos.
5. Uma vez que as peças são feitas sob condições de menor variabilidade de projeto de peças por trabalhadores que são mais especificamente treinados para as peças, o controle da qualidade é melhorado.
6. Com roteiros mais curtos e mais diretos ao longo da produção, e com redução dos custos de manuseio de materiais, o planejamento e o controle da produção são mais simples.

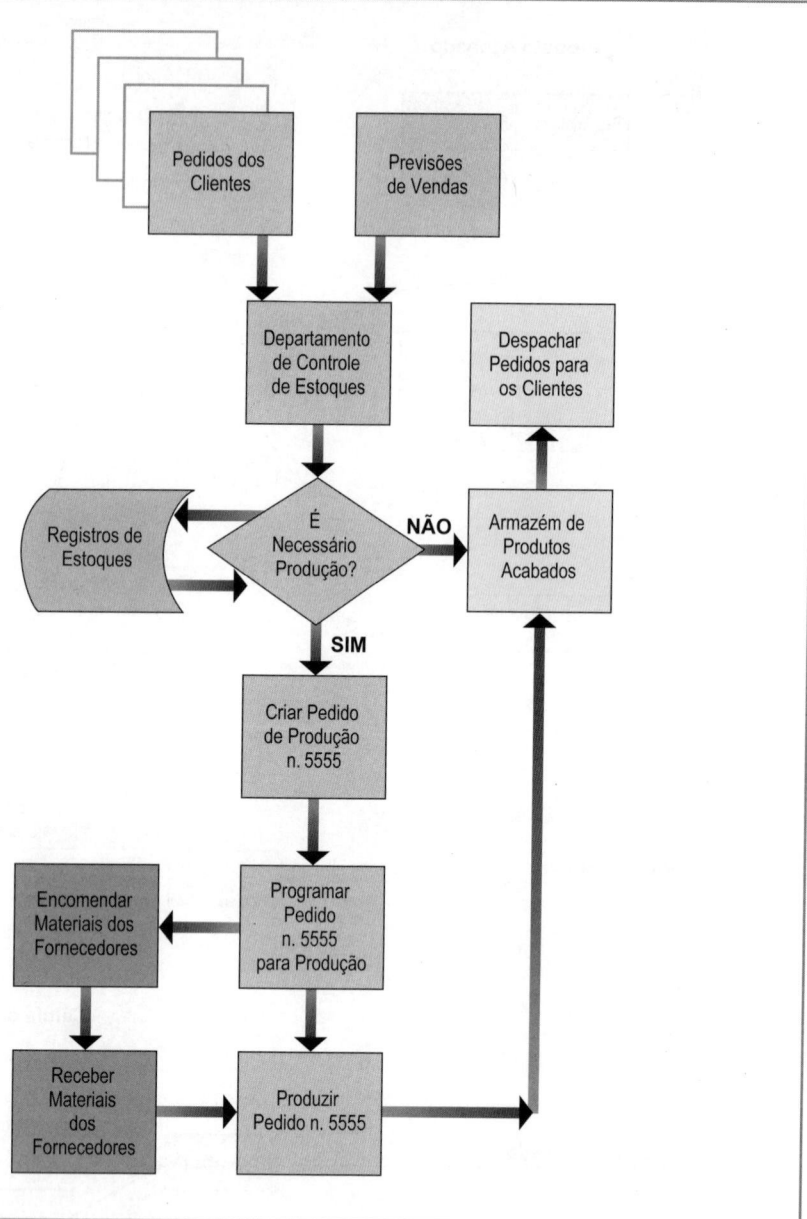

FIGURA 4.8 — O SISTEMA DE PRODUÇÃO PARA ESTOQUE

7. Em conseqüência da reduzida variedade de peças e similaridade de ferramentaria e máquinas dentro das células, a automação das células é muito simplificada. Portanto a formação de células pode ser vista como uma etapa intermediária na automação de job shops.

Como se poderia esperar, a GT/CM também tem algumas desvantagens. Por exemplo, equipamentos duplicados podem ser necessários a fim de que peças não tenham de ser transportadas entre as células. Além disso, já que nem todas as peças de uma job shop podem ser feitas nas células GT/CM, a produção das peças restantes numa job shop pode não ser tão eficiente, assim que as células GT/CM tiverem sido implantadas.

De acordo com as reivindicações da GT/CM, não veremos mais essa forma de produção no futuro, mas nem todas as job shops serão convertidas em GT/CM. Conforme discutiremos mais tarde, somente as job shops que possuem um elevado grau de padronização de peças e tamanhos médios de lote são candidatas à GT/CM.

Inter-Relações entre Projeto de Produtos, Projeto de Processos e Política de Estoques

No Capítulo 2 discutimos o conceito de estratégia de posicionamento para fabricantes. O posicionamento exige que os gerentes escolham um tipo básico de projeto de produção, como, por exemplo, focalizado no produto, focalizado no processo ou GT/CM, conforme discutimos anteriormente. De igual importância nas decisões de posicionamento, entretanto, são duas decisões inter-relacionadas sobre cada negócio:

1. Determinar o tipo de projeto de produto — personalizado ou padrão.
2. Decidir sobre a política de estoques de bens acabados — produzir para estoque ou produzir sob encomenda.

Essas duas decisões estão intimamente relacionadas, porque a decisão entre projetos personalizados ou padronizados necessariamente afeta o tipo de política de estoques acabados que é tanto prática como possível.

Os projetos de produto padrões normalmente estão vinculados a sistemas de estoques de bens acabados de produção para estoque. Examine a Figura 4.8 e veja se você pode dizer por quê. Essa figura ilustra os procedimentos usualmente seguidos nos sistemas de estoques de bens acabados de produção para estoque. Os pedidos dos clientes e as previsões de vendas dão aos departamentos de controle de estoques estimativas das demandas por produtos nas semanas ou meses seguintes. Depois de consultar os registros para determinar os níveis de estoques de bens acabados, é possível saber se será necessária a produção futura de um produto em particular. Se não, os pedidos de clientes por bens acabados podem ser despachados diretamente dos estoques do armazém de bens acabados. Se parecer provável uma escassez de estoques, uma ordem de produção é criada. Matérias-primas, componentes, submontagens e montagens são pedidos de fornecedores, e o pedido é programado para produção. Depois que são recebidos os materiais dos fornecedores e depois que o pedido é produzido, ele é enviado para o armazém de produtos acabados. Os pedidos dos clientes são despachados desse armazém.

Se projetos padrões forem escolhidos, o despacho de pedidos dos clientes a partir dos estoques de bens acabados normalmente tanto é possível como prático. Uma vez que os poucos projetos de produto padrões são bem conhecidos, é possível produzir produtos e colocá-los no estoque de produtos acabados antes do recebimento de pedidos dos clientes. Além disso, como existem somente alguns projetos de produto padrões, cada um com um volume relativamente elevado, é prático armazenar esses poucos projetos de produto e despachar os pedidos dos clientes diretamente do estoque de produtos acabados.

Os projetos de produto personalizados normalmente estão vinculados a sistemas de estoques de bens acabados de produção sob encomenda. Examine a Figura 4.9 e veja se você pode dizer por quê. Essa figura ilustra os procedimentos normalmente seguidos em sistemas de estoques de bens acabados de produção sob encomenda. Os pedidos dos clientes são recebidos em departamentos de planejamento e controle de produção. Depois que um pedido do cliente é criado, deve-se determinar se existe um projeto de produto para esse pedido. Se anteriormente já tiverem sido produzidos produtos que satisfaçam as especificações dos clientes, talvez os produtos não precisem ser projetados. O mesmo é verdadeiro em relação aos planos de processamento — os roteiros de produção ao longo da job shop. O projeto de produtos e o desenvolvimento de planos de processamento são chamados **planejamento da pré-produção** nas job shops. Depois de programar o pedido dos clientes para produção, notificar o cliente a respeito de uma data de entrega e pedir materiais dos fornecedores, o pedido aguarda numa **carteira de pedidos** até ser produzido e despachado para o cliente.

Como se pode ver na Figura 4.9, a produção de bens acabados normalmente tem início depois que o pedido do cliente é recebido, porque os detalhes de projeto do produto podem ser fornecidos pelo cliente. Além disso, não é incomum projetar-se totalmente um produto para um cliente *depois* de receber o pedido, se o cliente tiver submetido especificações de desempenho (uma descrição detalhada daquilo que o produto deve fazer). Nesses casos, portanto, talvez não seja possível produzir produtos antes que os pedidos dos clientes sejam recebidos. Além disso, devido ao grande número de projetos de produto, à pequena demanda por cada projeto e à infreqüência de demanda por cada projeto, talvez seja pouco prático armazenar produtos em estoques de produtos acabados enquanto se espera pelos pedidos dos clientes.

Não pressuponha que as empresas seguem somente estratégias puras de posicionamento. Consulte a Tabela 2.9 no Capítulo 2 para obter uma descrição das estratégias puras de posicionamento. Encontramos também estratégias mistas de posicionamento na prática. Como um exemplo de sistema de produção focalizado no produto, de produção sob encomenda, digamos que uma empresa tenha alguns projetos de produtos básicos altamente padronizados mas com opções ou acessórios que possam ser acrescentados para se adequar a clientes individuais. Os componentes podem ser produzidos antecipadamente e estocados antes dos pedidos dos clientes; então, os produtos podem ser montados no último instante de acordo com as especificações dos clientes. Algumas fábricas de automóveis têm essa forma de projeto de processo e podem construir um automóvel numa linha de montagem de acordo com o pedido do cliente. Como o Instantâneo da Indústria 4.4 ilustra, a Compaq Computer Corporation mudou sua linha de produção de computadores pessoais para o sistema de produção sob encomenda. A padronização de componentes, a padronização do projeto de produtos básicos e um sistema de informação e comunicação muito bom tornam essa combinação exeqüível.

Por outro lado, um fabricante de móveis pode usar um sistema focalizado no processo, de produção para estoque. Devido à natureza da tecnologia de preparo da madeira, lixamento e preparo da superfície, pintura, estofamento e embalagem, essas operações são mais compatíveis com um sistema focalizado no processo. Mas, devido aos projetos de produto padronizados, é usada uma política de estoques de produtos acabados de produção para estoque.

PROJETO DE PROCESSOS NOS SERVIÇOS

Conforme discutimos anteriormente, as dimensões do projeto de serviços são o grau de padronização, o grau de contato com o cliente e a combinação de bens físicos e serviços intangíveis. O projeto definitivo de um serviço estabelecerá cada uma dessas dimensões e será impulsionado pela estratégia de negócios da empresa. A estratégia de operações que decorre da estratégia de negócios também requer um plano para produzir os serviços.

Grande parte da discussão sobre como projetar processos de produção para produzir produtos também se aplica ao projeto de processos de produção para serviços. Alguns dos fatores importantes no projeto de processos para produtos também são importantes para os serviços e não são explicados aqui. Estes são a natureza da demanda por clientes (tanto em termos de nível como de padrão), o grau de integração vertical, a flexibilidade de produção, o grau de automação e a qualidade de serviço. A flexibilidade de volume é de especial importância em muitos serviços. A natureza fundamental de muitos serviços, como ilustra a Tabela 2.8, cria a necessidade de flexibilidade de volume, que é a capacidade de aumentar ou reduzir rapidamente o volume de produtos produzidos. Essa necessidade provém da incapacidade que muitos serviços têm de armazenar serviços acabados em antecipação à demanda por clientes. Para alguns serviços, essa incapacidade exige que processos de produção sejam projetados para gerar e entregar serviços quando isso for exigido pelos clientes ou por perda de vendas.

As técnicas usadas para decidir entre alternativas de processamento para produtos também se aplicaria aos serviços. Mas os tipos de processos de produção para os serviços são muito diferentes daqueles para os produtos. Para entender melhor os processos de produção para os serviços, é útil pensarmos sobre três diferentes esquemas para produzir e entregar serviços:

1. **Quase-manufatura.** Um exemplo dessa abordagem estaria no setor de apoio (*back-room*[2]) de lanchonetes como o McDonald's. Ou a produção focalizada no produto ou a focalizada no processo poderiam ser apropriadas, dependendo da natureza dos bens ou serviços a serem produzidos. Aqui,

---

[2]*Back-room:* expressão usada para designar um ambiente localizado na parte posterior de um estabelecimento, normalmente acessível somente a pessoal autorizado ou grupos privilegiados. Pode ser um local de reunião, para tomada de decisões, ou o setor operacional; por exemplo, os escritórios de um banco ou a cozinha de uma lanchonete.

FIGURA 4.9   O Sistema de Produção sob Encomenda

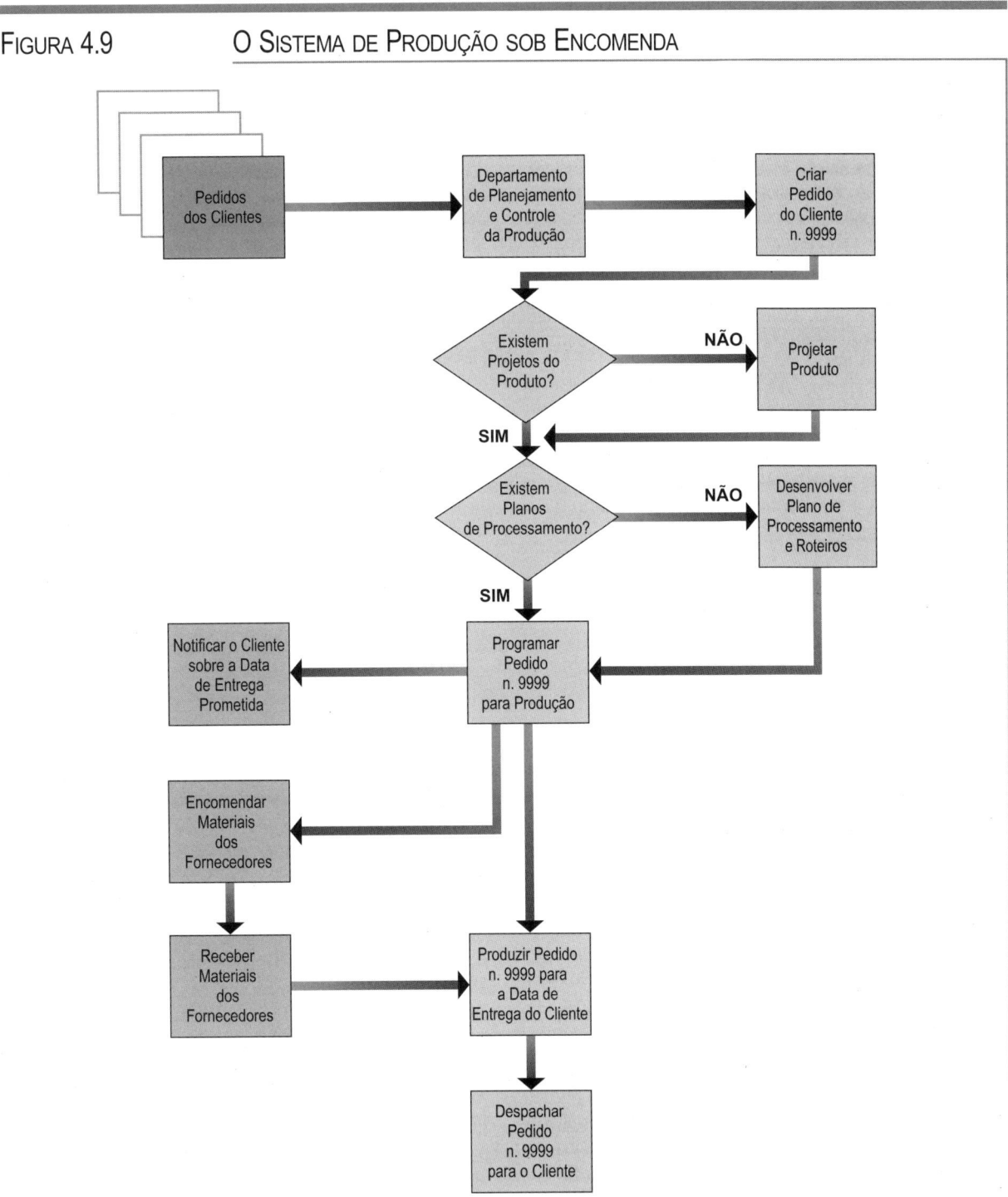

os bens físicos são predominantes sobre os bens intangíveis, e há pouco contato com o cliente. *A característica distintiva desse esquema é que a produção de bens se desenvolve ao longo de uma linha de produção com quase nenhum envolvimento na produção.*

2. **Cliente como participante.** Exemplos desta abordagem são os caixas automáticos, venda a varejo, postos de gasolina tipo *self-service* e restaurantes por quilo. Os bens físicos podem ser uma parte significativa do serviço, e os serviços podem ser ou padronizados ou personalizados. *A carac-*

> ## INSTANTÂNEO DA INDÚSTRIA 4.4
>
> ### A COMPAQ MUDA PARA PRODUÇÃO SOB ENCOMENDA
>
> A Compaq Computer Corporation se desfez de suas antigas linhas de montagem e agora faz seus computadores pessoais com células compostas de três pessoas que montam os computadores conforme a abordagem de produzir para estoque. Nesse arranjo, a equipe de três pessoas examina o pedido do próximo cliente num monitor para ver os atributos do computador a ser montado (periféricos, unidades de disco etc.) e monta o computador especificamente para esse cliente. Nas células de três pessoas, uma pessoa prepara todas as submontagens que entram num computador. A segunda pessoa instala essas submontagens no gabinete do computador. E a terceira pessoa executa todos os testes para certificar-se de que os circuitos estão conectados apropriadamente. Nesse método de produção, as peças e submontagens são estocadas antes que os pedidos dos clientes sejam recebidos, mas os produtos acabados não; a montagem final ocorre somente depois do recebimento do pedido. Isso permite que a Compaq combine a produção com os pedidos dos clientes e reduza o custo de cada etapa de produção — estoques, manuseio, frete e produtos não vendidos. A mudança para um sistema de produção sob encomenda também diminui a dependência de previsões de mercado por parte da Compaq. A Compaq afirma que a produção de cada empregado na célula de três pessoas aumentou em 23% e que a produção por metro quadrado aumentou 16% em comparação com as linhas de montagem de produção para estoque.
>
> *Fonte:* "Compaq Storms the PC Heights from Its Factory Floor". *The New York Times*, 13 de novembro de 1994.

terística distintiva dessa abordagem é o elevado grau de envolvimento com o cliente no processo de gerar o serviço.

3. **Cliente como produto.** Exemplos dessa abordagem são as clínicas médicas e os salões de cabeleireiros. Esses esquemas oferecem serviços especializados e um elevado grau de contato com o cliente. *A característica distintiva dessa abordagem é que o serviço é prestado através de atenção pessoal ao cliente.* Esse sistema pode proporcionar uma percepção de elevada qualidade.

Ao examinar esses tipos de processo para produzir serviços, o grau de contato com o cliente é especialmente relevante para o projeto do processo. Numa extremidade, os serviços que têm o cliente como produto, como os salões de cabeleireiro e as clínicas médicas, o serviço é realizado de fato *no* cliente. O cliente torna-se o foco central do projeto de processos de produção. Cada elemento do equipamento, o treinamento dos empregados e as construções devem ser projetados tendo o cliente em mente. Além disso, bom atendimento e instalações confortáveis devem ser oferecidos para receber, manter, processar e liberar clientes. No outro extremo, nos serviços de quase-manufatura, como nas operações de back-room de bancos, não há nenhum contato com os clientes, e essas operações podem ser altamente automatizadas para obter baixo custo e rapidez, com pouca ênfase nas relações com o cliente.

Há uma tendência para que os gerentes de operações de serviços deixem o projeto de processos de produção referente aos serviços nos níveis verbal e subjetivo. G. Lynn Shostack, vice-presidente sênior encarregado do Private Clients Group da Bankers Trust Company, insiste para que os gerentes desenvolvam uma abordagem mais quantificável e objetiva para projetar processos de serviços. Ele sugere os seguintes passos:

1. *Identifique processos.* Desenvolva fluxogramas ou diagramas que liguem as etapas de produção no sistema de produção global. Inclua etapas que o cliente não vê, como, por exemplo, a compra de suprimentos.

2. *Isole pontos falhos.* Assim que o processo for diagramado, determine os pontos de decisão onde o sistema de produção pode falhar. Incorpore passos corretivos que evitem as conseqüências de possíveis erros.

3. *Estabeleça um intervalo de tempo.* Estime a quantidade de tempo que cada etapa do serviço exigirá. Essas estimativas de tempo tornam-se padrões em relação às quais se pode medir o desempenho do sistema. Se os serviços forem fornecidos em mais tempo do que o padrão, a produtividade e a lucratividade serão menores do que o esperado.

4. *Analise a lucratividade.* Monitore continuamente a lucratividade do serviço. Essa monitoração permite que seja evitada a falta de lucratividade, que a produtividade seja medida, que a uniformidade seja mantida e que a qualidade seja controlada.

Abordagens como essas são necessárias para melhorar a competitividade dos serviços.

Outro conceito popularizado recentemente relacionado ao projeto de processos é a **reengenharia de processo**. Reengenharia de processo é o conceito de mudar *drasticamente* um projeto de processo existente, como se o estivéssemos projetando desde o início numa folha de papel em branco, em vez de simplesmente fazermos melhorias marginais. Um processo que sofreu reengenharia corretamente é, via de regra, mais eficiente, resultando muitas vezes em uma força de trabalho menor.

Discutimos os diferentes tipos de projetos de processo, mas como decidir entre eles?

DECIDINDO ENTRE ALTERNATIVAS DE PROCESSAMENTO

Ao escolher um processo de produção, diversos fatores devem ser considerados, como o tamanho do lote e a variedade de produto, as necessidades de capital e a análise econômica.

TAMANHO DO LOTE E VARIEDADE DE PRODUTO

A Figura 4.10 mostra que o projeto de processo apropriado depende do número de projetos de produto e do tamanho dos lotes a serem produzidos num sistema de produção.

À medida que nos movemos do Ponto A para o Ponto D na Figura 4.10, o custo de produção por unidade e a flexibilidade de produto aumentam. No Ponto A há um único produto, e a demanda correspondente ao produto é muito grande. Nesse caso extremo, uma organização focalizada no produto que seja dedicada somente a esse produto seria apropriada. Os custos de produção por unidade são muito baixos, mas esse tipo de organização de produção é muito inflexível, porque o equipamento para o produto e o treinamento específico para os empregados tornam pouco prático mudar para a produção de outros produtos. À medida que o número de projetos de produto aumenta e que o tamanho do lote dos produtos diminui, em algum ponto, digamos o Ponto B, um sistema de lotes focalizado no produto torna-se impróprio. Não obstante esse sistema ser relativamente inflexível, os empregados são treinados para deslocar-se para a produção de outros produtos, e o equipamento é projetado para ser mudado para outros produtos, mas com certa dificuldade.

No outro extremo, o Ponto D representa a produção de muitos produtos diferentes. Nesse caso, uma job shop que produz produtos únicos em lotes de um único item seria apropriada. Essa forma de produção é a mais moderna em termos de flexibilidade de produto. À medida que o número de produtos diminui e o tamanho do lote dos produtos aumenta a partir desse extremo, em algum ponto, digamos o Ponto C, a manufatura celular para parte da produção de peças dentro de uma job shop torna-se apropriada.

Seria útil consultarmos agora a Figura 2.3 do Capítulo 2, onde apresentamos o conceito de **ciclo de vida do processo**. Colocando de maneira simples, os sistemas de produção tendem a evoluir à medida que os produtos se movem ao longo de seus ciclos de vida de produto. Dois princípios são fundamentais para o conceito de ciclos de vida do processo. Os ciclos de vida do produto e os ciclos de vida do processo são interdependentes: um afeta o outro. Os processos de produção afetam os custos de produção, a qualidade e a capacidade de produção, que por sua vez afetam o volume de produtos que podem ser vendidos. Similarmente, o volume de produtos que são vendidos afeta o tipo de processo de produção que pode ser justificável.

Dessa forma, *quando estratégias de negócios são desenvolvidas para cada linha de produto, a determinação do volume de demanda esperada para cada produto e do número de modelos de produto necessários para atrair mercado é um fator importante na escolha do tipo de projeto de processo.* Outros fatores também têm impacto sobre essa decisão.

FIGURA 4.10   O Tipo de Projeto de Processo Depende da Diversidade de Produtos e do Tamanho do Lote

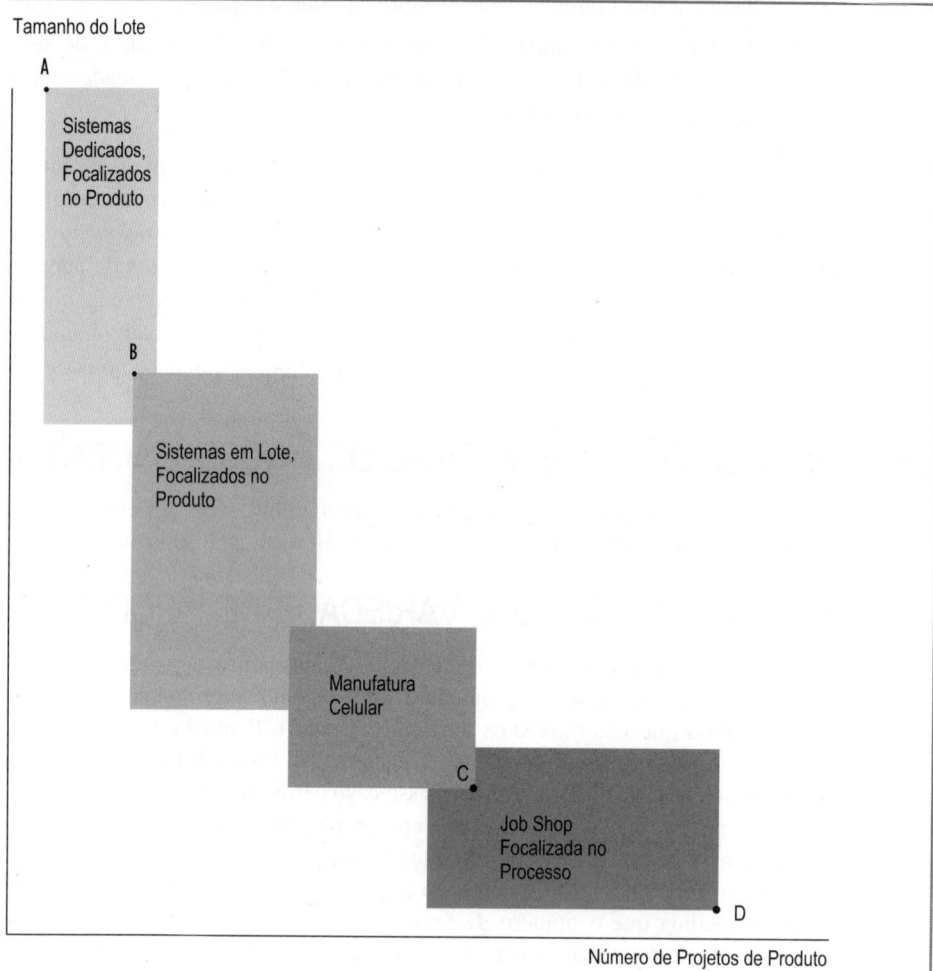

NECESSIDADES DE CAPITAL PARA PROJETOS DE PROCESSOS

A quantidade de capital necessário para os sistemas de produção tende a diferir para cada tipo de processo de produção. Na Figura 4.10, em geral, a quantidade de capital necessário é maior no Ponto A e diminui com o movimento para baixo à direita rumo ao Ponto D. A quantidade de capital disponível e o custo de capital para a empresa poderiam ser fatores importantes na escolha de um tipo de projeto de processo, e as estratégias de negócios teriam de ser ajustadas conseqüentemente.

ANÁLISE ECONÔMICA

Entre os fatores a serem considerados quando se decide entre os tipos de organizações de processamento da produção, o custo de produção de cada alternativa é importante. Nesta seção discutiremos as funções de custo das alternativas de processamento, o conceito de alavancagem operacional, análise de *break-even*[3] e análise financeira.

---

[3]*Break-even:* ponto de equilíbrio; não auferir lucro, nem sofrer prejuízo; terminar empatado.

FIGURA 4.11 — FUNÇÕES DE CUSTO DE ALTERNATIVAS DE PROCESSAMENTO

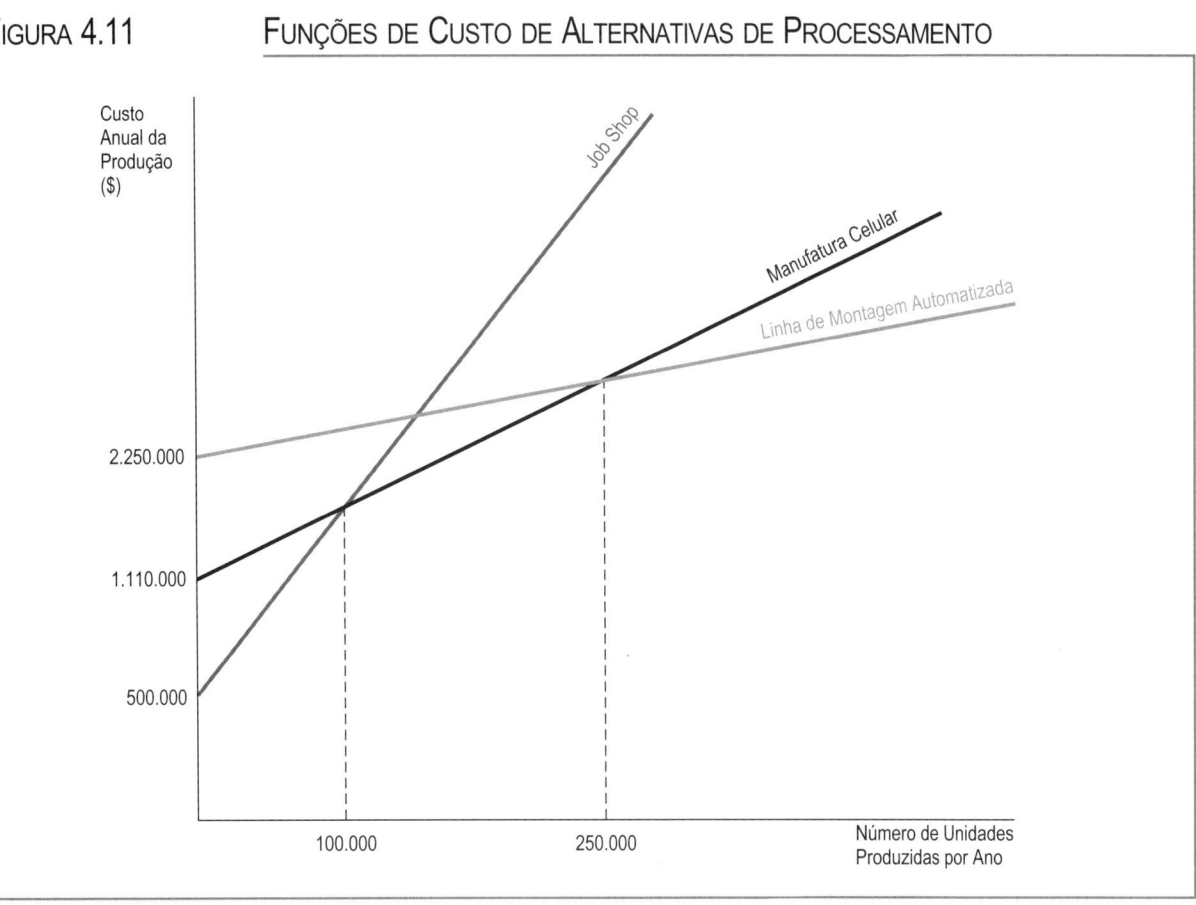

Funções de Custo de Alternativas de Processamento Conforme mencionamos anteriormente, cada tipo de projeto de processo tende a exigir uma quantidade diferente de capital. Os custos de capital normalmente são encargos fixos que ocorrem mensalmente e representam certa medida do custo de capital para a empresa. A Figura 4.11 ilustra graficamente que diferentes formas de projeto de processo para produzir um produto têm diferentes funções de custo. Quanto maior o custo inicial dos equipamentos, construções e outros ativos fixos, maiores serão os custos fixos. Além disso, diferentes formas de organizações de produção têm diferentes custos variáveis — aqueles custos que variam com o volume de produtos produzidos em cada mês.

Como se pode ver na Figura 4.11, a alternativa de linha de montagem automatizada tem custos anuais fixos de $ 2.250.000. Custos fixos são os custos anuais quando o volume produzido é igual a zero. Esses custos estão relacionados com a muito dispendiosa robótica, controles computadorizados e equipamentos de manuseio de materiais para uma linha de montagem automatizada. Pode-se ver também na Figura 4.11 que os custos variáveis (mão-de-obra, materiais e gastos gerais variáveis) para uma linha de montagem automatizada são muito baixos em relação às outras formas de projeto de processo, porque a inclinação (elevação acima do eixo horizontal) de sua função de custo é muito horizontal. Isso significa que os custos anuais não se elevam muito rapidamente quando o volume anual de produção cresce. A função de custo de uma job shop comumente exibe custos fixos muito baixos e custos variáveis muito elevados. Os custos fixos e variáveis da manufatura celular normalmente são intermediários em relação aos dos outros dois projetos de processo.

Uma importante conclusão a partir da Figura 4.11 é esta: *Se a disponibilidade de capital não for um fator e os custos de produção anual forem a consideração predominante, o projeto de processo que é preferível depende do volume de produção do produto.* No exemplo da Figura 4.11, se o volume de produção anual for menor do que 100 mil unidades, uma job shop seria preferível. Se um volume de produção

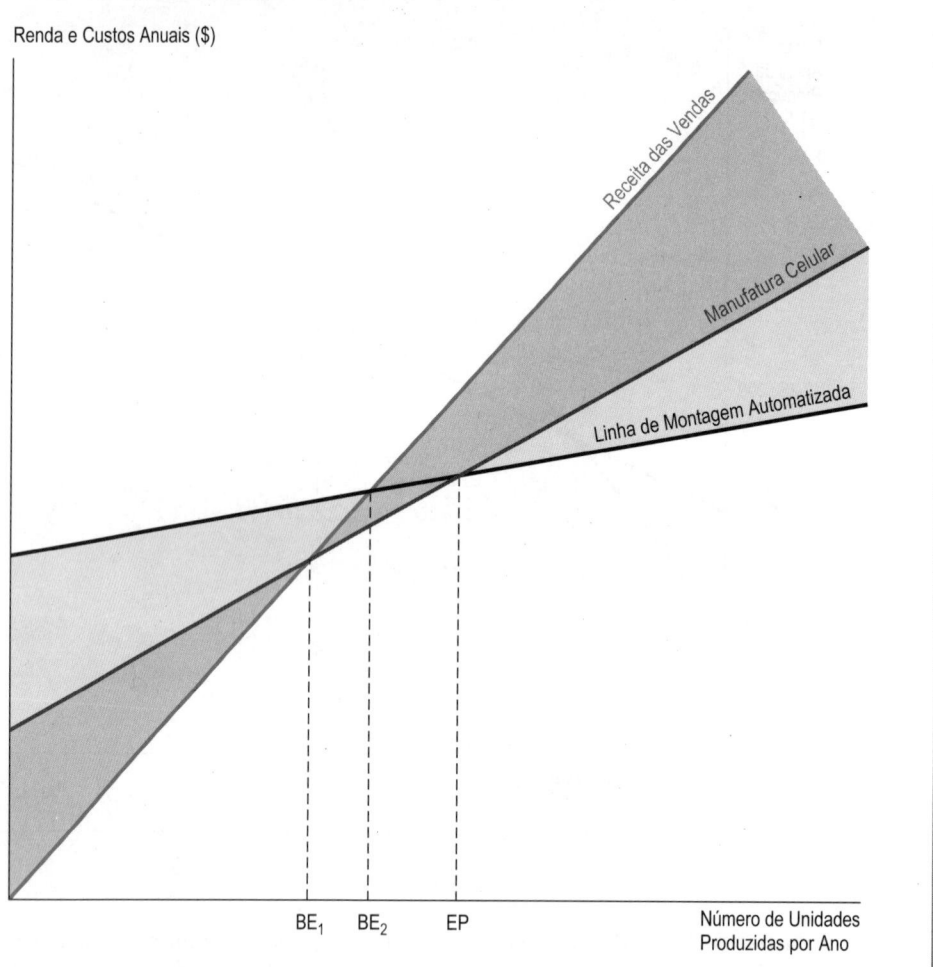

FIGURA 4.12   ALAVANCAGEM OPERACIONAL E ALTERNATIVAS DE PROJETO DE PROCESSO

entre 100 mil e 250 mil for esperado, a manufatura celular seria preferível. E se um volume de produção maior do que 250 mil unidades for esperado, uma linha de montagem automatizada seria preferível.

Alavancagem operacional é outro importante conceito relacionado com a análise econômica.

Conceito de Alavancagem Operacional   Quando examinamos funções de custo das alternativas de processamento, o conceito de alavancagem operacional tem importantes implicações. ***Alavancagem operacional*** *é uma medida da relação entre os custos anuais de uma empresa e suas vendas anuais. Se uma porcentagem elevada dos custos de uma empresa for fixa, diz-se que ela tem um grau elevado de alavancagem operacional. Um grau elevado de alavancagem operacional, quando as outras coisas permanecem constantes, implica que uma mudança percentual relativamente pequena nas vendas resultará numa grande mudança percentual na renda operacional (a diferença entre as vendas anuais e os custos de produção anuais).*

A Figura 4.12 ilustra o conceito de alavancagem operacional. No nível de produção BE_1, os custos de produção anuais da manufatura celular se igualam com as receitas das vendas anuais, que é o ponto de equilíbrio. As áreas sombreadas à direita e à esquerda de BE_1 representam os lucros e os prejuízos, respectivamente. O conceito de alavancagem operacional se relaciona com o ângulo entre a função de custo e as linhas das receitas de vendas. Se a alavancagem operacional e o ângulo forem pequenos, os lucros aumentarão lentamente para a direita do ponto de equilíbrio, e os prejuízos se elevarão lentamente para a

TABELA 4.3	DEFINIÇÕES DE VARIÁVEIS E FÓRMULAS PARA A ANÁLISE DE BREAK-EVEN

p = preço de venda por unidade	Q = número de unidades produzidas e vendidas por período
v = custo variável por unidade	P = lucros por período antes da dedução do imposto de renda
FC = custo fixo total por período	TR = receita total por período
TVC = custo variável total por período	TC = período de custo total
C = contribuição por período	c = contribuição por unidade

	No ponto de equilíbrio (P = 0)
1. $TR = pQ$	8. $FC = pQ - vQ = Q(p - v)$
2. $c = p - v$	9. $Q = FC/(p - v)$
3. $C = Q(p - v) = TR - vQ = FC + P$	10. $TVC = TR - FC = pQ - FC$
4. $TC = FC + TVC$	11. $v = \dfrac{TR - FC}{Q} = \dfrac{pQ - FC}{Q} = p - \dfrac{FC}{Q}$
5. $TVC = vQ$	
6. $P = TR - TC = pQ - (FC + vQ)$	12. $TR = FC + TVC = FC + vQ$
7. $Q = (P + FC)/(p - v)$	13. $p = (FC + vQ)/Q = FC/Q + v$

esquerda do ponto de equilíbrio. Se a alavancagem operacional e o ângulo forem grandes, os lucros e os prejuízos se elevarão rapidamente para a direita ou para a esquerda do ponto de equilíbrio, respectivamente.

Como se pode ver na Figura 4.12, a alavancagem operacional para linhas de montagem automatizadas é representada pelas áreas sombreadas à direita e à esquerda, respectivamente, do volume BE_2, o ponto de equilíbrio. A alavancagem operacional do projeto de processo de linha de montagem automatizada é maior do que a alavancagem operacional da manufatura celular. O conceito de alavancagem operacional tem as seguintes implicações importantes para a escolha do projeto de processo:

1. Lucros de longo prazo maiores podem ser realizados a partir de processos de produção com uma alavancagem operacional maior assim que o volume de produção atinge certo nível (Ponto EP na Figura 4.12).

2. Prejuízos de longo prazo maiores podem resultar de processos de produção com alavancagem operacional maior se o volume de produção for menor do que o ponto de equilíbrio (Ponto BE_2 na Figura 4.12).

3. Quanto maior a alavancagem operacional de um processo de produção, maior será a incerteza de lucros futuros.

4. Quanto maior a incerteza das previsões de vendas, maior o risco de prejuízos quando são usados processos de produção com elevada alavancagem operacional.

A importância prática dessas implicações é esta: se houver uma quantidade substancial de incerteza referente à previsão do número de produtos a ser produzido, projetos de processo com níveis menores de alavancagem operacional tendem a ser preferíveis.

Análise de Break-Even A análise de break-even comumente é usada para auxiliar na escolha entre alternativas de processamento. Aqui trabalhamos com um exemplo para refrescar nossa memória a respeito dos conceitos de pontos de equilíbrio e para demonstrar como a análise de break-even pode ser usada para comparar alternativas de processamento de produção.

A Tabela 4.3 contém as definições de variáveis e fórmulas para análise direta do ponto de equilíbrio. O Exemplo 4.1 compara as funções de custo de três alternativas de processamento de produção.

Exemplo 4.1

Análise de Break-Even: Escolhendo um Processo de Produção

Três processos de produção — automatizado (A), manufatura celular (C) e job shops (J) — têm a seguinte estrutura de custo:

Processo	Custo Fixo por Ano	Custo Variável por Unidade
A	$ 110.000	$ 2
C	80.000	4
J	75.000	5

a) Qual é o processo mais econômico para um volume de 10 mil unidades por ano?
b) Em qual volume cada um dos processos seria preferível?

Solução

a)
$$TC = FC + v(Q)$$
$$TC_A = FC_A + v_A(10.000) = \$ 110.000 + \$ 2(10.000) = \$ 130.000$$
$$TC_C = FC_C + v_C(10.000) = \$ 80.000 + \$ 4(10.000) = \$ 120.000$$
$$TC_J = FC_J + v_J(10.000) = \$ 75.000 + \$ 5(10.000) = \$ 125.000$$

O processo de produção com manufatura celular tem o custo mais baixo quando Q = 10.000 unidades.

b)
$$TC_J = TC_C$$
$$FC_J + v_J(Q) = FC_C + v_C(Q)$$
$$\$ 75.000 + \$ 5(Q) = \$ 80.000 + \$ 4(Q)$$
$$Q = 5.000 \text{ unidades}$$
$$TC_C = TC_A$$
$$FC_C + v_C(Q) = FC_A + v_A(Q)$$
$$\$ 80.000 + \$ 4(Q) = \$ 110.000 + \$ 2(Q)$$
$$\$ 2Q = \$ 30.000$$
$$Q = 15.000 \text{ unidades}$$

O processo de job shop seria preferível na faixa de volume anual de 0-5.000 unidades, a manufatura celular seria preferível na faixa de 5.000-15.000, e o processo automatizado seria preferível na faixa de 15.000 unidades ou mais. Estaríamos indiferentes entre o processo de job shop e manufatura celular e o processo automatizado na faixa de 15.000 unidades.

FIGURA 4.13 — ABORDAGEM GRÁFICA À ANÁLISE DE BREAK-EVEN

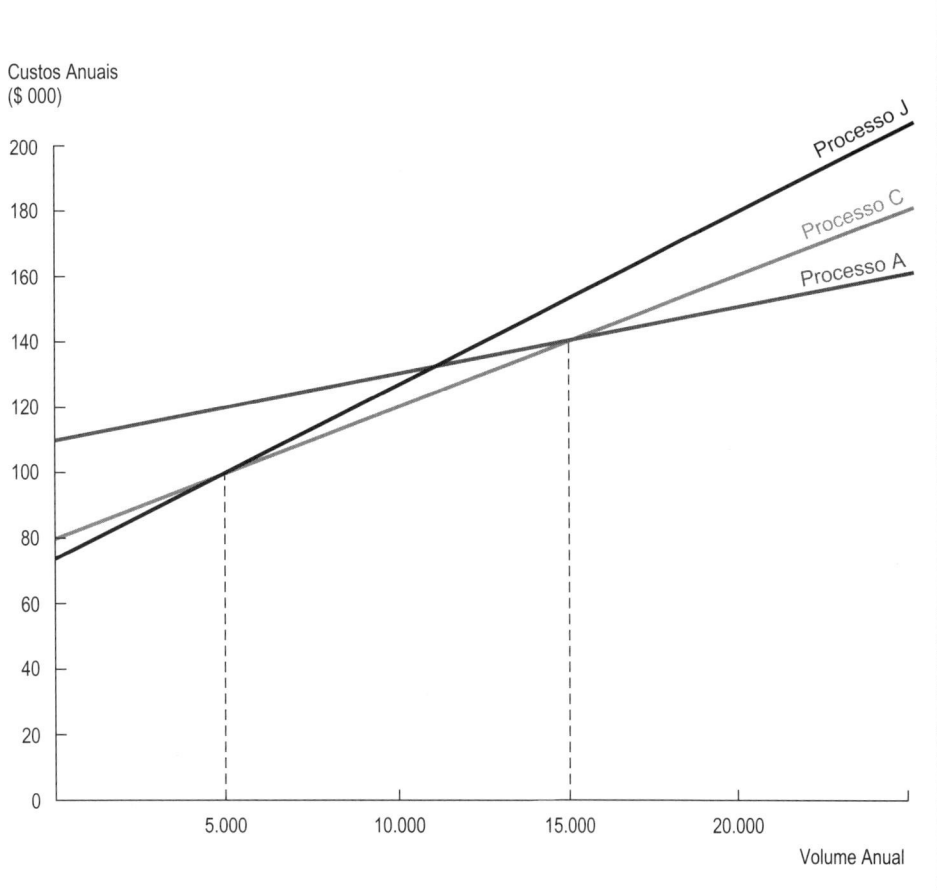

A **análise de break-even** é amplamente usada para analisar e comparar alternativas de decisão. Ela tem algumas fragilidades, entretanto, quando comparada com outros métodos. Uma fragilidade básica é a incapacidade que a técnica tem de lidar de maneira direta com a incerteza. Todos os custos, volumes e outras informações usadas na técnica devem ter a presunção de que são conhecidos com certeza. Outra desvantagem da ferramenta é que se presume que os custos se mantêm ao longo da faixa inteira de volumes possíveis. Adicionalmente, a análise de break-even não leva em consideração o valor temporal do dinheiro.

A análise de break-even pode ser exibida ou de forma algébrica, como no Exemplo 4.1, ou graficamente, como na Figura 4.13. Em qualquer das formas, os resultados são facilmente explicáveis. Essa é uma importante vantagem, porque *muitas vezes os gerentes preferem conviver com um problema que não conseguem resolver do que implementar uma solução que não entendem.*

Análise Financeira A grande quantidade de dinheiro a ser investida em alternativas de processamento de produção e o tempo que se espera que esses ativos perdurem tornam o valor temporal do dinheiro um importante conceito. O período de retorno do investimento, valor atual líquido, taxa interna de retorno e índice de lucratividade são métodos usados para analisar problemas APO que envolvem períodos de tempo longos.

Ainda que esteja além do escopo deste curso, essas técnicas são ferramentas valiosas para comparar alternativas de processamento.

Gráficos de Montagem

Gráficos de montagem geralmente são usados para fornecer uma *macrovisão* de como os materiais e submontagens se unem para formar produtos acabados. Esses gráficos relacionam todos os materiais importantes, componentes, operações de submontagem, inspeções e operações de montagem. A Figura 4.14 é um gráfico de montagem que mostra as etapas principais na montagem de uma calculadora eletrônica manual. Siga esses passos e tente visualizar as operações reais de produção.

Os gráficos de montagem, às vezes chamados **gráficos gozinto** (das palavras *goes* e *into*), são ideais para se obter uma visão detalhada do processo de produzir a maioria dos produtos montados. Eles também são úteis para planejar sistemas de produção para serviços quando esses serviços envolvem processar bens tangíveis, como em restaurantes tipo fast-food.

Gráficos de Processo

Os **gráficos de processo** fornecem mais detalhes para planejadores do processo do que os gráficos de montagem. A Figura 4.15 mostra os passos necessários para se processar 1.500 libras de materiais preparados por meio de mistura. Esse gráfico é uma análise detalhada de somente uma das operações necessárias para produzir comprimidos de aspirina. Essa ferramenta de planejamento divide a operação de mistura em 14 etapas elementares e as separa em cinco classes — operação, transporte, inspeção, atraso e armazenamento. A freqüência de ocorrência de cada classe, a distância percorrida e a descrição e o tempo correspondente a cada etapa são registrados. Quando o cabeçalho do gráfico é preenchido, o método de execução dessa operação de mistura é cuidadosamente documentado.

Gráficos de processo podem ser usados para comparar métodos alternativos de execução de operações individuais ou grupos de operações. A distância percorrida e o tempo para produzir produtos/serviços podem então ser reduzidos examinando-se gráficos de processos alternativos correspondentes a diferentes métodos de produção. Essa ferramenta de planejamento do processo pode ser usada tanto para produtos/serviços que sejam produzidos em sistemas contínuos como para aqueles produzidos em sistemas intermitentes. Além disso, ele é igualmente valioso para o planejamento do processo quando novos produtos/serviços são planejados ou quando operações existentes são analisadas para se obter melhorias. Os gráficos de processo voltarão à tona novamente no Capítulo 15, quando estudaremos a análise do desempenho humano em sistemas de produção.

Um Passeio pelas Instalações

Uma Fábrica Dedicada, Focalizada no Produto: Safety Products Corporation

A Safety Products Corporation é a maior fornecedora de produtos de segurança e sinalização de transportes dos Estados Unidos. Seus produtos são vendidos em quatro grandes mercados: rodoviário, ferroviário, marítimo e de construção. Para o mercado rodoviário, seus principais produtos são os sinalizadores de emergência (*flares*), refletores e sinais em veículos de movimento lento. Para os mercados ferroviário e marítimo, a empresa fornece uma variedade de sinalizadores de emergência. Para o mercado de construção, ela produz uma ampla variedade de sinais de aviso e dispositivos de sinalização.

Fundada em 1938, a empresa logo se tornou a principal fornecedora de sinalizadores de emergência para as rodovias do país. A partir daquela época, o tráfego rodoviário bloqueou o crescimento do tráfego ferroviário, e a empresa gradualmente acrescentou produtos de segurança e de sinalização a esse crescente mercado. Entre todos os produtos da empresa, os sinalizadores rodoviários de emergência são responsáveis por cerca de 60% de sua receita de vendas. Usados como dispositivos de sinalização quando emergências rodoviárias exigem a colocação de avisos de alerta ao tráfego que se aproxima, os sinalizadores rodoviários de emergência podem ser vistos facilmente pelos motoristas tanto durante o dia como à noite, faça sol, chuva ou neve. Os órgãos que aplicam as leis municipais e estaduais são responsáveis por uma grande parte das vendas desse produto. Mas as vendas de sinalizadores rodoviários de emergência para lojas de autopeças, lojas de ferragens e supermercados que vendem direto ao consumidor estão se aumentando. O crescimento das vendas de sinalizadores rodoviários de emergência foi tão grande que novas fábricas foram construídas em Richmond, na Virgínia, em Salinas, na Califórnia, e em Des Moines, no estado de Iowa.

Capítulo 4 – Projetando e Desenvolvendo Produtos e Processos de Produção

FIGURA 4.14   Gráfico de Montagem para a Calculadora Eletrônica Manual OK-20

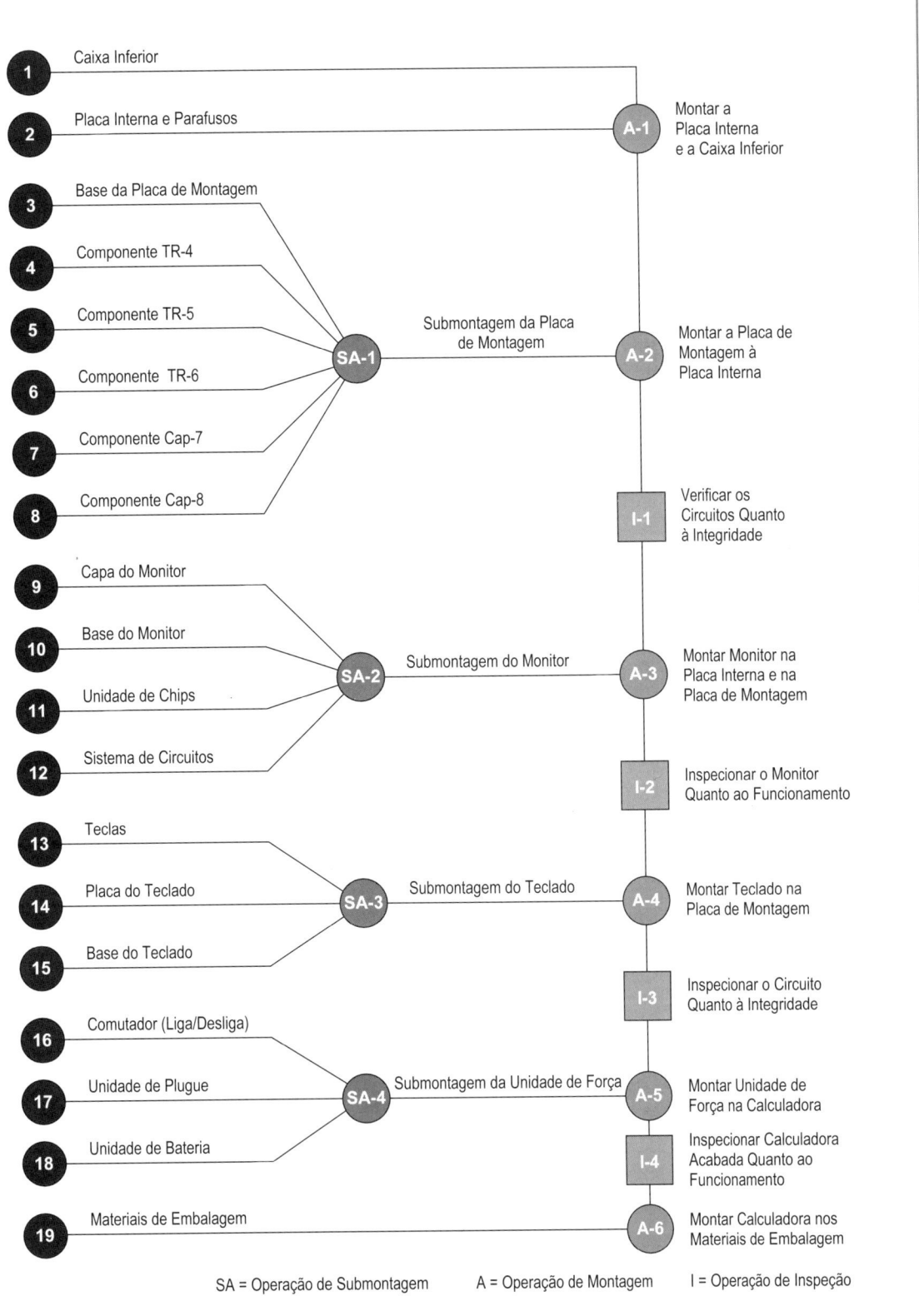

SA = Operação de Submontagem   A = Operação de Montagem   I = Operação de Inspeção

FIGURA 4.15 — Gráfico de Processo para Mistura da Aspirina

Operação: Misturar materiais de aspirina		**Folha** 1 **de** 1 **Folhas**	**Resumo**	
Produto: Aspirina Pronto (325)		**Gráfico traçado por:** B. Brown	○ Operação	5
Depto.: Mistura			⇨ Transporte	5
Desenho N.: — **Parte N.** 42200		**Data** 16-3	□ Inspeção	1
Quantidade: 1.500 libras de materiais misturados para a aspirina Pronto 325		**Aprovado por:** M. Sharp	D Atraso	1
			△ Armazenamento	2
Atual X **Proposta** ___		**Data** 17-3	Distância Vertical	—
			Distância Horizontal	212
			Tempo (Horas)	1,041

N.	Distância Deslocada (Pés)	Tempo de Trabalhador (Horas)	Símbolos	Descrição
1	15	0,200		Descarregar pacotes de materiais do caminhão para a área de carga/descarga e colocar no palete.
2	42	0,033		Transportar com caminhão os pacotes de materiais para a área de armazenamento.
3				Armazenar materiais até quando for necessário.
4	25	0,025		Mover pacotes até a rampa de carga.
5		0,330		Desempacotar materiais e despejar na rampa de carga.
6	20	0,030		Transportar carga até o misturador.
7		0,100		Carregar misturador e iniciar o ciclo de mistura.
8		0,083		Esperar até que o misturador encerre o ciclo.
9		0,017		Despejar a carga do misturador no veículo receptor.
10		0,020		Inspecionar materiais quanto à mistura apropriada.
11	50	0,033		Transportar veículo até o posto de pesagem e empacotamento.
12		0,167		Operar máquina para pesar e empacotar 1.500 libras de material misturado.
13	60	0,033		Transportar material para a área de carga/descarga.
14				Armazenar materiais até que o caminhão chegue.

Estratégia de Negócios A fábrica de Richmond, na Virgínia, foi construída como um elemento-chave da estratégia de negócios para o sinalizador rodoviário de emergência. Essa estratégia reforça os baixos custos de manufatura decorrentes da automação, os baixos custos de embarque e a superioridade tecnológica do produto. Os custos de manufatura e embarque são de importância estratégica, porque os órgãos que aplicam as leis compram cerca de 75% da produção, e vencer depende da capacidade da companhia para apresentar lances competitivos de baixo preço.

A localização da fábrica é de importância estratégica na manutenção de baixos custos de embarque. A localização na costa leste é uma excelente escolha para controlar os custos de remessa de matérias-primas que chegam, já que papéis da costa leste dos Estados Unidos e Canadá e produtos químicos da Europa são os principais materiais recebidos na fábrica. Os custos de remessa para o estrangeiro de produtos acabados se mantêm baixos devido à proximidade da fábrica com os centros populacionais da costa leste dos Estados Unidos.

A superioridade técnica dos sinalizadores rodoviários de emergência da empresa foi estabelecida através de superior formulação dos produtos químicos, extensos programas de pesquisa e desenvolvimento e serviço técnico aos clientes. A companhia criou uma valiosa reputação como a mais antiga fornecedora de sinalizadores ferroviários de emergência, com uma tradição de padrões estritos de segurança e desempenho. Extensos programas de pesquisa e desenvolvimento resultaram em projetos de produto robustos, que têm um desempenho conforme o esperado mesmo quando as condições de manufatura ou de campo se afastam daquilo que é comum. A empresa estimula os órgãos que aplicam as leis a realizarem testes de produtos concorrentes e fornece equipamentos e manuais para apoiá-los. Em conseqüência, os órgãos que aplicam as leis têm aprimorado seus critérios para a escolha de sinalizadores rodoviários de emergência, preferindo os produtos de melhor desempenho.

O Produto A Figura 4.16 ilustra um sinalizador rodoviário de emergência de 15 minutos. Esse produto, feito de um tubo de papel enrolado com uma mistura de produtos químicos chamada *flame mix* (mistura inflamável), tem na ponta uma mistura de produtos químicos chamada *ignitor button* (botão de ignição) e é adaptado com uma tampa, sendo que em uma de suas extremidades há uma superfície coberta com uma mistura de produtos químicos chamada *scratch mix* (mistura de raspagem). O sinalizador de emergência é acionado retirando-se a capa da superfície de raspagem e a tampa do corpo do sinalizador, segurando-se esse corpo com uma mão e a tampa com a outra, e esfregando-se levemente a superfície de raspagem no botão de ignição. Instruções de segurança e uso estão impressas no corpo do sinalizador.

A Fábrica A fábrica da Safety Products Corporation em Richmond, na Virgínia, embarca sinalizadores rodoviários de emergência de 15 minutos para 15 estados ao longo da costa leste. A fábrica custou aproximadamente US$ 50 milhões para ser construída, e suas vendas anuais são de aproximadamente US$ 25 milhões. A fábrica é chamada **fábrica dedicada**, ou seja, ela é dedicada a apenas um produto, o sinalizador rodoviário de emergência de 15 minutos, que é produzido continuamente na fábrica sem a necessidade de mudança para outros produtos. Existem dez operações de produção altamente automatizadas por meio das quais os produtos fluem sem parar. O único estoque de *work-in-process*[4] significativo consiste nos produtos que estão no transportador que atravessa a fábrica inteira. Os materiais via de regra fluem dos fornecedores de forma a coincidir com a programação da fábrica. Ainda que a demanda pelo produto seja sazonal, os níveis de emprego da empresa se mantêm bastante uniformes, permitindo que estoques de produtos acabados aumentem durante períodos de baixa demanda e caiam durante períodos de alta demanda. Dois turnos completos de oito horas são trabalhados diariamente durante o ano inteiro, e são feitas horas extras durante períodos de demanda muito elevada. Esse plano de produção exige uma cuidadosa previsão da demanda.

A força de trabalho na fábrica é composta de aproximadamente 150 empregados horistas. Uma divisão de um famoso sindicato de trabalhadores dos transportes representa os empregados. Cada empregado passa por um programa de treinamento de uma semana que inclui uma explanação dos programas e políticas da companhia, cursos em segurança de produto e qualidade de produto, e treinamento no trabalho. Há 16 empregados assalariados na fábrica: um gerente de fábrica, cinco pessoas de escritório, um superintendente de produção, seis supervisores de deslocamento de produção, dois empregados de engenharia e manutenção e um especialista em controle da qualidade.

---

[4] *Work-in-process:* trabalho em execução; produtos em curso de fabricação.

FIGURA 4.16   UM SINALIZADOR RODOVIÁRIO DE EMERGÊNCIA DE 15 MINUTOS

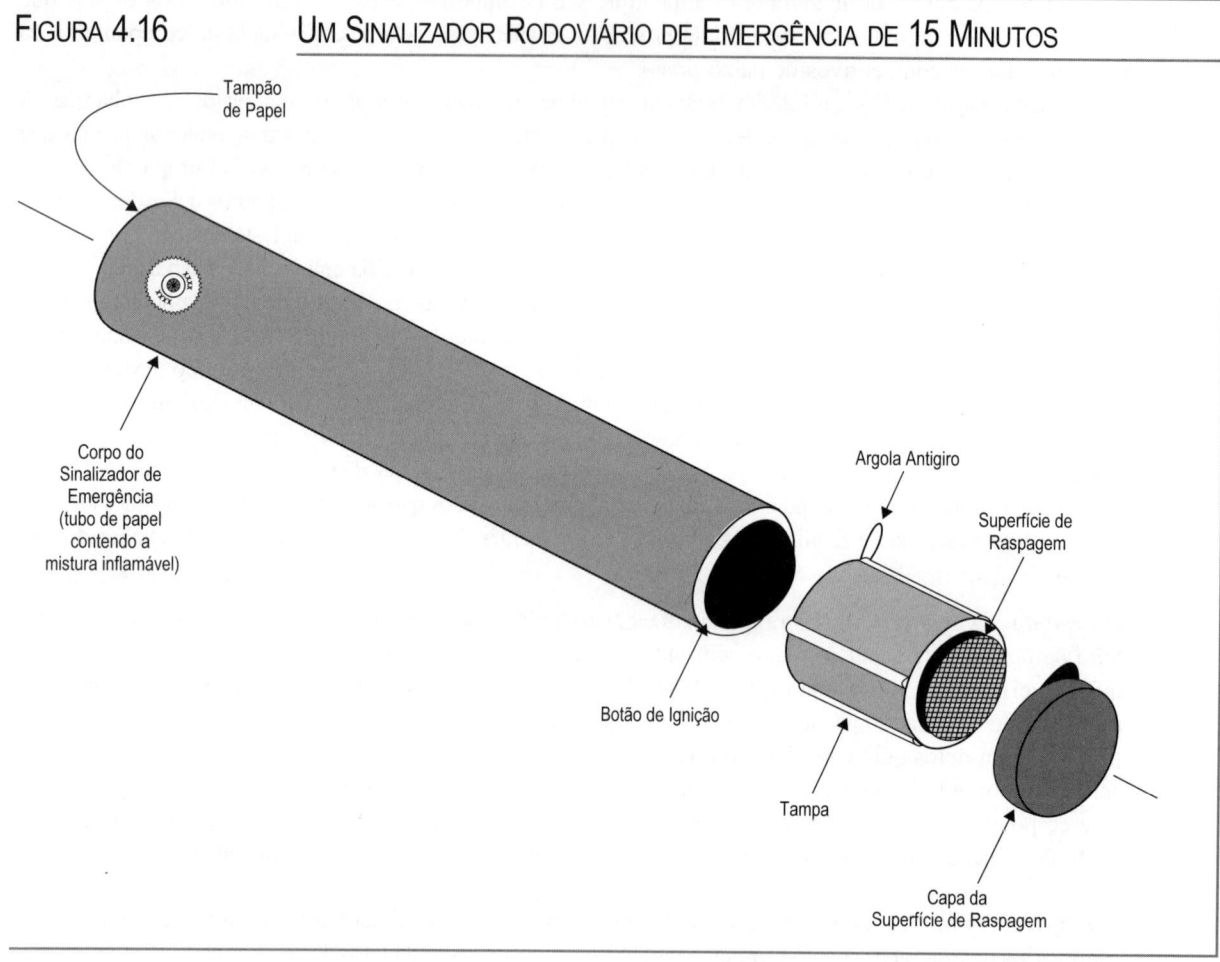

A Figura 4.17 ilustra como os sinalizadores rodoviários de emergência são manufaturados. As matérias-primas são recebidas de caminhões ou vagões de trem no armazém de matérias-primas e são então levadas do armazém em pequenas quantidades até a linha de produção conforme o necessário. Os produtos acabados são levados da linha de produção até o armazém de produtos acabados e guardados para embarque para os clientes em caminhões.

As principais operações de produção são descritas a seguir.

Enrolar Tubos   Grandes rolos de papel de cor vermelha são posicionados em *máquinas de enrolar tubos*. Essas máquinas puxam contínua e automaticamente o papel dos rolos, cortam-no no tamanho de um sinalizador de emergência, aplicam cola num lado, enrolam o papel com cola na forma de um tubo e colocam-no numa bandeja de contenção para secagem. Cada bandeja suporta 144 tubos, ou uma grosa. Os operadores dessa operação, à semelhança dos operadores de todas as operações da fábrica, monitoram o equipamento, fazem ajustes na máquina quando necessário, limpam as máquinas e a área de trabalho, e ligam e desligam as máquinas quando necessário.

Tapar e Dobrar os Tubos   As bandejas de tubos de papel secos são puxadas para as *máquinas de tapar e dobrar*, que agarram automaticamente os tubos de papel, inserem tampões de papel nas extremidades dos tubos, dobram os tubos em torno dos tampões que fecham as extremidades inferiores dos tubos e colocam as bandejas novamente no transportador.

Misturar o Composto Inflamável, de Raspagem e de Ignição   Produtos químicos são combinados numa formulação patenteada para cada uma das três misturas para o produto: a mistura inflamável, a mistura de

FIGURA 4.17   FLUXO DE PRODUTO NA SAFETY PRODUCTS CORPORATION

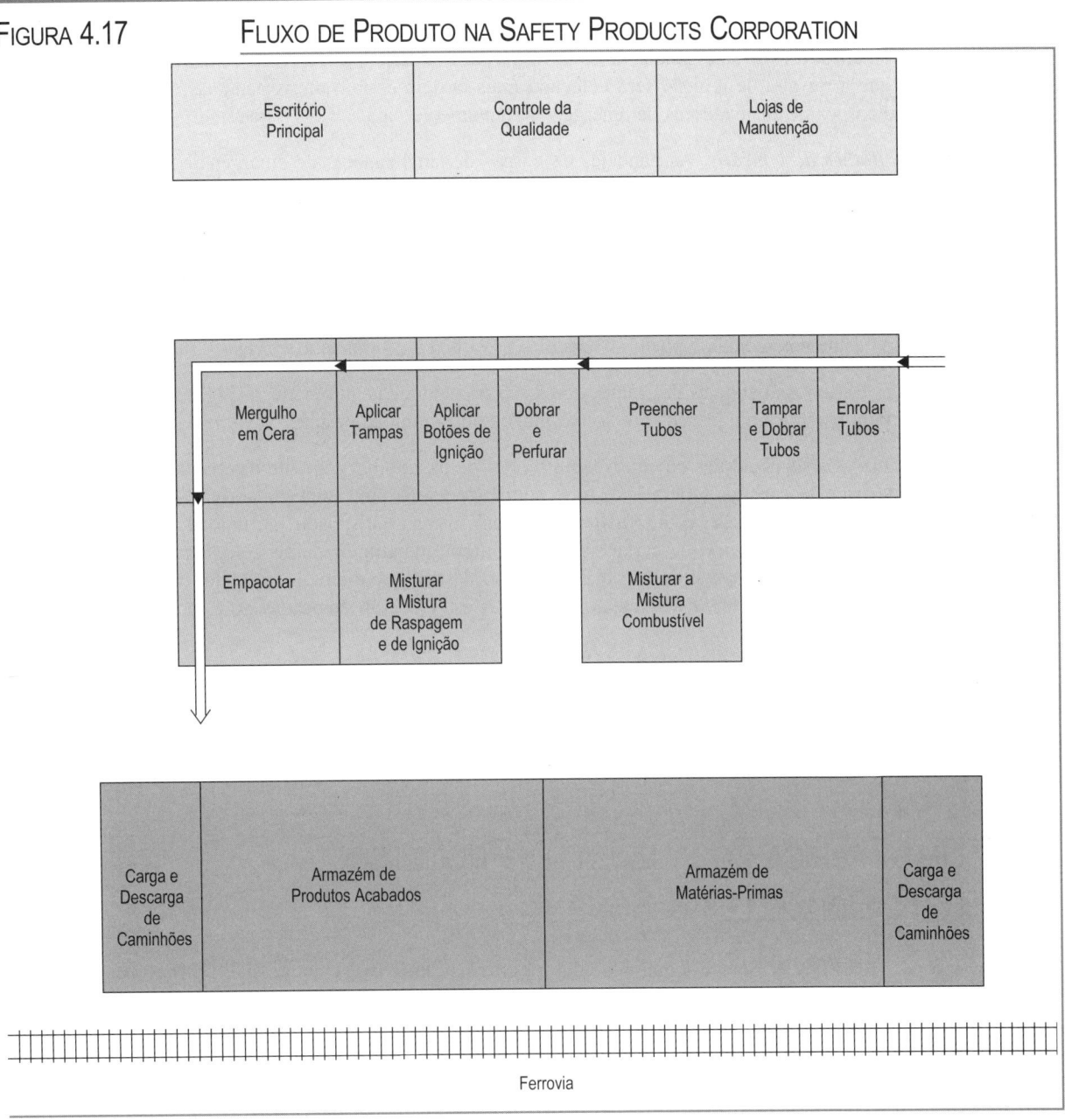

ignição e a mistura de raspagem. Os operadores seguem cuidadosamente os procedimentos de segurança e qualidade prescritos para assegurar uma operação segura e desempenho do produto. Os materiais são retirados de seus recipientes de embarque e colocados em *máquinas de misturar*, e instruções de mistura previamente programadas são codificadas nas máquinas. Depois que as misturas estão completas, elas são levadas por transportadores para as áreas da linha de produção. A principal responsabilidade dos operadores é manter condições de trabalho seguras, seguindo estritamente os procedimentos operacionais impressos e mantendo as áreas de mistura meticulosamente limpas. Além disso, os operadores devem seguir rigidamente as formulações químicas prescritas para o produto.

Preencher os Tubos   As bandejas de tubos de papel são puxadas automaticamente para *máquinas de preenchimento*, que preenchem os 144 tubos de papel com a mistura inflamável, compactam a coluna de mistura na densidade desejada e colocam as bandejas novamente no transportador.

Dobrar e Perfurar As bandejas de tubos de papel cheios se movem ao longo dos transportadores para *máquinas de dobrar e perfurar*. Essas máquinas posicionam as bandejas, dobram a parte superior dos corpos dos sinalizadores de emergência, fazem furos na parte superior dos corpos dos sinalizadores de emergência em que a mistura de ignição será colocada mais tarde e empurram as bandejas, cada qual com uma grosa de corpos de sinalizadores de emergência, novamente para o transportador.

Aplicar Botões de Ignição As bandejas de corpos de sinalizadores de emergência são colocadas automaticamente em *máquinas de dosagem da mistura de ignição*. Essas máquinas dosam automaticamente uma quantidade prescrita da grossa mistura de ignição líquida nas cavidades criadas na operação de dobrar e perfurar e colocam as bandejas de volta no transportador.

Aplicar Tampas Completamente automatizadas, *máquinas de tampar* puxam as bandejas de corpos de sinalizadores de emergência para a posição adequada, colocam montagens de capa plástica nos corpos dos sinalizadores de emergência e põem as bandejas novamente no transportador.

Banho de Cera As bandejas de sinalizadores são transportadas automaticamente por um banho de cera quente, para garantir uma proteção de longo prazo contra umidade e infiltração de água.

Empacotar Os sinalizadores de emergência são retirados automaticamente das bandejas e colocados em caixas de papelão corrugado para embarque com capacidade para uma grosa, ou 144 sinalizadores. As caixas de papelão são lacradas automaticamente, paletizadas e dispostas em unidades com *shrink wrap*. Paletes são estrados (*frames*) descartáveis que permitem que empilhadeiras coloquem seus garfos sob as cargas para transportá-las, e shrink wrap é um filme plástico que é envolto ao redor de uma carga inteira. Cada palete suporta 72 caixas de papelão. As cargas estão ou são colocadas no estoque ou são rotuladas para embarque imediato.

A fábrica de Richmond tem obtido um desempenho além das expectativas da Safety Products Corporation. Os custos de embarque e produção têm sido tão baixos que a empresa adquiriu posição de destaque em concorrências junto aos órgãos regionais que aplicam as leis. Adicionalmente, a qualidade e a superioridade tecnológica dos produtos da companhia têm sido fatores decisivos para seu sucesso.

UMA FÁBRICA FOCALIZADA NO PROCESSO: R. R. DONNELLEY & SONS

A R. R. Donnelley & Sons é a maior produtora mundial de livros. Uma de suas fábricas está localizada em Willard, no centro-norte rural de Ohio, num ponto quase eqüidistante entre Columbus, Cleveland e Toledo. A fábrica de Willard está em operação há cerca de 35 anos e se beneficia do fato de estar próxima à linha principal da Baltimore & Ohio Railroad e de ter uma força de trabalho local abundante. A R. R. Donnelley tem contratos com editoras para imprimir livros e produtos de documentação de software. Há muitos concorrentes locais e estrangeiros, e a estratégia de negócios da R. R. Donnelley é oferecer uma produção personalizada de livros com superior qualidade, de entregas no tempo certo, preços competitivos e flexibilidade de manufatura.

A qualidade superior é obtida através de muitos meios. Primeiro, a alta administração criou um ambiente no qual a atitude é "quase não é bom o bastante". Um departamento de controle da qualidade distinto supervisiona o programa da qualidade total na fábrica. Estritas especificações são seguidas para todos os materiais comprados. Equipes de empregados estudam e encontram soluções para problemas de produção relacionados com a qualidade ao longo do processo de produção. Padrões de qualidade extremamente elevados são aplicados aos produtos em cada etapa do processo de produção, e os empregados checam cada produto para se certificar de que eles seguem os padrões. Os empregados parecem sinceramente dedicados ao programa de controle da qualidade da companhia.

A fábrica tem mais de 93 mil metros quadrados de espaço de construção e mais de 1.400 empregados. Rumo à meta de fornecer entregas no tempo certo e preços competitivos, os pedidos de livros feitos pelos clientes são cuidadosamente planejados, produzidos, remetidos e controlados como lotes ou tarefas únicas. Por exemplo, se a South-Western College Publishing fizesse um pedido de 5 mil exemplares do livro *Administração da Produção e Operações*, de Gaither e Frazier, o pedido inteiro comumente seria produzido como um único lote que fluiria de departamento a departamento através da fábrica. Essa disposição freqüentemente é chamada **job shop** porque os pedidos dos clientes são tratados como tarefas (jobs) que fluem através da fábrica, e as tarefas tornam-se o foco do planejamento e controle da produção.

Uma vez que existe uma enorme variedade entre as tarefas que devem ser desenvolvidas pela fábrica, uma grande flexibilidade de manufatura é necessária. Isso significa que em qualquer departamento de produção em particular, os empregados, a maquinaria de produção e os materiais devem ser flexíveis o bastante para ser mudados de uma tarefa para outra. A flexibilidade de empregados é auxiliada pelo treinamento multifuncional em diversas tarefas, treinamento nos aspectos técnicos das tarefas e recompensas por iniciativa dos empregados. Máquinas de produção devem ser projetadas de forma que sejam máquinas de uso geral que possam ser rapidamente mudadas para outras tarefas, para que se acomodem à grande variedade de produtos. Uma vez que o grande número de materiais necessários para desenvolver a enorme variedade de tarefas deve ser pedido em grandes quantidades de fornecedores distantes que exigem até três meses para a entrega, grandes quantidades de materiais são armazenadas.

A fábrica se assemelha a todas as outras job shops em termos de que a produção é planejada e controlada concentrando-se em tarefas solicitadas pelos clientes. Em um aspecto, a fábrica é incomum quando comparada com outras job shops: todas as tarefas tomam o mesmo caminho básico através dos departamentos de produção — preparo da chapa de impressão, impressão, *slitting*[5] e intercalação, e encadernação. Na maioria das outras job shops, as tarefas tomam um grande número de roteiros através dos departamentos até o grau em que, para um olhar despreparado, os roteiros parecem quase aleatórios. Existem, entretanto, algumas diferenças de percurso entre as tarefas, porque tarefas podem ser atribuídas a diferentes centros de trabalho e a máquinas individuais dentro dos departamentos de produção.

Os processos de produção na fábrica são ilustrados na Figura 4.18. As principais etapas de produção são (1) recebimento, (2) preparo da chapa de impressão, (3) revisão da chapa de impressão, (4) impressão, (5) secagem, (6) slitting e intercalação, (7) encadernação e (8) embarque.

Recebimento Os materiais são recebidos na fábrica, vindos de fornecedores que podem estar próximos ou distantes. Esses materiais são estoques de papel e tintas, bem como suprimentos de manutenção, produção e material de escritório. O material mais pesado e que necessita maior espaço para armazenamento, entretanto, é o papel, que chega em grandes e pesados rolos. A fábrica usa 200 milhões de libras (10.718 toneladas) de papel anualmente, e recebe centenas de diferentes tipos de papel de mais de 25 diferentes fábricas. Imagine, se puder, o espaço necessário para armazenar essa quantidade de papel. Cada material recebido deve ser checado pelo pessoal de controle da qualidade para determinar se satisfaz as especificações e os padrões de qualidade prescritos. Somente depois de aprovados nessas inspeções os materiais podem ser colocados no armazém para ser preparados para uso.

Preparo da Chapa de Impressão Nessa operação são feitas as chapas de impressão usadas nas prensas de impressão para imprimir os livros. Essas chapas são produzidas por um processo fotográfico no qual uma imagem fotográfica de uma página original que é fornecida pelo editor é transferida para uma "chapa". Uma chapa é uma folha de metal com letras em relevo, de tal forma que quando se aplica tinta às letras e se faz a impressão em papel, a página pretendida do livro é transferida para o papel. O equipamento usado nesse processo é controlado por computador para se obter melhor controle da qualidade. Pessoal altamente capacitado é necessário nessa etapa de produção, pois, apesar dos recursos dos computadores, o preparo da chapa de impressão continua a ser manual.

Prova da Chapa de Impressão Essa operação consiste em verificar se as imagens nas chapas são duplicações exatas das páginas originais fornecidas pelo editor. As páginas originais contêm, por exemplo, texto, tabelas, fotografias e equações matemáticas. A revisão da chapa de impressão deve ser minuciosa, e até mesmo microscópios são usados para comparar as chapas de impressão com as páginas originais. Essa operação também usa mão-de-obra intensivamente e requer empregados comprometidos com os mais elevados padrões de qualidade de produto.

Impressão e Secagem Cada tarefa, dependendo de seu tamanho, é encaminhada para um tipo de impressão: uma prensa grande, uma prensa automatizada menor ou uma prensa alimentada por papel. Essas

---

[5]*Slitting:* (tip.) operação feita com o *slitter*, que é uma máquina de cortar bobinas; prelo cilíndrico com navalha rotativa que corta o papel em duas partes ao mesmo tempo em que efetua a impressão.

FIGURA 4.18 — FLUXO DAS TAREFAS DE PINTURA NA R. R. DONNELLEY & SONS

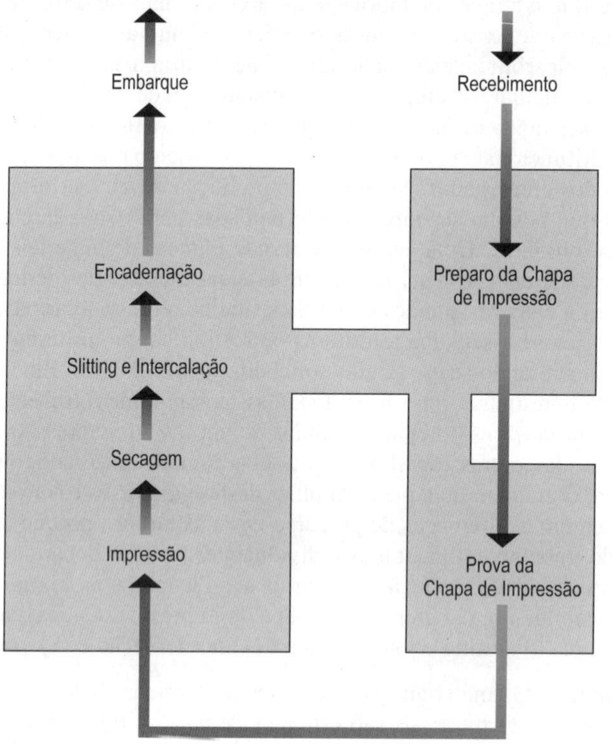

(Fluxograma: Recebimento → Preparo da Chapa de Impressão → Prova da Chapa de Impressão → Impressão → Secagem → Slitting e Intercalação → Encadernação → Embarque)

prensas incorporam a mais moderna tecnologia de impressão, com monitoração computadorizada contínua do estoque de papel, manipulação automatizada dos rolos de estoque de papel, scanners óticos e controle computadorizado de ajustes da máquina. A passagem de folhas de papel em prensas que chegam a 3 metros de largura a velocidades de 457 metros por minuto resulta em enormes índices de produção de páginas impressas. O estoque de papel impresso passa então por uma série de cilindros aquecidos e resfriados até secar. O equipamento de secagem exige uma grande quantidade de espaço. Essa etapa de produção requer uso intensivo de capital.

Slitting e Intercalação A operação de slitting envolve cortar as folhas de papel impresso em folhas no tamanho de página. Grandes máquinas de cisalhamento são usadas para cortar pilhas de folhas em folhas sucessivamente menores. Depois do slitting, as páginas são classificadas em seqüência e coladas em pequenos montes de 16 folhas ou 32 páginas, chamados *assinaturas*. As assinaturas são brevemente expostas a uma chama aberta para remover quaisquer partículas de recorte de papel em excesso, e conjuntos de assinaturas correspondentes a cada livro são reunidas para encadernação.

Encadernação As capas duras são montadas num processo distinto. As capas frontal e posterior são impressas numa única folha, coladas num suporte de papelão e dobradas de maneira adequada. As capas moles são impressas diretamente no estoque de papel da capa. Quando da encadernação, um equipamento de embalagem é usado para envolver capas em torno de pacotes previamente colados de assinaturas para formar livros acabados.

Embarque Os livros acabados são colocados ou em caixas e depois em paletes, ou diretamente em paletes. Paletes são estrados de madeira, papel, plástico ou fibra de vidro sobre os quais produtos são empilhados. Uma embalagem shrink wrap plástica é então envolta em torno da carga de cada palete para formar uma carga unificada. Paletes de livros são transportados por empilhadeiras do departamento de expedição até caminhões ou vagões de carga para ser embarcados até os armazéns regionais dos editores.

A estratégia da R. R. Donnelley é fornecer a seus clientes qualidade superior de produto, entregar no tempo certo e preços competitivos. O projeto, o layout e a operação de sua fábrica em Willard, Ohio, parecem bem adaptados para fornecer essas competências essenciais.

UMA OPERAÇÃO DE SERVIÇO: CENTRO DE DISTRIBUIÇÃO REGIONAL DA WAL-MART

A Wal-Mart Stores Inc. é uma cadeia de venda a varejo que opera em todos os estados americanos, com quartel-general em Bentonville, no Arkansas. As lojas oferecem compras *one-stop*[6] para a família, com uma variedade de mercadorias, inclusive produtos eletrônicos, brinquedos, tecidos, suprimentos para artesanato, suprimentos para automóveis, equipamentos para jardins, artigos esportivos, jóias, roupas e sapatos. A filosofia de comercialização declarada da Wal-Mart é oferecer mercadorias de marca registrada, de qualidade, a preços diariamente baixos, não somente durante as promoções.

A primeira loja da Wal-Mart foi aberta em Rogers, no Arkansas, em 1962, por Sam e Bud Walton. Suas ações foram negociadas pela primeira vez na Bolsa de Valores de Nova Iorque em 1972. Atualmente, nos Estados Unidos, a Wal-Mart tem cerca de 2 mil lojas de venda a varejo, mais de 35 centros de distribuição regionais, mais de 700 mil empregados (ou *associados*, como a Wal-Mart os chama), uma das maiores frotas particulares de caminhões nos Estados Unidos, mais de 100 mil fornecedores nos Estados Unidos e vendas anuais de mais de US$ 100 milhões.

A Wal-Mart usa centros de distribuição regionais para receber as remessas de mercadorias dos fornecedores, receber pedidos de mercadorias de suas lojas, preparar os pedidos para as lojas e carregar e embarcar os pedidos para as lojas. O centro de distribuição regional de New Braunfels, no Texas, foi construído em 1998 e atualmente serve a lojas espalhadas por todo o centro e sul do Texas. Depois de atingir sua capacidade, espera-se que ele atenda a 180 lojas e empregue cerca de 800 associados.

É difícil imaginar o tamanho desse centro de distribuição lendo a respeito dele num relato como este, mas considere estes fatos:

- O centro tem mais de 93.000 m² de área útil, o que equivale a aproximadamente 23 campos de futebol, ou mais de 9,30 hectares.
- O centro tem 96 portas de doca para carga e descarga de carretas.
- O centro tem 9,014 km de correias transportadoras para levar mercadoria dos caminhões que chegam para o armazenamento e do armazenamento para os caminhões que saem.
- O centro tem 69,934 km de largura de prateleiras e 83.980 diferentes localizações de endereço ou compartimentos (*slots*) de prateleira dentro do armazém onde a mercadoria pode ser armazenada. As prateleiras, sozinhas, pesam 1.632.924 kg.
- O centro possui mais de 1.200 vagas de estacionamento para carretas, 110 vagas de estacionamento para caminhões e 700 vagas de estacionamento para associados.

A instalação é organizada de acordo com funções como garantia da qualidade, manutenção, tráfego, distribuição, prevenção de prejuízos, processamento de dados e pessoal. A garantia da qualidade recebe grande ênfase no centro de distribuição. Seu principal propósito é certificar-se de que a quantidade e o tipo certos de mercadoria foram recebidos, que a mercadoria não foi danificada no embarque, e que a quantidade e o tipo certos de mercadoria foram embarcados para as lojas. O departamento de tráfego preocupa-se principalmente com a programação e a coordenação de caminhões de transporte comuns que chegam dos fornecedores. O departamento de distribuição preocupa-se com a programação e a coordenação de caminhões da empresa que saem para as lojas. O departamento de prevenção de prejuízos é responsável pela proteção e segurança.

A Figura 4.19 ilustra o layout geral do centro de distribuição. As demais operações da instalação serão discutidas a seguir: pedidos das lojas, mercadorias que chegam, atendimento dos pedidos, sistema transportador/classificador e mercadorias que saem.

---

[6]*One-stop:* literalmente, "uma única parada". Lojas onde é possível comprar uma grande variedade de mercadorias, sem ser necessário se deslocar por muitos lugares.

FIGURA 4.19   CENTRO DE DISTRIBUIÇÃO REGIONAL

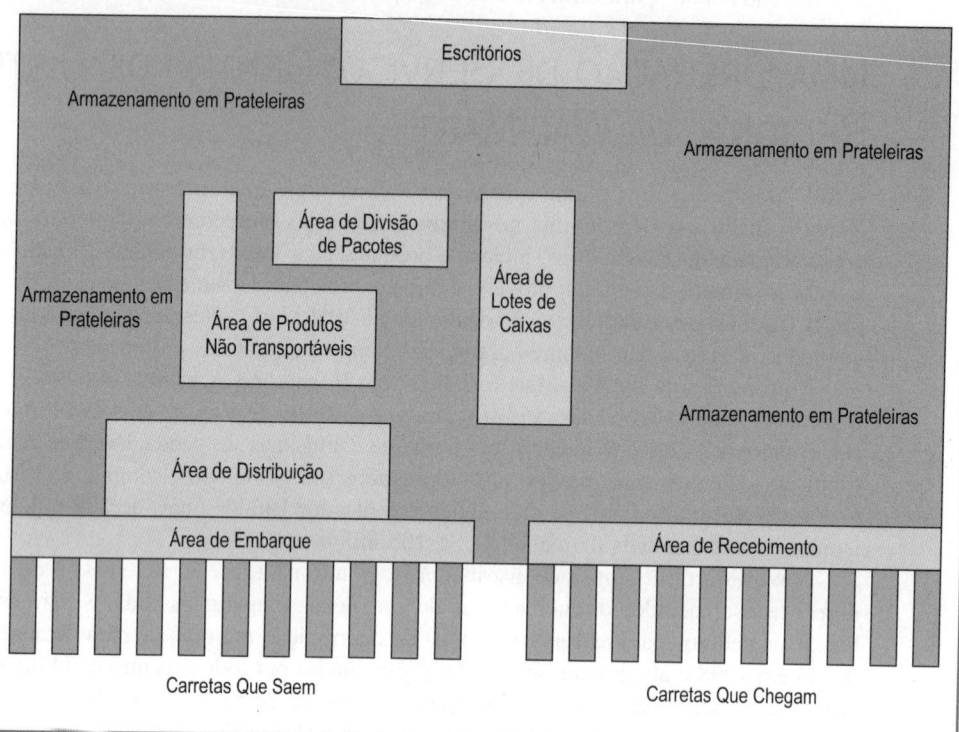

Pedidos das Lojas   Cada loja da Wal-Mart tem uma conexão computadorizada direta com o centro de operações em Bentonville. No final de cada dia de trabalho, os associados de cada loja enviam uma lista de pedidos de mercadorias por um terminal de computador a Bentonville. O sistema de computador do centro de operações divide a lista de pedidos e designa os pedidos a centros de distribuição regionais. Não obstante a maior parte das mercadorias ser embarcada do centro de distribuição regional mais próximo, certos produtos especiais são estocados em somente alguns dos centros. Um sistema de computador em cada um dos centros de distribuição regionais recebe os pedidos na manhã seguinte e lhes imprime os rótulos.

Os rótulos desempenham um papel crucial na operação do centro. Cada pacote de mercadoria que deve ser embarcado para uma loja deve ter um rótulo adesivo previamente impresso anexado. Esses rótulos estão na forma de código de barras, para que possam ser lidos por equipamentos de leitura ótica, e na forma impressa, para facilitar a leitura pelos associados. Um rótulo representa a autorização para despachar a mercadoria e contém todas as informações relativas ao pedido: destino da loja, nome da mercadoria, quantidade de mercadoria, nome do fornecedor e localização ou espaço de armazém.

Mercadorias Que Chegam   O departamento de compras no centro de operações de Bentonville compra mercadoria dos fornecedores em contratos de longo prazo. O departamento de compras mantém os departamentos de tráfego dos centros de distribuição regionais informados sobre qual fornecedor deve fornecer cada tipo de mercadoria. Quase todas as mercadorias são feitas nos Estados Unidos e literalmente vêm de todas as regiões do país. À medida que as mercadorias são embarcadas dos centros de distribuição regionais, os registros de estoques são continuamente revisados, a fim de que o departamento de tráfego saiba quando remessas de cada tipo de mercadoria são necessárias. O departamento de tráfego programa então para que remessas dos fornecedores cheguem antes que os centros de distribuição regionais esgotem cada tipo de mercado. Talvez igualmente importante é o fato de que as mercadorias não chegam cedo demais nos centros de distribuição, mantendo assim os níveis de estoque baixos e o investimento em estoques controlado.

Atendimento dos Pedidos O atendimento dos pedidos envolve usar os rótulos previamente impressos para localizar dentro do armazém cada pacote de mercadoria no pedido de uma loja, anexar o rótulo ao pacote e transportar o pacote para a área de embarque. Cada rótulo a ser embarcado diariamente é enviado a uma das quatro áreas da instalação: a área de lotes de caixas, a área de produtos não transportáveis, a área de divisão de pacotes ou a área de distribuição.

A área de lotes de caixas contém mercadorias que são embarcadas em múltiplos de caixas inteiras. Nessa área, associados com rolos de rótulos caminham entre as prateleiras de mercadoria e uma correia transportadora que se move continuamente. Os associados lêem o número de localização de compartimento da mercadoria, localizam o compartimento, verificam a exatidão da quantidade e o tipo de informação da mercadoria no rótulo do pedido, pegam uma caixa de mercadoria e colocam-na no transportador e anexam o rótulo adesivo no pacote. A partir daí, os pacotes são transportados para o sistema transportador/classificador elevado.

A área de produtos não transportáveis contém mercadorias pesadas ou volumosas demais para caber no sistema transportador/classificador. Essas mercadorias — sacos de 22,68 kg de ração canina, por exemplo — normalmente são recebidas, manipuladas, armazenadas e embarcadas em cargas unitizadas. Uma carga unitizada é um lote de mercadoria que é colocado num palete (um estrado de madeira quadrado de 1,20 m) e embalado a vácuo (shrink wrapped) com plástico transparente. O atendimento de pedidos de mercadorias não transportáveis é realizado anexando-se um rótulo à parte superior da carga unitizada e transportando-se a carga para a área de embarque com uma empilhadeira.

A área de divisão de pacotes contém mercadorias que devem ser embarcadas em quantidades menores do que o conteúdo de uma caixa inteira. Associados cortam o topo das caixas e colocam-nas em localizações de compartimento dentro de prateleiras que estão adjacentes a uma correia transportadora que se move continuamente. Os associados que fazem o atendimento de pedidos usam então os rótulos para localizar o compartimento, verificam a informação no rótulo, colocam a quantidade de mercadoria necessária no transportador e anexam o rótulo à mercadoria. No final do transportador, a mercadoria é carregada em caixas e checada pelo controle da qualidade. Os pacotes de mercadoria entram então no sistema transportador/classificador.

A área de distribuição contém mercadorias especiais que estão em promoção nacional atualmente. Por exemplo, mercadorias especiais a serem estocadas em lojas para a promoção do dia das mães são encontradas nessa área. Os pedidos de lojas são atendidos a partir dessa área, e as mercadorias ou entram no sistema transportador/classificador, ou são levadas para a área de embarque com empilhadeiras.

Sistema Transportador/Classificador O sistema transportador/classificador é usado para transportar pacotes das áreas de armazenamento do armazém, levá-las para a área de embarque e classificá-las para a seção de carga. Esse sistema consiste em uma rede de transportadores, scanners óticos e equipamentos de desvio de pacotes. Pacotes são transportados das áreas de atendimento de pedidos no chão do armazém para um sistema de esteiras transportadoras aéreas, com aproximadamente três andares de altura e situado logo abaixo do teto do armazém. Aqui, os pacotes são virados, para que os rótulos fiquem voltados para cima, e então são canalizados para scanners óticos. Esses scanners lêem todas as informações dos códigos de barras nos rótulos, enviam a informação para o sistema de registro de estoques e enviam para o equipamento de desvio de pacotes informações sobre qual seção de embarque deve receber cada pacote. O equipamento de desvio de pacotes empurra os pacotes do transportador principal para transportadores secundários que se dirigem para seções de carga específicas na área de embarque.

Mercadorias Que Saem Os pacotes de mercadorias saem do sistema transportador/classificador em esteiras rolantes que se estendem para os caminhões que chegam. Os associados fazem leitura ótica com bastões de leitura ótica manuais para verificar a informação dos scanners óticos do sistema transportador/classificador. Os pacotes do sistema transportador/classificador são colocados manualmente nos caminhões que saem, e as cargas de mercadorias não transportáveis são colocadas nos caminhões que saem com empilhadeiras. A instalação tem a capacidade de embarcar para as lojas aproximadamente 200 caminhões totalmente carregados por dia. Essa instalação regional, em combinação com o sistema de informação computadorizado nas lojas e no centro de operações de Bentonville, entrega pedidos para as lojas em no máximo 48 horas depois de feitos os pedidos. A divisão desse tempo de execução de 48 horas é a seguinte:

1. Os pedidos são transmitidos das lojas para o centro de operações no final do dia.
2. Os pedidos são designados a centros de distribuição regionais, e rótulos são impressos na manhã seguinte.

3. Os pedidos são atendidos, carregados em caminhões e embarcados no mesmo dia.
4. Os pedidos são transportados para as lojas em caminhões da própria companhia e chegam o mais tardar no dia seguinte, dependendo da distância entre a loja e o centro de distribuição regional.

Uma vez que as lojas não têm armazéns, os pedidos de mercadorias vão diretamente dos caminhões para as prateleiras das lojas. Esse sistema de entrega rápida de mercadorias dos centros de distribuição regionais permite que as lojas operem sem armazéns.

Além disso, as lojas podem esperar até que a mercadoria nas prateleiras esteja quase no fim antes de fazer o pedido, permitindo assim menores estoques de prateleira. Tudo isso se traduz em menores custos operacionais, maior produtividade e melhor serviço ao cliente.

Resumo Final

O Que os Fabricantes de Classe Mundial Estão Fazendo

Os fabricantes de classe mundial planejam e projetam produtos, serviços e processos de produção a fim de que os sistemas de produção possam ser usados como armas competitivas na captação de fatias de mercados mundiais. Isso exige que os processos de produção sejam planejados e projetados com capacidades específicas que coincidam com as prioridades competitivas de suas estratégias comerciais.

Cada vez mais os fabricantes americanos vêm a qualidade do produto e o serviço ao cliente como forças fundamentais, e a flexibilidade de produção e custos como fragilidades básicas em relação aos concorrentes. O desafio para o futuro é redesenhar processos de produção de forma que as potencialidades da qualidade do produto e do serviço ao cliente sejam mantidas e a flexibilidade da produção e custos seja melhorada. Com essa finalidade, os fabricantes de classe mundial estão fazendo o seguinte:

- Levando mais rapidamente produtos ao mercado, usando engenharia simultânea, CAD/CAM e equipes autônomas de desenvolvimento de novos produtos.
- Projetando produtos para obter facilidade de produção e para obter qualidade a fim de que os sistemas de produção possam ser usados como armas para competir em mercados globais, e melhorando projetos de produto com programas de melhoria contínua voltados a pequenas melhorias constantes.
- Aprimorando os esforços de previsão a fim de que as capacidades dos processos de produção se enquadrem de fato nas necessidades do mercado.
- Tornando-se menos verticalmente integradas ao se concentrar em seus negócios centrais, ficando assim menos vulneráveis a concorrentes menores e mais especializados, e desenvolvendo uma rede de fornecedores na qual estes são tratados mais como sócios do que como adversários.
- Reduzindo os custos de produção e tornando-se mais flexíveis ao adotar o conceito de *produção enxuta*, usando empregados altamente treinados em todas as etapas e adotando uma abordagem meticulosa em cada detalhe de produção. Esse conceito é imensamente diferente do conceito de produção em massa convencional, que simplifica cada tarefa a uma rotina descuidada ao mesmo tempo em que recorre a exércitos de supervisores para controlar os custos e limitar defeitos.
- Melhorando a flexibilidade ao substituir algumas linhas de produção manuais e *automação inflexível* (maquinaria automatizada, que é difícil de mudar para outros produtos) pela *automação flexível* (máquinas automatizadas auxiliadas por computador que são facilmente reprogramadas para outros produtos).
- Melhorando a flexibilidade ao redesenhar processos de produção para agilizar o fluxo de produtos ao longo da produção e reduzindo estoques de produtos em processo.
- Modificando algumas job shops para que incluam certa manufatura celular para melhorar os custos de produção, qualidade de produto e acelerar a produção.
- Instalando sistemas de controle de produção computadorizados melhorados para planejar e acompanhar melhor os pedidos dos clientes, fornecendo assim melhor serviço ao cliente, custos reduzidos e melhorada flexibilidade.

Questões de Revisão e Discussão

1. Cite e descreva os passos para desenvolver novos produtos. Quais as diferenças fundamentais entre um *protótipo* e um *projeto de produção?*
2. Explique três maneiras pelas quais as empresas americanas estão levando mais rapidamente novos produtos ao mercado.
3. Explique o significado de projetar produtos para obter facilidade de produção. Por que isso é importante?
4. Explique o significado de projetar produtos para obter qualidade. Por que isso é importante?
5. Compare o desenvolvimento de novos produtos e o desenvolvimento de novos serviços. Em que eles se assemelham? Em que diferem?
6. Explique o que se quer dizer com "evolução das estratégias de posicionamento para produtos". Qual a importância desse conceito para a estratégia de operações?
7. Discuta o papel do projeto de processo na estratégia de operações.
8. Descreva a relação entre projeto de processo e projeto de produto. O que é *engenharia simultânea?* Quais são suas vantagens?
9. Quais são os passos no projeto do processo? Quais entradas (inputs) são necessárias para o projeto do processo? Quais as saídas (outputs) do projeto do processo?
10. Explique como estes fatores afetam as decisões sobre projeto do processo: (a) natureza da demanda por produtos, (b) grau de integração vertical, (c) flexibilidade de produto e volume, (d) grau de automação, (e) qualidade de produto.
11. Explique por que os sistemas focalizados no produto às vezes são chamados: (a) produção contínua, (b) linhas de produção ou linhas de montagem. Explique a diferença entre: (a) manufatura discreta e manufatura por processo, (b) produção focalizada no processo e manufatura por processo.
12. Explique por que a produção focalizada no processo às vezes é chamada: (a) produção intermitente, (b) produção stop-and-go, (c) job shops.
13. Sob quais condições um gerente quereria formar células de manufatura numa job shop? O que é uma *família de peças?*
14. À medida que o número de projetos de produto aumenta e que os tamanhos de lote diminuem, explique o que acontece com: (a) o custo de produção por unidade, (b) a flexibilidade de produção. Apresente algumas razões para a existência dessa relação.
15. Explique brevemente como você se decidiria entre dois diferentes projetos de processo. Quais fatores consideraria? Quais ferramentas de análise usaria?
16. Dê as implicações importantes da seguinte afirmação: Diz-se que os sistemas de produção automatizados têm maior alavancagem operacional. Defina a expressão *alavancagem operacional*. Explique por que os sistemas de produção automatizados tendem a ter níveis mais elevados de alavancagem operacional.
17. Descreva um gráfico de montagem e um gráfico de processo. Em que eles diferem? Explique como eles são usados no projeto de processo.
18. Cite e descreva três classes de processos de produção para serviços. Dê um exemplo correspondente a cada classe.
19. Quais passos podem ser dados no projeto de processos de produção para um serviço para tornar essa atividade mais quantificável e objetiva? Discuta as dificuldades que poderiam ser encontradas.

Tarefas na Internet

1. Visite uma livraria na Internet e encontre livros sobre: (a) projeto de novos produtos, (b) projeto de serviços, (c) engenharia simultânea, (d) reengenharia de processo.
2. Procure na Internet um artigo sobre manufatura celular e faça um breve resumo.
3. Procure na Internet uma companhia que tenha uma job shop e descreva o que a empresa produz. Inclua o site da companhia.
4. Visite o site da Wal-Mart em **www.wal-mart.com.** Procure as duas lojas mais próximas de sua casa e escreva seu endereço.

PROBLEMAS

Gráficos de Montagem

1. Escolha um produto montado com pelo menos seis partes. Prepare um gráfico de montagem para o produto.

2. Ken Chang, um analista de produção da SharpEase Company, preparou a seguinte informação para a produção de um novo apontador elétrico de lápis. Prepare um gráfico de montagem para o produto.

Lista de Componentes para o Apontador Modelo D-41			
Descrição do Componente	Código do Componente	Código(s) do(s) Componente(s) Precedente(s)*	É Necessário Inspeção Depois Que o Componente É Instalado?
1. Motor	318	—	N
2. Unidade de esmerilhamento	290	318	N
3. Base	256	290	N
4. Invólucro	155	—	N
5. Cordão elétrico	310	155	N
6. Parafusos (3)	199	256, 310	N
7. Pés de borracha (4)	175	199	N
8. Bandeja de aparas	225	175	S
9. Embalagem	110	225	N

*O(s) código(s) do componente que deve(m) preceder imediatamente esse componente.

3. Cite uma atividade com a qual você tenha familiaridade e que tenha pelo menos seis passos — por exemplo, trocar o óleo de seu automóvel, recarregar um grampeador ou ligar e acessar um programa em seu computador pessoal. Prepare um gráfico de processo para a atividade.

4. a) Prepare um gráfico de processo a partir das informações que se seguem.
   b) Explique como esse gráfico de processo poderia ser usado.

Tarefas de Montagem do Termômetro Modelo 245B		
Descrição da Tarefa	Distância Deslocada (cm)	Tempo Necessário (min)
1. Pegar a base, orientar para a posição correta.	24	0,08
2. Pegar circuitos, anexar à base.	18	0,06
3. Pegar *harness* de fiação, conectar à base e aos circuitos.	20	0,17
4. Posicionar a unidade, conectar ao teste de circuito.	12	0,10
5. Aguardar o teste de circuito, interromper se a unidade falhar e soar o alarme.	—	0,15
6. Pegar montagem do mostrador (*display*), anexar à base.	18	0,06
7. Anexar harness de fiação à montagem do mostrador.	—	0,05
8. Pegar estojo externo, anexar à unidade base.	20	0,08
9. Posicionar unidade, conectar para o teste final.	12	0,10
10. Aguardar o teste final, interromper se a unidade falhar e soar o alarme.	—	0,20
11. Colocar a unidade na embalagem, fechar embalagem, colocar na rampa.	24	0,13

Análise Econômica

5. Uma companhia precisa substituir uma máquina antiga que é usada para produzir seu principal produto. O preço de venda do produto será $ 219 por unidade. Duas diferentes máquinas que poderiam produzir o produto estão sendo consideradas. A Máquina A teria um custo anual fixo de $ 9.500 e um custo variável por unidade de $ 119. A Máquina B teria um custo anual fixo de $ 7.900 e um custo variável por unidade de $ 128.

Capítulo 4 – Projetando e Desenvolvendo Produtos e Processos de Produção

a) Compare a quantidade de break-even para cada máquina.
b) Baseando-se no custo anual, em qual volume anual a companhia estaria indiferente a comprar a Máquina A ou B?

6. Uma companhia está tentando decidir se deve comprar uma peça de um fornecedor, produzir a peça enquanto usa montagem manual, ou produzir a peça com um sistema de montagem automatizado. Eis os dados sobre os quais a decisão será tomada:

	Comprar	Produzir – Montagem Manual	Produzir – Montagem Automatizada
Volume anual de peças	$ 250.000	250.000	250.000
Custo fixo por ano	0	$ 750.000	$ 1.250.000
Custo variável por parte	$ 10,50	$ 8,95	$ 6,40

a) Baseando-se nesses dados, qual é a melhor alternativa?
b) Em qual volume anual da peça a companhia estaria indiferente entre comprar a peça ou produzir a peça com montagem automatizada?
c) Em qual volume anual da peça a companhia estaria indiferente entre produzir a peça com montagem manual ou com montagem automatizada?
d) Quais outras considerações seriam importantes na decisão?

7. A Grey's Manufacturing produz peças usinadas para a indústria de construção naval em Boston. Sua fábrica agora é uma job shop focalizada no processo convencional com departamentos criados em torno dos tipos de maquinaria exigidos pelas peças. Depois de um estudo de engenharia, a administração da Grey's está considerando uma proposta para pegar uma família de peças da job shop e colocá-la numa nova célula de manufatura. A demanda para essa família de peças permanece bastante estável de ano a ano, e os pedidos dessas peças são em lotes de tamanho moderado. Espera-se que o custo de operação da job shop permaneça imutável. A decisão girará em torno de se a família de peças pode ser manufaturada de maneira mais econômica numa job shop ou num ambiente de manufatura celular.

	Job Shop Atual	Manufatura Celular Proposta
Volume de produção anual (peças da família)	80.000	80.000
Custos fixos anuais	$ 25.000	$ 220.000
Custo variável por peça	$ 10,40	$ 7,80

a) A proposta de manufatura celular deve ser aceita?
b) Quais devem ser as economias de custo anual se a proposta for aceita?
c) Em qual volume de peças a administração da Grey's estaria indiferente em relação à proposta?
d) Quais outras considerações afetariam as decisões de aceitar a proposta?

8. Um fabricante de móveis compra um produto de um fornecedor e o armazena para revendê-lo a seus clientes. O contrato de abastecimento entre o fabricante e o fornecedor estipula o seguinte:

Ano	Número de Produtos/Ano	Preço/Produto	Despesas de Usinagem
1	1.000	$ 350	$ 10.000
2	1.500	375	20.000
3	2.500	395	30.000
4	3.500	420	35.000
5	4.500	450	50.000

O fornecedor informou à empresa que não poderá honrar seu acordo de abastecimento anterior depois do primeiro ano. O fabricante acredita que poderá conseguir outro fornecedor para cumprir o restante do contrato de fornecimento, mas também quer considerar fazer o produto em casa (*in-house*). Ele desenvolveu dois planos para produzir o produto em casa: um processo de automação e um processo convencional. Os dois planos têm estes custos:

	Processo de Automação			Processo Convencional		
Ano	Primeiro Custo	Despesas de Usinagem	Custo/ Unidade	Primeiro Custo	Despesas de Usinagem	Custo/ Unidade
2	$ 1.000.000	$ 20.000	$ 125	$ 250.000	$ 30.000	$ 275
3		30.000	145		40.000	290
4		35.000	150		45.000	310
5		50.000	200		60.000	360

Suponha que o número de produtos por ano seja o mesmo que o projetado no contrato anterior de abastecimento.

a) Desenhe um gráfico de barras vertical mostrando o custo anual correspondente aos anos 2 a 5 para estas três alternativas: Fornecedor, Automação e Convencional. Como as três alternativas se comparam em termos de custos anuais?
b) Desenhe um gráfico mostrando os custos cumulativos para as três alternativas correspondentes aos anos 2 a 5. Durante quais anos o processo de automação começaria a mostrar uma vantagem de custo sobre as alternativas de projeto Fornecedor e Convencional?
c) Se a empresa seguir sua recomendação no item *b*, quanto dinheiro economizará em relação ao que teria sido pago para o fornecedor ao longo do período de quatro anos?

Estudo de Caso

Computer Products Corporation (CPC)

Abe Landers é planejador de produção da Computer Products Corporation (CPC) de Austin, no Texas. Ele estudou recentemente para seu exame de certificação da American Production and Inventory Control Society (APICS). Uma parte de seu exame exige que os candidatos tenham familiaridade com gráficos de montagem e de processo. Abe desenvolveu dois exemplos da planta da CPC para ilustrar o uso dessas ferramentas de planejamento da produção. Ele reuniu as seguintes informações sobre a montagem de um microprocessador que é usado em uma das unidades de disco flexível da CPC:

Lista de Componentes da Montagem do Microprocessador z44

Descrição do Componente	Código do Componente	Código do Componente Precedente	É Necessário Inspeção Depois Que o Componente É Instalado?
1. Placa de circuito impresso	pc551	—	Não
2. Conjunto de transistores	t6798	pc551	Sim
3. *Chip set*[7] da ROM	i8088	t6798	Sim
4. Chip set da RAM	j88000	i8088	Sim
5. Embalagem	p65	j88000	Não

---
[7]*Chip set:* um grupo de chips criados para funcionar como uma unidade e executar uma função. Por exemplo, um ship set de modem contém todos os circuitos primários para transmissão e recepção. Um chip set de PC contém os controladores de sistema, memória e barramento.

Tarefas de Montagem para Montagem do Microprocessador z44		
Descrição da Tarefa	Distância Deslocada	Tempo de Trabalhador
1. Pegar a placa de PC e colocá-la no gabarito	35,56 cm	0,05 min
2. Inserir conjunto de transistores na placa.	30,48	5,69
3. Assentar, dobrar e aparar.	—	1,55
4. Inspecionar montagem.	—	2,55
5. Inserir conjunto da ROM.	55,88	3,50
6. Assentar, dobrar e aparar.	—	1,25
7. Inspecionar montagem.	—	2,50
8. Inserir conjunto da RAM.	50,8	2,75
9. Assentar, dobrar e aparar.	—	1,25
10. Inspecionar montagem.	—	2,25
11. Colocar montagem na máquina de solda de fluxo e retirar.	396,24	6,35
12. Inspecionar montagem.	—	2,00
13. Colocar montagem na embalagem para transporte e colocá-la na caixa.	88,9	0,50

Tarefas

1. Prepare um gráfico de montagem para a montagem do microprocessador z44.
2. Prepare um gráfico de processo para a montagem do microprocessador z44.
3. Como esses gráficos poderiam ser aplicados no projeto de processo?

capítulo 5

TECNOLOGIA DE PRODUÇÃO
ESCOLHA E ADMINISTRAÇÃO

Introdução

Proliferação da Automação

Tipos de Automação
  Anexos de Máquina
  Máquinas de Controle Numérico
  Robôs
  Inspeção Automatizada do Controle da Qualidade
  Sistemas Automáticos de Identificação
  Controles Automatizados de Processo

Sistemas Automatizados de Produção
  Linhas Automatizadas de Fluxo
  Sistemas Automatizados de Montagem
  Sistemas Flexíveis de Manufatura
  Sistemas Automatizados de Armazenamento e Recuperação

Fábricas do Futuro
  CAD/CAM
  Manufatura Integrada por Computador
  Características das Fábricas do Futuro

Automação nos Serviços

Questões de Automação
  Produção de Alta, Média ou Baixa Tecnologia?
  Construindo Flexibilidade de Manufatura
  Justificando Projetos de Automação
  Administrando a Mudança Tecnológica
  Demissão, Treinamento e Retreinamento de Trabalhadores

Decidindo entre Alternativas de Automação
  Análise Econômica
  Abordagem da Escala de Classificação
  Abordagem da Escala Ponderada de Classificação

Resumo Final: O Que os Fabricantes de Classe Mundial Estão Fazendo

Questões de Revisão e Discussão

Tarefas na Internet

Problemas

VANTAGEM ESTRATÉGICA DA TECNOLOGIA

O que a Intel e a Wal-Mart têm em comum? Ambas têm sido muito bem-sucedidas em usar a tecnologia para melhorar suas operações.

Criar e aplicar nova tecnologia há muito tempo é um fator fundamental para o sucesso econômico. No mundo atual, entretanto, os homens de negócios sentem uma nova urgência em decorrência das aumentadas exigências de recursos para avanços tecnológicos, bem como da acelerada taxa de difusão tecnológica global. Isso exige uma reflexão estratégica sobre a tecnologia além do simples desenvolvimento de novos produtos ou serviços.

Considere a indústria de lentes óticas de alta precisão. Lentes de alta precisão são usadas numa ampla variedade de aplicações, de lasers e fibras óticas comerciais a equipamentos médicos e militares. A natureza dispendiosa de mão-de-obra intensiva na manufatura de lentes de alta precisão tornou difícil para as empresas americanas que fabricam essas lentes competirem com firmas localizadas em países com baixos custos de mão-de-obra. À medida que o processo de manufatura se torna mais automatizado, porém, ele consome mais capital intensivo em vez de mão-de-obra intensiva, e as companhias americanas podem competir de igual para igual. Com esse fim, o Center for Optics Manufacturing de Rochester, Nova Iorque, um consórcio tripartite que envolve o governo dos Estados Unidos, institutos acadêmicos e a indústria, passou os últimos anos desenvolvendo maneiras práticas e econômicas de automatizar a fabricação de lentes de alta precisão.

O uso da tecnologia para obter vantagem estratégica não se limita aos fabricantes. Os avanços nas tecnologias de computação e informação têm permitido que muitas organizações de serviço tirem proveito da tecnologia para se tornar mais competitivas.

Este é realmente o momento ideal para estudarmos a administração das operações. Ficamos otimistas quando lemos relatos sobre o uso de tecnologia de ponta em nossas fábricas e operações de serviços. Não obstante ser no chão de fábrica que a derradeira batalha por competitividade deve ser travada, é absolutamente fácil negligenciarmos os processos de produção do setor de fábrica no precipitado ambiente atual das fusões de muitos bilhões de dólares, programas de propaganda de muitos milhões de dólares, acordos comerciais internacionais e enormes mudanças nas taxas de câmbio da moeda. Todavia, é para o setor de fábrica que olharemos neste capítulo, quando exploraremos as importantes questões de como escolher e administrar novas tecnologias a fim de que os sistemas de produção possam servir como armas competitivas para captar mercados internacionais.

Fazer uso de *tecnologia avançada* ou *high-tech* significa aplicar as mais recentes descobertas científicas ou da engenharia ao projeto de processos de produção. Nova tecnologia pode significar uma ampla variedade de avanços tecnológicos ou da engenharia. Adicionalmente, nova tecnologia de produção quase sempre significa que uma tecnologia de informação e automação foi integrada aos processos de produção.

No passado, automação significava a substituição de esforço humano por esforço de máquina, mas a tecnologia de produção há muito superou esse antigo conceito. O uso do termo **automação** significa atualmente integrar uma ampla variedade de avançadas descobertas de informação e engenharia nos processos de produção para fins estratégicos.

PROLIFERAÇÃO DA AUTOMAÇÃO

As companhias americanas estão investindo enormes somas de dinheiro em projetos de automação de fábrica, mas ainda estão atrás de muitas fábricas japonesas em algumas indústrias. Os fabricantes americanos se atrasaram em reconhecer os amplos benefícios da automação. A princípio, pareciam pensar que a principal vantagem da automação eram economias de custo de mão-de-obra. As empresas americanas tendiam a deslocar a produção para o exterior: para Taiwan, Coréia, México e outros países com custos de mão-de-obra mais baixos, em vez de investir em projetos de automação em suas próprias fábricas. A busca de custos de mão-de-obra mais baixos no exterior resultou na transferência de tecnologia antiga para o exterior, em ficarem presos a taxas de câmbio desfavoráveis e no fracasso das empresas americanas em avançar suas tecnologias de produção. Durante certo tempo, portanto, os fabricantes americanos colheram economias de mão-de-obra a curto prazo, mas sacrificaram a oportunidade de obter as muitas vantagens de desempenho de longo prazo oferecidas pela automação. Hoje muitos projetos de automação visam não somente obter economias de custo de mão-de-obra, mas também melhorada qualidade de produto, produção e entrega rápidas de produtos, e, quando é usada automação flexível, aumentada flexibilidade de produto. O Instantâneo da Indústria 5.1 ilustra como a adoção da tecnologia de produção está influindo na produtividade dos trabalhadores nos Estados Unidos.

Neste capítulo discutiremos tipos de automação, sistemas automatizados de produção, fábricas do futuro, automação nos serviços e diversas outras questões de automação.

TIPOS DE AUTOMAÇÃO

O enorme crescimento no campo da automação industrial trouxe uma grande quantidade de máquinas automatizadas com recursos diversos. Esses tipos de automação são especialmente dignos de nota: anexos de máquina, máquinas de controle numérico, robôs, inspeção automatizada do controle da qualidade, sistemas automáticos de identificação e controles automatizados de processo. A Tabela 5.1 descreve cada um desses tipos e apresenta exemplos de cada tipo.

ANEXOS DE MÁQUINA

Os **anexos de máquina** são dispositivos relativamente baratos que reduzem a quantidade de esforço humano e tempo necessários para executar uma operação. Esses suplementos representam a mais antiga tecnologia de automação e comumente são encontrados em todos os sistemas de produção.

MÁQUINAS DE CONTROLE NUMÉRICO

As **máquinas de controle numérico (NC — numerically controlled machines)** foram as pioneiras entre as máquinas automáticas nas décadas de 1950 a 1980, quando uma ampla variedade de aplicações foi desenvolvida para essa importante realização tecnológica. Essas máquinas são previamente programadas por meio de fita magnética ou computadores para executar um ciclo de operações de maneira repetida. As máquinas têm um sistema de controle que lê as instruções e depois as converte em operações de máquina. As configurações de máquina são realizadas pelo sistema de controle, em lugar de por seres humanos.

No decorrer dos anos, as máquinas NC evoluíram. As primeiras máquinas NC usavam fita perfurada representando instruções de máquina. Posteriormente, algumas máquinas NC incorporaram mudança automática de ferramentas. Com os avanços na área de computação, vieram as máquinas de controle numérico computadorizadas (CNC). À medida que a computação ganhava em sofisticação foram desenvolvidas máquinas de controle numérico diretas (DNC) que colocavam diversas máquinas sob o controle de um único computador.

As máquinas NC são máquinas automatizadas importantes por si mesmas. Quando seus programas são produzidos de maneira eficiente, e quando suas ferramentas são projetadas de maneira eficiente, elas têm grande flexibilidade para ser mudadas para outros produtos e, portanto, são usadas extensivamente em job shops focalizadas no processo. Além disso, as máquinas de controle numérico representam uma importante etapa evolutiva no avanço rumo ao que há de mais moderno em termos de máquinas automatizadas — os robôs.

ROBÔS

Joseph Engleberger, aclamado como o pai dos robôs industriais, desenvolveu o primeiro robô para uso industrial, instalado em 1959 para descarregar uma máquina de fundição sob pressão numa fábrica da GM. A **robótica** é um campo em rápido desenvolvimento no qual máquinas semelhantes a humanos realizam tarefas de produção. O Robotic Institute of America define um **robô** da seguinte maneira: *Um robô industrial é um manipulador reprogramável, multifuncional, para movimentar materiais, peças, ferramentas ou dispositivos especializados por meio de movimentos programados variáveis para o desempenho de uma variedade de tarefas.* O cérebro dessas máquinas é um microcomputador que, quando programado, orienta a máquina por meio de operações predeterminadas.

INSTANTÂNEO DA INDÚSTRIA 5.1

IMPACTO DA TECNOLOGIA DE PRODUÇÃO SOBRE A PRODUTIVIDADE

Os trabalhadores americanos obtiveram recentemente o maior ganho de produtividade em cinco anos, quando as empresas puderam, finalmente, colher os benefícios de um forte investimento em novos equipamentos e tecnologia. Uma razão fundamental para o crescimento: uma explosão de 9,8% — a melhor em 15 anos — de produtividade nas empresas manufatureiras americanas, que são responsáveis por 18% do resultado total. O crescimento pode ser o resultado de bilhões de dólares gastos na modernização de fábricas, compra de equipamentos, atualização de computadores e adoção de programas de qualidade.

Por exemplo, a Bison Gear & Engineering de St. Charles, de Illinois, mudou-se para uma nova fábrica de US$ 8 milhões em maio, elevando a produção em 9% ano a ano desde então. A mudança agrupou 175 trabalhadores de três prédios em um único, com novo equipamento de ferramentaria e um sistema telefônico que "faz tudo, exceto torrar pão", nas palavras de Ron Bullock, CEO da Bison.

A produtividade da Ball-Foster Glass Container, de El Monte, Califórnia, elevou-se em 5% no ano passado, graças ao novo equipamento e a um programa de administração da qualidade total que, segundo o gerente de fábrica, Rich O'Neil, "elevou as expectativas de fazermos melhor do que fazíamos antes" para os 300 trabalhadores da fábrica.

O salto de produtividade em outubro reacende as esperanças de que os ganhos de produtividade retomem o crescimento de 2,5% ao ano, encerrando um período de 10 anos de fracos ganhos anuais de 1% na produtividade do trabalhador por hora.

Fonte: Belton, Beth. "U.S. Workers' Productivity Jumps 4,5%". *USA Today*, 14 de novembro de 1997.

TABELA 5.1 — TIPOS DE AUTOMAÇÃO

Tipos de Máquinas	Descrição	Exemplos
Anexos de máquina	Máquinas que substituem o esforço humano por esforço de máquina e tipicamente executam de algumas a muitas operações. despejam cargas de produtos	Anexos para avanço de magazine, dispositivos para centralização e fixação rápidas para tornos, alimentadores em tiras para máquinas de estampar, tremonhas vibratórias com balanças que químicos em contêineres receptores.
Máquinas de controle numérico (NC)	Máquinas com sistemas de controle que lêem instruções e as convertem para operações de máquina.	Tornos, tornos mecânicos verticais, máquinas de fabricação de pneus, máquinas de cura, máquinas de tecelagem.
Robôs	Manipuladores de uso geral, reprogramáveis, de múltiplas funções, que possuem algumas características semelhantes às humanas.	Máquinas que soldam, pintam, montam, inspecionam a qualidade, pegam, transportam e armazenam.
Inspeção automatizada do controle da qualidade	Máquinas automatizadas que executam parte ou todo o processo de inspeção.	Verificações de circuitos eletrônicos, verificações de funções ativadas por computador, robôs de pesagem, sistemas de inspeção flexível.
Sistemas automáticos de identificação (AIS)	Tecnologias usadas em aquisição automática de dados de produtos para entrada num computador.	Sistemas de código de barras, contabilidade de estoques, entrada de dados para controle de chão de fábrica, sistemas para ajustar configurações de máquinas de produção
Controles automatizados de processo	Sistemas de computador que recebem dados sobre o processo de produção e enviam ajustes para as configurações do processo.	Sistemas de controle para laminadores na manufatura de pneus, calandras no processamento de filme plástico, unidades de destilação fracionada (craqueamento) em refinarias de petróleo.

A variedade de robôs disponível atualmente é impressionante. E as coisas que os robôs podem fazer são realmente surpreendentes. Esses robôs podem movimentar seus braços nos eixos vertical, radial e horizontal e segurar ferramentas como pistolas de solda a pontos, ferramentas de soldagem por arco voltaico, pistolas de pintura de pulverização, fusos rotativos para máquinas de cortar metal, chaves de fenda, tochas de aquecimento e ferramentas de corte a jato de água.

Os robôs têm pegadores na extremidade de seus braços que são dispositivos a vácuo, magnetizados ou aderentes. Os robôs também têm sensores que permitem que os pegadores e os braços sejam posicionados em locais precisos quando executam seu trabalho. Os tipos comuns de sensores são os seguintes:

1. Os **sensores táteis** são de dois tipos: *contato* e *força*. Os sensores de contato indicam se foi feito contato, enquanto os de força indicam a magnitude da força do contato feito com o objeto.
2. Os **sensores de proximidade** indicam quando um objeto está próximo do sensor.
3. Os **sensores de visão de máquina** são usados para inspeção, identificação de peças, orientação e outros usos. Já os **sensores óticos** são usados para detectar a presença de objetos.

Os robôs podem operar em ambientes hostis aos seres humanos. Calor, ruído, poeira e escuridão, por exemplo, não constituem ameaça aos robôs. Além disso, em muitas aplicações os robôs podem produzir produtos de qualidade superior se comparados aos seres humanos, porque são mais previsíveis e executam as mesmas operações de maneira precisa e repetidamente, sem fadiga.

Cada vez mais os robôs podem ser reprogramados para executar outras tarefas. Alguns deles podem até ser reprogramados simplesmente anexando-se uma extensão entre o braço do robô e o braço de um operador experiente: o operador movimenta fisicamente o robô de acordo com as operações que este deve executar, reprogramando, assim, o robô. Mais tipicamente, entretanto, um programa é armazenado num disco ou outro meio magnético de armazenamento. Essa disposição permite que o robô seja reprogramado simplesmente inserindo-se o disco ou cartão num compartimento e retornando o robô ao "modo executar". Os robôs são os blocos de construção básicos para os sistemas automatizados de produção.

INSPEÇÃO AUTOMATIZADA DO CONTROLE DA QUALIDADE

Sistemas de inspeção automatizada do controle da qualidade são máquinas que foram integradas à inspeção de produtos para propósitos de controle da qualidade. Esses sistemas executam uma ampla variedade de testes e inspeções e são encontrados em muitas indústrias. Eles podem ser usados para tomar as dimensões físicas de peças, comparar as medições com os padrões e determinar se as peças cumprem as especificações da qualidade. E podem ainda ser usados para verificar o desempenho de circuitos eletrônicos — por exemplo, na indústria de computadores, softwares testam cada função que um computador deve executar. Conforme veremos no Capítulo 17, quando inspeções de controle da qualidade são executadas por máquinas automatizadas, a inspeção total se torna economicamente viável para muitos produtos. Essa tendência deve levar a uma qualidade de produto melhorada e custos de inspeção de controle da qualidade reduzidos.

SISTEMAS AUTOMÁTICOS DE IDENTIFICAÇÃO

Sistemas automáticos de identificação (AIS — automatic identification systems) usam códigos de barras, radiofreqüências, cintas magnéticas, reconhecimento ótico de caracteres e visão de máquina para sentir e introduzir dados em computadores. Os dados são lidos de produtos, documentos, peças e recipientes sem a necessidade de que os trabalhadores os leiam e interpretem. Um bom exemplo desses sistemas são as caixas registradoras em supermercados. O funcionário passa o código de barras do produto por um scanner. O sistema lê o número de identificação a partir do código de barras existente no item, acessa um banco de dados computadorizado, envia o preço do produto à caixa registradora, descreve o item para o cliente na tela e introduz o número de identificação do item no sistema de estoques.

Os AIS estão se tornando cada dia mais comuns em supermercados, chão de fábrica, lojas varejistas e atacadistas etc. O custo do hardware dos AIS não é elevado, ao contrário do custo para desenvolver software e bancos de dados para tornar o AIS eficaz.

CONTROLES AUTOMATIZADOS DE PROCESSO

Os **controles automatizados de processo** usam sensores para obter medidas do desempenho de processos industriais, controlam essas medidas com padrões contidos em softwares armazenados em computador, e, quando o desempenho varia de forma significativa, enviam sinais que mudam as configurações dos processos. Esses sistemas estão em uso há muitos anos nas indústrias de processamento químico, refinarias de petróleo e papel.

Um exemplo de controle de processo automatizado foi observado recentemente na indústria de papel. Uma grande calandra prensa polpa de madeira entre rolos para formar uma folha de papel contínua. Um grande scanner ótico é montado sobre a folha de papel para monitorar a espessura e a densidade do papel. As leituras do scanner ótico são alimentadas num sistema de computador especialista, o qual é um algoritmo lógico baseado em regras[1]. Esse sistema especialista decide se a espessura e a densidade do papel estão dentro de parâmetros prefixados. Se não estiverem, o sistema decidirá quais mudanças deverão ser feitas e enviará novas configurações à máquina de calandra, alterando assim a espessura e a densidade do papel.

Com o uso crescente dos sistemas de projeto auxiliado por computador e manufatura auxiliada por computador (CAD/CAM — computer aided design/computer aided manufacturing), os controles automatizados de processo se tornaram importantes em outras indústrias também. Até mesmo na manufatura discreta as configurações de máquinas individuais e grupos de máquinas agora podem ser sentidas e mudadas quando necessário para fornecer produtos de dimensões uniformes.

Como acontece com outras maquinarias automatizadas, quando são instalados controles automatizados de processo certa flexibilidade é perdida até que um software possa ser desenvolvido para acomodar diferentes características do produto. Além disso, não obstante o custo inicial do hardware desses sistemas não ser muito alto, o custo para desenvolver o software de suporte e a integração com o restante do sistema de produção pode ser muito elevado. Todavia, há que se ter em mente a qualidade de produto necessária para sustentar a estratégia de negócios.

As máquinas automatizadas descritas nesta seção são impressionantes, mas os benefícios finais da automação podem não ser obtidos até que as máquinas individuais sejam integradas a sistemas totalmente automatizados de produção.

SISTEMAS AUTOMATIZADOS DE PRODUÇÃO

À medida que a tecnologia de automação tornou-se mais sofisticada, o foco afastou-se das máquinas individuais e voltou-se a um conceito mais amplo. Hoje, sistemas inteiros de máquinas automatizadas interligadas para propósitos mais abrangentes estão se tornando mais comuns. Discutiremos quatro categorias gerais desses sistemas: linhas automatizadas de fluxo, sistemas automatizados de montagem, sistemas flexíveis de manufatura e sistemas automatizados de armazenamento e recuperação.

LINHAS AUTOMATIZADAS DE FLUXO

Uma **linha automatizada de fluxo** inclui diversas máquinas automatizadas unidas por máquinas automatizadas de transferência e manipulação de peças. A máquina automatizada na linha usa alimentadores automatizados de matéria-prima e executa automaticamente suas operações sem a necessidade de participação humana. Quando cada máquina conclui suas operações, peças parcialmente concluídas são automaticamente transferidas para a máquina seguinte na linha numa seqüência fixa até que o trabalho seja concluído. Esses sistemas, comuns na indústria automobilística, são normalmente usados para produzir um componente principal inteiro; por exemplo, caixas de câmbio para caminhões.

Esses sistemas são em geral chamados de **automação fixa** ou **automação dedicada**, o que significa que as linhas de fluxo são projetadas para produzir um tipo específico de componente ou produto. Tendo em vista seu elevado investimento inicial e a dificuldade de modificação para outros produtos, esses sistemas são usados quando a demanda é elevada, estável e se estende bastante no futuro. Se essas condições

---

[1] Um sistema especialista baseado em um conjunto de regras que um especialista humano seguiria durante o diagnóstico de um problema.

forem satisfeitas, o custo de produção por unidade será muito baixo. Em virtude, porém, dos breves ciclos de vida de certos produtos e das mudanças na tecnologia de produção, a popularidade da automação fixa vem declinando. Os sistemas de produção estão favorecendo cada vez mais equipamentos de produção que oferecem maior flexibilidade de produto. Falaremos mais sobre essa tendência quando estudarmos sistemas flexíveis de manufatura.

SISTEMAS AUTOMATIZADOS DE MONTAGEM

Um **sistema automatizado de montagem** consiste em um sistema de máquinas automatizadas de montagem ligadas por equipamentos automatizados de manipulação de materiais. Materiais são automaticamente manipulados em cada máquina, comumente algum tipo de robô (como um soldador robotizado ou uma unidade de inserção de componentes). Então o trabalho parcialmente concluído é automaticamente transferido para a máquina de montagem seguinte. Esse processo é repetido até que toda a montagem seja concluída. O propósito desses sistemas é produzir montagens principais ou mesmo produtos acabados.

Para que um sistema automatizado de montagem seja bem-sucedido, são necessárias grandes modificações de projeto de produtos. O projeto de produto apropriado para montagem por mãos humanas não pode ser aplicado diretamente a um sistema automatizado de montagem, porque as capacidades dos seres humanos não podem ser reproduzidas por robôs. Por exemplo, um trabalhador pode usar um parafuso, arruela de aperto e porca para unir duas peças, mas, na montagem automatizada, novos procedimentos e projetos de produto modificados são necessários.

Princípios como os que seguem são aplicados quando se redesenha produtos para montagem automatizada:

1. **Reduza a quantidade de montagens.** Por exemplo, use uma peça moldada de plástico em vez de duas peças de metal laminado que devem ser unidas.
2. **Reduza o número de fixadores.** Por exemplo, projete peças que se encaixem ou que possam ser soldadas uma à outra em vez de serem presas por parafusos, porcas e pinos.
3. **Projete componentes para que sejam automaticamente entregues e posicionados.** Isso significa projetar peças de forma que elas possam ser alimentadas e orientadas para entrega a partir de alimentadores de peças, rampas ranhuradas, bacias vibratórias e outros mecanismos de alimentação contínua de peças.
4. **Projete produtos para montagem em camadas e inserção vertical de peças.** Os produtos geralmente devem ser montados a partir de base ascendente em camadas até o topo. As peças devem ser projetadas de forma que possam ser inseridas verticalmente na montagem.
5. **Projete peças de forma que elas se alinhem automaticamente.** As peças devem ter recursos como ressaltos ou protuberâncias que se encaixem em recursos coincidentes existentes em peças adjacentes que posicionem e alinhem automaticamente as peças quando elas forem inseridas nas montagens.
6. **Projete produtos em módulos maiores para produção.** Um sistema automatizado de montagem seria então usado para montar cada módulo. Ao dividir a montagem do produto inteiro em diversos módulos de montagem, é reduzido o tempo de inatividade (*downtime*) do sistema.
7. **Aumente a qualidade dos componentes.** Componentes de alta qualidade evitam obstrução nos mecanismos de alimentação e montagem.

Os sistemas automatizados de montagem podem fornecer aos fabricantes baixos custos de produção por unidade, melhorada qualidade de produto e maior flexibilidade de produto. Uma vez que algumas das máquinas desses sistemas tendem a ser robôs padrões, que estão disponíveis em diversos fornecedores atualmente, o investimento inicial em equipamentos não é tão elevado como se poderia imaginar. Além disso, cada vez mais esses robôs podem ser reprogramados para outros produtos e operações, reduzindo assim a necessidade de que a demanda por produtos seja estável e se estenda muito no futuro.

SISTEMAS FLEXÍVEIS DE MANUFATURA

Sistemas flexíveis de manufatura (FMS — flexible manufacturing systems) são grupos de máquinas de produção organizados em seqüência, ligados por máquinas automatizadas de manuseio de materiais e transferência, e integrados por um sistema de computador. A Figura 5.1 ilustra esse sistema.

FIGURA 5.1 — UM SISTEMA FLEXÍVEL DE MANUFATURA

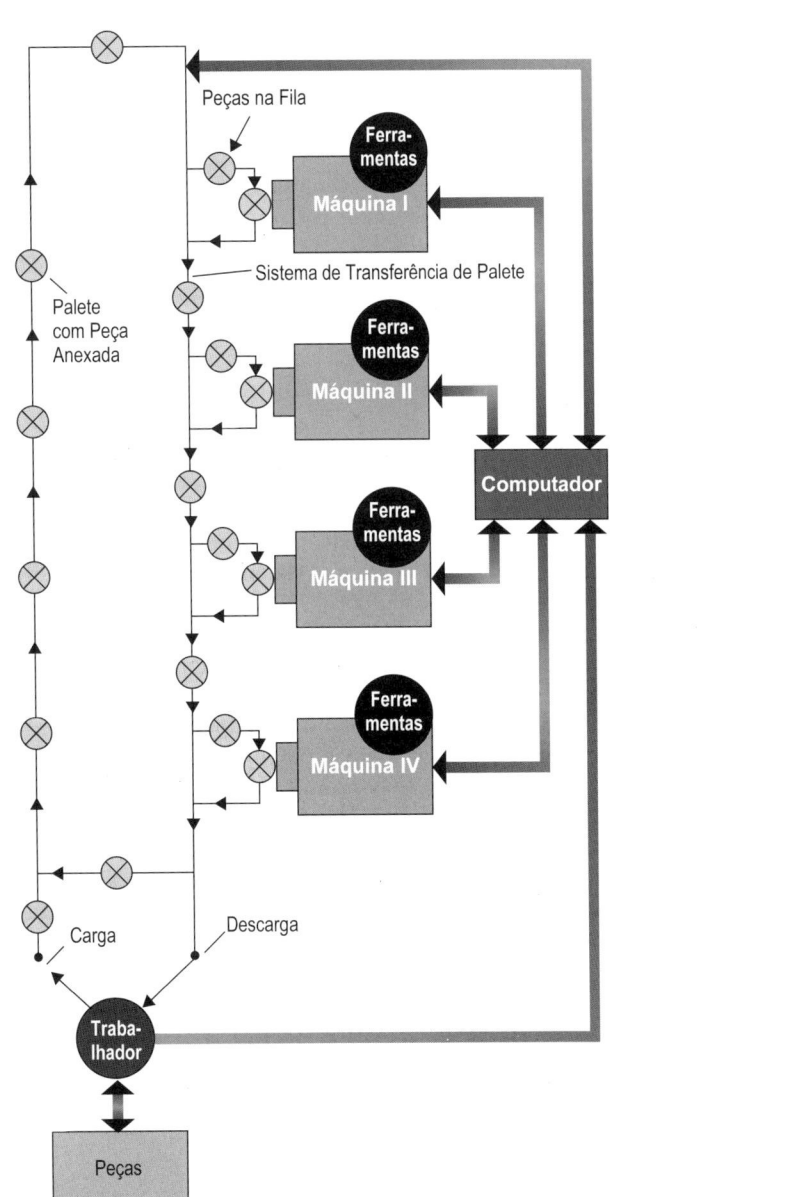

Fonte: Adaptado com autorização de "Computer-Managed Parts Manufacture", de Nathan H. Cook, SCIENTIFIC AMERICAN, fevereiro de 1975. Copyright © 1975 por SCIENTIFIC AMERICAN Inc. Todos os direitos reservados.

Nesses sistemas, às vezes chamados *sistemas flexíveis de máquina*, *kits* de materiais e peças para um produto são carregados no sistema de manipulação de materiais. Um código é então introduzido no sistema de computador, identificando o produto a ser produzido e a localização do produto na seqüência. Quando produtos parcialmente concluídos encerram seu ciclo numa máquina de produção, são automaticamente transferidos para a máquina de produção seguinte. Cada máquina de produção recebe suas configurações e instruções do computador, carrega e descarrega ferramentas automaticamente quando necessário, e conclui seu trabalho sem a necessidade de trabalhadores para cuidar de suas operações.

Não obstante o custo inicial desses sistemas ser elevado, os custos de produção por unidade são baixos, e tanto a qualidade como a flexibilidade dos produtos são elevadas. Os FMS estão crescendo em termos de importância, e muitas empresas estão considerando instalá-los. O Instantâneo da Indústria 5.2 discute o uso dos FMS por diversos fabricantes.

Sistemas Automatizados de Armazenamento e Recuperação

Sistemas automatizados de armazenamento e recuperação (ASRS — automated storage and retrieval systems) são sistemas para receber pedidos de materiais de qualquer parte em suas operações, coletar os materiais dentro de um armazém e entregá-los a estações de trabalho nas operações. Há três elementos importantes nos ASRS:

1. **Computadores e sistemas de comunicação.** Esses sistemas são usados para fazer pedidos de materiais, localizar os materiais no depósito, dar comandos para a entrega de materiais nos locais das operações e ajustar registros de estoques mostrando a quantidade e a localização de materiais.
2. **Sistemas automatizados de manipulação e entrega de materiais.** Esses sistemas são automaticamente carregados com contêineres de materiais, que são entregues no armazém. Similarmente, eles são automaticamente carregados com pedidos de materiais no armazém, que são entregues nas estações de trabalho nas operações. Correias controladas por computador de diversos tipos às vezes são usadas, mas **sistemas de veículos automatizados (AGVS — automated guided vehicle systems)** estão sendo usados em número maior para essa finalidade. Os AGVS comumente são trens não tripulados, caminhões com transportador mecânico e transportadores de carga unitizada. Os AGVS normalmente seguem fios de orientação ou faixas pintadas ao longo das operações até que seus destinos sejam alcançados.
3. **Sistemas de armazenamento e recuperação em armazéns.** Os armazéns guardam materiais em contêineres de tamanho padrão com quantidades fixas de cada material. Por exemplo, um contêiner de um tipo de peça injetada em particular sempre conteria 100 peças. Esses contêineres são organizados de acordo com um esquema que permite que a localização de cada material seja determinada de maneira precisa por um computador. Uma **máquina de armazenamento e recuperação (S/R — storage and retrieval)** recebe comandos de um computador, pega contêineres de materiais de um **ponto de coleta** no armazém, entrega materiais a suas localizações designadas no armazém e coloca-os em suas localizações. Similarmente, máquinas S/R localizam contêineres de materiais no depósito, retiram contêineres do depósito e os entregam em um **ponto de depósito** no armazém.

Os propósitos principais de instalar os ASRS são os seguintes:

1. **Aumentar a capacidade de armazenamento.** Os ASRS normalmente aumentam a densidade de estocagem nos armazéns, ou seja, o número máximo total de cargas individuais que podem ser armazenadas.
2. **Aumentar a produção do sistema.** Os ASRS aumentam o número de cargas por hora que o sistema de armazenamento pode receber e colocar no depósito e recuperar e entregar a estações de trabalho.
3. **Reduzir custos de mão-de-obra.** Ao automatizar os sistemas de recuperação, armazenamento e entrega de materiais, a mão-de-obra e os custos relacionados freqüentemente são reduzidos.
4. **Melhorar a qualidade do produto.** Em virtude de erros humanos na identificação de materiais, peças erradas muitas vezes são entregues e montadas em produtos. Em geral erros ocorrem devido à semelhança de diferentes materiais. Os sistemas automatizados que identificam peças com base em códigos de barras e outros métodos de identificação não estão sujeitos a esse tipo de erro de identificação.

Além de seu uso em ambientes de manufatura, os ASRS têm sido implementados de maneira bem-sucedida em algumas organizações de serviço.

Discutimos diversos sistemas automatizados de produção usados atualmente. Como serão os sistemas de produção no futuro?

Capítulo 5 – Tecnologia de Produção

INSTANTÂNEO DA INDÚSTRIA 5.2

FMS MUDA PARA OUTROS PRODUTOS EM SEGUNDOS

Trinta e cinco braços de robô seguram as peças principais do chassi de um Nissan Sentra num alinhamento virtualmente perfeito, e 16 outros soldam as peças em 62 pontos. Então, 45 segundos depois, tudo se modifica. O chassi do sedã de quatro portas se move, e um computador reajusta automaticamente o conjunto de robôs para montar o item seguinte da linha, um *hatchback*[2]. Depois que o computador faz seu trabalho novamente, os robôs montam o chassi de uma *station wagon*[3]. Mais adiante na linha, cada chassi será pintado numa cor diferente e receberá diferentes peças, tudo determinado pelo comando do computador. Cada carro porta um disco de identificação especialmente programado. Ele emite sinais de rádio captados por receptores em cada estação de trabalho, que diz ao robô ou trabalhador qual tipo de bateria, pára-choques ou sistema de som instalar. O novo sistema flexível de manufatura usa robôs programáveis por computador que podem produzir até quatro modelos diferentes e oito tipos de chassi. Novos modelos podem ser introduzidos, bastando para isso modificar os programas do robô, que vêm da atividade de projeto de produtos CAD/CAM. Os custos de reorganização da ferramentaria para novos produtos são drasticamente reduzidos, novos produtos podem ser introduzidos na metade do tempo, e é evitado um estoque excessivo de carros. A Nissan usa os FMS em suas fábricas de Zama e Tochigi e está instalando os FMS em duas outras fábricas no Japão e em sua fábrica em Smyrna, no Tennessee.

E a Nissan não é a única. A Toyota fabrica os modelos Supra, Lexus e Soarer na mesma linha em sua fábrica de Tahara. A Honda produz o Accords e o Integras numa única linha em Suzuka. E encontramos os FMS em outras indústrias além da automobilística. A Manufacturing Systems Division da Cincinnati Milacron instalou centenas desses sistemas nos Estados Unidos. E a Cummins Engine Company é um usuário destacado do FMS.

Fontes: "Japan's Industrial Robots Becoming More Flexible". *Houston Chronicle*, 16 de abril de 1990; Meredith, J., "Installation of Flexible Manufacturing System Teaches Management Lessons in Integration, Labor, Cost, Benefits". *Industrial Engineering*. Abril de 1988; Venkatesan, Ravi, "Cummins Engine Flexes Its Factory", *Harvard Business Review*, março-abril de 1990.

FÁBRICAS DO FUTURO

Para compreender a natureza da produção que provavelmente prevalecerá nas próximas décadas, devemos entender dois sistemas baseados em computador bastante complexos: projeto auxiliado por computador e manufatura auxiliada por computador (CAD/CAM) e manufatura integrada por computador (CIM).

CAD/CAM

CAD e CAM foram discutidos no Capítulo 2. Os termos CAD e CAM são assim definidos:

- **CAD:** Uso de computadores em desenho interativo de engenharia e armazenamento de projetos. Programas concluem o layout, transformações geométricas, projeções, rotações, ampliações e vistas de intervalos (corte transversal) de uma peça e sua relação com outras partes.
- **CAM:** Uso de computadores para programar, dirigir e controlar equipamentos de produção na fabricação de itens manufaturados.

O CAD preocupa-se com a automação de certas fases do projeto de produtos, e seu uso está crescendo, uma vez que um número cada vez maior de poderosos softwares de projeto de produtos é desenvolvido. A aumentada disponibilidade dessas estações de trabalho de projetos de engenharia está revolucionando a

---

[2] *Hatchback:* automóvel de dupla função (carga e passeio). Um automóvel cuja parte traseira possui uma portinhola que se abre para cima.

[3] *Station wagon:* carro espaçoso, para a família.

maneira como os produtos são projetados. Sistemas CAD são instalados para aumentar a produvididade de projetistas, melhorar a qualidade dos projetos, melhorar a padronização de produtos e documentação de projetos, e criar um banco de dados de manufatura. O software de CAD mais amplamente usado é o AutoCAD, que pode rodar em computadores pessoais. Produzido pela Autodesk Inc. (**www.autodesk.com**), ele está em sua versão n. 14. Introduzido no mercado em 1982, quase 2 milhões de cópias do AutoCAD foram remetidas para mais de 150 países, tornando a Autodesk a quinta maior companhia de softwares para PC no mundo.

A CAM preocupa-se com a automatização do planejamento e controle da produção. Ela avança mais lentamente do que o CAD, mas está progredindo. A capacidade de planejar a produção, preparar roteiros de produtos, gerar programas NC, fixar as configurações da maquinaria de produção, preparar programações de produção e controlar a operação de processos de produção com computadores — tudo isso, indubitavelmente, continuará a expandir-se à medida que os softwares de computador se tornarem mais sofisticados. Mas é a combinação dos sistemas CAD e CAM, no CAD/CAM, que fornecerá uma visão dos futuros sistemas de produção.

CAD/CAM implica uma fusão do CAD e da CAM e uma interação entre os dois sistemas. O importante resultado dessa fusão é a automação da transição do projeto de produtos para a manufatura. Novos produtos poderão ser projetados rapidamente à medida que as demandas por mercado mudarem. E, desde que esses novos projetos de produto são armazenados num banco de dados comum, através da CAM os novos produtos poderão ser introduzidos na produção muito mais rapidamente e com menos despesa. Dessa forma, o CAD/CAM promete grande flexibilidade de produto, baixos custos de produção e melhorada qualidade de produto.

Manufatura Integrada por Computador

Manufatura integrada por computador (CIM — computer integrated manufacturing) é definida como "a aplicação de um computador para atravessar e conectar vários sistemas computadorizados e uni-los num todo coerente e integrado". Como ilustra a Figura 5.2, orçamento, CAD/CAM, controles de processo, sistemas de tecnologia de grupo, MRP II, sistemas de relatório financeiro etc. seriam vinculados e conectados por meio de interface.

Segundo Mikell P. Groover, a CIM tem uma aplicação mais ampla do que o CAD/CAM:

O conceito de CIM é que todas as operações da empresa relacionadas com a função de produção [são] incorporadas num sistema de computador integrado para auxiliar, aumentar e/ou automatizar as operações. O sistema de computador abrange toda a empresa, alcançando todas as atividades que dão sustentação à manufatura. Nesse sistema integrado de computador, a saída de uma atividade serve como entrada para a atividade seguinte ao longo da cadeia de eventos que se inicia com o pedido de vendas e culmina com a remessa do produto.

Além dos abrangentes sistemas de computador descritos acima, o termo *CIM* passou a ser associado com o uso da mais moderna tecnologia de produção. Mas como destaca John J. Clancy, presidente da McDonnell-Douglas: "A CIM não é uma peça de equipamento; de fato, CIM não é uma tecnologia — é uma maneira de usar a tecnologia".

Quando os softwares de computador se tornaram mais sofisticados durante a década de 1990, os abrangentes pacotes de software mais recentes passaram a ser chamados sistemas de **planejamento dos recursos empresariais (ERP)**. Os sistemas ERP automatizam processos de manufatura, organizam livros contábeis, modernizam departamentos corporativos como recursos humanos e muito mais — eles são aplicações de software que tornaram a reengenharia possível.

Um sistema ERP é um complexo conjunto de programas que podem consumir diversos anos e muitos milhões de dólares para ser implementados. Para as grandes companhias, comprar e promover um sistema ERP pode custar centenas de milhões de dólares. A Chevron gastou cerca de US$ 160 milhões ao longo de cinco anos durante a década de 1990 para pôr em funcionamento seu sistema ERP.

As seis principais companhias produtoras do software ERP são a SAP, a Oracle, a J. D. Edwards, a PeopleSoft, a Baan e a SSA. Um dos primeiros ERP foi desenvolvido pela gigante alemã dos softwares,

SAP, fundada em 1972 por cinco exengenheiros da IBM. Com uma fatia de mercado de 33%, o software da SAP, chamado R/3, inicialmente destinava-se a tornar os processos de manufatura e contabilidade mais eficientes, mas atualmente a SAP oferece módulos R/3 para muitas outras funções de negócios como, por exemplo, logística e recursos humanos.

Com nosso entendimento do CAD/CAM e da CIM, vamos considerar a natureza das fábricas do futuro.

CARACTERÍSTICAS DAS FÁBRICAS DO FUTURO

Atualmente existem fábricas do tipo conhecido como **fábricas do futuro**, e um número cada vez maior dessas organizações será estabelecido no futuro e terá estas características:

1. **Elevada qualidade do produto.** A baixa qualidade e a variabilidade associadas com operações manuais serão evitadas. A automação permitirá uma qualidade do produto consistente e elevada. A demanda por produtos de elevada qualidade no mercado garantirá que essa característica receba a mais alta prioridade.
2. **Elevada flexibilidade.** Nova tecnologia flexível será usada no projeto de processos de produção. Muitos modelos de produto serão produzidos para atrair mercados que exigem variedade de produtos. Pequenos lotes de muitos modelos de produto serão produzidos, e os processos de produção serão econômicos para operar nessas condições.
3. **Rápida entrega de pedidos dos clientes.** Com tamanhos de lote pequenos, operações que podem ser rapidamente mudadas para outros produtos e altas cadências de produção, os pedidos dos clientes serão produzidos e remetidos com rapidez.
4. **Transformada economia de produção.** Na fábrica automatizada, os custos que anteriormente eram variáveis se tornarão fixos, e os custos que anteriormente eram fixos se tornarão variáveis. Os custos serão, em sua maioria, fixos. O único custo variável significativo será o de materiais e gastos gerais. Sejam quais forem os custos de mão-de-obra, como o de manutenção, eles serão considerados custos fixos. O custo predominante serão os custos com gastos gerais, como os de escritório e funcionários de escritório, engenharia, equipamentos, ferramentaria, manutenção, utilidades e software.
5. **Sistemas acionados por computador e integrados por computador.** O sistema CAD/CAM será a base para projetos de produtos e planejamento de processo. A CIM (ou ERP) integrará todas as fases do negócio a partir de um banco de dados comum.
6. **Mudanças na estrutura organizacional.** Na fábrica automatizada, o pessoal da linha de produção parecerá mais com o pessoal do staff, e vice-versa. Manutenção, qualidade do produto, engenharia, administração da mudança tecnológica, desenvolvimento e manutenção de software e projetos de robótica e automação se tornarão as principais atividades da organização.

Nas fábricas do futuro, as job shops evoluirão rumo à manufatura celular, com graus crescentes de automação flexível. A produção focalizada no produto evoluirá rumo a sistemas flexíveis de manufatura (FMS). Em ambas essas extremidades da continuação do presente, a flexibilidade do produto, baixos custos por unidade e elevada qualidade de produto prevalecerão.

Consideremos agora o uso da automação no florescente setor de serviços.

AUTOMAÇÃO NOS SERVIÇOS

As oportunidades para aplicar a automação são impressionantes quando consideramos a ampla variedade de serviços prestados por empresas das seguintes indústrias: seguros, setor imobiliário, caixas econômicas e bancos, transporte rodoviário, empresas aéreas e frete aéreo, construção, venda a varejo e no atacado, impressão e publicação, propaganda e radiodifusão, serviços comerciais, corretagem de valores e serviços financeiros, serviços de saúde, hospedagem e entretenimento, comunicações, ferrovias e serviços públicos.

A Tabela 5.2 apresenta alguns exemplos de automação em quatro indústrias de serviços. Talvez nenhuma outra indústria de serviços seja tão dominada pelo uso de computadores e equipamentos automati-

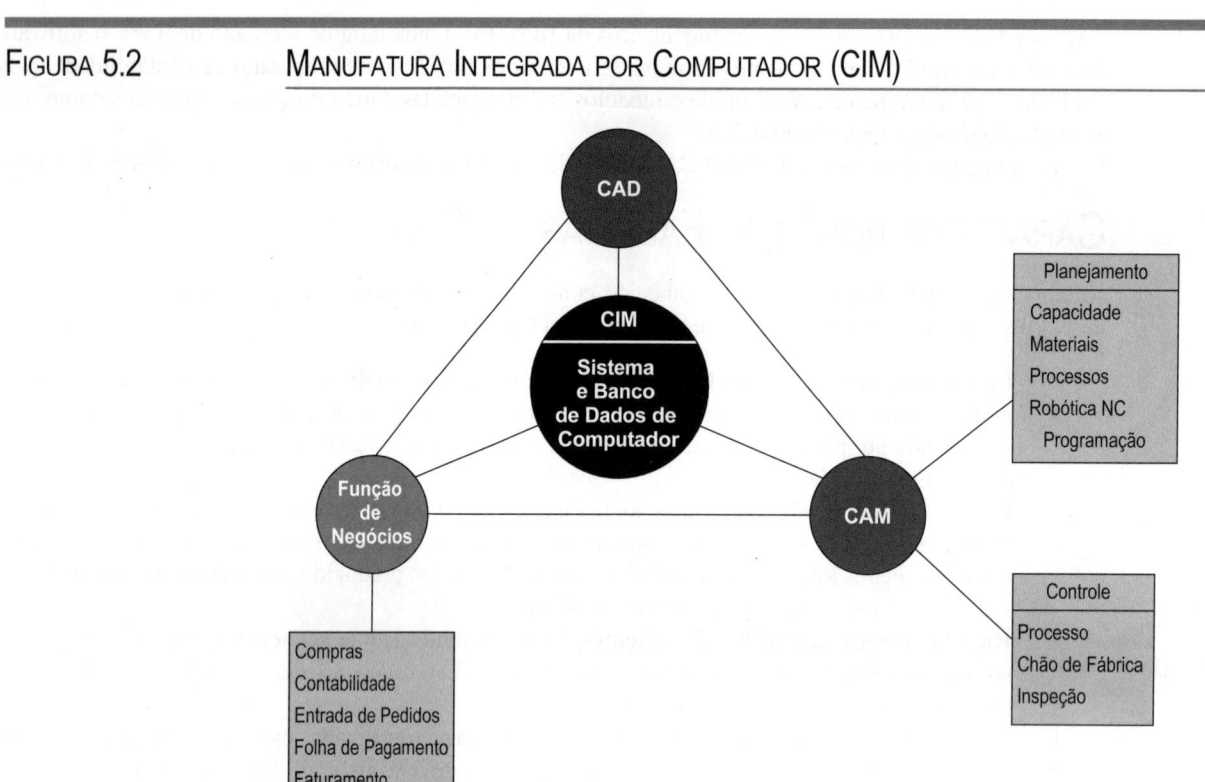

FIGURA 5.2 — MANUFATURA INTEGRADA POR COMPUTADOR (CIM)

zados quanto a de serviços bancários e caixas econômicas. Os caixas eletrônicos, os sistemas automáticos de transferência de fundos e extratos bancários computadorizados são somente a ponta do *iceberg*. Essa indústria inteira é tão dependente dos computadores e equipamentos relacionados para suas operações diárias que ela literalmente não operaria sem eles.

À medida que equipamentos e sistemas tecnológicos cada vez mais avançados são integrados às operações de serviços, uma interessante tendência rumo a serviços mais padronizados e menos contato com o cliente é observada. Uma vez que muitos equipamentos automatizados não podem operar em ambientes sujeitos às mudanças que estão presentes em alguns serviços, será necessário reduzir e padronizar muitos dos serviços oferecidos para que seja possível a introdução desses equipamentos. Essa padronização, entretanto, acarreta *trade-offs*[4]. Por um lado, a partir da perspectiva dos clientes, serviços padronizados não são tão atraentes, já que não têm um desenho personalizado para cada cliente. Por outro, o custo das operações e os preços dos serviços ou são reduzidos, ou não se elevam tão rapidamente, e podem ser mais convenientes para os clientes. Considere, por exemplo, a proliferação dos caixas eletrônicos — os clientes não podem obter uma variedade ampla de serviços bancários nos caixas eletrônicos, mas suas localizações são convenientes e seus serviços são imediatos.

De maneira geral, onde há maior contato com os clientes nos serviços, tende a haver menor uso de todos os tipos de equipamentos, inclusive os automatizados.

A Figura 5.3 ilustra a relação entre o grau de contato com o cliente e a quantidade de capital. A quantidade de capital se eleva à medida que nos movemos dos equipamentos manuais para os mecanizados e para os automatizados. Essa figura sugere que os equipamentos automatizados podem não ser apropriados para operações de serviços que têm um grau elevado de contato com o cliente. Mas, como discutimos anteriormente, algumas operações de serviços podem ser automatizadas em virtude de maior conveniência e

---

[4] *Trade-off*: troca ocasional ou transigência em face de duas alternativas, geralmente de igual valor; acordo, acerto; concessão.

TABELA 5.2 — ALGUNS EXEMPLOS DE AUTOMAÇÃO NOS SERVIÇOS

Indústrias de Serviços	Exemplos de Automação
Empresas aéreas	Sistemas de controle de tráfego aéreo Sistemas de piloto automático Sistemas de reserva Colocação de cargas em contêineres
Bancos, caixas econômicas e serviços financeiros	Caixas eletrônicos Transferência automática de fundos Códigos de reconhecimento de caracteres de tinta magnética Scanners óticos Extratos bancários computadorizados Serviços bancários telefônicos e on-line
Venda a varejo/no atacado	Terminais de ponto-de-venda Sistemas de código de barras Scanners óticos Armazéns automatizados Cabinas fotográficas automatizadas Sistemas automatizados de pagamento em postos de serviços
Atendimento à saúde	AGVS para remoção de lixo Scanners Sistemas de imagens de ressonância magnética Monitoração automatizada de pacientes Terminais junto ao leito Robôs domésticos e hospitalares

custos reduzidos. Além disso, em geral os serviços tipicamente não têm grande contato com o cliente em todas as partes de sua organização. Por exemplo, as operações de apoio nos bancos, para onde os clientes raramente vão, são ótimas candidatas à automação.

As operações de muitas companhias de serviços estão melhorando devido ao avanço das tecnologias de comunicações, à Internet e às intranets.

O Instantâneo da Indústria 5.3 descreve como uma empresa está usando a Internet para diminuir o tempo de execução necessário para desenvolver novo software.

A ampla disseminação dos serviços automatizados nas indústrias de manufatura e serviços levantou muitas questões que requerem um exame.

QUESTÕES DE AUTOMAÇÃO

Das questões de automação importantes a serem consideradas, discutiremos estas: produção de alta tecnologia (high-tech), média tecnologia (mid-tech) e baixa tecnologia (low-tech); construindo flexibilidade de manufatura; justificando projetos de automação; administrando a mudança tecnológica; e demissão, treinamento e retreinamento de trabalhadores.

PRODUÇÃO DE ALTA, MÉDIA OU BAIXA TECNOLOGIA?

Podemos citar exemplos de companhias muito bem-sucedidas que utilizam as mais antigas tecnologias manuais conhecidas. Também podemos citar exemplos de companhias que estão fracassando apesar de possuir a tecnologia avançada mais moderna. Mas não devemos concluir precipitadamente que a tecnologia usada por uma empresa não tem relação com sua produtividade ou sucesso. Uma cuidadosa reflexão sobre essas questões deve nos levar a estas conclusões:

| FIGURA 5.3 | GRAU DE CONTATO COM O CLIENTE NOS SERVIÇOS E O USO DE EQUIPAMENTOS AUTOMATIZADOS |

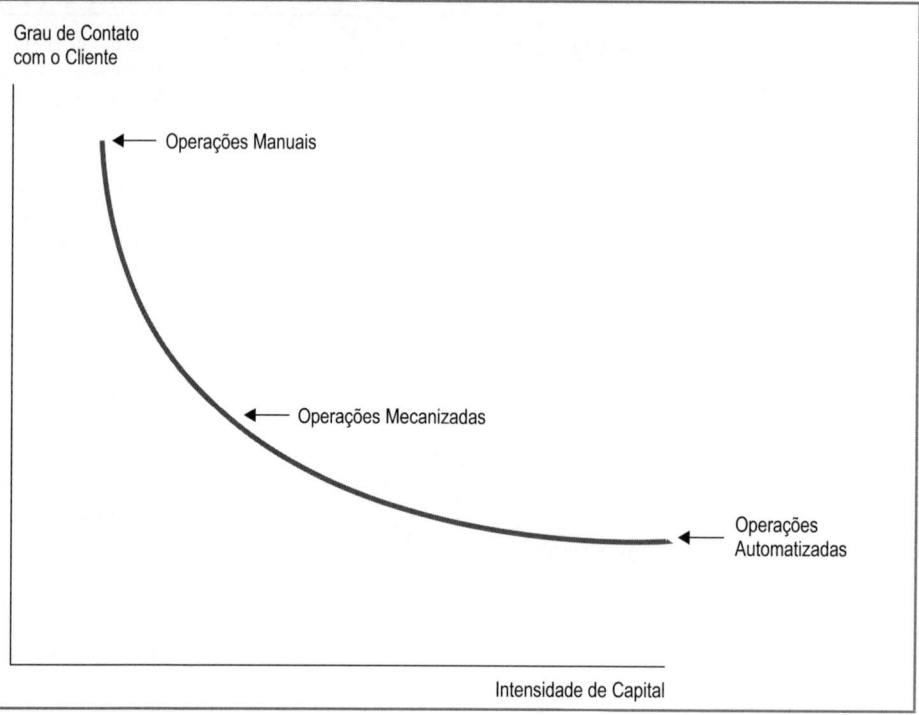

1. **Nem todos os projetos de automação são bem-sucedidos.** Algumas empresas lançam grandes projetos de automação mas administram mal a implementação da maquinaria automatizada, o que pode resultar em um desempenho pior depois da automação.
2. **A automação não pode compensar uma má administração.** Mesmo que a implementação da maquinaria automatizada seja bem-sucedida, a empresa pode ser tão mal administrada que fracasse de qualquer maneira.
3. **A análise econômica não pode justificar a automação de algumas operações.** Por exemplo, se o custo de mão-de-obra for muito baixo e o equipamento automatizado for muito caro, o custo extra para automatizar pode não ser suficientemente compensado pela qualidade de produto e outras melhorias. Essa é a razão pela qual encontramos tantas fábricas de roupas em ambos os lados da fronteira entre o México e os Estados Unidos.
4. **Não é tecnicamente viável automatizar algumas operações.** Na indústria de vestuário, por exemplo, a roupa que deve ser processada é tão elástica, flexível e frágil que certas operações de produção, como corte, montagem e costura, ainda não são automatizadas. Nessas operações, o principal obstáculo para a automação é o posicionamento impreciso do tecido em relação aos cortadores, aos cabeçotes de costura e outros dispositivos mecânicos.
5. **Os projetos de automação talvez tenham de esperar em novos e pequenos negócios.** Devido à escassez de capital e habilidades técnicas e de engenharia, parte da produção e distribuição de produto pode ser contratada junto a empresas fornecedoras, transportadoras e de distribuição. À medida que os produtos amadurecem, esses negócios tipicamente trazem a produção e/ou transporte e distribuição novamente para casa, mas a automação provavelmente ainda não está em perspectiva. Por fim, os processos de produção podem ser automatizados à medida que os produtos amadurecem e as empresas adquirem capacidades tecnológicas e de engenharia para projetar, instalar e integrar projetos de automação. Mas nem toda capacidade de automação deve residir dentro de uma empresa, porque há uma lista extensa de empresas que fornecem serviços de automação

INSTANTÂNEO DA INDÚSTRIA 5.3

A TECNOLOGIA DE COMUNICAÇÕES DERRUBA O TEMPO E A DISTÂNCIA

Um grupo de programadores de computador da Tsinghua University, em Beijing, está escrevendo software usando a tecnologia Java. Eles trabalham para a IBM. No final de cada dia, eles enviam seu trabalho pela Internet para uma instalação da IBM em Seattle. Lá, programadores desenvolvem o trabalho e usam a Internet para remetê-lo ao Institute of Computer Science, na Bielorrússia, e para o Software House Group, na Lituânia. De lá o trabalho é enviado para o leste, ao Tata Group, da Índia, que repassa o software para Tsinghua de manhã, em Beijing, novamente para Seattle e assim por diante, num grande giro global que nunca cessa até que o projeto esteja concluído.

"Nós o chamamos Java Around the Clock", diz John Patrick, vice-presidente de tecnologia de Internet da IBM. "É como se tivéssemos criado um dia de 48 horas através da Internet." A Internet e as redes de computador possibilitam que as empresas trabalhem globalmente de uma maneira que elas jamais poderiam fazer antes.

Fonte: Maney, Kevin. "Technology Is 'Demolishing' Time, Distance". *USA Today*, 24 de abril de 1997.

---

turnkey[5] tanto para pequenas como para grandes empresas. Embora sejam caras para novos e pequenos negócios, empresas como a Cincinnati Milacron, Cross & Trecker, Prab Robots, Mobot Corporation, United Technologies e General Electric são exemplos de empresas que oferecem serviços de automação.

Algumas operações de produção não foram automatizadas e, sem dúvida, jamais o serão. Mas, para empresas que estão comprometidas com o crescimento, sobrevivência e lucratividade de longo prazo, a principal razão para não automatizar não pode ser sua mente fechada sobre o assunto. *A verdade é que todas as empresas devem manter seus processos de produção atualizados à medida que a tecnologia de produção avança. Agir de outra maneira colocaria o futuro de suas empresas em risco, porque elas devem presumir que seus concorrentes agarrarão as vantagens estratégicas oferecidas ao mudar para uma tecnologia avançada.* Para muitas empresas atualmente a questão não é a automatização de suas operações. Ao contrário, as questões são: Quais operações serão automatizadas? Em qual seqüência elas serão automatizadas? Quando elas serão automatizadas?

CONSTRUINDO FLEXIBILIDADE DE MANUFATURA

A expressão **automação flexível** se contrapõe às expressões **sistemas fixos de manufatura** ou **automação dedicada**, como em linhas automatizadas de fluxo ou linhas convencionais de produção. Nos últimos anos, essa expressão passou a se referir a todos os tipos de equipamentos e sistemas de produção que fornecem a capacidade de reagir a necessidades mutáveis de mercado. **Flexibilidade de manufatura** é a capacidade de melhorar ou manter fatias de mercado em decorrência de:

1. Os pedidos dos clientes podem ser entregues logo depois de seu recebimento. Às vezes isso significa modificar programações de produção para responder a um pedido de rápida entrega de um cliente.
2. A produção pode ser rapidamente modificada de produto a produto, porque, numa semana em particular, clientes podem encomendar lotes relativamente pequenos de muitos modelos de produto.
3. A capacidade de produção pode ser aumentada rapidamente para responder a demandas por mercado em alta.
4. Novos produtos podem ser desenvolvidos e introduzidos rapidamente e de forma barata em resposta a necessidades mutáveis de mercado.

---

[5]*Turnkey:* refere-se a um sistema fechado, pronto. Um sistema completo de hardware e software entregue ao cliente pronto para funcionar.

Conforme observamos anteriormente, a flexibilidade de manufatura é de dois tipos gerais: flexibilidade de volume e flexibilidade de produto. A flexibilidade de volume normalmente é proporcionada pelo uso de trabalho em horas extras, estoques de produtos acabados extras e projeto de processos de produção, ou com **cadências variáveis de produção** ou **capacidade excessiva**. À medida que os sistemas de produção se tornaram mais receptivos às demandas por mercado, entretanto, aquilo que costumava ser capacidade excessiva passa a ser considerado unicamente *capacidade suficiente para responder a demandas por mercado de pico*. Mas, talvez a forma mais importante de flexibilidade de manufatura seja a flexibilidade de produto — a capacidade de mudar rapidamente e de maneira barata o sistema de produção para outros produtos.

Conforme discutimos anteriormente, os sistemas de produção focalizados no processo oferecem grande flexibilidade de produto, não obstante os custos de produção por unidade poderem ser elevados. Historicamente, o número de sistemas de produção focalizados no processo tem excedido em muito o de outras formas de produção. Mas atualmente muitos fabricantes estão procurando alternativas para as job shops, porque esses sistemas de produção focalizados no processo não permitirão que eles concorram com seus concorrentes estrangeiros em termos de custos de produção. Em virtude de melhorada tecnologia de produção, entretanto, há outras maneiras de obter flexibilidade de produção e ainda obter baixos custos de produção por unidade.

Eis algumas máquinas ou sistemas de produção que são entendidos como fornecedores de flexibilidade de produto:

- Máquinas NC
- Robôs programáveis e reprogramáveis
- Inspeção automatizada de controle da qualidade
- Sistemas automatizados de identificação (AIS)
- Controles automatizados de processo
- Sistemas automatizados de montagem
- Sistemas flexíveis de manufatura (FMS)
- Sistemas automatizados de armazenamento e recuperação (ASRS)
- Projeto auxiliado por computador e manufatura auxiliada por computador (CAD/CAM)
- Manufatura integrada por computador (CIM)

Essas máquinas e sistemas de produção representam o núcleo daquilo que denominamos *automação flexível*. Talvez seu maior mérito seja sua capacidade de produzir produtos a baixos custos unitários e, simultaneamente, oferecer grande flexibilidade de produto. *A flexibilidade de manufatura tornou-se a pedra angular da estratégia de operações na década de 1990, e os processos de produção projetados atualmente estão cada vez mais ancorados nessa pedra angular.*

A automação flexível e outras formas de automação exigem aumentado investimento, entretanto, e está se tornando cada vez mais patente que as abordagens tradicionais para justificar esses enormes investimentos são inadequadas.

JUSTIFICANDO PROJETOS DE AUTOMAÇÃO

Cresce a evidência de que durante diversas décadas as políticas administrativas e as abordagens de orçamento de capital americanas levaram somente a pequenas melhorias nos produtos e processos de produção existentes.

A taxa de rotatividade de nossos gerentes tem sido tão elevada que as melhorias de produto e mudanças de processos de produção de longo prazo têm sido evitadas. Muitas vezes são necessários cinco anos ou mais para modificar drasticamente projetos de produto e automatizar fábricas. Não tem havido muito incentivo para que gerentes que planejam permanecer por somente alguns anos numa empresa se comprometam com esses projetos de longo prazo.

Período de pagamento, valor atual líquido, taxa de rentabilidade interna e outras abordagens convencionais de orçamento de capital podem, quando tomadas isoladamente, ser ferramentas inadequadas sobre as quais basear importantes decisões de projeto e redesenho de produto e processo. Essas ferramentas têm muitas vezes levado os gerentes a expandir as instalações atuais com tecnologia existente, em vez de construírem novas instalações com nova tecnologia de produção. Levando essa abordagem ao extremo, as empresas acabam por ficar com instalações de produção enormes, pesadas e altamente centralizadas, baseadas numa tecnologia de produção desatualizada.

O investimento em inovação em tecnologia de produto e processo deve ser afastado do contexto das decisões de investimento de projeto a projeto. Ao contrário, o investimento em tecnologia de produto e processo deve ser visto como uma opção estratégica de longo prazo para a empresa. Essas opções, à semelhança de outras decisões comerciais importantes, não podem se basear somente numa única forma de pagamento. *Não obstante os retornos sobre o investimento serem um importante critério para essas decisões de investimento, o termo **retornos** assumirá um novo e ampliado significado. Melhorada qualidade de produto, entrega mais rápida dos pedidos dos clientes, aumentada flexibilidade de produto e volume, reduzidos custos de produção, aumentada fatia de mercado e outras vantagens terão de ser levados em conta nas decisões de orçamento de capital futuras.* O investimento em tecnologia de produto e processo deve ser visto como uma opção estratégica para transformar a fábrica numa arma competitiva que auxilie a corporação a captar fatias de mercado.

ADMINISTRANDO A MUDANÇA TECNOLÓGICA

As empresas que tentaram projetos de automação ambiciosos aprenderam que a implementação de grandes projetos de automação é muito mais difícil e complexa do que o imaginado os projetos de automação quase sempre requerem mais tempo e custam mais do que originariamente esperado.

Dada a dificuldade de gerenciar mudanças na tecnologia de produção, o que aprendemos sobre como administrar a implementação de grandes projetos de automação? Estas sugestões são apresentadas:

1. **Tenha um plano mestre para a automação.** O plano deve indicar quais operações automatizar, quando e em qual seqüência automatizar cada área do negócio, e como a organização e seus produtos, marketing e outras unidades empresariais terão de mudar por causa da automação.
2. **Reconheça os riscos de automatizar.** Há riscos associados com todo projeto de automação. Entre os que devem ser considerados estão: o risco de obsolescência radical, o perigo de que novas tecnologias não possam ser protegidas e sejam facilmente transferidas para os concorrentes, e a possibilidade de que uma nova tecnologia de produção não possa ser desenvolvida de maneira bem-sucedida.
3. **Estabeleça um novo departamento de tecnologia de produção.** Essa unidade disseminará informações sobre a nova tecnologia, se tornará uma defensora da adoção da nova tecnologia, dará o exemplo em termos de educar e treinar outros sobre a nova tecnologia e fornecerá a assistência técnica necessária para a instalação e a implementação de equipamentos de tecnologia avançada.
4. **Reserve um bocado de tempo para a conclusão de projetos de automação.** Tempo suficiente deve ser reservado para aprender como instalar, equipar, depurar, programar e colocar uma máquina automatizada na velocidade de produção. Há muito a ser aprendido, e sempre demandará mais tempo do que o esperado. Um especialista em automação sugeriu recentemente: "Avalie quanto tempo você espera que seja necessário, e depois multiplique por três". O ponto-chave: *O que se aprende sobre a implementação de um projeto de automação deve ser aplicado ao seguinte. Há uma nova tecnologia associada com a implementação de projetos de automação, e ela é mais bem aprendida aos poucos.*
5. **Não tente automatizar tudo de uma só vez.** Pequenas falhas em equipamentos automatizados são inevitáveis. Tente programar os projetos a fim de que aquilo que for aprendido de um projeto possa ser aplicado em outro. Quando se reserva tempo suficiente, a freqüência de prazos programados e não cumpridos, a frustração organizacional e a pressão para comprimir a programação são reduzidas. Ao programar os projetos, os recursos de uma organização poderão ser mais estritamente concentrados em um ou dois projetos de cada vez, aumentando assim a probabilidade de sucesso.
6. **Pessoas são a chave para tornar bem-sucedidos projetos de automação.** Se a automação for planejada no nível estratégico, o treinamento e a educação de todas as pessoas da organização a respeito da tecnologia avançada de produção devem ser uma constante. Participação freqüente e intensiva de todo o pessoal envolvido deve fazer parte dos projetos de automação. Representantes de sindicatos de trabalhadores devem ter papel ativo na automação. Os sindicatos de trabalhadores estão especialmente interessados em divulgar notícias de empregos afetados, retreinamento e readmissão de trabalhadores demitidos, e políticas de dispensa associadas com a automação.

7. **Se as empresas se movimentarem muito lentamente para adotar nova tecnologia de produção, poderão ser deixadas para trás.** Ser ponderada e cuidadosa quando se movimenta de um projeto de automação para outro não autoriza a empresa a arrastar-se. Fazer isso significa que ela será derrotada pela competição.

DEMISSÃO, TREINAMENTO E RETREINAMENTO DE TRABALHADORES

Uma conseqüência da automação industrial é a eliminação de certos empregos. Por exemplo, um trabalhador pode monitorar três robôs de soldagem elétrica em uma tarefa que antes exigia quatro trabalhadores. Ainda, uma secretária pode fazer o trabalho de três, graças aos modernos processadores de texto. Alguns economistas dizem que, a longo prazo, o número de empregos eliminados nas fábricas e escritórios em razão da automação será superado pelos recém-criados empregos em engenharia, manufatura, vendas e assistência técnica para produtos de nova tecnologia. Embora isso possa ser verdadeiro, a questão preocupante a curto prazo é: O que farão os trabalhadores de fábrica e de escritório que perderam seus empregos para a automação? A resposta é bastante simples: eles serão transferidos para outras funções dentro de suas empresas, ou irão para outras empresas, ou ficarão desempregados. E num primeiro momento nenhuma dessas alternativas é interessante.

Muitas empresas têm desenvolvido programas de treinamento domésticos (*in-house*) para lidar com essas questões, ao passo que outras recorrem a fontes externas de treinamento. Na década de 1980, quando muitos milhares de projetos de automação foram implementados nos Estados Unidos, inúmeras empresas perceberam que não se podiam dar ao luxo de *não* treinar ou retreinar seus atuais empregados.

Com uma economia forte, menos necessidade de trabalhadores com menor habilitação e escassez de empregados de manufatura mais bem habilitados e treinados em tecnologias de produção mais novas, as empresas estão oferecendo mais treinamento personalizado para seus trabalhadores do que antes. A Northeast Tool & Manufaturing Co., uma pequena empresa fabricante de moldes na periferia de Charlotte, Carolina do Norte, faz com que todos os seus empregados passem por exames de aptidão que medem tudo, de habilidades matemáticas e mecânicas a liderança e adaptabilidade. Esses testes são usados para desenvolver treinamento personalizado. Baseando-se nos resultados, alguns empregados se matriculam em cursos em sua cidade, seguem cursos utilizando os computadores instalados na fábrica ou freqüentam aulas na própria empresa.

Alguns trabalhadores da área administrativa e do setor de produção perderão seus empregos, e infelizmente muitos deles terão de optar por trabalhar na economia informal ou permanecer desempregados. Os programas de treinamento subsidiados e patrocinados pelo governo americano vêm aumentando, e está sendo estudada uma proposta que exige que as empresas gastem 1,5% de sua folha de pagamento em programas de treinamento. Mesmo assim, as empresas americanas ficarão atrás de muitos de seus concorrentes; por exemplo, as empresas alemãs gastam uma média de 4% de sua folha de pagamento em treinamento.

À medida que a tecnologia se intensificar nos próximos anos, o treinamento e o retreinamento de empregados se tornará uma responsabilidade inevitável e uma carga crescente para as empresas americanas.

Com a discussão precedente como pano de fundo, vamos estudar algumas maneiras de decidir entre alternativas de automação.

DECIDINDO ENTRE ALTERNATIVAS DE AUTOMAÇÃO

Quando os gerentes refletem a respeito de decisões de automação, diversas alternativas devem ser consideradas. Apresentamos aqui três abordagens comumente usadas na indústria: análise econômica, abordagem da escala de classificação e abordagem da escala ponderada de classificação.

ANÁLISE ECONÔMICA

A análise econômica sempre será um fator importante, se não predominante, na escolha entre alternativas de automação. Mas outros fatores também devem ser considerados. A incorporação de uma variedade de fatores nessas decisões requer o uso de diferentes abordagens.

ABORDAGEM DA ESCALA DE CLASSIFICAÇÃO

Os gerentes que tomam decisões de automação sabem que os seguintes fatores importantes devem ser considerados:

1. **Fatores econômicos.** Esses fatores dão aos gerentes alguma idéia do impacto *direto* das alternativas de automação sobre a lucratividade. Não obstante o foco poder estar no fluxo de caixa, custos fixos anuais, custo variável por unidade, custo médio de produção por unidade, ou custos anuais totais de produção nos níveis de produção previstos, a intenção é determinar o impacto direto sobre a lucratividade. Análise de break-even e análise financeira freqüentemente são usadas para essa finalidade.
2. **Efeito sobre a fatia de mercado.** Como as alternativas de automação provavelmente afetarão a fatia de mercado? Algumas alternativas exigem redesenho de produto e especialização de produto, o que pode afetar as vendas. Não obstante algumas alternativas permitirem mais variedade de produto e maior apelo ao cliente, o efeito líquido dessas mudanças sobre a fatia de mercado é uma medida difícil de obter. Todavia, os efeitos estão aí e devem ser levados em conta nessas decisões.
3. **Efeito sobre a qualidade de produto.** Como as alternativas de automação provavelmente afetarão a qualidade de produto? Medir esse efeito não é fácil. Taxas de produção de sucata, mudanças de fatia de mercado, custos de produção e outras medidas representam esforços para ligar *indiretamente* as mudanças de qualidade de produto resultantes das alternativas de automação com a lucratividade.
4. **Efeito sobre a flexibilidade de manufatura.** Como as alternativas de automação provavelmente afetarão a flexibilidade do produto e do volume? Esse fator está crescendo em termos de importância à medida que os ciclos de vida de produto se abreviam e as organizações concorrentes oferecem aos consumidores a oportunidade de encomendar produtos com características projetadas de forma personalizada. Medições da flexibilidade de manufatura são extremamente difíceis de desenvolver. O custo de comutações de máquinas, custos de trabalho extra e mudanças de fatia de mercado são medidas que podem ser usadas para avaliar o efeito das alternativas de automação sobre a flexibilidade de manufatura.
5. **Efeito sobre as relações do trabalho.** Como as alternativas de automação provavelmente afetarão os trabalhadores, seus sindicatos e a relação entre a administração e a força de trabalho? O número de trabalhadores que devem ser demitidos, a quantidade de treinamento e retreinamento necessários e a disponibilidade de trabalhadores com as habilidades necessárias para operar equipamento automatizado são fatores que afetam a escolha de alternativas de automação.
6. **Tempo necessário para a implementação.** Quanto tempo as alternativas de automação exigirão para implementar as máquinas e sistemas automatizados? As alternativas podem ter diferentes exigências de tempo para implementação, porque elas têm diferentes níveis de tecnologia, o pessoal organizacional pode não estar familiarizado com alguns tipos de tecnologia e as alternativas exigem diferentes tipos de mudanças no restante do sistema de produção.
7. **Efeito da implementação da automação sobre a produção em andamento.** Se a automação se destinar a substituir as operações de produção existentes, ou se a automação precisar compartilhar instalações com as operações existentes, como as alternativas de automação afetarão a produção existente? Acontece que a produção deve prosseguir, apesar de projetos de automação. Produtos devem ser entregues, pois os clientes não esperarão simplesmente por causa de projetos de automação. Algumas alternativas de automação afetam de forma menos intensa as operações existentes porque devem ser instaladas numa localização diferente, não exigem o uso de equipamentos de produção existentes ou, de outro modo, não interagem com a produção existente.
8. **Capital necessário.** Quanto capital será necessário para cada alternativa de automação? Se o capital estiver em escassez, como quase sempre está, esse fator poderá ser a consideração predominante nas decisões de automação.

Dado que fatores como esses poderiam ser todos importantes para se decidir entre alternativas de automação, como os gerentes podem considerar simultaneamente todos eles? A Tabela 5.3 ilustra como a **abordagem da escala de classificação** poderá ser usada quando o gerente tiver de se decidir entre duas alternativas de automação.

| TABELA 5.3 | ABORDAGEM DA ESCALA DE CLASSIFICAÇÃO PARA COMPARAR ALTERNATIVAS DE AUTOMAÇÃO |

Fatores de Automação	Linha Automatizada de Fluxo	Sistemas Flexíveis de Manufatura
Fatores econômicos		
Custos operacionais anuais	$ 4.955.900	$ 5.258.100
Custos de produção por unidade	$ 59,40	$ 63,02
Outros fatores		
Fatia de mercado	5	4
Qualidade do produto	4	4
Flexibilidade do produto	2	4
Flexibilidade do volume	4	2
Relações de trabalho	3	3
Tempo de implementação	3	4
Operações existentes	5	5
Exigências de capital	3	4

Observação: É usada uma escala de classificação de cinco pontos: 5 = excelente, 4 = bom, 3 = médio, 2 = abaixo da média e 1 = fraco.

Podemos ver na Tabela 5.3 que se somente os fatores econômicos forem levados em consideração, a linha automatizada de fluxo será preferível. Mas se outros fatores forem considerados, a escolha não será tão clara. O sistema flexível de manufatura se classifica melhor em termos de flexibilidade de produto, tempo de implementação e exigências de capital, e as linhas automatizadas de fluxo se classificam melhor em termos de fatores econômicos, fatia de mercado e flexibilidade de volume. Nos casos em que nenhuma alternativa é claramente superior em todos os fatores, a escolha apropriada dependerá de qual dos fatores tem maior importância para os gerentes que devem tomar a decisão.

A abordagem da escala de classificação exige que os tomadores de decisões pesem os fatores de cada alternativa, processem essa informação por meio de seus cálculos mentais únicos e cheguem a uma classificação global de cada alternativa de automação. Consideremos agora outra abordagem que desenvolve diretamente a classificação global de cada alternativa.

ABORDAGEM DA ESCALA PONDERADA DE CLASSIFICAÇÃO

A Tabela 5.4 ilustra uma abordagem da **escala ponderada de classificação** para a mesma decisão descrita na Tabela 5.3. Mas nessa abordagem as pontuações globais para cada alternativa de automação são desenvolvidas como parte da análise.

Podemos ver na Tabela 5.4 que o sistema flexível de manufatura parece ser uma escolha ligeiramente melhor — 0,818 contra 0,770. Essa abordagem exige que os gerentes declarem os fatores que serão considerados na decisão e os pesos de cada fator *antes que a decisão seja tomada*. Essas considerações representam uma estrutura de decisão imposta aos tomadores de decisão, a qual deve ser inerentemente superior a uma ponderação puramente subjetiva das alternativas. Presume-se que cada alternativa incluída na análise tenha passado pela exigência de cumprir certas qualificações. Por exemplo, se uma alternativa exigir tanto capital que seja pouco prático considerá-la, essa alternativa não deve ser incluída na análise. Em outras palavras, todas as alternativas sobreviventes até esse ponto da análise são fundamentalmente sólidas e viáveis, e nessa abordagem tentamos determinar qual alternativa é superior às outras.

As abordagens discutidas têm todas a presunção de que estamos tentando alcançar diversos objetivos simultaneamente. Uma série de técnicas matemáticas de programação foi desenvolvida nos últimos anos para analisar esses problemas.

TABELA 5.4 — ABORDAGEM DA ESCALA PONDERADA DE CLASSIFICAÇÃO PARA COMPARAR ALTERNATIVAS DE AUTOMAÇÃO

Fatores de Automação	Peso do Fator	Linha Automatizada de Fluxo			Sistema Flexível de Manufatura		
		Dados Econômicos	Pontuações	Pontuações Ponderadas	Dados Econômicos	Pontuações	Pontuações Ponderadas
Custos de produção por unidade	0,30	$ 59,40	1,000*	0,300	$ 63,02	0,943*	0,293
Fatia de mercado	0,10		1,000	0,100		0,800	0,080
Qualidade do produto	0,10		0,800	0,080		0,800	0,080
Flexibilidade do produto	0,20		0,400	0,080		0,800	0,160
Flexibilidade do volume	0,05		0,800	0,040		0,400	0,020
Relações de trabalho	0,05		0,600	0,030		0,600	0,030
Tempo de implementação	0,10		0,600	0,060		0,800	0,080
Operações existentes	0,05		1,000	0,050		1,000	0,050
Exigências de capital	0,05		0,600	0,030		0,700	0,035
	Pontuações globais			0,770			0,818

*Essas pontuações são determinadas dividindo-se o mais baixo custo de produção por unidade pelos custos de produção por unidade reais: $ 59,40/$ 59,40 = 1,000 e $ 59,40/$ 63,02 = 0,943; todas as outras pontuações de fatores são estimadas baseando-se numa pontuação máxima de 1,000, em que, quanto mais elevada, melhor.

RESUMO FINAL

O QUE OS FABRICANTES DE CLASSE MUNDIAL ESTÃO FAZENDO

Os fabricantes de classe mundial visualizam a tecnologia avançada de produção como uma arma competitiva que pode ser usada para captar fatias de mercados internacionais. Os fabricantes americanos usam a automação da produção para aumentar ainda mais suas potencialidades de qualidade de produto e serviço ao cliente e para tornar os sistemas de produção mais competitivos em termos de flexibilidade e custos.

Rumo a esse objetivo, fabricantes de classe mundial grandes e pequenos estão:

- Projetando produtos para serem *amigáveis à automação*: reduzindo a quantidade de montagens, reduzindo o número de prendedores, permitindo inserção vertical, auto-alinhamento de peças e aumentando a qualidade dos componentes.
- Usando CAD/CAM para projetar produtos e introduzir produtos na produção. O custo e o tempo necessários para projetar e introduzir produtos são grandemente reduzidos.
- Adotando sistemas automatizados de produção de maneira seletiva tão logo projetos de automação sejam cuidadosamente planejados e executados: sistemas automatizados de montagem, FMS e ASRS. Além disso, máquinas automatizadas avançadas são integradas com a produção tradicional: centros automatizados de usinagem, grupos de robôs de soldagem e pintura automatizada.
- Convertendo sistemas de *automação rígida* para automação mais flexível.
- Contestando a antiga crença de que estoques de alto volume de produtos idênticos são necessários para se obter baixo custo e movendo-se rumo ao ideal de sistemas flexíveis de produção capazes de produzir pequenos lotes de produtos feitos sob medida conforme as exigências de clientes especiais a curto prazo.
- Adotando um sistema CIM abrangente. Todas as fases do negócio são integradas a partir de um banco de dados comum.
- Desfrutando de muitas das características de desempenho da *fábrica do futuro*: elevada qualidade de produto, elevada flexibilidade, rápida entrega dos pedidos dos clientes, capacidade de mudar o sistema de produção e sistemas acionados e integrados por computador.

- Melhorando sistemas de controle computadorizados da produção para melhor planejar e acompanhar os pedidos dos clientes, fornecendo assim melhor serviço ao cliente, custos reduzidos e melhorada flexibilidade.
- Operando a partir de um plano de automação: reconhecendo os riscos da automação, tendo um departamento de tecnologia de produção, reservando bastante tempo para a conclusão de projetos de automação, não tentando automatizar tudo, ou tudo de uma só vez, reconhecendo que são as pessoas que tornam projetos de automação bem-sucedidos e não se deslocando muito lentamente ao adotar novas tecnologias de produção.
- Justificando projetos de automação baseados em múltiplos fatores. A economia, fatias de mercado, qualidade, flexibilidade, relações de trabalho, tempo necessário, efeito sobre a produção existente e quantidade de capital necessário — todos podem ser importantes.
- Treinando e criando equipes capazes de idealizar, projetar e usar nova tecnologia de produto, e fomentando a capacidade da administração para desenvolver e implementar novos processos de produção.

QUESTÕES DE REVISÃO E DISCUSSÃO

1. Automação tradicionalmente significou a substituição de esforço humano por esforço de máquina. Critique essa visão tradicional da automação.
2. Quais benefícios devem ser esperados de projetos de automação? Discuta o impacto global que as economias de mão-de-obra decorrentes da automação têm sobre as organizações.
3. Quais são as diferenças entre máquinas NC, CNC e DNC?
4. Descreva as condições que justificariam a instalação de um robô de pintura de automóvel.
5. Descreva e dê um exemplo de cada um destes tipos de máquinas automatizadas: (a) anexos automáticos, (b) de controle numérico (NC), (c) robôs, (d) inspeção automatizada do controle da qualidade, (e) sistemas automáticos de identificação e (f) controles automatizados de processo.
6. Descreva e dê um exemplo de cada um destes tipos de sistemas automatizados de produção: (a) linhas automatizadas de fluxo, (b) sistemas automatizados de montagem, (c) sistemas flexíveis de manufatura (FMS) e (d) sistemas automatizados de armazenamento e recuperação (ASRS).
7. O que se pretende dizer com a expressão *automação rígida*? Explique a diferença entre automação rígida e *automação flexível*.
8. Explique por que os produtos deverão ser redesenhados se os sistemas automatizados de montagem precisarem ser usados na produção.
9. Defina e descreva: (a) CAD, (b) CAM, (c) CAD/CAM, (d) CIM e (e) características das fábricas do futuro.
10. Quais companhias são as principais produtoras do software ERP?
11. Dê três exemplos do uso da automação nos serviços que você conhece a partir de sua experiência pessoal.
12. O que se pretende dizer com a expressão *automação flexível*? Quais as quatro principais razões pelas quais a fatia de mercado pode ser aumentada devido à *flexibilidade de manufatura*? Cite três máquinas de sistemas de produção que ofereçam flexibilidade de produto.
13. Explique as dificuldades para implementar projetos de automação em pequenos e novos negócios. Como as dificuldades podem ser superadas?
14. Se você pudesse dar a gerentes que estão considerando projetos de automação um conselho sobre como justificar esses projetos, o que diria a eles?
15. Dê sete sugestões sobre como administrar melhor a implementação de grandes projetos de automação.
16. Defina *demissão, treinamento* e *retreinamento de trabalhadores* no contexto da automação. Descreva programas de treinamento patrocinados por empresas e explique seu conteúdo e funcionamento.
17. Cite e descreva duas maneiras de analisar alternativas de automação.
18. Quais são as potencialidades e fragilidades de cada uma das duas maneiras de analisar as alternativas de automação apresentadas neste capítulo?
19. Identifique as condições dos negócios que justificariam o uso de um sistema flexível de manufatura.

TAREFAS NA INTERNET

1. Procure na Internet por um fabricante de robôs. Descreva a linha de produtos de robôs da empresa e inclua seu site.
2. Procure na Internet por uma empresa que seja especializada em auxiliar fabricantes na automação de fábrica. Descreva os produtos ou serviços da empresa e inclua seu site.
3. Visite o site da Autodesk, a empresa que produz o software AutoCAD (**www.autodesk.com**). Explore-o e encontre suas páginas de notícias e *press release*. Encontre e resuma um *press release* interessante e recente. Forneça o título e a data do *press release*.
4. Visite o site da produtora alemã de software SAP (**www.sap.com**). Explore o site para obter informações sobre a versão mais recente do sistema de software R/3. Descreva brevemente alguns de seus novos recursos.
5. Procure na Internet por um artigo que descreva o uso de nova tecnologia numa organização de serviços. Resuma como a nova tecnologia está levando a melhorias nas operações da organização.

PROBLEMAS

Projetos em Campo

1. Visite uma empresa de serviços que tenha equipamentos ou processos automatizados. Relacione as tecnologias ou processos automatizados que observar. Descubra qual é a peça de equipamento automatizado ou processo automatizado mais recente que esteja atualmente em operação. Obtenha as respostas para estas perguntas: Quais são as principais razões ou justificativas da empresa para automatizar o processo? Essa automação de processo atingiu as expectativas de desempenho e custo da empresa? Houve alguma dificuldade para implementar a automação? Quanto tempo foi necessário para implementar a automação? Empregados foram demitidos por causa da automação? Em caso afirmativo, eles foram readmitidos?

Análise Econômica

2. O Great State Bank necessita de uma nova máquina de classificação de cheques e está considerando duas marcas: Vandine e Murcheck. A máquina Vandine é altamente automatizada e teria um custo fixo anual de $ 8.500 e um custo variável de $ 35 por classificação. A máquina Murcheck é menos automatizada, exigindo mais tempo de empregado, com um custo fixo anual de $ 7.000 e um custo variável de $ 55 por classificação. O banco executa somente uma classificação por dia e opera durante 248 dias anualmente. Use análise de break-even para resolver esse problema.
   a) Compute o custo anual total para cada máquina. Baseando-se somente no custo anual, qual máquina é a preferível?
   b) Para quantas classificações por ano o banco estaria indiferente entre comprar qualquer uma das duas máquinas?
   c) Quais outros fatores seriam considerados nessa tomada de decisão?

3. A KinderRead Inc. produz materiais para ajudar os pais a ensinar alunos de jardim de infância a ler. A máquina de empacotamento da empresa não pode mais manipular o volume de produção atual; desse modo, duas novas máquinas estão sendo consideradas. A Máquina A é mais automatizada do que a B, e também custa mais inicialmente. O custo fixo anual é $ 5.500 para a Máquina A e $ 4.000 para a B. O custo variável por unidade empacotada é $ 1,60 para a Máquina A e $ 1,80 para a B.
   a) Se o volume de produção anual for 9 mil unidades, qual máquina seria preferível baseando-se somente no custo anual?
   b) Para qual faixa de volume de produção anual cada máquina seria preferível baseando-se somente no custo anual?
   c) Se for esperado um volume de produção anual de 7.500 unidades, como a empresa deve decidir qual máquina deve comprar?

4. A Prestige Machine Works manufatura peças para a indústria aeronáutica. Para tornar-se mais competitiva, a empresa decidiu atualizar sua tecnologia de produção. Três tecnologias alternativas estão sendo consideradas: manufatura celular (MC), máquinas de controle numérico (NC) e um sistema flexível de manufatura (FMS). Espera-se que o volume de produção anual seja no mínimo de 65 mil unidades por ano durante os próximos anos, mas que poderia chegar a 85 mil unidades por ano. Os custos para as três alternativas são:

	MC	N/C	FMS
Custo fixo anual ($)	85.000	230.000	410.000
Custo variável por unidade ($)	42,50	40,30	39,10

a) Baseando-se no custo anual, a qual volume anual a empresa estaria indiferente entre as alternativas MC e NC? Entre as alternativas NC e FMS?
b) Determine o custo anual total correspondente a cada alternativa se o volume anual for 65 mil e se o volume anual for 85 mil.
c) Baseando-se somente na informação fornecida, qual tecnologia de produção você recomendaria para a empresa? Por quê?
d) Quais outros fatores devem ser considerados quando se toma essa decisão?

5. A Crystal Machining Company produz componentes de titânio para satélites. Em virtude do aumento da competição, a empresa decidiu modernizar suas instalações de produção. Três tecnologias de produção alternativas estão sendo consideradas: manufatura celular (MC), máquinas de controle numérico (NC) e um sistema flexível de manufatura (FMS). Espera-se que o volume de produção seja algo entre 15 mil e 20 mil unidades por ano durante os próximos anos. Os custos para as três alternativas são:

	MC	N/C	FMS
Custo fixo anual ($)	58.000	113.000	250.000
Custo variável por unidade ($)	189	175	168

a) Baseando-se no custo anual, a qual volume anual a empresa estaria indiferente entre as alternativas MC e NC? Entre as alternativas NC e FMS?
b) Determine o custo anual total correspondente a cada alternativa se o volume anual for 15 mil e o volume anual for 20 mil.
c) Baseando-se somente na informação fornecida, qual tecnologia de produção você recomendaria para a empresa? Por quê?
d) Quais outros fatores devem ser considerados quando se toma essa decisão?

6. Henry Hughes é o gerente de operações de uma clínica de saúde. Henry está tentando decidir qual de duas máquinas de exame de sangue comprar. O Modelo A realiza exames de sangue mais rápido, com menos envolvimento de empregados. O Modelo B é menos automatizado e requer mais tempo de empregado para realizar os exames de sangue. Cada máquina tem um tempo de vida esperado de cinco anos. A máquina A custaria inicialmente $ 8.000, e a Máquina B custaria inicialmente $ 5.000. As economias de custo para a clínica, correspondentes a cada máquina em cada ano, são mostradas a seguir. (Todas as estimativas são feitas após a dedução dos impostos. Talvez você queira revisar o método de pagamento a partir de um texto financeiro ou outra fonte antes de tentar resolver este problema.)

	Economias Anuais	
Ano	Máquina A	Máquina B
1	$ 3.000	$ 2.000
2	2.300	1.800
3	2.000	1.300
4	1.800	1.000
5	1.600	600

a) Compute o período de retorno do investimento para cada máquina.
b) Durante os próximos cinco anos, quais seriam as economias líquidas totais para a empresa com cada máquina?
c) Baseando-se nessa análise econômica, qual máquina você recomendaria? Por quê?
d) Quais outros fatores devem ser considerados quando se toma essa decisão?

Abordagem da Escala de Classificação

7. A Missoula Steel Company corta peças de aço laminado projetadas pelo cliente. A tecnologia atual da empresa permite que ela corte chapas de aço de até 0,635 cm de espessura. A companhia gostaria de comprar uma nova máquina de corte usando uma tecnologia diferente que lhe permitiria cortar chapas de aço de até 1,27 cm de espessura. Carl Lefleur, o gerente de produção, reduziu a decisão a duas alternativas: uma tecnologia baseada em chama e uma outra baseada em plasma. Cada tecnologia tem suas próprias potencialidades e fragilidades. Foram preparadas as seguintes informações para auxiliar na avaliação:

Capítulo 5 – Tecnologia de Produção

Fatores	Baseada em Chama	Baseada em Plasma
Fator econômico:		
Custo operacional anual	$ 110.000	$ 215.000
Outros fatores:		
Qualidade de produto	3	5
Flexibilidade de produto	4	5
Fatia de mercado	4	5
Flexibilidade de volume	5	2
Exigências de manutenção	5	3
Exigências de treinamento	4	3
Tempo de implementação	4	2
Exigências de capital	4	2

Nota: É usada uma escala de classificação de cinco pontos:
5 = excelente, 4 = bom, 3 = médio, 2 = abaixo da média e 1 = ruim.

Qual alternativa tecnológica você acha que o sr. Lefleur deve recomendar? Por quê?

Abordagem da Escala Ponderada de Classificação

8. A Superior Insurance Company decidiu substituir seu desatualizado sistema de correio de voz telefônico por um sistema moderno. Sally Billings, vice-presidente de operações, reduziu as opções a dois sistemas de correio de voz: Gamma e Omega. O sistema Gamma, bastante básico, permite que os empregados obtenham suas correspondências somente a partir de seus escritórios. O sistema Omega, mais avançado tecnologicamente, oferece mais opções de mensagens a quem faz chamadas, e permite que os empregados obtenham suas correspondências a partir de qualquer telefone de tom. O sistema Omega também oferece capacidades de chamada (*paging*) remotas. Para auxiliar na avaliação, a sra. Billings preparou as seguintes informações:

Fatores	Peso do Fator	Pontuações	
		Gamma	Omega
Fator econômico:			
Custo operacional anual	0,15	$ 30.000	$ 50.000
Outros fatores:			
Qualidade percebida do sistema	0,10	0,6	1,0
Recursos do sistema	0,30	0,4	1,0
Facilidade de uso	0,05	1,0	0,6
Capacidade de armazenamento de mensagens	0,10	0,6	1,0
Exigências de treinamento	0,05	1,0	0,4
Tempo de implementação	0,05	0,8	0,6
Exigências de capital	0,20	0,8	0,6

Nota: Uma pontuação mais elevada é melhor.

Use a abordagem da escala ponderada de classificação para comparar as duas alternativas de automação. Qual alternativa você recomendaria à sra. Billings? Por quê?

9. Carl Lefleur, gerente de produção da Missoula Steel Company no Problema 7, decidiu usar a abordagem da escala ponderada de classificação para comparar as duas tecnologias de corte de aço. Para usar essa abordagem, o sr. Lefleur preparou as seguintes informações:

Fatores	Peso do Fator	Pontuações	
		Baseada em Chama	Baseada em Plasma
Fator econômico:			
Custo operacional anual	0,10	$ 110.000	$ 215.000
Outros fatores:			
Qualidade de produto	0,30	0,6	1,0
Flexibilidade de produto	0,10	0,8	1,0
Fatia de mercado	0,20	0,8	1,0
Flexibilidade de volume	0,05	1,0	0,4
Exigências de manutenção	0,05	1,0	0,6
Exigências de treinamento	0,05	0,8	0,6
Tempo de implementação	0,05	0,8	0,4
Exigências de capital	0,10	0,8	0,4

Nota: Uma pontuação mais elevada é melhor.

Use a abordagem da escala ponderada de classificação para comparar as duas alternativas tecnológicas. Qual alternativa você recomendaria ao sr. Lefleur? Por quê?

capítulo 6

Planejamento da Capacidade de Longo Prazo e Localização de Instalações

Introdução

Planejamento da Capacidade de Longo Prazo
  Definição da Capacidade de Produção
  Medições da Capacidade
  Prevendo a Demanda por Capacidade
  Maneiras de Mudar a Capacidade
  Economias de Escala
    Redes de Subcontratados • Produção Focalizada • Economias de Escopo
  Analisando Decisões Quanto ao Planejamento da Capacidade
  Análise da Árvore de Decisões

Localização de Instalações
  Fatores Que Afetam as Decisões Quanto à Localização
  Tipos de Instalações e Seus Fatores Predominantes de Localização
  Dados, Políticas, Incentivos e Táticas de Preempção
  Analisando Localizações de Venda a Varejo e de Outros Serviços
  Analisando Localizações de Instalações Industriais
  Fatores Quantitativos e Qualitativos nas Decisões Quanto à Localização

Resumo Final: O Que os Fabricantes de Classe Mundial Estão Fazendo

Questões de Revisão e Discussão

Tarefas na Internet

Problemas

Estudo de Caso
  Integrated Products Corporation

Introdução

A Bolsa de Valores de Nova Iorque e uma Fazenda de Criação de Porcos?

O que a Bolsa de Valores de Nova Iorque possivelmente teria em comum com uma fazenda de criação de porcos? Resposta: Ambas precisam aumentar sua capacidade de produção ou operações de longo prazo. Os dois relatos seguintes descrevem como duas organizações muito diferentes, sendo a primeira uma organização de serviços e a outra uma produtora de carne, devem planejar como expandir suas capacidades para atender suas necessidades para os próximos anos.

Como a quebra de um recorde, o recente dia de negócios de um bilhão de ações foi um feito previsto há muito tempo, mas não totalmente esperado. O registro anterior de 750 milhões de ações negociadas caiu por terra quando o volume ultrapassou 1,2 bilhão de ações. E agora os executivos de Wall Street estão acelerando seus planos de aumentar a capacidade de seus sistemas de computador.

"Se você me perguntasse antes da semana passada, eu teria dito que daqui a três anos precisaremos ter a capacidade de negociar 3,5, talvez 4,25 bilhões de ações", disse Richard A. Grasso, presidente e superintendente da Bolsa de Valores de Nova Iorque. "Agora acho que está mais próximo de 5 ou 5,5 bilhões. Queremos ter a capacidade de negociar cinco vezes nosso volume médio diário. Se presumirmos que atingiremos uma média de 1 bilhão de ações por dia em três anos, e isso talvez seja um pouco agressivo, precisamos ser capazes de negociar 5 bilhões de ações." Neste ano, o volume médio diário tem sido de 520 milhões de ações, e a capacidade estabelecida é de 2,5 bilhões de ações por dia.

A Nippon Meat Packers Inc., do Japão, está se movimentando para duplicar seus planos originais referentes a uma gigantesca fazenda de produção de carne suína próxima a Perryton, Texas. A empresa revelou recentemente em Tóquio que investirá um total de US$ 240 milhões para construir 175 criadouros, uma usina de alimentação e um matadouro. A operação, conhecida como Texas Farm Inc., planeja produzir 55 mil toneladas de carne de porco anualmente para embarque para o Japão, onde a demanda por carne está se elevando em meio a uma minguante oferta.

A Texas Farm adquiriu 10 mil acres de terra ao sul de Perryton, ao norte do Texas Panhandle[1], e planeja a produção com 55 mil matrizes. Cada criadouro pode produzir centenas de animais uniformes, confinados e alimentados de maneira automática. Esses tipos de operações se proliferaram no sudeste e no meio-oeste, mas entraram no Texas somente nos últimos anos.

Ao escrevermos este livro, a Texas Farm contava com 70 criadouros, com um número entre 6 mil e 7 mil fêmeas, e 135 empregados. A empresa, que já investiu até agora US$ 47 milhões em terras e instalações, registrou quatro pedidos de autorização para expansão na Texas Natural Resource Conservation Commission e está esperando aprovação de três.

Os relatos precedentes enfatizam a importância das decisões de planejamento das instalações na estratégia de uma empresa para competir em mercados internacionais. *O planejamento das instalações inclui determinar quanta capacidade de produção a longo prazo é necessária, quanta capacidade adicional é necessária, onde as instalações de produção devem estar localizadas, e o layout e características das instalações.*

O planejamento das instalações baseia-se num plano estratégico de longo prazo para a empresa, o qual delineia as linhas de produto a serem produzidas em cada período de tempo do plano. Para muitas empresas, planos de capacidade de longo prazo e localização das instalações são as decisões estratégicas mais importantes a serem tomadas.

Essas decisões são cruciais porque, primeiro, o investimento de capital em maquinaria, tecnologia, terras e prédios para manufatura e serviços é enorme. Assim que uma empresa tiver investido milhões de dólares numa instalação, ela viverá com essa decisão por muito tempo. Essas decisões, portanto, são alvo de um es-

---

[1]*Panhandle:* o cabo de uma panela; (fig.) região de um estado (por exemplo, Flórida, Texas, Idaho) cujo mapa sugere a forma de um cabo de panela. (N. do T.)

tudo intenso e são tomadas no nível mais alto da empresa. Em segundo lugar, as estratégias de longo prazo são incorporadas aos planos de instalações de uma empresa. Questões como quais linhas de produto devem ser produzidas, onde eles devem ser vendidos e quais tecnologias serão empregadas refletem os planos estratégicos da companhia e também são resolvidas no nível mais elevado da empresa. Em terceiro lugar, a eficiência operacional das operações depende da capacidade das instalações. Custos de manutenção, facilidade de programação e economia de escala estão entre os fatores afetados pela capacidade das instalações. Em quarto lugar, a capacidade das instalações torna-se uma restrição a muitas outras decisões da APO. A quantidade de um produto que pode ser economicamente produzida num período de tempo específico é um fator limitador no planejamento da produção a curto prazo.

Neste capítulo desenvolveremos uma estrutura para planejar capacidades de instalação de longo prazo, exploraremos algumas das questões importantes no planejamento da capacidade e estudaremos alguns dos métodos usados para analisar as decisões de localização de instalações na APO.

Planejamento da Capacidade de Longo Prazo

As decisões de planejamento da capacidade normalmente envolvem as atividades relacionadas a seguir:

1. Estimar as capacidades das instalações atuais.
2. Prever as necessidades de capacidade futura de longo prazo para todos os produtos e serviços.
3. Identificar e analisar fontes de capacidade para atender necessidades de capacidade futuras.
4. Escolher dentre as fontes alternativas de capacidade.

Definição da Capacidade de Produção

Em geral, **capacidade de produção** é a cadência máxima de produção de uma organização. Diversos fatores subjacentes ao conceito de capacidade tornam seu uso e entendimento um tanto complexos. Primeiro, variações diárias como ausências e férias de empregados, quebra de equipamentos e atrasos na entrega de materiais se combinam para tornar incerta a capacidade de produção das instalações. Em segundo lugar, as cadências de produção de diferentes produtos e serviços não são as mesmas. Dessa forma, 50 mil As ou 20 mil Bs podem ser produzidos por mês, ou alguma combinação de As e Bs pode ser produzida. A combinação de produtos pode, portanto, ser levada em conta quando a capacidade é estimada. Em terceiro lugar, de qual nível de capacidade estamos falando? O maior possível, que é a capacidade baseada num esquema de trabalho de cinco dias por semana, sendo a capacidade prática baseada no uso de instalações existentes sem a necessidade de reativar instalações desativadas, ou algum outro nível?

O Federal Reserve Board mede e acompanha a produção e a capacidade industriais nos Estados Unidos (**www.bog.frb.fed.us**). Ele define **capacidade prática sustentável** como "o maior nível de produção que uma empresa pode manter dentro da estrutura de uma programação de trabalho realista, levando em conta um período de inatividade (downtime) normal e supondo uma disponibilidade suficiente de entradas para operar a maquinaria e o equipamento existentes".

Medições da Capacidade

Para empresas que produzem somente um produto ou alguns produtos homogêneos, as unidades para medir a **capacidade de produção** são diretas: automóveis por mês, toneladas de carvão por dia e barris de cerveja por trimestre são exemplos dessas medidas. Quando uma combinação consistente de produtos como cortadores de grama, semente de grama e móveis para jardins é produzida numa instalação, entretanto, a diversidade dos produtos constitui um problema na capacidade de medição. Nesses casos, uma **unidade agregada de capacidade** deve ser estabelecida. Essa medida agregada da capacidade deve permitir que os índices de produção dos vários produtos sejam convertidos para uma unidade comum de medição da produção. Por exemplo, medições como toneladas por hora e dólares de vendas por mês freqüentemente são usadas como medidas agregadas da capacidade entre produtos diversos.

No planejamento da capacidade para serviços, é especialmente difícil a realização de medições da produção. Nesses casos, **medidas da capacidade de entrada** podem ser usadas. Por exemplo, as empresas aéreas usam milhagens por assentos disponíveis por mês, os hospitais usam leitos disponíveis por mês, os serviços de arrecadação tributária usam dias de liquidação de contas por mês e as empresas de serviços de engenharia usam horas de mão-de-obra por mês.

"A utilização da capacidade instalada nos Estados Unidos atingiu 85% em dezembro, o mais alto índice desde 1985." O que isso significa? As medições da **porcentagem de utilização da capacidade** relacionam medidas da produção com as entradas disponíveis. Por exemplo, um serviço de arrecadação tributária que tinha 10 mil horas de mão-de-obra disponíveis durante o mês de março usou 8.200 horas de mão-de-obra para satisfazer as exigências de seus clientes. Dividimos as horas de mão-de-obra reais usadas pelas horas de mão-de-obra máximas disponíveis durante uma programação normal para chegar à porcentagem de utilização da capacidade, ou 82%, neste exemplo. Outros cálculos da porcentagem de utilização da capacidade comumente usados são os automóveis efetivamente produzidos por trimestre divididos pela capacidade trimestral de produção de automóveis, e os assentos de avião ocupados por mês divididos pela capacidade mensal de assentos de avião.

PREVENDO A DEMANDA POR CAPACIDADE

Fornecer capacidade de longo prazo significa tornar instalações de produção disponíveis — terras, prédios, máquinas, ferramentas, materiais, pessoal e utilidades. As atividades de planejamento, compras, construção, início e treinamento necessárias para a nova instalação de produção poderiam tomar de 5 a 10 anos, e normalmente se esperaria que essa instalação permanecesse economicamente produtiva por outros 15 a 20 anos. A previsão da demanda para os produtos ou serviços que essa instalação vai produzir, portanto, necessariamente deve cobrir de 10 a 30 anos. Previsões que cobrem esses longos períodos de tempo são difíceis porque podem ocorrer mudanças fundamentais na economia, mudanças nas preferências de consumo, desenvolvimentos tecnológicos, deslocamentos demográficos, mudanças nas regulamentações do governo, eventos políticos e militares e outros desenvolvimentos.

Em virtude da vida relativamente longa de uma instalação de produção, os ciclos de vida de produto (introdução, crescimento, maturidade e declínio) terão de ser considerados. À medida que um produto atravessa seu ciclo de vida de produto, a capacidade de produção necessária também tem de mudar, e medidas devem ser tomadas para expandir ou reduzir a capacidade. Desenvolvimentos tecnológicos devem ser antecipados e integrados ao planejamento de instalações, porque eles podem afetar drasticamente a maneira pela qual um produto é produzido, e isso afeta a capacidade.

A previsão da capacidade de produção de um produto ou serviço normalmente envolve quatro passos. Primeiro, a demanda total por um produto ou serviço em particular de todos os fornecedores é estimada. Segundo, a fatia de mercado (porcentagem da demanda total) para uma única empresa é estimada. Terceiro, a fatia de mercado é multiplicada pela demanda total para se obter a demanda estimada. Finalmente, a demanda por produto ou serviço é convertida nas necessidades de capacidade. Assim que uma empresa obtém suas melhores estimativas da demanda para seus produtos e serviços, ela deve determinar quanta capacidade de produção deve ser fornecida para cada produto ou serviço.

Por vários motivos a capacidade de produção a ser fornecida não se iguala necessariamente à quantidade de produtos e serviços que se espera que sejam a demanda. Primeiro, capital suficiente e outros recursos podem não estar economicamente disponíveis para satisfazer toda a demanda. Segundo, devido à incerteza das previsões e à necessidade de vincular a capacidade de produção às estratégias de operações em termos de prioridades competitivas, uma capacidade contingencial pode ser estabelecida. Uma **capacidade contingencial** é uma quantidade adicional de capacidade de produção acrescentada à demanda esperada para permitir:

- Capacidade extra para o caso de ocorrer mais demanda do que o esperado.
- Capacidade de satisfazer a demanda durante períodos de demanda de pico.
- Menores custos de produção; instalações de produção operadas muito próximo da capacidade máxima experimentam custos mais elevados.
- Flexibilidade de produto e volume; é possível responder às necessidades dos clientes quanto a produtos diferentes e volumes mais elevados devido à capacidade extra.
- Melhorada qualidade de produtos e serviços; instalações de produção operadas muito próximo da capacidade máxima experimentam uma degradação da qualidade.

Outra consideração importante ao determinar quanta capacidade de longo prazo para produtos e serviços uma única empresa deve fornecer é quanta capacidade seus concorrentes provavelmente acrescentarão. Se os concorrentes tiverem acrescentado ou se for esperado que eles adicionem uma capacidade que criará uma situação de supercapacidade numa empresa, esta deve repensar quanta capacidade, se for o caso, ela própria deve acrescentar. Semicondutores, automóveis e computadores pessoais são exemplos de como a capacidade industrial excessiva pode levar a preços aviltados e pouca lucratividade.

Maneiras de Mudar a Capacidade

Assim que as necessidades de capacidade de longo prazo forem estimadas através de previsões de longo prazo, existirão muitos caminhos para fornecer a capacidade. As empresas podem se ver, elas próprias, numa situação de escassez de capacidade, em que a capacidade atual é insuficiente para cumprir a demanda prevista para seus produtos e serviços, ou podem ter uma capacidade atual excessiva das necessidades futuras esperadas. A Tabela 6.1 mostra como os gerentes podem acomodar as mutantes necessidades de capacidade de longo prazo das organizações. O Instantâneo da Indústria 6.1 ilustra como algumas companhias enfrentam a escassez e o excesso de capacidade.

Um caminho normalmente preferido pelos gerentes de operações para manterem níveis elevados de utilização das instalações, apesar da demanda em queda no longo prazo para seus produtos e serviços atuais, é a introdução gradual de novos produtos para substituir os antigos e os que estão em queda. A Figura 6.1 mostra como uma empresa poderia projetar e desenvolver novos produtos à medida que os antigos declinassem ao longo do tempo. Essa introdução gradual pode ser a força motivadora fundamental por trás do desenvolvimento de novos produtos e serviços.

Se os gerentes de operações decidirem construir novas instalações como a melhor fonte alternativa de capacidade adicional, a maneira pela qual programam no tempo a capacidade é uma questão importante.

Economias de Escala

Para determinadas empresas, há um volume anual de saídas que resulta no menor custo unitário médio. Esse nível de saída é chamado **melhor nível operacional**. A Figura 6.2 ilustra esse conceito. Note que à medida que o volume anual de saídas se eleva, afastando-se de zero numa dada empresa, os custos unitários médios caem. Esses custos em queda resultam dos custos fixos que se distribuem por um número cada vez maior de unidades, turnos de produção mais longos que resultam em menos mão-de-obra, que é alocada para configurações e trocas de máquina, proporcionalmente menos sucata de materiais e outras economias. Essas economias, chamadas **economias de escala**, continuam a acumular-se à medida que o volume de saídas se eleva, até atingir o melhor nível operacional para essa instalação em particular.

TABELA 6.1 — MANEIRAS DE MUDAR A CAPACIDADE DE LONGO PRAZO

Tipo de Mudança de Capacidade	Maneiras de Acomodar Mudanças de Capacidade de Longo Prazo
Expansão	1. Subcontratar outras empresas para que se tornem fornecedores de componentes ou produtos inteiros da empresa em expansão. 2. Adquirir outras empresas, instalações ou recursos. 3. Desenvolver locais, construir prédios, comprar equipamentos. 4. Expandir, atualizar ou modificar instalações existentes. 5. Reativar instalações em estado de espera (*standby*).
Redução	1. Vender instalações existentes e estoques e demitir ou transferir empregados. 2. Desativar instalações e colocá-las no estado de espera (standby), vender estoques e demitir ou transferir empregados. 3. Desenvolver e dividir em fase novos produtos à medida que outros produtos declinam.

INSTANTÂNEO DA INDÚSTRIA 6.1

FALTA E EXCESSO DE CAPACIDADE

Os relatos a seguir ilustram como as empresas lutam ora para aumentar a capacidade, ora para diminuí-la.

O negócio está tão bem na Boeing que ela está perdendo dinheiro. Há exatamente três anos, a Boeing Co., a maior fabricante mundial de jatos comerciais, reduziu sua capacidade de produção e demitiu 12 mil funcionários. Agora a Boeing foi pega de surpresa por súbita reviravolta nos pedidos e contratou recentemente mais 32 mil pessoas, e tem planos para contratar ainda mais.

Ironicamente, a recente duplicação de pedidos de jatos vai custar à Boeing US$ 2,6 bilhões, sendo que essas notícias fizeram com que os preços de suas ações caíssem mais de 7%. Num esforço para atender todos os novos pedidos, a Boeing mais do que dobrou sua capacidade de produção — de 18 aviões por mês para 43. Ela tentou aumentar a capacidade o mais rapidamente possível. Infelizmente, o mau planejamento para elevar sua capacidade de produção lhe causou muitos problemas, como falta de mão-de-obra, escassez de peças, linha de montagem insatisfeita e atraso na entrega de aviões. Para tentar resolver os problemas, a Boeing precisou suspender a produção de alguns modelos de jatos e desacelerar a produção de outros. Ela estima que talvez sejam necessários de seis a nove meses para que todos os problemas sejam solucionados.[a]

Os fabricantes mundiais de automóveis, duramente atingidos pela recente crise econômica do Brasil, estão respondendo rapidamente. Até a crise econômica, esperava-se que as vendas de automóveis brasileiros tivessem um *boom*. A GM, a Ford, a Chrysler, a Toyota e a Mercedes têm, todas, novas instalações. Mas agora, espera-se que as vendas de automóveis caiam.

Em resposta, os fabricantes de automóveis tentaram rapidamente reduzir a produção e a capacidade. A GM está cortando a produção em 25%. A Ford fechou sua fábrica brasileira por duas semanas. A Volkswagen começou a reduzir a semana de trabalho em duas de suas fábricas em São Paulo, operando somente três dias por semana em vez de cinco. Os analistas dizem que as rápidas mudanças dos fabricantes de automóveis são sábias, dada a volatilidade da economia brasileira.[b]

Fontes:
a. "Boeing Hitting Turbulence: 747 Production to Halt 20 Days; 737 Slowdown". *Houston Chronicle*, 4 de outubro de 1997; "Boeing Victimized by Success". *Houston Chronicle*, 23 de outubro de 1997.
b. Maynard, Micheline. "Auto Industry Reacts Quickly". *USA Today*, 17 de novembro de 1997.

FIGURA 6.1   EFEITOS DE SE INTRODUZIR GRADUALMENTE PRODUTOS NA UTILIZAÇÃO DA CAPACIDADE DA INSTALAÇÃO

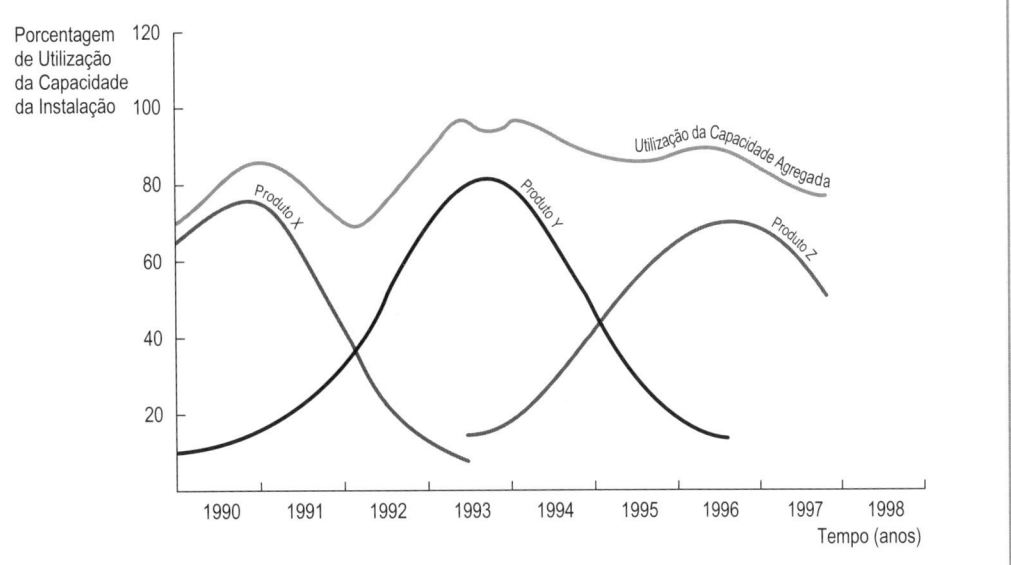

FIGURA 6.2 — ECONOMIAS E DESECONOMIAS DE ESCALA

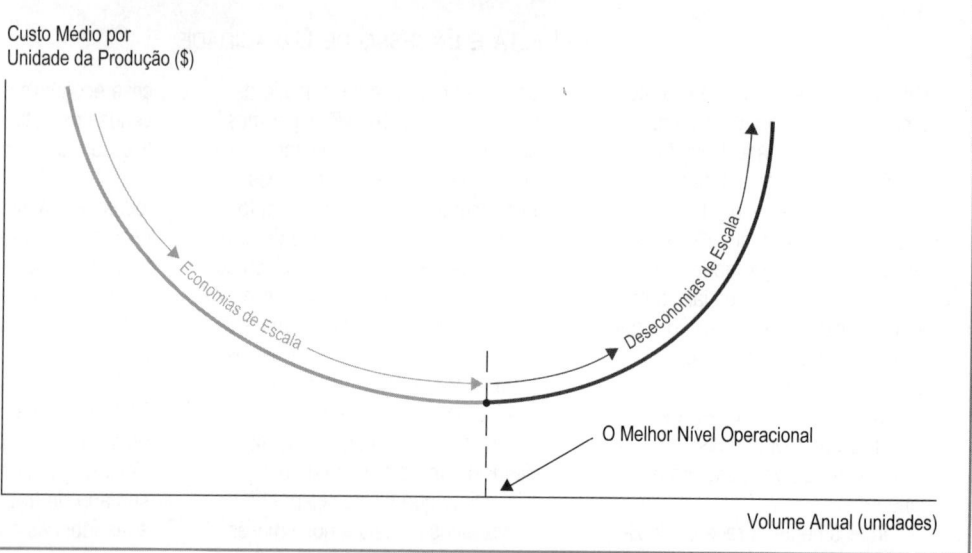

Depois desse ponto, entretanto, um volume adicional de saídas resulta em custos médios por unidade sempre crescentes. Esses custos crescentes surgem do aumentado congestionamento de materiais e trabalhadores, o que contribui para elevar a ineficiência, a dificuldade para planificar, produtos danificados, moral reduzido, maior uso de trabalho em horas extras e outras deseconomias. O impacto desses fatores, chamados **desceconomias de escala**, eleva-se a uma taxa acelerada acima do melhor nível operacional para a instalação.

Uma vez que cada instalação tem seu próprio melhor nível operacional particular, sendo todas as outras coisas iguais, e que instalações que têm níveis operacionais mais elevados exigem maiores investimentos, os gerentes de operações devem decidir entre duas abordagens gerais para expandir a capacidade de longo prazo:

1. Investir fortemente numa grande instalação que exige um grande investimento inicial, mas que terá um nível operacional mais elevado e que, por fim, atenderá as necessidades de capacidade da empresa. Em outras palavras, construir uma instalação definitiva agora e se desenvolver nela.
2. Planejar para investir num projeto de instalação inicial agora e expandir ou modificar essa instalação quando necessário para elevar os melhores níveis operacionais para atender a demanda de longo prazo por produtos e serviços. Em outras palavras, expandir a capacidade de longo prazo incrementalmente quando necessário para atender as demandas por capacidade futuras.

A Figura 6.3 compara essas estratégias. Note que os Projetos A, B e C exibem os melhores níveis operacionais nos volumes anuais de 240 mil, 450 mil e 640 mil, respectivamente. Suponhamos, por exemplo, que nossas necessidades de capacidade de longo prazo fossem estimadas como um volume anual de 640 mil em 10 anos a partir de agora. Qual a melhor maneira de provermos para essa capacidade de longo prazo: incrementalmente ou tudo de uma vez?

Como mostra a Figura 6.3, a estratégia de escolhermos inicialmente o Projeto A e subseqüentemente modificarmos esse projeto para o Projeto B e depois para o Projeto C parece fazer sentido, porque o custo médio por unidade tende a ser o menor. Adicionalmente, essa abordagem incremental pode ser menos arriscada, porque, se nossas necessidades de capacidade previstas não se materializarem, o programa de expansão poderá ser interrompido em tempo de evitar investimentos desnecessários em expansão desnecessária. Por outro lado, um grande projeto de construção provavelmente envolverá menos investimento e custos do que diversos projetos pequenos, porque não haveria qualquer construção redundante ou interrupções de produção. Devido à inflação, os custos de construção podem ser menores se construirmos toda a capacidade necessária agora. Além do mais, evitamos o risco de precisar desativar negócios futuros se nossa previsão de longo prazo vir a ser muito baixa e nossa capacidade for inadequada. *Mas uma das prin-*

FIGURA 6.3 — ELEVAÇÕES NA CAPACIDADE INCREMENTAL DA INSTALAÇÃO

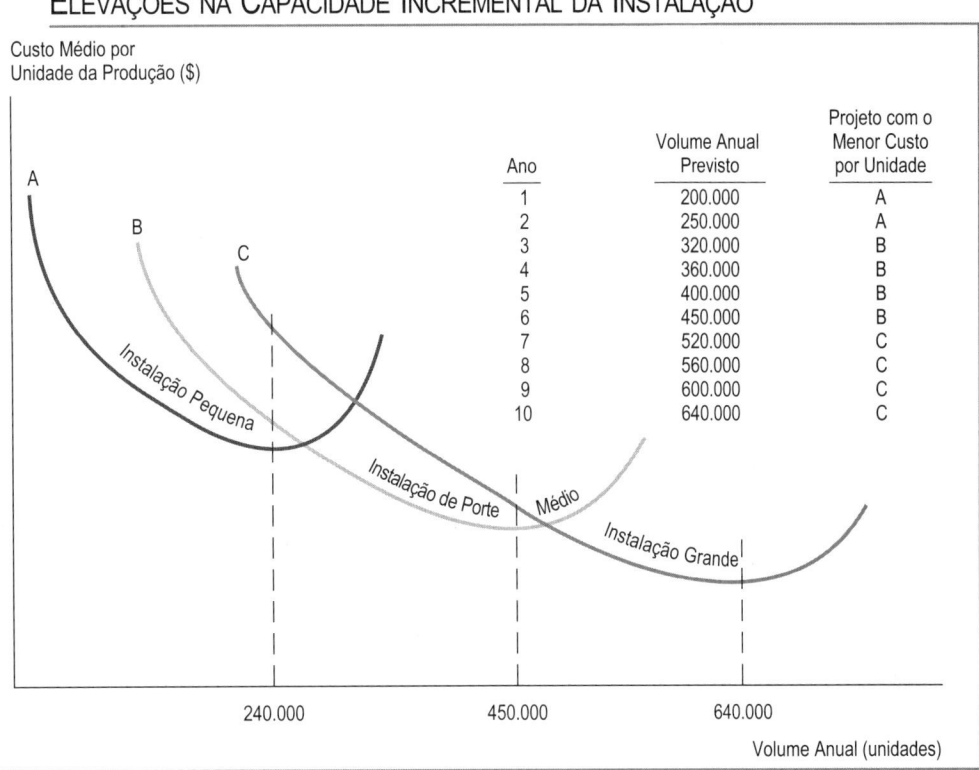

cipais causas de supercapacidade industrial é o argumento segundo o qual instalações maiores realizam maiores economias de escala. Uma grande preocupação a respeito de construirmos a grande instalação agora é porque investimentos estarão presos à capacidade excessiva, na qual nenhum retorno será realizado por diversos anos. Isso resulta ou num grande dispêndio adicional em juros, ou em renda perdida devido a não se ter o capital comprometido com outros tipos de investimentos que gerariam receita.

Escolher entre expandir a capacidade de uma só vez ou incrementalmente não é uma opção clara para a maioria das empresas. Nos casos de produtos maduros com padrões de demanda estáveis e previsíveis, as empresas são mais receptivas a construir a instalação definitiva agora. Com novos produtos, entretanto, elas se voltam para uma estratégia de expansão incremental devido ao risco das previsões e à natureza imprevisível de suas demandas de longo prazo. A escolha final diferirá de empresa para empresa devido à natureza de seus produtos, à disponibilidade de fundos de investimento e suas atitudes em relação ao risco, e outros fatores.

Redes de Subcontratados Uma alternativa viável para as instalações de produção de maior capacidade é desenvolver **redes de subcontratados e fornecedores**. Ao recorrer a menos integração vertical, os fabricantes desenvolvem relações contratuais de longo prazo com fornecedores de peças, componentes e montagens. Essa abordagem permite que os fabricantes operem com menos capacidade dentro de suas instalações porque grande parte de suas necessidades de capacidade foi transferida a seus fornecedores. Essa abordagem não somente exige menos capital para instalações de produção, mas os fabricantes também podem variar mais facilmente suas capacidades durante períodos de demanda menos intensos ou de pico. Uma vez que as elevações ou quedas de capacidade podem ser parcialmente absorvidas pelos fornecedores, os fabricantes podem oferecer melhores políticas de emprego permanente para suas forças de trabalho.

Produção Focalizada Dois conceitos importantes entram em conflito quando a capacidade de produção é planejada: economias de escala e produção focalizada. **Produção focalizada** é o conceito segundo o qual cada instalação de produção deve ser especializada de alguma maneira para se tornar menos vulnerável à competição. Embora as economias de escala possam levar a instalações de produção maiores, de certa forma, a produção focalizada leva a instalações menores. Portanto, enquanto procuram pelo melhor nível operacional para cada instalação, as empresas devem, ao mesmo tempo, desenvolver planos relativos a como a instalação pode ser especializada. À semelhança de suas concorrentes estrangeiras, os fabricantes americanos estão tendendo para instalações de produção menores e mais especializadas.

Economias de Escopo   Outro conceito importante que deve ser levado em conta quando consideramos as economias de escala e a produção focalizada são as **economias de escopo**. A expressão economias de escopo refere-se à capacidade de produzir muitos modelos de produto numa instalação de produção altamente flexível a um custo mais baixo do que em instalações de produção separadas. O pensamento tradicional supunha que à medida que os investimentos de capital, mecanização e automação são aumentados, a flexibilidade de produção deve diminuir, e que a produção automatizada pode ser justificada somente por produtos de volume elevado devido a economias de escala. Mas os avanços tecnológicos no desenvolvimento da automação e programação, descritos no Capítulo 5, transformaram essa maneira de pensar. Agora, uma automação altamente flexível e programável permite que sistemas de produção mudem para outros produtos rapidamente e a baixo custo, com o resultado de que economias de escala são criadas espalhando-se o custo de instalações automatizadas por muitas linhas de produto.

ANALISANDO DECISÕES QUANTO AO PLANEJAMENTO DA CAPACIDADE

As decisões quanto ao planejamento da capacidade podem ser analisadas usando-se diversas abordagens diferentes. A **análise de break-even,** discutida no Capítulo 4, comumente é usada para comparar funções de custo de duas ou mais alternativas de instalação. A **análise do valor presente** também é especialmente útil no planejamento da capacidade de longo prazo. A **simulação por computador** e a **teoria das filas**, ilustradas no Capítulo 12, também podem ser usadas para analisar as decisões sobre planejamento da capacidade. A **programação linear** também é usada nessas decisões; essa abordagem será usada ainda neste capítulo para analisar as decisões quanto à localização de instalações.

Além dessas técnicas, as árvores de decisões são especialmente úteis para analisar as decisões quanto ao planejamento de instalações.

ANÁLISE DA ÁRVORE DE DECISÕES

As decisões quanto ao planejamento de instalações são complexas. Freqüentemente elas são difíceis de organizar, porque são **decisões multifásicas**, ou seja, envolvem diversas decisões interdependentes que devem ser tomadas em seqüência. As árvores de decisões foram desenvolvidas para decisões multifásicas como um auxílio para os analistas que devem ver claramente quais decisões devem ser tomadas, em qual seqüência as decisões devem ocorrer e a interdependência das decisões. Essa capacidade de estruturar a maneira de pensarmos a respeito das decisões multifásicas simplifica a análise.

O Exemplo 6.1 demonstra os aspectos fundamentais da **análise da árvore de decisões**. Essa forma de análise dá aos gerentes:

- Uma maneira de estruturar decisões multifásicas complexas ao relacionar decisões do presente com o futuro.
- Uma maneira direta de lidar com eventos incertos.
- Uma maneira objetiva de determinar o valor relativo de cada alternativa de decisão.

Um lembrete de cuidado deve ser observado com respeito à interpretação do valor esperado (VE) na análise de decisões. Um erro que poderíamos cometer é interpretar o VE para cada decisão de maneira literal e absoluta. Os VEs são somente **medidas relativas** do valor, e não **medidas absolutas**. Considere os lucros (prejuízos) do Exemplo 6.1. Eles são resultados possíveis para a alternativa de estudo: $ 30.000, $ 490.000, ($ 110.000) ou $ 2.000. Somente um desses valores será retornado finalmente a quem toma as decisões. O VE de $ 66.000 jamais será retornado à empresa. O VE é somente uma medida do valor dessa alternativa em relação às outras alternativas.

Exemplo 6.1

Árvore de Decisões: Manufaturar ou Não Manufaturar?

A Biltmore Manufacturing desenvolveu um novo produto promissor. A administração da empresa tem à frente três opções: vender a idéia do novo produto por $ 20.000, contratar um consultor para estudar o mercado e depois tomar uma decisão ou arranjar financiamento para construir uma fábrica e depois manufaturar e comercializar o produto.

O estudo custará à Biltmore $ 10.000, e sua administração acredita que tem 50% de chance de encontrar um mercado favorável. Se o estudo for desfavorável, a administração calcula que poderá vender a idéia por $ 12.000. Se o estudo for favorável, ela calcula que poderá vender a idéia por $ 40.000. Mas, mesmo que um mercado favorável seja encontrado, a chance de um produto definitivamente bem-sucedido é de aproximadamente 2 em 5. Um produto bem-sucedido retornará $ 500.000. Mesmo com um estudo desfavorável, pode-se esperar um produto bem-sucedido aproximadamente uma vez em cada dez introduções de novos produtos. Se a administração da Biltmore decidir manufaturar o produto sem um estudo, haverá somente a chance de 1 para 4 de ser bem-sucedida. Um fracasso de produto custa $ 100.000. O que a Biltmore deve fazer?

Solução

1. Desenhe uma árvore da esquerda para a direita com quadrados (□) para as decisões e (○) para os eventos aleatórios. Essas decisões e eventos aleatórios muitas vezes são chamados **nós** ou **garfos**. Escreva os valores do resultado (lucros ou prejuízos) na margem direita e escreva a probabilidade de eventos aleatórios entre parênteses nas ramificações à direita dos círculos.

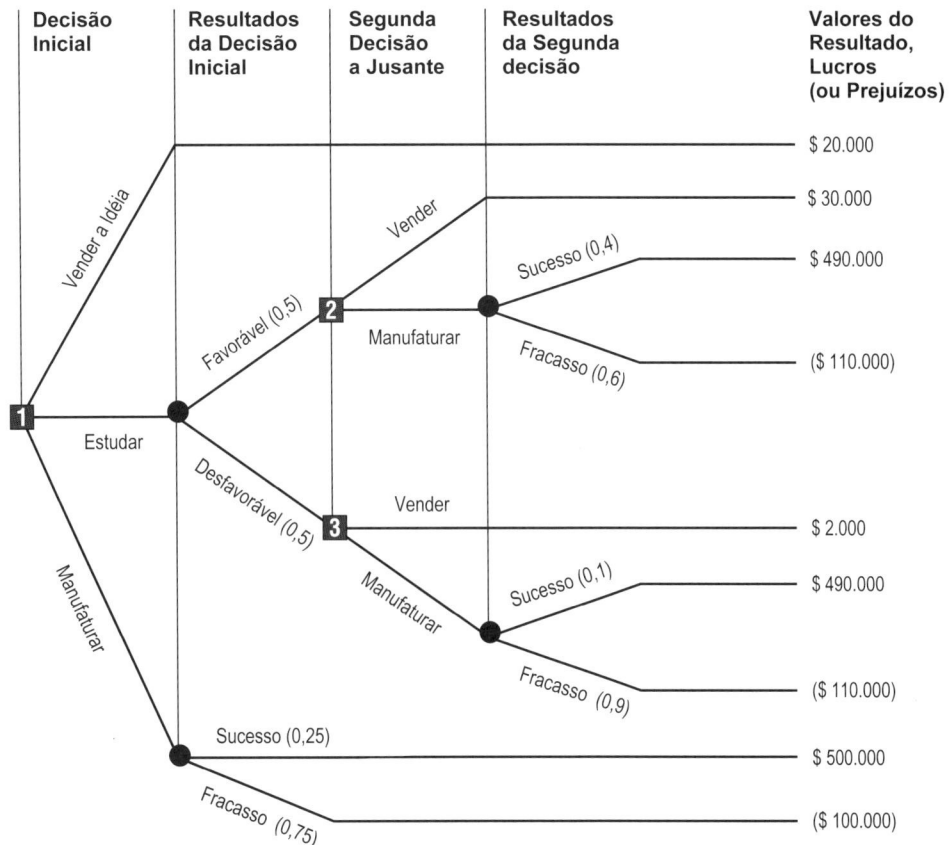

2. Trabalhando da direita para a esquerda, compute o valor esperado (VE) para as segundas decisões a jusante em cada círculo correspondente a eventos aleatórios. Escreva os VEs à direita de cada círculo. Por exemplo, o VE dos eventos aleatórios para a decisão de manufaturar — decisão 2 — é computado como VE = 0,4($ 490.000) + 0,6(–$ 110.000) = $ 130.000. Continuando a trabalhar da direita para a esquerda, decida qual alternativa das segundas decisões a jusante (2 e 3) tem o VE mais elevado. Escreva o VE escolhido à direita das caixas de decisão e corte (—/ /—) todos os outros ramos. Continue a trabalhar da direita para a esquerda como antes e compute o VE para a decisão inicial. Por exemplo, o VE para a alternativa de estudo é computado como: VE = 0,5($ 130.000) + 0,5($ 2.000) = $ 66.000.

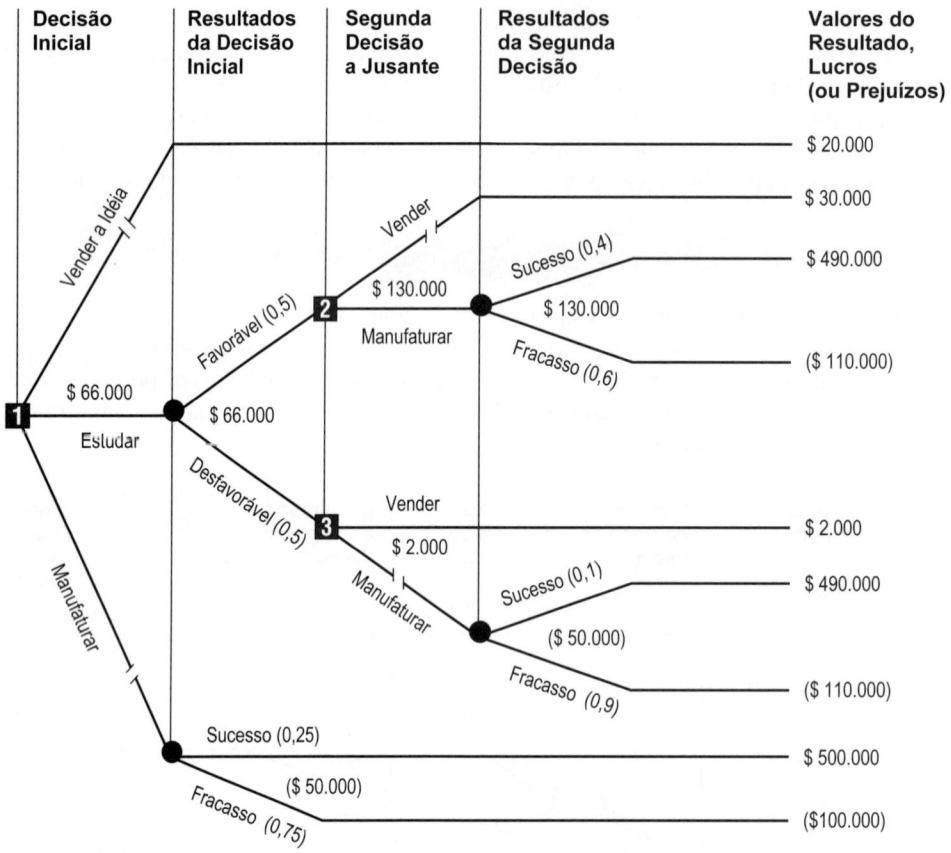

3. O VE para a decisão inicial é $ 66.000. A seqüência das decisões é deduzida seguindo-se os ramos cortados da árvore, da esquerda para a direita: estude e, se for favorável, manufature; se for desfavorável, venda.

O **valor esperado como um critério de decisão** varia em termos de eficácia, dependendo da situação de decisão. Com uma decisão tomada uma só vez, o que normalmente acontece com as decisões de planejamento de instalações na APO, o valor esperado é o melhor, no máximo, somente como uma medida relativa do valor.

Mas, mesmo que os valores esperados ou probabilidades não sejam incluídos nas árvores de decisões, o valor dessas árvores como uma maneira útil de organizar a forma pela qual pensamos a respeito das decisões multifásicas complexas deve ser reconhecido. Essa ferramenta permite que os tomadores de decisões vejam claramente quais decisões devem ser tomadas, em qual seqüência elas devem ocorrer, e suas interdependências. O valor esperado, se interpretado corretamente, é um benefício adicional.

Apesar das técnicas específicas empregadas para analisar as decisões de planejamento da capacidade de longo prazo, você pode estar certo de que essas decisões estão entre as decisões mais analisadas que envolvem os gerentes de operações. As razões para esse envolvimento residem na importância que essas decisões representam para esses gerentes.

Quando as capacidades de instalações existentes forem inadequadas para atender as necessidades de capacidade de longo prazo e novas instalações precisarem ser construídas, alugadas ou compradas, uma questão importante que deve ser resolvida é onde localizar as novas instalações.

LOCALIZAÇÃO DE INSTALAÇÕES

As decisões quanto à localização de instalações não são tomadas de maneira apressada. Ao contrário, elas envolvem longos e custosos estudos de localizações alternativas antes que o local definitivo seja escolhido. Aqueles que já passaram por diversos desses estudos de localizações geralmente concluem que não existe nenhuma melhor localização definitiva, mas que, ao contrário, há diversas localizações boas. Se um local for claramente superior a todos os outros em todos os sentidos, a decisão quanto à localização será fácil. Tipicamente, entretanto, diversos locais possíveis, cada um com suas potencialidades e fragilidades, surgem como boas opções, e a decisão quanto à localização torna-se uma **decisão meio-termo (*trade-off*)**: você poderá ganhar um tipo de benefício somente abrindo mão de outro. Essas decisões meio-termo relativas à escolha de pontos estratégicos podem ser aflitivas, e normalmente são resolvidas somente depois de uma longa e cuidadosa ponderação dos prós e contras de cada localização.

As decisões quanto à localização podem ser mais bem entendidas examinando-se os fatores que comumente afetam a escolha final das localizações de instalações.

FATORES QUE AFETAM AS DECISÕES QUANTO À LOCALIZAÇÃO

A escolha de uma localização para as instalações normalmente envolve uma seqüência de decisões. Essa seqüência pode incluir uma decisão quanto a um país, uma região, uma comunidade ou um local estratégico. A Figura 6.4 mostra essa seqüência de decisões quanto a uma localização.

Primeiro, a administração deve decidir se a instalação será localizada *internacionalmente* ou *domesticamente*. Há apenas alguns anos essa escolha teria recebido somente uma pequena consideração. Hoje, entretanto, com a internacionalização dos negócios, os gerentes estão considerando rotineiramente *em qual parte do mundo* suas instalações devem estar localizadas. O Instantâneo da Indústria 6.2 ilustra como as decisões referentes à localização de instalações transcendem as fronteiras nacionais.

As recentes experiências das empresas americanas em localizarem instalações em países estrangeiros têm sido às vezes doces e às vezes amargas. Instabilidade política, militar, social e econômica podem tornar essas decisões arriscadas. Considere também o efeito nas mudanças das taxas de câmbio estrangeiras na década de 1980 sobre essas decisões. Empresas americanas como a Ford, GE e Cincinnati Milacron localizaram instalações de produção fora do país para aproveitar os custos de mão-de-obra mais baixos nos países estrangeiros. Mas, embarcar os bens das fábricas no exterior de volta para os Estados Unidos significava converter o valor dos bens em moeda estrangeira em dólares. Com a drástica queda do dólar em relação às moedas estrangeiras na última metade da década de 1980, o custo desses bens em dólares foi, de fato, maior do que aquilo que custariam se fossem manufaturados nos Estados Unidos.

Resolvida a questão internacional *versus* doméstico, a administração deve decidir em qual região dentro do país a instalação deve ser localizada. Essa **decisão regional** pode envolver escolher entre algumas regiões nacionais, como na Figura 6.4, ou entre diversas regiões dentro de uma área geográfica muito menor.

FIGURA 6.4   A DECISÃO QUANTO À LOCALIZAÇÃO DE INSTALAÇÕES

A Seqüência de Decisões Quanto à Localização

1 → Decisão Nacional
2 → Decisão Regional
3 → Decisão Comunitária
4 → Decisão quanto ao Local

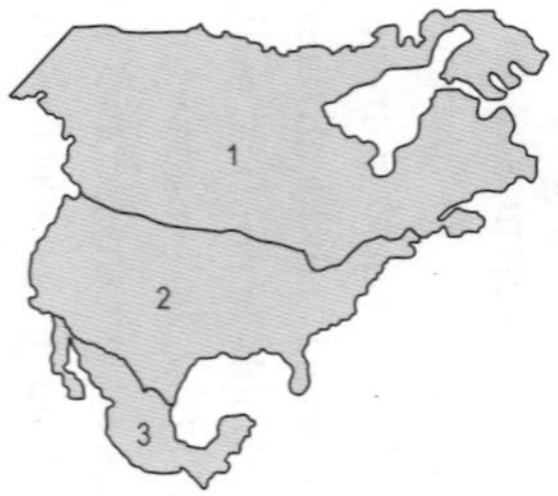

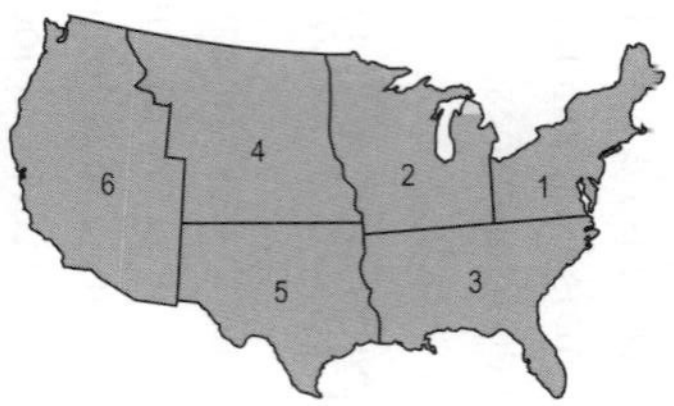

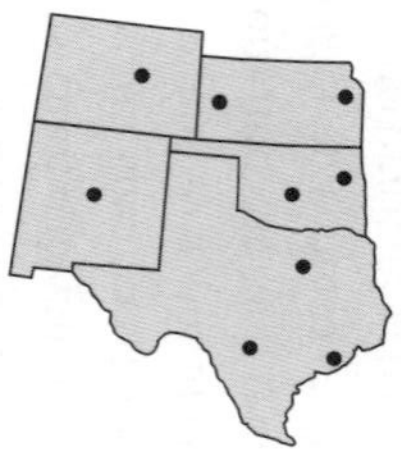

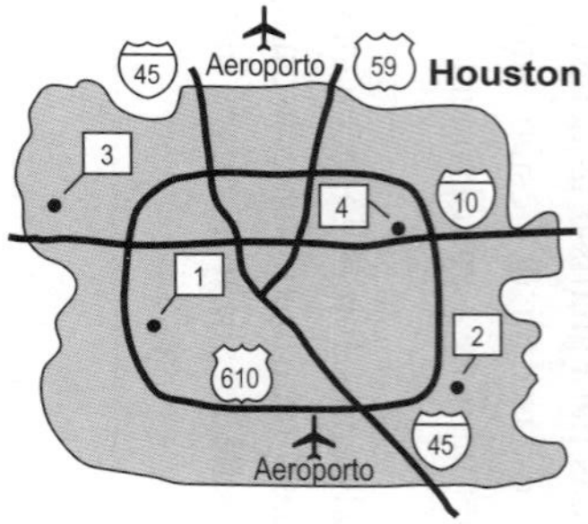

Alguns Fatores Que Afetam as Decisões Quanto à Localização

Decisão Nacional
1. Estabilidade do Governo, Economia e Sistema Político
2. Disponibilidade e Custos de Mão-de-Obra
3. Cotas de Exportação e Importação, Taxas Alfandegárias e Comissões
4. Taxas de Câmbio da Moeda
5. Sistema de Transporte
6. Oferta de Energia
7. Sistema de Telecomunicações
8. Disponibilidade e Custos de Materiais e Suprimentos
9. Clima
10. Incentivos e Restrições Governamentais
11. Peculiaridades Culturais e Econômicas
12. Regulamentação Quanto às Operações

Decisão Regional
1. Concentrações e Tendências de Clientes e Cidadãos
2. Disponibilidade e Custos de Mão-de-obra
3. Grau de Organização Sindical
4. Custos de Construção e de Terras
5. Oferta e Custos de Serviços Públicos
6. Disponibilidade de Sistemas de Transporte
7. Custos dos Transportes
8. Disponibilidade e Custos de Materiais e Suprimentos
9. Clima
10. Incentivos Governamentais
11. Regulamentação Ambiental

Decisão Comunitária
1. Concentrações e Tendências de Clientes e Cidadãos
2. Preferência da Administração
3. Serviços Comunitários e Impostos
4. Atitudes Comunitárias em Relação a Localizações de Novas Instalações
5. Disponibilidade e Custos de Mão-de-obra
6. Disponibilidade e Custos de Locais
7. Custos de Construção
8. Disponibilidade de Sistemas de Transporte
9. Custos dos Transportes
10. Disponibilidade e Custos de Materiais e Suprimentos
11. Serviços Bancários
12. Regulamentação e Impactos Ambientais
13. Incentivos Governamentais

Decisão quanto ao Local
1. Concentrações e Tendências de Clientes e Cidadãos
2. Custos de Locais
3. Tamanho dos Locais
4. Proximidade a Sistemas de transporte
5. Disponibilidade de Serviços Públicos
6. Restrições de Zoneamento
7. Proximidade a Indústrias de Serviço Relacionadas
8. Impacto Ambiental
9. Disponibilidade e Custos de Materiais e Suprimentos

> ## INSTANTÂNEO DA INDÚSTRIA 6.2
>
> ### LOCALIZAÇÃO GLOBAL DE INSTALAÇÕES NA DEC
>
> A Digital Equipment Corporation (DEC) é uma grande fabricante de computadores sediada nos Estados Unidos. Mais da metade de suas receitas vem de mais de 80 países, principalmente da Europa. A DEC opera mais de 30 fábricas em mais de uma dúzia de países.
>
> Ao decidir-se quanto a localizações internacionais de novas fábricas e centros de distribuição, a DEC considera uma série de fatores:
> - Localização de clientes e fornecedores.
> - Localização e disponibilidade de mão-de-obra qualificada e barata.
> - Tamanho do canal de distribuição de materiais em termos de distância e tempo.
> - Tempo de trânsito e custo de vários meios de transporte.
> - Custo de materiais em diferentes nações.
> - Importância e localização de zonas francas (zonas comerciais com isenção de impostos).
> - Comércio recíproco (*offset*) (valor de bens e serviços comprados num país para equilibrar a venda de produtos nesse país).
> - Alvos de conteúdo locais (porcentagem de componentes, em valor, para um produto).
> - Regulamentação de exportações, taxas alfandegárias e políticas de *drawback*[2].
>
> Baseando-se nesses fatores, a DEC usa uma abordagem fundamentada na programação linear para desenvolver planos de 18 meses e 5 anos para localizações de instalações, planos de capacidade e estratégias de abastecimento em todo o mundo.
>
> *Fonte:* Arntzen, Bruce C., Gerald G. Brown, Terry P. Harrison e Linda L. Trafton. "Global Supply Chain Management at Digital Equipment Corporation". *Interfaces* 25, n. 1 (janeiro-fevereiro de 1995).

A Figura 6.5 ilustra a classificação de regiões e estados dos Estados Unidos como localizações de manufatura desejáveis, preparadas por uma empresa de contabilidade e consultoria administrativa internacional sediada em Chicago.

Assim que a decisão quanto à região geográfica tiver sido tomada, a administração deve decidir-se entre diversas comunidades dentro dessa região. A Figura 6.4 também relaciona alguns dos fatores que afetam a decisão quanto à comunidade. A maioria dos fatores levados em consideração na decisão quanto à região também está presente na decisão quanto à comunidade.

A **decisão comunitária** tem alguns fatores adicionais que afetam a escolha da localização. Serviços comunitários e impostos, atitudes e incentivos para criação de novas instalações, disponibilidade e custos de locais, impacto ambiental, serviços bancários e preferências administrativas são fatores importantes para se decidir entre comunidades. Finalmente, feita a opção por uma comunidade, um ponto estratégico dentro dessa comunidade deve ser escolhido. Alguns fatores adicionais surgem na **escolha do local estratégico**: tamanho e custo de cada local, proximidade a sistemas de transporte e indústrias ou serviços relacionados, disponibilidade de serviços públicos e materiais e suprimentos, e restrições de zoneamento.

TIPOS DE INSTALAÇÕES E SEUS FATORES PREDOMINANTES DE LOCALIZAÇÃO

Você já pensou por que:

- Muitos fabricantes de automóveis estão em Detroit?
- Muitas empresas de pesquisa e desenvolvimento (P&D) de computadores high-tech estão no Vale do Silício no norte da Califórnia?
- Diversos fabricantes de computadores pessoais e chips estão em Austin, Texas?
- Diversos estabelecimentos que atendem encomendas postais de produtos comercializados em massa estão em Chicago?
- Pequenas mercearias parecem estar em quase todas as esquinas de sua cidade?

Por que certas empresas estão localizadas próximo de suas matérias-primas, enquanto outras estão perto de seus consumidores? E por que empresas concorrentes se localizam tão perto umas das outras? Essas per-

---

[2] Política de *drawback:* reintegração de direitos pagos à alfândega. Faculdade que tem o importador de obter a devolução dos direitos alfandegários pagos pela matéria-prima, quando é reexportada, já industrializada.

guntas sugerem que cada tipo de empresa tem alguns fatores predominantes que, por fim, determinam a decisão quanto à localização das instalações.

A Tabela 6.2 classifica a importância relativa de alguns dos fatores que afetam as decisões quanto à localização para diferentes tipos de instalações. As atividades de mineração, lavra e manufatura pesada têm instalações que consomem **capital intensivamente** e que são dispendiosas para construir, cobrem grandes áreas geográficas e usam grandes quantidades de matérias-primas pesadas e volumosas. Adicionalmente, seus processos de produção se desfazem de grandes quantidades de refugo, o total de saídas acabadas pesa muito menos do que as entradas totais de matéria-prima, enormes quantidades de serviços públicos são absorvidas, e os produtos são embarcados somente para alguns clientes. Conseqüentemente, essas instalações tendem a ser localizadas próximo de suas fontes de matéria-prima e não de seus mercados, de forma a minimizar os custos de transporte totais das entradas e saídas. Adicionalmente, elas tendem a escolher locais em que os custos de terrenos e construções são relativamente baratos e onde se espera que o tratamento de refugo não prejudique o meio ambiente. A disponibilidade de abundante oferta de serviços públicos e a proximidade de um serviço ferroviário também são importantes.

Instalações de manufatura leve fabricam itens como componentes eletrônicos e, necessariamente pequenas, localizam-se perto ou de fontes de matéria-prima ou de seus mercados. De preferência, elas procuram um equilíbrio entre os custos de transporte das entradas e saídas, e outros fatores relativos à localização tendem, portanto, a dominar a decisão a respeito de onde localizar. A disponibilidade e o custo da mão-de-obra são importantes nas decisões quanto à localização dessas instalações, ao passo que o custo de transporte tem menos importância. Se a tendência rumo a uma maior automação de fábrica se elevar, como se espera, o custo de mão-de-obra poderia tornar-se menos importante nas decisões quanto à localização de fábrica no futuro. A tendência poderia ser rumo a sistemas de produção mais dispersos, descentralizados, com muitas pequenas fábricas que utilizam automação flexível.

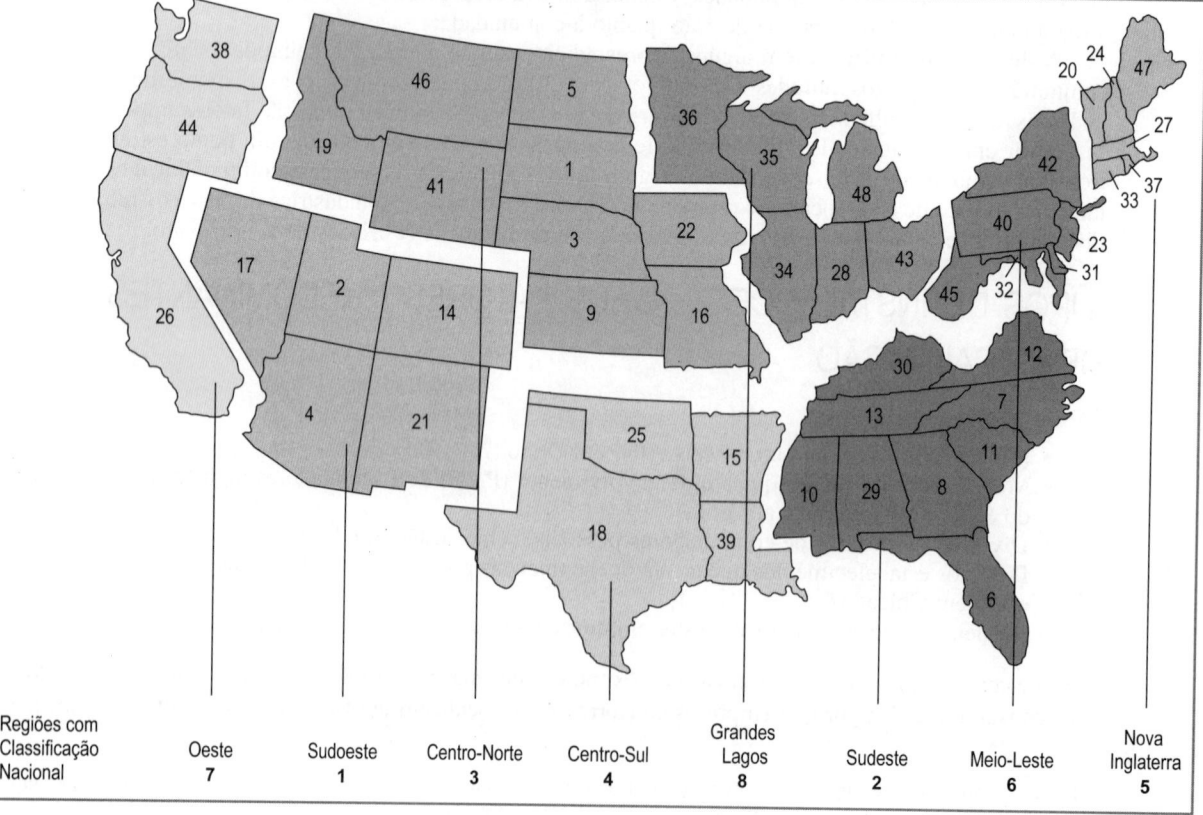

FIGURA 6.5 — CLASSIFICAÇÕES DE REGIÕES E ESTADOS AMERICANOS COMO LOCALIZAÇÕES DESEJÁVEIS DE MANUFATURA

TABELA 6.2 — Importância Relativa dos Fatores de Localização em Diferentes Instalações

Fator Que Afeta a Decisão Quanto à Localização	Mineração, Lavra, Manufatura Pesada	Manufatura Leve	P&D e Manufatura High-Tech	Armazenamento	Venda a Varejo	Serviços ao Cliente com Fins Lucrativos	Serviços do Governo Municipal	Serviços de Saúde e Emergência
1. Proximidade de concentrações de clientes e cidadãos	C	C	B	B	A	A	A	A
2. Disponibilidade e custos de mão-de-obra	B	A	B	B	B	A	B	B
3. Atratividade da comunidade para recrutar profissionais	C	B	A	C	C	C	C	C
4. Grau de organização sindical	A	A	C	B	B	B	C	B
5. Custos de construção e terrenos	A	B	B	B	B	B	B	B
6. Proximidade de instalações de transporte	A	B	C	A	B	C	C	C
7. Custos de transporte das entradas	A	B	C	A	B	C	C	C
8. Custos de transporte das saídas	B	B	C	A	C	C	C	C
9. Disponibilidade e custos de serviços públicos	A	B	C	C	C	C	C	C
10. Proximidade de matérias-primas e suprimentos	A	B	C	C	C	C	C	C
11. Restrições de zoneamento e impacto ambiental	A	B	C	C	C	B	C	C

Observação: A = muito importante, B = importante, C = menos importante.

A localização dos armazéns é de grande importância. Os fatores predominantes são aqueles que afetam os custos de transporte. Não obstante ser desejável e freqüentemente necessário estar bastante próximo de mercados, tanto para comunicar-se eficazmente com os destinatários dos produtos que saem como para reagir rapidamente aos pedidos dos clientes, o custo de transporte é o fator de localização máximo para os armazéns. Essas instalações são, portanto, objetos de avaliações econômicas quantitativas, como, por exemplo, programação linear.

O sucesso e a sobrevivência das empresas de P&D e de manufatura high-tech dependem em grande parte de sua capacidade de recrutar e manter cientistas, engenheiros e outros profissionais. A atratividade do estilo de vida da comunidade e a proximidade de universidades são fatores preponderantes no recrutamento desses empregados. E quando diversas empresas com interesses tecnológicos similares se localizam perto umas das outras, uma comunidade de associações científicas e uma força de trabalho comunitária mais bem treinada se beneficiam. Por esses motivos, vemos que comunidades como as seguintes são atraentes:

- Laser Lane, lasers e eletroótica em Orlando, Flórida.
- Silicon Prairie, desenvolvimento de software em Champaign/Urbana, Illinois.
- Medical Alley, instrumentos médicos, atendimento à saúde em Mineápolis/St. Paul, Minnesota.
- Biomed Mountais, dispositivos médicos, órgãos artificiais em Salt Lake City, Utah.

As instalações de venda a varejo e os serviços ao cliente com fins lucrativos são localizados próximo a concentrações de clientes alvos. Todos os outros fatores relativos à localização estão subordinados a esse fator único. Os estudos dessas localizações de instalações tipicamente envolvem a identificação de concentrações residenciais de clientes alvos, dados sobre o trânsito em ruas vizinhas, tendências de crescimento de comunidades e subúrbios, níveis de gasto discricionário da vizinhança e outras informações demográficas. Uma vez que algumas instalações de serviços como estabelecimentos de lavagem a seco, clínicas médicas e laboratórios fotográficos podem se desfazer de grandes quantidades de refugo de papel, produtos químicos e suprimentos gastos, restrições de zoneamento e impacto ambiental podem desempenhar um papel mais importante do que nas decisões referentes às localizações de vendas a varejo.

Os serviços de governos municipais, em geral localizados próximo a concentrações de seus cidadãos, freqüentemente são agrupados a fim de que seus cidadãos possam economizar tempo, esforço e custos de transporte. Adicionalmente, esses serviços são agrupados a fim de permitir interação entre agências.

Os serviços de saúde e emergência tradicionalmente são localizados próximo a concentrações de cidadãos, porque a consideração fundamental ao escolher localizações é que elas resultem nos mais baixos tempos de resposta globais entre os cidadãos e os serviços. A minimização de perdas de propriedades e perdas de vidas é a consideração preponderante nessas localizações. Os postos de bombeiros tipicamente estão localizados perto de concentrações de residências para minimizar o tempo necessário para os carros do corpo de bombeiros chegarem ao cenário do incêndio. Os serviços de ambulância são localizados similarmente perto desses centros populacionais para minimizar o tempo necessário para transportar pacientes para hospitais e clínicas de saúde. Os hospitais comumente são localizados próximo das grandes concentrações humanas.

O tipo de instalação, a natureza de seus produtos e serviços e a natureza das atividades diárias afetam a importância que cada fator de localização desempenha nas decisões referentes a localizações. Cada decisão quanto à localização é única, porque a natureza de cada instalação e sua operação diária é única. O entendimento dos fatores que afetam essas decisões e sua importância relativa para localizar diversas classes de instalações constitui uma útil estrutura para análise.

DADOS, POLÍTICAS, INCENTIVOS E TÁTICAS DE PREEMPÇÃO

A quantidade de dados necessários para comparar alternativas de localização de instalações pode ser enorme, e as fontes desses dados são numerosas. Uma fonte é o IBGE. Outras fontes valiosas de dados sobre localização são as câmaras de comércio das cidades que estão em consideração. Outra maneira infalível para que uma empresa seja inundada com dados sobre localização de instalações é preparar um *press release* para que os meios de comunicação divulguem sua intenção de localizar uma nova instalação que empregará quinhentas pessoas e terá uma folha de pagamento anual de US$ 10 milhões.

Assim que governos, câmaras de comércio e comunidades se inteirarem de que uma nova instalação está sendo planejada, os aspectos políticos das decisões quanto à localização das instalações se tornarão patentes. Parece não haver um fim nos extremos a que o governo e as organizações civis chegam para atrair novas instalações para suas comunidades. Por exemplo, quando a Chrysler-Mitsubishi procurava um lugar para instalar uma montadora para seu automóvel Diamond-Star, os meios de comunicação apresentavam relatos detalhados e quase diários dos lugares visitados pela equipe de pesquisa, de quais comunidades tinham feito apresentações para a companhia e de quais políticos estaduais haviam visitado os escritórios da empresa. Uma comunidade atrás da outra desenrolava o tapete vermelho para a equipe visitante, e a lista de incentivos oferecidos à companhia crescia. A instalação foi finalmente localizada em Bloomington, Illinois. Esse relato ilustra que incentivos econômicos na forma de redução de imposto de renda, IPTU e outros impostos, rodovias, estacionamentos e outras concessões são fatores poderosos nas decisões quanto à localização de instalações. Outros exemplos incluem a decisão da Packard Bell Computer de mudarse de Los Angeles para a região de Sacramento, a decisão da McDonnell Douglas de construir um novo avião em Dallas em vez de em Long Beach, e a decisão da Texas Instruments de construir uma fábrica de semicondutores de US$ 1 bilhão em Dallas e uma fábrica de pastilhas semicondutoras de US$ 500 milhões em Avezzano, Itália.

Assim que uma empresa anuncia que pretende localizar uma instalação em algum lugar, iniciam-se conversações nos vários centros de operação de seus concorrentes. Esse anúncio é o primeiro passo numa **tática de preempção**, e ela normalmente tem no mínimo dois efeitos. Primeiro, se os concorrentes estiverem considerando expandir suas capacidades, eles podem temer uma supercapacidade dentro da indústria e se atemorizarem. Segundo, se for anunciada uma escolha de localização específica, os concorrentes podem ser dissuadidos de se localizar na mesma região. Essa tática de preempção é, dessa forma, voltada a desestimular a competição.

As decisões a respeito de localizações são muito complexas. Tantas variáveis estão relacionadas de forma complicada e tanta incerteza está presente que é difícil entender todas as informações simultaneamente. Devido a essa complexidade, as técnicas de análise tendem a considerar somente parte das informações relevantes, às vezes de maneira bastante simples; dessa forma, ao tomar a decisão, a pessoa responsável por ela fica com a tarefa de integrar de maneira inteligente os resultados da análise com o restante da informação.

As técnicas de análise apresentadas nas seções seguintes devem ser vistas com esta perspectiva: elas constituem uma maneira organizada de analisar parte da informação relevante presente numa decisão de localização. Cabe à administração usar os resultados da análise juntamente com outras informações para tomar a decisão final quanto à localização.

ANALISANDO LOCALIZAÇÕES DE VENDA A VAREJO E DE OUTROS SERVIÇOS

A Tabela 6.2 mostrou que o fator predominante nas decisões quanto à localização de algumas instalações é a proximidade de concentrações de clientes. Instalações como, por exemplo, venda a varejo, serviços ao cliente com fins lucrativos e serviços de saúde/ emergência são tipos de instalações que tentam localizar-se perto de seus clientes/cidadãos.

A venda a varejo e outras organizações de serviço tipicamente realizam estudos, fundamentados empiricamente, de localizações de instalações alternativas. A Tabela 6.3 mostra os passos básicos nesses estudos. Primeiro, a administração de uma organização deve entender por que os clientes compram seus pro-

TABELA 6.3	PASSOS PARA ANALISAR AS DECISÕES QUANTO À LOCALIZAÇÃO DE INSTALAÇÕES DE SERVIÇOS
	1. **Pesquisa do comportamento do cliente:** Por que os clientes compram nossos produtos e serviços?
	2. **Pesquisa de mercado:** Quem são nossos clientes e quais são suas características?
	3. **Coleta de dados para cada alternativa de localização:** Onde estão as concentrações de clientes visados? Quais são seus padrões de gastos? Quais são as tendências de crescimento e o grau de competição atual e projetado?
	4. **Projeções das receitas para cada alternativa de localização:** Quais são as projeções econômicas relevantes, as projeções de dispêndios discricionários, a atividade da competição e a receita da localização programada no tempo?
	5. **Projeções de lucros para cada alternativa de localização:** Quais são as receitas projetadas menos os custos operacionais programados no tempo?

dutos e serviços. Em seguida, uma pesquisa de mercado deve ser executada para determinar as características dos clientes visados. Quando grandes concentrações de clientes visados são identificadas, localizações alternativas próximas a essas concentrações podem ser consideradas. Enormes atividades de coleta de dados podem ocorrer neste ponto do estudo. Padrões de trânsito, dados de dispêndios e rendimentos locais, competição e tendências de crescimento projetadas são estimados para cada localização. Receitas e custos operacionais são projetados para cada localização. Os lucros projetados baseados em dados empíricos tornam-se a base para comparar as alternativas de localização sob consideração.

Os antigos estudos sobre a localização de pontos-de-venda a varejo baseavam-se no **modelo do centro de gravidade**, estruturado em dois princípios: (1) clientes são atraídos para uma localização em proporção direta com a população existente na região imediata à localização, e (2) clientes são atraídos para uma localização na proporção inversa do quadrado da distância que os clientes devem percorrer até uma localização. Estudos mais recentes da venda a varejo baseiam-se em variações modernas desses princípios do modelo do centro de gravidade. Tomemos, por exemplo, o modelo de venda a varejo de Huff para avaliar a utilidade dos shopping centers:

$$E_{ij} = P_{ij}C_i$$

em que

E_{ij} = número esperado de clientes em i que provavelmente se dirigirão ao shopping center j
C_i = número de clientes em i
P_{ij} = probabilidade de um cliente num ponto de origem i que se dirige ao shopping center j. Pij é uma função do tamanho do shopping center j, do tempo de percurso de um cliente no ponto de origem i para se dirigir ao shopping center j, e do efeito do tempo de percurso sobre vários tipos de viagens.

Esse modelo de venda a varejo e outros similares destinam-se a estimar a demanda por clientes nas localizações de venda a varejo; dessa forma, as receitas de venda a varejo em localizações alternativas podem ser estimadas. O Instantâneo da Indústria 6.3 descreve um software de computador muito bem-sucedido para localizar instalações de venda a varejo.

Instantâneo da Indústria 6.3

Software do McDonald's de Localização de Pontos Estratégicos

O McDonald's é provavelmente o líder mundial em instalações de venda a varejo construídas anualmente. Para auxiliá-los em termos de onde essas instalações serão localizadas, eles usam um poderoso software.

Esse software, que precisa de estações de trabalho de engenharia mais poderosas que os PCs para poder rodar, integra um censo demográfico e informações adicionais que o McDonald's coletou sobre pontos estratégicos em todas as partes dos Estados Unidos.

Os usuários desse software podem mover um mouse sobre um mapa fornecido pelo U.S. Census Bureau Data e ver na tela do computador os dados correspondentes à localização do mouse. Por exemplo, se o mouse for colocado na intersecção de uma rua movimentada, o número de famílias, renda discricionária, tamanho da população visada e outros dados de marketing correspondentes à vizinhança aparecem na tela.

O software inclui um enorme banco de dados que o McDonald's construiu a partir de estudos feitos sobre a localização e a partir de pesquisas dos clientes sobre o número de transeuntes e pessoas que moram ou trabalham regularmente em cada localização de ponto estratégico possível.

O programa, comercializado pela Dakota Marketing sob o nome *Quintillion*, se destina a bancos, grandes comerciantes, lojas varejistas, supermercados, lojas de departamentos e outras redes de cadeias de lojas.

Fonte: "McDonald's Markets Site-Location Software". *Houston Chronicle*, 8 de dezembro de 1991.

ANALISANDO LOCALIZAÇÕES DE INSTALAÇÕES INDUSTRIAIS

A Tabela 6.4 classifica os problemas de localização em quatro classes básicas, da mais simples para a mais complexa. Na primeira classe, presume-se que uma única instalação receba materiais de diversas fontes e remeta produtos acabados a diversos destinos. Essa classe de problema comumente é analisada com **análise convencional de custos**.

A Tabela 6.5 é uma análise de custos para três localizações alternativas de uma usina siderúrgica. A vantagem desse tipo de análise é sua facilidade de comunicação e entendimento. Uma desvantagem dessa abordagem é que os custos de 1, 5 e 10 anos no futuro são comparados sem se considerar o valor temporal do dinheiro. Deve-se também reconhecer que fatores qualitativos relevantes não são considerados nessa análise.

Quando uma ou mais instalações devem ser localizadas juntamente com instalações existentes similares, como nas Classes 2 e 3 da Tabela 6.4, as análises se tornam mais complexas. Alguma forma de programação linear comumente é empregada nesses problemas para investigar simultaneamente todas as combinações possíveis de remessas de material. Este é um **problema de transporte** da programação linear (PL), e o objetivo é minimizar os custos totais anuais de transporte e manuseio para operar os três armazéns. Embora essa abordagem identifique a localização de armazém que tem o menor custo, fatores qualitativos relevantes não são considerados.

Por exemplo, Markland usou simulação por computador para estudar os complexos fluxos de produtos da Purina Company entre plantas, armazéns de campo, atacadistas e mercearias. A simulação por computador será discutida no Capítulo 12 deste livro.

A Classe 4 da Tabela 6.4, muitas vezes denominada **problema de transbordo**[3], tem uma ordem de magnitude mais complexa do que os outros tipos de decisões quanto à localização considerados até aqui. Há diversas abordagens de solução para estes e outros problemas de localização complexos. Wagner e Geoffrion e Graves desenvolveram técnicas de solução avançadas para esses problemas.

TABELA 6.4 — ALGUNS TIPOS COMUNS DE PROBLEMAS DE LOCALIZAÇÃO

Classe de Problema de Localização	Objetivo da Análise
1. Localização de *uma instalação de fábrica única* que será atendida por uma ou mais fontes e que, por sua vez, abastecerá um ou mais destinos.	Minimizar os custos anuais totais (custos de transporte das entradas e das saídas e custos operacionais) ou maximizar os lucros anuais enquanto considera todos esses custos.
2. Localização de *uma ou mais instalações fontes* que se combinarão com instalações fontes existentes para abastecer diversos destinos existentes.	Minimizar os custos anuais totais (custos de transporte das saídas e custos operacionais) ou maximizar os lucros enquanto considera todos esses custos.
3. Localização de *uma ou mais instalações de destino* que se combinarão com instalações de destino existentes para serem atendidas por uma ou mais fontes existentes.	Minimizar os custos anuais totais (custos de transporte das entradas e custos operacionais) ou maximizar os lucros enquanto considera todos esses custos.
4. Localização de *uma ou mais instalações* que se combinarão com as instalações de fábrica existentes para serem atendidas por uma ou mais fontes existentes e que, por sua vez, abastecerão um mais destinos existentes.	Minimizar os custos anuais totais (custos de transporte das entradas e das saídas e custos operacionais) ou maximizar os lucros anuais enquanto considera todos esses custos.

---

[3]*Transbordo:* transferência de carga de um transporte para outro; baldeação.

TABELA 6.5 — COMPARAÇÕES DE CUSTO: TRÊS LOCALIZAÇÕES ALTERNATIVAS PARA UMA USINA SIDERÚRGICA

	St. Louis, Missouri			Cleveland, Ohio			Milwaukee, Wisconsin		
Elemento de Custo	Ano 1	Ano 5	Ano 10	Ano 1	Ano 5	Ano 10	Ano 1	Ano 5	Ano 10
Transporte das Entradas	$ 18,5	$ 22,9	$ 28,4	$ 17,4	$ 21,5	$ 26,8	$ 16,4	$ 19,9	$ 24,6
Transporte das Saídas	6,1	7,6	10,2	6,0	7,6	10,0	6,1	7,6	10,1
Mão-de-Obra	14,7	19,4	26,2	18,6	22,7	30,5	21,5	25,4	33,9
Matéria-Prima	30,3	39,4	57,1	29,5	39,1	56,3	28,9	38,6	55,2
Suprimentos	4,2	4,5	5,9	4,4	4,9	5,9	4,6	4,9	6,2
Serviços Públicos	6,0	9,2	18,5	8,4	12,6	29,2	10,1	16,3	32,1
Gastos Gerais Variáveis	5,9	6,8	7,5	6,1	7,2	8,2	6,0	7,6	8,6
Gastos Gerais Fixos	9,6	10,5	14,2	10,2	11,6	14,9	10,4	12,3	15,3
Custo Operacional Total	95,3	120,3	168,0	100,6	127,2	181,8	104,0	132,6	186,0
Volume Projetado	1,201	1,489	2001	1,201	1,489	2,001	1,201	1,489	2,001
Custo de Produção por Unidade (US$/tonelada)	$ 79,4	$ 80,8	$ 840	$ 83,8	$ 85,4	$ 90,4	$ 86,6	$ 89,1	$ 93,0

Observação: Os custos são em milhões de dólares, e o volume é em milhões de toneladas.

FATORES QUANTITATIVOS E QUALITATIVOS NAS DECISÕES QUANTO À LOCALIZAÇÃO

As técnicas para analisar e comparar localizações alternativas até agora se basearam em localizar concentrações de clientes, como no caso da maioria das organizações de serviços, ou em minimizar o tempo de percurso, a distância ou custos, como no caso das fábricas e armazéns. Essas análises quantitativas fornecem valiosas entradas quantitativas para as decisões quanto à localização, mas muitas dessas decisões também podem envolver fatores não facilmente quantificáveis.

TABELA 6.6 — ABORDAGEM DE ESCALA DE CLASSIFICAÇÃO PARA COMPARAR LOCALIZAÇÕES ALTERNATIVAS PARA UMA USINA SIDERÚRGICA

Fatores de Localização	St. Louis, Missouri	Cleveland, Ohio	Milwaukee, Wisconsin
Fatores Econômicos			
Custos operacionais anuais	$ 95.300.000	$ 100.600.000	$104.000.000
Custos de produção por unidade	$ 79,40/ton	$ 83,80/ton	$ 86,60/ton
Fatores Qualitativos			
Disponibilidade de moradias	3	3	4
Custo de vida	3	3	2
Disponibilidade de mão-de-obra	3	3	5
Atividades comunitárias	3	2	4
Serviços de educação e saúde	3	3	4
Lazer	4	2	5
Atividades sindicais	3	1	3
Sistemas de transporte locais	3	5	3
Proximidade de indústria similar	3	4	4
Atitudes comunitárias	5	5	5

Observação: É usada uma escala de classificação de cinco pontos: 5 = excelente, 4 = bom, 3 = médio, 2 = abaixo da média, 1 = fraco.

Os gerentes que tomam decisões quanto à localização sabem que em alguns casos os fatores qualitativos podem ser predominantes quando comparados com os quantitativos. Alguns desses fatores qualitativos são moradia, custo de vida, disponibilidade de mão-de-obra, clima, atividades comunitárias, serviços de educação e saúde, lazer, igrejas, atividades sindicais, sistemas de transporte locais, proximidade de instalações industriais similares e atitudes comunitárias. Esses fatores trabalham em conjunto com fatores quantitativos, como, por exemplo, custos anuais das operações para determinar a aceitabilidade de uma localização em particular.

Os gerentes freqüentemente lutam com a tarefa de buscar uma compensação entre fatores qualitativos e quantitativos. Os métodos para exibir sistematicamente as vantagens e desvantagens relativas de cada alternativa de localização, tanto quantitativas como qualitativas, evoluíram. Duas abordagens foram discutidas no Capítulo 5: escala de classificação e escala ponderada de classificação.

A Tabela 6.6 ilustra a abordagem de escala de classificação. Os gerentes devem processar essas comparações por meio de seus cálculos mentais únicos e chegar a uma classificação relativa para cada uma das alternativas de localização. A Tabela 6.7 ilustra a abordagem da escala ponderada de classificação. Abordagens como essas podem ser úteis para comparar alternativas de localização, especialmente quando fatores qualitativos forem importantes nas decisões quanto à localização.

Os conceitos, fatores de localização e técnicas de análise para abordar as decisões quanto à localização de instalações apresentados neste capítulo não esgotam o assunto. Aquilo que é apresentado aqui serve somente como uma introdução a um tema amplo.

TABELA 6.7 — ABORDAGEM DA ESCALA PONDERADA DE CLASSIFICAÇÃO PARA COMPARAR LOCALIZAÇÕES ALTERNATIVAS PARA UMA USINA SIDERÚRGICA

Fator de Localização Relevante	Peso do Fator	St. Louis, Missouri			Cleveland, Ohio			Milwaukee, Wisconsin		
		Dados Econômicos	Pontuação	Pontuação Ponderada	Dados Econômicos	Pontuação	Pontuação Ponderada	Dados Econômicos	Pontuação	Pontuação Ponderada
Custo de produção por tonelada	0,60	$ 79,40	1,000*	0,600	$ 83,80	0,948*	0,569	$ 86,80	0,917*	0,550
Custo de vida	0,05		0,600†	0,030		0,650	0,033		0,500	0,025
Disponibilidade de mão-de-obra	0,20		0,650	0,130		0,600	0,120		0,950	0,190
Atividades sindicais	0,10		0,700	0,070		0,700	0,070		0,650	0,065
Proximidade de indústria similar	0,03		0,600	0,018		0,650	0,020		0,850	0,026
Transporte local	0,02		0,600	0,012		0,700	0,014		0,700	0,014
Pontuação Total da Localização				0,860			0,826			0,870

*Essas pontuações são determinadas dividindo-se o mais baixo custo por tonelada pelo custo por tonelada real:

$$\frac{79,40}{79,40} = 1,000 \qquad \frac{79,40}{83,80} = 0,947 \qquad \frac{79,40}{86,60} = 0,917$$

†As pontuações qualitativas do fator são estimadas baseando-se numa pontuação máxima de 1,000.

RESUMO FINAL

O QUE OS FABRICANTES DE CLASSE MUNDIAL ESTÃO FAZENDO

Os fabricantes de classe mundial reconhecem que as decisões quanto à capacidade de longo prazo e à localização de instalações estão entre as mais importantes de suas decisões estratégicas. O investimento de capital em instalações de produção é enorme, e a capacidade de produção a ser usada como uma arma competitiva para captar mercados internacionais se pendura na balança. O planejamento da capacidade cobre períodos de tempo tão longos que mudanças fundamentais podem ocorrer na economia, nas preferências de consumo, na tecnologia, nos aspectos demográficos e nas regulamentações governamentais. Esse planejamento está, portanto, sujeito a uma grande incerteza e risco.

Todavia, os fabricantes de classe mundial distinguem-se com um notável planejamento de negócios de longo prazo, e segue-se necessariamente que eles também se sobressaem na realização de estudos da capacidade de longo prazo. Eles não somente levam em conta as previsões de longo prazo da demanda por seus produtos e serviços, mas também consideram esses fatores como mudanças esperadas nos ciclos de vida do produto e nos ciclos de vida do processo, disponibilidade de capital e outros recursos, tecnologia de produção e de produto e supercapacidade industrial. De especial importância é a medida de capacidade extra na forma de capacidade contingencial para levar em conta uma demanda inesperada, picos sazonais de demanda, a anulação de deseconomias de escala e a combinação de prioridades competitivas de instalações de produção.

Os fabricantes de classe mundial justificam os enormes investimentos em instalações de produção baseando-se menos no quanto economizam e em outras fórmulas de retornos financeiros convencionais e mais no quanto essas instalações posicionam suas empresas para capitalizar as oportunidades estratégicas de captar fatias de mercado internacionais. A redução da integração vertical através do desenvolvimento de uma rede eficaz de subcontratados pode melhorar o desempenho global da empresa. Melhorada tecnologia de produção, reduzido investimento de capital, aumentada flexibilidade e aumentada capacidade e níveis de emprego mais estáveis são vantagens freqüentemente citadas da maior confiança em fornecedores. Os fabricantes de classe mundial estão optando por estreitar o foco de suas instalações de produção, tornando-as assim menos vulneráveis a concorrentes menores e mais especializados. Isso significa que as instalações de produção em geral tendem a ser menores, mais amplamente dispersas e localizadas mais perto dos clientes. A introdução da automação flexível na produção permitiu as economias de escopo, espalhando o custo da automação entre muitos produtos diferentes.

As decisões quanto à localização de instalações nos fabricantes de classe mundial envolvem cada vez mais uma procura mundial por pontos estratégicos. As fronteiras nacionais constituem um obstáculo menor do que no passado. Uma grande quantidade de fatores é considerada nas decisões quanto à localização, e a importância desses fatores varia conforme o tipo de instalação. O tipo de instalação — da manufatura pesada a serviços de saúde — tem seu próprio conjunto de fatores, que deve ser cuidadosamente comparado com aqueles que são apresentados por localizações de pontos estratégicos potenciais. Grandes quantidades de dados são coletadas e analisadas para cada localização considerada. Programação linear, análise de custos e outras técnicas podem ser usadas nessas análises.

Os incentivos oferecidos pelos governos das comunidades que estão em consideração são importantes para a escolha da localização. Além disso, a atenção que se mantém sobre a concorrência deve considerar os anúncios de escolhas de localização para propósitos de preempção. A escolha final da localização da instalação envolverá a necessidade de se considerar de maneira simultânea muitos fatores econômicos e qualitativos.

QUESTÕES DE REVISÃO E DISCUSSÃO

1. Cite quatro atividades usualmente envolvidas em qualquer decisão de planejamento da capacidade de longo prazo.
2. Como a medição da capacidade dos serviços provavelmente difere da medição da capacidade de manufatura?
3. Defina estas expressões: *capacidade de produção, unidade agregada de capacidade, capacidade de entrada, porcentagem de utilização da capacidade, capacidade contingencial*.
4. Cite três maneiras pelas quais as empresas podem ampliar a capacidade de longo prazo.
5. Defina estas expressões: *o melhor nível operacional, economias de escala, deseconomias de escala, economias de escopo, redes de fornecedores*.
6. Cite cinco técnicas usadas para analisar decisões quanto à capacidade de longo prazo.
7. Cite quatro passos seqüenciais nas decisões quanto à localização.
8. Quais fatores afetam as decisões quanto à localização nacional?
9. Quais fatores afetam as decisões quanto à localização numa comunidade?
10. Quais fatores afetam as decisões quanto à localização de um ponto estratégico?
11. Relacione os fatores predominantes que afetam a localização destas instalações:
    a) Mineração, lavra e instalações de manufatura pesada.
    b) Instalações de manufatura leve.
    c) Pesquisa e desenvolvimento e manufatura high-tech.
    d) Armazéns.
    e) Instalações de varejo e serviço.

f) Serviços do governo local e instalações de serviços de saúde e emergência.
12. Cite cinco passos na análise de localizações de instalações de venda a varejo e serviços.
13. Descreva quatro classes de problemas de localização.
14. Com qual classe de problema de localização as comparações de custos convencionais e a análise de break-even podem ser apropriadamente usadas?
15. Cite cinco fatores quantitativos comumente considerados nas decisões quanto à localização de instalações.
16. Descreva como os gerentes podem considerar simultaneamente tanto fatores quantitativos como qualitativos na análise de localização de instalações.
17. Descreva como os fabricantes de classe mundial abordam as decisões quanto à capacidade de longo prazo e localização de instalações.

TAREFAS NA INTERNET

1. O Office of System Capacity é um departamento dentro da Federal Aviation Administration. Visite e explore seu site (**asc-www.hq.faa.gov/**). Qual é o propósito ou o papel desse departamento (isto é, o que o departamento faz)?
2. Um fator na decisão quanto à localização de uma instalação de alta tecnologia que empregará muitas pessoas altamente treinadas é o custo de vida na região. O ACCRA Cost of Living Index é computado para as áreas metropolitanas dos Estados Unidos com população acima de 1,5 milhão. Encontre o ACCRA Cost of Living Index na Internet. Quais são as cinco regiões metropolitanas mais caras e quais são as cinco menos caras para se viver nos Estados Unidos? Anote o site onde você encontrou essa informação.
3. O Federal Reserve Board publica freqüentes relatórios sobre "Produção Industrial e Utilização da Capacidade" nos Estados Unidos. Encontre um relatório recente na Internet e anote o site do relatório. Qual é a mais recente porcentagem de utilização da capacidade apresentada, e para qual período de tempo?
4. A Economic Development Commission, da Flórida, fornece informações na Internet sobre localização de instalações para a região de Orlando (**www.business-orlando.org**). Encontre informações sobre os custos de construção contra os custos de aluguel por pé quadrado para diferentes tipos de instalações. Encontre as porcentagens de índice de ocupação recentes para diferentes tipos de instalações. Resuma essas informações.

PROBLEMAS

Decisões Quanto ao Planejamento de Longo Prazo das Instalações

1. A Hardhead Lids Company planeja produzir capacetes para motociclistas. Espera-se que o custo fixo anual para o processo de produção seja $ 185.000. Espera-se que o custo variável por capacete seja $ 76. A companhia espera vender cada capacete por $ 99.
   a) Quantos capacetes devem ser vendidos a cada ano para se atingir o ponto de equilíbrio (break-even)?
   b) Quanta receita anual é necessária para se atingir o ponto de equilíbrio?
   c) Se 15 mil capacetes forem vendidos anualmente, quanto lucro será obtido?
   d) Se forem esperadas vendas anuais de 15 mil capacetes, qual deve ser o preço de venda para que se obtenha um lucro de $ 300.000?
2. Uma empresa formulou um conceito de novo produto e agora deve decidir se é oportuno prover capacidade de produção de longo prazo em seu plano qüinqüenal. A empresa tem três oportunidades

para lucrar com o novo produto: vender a idéia definitivamente para outra companhia, arrendar o conceito recebendo direitos autorais (*royalties*), ou desenvolver o produto em casa. Se o conceito for vendido de maneira definitiva, isso trará um lucro de $ 1.500.000. Uma empresa de consultoria pesquisou os mercados potenciais para a idéia. Se o conceito for arrendado por royalties, duas empresas apresentaram propostas e se aplicam estas informações:

Tamanho do Mercado	Probabilidade	Compensações
Empresa A		
Grande	0,5	$ 2.800.000
Marginal	0,5	2.200.000
Empresa B		
Grande	0,5	2.600.000
Marginal	0,5	2.300.000

Se a empresa desenvolver o conceito num novo produto, ela poderá vender os direitos do produto. Se essa alternativa for escolhida, estas informações se aplicarão:

Tamanho do Mercado	Probabilidade	Compensações
Grande	0,5	$ 2.500.000
Marginal	0,5	2.200.000

Se a empresa desenvolver o novo produto e depois produzi-lo e comercializá-lo, estas informações se aplicarão:

Tamanho do Mercado	Probabilidade	Compensações
Grande	0,5	$ 3.000.000
Marginal	0,5	1.800.000

a) Use uma árvore de decisões e recomende um curso de ação para essa idéia de novo produto.
b) Se a empresa seguir suas recomendações, que retornos poderia obter?

3. A BuiltRite Manufacturing Company desenvolveu um novo produto e agora deve decidir-se entre dois planos de instalações. A primeira alternativa é construir uma nova grande instalação imediatamente. A segunda é construir uma fábrica pequena inicialmente e considerar ampliá-la para uma instalação maior 3 anos depois, somente se o mercado tiver se mostrado favorável durante os 3 primeiros anos. O marketing apresentou as seguintes estimativas de probabilidade para o plano de 10 anos:

(A) Demanda para os 3 primeiros anos	Probabilidade de A P(A)	(B) Demanda para os 7 próximos anos	Probabilidade de B, Dado A P(B|A)
Desfavorável	0,2	Desfavorável	1,0
Desfavorável	0,2	Favorável	0
Favorável	0,8	Favorável	0,5
Favorável	0,8	Desfavorável	0,5

Estas compensações para cada resultado foram apresentadas pelo departamento de contabilidade:

Capítulo 6 – Planejamento da Capacidade de Longo Prazo e Localização de Instalações

Demanda	Plano da instalação	Compesação (milhões)
Favorável-favorável	Fábrica grande	$ 10,0
Favorável-desfavorável	Fábrica grande	5,0
Desfavorável-desfavorável	Fábrica grande	3,0
Favorável-favorável	Fábrica pequena – expandida	7,0
Favorável-desfavorável	Fábrica pequena – expandida	2,0
Favorável-favorável	Fábrica pequena – não expandida	1,0
Favorável-desfavorável	Fábrica pequena – não expandida	2,0
Desfavorável-desfavorável	Fábrica pequena – não expandida	1,0

Com essas estimativas, analise a decisão da BuiltRite quanto a instalações e:
a) Realize uma análise da árvore de decisões completa.
b) Recomende uma estratégia para a BuiltRite.
c) Determine quais compensações resultarão de sua recomendação.

4. Uma empresa manufatura produtos de aço estampado. Cada vez mais, fabricantes estrangeiros estão solapando os preços da companhia para esses estampos, e a empresa está estudando a tecnologia de sua capacidade de produção para determinar se ela deve ser atualizada para se tornar competitiva entre as empresas estrangeiras. Se os processos de produção forem automatizados, o valor presente líquido dos retornos (valor presente líquido significa que os retornos são expressos em termos de moeda de hoje) para a companhia dependerá do mercado para os produtos da fábrica:

Processo	Nível de Mercado	Probabilidade	Retorno
Automatizado	Elevado	0,1	$ 4.000.000
	Médio	0,5	2.600.000
	Baixo	0,4	1.500.000

Se a empresa decidir não fazer nada agora e rever a situação em 5 anos, duas alternativas provavelmente estarão presentes — continuar operando com os processos de produção existentes ou desativar a fábrica e liquidar seus ativos. Se a fábrica continuar a ser operada em suas condições existentes depois de 5 anos, o valor presente líquido dos retornos dependerá do mercado para os produtos da fábrica na época:

Alternativa	Nível de Mercado	Probabilidade	Retorno
Não fazer nada agora,	Elevado	0,3	$ 3.000.000
continuar operando de acordo	Médio	0,4	2.500.000
com as condições existentes	Baixo	0,3	2.000.000

Se a fábrica for desativada e liquidar seus ativos depois de 5 anos, o valor presente líquido dos retornos será estimado como $ 2.000.000.
a) Use uma análise da árvore de decisões e recomende um curso de ação para a companhia.
b) Quais retornos a empresa deve esperar de fato em conseqüência de seguir suas recomendações?

5. Os sócios de uma clínica médica desejam se instalar mais perto do hospital municipal. Um corretor imobiliário tem um prédio comercial de acordo com o gosto deles próximo ao hospital, e propôs a compra do imóvel ou uma locação por 50 anos. Aqui estão as informações que afetam a análise:

	Alugar	Comprar
Valor recuperado	—	0
Custo inicial	—	$ 50.000
Vida econômica	30 anos	30 anos
Depreciação anual	—	$ 15.000
Compensação do aluguel anual	$ 45.000	—
Taxa tributária	0,4	0,4

Se o período de compensação depois da dedução dos impostos for inferior a seis anos, a clínica comprará o prédio; se o período for maior do que seis anos, ela alugará o prédio. O que a clínica deve fazer?

6. Duas localizações são examinadas para a construção de uma nova fábrica. Dois processos de produção, A e B, são estudados. Os custos operacionais anuais para cada processo nas duas localizações são:

Localização	Processo A		Processo B	
	Custos Fixos	Custo Variável por Unidade	Custos Fixos	Custo Variável por Unidade
Phoenix	$ 2.500.000	$ 7,90	$ 5.400.000	$ 3,80
Denver	1.750.000	9,40	3.000.000	5,10

Em que intervalos, isto é, limites superior e inferior, de produção cada localização e processo seriam preferíveis?

7. Uma empresa está estudando três localizações para uma nova instalação de produção para produzir scanners de código de barras. A companhia desenvolveu estas estimativas para as três localizações:

Alternativa de Localização	Custos Fixos Anuais (milhões)	Custo Variável por Scanner de Código de Barras
Dallas	$ 4,9	$ 2.400
San Antonio	3,6	2.700
Houston	4,1	2.500

A empresa estima que as vendas dos scanners de código de barras será de 5 mil scanners no primeiro ano, 10 mil no terceiro ano e 15 mil no quinto ano.

a) Use uma análise de break-even para determinar qual localização seria preferível nos anos 1, 3 e 5.
b) Para que intervalos, isto é, limites superior e inferior, de produção cada uma das localizações seria preferível?

8. Uma companhia está estudando as localizações alternativas de uma nova instalação para manufaturar computadores para pequenos negócios. Duas alternativas parecem ter surgido: Kansas City e Atlanta. Um analista preparou estas informações para a decisão quanto à localização:

Fatores de Classificação	Localização	
	Kansas City	Atlanta
Fator Econômico		
Custos Operacionais Anuais ($ 000.000)	54,1	47,4
Fatores Qualitativos		
Disponibilidade de moradias	3	4
Custo de vida	4	4
Disponibilidade de mão-de-obra	4	4
Atividades comunitárias	3	5
Serviços educacionais e de saúde	4	4
Lazer	3	4
Atividades sindicais	3	4
Sistemas de transporte locais	4	4
Proximidade de indústria similar	4	3
Atividades comunitárias	5	4
Restrições de zoneamento	5	4

Observação: É usada uma escala de classificação de cinco pontos: 5 = excelente, 4 = bom, 3 = médio, 2 = abaixo da média e 1 = fraco.

Qual localização você recomendaria? Por quê?

9. A Kansas Roofing Materials Company planeja localizar uma nova instalação de produção em Kansas City, Topeka ou Wichita. Seis fatores de localização são importantes — custo por quadrado (9,29 me-

Capítulo 6 – Planejamento da Capacidade de Longo Prazo e Localização de Instalações

tros quadrados de cobertura de telhados), disponibilidade de mão-de-obra, atividades sindicais, transporte local, proximidade de indústria similar e proximidade a matérias-primas.

Fator de Localização	Peso	Kansas City	Topeka	Wichita
Custo por quadrado	0,65	$ 13,25	$ 11,93	$ 12,63
Disponibilidade de mão-de-obra	0,10	0,90	0,70	0,70
Atividades sindicais	0,10	0,80	0,40	0,60
Transporte local	0,05	0,80	0,50	0,60
Proximidade de indústria similar	0,05	0,80	0,40	0,50
Proximidade a matérias-primas	0,05	0,70	0,60	0,50

Use a abordagem da escala ponderada de classificação para comparar as três localizações alternativas. Qual localização é preferível?

ESTUDO DE CASO

INTEGRATED PRODUCTS CORPORATION

A Integrated Products Corporation (IPC) está avaliando os aspectos econômicos de instalar uma fábrica em duas localizações alternativas: Flagstaff e Tulsa. A empresa necessita de mais capacidade de produção para sua linha de computadores pessoais do que aquilo que suas duas fábricas atuais em Atlanta e El Paso podem oferecer. Um dos fatores mais importantes nessa decisão é qual localização resultará no menor custo anual de embarque das três fábricas para os cinco armazéns regionais. As seguintes estimativas de custo de embarque e capacidade de produção se aplicam:

Fábrica	Capacidade Anual (computadores)	Armazém	Exigência Anual (computadores)
Atlanta	3.400	Chicago	2.350
El Paso	4.600	Dallas	2.800
Flagstaff ou Tulsa	5.000	Denver	1.450
		Nova Iorque	3.700
		San Jose	2.700

Fábrica	Armazém	Custo de Embarque por Computador	Fábrica	Armazém	Custo de Embarque por Computador
Atlanta	Chicago	$ 45	Flagstaff	Chicago	$ 70
	Dallas	50		Dallas	45
	Denver	70		Denver	40
	Nova Iorque	55		Nova Iorque	100
	San Jose	100		San Jose	50
El Paso	Chicago	$ 60	Tulsa	Chicago	$ 50
	Dallas	40		Dallas	30
	Denver	45		Denver	50
	Nova Iorque	105		Nova Iorque	100
	San Jose	50		San Jose	70

Tarefas
1. Formule dois problemas de programação linear para determinar o plano de embarque ótimo para cada uma das alternativas de localização propostas.
2. O que a solução significa em termos do problema original?

capítulo 7

LAYOUT DAS INSTALAÇÕES MANUFATURA E SERVIÇOS

Introdução

Layouts de Instalações de Manufatura
Manuseio de Materiais
Layouts por Processo
Layouts por Produto
Layouts de Manufatura Celular
Layouts por Posição Fixa
Layouts Híbridos
Novas Tendências nos Layouts de Manufatura

Analisando Layouts de Instalações de Manufatura
Planejando Layouts por Processo e Armazenamento
  Análise da Seqüência de Operações • Análise de Diagrama de Blocos • Análise de Distância da Carga • Analisando Layouts com Computador
Planejando Layouts por Produto
  Balanceamento de Linha • Balanceamento de Linha de Modelo Misto • Planejando Layouts de Manufatura Celular

Layout de Instalações de Serviço
Tipos de Layouts de Instalações de Serviço
Analisando Layouts de Instalações de Serviço

Resumo Final: O Que os Fabricantes de Classe Mundial Estão Fazendo

Questões de Revisão e Discussão

Tarefas na Internet

Problemas

Estudo de Caso
Integrated Products Corporation

Layouts Modernos: Compactos e Flexíveis

Os layouts de instalações atuais são projetados com a meta última de produzir produtos e serviços que atendam as necessidades dos clientes. Isso significa que os layouts devem ser capazes de produzir produtos rapidamente e entregá-los no tempo certo. Os layouts atuais têm cerca de 1/3 do tamanho dos do passado. Para economizar espaço, os estoques são drasticamente reduzidos, equipamentos menores são projetados e corredores e centros de trabalho são estreitados. Então, os trabalhadores são treinados para fazer mais de um trabalho, a fim de poderem usar o espaço do chão de fábrica para mais de um propósito. Esses layouts compactos têm um grande efeito estratégico sobre o desempenho das fábricas. Os materiais percorrem distâncias mais curtas, os produtos atravessam a fábrica mais rápido, os clientes são servidos com mais eficiência. Semelhantemente, o custo do espaço, do manuseio de materiais e da manutenção de estoques é reduzido. Isso torna as fábricas e as operações de serviço mais flexíveis, porque mudanças podem ser feitas mais rapidamente. Além disso, os trabalhadores estão mais próximos, o que ajuda a acelerar as mudanças devido à melhorada comunicação e aumento do moral resultantes de grupos de trabalho mais próximos.

*Planejar o **layout da instalação** significa planejar a localização de todas as máquinas, utilidades, estações de trabalho, áreas de atendimento ao cliente, áreas de armazenamento de materiais, corredores, banheiros, refeitórios, bebedouros, divisórias internas, escritórios e salas de computador, e ainda os padrões de fluxo de materiais e de pessoas que circulam nos prédios.* O planejamento do layout das instalações deve ser visto como uma extensão natural da discussão a respeito do planejamento de processo vista no Capítulo 4. No planejamento do processo, escolhemos ou projetamos a maquinaria de processamento; em conjunto com o projeto de produtos, determinamos as características dos materiais que compõem os produtos, e introduzimos nova tecnologia nas operações. Através dos layouts de instalações, a disposição física desses processos dentro e ao redor dos prédios, o espaço necessário para a operação desses processos e o espaço necessário para as funções de apoio são fornecidos. À medida que o planejamento do processo e o planejamento do layout das instalações progridem, há um contínuo intercâmbio de informações entre essas duas atividades de planejamento, porque uma afeta a outra.

A Tabela 7.1 relaciona alguns objetivos de layouts de instalações para operações de manufatura, armazenamento, serviços e escritório. A tabela é organizada de forma a mostrar primeiro os objetivos das operações de manufatura, os quais também se aplicam a operações de armazenamento, serviços e escritório, e, então, os objetivos adicionais.

Uma cuidadosa leitura dos objetivos dos layouts de instalações apresentados na Tabela 7.1 sugere que o planejamento do layout das instalações deve estar vinculado à estratégia de operações. Lembre-se do Capítulo 2 que as prioridades competitivas que a função de operações pode fornecer são: baixos custos de produção, entregas rápidas e no tempo certo, produtos e serviços de alta qualidade e flexibilidade de produto e volume. Os objetivos apresentados na Tabela 7.1 que motivam nossos layouts de instalações devem refletir uma combinação apropriada dessas prioridades competitivas, que são incorporadas em nossa estratégia de operações. *A estratégia de operações impulsiona o planejamento do layout das instalações, e os layouts de instalações servem como um meio para realizarmos as estratégias de operações.*

Layouts de Instalações de Manufatura

Entre os muitos objetivos dos layouts de instalações, o foco central da maioria dos layouts de manufatura é minimizar o custo de processamento, transporte e armazenamento de materiais ao longo do sistema de produção.

Manuseio de Materiais

Os materiais usados na manufatura são muitos: matérias-primas, componentes comprados, materiais em processo, produtos acabados, materiais de embalagem, suprimentos de manutenção e conserto, sucata e resíduos. Esses materiais variam muito em termos de tamanho, forma, propriedades químicas e características especiais.

TABELA 7.1 — ALGUNS OBJETIVOS DOS LAYOUTS DE INSTALAÇÕES

Objetivos para os Layouts da Operação de Manufatura

Fornecer suficiente capacidade de produção.
Reduzir o custo de manuseio de materiais.
Adequar-se a restrições do lugar e do prédio.
Garantir espaço para as máquinas de produção.
Permitir elevada utilização e produtividade da mão-de-obra, das máquinas e do espaço.
Fornecer flexibilidade de volume e produto.
Garantir espaço para banheiros e outros cuidados pessoais dos empregados.
Garantir segurança e saúde para os empregados.
Permitir facilidade de supervisão.
Permitir facilidade de manutenção.
Atingir os objetivos com o menor investimento de capital.

Objetivos Adicionais para os Layouts da Operação de Armazenamento

Promover carga e descarga eficiente de veículos de transporte.
Fornecer eficaz retirada de estoques, atendimento de encomendas e carga unitizada.
Permitir facilidade de contagem de estoques.
Promover acurados registros dos estoques.

Objetivos Adicionais para Layouts da Operação de Serviços

Proporcionar conforto e conveniência para o cliente.
Fornecer um ambiente atraente para os clientes.
Permitir uma exposição atraente das mercadorias.
Reduzir o tempo de locomoção do pessoal ou dos clientes.
Proporcionar privacidade nas áreas de trabalho.
Promover a comunicação entre as áreas de trabalho.
Proporcionar rotação de estoques para os produtos que estão na prateleira.

Objetivos Adicionais para os Layouts da Operação de Escritório

Reforçar a estrutura da organização.
Reduzir o tempo de locomoção do pessoal ou dos clientes.
Proporcionar privacidade nas áreas de trabalho.
Promover a comunicação entre as áreas de trabalho.

A maior parte dessa variedade nas características dos materiais é determinada pelas decisões quanto ao projeto do produto. O layout das instalações é diretamente afetado pela natureza desses materiais. Materiais grandes e volumosos, pesados, fluidos, sólidos, flexíveis e não flexíveis e os que exigem manuseio especial para protegê-los de condições como calor, frio, umidade, luz, poeira, fogo e vibração — todos afetam o layout das instalações para manuseio, armazenamento e processamento desses materiais.

*Um **sistema de manuseio de materiais** é a rede inteira de transportes que recebe materiais, armazena materiais em estoques, movimenta-os entre pontos de processamento dentro de prédios e entre prédios, e finalmente deposita os produtos acabados nos veículos que os entregarão aos clientes.*

O projeto e o layout de prédios devem estar integrados com o projeto do sistema de manuseio de materiais. Por exemplo, se for necessário o uso de esteiras transportadoras aéreas, a estrutura do prédio deve ser forte o bastante para suportar a operação desses dispositivos. Similarmente, se cargas pesadas precisarem ser transportadas em caminhões, os pisos devem ter uma sustentação adequada para suportar a constante pressão do peso dessas cargas. Adicionalmente, os corredores devem ser suficientemente largos para acomodar empilhadeiras e outros dispositivos que percorrerão as áreas.

Dispositivos fixos, como, por exemplo, correias transportadoras, também devem ter espaço de piso garantido.

Certos princípios foram desenvolvidos para guiar o layout das instalações a fim de garantir o manuseio eficiente dos materiais. A Tabela 7.2 resume alguns desses fundamentos. A Tabela 7.3 descreve alguns dispositivos de manuseio de materiais. Cada um desses dispositivos tem suas próprias características e vantagens e desvantagens particulares. Os transportadores, por exemplo, são dispendiosos para comprar e tipicamente não requerem operadores, seguem rotas fixas e servem como dispositivos de armazenamento e contenção temporários. Os caminhões, por outro lado, são relativamente baratos para comprar, não seguem rotas fixas e fornecem maior flexibilidade de manuseio de materiais.

Capítulo 7 – Layout das Instalações

TABELA 7.2 — PRINCÍPIOS DO MANUSEIO DE MATERIAIS

1. Os materiais devem movimentar-se por entre a instalação em fluxos lineares, minimizando ziguezagues ou recuos.
2. Processos de produção relacionados devem ser organizados a fim de proporcionar fluxos lineares de materiais.
3. Dispositivos mecânicos de manuseio de materiais devem ser projetados e localizados, e localizações de armazenamento de materiais devem ser escolhidas a fim de que o esforço humano despendido em dobrar, alcançar, levantar e caminhar seja minimizado.
4. Materiais pesados ou volumosos devem ser movimentados na distância mais curta quando da localização dos processos que os usam próximo às áreas de recebimento e embarque.
5. O número de vezes que cada material é movimentado deve ser minimizado.
6. A flexibilidade do sistema deve prever situações inesperadas, como, por exemplo, quebras de equipamentos de manuseio de materiais, mudanças na tecnologia do sistema de produção e expansão futura de capacidades de produção.
7. O equipamento móvel deve transportar cargas completas todas as vezes; cargas vazias ou parciais devem ser evitadas.

Os quatro tipos básicos de layouts para instalações de manufatura são: processo, produto, manufatura celular (MC) e posição fixa.

LAYOUTS POR PROCESSO

Layouts por processo, layouts funcionais ou job shops, como às vezes são chamados, são projetados para acomodar a variedade de projetos de produto e etapas de processamento. Veja a Figura 4.5 no Capítulo 4. *Se a instalação de manufatura produzir uma variedade de produtos personalizados em lotes relativamente pequenos, a instalação provavelmente usará um layout por processo.*

TABELA 7.3 — EQUIPAMENTOS DE MANUSEIO DE MATERIAIS

Dispositivos automáticos de transferência — Máquinas que agarram materiais automaticamente, seguram-nos firmemente enquanto operações são executadas e movem-nos para outros locais.

Contêineres e dispositivos manuais

Carros manuais — Vagões não motorizados, carrinhos de mão e carretas empurradas por trabalhadores.

Paletes — Estruturas básicas sobre as quais materiais são empilhados e movimentados por veículos de manuseio de materiais.

Caixas de carga — Recipientes para peças soltas ou materiais para armazenamento e movimento entre as operações.

Caixas de arame — Recipientes para armazenar peças soltas de materiais em estoque.

Transportadores

Correia — Correia motorizada, usualmente feita de tecido emborrachado ou tecido ou trama de metal sobre uma estrutura rígida.

Corrente — Corrente motorizada que arrasta materiais ao longo de uma base inclinada.

Pneumático — Um elevado volume de ar flui através de um tubo, carregando os materiais ao longo do fluxo de ar.

Roletes — Caixas, peças grandes ou cargas unificadas rolam sobre uma série de cilindros montados sobre uma estrutura rígida. Os cilindros podem ser motorizados ou não.

Tubo — Correntes com lâminas raspadeiras circulares que arrastam materiais dentro de um tubo.

Guindastes — Guinchos montados sobre trilhos aéreos, rodas ou trilhos ao nível do chão; eles levantam, pesam e transportam materiais grandes e pesados.

Elevadores — Um tipo de guindaste que, embora numa posição fixa, eleva materiais, usualmente entre andares de prédios.

Tubulações — Tubos fechados que transportam líquido por meio de bombas ou da gravidade.

Plataformas giratórias — Dispositivos que seguram, preparam ou giram materiais ou peças de operação a operação.

Caminhões — Veículos impulsionados por energia elétrica, diesel, gasolina ou gás liquefeito de petróleo equipados com caçambas, garfos, braços ou outros dispositivos de contenção.

Sistemas de veículos automatizados — Trens não tripulados, caminhões com transportador mecânico e transportadores de carga unitizada (veja o Capítulo 5).

Os layouts por processo tipicamente usam máquinas de uso geral que podem ser mudadas rapidamente para novas operações para diferentes projetos de produto. Essas máquinas normalmente são organizadas de acordo com o tipo de processo que é executado. Por exemplo, toda a usinagem seria feita em um departamento, toda a montagem em outro departamento e toda a pintura em outro. O equipamento de manuseio de material geralmente consiste em empilhadeiras e outros veículos móveis que levam em conta a variedade de caminhos seguidos ao longo das instalações pelos produtos produzidos. Os trabalhadores em layouts por processo devem mudar e adaptar-se rapidamente ao grande número de operações a serem executadas em cada lote de produtos em particular que é produzido. Esses trabalhadores devem ser altamente habilitados e requerem instruções de trabalho e supervisão técnica intensivas. Os layouts por processo exigem planejamento contínuo, programação e funções de controle para assegurar uma quantidade ótima de trabalho em cada departamento e em cada estação de trabalho. Os produtos permanecem no sistema de produção por períodos de tempo relativamente longos, e grandes estoques de produtos em processo estão presentes.

LAYOUTS POR PRODUTO

Layouts por Produto são idealizados para acomodar somente alguns poucos projetos de produto. Veja a Figura 4.4 do Capítulo 4. Esses layouts são projetados para permitir um fluxo linear de materiais ao longo da instalação que faz os produtos. As montadoras de automóveis são bons exemplos de instalações que usam um layout por produto.

Os layouts por produto tipicamente usam máquinas especializadas que são configuradas uma única vez para executar uma operação específica durante um longo período de tempo em um produto. A mudança dessas máquinas para um novo projeto de produto requer longos períodos de inatividade e é dispendiosa. As máquinas normalmente são organizadas em departamentos de produção. Dentro de um departamento de produção, diversos processos, como, por exemplo, estamparia, usinagem e montagem, poderiam ser executados.

Os trabalhadores em layouts por produto executam repetidamente uma estreita variedade de atividades em somente alguns projetos de produto. A quantidade de habilidade, treinamento e supervisão necessária é pequena. Não obstante as atividades de planejamento e a planificação de tarefas associadas com esses layouts serem complexas, elas não são contínuas. Ao contrário, o planejamento e planificação de tarefas tendem a ser feitos intermitentemente à medida que as mudanças ocorrem.

LAYOUTS DE MANUFATURA CELULAR

Na **manufatura celular (MC)** as máquinas são agrupadas em células, e as células funcionam de uma forma bastante semelhante a uma ilha de layout de produção dentro de uma job shop maior ou layout por processo. A Figura 4.7 no Capítulo 4 ilustra um layout de MC. Cada célula num layout de MC é formada para produzir uma única **família de peças** — algumas peças, tendo todas características comuns, o que comumente significa que elas exigem as mesmas máquinas e têm configurações similares. O Instantâneo da Indústria 7.1 descreve a natureza das células de manufatura na indústria atual.

Não obstante o layout de uma célula poder assumir muitas formas diferentes, o fluxo de peças tende a ser mais similar a um layout por produto do que a uma job shop. Um layout de MC seria tentado por estas razões:

- As mudanças de máquinas são simplificadas.
- Os períodos de treinamento para os trabalhadores são abreviados.
- Os custos de manuseio de materiais são reduzidos.
- Peças podem ser feitas e embarcadas mais rapidamente.
- É necessário menos estoque de produtos em processo.
- A produção é mais fácil de automatizar.

Ao desenvolver um layout de MC, o primeiro passo é a **decisão quanto à formação da célula**, que é a decisão inicial sobre quais máquinas de produção e quais peças agrupar numa célula. Em seguida, as máquinas são organizadas dentro de cada célula.

INSTANTÂNEO DA INDÚSTRIA 7.1

A NATUREZA DAS CÉLULAS DE MANUFATURA

1. A maioria das aplicações de MC está na produção metalúrgica, em ferramentarias e em operações de fabricação de equipamentos metálicos.
2. As células normalmente são formadas tomando-se a produção de peças de uma job shop existente.
3. O número de peças produzidas nas células é uma porcentagem relativamente pequena da produção total. A produção nas células tem uma média de apenas 10% do total. Cerca da metade das empresas relata que 5% ou menos de suas horas de máquina foram gastas em células. As células usualmente aparecem como ilhas dentro de job shops maiores.
4. Tanto empresas pequenas como grandes usam células de manufatura. Os usuários têm um total de 300 a 17 mil empregados e de 90 a 3 mil máquinas.
5. Tamanhos moderados de lote de peças são produzidos nas células: uma média de aproximadamente 6 mil peças de cada tipo por ano e um tamanho de lote médio em torno de 750 peças.
6. O número de células num layout de MC é relativamente pequeno. A média é de aproximadamente cinco ou seis, e cerca de 1/3 das empresas tem três ou menos células.
7. O número de máquinas de produção por célula é relativamente pequeno. A média é de seis, e aproximadamente a metade das empresas tem entre quatro e seis máquinas por célula. As peças raramente são encaminhadas para todas as máquinas numa célula.
8. Há relativamente poucos trabalhadores dentro das células. Para as células que têm trabalhadores, a faixa é de 2 a 15.

Fonte: Gaither, N., G. V. Frazier e J. C. Wei. "From Job Shops to Manufacturing Cells". *Production and Inventory Management Journal*, n. 4 (quarto trimestre de 1990).

LAYOUTS POR POSIÇÃO FIXA

Algumas empresas de manufatura e construção usam um layout para organizar o trabalho, o qual localiza o produto numa posição fixa e transporta trabalhadores, materiais, máquinas e subcontratados até o produto e a partir do produto. A Figura 7.1 demonstra esse tipo de layout. Montagem de mísseis e de grandes aeronaves, construção naval e construção de pontes são exemplos de **layouts por posição fixa**. Layouts por posição fixa são usados quando um produto é muito volumoso, grande, pesado ou frágil. A natureza de posição fixa do layout minimiza a quantidade necessária de movimento de produto.

LAYOUTS HÍBRIDOS

A maioria das instalações de manufatura usa uma combinação de tipos de layout. A Figura 7.2 mostra esse **layout híbrido** em que os departamentos são organizados de acordo com os tipos de processos, mas o produto flui através de um layout por produto. Como outro exemplo de layout híbrido, considere a montagem final do avião comercial da Boeing (modelos 737, 747, 757, 767 e 777). Durante a montagem final, cada unidade de aeronave é localizada num espaço de montagem de posição fixa. Entretanto, a cada dois ou três dias, cada aeronave é retirada de seu espaço e empurrada até o espaço de montagem seguinte, onde diferentes tarefas de montagem são executadas. Desse modo, não obstante um avião ser montado durante dois ou três dias numa localização fixa, ele percorre de seis a oito diferentes espaços de montagem, numa forma de layout por produto.

É importante entender as características, vantagens e desvantagens de cada tipo básico de layout.

NOVAS TENDÊNCIAS NOS LAYOUTS DE MANUFATURA

A Tabela 7.4 compara e contrasta layouts tradicionais com layouts modernos. *Em geral, os layouts de fabricantes americanos tradicionalmente têm sido projetados para produzir elevada utilização de trabalhador e de máquina, ao passo que os layouts modernos são projetados para obter qualidade e flexibilidade, que é a capacidade de mudar rapidamente para diferentes modelos de produto ou para diferentes volumes de produção.*

À medida que as instalações americanas se movem rumo a layouts modernos, estas tendências podem ser observadas:

- Layouts de manufatura celular dentro de layouts por processo maiores.

Parte II – Decisões Estratégicas

FIGURA 7.1   LAYOUT POR POSIÇÃO FIXA

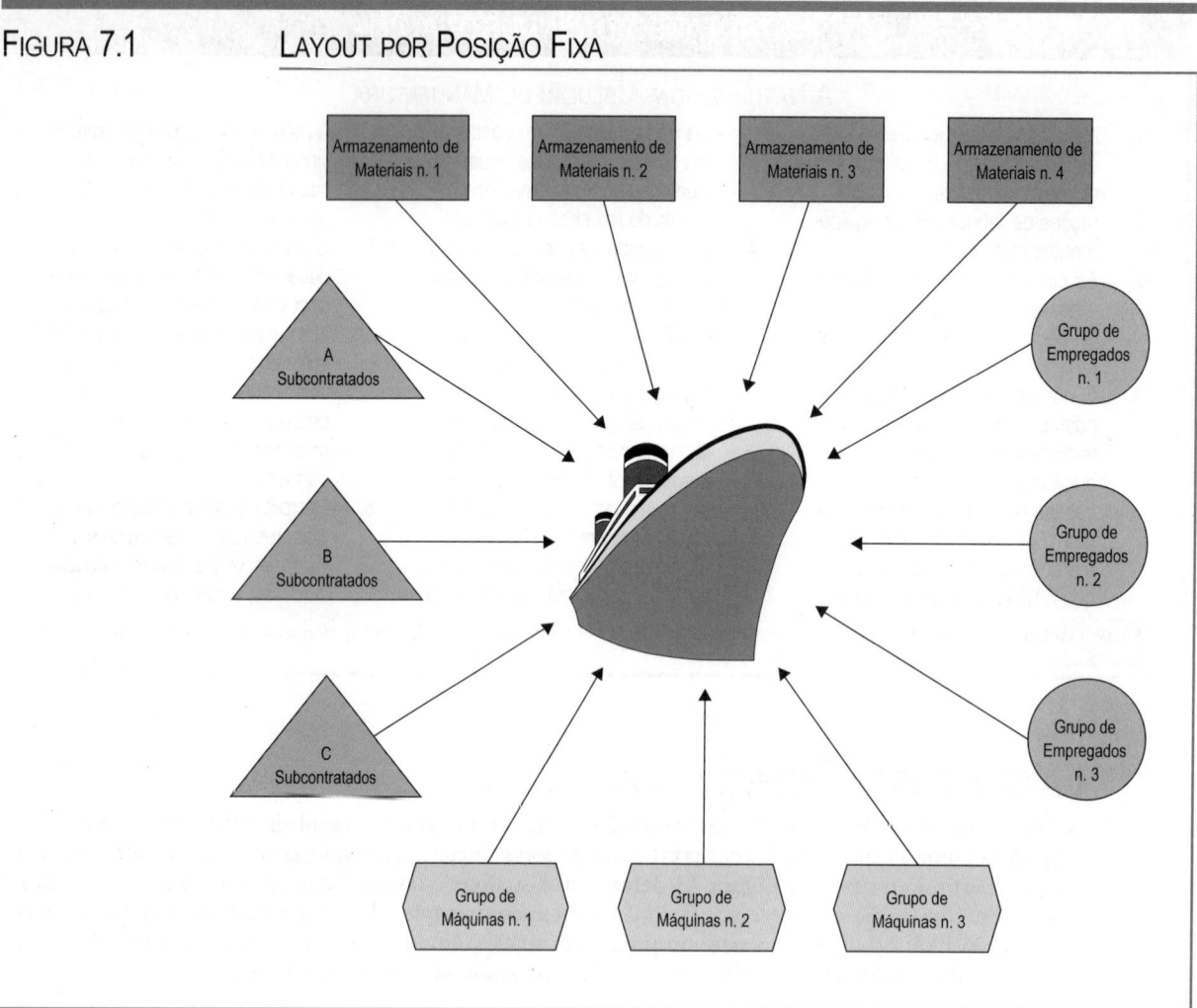

FIGURA 7.2   LAYOUT HÍBRIDO PARA PRODUZIR OS PRODUTOS X E Y

TABELA 7.4 — LAYOUTS AMERICANOS TRADICIONAIS *VERSUS* LAYOUTS MODERNOS

Características dos Layouts Tradicionais

Objetivo principal: Elevada utilização de máquina e trabalhador.

Meios de atingir o objetivo: Longos turnos de produção, atribuição de tarefas fixas para os trabalhadores a fim de obter os benefícios da especialização de mão-de-obra, estoques para se resguardar de quebras de máquinas, taxas de produção constantes e produtos com defeitos separados para posterior retrabalho, e grandes máquinas de produção que são mantidas em sua capacidade de utilização total.

Aparência dos layouts: Plantas da instalação de manufatura muito grandes, extensas áreas reservadas para estoques, muito espaço usado para longas esteiras transportadoras e outros dispositivos de manuseio de materiais, grandes máquinas de produção que exigem muito espaço de piso, linhas de produção lineares ou em forma de L e espaço de piso geralmente subutilizado.

Características dos Layouts Modernos

Objetivo principal: Qualidade do produto e flexibilidade, que é a capacidade de modificar volumes de produção rapidamente e mudar para modelos de produto diferentes.

Meios de atingir o objetivo: Trabalhadores treinados em muitas tarefas, forte investimento em manutenção preventiva, máquinas pequenas facilmente mudadas para diferentes modelos de produto, trabalhadores estimulados a exercer a iniciativa de resolver problemas de qualidade e outros problemas de produção quando eles ocorrem, trabalhadores e máquinas mudados quando necessário para resolver problemas de produção, linhas de produção desaceleradas e quebras de máquina ou problemas de qualidade resolvidos quando ocorrem, manutenção de pouco estoque e estações de trabalho dispostas próximo umas das outras.

Aparência dos layouts: Plantas da instalação de manufatura relativamente pequenas, layouts compactos e estreitamente dispostos, grande porcentagem de espaço de piso usado para produção, menos espaço de piso ocupado por estoques ou dispositivos de manuseio de materiais e linhas de produção em forma de U.

- Equipamentos de manuseio de materiais automatizados, especialmente sistemas automatizados de armazenamento e recuperação, sistemas de veículos automatizados, dispositivos automáticos de transferência e plataformas giratórias.
- Linhas de produção em forma de U que permitem que os trabalhadores vejam a linha inteira e se desloquem facilmente entre as estações de trabalho. Essa forma permite a rotação de trabalhadores entre as estações de trabalho ao longo das linhas para aliviar o tédio e equilibrar o trabalho realizado por cada operador entre as estações de trabalho. Adicionalmente, um trabalho em equipe e moral elevado tendem a surgir, porque os trabalhadores são agrupados em áreas menores e a comunicação e o contato social são encorajados.
- Mais áreas de trabalho abertas com um número menor de divisórias ou outros obstáculos, para dar visão das estações de trabalho adjacentes.
- Layouts de fábrica menores e mais compactos. Com mais automação, como, por exemplo, robôs, menos espaço precisa ser fornecido aos trabalhadores. As máquinas podem ser dispostas mais perto umas das outras, e os materiais e produtos percorrem distâncias mais curtas.
- Menos espaço é fornecido para armazenamento de estoques no layout.

O Instantâneo da Indústria 7.2 descreve como uma empresa economizou espaço de piso convertendo-se para um moderno layout de fábrica.

ANALISANDO LAYOUTS DE INSTALAÇÕES DE MANUFATURA

Talvez a técnica de layout de instalação mais comum seja a de usar **gabaritos** ou **modelos** bi ou tridimensionais numa planta do piso do prédio. Os analistas deslocam esses modelos de máquinas, escrivaninhas e outros equipamentos — os quais são colocados na mesma escala que a planta do piso do prédio — para várias posições. Eles obtêm um layout detalhado no qual materiais e pessoal podem fluir de um lugar para outro com poucas viagens. O método da planta/gabarito de piso é especialmente útil quando se desenvolve um layout de um departamento ou prédio existente ou quando a configuração do prédio é conhecida.

Outras técnicas de layout diferem entre três tipos de layout: layouts por processo e armazenamento, layouts por produto e layouts de MC.

Instantâneo da Indústria 7.2

Fábrica da Boeing Economiza Espaço

A Boeing Company tem uma fábrica em Spokane, Washington, que produz principalmente painéis de assoalho e dutos de ar para seus jatos comerciais. Em 1996, a Boeing fez substanciais mudanças nos projetos de processo e layout de instalações nessa fábrica. Como parte de uma transformação global na empresa para modernas abordagens de produção, a fábrica de Spokane foi convertida para uma instalação de manufatura enxuta. Grande parte do estoque de produtos em processo foi eliminada, os fluxos de peças foram redesenhados e as máquinas foram deslocadas para mais perto umas das outras.

Além dos tempos de execução mais breves e custos operacionais mais baixos, um resultado foi a liberação de espaço de piso no prédio.

Antes da conversão para a manufatura enxuta, o prédio inteiro era utilizado. Depois da conversão, cerca da metade do espaço de piso de manufatura foi liberado. Vários meses depois, metade do prédio ainda estava vazia e apresentava um dilema interessante para o gerente de fábrica e para a Boeing: o que fazer com o espaço vazio.

Planejando Layouts por Processo e Armazenamento

Análise da seqüência de operações, análise de diagrama de blocos e análise de distância da carga freqüentemente são usadas para desenvolver esses layouts.

Análise da Seqüência de Operações *A análise da seqüência de operações desenvolve um bom esquema para a organização de departamentos, analisando graficamente o problema de layout.* O Exemplo 7.1 desenvolve a organização de 10 departamentos numa instalação de manufatura. Ele mostra como determinamos a localização de departamentos operacionais em relação uns aos outros quando a forma externa ou dimensões do prédio não são fatores limitadores.

Exemplo 7.1

Análise da Seqüência de Operações

A Red Crystal Glass Products Company produz seis produtos que são transportados entre 10 departamentos operacionais dentro de sua planta de produção. A Red Crystal planeja construir uma nova instalação. É dada a Bill Dewey essa importante tarefa de layout. O número total de produtos que percorrem os departamentos operacionais da Red Crystal por mês é crucial para o novo layout:

Código do Departamento	Descrição do Departamento	Esmeril 5	Pintura 6	Furadeira 7	Retrabalho 8	Envernizamento 9	Expedição e Recepção 10
1	Sopro e moldagem	1.000		5.000		3.000	3.000
2	Tratamento térmico	2.000	2.000				3.000
3	Gargalo		2.000			2.000	
4	Embalagem	1.000		4.000			5.000
5	Esmeril		2.000				
6	Pintura					2.000	
7	Furadeira				1.000		
8	Retrabalho						1.000
9	Envernizamento						
10	Expedição e Recebimento						

Bill quer desenvolver um diagrama esquemático dos fluxos de produto entre os departamentos operacionais.

Solução

Primeiro, desenvolva um diagrama esquemático inicial com círculos representando os departamentos e linhas representando a viagem do produto entre os departamentos. O número de produtos que viajam por mês entre os departamentos é escrito nas linhas:

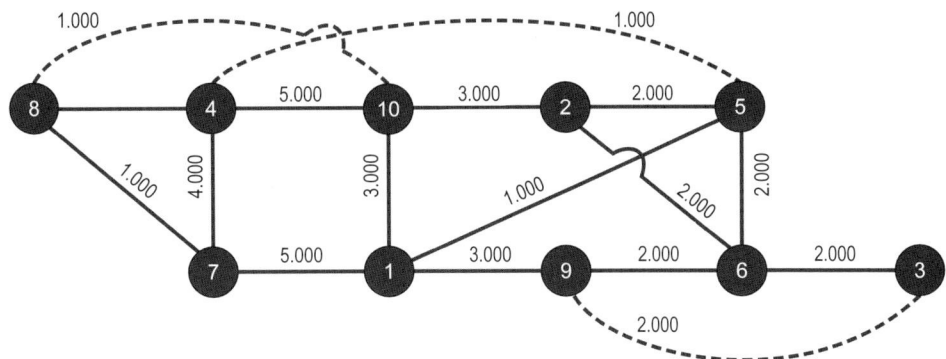

Em seguida, reestruture o diagrama esquemático inicial para mover os departamentos para mais perto um do outro quando o número de movimentos de produto entre eles for elevado, e mova departamentos para formar uma figura quase retangular. Por exemplo, no diagrama acima, o Departamento 3 poderia ser movido para mais perto do Departamento 9, e os Departamentos 8, 9 e 6 poderiam ser deslocados para formar uma figura retangular:

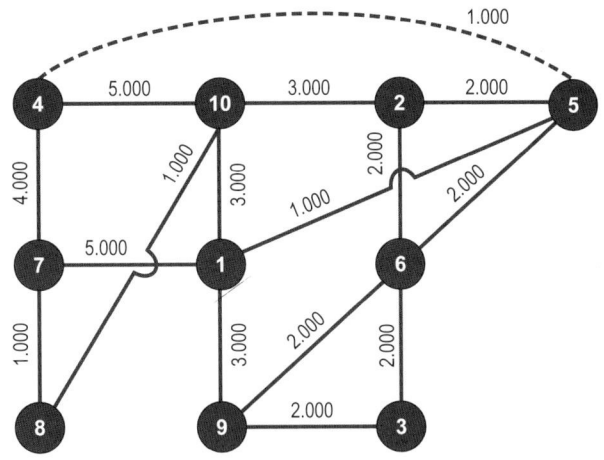

Uma inspeção adicional desse diagrama esquemático não revela qualquer outra mudança nas localizações de departamentos que melhore substancialmente o layout.

Análise de Diagrama de Blocos O Exemplo 7.2 pega o diagrama esquemático final do Exemplo 7.1 e desenvolve *uma **análise de diagrama de blocos**, a qual define a forma e as dimensões gerais do prédio e a localização das fronteiras departamentais interiores.*

Exemplo 7.2

Análise de Diagrama de Blocos

Bill Dewey, da Red Crystal Glass Products Company, deseja desenvolver um layout departamental a partir do diagrama esquemático do Exemplo 7.1. Embora o diagrama esquemático final desse exemplo mostre as relações gerais entre os departamentos operacionais, Bill deve determinar agora as dimensões do prédio e onde as fronteiras departamentais internas se situarão. As áreas necessárias para cada departamento são cruciais para o layout desse prédio:

Departamento	Área Necessária (m²)	Departamento	Área Necessária (m²)
1. Sopro e moldagem	20	6. Pintura	20
2. Tratamento térmico	20	7. Furadeira	40
3. Gargalo	40	8. Retrabalho	20
4. Embalagem	40	9. Envernizamento	20
5. Esmeril	90	10. Remessa e recebimento	20

Bill deseja usar uma análise de diagrama de blocos para desenvolver um layout departamental para o novo prédio da Red Crystal.

Solução

Primeiro, use o diagrama esquemático final do Exemplo 7.1 e coloque cada círculo que representa departamentos no centro de um quadrado com a mesma área relativa mostrada na tabela acima:

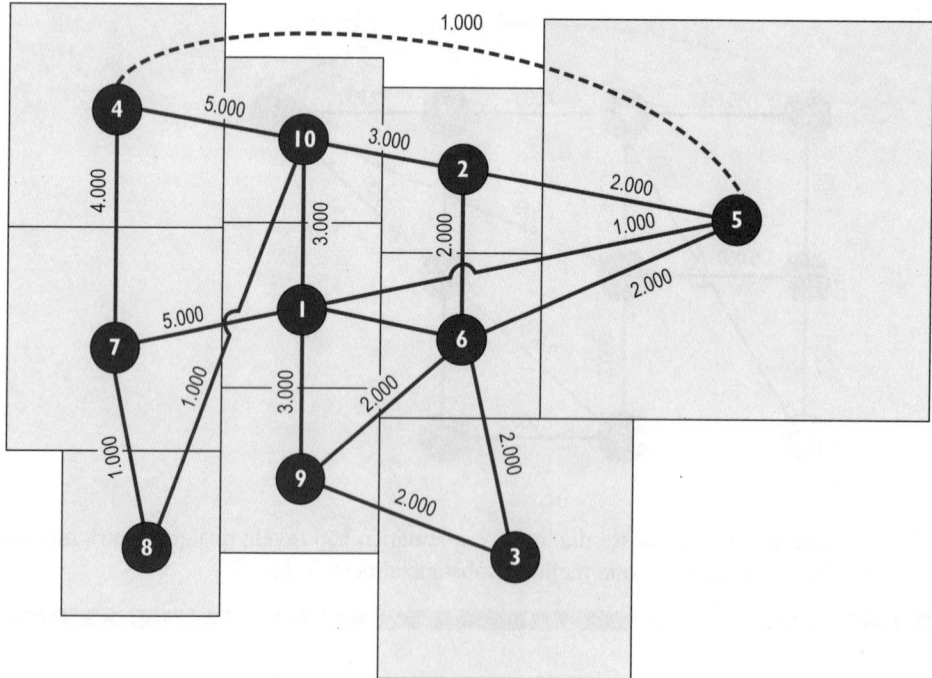

Note que esse layout mantém as mesmas relações gerais entre os departamentos, mas a fronteira externa da instalação é demasiadamente irregular para um projeto de prédio prático.

Capítulo 7 – Layout das Instalações

Em seguida, varie as formas dos departamentos para encaixar o sistema num prédio retangular enquanto mantém a área necessária de cada departamento e as mesmas relações entre departamentos:

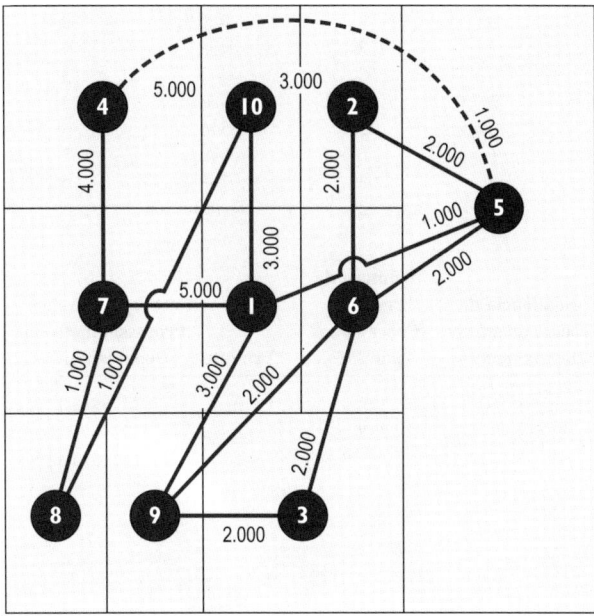

Esse diagrama de blocos é o layout departamental proposto por Bill para o novo prédio.

Análise de Distância da Carga A análise de seqüência de operações e a análise de diagrama de blocos não desenvolvem layouts ótimos — *os melhores* —, mas somente bons layouts. Não é incomum que essas análises desenvolvam dois ou mais diagramas de blocos alternativos, cada um dos quais aparentemente bom. *A **análise de distância da carga** é útil para comparar layouts alternativos para identificar aquele no qual os produtos ou materiais fazem a menor viagem por período de tempo.*

O Exemplo 7.3 compara duas dessas alternativas de layout.

EXEMPLO 7.3

ANÁLISE DE DISTÂNCIA DA CARGA

Duas alternativas de layout são mostradas a seguir. Os produtos da instalação, a viagem deles por entre os departamentos e as distâncias entre departamentos para cada alternativa de layout também são exibidos. Qual alternativa de layout minimiza a viagem de produtos ao longo da instalação?

Layout A

8	4	10	2	5
3	7	1	9	6

Layout B

7	1	9	6	3
4	10	2	5	8

Combinação de Movimento Departamental	Distância entre Departamentos (metros)		Combinação de Movimento Departamental	Distância entre Departamentos (metros)	
	Layout A	Layout B		Layout A	Layout B
1–5	9	9	3–9	9	6
1–7	3	3	4–5	9	9
1–9	3	3	4–7	3	3
1–10	3	3	4–10	3	3
2–5	3	3	5–6	3	3
2–6	6	6	6–9	3	3
2–10	3	3	7–8	6	15
3–6	12	3	8–10	6	9

Produto	Seqüência de Processamento nos Departamentos	Número de Produtos Processados por Mês	Produto	Seqüência de Processamento nos Departamentos	Número de Produtos Processados por Mês
a	1–5–4–10	1.000	d	1–7–8–10	1.000
b	2–6–3–9	2.000	e	2–5–6–9	2.000
c	2–10–1–9	3.000	f	1–7–4–10	4.000

Solução

1. Primeiro, compute o total de viagens para cada produto ao longo de cada alternativa de layout:

Produto	Seqüência de Processamento nos Departamentos	Compute a Distância para Cada Produto (metros)	
		Layout A	Layout B
a	1–5–4–10	9 + 9 + 3 = 21	9 + 9 + 3 = 21
b	2–6–3–9	6 + 12 + 9 = 27	6 + 3 + 6 = 15
c	2–10–1–9	3 + 3 + 3 = 9	3 + 3 + 3 = 9
d	1–7–8–10	3 + 6 + 6 = 15	3 + 15 + 9 = 27
e	2–5–6–9	3 + 3 + 3 = 9	3 + 3 + 3 = 9
f	1–7–4–10	3 + 3 + 3 = 9	3 + 3 + 3 = 9

2. Em seguida, compute a distância total que cada produto percorre por mês ao longo de cada alternativa de layout:

Produto	Número de Produtos Processados por Mês	Distância por Produto (metros)		Distância por Produto (metros)	
		Layout A	Layout B	Layout A	Layout B
a	1.000	21	21	21.000	21.000
b	2.000	27	15	54.000	30.000
c	3.000	9	9	27.000	27.000
d	1.000	15	27	15.000	27.000
e	2.000	9	9	18.000	18.000
f	4.000	9	9	36.000	36.000
			Total	171.000	159.000

3. O Layout B resulta na menor distância total percorrida por mês pelos produtos ao longo das instalações.

As três técnicas de análise de layout apresentadas — análise da seqüência de operações, de diagrama de blocos e de distância da carga — podem ser usadas quer o analista deva ou não restringir-se à configuração do prédio. Essas análises iniciam com os processos de produção e desenvolvem um layout que define a configuração do prédio. Mas em geral devemos iniciar com um prédio e desenvolver um layout dentro dessas dimensões. Os locais às vezes são tão pequenos ou tão incomuns que somente alguns tipos de prédios são possíveis. Os departamentos existentes devem ser expandidos. Todos esses são apenas exemplos de *relayouts*. Em casos como esses, é inevitável que iniciemos com a configuração do prédio e retornemos ao projeto de layout.

Analisando Layouts com Computador Muitos programas de computador têm sido escritos para desenvolver e analisar layouts por processo. Três das análises de computador mais conhecidas são os ALDEP, o CORELAP e o CRAFT.

Os ALDEP — programas automatizados de projeto de layouts — e o CORELAP — planejamento computadorizado do layout da relação — usam essencialmente os mesmos procedimentos e a mesma lógica. Em vez de considerar o número de produtos que fluem entre os departamentos, esses programas usam **classificações de proximidade**, que é uma medida relativa de quão desejável é que os departamentos fiquem próximos entre si. Esses programas maximizam a classificação da proximidade total para todos os departamentos ao mesmo tempo que obedecem as características necessárias do prédio. Problemas de layout muito grandes e complexos são exeqüíveis, e cada análise produz um layout de blocos plotado da planta do piso.

O CRAFT — alocação relativa computadorizada de instalações — usa o mesmo procedimento básico e a mesma lógica que as análises de seqüência de operações e diagrama de blocos. O CRAFT minimiza o custo total de manuseio de materiais por período de tempo para o layout. Os movimentos de materiais por período de tempo são convertidos para custo por período de tempo para os movimentos de cada material entre os departamentos. Os analistas introduzem um layout de blocos inicial, e o CRAFT modifica o layout inicial até que nenhuma melhoria de custo seja possível. Novos layouts iniciais produzem diferentes layouts CRAFT, de forma que alguma experimentação é aconselhável. O programa também pode manipular problemas de layout grandes e complexos ao mesmo tempo que se atém às características complexas do prédio. As saídas do programa são um layout de blocos plotado da planta do piso e o custo dos layouts.

Estes e outros programas de computador podem poupar tempo e esforço em problemas de layout grandes e complexos, mas suas saídas são somente o início de um layout acabado. Seus layouts devem ser aprimorados manualmente e verificados quanto à lógica, e as máquinas e outros elementos do layout normalmente devem ser ajustados manualmente com gabaritos e recortes (*cutouts*).

PLANEJANDO LAYOUTS POR PRODUTO

A análise de linhas de produção é o foco central da análise de layouts por produto. O projeto de produto e a demanda por mercado para os produtos determinam, em última análise, as etapas do processo tecnológico e a capacidade de produção necessária das linhas de produção. O número de trabalhadores, máquinas assistidas ou não assistidas e ferramentas necessárias para atender a demanda por mercado devem então ser determinados. Essa informação é fornecida pelo balanceamento de linha.

Balanceamento de Linha O **balanceamento de linha** é a análise de linhas de produção que divide igualmente o trabalho a ser feito entre estações de trabalho, a fim de que o número de estações de trabalho necessário na linha de produção seja minimizado. A Tabela 7.5 resume alguns dos termos freqüentemente usados no balanceamento de linha, e a Tabela 7.6 descreve o procedimento de balanceamento de linha.

As linhas de produção têm estações de trabalho e centros de trabalho organizados em seqüência ao longo de uma linha reta ou curva. Uma estação de trabalho é uma área física onde um trabalhador com ferramentas, um trabalhador com uma ou mais máquinas, ou uma máquina não assistida, como um robô, executa um dado conjunto de tarefas. Um centro de trabalho é um pequeno agrupamento de estações de trabalho idênticas, com cada estação de trabalho executando o mesmo conjunto de tarefas. A meta da análise de linhas de produção é determinar quantas estações de trabalho ter e quais tarefas atribuir a cada uma a fim de que o número mínimo de trabalhadores e a quantidade mínima de máquinas sejam usados para fornecer a quantidade necessária de capacidade.

TABELA 7.5	TERMINOLOGIA DA ANÁLISE DE LINHA DE PRODUÇÃO
	Tarefas — Elementos de trabalho. *Pegar um lápis, posicionar o lápis sobre um papel para escrever e escrever um número* é um exemplo de tarefa.
	Precedência da tarefa — A seqüência ou ordem em que as tarefas devem ser executadas. A precedência de cada tarefa é conhecida a partir de uma lista das tarefas que devem precedê-la imediatamente.
	Duração de tarefa — A quantidade de tempo necessária para que um trabalhador bem treinado ou máquina não assistida executem uma tarefa. As durações de tarefas normalmente são expressas em minutos.
	Tempo de ciclo — O tempo em minutos entre cada produto que sai no final de uma linha de produção.
	Tempo produtivo por hora — O número de minutos que uma estação de trabalho opera em média a cada hora. Uma estação de trabalho pode não estar em operação devido a coisas como almoço, tempo pessoal, quebras, troca de ferramental e paralisações.
	Estação de trabalho — Localização física onde um conjunto particular de tarefas é executado. As estações de trabalho normalmente são de dois tipos: uma estação de trabalho tripulada, que contém um trabalhador que opera máquinas e/ou ferramentas, e uma estação de trabalho não tripulada, que contém máquinas não assistidas, como robôs.
	Centro de trabalho — Uma localização física onde duas ou mais estações de trabalho idênticas estão localizadas. Se for exigido que mais de uma estação de trabalho ofereça capacidade de produção suficiente, elas serão combinadas para formar um centro de trabalho.
	Número de estações de trabalho em funcionamento — A quantidade de trabalho a ser feita no centro de trabalho, expressa em número de estações de trabalho. Vinte e oito horas de trabalho num centro de trabalho durante um turno de 8 horas seria equivalente a 28/8, ou 3,5 estações de trabalho operando.
	Número mínimo de estações de trabalho — O menor número de estações de trabalho que podem fornecer a produção exigida, calculada por: $$\frac{\text{Soma de todos os tempos de tarefas}}{\text{Tempo de ciclo}} = \frac{\text{Soma de todos os tempos de tarefas} \times \text{Demanda por hora}}{\text{Tempo produtivo por hora}}$$
	Número real de estações de trabalho — O número total de estações de trabalho necessárias na linha de produção inteira, calculadas como o próximo valor inteiro mais alto do número de estações de trabalho em funcionamento.
	Utilização — A porcentagem de tempo que uma linha de produção trabalha. Isso normalmente é calculado por: $$\frac{\text{Número mínimo de estações de trabalho}}{\text{Número real de estações de trabalho}} \times 100$$

TABELA 7.6	PROCEDIMENTO DE BALANCEAMENTO DE LINHA
	1. Determine quais tarefas devem ser executadas para concluir uma unidade de um produto em particular.
	2. Determine a ordem ou seqüência na qual as tarefas devem ser executadas.
	3. Trace um diagrama de precedência. Este é um fluxograma em que círculos representam tarefas e setas interligadas representam a precedência.
	4. Estime as durações das tarefas.
	5. Calcule o tempo de ciclo.
	6. Calcule o número mínimo de estações de trabalho.
	7. Use uma regra heurística para atribuir tarefas a estações de trabalho de forma que a linha de produção seja balanceada.

Se um produto precisa chegar ao final de uma linha de produção a cada 5 minutos, então o tempo de ciclo será de 5 minutos. Isso significa que deve haver um produto saindo de cada estação de trabalho a cada 5 minutos ou menos. Se o tempo necessário para realizar as tarefas numa estação de trabalho fosse 10 minutos, então duas estações de trabalho seriam combinadas num centro de trabalho a fim de que dois produtos saíssem do centro a cada 10 minutos, ou o equivalente a um produto a cada 5 minutos. Por outro

FIGURA 7.3 — Passos na Regra Heurística de Utilização* Incremental

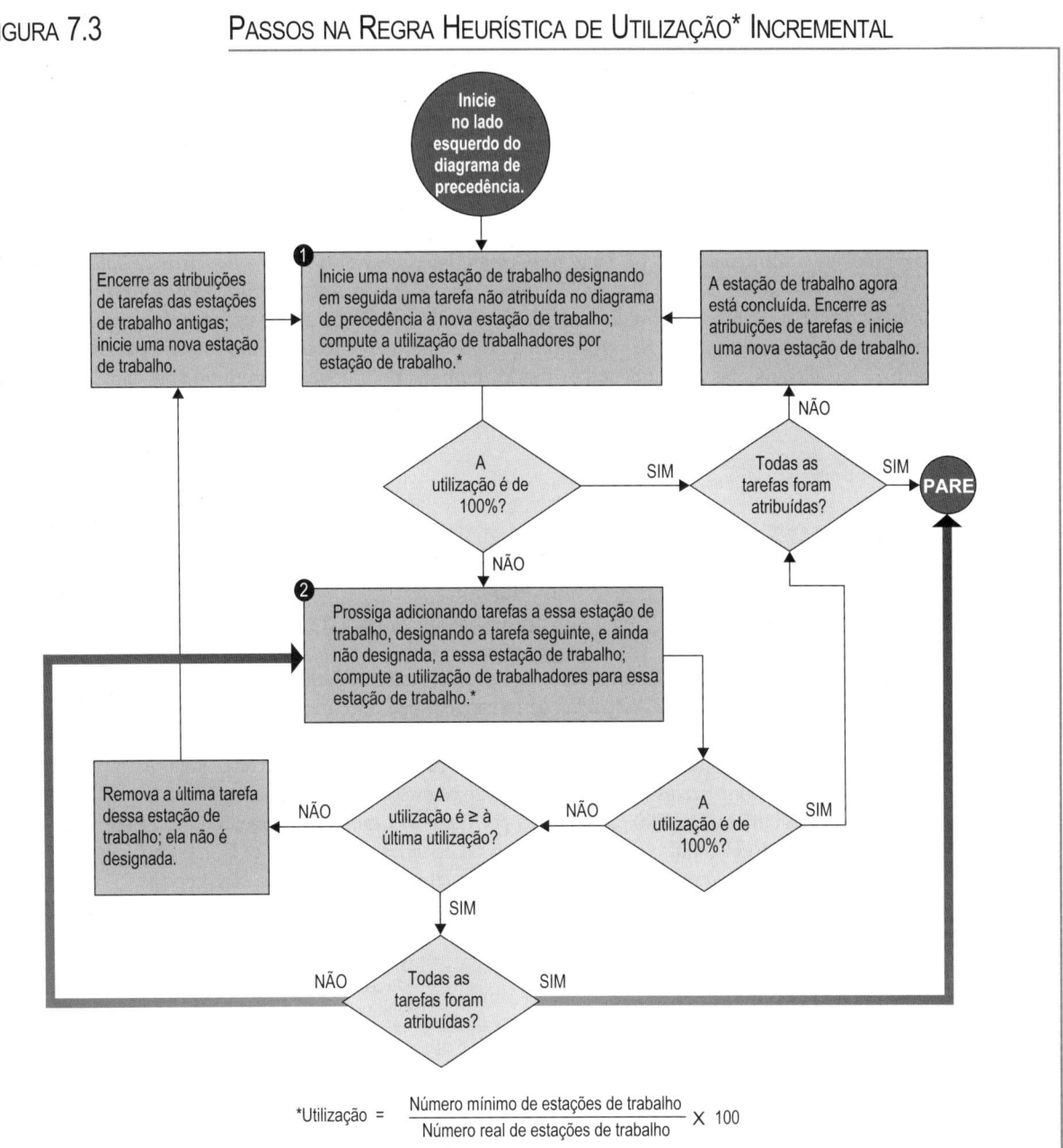

*Utilização = $\dfrac{\text{Número mínimo de estações de trabalho}}{\text{Número real de estações de trabalho}} \times 100$

lado, se a quantidade de trabalho atribuída a uma estação de trabalho fosse somente 4 minutos, essa estação de trabalho trabalharia 4 minutos e permaneceria ociosa 1 minuto. É praticamente impossível atribuir tarefas a estações de trabalho de forma que cada uma produza um produto em exatamente 5 minutos. Ao balancear a linha, nosso objetivo é atribuir tarefas a estações de trabalho a fim de que haja menos tempo ocioso. Isso significa designar tarefas a estações de trabalho e centros de trabalho de forma que um produto acabado seja concluído muito próximo do tempo de ciclo, mas sem ultrapassá-lo.

Regras Heurísticas do Balanceamento de Linha Os pesquisadores têm usado a programação linear, a programação dinâmica e outros modelos matemáticos para estudar problemas de balanceamento de linha. Mas esses métodos estão além do escopo deste livro e normalmente não são úteis para resolver grandes problemas. Métodos heurísticos, ou baseados em regras simples, têm sido usados para desenvolver boas soluções para esses problemas — não soluções ótimas, mas soluções muito boas. Entre esses métodos estão a regra heurística de utilização incremental (IU) e a regra heurística da tarefa de mais longa duração (LTT).

A **regra heurística de utilização incremental** simplesmente acrescenta tarefas a uma estação de trabalho em ordem de precedência de tarefa, uma de cada vez, até que a utilização seja de 100% ou se observe que tal utilização caia. Então, esse procedimento é repetido na estação de trabalho seguinte para as tarefas restantes.

A Figura 7.3 ilustra os passos seguidos na regra heurística de utilização incremental, e o Exemplo 7.4 usa essa regra heurística para balancear uma linha de produção que monta calculadoras manuais. *A regra heurística de utilização incremental é apropriada quando uma ou mais durações de tarefas são iguais ou maiores do que a duração do ciclo. Uma importante vantagem dessa regra heurística é que ela é capaz de resolver problemas de balanceamento de linha independentemente da duração das tarefas em relação à duração do ciclo.* Sob certas circunstâncias, entretanto, essa regra heurística cria a necessidade de ferramentas e equipamentos extras. Se o foco principal da análise for minimizar o número de estações de trabalho ou se as ferramentas e equipamentos usados na linha de produção forem ou abundantes ou baratos, essa regra heurística será apropriada.

EXEMPLO 7.4

BALANCEAMENTO DE LINHA COM A REGRA HEURÍSTICA DE UTILIZAÇÃO INCREMENTAL

A Textech, uma grande fabricante de produtos eletrônicos, monta calculadoras manuais Modelo AT75 em sua fábrica de Midland, Texas. As tarefas de montagem que devem ser executadas em cada calculadora são mostradas a seguir. O abastecimento das peças usadas nessa linha de montagem é feito pelo pessoal do setor de manuseio de materiais em caixas de peças usadas em cada tarefa. As montagens são transportadas por correias transportadoras entre as estações de trabalho. A Textech quer que essa linha de montagem produza 540 calculadoras por hora: **a)** Compute a duração do ciclo por calculadora em minutos. **b)** Compute o número mínimo de estações de trabalho. **c)** Como você combinaria as tarefas em estações de trabalho para minimizar o tempo ocioso? Avalie sua proposta.

Tarefa	Tarefas Que Devem Preceder Imediatamente	Tempo para Executar a Tarefa (Minutos)
A. Colocar quadro (*frame*) de circuitos num gabarito.		0,18
B. Colocar o Circuito n. 1 no quadro.	A	0,12
C. Colocar Circuito n. 2 no quadro.	A	0,32
D. Colocar Circuito n. 3 no quadro.	A	0,45
E. Anexar circuitos ao quadro.	B,C,D	0,51
F. Soldar conexões de circuito ao controle de circuito central.	E	0,55
G. Colocar montagem de circuito no quadro interno da calculadora.	F	0,38
H. Anexar montagem de circuito ao quadro interno da calculadora.	G	0,42
I. Colocar e anexar mostrador no quadro interno.	H	0,30
J. Colocar e anexar teclado no quadro interno.	I	0,18
K. Colocar e anexar a parte superior da calculadora no quadro interno.	J	0,36
L. Colocar e anexar montagem de força no quadro interno.	J	0,42
M. Colocar e anexar parte inferior da calculadora no quadro interno.	K,L	0,48
N. Testar integridade do circuito.	M	0,30
O. Colocar a calculadora e o material impresso na caixa.	N	0,39
	Total	5,36

Solução

a) Compute o tempo de ciclo por calculadora:

$$\text{Tempo de ciclo} = \frac{\text{Tempo produtivo/hora*}}{\text{Demanda/hora}} = \frac{54 \text{ minutos/hora}}{540 \text{ calculadoras/hora}} = 0{,}100 \text{ minuto/calculadora}$$

b) Compute o número mínimo de estações de trabalho:

$$\text{Número mínimo de estações de trabalho} = \frac{\text{Soma das durações das tarefas} \times \text{Demanda por hora}}{\text{Tempo produtivo por hora}}$$

$$= \frac{5{,}36 \text{ minutos/calculadora} \times 540 \text{ calculadoras/hora}}{54 \text{ minutos por hora}}$$

$$= 53{,}60 \text{ estações de trabalho}$$

c) Balanceie a linha:

1. Primeiro, trace um diagrama de precedência para a linha de produção. Esse diagrama usa círculos para representar as tarefas e setas para mostrar relações de precedência.

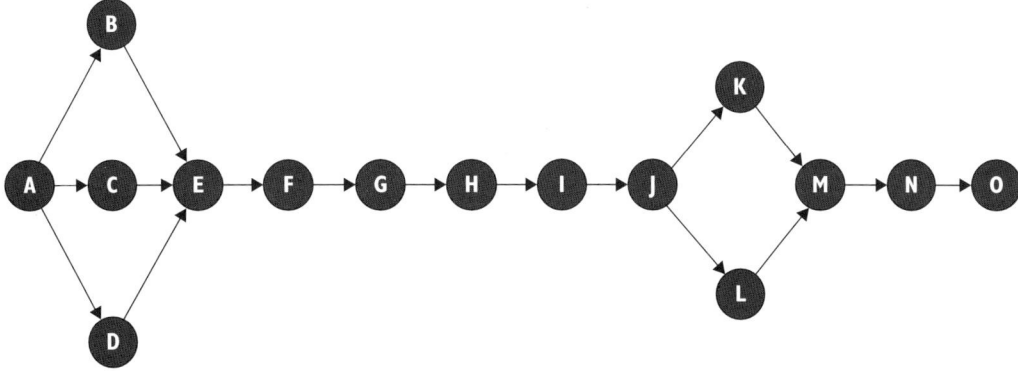

2. Em seguida, atribua tarefas a centros de trabalho. Isto é feito seguindo-se a seqüência de tarefas (D deve suceder A, G deve suceder F e assim por diante), e a regra heurística de utilização incremental é usada para agrupar as tarefas em centros de trabalho. Nesse método, as tarefas são combinadas em seqüência até que a utilização do centro de trabalho seja 100% ou até que se observe que a utilização do centro de trabalho caia, e então um novo centro de trabalho é iniciado. Examine o Centro de Trabalho 1 e note que consideramos primeiro a Tarefa A isoladamente [(1,8 ÷ 2,0) × 100 = 90%]; consideramos em seguida a Tarefa A e a Tarefa B juntas [(3,0 ÷ 3,0) × 100 = 100%]. Uma vez que essa combinação tem uma utilização de 100%, as Tarefas A e B são combinadas no Centro 1 e agora nos mudamos para o Centro 2. No Centro 2, quando as Tarefas C, D e E são combinadas uma tarefa de cada vez, a utilização do centro de trabalho se eleva de 80% para 96,3% e para 98,5%; mas, quando a Tarefa F é adicionada a C, D e E, a utilização cai para 96,3%. O Centro de Trabalho 2 inclui, portanto, as Tarefas C, D e E, e passamos ao Centro de Trabalho 3.

(1) Centro de Trabalho	(2) Tarefa	(3) Minutos/Calculadora	(4) Número de Estações de Trabalho em Funcionamento [(3) ÷ tempo de ciclo]	(5) Número Real de Estações de Trabalho Necessárias	(6) Utilização de Estações de Trabalho [(4) ÷ (5)] × 100
1	A	0,18	1,8	2	90,0%
	A,B	0,18 + 0,12 = 0,30	3,0	3	100,0

(1) Centro de Trabalho	(2) Tarefa	(3) Minutos/Calculadora	(4) Número de Estações de Trabalho em Funcionamento [(3) ÷ tempo de ciclo]	(5) Número Real de Estações de Trabalho Necessárias	(6) Utilização de Estações de Trabalho [(4) ÷ (5)] × 100
2	C	0,32	3,2	4	80,0
2	C,D	0,32 + 0,45 = 0,77	7,7	8	96,3
2	C,D,E	0,32 + 0,45 + 0,51 = 1,28	12,8	13	98,5
2	C,D,E,F	0,32 + 0,45 + 0,51 + 0,55 = 1,83	18,3	19	96,3
3	F	0,55	5,5	6	91,7
3	F,G	0,55 + 0,38 = 0,93	9,3	10	93,0
3	F,G,H	0,55 + 0,38 + 0,42 = 1,35	13,5	14	96,4
3	F,G,H,I	0,55 + 0,38 + 0,42 + 0,30 = 1,65	16,5	17	97,0
3	F,G,H,I,J	0,55 + 0,38 + 0,42 + 0,30 + 0,18 = 1,83	18,3	19	96,3
4	J	0,18	1,8	2	90,0
4	J,K	0,18 + 0,36 = 0,54	5,4	6	90,0
4	J,K,L	0,18 + 0,36 + 0,42 = 0,96	9,6	10	96,0
4	J,K,L,M	0,18 + 0,36 + 0,42 + 0,48 = 1,44	14,4	15	96,0
4	J,K,L,M,N	0,18 + 0,36 + 0,42 + 0,48 + 0,30 = 1,74	17,4	18	96,7
4	J,K,L,M,N,O	0,18 + 0,36 + 0,42 + 0,48 + 0,30 + 0,39 = 2,13	21,3	22	96,8
				Total 55	

3. Resuma a designação de tarefas a estações de trabalho na linha de produção:

Tarefas em centros de trabalho	A,B	C,D,E	F,G,H,I	J,K,L,M,N,O	
Centros de trabalho	①→	②→	③→	④	
Número real de estações de trabalho	3,0	13,0	17,0	22,0	55,0 Total

4. Em seguida, compute a eficiência do balanceamento:

$$\text{Utilização} = \frac{\text{Número mínimo de estações de trabalho}}{\text{Número real de estações de trabalho}} = \frac{53,6}{55} = 0,975 \text{ ou } 97,5\%$$

* Uma média de seis minutos por hora, neste exemplo, não é produtiva devido a horários de almoço, tempo pessoal, quebra de máquinas e tempos de preparação e paralisação.

TABELA 7.7   PASSOS NA REGRA HEURÍSTICA DA TAREFA DE MAIS LONGA DURAÇÃO

1. Admitamos que i = 1, onde *i* é o número da estação de trabalho que está sendo formada.

2. Faça uma lista de todas as tarefas candidatas a serem designadas a essa estação de trabalho. Para que uma tarefa esteja nessa lista, ela deve satisfazer a todas estas condições:
   a) Ela não pode ter sido designada anteriormente a essa ou a qualquer outra estação de trabalho.
   b) Suas predecessoras imediatas devem ter sido atribuídas a essa estação de trabalho ou a uma anterior.
   c) A soma dessa duração de tarefa e de todas as outras durações de tarefa já designadas à estação de trabalho deve ser inferior ou igual à duração do ciclo. Se nenhuma candidata puder ser encontrada, vá para o Passo 4.

3. Designe a tarefa da lista que tem a mais longa duração à estação de trabalho.

4. Encerre a atribuição de tarefas à Estação de Trabalho *i*. Isso pode ocorrer de duas maneiras. Se não houver qualquer tarefa na lista de candidatas para a estação de trabalho mas ainda houver tarefas a serem designadas, defina i = i + 1 e retorne ao Passo 2. Se não houver mais tarefas não designadas, o procedimento estará completo.

A **regra heurística da tarefa de mais longa duração** adiciona tarefas a uma estação de trabalho, uma de cada vez, na ordem de precedência das tarefas. Se for necessário que a escolha seja entre duas ou mais tarefas, aquela que tem a mais longa duração será adicionada. Isso tem o efeito de designar o mais rápido possível as tarefas que são mais difíceis de encaixar numa estação de trabalho. Tarefas com durações menores são então reservadas para se aprimorar a solução.

Essa regra heurística segue os passos mostrados na Tabela 7.7, e o Exemplo 7.5 usa essa regra heurística para balancear uma linha de produção.

Exemplo 7.5

Balanceamento de Linha com a Regra Heurística da Tarefa de Mais Longa Duração

Tarefa	Predecessora Imediata	Tempo de Tarefa (minutos)
a	—	0,9
b	a	0,4
c	b	0,6
d	c	0,2
e	c	0,3
f	d,e	0,4
g	f	0,7
h	g	1,1
	Total	4,6

Usando a informação contida na tabela acima:

a) Trace um diagrama de precedência.
b) Supondo que 55 minutos por hora sejam produtivos, compute o tempo de ciclo necessário para obter 50 unidades por hora.
c) Determine o número mínimo de estações de trabalho.
d) Atribua tarefas a estações de trabalho usando a regra heurística da tarefa de mais longa duração.
e) Calcule a utilização da solução em *d*.

Solução

a) Trace um diagrama de precedência:

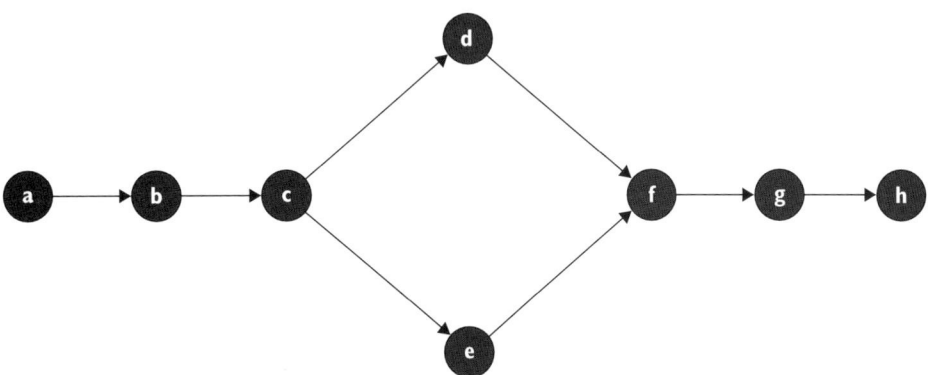

b) Supondo que 55 minutos por hora sejam produtivos, compute a duração do ciclo necessário para obter 50 unidades por hora:

$$\text{Duração do ciclo} = \frac{\text{Tempo produtivo por hora}}{\text{Demanda por hora}} = \frac{55 \text{ minutos por hora}}{50 \text{ produtos por hora}}$$

$$= 1,1 \text{ minuto por produto}$$

c) Determine o número mínimo de estações de trabalho:

$$\frac{\text{Número mínimo de}}{\text{estações de trabalho}} = \frac{\text{Soma de todas as durações de tarefa} \times \text{Demanda por hora}}{\text{Tempo produtivo por hora}}$$

$$= \frac{4,6 \text{ minutos/produto} \times 50 \text{ produtos/hora}}{55 \text{ minutos/hora}}$$

$$= 4,2 \text{ estações de trabalho}$$

d) Atribua tarefas a estações de trabalho usando a regra heurística da tarefa de mais longa duração:

(1) Estação de Trabalho	(2) Lista de Candidatas	(3) Tarefa Atribuída Tarefa	(4) Duração de Tarefa	(5) Soma das Durações de Tarefa	(6) Duração de Tarefa Não Atribuída na Estação de Trabalho [1,1 − (5)]
1	a	a	0,9	0,9	0,2
2	b	b	0,4	0,4	0,7
2	c	c	0,6	1,0	0,1
3	d,e*	e	0,3	0,3	0,8
3	d	d	0,2	0,5	0,6
3	f	f	0,4	0,9	0,2
4	g	g	0,7	0,7	0,4
5	h	h	1,1	1,1	0

*A tarefa *e* é escolhida em vez de *d* porque sua duração é mais longa.

Resuma a designação de tarefas a estações de trabalho na linha de produção:

Tarefa nas Estações de Trabalho	Estação de Trabalho
a	1
b,c	2
e,d,f	3
g	4
h	5

e) Calcule a utilização da solução em *d*:

$$\text{Utilização} = \frac{\text{Número mínimo de estações de trabalho}}{\text{Número real de estações de trabalho}} \times 100$$

$$= \frac{4,2}{5} \times 100$$

$$= 84\%$$

Capítulo 7 – Layout das Instalações

As condições de uso da regra heurística da tarefa de mais longa duração são:

1. Ela somente pode ser usada quando cada uma e todas as durações de tarefa forem inferiores ou iguais à duração do ciclo.
2. Não pode haver quaisquer estações de trabalho duplicadas.

Uma vez que não há qualquer estação de trabalho duplicada, a quantidade de ferramentas e equipamentos necessária é baixa. Essa restrição também reduz a flexibilidade, entretanto. *Se cada uma e todas as durações de tarefa forem inferiores ou iguais à duração do ciclo, e se o foco principal da análise de linhas de produção for minimizar o número de estações de trabalho e a quantidade necessária de ferramentas e equipamentos, então essa regra heurística seria apropriada.* Felizmente, há modificações dessa regra heurística que permitem que as durações de tarefa sejam maiores do que a duração do ciclo.

As duas regras heurísticas de balanceamento de linha aqui discutidas são representativas de um grande grupo dessas regras. Desse modo, qual delas você deve usar ao analisar um problema de balanceamento de linha em particular? Em algumas circunstâncias, talvez você não possa fazer uma escolha, porque somente uma regra heurística pode acomodar as condições que se enquadram em seu problema de balanceamento de linha. Por exemplo, se uma ou mais durações de tarefa forem iguais ou maiores do que a duração do ciclo, talvez você tenha de escolher a regra heurística de utilização incremental. Outras vezes, se o uso de mais de uma regra heurística parecer apropriado, seria aconselhável que você usasse diversas regras heurísticas de balanceamento de linha no mesmo problema para determinar qual produz a melhor solução.

Questões de Balanceamento de Linha Antigamente as linhas de produção eram projetadas de forma que as correias transportadoras acompanhassem a velocidade do trabalho dos empregados. Pesquisa e o bom senso mostraram que os trabalhadores não gostam desse arranjo. Eles tendem a se tornar mais irritáveis no trabalho, ausentam-se mais freqüentemente, produzem produtos de qualidade inferior e são menos saudáveis dentro e fora do trabalho. Poucas empresas atualmente colocam propositadamente trabalhadores sob o controle de máquinas; os trabalhadores devem estar no controle.

Os problemas de balanceamento de linha desta seção forneceram a demanda por mercado ou volume de produção como um dado. Se o volume de produção for conhecido, o tempo de ciclo pode ser calculado, e esse valor impulsiona as regras heurísticas de balanceamento de linha que determinam o número de estações de trabalho necessário. Esta nem sempre é a natureza dos problemas reais na indústria. Às vezes o número de estações de trabalho é dado, e a duração de ciclo é deduzida. Isso poderia ser feito experimentando-se diversos valores de duração do ciclo com uma das regras heurísticas de balanceamento de linha até que o número de estações de trabalho na solução coincidisse com o número de estações de trabalho desejado. Em outros momentos é usada uma faixa de valores para a duração do ciclo para orientar o balanceamento de linha numa busca por uma solução que minimize o tempo ocioso.

Variar a duração do ciclo pode ter importantes resultados no balanceamento. Uma duração de ciclo mais longa — a mesma coisa que um volume de produção mais baixo — pode resultar num número menor de estações de trabalho e menos usinagem e maquinaria, o que pode levar a custos de produção mais baixos. Essa tática pode exigir a manutenção de um estoque maior de produtos acabados, que pode esgotar-se em períodos de pico de demanda. Uma duração de ciclo mais breve — a mesma coisa que um volume de produção mais elevado — poderia, supostamente, levar a menos tempo ocioso e menores custos de produção. Dessa forma, é aconselhável uma experimentação com diferentes durações de ciclo a fim de que eles resultem em baixos custos de produção e menos investimento de capital em máquinas e ferramentas.

Mudanças na demanda por produto, modificações de máquinas, variações no aprendizado e treinamento de empregados e outras mudanças podem levar a linhas de produção desbalanceadas ou com capacidade insuficiente ou excessiva. Em todos esses casos, as linhas de produção devem ser rebalanceadas. **Rebalancear uma linha de produção** é uma ocorrência comum, porque mudar é um fato da vida. A maioria das linhas de produção é rebalanceada diversas vezes por ano. Esse rebalanceamento significa certa dose de interrupção na produção, porque são afetados os layouts e empregos dos trabalhadores. Mas continuar operando uma linha de produção desatualizada e desbalanceada com a capacidade incorreta pode causar custos de produção elevados, mau serviço ao cliente e estoques excessivos.

Balanceamento de Linha de Modelo Misto Até agora em nosso estudo supomos que cada linha de montagem produz somente um modelo de produto. Se mais de um modelo precisar ser produzido na mesma linha de produção, surgem estas questões:

1. Quanto de cada modelo de produto devemos produzir quando ele for colocado em produção (qual deve ser o tamanho do lote de produção)?
2. Em qual seqüência ou ordem os lotes de produção dos modelos devem ser colocados em produção?

Se os lotes de produção forem muito grandes, os modelos serão colocados em produção infreqüentemente, os estoques em processo de alguns modelos serão muito elevados, e o estoque dos outros modelos poderá se exaurir antes de ser colocado em produção. Se os lotes de produção forem demasiadamente pequenos, o constante tumulto de tantas mudanças de modelos poderá elevar os custos de manufatura.

Algumas companhias dividem o número de cada modelo de produto incluído no plano de produção mensal pelo número de dias de trabalho no mês. Isso dá o número médio de cada modelo a ser produzido a cada dia. Esse número é então dividido diversas vezes durante o dia e colocado em seqüência com os outros modelos. Como uma ilustração simples, digamos que precisemos produzir 300 modelos A e 200 modelos B por dia e que a duração do ciclo para A seja 45 segundos e para B seja 65 segundos. Considerando que as mudanças de máquina sejam desprezíveis, eis um esquema de balanceamento de modelo fixo para essa ilustração:

Seqüência do Modelo	20 Bs	30 As
Tempo de produção (minutos)	21,67	22,50
Tempo de seqüência (minutos)	44,17	
Seqüências por turno de 8 horas	10	
Tempo de funcionamento da linha de produção por turno (minutos)	441,7	
Tempo de inatividade da linha de montagem por turno (minutos)	38,3	

Nesse esquema, 20 modelos B seriam seguidos por 30 modelos A, e essa seqüência seria repetida a cada 44,17 minutos, 10 vezes durante um turno de 8 horas. A linha de montagem operaria 441,7 minutos em 8 horas, deixando 38,3 minutos para manutenção, pausas de empregados e outros propósitos. Ao fornecer 10 seqüências de 20 modelos B e 30 modelos A em cada turno de 8 horas, é garantido aos empregados uma variedade em seu trabalho quando eles mudam de modelo. Além disso, desde que os lotes de produção de cada modelo são relativamente pequenos, não ocorrem excessivos estoques em processo.

Planejando Layouts de Manufatura Celular Conforme discutimos anteriormente, a questão inicial que deve ser resolvida nos layouts de MC é a decisão quanto à formação da célula: quais máquinas são designadas a células de manufatura e quais peças serão produzidas em cada célula? Se as vantagens da manufatura celular se materializarem, essa decisão inicial será crucial. O Exemplo 7.6 ilustra os elementos essenciais dessas decisões.

Há duas exigências fundamentais para que as peças sejam feitas em células:

1. A demanda para as peças deve ser suficientemente elevada e estável, de forma que tamanhos de lote moderados das peças possam ser produzidos periodicamente.
2. As peças que estão em consideração devem ser capazes de ser agrupadas em famílias de peças. Dentro de uma família de peças, as peças devem ter características físicas similares e, dessa forma, elas exigem operações de produção similares.

No Exemplo 7.6 supomos que cinco peças sofreram um exame detalhado a fim de que a natureza da demanda das mesmas cumprisse o primeiro requisito acima. Além disso, supomos que as peças foram escolhidas de forma a exigir operações de produção similares. A exigência das mesmas máquinas é talvez o mais forte indício de que as peças têm operações de produção similares.

A solução do Exemplo 7.6 resultaria em quatro das peças e cinco das máquinas serem atribuídas a duas células. Uma das peças, a 5, é uma peça excepcional, o que significa que ela não pode ser feita inteiramente dentro de uma única célula. As alternativas para produzir essa peça são:

1. **Produzir a Peça 5 transportando lotes da peça entre as duas células.** A vantagem dessa alternativa é que a utilização de máquina (a porcentagem de tempo em que as máquinas operam) das células seria mais elevada. As desvantagens são o custo adicional de manuseio de material e a complexidade adicional para coordenar a programação da produção entre as células.
2. **Subcontratar a produção da Peça 5 a fornecedores fora da empresa.** A vantagem dessa alternativa é que ela evita o custo adicional de manuseio de materiais e a complexidade da programação causada ao transportar lotes da peça entre as células. A desvantagem é que essa subcontratação pode custar mais do que para fazer a peça em casa.
3. **Produzir a Peça 5 na job shop, fora das células de MC.** A vantagem dessa alternativa é que ela evita o custo adicional de manuseio de materiais e a complexidade da programação causada ao transportar lotes da peça entre as células e qualquer custo adicional de subcontratação. A principal desvantagem dessa alternativa é que as máquinas nas quais a Peça 5 é feita (A, B, C e E) já estão nas células do layout MC. Se a Peça 5 tivesse de ser enviada novamente agora para a job shop para produção, máquinas adicionais talvez tivessem de ser compradas.
4. **Comprar uma Máquina A adicional para produzir a Peça 5 na segunda célula.** Essa alternativa atribuiria as Máquinas A e D e as Peças 1 e 2 à primeira célula e as Máquinas A, B, C e E e as peças 3, 4 e 5 à segunda célula. A vantagem dessa alternativa é que o custo adicional de manuseio de materiais e a complexidade de programação de transportar lotes da Peça 5 entre células são evitados. A desvantagem é o custo adicional de comprar outra Máquina A.

EXEMPLO 7.6

DECISÕES QUANTO À FORMAÇÃO DA CÉLULA NOS LAYOUTS DE MANUFATURA CELULAR

A Acme Machine Shop produz peças usinadas numa job shop. A Acme implementou recentemente um programa de tecnologia de grupo (GT — group technology) em sua fábrica, e agora está preparada para desenvolver células de manufatura celular em seu chão de fábrica. Os analistas de produção identificaram cinco peças que parecem cumprir os requisitos das peças apropriadas à MC: tamanhos de lote moderados, demanda estável e características físicas comuns. A matriz de peças-máquinas a seguir identifica as cinco peças (1 a 5) e as máquinas (A a E) nas quais as peças são produzidas atualmente na job shop. Os Xs nas células da matriz indicam as máquinas nas quais as peças devem ser produzidas. Por exemplo, a Peça 1 exige operações nas Máquinas A e D.

	Peças				
	1	2	3	4	5
A	X		X		X
B		X		X	X
C		X		X	X
D	X		X		
E		X		X	X

A Acme deseja designar as máquinas (e as peças que as máquinas fazem) a células de forma que, se uma peça for atribuída a uma célula, todas as máquinas necessárias para fazer a peça também estejam na mesma célula. Por exemplo, se a Peça 1 for designada a uma célula, as Máquinas A e D também deverão ser designadas a essa célula. Organize as máquinas e as peças nas células.

Solução

1. **Reorganize as linhas.** Primeiro, coloque as máquinas que produzem as mesmas peças em filas adjacentes. Note que as Máquinas A e D são exigidas pelas Peças 1 e 3; coloque essas duas máquinas nas duas primeiras linhas. Note também que as Máquinas B, C e E são exigidas pelas Peças 2, 4 e 5; coloque essas três máquinas nas três linhas seguintes.

Peças

		1	2	3	4	5
	A	X		X		X
	D	X		X		
Máquinas	B		X		X	X
	C		X		X	X
	E		X		X	X

2. **Reorganize as colunas.** Em seguida, reorganize as colunas de forma que as mesmas máquinas sejam colocadas em colunas adjacentes. Note que as Peças 1 e 3 exigem as Máquinas A e D; coloque essas duas peças nas duas primeiras colunas. Note também que as Peças 2, 4 e 5 exigem as Máquinas B, C e E; coloque essas três peças nas três colunas seguintes.

Peças

		1	3	2	4	5*
	A	X	X			X
	D	X	X			
Máquinas	B			X	X	X
	C			X	X	X
	E			X	X	X

Essa matriz de peças-máquinas contém a solução para esse problema de formação de célula. As Peças 1 e 3 devem ser produzidas na Célula 1 nas Máquinas A e D. As Peças 2 e 4 devem ser produzidas na Célula 2 nas Máquinas B, C e E. A Peça 5^* é chamada **peça excepcional**, porque não pode ser produzida dentro de uma única célula: ela exige a Máquina A, que está na Célula 1, e as Máquinas B, C e E, que estão na Célula 2.

A decisão quanto à formação de células que é analisada no Exemplo 7.6 não é muito complexa, mas vários problemas reais na indústria são resolvidos dessa maneira. Por exemplo, diversas células da Divisão de Sistemas de Defesa da Texas Instruments de Dallas, no Texas, foram formadas de uma maneira muito semelhante ao Exemplo 7.6. Em problemas mais complexos, questões como as seguintes devem ser resolvidas:

1. Se todas as peças não puderem ser divididas uniformemente entre as células e tivermos de escolher entre diversas peças aquelas que serão peças excepcionais, como decidiremos? Como decidir entre as peças? Na prática, a peça que tem o menor custo adicional de subcontratação ou o menor custo adicional para produzi-la na job shop é escolhida.
2. Se uma capacidade de produção inadequada estiver disponível para produzir todas as peças em células, quais peças devem ser feitas fora das células? Geralmente, as que exigem a menor capacidade e o maior custo adicional para subcontratar ou para fazer na job shop são escolhidas para permanecer nas células.

Acabamos de discutir diversas técnicas para desenvolver layouts para operações de manufatura. Vamos considerar agora os layouts para operações de serviço.

LAYOUTS DE INSTALAÇÕES DE SERVIÇO

Nos Capítulos 2 e 4 discutimos as características dos serviços e os processos usados para produzi-los. Três pontos resumem as discussões anteriores:

1. Talvez a característica mais distinta dos serviços seja sua diversidade.
2. Há três dimensões quanto ao tipo de serviço — projeto padrão ou personalizado, quantidade de contato com o cliente, e a combinação de bens físicos e serviços intangíveis.
3. Há três tipos de operações de serviços — quase-manufatura, o cliente como participante e o cliente como produto.

O entendimento desses três pontos nos prepara para uma discussão a respeito dos tipos de layouts para instalações de serviços.

TIPOS DE LAYOUTS DE INSTALAÇÕES DE SERVIÇO

Considere a natureza do serviço e a maneira pela qual esses negócios entregam ou conduzem seus serviços — empresas aéreas, bancos, varejistas, hospitais, restaurantes, seguros, negócios imobiliários, transporte rodoviário, lazer, telefonia e serviços públicos. Uma vez que há muita diversidade entre esses serviços, também tende a haver uma variedade nos tipos de layouts para as instalações de serviços.

Para a maioria dos negócios de serviços, uma característica torna no mínimo parte de suas operações diferente da maioria das operações de manufatura: o encontro entre o cliente e o serviço deve ser garantido. Esse encontro pode ser intenso, porque o cliente de fato torna-se parte do processo de produção, como nos hospitais, onde o serviço é realizado realmente no cliente. Ou o encontro pode ser menos intenso, como no comércio varejista, onde os clientes escolhem, pagam e levam bens físicos. Mas, independentemente da natureza e intensidade desse encontro, os layouts de instalações de serviços são drasticamente afetados.

Os layouts de instalações de serviços geralmente oferecem fácil acesso a essas propriedades e estacionamentos grandes, bem organizados e amplamente iluminados. Adicionalmente, essas instalações em geral têm passarelas amplas e bem projetadas para que as pessoas entrem e saiam dos estacionamentos. As entradas e saídas são bem marcadas, facilmente localizáveis e projetadas para acomodar um número grande de clientes durante os horários de pico. Portas automáticas e elevadores muitas vezes são oferecidos para facilitar o esforço físico de abrir portas e subir escadas quando as mercadorias precisam ser transportadas. Saguões ou outras áreas de recepção ou de guarda-volumes para clientes, filas de espera de clientes, balcões de serviço, caixas registradoras, estações de trabalho de empregados, exposições de mercadorias, corredores e decoração e iluminação atraentes devem ser oferecidos.

O grau em que as instalações de serviços devem oferecer esses recursos relacionados com o cliente nas instalações varia com a quantidade de envolvimento e contato com o cliente inerente ao serviço. Numa extremidade estão as operações de frente ou balcão de atendimento (*front-room*) de um banco, onde o layout inteiro da instalação deve ser projetado tendo em vista o cliente — estacionamento, facilidade de entrada e saída, áreas de espera agradáveis e áreas individualizadas para atendimento de clientes de contas de poupança e de empréstimos. Na outra extremidade estão as operações de retaguarda (*back-room*) de um banco, onde o layout das instalações deve ser projetado somente para as atividades de processamento das transações financeiras, atualização de registros de contas e geração de extratos bancários e relatórios, em que o foco principal são as tecnologias ou materiais físicos em processamento e a eficiência de produção. Esta é uma operação de serviço de quase-manufatura.

Esses dois extremos nos layouts das instalações de serviços são quase pontos finais de um *continuum*. Outras instalações de serviços mesclam as características desses dois layouts. Os layouts de restaurantes luxuosos, por exemplo, tipicamente enfatizam a recepção ao cliente e o atendimento individualizado, talvez mais do que o processamento e a preparação dos alimentos. Por outro lado, os layouts de restaurantes de fast-food tendem a enfatizar o processamento e a preparação dos alimentos em vez da recepção ao cliente e do atendimento individual.

A combinação de ênfase no cliente ou na tecnologia, processamento de materiais físicos e ênfase na eficiência de produção varia de acordo com o tipo de serviço oferecido e as estratégias de operação de cada organização.

ANALISANDO LAYOUTS DE INSTALAÇÕES DE SERVIÇO

Para muitas instalações de serviço, as técnicas para o layout de instalações de manufatura podem ser aplicadas diretamente. Para serviços que são do tipo quase-manufatura, como, por exemplo, os restaurantes de fast-food, operações de apoio de bancos, operações de manutenção de empresas aéreas, operações de armazenagem do comércio varejista e instalações de geração de eletricidade, estes tópicos são especialmente importantes:

- Os princípios de manuseio de materiais e equipamentos de manuseio de materiais, para todos os tipos de serviços em que o manuseio de bens físicos é significativo.
- O uso de gabaritos e modelos físicos para desenvolver plantas de piso de construção para todos os tipos de serviços.
- O uso de análise da seqüência de operações, análise de distância da carga e análise de layouts com computador para operações de serviço com produção focalizada no processo.
- O uso de balanceamento de linha para operações de serviço com produção focalizada no produto.

Para muitos serviços de todos os tipos, um elemento importante do layout das instalações são as filas de espera para os clientes. De especial importância é a questão da quantidade de espaço para os balcões de atendimento e para os clientes que esperam, e a previsão de filas de espera nos layouts de toda a instalação.

Essas questões são de importância crucial para os layouts de instalações de serviços. Estudaremos essas e outras questões relacionadas às filas de espera no Capítulo 12.

Para várias outras operações de serviços, os layouts de instalações são muito semelhantes aos layouts por processo na manufatura, porque eles devem permitir que os clientes sigam uma variedade de caminhos ao longo das instalações. Os layouts de hospitais, por exemplo, tipicamente permitem uma grande variedade nos passos que os pacientes seguem — cirurgia, radiologia, exames de laboratório, fisioterapia, tratamento intensivo, consultórios médicos, farmácia, salas de emergência, quartos dos pacientes e administração. Os departamentos dos hospitais são agrupados e localizados de acordo com seus processos, de uma maneira muito semelhante àquela como uma seção de máquinas dedicadas disporia suas máquinas e estações de trabalho.

Nos Exemplos 7.1 e 7.2 usamos a análise da seqüência de operações e a análise de diagrama de blocos para desenvolver bons layouts por processo na manufatura. Essa abordagem normalmente tenta minimizar:

- A distância total percorrida mensalmente pelos produtos entre os departamentos, ou
- O custo mensal do manuseio de materiais entre os departamentos.

Em muitos serviços, as razões para se colocar departamentos próximos uns dos outros são mais complexas, e muitas vezes elas têm objetivos múltiplos e são subjetivas. Num hospital, por exemplo, o centro radiológico deve ficar perto da sala de emergência, para permitir um diagnóstico rápido nos casos de emergência, e a farmácia deve ficar perto dos quartos dos pacientes, para permitir uma pronta distribuição de medicamentos. Similarmente, usar o mesmo equipamento ou pessoal, facilidade de comunicação, movimento lógico dos clientes, rapidez, segurança, contaminação ou outros fatores poderia ser uma razão legítima para esperar que dois departamentos estivessem próximos um do outro. Nesses casos, **classificações**

de proximidade são usadas para refletir a conveniência de se ter um departamento próximo ao outro. Métodos de tentativas, análise da seqüência de operações ou análise de diagrama de blocos poderiam então usar as classificações de proximidade para desenvolver bons layouts de instalações.

Ao usar essas abordagens, diversos objetivos podem ser estabelecidos: minimizar a soma de pares de classificações de proximidade, minimizar a distância total entre departamentos, ponderada pelo inverso das classificações de proximidade, e assim por diante.

O Exemplo 7.7 ilustra o uso de classificações de proximidade para desenvolver um layout de instalações. O método empregado nesse exemplo é explicado na Tabela 7.8.

TABELA 7.8 — PROCEDIMENTO PARA USAR CLASSIFICAÇÕES DE PROXIMIDADE

1. $m = 1$ e $n = 6$.
2. Identifique pares de departamentos com classificações de proximidade iguais a m.
3. Desenvolva um layout experimental com os pares de departamentos identificados no Passo 1 adjacentes um ao outro.
4. Identifique pares de departamentos com classificações de proximidade iguais a n.
5. Encaixe os pares de departamentos identificados no Passo 4 no layout experimental do Passo 3.
6. Examine o layout experimental do Passo 5. Se alguma classificação de proximidade dos pares de departamentos tiver sido violada, reorganize os departamentos para que satisfaçam todas as classificações de proximidade.
7. $m = 3$ e $n = 4$? Se assim for, vá ao Passo 8. Se não, $m = m + 1$ e $n = n - 1$, vá ao Passo 2.
8. Saia.

EXEMPLO 7.7

USANDO CLASSIFICAÇÕES DE PROXIMIDADE PARA DESENVOLVER LAYOUTS DE INSTALAÇÕES DE SERVIÇO

Estas classificações de proximidade são usadas com a finalidade de indicar a conveniência de se ter departamentos próximos uns dos outros:

Classificações de Proximidade	Significado da Classificação
1	Necessário
2	Muito importante
3	Importante
4	Ligeiramente importante
5	Indiferente
6	Indesejável

Aqui estão seis departamentos e suas classificações de proximidade. A classificação de proximidade entre um par de departamentos é encontrada entre suas intersecções na grade a seguir.

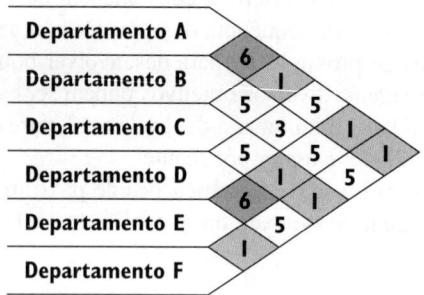

Use o método da Tabela 7.8 para distribuir os seis departamentos num prédio retangular, com dois departamentos de profundidade e três departamentos de largura.

Solução

Primeiramente, note que os pares de departamentos com classificações de proximidade iguais a 1 (necessários) são: A-C, A-E, A-F, C-E, C-F e E-F. A deve tocar C, E e F; C deve tocar E e F; e E deve tocar F. Como uma primeira tentativa, experimente um layout com A, C, E e F, todos contíguos. O layout abaixo satisfaz todos os emparelhamentos de departamentos com classificações iguais a 1.

A	C
E	F

Em seguida, note que os pares de departamentos com classificações de proximidade iguais a 6 (indesejáveis) são A-B e D-E. A não deve ser contíguo a B, e D não deve ser contíguo a E. Colocando-se os departamentos D e E nos dois espaços restantes, o layout a seguir satisfaz todos os emparelhamentos de departamentos com classificações de proximidade iguais a 6.

A	C	B
E	F	D

Note que, nesse último passo, satisfazer as classificações de proximidade de 6 simultaneamente satisfez as classificações de proximidade de 1. Os problemas podem não ser sempre assim tão simples, e alguns malabarismos com os departamentos podem ser necessários para verificar se melhorias podem ser feitas.

Resumo Final

O Que os Fabricantes de Classe Mundial Estão Fazendo

O layout das instalações afeta muito o desempenho dos sistemas de produção. Os fabricantes de classe mundial dedicam um grande esforço para desenvolver layouts projetados para cumprir as prioridades competitivas para os produtos em seus planos de negócios. E os *relayouts* recebem uma grande atenção quando as condições operacionais se modificam. A manufatura, operações de armazenamento, operações de serviço e operações de escritório compartilham muitos objetivos de layout. Os principais entre eles são a provisão para suficiente capacidade de produção, baixos custos de manuseio de materiais, provisão para as necessidades pessoais e de segurança dos trabalhadores, baixo investimento de capital e baixos custos de produção.

Os fabricantes de classe mundial lutam por flexibilidade em seus layouts que lhes permita mudar os volumes de produção e mudar rapidamente para outros modelos de produto. Para atingir esse objetivo, essas empresas têm treinamento intensivo e em múltiplas funções para os trabalhadores, sofisticados programas de manutenção preventiva, pequenas máquinas flexíveis, trabalhadores com iniciativa própria que são treinados para resolver problemas, pouco estoque desnecessário e estações de trabalho colocadas próximas entre si. Seus layouts são relativamente pequenos, compactos e estreitamente concentrados, com uma porcentagem maior de espaço de piso usado para a produção e uma porcentagem menor de estoques. Os fabricantes de classe mundial estão usando mais layouts de manufatura celular, mais equipamentos automatizados de manuseio de materiais, como, por exemplo, armazéns automatizados e sistemas de veículos automatizados, mais linhas de produção em forma de U, que permitem maior interação e rotação de trabalho dos trabalhadores, e mais áreas abertas com um número menor de divisórias e visão clara de estações de trabalho adjacentes.

Os fabricantes de serviço de classe mundial estão projetando layouts de operações de apoio de uma maneira muito semelhante à dos fabricantes de classe mundial. Aqui, as tecnologias de produção, processamento de materiais físicos, custos de produção e flexibilidade orientam o desenvolvimento dos layouts. Adicionalmente, enquanto competem por clientes, os fabricantes de classe mundial projetam seus layouts de instalações tendo em mente seus clientes. Estacionamento, recepção e conforto para os clientes orientam o desenvolvimento de layouts de serviço.

Os fabricantes de classe mundial usam consultores, programas de computador e especialistas do staff interno para desenvolver layouts de instalações. Muitas grandes corporações têm departamentos em suas sedes corporativas que fornecem assistência no projeto, construção, localização e layout das instalações para todas as divisões da empresa. A maioria das empresas tem grupos de analistas internos que fornecem análise dos problemas de layout e recomendam layouts de instalações para processo, produto, manufatura celular e layouts de serviço. Programas de computador como os ALDEP, o CORELAP e o CRAFT, e programas de computador para regras heurísticas de balanceamento de linha são usados para fornecer layouts de instalações.

Questões de Revisão e Discussão

1. Defina *layout de instalação*.
2. Cite três objetivos para estes tipos de layout:
    a) Operações de manufatura
    b) Operações de armazenamento
    c) Operações de serviço
    d) Operações de escritório
3. Qual é o objetivo predominante para estes tipos de layout?
    a) Operações de manufatura
    b) Operações de armazenamento
    c) Operações de serviço
    d) Operações de escritório
4. Cite quatro princípios do manuseio de materiais.
5. Cite e descreva cinco tipos de dispositivos de manuseio de materiais.
6. O que é um AGVS? Descreva-o e discuta suas utilizações.
7. Cite e descreva quatro tipos de layouts para operações de manufatura.

8. Quais são as principais decisões que devem ser tomadas num layout de MC? Defina e descreva o problema de formação de células.
9. Quais são os objetivos nas decisões quanto à formação de células? Descreva como os problemas de formação de células são analisados. O que é uma peça excepcional? O que é feito com as peças excepcionais?
10. Compare e contraste o layout de um banco com o layout de um hospital. Em que eles se assemelham e em que diferem?
11. Explique por que balanceamos as linhas de produção. Descreva o procedimento geral de balanceamento de linha.
12. Cite duas regras heurísticas de balanceamento de linha. Explique a regra heurística de utilização incremental. Explique a regra heurística da tarefa de mais longa duração. Sob quais condições cada regra heurística seria usada?
13. Descreva a abordagem moderna para os layouts de manufatura. Compare e contraste as abordagens moderna e tradicional.
14. Cite cinco tendências nos layouts de manufatura.

Tarefas na Internet

1. Procure na Internet por uma empresa que forneça sistemas de esteiras transportadoras. Descreva alguns dos sistemas de esteiras transportadoras que a empresa pode fornecer. Inclua o site da empresa.
2. A Crown Equipment Corporation (**www.crownlift.com**) manufatura empilhadeiras *heavy-duty*[1], usadas para transportar materiais e produtos em armazéns e centros de distribuição internacionais. Descreva as três diferentes empilhadeiras da linha de produtos da Crown. Descreva a função e a finalidade do produto da Crown chamado Wave.
3. Visite o site de jatos comerciais da Boeing (**www.boeing.com/commercial/**). Qual é o papel no mercado do novo jato Modelo 717 da Boeing? Escolha um dos outros modelos de jatos comerciais da Boeing (737, 747, 757, 767 ou 777) e encontre e imprima um diagrama do layout ou configuração dos assentos. Descreva as opções de capacidade de assentos desse modelo de jato.
4. Visite uma livraria on-line. Encontre um livro recente sobre layout de instalações ou layout de fábrica. Relacione o título, autores, data de publicação e editora.

Problemas

1. A fábrica da Computer Products Corporation (CPC) em Los Angeles planeja adicionar uma nova ala a sua planta de produção existente. A nova ala abrigará a manufatura de montagens eletrônicas para próprio uso interno na CPC e para outras empresas das indústrias de produtos eletrônicos e de computadores. Praticamente toda a produção da nova ala será representada por cinco montagens: P55 Power Unit, Z4 Converter, U69 Equalizer, K5 Audio e T22 Stabilizer. O layout da nova ala se baseará no processo utilizado para manufaturar as montagens. As estimativas seguintes foram desenvolvidas para o número de viagens dos lotes de montagens entre os departamentos de produção durante o próximo ano.

Código do Departamento	Departamento	\.	\.	Código do Departamento	\.	\.	\.
		1	2	3	4	5	6	7
1	Recebimento		1.600	1.500	200			
2	Preparo de kits			1.400	200			
3	Inspeção				2.900			
4	Inserção					3.300		
5	Soldagem						3.000	
6	Acabamento							300
7	Embalagem e embarque							3.000

---

[1] *Heavy-duty*: para trabalho pesado; para demanda pesada.

Capítulo 7 – Layout das Instalações

Desenvolva um diagrama esquemático das relações gerais entre os departamentos de produção, usando análise da seqüência de operações.

2. A ABC Food Market acaba de comprar um prédio com 60 x 140 m de área útil e um amplo estacionamento. A administração da ABC solicitou ajuda de um consultor para auxiliá-la no projeto de um layout de instalação para essa loja. O consultor recebeu estas informações:

Média Diária de Tráfego de Clientes entre Departamentos

Departamento	A	B	C	D	E	F	G	H
A	—	2.000	1.000	0	500	1.500	200	300
B		—	500	1.000	500	500	0	500
C			—	500	1.500	200	0	300
D				—	0	500	500	500
E					—	0	500	0
F						—	500	1.000
G							—	500
H								—

Departamento	Área Necessária (m²)	Departamento	Área Necessária (m²)	Departamento	Área Necessária (m²)
A	600	D	800	G	1.600
B	600	E	500	H	1.200
C	1000	F	2.100		

A administração da ABC indicou ainda que o consultor poderia organizar os departamentos em qualquer configuração dentro do prédio e que as entradas e saídas atuais poderiam ser modificadas para atender as necessidades do layout. A empresa deseja minimizar a viagem dos clientes entre os departamentos.

a) Desenvolva um diagrama esquemático inicial para a disposição dos departamentos dentro da instalação da loja de produtos alimentícios.
b) Use a análise da seqüência de operações para desenvolver um "excelente" diagrama esquemático para os departamentos.
c) Use a análise de diagrama de blocos para desenvolver um layout departamental final. (*Observação:* As áreas para os departamentos relacionados anteriormente incluem provisões para corredores.)

3. A fábrica da Yellow Bird está acrescentando uma nova ala a seu prédio para manufaturar uma nova linha de produtos com cinco modelos: *a*, *b*, *c*, *d* e *e*. Duas alternativas de layout são mostradas a seguir.

Layout A

1	2	5
4	6	3

Layout B

4	5	6
1	2	3

Os modelos de produto da nova ala, seus movimentos ao longo dos seis departamentos e as distâncias entre os departamentos são mostrados na tabela a seguir:

Modelo do Produto	Caminhos de Processamento do Modelo de Produto	Número de Produtos Produzidos Mensalmente	Movimentos do Modelo de Produto	Distância entre Departamentos (metros)	
				Layout A	Layout B
a	4–5–6	5.000	1–2	3	3
b	1–2–3	5.000	2–3	8	5
c	1–2–6	4.000	2–5	5	5
d	1–2–5	2.000	2–6	3	9
e	3–4–5	4.000	3–4	8	10
			3–5	3	6
			4–5	10	5
			5–6	8	5

Qual alternativa de layout minimiza a viagem mensal de produto ao longo da nova ala proposta? (Use a análise de distância da carga.)

4. A Computer Products Corporation adicionará uma nova ala a suas instalações para manufaturar montagens eletrônicas. A administração está considerando dois layouts alternativos:

Layout I

Layout II

As montagens eletrônicas da fábrica, as viagens que os lotes de montagens eletrônicas fazem entre os departamentos e as distâncias entre os departamentos são mostradas a seguir:

Viagens entre os Departamentos	Distância entre os Departamentos (metros)	
	Layout I	Layout II
1–2	7	15
1–3	7	9
1–4	12	14
2–3	13	6
2–4	9	22
3–4	13	16
4–5	15	12
5–6	15	13
5–7	15	18
6–7	12	12

	Seqüência de Processamento das Montagens nos Departamentos	
Montagens Eletrônicas	Seqüência de Processamento nos Departamentos	Lotes de Montagens a Serem Produzidas por Ano
P55 Power Unit	1–2–3–4–5–6–7	1.400
Z4 Converter	1–2–4–5–6–7	200
U69 Equalizer	1–3–4–5–6–7	1.200
K5 Audio	1–3–4–5–7	300
T22 Stabilizer	1–4–5–6–7	200

Use a análise de distância da carga para determinar qual layout minimiza a distância anual que os lotes de montagens percorrem ao longo da nova ala.

5. Uma empresa monta e envia pelo correio pacotes de propaganda para clientes, em base contratual. Um desses contratos foi assinado recentemente, e a empresa está desenvolvendo um layout para a linha de montagem. Essas tarefas, suas tarefas precedentes e as durações das tarefas foram identificadas e estimadas, como é mostrado a seguir. O contrato especifica que 50 mil correspondências devem ser processadas em cinco dias úteis, a empresa trabalha somente um turno de 8 horas por dia, e os empregados têm permissão para duas pausas de 15 minutos por turno para o café.

a) Trace o diagrama das relações de precedência.
b) Compute a duração de ciclo em minutos.
c) Compute o número mínimo de estações de trabalho para o contrato.

Tarefa	Tarefas Precedentes	Duração das Tarefas (minutos/correspondência)
A. Inspecionar materiais quanto à qualidade	—	0,30
B. Preparar kits para montagem	A	0,20
C. Montar e colar envelopes	B	0,15
D. Pegar e dobrar circular	B	0,10
E. Anexar endereço ao envelope	C	0,10
F. Colocar circular no envelope e selar envelope	D,E	0,15
G. Preparar capa plástica para encaixar o envelope	F	0,05
H. Selar pacote na capa plástica	G	0,15
I. Processar correspondências endereçadas através de máquina de postagem	H	0,15
J. Entregar correspondências na caixa de correspondência	I	0,05

6. As operações de apoio de um restaurante de fast-food têm estas tarefas:

Tarefa	Tarefas Precedentes	Tempo para Executar a Tarefa (minutos)	Tarefa	Tarefas Precedentes	Tempo para Executar a Tarefa (minutos)
A	—	0,39	H	—	0,90
B	—	0,25	I	—	0,60
C	—	0,40	J	H,I,G	0,40
D	—	0,05	K	J	0,30
E	A,B	0,49	L	K	0,25
F	C,D	0,65			Total 5,07
G	E,F	0,39			

Se 100 hambúrgueres por hora precisarem ser preparados pelo pessoal e 50 minutos por hora forem produtivos:
a) Trace um diagrama das relações de precedência.
b) Compute a duração do ciclo por hambúrguer, em minutos.
c) Compute o número mínimo de estações de trabalho necessário.
d) Como você combinaria tarefas em estações de trabalho para minimizar o tempo ocioso? Use a regra heurística de utilização incremental. Avalie sua proposta. Você poderia usar a regra heurística da tarefa de mais longa duração? Por que a usaria? Por que não?

7. O tempo para executar cada tarefa e as tarefas precedentes é mostrado a seguir:

Tarefa	Tarefas Precedentes	Tempo para Executar a Tarefa (minutos)
A	—	0,07
B	—	0,15
C	A,B	0,08
D	C	0,05
E	C	0,18
F	—	0,12
G	—	0,06
H	F,G	0,10
I	D,E	0,15
J	H,I	0,11
K	J	0,06
L	K	0,19

Se 220 produtos forem necessários por hora e 55 minutos por hora forem produtivos:
a) Trace um diagrama das relações de precedência.
b) Compute a duração do ciclo por hambúrguer em minutos.
c) Compute o número mínimo de estações de trabalho necessário.
d) Use a regra heurística da tarefa de mais longa duração para balancear a linha de produção. Avalie sua solução.

8. Estas classificações de proximidade são usadas com a finalidade de indicar a conveniência de se ter departamentos contíguos:

Classificações de Proximidade	Significado da Classificação
1	Necessário
2	Muito importante
3	Importante.
4	Ligeiramente importante
5	Indiferente
6	Indesejável

Aqui estão seis departamentos e suas classificações de proximidade. A classificação de proximidade entre dois departamentos é encontrada entre suas intersecções na grade a seguir.

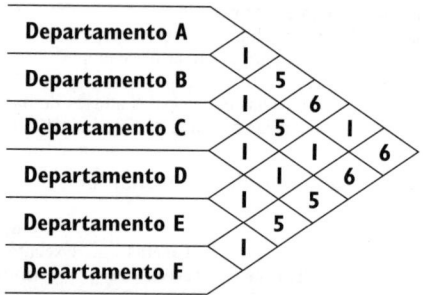

Eis um layout de seis departamentos. Sugira melhorias no layout para que cumpram de maneira mais estreita as classificações de proximidade acima.

A	E	B
F	C	D

9. Estas classificações de proximidade são usadas com a finalidade de indicar a conveniência de se ter departamentos contíguos:

Classificações de Proximidade	Significado da Classificação
1	Necessário
2	Muito importante
3	Importante
4	Ligeiramente importante
5	Indiferente
6	Indesejável

Aqui estão nove departamentos e suas classificações de proximidade. A classificação de proximidade entre dois departamentos é encontrada entre suas intersecções na grade a seguir.

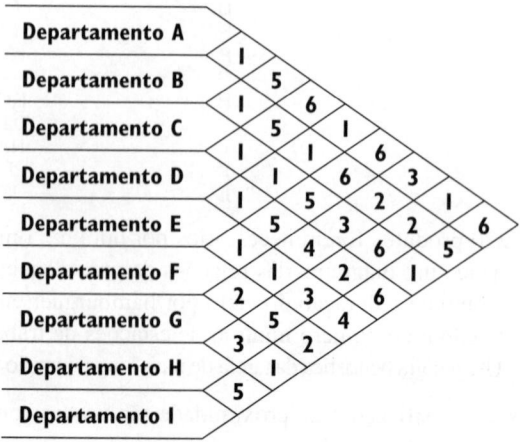

Capítulo 7 – Layout das Instalações

Eis um layout de nove departamentos. Sugira melhorias no layout para que cumpram de maneira mais estreita as classificações de proximidade acima.

A	C	H
D	B	I
F	G	E

Estudo de Caso

Integrated Products Corporation

Um analista de métodos da Integrated Products Corporation (IPC) tem estudado a linha de montagem que produz scanners de códigos de barra. O objetivo dessa análise é reduzir o tempo ocioso dos trabalhadores na linha de montagem para reduzir o custo de mão-de-obra dos scanners. Essa informação se aplica:

Tarefa	Tarefas Precedentes	Duração da Tarefa (minutos)
A. Preparar kits das montagens compradas	—	1,35
B. Inspecionar as montagens dispostas em kits	A	2,20
C. Processar placa controladora através da linha de equipamentos de auto-inserção	—	1,90
D. Processar placa controladora através da linha de equipamentos de soldagem	C	2,39
E. Aparar e fazer acabamento na placa controladora	D	1,75
F. Montar unidade de força no chassi	B	1,25
G. Montar unidade de leitura no chassi	F	0,90
H. Montar placa controladora no chassi	E,G	2,49
I. Montar unidade de vídeo no chassi	H	2,19
J. Inspecionar e testar scanner acabado	I	2,40
K. Embalar scanner acabado	J	0,69
		Total 19,58

Vinte scanners de código de barra devem ser produzidos pela linha de produção por hora. Em média 50 minutos por hora são produtivos, devido ao tempo pessoal, quebras de máquina e tempos de inicialização e paralisação. Uma vez que o contrato com o sindicato de trabalhadores restringe os tipos de tarefas que podem ser combinadas em estações de trabalho, as tarefas podem ser agrupadas somente dentro destes grupos de compatibilidade:

Grupo de Compatibilidade	Tarefas
Grupo I	A,B
Grupo II	C
Grupo III	D
Grupo IV	E
Grupo V	F,G,H,I,J,K

Por exemplo, as Tarefas F e G poderiam ser combinadas numa estação de trabalho, mas as Tarefas E e F não. As tarefas dentro de grupos de compatibilidade podem ser combinadas enquanto se observam as relações de precedência; em outras palavras, as tarefas adjacentes ao longo do diagrama de rede podem ser combinadas. O trabalho do Grupo I é essencialmente um trabalho manual que exige somente ferramentas baratas e abundantes.

Tarefas

1. Trace um diagrama das relações de precedência.
2. Compute a duração do ciclo por scanner de código de barra.
3. Compute o número mínimo de estações de trabalho necessário.
4. Compare e explique a solução da regra heurística de utilização incremental e a da regra heurística da tarefa de mais longa duração.
5. Discuta como você implementaria sua solução num ambiente de manufatura real. Quais obstáculos você esperaria encontrar? Como você superaria esses obstáculos?

PARTE III

DECISÕES OPERACIONAIS
Planejando a Produção para Atender a Demanda

CAPÍTULO 8
Sistemas de Planejamento da Produção

CAPÍTULO 9
Sistemas de Estoques com Demanda Independente

CAPÍTULO 10
Sistemas de Planejamento das Necessidades de Recursos

CAPÍTULO 11
Planejamento e Controle do Chão de Fábrica na Manufatura

CAPÍTULO 12
Planejamento e Programação de Operações de Serviço

CAPÍTULO 13
Manufatura Just-in-Time

CAPÍTULO 14
Administração da Cadeia de Suprimentos

Na Parte II deste livro exploramos como os gerentes de operações abordam e analisam decisões estratégicas nas operações. Planejamento e desenvolvimento de processos de produção, planejamento e implementação de nova tecnologia de produção, alocação de recursos escassos a unidades de negócios e planejamento de longo prazo da capacidade e das instalações requerem grande atenção e evidência. Por mais importantes que essas decisões estratégicas sejam, entretanto, não devemos permitir que elas ofusquem outras decisões em andamento na APO que, sob certas condições, podem ser de igual importância.

Quando visitamos gerentes de operações, eles dizem que a maior fonte de pressão e tensão em seus empregos é o constante impulso para produzir produtos e serviços de alta qualidade que cumpram as promessas de entrega a clientes ao mesmo tempo que mantêm o controle sobre os custos. Os produtos e serviços devem ser entregues no tempo certo e dentro dos orçamentos de custo. Com essa finalidade, os gerentes de operações se envolvem em atividades de planejamento da produção como estas:

1. Desenvolver planos agregados de capacidade que normalmente cobrem de 6 a 18 meses. Esses planos de médio alcance devem fornecer a capacidade de produção necessária para cumprir a demanda dos clientes por produtos e serviços.
2. Estabelecer sistemas de planejamento da produção que orientem as organizações para manter as promessas de entrega aos clientes, cumprir metas de estoque e manter baixos custos de produção.
3. Garantir suficiente estoque de produtos acabados para atingir o objetivo duplo de baixos custos operacionais e pronta entrega de produtos aos clientes.
4. Programar a produção de produtos e serviços necessários para cumprir as promessas de entrega aos clientes e das cargas de trabalho às instalações de produção de forma que os custos de produção sejam baixos.
5. Planejar a compra, armazenagem e embarque de materiais a fim de que os materiais certos estejam disponíveis na quantidade certa e na hora certa para suportar os programas de produção.

Uma vez que o efeito cumulativo desses planos, questões e decisões de médio e curto prazo é enorme, eles são enfatizados na Parte III.

capítulo 8

SISTEMAS DE PLANEJAMENTO DA PRODUÇÃO

Introdução

Hierarquia do Planejamento da Produção

Planejamento Agregado
  Demanda Agregada
  Dimensões da Capacidade de Produção
  Fontes de Capacidade de Produção de Médio Prazo
  Alguns Planos Agregados Tradicionais
    Acompanhar a Demanda • Nivelar a Capacidade Produtiva
  Critérios para Escolher Planos Agregados
  Planos Agregados para Serviços
  Modelos Matemáticos para o Planejamento Agregado
  Táticas de Preempção

Programa Mestre de Produção
  Objetivos do Programa Mestre de Produção
  Período de Congelamento em Programas Mestres de Produção
  Procedimentos para Desenvolver Programas Mestres de Produção
  Administração da Demanda
  Atualização Semanal do MPS
  O MPS em Empresas de Produção para Estoque e de Produção sob Encomenda
  Extensão dos Horizontes de Planejamento
  MPS Computadorizado

Tipos de Sistemas de Planejamento e Controle da Produção
  Sistemas de Estoque de Reserva
  Sistemas Empurrar
  Sistemas Puxar
  Concentrando-se nos Gargalos
    Teoria das Restrições

Questões de Revisão e Discussão

Tarefas na Internet

Problemas

Estudo de Caso
  Planejamento Agregado na Bell Computers

Introdução

PLANEJAMENTO AGREGADO NA NEW GENERATION COMPUTERS

Um gerente de operações da New Generation Computers (NGC) está desenvolvendo um plano agregado de produção de seis meses para produzir uma família de impressoras de computador. O departamento de marketing da NGC estimou a demanda para as impressoras para o período de seis meses. Há diversos modelos de impressora, e a quantidade de mão-de-obra necessária para produzir cada impressora depende das características do modelo. Não obstante haver a possibilidade de fazerem horas extras, a NGC tem uma política que limita a quantidade mensal de horas extras a 10% do trabalho em horário normal. O trabalho em horas extras é mais dispendioso do que o trabalho em horário normal, e o sindicato de trabalhadores do qual a NGC faz parte tem resistido ao uso de trabalho em horas extras. A NGC tem uma política de não demitir seus trabalhadores; desse modo, o mesmo número de horas de trabalho em horário normal está disponível para produzir as impressoras em cada mês. A operação de soldagem por fluxo trabalha três turnos por dia e pode produzir no máximo 200 impressoras por dia. A NGC incorre num custo de transporte todas as vezes que uma impressora é produzida num mês e despachada no mês seguinte. Os objetivos do plano agregado de produção são utilizar plenamente a força de trabalho, não ultrapassar a capacidade de máquina, despachar os pedidos para o cliente prontamente e minimizar os custos do trabalho em horas extras e de manutenção em estoque.

O relato precedente é um exemplo daquilo que é chamado **planejamento agregado**. Nesse planejamento, os gerentes de operações desenvolvem planos de médio alcance de como produzirão produtos durante as semanas seguintes. Esses planos especificam a quantidade de mão-de-obra, de subcontratação e de outras fontes de capacidade a serem usadas. Os gerentes de operação também se envolvem no preparo de **programas mestres de produção**, desenvolvendo planos de produção de curto prazo de quais produtos acabados produzir nas próximas semanas. Neste capítulo estudaremos tanto o planejamento de médio prazo como o de curto prazo.

HIERARQUIA DO PLANEJAMENTO DA PRODUÇÃO

A Figura 8.1 ilustra o planejamento de produção de longo, médio e curto prazo. Estudamos o planejamento da capacidade de longo prazo no Capítulo 6; esses planos são necessários para desenvolver instalações e equipamentos, grandes fornecedores e processos de produção, e se tornam embaraços nos planos de médio e curto prazos. O planejamento agregado desenvolve planos de produção de médio prazo referentes a emprego, estoque agregado, utilidades, modificações de instalações e contratos de fornecimento de materiais. Esses planos agregados impõem restrições aos planos de produção de curto prazo que se seguem. Estudaremos em seguida o planejamento agregado da produção.

Programas mestres de produção são planos de curto prazo para produzir produtos acabados ou itens finais, os quais são usados para impulsionar sistemas de planejamento e controle. Esses sistemas desenvolvem programas de produção de curto prazo de peças e montagens, programas de compra de materiais, programas do setor de produção e cronogramas da força de trabalho. Os Capítulos 9 a 14 preocupam-se com os sistemas de planejamento e controle da produção, no curto prazo. Uma vez que o programa mestre de produção impulsiona esses sistemas, este capítulo é crucial para entendermos os capítulos restantes da Parte III. Por esse motivo, discutiremos os programas mestres de produção posteriormente.

PLANEJAMENTO AGREGADO

O planejamento agregado é necessário na APO porque ele proporciona:

- Instalações amplamente carregadas e minimiza a sobrecarga e a subcarga, reduzindo assim os custos de produção.
- Um plano para mudança sistemática da capacidade de produção para atender os picos e momentos de baixa da demanda esperada.

FIGURA 8.1 — PLANEJAMENTO DA PRODUÇÃO NA MANUFATURA

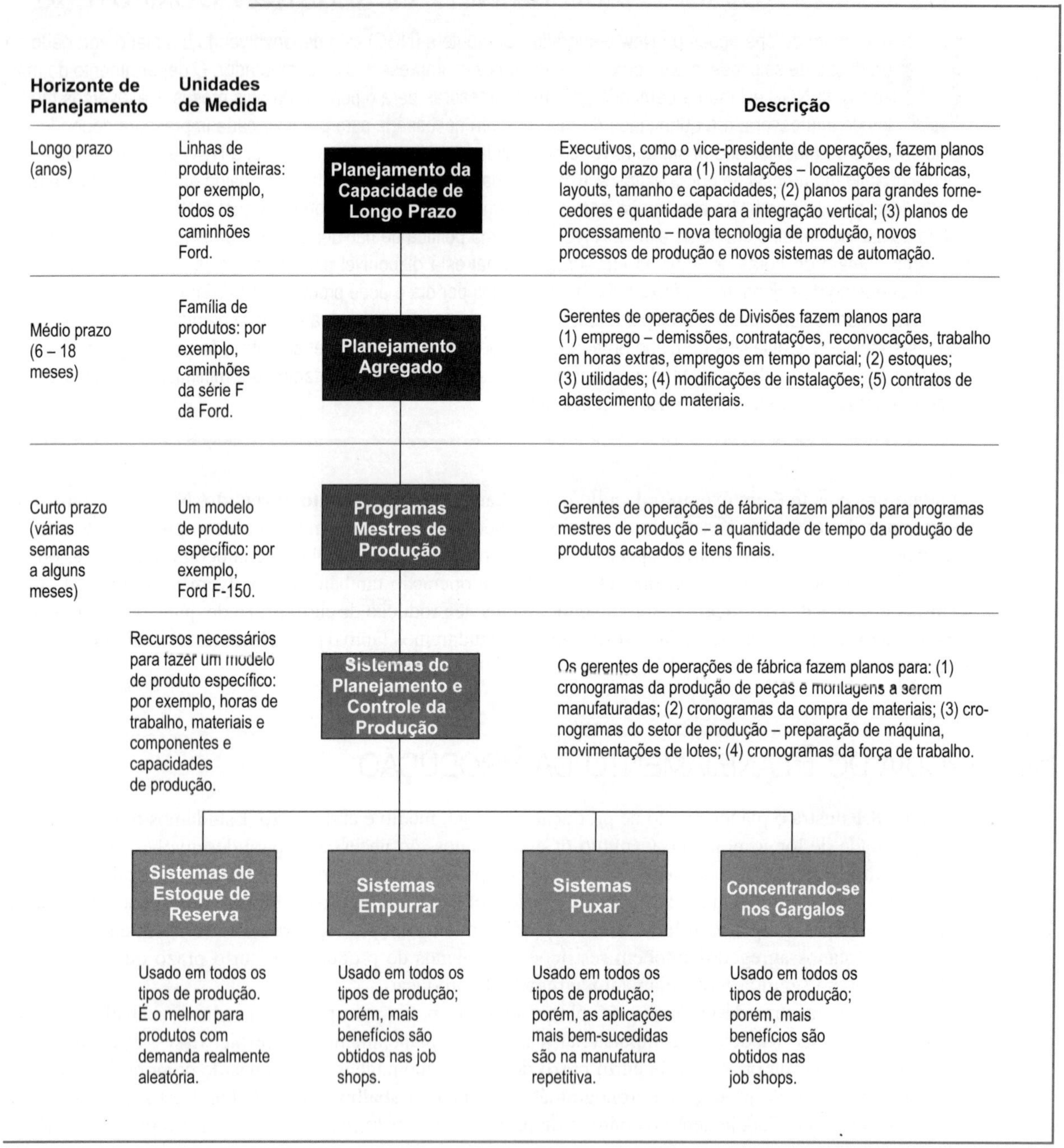

Horizonte de Planejamento	Unidades de Medida		Descrição
Longo prazo (anos)	Linhas de produto inteiras: por exemplo, todos os caminhões Ford.	**Planejamento da Capacidade de Longo Prazo**	Executivos, como o vice-presidente de operações, fazem planos de longo prazo para (1) instalações – localizações de fábricas, layouts, tamanho e capacidades; (2) planos para grandes fornecedores e quantidade para a integração vertical; (3) planos de processamento – nova tecnologia de produção, novos processos de produção e novos sistemas de automação.
Médio prazo (6 – 18 meses)	Família de produtos: por exemplo, caminhões da série F da Ford.	**Planejamento Agregado**	Gerentes de operações de Divisões fazem planos para (1) emprego – demissões, contratações, reconvocações, trabalho em horas extras, empregos em tempo parcial; (2) estoques; (3) utilidades; (4) modificações de instalações; (5) contratos de abastecimento de materiais.
Curto prazo (várias semanas a alguns meses)	Um modelo de produto específico: por exemplo, Ford F-150.	**Programas Mestres de Produção**	Gerentes de operações de fábrica fazem planos para programas mestres de produção – a quantidade de tempo da produção de produtos acabados e itens finais.
	Recursos necessários para fazer um modelo de produto específico: por exemplo, horas de trabalho, materiais e componentes e capacidades de produção.	**Sistemas de Planejamento e Controle da Produção**	Os gerentes de operações de fábrica fazem planos para: (1) cronogramas da produção de peças e montagens a serem manufaturadas; (2) cronogramas da compra de materiais; (3) cronogramas do setor de produção – preparação de máquina, movimentações de lotes; (4) cronogramas da força de trabalho.

Sistemas de Estoque de Reserva	**Sistemas Empurrar**	**Sistemas Puxar**	**Concentrando-se nos Gargalos**
Usado em todos os tipos de produção. É o melhor para produtos com demanda realmente aleatória.	Usado em todos os tipos de produção; porém, mais benefícios são obtidos nas job shops.	Usado em todos os tipos de produção; porém, as aplicações mais bem-sucedidas são na manufatura repetitiva.	Usado em todos os tipos de produção; porém, mais benefícios são obtidos nas job shops.

- Capacidade de produção adequada para atender a demanda agregada esperada.
- Obter a máxima produção para a quantidade de recursos disponíveis, o que é importante em tempos de recursos escassos de produção.

O planejamento agregado é a chave para se administrar a mudança na APO, porque os padrões mutáveis de necessidades dos clientes e os planos para prover recursos de produção que se adaptem a essas mudanças são fundamentais para o planejamento agregado.

O planejamento agregado, enquanto processo, geralmente segue os passos mostrados na Tabela 8.1.

TABELA 8.1	PASSOS NO PLANEJAMENTO AGREGADO
	1. Inicie com uma previsão de vendas para cada produto que indique as quantidades a serem vendidas em cada período de tempo (normalmente semanas, meses ou trimestres) durante o horizonte de planejamento (normalmente 6 a 18 meses).
	2. Totalize todas as previsões de produtos ou serviços individuais numa demanda agregada. Se os produtos não forem aditivos devido a unidades heterogêneas, uma unidade de medida heterogênea deverá ser escolhida que tanto permita que previsões sejam acrescentadas como vincule saídas agregadas à capacidade de produção.
	3. Transforme a demanda agregada para cada período de tempo em trabalhadores, materiais, máquinas e outros elementos de capacidade de produção necessários para satisfazer a demanda agregada.
	4. Desenvolva esquemas de recursos alternativos para fornecer a capacidade de produção necessária para suportar a demanda agregada cumulativa.
	5. Escolha o plano dentre as alternativas consideradas que satisfaça a demanda agregada e atinja da melhor maneira os objetivos da organização.
	Observação: O Passo 5 supõe que o sistema da produção seja orientado pela política administrativa para produzir a previsão de vendas. Há ocasiões em que a capacidade não pode ser suficientemente aumentada, e há ocasiões em que seria mais lucrativo produzir menos do que a previsão de vendas. Presumimos, para as finalidades deste capítulo, que essas questões já foram resolvidas e que a previsão de vendas seja a meta de produção.

DEMANDA AGREGADA

O planejamento de médio prazo da produção inicia-se com previsões da demanda. Métodos como os discutidos no Capítulo 3 são usados para avaliar a quantidade de produtos ou serviços que provavelmente terão uma demanda em cada período de tempo do horizonte de planejamento.

A Figura 8.2 mostra como a Sherman-Brown Chemical Company desenvolve uma demanda agregada com um horizonte de planejamento de um ano.

As previsões trimestrais para os três produtos individuais são reunidas para formar a demanda agregada para todos os produtos, expressa em galões por trimestre. As capacidades de produção também são expressas nessa mesma unidade de medida — galões por trimestre. Uma vez que o plano agregado também é expresso em galões por trimestre, as capacidades de produção podem então ser ajustadas para cima ou para baixo para atender de maneira aproximada a demanda agregada.

Quando produtos diversos são produzidos, agregar a demanda pode não ser algo tão direto — por exemplo, uma empresa que produz tanto cortadores de grama como ceifadeiras rotativas (*rototillers*). Uma vez que é improvável que um cortador de grama requeira a mesma quantidade de mão-de-obra e capacidade de máquina que uma ceifadeira rotativa, a produção deve ser expressa em unidades que não sejam produtos por mês. Nesse casos, a produção pode ser convertida de produtos por mês para unidades como horas de trabalho, horas de máquina, dólares de vendas ou outras unidades que sejam uma boa medida da capacidade de produção.

A produção de cortadores de grama e ceifadeiras rotativas poderia ser convertida em horas de trabalho usando-se um padrão de trabalho: um cortador de grama requer 21 horas de trabalho, e uma ceifadeira rotativa requer 17 horas de trabalho. O plano agregado para os dois produtos seria o total de horas de trabalho para cada período de tempo necessário para produzir a quantidade prevista dos dois produtos.

DIMENSÕES DA CAPACIDADE DE PRODUÇÃO

Uma parte essencial do planejamento agregado é um entendimento abrangente de cada uma das capacidades do sistema de produção. De especial importância são as respostas às seguintes perguntas:

1. **Quanto de cada recurso de produção está disponível?** A capacidade de produção em cada período de tempo pode ser restrita por fatores como o número de trabalhadores ou o número de máquinas.

FIGURA 8.2   AGREGANDO PREVISÕES DE PRODUTOS INDIVIDUAIS À DEMANDA AGREGADA: SHERMAN-BROWN CHEMICAL COMPANY

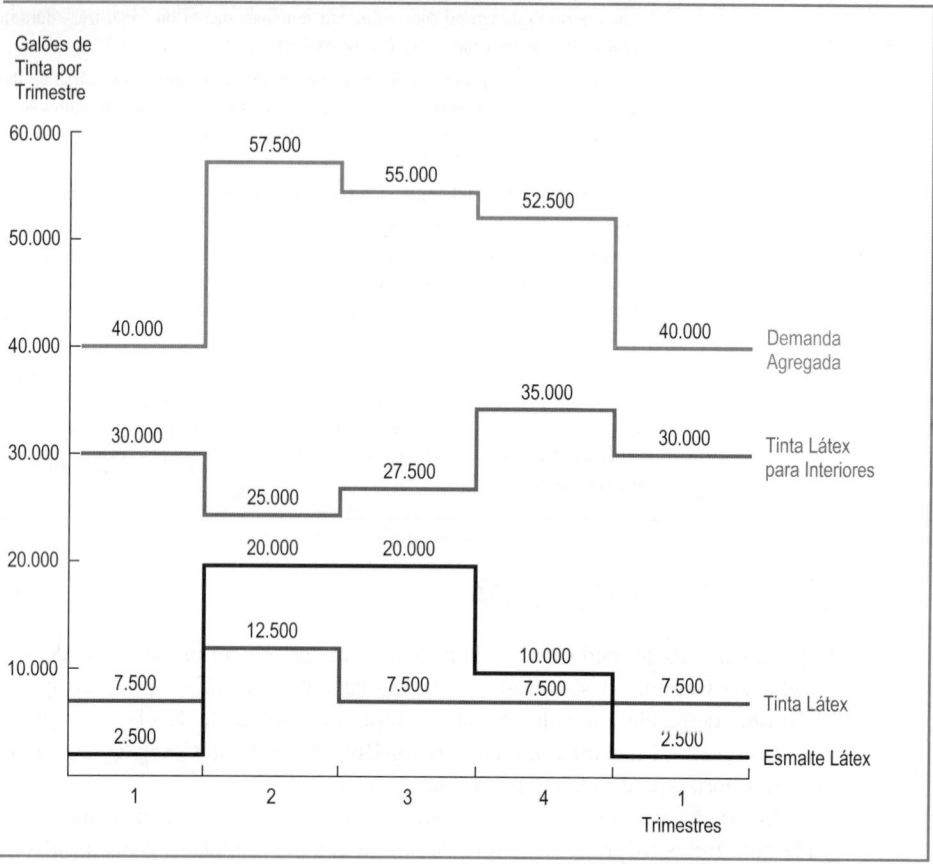

2. **Quanta capacidade cada tipo de produto fornece?** A quantidade de recursos necessários para produzir um único produto permite a transformação da demanda em necessidades de capacidade de produção. Padrões de trabalho (horas de trabalho por produto) e padrões de máquina (horas de máquina por produto) comumente são usados para transformar a demanda no número de trabalhadores e máquinas necessários.
3. **Em qual etapa de produção determinamos a capacidade?** Na produção focalizada no produto, a capacidade pode ser determinada pela **operação de entrada** (*gateway*), ou a primeira operação numa linha de produção. Na produção focalizada no processo, a capacidade pode ser determinada por uma **operação gargalo**, ou a operação que tem a menor capacidade por produto. Em outros tipos de produção, a capacidade pode ser determinada pelo número de horas de trabalho ou horas de máquina num departamento de produção em particular ou numa fábrica inteira.
4. **Quanto custa ajustar a capacidade para cima ou para baixo?** O custo de contratar, demitir e reconvocar empregados, por exemplo, pode afetar os planos para fornecer capacidade de produção.

Essas complexidades da capacidade de produção levaram os sistemas de produção a identificar diversas fontes práticas de fornecimento de capacidade de produção de médio prazo.

FONTES DE CAPACIDADE DE PRODUÇÃO DE MÉDIO PRAZO

Uma vez que o planejamento agregado abrange períodos de somente 6 a 18 meses, não há tempo suficiente disponível para aumentar a capacidade acrescentando prédios, máquinas e outros bens de capital.

Isso desvia o foco para outras fontes de capacidade de produção quando são desenvolvidos planos para sustentar as necessidades dos clientes. Diversas variáveis podem ser alteradas para mudar a capacidade de produção de mês a mês. Entre essas variáveis estão:

1. **Trabalho em horas normais.** Produção por trabalhadores paga de acordo com taxas de trabalho em horas normais, o que normalmente significa 44 horas. As fontes de trabalho são os empregados que trabalham em tempo integral e parcial, novas contratações e trabalhadores demitidos e que podem ser reconvocados. O mercado de trabalho local pode ser um fator limitador, e os contratos com sindicatos de trabalhadores podem limitar a flexibilidade que a administração tem para contratar novos empregados e demitir trabalhadores experientes.
2. **Trabalho em horas extras.** Produção por trabalhadores pagos de acordo com taxas de trabalho em horas extras, o que normalmente significa mais de 44 horas por semana. O trabalho em horas extras pode ser limitado por políticas sindicais ou da empresa.
3. **Estoques.** A produção em períodos anteriores que é estocada para embarque em períodos posteriores.
4. **Subcontratação.** Produção de produtos ou serviços por fornecedores.

O trabalho em horas normais é a fonte preferida de capacidade de produção e é usada para fornecer uma capacidade de produção básica. Quando a demanda ultrapassa a capacidade da força de trabalho existente, novas contratações, trabalho em horas extras, estoques e subcontratação podem ser usados, mas isso tudo pode custar mais e causar outras dificuldades. As empresas abordam com cautela a decisão de como fornecer a melhor capacidade de produção para os picos de demanda.

ALGUNS PLANOS AGREGADOS TRADICIONAIS

Dadas as fontes de capacidade de produção acima, certos planos tradicionais para fornecer capacidade de produção para atender as necessidades dos clientes evoluíram. O plano de acompanhar a demanda e o plano de nivelar a capacidade, usados em conjunto com estoques, *backlog*[1], trabalho em horas extras, trabalho em tempo parcial ou subcontratação comumente são observados na prática da APO.

Acompanhar a Demanda No tipo de plano agregado **acompanhar a demanda**, a capacidade de produção em cada período de tempo é variada para coincidir exatamente com a demanda agregada prevista nesse período. Essa abordagem altera o nível da força de trabalho em cada período de tempo, o que implica novas contratações ou demissões de trabalhadores. A Figura 8.3 mostra como a força de trabalho na Sherman-Brown Chemical Company flutuaria com esse tipo de plano agregado.

O padrão de trabalho na Sherman-Brown são 2,311 homens.hora por galão de tinta. O número de trabalhadores necessário em cada trimestre é determinado, portanto, da seguinte maneira:

$$\text{Trabalhadores} = \frac{\text{Galões de tinta por trimestre} \times \text{Padrão de trabalho por galão}}{\text{Dias de trabalho por trimestre por galão} \times \text{Horas por dia}}$$

1° *trimestre* = $(40.000 \times 2,311) \div (65 \times 8)$ = 178 trabalhadores

2° *trimestre* = $(57.500 \times 2,311) \div (65 \times 8)$ = 256 trabalhadores

3° *trimestre* = $(55.000 \times 2,311) \div (65 \times 8)$ = 245 trabalhadores

4° *trimestre* = $(52.500 \times 2,311) \div (65 \times 8)$ = 234 trabalhadores

A principal vantagem desse plano é que quase nenhum estoque de produtos acabados é necessário, e, portanto, grande parte do custo para manter ou carregar estoques é evitada. Os custos de mão-de-obra e materiais, porém, tendem a ser mais elevados em virtude das rupturas causadas pelo freqüente ajustamento para cima e para baixo da força de trabalho e das capacidades de suprimento de materiais.

---

[1] *Backlog:* pedidos em carteira; registro de pedidos para entrega futura.

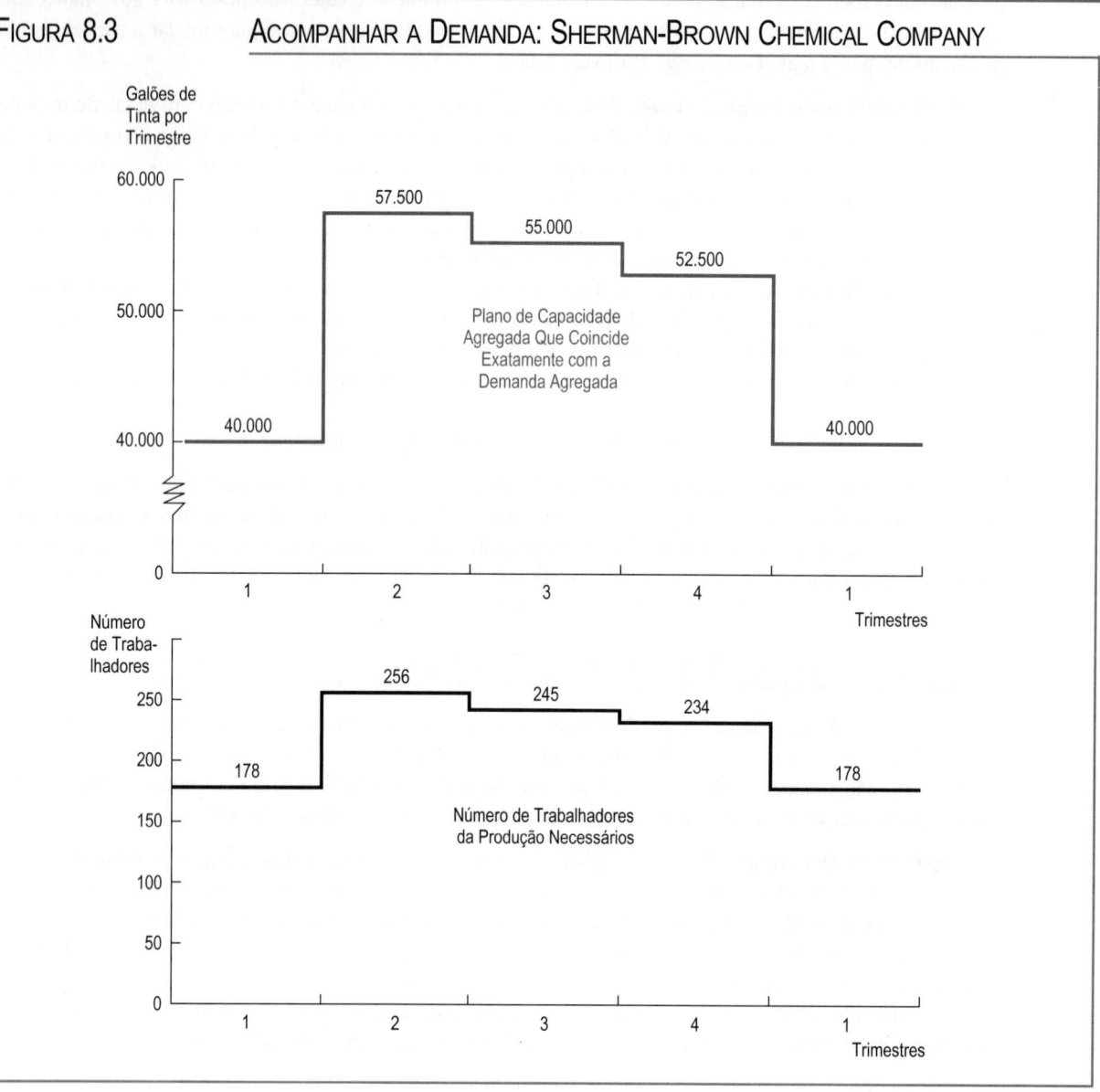

FIGURA 8.3 — ACOMPANHAR A DEMANDA: SHERMAN-BROWN CHEMICAL COMPANY

Nivelar a Capacidade Produtiva Na abordagem *nivelar a capacidade*, a capacidade de produção é mantida constante ao longo do horizonte de planejamento. A diferença entre a taxa de produção constante e a taxa de demanda variável é composta por estoques, backlog, trabalho em tempo parcial ou subcontratações. A Figura 8.4 ilustra como essa diferença é compensada com cada uma dessas fontes de capacidade.

Compensando com Estoques. Se uma empresa é de produção sob encomenda, o estoque de produtos acabados compensa a diferença entre a demanda variável e a capacidade de produção constante. A Figura 8.5 mostra como essa abordagem funcionaria se a Sherman-Brown Chemical Company fosse uma empresa de produção para estoque. A companhia definiria sua capacidade de produção constante como igual à demanda trimestral média de 51.250 galões, e permitiria estoques para suprir a capacidade em trimestres em que a demanda ultrapassasse a capacidade.

O estoque final de cada trimestre é computado pela seguinte fórmula:

$$EF_t = EF_{t-1} + (P_t - D_t)$$

FIGURA 8.4 — Nivelar a Capacidade: Com Estoques, com Backlog e com Trabalho em Horas Extras e Subcontratações

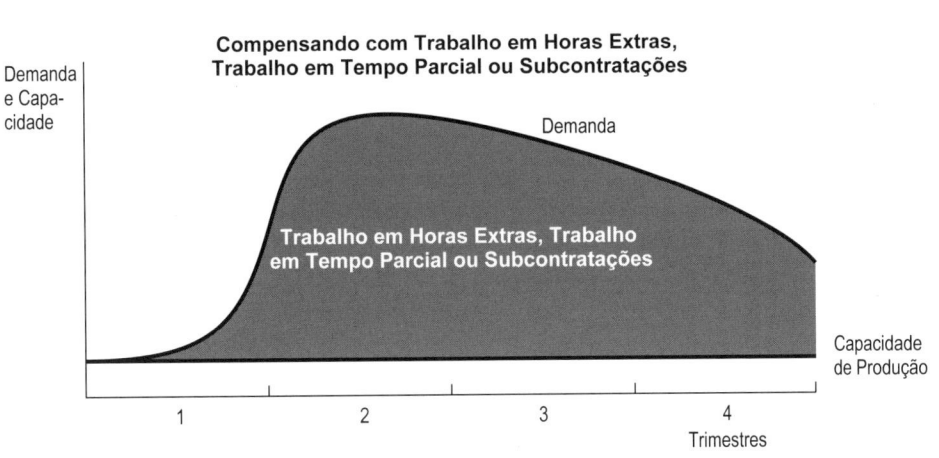

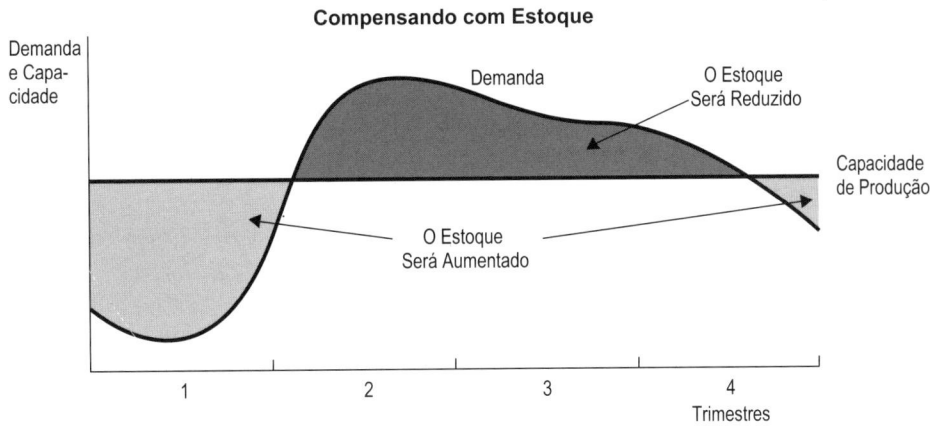

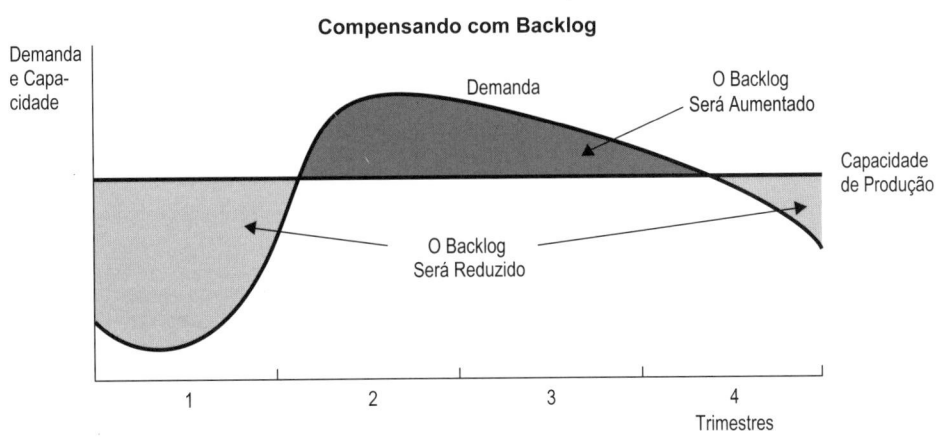

FIGURA 8.5 — NIVELAR A CAPACIDADE: SHERMAN-BROWN CHEMICAL COMPANY — PRODUÇÃO PARA ESTOQUE

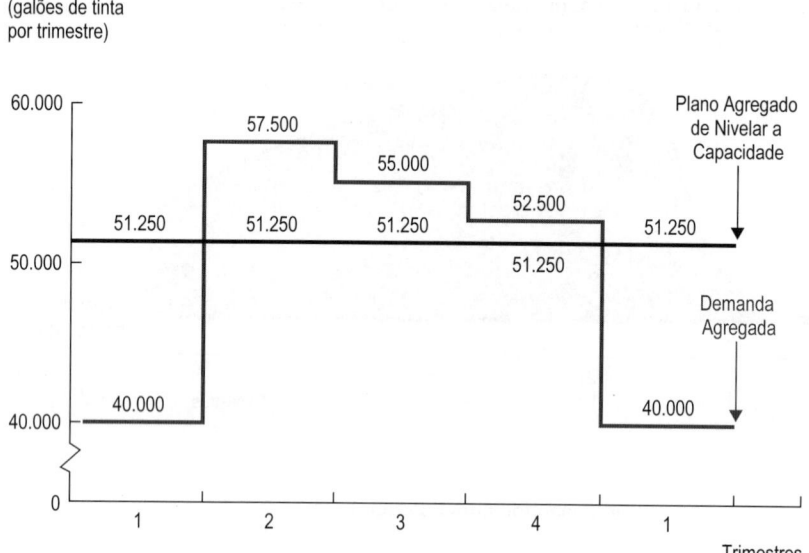

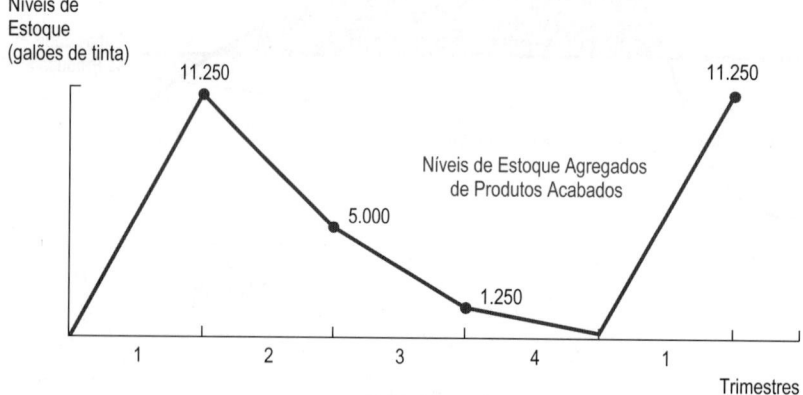

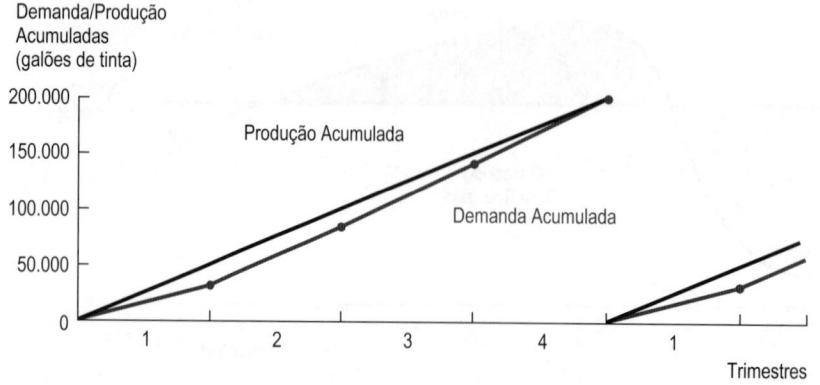

onde:

$$EF_t = \text{estoque final no trimestre } t$$
$$EF_{t-1} = \text{estoque final no trimestre } t - 1, \text{ o trimestre anterior}$$
$$P_t = \text{produção no trimestre } t$$
$$D_t = \text{demanda no trimestre } t$$

Se presumirmos que o estoque seja zero no início do trimestre 1, o estoque final em cada um dos trimestres será computado da seguinte maneira:

$$EF_1 = EI_0 + (P_1 - D_1)$$
$$= 0 + (51.250 - 40.000)$$
$$= 11.250 \text{ galões}$$

$$EF_2 = EF_1 + (P_2 - D_2)$$
$$= 11.250 + (51.250 - 57.500)$$
$$= 5.000 \text{ galões}$$

$$EF_3 = EF_2 + (P_3 - D_3)$$
$$= 5.000 + (51.250 - 55.000)$$
$$= 1.250 \text{ galões}$$

$$EF_4 = EF_3 + (P_4 - D_4)$$
$$= 1.250 + (51.250 - 52.500)$$
$$= 0 \text{ galão}$$

O estoque de produtos acabados se eleva até alcançar um pico de 11.250 galões no final do primeiro trimestre. No segundo e terceiro trimestres, os estoques cairão, porque a produção é menor do que a demanda agregada. No quarto trimestre, o estoque decresce ainda mais, até ser completamente esvaziado, porque a demanda ainda ultrapassa a produção. Com os níveis de produção mantidos constantes, os estoques de produtos acabados se elevam e caem para compensar as diferenças entre a demanda agregada e os níveis de produção de período a período.

A principal vantagem de nivelar a capacidade com estoques é que essa abordagem normalmente promove baixos custos de produção. Isso ocorre porque (1) os custos para contratar, treinar e demitir trabalhadores e usar trabalho em horas extras são praticamente eliminados; (2) o custo para localizar e desenvolver novas fontes de suprimentos de materiais é minimizado; (3) somente a maquinaria de produção mais eficiente é usada; (4) os custos de mão-de-obra e materiais por produto são baixos, uma vez que a operação com produção constante eliminou o contínuo início e interrupção de operações; (5) a supervisão é simplificada e as taxas de sucata são baixas, porque os trabalhadores são experientes em suas funções; (6) a rotatividade voluntária e o absenteísmo podem ser mais baixos. Os japoneses usam o conceito de nivelar a capacidade ao máximo, resultando em níveis de emprego estáveis, reduzida rotatividade e absenteísmo, melhorados níveis de qualidade e maior compromisso do empregado para com as metas da empresa. Em suma, *os gerentes de operações gostam dessa abordagem porque os custos operacionais tendem a ser mais baixos, a qualidade dos produtos tende a ser mais alta e consistente, e as taxas de produção normalmente são confiáveis. Os gerentes financeiros, entretanto, tipicamente não preferem essa alternativa, porque essa abordagem resulta em níveis de estoque de produtos acabados mais elevados, prendendo, desse modo, dinheiro, e aumentando o custo de manutenção desses estoques.* Os custos de manutenção em estoque são reais, e a resolução desse conflito normalmente depende, enfim, do acerto (trade-off) entre os custos adicionais de manutenção em estoque e as economias em custos de mão-de-obra e materiais que resultam de nivelar a capacidade como um plano agregado.

Compensando com Backlog. Nas empresas de produção sob encomenda, o backlog visa compensar a diferença entre uma taxa de demanda variável e uma taxa de demanda constante. Um backlog de pedidos do cliente é simplesmente uma pilha de pedidos do cliente recebidos mas ainda não produzidos ou embarcados.

A Figura 8.6 mostra como um plano de nivelar a capacidade funcionaria se a Sherman-Brown Chemical Company fosse uma empresa de produção sob encomenda. A companhia definiria sua capacidade de produção constante como igual à demanda trimestral média de 51.250 galões, e permitiria que o backlog compusesse a diferença entre a taxa de demanda variável e a taxa de produção constante.

FIGURA 8.6 NIVELAR A CAPACIDADE: SHERMAN-BROWN CHEMICAL COMPANY — PRODUÇÃO SOB ENCOMENDA

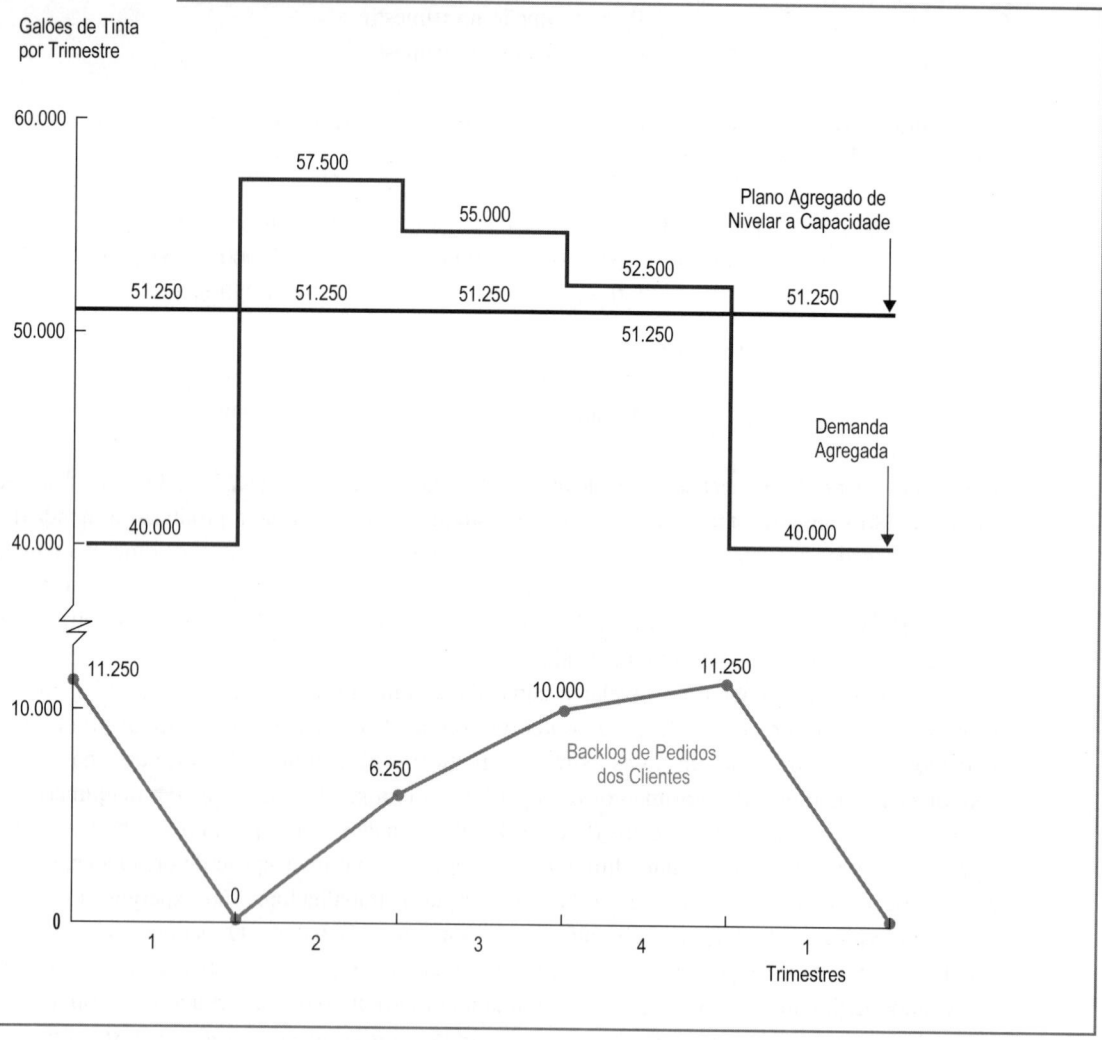

O backlog final de cada trimestre é computado por esta fórmula:

$$BF_t = BF_{t-1} + (D_t - P_t)$$

onde:

BF_t = backlog final no trimestre t
BF_{t-1} = backlog final no trimestre $t - 1$, o trimestre anterior
P_t = produção no trimestre t
D_t = demanda no trimestre t

Presume-se que o backlog seja 11.250 galões no início do trimestre 1, sendo que o backlog final em cada trimestre é computado da seguinte maneira:

$$BF_1 = BF_0 + (D_1 - P_1) \qquad BF_2 = BF_1 + (D_2 - P_2)$$
$$= 11.250 + (40.000 - 51.250) \qquad = 0 + (57.500 - 51.250)$$
$$= 0 \text{ galão} \qquad = 6.250 \text{ galões}$$

$$BF_3 = BF_2 + (D_3 - P_3)$$
$$= 6.250 + (55.000 - 51.250)$$
$$= 10.000 \text{ galões}$$

$$BF_4 = BF_3 + (D_4 - P_4)$$
$$= 10.000 + (52.500 - 51.250)$$
$$= 11.250 \text{ galões}$$

Durante o primeiro trimestre, o backlog cairia, porque a demanda é inferior à capacidade de produção. Nos trimestres restantes, o backlog se elevaria, porque a demanda ultrapassa a capacidade de produção.

A capacidade de produção com backlog é preferida pelos gerentes de operações pelas mesmas razões da abordagem nivelar a capacidade com estoques — porque ela resulta em baixos custos de produção, qualidade de produção elevada e consistentes e confiáveis volumes de produção. As empresas de produção sob encomenda comumente produzem produtos projetados de forma personalizada. Essas empresas podem ter dificuldades para desenvolver planos agregados em razão da diversidade de produtos.

O problema se torna um pouco mais fácil se a empresa tiver um backlog grande de pedidos do cliente, porque os produtos poderão ser projetados e a produção poderá ser planejada tão antecipadamente que uma produção agregada poderá ser planejada.

Compensando com Trabalho em Horas Extras ou Subcontratações. Outra abordagem ao planejamento agregado da capacidade é o uso do trabalho em horas normais para fornecer uma capacidade de produção que se iguale à taxa de demanda mínima prevista durante o horizonte de planejamento. Então, trabalho em horas extras ou subcontratação é usado para suprir qualquer demanda acima do mínimo.

Essa abordagem do planejamento agregado da capacidade pode ser usada ou em empresas de produção para estoque ou em empresas de produção sob encomenda.

Há duas vantagens principais nessa abordagem: nenhum estoque de produtos acabados é carregado, e não há contratações, demissões ou reconvocações de trabalhadores. Isso resulta em baixos custos de manutenção de estoque e níveis de emprego estáveis para a força de trabalho. Mas pode haver desvantagens. A quantidade de trabalho em horas extras disponível pode ser insuficiente para atender a demanda se os picos de demanda forem muito elevados.

Além disso, o uso contínuo de trabalho em horas extras pode esgotar os trabalhadores, o que, por sua vez, pode levar à deterioração do moral, problemas com a qualidade de produtos e serviços e outras dificuldades.

CRITÉRIOS PARA ESCOLHER PLANOS AGREGADOS

Os **custos de contratação** tipicamente incluem os custos em que se incorre no processo de contratação, treinamento de novos trabalhadores e o custo de produtos descartados enquanto os trabalhadores estão aprendendo suas funções.

Os **custos de demissão** normalmente incluem o pagamento de rescisão de contratos trabalhistas, benefícios empregatícios etc.

O Exemplo 8.1 compara dois planos agregados alternativos para a Sherman-Brown. Os dois planos usam ou trabalho em horas extras ou subcontratações para aumentar uma força de trabalho em horas normais constante.

Conforme o exemplo ilustra, muitos fatores, alguns com efeitos sobre os custos e lucros difíceis de quantificar, podem ser usados para avaliar planos agregados.

PLANOS AGREGADOS PARA SERVIÇOS

Alguns sistemas de serviços realizam planejamento agregado quase da mesma maneira que a Sherman-Brown. De fato, em alguns sistemas de serviços que oferecem serviços padronizados para clientes, o planejamento agregado pode ser ainda mais simples do que em sistemas que produzem produtos. Exemplos dessas situações de planejamento agregado em sistemas de serviços são os restaurantes, empresas de transporte em caminhões, empresas aéreas e bancos.

O Exemplo 8.2 ilustra o planejamento agregado da capacidade numa companhia de fretes aéreos.

EXEMPLO 8.1

NIVELAR A CAPACIDADE COM TRABALHO EM HORAS EXTRAS OU COM SUBCONTRATAÇÕES

A Sherman-Brown Chemical Company tem considerado manter somente o número suficiente de trabalhadores em horas normais por trimestre para produzir 40 mil galões. Ou subcontratações ou trabalho em horas extras seriam usados para preencher a diferença entre a capacidade de produção de 40 mil galões por trimestre, trabalhando em horas normais, e a demanda trimestral altamente variável. A Sherman-Brown fornecerá os materiais, e tem uma proposta de um fornecedor por um preço de US$ 19,50 para cada galão fornecido, e o fornecedor dá a garantia de que poderia suprir até 20 mil galões por trimestre. O sindicato de trabalhadores da Sherman-Brown quer trabalhar o máximo de horas extras para evitar o uso do fornecedor. O custo do trabalho em horas extras é US$ 9,50 por hora extra trabalhada. **a)** Compute o custo das horas extras e o custo de subcontratação por trimestre para os dois planos agregados. **b)** Quais fatores seriam importantes na decisão entre os dois planos?

SOLUÇÃO

a) Primeiramente, compute a quantidade de tinta que teria de ser fornecida ou pelo trabalho em horas extras ou pela subcontratação e determine o custo de cada um dos planos alternativos:

(1) Trimestre	(2) Demanda Agregada (galões)	(3) Galões a Serem Fornecidos pelo Trabalho em Horas Extras ou Subcontratação [(2) − 40.000]	(4) Custo do Trabalho em Horas Extras [(3) × 2,311 × 9,50]	(5) Custo da Subcontratação [(3) × 19,50]
1	40.000	0	$ 0	$ 0
2	57.500	17.500	384.204	341.250
3	55.000	15.000	329.318	292.500
4	52.500	12.500	274.431	243.750
		Total	$ 987.953	$ 877.500

b) Quais fatores seriam importantes na decisão entre os dois planos?

1. Os custos desenvolvidos na tabela acima são certamente um fator importante.
2. Manter relações cordiais entre a administração e o sindicato de trabalhadores também é importante. Se os trabalhadores disserem que querem trabalhar a quantidade de horas extras que seriam necessárias, permitir que eles trabalhem em horas extras poderia ser um fator positivo nas negociações futuras. Os benefícios desse fator teriam de ser ponderados em relação ao custo adicional do trabalho em horas extras sobre o de subcontratação.
3. Cansaço, moral baixo e custos elevados seriam o resultado final de se trabalhar demasiadamente em horas extras. Esse fator seria um custo adicional que teria de ser acrescentado ao fator 2 acima.
4. A qualidade do produto poderia ser ou não ser melhor com o plano de trabalho em horas extras, porque toda produção seria feita em casa (*in-house*) e sob controle direto da Sherman-Brown.
5. A flexibilidade de aumentar ou diminuir os níveis de produção em qualquer trimestre parece ser quase a mesma com ambas as alternativas. Porém, se a alternativa de subcontratar for escolhida, trabalho em horas extras poderia ser usado para aumentar ainda mais a produção. Por outro lado, se a alternativa de trabalho em horas extras for escolhida, diminuir os níveis de produção poderia ser mais fácil simplesmente reduzindo-se o trabalho em horas extras.

Capítulo 8 – Sistemas de Planejamento da Produção

EXEMPLO 8.2

PLANEJAMENTO AGREGADO DA CAPACIDADE NA QUICK CARGO AIR FREIGHT COMPANY

O terminal central da Quick Cargo Air Freight Company recebe fretes aéreos de aviões que chegam de todos os pontos dos Estados Unidos e os redistribui para embarque para todos os destinos nos Estados Unidos. A empresa garante remessa noturna de todos os pacotes; desse modo, pessoal suficiente deve estar disponível para processar toda a carga quando ela chega. A empresa agora tem 24 empregados que trabalham no terminal. A demanda prevista para os trabalhadores de armazéns durante os próximos sete meses é 24, 26, 30, 28, 28, 24 e 24. Os custos são $ 2.000 para contratar e $ 3.500 para demitir cada trabalhador. Se for usado trabalho em horas extras para suprir mão-de-obra além da força de trabalho atual, isto custará o equivalente a $ 2.600 a mais para cada trabalhador adicional. A empresa deve usar uma estratégia de nivelar a capacidade com trabalho em horas extras ou um plano de acompanhar a demanda durante os próximos seis meses?

SOLUÇÃO

O custo do trabalho em horas normais pode ser desconsiderado para a finalidade de comparar os dois planos, porque ele seria incluído em ambos os planos. A análise gira em torno do custo do trabalho em horas extras para nivelar a capacidade contra o custo de contratar e demitir trabalhadores no plano de acompanhar a demanda.

Primeiramente, determine o custo do trabalho em horas extras no plano de nivelar a capacidade:

(1) Mês	(2) Número Previsto de Trabalhadores	(3) Custo do Trabalho em Horas Extras [(2) − 24] × $ 2.600
1	24	0
2	26	$ 5.200
3	30	15.600
4	28	10.400
5	28	10.400
6	24	0
7	24	0
	Custo das horas extras	$ 41.600

Em seguida, determine o custo para contratar e demitir do plano de acompanhar a demanda:

(1) Mês	(2) Número Necessário de Trabalhadores	(3) Número de Trabalhadores Contratados	(4) Número de Trabalhadores Demitidos	(5) Custo de Trabalhadores Contratados [(3) × $ 2.000]	(6) Custo de Trabalhadores Demitidos [(4) × $ 3.500]
0	24				
1	24	0	0	0	0
2	26	2		$ 4.000	
3	30	4		8.000	
4	28		2		$ 7.000
5	28	0	0	0	0
6	24		4		14.000
7	24				
			Custo	$ 12.000	$ 21.000

> O custo total do plano de acompanhar a demanda é o custo de contratar e demitir trabalhadores, ou $ 12.000 + $21.000 = $ 33.000. O custo do plano de acompanhar a demanda é menor que o plano de nivelar a capacidade com horas extras e deve ser preferido.

Alguns sistemas que fornecem serviços personalizados a clientes enfrentam a mesma dificuldade que as job shops ao especificar a natureza e a extensão dos serviços a serem executados para cada cliente. Exemplos desses sistemas são os hospitais, centros de serviço de computação e oficinas de funilaria de automóveis. Outro fator complicador com muitos desses sistemas de serviços personalizados é que, diferentemente das job shops, o cliente pode ser uma parte integrante do sistema de produção, e ajustar a capacidade de produção para cima ou para baixo pode alterar diretamente a qualidade percebida dos serviços prestados. Exemplos desses serviços são os pequenos colégios e universidades particulares, clubes de campo privados e clínicas de saúde particulares.

Também especialmente preocupante para os gerentes que devem planejar níveis de capacidade para sistemas de serviço é a ausência de estoques de produtos acabados como um amortecedor entre a capacidade do sistema e as necessidades dos clientes. Porém, planos de nivelar a capacidade ainda podem ser usados se empregados trabalhando em horas extras ou em tempo parcial puderem ser utilizados para ajustar a diferença entre a taxa de demanda variável e a taxa de produção constante. Isso é especialmente verdadeiro nos serviços diretos do trabalhador para o cliente em que nenhum produto é processado, armazenado ou transferido. Exemplos desses sistemas são os serviços de imposto de renda, serviços jurídicos e serviços de ambulância de emergência e de combate a incêndios. Outras técnicas também encorajam o uso de planos de nivelar a capacidade. Por exemplo, o uso de horários de consulta tende a nivelar as alterações na demanda nas clínicas médicas, promovendo assim os planos de nivelar a capacidade. Similarmente, os guichês de atendimento depois do expediente nos bancos promovem os planos de nivelar a capacidade. Apesar dessas inovações, entretanto, muitos desses sistemas devem desenvolver planos de capacidade que quase coincidam com a demanda agregada esperada.

Em sistemas que prestam serviços padronizados, realizaríamos um planejamento agregado da capacidade, como no Exemplo 8.2. Em serviços projetados de forma personalizada, sugeriríamos uma abordagem de dois passos ao planejamento agregado. Primeiro, desenvolva previsões de demanda agregada em algumas unidades homogêneas de medição, como, por exemplo, horas de trabalho, capacidade de máquina ou dólares de vendas. Segundo, tente descobrir unidades de capacidade com denominador comum que sejam úteis para transformar demanda agregada em necessidades de recursos de produção. Essa experimentação pode ser necessária para desenvolver esses fatores de transformação. Em seguida, especialmente se a primeira sugestão for inviável, desenvolva inovações alternativas para ampliar a flexibilidade das capacidades dos recursos de produção. Exemplos dessas inovações são os trabalhadores em disponibilidade (standby), que são convocados em períodos de demanda de pico, máquinas e prédios que podem ser ativados durante períodos de demanda de pico, subcontratados que respondem rapidamente e aposentados que desejam trabalhar somente em tempo parcial e podem ser reconvocados por períodos breves. Esses recursos de reserva fornecem aos gerentes de operações um plano agregado da capacidade quase nivelada com a capacidade extra necessária para responder a súbitas elevações de demanda.

MODELOS MATEMÁTICOS PARA O PLANEJAMENTO AGREGADO

Diversos métodos de planejamento agregado foram desenvolvidos à medida que o uso de computadores e a disciplina de Pesquisa Operacional cresceram. Esses métodos procuram projetar planos de capacidade para sistemas de produção que atinjam os objetivos das organizações dentro da disponibilidade de seus recursos de produção e restrições de demanda agregada. Uma breve descrição de três desses métodos encontra-se na Tabela 8.2.

Os modelos matemáticos no planejamento agregado não predominam na prática da APO — não ainda, pelo menos. Mas você deve saber a respeito dessas técnicas, porque suas abordagens são úteis para reestruturarmos a maneira pela qual pensamos e abordamos esses problemas complexos. E os modelos podem tornar-se mais importantes no planejamento da capacidade no futuro.

Capítulo 8 – Sistemas de Planejamento da Produção

TABELA 8.2	MODELOS MATEMÁTICOS PARA PLANEJAMENTO AGREGADO

1. **Programação linear.** E. H. Bowman foi um dos primeiros a aplicar programação linear ao planejamento agregado.[a] Os modelos de programação linear procuram minimizar os custos operacionais totais ao longo do horizonte de planejamento, e incluem custos como o do trabalho em horas normais, em horas extras, custos de subcontratação, custos da contratação de trabalhadores, custos da demissão de trabalhadores e custos de manutenção em estoque. As restrições dos modelos normalmente incluem fatores como a capacidade máxima disponível em cada período de tempo dos trabalhadores em horas normais, em horas extras e novos trabalhadores, e a demanda agregada cumulativa mínima ao longo do horizonte de planejamento.

2. **Regras de decisão lineares (LDRs — linear decision rules).** Holt, Modigliani, Muth e Simon, do Carnegie Institute of Technology, foram os primeiros a usar essa abordagem.[b] As LDRs desenvolvem uma função matemática quadrática de custo que inclui — folha de pagamento normal, contratação, demissão, horas extras, manutenção em estoque, pedidos pendentes ou escassez de produtos, e preparação. A função matemática quadrática composta de custo é resolvida por meio de cálculo ou métodos de programação quadráticos. A solução fornece o número de trabalhadores a serem contratados ou demitidos, o número necessário de horas extras, flutuações de estoque esperadas e preparação de máquina.

3. **Pesquisa computadorizada.** Essa abordagem examina seqüencialmente milhares de combinações de recursos de produção (trabalho em horas normais, horas extras, demissões, contratações e subcontratações) em cada período de tempo para atender a demanda agregada cumulativa ao longo de um horizonte de planejamento. Esse método usa regras previamente programadas que controlam a maneira pela qual recursos podem ser combinados para se escolher um plano de capacidade de baixo custo para cada período de tempo.

[a]Bowman, E. H. "Production Planning by the Transportation Method of Linear Programming". *Journal of Operations Research Society*, 4 de fevereiro de 1956.

[b]Holt, Charles C., Franco Modigliani, John F. Muth e Herbert A. Simon. *Planning Production, Inventories, and Work Force.* Englewood Cliffs, NJ: Prentice Hall, 1960.

TÁTICAS DE PREEMPÇÃO

A partir de nossa discussão a respeito do planejamento agregado, pode parecer que a administração não pode afetar os padrões de demanda e que lidar com alterações na demanda é uma parte necessária do planejamento agregado. Embora isso seja parcialmente verdadeiro, a administração pode envolver-se em atividades que terão grandes alterações na demanda. As empresas freqüentemente publicam **preços com desconto** que entram em vigor durante as baixas de demanda, e **preços de pico** (ou preços de temporada) que entram em vigor durante picos de demanda. Essas táticas de preços tendem a motivar os clientes a fazerem um número menor de pedidos durante períodos de pico de demanda e mais pedidos durante períodos com baixas de demanda. Similarmente, as empresas podem influenciar padrões de demanda com táticas como as das promoções "pague 2 e leve 3", "compre agora e só pague no próximo mês" e remessas com frete gratuito durante períodos de baixa demanda. Dessa maneira, a demanda torna-se mais uniforme e o planejamento agregado, mais direto.

Discutimos os principais conceitos, questões e técnicas do planejamento agregado — o desenvolvimento de planos de capacidade de médio prazo para sistemas de produção. Esses planos entram diretamente na programação diária de produtos e serviços. O programa mestre de produção é o ponto de partida para essas programações do dia-a-dia.

PROGRAMA MESTRE DE PRODUÇÃO

O **programa mestre de produção (MPS — master program schedule)** define a quantidade de cada item final a ser concluída em cada semana do horizonte de planejamento de curto prazo. Itens finais são produtos acabados, ou peças que são embarcadas como itens finais. Itens finais podem ser embarcados para os clientes ou colocados em estoque. *Os gerentes de operações se reúnem semanalmente para revisar pre-*

visões de mercado, pedidos dos clientes, níveis de estoque, carga de instalações e informações sobre a capacidade, a fim de que programas mestres de produção possam ser desenvolvidos. O MPS é um plano para produção futura de itens finais ao longo de um horizonte de planejamento de curto prazo que normalmente abrange de algumas semanas a vários meses.

Objetivos do Programa Mestre de Produção

Como é ilustrado na Figura 8.1, a capacidade de produção de curto prazo é restrita pelo plano agregado de capacidade. O programa mestre de produção pega essa capacidade de produção de curto prazo que foi determinada pelo plano agregado e a aloca para pedidos de itens finais. Os objetivos do programa mestre de produção são duplos:

1. Programar itens finais para serem concluídos prontamente e quando prometido aos clientes.
2. Evitar sobrecarregar ou gerar ociosidades na produção, a fim de que a capacidade de produção seja utilizada eficientemente e resulte em baixos custos de produção.

Período de Congelamento em Programas Mestres de Produção

Os programas mestres de produção podem ser vistos como divididos em quatro seções, cada uma separada por um ponto no tempo chamado **período de congelamento (*time fence*[2])**. A primeira seção inclui as primeiras semanas do programa e nos referimos a ela como *congelada*; a segunda seção de algumas semanas é denominada *firme*; a seção seguinte de algumas semanas é chamada *cheia*; e a última seção de algumas semanas é chamada *aberta*.

Congelada significa que essa primeira parte do MPS não pode ser modificada, a não ser sob circunstâncias extraordinárias e somente com autorização dos mais altos níveis da organização. Modificações nessa parte do programa normalmente são proibidas, porque seria dispendioso inverter os planos para comprar materiais e produzir as peças que entram nos produtos. Além disso, quando mudamos o MPS, deslocamos um pedido, colocando-o na frente de outro — por que tornarmos um cliente satisfeito à custa de tornarmos outro insatisfeito? *Firme* significa que podem ocorrer mudanças nessa seção do programa, mas somente em situações excepcionais. Resiste-se a mudanças nessa seção do programa pelas mesmas razões que na seção "congelada". *Cheia* significa que toda a capacidade de produção disponível foi alocada aos pedidos. Mudanças podem ser feitas na seção "cheia" do programa, e os custos de produção serão apenas ligeiramente afetados, mas o efeito sobre a satisfação do cliente é incerto. *Aberta* significa que nem toda a capacidade de produção foi alocada, e é nessa seção do programa que novos pedidos comumente são encaixados.

Procedimentos para Desenvolver Programas Mestres de Produção

A Figura 8.7 ilustra o processo para desenvolvermos o programa mestre de produção. Trabalhando a partir dos pedidos dos clientes, previsões, relatórios da situação do estoque e informações sobre a capacidade de produção, os programadores de produção colocam os pedidos mais urgentes no primeiro encaixe aberto disponível do MPS. Diversas atividades importantes ocorrem nesse ponto. Primeiro, os programadores devem estimar a demanda total para os produtos de todas as fontes, designar pedidos a brechas (slots) de produção, fazer promessas de entrega a clientes e fazer os cálculos detalhados para o MPS. O Exemplo 8.3 ilustra como um programador da produção poderia totalizar as demandas e executar os cálculos detalhados para um MPS. As atividades de entrada de pedidos e promessa de entrega dos pedidos serão discutidas na seção sobre administração da demanda.

---

[2] A expressão *time fence* tem surgido na literatura técnica brasileira traduzido por: período de congelamento, horizonte firme e até mesmo por "cerca de tempo". (N. do R.T.)

Capítulo 8 – Sistemas de Planejamento da Produção

FIGURA 8.7   O Processo do Programa Mestre de Produção

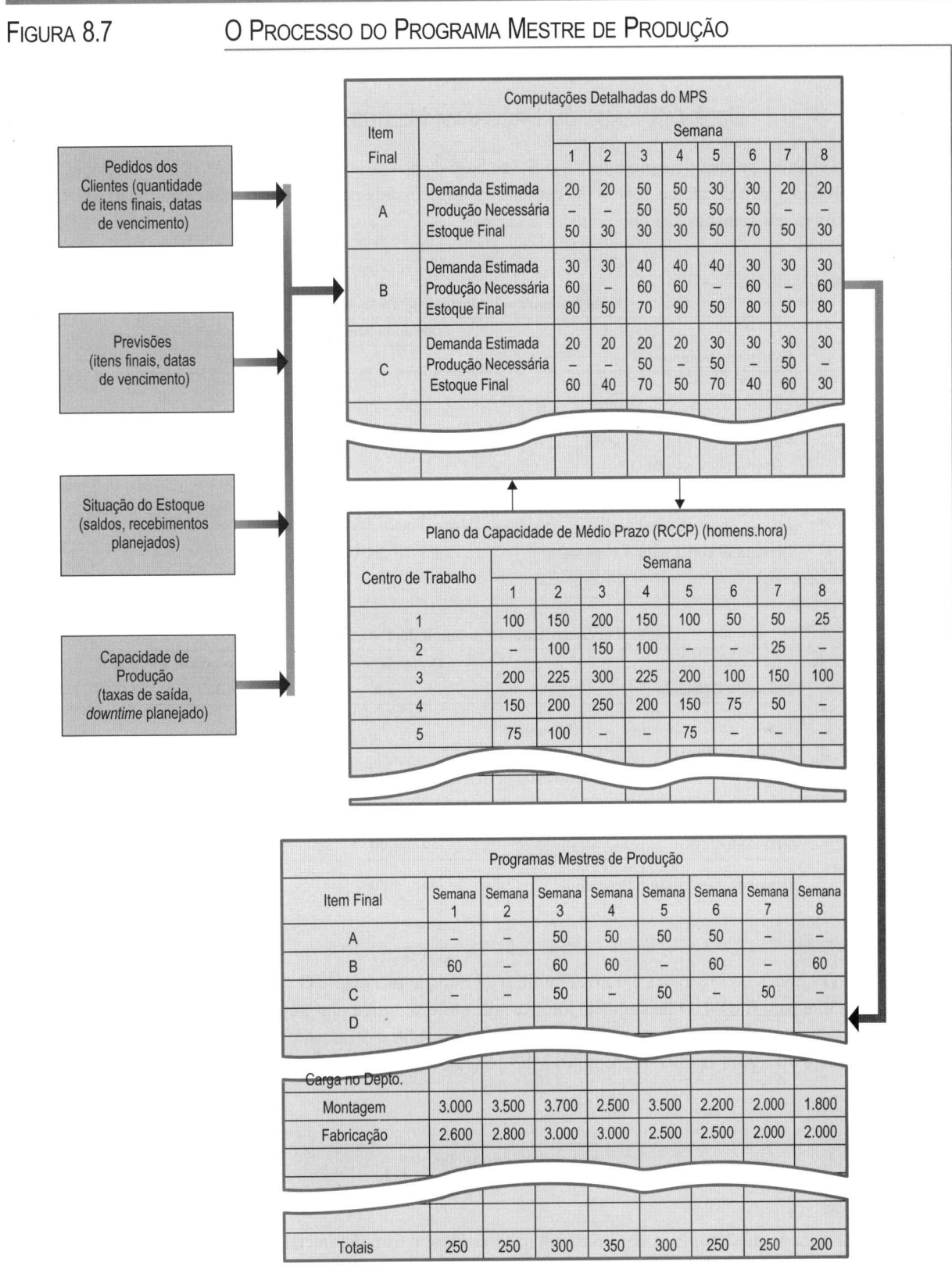

Exemplo 8.3

Desenvolvendo um Programa Mestre de Produção

Uma empresa produz dois produtos, A e B, em base de produção para estoque. As demandas para os produtos vêm de muitas fontes. As estimativas de demanda para os dois produtos ao longo das próximas seis semanas são apresentadas a seguir.

Demanda para o Produto A de Todas as Fontes

Fontes da Demanda	Demanda Semanal (número de produtos A)					
	1	2	3	4	5	6
Pedidos internos da empresa (*intercompany*)				20	10	10
Pedidos de armazéns filiais			20			
Pedidos do departamento de pesquisa e desenvolvimento (P&D)				10	10	
Necessidades do cliente (previsões e pedidos em mãos)	20	20	20	20	20	20
Demandas Totais para o Produto A	20	20	50	50	30	30

Demandas para o Produto B de Todas as Fontes

Fontes de Demanda	Demanda Semanal (número de produtos B)					
	1	2	3	4	5	6
Pedidos internos da empresa (*intercompany*)			10		10	
Pedidos de armazéns filiais				20		
Pedidos do departamento de pesquisa e desenvolvimento (P&D)					10	10
Necessidades do cliente (previsões e pedidos em mãos)	30	30	30	20	20	20
Demanda Total para o Produto B	30	30	40	40	40	30

O estoque de segurança é o nível mínimo de estoque planejado. O estoque de segurança para A é 30 e para B é 40. O tamanho de lote fixo (um **lote** significa um grupo, e um tamanho de lote é produzido quando ocorre a produção do produto) para A é 50 e para B é 60. O estoque inicial para A é 70 e para B é 50. Prepare um MPS para esses dois produtos.

Solução

Para cada produto, tome as demandas totais, considere o estoque inicial, determine em quais semanas o estoque final cairia abaixo do estoque de segurança (ES), e, dessa forma, exigiria produção, e programe um lote do produto a ser produzido durante essas semanas.

Capítulo 8 – Sistemas de Planejamento da Produção

Programa Mestre de Produção (Número de Produtos A e B)

Item Final		Semanas					
		1	2	3	4	5	6
A	Demanda total	20	20	50	50	30	30
	Estoque inicial	70	50	30	30	30	50
	Produção necessária	—	—	50	50	50	50
	Estoque final	50	30	30	30	50	70
B	Demanda total	30	30	40	40	40	30
	Estoque inicial	50	80	50	70	90	50
	Produção necessária	60	—	60	60	—	60
	Estoque final	80	50	70	90	50	80

Observação: Os estoques de segurança são 30 para A e 40 para B, os tamanhos de lote fixos são 50 para A e 60 para B, e o estoque inicial na semana 1 é 70 para A e 50 para B.

Olhemos mais de perto os cálculos correspondentes ao produto A no MPS acima. Percorra essas computações e compare-as com o MPS:

(1) Semana	(2) Estoque Inicial	(3) Demanda Total	(4) Saldo [(2) − (3)]	(5) Produção Necessária [tamanho de lote fixo se a coluna (4) for menor do que o estoque de segurança; se não, será igual a zero]	(6) Estoque Final [(2) + (5) − (3)]
1	70	20	50	—	50
2	50	20	30	—	30
3	30	50	(20)	50	30
4	30	50	(20)	50	30
5	30	30	0	50	50
6	50	30	20	50	70

Observação: Para o produto A, o estoque de segurança é 30, o tamanho de lote fixo é 50 e o estoque inicial na semana 1 é 70.

Na semana 1 o saldo ultrapassa o estoque de segurança desejado (50 > 30); portanto, nenhuma produção de A é necessária. Na semana 2 o saldo também é suficiente para fornecer o estoque de segurança desejado (30 = 30), e nenhuma produção de A é necessária. Mas, nas semanas 3 e 4, os saldos seriam de fato negativos se a produção de A não fosse programada; portanto, um tamanho de lote fixo de 50 produtos A é programada em ambas essas semanas. As semanas 5 e 6 são computadas similarmente.

Quando pedidos são encaixados no MPS, os efeitos sobre a carga dos centros de trabalho de produção são verificados. Essa verificação preliminar do MPS às vezes é chamada **planejamento da capacidade de médio prazo (RCCP — rough-cut capacity planning)**. A meta principal do planejamento da capacidade de médio prazo é identificar qualquer semana no MPS em que ocorra subcarga ou sobrecarga da capacidade de produção e revisar o MPS quando necessário. **Subcarga** (*underloading*) significa que uma produção não suficiente de itens finais foi programada para carregar plenamente a instalação. **Sobrecarga** (*overloading*) significa que demasiada produção de itens finais foi programada na instalação e que existe uma capacidade insuficiente para produzir o MPS. O Exemplo 8.4 ilustra como o planejamento da capacidade de médio prazo (RCCP) pode ser executado.

Exemplo 8.4

Planejamento da Capacidade de Médio Prazo

A empresa do Exemplo 8.3 agora deseja determinar se o MPS que foi desenvolvido subcarrega ou sobrecarrega a linha de montagem final que produz tanto o produto A como o produto B. A linha de montagem final tem uma capacidade semanal disponível de 100 horas. Cada produto A requer 0,9 hora, e cada produto B requer 1,6 hora de capacidade de montagem final. **a)** Compute as horas de montagem final reais necessárias para produzir o previsto no MPS para ambos os produtos; isso muitas vezes é chamado *carga*. Compare a carga com a capacidade de montagem final disponível em cada semana e para o total de 6 semanas; isso muitas vezes é chamado *planejamento da capacidade de médio prazo* (RCCP). **b)** Existe uma capacidade de montagem final suficiente para produzir o MPS? **c)** Quais mudanças no MPS você recomendaria?

Solução

a) Compute a carga em cada semana e durante as 6 semanas, e compare as cargas com a capacidade de montagem final:

Item Final		Horas Semanais de Montagem Final						
		1	2	3	4	5	6	Total
A	Produção	—	—	(50)	(50)	(50)	(50)	
	Horas de montagem final	—	—	45	45	45	45	
B	Produção	(60)	—	(60)	(60)	—	(60)	
	Horas de montagem final	96	—	96	96	—	96	
Carga (horas)		96	—	141	141	45	141	564
Capacidade (horas)		100	100	100	100	100	100	600

Observação: Os números entre parênteses são os números dos itens finais a serem produzidos em cada semana. Eles vêm do MPS do Exemplo 8.3.

b) Um total de 600 horas de capacidade de montagem final está disponível durante o programa de 6 semanas, e o MPS requer somente um total de 564 horas. Entretanto, o MPS sobrecarrega a montagem final nas semanas 3, 4 e 6 e subcarrega a montagem final nas semanas 1, 2 e 5.

c) Um balanceamento melhor da capacidade de montagem final semanal é possível se alguns dos lotes de produção forem deslocados para semanas anteriores do programa. Desloque lotes do produto A das semanas 4 e 6 para as semanas 3 e 5, e desloque o lote do produto B da semana 3 para a semana 2:

Item Final		Horas Semanais de Montagem Final						
		1	2	3	4	5	6	Total
A	Produção	—	—	(100)	—	(100)	—	
	Horas de montagem final	—	—	90	—	90	—	
B	Produção	(60)	(60)	—	(60)	—	(60)	
	Horas de montagem final	96	96	—	96	—	96	
Carga (horas)		96	96	90	96	90	96	564
Capacidade (horas)		100	100	100	100	100	100	600

Observação: Os números entre parênteses são os números dos itens finais a serem produzidos em cada semana.

Esse MPS revisado carregaria melhor a linha de montagem final, mas certo estoque adicional seria criado produzindo-se esses lotes mais cedo.

ADMINISTRAÇÃO DA DEMANDA

Estimar a demanda futura é uma parte crucial do programa mestre de produção. A American Production and Inventory Control Society (APICS) descreve isso como **administração da demanda**, que é definida como "a função de reconhecer todas as demandas por produtos e serviços para sustentar o mercado. Ela envolve fazer aquilo que é necessário para ajudar a fazer a demanda acontecer e priorizar a demanda quando a oferta estiver em falta. A apropriada administração da demanda facilita o planejamento e a utilização de recursos para se obter resultados comerciais lucrativos. Ela abrange as atividades de previsão, entrada de pedidos, promessa de entrega de pedidos e determinação das necessidades de armazéns, pedidos entre fábricas e necessidades de peças de manutenção". A administração da demanda inclui estabelecer um sistema de previsão eficaz para os itens finais, monitorar as previsões e modificar o sistema quando necessário para melhorar as previsões.

A **entrada de pedidos** e a **promessa de entrega de pedidos** são funções importantes no programa mestre de produção. Os programas mestres devem revisar os pedidos dos clientes, checar as datas de entrega solicitadas em relação às brechas de produção abertas no MPS, determinar a prioridade dos pedidos, designar brechas de produção no MPS para os pedidos e comunicar as datas prometidas aos clientes. Cada data prometida orienta um pedido ao longo dos processos de produção e torna-se uma meta importante dos gerentes de operações até que o pedido seja entregue ao cliente. Os pedidos vêm de dentro da empresa. O departamento de marketing pede produtos como amostras para dar aos clientes como promoção, o departamento de P&D pede produtos para serem usados em testes, e armazéns filiais pedem produtos. Peças de manutenção comumente são pedidas por distribuidores para ser usadas em trabalho de garantia ou conserto. Os pedidos dessas peças são tratados no programa mestre de produção como outros pedidos de clientes, exceto que as peças são tratadas como itens finais e, dessa forma, tornam-se parte do MPS.

ATUALIZAÇÃO SEMANAL DO MPS

Para entender realmente a natureza da administração da demanda, devemos entender a natureza dinâmica do MPS. O MPS em geral é atualizado semanalmente, o que quer dizer que, passada uma semana, uma semana é retirada da parte da frente do MPS, uma semana é acrescentada à parte de trás, e as demandas correspondentes ao MPS inteiro são estimadas novamente. Uma vez que as demandas que estão muito distantes nos últimos períodos do MPS provavelmente serão modificadas quando sofrerem muitas atualizações ao se mover rumo à parte anterior, congelada, do programa, a precisão das previsões na última parte do MPS não será tão crucial como na parte anterior. Além disso, a parte anterior do MPS tende a ser dominada por pedidos reais presentes feitos por clientes, ao passo que a última parte do programa tende a ser dominada por previsões. Dessa forma, as previsões de demanda da primeira parte do MPS são, por natureza, mais acuradas.

A Figura 8.8 ilustra esse princípio. Nas semanas 1 e 2 a estimativa de demanda é composta inteiramente por pedidos. Na semana 8 a estimativa de demanda é composta inteiramente por previsões. No meio do programa, a estimativa de demanda é uma combinação de pedidos reais e previsões, mas previsões se tornam mais predominantes à medida que nos movemos para períodos posteriores. Através do processo de atualização semanal, as estimativas de demanda nos últimos períodos do MPS, que se baseiam principalmente em previsões, movem-se para a frente no MPS, e essas estimativas de demanda tornam-se mais acuradas por duas razões. Primeiro, grande parte da demanda baseada em previsões torna-se baseada mais em pedidos de clientes, e, em segundo lugar, as previsões tornam-se aprimoradas através do processo de atualização semanal. De semana a semana, à medida que o MPS é atualizado, os pedidos permanecem fluindo e as previsões são modificadas, e tudo isso ocorre antes que capital deva ser comprometido com pedido de materiais, programação de trabalhadores e programação de preparação de máquina. No momento em que um pedido se move para a parte anterior, congelada, do MPS, e capital deve ser comprometido com o pedido, os gerentes de operações são capazes de colocar muita confiança na precisão das estimativas de demanda.

FIGURA 8.8 — ESTIMATIVAS DA DEMANDA: UMA COMBINAÇÃO DE PEDIDOS E PREVISÕES

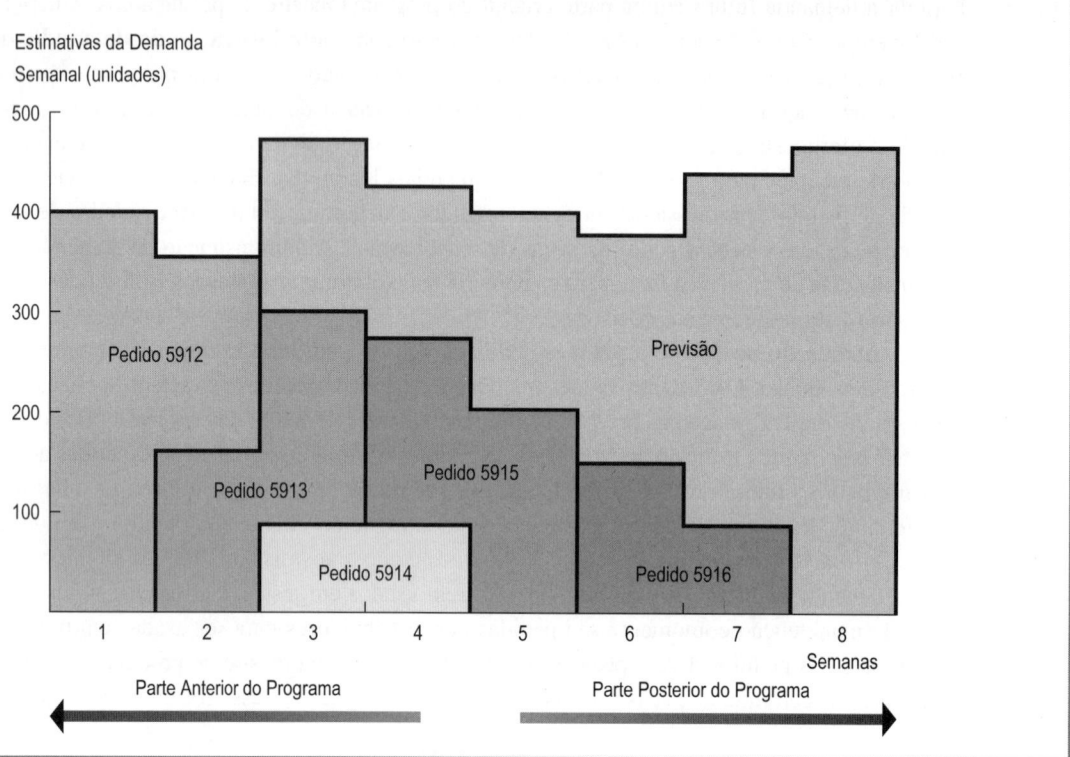

O MPS EM EMPRESAS DE PRODUÇÃO PARA ESTOQUE E DE PRODUÇÃO SOB ENCOMENDA

Os procedimentos do programa mestre de produção diferem para empresas de produção para estoque ou sob encomenda. Os elementos do MPS mais afetados pelo tipo de sistema de produção são a **administração da demanda**, a **determinação do tamanho de lote** e o **número de produtos a programar**.

Em sistemas de produção sob encomenda, os pedidos dos clientes constituem o foco predominante na administração da demanda. O programador da produção normalmente trabalha a partir de um backlog de pedidos de clientes, e as previsões de demanda por produtos podem não ser usadas. Os pedidos dos clientes no backlog são designados a espaços de produção abertos. O tamanho do lote, o número de produtos a serem produzidos num pedido, normalmente é determinado pelo pedido do cliente. Se um cliente pedir 500 unidades de um produto em particular, comumente 500 unidades dos produtos serão produzidas num pedido. Essa abordagem de determinação do tamanho de lote é denominada **lote por lote (LFL — lot-for-lot)**.

Em empresas de produção para estoque, os pedidos de produtos vêm principalmente de pedidos feitos por armazéns de dentro da empresa. Esses pedidos baseiam-se em previsões da demanda futura por produtos procurados por muitos clientes. As previsões, portanto, tendem a desempenhar um papel mais importante na administração da demanda em empresas de produção para estoque. Na primeira parte do MPS, esses pedidos de armazéns que se baseavam em previsões podem ser sustentados pelos pedidos reais dos clientes. Porém, em empresas de produção para estoque, os pedidos dos clientes afetam apenas indiretamente a administração ao afetar os pedidos feitos por armazéns.

Os tamanhos de lote dos pedidos em empresas de produção para estoque são uma questão de economia. Quanto de um produto em particular deve ser produzido a fim de que o custo de produção médio por unidade seja baixo? Se produzirmos muito pouco do produto, o custo fixo de preparar-se para produzir o pedido será dividido entre um número muito pequeno de produtos, e o custo de produção médio por unidade será elevado. Se produzirmos muito do produto, o estoque do produto se tornará muito grande à medida que produzirmos o pedido, o custo de manutenção em estoque se tornará muito elevado, e o custo de produção médio por unidade será também muito elevado. Deve-se descobrir um equilíbrio entre esses custos ao determinar tamanhos de lote econômicos em empresas de produção para estoque.

Extensão dos Horizontes de Planejamento

Os horizontes de planejamento no programa mestre podem variar de apenas algumas semanas, em algumas empresas, a mais de um ano em outras. Como uma empresa decide quão longo deve ser seu horizonte de planejamento? Não obstante diversos fatores se imporem nessa decisão, um fator tende a ser predominante: *o horizonte de planejamento deve ser no mínimo igual ao mais longo lead time cumulativo do item final.* **Lead time cumulativo do item final** significa a quantidade de tempo para receber o material dos fornecedores, produzir todas as peças e montagens, ter o item final montado e pronto para expedição, e entregá-lo aos clientes. O item final com o maior lead time determina, portanto, a menor quantidade de tempo em que um horizonte de planejamento deve estender-se. Na prática, os horizontes de planejamento normalmente são maiores do que este mínimo.

A descrição do MPS acima mencionou com freqüência as atividades dos programadores de produção. Em algumas aplicações do MPS atualmente, algumas dessas atividades são executadas por computador.

MPS Computadorizado

O MPS pode ser preparado com o auxílio de um sistema computadorizado. Nesses casos, as informações sobre demanda de itens finais, informações sobre situação de estoques, restrições de capacidade, previsões da demanda, tamanhos de lote e níveis de estoque de segurança desejados são usados pelo computador para executar os cálculos de MPS detalhados, comparar esses valores com as cargas do centro de trabalho e restrições de capacidade e, finalmente, gerar um MPS. Quando itens finais são produzidos em diversos departamentos de produção, o computador não somente é econômico; ele é absolutamente necessário para processar todos os dados.

O MPS certamente é o foco central na maioria dos sistemas de programação computadorizados, independentemente de se os programas são projetados de forma personalizada para um sistema de produção ou se são um sistema padrão de uma das empresas produtoras de hardware ou software de computador.

O *Communications Oriented Production Information and Control Systems* (COPICS) da IBM, como ilustra a Figura 8.9, é um exemplo desses sistemas de programação computadorizados. Não obstante o COPICS ter evoluído e trocado de nome ao longo dos anos, ele ainda ilustra a utilidade dos computadores na programação, planejamento e controle de produção. O COPICS e sistemas similares são mais do que apenas sistemas de programação computadorizados, porque eles integram decisões de previsão, programação, estoques e compras num grande sistema de informação para planejar e controlar todas as facetas do sistema de produção.

Quando o programa mestre de produção é feito de maneira apropriada, relações positivas com o cliente são desenvolvidas, os níveis de estoques são baixos porque os itens finais certos são produzidos em quantidades exatas, e os recursos de produção são plenamente utilizados. Adicionalmente, o MPS impulsiona todos os sistemas do planejamento e controle da produção que discutiremos agora.

Tipos de Sistemas de Planejamento e Controle da Produção

Assim que um programa mestre de produção é concluído, sabe-se quando e quantos produtos de cada tipo serão expedidos. Como uma organização de produção planeja e controla a compra de materiais, a produção de peças e montagens e todos os outros trabalhos necessários para produzir os produtos depende do tipo de sistema de planejamento e controle da produção usado. Aqui, descreveremos quatro abordagens ao

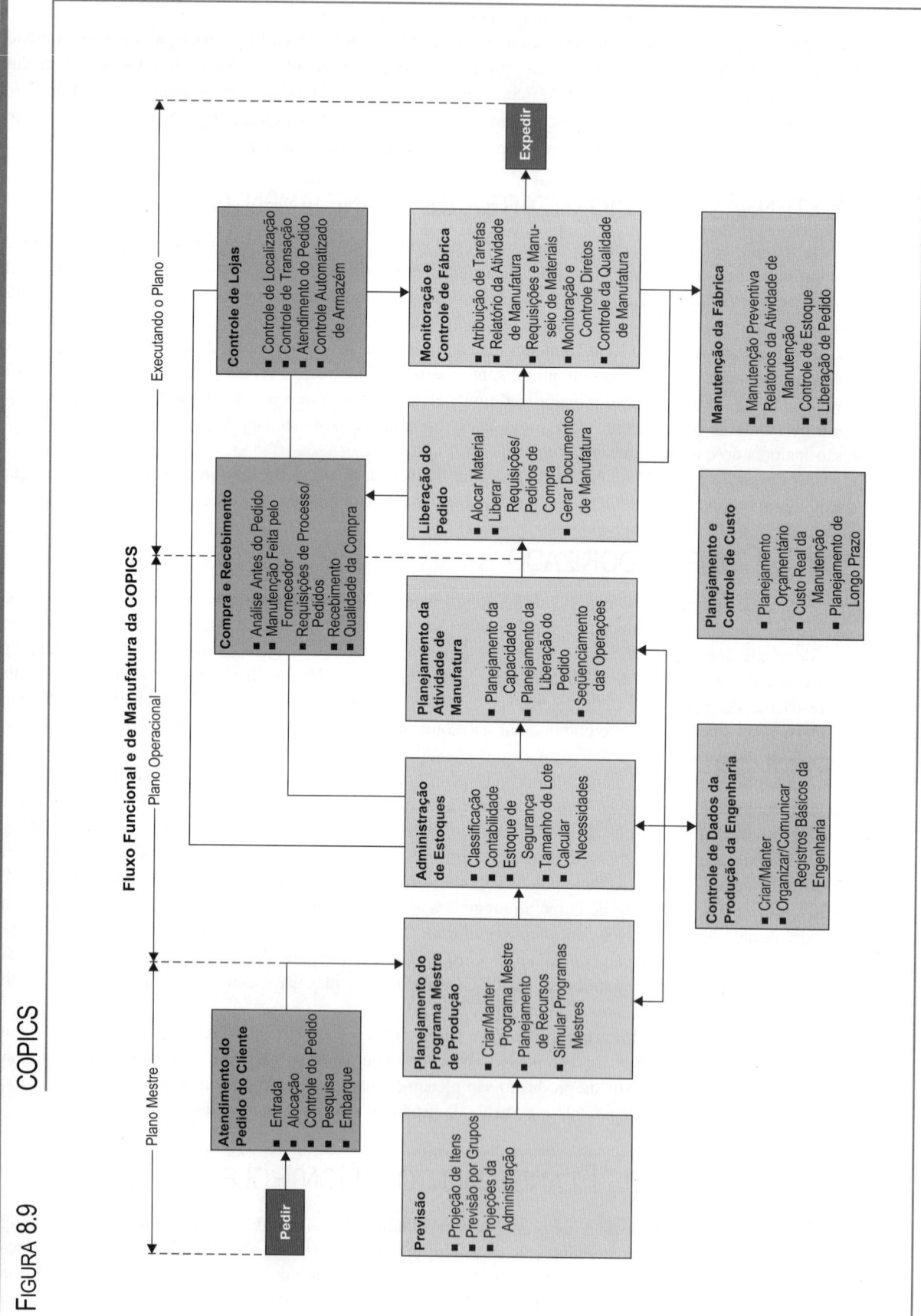

FIGURA 8.9 COPICS

planejamento e controle da produção: estoque de reserva, sistemas empurrar, sistemas puxar e a abordagem que se concentra nos gargalos.

SISTEMAS DE ESTOQUE DE RESERVA

Na **abordagem do estoque de reserva** para planejamento e controle da produção, a ênfase está na manutenção de depósitos de materiais para sustentar a produção. A Figura 8.10 descreve talvez o mais simples dos sistemas de planejamento e controle da produção. A abordagem do estoque de reserva opera com pouca informação percorrendo a cadeia do sistema de produção, dos clientes para a produção e desta para os fornecedores. Uma vez que os fabricantes podem não saber o momento de ocorrência (*timing*) e a quantidade da demanda por clientes, muitos produtos de cada tipo são produzidos de antemão e armazenados no estoque de produtos acabados. Quando são feitos embarques para os clientes, o tanque "estoque de produtos acabados" tem seus produtos drenados, e a montagem final faz mais unidades deles drenando as peças e submontagens que foram feitas antecipadamente e guardadas no estoque de produtos em processo. À medida que os estoques de produtos em processo se exaurem, mais peças e submontagens são produzidas drenando-se o estoque de matérias-primas. À medida que o estoque de matérias-primas se esvazia, pedidos de mais matérias-primas são feitos aos fornecedores. Se uma empresa operar em base de produção sob encomenda em vez de produção para estoque, como descreve a Figura 8.10, um backlog de pedidos de clientes substituiria o tanque "estoque de produtos acabados".

Embora provavelmente seja verdadeiro que os sistemas de informação e comunicação modernos tornaram essa forma simplista de planejamento e controle da produção um tanto obsoleta, os conceitos dessa abordagem ainda são aplicados por algumas empresas. *Um sistema de estoque de reserva pode ser usado ou na produção focalizada no produto ou na focalizada no processo e exige pouca informação sofisticada sobre clientes, fornecedores e produção. Por outro lado, esse tipo de sistema pode levar a estoques excessivos e é bastante inflexível em sua capacidade de responder às necessidades dos clientes.* Essa abordagem tende a funcionar melhor quando a demanda por produtos é verdadeiramente aleatória. As políticas de pedidos de matérias-primas e estoques de produtos acabados são cruciais para sistemas de estoque de reserva. Estudaremos essas políticas no Capítulo 9. Esse tipo de sistema forma um quadro de referência para discutirmos outros tipos de sistemas de planejamento e controle da produção.

SISTEMAS EMPURRAR

Num sistema empurrar (push), a ênfase se desloca para o uso de informações sobre clientes, fornecedores e produção para administrar fluxos de materiais. Lotes de matérias-primas são planejados para chegar a uma fábrica aproximadamente no prazo necessário para se fazer lotes de peças e submontagens. Peças e submontagens são feitas e entregues para montagem final aproximadamente quando necessário, e produtos acabados são montados e embarcados mais ou menos quando os clientes necessitam deles. *Lotes de materiais são empurrados pelas portas dos fundos das fábricas, um após outro, os quais, por sua vez, empurram outros lotes ao longo de todas as etapas de produção. Esses fluxos de materiais são planejados e controlados por uma série de programas de produção que estabelecem quando lotes de cada produto em particular devem sair de cada etapa da produção.* "Isto é um **sistema empurrar**: fazer as peças e enviá-las para onde elas serão necessárias em seguida, ou para estoque, empurrando, assim, materiais ao longo da produção de acordo com o programa."

Vejamos como esse programa se pareceria. Se um pedido de 500 produtos tivesse de ser expedido para um cliente em 30 de agosto e fosse necessário somente uma semana para atravessar cada uma das quatro etapas de produção, o programa seria o seguinte:

Etapa de Produção	Data de Início	Data de Encerramento
Comprar materiais	3 de agosto	9 de agosto
Produzir kits de peças	10 de agosto	16 de agosto
Fazer submontagens	17 de agosto	23 de agosto
Montagem final	24 de agosto	30 de agosto

FIGURA 8.10   A Abordagem do Estoque de Reserva para Planejamento e Controle da Produção

(Diagrama: Fornecedores → Estoque de Matéria-Prima → Produzir Peças e Submontagens → Estoque de Produtos em Processo → Montar Produtos Acabados → Estoque de Produtos Acabados → Clientes)

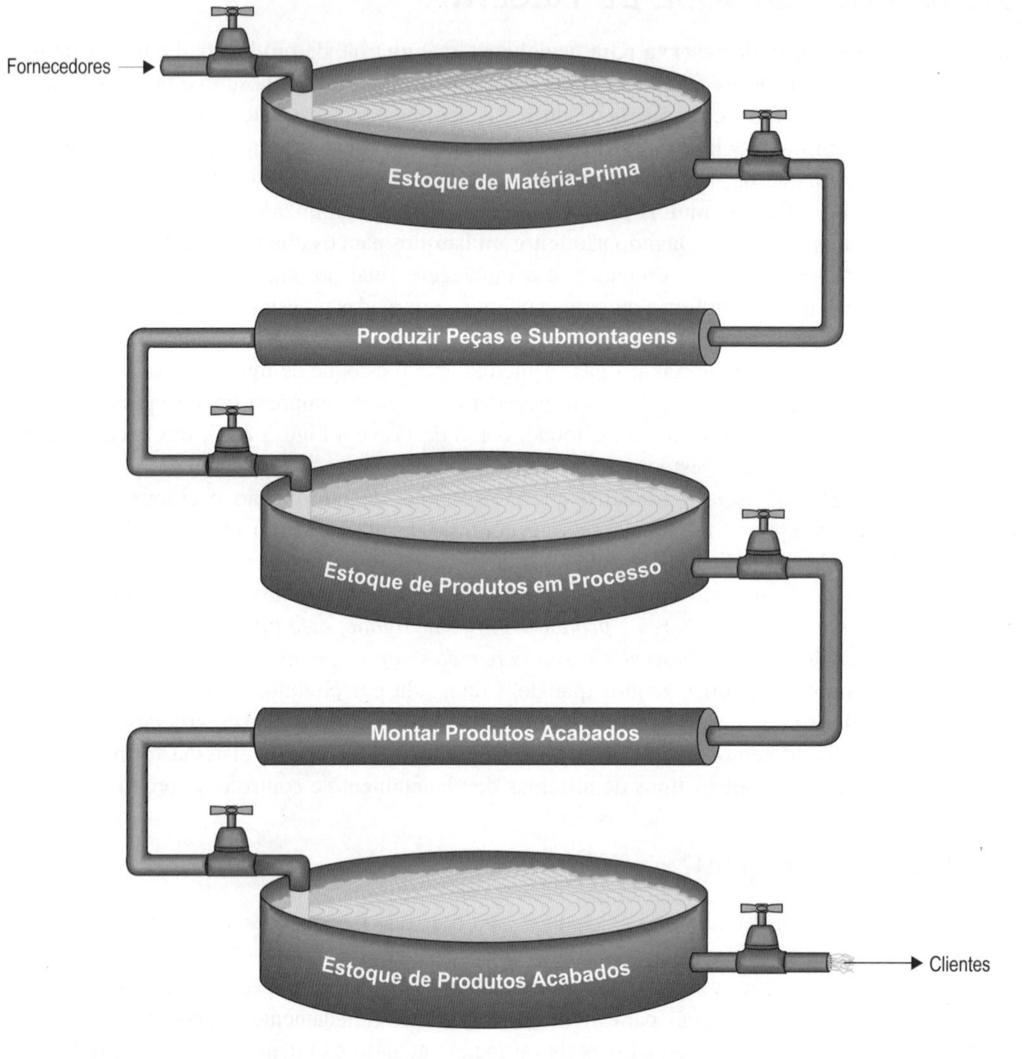

Em sistemas empurrar, a capacidade de produzir produtos no prazo prometido aos clientes depende muito da precisão dos programas. Por sua vez, a precisão dos programas depende muito da precisão das informações sobre a demanda por clientes e dos lead times — quanto tempo será necessário para que os pedidos se movam entre as etapas de produção. Estudaremos mais sobre como preparar esses programas no Capítulo 10.

Os sistemas empurrar têm resultado em grandes reduções de estoques de matérias-primas e maior utilização de trabalhadores e máquinas, em comparação com os sistemas de estoque de reserva, especialmente na produção focalizada no processo.

SISTEMAS PUXAR

Em sistemas puxar (pull) de planejamento e controle da produção, a ênfase está na redução dos níveis de estoque em cada etapa da produção. Nos sistemas empurrar, olhamos para o programa para determinar o que produzir em seguida. Em sistemas puxar, olhamos somente para etapa de produção seguinte e determinamos o que é necessário aí, e então produzimos somente isso. Conforme Hall afirma: "Não é possível *enviar* algo para lugar nenhum. Alguém terá de vir pegá-lo". Os produtos caminham diretamente das etapas de produção a montante (*upstream*) para etapas de produção a jusante (*downstream*) com pouco estoque entre as etapas. Dessa forma, matérias-primas e peças são puxadas do fundo da fábrica rumo à parte da frente da fábrica, onde se tornam produtos acabados. Embora conhecida por muitos nomes, o nome comumente aceito hoje é **manufatura just-in-time (JIT)**.

O JIT exige que os gerentes de operações se envolvam intensamente em resolver problemas do chão de fábrica. Com estoques de itens em processo divididos, todo material deve cumprir padrões da qualidade, toda peça deve chegar exatamente no tempo prometido e exatamente no lugar que se espera que ela esteja, e toda máquina deve funcionar conforme é esperado, sem quebras. Se isso não acontecer, as interrupções na produção serão intoleráveis.

Em sistemas JIT, portanto, um esforço enorme é dedicado a eliminar permanentemente cada problema surgido a fim de que a produção não seja interrompida novamente por esse problema. Por esse motivo, os gerentes de operações não se responsabilizam pelo JIT de maneira superficial.

Certas mudanças na fábrica e na maneira pela qual ela é administrada devem ocorrer antes que o JIT possa ser bem-sucedido. Para simplificar a produção, os níveis de produção devem permanecer relativamente constantes por longos períodos. Isso pode ser obtido por meio da utilização de estoques para compensar a diferença entre a variabilidade de demanda e a capacidade nivelada de produção, ou os gerentes devem envolver-se em táticas de preempção para nivelar a demanda por produtos por parte dos clientes.

Discutimos essas táticas anteriormente neste capítulo. Além disso, a quantidade de trabalho necessária para preparar máquinas para outros produtos deve ser drasticamente reduzida. Se isso não for realizado, o grande número de pequenos lotes de produtos necessários no JIT resultaria em exorbitantes custos de preparação.

As aplicações bem-sucedidas do JIT têm sido predominantemente em fábricas menores, mais focalizadas, e na manufatura repetitiva. Manufatura repetitiva significa produzir produtos padronizados nas linhas de produção. A complexidade das job shops é um obstáculo ao uso do JIT. Os proponentes do JIT argumentam que o JIT pode ser bem-sucedido em job shops porque muitas operações podem ser feitas de forma a se comportar como manufatura repetitiva. A presença de aplicações JIT bem-sucedidas em job shops parecer sustentar essa alegação.

Os benefícios dos programas JIT são de tal maneira convincentes que não se admira que o JIT seja tão popular atualmente. Estoques reduzidos, rápida entrega de produtos, melhorada qualidade de produto e custos de produção mais baixos são argumentos fortes para se transformar alguns sistemas empurrar em sistemas puxar.

O JIT é uma abordagem tão importante para a manufatura atual que o Capítulo 13 é dedicado inteiramente ao tema.

CONCENTRANDO-SE NOS GARGALOS

Alguns sistemas de planejamento e controle da produção concentram-se nos gargalos de produção — operações, máquinas ou etapas de produção que impedem a produção porque têm menos capacidade do que as etapas a montante ou a jusante. Em operações gargalo, lotes de produtos chegam mais rápido do que podem ser concluídos. Dessa forma, essas operações controlam a capacidade de uma fábrica inteira.

Teoria das Restrições (TOC — Theory of Constraints) A abordagem de administrar gargalos, ou administração das restrições, para controlar a produção foi popularizada pelo dr. Eliyahu Goldratt, que se refere a essa abordagem ou filosofia como **teoria das restrições (TOC)** e tem apresentado seminários sobre a TOC nos Estados Unidos a todos os tipos de indústria e grupos acadêmicos. Algumas pessoas referem-se a essa filosofia da TOC como **manufatura síncrona**, porque todas as partes da organização trabalham juntas para atingir as metas desejadas.

Os conceitos da TOC foram desenvolvidos pelo dr. Goldratt no software chamado **tecnologia otimizada de produção (OPT — optimized production technology)**. A OPT continua a ser melhorada e comercializada pelo Scheduling Technology Group Ltd. (**www.stg.co.uk**), de Londres, Inglaterra, com uma nova sede americana em Dallas, Texas.

A OPT é um sistema de informação de planejamento e controle da produção completo especialmente apropriado para ambientes de job-shop complexos. Ao desenvolver a quantidade de trabalho a ser feita em cada centro de trabalho, a OPT, dada uma combinação (mix) de produtos, localiza os gargalos nos processos de produção.

Se for necessário que um produto percorra uma série de operações, não importa quão rápidas sejam outras operações da série, a capacidade do gargalo determina a capacidade da série. É nesse ponto que a OPT exibe sua vantagem sobre outros sistemas. Uma vez que os gargalos tenham sido localizados, a OPT usará um grupo de algoritmos proprietários para programar trabalhadores, máquinas e ferramentas nos centros de trabalho que sejam gargalo.

Para ilustrar os efeitos da TOC, o dr. Goldratt e Jeff Cox escreveram uma obra de ficção fascinante e altamente recomendável, *The Goal: A Process of Ongoing Improvement*, que ilustra de maneira dramática a implementação da TOC numa fábrica. Alex Rogo, a personagem principal em *The Goal*, é um gerente de fábrica que procura uma maneira de salvar sua fábrica, que está prestes a ser enterrada por uma alta administração desatenciosa e ignorante. Seguindo o conselho de Jonah, um consultor que faz continuamente perguntas que são facilmente entendidas e que têm respostas muito difíceis, a fábrica sobrevive.

O dr. Goldratt escreveu posteriormente *It's Not Luck*, outra obra de ficção altamente recomendável que é um livro que acompanha *The Goal*. Ele também escreveu *Critical Chain*, que aplica conceitos TOC à administração de projetos.

O processo seguido pelo gerente de fábrica em *The Goal* está no âmago da TOC. Primeiro, o gerente de fábrica mede as taxas de produção das principais operações na fábrica. Ele descobre uma operação que é muito mais lenta do que todas as outras — um gargalo. Em seguida, ele pede a uma equipe de seu melhor pessoal para descobrir maneiras de aumentar a taxa de produção da operação gargalo. Então, depois que a taxa de produção da operação gargalo é aumentada, observa-se que a taxa de produção da fábrica inteira é aumentada. A equipe passa então para a operação mais lenta seguinte e repete o processo. A produção da fábrica aumenta à medida que a taxa de produção de cada operação gargalo é aumentada. Esse procedimento resulta em um aumento substancial da taxa de produção da fábrica, com pouco custo adicional e com uma conseqüente elevação dos lucros.

Um aspecto fundamental da filosofia da TOC é a melhoria contínua do desempenho da produção. Em vez de usar as medições contábeis tradicionais de custo por unidade e utilização de trabalhadores e equipamentos, as novas medidas de **throughput** (a taxa em que dinheiro é gerado pela venda de produtos), *estoque* (dinheiro investido em estoques) e **despesas operacionais** (dinheiro gasto em converter estoques em throughput) são usadas para medir o desempenho da produção. A idéia é aumentar o throughput e reduzir tanto as despesas de estoque como as operacionais.

O sistema de controle se baseia nos conceitos de tambor, pulmão (*buffer*[3]) e corda. A produção é controlada em pontos de controle, ou gargalos, que são coletivamente chamados **tambor** (*drum*), porque estabelecem o ritmo ou cadência a ser seguido por todas as outras operações. O tambor fornece o MPS que é coerente com os gargalos de produção. Um **pulmão** na forma de estoque é mantido antes de um gargalo, a fim de que sempre haja material no qual trabalhar. Esses pulmões garantem a segurança de que as promessas de entrega aos clientes possam ser feitas com elevada confiabilidade. Uma **corda** (*rope*) é alguma forma de comunicação, como, por exemplo, uma programação, que é comunicada no sentido inverso do processo para impedir que os estoques se elevem e para coordenar as atividades necessárias para sustentar o MPS. A corda garante que toda etapa de produção esteja sincronizada com o MPS.

Os princípios, a teoria e a filosofia da TOC constituem um avanço nos sistemas de planejamento e controle da produção.

---

[3]*Buffer*: (inf.) área usada para armazenamento temporário; pulmão.

Questões de Revisão e Discussão

1. Quais planos resultam do planejamento de longo prazo da capacidade? Quem prepara esses planos?
2. Quais planos resultam do planejamento de médio prazo da capacidade? Quem prepara esses planos?
3. Quais são os principais planos de produção de curto prazo? Como eles se relacionam? Quem prepara esses planos?
4. Explique as relações entre os planos de produção de longo, médio e curto prazo.
5. Defina e descreva *planejamento agregado*.
6. Cite e descreva quatro fontes de capacidade de produção de médio prazo.
7. Descreva como os seguintes recursos de produção podem ser aumentados ou diminuídos para ampliar ou reduzir a capacidade de produção: (a) força de trabalho, (b) materiais e (c) máquinas.
8. Relacione as vantagens e desvantagens destes planos agregados tradicionais: (a) acompanhar a demanda, (b) nivelar a capacidade com estoque, (c) nivelar a capacidade com backlog, (d) nivelar a capacidade com trabalho em horas extras, (e) nivelar a capacidade com subcontratações e (f) nivelar a capacidade com trabalhadores em tempo parcial.
9. Por que o planejamento agregado em empresas de produção sob encomenda é difícil? O que os gerentes de operações podem fazer para superar essas dificuldades?
10. Apresente três motivos pelos quais o planejamento agregado nos serviços é difícil. O que os gerentes de operações fazem para superar essas dificuldades?
11. Explique como a programação linear pode ser usada no planejamento agregado.
12. Explique como o planejamento agregado difere entre empresas de produção para estoque e produção sob encomenda.
13. Quais critérios seriam usados para decidir-se entre dois planos agregados?
14. O que é um programa mestre de produção? Quais entradas são necessárias? Descreva o processo de preparação de um programa mestre de produção.
15. Explique estes termos do programa mestre de produção: (a) congelado, (b) firme, (c) cheio, (d) aberto, (e) tamanho de lote, (f) planejamento da capacidade de médio prazo (RCCP), (g) atualização, (h) administração da demanda, (i) entrada de pedidos e (j) promessa de entrega de pedidos.
16. Explique o processo de atualizar semanalmente o programa mestre de produção.
17. Explique por que os gerentes de operações têm confiança nas estimativas de demanda incluídas na primeira parte do programa mestre de produção. Por que a atualização do MPS tende a elevar essa confiança?
18. Explique as diferenças no programa mestre de produção entre empresas de produção para estoque e de produção sob encomenda.
19. O que determina a extensão dos horizontes de planejamento no programa mestre da produção?
20. Cite e descreva quatro tipos de sistemas de planejamento e controle da produção.

Tarefas na Internet

1. Visite o site da Internet para o software Optimized Production Technology (OPT) (**www.stg.co.uk**). Encontre informações sobre a versão mais recente desse software e descreva alguns de seus recursos.
2. Use um mecanismo de busca como, por exemplo, o AltaVista (**www.altavista.com**), para encontrar um documento ou artigo sobre *planejamento agregado*. Resuma brevemente o documento e inclua a citação bibliográfica e o site.
3. Procure na Internet por um software que faça *programação mestre de produção*. Descreva alguns dos recursos do software e inclua o site.
4. As empresas algumas vezes contratam empregados temporários para auxiliá-las em suas necessidades em picos de demanda. A Kelly Services Inc. é uma das maiores fornecedoras de empregados temporários para empresas nos Estados Unidos. Visite seu site em **www.kellyservices.com** e explore-o para obter informações sobre contratação de pessoal temporário na manufatura. Resuma algumas das vantagens estabelecidas de usar pessoal temporário na manufatura da Kelly Services.

PROBLEMAS

Planejamento Agregado

1. A Blaze Advertising é uma agência de propaganda que presta serviços a varejistas. Os serviços da empresa situam-se em três categorias — televisão, mídia impressa e rádio. A Blaze está planejando sua força de trabalho para o próximo ano e estima que para cada dólar de vendas será necessário 0,01 hora de empregado. A previsão das vendas do próximo ano para cada categoria é:

Categoria de Propaganda	Vendas (milhares de dólares)			
	1º Trimestre	2º Trimestre	3º Trimestre	4º Trimestre
Televisão	$ 4.200	$ 4.500	$ 5.200	$ 4.000
Mídia impressa	3.700	3.500	5.000	3.500
Rádio	1.500	1.000	2.000	1.000

    Se a relação for 2 mil horas por ano para cada empregado, compute o número de empregados necessários para cada categoria de propaganda em cada trimestre e o número total de empregados necessários em cada trimestre.

2. Uma empresa planeja a capacidade de produção agregada necessária para produzir a previsão de vendas apresentada nesta tabela:

Resina	Previsão de Vendas (milhares de toneladas)			
	1º Trimestre	2º Trimestre	3º Trimestre	4º Trimestre
A	9,0	10,0	12,0	14,0
B	7,0	8,0	5,0	10,0
C	6,0	3,0	4,0	7,0

    Existe ampla capacidade de máquina para produzir a previsão, e cada tonelada de resina exige cinco horas de trabalho.
    a) Compute a demanda agregada para resinas em cada trimestre.
    b) Compute o número agregado de horas de trabalho em cada trimestre.
    c) Se cada trabalhador trabalhar 520 horas por trimestre, quantos trabalhadores serão necessários em cada trimestre?

3. A Steel Fabricators está tentando decidir-se entre dois planos agregados de capacidade, o n. 1 e o n. 2. O número de trabalhadores por trimestre e o estoque anual médio de bens acabados em milhares de libras correspondentes aos dois planos são mostrados a seguir. Se os custos de contratação forem $ 5.500 por trabalhador contratado, os custos de demissão forem $ 1.800 por trabalhador demitido, e o custo de manutenção em estoque for $ 0,10 por libra por ano, compute os custos de contratação, demissão, manutenção em estoque e os custos incrementais totais correspondentes a cada plano. Qual plano você preferiria? Por quê?

Plano Agregado	Trimestre	Trabalhadores Necessários	Estoque Anual Médio (milhares de libras)
N. 1	1	210	2.500
	2	200	
	3	190	
	4	200	
N. 2	1	200	3.950
	2	200	
	3	200	
	4	200	

4. A Fabric Inc. faz meias infantis de tamanho único. A Fabric está considerando atualmente dois planos de capacidade para o próximo ano: nivelar a capacidade com estoque e acompanhar a demanda. A demanda agregada trimestral correspondente aos dois planos é mostrada a seguir. O padrão de trabalho por par de meias é 0,3 hora, o custo de contratação é $ 500 por trabalhador contratado, o custo de demissão é $ 250 por trabalhador demitido, o custo de manutenção em estoque para produtos acabados é $ 1 por par de meias por ano, e os dias úteis por trimestre são 60.

Trimestre	Demanda Agregada (milhares de pares de meias)
1	350
2	500
3	900
4	400

O estoque inicial no primeiro trimestre é de 137.500 pares de meias para o plano de nivelar a capacidade. O estoque inicial no primeiro trimestre é zero para o plano de acompanhar a demanda. Qual plano exibe os custos operacionais incrementais totais mais baixos? Suponha que o padrão de demanda trimestral se repita de ano a ano.

5. Uma empresa está desenvolvendo um plano agregado de capacidade a partir da previsão de vendas que se segue:

Produto	Previsão de Vendas (produtos)			
	1º Trimestre	2º Trimestre	3º Trimestre	4º Trimestre
1	2.000	1.500	1.600	1.800
2	1.200	1.000	800	1.000

Existe ampla capacidade de máquina para produzir a previsão. Cada produto 1 consome uma média de 20 horas de trabalho e cada produto 2 consome uma média de 15 horas de trabalho.

a) Compute o número agregado de horas de trabalho em cada trimestre.
b) Se cada trabalhador trabalhar 520 horas por trimestre, quantos trabalhadores serão necessários em cada trimestre?

6. Um fabricante é um produtor cuja empresa é de produção sob encomenda, focalizada no processo. Dois planos agregados são avaliados pela empresa: acompanhar a demanda e nivelar a capacidade com backlog. No plano de nivelar a capacidade, foram considerados os custos trimestrais do backlog:

Custos trimestrais do backlog = $ 0,20 (DVT − DPT)

onde DVT são os dólares das vendas trimestrais e DPT são os dólares da produção trimestral. Não há custos de produção quando DPT ≥ DVT. No plano de acompanhar a demanda, o custo para contratar e demitir trabalhadores deve ser considerado. Custa $ 2.000 para contratar um trabalhador e $ 3.000 para demitir um trabalhador. A informação desenvolvida para essa análise é apresentada a seguir:

Plano	Trimestre	Trabalhadores Contratados	Trabalhadores Demitidos	Milhares de Dólares da Produção	Milhares de Dólares das Vendas
Acompanhar a demanda	Q_1	10		$ 1.200	$ 1.200
	Q_2	20		1.600	1.600
	Q_3		5	1.500	1.500
	Q_4		25	1.000	1.000
Nivelar a produção	Q_1	0	0	$ 1.325	$ 1.200
	Q_2	0	0	1.325	1.600
	Q_3	0	0	1.325	1.500
	Q_4	0	0	1.325	1.000

Qual plano agregado de capacidade você preferiria? Por quê?

Programa Mestre de Produção

7. Uma empresa manufatura uma linha de impressoras de computador em base de produção sob encomenda. Cada impressora exige uma média de 30 horas de trabalho, e a fábrica usa um backlog de pedidos para permitir um plano agregado de capacidade. Esse plano fornece uma capacidade semanal de 9 mil horas de trabalho. A empresa preparou este MPS de cinco semanas:

	Produção Semanal (impressoras)				
Produto	1	2	3	4	5
Impressoras	200	275	275	300	360

   a) Compute as horas de trabalho reais necessárias em cada semana e para o total de cinco semanas para produzir o MPS (isso, muitas vezes, é chamado *carga*). Compare a carga com a capacidade de horas de trabalho em cada semana e para o total de cinco semanas (isso, muitas vezes, é chamado *planejamento da capacidade de médio prazo* — RCCP).
   b) Existe suficiente capacidade de produção para produzir o MPS?
   c) Quais mudanças no MPS você recomendaria?

8. Uma empresa manufatura scanners de código de barras em base de produção sob encomenda. A empresa manufatura três modelos dos scanners na mesma linha de montagem final. A linha de montagem final tem 20 mil horas de capacidade semanal. O MPS de seis semanas e o padrão de montagem final para cada modelo são:

Produto	Padrão de Montagem Final (horas por scanner)	Produção Semanal (scanners)					
		1	2	3	4	5	6
A	25	200	150	200	250	150	250
B	30	100	200	350	250	150	250
C	35	150	150	150	200	250	250

   a) Compute as horas de montagem final necessárias em cada semana e para o total de seis semanas para produzir o MPS (carga). Compare a carga com a capacidade de horas de trabalho em cada semana e para o total de seis semanas (RCCP).
   b) Existe suficiente capacidade de produção para produzir o MPS?
   c) Quais mudanças no MPS você recomendaria?

9. Uma fábrica está no processo de atualizar o programa mestre de produção para seus produtos. A fábrica produz para estoque. A tabela a seguir mostra as estimativas de demanda para o produto durante as próximas seis semanas.

Tipo de Demanda	Semana					
	1	2	3	4	5	6
Clientes (previsões e pedidos)	700	1.200	700	500	400	1.200
Armazéns filiais	100	100	400	500	200	100
Pesquisa de mercado		50			10	
Pesquisa de produção	10					

O nível de estoque de segurança (o estoque não pode cair abaixo do nível de estoque de segurança), o tamanho de lote mínimo (o mínimo em que o tamanho de lote deve ser produzido quando a produção do produto ocorre) e o nível de estoque inicial para o produto são:

Tamanho de Lote Mínimo	Estoque de Segurança	Estoque Inicial
2.000	500	1.500

Prepare um MPS de seis semanas para o produto. Suponha que haja uma ampla capacidade de produção na fábrica.

10. Uma empresa produz três produtos para estoque. As demandas (em caixas) para esses produtos ao longo do horizonte de planejamento de oito semanas são:

Demanda do Produto	Semana							
	1	2	3	4	5	6	7	8
Clientes (Previsões e Pedidos)								
A	1.000	2.000	2.000	500	1.000	2.000	1.500	500
B	3.000	2.000	2.000	5.000	7.000	6.000	4.000	4.000
C	1.500	500	500	1.500	1.000	500	500	500

Demanda do Produto	Semana							
	1	2	3	4	5	6	7	8
Armazéns Filiais								
A	1.500		1.500			2.000		
B	1.500		2.000			3.000		
C		1.000					500	
Pesquisa de Mercado								
A	50			50			50	
B		50			50			50
C			50		50			

Os níveis do estoque de segurança (os níveis de estoque não podem cair abaixo do nível do estoque de segurança), os tamanhos de lote mínimos (o mínimo em que um tamanho de lote deve ser produzido quando a produção do produto ocorre) e o nível de estoque inicial para os produtos são:

Produto	Tamanho de Lote Mínimo (caixas)	Estoque de Segurança (caixas)	Estoque Inicial (caixas)
A	5.000	3.000	4.000
B	8.000	5.000	4.000
C	2.000	1.000	2.000

Prepare o MPS das oito semanas seguintes. Suponha que exista uma ampla capacidade de produção.

Estudo de Caso

Planejamento Agregado na Bell Computers

A Bell Computers está desenvolvendo um plano agregado de produção para os dois primeiros trimestres do próximo ano para produzir monitores AB1200. O departamento de marketing estimou que 800 dos AB1200s precisarão ser embarcados para os clientes no primeiro trimestre e 1.200 no segundo trimestre. São necessárias 8 horas de trabalho para produzir cada impressora e somente 8 mil horas de trabalho em horas normais estão disponíveis em cada primeiro e segundo trimestre. Trabalho em horas extras pode ser usado para produzir as impressoras, mas a fábrica tem uma política que limita a quantidade de horas extras em 10% do trabalho em horas normais disponível. A mão-de-obra custa $ 12 por hora no trabalho em horas normais e $ 18 por hora no trabalho em horas extras. Se uma impressora for produzida no primeiro trimestre e embarcada no segundo, a fábrica incorrerá num custo de manutenção em estoque igual a $ 150 por impressora. Quantas impressoras devem ser produzidas num regime de trabalho em hora normal e num regime de trabalho em horas extras em cada primeiro e segundo trimestre para minimizar o custo do trabalho em hora normal e em horas extras e os custos de manutenção em estoque? As necessidades de mercado e a disponibilidade de mão-de-obra em horas normais e em horas extras devem ser levadas em consideração.

Tarefa

1. Formule este problema de planejamento agregado como um problema de programação linear. Formule a função objetiva e as funções de restrição. Defina as variáveis de decisão.

Sistemas de Estoques com Demanda Independente

Introdução

Pontos de Vista Opostos sobre Estoques
Por Que Queremos Manter Estoques
Por Que Não Queremos Manter Estoques

Natureza dos Estoques

Sistemas do Lote Padrão
Determinando as Quantidades Pedidas
  Modelo I — Lote Econômico de Compra (LEC) •
  Modelo II — LEC para Lotes de Produção • Modelo III
  — LEC com Descontos por Quantidade
Determinando Pontos de Pedido
  Definindo Pontos de Pedido nos Níveis de Serviço •
  Alguns Princípios Básicos para Definir Pontos de
  Pedido

Sistemas do Intervalo Padrão

Outros Modelos de Estoques
Modelos Híbridos de Estoque
Modelos de Estoque de Período Único

Algumas Realidades do Planejamento de Estoques
Classificação ABC de Materiais
LEC e Incerteza
Dinâmica do Planejamento de Estoques
Outros Fatores Que Afetam o Planejamento de Estoques
Computadores e o Planejamento de Estoques

Resumo Final: O Que os Fabricantes de Classe Mundial Estão Fazendo

Questões de Revisão e Discussão

Tarefas na Internet

Problemas

Estudo de Caso
Níveis de Estoque de Segurança na Bell Computers

Introdução

Definição das Políticas de Estoques na Airco Division

A reunião foi realizada na sede da Airco Division em St. Louis, e todos os gerentes de fábrica e de armazém da divisão, seu vice-presidente de operações e seu vice-presidente de marketing estavam presentes. Desnecessário dizer que a reunião foi um desfile de autoridades. Todos deviam estar presentes a fim de que um acordo sobre as políticas de estoques para a divisão pudesse ser alcançado.

O vice-presidente corporativo e o gerente geral da divisão, o sr. Milligan, deram início à reunião e abriram a discussão.

O sr. Milligan declarou que os investimentos em estoques devem ser reduzidos, mas que, ao mesmo tempo, alguns clientes indicaram nos últimos meses que seus pedidos não puderam ser entregues imediatamente porque os armazéns da Airco estavam sem estoque. O vice-presidente de marketing declarou que a divisão tinha uma grande quantidade de produtos nos armazéns, mas que eram os produtos errados. Além disso, ele achava que a divisão estava se excedendo quanto à quantidade de estoque de segurança nos armazéns. O vice-presidente de operações declarou que o motivo pelo qual produtos errados estavam nos armazéns era que as previsões de marketing sempre estavam erradas. Ele perguntou ao vice-presidente de marketing qual porcentagem do tempo os armazéns devem permanecer sem produtos quando os pedidos dos clientes são recebidos. O vice-presidente de marketing respondeu que suficiente estoque de produtos sempre deve estar disponível para atender os pedidos dos clientes quando estes são recebidos.

As políticas de estoques são suficientemente importantes para que gerentes de produção, de marketing e de finanças trabalhem juntos com a finalidade de alcançar um acordo sobre essas políticas. O fato de haver pontos de vista conflitantes no que se refere a políticas de estoques ressalta o equilíbrio que deve ser buscado entre metas conflitantes — reduzir custos de produção, reduzir investimentos em estoques e aumentar a receptividade do cliente.

Este capítulo preocupa-se com a integração desses pontos de vista aparentemente irreconciliáveis na definição de políticas de estoques. Examinaremos a natureza dos estoques e o funcionamento interno dos sistemas de estoques, e desenvolveremos um entendimento das questões fundamentais no planejamento de estoques e diversas técnicas para analisar problemas de estoque.

Pontos de Vista Opostos sobre Estoques

Os estoques têm atualmente uma imagem de menino bom e menino mau. Há muitas razões pelas quais gostamos de ter estoques, mas também há razões pelas quais a manutenção de estoques é considerada imprudente.

Por Que Queremos Manter Estoques

Estoques são necessários, mas a questão importante é quanto estoque manter. A Tabela 9.1 resume os motivos para se manter estoques de bens acabados, em processo e de matérias-primas.

Além da importância estratégica de provermos estoques de bens acabados a fim de que o serviço ao cliente seja melhorado através do rápido embarque dos pedidos dos clientes, também mantemos estoques porque, ao fazê-lo, certos custos são reduzidos:

1. **Custos de emissão do pedido.** Cada vez que compramos um lote de matéria-prima de um fornecedor, incorremos num custo para processar o pedido de compra, expedir, fazer registros contábeis e receber o pedido no armazém. Cada vez que produzimos um lote de produção, incorremos num custo de mudança para modificarmos a produção de um produto anterior para o seguinte. Quanto maiores os tamanhos de lote, mais estoques mantemos, mas pedimos menos vezes durante o ano, e os custos anuais de emissão de pedidos são menores.

TABELA 9.1 — POR QUE QUEREMOS MANTER ESTOQUES?

Bens acabados	1. Fundamental nas estratégias de posicionamento de produção para estoque, de importância estratégica.
	2. Necessário em planos para nivelar a capacidade agregada.
	3. Produtos podem ser exibidos aos clientes.
Em processo	1. Necessário na produção focalizada no processo; desvincula as etapas de produção; aumenta a flexibilidade.
	2. A produção e o transporte de lotes maiores de produtos criam mais estoques, mas pode reduzir os custos de manuseio de materiais e de produção.
Matérias-primas	1. Os fornecedores produzem e embarcam algumas matérias-primas em lotes.
	2. Compras maiores resultam em mais estoques, mas podem resultar em descontos por quantidade e custos reduzidos de frete e manuseio de material.

2. **Custos do *stockout*[1].** Cada vez que ficamos sem estoque de matérias-primas ou bens acabados podemos incorrer em custos. Em termos de estoque de bens acabados, os custos de stockout podem incluir vendas perdidas e clientes insatisfeitos. Em termos de estoques de matérias-primas, os custos de stockout podem incluir o custo de interrupções na produção e, às vezes, até vendas perdidas e clientes insatisfeitos. Um estoque adicional, chamado **estoque de segurança**, pode ser preenchido para garantir segurança contra stockouts excessivos.
3. **Custos de aquisição.** Para materiais comprados, pedir lotes maiores pode aumentar os estoques de matérias-primas, mas os custos unitários podem ser menores por causa dos descontos por quantidade e dos menores custos de frete e manuseio de materiais. Para materiais produzidos, tamanhos de lote maiores aumentam os estoques em processo e de bens acabados, mas os custos médios por unidade podem ser menores porque os custos de mudança são amortizados entre lotes maiores (veja a Figura 9.1).
4. **Custos da qualidade na partida (*start up*).** Quando iniciamos pela primeira vez um lote de produção, o risco de produtos defeituosos é grande. Os trabalhadores podem estar aprendendo, materiais podem não ser abastecidos apropriadamente, configurações de máquinas podem precisar de ajustes, e poucos produtos podem precisar ser produzidos antes que as condições se estabilizem. Tamanhos de lote maiores significam um número menor de mudanças por ano e menos sucata.

Estoques podem ser indispensáveis para a operação eficiente e eficaz dos sistemas de produção. Mas há boas razões pelas quais não queremos manter estoques.

Por Que Não Queremos Manter Estoques

Certos custos se elevam com níveis de estoques mais elevados:

1. **Custos da manutenção em estoque.** Juros sobre a dívida, juros da renda não auferida, aluguel de armazém, resfriamento, aquecimento, iluminação, limpeza, conserto, proteção, embarque, recebimento, manuseio de materiais, impostos, seguro e administração são alguns dos custos em que se incorre para segurar, financiar, armazenar, manusear e administrar estoques maiores.
2. **Custos da receptividade do cliente.** Grandes estoques em processo obstruem os sistemas de produção. O tempo necessário para produzir e receber pedidos dos clientes é aumentado, e nossa capacidade para reagir às mudanças nos pedidos dos clientes diminui.

---

[1] *Stockout:* redução a zero do nível de estoque de um material.

FIGURA 9.1 — CUSTO POR UNIDADE *VERSUS* TAMANHO DO LOTE DE PRODUÇÃO

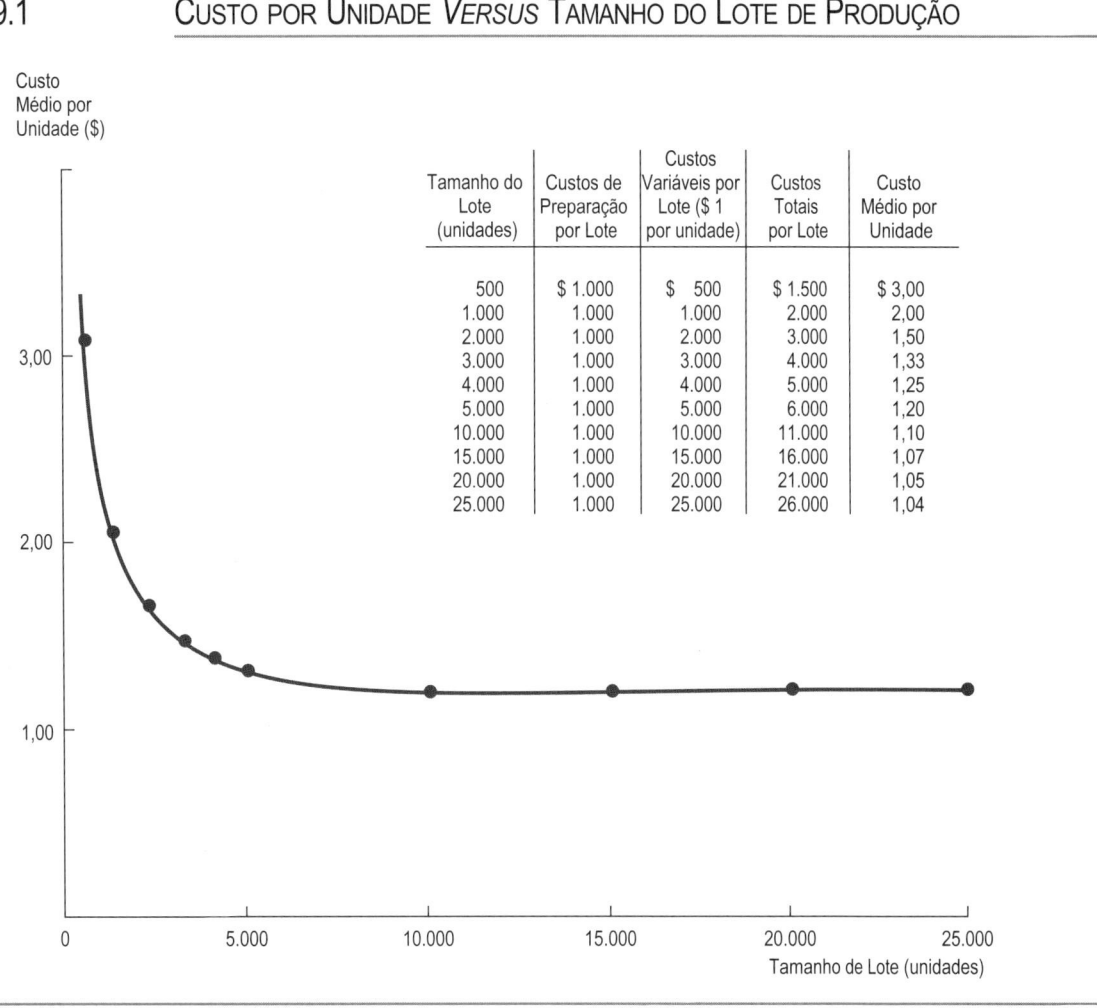

Tamanho do Lote (unidades)	Custos de Preparação por Lote	Custos Variáveis por Lote ($ 1 por unidade)	Custos Totais por Lote	Custo Médio por Unidade
500	$ 1.000	$ 500	$ 1.500	$ 3,00
1.000	1.000	1.000	2.000	2,00
2.000	1.000	2.000	3.000	1,50
3.000	1.000	3.000	4.000	1,33
4.000	1.000	4.000	5.000	1,25
5.000	1.000	5.000	6.000	1,20
10.000	1.000	10.000	11.000	1,10
15.000	1.000	15.000	16.000	1,07
20.000	1.000	20.000	21.000	1,05
25.000	1.000	25.000	26.000	1,04

3. **Custos para coordenar a produção.** Uma vez que grandes estoques obstruem o processo de produção, mais pessoas são necessárias para desembaraçar engarrafamentos, resolver problemas de produção relacionados com o congestionamento e coordenar programas.
4. **Custos de redução do retorno sobre o investimento (ROI).** Estoques são ativos, e grandes estoques reduzem o retorno sobre o investimento. Um reduzido retorno sobre o investimento se soma aos custos financeiros da empresa ao elevar as taxas de juros sobre a dívida e reduzir os preços das ações.
5. **Custos da capacidade reduzida.** Estoques representam uma forma de desperdício. Materiais pedidos, guardados e produzidos antes que sejam necessários desperdiçam capacidade de produção.
6. **Custos da qualidade de lotes grandes.** Produzir grandes lotes de produção resulta em grandes estoques. Em raras ocasiões, algo sai errado e uma grande parte de um lote de produção tem defeitos. Nessas situações, tamanhos de lote menores podem reduzir o número de produtos com defeito.
7. **Custos de problemas de produção.** Estoques em processo mais elevados camuflam os problemas de produção subjacentes. Problemas como quebras de máquina, má qualidade de produto e escassez de materiais nunca são resolvidos.

A princípio, esses custos podem parecer indiretos, difusos e até mesmo irrelevantes, mas a redução desses custos ao manter menos estoques pode ser crucial na luta para competir por mercados mundiais.

Natureza dos Estoques

Duas importantes questões fundamentam todo o planejamento de estoques:

- Quanto de cada material pedir quando pedidos forem feitos a fornecedores externos ou a departamentos de produção dentro da organização.
- Quando fazer os pedidos.

As **quantidades pedidas**, ou **tamanhos do lote**, e quando fazer esses pedidos, ou **pontos de pedido**, determinam em grande parte a quantidade de materiais em estoque em qualquer instante dado.

O estudo do **ciclo de estoque** — materiais são pedidos, recebidos, usados, e o processo se repete — usa uma terminologia toda própria. Esses termos estão incluídos no glossário no final deste livro.

Os estoques podem conter materiais de **demanda dependente** ou de **demanda independente**. *Em estoques com demanda independente, a demanda para um item mantido em estoque é independente da demanda para qualquer outro item mantido em estoque.* Bens acabados embarcados para os clientes é um exemplo de estoques com demanda independente. As demandas para esses itens são estimadas a partir de previsões ou pedidos reais dos clientes. O restante deste capítulo é dedicado às decisões referentes à quantidade pedida e pontos de pedido dos estoques com demanda independente. *Estoques com demanda dependente consistem em itens cuja demanda depende das demandas de outros itens também mantidos em estoque.* Por exemplo, a demanda para uma caixa de calculadora e para um contêiner de embarque, que são componentes, dependem ambos da demanda para a calculadora, que é um bem acabado. Tipicamente, a demanda por matéria-prima e componentes pode ser calculada se estimarmos a demanda para os bens acabados em que entram esses materiais. As decisões referentes à quantidade pedida e ponto de pedido para estoques com demanda dependente são, por conseguinte, distintamente diferentes daquelas dos estoques com demanda independente; essas decisões serão tratadas no Capítulo 10.

Em estoques com demanda independente, quanto devemos pedir de um material ao tornarmos a suprir um estoque? A resposta depende dos custos de pedir demasiadamente e de pedir muito pouco. Os custos de pedir demasiadamente são, todos, custos que fazem com que não queiramos manter estoques, conforme discutimos anteriormente: manutenção em estoque, receptividade do cliente, coordenação da produção, redução do retorno sobre o investimento (ROI), capacidade reduzida, qualidade de lotes grandes e problemas de produção. Os custos de pedir pouco são, todos, custos que fazem com que queiramos manter estoques, conforme discutimos anteriormente: custos da emissão do pedido, stockout, aquisição e qualidade na partida.

Materiais são pedidos de forma que o custo de se pedir pouco seja equilibrado em relação ao custo de se pedir muito de cada produto. Na Figura 9.2, duas classes de custos estão traçadas graficamente. Os custos de manutenção de estoque representam todos os custos anuais associados com pedir demasiadamente. Esses custos sobem à medida que as quantidades pedidas se elevam, porque os níveis médios de estoque se elevam à medida que as quantidades pedidas se elevam. Os custos de pedido todos os custos anuais associados com o pedido. Esse custo cai à medida que as quantidades pedidas aumentam, porque o número de pedidos emitidos diminui e, conseqüentemente, o nível médio de estoque aumenta.

Como mostra a Figura 9.2, quando a curva dos custos anuais de manutenção em estoque é adicionada à curva dos custos anuais de emissão de pedidos, resulta uma curva dos custos anuais totais de estocagem. *Essa curva dos custos totais demonstra um conceito importante no planejamento de estoques: para todo material mantido em estoque existe uma quantidade ótima do pedido em que os custos anuais totais de estocagem atingem um mínimo.* Nesse cálculo, a quantidade ótima do pedido, tradicionalmente chamado **lote econômico de compra (LEC)**, é de aproximadamente 524 unidades por pedido.

Esse conceito é útil para os gerentes de operações, especialmente se for usado o sistema do lote padrão.

Sistemas do Lote Padrão

Os **sistemas do lote padrão** fazem pedidos da mesma quantidade de material cada vez que esse material é pedido. Entretanto, *quando* o pedido é feito, é permitido variar. O estoque cai até que um nível de estoque crítico, o ponto de pedido, acione um pedido. O **ponto de pedido (PP)** é determinado estimando-se

| FIGURA 9.2 | BALANCEANDO OS CUSTOS DE MANUTENÇÃO EM ESTOQUE CONTRA OS CUSTOS DE EMISSÃO DE PEDIDOS |

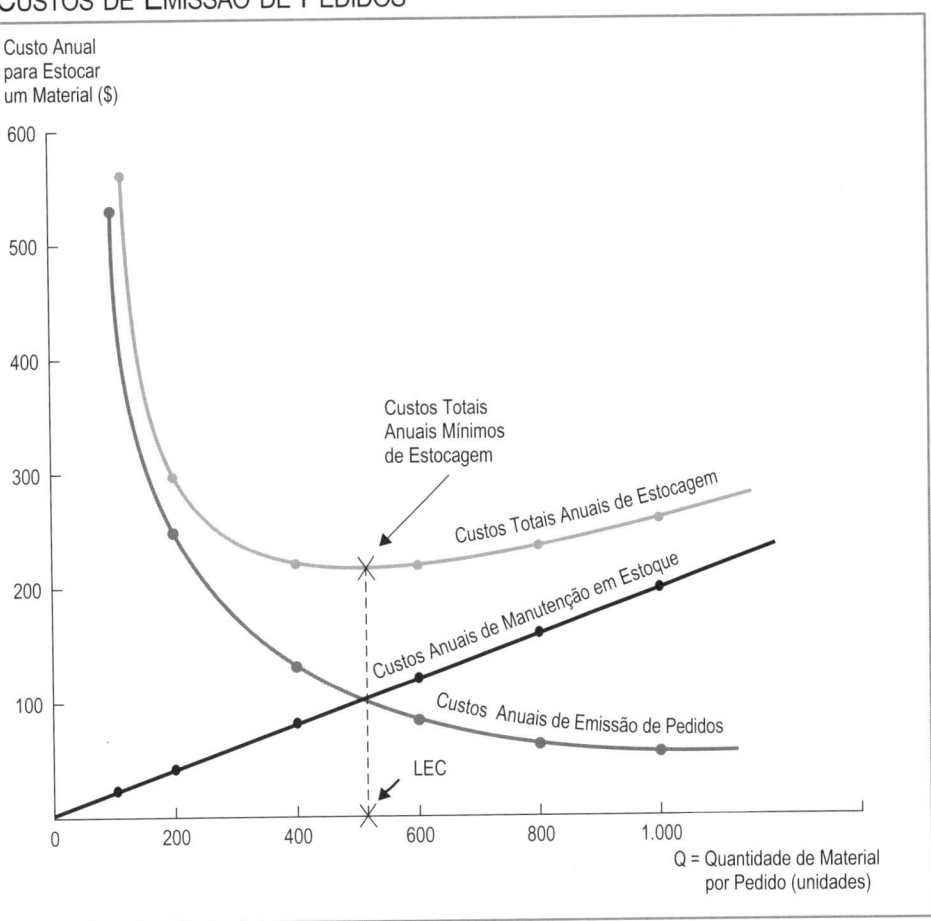

o quanto esperamos usar de um material entre o tempo em que fazemos o pedido e recebemos outro lote desse material. Quando o lote é recebido e o estoque é novamente preenchido, o lote padrão é colocado em estoque.

O **sistema de duas gavetas** de controle de estoque é uma aplicação simples desse tipo de sistema. No sistema de duas gavetas, cada material tem duas gavetas que guardam fisicamente o material num armazém. À medida que o material é usado, material é retirado de uma gaveta grande até que essa gaveta grande se torne vazia. No fundo da gaveta grande há uma requisição previamente impressa de outro pedido do material. Essa requisição de renovação é enviada e, enquanto isso, são usados materiais contidos na gaveta pequena, que contém apenas o material suficiente para durar até a próxima renovação de estoque. Quando o estoque é renovado, uma requisição é colocada no fundo da gaveta grande, ambas as gavetas são preenchidas, e o ciclo é repetido. A quantidade pedida é o volume necessário para preencher ambas as gavetas. O ponto de pedido é o volume necessário para preencher a gaveta pequena.

Nesses sistemas, normalmente assumimos uma permanente contagem de estoques. No **sistema de inventário permanente**, adições e subtrações dos registros de estoque são feitas no momento em que materiais são adicionados ou removidos do estoque. Com esse método, podemos determinar a quantidade de material em estoque em qualquer instante olhando para seu **registro de estoque**, uma exposição de todas as transações de estoque que afetaram esse material. Hoje, essas exposições comumente fazem parte do sistema de computador da empresa e aparecem no vídeo do terminal de computador quando chamadas.

Duas decisões são fundamentais para o sistema do lote padrão: quantidades pedidas e pontos de pedido.

Determinando as Quantidades Pedidas

Quando gerentes de operações precisam decidir-se a respeito da quantidade de materiais a ser pedida em sistemas do lote padrão, não há uma fórmula única que se aplique a todas as situações. Cada situação exige uma análise baseada nas características desse sistema de estoque em particular. Aqui, desenvolvemos estimativas das quantidades ótimas de pedido para três modelos de estoque: Modelo I — lote econômico de compra (LEC), Modelo II — LEC para lotes de produção, e Modelo III — LEC com descontos por quantidade.

Modelo I — Lote Econômico de Compra (LEC) A Tabela 9.2 descreve as suposições, as definições de variáveis, as fórmulas de custo e a derivação da fórmula LEC para o Modelo I. A questão fundamen-

---

TABELA 9.2 — MODELO I — LOTE ECONÔMICO DE COMPRA (LEC)

Suposições

1. A demanda anual, o custo de manutenção em estoque e o custo de emissão do pedido podem ser estimados.
2. O nível médio de estoque para determinado material é a quantidade pedida dividida por 2. Isso supõe implicitamente que nenhum estoque de segurança é utilizado, que os pedidos são recebidos todos de uma vez, que os materiais são usados a uma taxa uniforme e que os materiais foram usados completamente quando o pedido seguinte chega.
3. Stockout, receptividade do cliente e outros custos são irrelevantes.
4. Não existem descontos por quantidade.

Definições de Variáveis

D = demanda anual para determinado produto (unidades por ano)*
Q = quantidade de material pedida em cada ponto de pedido (unidades por pedido)
C = custo para manter uma unidade em estoque durante um ano ($ por unidade por ano)*
S = custo médio para emitir um pedido de um material ($ por pedido)
CTE = custo total anual de estocagem de um material ($ por ano)

Fórmulas de Custo

Custo anual de manutenção em estoque = Nível médio de estoque × Custo de manutenção em estoque = $(Q/2)C$
Custo anual de emissão de pedidos = Pedidos por ano × Custo para emitir um pedido = $(D/Q)S$
Custo total anual de estocagem (CTE) = Custo anual de manutenção em estoque + Custo anual de emissão de pedidos
$= (Q/2)C + (D/Q)S$

Derivação da Fórmula do Lote Econômico de Compra

A quantidade ótima do pedido é encontrada definindo-se a derivada de CTE em relação a Q como igual a 0 e resolvendo-se Q:

1. A fórmula para CTE é: $\quad CTE = (Q/2)C + (D/Q)S$
2. A derivada de CTE com respeito a Q é: $\quad d(CTE)/d(Q) = C/2 + (-DS/Q^2)$
3. Defina a derivada de CTE como igual a zero e resolva Q:

$$C/2 + (-DS/Q^2) = 0$$
$$-DS/Q^2 = -C/2$$
$$Q^2 = 2DS/C$$
$$Q = \sqrt{2DS/C}$$

4. Portanto, o LEC é: $\quad LEC = \sqrt{2DS/C}$

---

*Nos casos em que um material tem demanda sazonal, D representaria a demanda trimestral e C representaria o custo de manutenção em estoque durante um trimestre. Desse modo, as políticas de pedido variariam de trimestre a trimestre quando a demanda sazonal variasse.

Capítulo 9 – Sistemas de Estoques com Demanda Independente

FIGURA 9.3   NÍVEL MÉDIO DE ESTOQUE NO MODELO I

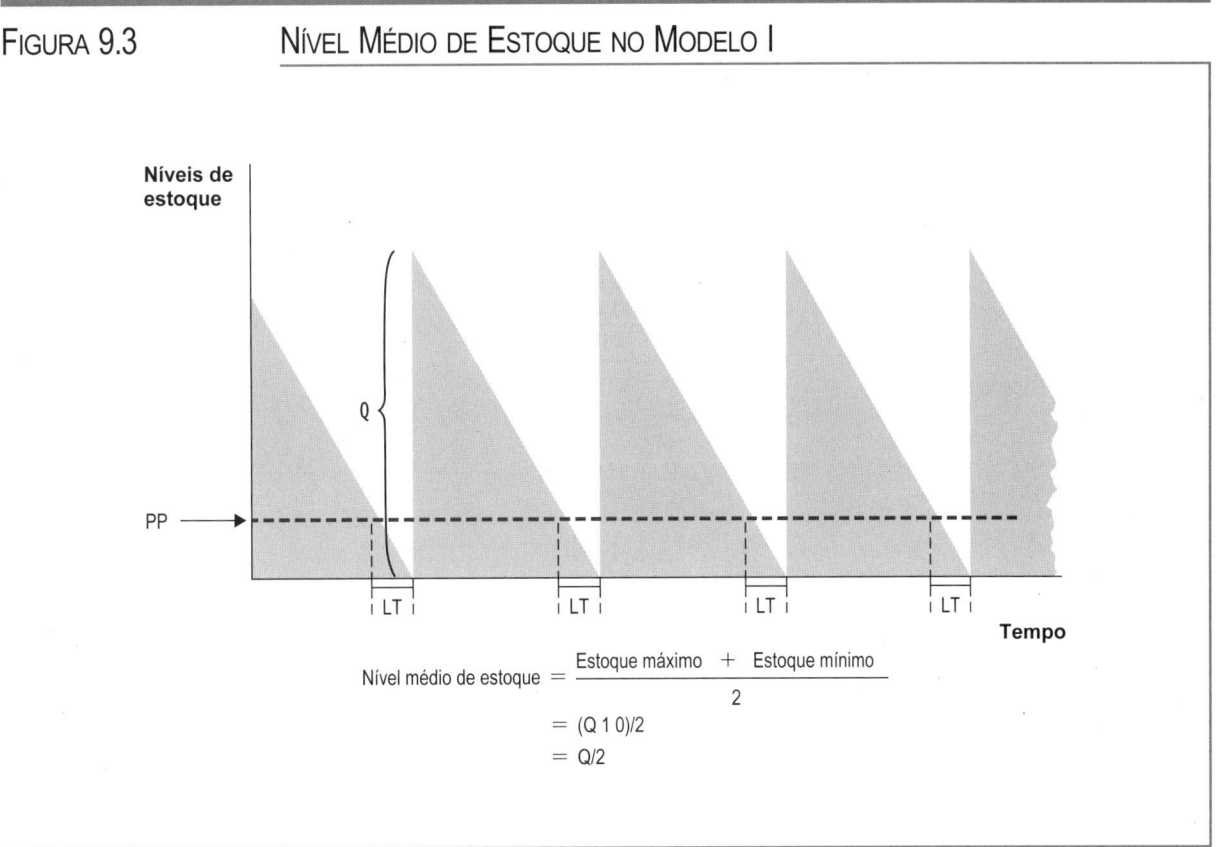

tal na aplicação desse modelo é: As suposições se enquadram em nossa situação de estoque, ou os desvios dessas suposições são apenas pequenos?

Como demonstra a Figura 9.3, um estoque médio igual a $Q/2$ implica que não há qualquer estoque de segurança, os pedidos são recebidos todos de uma só vez, os materiais são usados a uma taxa uniforme, e os materiais foram usados completamente quando o pedido seguinte chega. A presença de todas essas características é rara, na prática; mas apesar de pequenos desvios $Q/2$ pode ser ainda uma estimativa razoável dos níveis de estoque médios para alguns materiais.

O Exemplo 9.1 aplica as fórmulas de custo e de LEC a um material comprado por uma empresa de suprimentos hidráulicos.

EXEMPLO 9.1

USO DO MODELO I NUMA EMPRESA DE SUPRIMENTOS HIDRÁULICOS

A Call-Us Plumbing Supply Company armazena milhares de itens hidráulicos vendidos a encanadores, empreiteiros e varejistas. O sr. Swartz, o gerente geral da empresa, pondera a respeito de quanto dinheiro poderia ser economizado anualmente se fosse usado o LEC em vez das regras empíricas atuais da empresa. Ele instrui Mary Ann Church, uma analista de estoques, a realizar uma análise somente de um material (material n. 3925, uma válvula de latão) para verificar se economias significativas poderiam resultar da utilização do LEC. Mary Ann desenvolve as seguintes estimativas a partir de informações contábeis: $D = 10.000$ válvulas por ano, $Q = 400$ válvulas por pedido (quantidade pedida atual), $C = \$\,0,40$ por válvula por ano, e $S = \$\,5,50$ por pedido.

> ## Solução
>
> 1. Mary Ann calcula os custos anuais totais de estocagem presentes:
>
> $$CTE_1 = (Q/2)C + (D/Q)S = \left(\frac{400}{2}\right)0,4 + \left(\frac{10.000}{400}\right)5,5 = 80 + 137,50 = \$\,217,50$$
>
> 2. O LEC é calculado:
>
> $$LEC = \sqrt{\frac{2DS}{C}} = \sqrt{\frac{2(10.000)(5,5)}{0,4}} = \sqrt{275.000} = 524,4 \text{ válvulas}$$
>
> 3. Os custos anuais totais de estocagem, se fosse empregado o LEC, são calculados:
>
> $$CTE_2 = (Q/2)C + (D/Q)S = \left(\frac{524,4}{2}\right)0,4 + \left(\frac{10.000}{524,4}\right)5,5$$
>
> $$= 104,88 + 104,88 = \$\,209,76$$
>
> 4. As economias anuais estimadas em termos de custos de estocagem são calculadas:
>
> $$\text{Economias} = CTE_1 - CTE_2 = 217,50 - 209,76 = \$\,7,74$$
>
> 5. Mary Ann conclui que se as economias anuais desse material forem aplicadas aos milhares de itens contidos no estoque, as economias do LEC seriam significativas.

Modelo II — LEC para Lotes de Produção O Modelo II, LEC para lotes de produção, é útil para determinar o tamanho dos pedidos se um material for produzido numa etapa de produção, armazenado em estoque e depois enviado para a etapa seguinte de produção ou enviado para os clientes. A produção ocorre e flui para o estoque a uma taxa (p) que é maior do que a taxa de uso ou de demanda (d) na qual o material flui para fora do estoque. Portanto esse modelo é apropriado para planejar o tamanho de **lotes de produção** para manufatura de produtos internamente na empresa (in-house).

Esse modelo tem somente uma leve modificação em relação ao Modelo I: presume-se que os pedidos sejam fornecidos ou produzidos a uma taxa uniforme em vez de tudo de uma só vez. A Tabela 9.3 apresenta as suposições, as definições de variáveis, as fórmulas de custo e a derivação do LEC para o Modelo II. A Figura 9.4 mostra que os pedidos são produzidos a uma taxa uniforme (p) durante a primeira parte do ciclo de estoque e são usadas a uma taxa (d) ao longo do ciclo. Os níveis de estoque crescem a uma taxa igual a (p – d) durante a produção e nunca atingem o nível Q como no Modelo I. O Exemplo 9.2 ilustra o uso do Modelo II na determinação do tamanho de lotes de produção.

> ## Exemplo 9.2
>
> ### Uso do Modelo II na Determinação do Tamanho de Lotes de Produção
>
> A Call-Us Plumbing Supply Company tem um departamento de produção adjacente que poderia produzir a válvula n. 3925. Se as válvulas fossem produzidas internamente na empresa em lotes de produção, elas fluiriam gradualmente para estoque no armazém principal para ser usadas. O custo de manutenção de estoque, o custo de emissão do pedido ou de colocação, e a demanda anual permaneceriam aproximadamente os mesmos. Uma vez que as válvulas fluem de fato para o es-

toque em vez de ser recebidas todas de uma vez, como um lote, o sr. Swartz pondera como isso afetaria a quantidade pedida e o custo anual de estocagem. Mary Ann Church desenvolve estas estimativas: D = 10.000 válvulas por ano, C = $ 0,40 por válvula por ano, S = $ 5,50 por pedido, d = 40 válvulas por dia (10.000 válvulas por ano ÷ 250 dias úteis), e p = 120 válvulas por dia.

Solução

1. Mary Ann calcula o LEC:

$$\text{LEC} = \sqrt{\frac{2DS}{C}\left(\frac{p}{p-d}\right)} = \sqrt{\frac{2(10.000)(5,5)}{0,4}\left(\frac{120}{120-40}\right)} = 642,26 \text{ válvulas}$$

2. Os novos custos anuais totais de estocagem são calculados:

$$\text{CTE}_3 = (Q/2)\left(\frac{p-d}{p}\right)C + (D/Q)S = \frac{642,26}{2}\left(\frac{120-40}{120}\right)0,4 + \left(\frac{10.000}{642,26}\right)5,5$$

$$= 85,63 + 85,63 = \$ \; 171,26 \text{ por ano}$$

3. O LEC e os custos anuais totais de estocagem do Exemplo 9.1, quando as válvulas n. 3925 eram entregues todas de uma só vez, eram LEC = 524,4 e CTE_2 = $ 209,76.
4. As economias estimadas são calculadas:

$$\text{Economias} = \text{CTE}_2 - \text{CTE}_3 = 209,76 - 171,26 = \$ \; 38,50 \text{ por ano}$$

Modelo III — LEC com Descontos por Quantidade Os fornecedores podem oferecer seus produtos a preços unitários mais baixos se quantidades maiores forem pedidas. Essa prática é denominada **desconto por quantidade** e ocorre porque quantidades maiores de pedido podem ser menos dispendiosas para produzir e expedir. Uma preocupação crucial na maioria das decisões a respeito de quantidades pedidas é encomendar material suficiente em cada pedido para qualificar-se para o melhor preço possível, mas não comprar tanto a ponto de que os custos da manutenção em estoque consumam as economias nos custos de compra. O Modelo III tenta atingir esse objetivo. A quantidade comprada não tem necessariamente de ser a quantidade LEC, conforme foi formulado no Modelo I ou Modelo II; ao contrário, é a quantidade que minimiza a soma dos custos anuais de manutenção em estoque, pedidos e aquisições. A Tabela 9.4 relaciona as suposições, as definições de variáveis, as fórmulas e os procedimentos desse modelo.

O Modelo III utiliza ou as fórmulas do Modelo I, ou do Modelo II. Se as entregas dos pedidos ocorrerem de uma só vez, serão usadas as fórmulas do Modelo I; se elas forem graduais, serão usadas as fórmulas do Modelo II. É especialmente importante reconhecer que as quantidades fundamentais a serem consideradas são qualquer LEC viável (o LEC está na faixa de quantidade para seu preço?) e a quantidade em qualquer quebra de preço com preços mais baixos. A Tabela 9.5 apresenta quatro diferentes situações em que se deve tomar decisões referentes a descontos por quantidade/quantidade pedida para demonstrar os procedimentos para identificar as quantidades a serem investigadas ao comparar os custos anuais totais de materiais (CTM).

O Exemplo 9.3 aplica o Modelo III a nossos antigos amigos da empresa de suprimentos hidráulicos. Nesse exemplo, o gerente deve decidir-se tanto sobre a quantidade como sobre o método de entrega — ou entregas parceladas, ou pedidos recebidos de uma só vez — para um material. Siga os passos desse exemplo; ele demonstra os procedimentos do Modelo III.

TABELA 9.3 — MODELO II — LEC PARA LOTES DE PRODUÇÃO

Suposições

1. A demanda anual, o custo de manutenção de estoque e o custo de emissão do pedido podem ser estimados.
2. Nenhum estoque de segurança é utilizado, os materiais são fornecidos a uma taxa uniforme (p) e usados a uma taxa uniforme (d), e os materiais foram usados completamente quando o pedido seguinte começa a chegar.
3. Os custos de stockout, receptividade do cliente e outros custos são irrelevantes.
4. Não existem descontos por quantidade.
5. A taxa de suprimento (p) é maior do que a taxa de uso (d).

Definições de Variáveis

Todas as definições do Modelo I também são aplicadas ao Modelo II*. Adicionalmente:

d = taxa na qual unidades são retiradas do estoque para ser usadas (unidades por período de tempo).
p = taxa na qual unidades são supridas no estoque (mesmas unidades que d).

Fórmulas de Custo

Nível de estoque mínimo = Taxa de crescimento do estoque × Período de entrega
$$= (p - d)(Q/p)$$
Nível de estoque mínimo = 0
Nível médio de estoque = 1/2(Nível de estoque máximo + Nível de estoque mínimo)
$$= 1/2[(p - d)(Q/p) + 0] = (Q/2)[(p - d)/p]$$
Custo anual de manutenção em estoque = Nível médio de estoque × Custo de manutenção de estoque
$$= (Q/2)[(p - d)/p]C$$
Custo anual de emissão do pedido = Pedidos por ano × Custo de emissão do pedido = $(D/Q)S$
Custo anual total de estocagem (CTE) = Custo anual de manutenção de estoque × Custo anual de emissão de pedidos
$$= (Q/2)[(p - d)/p]C + (D/Q)S$$

Derivação da Fórmula do Lote Econômico de Compra

Novamente, como no Modelo I, defina a derivada do CTE com respeito a Q como igual a zero e resolva Q:
1. A fórmula para CTE é: $\quad CTE = (Q/2)[(p - d)/p]C + (D/Q)S$
2. A derivada de CTE com respeito a Q é: $\quad d(CTE)/d(Q) = [(p - d)/2p]C - DS/Q^2$
3. Defina a derivada de CTE como igual a zero e resolva Q:
$$[(p - d)/2p]C - DS/Q^2 = 0$$
$$Q^2 = (2DS/C)[p/(p - d)]$$
$$Q = \sqrt{(2DS/C)[p/(p - d)]}$$
4. O LEC é, portanto: $\quad LEC = \sqrt{(2DS/C)[p/(p - d)]}$

*Veja a nota na Tabela 9.2.

Os descontos por quantidades, quando usados com fórmulas LEC, começam por dar mais realismo a esses métodos de análise. Não obstante algumas suposições restritivas ainda estarem presentes no Modelo III, um número suficiente de decisões reais a respeito de estoques aborda as suposições desse modelo para torná-lo uma técnica valiosa na APO.

FIGURA 9.4   NÍVEL MÉDIO DE ESTOQUE NO MODELO II

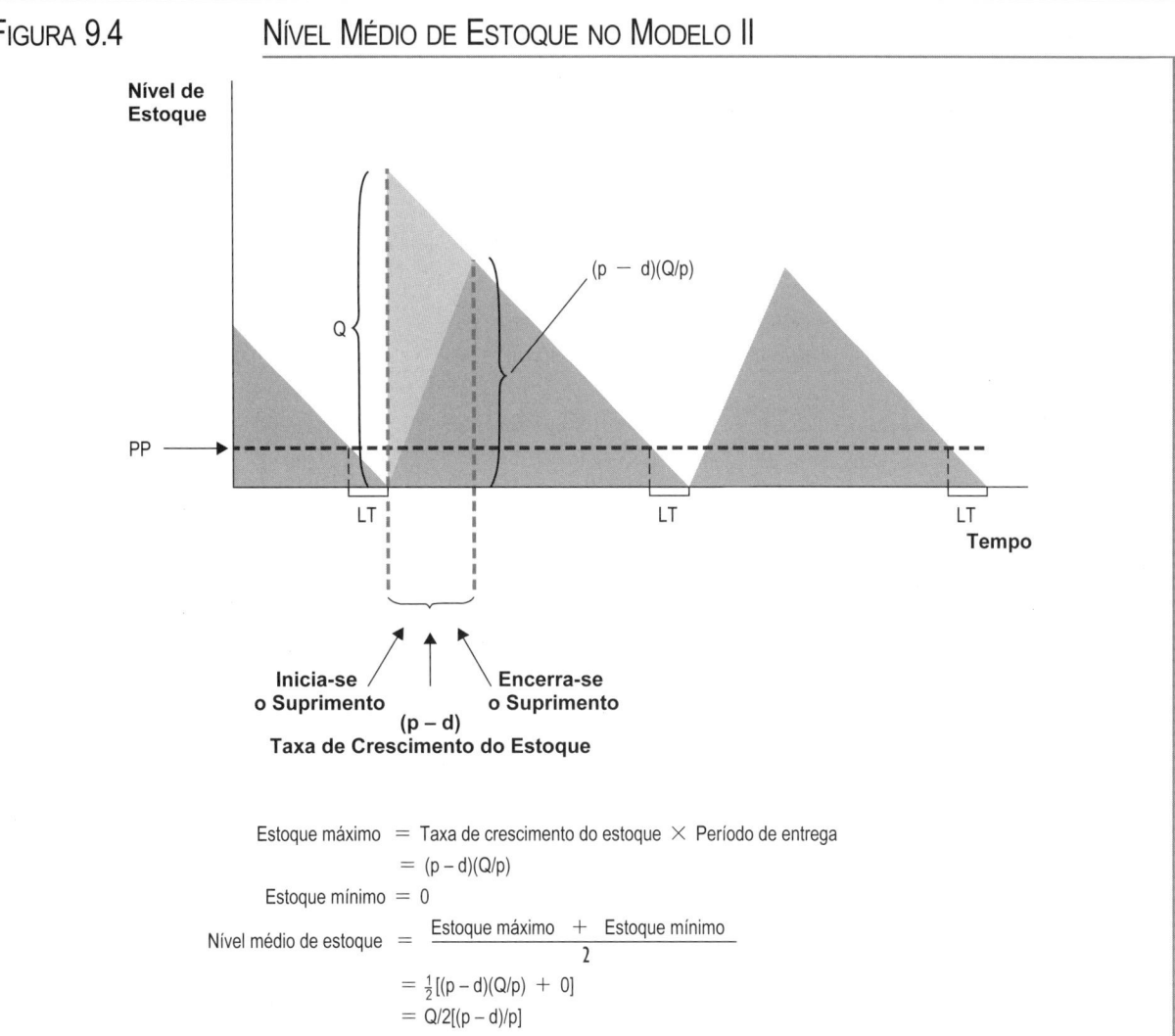

DETERMINANDO PONTOS DE PEDIDO

A Tabela 9.6 contém muitos termos freqüentemente usados na definição de pontos de pedido. Talvez você ache útil consultar ocasionalmente a tabela à medida que avançarmos nesta seção. Quando definem pontos de pedido num sistema do lote padrão, os gerentes de operações são confrontados com uma demanda incerta durante o lead time. **Demanda durante o lead time (DDLT)** significa a quantidade de um material que será demandado enquanto estamos esperando que um pedido de um material chegue e renove o estoque. A variação da demanda durante o lead time vem de duas fontes. Primeiro, o lead time necessário para receber um pedido está sujeito a variações. Por exemplo, os fornecedores podem encontrar dificuldades para processar pedidos, e as empresas de transporte em caminhões podem ter falhas de equipamento ou greves que retardem as entregas. Segundo, as demandas dos clientes por produtos acabados são conhecidas como sujeitas a grandes variações diárias, e as demandas dos departamentos de produção por matérias-primas podem variar devido a mudanças nas programações de produção. *O que torna essa variação de demanda durante o lead time especialmente preocupante para os gerentes de operações é que essa incerteza os atinge quando eles são mais vulneráveis — quando estão esperando que um pedido de materiais chegue e os níveis de estoque estão baixos.*

TABELA 9.4   MODELO III — LEC COM DESCONTOS POR QUANTIDADE

Suposições

1. A demanda anual, o custo de manutenção de estoque e o custo de pedido de um material podem ser estimados.
2. Os níveis de estoque médios podem ser estimados em:

   $Q/2$ — se as suposições do Modelo I prevalecerem: nenhum estoque de segurança, os pedidos são recebidos todos de uma só vez, os materiais são usados a uma taxa uniforme, e os materiais foram usados completamente quando o pedido seguinte chega.

   $Q/2[(p - d)/p]$ — se as suposições do Modelo II prevalecerem: nenhum estoque de segurança, os materiais são fornecidos a uma taxa uniforme (p) e usados a uma taxa uniforme (d), e os materiais foram usados completamente quando o pedido seguinte chega.

3. Os custos de stockout, receptividade do cliente e outros custos são irrelevantes.
4. Existem descontos por quantidade. Quando quantidades maiores são pedidas, descontos no preço se aplicam a todas as unidades pedidas.

Definições de Variáveis

Todas as definições nos modelos anteriores se aplicam ao Modelo III*. Adicionalmente:

   CTM = custos anuais totais de materiais ($ por ano)
   ac = custo de aquisição para comprar ou produzir uma unidade de um material ($ por unidade)

Fórmulas

As fórmulas do LEC e do CTE do Modelo I ou do Modelo II são aplicadas ao Modelo III, dependendo de quais suposições se enquadram melhor na situação de estoque.

Custos anuais de aquisição = Demanda anual × Custo das aquisições = (D)ac

Custos anuais totais de materiais (CTM) = Custos anuais totais de estocagem + Custos anuais de aquisição = CTE + (D)ac

Modelo I — Pedido entregue de uma só vez

$LEC = \sqrt{2DS/C}$

$CTM = (Q/2)C + (D/Q)S + (D)ac$

Modelo II — Entregas parceladas

$LEC = \sqrt{(2DS/C)[p/(p - d)]}$

$CTM = (Q/2)[(p - d)/p]C + (D/Q)S + (D)ac$

Procedimentos

1. Compute o LEC usando cada um dos preços de venda. Observe que C normalmente é uma função do preço de venda ou do custo de produção. Por exemplo, C pode ser definido como 20% do preço de venda. Portanto, o LEC se modificará à medida que C e ac mudarem.
2. Determine qual LEC a partir do Passo 1 acima é viável. Ou seja, o LEC computado está na faixa de quantidade para seu preço?
3. O custo anual total de materiais (CTM) é computado para o LEC viável e a quantidade em qualquer quebra de preço com preços de venda mais baixos.
4. A quantidade pedida que tem o menor custo anual total de materiais (CTM) é o lote econômico de compra para o material.

*Veja a nota da Tabela 9.2.

TABELA 9.5   IDENTIFICANDO QUANTIDADES-CHAVES A SEREM INVESTIGADAS QUANDO EXISTEM DESCONTOS POR QUANTIDADE

Quantidade	Preço	LEC Viável	Quantidade-Chave a Ser Investigada	Quantidade	Preço	LEC Viável	Quantidade-Chave a Ser Investigada
1–399	$ 2,20			1–499	$ 6,95		
400–699	2,00	524,4	524,4*	500–999	6,50		
700+	1,80		700*	1.000–1.999	6,25	1.700	1.700
				2.000+	6,10		2.000
1–699	$ 43,50	590	590	1–599	$ 10,50		
700–1.499	36,95		700	600–749	7,50		
1.500+	35,50		1.500	750–999	7,25		
				1.000+	7,15	1.200	1.200

*Veja o Exemplo 9.3 e a Figura 9.5.

FIGURA 9.5 — CURVAS CTM DE DESCONTO POR QUANTIDADE

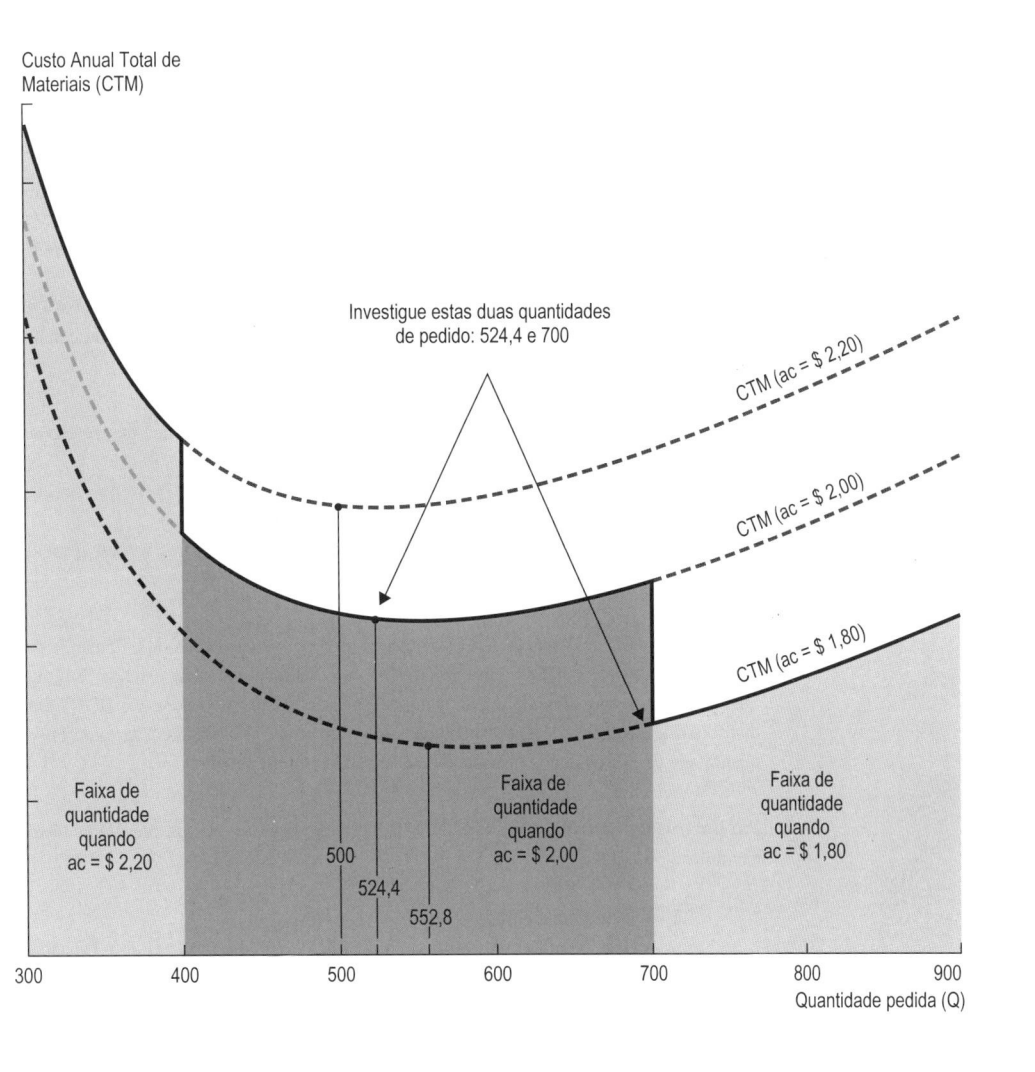

Se os pedidos chegarem atrasado ou se a demanda para os materiais for maior do que o esperado enquanto estamos esperando que um pedido chegue, poderá ocorrer um stockout. Um **stockout** significa que há estoques insuficientes para cobrir as demandas para um material durante o lead time.

Se mantivermos demasiado estoque de segurança, o custo de manutenção desses materiais em estoque será alto; entretanto, quando pouco estoque de segurança é mantido, o custo dos stockouts torna-se alto. Os gerentes de operações querem equilibrar esses dois custos quando definem pontos de pedido.

A Figura 9.6 ilustra as relações entre as variáveis envolvidas na definição dos pontos de pedido e do estoque de segurança.

A relação mais importante que você deve conhecer é:

Ponto de pedido = Demanda esperada durante o lead time + Estoque de segurança

$$PP = DEDLT + ES$$

| TABELA 9.6 | TERMOS FREQÜENTEMENTE USADOS EM ANÁLISES NO PLANEJAMENTO DE ESTOQUES SOB INCERTEZA |

Distribuições DDLT Contínuas — Distribuições de probabilidade de toda a demanda possível durante valores de lead time (DDLT), em que a DDLT é uma variável aleatória contínua. Em outras palavras, a DDLT pode assumir qualquer valor continuamente entre os valores de DDLT extremos da distribuição. Exemplos dessas distribuições são a normal, a t de Student e a exponencial.

Parâmetros da Distribuição DDLT — As medidas que descrevem as distribuições DDLT. Por exemplo:

DEDLT — Demanda esperada durante o lead time é a média das distribuições DDLT. Por exemplo:
σ_{DDLT} — Desvio padrão da demanda durante o lead time, a medida de como os valores DDLT estão dispersos nas proximidades de sua média.

Parâmetros da Distribuição (d) Demanda por Dia — As medidas que descrevem as distribuições d. Por exemplo:

$\bar{d}$ — Demanda média por dia.
σ_d — Desvio padrão da demanda por dia, a medida de como os valores d estão dispersos nas proximidades de sua média.

Distribuição DDLT Discreta — Distribuições da probabilidade de toda a demanda possível durante valores de lead time (DDLT), em que DDLT é uma variável aleatória discreta. Em outras palavras, a DDLT pode assumir somente alguns valores específicos entre os valores de DDLT extremos da distribuição. Exemplos dessas distribuições são a binomial, a hipergeométrica, de Poisson, e uma grande quantidade de outros dados históricos determinados empiricamente.

Parâmetros da Distribuição Lead Time (LT) — As medidas que descrevem as distribuições LT. Por exemplo:

$\overline{LT}$ — Lead time médio.
σ_{LT} — Desvio padrão do lead time, a medida de como os valores de LT estão dispersos — nas proximidades de sua média.

Nível Ótimo de Estoque de Segurança — A quantidade de estoque de segurança, a qual é o ponto de pedido (PP) menos a demanda esperada durante o lead time (DEDLT), que equilibra os custos esperados a longo prazo e os custos esperados a curto prazo durante o lead time.

Tabelas de Custos Esperados (*payoff*) — Uma forma de análise do nível do estoque de segurança e de problemas do ponto de pedido no planejamento de estoque sob incerteza. Essa técnica computa o total de custos esperados para longo e curto prazo por lead time para cada estratégia de ponto de pedido. O ponto de pedido que tem o mínimo custo esperado total é o ponto de pedido ótimo. O estoque de segurança ótimo é então deduzido (ES = PP − DEDLT).

Risco de Stockouts — A probabilidade de que todos os pedidos dos clientes ou de departamentos de produção não possam ser completamente atendidos a partir dos estoques durante o lead time. Se houver 10% de risco de stockout, o nível de serviço será de 90%.

Nível de Serviço — A probabilidade de que um stockout não ocorrerá durante o lead time. Por exemplo, um nível de serviço de 90% significa que há uma probabilidade de 10% de que *todos* os pedidos não poderão ser atendidos a partir do estoque durante o lead time.

Capítulo 9 – Sistemas de Estoques com Demanda Independente

EXEMPLO 9.3

LEC COM DESCONTO POR QUANTIDADE NUMA EMPRESA DE SUPRIMENTOS HIDRÁULICOS

Um fornecedor da válvula n. 3925 ofereceu ao sr. Swartz descontos por quantidade se ele comprar mais do que seus pedidos atuais. Os novos volumes e preços são:

Faixa de Quantidades Pedidas	Custo de Aquisição por Válvula (ac)
1–399	$ 2,20
400–699	2,00
700+	1,80

O sr. Swartz pede a Mary Ann Church para investigar os novos preços sob dois conjuntos de suposições: os pedidos são recebidos todos de uma vez e as entregas são parceladas.

SOLUÇÃO

Os Pedidos São Recebidos de uma Só Vez

1. Mary Ann desenvolveu estas estimativas: D = 10.000 válvulas por ano, C = 0,2(ac) dólares por válvula por ano, e S = $ 5,50 por pedido.
2. Os LECs são computados para cada um dos custos de aquisição:

$$LEC_{2,20} = \sqrt{\frac{2DS}{C}} = \sqrt{\frac{2(10.000)(5,5)}{0,2(2,2)}} = 500$$

$$LEC_{2,00} = \sqrt{\frac{2DS}{C}} = \sqrt{\frac{2(10.000)(5,5)}{0,2(2,0)}} = 524,4$$

$$LEC_{1,80} = \sqrt{\frac{2DS}{C}} = \sqrt{\frac{2(10.000)(5,5)}{0,2(1,8)}} = 552,8$$

3. Mary Ann traça graficamente o CTM para cada custo de aquisição (veja a Figura 9.5). Por exemplo, $CTM_{2,2}$ pode ser traçado graficamente substituindo-se diversos valores de Q nessa fórmula de CTM:

$$CTM = \left(\frac{Q}{2}\right)C + \left(\frac{D}{Q}\right)S + (D)ac$$

$$CTM_{2,2} = \left(\frac{Q}{2}\right)(2,2)(0,2) + \left(\frac{10.000}{Q}\right)5,5 + (10.000)2,2$$

Mary Ann nota que somente $LEC_{2,00}$ é viável, porque 524,4 válvulas por pedido podem ser compradas a $ 2,00 por válvula. O CTM nas duas quantidades, portanto, é investigado: 524,4 unidades por pedido (cada uma a $ 2,00) e 700 unidades por pedido (cada uma a $ 1,80):

Q = 524,4: $CTM = \left(\frac{Q}{2}\right)C + \left(\frac{D}{Q}\right)S + (D)ac$

$= \left(\frac{524,4}{2}\right)0,4 + \left(\frac{10.000}{524,4}\right)5,5 + (10.000)2$

$= 104,88 + 104,88 + 20.000 = $ 20.209,76$ por ano

$$Q = 700: \quad CTM = \left(\frac{Q}{2}\right)C + \left(\frac{D}{Q}\right)S + (D)ac$$

$$CTM = \left(\frac{700}{2}\right)(0,2 \times 1,8) + \left(\frac{10.000}{700}\right)5,5 + (10.000)1,8$$

$$= 126,00 + 78,57 + 18.000 = \$ 18.204,57 \text{ por ano}$$

4. Mary Ann conclui que se os pedidos forem entregues de uma só vez, 700 válvulas devem ser pedidas em cada renovação de estoque.

Entregas Parceladas

1. Mary Ann desenvolveu estas estimativas: D = 10.000 válvulas por ano, S = $ 5,50 por pedido, C = 0,2 (ac) dólares por válvula por ano, p = 120 válvulas por dia, e d = 40 válvulas por dia.
2. O LEC agora é computado:

$$LEC_{2,20} = \sqrt{\frac{2DS}{C}\left(\frac{p}{p-d}\right)} = \sqrt{\frac{2(10.000)(5,5)}{0,2(2,2)}\left(\frac{120}{120-40}\right)} = 612,4$$

$$LEC_{2,00} = \sqrt{\frac{2DS}{C}\left(\frac{p}{p-d}\right)} = \sqrt{\frac{2(10.000)(5,5)}{0,2(2,0)}\left(\frac{120}{120-40}\right)} = 642,3$$

$$LEC_{1,80} = \sqrt{\frac{2DS}{C}\left(\frac{p}{p-d}\right)} = \sqrt{\frac{2(10.000)(5,5)}{0,2(1,8)}\left(\frac{120}{120-40}\right)} = 677,0$$

3. Mary Ann nota que somente o $LEC_{2,00}$ é viável, porque 642,3 válvulas por pedido podem ser compradas a $ 2,00 por válvula. Duas quantidades são investigadas, 642,3 e 700 unidades por pedido:

$$Q = 642,3: \quad CTM = \frac{Q}{2}\left(\frac{p-d}{p}\right)C + \left(\frac{D}{Q}\right)S + (D)ac$$

$$= \frac{642,3}{2}\left(\frac{120-40}{120}\right)(0,2 \times 2,0) + \left(\frac{10.000}{642,3}\right)5,5 + (10.000)2,0$$

$$= 85,63 + 85,63 + 20.000 = \$ 20.171,26 \text{ por ano}$$

$$Q = 700: \quad CTM = \frac{Q}{2}\left(\frac{p-d}{p}\right)C + \left(\frac{D}{Q}\right)S + (D)ac$$

$$= \frac{700}{2}\left(\frac{120-40}{120}\right)(0,2 \times 1,8) + \left(\frac{10.000}{700}\right)5,5 + (10.000)1,8$$

$$= 84,00 + 78,57 + 18.000 = \$ 18.162,57 \text{ por ano}$$

Mary Ann conclui que se forem usadas entregas parceladas, 700 unidades por pedido devem ser compradas.

4. Dada uma escolha, o sr. Swartz preferiria ter entregas parceladas de válvulas n. 3925 em quantidades de 700 unidades por pedido, porque o CTM de entregas parceladas é ligeiramente menor do que para os pedidos entregues de uma só vez.

| FIGURA 9.6 | RELAÇÕES ENTRE DDLT, DEDLT, ES, PP E POSSIBILIDADE DE STOCKOUTS PARA CADA CICLO DE NOVO PEDIDO |

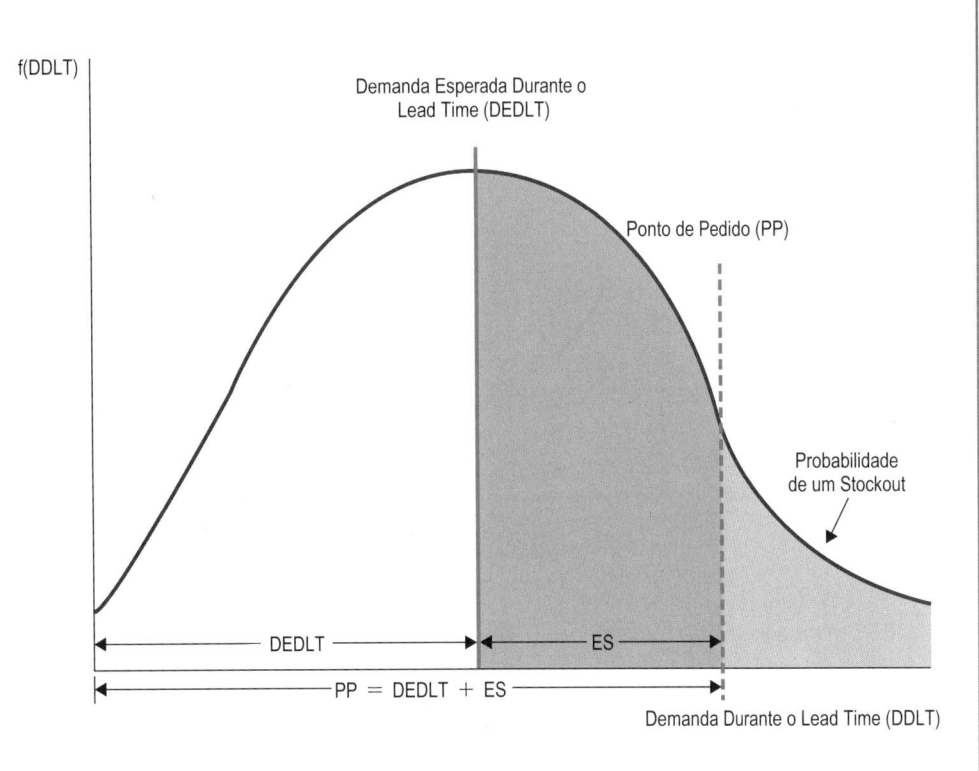

Como se pode ver na demanda durante a distribuição do lead time na Figura 9.6, estoque de segurança é adicionado à demanda esperada durante o lead time para determinar o ponto de pedido. Se presumirmos que podemos estimar acuradamente o valor da demanda esperada durante o lead time a partir de registros históricos ou de outras fontes, a definição do estoque de segurança também definirá o ponto de pedido. Desse modo, quando definimos o nível do estoque de segurança para um material, também definimos simultaneamente o ponto de pedido. Como podemos ver na Figura 9.6, aumentar o estoque de segurança para um material reduz a probabilidade de um stockout durante o lead time. Isso reduz o custo dos stockouts, mas tem a desvantagem de aumentar os custos de manutenção de estoque.

Ao tentar equilibrar os custos de manter demasiado ou pouco estoque de segurança para cada material, os analistas têm procurado soluções ótimas para esse problema. O principal obstáculo para determinarmos níveis de estoque ótimos é estimarmos os custos de stockouts. Sabemos que os stockouts custam, mas quanto? Quanto lucro é perdido quando perdemos ou desapontamos clientes devido a stockouts? Quanto custa quando os departamentos de produção precisam mudar programas de produção ou encerrar a produção quando enfrentam stockouts de matérias-primas? Em razão da dificuldade de determinar com precisão os custos de stockouts, os analistas tomaram outra abordagem para definir estoques de produção — definir pontos de pedido nos níveis de serviço determinados pela política administrativa.

Definindo Pontos de Pedido nos Níveis de Serviço A expressão **nível de serviço** refere-se à probabilidade de que um stockout não ocorrerá durante o lead time. Os gerentes poderiam dizer, por exemplo: "Queremos uma probabilidade de 90% de que *todos* os pedidos dos clientes podem ser enviados imediatamente do estoque".

Figura 9.7   Distribuição DDLT

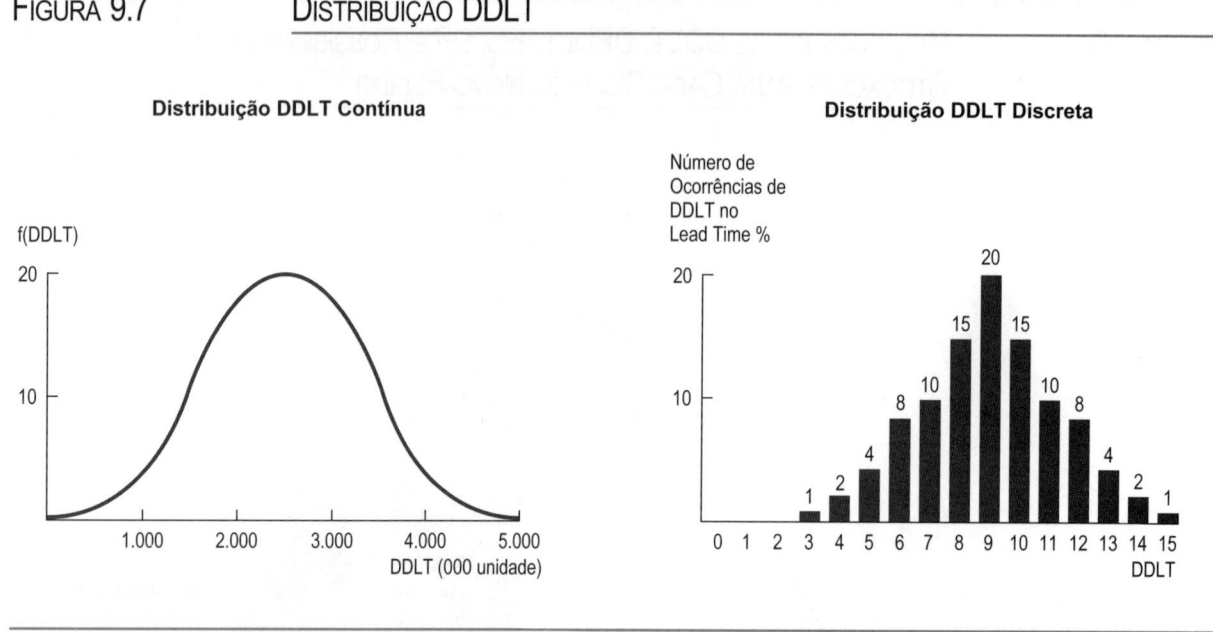

Distribuições DDLT Discretas e Contínuas. Quando a DDLT varia de 3 a 15 unidades, como é mostrado no lado direito da Figura 9.7, uma **distribuição DDLT discreta** pode descrever mais acuradamente a ocorrência da DDLT, uma vez que seus valores somente podem ser valores inteiros de 3 a 15 unidades. Quando o número de unidades em DDLT for muito grande, como é mostrado no lado esquerdo da Figura 9.7, ou quando as unidades forem divisíveis, como no caso de barris de petróleo bruto, as **distribuições DDLT contínuas** descrevem acuradamente a ocorrência de DDLT. Quando existem suficientes dados históricos correspondentes à demanda durante o lead time para o material, a definição dos níveis de estoque de segurança é direta.

O Exemplo 9.4 define o nível de estoque de segurança para um material cuja DDLT foi classificada em classes discretas.

Exemplo 9.4

Definindo o Estoque de Segurança nos Níveis de Serviço para uma Distribuição DDLT Discreta

A Whipple Manufacturing Company fabrica produtos de escritório. Um desses produtos, um computador para processamento de texto, é produzido para estoque e guardado num estoque de produtos acabados até ser pedido por clientes. Quando o estoque de produtos acabados cai até o ponto de pedido, um pedido de um lote de produção é feito ao departamento de produção da Whipple. A administração da Whipple quer determinar quanto estoque de segurança deve ser mantido para esse item e obteve as seguintes informações: a demanda média por dia é de 6,0 unidades, o lead time médio da produção é de 10 dias, e os registros históricos mostram esta freqüência do lead time real da demanda:

DDLT Real	Freqüência
21–30	0,05
31–40	0,10
41–50	0,15
51–60	0,20
61–70	0,20
71–80	0,15
81–90	0,10
91–100	0,05

Se a administração da Whipple quiser oferecer um nível de serviço de 80% durante o lead time:
a) Qual é o ponto de pedido? **b)** Qual é o estoque de segurança?

Solução

a) Primeiro, use os dados da DDLT para desenvolver uma distribuição cumulativa de probabilidade do nível de serviço:

DDLT Real	Freqüência	Nível de Serviço (probabilidade de DDLT ou menos)
11–20	0	0
21–30	0,05	0,05
31–40	0,10	0,15
41–50	0,15	0,30
51–60	0,20	0.50
61–70	0,20	0,70
71–80	0,15	0,85
81–90	0,10	0,95
91–100	0,05	1,00

Em seguida, trace graficamente esta distribuição cumulativa:

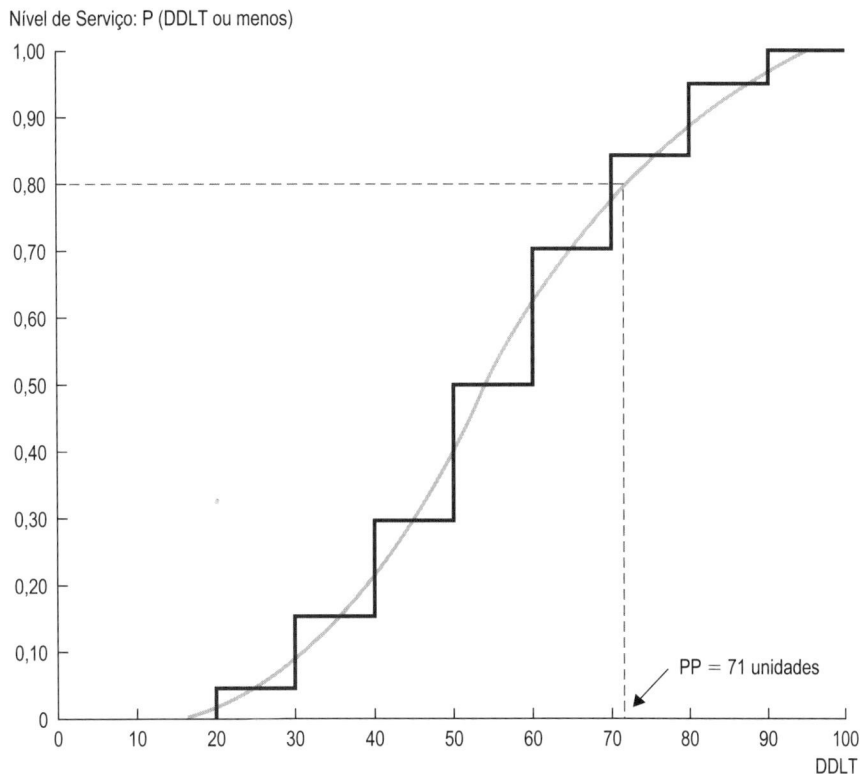

O gráfico de dados discretos é convertido num gráfico de dados contínuos, desenhando uma linha curva que atravessa os pontos médios dos topos dos degraus. Como se pode ver nesse gráfico, o ponto de pedido é de 71 unidades. Se a Whipple iniciar um lote de produção quando o estoque cair até 71 unidades, ocorrerão stockouts (DDLT > 71) aproximadamente 20% do tempo.

b) Determine o nível de estoque de segurança:

$$PP = DEDLT + \text{Estoque de segurança}$$

Estoque de segurança = PP − DEDLT = PP − [(Demanda média por dia) × (Lead time médio)]

$$= 71 - (6{,}0 \times 10) = 71 - 60 = 11 \text{ unidades}$$

Observação: Essa abordagem de classificar valores da DDLT históricos em classes discretas tem a vantagem de não ter de supor uma forma em particular (por exemplo, normal) para a função DDLT de probabilidade.

O Exemplo 9.5 demonstra como definir os níveis de estoque de segurança quando a DDLT é descrita por uma distribuição contínua. Esse exemplo supõe que a DDLT histórica para uma matéria-prima é, de fato, de uma distribuição normal. Lembre-se de que definimos anteriormente ponto de pedido como:

Ponto de pedido = Demanda esperada durante o lead time + Estoque de segurança

EXEMPLO 9.5

DEFININDO O ESTOQUE DE SEGURANÇA NOS NÍVEIS DE SERVIÇO PARA UMA DDLT QUE É NORMALMENTE DISTRIBUÍDA

Billie Jean Bray, a gerente de materiais da INJECTO Wholesale Plastics, está tentando definir o nível de estoque de segurança para a resina n. 942. Esse material é vendido para clientes da INJECTO, e acredita-se que sua demanda durante o lead time seja normalmente distribuída, com uma média de 693,7 libras e um desvio padrão de 139,27 libras. **a)** Qual é a DEDLT para a resina n. 942? **b)** Qual é a σ_{DDLT} para a resina n. 942? **c)** Se o gerente de produção especificar um nível de serviço de 95% para a resina n. 942 durante o lead time, qual estoque de segurança deve ser mantido?

SOLUÇÃO

a) A média da distribuição DEDLT é

$$DEDLT = 693{,}7 \text{ libras}$$

b) O desvio padrão da DDLT é

$$\sigma_{DDLT} = 139{,}27 \text{ libras}$$

Portanto temos uma distribuição normal de DDLT com uma média de 693,7 libras e um desvio padrão de 139,27 libras (veja a figura a seguir).

c) Compute o estoque de segurança (ES) para que forneça um nível de serviço de 95%; em outras palavras, qual é o nível de DDLT que tem uma probabilidade de somente 5% de ser ultrapassado? Este é o ponto de pedido:

$$PP = DEDLT + Z(\sigma_{DDLT})$$

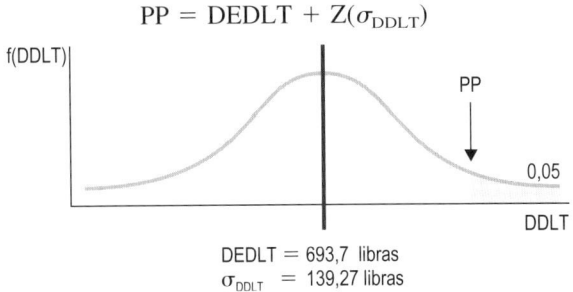

DEDLT = 693,7 libras
σ_{DDLT} = 139,27 libras

(O valor Z encontra-se na Tabela de Distribuição Normal, no final do livro.) Localize 0,95 (a área à esquerda do PP) no corpo da tabela, e leia o valor Z igual a 1,64. Esse é o número de desvios padrões em que o PP está afastado da DEDLT:

$$PP = 693,7 + 1,64\,(139,27) = 922,1 \text{ libras}$$

O estoque de segurança é então deduzido:

$$ES = PP - DEDLT = 922,1 - 693,7 = 228,4 \text{ libras}$$

Lead Time Constante e Demanda por Dia Normalmente Distribuída. Há momentos em que é difícil se obter dados sobre a DDLT. Nesses casos, muitas vezes é satisfatório obter dados sobre a demanda por dia e supor um lead time constante. Uma vez que os dados históricos da demanda por dia em geral estão abundantemente disponíveis e o lead time comumente está sujeito a menos variações do que a demanda diária, essa abordagem pode ser útil.

O Exemplo 9.6 desenvolve níveis de estoque de segurança para um material enquanto presume um lead time constante e uma demanda por dia normalmente distribuída. Uma distribuição DDLT normal é desenvolvida computando-se a demanda esperada durante o lead time (DEDLT) e o desvio padrão da demanda durante o lead time (σ_{DDLT}):

$$DEDLT = LT(\bar{d}) \quad e \quad \sigma_{DDLT} = \sqrt{LT(\sigma_d)^2}$$

A distribuição normal DDLT é então analisada para calcular o valor da DDLT que fornece o nível de serviço especificado, e esse valor é o ponto de pedido (PP).

Exemplo 9.6

Definindo Níveis de Estoque de Segurança nos Níveis de Serviço para Lead Time Constante e para Demanda por Dia Normalmente Distribuída

Bob Fero é analista de operações da Sell-Rite Discount Stores de Washington. Ele está estudando atualmente as políticas de pedido e de estoques no armazém central da Sell-Rite para um de seus itens de maior demanda: um brinquedo infantil. Um exame dos dados de suprimento e demanda históricos para esse item indicou um lead time (LT) de 10 dias quase constante, e uma alta capacidade produtiva permitia tempos de produção e entrega muito consistentes. Bob também descobriu que a demanda por dia (d) era quase que normalmente distribuída com uma média ($\bar{d}$) de 1.250 brinquedos por dia com um desvio padrão (σ_d) de 375 brinquedos por dia. **a)** Compute o ponto de pedido para o brinquedo se o nível de serviço for especificado em 90% durante o lead time. **b)** Quanto estoque de segurança é fornecido em sua resposta na parte *a*?

Solução

a) Compute o ponto de pedido:

1. Primeiro, compute a média e o σ_{DDLT}:

$$\text{Média} = \text{Lead time} \times \text{Demanda média por dia} = LT(\bar{d}) = 10(1.250)$$
$$= 12.500 \text{ brinquedos durante o lead time}$$
$$\sigma_{DDLT} = \sqrt{LT(\sigma_d)^2} = \sqrt{10(375)^2} = 1.185,85 \text{ brinquedos durante o lead time}$$

2. A média e o σ_{DDLT} descrevem totalmente a distribuição DDLT:

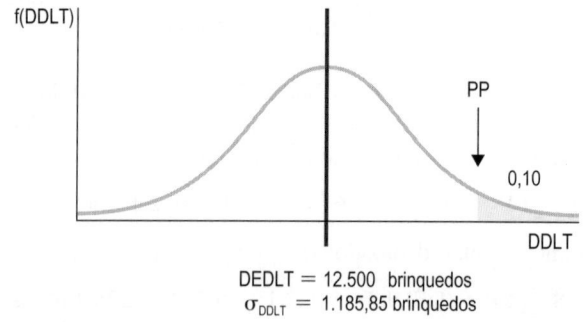

DEDLT = 12.500 brinquedos
σ_{DDLT} = 1.185,85 brinquedos

3. Em seguida, devemos determinar Z, o número de desvios padrões em que PP está afastado da média.
4. Em seguida, compute o ponto de pedido:

$$PP = DEDLT + Z(\sigma_{DDLT}) = 12.500 + 1,28(1.185,85) = 12.500 + 1.517,89$$
$$= 14.017,89 \text{ brinquedos}$$

Os pedidos seriam feitos quando o nível de estoque caísse para 14.018 brinquedos.

b) Compute o estoque de segurança (ES):

$$ES = PP - DEDLT = 14.018 - 12.500 = 1.518 \text{ brinquedos}$$

Todas essas abordagens para lidar de maneira explícita com a incerteza no planejamento de estoques contam com os gerentes para especificar níveis de serviço que cumpram ou a política de manufatura ou a política de marketing. Examinemos agora alguns princípios básicos para determinar pontos de pedido e níveis de estoque de segurança.

Alguns Princípios Básicos para Definir Pontos de Pedido Talvez o princípio básico mais comum envolva definir níveis de estoque de segurança numa **porcentagem da DEDLT**:

Ponto de pedido = DEDLT + j(DEDLT), em que *j* é um fator que varia de 0 a 3,00.

Os materiais comumente são classificados de acordo com as classes:

Classe	Descrição	j
1	Não crítico	0,10
2	Incerto — não crítico	0,20
3	Crítico	0,30
4	Incerto — crítico	0,50
5	Supercrítico	1,00
6	Incerto — supercrítico	3,00

Capítulo 9 – Sistemas de Estoques com Demanda Independente

Essas classificações seriam idealizadas de forma personalizada para o sistema de estoque de uma empresa e aplicadas uniformemente à maioria dos materiais em estoques de bens acabados e de matérias-primas.

Outra abordagem define o estoque de segurança na **raiz quadrada da DEDLT**:

Ponto de pedido = DEDLT + $\sqrt{\text{DEDLT}}$

Esse método escolhe níveis de estoque de segurança que sejam grandes em relação à DEDLT quando a DEDLT for pequena e que sejam relativamente pequenos quando a DEDLT for grande. Essa abordagem normalmente é aplicada quando stockouts não são especialmente indesejáveis ou custosos.

A porcentagem de DEDLT e a raiz quadrada de métodos DEDLT para definir pontos de pedido são demonstradas no Exemplo 9.7. Nesse exemplo, os dois métodos para computar pontos de pedido desenvolvem estoques de segurança de 12 e 8 unidade de peças fundidas. Qual é o correto? Ambos estão matematicamente corretos, mas a exatidão de cada ponto de pedido pode ser testada somente por meio de experimentação — escolha um e faça registros sobre a DDLT à medida que o tempo passar. Esse é o único teste verdadeiro de um ponto de pedido: O estoque de segurança oferece o nível desejado de proteção contra stockouts?

EXEMPLO 9.7

USANDO PRINCÍPIOS BÁSICOS PARA DEFINIR PONTOS DE PEDIDO

A Dapple Manufacturing Company produz peças fundidas em bronze. Um tipo de peça fundida, n. 699, é guardado em estoque até que clientes a encomendem da Dapple. George Dapple, gerente de materiais da Dapple, está se interessando por várias abordagens para definir pontos de pedido para materiais. A peça n. 699 é escolhida como material de investigação. Foram coletados os seguintes dados sobre a peça n. 699: a demanda média por dia é de 6 peças, e o lead time médio é de 10 dias, o tempo necessário para produzir um lote de peças. O estudo de George exige o seguinte: **a)** Se o estoque de segurança for definido em 20% da DEDLT, qual é o ponto de pedido? **b)** Se o estoque de segurança for definido na raiz quadrada de DEDLT, qual será o ponto de pedido?

SOLUÇÃO

a) Ponto de pedido = DEDLT + 0,2 (DEDLT)

   = Demanda média por dia × Lead time médio + 0,2 (DEDLT)

   = 6,0(10) + 0,2(6,0 × 10) = 60 + 12 = 72 peças fundidas

b) Ponto de pedido = DEDLT + $\sqrt{\text{DEDLT}}$ = 60 + $\sqrt{60}$ = 60 + 7,75 = 67,75, ou 68 peças fundidas

Como a utilização de estoques de segurança afeta a quantidade pedida (LEC) num sistema do lote padrão? Minimamente, se tanto! Porém, os custos anuais totais de estocagem são afetados, porque os estoques de segurança causam estes eventos:

- **Aumentados Custos Anuais de Manutenção em Estoque.** Isso resulta do fato de que os estoques de segurança são considerados estoque morto: em média, eles nunca são usados. O estoque adicional, portanto, resulta em custos anuais de manutenção em estoque mais elevados.
- **Menores Custos Anuais de Stockout.** Os modelos LEC básicos não incluem custos de stockout, e por uma boa razão: eles são difíceis de estimar. Mas, de maneira conceitual, sabemos que os custos dos stockouts são reais, e estes seriam reduzidos pelos estoques de segurança.

Consideramos a determinação das quantidades pedidas e os pontos de pedido em sistemas do lote padrão. Consideremos agora os sistemas de estoque do intervalo padrão.

Sistemas do Intervalo Padrão

Os **sistemas do intervalo padrão** revisam os níveis de estoque em intervalos de tempo fixos, e são feitos pedidos de material suficiente para devolver os níveis de estoque a certo nível previamente determinado. Os pedidos são feitos em intervalos de tempo igualmente espaçados, e a quantidade pedida em cada ciclo é computada com esta fórmula:

Quantidade pedida = Meta de estoque máximo − Nível de estoque + DEDLT

O nível de estoque máximo normalmente é determinado pela quantidade de espaço alocada a um material ou num armazém ou nas prateleiras das lojas. Se no momento da revisão o nível de estoque estiver relativamente baixo, quantidades de pedido maiores serão pedidas. Se, por outro lado, os estoques estiverem elevados quando da revisão, quantidades menores serão pedidas.

O sistema do intervalo padrão se presta a estoques em que é desejável contar o estoque fisicamente em base periódica regular, como em algumas lojas de venda a varejo. Nessas situações, especialmente com bens que estejam em exposição em lugares onde talvez não seja viável a contabilidade permanente de estoques, contagens periódicas dos materiais presentes podem ser o sistema mais prático a ser usado, e o sistema do intervalo padrão seria apropriado.

Assim que o intervalo entre pedidos tiver sido fixado e soubermos as datas de revisões dos estoques, o nível de estoque não necessitará ser monitorado até a próxima revisão. Entre essas revisões, as incertezas relativas tanto à demanda como ao lead time se combinam para colocar esse sistema num risco maior de stockouts do que o sistema do lote padrão. Em sistemas do intervalo padrão, sem nenhuma revisão per-

---

Tabela 9.7 — Modelo IV — Intervalo Econômico de Pedido

Suposições

1. A demanda anual, o custo de manutenção em estoque e o custo de emissão do pedido de um material podem ser estimados.
2. O estoque médio é o tamanho médio do lote dividido por 2. Isso supõe implicitamente que não há qualquer estoque de segurança, os pedidos são recebidos de uma só vez, os materiais são usados a uma taxa uniforme, e os materiais, em média, foram completamente utilizados quando o pedido seguinte é recebido.
3. Os custos de stockout, receptividade do cliente e outros custos são irrelevantes.
4. Não existem descontos por quantidade.

Definições de Variáveis

As definições de variáveis do Modelo I se aplicam aqui.* Adicionalmente:

T = Tempo entre os pedidos expresso como uma fração de um ano.

Fórmulas de Custo

Custos anuais de manutenção em estoque = Estoque médio × Custo de manutenção em estoque = $(DT/2)C$

Custos anuais de realização de estoques = Número de pedidos por ano × Custo por pedido = $(D/DT)S = S/T$

Custo anual total de estocagem (CTE) = Custos anuais de manutenção em estoque + Custos anuais de emissão de pedidos = $(DT/2)C + S/T$

Derivação da Fórmula do Intervalo Ótimo de Compra

Defina a derivada de CTE com respeito a T como igual a zero e resolva T:

1. A fórmula para CTE é: $\quad CTE = (DT/2)C + S/T$
2. A derivada de CTE com respeito a T é: $\quad d(CTE)/d(T) = (D/2)C - (S/T^2)$
3. Defina a derivada de CTE com respeito a T como igual a zero e resolva T: $\quad (D/2)C - (S/T^2) = 0$
$$T^2 = 2S/DC$$
4. O T ótimo é, portanto: $\quad T = \sqrt{2S/DC}$

*Veja a nota da Tabela 9.2.

manente dos níveis de estoque, stockouts podem ocorrer quase que a qualquer momento. O sistema do intervalo padrão normalmente exige, portanto, mais estoque de segurança para acomodar esse aumentado risco de stockouts.

Escolher um ponto de pedido para materiais é a decisão-chave nos sistemas do intervalo padrão. Se os materiais forem revisados com demasiada freqüência, os custos anuais de emissão de pedidos serão excessivos. Mas, se eles forem revisados muito infreqüentemente, as quantidades pedidas e os níveis de estoque serão muito elevados, e a probabilidade de stockouts será aumentada. Portanto o intervalo de tempo entre as revisões deve ser tal que os custos anuais de manutenção de estoque sejam balanceados em relação aos custos anuais de emissão de pedidos. A Tabela 9.7 apresenta as suposições e as definições de variáveis e fórmulas correspondentes ao Modelo IV — intervalo padrão.

O Exemplo 9.8 aplica as fórmulas para o intervalo ótimo de compra e a quantidade pedida desse modelo a um material de uma companhia de venda por atacado. Observe que T, o intervalo de tempo ótimo para revisar a situação de um material e fazer o pedido de um material, é expresso como uma fração de um ano. Observe também que T é um cálculo que seria feito somente uma vez por ano aproximadamente, ao passo que cálculos da quantidade pedida devem ser feitos para cada pedido. Em outras palavras, T permanece fixo por um longo tempo, e é permitido que Q varie de pedido a pedido.

Exemplo 9.8

Intervalo Ótimo entre Pedidos num Sistema de Estoque do Intervalo Padrão

A C, D, & F Retailing Company faz revisões mensais dos níveis de estoque de seus produtos em exposição e faz pedidos desses produtos, se necessário, a seus fornecedores. O gerente regional pondera se revisões mensais são ótimas quando considera tanto os custos de manutenção em estoque como os custos de preparação de pedidos.

Um produto é escolhido para ser o foco de investigação — Goo-Goo, um alimento infantil feito de cereais e vendido em potes. Estão disponíveis as seguintes informações relativas ao Goo-Goo: D = 29.385 potes por ano, C = 30% do custo de aquisição, ac = $ 0,29 por pote, e S = $ 10,90 por pedido. **a)** Quão freqüentemente o Goo-Goo deve ser pedido? **b)** Na primeira revisão depois que T foi computado na parte *a*, se o nível de estoque for igual a 985 potes, a meta máxima de estoque (incluindo o estoque de segurança) for igual a 3.220 potes, e a demanda esperada durante o lead time for igual a 805 potes, quantos potes devem ser pedidos?

Solução

a) C = 0,3 × 0,29

$$T = \sqrt{\frac{2S}{DC}} = \sqrt{\frac{2(10,9)}{(29,385)(0,3 \times 0,29)}} = 0,0923 \text{ ano} = 33,7 \text{ dias}$$

b) Quantidade pedida = Meta máxima de estoque − Nível de estoque + DEDLT

$$= 3.220 - 985 + 805 = 3.040 \text{ potes}$$

A seguinte generalização pode ser deduzida da fórmula para T:

1. Materiais mais caros são revisados mais freqüentemente.
2. Materiais com consumo mais elevado são revisados mais freqüentemente.
3. Materiais com custos de pedido mais elevados são pedidos menos freqüentemente.

Esses, parecem ser critérios racionais para determinar outros intervalos para materiais.

OUTROS MODELOS DE ESTOQUES

Embora os modelos do lote padrão e os sistemas do intervalo padrão sejam bem conhecidos, outros modelos de estoque também estão em uso. Entre eles, os modelos híbridos e os de período único são dignos de nota.

MODELOS HÍBRIDOS DE ESTOQUE

Alguns modelos híbridos incluem diversos mas não todos os recursos dos modelos do lote padrão e do intervalo padrão. Um desses modelos é o **modelo opcional de renovação de estoque**. À semelhança do sistema do intervalo padrão, os níveis de estoque são revisados num intervalo de tempo fixo, e um pedido suficientemente grande é feito para elevar o estoque a uma meta máxima de estoque. Mas, diferentemente dos sistemas do intervalo padrão, a menos que o estoque tenha caído abaixo de certo nível mínimo no momento da revisão, nenhum pedido de renovação de estoque é feito. Esse modelo protege contra fazermos pedidos muito pequenos, e seria atraente quando os custos de revisão e emissão de pedidos são grandes.

Um **modelo básico de estoque** é um sistema de planejamento de estoques muito simples. Ele inicia com certo nível de estoque e depois, quando quer que seja feita uma retirada do estoque, é feito um pedido de renovação que é igual à retirada. Esse modelo assegura que o estoque seja mantido num nível aproximadamente constante. O estoque inicial comumente é igual à DEDLT mais o estoque de segurança, e muitas renovações de estoque são feitas para pedidos relativamente pequenos. Esse sistema seria apropriado para itens muito caros com custos de pedido pequenos.

Algumas empresas são famosas por usar mais de um dos modelos opcionais de renovação, estoque básico, lote padrão e intervalo padrão ao mesmo tempo, mas em diferentes departamentos de produção. Por exemplo, um varejista poderia usar um intervalo padrão no balcão do negócio no piso de exposição, onde a contagem física é a única maneira de determinar níveis de estoque acurados. Mas o lote padrão poderia ser usado na retaguarda do negócio, no armazém, onde um sistema computadorizado de contabilidade de estoque permanente poderia estar em operação. Dessa forma, diversos modelos de estoque poderiam ser usados ao mesmo tempo, cada um adaptado da melhor maneira a sua aplicação especial.

MODELOS DE ESTOQUE DE PERÍODO ÚNICO

Alguns problemas de estoque envolvem determinar uma quantidade pedida para um item para cobrir a demanda somente para um único período. Esse tipo de problema é comum para materiais de vida curta, como, por exemplo, produtos da moda, alimentos perecíveis e matérias publicadas em revistas e jornais. Esse tipo de problema de estoque tem sido tradicionalmente chamado **problema do jornaleiro**. A estrutura desse problema é especialmente bem adequada para ser usada em tabelas de custos esperados.

As tabelas de custos esperados são aplicadas numa ampla variedade de problemas de estocagem em que os gerentes de operações enfrentem uma demanda incerta e seja custoso para estocar demasiadamente ou muito pouco. Por exemplo, os varejistas devem decidir-se a respeito de quantas unidades de um produto em particular estocar para a semana seguinte, dados os muitos níveis de demanda possíveis para o produto. Nessas situações, os gerentes de operações devem avaliar as muitas alternativas disponíveis para atender a níveis de demanda (*estados da natureza*) incertos.

Como os gerentes de operações escolhem dentre as alternativas? Normalmente eles usam uma destas regras ou critérios: (1) Escolha a alternativa que tenha os maiores lucros esperados. (2) Escolha a alternativa que tenha os menores custos totais esperados a curto e longo prazo. (3) Escolha a alternativa que tenha os menores custos totais esperados. Uma vez que os gerentes de operações em geral preferem maximizar os lucros esperados, a Regra 1 comumente é a preferida. A Regra 2 também é usada com freqüência pelos gerentes de operações, e se lucros estiverem envolvidos, ela dá resultados equivalentes à Regra 1. Quando receitas não estão envolvidas, como em agências governamentais e organizações sem fins lucrativos, ou quando receitas não podem ser atribuídas com precisão a produtos ou unidades específicas que são estocadas, a Regra 3 freqüentemente é usada.

Uma vez que a escolha da regra ou critério usado para decidir-se entre as alternativas pode eventualmente afetar a alternativa escolhida, é importante refletir com cuidado sobre qual é a regra mais apropriada para a situação de decisão em análise. O Exemplo 9.9 demonstra como as tabelas de custos esperados são usadas pelos gerentes de operações quando diferentes critérios de decisão são utilizados.

Capítulo 9 – Sistemas de Estoques com Demanda Independente

Uma complicação que os estudantes normalmente encontram é a presença de **custos de oportunidade**. Incorre-se nesses custos, por exemplo, quando unidades não suficientes são estocadas no início do período e a demanda ultrapassa o número de unidades estocadas em algum momento durante o período. Esses custos estão na forma de lucros não auferidos. Nesse tipo de problema, muitas vezes nos confundimos a respeito de como incorporar esses custos de oportunidade em nossa tabela de custos esperados. Duas abordagens igualmente aceitáveis para esses problemas são demonstradas no Exemplo 9.9.

1. Minimize os custos totais esperados de longo e curto prazo em que os custos de curto prazo representam o lucro por unidade. Os custos de longo prazo são incorporados, como sempre.

2. Maximize os lucros totais esperados. Note no Exemplo 9.9 que os lucros por unidade são $ 5 e que para a estratégia de estocagem de 200 unidades, quando quer que a demanda seja 200, 300, 400 ou 450, os lucros são $ 1.000. Nesse tratamento, quando quer que a demanda ultrapasse a oferta, o número de unidades vendidas será o número de unidades estocadas, e os lucros serão implicitamente penalizados ao permanecer os mesmos, independentemente da aumentada demanda. Portanto o custo de curto prazo por unidade implícito é o lucro por unidade inteiro. Os custos de longo prazo são incorporados, como sempre.

EXEMPLO 9.9

TABELAS DE CUSTOS ESPERADOS (PAYOFF): UMA DECISÃO A RESPEITO DE ESTOCAGEM NA VENDA A VAREJO

A Fashion Retailers Inc. está tentando decidir-se a respeito de quantos xales de seda n. 325 estocar para a próxima estação. O histórico de vendas desse item é o seguinte:

Número de estações	Xales em Demanda (SN)	Probabilidade de Xales Demandados P(SN)
1	100	0,1
1	200	0,1
4	300	0,4
3	400	0,3
1	450	0,1
Total 10		1,0

O xale n. 325 é vendido a $ 15 por unidade e tem um custo igual a $ 10 por unidade. Se um desses xales for estocado para venda, mas não for vendido durante a estação, o desconto para ele na próxima estação será de $ 2, ou um custo de longo prazo. **a)** Use tabelas de custos esperados para minimizar os custos totais esperados de longo e curto prazo. Qual é o valor esperado da informação perfeita (VEIP)? Explique seu significado. **b)** Use tabelas de custos esperados para maximizar os lucros totais esperados. Compute o VEIP. **c)** Qual estratégia de estocagem é a melhor para o xale n. 325? Explique a equivalência das soluções das partes *a* e *b* acima.

SOLUÇÃO

a) Use tabelas de custos esperados para minimizar os custos totais esperados de longo e curto prazo. Qual é o VEIP? Explique seu significado.

Primeiramente, preencha uma tabela de custos esperados que minimize os custos totais esperados de longo e curto prazo em que os custos de longo prazo sejam $ 2 por unidade e os custos de curto prazo sejam $ 5 por unidade, o lucro perdido sobre vendas não realizadas.

	\ SN$_i$	Estados da Natureza					Custos Totais Esperados de Longo e Curto Prazo
	S$_j$ \	100	200	300	400	450	CE = Σ[P(SN$_i$)c$_{ij}$]
	100	$ 0	$ 500	$ 1.000	$ 1.500	$ 1.750	$ 1.075
	200	200	0	500	1.000	1.250	645
Estratégias	300	400	200	0	500	750	285
	400	600	400	200	0	250	205
	450	700	500	300	100	0	270
	P(SN$_i$)	0,1	0,1	0,4	0,3	0,1	

Os procedimentos das tabelas de custos esperados podem ser ilustrados explicando-se detalhadamente três dos elementos da tabela, usando-se S$_j$ com o significado de *estratégias de estocagem* e SN$_i$ com o significado de *estados da natureza*, ou níveis de demanda incertos:

- **S igual a 200 e SN igual a 400:** Os $ 1.000 encontrados nessa posição indicam que se for escolhida uma estratégia de estocagem de 200 unidades e se for experimentada uma demanda de 400 unidades, isso provocará uma falta de 200 unidades durante a estação. Os custos de curto prazo são $ 5 por unidade vezes 200 unidades, o que é igual a $ 1.000.
- **S igual a 300 e SN igual a 300:** O zero encontrado nessa posição indica que desde que a estratégia cumpra exatamente o estado da natureza, não há nem custos de curto nem de longo prazo.
- **S igual a 400 e SN igual a 100:** Os $ 600 encontrados nessa posição indicam que se for escolhida uma estratégia de estocagem de 400 unidades e se for experimentada uma demanda de 100 unidades, isso produzirá um excesso de 300 unidades em estoque no final da estação. O custo de longo prazo para a estação é de 300 unidades vezes $ 2 por unidade, o que é igual a $ 600.

Todos os outros elementos da tabela de custos esperados são computados similarmente. A coluna de custos esperados (CE) da tabela é preenchida somando-se ao longo de cada linha de estratégia (S$_j$) os produtos da probabilidade dos estados da natureza P(SN$_i$) e seus C$_{ij}$. Por exemplo, o CE de S$_j$ = 400 unidades é computado desta maneira:

$$CE = 0,1(600) + 0,1(400) + 0,4(200) + 0,3(0) + 0,1(250)$$
$$= 60 + 40 + 80 + 0 + 25 = 205$$

Agora, qual é o VEIP e qual é seu significado? O VEIP é $ 205, o valor dos custos mínimos totais esperados de longo e curto prazo derivados da tabela de custos esperados acima. O VEIP significa que se toda a incerteza do problema pudesse ser removida através de uma pesquisa de mercado perfeita ou de algum outro meio, uma média de $ 205 por estação poderia ser economizada, eliminando completamente os custos de longo e curto prazo. Em outras palavras, até $ 205 por estação poderiam ser gastos para se obter informações de mercado perfeitas para remover a incerteza. Os custos de longo e curto prazo para cada nível de demanda sob a condição de informação perfeita se encontram na diagonal da tabela de custos esperados. Uma vez que todos esses valores na diagonal são iguais a zero, os custos totais esperados de longo e curto prazo também são iguais a zero. A diferença entre os custos totais esperados de longo e curto prazo sob condições de informação perfeita ($ 0) e sob condições de informação imperfeita ou incerteza ($ 205) é o VEIP.

b) Use tabelas de custos esperados para maximizar os lucros totais esperados. Compute o VEIP.

Primeiro, preencha a tabela de custos esperados que maximize os lucros totais esperados (veja a tabela de custos esperados). Os elementos coloridos da tabela são explicados da seguinte maneira:

- **S igual a 200 e SN igual a 400:** Os $ 1.000 encontrados nessa posição indicam que se for escolhida a estratégia de 200 unidades e se for experimentada uma demanda de 400 unidades, as receitas serão igual a $ 15(200) ou $ 3.000, e o custo de bens vendidos será $ 10(200), ou $ 2.000, para um lucro de $ 1.000 para a estação.

- **S igual a 300 e SN igual a 300:** Os $ 1.500 encontrados nessa posição indicam que a estratégia cumpre exatamente o estado da natureza; as receitas seriam de $ 15(300), ou $ 4.500, e o custo dos bens vendidos seria $ 10(300), ou $ 3.000, para um lucro de $ 1.500 para a estação.

	Estados da Natureza					Lucros Totais Esperados
S_j \ SN_i	100	200	300	400	450	$LE = \Sigma[P(SN_i) \times \pi_{ij}]$
100	$ 500	$ 500	$ 500	$ 500	$ 500	$ 500
200	300	1.000	1.000	1.000	1.000	930
300	100	800	1.500	1.500	1.500	1.290
400	(100)	600	1.300	2.000	2.000	1.370 ←
450	(200)	500	1.200	1.900	2.250	1.305
$P(SN_i)$	0,1	0,1	0,4	0,3	0,1	

Estratégias

Observação: π_{ij} é o lucro de S_j e SN_i.

- **S igual a 400 e SN igual a 100:** O ($ 100) significa que se for escolhida uma estratégia de 400 unidades e se for experimentada uma demanda de 100 unidades, as receitas serão $ 15(100), ou $ 1.500; o custo de bens vendidos será $ 10(100), ou $ 1.000; e os custos de longo prazo serão $ 2(300), ou $ 600. Os lucros serão ($ 100) para a estação.

Todos os outros elementos da tabela de custos esperados são computados similarmente. A coluna de lucros esperados (LE) é preenchida somando-se ao longo de cada linha de estratégia (S_j) os produtos da probabilidade dos estados da natureza $P(SN_i)$ e seu π_{ij}. Por exemplo, o LE de $S_j = 400$ unidades é computado desta maneira:

$$LE = 0{,}1(-100) + 0{,}1(600) + 0{,}4(1.300) + 0{,}3(2.000) + 0{,}1(2.000)$$

$$= -10 + 60 + 520 + 600 + 200 = 1.370$$

Agora, compute o VEIP:

$$VEIP = [0{,}1(500) + 0{,}1(1.000) + 0{,}4(1.500) + 0{,}3(2.000) + 0{,}1(2.250)] - 1.370 = \$ 205$$

Os lucros correspondentes a cada nível de demanda sob condições de informação perfeita são encontrados na diagonal da tabela de custos esperados. Os lucros totais esperados sob condições de informação perfeita menos os lucros máximos totais esperados sob condições de informação imperfeita ou incerteza é o valor do VEIP.

c) Qual estratégia de estocagem é a melhor para o xale n. 325? Explique a equivalência das soluções das partes *a* e *b* acima.

A melhor estratégia de estocagem é de 400 unidades dos xales n. 325. Essa alternativa é preferível, independentemente de se é usado o critério dos custos totais esperados ou o dos custos totais esperados de longo e curto prazo. A equivalência das duas análises é clara a partir de uma comparação de suas tabelas de custos esperados. Por exemplo, pode-se ver que a diferença entre a estratégia ótima de 400 unidades e qualquer outra estratégia de estocagem é a mesma em ambas as análises. Para uma estratégia de 200 unidades, os custos se elevam ($ 645 – $ 205 = $ 440) e os lucros decrescem ($ 1.370 – $ 930 = $ 440) no mesmo valor. O critério de minimizar os custos totais esperados (custo de bens vendidos, custos de longo e curto prazo) seria impróprio neste exemplo devido à presença de receitas.

Tabelas de custos esperados são uma ferramenta eficaz para analisar decisões a respeito de períodos únicos sob condições de incerteza. Sua flexibilidade para avaliar uma grande quantidade de decisões APO sobre estocagem é, talvez, sua maior força. Capital, peças de manutenção, trabalhadores, itens de estoque, capacidade de produção, máquinas de reserva (standby) e capacidade de serviço são, todos, decisões sobre estocagem de período único que podem ser analisadas por meio de tabelas de custos esperados quando os níveis de demanda ou estados da natureza forem incertos.

Algumas Realidades do Planejamento de Estoques

Discutimos diversas abordagens analíticas para planejamento de estoques. Agora precisamos considerar a magnitude do problema e algumas das dificuldades práticas que os gerentes de operações têm ao tomar essas decisões.

Classificação ABC de Materiais

Devido ao grande número de materiais usado na produção em muitas fábricas, pode ser desejável classificar materiais de acordo com a quantidade de análises que podem ser justificadas. Um esquema para classificar materiais é o método ABC, baseado na idéia de que somente uma pequena porcentagem dos materiais representa a maior parte do valor do estoque. A Figura 9.8 ilustra o método ABC de classificação de materiais.

Estas observações a respeito da classificação ABC explicam a interpretação da Figura 9.8:

1. Os materiais A representam somente 20% dos materiais em estoque e 75% do valor do estoque.
2. Os materiais B representam 30% dos materiais em estoque e 20% do valor do estoque.
3. Os materiais C representam 50% dos materiais em estoque e somente 5% do valor do estoque.

FIGURA 9.8   Classificação ABC de Materiais

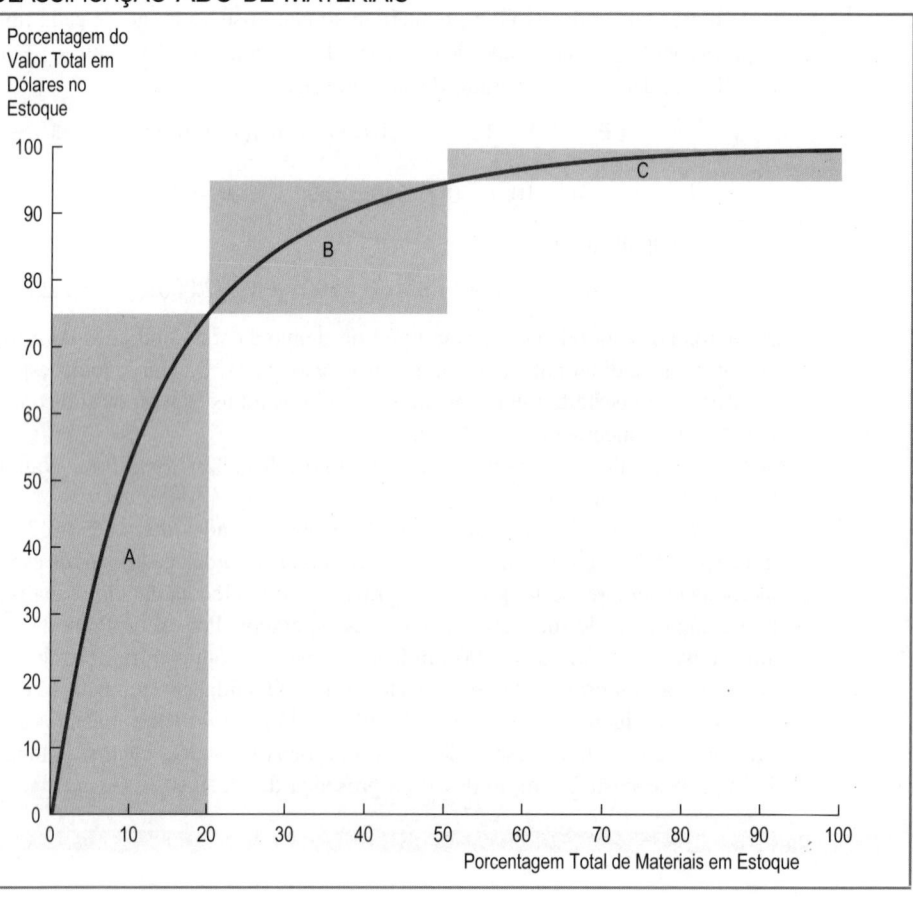

Essa classificação sugere que quanto maior o valor de estoque de um material, mais análise deve ser aplicada a esse material. Comumente, os materiais Classe A seriam analisados extensamente, e os materiais Classe C seriam pouco analisados.

Entretanto, deve-se ter critério na aplicação dessa abordagem ou de qualquer um dos modelos de estoque deste capítulo, porque outros fatores práticos podem ser cruciais nas decisões relativas a estoques. Exceções devem ser feitas para certos tipos de materiais:

- **Materiais críticos para a produção.** Uma vez que stockouts desses materiais podem paralisar linhas de produção inteiras, estoques maiores podem se justificar.
- **Materiais com vida mais breve na prateleira.** Uma vez que esses materiais podem estar sujeitos a obsolescência ou deterioração muito rápidas, estoques menores podem se justificar.
- **Materiais que são muito grandes e volumosos.** Uma vez que esses materiais exigem muito espaço de armazém, estoques menores podem se justificar.
- **Materiais valiosos sujeitos a roubo.** Para reduzir riscos de perda, estoques menores podem se justificar.
- **Materiais com lead times altamente irregulares.** Pedidos maiores desses materiais reduzem o número de pedidos durante o ano e mitigam a incerteza de oferta.
- **Materiais com demanda altamente irregular.** Grandes quantidades pedidas e grandes pontos de pedido podem se justificar para materiais com demandas imprevisíveis.
- **Embalagem, contêiner de embarque ou tamanho de veículo padrões.** Quantidades que não sejam o LEC podem se justificar devido aos custos extras se o tamanho do pedido se afastar da norma.

LEC E INCERTEZA

Quantidades pedidas e pontos de pedido exigem o uso de informações sujeitas a incerteza. Examine a Figura 9.2 novamente. Observe que erros de estimativa da demanda (D), custo de manutenção em estoque (C), ou custo de emissão do pedido (S) nos levariam para a direita ou para a esquerda do LEC ao longo da curva dos custos anuais totais de estocagem. Deslocar-se em qualquer uma das direções eleva os custos anuais para estocar um material. Observe, entretanto, que essa curva tende a ser um tanto plana próximo ao LEC — isto é considerado típico. O impacto total dos erros para estimar a quantidade de um material comumente não é significativo. Entretanto, quando dezenas de milhares de itens são mantidos em estoque, o impacto dos erros de estimativa se elevam enormemente.

O que talvez seja uma preocupação maior para as decisões referentes a estoques na APO sejam os custos que não são incluídos nas fórmulas LEC. Custos de stockout, qualidade na partida (start-up), receptividade do cliente, coordenação de produção, ROI diluído, capacidade reduzida, qualidade de lotes grandes e custos de problemas da produção são reais e substanciais e devem afetar as decisões relativas à emissão de pedidos. Mas os modelos LEC não incorporam diretamente esses custos. Na prática, quando estes custos são fatores importantes, as decisões relativas à emissão de pedidos são ajustadas conseqüentemente. Por exemplo, se os custos de stockout predominarem, as quantidades pedidas e os pontos de pedidos se tornarão grandes. A filosofia LEC ainda se aplica nessas situações; porém, mais tipos de custos podem ser incluídos implicitamente nos modelos.

Outra tática APO pragmática para todos os tipos de produção é estabelecer procedimentos de emergência para renovar estoques rapidamente. Esses procedimentos de emergência têm como objetivo evitar stockouts e permitir níveis de estoque de segurança mais baixos. Um bom exemplo da utilização de procedimentos de emergência para renovação de estoques é encontrado em hospitais, muitos dos quais têm helicópteros disponíveis para suprir materiais críticos, quando necessário, de outros hospitais ou de armazéns de suprimentos hospitalares.

DINÂMICA DO PLANEJAMENTO DE ESTOQUES

Quase todos os sistemas de estoque revisam continuamente suas práticas de emissão de pedidos e modificam suas quantidades de pedido, pontos de pedido e intervalos de tempo, quando necessário, para obter o tipo de desempenho de estoque desejado. Quando vemos o planejamento de estoques como um sistema dinâmico que é modificado continuamente quando necessário, menos ênfase precisamos dar a qualquer um dos cálculos. De fato, em vez de usar o LEC, muitas empresas definem quantidades pedidas *iniciais* com base na tradição, em estimativas grosseiras ou em outros fatores. Depois, elas aumentam ou diminuem as quantidades pedidas para que se enquadrem em seus padrões de demanda e oferta. Desse modo, os sistemas de estoque desenvolvem empiricamente quantidades de pedido e pontos de pedido de forma que não resultem nem em stockouts excessivos nem em estoques excessivos.

Outros Fatores Que Afetam o Planejamento de Estoques

A quantidade de um material que *pode* ser pedida pode ser restringida. Por exemplo, a capacidade de armazém pode limitar a quantidade pedida de um material. Além disso, a capacidade de produção e os programas de produção de outros produtos podem limitar o tamanho das quantidades pedidas.

Compras especiais de materiais são um fator que faz com que as quantidades pedidas sejam maiores do que o LEC. Quando o departamento de compras descobre uma compra especial, as economias dos descontos por quantidade podem ser tão espetaculares que a empresa comprará tudo o que puder adquirir desse material. Não obstante isso tender a representar um massacre para a capacidade de armazenamento e aumentar outros custos, as economias nos custos de compra podem ser tão grandes que as empresas ocasionalmente fazem essas compras especiais.

Computadores e o Planejamento de Estoques

Uma das primeiras áreas dos negócios a beneficiar-se da informática foi o planejamento de estoques. O Instantâneo da Indústria 9.1 ilustra que atualmente registros dos itens em estoque são mantidos rotineiramente com a utilização de computadores. Quando ocorrem mudanças nos níveis de estoque, os arquivos de computador são modificados para refletir as transações de estoque mais recentes. Os gerentes podem pesquisar estes arquivos e determinar instantaneamente quanto de um material está em estoque, quanto de um material deve ser pedido, quando se espera que certos pedidos sejam recebidos, e outras informações cruciais para a administração de estoques. Computar quantidades pedidas, determinar quando pedidos devem ser feitos e imprimir requisições de compra e ordens de compra são tarefas rotineiramente executadas por computadores.

Instantâneo da Indústria 9.1

Gerentes Usam Computadores para Tomar Decisões a Respeito de Estoques

Empresas como a Hallmark Cards, Wal-Mart, Dayton Hudson e Kmart estão usando informações de computador para administrar cada aspecto dos estoques atualmente. Eis alguns casos interessantes que ilustram como os computadores são usados:

- A Hallmark Cards introduziu um novo enfeite de árvore de Natal de US$ 24. Informações computadorizadas permitiram que a empresa deslocasse estoques de lojas que possuíam estoque excessivo para lojas que estavam com falta de produtos.
- Numa loja Kmart, informações computadorizadas indicaram que as vendas de cones de pinho perfumados numa cesta de vime estavam abaixo das vendas em outras lojas Kmart. O computador indicou que o custo da Kmart era US$ 4,68, de forma que o preço da cesta foi reduzido de US$ 9,99 para US$ 7,99, e as vendas para esse item se aceleraram.
- Os compradores da Kmart observaram a partir de informações computadorizadas que as vendas de um cavalinho de balanço eram aproximadamente o dobro das vendas do último ano nesse ponto da estação. Eles rapidamente duplicaram seus pedidos para a estação feitos ao fabricante do item.
- Também na Kmart. No passado, se um item tivesse vendas mais lentas do que o esperado, ele teria descontos em todas as lojas. Agora, com informações computadorizadas a respeito das vendas, um item terá descontos somente nas lojas com vendas lentas.
- Com informações computadorizadas sobre as vendas diárias, o pensamento a respeito de estoques na Kmart modificou-se. Agora, desde que as vendas de cada item do Dia dos Namorados[6] serão conhecidas diariamente, à medida que o dia 14 de fevereiro se aproxima, as decisões quanto a dar descontos para itens com vendas mais lentas são tomadas mais tarde. Dessa forma, itens não têm descontos desnecessários.
- Também na Kmart, o computador desenterrou fatos demográficos interessantes. Eles descobriram que a venda de confetes era maior nos bairros hispânicos na Páscoa; dessa forma, estoques maiores de confete eram armazenados nas lojas em bairros hispânicos.
- A partir da informação computadorizada descobriu-se que as pessoas que compram fraldas descartáveis a partir das 5 da tarde em muitas das cidades do meio-oeste tendem a comprar uma caixa de cerveja com 6 unidades. Para impulsionar as vendas de salgadinhos, a loja passou a expô-los próximo ao corredor das fraldas. As vendas de salgadinhos subiram 17%.

Fonte: "Computers Manage Holiday Stock". *Wall Street Journal*, 23 de dezembro de 1992.

---

[6] Dia de São Valentim, 14 de fevereiro: data em que se comemora o Dia dos Namorados nos Estados Unidos. (N. do T.)

A seguir listamos alguns exemplos de sistemas de informação sobre assuntos administrativos com software de administração de estoques incorporado: Paragon Applications (**www.paragonms.com**), SKEP (**www.adaptasolutions.com**), Glovia (**www.glovia.com**), Macola (**www.macola.com**), SAP (**www.sap.com**) e Baan (**www.baan.com**).

Resumo Final

O que os Fabricantes de Classe Mundial Estão Fazendo

O ciclo de estoque é o foco central dos sistemas de estoque com demanda independente. Materiais são pedidos, recebidos e usados, e o ciclo então se repete. As decisões fundamentais dizem respeito a quanto pedir de cada material e quando fazer os pedidos.

As fórmulas e definições de variáveis correspondentes aos modelos de estoque deste capítulo são dadas na Tabela 9.8.

Sob quais circunstâncias esses modelos seriam apropriados? Muitas operações de venda a varejo, venda por atacado e armazenagem usam rotineiramente esses modelos. Estoques constituem o meio de atenderem a uma demanda altamente variável para seus produtos e à necessidade de realizar entregas instantâneas.

Se um gerente usar o método de estoque de reserva para planejamento e controle da produção, como descrevemos no Capítulo 8, os modelos de estoque serão usados em todo o sistema de produção.

Se for usado o sistema *empurrar* de planejamento e controle da produção, entretanto, os modelos não serão usados para a maioria dos materiais em estoques de matérias-primas, mas poderiam ser usados para determinar tamanhos de lote de produção e estoques de bens acabados na produção para estoque.

No sistema *puxar* de planejamento e controle da produção, dados tamanhos de lote de produção pequenos e predeterminados, os modelos poderiam ser usados para determinar tempos de preparação. *Mas, atualmente, todos os tipos de empresas americanas de classe mundial estão lutando para ser **mais enxutas** quanto a estoques.*

Com essa finalidade, os tipos de sistemas de planejamento e controle da produção que as empresas americanas usam estão se modificando. O fato básico a respeito dos sistemas de quantidade pedida e ponto de pedido do planejamento de estoques é que eles se baseiam na ausência de informações a respeito de quanto de cada produto será demandado e quão rápido os fornecedores poderão fornecer os materiais.

As empresas de classe mundial estabeleceram sistemas de informação que as ligam eletronicamente com seus fornecedores e clientes. A disponibilidade de informações em tempo real sobre pedidos dos clientes e entregas dos fornecedores tem permitido que essas empresas mudem de sistemas de estoques de reserva para sistemas *empurrar* e para sistemas *puxar* para se concentrar nos gargalos. Não obstante algumas empresas ainda usarem abordagens do estoque de reserva, a maioria das empresas usa sistemas *empurrar*, muitas empresas adotaram sistemas *puxar*, e algumas empresas estão se concentrando em abordagens de concentração nos gargalos.

A combinação de melhorada informação sobre a demanda futura do cliente e um sistema de produção enxuto quanto a estoques tem permitido que algumas empresas mudem do sistema de produção para estoque para a produção sob encomenda.

Com menos estoque de itens em processo, os pedidos podem ser produzidos tão rapidamente que estoques de bens acabados são desnecessários para que se efetue rápida entrega dos pedidos aos clientes. O Instantâneo da Indústria 9.2 ilustra como alguns fabricantes de computadores estão mudando para a produção sob encomenda a fim de permanecer competitivos.

Para algumas empresas de classe mundial, a redução dos níveis de estoque em todo o sistema de produção é citada como um fator fundamental para seu sucesso.

O fato de serem enxutas quanto a estoques tem reduzido seus custos de produção e outros custos e tem melhorado a qualidade de produto e a receptividade do cliente.

TABELA 9.8 — RESUMO DOS MODELOS DE PLANEJAMENTO DE ESTOQUES

Definições de variáveis

- ac = custo da aquisição — custo para produzir ou comprar uma unidade de um material ($ por unidade)
- C = custo da manutenção em estoque — custo para manter uma unidade em estoque durante um ano ($ por unidade por ano); proporção do valor que está transmitindo custo vezes ac
- D = Demanda anual para um material (unidades por ano)
- d = taxa na qual os materiais saem do estoque (unidades por período de tempo)
- $\bar{d}$ = média de d, a demanda por unidade de tempo (unidades por período de tempo)
- DDLT = demanda durante o lead time (unidades)
- DEDLT = demanda esperada durante o lead time (unidades)
- LEC = lote econômico de compra — quantidade ótima de material a ser pedida (unidades por pedido)
- j = porcentagem de DEDLT como estoque de segurança
- LT = lead time (número de períodos de tempo)
- PP = ponto de pedido — ponto no qual materiais devem ser pedidos (unidades ou ponto no tempo)
- p = taxa na qual materiais são supridos para estoque (mesmas unidades que d)
- Q = quantidade de material pedida em cada ponto de pedido (unidades por pedido)
- σ_{DDLT} = desvio padrão de DDLT
- σ_d = desvio padrão de d
- S = custo médio para emissão de um pedido de um material ($ por pedido)
- ES = estoque de segurança (unidades)
- T = intervalo de tempo entre pedidos de um material (fração de um ano)
- CTM = custos anuais totais de materiais — custos anuais totais de estocagem e manutenção de um material em estoque ($ por ano)
- CTE = custos anuais totais de estocagem — custos anuais totais e custos anuais de emissão de pedidos de um material ($ por ano)
- Z = fator da curva de distribuição normal

Fórmulas

Sistemas de Estoque do Lote Padrão

Modelo I — LEC Básico (veja o Exemplo 9.1)

LEC = $\sqrt{2DS/C}$ CTE = (Q/2)C + (D/Q)S

Modelo II — LEC para Lotes de Produção (veja o Exemplo 9.2)

LEC = $\sqrt{(2DS/C)[p/(p-d)]}$
CTE = (Q/2)[(p − d)/p]C + (D/Q)S
Pontos de pedido (veja os Exemplos 9.4, 9.5, 9.6 e 9.7)
PP = DEDLT + ES
PP = DEDLT + j(DEDLT)   Porcentagem da DEDLT
PP = DEDLT + $\sqrt{DEDLT}$ Raiz quadrada da DEDLT
PP = DEDLT + Z(σ_{DDLT})   DDLT normal
PP = LT($\bar{d}$) + Z$\sqrt{LT(\sigma_d)^2}$ LT constante e d normal

Modelo III — LEC com Descontos por Quantidade (veja o Exemplo 9.3)

Quando as suposições do Modelo I se aplicarem:

LEC = $\sqrt{2DS/C}$ CTM = (Q/2)C + (D/Q)S + (D)ac

Quando as suposições do Modelo II se aplicarem:

LEC = $\sqrt{(2DS/C)[p/(p-d)]}$
CTM = (Q/2)[(p − d)/p]C + (D/Q)S + (D)ac

Em qualquer um dos casos, os procedimentos da Tabela 9.4 devem ser seguidos.

Sistema do Lote Padrão

Modelo IV — Lote Econômico de Compra (veja o Exemplo 9.8)
T = $\sqrt{2S/DC}$ CTE = (DT/2)C + S/T
Q = Meta máxima de estoque − Nível de estoque + DEDLT

Instantâneo da Indústria 9.2

Fabricantes de Computadores Adotam Estratégias de Produção sob Pedido

Quer saber o por que todo grande fabricante de computadores pessoais está se apressando para ser como a Dell Computer, o visionário grupo que inventou a venda direta de PCs? Simplesmente pergunte a um concorrente. "No mundo ideal", diz Jim McDonnell, principal executivo de marketing do grupo de PCs da Hewlett-Packard, "seu cliente quer comprar um PC, você obtém de uma fonte todas as peças nesse dia, embarca-as nesse dia e faz com que elas cheguem ao cliente nesse dia. Não há nenhuma proteção de preços. Não há nenhum estoque. Michael Dell provavelmente está mais próximo disso do que ninguém".

A estratégia de construir sob encomenda posta em prática pela Dell Computer Corporation transformou a Dell na companhia mais "quente" e de mais rápido crescimento da indústria. Sua fórmula: contornar (*bypass*) distribuidores e outros revendedores e vender diretamente para os clientes. Isso possibilita que a Dell crie uma configuração personalizada para todo comprador e venda seus PCS a preços inferiores aos dos varejistas. A Compaq, a Hewlett-Packard, a IBM e a Packard Bell NEC têm, todas, mexido em suas estratégias para incluir alguma forma de produção sob encomenda.

Na Dell, o processo inteiro, desde o momento em que o pedido do cliente, feito por telefone, é recebido até o carregamento do PC acabado num caminhão de entrega toma exatamente 36 horas. Os pedidos são repassados instantaneamente a uma das três fábricas da Dell — em Austin, Texas; em Penang, Malásia; ou Limerick, Irlanda[7]. Todavia, você não encontrará qualquer estoque lá. "Todos os nossos fornecedores sabem que nossos componentes devem ser entregues em uma hora", diz o gerente da fábrica de Austin, John Varol. Chips, placas e unidades de disco são mantidos em caminhões guardados em baias a 15 metros do início da linha de produção. Não há estoques de bens acabados tampouco. Para grandes clientes, a Dell tem um plano de rápido embarque, em que computadores são *entregues* na porta do cliente dentro de 48 horas a partir do pedido.

Fontes: "And Give Me an Extra-Fast Model With That, Please", *Business Week*, 29 de setembro de 1997; Serwer, Andrew E., "Michael Dell Turns the PC World Inside Out", *Fortune*, 8 de setembro de 1997; Kirkpatrick, David, "Now Everyone in PCs Wants to Be Like Mike", *Fortune*, 8 de setembro de 1997.

Questões de Revisão e Discussão

1. Cite dois propósitos de manter estes estoques: a) bens acabados, b) itens em processo e c) matérias-primas.
2. Defina estes termos: *backlogging, produção sob encomenda, produção para estoque, quantidade pedida, ponto de pedido, ciclo de estoque, preparações de máquina, tamanho de lote, intervalo do pedido, sistema de duas gavetas.*
3. Cite e descreva quatro custos que são reduzidos ao manter-se estoques.
4. Cite e descreva sete custos que são aumentados ao manter-se estoques.
5. Explique o que se quer dizer por material com demanda independente. Dê um exemplo e explique por que sua demanda é independente.
6. Explique o que se quer dizer por material com demanda dependente. Dê um exemplo e explique por que sua demanda é dependente.
7. Compare e coloque em contraste os sistemas do lote padrão com os sistemas do intervalo padrão.
8. Defina estes termos: *custos da manutenção em estoque, custos de emissão de pedidos, custos anuais da manutenção de estoque, custos do stockout, custos anuais de emissão de pedidos, custos anuais totais de estocagem.*
9. Relacione os custos incluídos nos custos anuais da manutenção de estoque na Figura 9.2.
10. Relacione os custos incluídos nos custos anuais de emissão de pedidos na Figura 9.2.
11. Cite quatro suposições do LEC básico — Modelo I.
12. Cite quatro suposições do LEC para lotes de produção — Modelo II.
13. Em quais unidades estão estas variáveis: D, S, C, Q, LEC, p e d?
14. Explique por que o nível máximo de estoque de um

---

[7] A Dell já está operando no Brasil com esquema semelhante (www.dell.com.br). (N. do T.)

material é maior quando os pedidos são recebidos todos de uma vez do que quando eles são recebidos gradualmente.
15. Quais são os propósitos do estoque de segurança? Como a utilização do estoque de segurança afetará o LEC? Como a utilização do estoque de segurança afetará o CTE?
16. Explique o que se quer dizer com esta afirmação: "As incertezas do planejamento de estoques quase sempre afetam os gerentes de operações quando eles estão mais vulneráveis — quando os níveis de estoque estão em seus pontos mais baixos".
17. Apresente uma breve explicação para cada um dos seguintes itens: a) DDLT, b) DEDLT, c) distribuições DDLT discretas, d) σ_{DDLT}, e) distribuições DDLT contínuas, f) LT, e g) σ_{LT}.
18. Defina *níveis de serviço*.
19. Supondo que a DDLT seja uma distribuição normal, escreva uma fórmula para computar a) DEDLT e b) σ_{DLT}.
20. Explique a relação entre estas variáveis: ponto de pedido, estoque de segurança e DEDLT.
21. Quais outros fatores além dos custos anuais totais de estocagem tipicamente afetam Q e T na prática?
22. O que os fabricantes de classe mundial estão fazendo com respeito à administração de estoques?

Tarefas na Internet

1. Procure na Internet por um fornecedor de software de controle de estoque. Descreva o que o software pode fazer. Inclua o site da empresa.
2. Procure na Internet por uma empresa que ofereça um desconto por quantidade (ou desconto por volume) para seus produtos. Descreva os descontos de preços e relacione o nome e o site da empresa.
3. O Paragon Applications (**www.paragonms.com**) é um pacote de software integrado para administrar o fluxo de materiais. Visite e explore o site. Descreva de maneira breve os diferentes módulos de software que fazem parte do Paragon Applications.

Problemas

1. Se D = 500.000 unidades por ano, C = 40% do custo de aquisição por unidade por ano, S = $ 59,50 por pedido, e ac = $ 5,50 por unidade:
   a) Qual é o LEC?
   b) Qual é o CTE no LEC?
   c) De quanto seria o aumento do CTE se a quantidade pedida precisasse ser 6.000 unidades devido a um tamanho de contêiner de embarque padrão?

2. O Lendmore Bank pede dinheiro a seu escritório central para cumprir suas contratransações diárias. Se o Lendmore estimar que $ 25.000.000 serão necessários no próximo ano, cada solicitação de dinheiro custará $ 2.650 (o que inclui os custos com funcionários e entrega em carros-fortes), e o dinheiro parado custará 8%:
   a) Quais quantidades de dinheiro o Lendmore deve incluir em cada pedido?
   b) Quais custos anuais totais de estocagem resultariam se o Lendmore seguisse a recomendação apresentada por você na parte *a*?
   c) Quantos dias o Lendmore poderia operar com cada pedido de dinheiro se permanecesse aberto 260 dias por ano e o dinheiro fosse pedido no sistema LEC?

3. A taxa de produção da montagem final são 800 CDs por dia. Depois que os CDs são montados, eles vão diretamente para o estoque de bens acabados. A demanda do cliente é de 400 CDs em média por dia e aproximadamente 50 mil CDs por ano. Se custar $ 500 para preparar a linha de montagem para os CDs e $ 1,00 por CD por ano para mantê-los em estoque:
   a) Quantos CDs devem estar num lote de produção na montagem final?
   b) Qual é o CTE do LEC?

4. Uma refinaria de petróleo compra petróleo bruto mediante um contrato de oferta de longo prazo por $ 22,50 por barril. Quando remessas de petróleo bruto são feitas para a refinaria, elas chegam à taxa de 10 mil barris por dia. A refinaria usa o petróleo a uma taxa de 5 mil barris por dia e planeja comprar 500 mil barris de petróleo bruto no próximo ano. Se o custo de manutenção em estoque for 25% do custo de aquisição por unidade por ano e o custo de emissão do pedido for $ 7.500 por pedido:
   a) Qual é o LEC para o petróleo bruto?
   b) Qual é o CTE no LEC?
   c) Quantos dias de produção são suportados por cada pedido de petróleo bruto?
   d) Quanta capacidade de armazenagem é necessária para o petróleo bruto?

5. Um atacadista de materiais de construção vende janelas. Estima-se que uma janela popular, número de peça 3060 BDP, tenha uma demanda de 50 mil no próximo ano. Para o armazém, custa $ 200 para fazer e receber um pedido, e os custos de manutenção em estoque são 30% do custo de aquisição. O fornecedor cota estes preços para essa janela:

Q	ac
1–999	$ 41,60
1.000–1.999	40,95
2.000+	40,92

   a) Qual é o LEC do armazém?
   b) Qual é o CTM mínimo?
   c) Quanto tempo transcorrerá entre os pedidos?

6. Se D = 150.000 unidades por ano, S = $ 500 por pedido, C = 0,35 (ac) dólares por unidade por ano, p = 600 unidades por dia, d = 300 unidades por dia, ac_1 = $ 15 por unidade para 1 a 9.999 unidades por pedido, ac_2 = $ 14,60 por unidade para 10.000 a 19.999 unidades por pedido e ac_3 = $ 14,40 por unidade para mais de 20 mil unidades por pedido:
   a) Qual é o CTM mínimo?
   b) Qual é o LEC?
   c) Quantos pedidos por ano devem ser feitos?
   d) Qual é o nível máximo de estoque?

7. A Computer Store vende suprimentos de computador. Um de seus produtos é papel para impressoras a laser, número de estoque 208511W. A loja compra o papel de um armazém regional que possui caminhões de entrega que circulam diariamente por todos os clientes de sua região. A loja utiliza 40 caixas do papel por dia numa operação de 5 dias por semana. O fornecedor cobra da loja $ 21,00 por caixa e entrega 100 caixas de papel por dia durante os períodos de renovação de estoque. Custa à loja $ 100 para fazer um pedido de papel, e os custos de manutenção de estoque são 25% do custo de aquisição. O fornecedor ofereceu recentemente um desconto de 1% se seus clientes aceitarem 200 ou mais caixas por dia de entrega. O fornecedor entregará menos de 100 ou 200 caixas no último dia de entrega de um pedido.
   a) Qual é o LEC atual para o papel?
   b) Qual é o CTM atual para o papel?
   c) Qual seria o LEC se a oferta de desconto do fornecedor fosse aceita?
   d) A Computer Store deve aceitar a proposta?

8. O departamento de manutenção de uma fábrica necessita planejar estoques de um produto de manutenção usado com freqüência, o rolamento n. 6691. Está em consideração o ponto de pedido para esse item e o nível apropriado do estoque de segurança. A demanda média por semana é de 15,4 rolamentos, e o lead time médio é de 5,1 semanas. Estes dados sobre a utilização deste rolamento foram obtidos do computador:

DDLT Real	Ocorrências	DDLT Real	Ocorrências
60–79	7	100–109	3
80–89	9	110–119	2
90–99	5	120–129	1

a) Compute o ponto de pedido usando o nível de serviço de 90%.
b) Qual estoque de segurança deve ser estabelecido com sua resposta para a parte *a*?

9. Se a DEDLT = 65,5 unidades, σ_{DDLT} = 10,5 unidades, a DDLT for normalmente distribuída e o nível de serviço for 95%:
a) Qual é o ponto de pedido?
b) Qual é o nível de estoque de segurança?

10. Uma peça usada para consertar máquinas tem uma demanda mensal normalmente distribuída com uma média de 65,0 e um desvio padrão de 5,2. Se o lead time for tão previsível a ponto de poder ser considerado constante 0,25 de um mês e o nível de serviço for 90%:
a) Qual é o ponto de pedido?
b) Qual é o nível de estoque de segurança?

11. Um departamento de manutenção de uma empresa necessita planejar estoques de um produto de manutenção usado com freqüência, o rolamento n. 6691. Está em consideração o ponto de pedido para esse item e o nível apropriado do estoque de segurança. A demanda média por semana é de 15,4 rolamentos, e o lead time médio é de 5,1 semanas. A fábrica opera sob uma política de manter 50% da DEDLT com o estoque de segurança para todos os itens da mesma classe desse rolamento.
a) Quanto estoque de segurança deve ser mantido para esse rolamento?
b) Em qual nível de estoque deve ser processado um pedido desse rolamento?

12. Um armazém de suprimentos de escritório está revisando suas políticas de emissão de pedidos para seus itens de estoque. O armazém realiza contagens periódicas dos itens de seu estoque e faz pedidos de materiais quando necessário. Um de seus itens é um calendário de mesa, com número de estoque 2436B. Foram feitas contagens hoje, e o nível de estoque foi de 3.395 unidades desse calendário. A meta máxima de estoque é de 10 mil unidades, e a DEDLT é igual a 1 mil. A demanda anual na região é de aproximadamente 100 mil, o custo de emissão de pedido é de $ 200 por pedido, o custo de aquisição é de $ 3,95, e o custo de manutenção de estoque é de 35% do custo de aquisição.
a) Quando deve ser feita a próxima contagem física do estoque?
b) Quantos calendários devem ser pedidos hoje?

13. Um fabricante de produtos eletrônicos usa uma liga de ouro para folhear. Quando ocorre um stockout, custa $ 60 para acelerar a entrega de um pedido. Qualquer ouro não utilizado em qualquer semana custa $ 30 a onça para financiar, proteger e segurar. Um padrão de demanda semanal por ouro foi determinado ao estudarem os registros recentes de produção na fábrica:

Demanda Semanal por Ouro (onças)	Probabilidade de Demanda Semanal
100	0,1
150	0,2
200	0,3
300	0,3
500	0,1

a) Quantas onças de ouro devem ser estocadas em cada semana com o objetivo de minimizar os custos esperados de longo e curto prazo para o material?
b) Qual é o VEIP?

14. Um banco mantém dinheiro em caixa para atender suas necessidades diárias. Se muito dinheiro estiver à mão, o banco deixará de ganhar certa renda de juros que poderia ter ganho com investimentos alternativos; ou seja, o dinheiro parado tem um custo de oportunidade, ou custo de longo prazo. Se o banco mantiver pouco dinheiro em caixa, precisará buscar dinheiro em outras instituições de empréstimo, e isso resultará em custos operacionais extras (custos de curto prazo). As estimativas de demanda para o próximo período são:

Demanda ou SN (milhares)	Freqüência	P(SN)
$ 100	1/10	0,1
200	1/10	0,1
250	2/10	0,2
300	3/10	0,3
400	3/10	0,3

As estimativas de custos de longo e curto prazo para a empresa são:

$$SC = \$\,1.000 + 0,8X \qquad LC = \$\,500 + 1,0Y$$

em que:

SC = custos de curto prazo totais para o período

LC = custos de longo prazo totais para o período

X = número total de unidades com custo de curto prazo (milhares de $) durante o período

Y = número total de unidades com custo de longo prazo (milhares de $) durante o período

Quanto dinheiro o banco deve manter à mão para o próximo período para minimizar os custos esperados de longo e curto prazo?

Estudo de Caso

Níveis de Estoque de Segurança na Bell Computers

A Bell Computers produz e armazena impressoras de computador em seu armazém de produtos acabados. Acredita-se que estes dados históricos sobre a DDLT sejam representativos da demanda futura de um modelo de impressora:

DDLT Real	Freqüência	DDLT Real	Freqüência
0–29	0	70–79	0,25
30–39	0,10	80–89	0,10
40–49	0,10	90–99	0,05
50–59	0,15	100–109	0,05
60–69	0,20	110–120	0

Tarefas

1. Se um nível de serviço de 90% no mínimo deve ser oferecido para essas impressoras: a) Qual é o ponto de pedido? b) Qual é o estoque de segurança?
2. Se a DDLT para a impressora for, de fato, normalmente distribuída, com uma média igual a 65 e um desvio padrão igual a 10, e um nível de serviço de 90% deve ser oferecido para essas impressoras: a) Qual é o ponto de pedido? b) Qual é o estoque de segurança?
3. Se o lead time para estas impressoras for tão estável a ponto de poder ser presumido como constante 6,5 dias, se a demanda por dia for normalmente distribuída com uma média igual a 10 e um desvio padrão igual a 2, e um mínimo de nível de serviço de 90% deve ser oferecido para essas impressoras: a) Qual é o ponto de pedido? b) Qual é o estoque de segurança?

capítulo 10

SISTEMAS DE PLANEJAMENTO DAS NECESSIDADES DE RECURSOS

Introdução

Planejamento das Necessidades de Materiais
Objetivos do MRP
Elementos do MRP
  Programa Mestre de Produção • Arquivo Lista de Materiais • Arquivo Situação do Estoque • Programa MRP de Computador • Saídas do MRP
Green Thumb Water Sprinkler Company
Dimensionamento de Lotes no MRP
Questões sobre o MRP
  Dimensionamento de Lotes • Sistemas de MRP de Mudança Líquida Versus MRP Regenerativo • Estoque de Segurança • MRP em Empresas de Montagem sob Encomenda
Do MRP I para o MRP II e para o ERP
Como o MRP Se Adapta a Mudanças
Avaliação do MRP

Planejamento das Necessidades de Capacidade
Programas de Carga

Resumo Final: O Que os Fabricantes de Classe Mundial Estão Fazendo

Questões de Revisão e Discussão

Tarefas na Internet

Problemas

Estudos de Caso
Integrated Products Corporation
Blanco Foods

Introdução 309

REDUÇÃO DE ESTOQUES NA SC CORPORATION

Na SC Corporation, a maior produtora mundial de refrigeradores por evaporação, as vendas haviam se elevado de US$ 5 milhões para US$ 20 milhões durante os 15 anos anteriores. Esse crescimento resultara da eficiência que os refrigeradores por evaporação tiveram sobre os sistemas de refrigeração convencionais quando o custo da eletricidade subiu. O sr. Gentry possuía a SC há mais de 30 anos, mas vendeu a empresa recentemente para uma grande e diversificada companhia fabricante de maquinaria elétrica. O novo proprietário enviou uma equipe de jovens e agressivos gerentes de operações para assumirem o controle da fábrica, e a impressão inicial que eles tiveram não foi favorável. A fábrica estava supercarregada com estoques: US$ 20 milhões em estoques de matérias-primas para sustentar US$ 20 milhões em vendas por ano pareciam fora de propósito. Os estoques ocupavam tanto espaço na fábrica que a capacidade de produção estava sendo prejudicada. Com vendas previstas para atingir US$ 30 milhões no ano seguinte, era evidente que algo deveria ser feito para aumentar a capacidade de produção. A equipe de gerentes de operações iniciou um planejamento das necessidades de materiais (MRP — material requirements planning) para reduzir os níveis de estoques. Ela também esperava que, ao liberar espaço de fábrica através da redução dos estoques, outra linha de montagem poderia ser instalada sem que fosse necessário ampliar a fábrica. Dois anos depois, os resultados do projeto MRP são espetaculares. As vendas anuais são de US$ 40 milhões, o estoque total de materiais é de US$ 9,8 milhões, os lucros se quintuplicaram, e a fábrica agora tem suficiente capacidade para sustentar vendas de aproximadamente US$ 50 milhões. Tudo isso foi realizado com menos investimento. A maquinaria necessária para a nova linha de montagem exigiu menos investimento do que a redução nos níveis de estoque atribuídos ao MRP.

Conforme a história de sucesso acima indica, o planejamento das necessidades de materiais (MRP) é usado cada vez mais, quando os fabricantes lutam para reduzir níveis de estoques, aumentar a capacidade de produção e aumentar os lucros. Este capítulo é sobre sistemas de planejamento das necessidades de recursos, e o MRP é uma parte importante desses sistemas.

No Capítulo 8 estudamos os planos de capacidade agregados, programas mestres de produção e sistemas de planejamento e controle da produção do tipo empurrar. Nesses sistemas, a ênfase se desloca para a utilização de informações sobre clientes, fornecedores e produção para administrar fluxos de materiais. Lotes de matérias-primas são planejados para chegar a uma fábrica mais ou menos quando necessário para fazer lotes de peças e submontagens. Peças e submontagens são feitas e entregues para montagem final mais ou menos quando necessário, e produtos acabados são montados e embarcados mais ou menos quando os clientes necessitam deles. Lotes de materiais são empurrados a partir dos fundos das fábricas um após o outro, o que por sua vez empurra outros lotes através de todas as etapas de produção. Esses fluxos de materiais são planejados e controlados por uma série de programas de produção. Esses programas estabelecem quando lotes de cada produto em particular devem sair de cada etapa da produção.

O planejamento das necessidades de recursos tem uma linguagem que se desenvolveu com sua crescente utilização na indústria. Os termos e suas definições que fazem parte dessa linguagem são encontrados no glossário ao final deste livro. A Figura 10.1 ilustra como as áreas funcionais de um negócio trabalham juntas para planejar e controlar as necessidades de recursos de uma empresa. Todas essas funções fornecem informações que fazem o sistema de planejamento das necessidades de recursos funcionar. A Figura 10.2 ilustra os principais elementos dos sistemas de planejamento de recursos. A demanda estimada de itens finais, a situação do estoque de itens finais, as políticas de definição de tamanho de lotes e estoques de segurança de itens finais, bem como o planejamento da capacidade de médio prazo (RCCP — rough-cut capacity planning), são integradas num programa mestre de produção (MPS). Esse MPS experimental é testado pelo planejamento das necessidades de materiais e pelo planejamento das necessidades de capacidade (CRP — capacity requirements planning). Em outras palavras, suficientes materiais podem ser comprados e existe suficiente capacidade extra para produzir os itens finais no MPS? Se os materiais comprados ou a capacidade de produção não estiver economicamente disponível, o MPS deve ser mudado. Depois que o MRP e o CRP determinam que um MPS é exeqüível, o MPS torna-se o núcleo de um plano de produção de curto prazo.

No restante deste capítulo estudaremos os dois elementos principais dos sistemas de planejamento das necessidades de recursos: planejamento das necessidades de materiais e planejamento das necessidades de capacidade.

FIGURA 10.1   ENTRADAS E SAÍDAS DE UM SISTEMA DE PLANEJAMENTO DAS NECESSIDADES DE RECURSOS

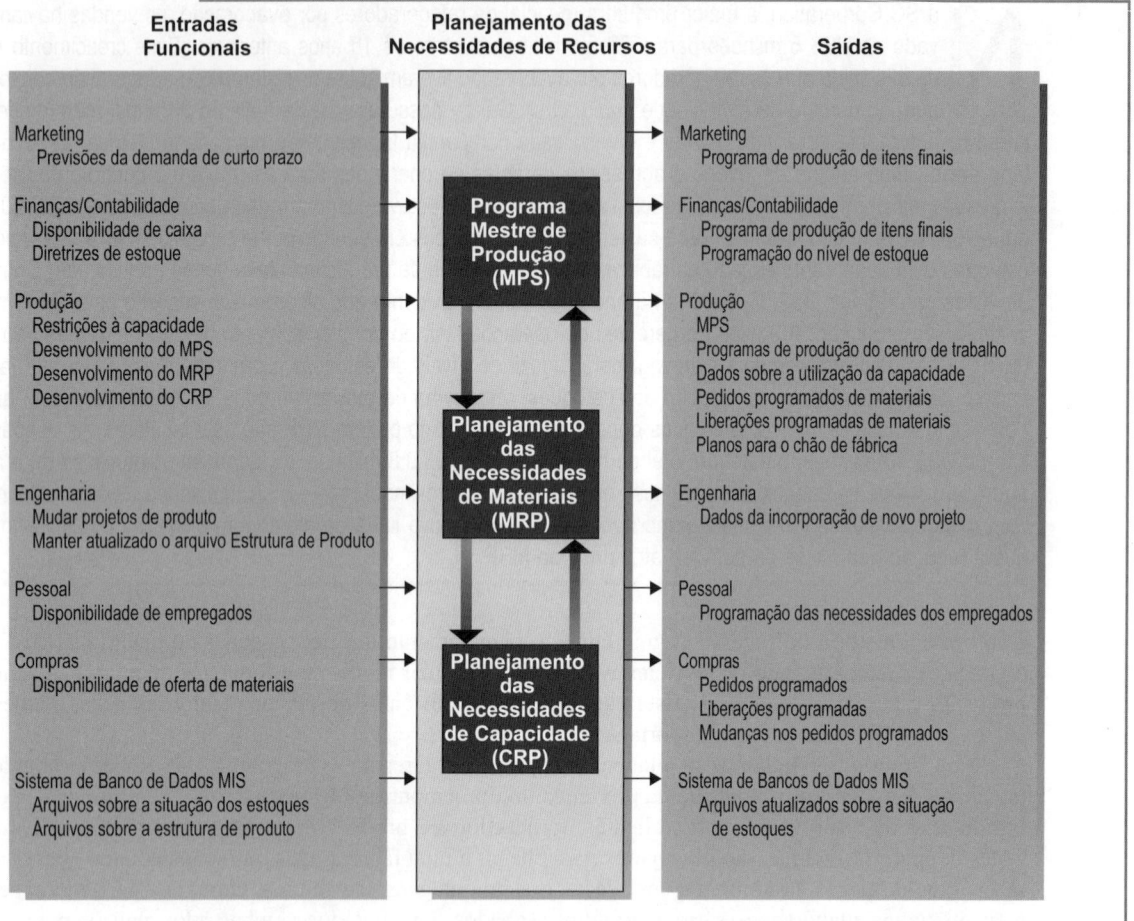

PLANEJAMENTO DAS NECESSIDADES DE MATERIAIS

O planejamento das necessidades de materiais (MRP) inicia-se com o princípio de que muitos materiais mantidos em estoque têm demandas dependentes, conceito esse apresentado no Capítulo 9. Materiais mantidos em estoques de matérias-primas e produtos parcialmente concluídos mantidos em estoques em processo são materiais com demanda dependente. A quantidade de um material em particular com demanda dependente e que é necessário em qualquer semana depende do número de produtos a serem produzidos que exigem esse material. A demanda por matérias-primas e produtos parcialmente concluídos não tem de ser prevista, portanto, porque, se for conhecido quais produtos devem ser produzidos numa semana, a quantidade de material necessário para produzir estes produtos acabados pode ser calculada.

O MRP é um sistema computadorizado que toma o MPS como um dado; ele explode o MPS na quantidade exigida de matérias-primas, peças, submontagens e montagens necessárias em cada semana do horizonte de planejamento; reduz essas necessidades de materiais para considerar os materiais que estão em estoque ou sob encomenda; e desenvolve um programa de pedidos de materiais comprados e peças produzidas durante o horizonte de planejamento.

Por que tantas organizações de produção atuais adotaram sistemas MRP? Os objetivos do MRP ajudam a explicar por que sua utilização cresceu com extrema rapidez.

FIGURA 10.2   SISTEMA DE PLANEJAMENTO DAS NECESSIDADES DE MATERIAIS

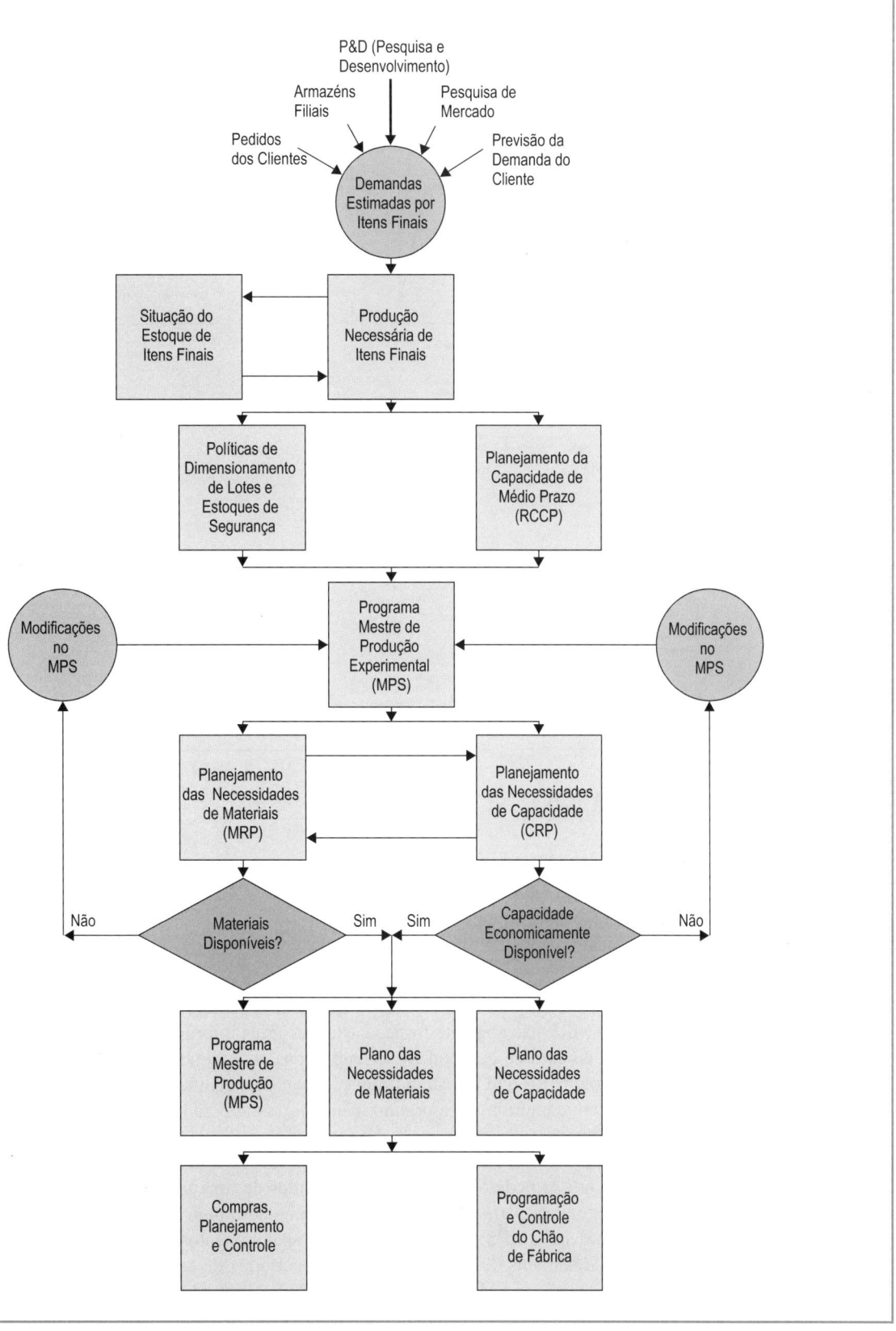

| FIGURA 10.3 | NÍVEIS DE ESTOQUE DE MATÉRIAS-PRIMAS NO MRP *VERSUS* SISTEMAS DO LOTE PADRÃO E PONTO DE PEDIDO |

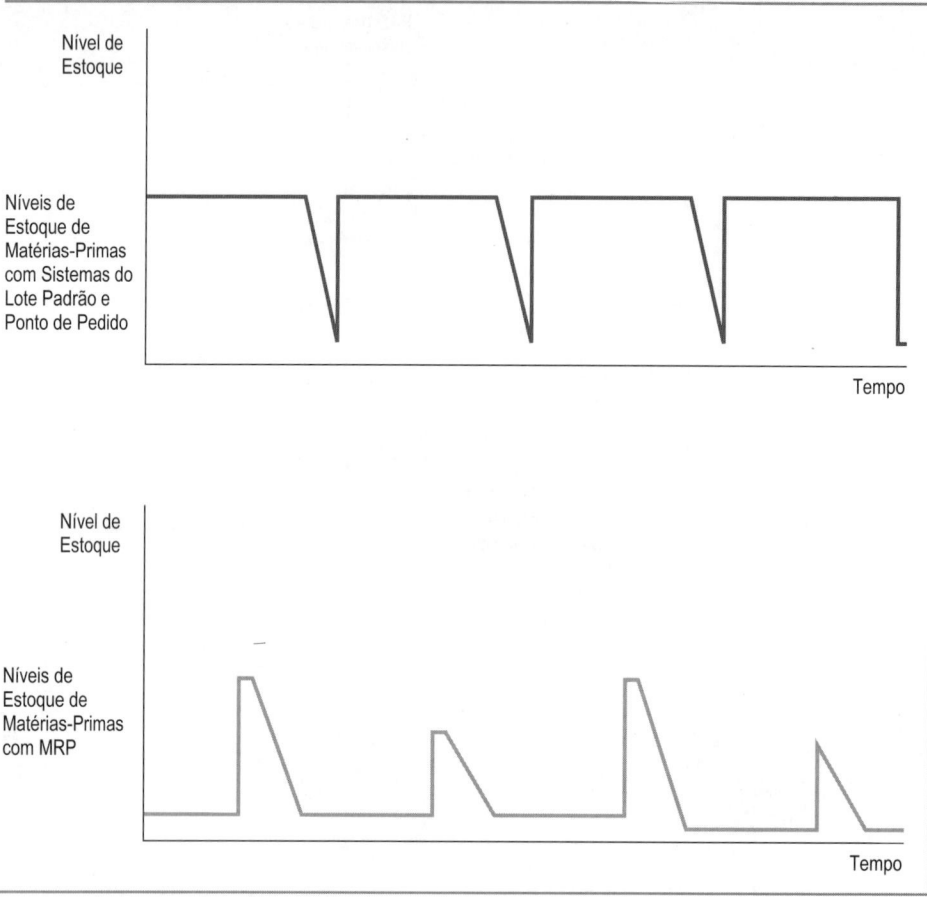

OBJETIVOS DO MRP

Os gerentes de operações adotam o MRP por estas razões:

- Melhorar o serviço ao cliente.
- Reduzir investimentos em estoques.
- Melhorar a eficiência operacional da fábrica.

Melhorar o serviço ao cliente significa mais do que apenas ter produtos disponíveis quando pedidos dos clientes são recebidos. Ter clientes satisfeitos significa também cumprir promessas de entrega e abreviar tempos de entrega. O MRP não somente fornece as necessárias informações administrativas para que se possa fazer promessas de entrega que podem ser cumpridas, mas também as promessas são incorporadas ao sistema de controle MRP que orienta a produção. Por conseguinte, as datas de entrega prometidas tornam-se metas a serem cumpridas pela organização, e a probabilidade de cumprimento das datas de entrega prometidas é melhorada.

A Figura 10.3 ilustra por que o MRP tende a reduzir os níveis de estoque. Quando são usados sistemas do lote padrão e ponto de pedido para programar pedidos de uma matéria-prima, a quantidade pedida mais o estoque de segurança permanecem em estoque até que o item final da matéria-prima apareça no programa mestre de produção (MPS). Uma vez que esses aparecimentos podem estar separados por diversas semanas, o padrão dos níveis de estoque tem longos períodos de estoques cheios intercalados por breves períodos de níveis baixos. No MRP, por outro lado, os pedidos de matérias-primas são programados para chegar aproximadamente no tempo em que o item final da matéria-prima vier a aparecer no MPS.

O padrão dos níveis de estoque no MRP tem longos períodos de baixos níveis de estoque intercalados por breves períodos de estoques cheios. O impacto do MRP nos níveis de estoques de matérias-primas é, portanto, a redução drástica dos níveis médios de estoque.

Uma vez que o MRP controla melhor a quantidade e os tempos de entrega de matérias-primas, peças, submontagens e montagens para as operações de produção, os materiais certos são entregues à produção na hora certa. Adicionalmente, o recebimento de materiais pode ser desacelerado ou acelerado em resposta a mudanças nos programas de produção. Esses controles de MRP resultam em reduzidos custos de mão-de-obra, materiais e gastos indiretos pelas seguintes razões:

- A diminuição no número de stockouts e atrasos na entrega de materiais resultam em mais produção sem elevações no número de empregados e máquinas.
- Redução da incidência de submontagens, montagens e produtos refugados resultantes da utilização de peças incorretas.
- A capacidade dos departamentos de produção é aumentada em conseqüência do diminuído tempo ocioso de produção, aumentada eficiência da movimentação física dos materiais, e reduzida confusão e atrasos de planejamento.

Todos esses benefícios resultam principalmente da **filosofia dos sistemas MRP**. Colocando-se de maneira simples, os sistemas MRP se baseiam na filosofia segundo a qual cada matéria-prima, peça e montagem necessária à produção devem chegar simultaneamente na hora certa para produzir os itens finais no MPS. Essa filosofia resulta no apressamento de materiais que irão se atrasar e no retardamento da entrega de materiais que irão chegar cedo. Por exemplo, se um material for chegar atrasado e nada puder ser feito a respeito, os outros materiais necessários para montar o item final não serão necessários até que o material atrasado chegue. O sistema MRP modifica as datas de vencimento de todos os materiais a fim de que eles cheguem simultaneamente para montar o item final. Um grande benefício dos sistemas MRP é que as operações de produção trabalham em peças que são realmente necessárias em suas datas de vencimento a fim de que a capacidade de produção suporte diretamente o MPS. Isso evita que se acelere a produção de peças através da fábrica para que elas cheguem à montagem final e se descubra que os itens finais das peças não poderão ser montados.

O MRP tornou-se uma valiosa ferramenta de planejamento para milhares de fábricas em todo o mundo. Depois da implementação do MRP, os benefícios comuns são os aumentados giros de estoque, mais promessas de entrega cumpridas, um número menor de pedidos que precisam ser divididos devido à escassez de materiais, necessidade de um número menor de expedidores, e lead times menores do pedido do cliente até a entrega dos produtos acabados. Examinemos agora os recursos dos sistemas MRP.

ELEMENTOS DO MRP

A Figura 10.4 descreve a operação do sistema MRP. O programa mestre de produção guia o sistema MRP inteiro. Ele é aceito como um dado. O arquivo situação do estoque e o arquivo lista de materiais fornecem informações adicionais sobre produtos incluídos no programa mestre de produção. Essas entradas são introduzidas no programa MRP de computador, que gera as saídas. As transações de estoques resultantes das ações do MRP são colocadas novamente no arquivo situação do estoque a fim de que sejam mantidos registros atualizados do estoque. A programação de pedidos e as mudanças e ajustes nos pedidos programados são as principais saídas do MRP. Relatórios de exceções, desempenho e planejamento também são gerados para ser utilizados pela administração.

Programa Mestre de Produção Um programa mestre de produção (MPS) é desenvolvido ou para renovar estoques de itens acabados ou para atender pedidos de clientes. Um MPS se inicia como um programa experimental a ser testado quanto à viabilidade através do MRP e CRP. À medida que esses programas se mostram viáveis, eles se tornam o MPS que será posto em ação. O MRP não pode distinguir entre programas mestres de produção exeqüíveis e inexeqüíveis. Isso equivale a dizer que o MRP supõe que o MPS possa ser produzido dentro das restrições à capacidade de produção. O MRP explode o programa mestre em necessidades de materiais. Se essas necessidades não puderem ser satisfeitas pelos materiais disponíveis no estoque ou pelos materiais pedidos, ou se não houver tempo suficiente para novos pedidos, então o MPS precisará ser modificado para um novo MPS.

FIGURA 10.4 — O SISTEMA MRP

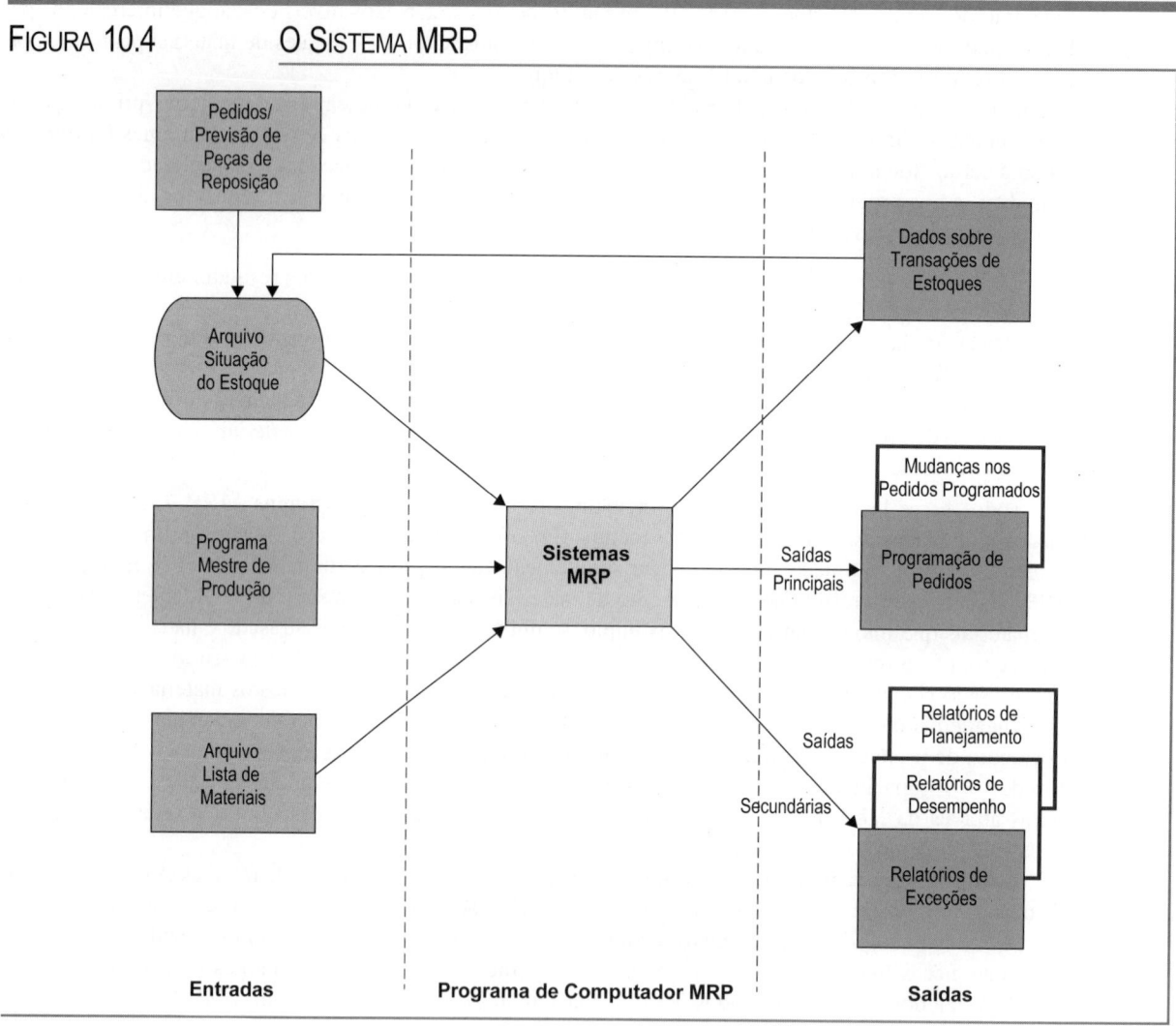

O MPS guia o sistema MRP, e, à medida que o MPS é atualizado, os resultados do MRP também são modificados. Pedidos de materiais são agilizados, desacelerados ou cancelados. Quando o MPS está congelado, o plano para recebimento de materiais decorrente do MRP também é congelado.

Arquivo Lista de Materiais (Bill of Materials) Uma **lista de materiais** é uma lista dos materiais e suas quantidades necessários para produzir uma unidade de um produto, ou **item final**. Cada produto tem, portanto, uma lista de materiais. Um **arquivo lista de materiais**, ou **arquivo estrutura analítica do produto** como às vezes é chamado, é uma lista completa de todos os produtos acabados, a quantidade de cada material em cada produto, e a estrutura (montagens, submontagens, peças e matérias-primas e suas relações) dos produtos. Outro termo para lista de materiais é **lista estruturada de materiais**, uma lista na qual o material original está na margem e seus componentes estão recuados para mostrar a estrutura (veja a Tabela 10.3).

O arquivo lista de materiais é um arquivo computadorizado atualizado que deve ser revisado à medida que os produtos são reprojetados. A precisão do arquivo lista de materiais é um grande obstáculo que deve ser superado na maioria das aplicações MRP. Confiando que o arquivo é atual, assim que o MPS é preparado, itens finais no MPS podem ser *explodidos* nas montagens, submontagens, peças e matérias-primas necessárias. Essas unidades podem ser ou compradas de fornecedores externos ou produzidas em departamentos de produção internos da empresa (in-house).

Arquivo Situação do Estoque O **arquivo situação do estoque** é um arquivo computadorizado com um registro completo de cada material mantido em estoque. Cada material, não importa em quantos níveis seja usado num produto ou em quantos produtos, tem um e somente um **registro de material**. Um registro de material inclui o **código do material**, estoque disponível, materiais sob encomenda e pedidos de clientes para o item. Esses registros são mantidos atualizados por transações de estoques, como, por exemplo, recibos, desembolsos, materiais sucateados, pedidos programados e liberações de pedidos.

Outra parte do arquivo inclui fatores de planejamento que são usados pelo sistema MRP. Esses fatores incluem informações como tamanhos de lote, lead times, níveis de estoque de segurança e taxas de produção de sucata.

Algumas peças, montagens e submontagens são mantidas como itens finais fornecidos aos clientes como peças de reposição. Esses materiais podem não fazer parte do MPS porque são comprados diretamente de fornecedores e colocados diretamente em estoque para demanda do cliente; em outras palavras, eles não são *produzidos* e, desse modo, não são incluídos no MPS. Os pedidos firmes ou pedidos previstos desses materiais, portanto, são lançados diretamente no arquivo situação do estoque, que se torna parte do sistema MRP.

O arquivo situação do estoque não só fornece ao sistema MRP um registro completo da situação de cada material em estoque mas também os elementos de planejamento que são usados no programa MRP de computador para projetar datas de entrega de pedidos, quantidades de cada material a ser pedido e quando fazer os pedidos.

Programa MRP de Computador O programa MRP de computador opera desta maneira:

1. Primeiro, com o MPS ele começa a determinar o número de itens finais necessários em cada período de tempo. Períodos de tempo (ou intervalos de tempo) às vezes são chamados **buckets** na terminologia do MRP.
2. Em seguida, as numerações das peças de reposição não incluídas no MPS, mas deduzidas dos pedidos dos clientes, são incluídas como itens finais.
3. O MPS e as peças de reposição são então explodidos em necessidades brutas para todos os materiais por período de tempo no futuro consultando-se o arquivo lista de materiais.
4. Em seguida, as necessidades brutas de materiais são modificadas pela quantidade de materiais disponíveis e já pedidos para cada período consultando-se o arquivo situação do estoque. As necessidades líquidas de cada material para cada intervalo de tempo são computadas da seguinte maneira:

$$\text{Necessidades líquidas} = \text{Necessidades brutas} - \left[\text{Estoque disponível} - \text{Estoque de segurança} - \text{Estoque alocado para outros usos} \right]$$

Se as necessidades líquidas forem maiores do que zero, pedidos do material devem ser feitos.
5. Finalmente, os pedidos são contrabalançados para períodos de tempo mais antecipados para levar em conta os lead times em cada etapa do processo de produção e os lead times dos fornecedores.

Esse procedimento resulta em dados sobre transações de estoques (pedidos liberados, mudanças nos pedidos etc.), os quais são usados para atualizar o arquivo situação do estoque, os registros de saída principais e os registros de saída secundários.

Saídas do MRP As saídas dos sistemas MRP fornecem dinamicamente o programa de materiais para o futuro — quantidade de cada material necessária em cada período de tempo para sustentar o MPS. Resultam duas saídas principais:

1. **Programação de pedidos** — um programa da quantidade de cada material a ser pedida em cada período de tempo. Esse programa é usado pelo departamento de compras para fazer pedidos a fornecedores e pela produção para pedir peças, submontagens ou montagens de departamentos de produção de estágios anteriores do processo produtivo. Os pedidos programados tornam-se um guia para produção futura nos fornecedores e para programas de produção in-house.
2. **Mudanças nos pedidos programados** — modificação de pedidos programados anteriormente. As quantidades pedidas podem ser mudadas, pedidos podem ser cancelados, ou podem ser atrasados ou adiantados para diferentes períodos de tempo por meio do processo de atualização.

As saídas de MRP secundárias fornecem estas informações:

1. **Relatórios das exceções** — relatórios que destacam itens que exigem atenção da administração a fim de fornecerem a quantidade certa de materiais em cada período de tempo. Exceções típicas observadas são o relato de erros, pedidos atrasados e excessiva produção de sucata.
2. **Relatórios do desempenho** — relatórios que indicam quão bem o sistema está operando. Exemplos de medidas do desempenho utilizadas são os giros de estoque, porcentagem das promessas de entrega mantidas e incidências de stockout.
3. **Relatórios do planejamento** — relatórios para serem usados em atividades futuras de planejamento de estoques. Exemplos dessas informações de planejamento são as previsões de estoques, relatórios de compromisso de compra, rastreamentos de fontes de demanda (*pegging*[1]) e planejamento das necessidades de materiais de longo prazo.

Estes são os principais elementos do MRP — as entradas, o programa MRP de computador e as saídas. Vamos examinar agora um exemplo para ver como o planejamento de estoques pode ser afetado pela utilização do MRP.

GREEN THUMB WATER SPRINKLER COMPANY

O Instantâneo da Indústria 10.1 demonstra como o MRP pode ser aplicado a um produto, um pulverizador de água. A Figura 10.5 ilustra esse produto. Leia o relato e examine a Figura 10.7, o programa MRP. Certifique-se de entender como cada informação é tirada do MPS (Tabela 10.1), da lista de materiais (Tabela 10.2) e do relatório da situação do estoque (Tabela 10.4) para ser usada nos cálculos do programa MRP.

INSTANTÂNEO DA INDÚSTRIA 10.1

GREEN THUMB WATER SPRINKLER COMPANY

James Verde, presidente da Green Thumb Water Sprinkler Company, acaba de convocar uma reunião de seu pessoal-chave para discutir novas abordagens do planejamento de estoques na Green Thumb. O sr. Verde inicia a reunião:

Sr. Verde: Convoquei esta reunião para explorarmos novos rumos para o planejamento de estoques em nossa organização. As incidências de stockouts em nossos estoques de matérias-primas levaram-nos a perder negócios a um ponto simplesmente insuportável. E a resposta não é quantidades de pedido maiores e estoques de segurança mais elevados, porque os juros cobrados para mantermos nosso estoque estão nos devorando vivos. De alguma forma, temos de planejar nossa aquisição de materiais para que se combinem mais estreitamente com os pedidos de produtos acabados feitos por nossos clientes.

Bonnie Buck: Concordo plenamente, sr. Verde. Como gerente de produção, posso dizer que quando nós, da produção, fazemos pedidos de materiais ao almoxarifado, parece que ele está sempre sem estoque. Os almoxarifados estão cheios — mas dos materiais errados. Alguma coisa tem de ser feita.

Bill Compton: Bem, como gerente de materiais, evidentemente estou na "cadeira elétrica" aqui. Nós já concluímos que nosso sistema tradicional de lotes padrões e pontos de pedido não está fazendo seu trabalho. Nossos pedidos de clientes individuais são simplesmente muito grandes e muito separados para que se adaptem às suposições de nosso sistema atual. Em antecipação a esse problema, Joe Johnson, nosso analista de sistema de estoque, freqüenta um curso de planejamento das necessidades de materiais (MRP) na universidade. Joe escolheu o pulverizador de gramados n. 377 (Figura 10.5) para demonstrar a técnica do MRP. Joe, quer nos mostrar os resultados de sua análise?

Joe Johnson: Obrigado, sr. Compton. Preparei um programa MRP para o n. 377 baseado em nosso programa mestre de produção mais recente e a situação de estoque do n. 377 e seus componentes. A programação dos pedidos resume o tempo e o tamanho dos pedidos de componentes do n. 377.

Depois que o grupo estuda os resultados da análise MRP, Bonnie

---
[1] *Pegging:* controle de ações. (N. do T.)

FIGURA 10.5 — PULVERIZADOR DE GRAMADOS N. 377

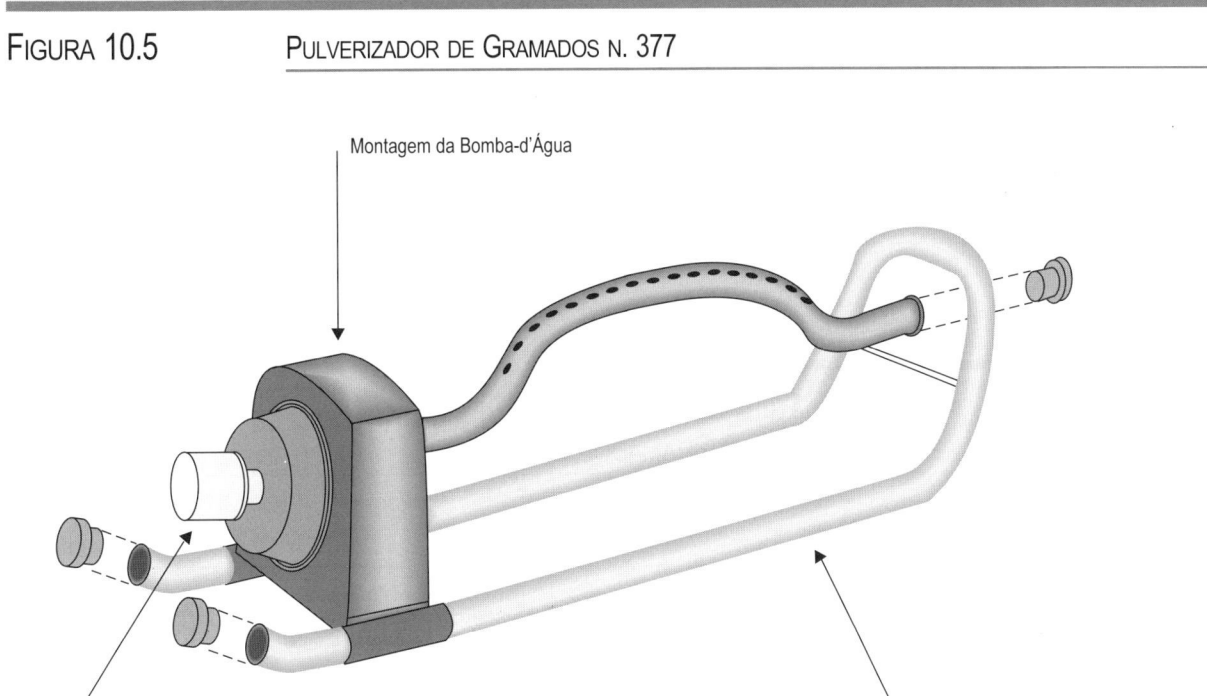

Montagem da Bomba-d'Água

Montagem do Engate da Mangueira n. 699

Montagem da Estrutura

Buck tem algumas perguntas a fazer:

Bonnie Buck: Joe, para que eu entenda a mecânica do MRP, você poderia pegar apenas um componente do programa MRP e explicar seus cálculos?

Joe Johnson: Claro, Bonnie. Vamos nos concentrar no componente C — a bomba-d'água. Primeiro, note que nossa análise dos pedidos dos clientes e previsões de pedidos resultou na Tabela 10.1, o programa mestre de produção do pulverizador de gramados n. 377. Mil unidades são necessárias na semana 4 e 2.000 unidades são necessárias na semana 8. Em seguida, a partir da lista de materiais para o n. 377 (Tabela 10.2), podemos ver que uma unidade do componente C entra em cada unidade do componente M (montagem da bomba-d'água) e uma unidade do componente M entra em cada n. 377. Essa relação pode, talvez, ser vista mais claramente na Figura 10.6 e na Tabela 10.3. Em seguida, examinando o programa MRP para o n. 377 na Figura 10.7, observe que na semana 4 entram 200 unidades do n. 377 (a diferença entre o saldo de estoque disponível e o estoque de segurança). Já que precisamos de 1.000 unidades do n. 377 na semana 4 e 200 unidades estão disponíveis em estoque, temos uma necessidade líquida de 800 unidades na semana 4. Uma vez que é necessário uma semana para processar um lote de unidades do n. 377 através das operações de montagem finais, as 800 unidades devem ser iniciadas através da montagem final na semana 3, um semana mais cedo.

Se 800 unidades do n. 377 precisarem iniciar a montagem final na semana 3, serão necessárias 800 unidades do componente M na semana 3, e isso precisa mostrar-se como uma necessidade bruta para o componente M na semana 3. Quando essa mesma lógica é aplicada ao componente M, 600 unidades do componente M devem ter sua produção iniciada na semana 2, e isso cria uma necessidade bruta de 600 unidades do componente C na semana 2. A necessidade bruta de 2.000 unidades do componente C na semana 6, de maneira semelhante, resulta diretamente da necessidade bruta do n. 377 na semana 8. A necessidade bruta de 1.000 unidades do componente C na semana 4 resulta da necessidade de expedir peças de reposição para os clientes. Essa informação é encontrada na Tabela 10.4. Isso explica como a necessidade bruta do componente C foi determinada. Uma explicação adicional de todas as necessidades brutas no programa MRP da Figura 10.7 está contida na Tabela 10.5. Veja a observação na parte inferior da Figura 10.7 para computar Disponível na semana 1.

A necessidade bruta de 600 unidades do componente C na se-

TABELA 10.1 — PROGRAMA MESTRE DE PRODUÇÃO: PULVERIZADOR DE GRAMADOS N. 377

	\multicolumn{8}{c}{Semana}
	1	2	3	4	5	6	7	8
Necessidade Bruta				1.000				2.000

TABELA 10.2 — LISTA DE MATERIAIS: PULVERIZADOR DE GRAMADOS N. 377

Código do Material Original	Código do Componente	Código do Nível	Descrição	Componentes Necessários por Material Pai[2]
	377	0	Pulverizador de Gramados n. 377	
377	M	1	Montagem da bomba-d'água	1
	F	1	Montagem da estrutura	1
	H	1	Montagem do engate da mangueira n. 699	1
M	A	2	Tubo de alumínio de 1/32" com 1/2" de diâmetro	10
	B	2	Parafusos de metal de 1/2" x 1/16"	3
	C	2	Bomba-d'água	1
F	A	2	Tubo de alumínio de 1/32" com 1/2" de diâmetro	40
	D	2	Tampa plástica n. 115 1/2" x 1/2"	3
	B	2	Parafusos de metal de 1/2" x 1/16"	3

TABELA 10.3 — LISTA ESTRUTURADA DE MATERIAIS: PULVERIZADOR DE GRAMADOS N. 377

\multicolumn{3}{c}{Nível}	
0	1	2	Quantidade
377			1
	M		1
		A	10
		B	3
		C	1
	F		1
		A	40
		D	3
		B	3
	H		1

---

[2] Os termos pai e filho são de uso corrente na terminologia do MRP. Assim, temos itens pai, itens filho etc. (N. do R.T.)

Capítulo 10 – Sistemas de Planejamento das Necessidades de Recursos

FIGURA 10.6 ESTRUTURA DE PRODUTO:
PULVERIZADOR DE GRAMADOS N. 377

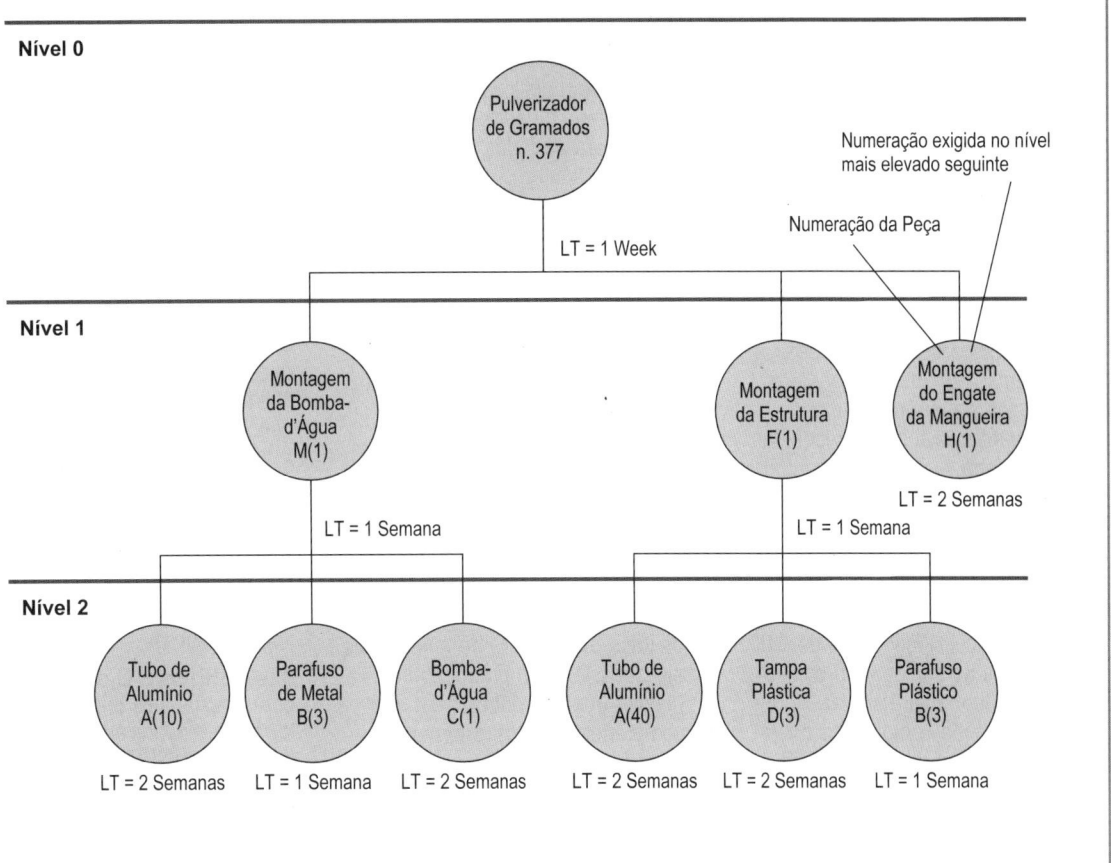

TABELA 10.4 RELATÓRIO DA SITUAÇÃO DO ESTOQUE:
PULVERIZADOR DE GRAMADOS N. 377

Código do Item	Dis-ponível	Estoque de Segurança	Alocado	Tamanho do Lote*	Lead Times (semanas)	Recebimento Programado		Pedidos de Peças de Reposição	
						Quantidade	Semana	Quantidade	Semana
377	500	300		LFL	1				
M	200	0		LFL	1				
F	300	0		LFL	1				
H	1.500	200	1.000	1.000+	2				
A	30.000	5.000	15.000	50.000+	2	50.000	1		
B	5.000	0	2.500	10.000+	1				
C	1.000	500	800	1.000+	2	1.000	1	1.000	4
D	3.000	0	2.000	10.000+	2	10.000	1		

*O sinal de adição (+) indica que qualquer quantidade acima do mínimo pode ser pedida. Por exemplo, 1.000+ indica que 1.000 ou mais itens podem ser pedidos.

mana 2 é satisfeita pelo recebimento programado de 1.000 unidades na semana 1, não obstante somente 700 dessas unidades estarem disponíveis para uso na semana 2, uma vez que estávamos com falta de 300 unidades ao entrarmos na semana 1 devido a uma alocação excessiva do estoque disponível além do estoque de segurança. A necessidade bruta de 600 unidades na semana 2 combinada com as 700 unidades disponíveis na semana 2 resulta em 100 unidades disponíveis para atender a necessidade bruta de 1.000 unidades na semana 4. Isso deixa uma necessidade líquida de 900 unidades na semana 4, e 1.000 unidades, o tamanho de lote mínimo, são planejadas para serem recebidas na semana 4. Depois de contrabalançarmos para as duas semanas de lead times até recebermos a remessa do componente C, devemos liberar o pedido de 1.000 unidades na semana 2.

A necessidade bruta de 2.000 unidades na semana 6 é computada de maneira similar. Agora você percebe como chegamos à Figura 10.7, o programa MRP?

Bonnie Buck: Sim. Como você sabe que o MPS e a programação de pedidos são exeqüíveis? Em outras palavras, como você sabe que temos a capacidade de produção para produzirmos o MPS, e como você sabe que os materiais estarão disponíveis em tempo para que possamos produzir o MPS?

Joe Johnson: Essa é uma boa pergunta, Bonnie. Sabemos que os materiais comprados estarão disponíveis em quantidades suficientes e em tempo para cumprir a programação de pedidos (Tabela 10.6) porque fizemos uma dupla checagem com nossos fornecedores. Esse método para verificar se materiais poderão ser fornecidos em tempo de tornarmos a produção do MPS exeqüível será uma necessidade contínua no MRP. Se descobríssemos que um material não poderia ser fornecido em tempo ou em quantidade suficiente para cumprir a programação de pedidos, teríamos somente duas alternativas: acelerar o pedido e talvez pagar a mais para fazermos com que ele fosse processado mediante um trabalho em horas extras em nossos fornecedores, ou modificar o MPS e refazer o processo de MRP. Se o MPS fosse modificado, o item final afetado teria de ser empurrado para frente, para períodos posteriores no MPS.

O MPS também foi checado quanto à viabilidade da capacidade de produção. Programas de carga foram desenvolvidos para cada departamento de produção da fábrica. Todos os produtos no MPS foram incluídos, e tornou-se claro que existe suficiente capacidade de produção em cada departamento para que possamos produzir o MPS. Isso suscita um ponto interessante: como desenvolver programas de produção semanais detalhados a partir do programa MRP mostrado na Figura 10.7? Somente os itens 377, M e F, de níveis mais elevados, exigem produção in-house; todos os outros itens são comprados de nossos fornecedores.

Os departamentos de produção em que os itens 377, M e F serão produzidos incluem as liberações de pedidos programados para esses itens em seus programas de carga. Por exemplo, 600 e 2.000 unidades do componente M devem entrar em produção no Departamento de Fabricação Mecânica e Montagem nas semanas 2 e 6, respectivamente. A quantidade de mão-de-obra por unidade e a quantidade de horas de máquinas por unidade são multiplicadas por essas quantidades, e o resultado é a quantidade da capacidade de produção necessária no departamento responsável pelo componente M. Quando esse mesmo processo é seguido para todos os nossos produtos, o carregamento pode ser comparado com a capacidade de mão-de-obra e de máquina do departamento. A mesma análise de carregamento também se aplicaria ao Departamento de Montagem Final e ao Departamento de Fabricação Metálica e Montagem.

Como se pode ver, o planejamento das necessidades de capacidade (CRP), como essa análise é chamada, é uma parte necessária do processo global de produção e planejamento de estoques. Adicionalmente, os programas de produção detalhados dos departamentos de produção são retirados dos programas MRP. Quando todas as liberações de pedidos programados são retiradas de todos os componentes do programa MRP que devem ser produzidos in-house e classificados de acordo com seus departamentos de produção, o resultado são programas de produção departamentais.

Você consegue ver a ligação entre o MRP e os programas de produção departamentais?

Bonnie Buck: Sim. Agora você poderia resumir como o MRP seria aplicado a todos os nossos produtos na prática?

Joe Johnson: O procedimento para nossos seis principais produtos seria mecanicamente o mesmo que o demonstrado para o item n. 377. A grande diferença seria informatizar o processo inteiro. Os números que vimos aqui hoje foram todos calculados manualmente. Estas poderiam ser as principais tarefas para tornarmos um sistema MRP operativo: (1) Criar um acurado arquivo computadorizado da situação do estoque de todos os nossos produtos. (2) Melhorar nossos métodos de previsão a fim de podermos combinar previsões com pedidos de clientes para formarmos uma base confiável para um programa mestre de produção acurado. (3) Criar um atualizado arquivo computadorizado lista de materiais de todos os nossos produtos. (4) Comprar os serviços da ABM Computer Services para auxiliar-nos a instalar o programa MRP de computador e depurar o sistema MRP depois que ele for instalado. Eu estimo que poderíamos ter um sistema MRP operando para todos os nossos produtos em aproximadamente seis meses.

Capítulo 10 – Sistemas de Planejamento das Necessidades de Recursos

FIGURA 10.7 — PROGRAMA MRP: PULVERIZADOR DE GRAMADOS N. 377

Código do Item	Código do Nível	Tamanho do Lote	Semanas de Lead Time	À Mão	Estoque de segurança	Alocado		Semana 1	Semana 2	Semana 3	Semana 4	Semana 5	Semana 6	Semana 7	Semana 8
377	0	LFL	1	500	300		Necessidades Brutas				1.000				2.000
							Recebimentos Programados								
							Disponível	200	200	200	200				
							Necessidades Líquidas				800				2.000
							Recebimentos de Pedidos Programados				800				2.000
							Liberações de Pedidos Programados				800			2.000	
M	1	LFL	1	200			Necessidades Brutas				800				2.000
							Recebimentos Programados								
							Disponível	200	200	200					
							Necessidades Líquidas				600				2.000
							Recebimentos de Pedidos Programados				600				2.000
							Liberações de Pedidos Programados			600			2.000		
F	1	LFL	1	300			Necessidades Brutas				800				2.000
							Recebimentos Programados								
							Disponível	300	300	300					
							Necessidades Líquidas				500				2.000
							Recebimentos de Pedidos Programados				500				2.000
							Liberações de Pedidos Programados			500			2.000		
H	1	1.000+	2	1.500	200	1.000	Necessidades Brutas				800				2.000
							Recebimentos Programados								
							Disponível	300	300	300		500	500	500	500
							Necessidades Líquidas				500				1.500
							Recebimentos de Pedidos Programados				1.000				1.500
							Liberações de Pedidos Programados		1.000				1.500		
A	2	50.000+	2	30.000	5.000	15.000	Necessidades Brutas	50.000	26.000				100.000		
							Recebimentos Programados								
							Disponível	60.000	60.000	34.000	34.000	34.000	34.000		
							Necessidades Líquidas						66.000		
							Recebimentos de Pedidos Programados						66.000		
							Liberações de Pedidos Programados				66.000				
B	2	10.000+	1	5.000		2.500	Necessidades Brutas		3.300				12.000		
							Recebimentos Programados								
							Disponível	2.500	2.500	9.200	9.200	9.200	9.200	7.200	7.200
							Necessidades Líquidas		800				2.800		
							Recebimentos de Pedidos Programados		10.000				10.000		
							Liberações de Pedidos Programados	10.000				10.000			
C	2	1.000+	2	1.000	500	800	Necessidades Brutas	1.000	600		1.000		2.000		
							Recebimentos Programados								
							Disponível	700	700	100	100	100	100		
							Necessidades Líquidas				900		1.900		
							Recebimentos de Pedidos Programados				1.000		1.900		
							Liberações de Pedidos Programados		1.000		1.900				
D	2	10.000+	2	3.000		2.000	Necessidades Brutas	10.000	1.500				6.000		
							Recebimentos Programados	11.000							
							Disponível	11.000	11.000	9.500	9.500	9.500	9.500	3.500	3.500
							Necessidades Líquidas								
							Recebimentos de Pedidos Programados								
							Liberações de Pedidos Programados								

Observação: Semana 1 Disponível = À Mão − Estoque de Segurança − Alocado + Necessidades Líquidas dos Recebimentos Programados = Necessidades Brutas − Disponível

TABELA 10.5 CÁLCULOS DAS NECESSIDADES BRUTAS: PULVERIZADOR DE GRAMADOS N. 377

Código do Componente	Código do Material Pai	Componentes Necessários por Material Pai	Componentes Necessários para Produção dos Materiais Pais		Peças de Reposição Necessárias		Necessidade Bruta Total	
			Quantidade	Semana	Quantidade	Semana	Quantidade	Semana
M	377	1	800	3			800	3
M	377	1	2.000	7			2.000	7
F	377	1	800	3			800	3
F	377	1	2.000	7			2.000	7
H	377	1	800	3			800	3
H	377	1	2.000	7			2.000	7
A	M	10	6.000	2				
A	F	40	20.000	2			26.000	2
A	M	10	20.000	6				
A	F	40	80.000	6			100.000	6
B	M	3	1.800	2				
B	F	3	1.500	2			3.300	2
B	M	3	6.000	6				
B	F	3	6.000	6			12.000	6
C	M	1	600	2			600	2
C	—	—			1.000	4	1.000	4
C	M	1	2.000	6			2.000	6
D	F	3	1.500	2			1.500	2
D	F	3	6.000	6			6.000	6

TABELA 10.6 PROGRAMAÇÃO DE PEDIDOS: PULVERIZADOR DE GRAMADOS N. 377

Código do Item	Semana							
	1	2	3	4	5	6	7	8
377			800				2.000	
M		600				2.000		
F		500				2.000		
H	1.000				1.500			
A				66.000				
B	10.000				1.000			
C		1.000		1.900				
D								

Sr. Verde: Joe, quais são as principais vantagens do MRP sobre nosso sistema atual de planejamento de estoques, ligado a lotes padrões e a pontos de pedido?

Joe Johnson: (1) Melhor serviço ao cliente, (2) menores níveis de estoque e (3) maior eficiência operacional em nossos departamentos de produção.

Todo o grupo concordou em fazer uma experiência com o MRP executando o novo sistema paralelamente com o sistema atual durante seis meses. Eles consideraram que essa abordagem deve fornecer uma comparação prática dos resultados do MRP com o sistema de planejamento de estoques atual.

A programação de pedidos (Tabela 10.6) é a principal saída do MRP. A **programação de pedidos** é um programa de liberações de pedidos futuros programados ao longo de todo o horizonte de planejamento. Esse relatório indica ao departamento de compras e aos programadores da produção quais materiais pedir, quais quantidades de materiais pedir e quando fazer pedidos de cada material do sistema de produção.

DIMENSIONAMENTO DE LOTES NO MRP

No MRP, quando quer que haja uma necessidade líquida de um material, deve-se tomar uma decisão referente a quanto desse material pedir. Essas decisões comumente são chamadas **decisões de dimensionamento de lotes**. Em empresas de produção sob encomenda, o tamanho do pedido feito pelo cliente normalmente é o tamanho do lote que será produzido, porque não se pode supor que haverá outros pedidos do produto projetado de forma personalizada no futuro. Por outro lado, em empresas de produção para estoque, desde que somente alguns projetos de produto padrão são produzidos para estoque, o tamanho dos lotes de produção é, antes de mais nada, uma questão de economia. Os gerentes de operações geralmente gostam de pedir e produzir grandes lotes de materiais por estas razões:

1. O custo anual para fazer preparação de máquina entre lotes de produção é menor e a capacidade de produção é maior devido ao menor tempo ocioso (downtime) causado pelas preparações de máquina.
2. O custo anual de emissão de pedidos de compra é menor porque somente alguns pedidos de grandes lotes de materiais são feitos aos fornecedores.
3. Ao pedir grandes lotes de materiais dos fornecedores podemos tirar proveito de descontos de preço e de transporte, resultando em menores custos de compra dos materiais.

Por outro lado, os gerentes de operações geralmente gostariam de produzir pequenos lotes de materiais por estas razões:

1. Lotes menores de materiais resultam em níveis de estoque médios mais baixos, e o custo anual de manutenção em estoque é mais baixo.
2. Níveis de estoque mais baixos podem reduzir o risco de obsolescência quando são modificados projetos de produto.
3. Lotes menores resultam em menos estoque em processo, e os pedidos dos clientes podem ser produzidos mais rapidamente.

Os gerentes de operações não podem usufruir dos benefícios tanto de lotes pequenos como de grandes lotes. Eles devem buscar um equilíbrio entre lotes que não sejam muito pequenos e lotes que não sejam demasiadamente grandes. Muita pesquisa tem sido realizada para desenvolver métodos de determinação de tamanhos de lote. Por exemplo, no Capítulo 9 foi usado o LEC para computar tamanhos de lote, mas duas suposições restritivas do LEC tornam seu uso no MPS e no MRP custoso.

Primeiro, o LEC básico supõe que o custo por unidade não depende da quantidade de um material pedido, mas sabemos que os fornecedores freqüentemente oferecem descontos dependendo do volume comprado. De maneira semelhante, para materiais produzidos em casa (in-house), como ilustra a Figura 9.1 no Capítulo 9, o tamanho do lote afeta o custo por unidade do material. Portanto, os gerentes de operações ou usam o LEC com descontos por quantidade, ou, talvez mais comumente, especificam **tamanhos de lote mínimos**. Para materiais comprados, esses lotes mínimos tipicamente têm descontos, e para materiais produzidos internamente na empresa o lote mínimo está num ponto igual às 5.000 unidades indicadas na Figura 9.1, em que o custo por unidade sobe abruptamente quando uma quantidade menor do que esse número de unidades é produzida. Por exemplo, um lote mínimo de 5.000 unidades significa que qualquer quantidade maior ou igual a 5.000 unidades pode ser pedida, mas nunca menos do que 5.000 unidades. Se houvesse uma necessidade líquida de 2.000 unidades desse material, um lote de 5.000 unidades seria pedido. Por outro lado, se houvesse uma necessidade líquida de 9.999 unidades, um lote de 9.999 unidades seria pedido.

Em segundo lugar, o LEC supõe que a demanda para o material seja uniforme de semana a semana. *No MRP e no MPS, as necessidades líquidas de materiais têm sido descritas como demandas instáveis (lumpy).* **Demanda instável** *significa que a demanda varia muito de semana a semana.* Na presença de demandas instáveis, outros métodos de dimensionamento de lotes são o **método do lote por lote** e o **método**

do período padrão (POQ). O Exemplo 10.1 demonstra o uso desses métodos quando aplicados a um programa de necessidades líquidas. Outras abordagens também têm sido experimentadas. Os métodos do menor custo total, do menor custo por unidade e do balanceamento periódico de peças são discutidos e descritos no livro de Orlicky. Os métodos heurísticos de Gaither, Groff, e Silver e Meal proporcionam um bom desempenho de custo e são muito eficientes. O método de Wagner e Within produz ótimos resultados, mas se baseia em programação dinâmica, é difícil de entender e pode não apresentar bom desempenho de custo quando ocorrerem muitas mudanças nas necessidades líquidas semanalmente.

É importante entender que o método de dimensionamento de lotes resultante no menor custo depende dos dados — padrões de custo e demanda. Aconselhamos que se faça experimentação antes que um método seja escolhido para sistemas de produção específicos.

Exemplo 10.1

Decisões Quanto ao Dimensionamento de Lotes para Materiais com Demandas Instáveis

As necessidades líquidas de um material a partir de um programa MRP são:

	Semana							
	1	2	3	4	5	6	7	8
Necessidades líquidas	300	500	1.000	600	300	300	300	1.500

A demanda anual para esse item final é estimada em 30 mil unidades durante um programa de 50 semanas por ano, ou uma média de 600 unidades por semana. Custa $ 500 para preparar as máquinas no departamento de montagem final para esse item final quando um lote de produção foi iniciado. Custa $ 0,50 por unidade quando uma unidade desse produto precisa ser mantida em estoque de uma semana para outra; portanto, quando uma unidade desse produto está num estoque final, ela deve ser transportada como estoque inicial na semana seguinte e incorre no custo de manutenção de estoque de $ 0,50 por unidade. Determine qual destes métodos de dimensionamento de lotes resulta nos menores custos de manutenção de estoque e preparação (ou pedido) para o programa de oito semanas: **a)** lote por lote (LFL), **b)** lote econômico de compra (LEC) ou **c)** método do período padrão (POQ).

Solução

a) Desenvolva os custos totais de manutenção de estoque e emissão de pedidos ao longo do programa de oito semanas para o método do lote por lote. *Os lotes de produção lote por lote (LFL) equivalem às necessidades líquidas em cada período.*

	Semana								Custos		
	1	2	3	4	5	6	7	8	Manutenção de Estoque	Emissão de Pedidos	Total
Necessidades Líquidas	300	500	1.000	600	300	300	300	1.500			
Estoque Inicial	0	0	0	0	0	0	0	0			
Lotes de Produção	300	500	1.000	600	300	300	300	1.500	$ 0	$ 4.000	$ 4.000
Estoque Final	0	0	0	0	0	0	0	0			

Custos de emissão de pedidos = Números de pedidos × $ 500 = 8 × $ 500 = $ 4.000

b) Desenvolva os custos totais de manutenção de estoque e emissão de pedidos ao longo do programa de oito semanas para o método de dimensionamento de lotes LEC. *Os lotes de produção LEC equivalem ao LEC computado.*

Primeiro, compute o LEC:

$$\text{LEC} = \sqrt{2DS/C} = \sqrt{2(30.000)(500)/(0,50)(50)} = 1.095,4, \text{ ou } 1.095 \text{ unidades}$$

	Semana								Custos		
	1	2	3	4	5	6	7	8	Manutenção de Estoque	Emissão de Pedidos	Total
Necessidades Líquidas	300	500	1.000	600	300	300	300	1.500			
Estoque Inicial	0	795	295	390	885	585	285	1.080			
Lotes de Produção	1.095	—	1.095	1.095	—	—	1.095	1.095	$ 2.495	$ 2.500	$ 4.995
Estoque Final	795	295	390	885	585	285	1.080	675			

Custos de manutenção de estoque = Soma dos estoques finais × $ 0,50 = 4.990 × $ 0,50 = $ 2.495

Custos de emissão de pedidos = Número de pedidos × $ 500 = 5 × $ 500 = $ 2.500

c) Desenvolva os custos totais de manutenção de estoque e de emissão de pedidos durante o programa de oito semanas para o método do período padrão (POQ). *Os lotes de produção equivalem às necessidades líquidas correspondentes aos períodos padrões computados.*

Primeiro, compute o POQ:

$$\text{POQ} = \frac{\text{Número de semanas por ano}}{\text{Número de pedidos por ano}} = \frac{50}{D/\text{LEC}} = \frac{50}{30.000/1.095,4}$$

$$= 1,83, \text{ ou } 2 \text{ semanas por pedido}$$

	Semana								Custos		
	1	2	3	4	5	6	7	8	Manutenção de Estoque	Emissão de Pedidos	Total
Necessidades Líquidas	(300	500)	(1.000	600)	(300	300)	(300	1.500)			
Estoque Inicial	0	500	0	600	0	300	0	1.500			
Lotes de Produção	800	—	1.600	—	600	—	1.800	—	$ 1.450	$ 2.000	$ 3.450
Estoque Final	500	0	600	0	300	0	1.500	0			

Custos de manutenção de estoque = Soma dos estoques finais × $ 0,50 = 2.900 × $ 0,50 = $ 1.450

Custos de emissão de pedidos = Número de pedidos × $ 500 = 4 × $ 500 = $ 2.000

Entre os métodos de dimensionamento de lotes considerados para esses dados, o método do período padrão exibe os menores custos de manutenção de estoque e emissão de pedidos durante o programa de necessidades líquidas de oito semanas.

A linha de necessidades líquidas no programa MRP correspondente a cada componente é analisada para determinar o tempo e o tamanho de lotes de produção ou lotes comprados usando-se uma das técnicas de dimensionamento de lotes mencionadas anteriormente. A linha Recebimentos de Pedidos Programados no programa MRP é o resultado final dessas decisões de dimensionamento de lotes.

QUESTÕES SOBRE O MRP

Qualquer tratamento no MRP deve incluir uma discussão a respeito de importantes questões que ainda devem ser resolvidas.

Dimensionamento de Lotes Diz-se que existe um problema potencial quando são aplicadas técnicas de dimensionamento de lotes em cada nível da estrutura de produto. Usar dimensionamento de lotes em componentes de nível mais baixo (matérias-primas e peças) não constitui um problema sério, mas com tamanhos de lote econômicos para componentes de níveis mais elevados (itens finais e submontagens), alguns usuários do MRP acreditam que pode resultar em excessivas elevações de estoque de componentes de nível mais baixo. Por exemplo, três componentes estão relacionados da seguinte maneira:

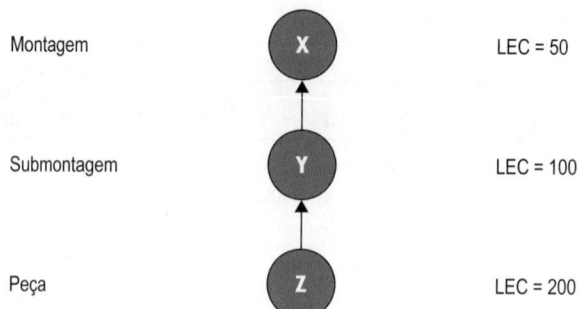

Se for recebido de um cliente um pedido de 25 unidades da peça X, se nenhum estoque das peças X, Y e Z estiver disponível, e se pedidos iguais ao LEC forem feitos, o estoque disponível para uso imediatamente depois da remessa do pedido do cliente será:

$$\text{Estoque da peça X} = 25 \text{ unidades}$$
$$\text{Estoque da peça Y} = 75 \text{ unidades}$$
$$\text{Estoque da peça Z} = 175 \text{ unidades}$$

Alguns usuários do MRP argumentam, entretanto, que níveis de estoque excessivos não são atingidos. O menor custo por unidade dos componentes de nível mais baixo leva a tamanhos de lote maiores e, conseqüentemente, a níveis de estoque mais elevados. Esses usuários do MRP sustentam que níveis de estoque mais elevados de componentes de nível mais baixo não devem causar surpresa ou perturbação: o dimensionamento de lote econômico de todos os níveis é, portanto, recomendado.

A tendência, na prática, é usar o lote por lote (LFL) em todos os níveis para empresas de produção sob encomenda. Além disso, o LFL comumente é usado em empresas de produção para estoque para itens finais e montagens, e tamanhos de lote mínimos são usados para componentes de nível mais baixo, como, por exemplo, matérias-primas e peças. A utilização do LFL em itens finais e montagens evita as grandes elevações de estoque de componentes de nível mais baixo descritas acima. Nas fábricas de amanhã, as operações serão mais enxutas, mais flexíveis e mais automatizadas. Nesses ambientes, o uso do LFL será mais comum para todos os materiais.

Sistemas de MRP de Mudança Líquida *Versus* MRP Regenerativo Algumas organizações usam aquilo que chamamos **MRP de mudança líquida**. Esses sistemas atualizam o programa mestre de produção quando ocorrem mudanças no MRP. O sistema MRP é então ativado para gerar um conjunto de saídas MRP. Essas saídas, entretanto, são somente as mudanças líquidas em séries de MRP passadas e não num conjunto inteiro de saídas MRP. O relatório de programação de pedidos, por exemplo, indicaria somente as mudanças na programação de pedidos anteriores, não um programa inteiramente novo. Não obstante esse conceito ser tentador do ponto de vista teórico, a ocorrência de sua aplicação tem sido desapontadora, porque ele tende a gerar um número demasiado de avisos de ação.

Muitas organizações continuam a usar aquilo que é chamado **MRP regenerativo**. Nesses sistemas, uma série MRP completa é processada periodicamente, em geral toda semana. Nesses momentos, um MPS novo, um arquivo situação do estoque atualizado e um arquivo lista de materiais atualizado são introduzidos no programa MRP de computador, que gera um conjunto completo de saídas. Não obstante os sistemas MRP regenerativos serem ligeiramente mais custosos de preparar e processar, aparentemente eles são mais fáceis de implementar e administrar.

Estoque de Segurança As opiniões dos usuários do MRP divergem no tocante ao uso de estoque de segurança no MRP. Os que defendem o uso de estoque de segurança no MRP argumentam que ele desempenha a mesma função nos sistemas MRP que em outros sistemas de planejamento de estoques — impedir os stockouts excessivos provocados por lead times e demandas diárias incertos. Aqueles que se opõem ao uso de estoque de segurança no MRP argumentam que, desde que os sistemas MRP se adaptam a condições mutáveis que afetam a demanda e os lead times, o estoque de segurança não será usado de fato sob a maioria das circunstâncias no MRP.

O uso de estoques de segurança pode ser justificado somente pelas fontes de incerteza presentes durante os lead times. Para itens de níveis mais elevados, como, por exemplo, itens finais, a incerteza da demanda se compara com qualquer outro item de estoque que tenha demanda independente. A incerteza de lead times para esses itens parece mais controlável se eles forem produzidos internamente na empresa. Para equilibrar, o uso de estoques de segurança para itens finais em sistemas MRP pode ser justificado na mesma base que em qualquer outro sistema — a presença de demanda incerta e lead times incertos.

Para itens de nível mais baixo, como, por exemplo, matérias-primas e peças, a incerteza de demanda é mais controlada porque a demanda é dependente. O MPS define a demanda semanal para esses itens. As únicas grandes incertezas presentes durante os lead times são a produção de sucata e a incerteza de lead time e demanda que ocorre devido a mudanças no MPS. Parece que algum estoque de segurança certamente pode ser justificado, mesmo de matérias-primas, peças e outros itens de nível mais baixo, ainda que em níveis significativamente reduzidos.

MRP em Empresas de Montagem sob Encomenda A **empresa de montagem sob encomenda** é um tipo especial de empresa de produção sob encomenda. Nela podemos encontrar milhões de itens finais únicos, porque os clientes podem escolher itens opcionais e acessórios. Uma fábrica de automóveis é um exemplo de empresa de montagem sob encomenda. Embora somente alguns modelos padrões sejam oferecidos aos clientes, os revendedores podem especificar cores, tipos de motor, tipos de transmissão, opções de acabamento, condicionadores de ar, vidros e travas de porta elétricos, piloto automático[3] e uma grande variedade de outras opções. Nesses casos, há somente algumas opções e modelos de produto básicos, mas há literalmente milhares de produtos acabados únicos possíveis. Um sistema MRP que tentasse desenvolver um MPS para esses itens finais exclusivos se veria sobrecarregado ao tentar explodir milhões de listas de materiais de itens finais nos recursos necessários para produzir o MPS.

Em empresas de montagem sob encomenda, portanto, o MPS e o MRP são tratados separadamente do **programa de montagem final (PMF)**. O PMF, habitualmente preparado com somente uma ou duas semanas de antecedência, programa os produtos exclusivos pedidos pelos clientes. Isso é necessário porque deve ser remetido aos clientes produtos que incluam suas opções específicas. Mas o MPS, o MRP e todos os outros elementos do sistema de planejamento das necessidades de recursos exigem um lead time muito mais longo e não se baseiam em pedidos exclusivos dos clientes. Ao contrário, o MPS *explode* listas de materiais moduladas, as quais podem ser imaginadas como famílias de produtos. Uma **lista de materiais modulada** de uma família de produtos em particular listará a porcentagem prevista de pedidos de clientes que exigem a inclusão de cada opção juntamente com o kit de peças que é comum a todos os pedidos de clientes. Essas famílias de produtos não montados, com todas as suas opções e kits de peças comuns, são programadas através das operações de produção de tal forma que as famílias de produtos cheguem à montagem final prontas para ser montadas nos produtos específicos dos pedidos dos clientes. Isso reduz muito a carga computacional no sistema MRP, não obstante criar a necessidade de se modificar a maneira pela qual os programas de montagem final (PMF) e as listas de materiais são preparados.

Do MRP I para o MRP II e para o ERP

Os sistemas de planejamento das necessidades de recursos estão em um estado de evolução contínua. Os primeiros sistemas eram muito simples e pouco sofisticados, e o valor da informação que era gerada para as operações era limitado. Em sua forma mais primitiva, o MRP simplesmente explodia o MPS nos materiais necessários.

Então, no final da década de 1970, Oliver Wight, George Plossl e outros começaram a conversar sobre como fechar o loop nos sistemas MRP. O termo **MRP de loop fechado** significa:

Um sistema construído em torno do planejamento das necessidades de materiais que inclui as funções adicionais de planejamento da produção (planejamento agregado), programa mestre de produção e planejamento das necessidades de capacidade. Assim que essa fase de planejamento é concluída e os planos são aceitos como realistas e realizáveis, as funções de execução entram em cena. As funções de execução incluem as funções de controle da manufatura, como a medição da entrada e saída (capacidade), programação e expedição detalhadas, além de relatórios de atrasos previstos tanto da fábrica como de fornecedores, programação do fornecedor etc. A expressão "loop fechado" implica que não somente esses elementos são incluídos no sistema global, mas que também há um retorno (feedback) das funções de execução a fim de que o planejamento possa se manter válido o tempo todo.

---

[3] Piloto automático, ou controle de cruzeiro (*cruise control*): sistema de controle automático que controla a velocidade fixa do automóvel.

Mais tarde, a necessidade de sistemas MRP mais sofisticados levou Wight, Plossl e outros a sugerirem uma mudança do MRP I para o planejamento dos recursos de manufatura (MRP II). A expressão **planejamento dos recursos de manufatura** significa:

> *Um método para o efetivo planejamento de todos os recursos de uma empresa manufatureira; ele encaminha o planejamento operacional em unidades, o planejamento financeiro em dólares, e tem uma capacidade de simulação para responder a perguntas do tipo "O que acontecerá se...?". Ele é composto de uma variedade de funções, ligadas umas às outras: planejamento dos negócios, planejamento de vendas e operações, planejamento da produção, programa mestre de produção, planejamento das necessidades de materiais, planejamento das necessidades de capacidade e sistemas de suporte à execução para capacidade e materiais. A saída desses sistemas é integrada com relatórios financeiros, como, por exemplo, o plano de negócios, relatório de compromisso de compra, orçamento de embarque, projeções de estoques em dólares etc. Planejamento dos Recursos de Manufatura é uma conseqüência natural e uma extensão do MRP de loop fechado.*

A evolução dos sistemas de planejamento das necessidades de recursos ainda está em curso. A novidade nessa evolução, o planejamento dos recursos empresariais (ERP), é ainda mais abrangente do que o MRP II. A expressão **planejamento dos recursos empresariais** significa:

> *Um sistema de informação orientado para a contabilidade para identificar e planejar os recursos empresariais necessários para aceitar, fazer, remeter e cuidar dos pedidos dos clientes. Um sistema ERP difere do sistema MRP II em termos de requisitos técnicos, como, por exemplo, interface do usuário, banco de dados relacional, uso de linguagem de quarta geração e ferramentas de engenharia auxiliada por computador no desenvolvimento, arquitetura cliente/servidor e portabilidade de sistema aberto.*

Os sistemas ERP consistem em muitos módulos de software que podem ser comprados separadamente para ajudar a administrar várias atividades diferentes em diversas áreas funcionais de um negócio. Por exemplo, o software R/3 da SAP, a maior vendedora do software ERP, oferece módulos para vendas e distribuição, contabilidade financeira, controle financeiro, administração de ativos fixos, recursos humanos, fluxo de trabalho, soluções industriais, administração de materiais, planejamento da produção (inclusive o MRP e CRP), administração da qualidade, manutenção de fábrica e sistemas de projeto. Os sistemas ERP exigem um grande compromisso e investimento, muitas vezes exigem que as empresas modifiquem alguns de seus processos para acomodar o software, e às vezes são necessários muitos anos para implementá-lo. Três dos sistemas de software ERP mais vendidos são o R/3 da SAP (**www.sap.com**), o Baan (**www.baan.com**) e o PeopleSoft (**www.peoplesoft.com**).

COMO O MRP SE ADAPTA A MUDANÇAS

Pode-se ter a impressão que assim que o sistema MRP entra em ação é difícil mudar o sistema. Pelo contrário, uma das pedras angulares do MRP é que ele deve ser um sistema dinâmico e que deve adaptar-se a mudanças. Por sua própria natureza, o MRP reflete as informações mais recentes em suas liberações de pedidos programados. Nos procedimentos de atualização do MPS, uma semana é adicionada ao fim do programa e uma semana é retirada do início, e todas as demandas semanais são novamente estimadas. Essa atualização do MPS tem como objetivo tornar o sistema MRP adaptável às mudanças na demanda por itens finais.

Uma vez que o MPS é atualizado semanalmente, os programas MRP também são atualizados semanalmente. Outro motivo para atualizar os programas MRP semanalmente é permitir que quaisquer mudanças nas entradas no MRP sejam refletidas nos programas. Uma vez que o arquivo situação do estoque e seus registros de materiais podem ter sido mudados desde a última atualização, os programas MRP captam essas mudanças. Por exemplo, digamos que tenhamos mudado os fornecedores de certo material e o lead time de compra para o material tenha se modificado. A atualização seguinte dos programas MRP refletirá essa mudança. Similarmente, se a engenharia mudasse o arquivo lista de materiais para efetuar mudanças de projeto de produto, depois da atualização seguinte os programas MRP refletiriam essas mudanças.

Uma das grandes melhorias dos sistemas MRP sobre os métodos de quantidade pedida e ponto de pedido tradicionais de planejamento das necessidades de materiais é sua natureza dinâmica. O MRP se adapta efetivamente a mudanças, e são fornecidas aos gerentes de operações informações baseadas nas condições atuais em vez de informações sobre quais eram as condições há várias semanas ou meses.

TABELA 10.7	CARACTERÍSTICAS DESEJÁVEIS DOS SISTEMAS DE PRODUÇÃO QUE SÃO ADEQUADAS AO MRP

1. Um sistema eficiente de computador.
2. Arquivos listas de materiais e situação do estoque acurados e computadorizados de todos os itens finais e materiais.
3. Um sistema discreto de produção que manufature produtos compostos de matérias-primas, peças, submontagens e montagens que sejam processadas através de muitas etapas de produção.
4. Processos de produção que exijam longos tempos de processamento.
5. Lead times relativamente confiáveis.
6. O programa mestre congelado durante um período de tempo suficiente para adquirir materiais sem excessiva pressa e confusão.
7. Apoio e compromisso da alta administração.

AVALIAÇÃO DO MRP

As vantagens reivindicadas para o MRP sobre as abordagens mais tradicionais do planejamento de estoques, como, por exemplo, lotes padrões e pontos de pedido, foram demonstradas aqui e em outros lugares na APO — melhorado serviço ao cliente, reduzidos níveis de estoque e melhorada eficiência operacional dos departamentos de produção. Isso parece tão bom que nos perguntamos: por que o mundo inteiro não foi envolvido pelo MRP? Há bons motivos para que isso não tenha acontecido.

A Tabela 10.7 relaciona as características de sistemas de produção que sustentam a implementação bem-sucedida do MRP. A presença de um sistema de computador eficiente é uma necessidade absoluta. Duas outras características que similarmente parecem quase automáticas são arquivos lista de materiais e situação do estoque acurados. A ausência desses arquivos e um sistema de computador ineficiente representam as maiores dores de cabeça para a implementação do MRP na prática. A correção de deficiências como essas pode consumir a maior parte do tempo de implementação.

O MRP é convencionalmente aplicado somente a sistemas de manufatura. Essas organizações processam produtos discretos para os quais listas de materiais são possíveis — um requisito do MRP. Isso significa que o MRP raramente é aplicado a sistemas de serviço, refinarias de petróleo, sistemas de venda a varejo, empresas de transporte e outros sistemas de não manufatura. Muitos acreditam que o MRP pode ser aplicado de maneira bem-sucedida a alguns desses sistemas de não manufatura. Quando sistemas de serviço exigem conjuntos de matérias-primas para entregar uma unidade de serviço (uma pseudolista de materiais), o MRP potencialmente pode ser aplicado.

O MRP proporciona os maiores benefícios a sistemas focalizados no processo que têm tempos de processamento longos e complexos passos de produção de múltiplas etapas porque o planejamento de estoques e da produção é mais complexo. Imagine um sistema de produção hipotético que converta matérias-primas em itens acabados simultaneamente, como acontece em alguns sistemas simples focalizados no produto. As matérias-primas seriam pedidas para se adaptar *exatamente* às necessidades de itens acabados. Na maioria dos sistemas focalizados no processo, entretanto, os lead times de processamento in-house podem ultrapassar os lead times necessários para se obter as matérias-primas dos fornecedores. A capacidade que o MRP tem para contrabalançar os recebimentos de pedidos programados com suas liberações, considerando lead times longos e etapas de processamento complexas, em muito simplifica o planejamento da produção e de estoques.

Para que o MRP seja eficiente, os lead times devem ser confiáveis. Além disso, o MRP deve permanecer *congelado* durante algum tempo antes que a produção real para o MPS se inicie, significando que aquilo que deve ser produzido, o MPS, deve ser conhecido com certeza, e o tempo e a quantidade de recebimentos de matérias-primas devem ser confiáveis. Quando os tamanhos de lote de matérias-primas são grandes e a variabilidade da demanda é pequena, os sistemas convencionais de tamanho de lote econômico e planejamento de estoque com ponto de pedido tendem a funcionar bem, porque suas suposições de demanda uniforme se aplicam. O MRP oferece, portanto, mais melhorias no planejamento de estoques quando o tamanho do lote é pequeno e a variabilidade da demanda é grande.

O MRP não foi e não será aplicado a todos os sistemas de produção. Em algumas aplicações APO, o MRP ou é desnecessário ou é economicamente injustificável. A freqüência de utilização do MRP, entretanto, encontra-se definitivamente numa drástica tendência de ascensão. À medida que ganhamos mais experiência com o MRP, percebemos que ele não é uma panacéia. Ele não resolve todos os nossos problemas de planejamento de estoques. Basicamente, o MRP é um sistema computadorizado de informação APO. Quando os sistemas de computador são ineficientes, os arquivos situação do estoque e lista de materiais são inexatos, os programas mestre de produção são pouco confiáveis, e quando o restante da organização é, de qualquer forma, mal administrado, o MRP — ou qualquer outra técnica — não é de muita ajuda. Ele gera maiores volumes de informações inexatas e não usadas do que aquilo que anteriormente se considerava possível. O MRP é mais bem aplicado quando os sistemas de produção são basicamente bem administrados e um sistema de planejamento da produção e de estoques mais abrangente se faz necessário.

A implementação de um sistema MRP não é um processo indolor. Uma vez que o MRP é um sistema de informação dependente de informação, simplesmente comprar software e talvez algum hardware não garante um sistema MRP bem-sucedido. Existem alguns custos iniciais significativos e alguns custos na implementação de um sistema MRP. Muitos desses custos estão associados com uma má correção ou informação inadequada, bem como com a instituição de uma disciplina de sistema para assegurar que a informação correta continue fluindo para o sistema MRP. Esses geralmente são custos ocultos que muitas vezes não são reconhecidos formalmente quando a proposta de um sistema MRP é apresentada.

Planejamento das Necessidades de Capacidade

O planejamento das necessidades de capacidade (CRP) é a parte do planejamento das necessidades de recursos que testa o programa mestre de produção (MPS) quanto à praticabilidade da capacidade. No processo de realização desse teste é desenvolvido um plano para a atribuição de pedidos a centros de trabalho, utilização de trabalho em horas extras, equipamento de reserva e subcontratação. A Figura 10.8 ilustra esse processo. O CRP pega as **liberações de pedidos programados** dos programas MRP e atribui os pedidos a centros de trabalho, consultando os roteiros de produção. Os **roteiros de produção** especificam a seqüência dos processos de produção que cada pedido exige. Em seguida, os lotes de materiais são transformados em necessidades de capacidade usando padrões de mão-de-obra e de máquina, e então programações das cargas semanais são preparadas para cada centro de trabalho que inclui todos os pedidos. Se suficiente capacidade estiver disponível em todos os centros de trabalho todas as semanas, então o MPS será confirmado. Se não, deve-se determinar se a capacidade pode ser economicamente mudada. Se trabalho em horas extras, subcontratação, máquinas de reserva ou outros meios puderem ser usados para aumentar a capacidade, então o MPS poderá ser confirmado. Se a capacidade não puder ser economicamente mudada, ou o roteiro ou a atribuição de pedidos a centros de trabalho deve ser mudado para melhorar a capacidade, ou o MPS deve ser mudado reprogramando-se os pedidos para se obter uma capacidade nivelada, e o processo é repetido.

O principal meio de testar a capacidade do MPS é através de programas de carga de centros de trabalho.

Programas de Carga

Um **programa de carga** é um dispositivo para comparar as horas de trabalho e as horas de máquina reais necessárias para produzir o MPS com as horas de trabalho e as horas de máquina disponíveis em cada semana. Os programas de carga geralmente são preparados numa hierarquia que parte de centros de trabalho no início do sistema de manufatura e percorre etapas sucessivas até o final do sistema de manufatura.

A Figura 10.9 demonstra que quando itens finais são incluídos no MPS, essa inclusão faz com que atividades sejam realizadas em etapas no sistema de produção. Os programas MRP determinam as liberações de pedidos programados, que é a base para a produção em todos os centros de trabalho. Iniciando pelo topo da figura na semana 5 no centro de trabalho Montagem Final, descobrimos que 600 unidades devem ser finalizadas na Montagem Final na semana 5. Uma semana antes, na semana 4, 600 unidades devem ser finalizadas no centro de trabalho Montar Estrutura. O lead time de uma semana é necessário para executar as operações no centro de trabalho Montar Estrutura e transportar as unidades para a Montagem Final.

Na semana 3, devem ser pedidas 1.800 peças n. 115 ao fornecedor. Não obstante o pedido de peças poder não exigir qualquer capacidade de produção, a atividade deve iniciar-se na semana 3, demonstrando

FIGURA 10.8 — O Processo de Planejamento das Necessidades de Capacidade

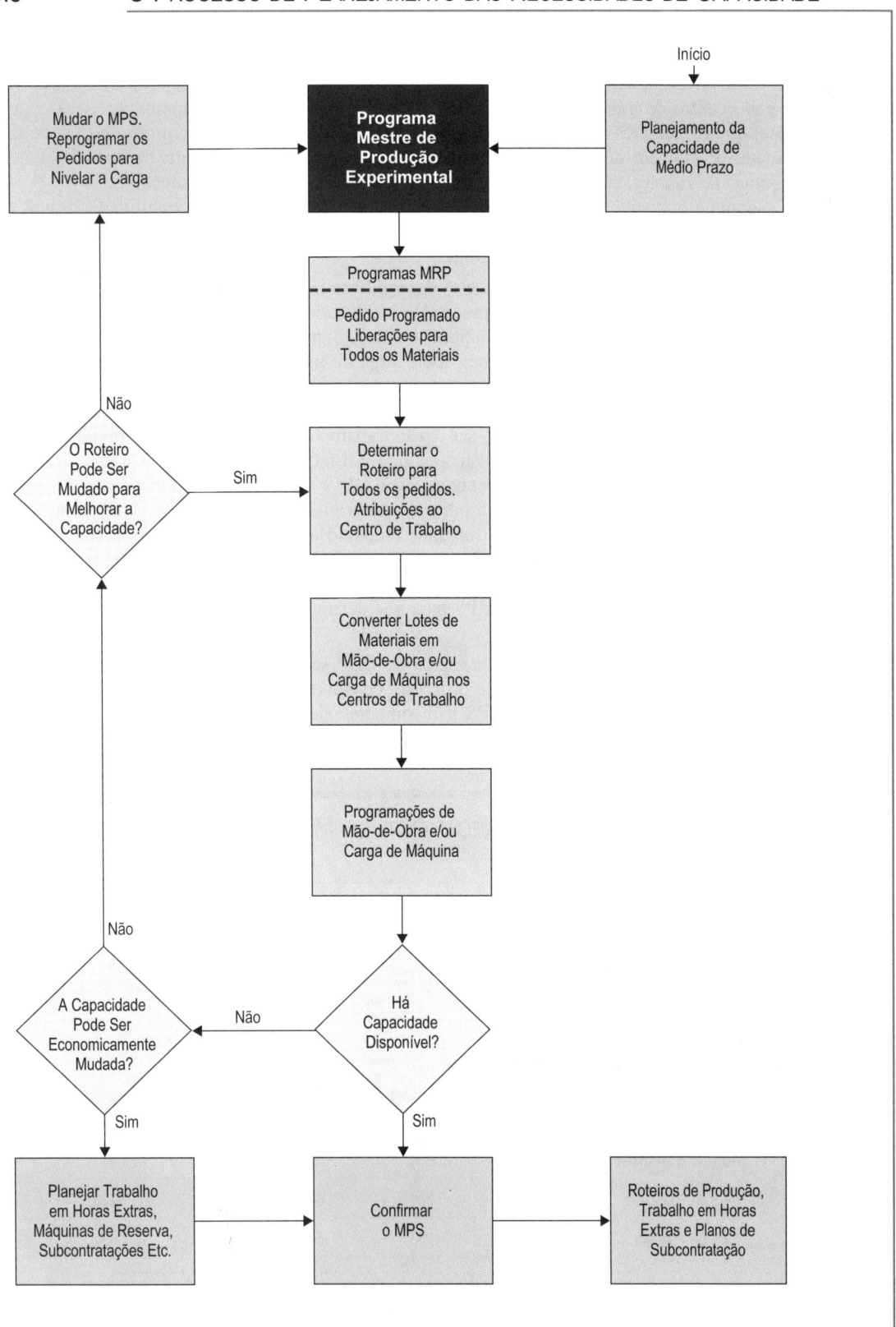

assim a necessidade de contrabalançarmos a atividade de emissão do pedido por um lead time de uma semana a partir de Montar Estrutura. A **compensação por lead times** entre sucessivas etapas do sistema de produção é fundamental para o planejamento das necessidades de recursos.

Observe na Figura 10.9 que podemos determinar o número real de horas de trabalho e horas de máquina que o MPS exigirá semanalmente em cada centro de trabalho para esse produto. Quando todos os itens finais do MPS estiverem incluídos, as horas de trabalho e as horas de máquina necessárias semanalmente em cada centro de trabalho poderão ser comparadas com o número disponível. Essas comparações permitem que os gerentes de operações determinem a viabilidade do MPS em cada centro de trabalho semanalmente e também dêem respostas a perguntas operacionais a respeito de trabalho em horas extras, máquinas de reserva, subcontratação e outras questões de sobrecarga e subcarga.

Suponha que você tenha um MPS experimental e deseje testar sua viabilidade através do CRP. Programas de carga como os ilustrados na Figura 10.10 podem ser usados para essa finalidade. A partir desses programas podemos determinar o seguinte:

1. A carga de horas de trabalho está desequilibrada no Departamento de Fabricação. Parece que algum trabalho de fabricação precisa ser deslocado das semanas 3, 4 e 8 para as semanas 5, 6 e 7. Uma revisão da carga de máquina no Departamento de Fabricação nessas semanas indica que esse deslocamento não provoca sobrecarga de máquina.
2. A mudança sugerida no Departamento de Fabricação acima não afetaria de maneira adversa a Montagem Final porque todas as unidades de Fabricação se movem para Montagem Final uma semana mais tarde, e poderia ser usado trabalho em horas extras para aliviar as horas de trabalho que causam sobrecarga nas semanas 6, 7 e 8 na Montagem Final. A carga de horas de máquina em todas as semanas na Montagem Final não é um fator limitador.
3. No nível da fábrica, a última parte do programa é sobrecarregada tanto em termos de horas de máquina como de horas de trabalho. Trabalho em horas extras poderia ser usado para aliviar a sobrecarga de horas de trabalho, e subcontratação ou a utilização de máquinas de reserva poderiam reduzir a sobrecarga de horas de máquina. Outra alternativa sempre está presente, entretanto, que é a de modificarmos o MPS para que desloque itens finais da última parte do programa para as semanas mais recentes.

Se o MPS for modificado, então a lógica do CRP seria aplicada novamente através de um conjunto revisado de programas de carga. Nesse processo, desenvolvemos um MPS experimental e depois o modificamos através do CRP até que o MPS não somente seja exeqüível, mas também os centros de trabalho sejam economicamente carregados. Isso promove eficiência operacional interna e baixos custos por unidade em todo o sistema de manufatura.

FIGURA 10.9 — EFEITOS DO CARREGAMENTO DO MPS SOBRE AS CAPACIDADES DO CENTRO DE TRABALHO

					Semanas				
	−2	−1	1	2	3	4	5	6	7	8
Montagem Final (unidades)			800		1.600		600		1.800	
Horas de Trabalho			400		800		300		900	
Horas de Máquina			240		480		180		540	
Montar Estrutura (unidades)		800		1.600		600		1.800		
Horas de Trabalho		320		640		240		720		
Horas de Máquina		280		560		210		630		
Pedir Peça n. 115 (peças)	2.400		4.800		1.800		5.400			

FIGURA 10.10   HIERARQUIA DA CAPACIDADE DE CARGA

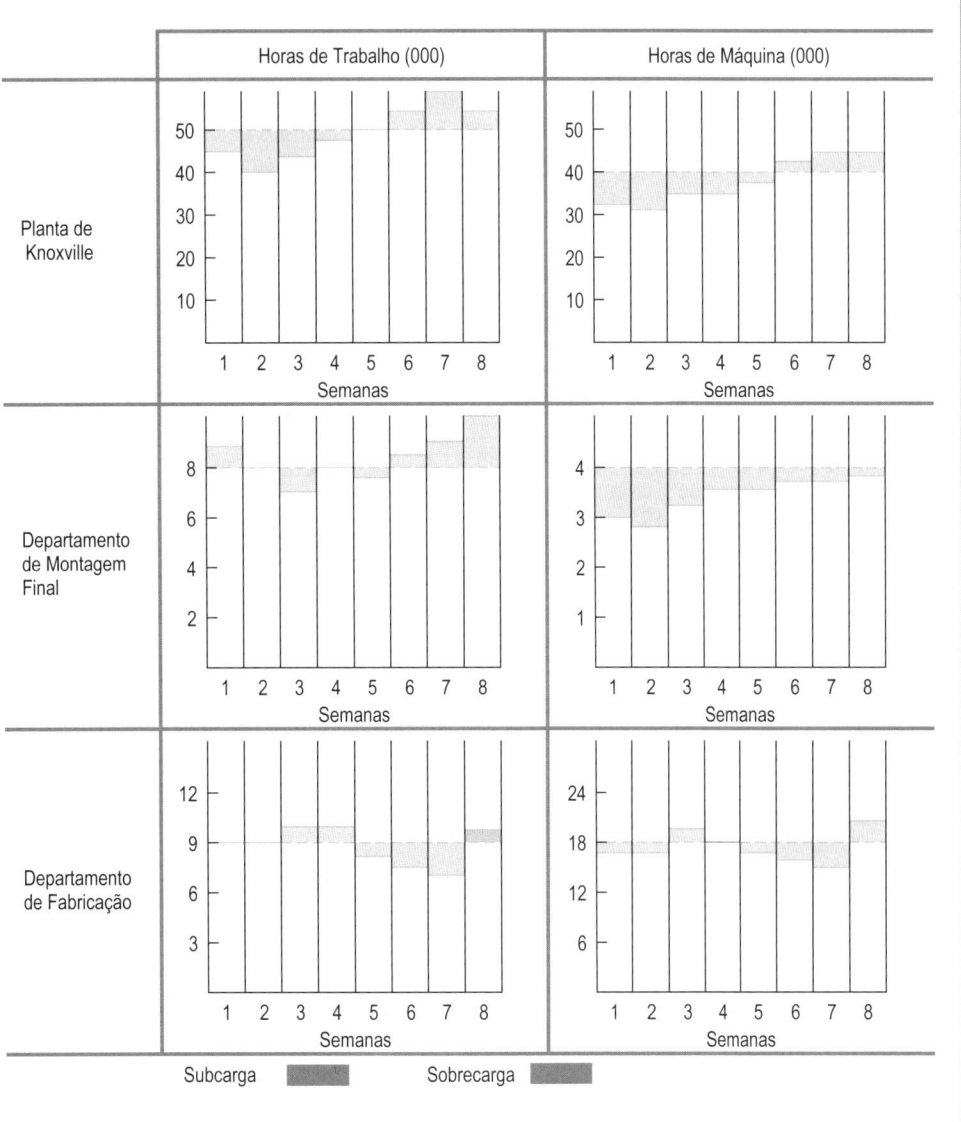

RESUMO FINAL

O QUE OS FABRICANTES DE CLASSE MUNDIAL ESTÃO FAZENDO

Os fabricantes de classe mundial há muito deixaram de usar sistemas de planejamento e controle da produção do tipo estoque de reserva para sistemas MRP e CRP. Provavelmente eles iniciaram como usuários Classe D do MRP: aqueles que usavam explosões de peças simples para pedir materiais. Então, quando esses fabricantes aprenderam, eles passaram a incorporar cada vez mais recursos de MRP até se tornarem usuários Classe A, aqueles que adotaram o planejamento dos recursos de manufatura (MRP II) ou o planejamento dos recursos empresariais (ERP). Para esses usuários, seus sistemas MRP são sistemas de informação completos e abrangentes. Esses sistemas de informação que envolvem a organização inteira fornecem planos de curto prazo que orientam as empresas rumo a maior produtividade, custos mais baixos e melhor serviço ao cliente.

Os fabricantes de classe mundial estão melhorando continuamente seus sistemas MRP. Eis alguns exemplos de recursos interessantes que estão sendo incluídos:

- Eles desenvolveram um sistema de fixação de lead times que reage a condições operacionais e econômicas. Se o backlog e o estoque em processo forem elevados, lead times mais longos são usados, e vice-versa. Além disso, se a economia estiver em alta e as lojas dos fornecedores estiverem cheias, lead times de entrega mais longos são usados, e o inverso também é verdadeiro.
- A Compaq Computer Corporation tem um sistema MRP muito eficiente que é convencional sob muitos aspectos. O sistema cobre 18 meses em intervalos de tempo de uma semana com um período de congelamento de 30 dias. O que diferencia o sistema da Compaq, entretanto, é que as atividades necessárias para desenvolver novos produtos são incluídas como níveis na árvore de estrutura de produtos para planejar quando lançar projetos de desenvolvimento para os novos produtos. As atividades são contrabalançadas por lead times a fim de que os gerentes saibam quando cada atividade deve iniciar e encerrar para que a necessária introdução dos novos produtos ocorra no programa. Essa abordagem seria útil em indústrias com ciclos de vida de produto muito breves e projetos de produto rapidamente mutáveis.
- Sofisticados algoritmos são usados para ajustar lead times para levar em consideração a carga em operações gargalo e o impacto que essas operações terão sobre os lead times dos produtos.
- Os relatórios gerados a partir de sistemas MRP são compartilhados com fornecedores e clientes para informá-los a respeito de quando materiais serão necessários e quando pedidos serão acabados e expedidos.
- Ao melhorar a comunicação com fornecedores e clientes e ter lead times que são adaptáveis às condições operacionais, há uma tendência geral rumo a lotes menores, e lead times mais curtos têm resultado em menos estoque em processo e produção mais rápida dos pedidos de clientes.

Melhorias como essas diferenciam os fabricantes de classe mundial de seus concorrentes, porque seus sistemas de planejamento e controle da produção são, em grande parte, responsáveis pela maior qualidade do produto, menores custos de produção e maior receptividade às necessidades dos clientes que têm permitido a essas empresas aumentar a fatia de mercado mesmo num ambiente de feroz competição internacional.

QUESTÕES DE REVISÃO E DISCUSSÃO

1. O que é planejamento das necessidades de recursos?
2. Identifique os principais elementos do planejamento das necessidades de recursos.
3. Descreva o papel do MPS, do MRP e do CRP no planejamento das necessidades de recursos.
4. Descreva as relações entre o MPS, o MRP e o CRP.
5. Descreva o processo do MRP.
6. Defina estes termos: *arquivo lista de materiais, arquivo situação do estoque, programa mestre de produção, programação de pedidos, mudanças nos pedidos programados, programas MRP, compensação por lead time.*
7. Quais são os objetivos do MRP? Explique como cada um desses objetivos é atingido.
8. O que é demanda instável? Cite três métodos de definição de tamanhos de lote que são usados quando a demanda é instável. Como um tamanho de lote mínimo funciona?
9. Explique como as necessidades líquidas de um material num intervalo de tempo são computadas.
10. Explique as diferenças entre sistemas MRP regenerativos e de mudança líquida. Quais são as vantagens e desvantagens de cada tipo de sistema MRP?
11. Explique estes termos: *MRP I, MRP de loop fechado, MRP II, ERP.*
12. Descreva o processo de CRP.
13. Cite as características dos sistemas de produção adequados ao MRP.
14. Resuma o que os fabricantes de classe mundial estão fazendo em seus sistemas MRP.

TAREFAS NA INTERNET

1. A PeopleSoft é uma das maiores produtoras de software de planejamento de recursos empresariais (ERP). Visite e explore seu site: **www.peoplesoft.com**. Descreva brevemente os módulos de software que fazem parte do software Enterprise Solutions ERP da PeopleSoft.
2. Use um índice de busca na Internet, como o Yahoo (**www.yahoo.com**), para encontrar uma empresa que produza o software MRP II para computadores pessoais. Descreva os recursos do software MRP II e inclua o site da empresa.
3. Visite uma livraria on-line para encontrar um livro recente sobre o software R/3 da SAP. Forneça a citação bibliográfica completa.
4. Procure na Internet por uma empresa de consultoria que ajude empresas a implementar o software MRP ou ERP. Descreva brevemente os serviços que ela oferece.

PROBLEMAS

Planejamento das Necessidades de Materiais (MRP)

1. Se o estoque inicial de um produto for 500 unidades, o estoque de segurança for 200 unidades e a demanda semanal estimada for 300, 400, 300, 800, 1.000 e 500 unidades durante um horizonte de planejamento de seis semanas, desenvolva um programa das necessidades líquidas para o produto.

2. O produto A é composto de uma montagem B, duas montagens C e uma montagem D. Cada montagem B é composta de duas peças E e três peças F. Cada montagem C é composta de uma submontagem G e três submontagens H. Cada montagem D é composta de duas peças I. Cada submontagem G é composta de uma peça E. Cada submontagem H é composta de duas peças F.
   a) Construa a árvore da estrutura do produto A.
   b) Prepare uma lista estruturada de materiais para o produto A.

3. Conclua o programa MRP para um componente:

Tamanho do Lote	Tempo (semanas)	À Mão	Estoque de Segurança	Alocado		Semanas				
						1	2	3	4	5
2.000+	1	2.000	1.000	1.000	Necessidades brutas			5.000		6.500
					Recebimentos programados	3.000				
					Disponível					
					Necessidades líquidas					
					Recebimentos de pedidos programados					
					Liberações de pedidos programados					

4. Um produto tem uma lista estruturada de materiais:

Nível				Quantidade
0	1	2	3	
500				1
	10			1
		11		2
		12		1
	20			1
		21		1
		22		2
	30			2

Este relatório sobre a situação do estoque foi publicado há pouco para o projeto:

Código do Item	À Mão	Estoque de Segurança	Alocado	Tamanho do Lote	Lead Time (semanas)
500	300	200	—	LFL	1
10	200	100	50	LFL	1
20	400	100	50	LFL	1
30	400	100	50	LFL	1
11	500	100	100	500+	1
12	400	100	100	500+	1
21	400	200	200	1.000+	1
22	400	200	200	1.000+	1

a) Prepare um programa MRP para todos os componentes do produto que cubra um horizonte de planejamento de cinco semanas se o MPS para o produto mostrar uma demanda estimada ou necessidade bruta de 500 unidades nas semanas 4 e 5.
b) O MPS é exeqüível a partir da perspectiva da oferta de materiais?

5. Um produto tem esta lista estruturada de materiais:

Nível				Quantidade
0	1	2	3	
3.650				1
	100			1
		110		1
		120		1
		130		1
	200			1
		210		1
			211	1
			212	1
		220		2
	300			1
		310		1

Este relatório sobre a situação do estoque foi publicado para o projeto:

Código do Item	À Mão	Estoque de Segurança	Alocado	Tamanho do Lote	Lead Time (semanas)	Recebimentos Programados Quantidade	Recebimentos Programados Semanas	Pedidos de Peças de Reposição Quantidade	Pedidos de Peças de Reposição Semanas
3.650	600	500	600	LFL	1	1.200	1		
100	1.000	600	100	LFL	1			300	3
200	1.600	600	400	LFL	1				
300	2.000	1.000	600	LFL	1				
110	1.500	200	800	LFL	1				
120	1.500	400	1.100	LFL	1				
130	1.200	400	400	LFL	1				
210	1.400	1.000	200	LFL	2				
220	1.200	500	200	LFL	2				
310	1.000	200	200	LFL	1				
211	1.000	500	200	LFL	1				
212	3.000	400	200	LFL	1				

a) Prepare um programa MRP para todos os componentes do produto que cubra um horizonte de planejamento de seis semanas se o MPS do produto mostrar uma demanda estimada ou necessidade bruta de 1.000 unidades nas semanas 4 e 5 e 1.500 unidades na semana 6.
b) O MPS é exeqüível a partir da perspectiva da oferta de materiais?
c) Se o MPS não for exeqüível, quais ações poderiam ser tomadas para torná-lo exeqüível?

6. No exemplo da Green Thumb Water Sprinkler Company apresentado neste capítulo, o MPS é mudado para 1.000 unidades na semana 4 e 2.000 unidades na semana 8, e para 2.500 unidades nas semanas 4, 5 e 7. Se todos os outros dados no caso permanecerem imutáveis:
   a) Prepare um programa MRP.
   b) O MPS é exeqüível a partir da perspectiva da oferta de materiais (componentes comprados ou produzidos)?
   c) Quais ações poderiam ser tomadas para permitir que a Green Thumb cumpra as exigências de oferta de materiais do MPS?

7. Você recebe este programa das necessidades líquidas:

Semana	1	2	3	4	5	6	7	8
Necessidades líquidas (unidades)	500	500	1.000	3.000	1.500	2.500	2.000	1.000

Se custar $ 6.000 para preparar o Departamento de Montagem Final para montar lotes desse produto, se custar $ 30 para manter uma unidade em estoque durante um ano e o Departamento de Montagem trabalhar 52 semanas por ano, desenvolva um programa de lotes de produção concluídos para o produto e calcule o custo de seu programa usando estes métodos:
   a) Lote por lote (LFL).
   b) Lote econômico de compra (LEC).
   c) Método do lote padrão (POQ).
Você pode desconsiderar o efeito do estoque inicial e do estoque de segurança sobre seus cálculos.

Planejamento das Necessidades de Capacidade (CRP)

8. A Ever-Pure Water Company situa-se sobre uma fonte de água mineral em Blackwater, Arkansas. A empresa engarrafa a água para ser expedida aos clientes através de uma rede de distribuidores. A administração da Ever-Pure desenvolveu este programa mestre de produção para as próximas seis semanas:

	Semana					
	1	2	3	4	5	6
Água (galões)	100.000	150.000	200.000	150.000	150.000	100.000

As horas de trabalho e as horas de máquina da Ever-Pure disponíveis e seus padrões de produção são os seguintes:

	Mão-de-Obra	Máquina
Capacidade mensal disponível (horas)	17.333	25.000
Padrão de produção (horas/galão)	0,10	0,15

   a) Determine a utilização percentual (horas padrões × 100 ÷ horas de capacidade) da capacidade de mão-de-obra e máquina em cada semana.
   b) Quais sugestões você apresentaria à administração da Ever-Pure referente a seu MPS?

9. A Silver Streak Iron Works produz três diferentes modelos de válvulas de poço para a indústria petrolífera. Cada válvula deve ser processada através de três departamentos de produção: Fundição, Fabricação e Montagem. Aproximadamente uma semana é necessário para que uma válvula seja completamente processada através de cada departamento. A Silver Streak agora está no processo de planejamento das necessidades de capacidade (CRP) e desenvolveu há pouco este MPS:

	Semana							
Modelo	1	2	3	4	5	6	7	8
X-100	300	500	500	600	700	500	200	300
Y-101	500	300	400	200	300	500	300	400
Z-102	600	500	700	700	800	600	800	600

As capacidades semanais de mão-de-obra e de máquina para os departamentos de produção são:

	Fundição		Fabricação		Montagem	
Modelo	Padrão de Mão-de-Obra (horas/unidade)	Padrão de Máquina (horas/unidade)	Padrão de Mão-de-Obra (horas/unidade)	Padrão de Máquina (horas/unidade)	Padrão de Mão-de-Obra (horas/unidade)	Padrão de Máquina (horas/unidade)
X-100	2,0	3,0	1,5	2,0	1,5	1,0
Y-101	2,5	3,5	2,0	2,5	1,5	1,5
Z-102	3,0	3,5	1,5	2,5	2,0	1,5

a) Desenvolva programas de carga de trabalho e de máquina para cada departamento e para a fábrica durante as seis primeiras semanas do MPS (lembre-se de contrabalançar os lead times entre os departamentos).

b) Interprete o significado de seu programa de carga: o MPS é exeqüível? Os departamentos de produção são eficientemente carregados? Você pode apresentar sugestões para mudar o MPS para mudar a carga?

Estudos de Caso

Integrated Products Corporation

A Integrated Products Corporation (IPC) produz placas gráficas e modems internos para computadores pessoais e de pequenos negócios. Cada um desses produtos deve ser processado através de dois departamentos de produção: primeiramente, através da Fabricação de Componentes; depois, através da Montagem. Aproximadamente uma semana é necessário para processar uma placa gráfica ou modem através de cada um dos dois departamentos de manufatura. Eis o programa mestre de produção (MPS) de seis semanas para os produtos:

	Semana					
	1	2	3	4	5	6
Placa gráfica	500	600	700	900	1.000	800
Modem	290	900	810	600	600	600

As capacidades de mão-de-obra e de máquina para os departamentos de produção são:

Departamento	Capacidade de Horas de Trabalho (horas de trabalho por semana)	Capacidade de Horas de Máquina (horas de de trabalho por semana)
Fabricação	16.000	9.000
Montagem	10.000	3.000

Os padrões de trabalho e de máquina para cada um dos produtos no departamento de manufatura são:

	Fabricação		Montagem	
Produto	Padrão de Trabalho (horas/unidade)	Padrão de Máquina (horas/unidade)	Padrão de Trabalho (horas/unidade)	Padrão de Máquina (horas/unidade)
Placa gráfica	9,0	5,0	8,0	2,0
Modem	8,0	6,0	6,0	2,0

A política de pessoal da fábrica não permite transferências de pessoal entre departamentos, e o tempo de trabalho em horas extras não pode ultrapassar 10% das horas de trabalho em tempo contínuo.

Tarefas

1. Desenvolva programas de carga de trabalho e de máquina para cada departamento para as cinco primeiras semanas do programa mestre de produção (lembre-se de contrabalançar os lead times entre os departamentos).

Capítulo 10 – Sistemas de Planejamento das Necessidades de Recursos

2. Interprete o significado de seu programa de carga: o MPS é exeqüível? Você pode apresentar sugestões para mudar o MPS para melhorar a carga?
3. Avalie sua proposta no Problema 2.

BLANCO FOODS: PLANEJAMENTO DAS NECESSIDADES DE MATERIAIS NA INDÚSTRIA DE PROCESSAMENTO

A Blanco Foods manufatura produtos alimentícios. Dentre seus muitos produtos há um pão de fôrma muito popular, o Bright & Early, usado para fazer torradas no café da manhã. A empresa usa um horizonte de planejamento de seis semanas em seus planos de marketing e de produção e agora está no processo de desenvolver um plano das necessidades de materiais. Seu departamento de planejamento da produção reuniu há pouco estas informações para serem usadas nesses planos:

1. As demandas semanais estimadas ou necessidades brutas para o produto Bright & Early são 1.200, 1.500, 900, 1.800, 2.000 e 1.500.
2. A lista de materiais para o produto Bright & Early é:

Código do Material Pai	Código do Componente	Código do Nível	Descrição	Quantidade de Componente por Unidade do Material Pai
	B&E	0	Pão de forma para torradas do café da manhã	
B&E	A	1	Mistura para batedeira	1,0 libra
B&E	B	1	Cobertura de açúcar cristalizado	0,1 libra
B&E	C	1	Uvas secas	0,2 libra
A	D	2	Farinha	0,6 libra
A	E	2	Fermento, sal, açúcar	0,15 libra
A	F	2	Leite e ovos	0,35 libra

3. A capacidade de produção atual é adequada para produzir o produto Bright & Early.
4. Os lead times de compra para produtos comprados são: B = 1 semana, C = 1 semana, D = 2 semanas, E = 2 semanas e F = 2 semanas. D, E e F podem ser abreviados para 1 semana com agilização e custos de frete adicionais.
5. O relatório sobre a situação de estoque para o produto Bright & Early é:

Código do Item	À Mão	Estoque de Segurança	Alocado	Tamanho do Lote	Recebimentos Programados Quantidade	Recebimentos Programados Semana
B&E	500	250		LFL		
A	1.600#		1.500#	LFL		
B	1.050#		1.000#	LFL	1.500#	1
C	1.200#		2.000#	LFL	1.000#	1
D	1.900#	1.000#	2.000#	2.000#+	2.000#	1
E	1.500#	1.000#	1.000#	1.000#+	1.000#	1
F	1.800#	1.000#	1.000#	1.000#+	1.000#	1

Tarefas

1. Prepare um programa MRP para o produto Bright & Early. O plano é viável a partir da perspectiva de disponibilidade de materiais? Qual agilização, se for o caso, é necessária para permitir que a Blanco Foods atenda as necessidades de materiais do MPS?
2. Resuma seu plano das necessidades de materiais para o produto Bright & Early e esboce quaisquer medidas extraordinárias necessárias para tornar o plano exeqüível.

capítulo 11

Planejamento e Controle do Chão de Fábrica na Manufatura

Introdução

Programando a Manufatura Focalizada no Processo
Planejamento e Controle do Chão de Fábrica
   Controle de Entrada e Saída • Gráficos de Gantt • Carga Finita e Infinita • Programação Progressiva e Regressiva
Problemas de Seqüenciamento de Pedidos
   Regras de Seqüenciamento • Critérios para Avaliar Regras de Seqüenciamento • Uma Comparação das Regras de Seqüenciamento • Controlando os Custos de Preparação • Minimizando o Tempo Total de Produção
Problemas de Designação

Programando a Manufatura Focalizada no Produto
Programação em Lote
   LEC para Lotes de Produção • Método do Esgotamento (run-out)
Programas de Entrega: Método da Linha de Balanceamento

Sistemas Computadorizados de Programação

Resumo Final: O Que os Fabricantes de Classe Mundial Estão Fazendo

Questões de Revisão e Discussão

Tarefas na Internet

Problemas

Estudo de Caso
Integrated Products Corporation

DECISÕES REFERENTES À PROGRAMAÇÃO DA PRODUÇÃO NA MICRO-SCANNERS CORPORATION

Era segunda-feira de manhã, cinco minutos depois do início do turno do dia na Micro-Scanners Corporation, e Lisa Johnson examinava os pedidos que esperavam para ser trabalhados em sua máquina. Ela e seu supervisor estudavam os seis pedidos à espera, tentando decidir-se em qual seqüência Lisa deveria produzir os pedidos. Primeiro, eles examinaram as programações de pedidos no programa MRP mais recente. Um pedido havia chegado cedo e não estava programado para ser liberado (iniciado) para o centro de trabalho até a próxima semana — esse pedido foi colocado no fim da fila. Outro pedido estava atrasado, porque estava programado para ter sido liberado para o centro de trabalho na semana passada — esse pedido foi colocado na frente da fila. Agora Lisa e seu supervisor tinham de decidir em qual seqüência produzir os quatro pedidos restantes. O supervisor sabia que coisas como custos de produção, utilização da capacidade e promessas de entrega a clientes poderiam ser afetadas pelas decisões que eles tomassem. Embora os quatro pedidos pudessem ser produzidos baseando-se na regra "primeiro a entrar, primeiro a ser atendido", Lisa preferia trabalhar nos pedidos que poderiam ser finalizados mais rápido, porque então mais pedidos poderiam ser finalizados por turno, e isso poderia fazer com que ela se destacasse. O supervisor acreditava que os pedidos com datas de entrega prometidas mais urgentes e a maioria do trabalho restante deveriam ser produzidos primeiro. Eles voltaram-se para a página 5 do relatório MRP para localizar as razões críticas para os quatro pedidos: 0,95, 1,05, 1,25 e 1,30. O supervisor explicou para Lisa que essas razões foram computadas dividindo-se o tempo restante para a data de entrega pelo tempo restante de produção; portanto, aqueles pedidos com baixas razões críticas deveriam ser produzidos primeiro. Lisa agora tem suas instruções e a seqüência na qual produzir os pedidos. O supervisor ponderou quais efeitos sua decisão teria sobre o custo de produção e a utilização da capacidade.

Na Parte III estudamos até agora o planejamento agregado, o programa mestre de produção (MPS), os sistemas de estoque com demanda independente e o planejamento das necessidades de materiais (MRP). Esses elementos do planejamento da produção fornecem informações sobre quais produtos e componentes devem ser produzidos em cada semana do horizonte de planejamento. Mas as questões fundamentais e diárias referentes ao chão de fábrica descritas no relato acima ainda precisam ser resolvidas.

Neste capítulo consideraremos questões referentes ao chão de fábrica, discutindo a manufatura focalizada no processo e a manufatura focalizada no produto.

PROGRAMANDO A MANUFATURA FOCALIZADA NO PROCESSO

As fábricas focalizadas no processo muitas vezes são chamadas job shops. Uma **job shop** é uma organização na qual os centros de trabalho ou departamentos são organizados em torno de tipos de funções ou similares ou especialidades departamentais, como, por exemplo, forja, usinagem, torneamento, tratamento térmico, perfuração e montagem. As tarefas geralmente são processadas em lotes, sendo que o tamanho do lote se baseia ou no tamanho do pedido do cliente ou em alguma quantidade econômica. Cada tarefa ou pedido segue um roteiro distinto através de vários centros de trabalho, e tipicamente existem muitas escolhas de roteiros numa job shop devido a uma variedade de tarefas processadas.

As job shops comumente usam sistemas empurrar de planejamento e controle da produção, e o MRP é uma parte fundamental desses sistemas. A Figura 11.1 ilustra que as decisões quanto à programação e chão de fábrica em operações ou job shops focalizadas no processo iniciam-se com o relatório da programação de pedidos de um sistema MRP. Um pedido é definido como a quantidade de uma única peça. Uma vez que uma peça recebe uma diferente numeração quando passa por sucessivas etapas de produção, um pedido correspondente a uma única peça pode ser vinculado a centros de trabalho específicos dentro da fábrica. A partir do relatório da programação de pedidos do sistema MRP, pode-se determinar quando pedidos de cada numeração de peça devem ser liberados (a produção é autorizada), e a partir do sistema CRP pode-se determinar para qual centro de trabalho o pedido deve ir. De posse dessas informações, os gerentes de operações podem tomar as decisões diárias quanto à programação e chão de fábrica, as quais

FIGURA 11.1   DECISÕES QUANTO À PROGRAMAÇÃO DE CHÃO DE FÁBRICA EM OPERAÇÕES FOCALIZADAS NO PROCESSO

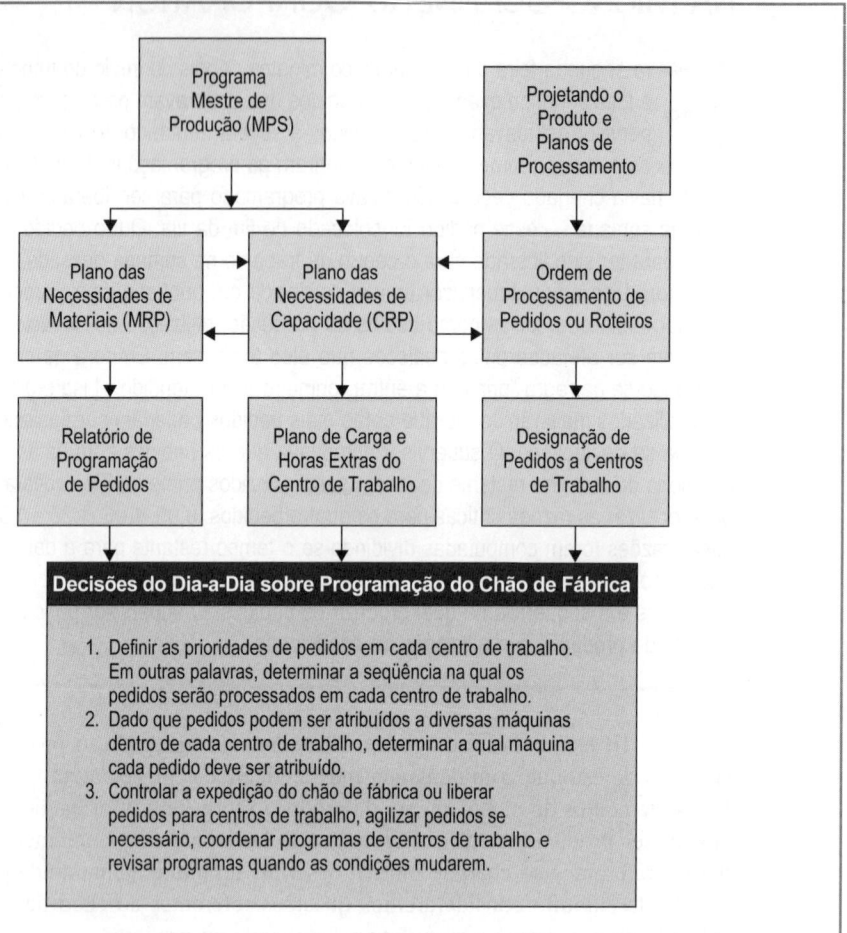

incluem decidir em qual seqüência os pedidos devem ser produzidos nos centros de trabalho, designar pedidos a máquinas dentro dos centros de trabalho e tomar decisões quanto ao controle do chão de fábrica.

A Tabela 11.1 descreve algumas das características da manufatura focalizada no processo e suas implicações quanto à programação. Uma coisa deve ficar clara a partir do estudo dessa tabela: essas características tornam as job shops complexas para programas. Uma vez que as job shops comumente produzem pedidos para clientes aos quais foram feitas promessas de entrega, os clientes são diretamente afetados pela produção. Além disso, desde que os lotes de produção nas job shops tendem a ser pequenos, numerosas preparações de máquina são necessárias. A relação de centros de trabalho para a qual um pedido é atribuído determina o roteiro para o pedido, e o número de possibilidades pode ser grande. *Trabalhadores e máquinas são tão flexíveis que são capazes de ser atribuídos e reatribuídos a muitos pedidos diferentes. Nesse ambiente flexível, variável e mutável, os programas devem ser específicos e detalhados em cada centro de trabalho para trazer ordem a uma situação potencialmente agitada.*

Se você tiver uma idéia a respeito de como os pedidos realmente se movem por uma shop shop será mais fácil entender como os programas do centro de trabalho se enquadram no esquema global da administração do chão de fábrica. Em job shops, os dois tipos seguintes de **planejamento de pré-produção** talvez tenham de ocorrer antes que a produção de um pedido possa ter início:

1. Projetar o produto de um pedido do cliente.
2. Planejar a relação de centros de trabalho através da qual o pedido deve passar antes de ser concluído; este é o **roteiro** de um pedido.

TABELA 11.1 — MANUFATURA FOCALIZADA NO PROCESSO: CARACTERÍSTICAS E SUAS IMPLICAÇÕES PARA A PROGRAMAÇÃO

Características	Implicações para a Programação
As operações similares são agrupadas com supervisão comum.	Numerosos programas individuais de centros de trabalho devem ser desenvolvidos e coordenados dentro dos departamentos de produção.
Os produtos são diversos e às vezes projetados de forma personalizada.	Muito planejamento de pré-produção é necessário para estabelecer roteiros, processamento e projetos de produto.
Os passos de processamento são desvinculados, e os pedidos podem seguir um grande número de caminhos através dos sistemas de produção.	Um sistema complexo de controle da produção deve planejar e controlar a movimentação dos pedidos através do sistema de produção.
Estoques em processo formam-se entre as etapas de processamento. Os trabalhadores possuem várias habilidades. As máquinas podem adaptar-se a uma variedade de produtos e operações.	Há uma grande flexibilidade para deslocar trabalhadores e máquinas de pedido a pedido.
As cargas de trabalho tipicamente não são balanceadas entre as etapas de processamento.	Uma sobrecarga extra é imposta aos programadores para que carreguem plenamente as instalações e minimizem o tempo ocioso e a subcarga.
Quando ocorrem quebras de equipamentos, a entrega de materiais se atrasa e outras interrupções ocorrem, as operações subseqüentes não são afetadas imediatamente.	Um número menor de concessões para tempo ocioso precisa ser incluído nos programas.
Numerosos pedidos podem acumular-se em cada etapa de processamento.	Deve ser estabelecido um sistema de prioridades que determine qual pedido deve ser programado primeiro em cada centro de trabalho.
Os produtos geralmente são do tipo produção sob encomenda.	Lead times longos são necessários para a manufatura e entrega de materiais. São usados programas de entrada de matérias-primas e programas de saída de produtos.

Os departamentos de controle da produção orientam então o movimento do pedido entre os centros de trabalho no roteiro. Os preparadores de materiais são notificados para mover o pedido para o centro de trabalho seguinte por meio de um **cartão de movimentação** (*move ticket*). O pedido pode ser acompanhado por meio de desenhos de engenharia, pelas especificações ou por instruções de trabalho a fim de que os trabalhadores de um centro de trabalho tenham as informações necessárias sobre como fazer seu trabalho. Um programa detalhado fornece informações ao supervisor de produção sobre qual pedido deve ser produzido primeiro em cada centro de trabalho ou quando cada pedido deve ser finalizado. Quando um pedido é concluído, o trabalhador notifica o departamento de planejamento e controle da produção, um cartão de movimentação é emitido para o centro de trabalho seguinte no roteiro do pedido, e os programas detalhados são atualizados. Torna-se claro, então, que os programas dos centros de trabalho são uma parte importante da administração do chão de fábrica.

Tendo essa descrição do ambiente de programação nas job shops como pano de fundo, discutiremos agora o planejamento e controle do chão de fábrica.

PLANEJAMENTO E CONTROLE DO CHÃO DE FÁBRICA

O controle do chão de fábrica inclui estas atividades:

1. Designar uma **prioridade** a cada pedido, uma medida da importância relativa de cada pedido. Isso ajuda a definir a seqüência de produção nos centros de trabalho.

2. Emitir **listas de remessa** para cada centro de trabalho. Essas listas permitem que os supervisores de produção saibam quais pedidos devem ser produzidos em um centro de trabalho, suas prioridades, e quando devem ser concluídos.
3. Manter o estoque de produtos em processo (WIP — work-in-process) atualizado. Isso inclui saber a localização de cada pedido e a quantidade de peças em cada pedido no sistema, rastrear a movimentação de pedidos entre centros de trabalho quando são usados cartões de movimentação, e saber o número de peças boas que sobrevivem em cada etapa de produção, a quantidade de sucata, a quantidade de retrabalho necessária e as unidades que faltam em cada pedido.
4. Fornecer controle de entrada e saída em todos os centros de trabalho. Isso significa desenvolver informações sobre como as tarefas estão fluindo entre os centros de trabalho.
5. Medir a eficiência, a utilização e a produtividade de trabalhadores e máquinas em cada centro de trabalho.

Os departamentos de planejamento e controle da produção executam essas atividades e relatam os resultados aos gerentes de operações a fim de que ações corretivas possam ser tomadas quando os pedidos se atrasarem ou quando ocorrem problemas de capacidade ou de carga de trabalho nos centros de trabalho.

Controle de Entrada e Saída   *O controle de entrada e saída é uma atividade fundamental que permite que os gerentes de operações identifiquem problemas como insuficiência de capacidade, capacidade excessiva e dificuldades de produção entre um grupo de estações de trabalho ligadas entre si.* O Exemplo 11.1 apresenta uma análise de um relatório de controle de entrada e saída. A partir desses relatórios, os gerentes de operações podem determinar se a quantidade de trabalho que flui para um centro de trabalho é a quantidade planejada e se a capacidade do centro de trabalho está em conformidade com o plano. Se demasiado trabalho estiver fluindo para um centro de trabalho em comparação com sua capacidade, então ocorrerá um excessivo estoque de produtos em processo precedendo o centro de trabalho. Quando tarefas se empilham nos centros de trabalho, não somente o centro de trabalho torna-se desordenado e abarrotado, como também os centros de trabalho subseqüentes podem tornar-se subalimentados de tarefas. Se, por outro lado, muito pouco trabalho estiver fluindo para um centro de trabalho em comparação com sua capacidade, ele será subutilizado, o que pode resultar em máquinas e trabalhadores parados.

Exemplo 11.1

Analisando Relatórios de Entrada e Saída

Relatório de Entrada e Saída no Final da Semana 5 para o Centro de Trabalho 240

	Semana					
	−1	1	2	3	4	5
Entrada planejada – horas de trabalho		300	300	300	300	300
Entrada real – horas de trabalho		250	220	260	180	150
Desvio cumulativo		−50	−130	−170	−290	−440
Saída planejada – horas de trabalho		300	300	300	300	300
Saída real – horas de trabalho		300	270	260	180	150
Desvio cumulativo		0	−30	−70	−190	−340
Estoque de produtos em processo final planejado – horas de trabalho		50	50	50	50	50
Estoque de produtos em processo final real – horas de trabalho	100	50	0	0	0	0

Mostramos acima um relatório de entrada e saída do Centro de Trabalho 240 no final da quinta semana. Todos os valores contidos no relatório estão em horas de trabalho. As tarefas que entram no centro de trabalho (entrada) foram transformadas para horas de trabalho, e as tarefas que saem do centro de trabalho (saída) também foram transformadas para horas de trabalho por meio do uso de padrões de trabalho. Essa transformação nos permite comparar diferentes tarefas usando uma medida comum que se relaciona diretamente com a capacidade.

Observe que a entrada planejada no centro de trabalho (tarefas que chegam ao centro de trabalho) é de 300 horas de trabalho em cada cinco semanas passadas, ou seja, é igual à saída planejada (tarefas que saem dos centros de trabalho). A saída real do centro de trabalho é bem menor do que a planejada, o que comumente poderia indicar que problemas de produção fizeram com que a capacidade do centro de trabalho fosse insuficiente. Uma olhada mais de perto na parte de entrada do relatório, entretanto, conta uma história diferente. Um número insuficiente de tarefas está saindo dos centros de trabalho antecedentes para manter o centro de trabalho plenamente utilizado. O estoque de produtos em processo no centro de trabalho era de 100 horas de trabalho no final da semana –1 ou no início da semana 1, mas isso se esvaziou no final da segunda semana para compensar a entrada insuficiente no centro de trabalho.

A causa dos problemas de produção nos centros de trabalho antecedentes deve ser encontrada e corrigida a fim de que um aumentado fluxo de tarefas possa entrar no Centro de Trabalho 240 para balancear sua capacidade.

A coordenação de programas de centros de trabalho auxilia na manutenção do fluxo de tarefas entre os centros de trabalho, e os gráficos de Gantt são úteis para esse propósito.

Gráficos de Gantt Os **gráficos de Gantt** podem ser usados para exibir visualmente as cargas de trabalho em cada centro de trabalho num departamento. A Figura 11.2 é um exemplo de gráfico de Gantt usado para comparar o programa semanal de cinco centros de trabalho numa oficina (*shop*) modelo (uma oficina usada para produzir produtos experimentais). As tarefas programadas para serem trabalhadas durante a semana são exibidas com seus nomes ou números de código (A, B, C etc.) e tempos de início e de encerramento, representados por uma barra aberta. À medida que o trabalho progride numa tarefa, uma barra sólida mostra como o centro está se comportando em relação ao programa. O tempo da revisão é indicado por uma seta vertical.

Preparações de máquina, manutenção de máquina e outros trabalhos planejados de não-produção são indicados por um X. Espaços em branco indicam tempo ocioso no centro de trabalho; equipes de trabalho não são necessárias durante esses períodos e podem ser deslocadas para outros centros de trabalho, ou outras tarefas podem ser programadas nesses espaços de tempo posteriormente. Os supervisores e planejadores da produção podem ver rapidamente no gráfico de Gantt o progresso dos centros de trabalho rumo a suas programações. Por exemplo, a Figura 11.2 mostra que a revisão é feita no meio da tarde de quarta-feira. Nessa hora, o centro de trabalho de usinagem está adiantado no programa cerca de meio dia na tarefa E, porque sua barra sombreada se estende para a direita da seta vertical, o centro de trabalho está adiantado no programa cerca de três horas na tarefa B, os centros de trabalho de teste e montagem estão dentro do programa, e o centro de trabalho de fabricação está cerca de duas horas atrasado no programa na tarefa D. *Os gráficos de Gantt são encontrados na maioria das fábricas e operações de serviço, e são muito úteis para coordenar uma diversidade de programas de equipes de trabalho, centros de trabalho e atividades de projetos.*

Carga Finita e Infinita Duas abordagens a respeito de como tarefas são atribuídas a centros de trabalho às vezes são usadas — carga finita e infinita.

A abordagem da **carga infinita** é usada quando tarefas são atribuídas a centros de trabalho sem considerar as capacidades desses centros. Essa abordagem abandona o planejamento das necessidades de capacidade (CRP) e seus programas de carregamento. A menos que a empresa tenha excessiva capacidade de produção, inaceitáveis filas de tarefas à espera ocorrem nos centros de trabalho.

A abordagem da **carga finita** é usada quando as capacidades de centros de trabalho são alocadas dentre uma lista de tarefas. Usando-se um modelo de simulação computadorizado ou outros meios, a ca-

FIGURA 11.2   GRÁFICO DE GANTT PARA COORDENAR PROGRAMAS DE CENTROS DE TRABALHO

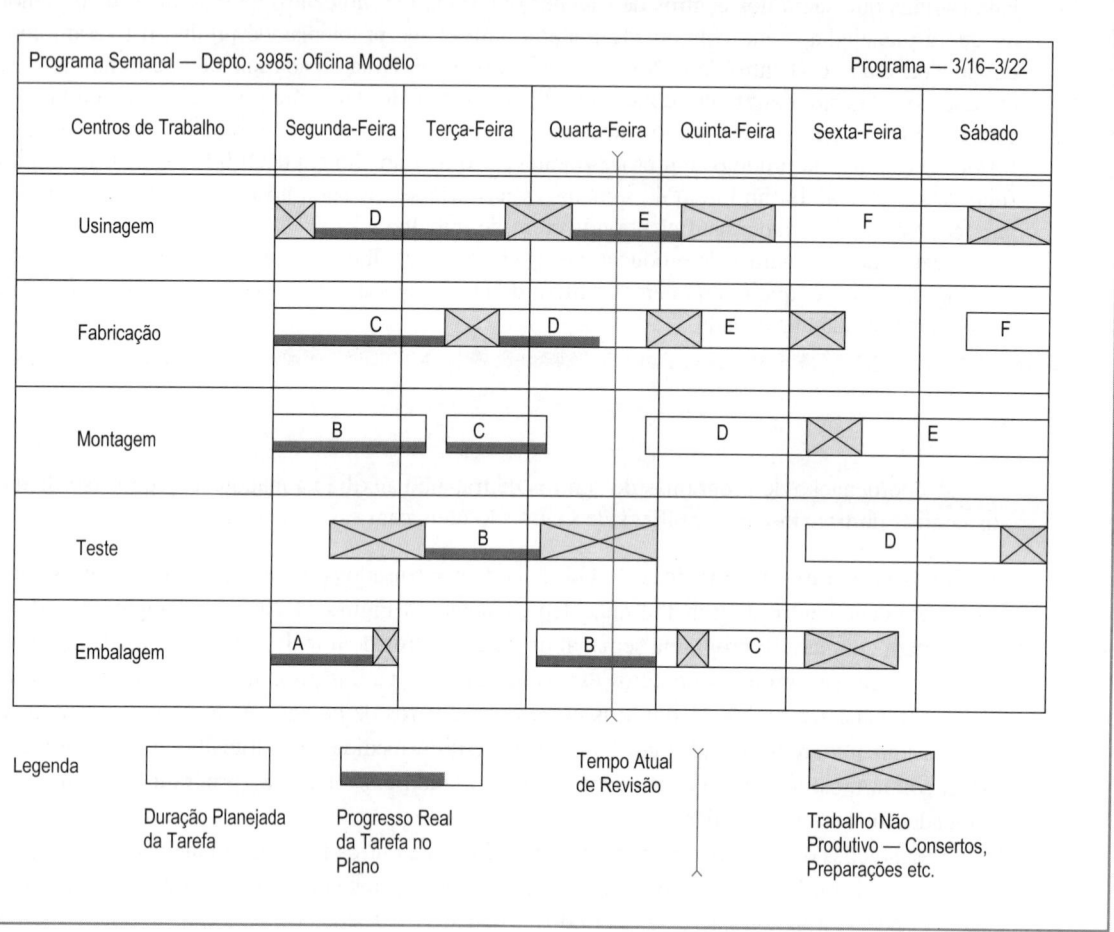

pacidade de cada centro de trabalho é alocada a tarefas de hora em hora, variando-se os tempos de início e de conclusão das tarefas. O resultado final dessa abordagem é que nenhum outro trabalho é programado para um centro de trabalho durante qualquer horário além da capacidade do centro de trabalho. Essa abordagem é parte integrante do CRP e é usada por muitas empresas atualmente.

Programação Progressiva e Regressiva   Ao preparar gráficos de Gantt como na Figura 11.2 ou programas de carga como na Figura 10.10 no Capítulo 10, há duas maneiras de determinar quais grades de programação (*time slots*) são atribuídas dentro dos centros de trabalho: programação progressiva e programação regressiva.

Na **programação progressiva**, as tarefas são atribuídas aos intervalos livres nos centros de trabalho no instante mais cedo possível. Essa abordagem supõe que os clientes queiram que suas tarefas sejam entregues o mais breve possível. Ainda que simples de usar, geralmente resulta em excessivos estoques em processo, porque as tarefas tendem a permanecer esperando suas novas atribuições a centros de trabalho.

No **planejamento regressivo**, o ponto de partida para o planejamento é uma data de entrega prometida ao cliente. Essa data é então tomada como um dado, e os programadores trabalham em sentido regressivo através da fábrica usando lead times para determinar quando as tarefas devem passar por cada etapa de produção. Tarefas são atribuídas às folgas na programação nos centros de trabalho o mais tarde possível para cumprir a data de entrega prometida. Não obstante essa abordagem exigir lead times acurados, ela tende a reduzir os estoques em processo, porque as tarefas não são concluídas até que sejam necessárias nos centros de trabalho seguintes em seus roteiros. Por esse motivo, a programação regressiva é a abordagem predominante nas empresas atualmente.

Os controles de entradas e saídas e os gráficos de Gantt fornecem aos gerentes de operações uma maneira sistemática de coordenarem o fluxo de tarefas entre centros de trabalho. Consideremos agora algumas maneiras de definir prioridades para tarefas em centros de trabalho.

PROBLEMAS DE SEQÜENCIAMENTO DE PEDIDOS

Nos problemas de seqüenciamento de pedidos queremos determinar a seqüência na qual produziremos um grupo de pedidos à espera num centro de trabalho. Analisamos esses problemas discutindo as várias regras de seqüenciamento, os critérios para avaliar essas regras, uma comparação dessas regras, o controle de custos de preparação e a minimização dos custos de produção.

Regras de Seqüenciamento Muitas regras podem ser seguidas para se definir as prioridades entre pedidos ou tarefas à espera nos centros de trabalho. Entre as mais comuns estão:

- **Primeiro a entrar, primeiro a ser atendido (PEPS)** — A tarefa seguinte a ser produzida é aquela que chegou primeiro entre as tarefas que estão à espera.
- **Menor tempo de processamento (MTP)** — A tarefa seguinte a ser produzida é aquela com o menor tempo de processamento entre as tarefas à espera.
- **Mais urgente data de vencimento (MUDV)** — A tarefa seguinte a ser produzida é aquela com a data de vencimento mais urgente (a data prometida ao cliente) entre as tarefas à espera.
- **Menor folga (MF)** — A tarefa seguinte a ser produzida é aquela com a menor folga (tempo até a data de vencimento menos tempo total de produção restante) entre as tarefas à espera.
- **Razão crítica (RC)** — A tarefa seguinte a ser produzida é aquela com a menor razão crítica (tempo até a data de vencimento dividido pelo tempo total de produção restante) entre as tarefas à espera.
- **Menor custo de preparação (MCP)** — Uma vez que as tarefas seguem logicamente umas às outras devido à facilidade de preparação, a seqüência das tarefas à espera é determinada analisando-se o custo total de realização de todas as preparações de máquina entre as tarefas.

Outras regras, como, por exemplo, o cliente mais valorizado, a tarefa mais lucrativa e a fila de espera mais curta na operação seguinte, também podem ser aplicadas.

Critérios para Avaliar Regras de Seqüenciamento Para se saber qual regra de seqüenciamento tem o melhor desempenho para um grupo de tarefas à espera, comumente são usados diversos critérios:

- **Tempo médio de fluxo** — A quantidade média de tempo que as tarefas gastam na oficina (*shop*).
- **Número médio de tarefas no sistema** — O número médio de tarefas na oficina.
- **Atraso médio de tarefa** — A quantidade média de tempo que a data de conclusão de uma tarefa ultrapassa sua data de entrega prometida.
- **Custo da preparação** — O custo total para fazer todas as preparações de máquina num grupo de tarefas.

Uma Comparação das Regras de Seqüenciamento Vamos demonstrar a utilização de regras de seqüenciamento e critérios de avaliação num sistema de produção de um centro de trabalho. O Exemplo 11.2 compara as regras de seqüenciamento do menor tempo de processamento e da razão crítica com a política do "primeiro a entrar, primeiro a ser atendido" atualmente em uso na empresa.

Exemplo 11.2

Avaliando Regras de Seqüenciamento

A Precision Machining realiza usinagem personalizada para seus clientes. A empresa usa atualmente a regra de seqüenciamento "primeiro a entrar, primeiro a ser atendido". Uma vez que a empresa quer finalizar as tarefas dos clientes mais rápido, ela está considerando duas outras regras: menor tempo de processamento e razão crítica. A empresa acha que estes critérios são importantes na escolha de uma regra de seqüenciamento: tempo médio de fluxo, número médio de tarefas no sistema e atraso médio de tarefa. Estude a situação da Precision e recomende uma regra de seqüenciamento.

Solução

Seis tarefas são recebidas na Precision, seus tempos de produção são estimados, e datas de entrega são prometidas aos clientes. Use as três regras para definir a seqüência das tarefas e avalie as regras de acordo com os três critérios.

1. Para a regra do "primeiro a entrar, primeiro a ser atendido", a seqüência para as tarefas é A, B, C, D, E e F — a seqüência na qual as tarefas foram recebidas na Precision. O tempo de produção e o tempo de entrega prometido são dados a seguir. O tempo de fluxo é computado somando-se o tempo de fluxo para a tarefa precedente e o tempo de produção para a tarefa atual. Se uma tarefa se atrasar, seu atraso será a diferença entre seu tempo de fluxo e seu tempo de entrega prometido

Primeiro a Entrar, Primeiro a Ser Atendido

(1) Seqüência da Tarefa	(2) Tempo de Produção (horas)	(3) Tempo de Entrega Prometido (horas)	(4) Tempo de Fluxo (horas)	(5) Atraso (horas) [(4) − (3)]
A	2	4	2	0
B	5	18	7	0
C	3	8	10	2
D	4	4	14	10
E	6	20	20	0
F	4	24	24	0

2. Para a regra do menor tempo de processamento, a seqüência é determinada pelos tempos de produção das tarefas: a tarefa a ser produzida em seguida é aquela com o menor tempo de processamento entre as tarefas à espera. O tempo de produção e o tempo de entrega prometido são dados a seguir. O tempo de fluxo e o atraso são computados no Passo 1.

O Menor Tempo de Processamento (MTP)

(1) Seqüência da Tarefa	(2) Tempo de Produção (horas)	(3) Tempo de Entrega Prometido (horas)	(4) Tempo de Fluxo (horas)	(5) Atraso (horas) [(4) − (3)]
A	2	4	2	0
C	3	8	5	0
D	4	4	9	5
F	4	24	13	0
B	5	18	18	0
E	6	20	24	4

3. Para a regra da razão crítica, a seqüência é determinada computando-se as razões críticas de todas as tarefas: a tarefa a ser produzida em seguida é aquela com a menor razão crítica (o tempo de entrega prometido dividido pelo tempo de produção) entre as tarefas à espera. O tempo de produção e o tempo de entrega prometido são dados a seguir. O tempo de fluxo e o atraso são computados conforme a descrição apresentada no Passo 1.

		Razão Crítica (RC)			
(1)	(2)	(3)	(4)	(5)	(6)
Seqüência da Tarefa	Tempo de Produção (horas)	Tempo de Entrega Prometido (horas)	Razão Crítica [(3)/(2)]	Tempo de Fluxo (horas)	Atraso (horas) [(5) − (3)]
D	4	4	1,00	4	0
A	2	4	2,00	6	2
C	3	8	2,67	9	1
E	6	20	3,33	15	0
B	5	18	3,60	20	2
F	4	24	6,00	24	0

Avalie as três regras usando estes critérios: tempo médio de fluxo, número médio de tarefas no sistema e atraso médio de tarefa.

1. O tempo médio de fluxo é computado somando-se os tempos de fluxo correspondentes às tarefas e dividindo-se pelo número de tarefas.

Regra de Seqüenciamento	Tempo Médio de Fluxo	Classificação
PEPS	(2 + 7 + 10 + 14 + 20 + 24)/6 = 12,83 horas	2
MTP	(2 + 5 + 9 + 13 + 18 + 24)/6 = 11,83 horas	1
RC	(4 + 6 + 9 + 15 + 20 + 24)/6 = 13,00 horas	3

2. O número médio de tarefas no sistema é computado tirando-se a média ponderada do número de tarefas existentes no sistema, em que os pesos são os tempos de produção para as tarefas. Por exemplo, o número médio de tarefas no sistema correspondente à regra do "primeiro a entrar, primeiro a ser atendido" é determinado por: 6 tarefas estão no sistema enquanto a tarefa A é produzida durante 2 horas, 5 tarefas estão no sistema enquanto a tarefa B é produzida durante 5 horas, 4 tarefas estão no sistema enquanto a tarefa C é produzida durante 3 horas, 3 tarefas estão no sistema enquanto a tarefa D é produzida durante 4 horas, 2 tarefas estão no sistema enquanto a tarefa E é produzida durante 6 horas, e 1 tarefa está no sistema enquanto a tarefa F é produzida durante 4 horas. A tarefa F é a última tarefa, e ela permanece no sistema durante um total de 24 horas.

Regra de Seqüenciamento	Número Médio de Tarefas no Sistema	Classificação
PEPS	[2(6) + 5(5) + 3(4) + 4(3) + 6(2) + 4(1)]/24 = 3,21 tarefas	2
MTP	[2(6) + 3(5) + 4(4) + 4(3) + 5(2) + 6(1)]/24 = 2,96 tarefas	1
RC	[4(6) + 2(5) + 3(4) + 6(3) + 5(2) + 4(1)]/24 = 3,25 tarefas	3

3. O atraso médio de tarefas é computado somando-se o atraso correspondente a todas as tarefas e dividindo-se pelo número de tarefas.

Regra de Seqüenciamento	Atraso Médio de Tarefas	Classificação
PEPS	(0 + 0 + 2 + 10 + 0 + 0)/6 = 2,00 horas	3
MTP	(0 + 0 + 0 + 5 + 4 + 0)/6 = 1,50 hora	2
RC	(2 + 2 + 1 + 0 + 0 + 0)/6 = 0,83 hora	1

A regra de seqüenciamento que deve ser escolhida neste exemplo depende do tipo de desempenho que é o mais importante para a Precision Machining. Se o cumprimento das datas de vencimento dos clientes for o mais importante, então a regra preferível seria a da razão crítica. Por outro, se a manutenção de baixos estoques de trabalho em processo for o mais importante, então o menor tempo de processamento seria a regra preferível.

No exemplo da Precision Machining, nenhuma regra de seqüenciamento em particular se classifica em primeiro lugar em todos os critérios de avaliação. Isso é o que encontramos nas aplicações do mundo real. Sabemos por experiência que:

1. **A regra do primeiro a entrar, primeiro a ser atendido não se comporta especialmente bem na maioria dos critérios de avaliação comumente usados.** Entretanto, ela dá aos clientes uma sensação de jogo limpo, e essa pode ser uma consideração importante para os clientes.

2. **O menor tempo de processamento não se comporta bem na maioria dos critérios de avaliação.** Ele é ótimo no tempo médio de fluxo e tende a comportar-se bem no número médio de tarefas no sistema. Mas pode não se comportar tão bem como razão crítica no atraso médio de tarefas. Uma deficiência da regra do menor tempo de processamento é que tarefas de longa duração são continuamente empurradas de volta no programa. A regra, portanto, deve ser deixada de lado periodicamente, a fim de que tarefas de longa duração possam ser movidas para a frente e trabalhadas.

3. **A razão crítica geralmente se comporta bem somente no critério de atraso médio da tarefa.** O índice médio é intrinsecamente atraente: queremos trabalhar primeiro nas tarefas com maior probabilidade de serem necessárias antes que possam ser finalizadas.

Os departamentos de programação geralmente analisam o desempenho de diferentes regras de seqüenciamento em grupos representativos de tarefas, como no exemplo da Precision Machining. Assim que eles escolhem a regra que tende a comportar-se melhor nos critérios mais importantes, está feita a parte de seus sistemas de programação e chão de fábrica, mas ela é revisada periodicamente.

Controlando os Custos de Preparação *Custos de preparação são os custos para mudar uma etapa num sistema de produção de uma tarefa para outra. Eles incluem custos como o de mudança de configurações de máquina, obtenção de instruções de trabalho e mudança de materiais e ferramentas. Geralmente, as tarefas devem ser produzidas numa seqüência que minimize o custo dessas preparações.* Por exemplo, quando duas tarefas usam quase as mesmas configurações de máquina, ferramentas e materiais, a mudança da primeira tarefa para a segunda é muito rápida e barata. O Exemplo 11.3 demonstra uma regra simples para determinar uma seqüência de trabalho que reduzirá o custo das preparações entre um grupo de tarefas à espera. O procedimento escolhe a primeira e a segunda tarefa na seqüência localizando o mais baixo custo de preparação dentre todas as preparações possíveis. Da segunda tarefa em diante, a tarefa seguinte é sempre determinada escolhendo-se o menor custo de preparação dentre as tarefas restantes. Essa regra pode não ser ótima, mas ela geralmente se comporta bem na prática.

EXEMPLO 11.3

CUSTOS DE PREPARAÇÃO E SEQÜÊNCIA DE TAREFA

A Sure Print Company faz trabalhos de impressão personalizados para empresas, políticos e escolas. A Sure Print está em meio ao *boom* de um ano eleitoral, e inúmeros cartazes de políticos estão esperando para ser processados na máquina de *offset*. Alicia Smith, que faz o planejamento de tarefas da Sure Print, está desenvolvendo atualmente um programa de impressão semanal para a máquina de offset. Ela desenvolveu esses custos de preparação para as seis tarefas à espera. Todas as tarefas portam igual prioridade; sendo assim, o fator decisivo para escolher uma seqüência de tarefas é o custo total de preparação para as seis tarefas.

Tarefas Que Precedem

		A	B	C	D	E	F
Tarefas Que Sucedem	A	—	$ 12	$ 15	$ 10	$ 35	$ 20
	B	$ 25	—	20	20	25	20
	C	27	15	—	12	20	15
	D	16	30	10	—	25	30
	E	35	20	25	30	—	30
	F	20	25	15	25	30	—

Alicia usa esta regra para desenvolver uma seqüência de tarefas de baixo custo: *Primeiro, escolha o menor custo de preparação dentre todas as preparações. A tarefa seguinte a ser escolhida terá o menor custo de preparação entre as tarefas restantes que sucedem à tarefa anteriormente escolhida.* Uma vez que há um elo com as tarefas iniciais (D-A e C-D), Alicia desenvolve duas seqüências:

1. A sucede D ($ 10 é o custo mínimo de preparação, D é o primeiro e A é o seguinte).
   F sucede A (leia-se coluna A; a tarefa F tem o menor custo de preparação entre as tarefas restantes).
   C sucede F (leia-se coluna F; a tarefa C tem o menor custo de preparação entre as tarefas restantes).
   B sucede C (leia-se coluna C; a tarefa B tem o menor custo de preparação entre as tarefas restantes).
   E sucede B (leia-se coluna B; a tarefa E tem o menor custo de preparação entre as tarefas restantes).
   A seqüência de tarefas é DAFCBE; seu custo total de preparação é 10 + 20 + 15 + 20 + 20 = $ 85.
2. Uma vez que há um elo entre as tarefas iniciais acima, a segunda seqüência de tarefas agora é desenvolvida: D sucede C, A sucede D, F sucede A, B sucede F, e E sucede B. A seqüência de tarefas é CDAFBE; seu custo de preparação é 10 + 10 + 20 + 20 + 20 = $ 80.

Das duas seqüências, CDAFBE é preferível, porque seu custo total de preparação é mais baixo.

Agora, Alicia sabe que este não é necessariamente o menor custo total de preparação possível para as seis tarefas. Em outras palavras, o método não garante uma solução ótima. Mas a regra simples é fácil de entender e apresenta resultados satisfatórios.

Outros procedimentos matematicamente mais sofisticados podem obter resultados ótimos. A **programação linear inteira** tem sido usada para minimizar os custos de preparação dentro de um conjunto de restrições que exigem que todas as tarefas sejam atribuídas à seqüência uma e somente uma vez.

Minimizando o Tempo Total de Produção Talvez queiramos determinar uma seqüência de tarefas que minimize o tempo total para produzir um grupo de tarefas. Esse objetivo comumente resultaria em baixos custos de produção e elevada utilização de trabalhador e máquina.

Seqüenciando n *Tarefas Através de Centros de Trabalho* Quando diversas tarefas precisam ser seqüenciadas através de dois centros de trabalho, freqüentemente queremos escolher uma seqüência de tarefas que valha para ambos os centros. Essa situação pode ser eficazmente analisada usando-se a regra de Johnson.

O Exemplo 11.4 demonstra o uso da regra de Johnson num sistema de produção de dois centros de trabalho — Precision Machining. As tarefas dos clientes devem passar pela usinagem (Centro de Trabalho 1) e acabamento (Centro de Trabalho 2) *na mesma seqüência de trabalho*. A seqüência de trabalho resultante tem o mínimo tempo total de produção através de ambos os centros de trabalho para todas as tarefas.

Exemplo 11.4

Seqüenciamento de Tarefas em Dois Centros de Trabalho com a Regra de Johnson

Há dois centros de trabalho na Precision Machining: usinagem e acabamento. A administração da Precision deseja adotar um procedimento que defina rotineiramente a seqüência na qual as tarefas passariam por ambos os centros de trabalho. Jane Bergland tem experimentado a regra de Johnson; ela acredita que a situação da Precision pode ser analisada de maneira eficiente com essa técnica. A administração da Precision quer que ambos os centros de trabalho façam a preparação para novas tarefas ao mesmo tempo. Em outras palavras, se o Centro de Trabalho 1 concluir seu trabalho numa tarefa, ele deve esperar até que o Centro de Trabalho 2 tenha concluído a tarefa na qual esteve trabalhando a fim de que ambos os centros de trabalho iniciem novas tarefas simultaneamente. A razão para essa exigência é que os supervisores poderão dar instruções de trabalho ao mesmo tempo a ambos os centros de trabalho a respeito de como fazerem as tarefas.

Jane visita o centro de computação, observando que seis tarefas estão à espera.

a) Estes dados foram desenvolvidos para as seis tarefas:

Trabalho de Computação	Tempo Estimado de Processamento (horas)	
	Centro de Trabalho 1 — Usinagem	Centro de Trabalho 2 — Acabamento
A	1,50	0,50
B	4,00	1,00
C	0,75	2,25
D	1,00	3,00
E	2,00	4,00
F	1,80	2,20

b) A regra de Johnson é:

1. Escolha o menor tempo de processamento em qualquer um dos centros de trabalho.
2. Se o menor tempo estiver no primeiro centro de trabalho, faça a primeira tarefa do programa. Se estiver no segundo centro de trabalho, faça a última tarefa do programa.
3. Elimine a tarefa atribuída no Passo 2.
4. Repita os Passos 1, 2 e 3, preenchendo o programa a partir do início e a partir do fim até que todas as tarefas tenham sido designadas a uma posição no programa.

Jane começa então a seguir os passos da regra:

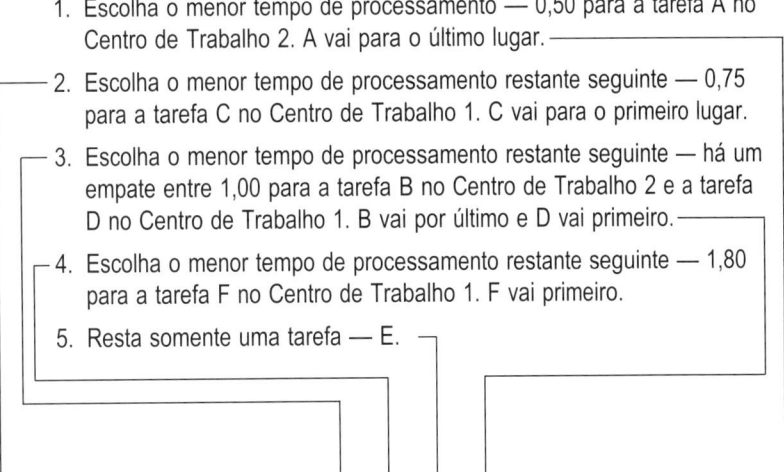

c) A seqüência de tarefas CDFEBA é estudada adicionalmente, desenvolvendo-se o tempo cumulativo para fazer todas as seis tarefas em ambos os centros de trabalho. Jane sabe que a administração da Precision quer que as tarefas iniciem ao mesmo tempo em ambos os centros de trabalho:

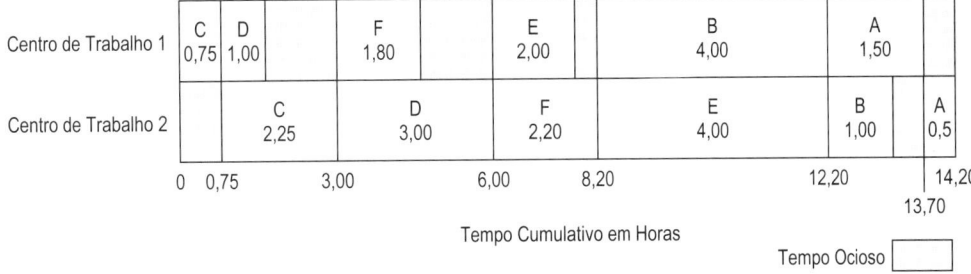

d) Jane pode ver que a seqüência de tarefas CDFEBA permite que ambos os centros de trabalho façam todas as tarefas em 14:20 horas. Ela pondera a respeito do quanto esse tempo cumulativo poderia ser reduzido se a administração da Precision afrouxasse a exigência segundo a qual as tarefas devem iniciar ao mesmo tempo em ambos os centros de trabalho.

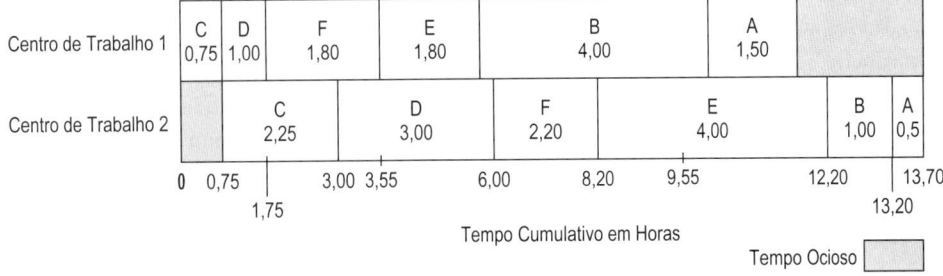

e) Quando as tarefas não precisam iniciar ao mesmo tempo em ambos os centros de trabalho, o tempo cumulativo é de 13:70 horas.

f) Jane usará este exemplo para demonstrar à administração da Precision a aplicação da regra de Johnson.

Observe no Exemplo 11.4 que, se ocorrer uma ligação com o menor tempo de processamento em diferentes centros de trabalho, não será encontrada nenhuma dificuldade para determinar a seqüência de tarefas. Se uma ligação precisar ocorrer dentro do mesmo centro de trabalho, entretanto, duas seqüências de trabalho terão de ser avaliadas comparando-se seus tempos cumulativos de produção, como na Parte c do exemplo. A seqüência de tarefas que tem o menor tempo cumulativo seria a recomendada. Observe também no exemplo que a regra de Johnson pode ser usada com ou sem a necessidade de que as preparações ocorram simultaneamente nos centros de trabalho.

Seqüenciamento de n tarefas através de m centros de trabalho As job shops geralmente precisam seqüenciar muitas tarefas através de muitos centros de trabalho, um problema para o qual não há soluções analíticas fáceis. Não obstante os gerentes de produção e programadores tomarem essas decisões de seqüenciamento diariamente, como eles trabalham para tomar essas decisões complexas? Geralmente, uma regra de seqüenciamento como o menor tempo de processamento, razão crítica ou data de vencimento mais breve é uniformemente aplicada. As seqüências de tarefas são modificadas para que se possa aproveitar as economias existentes nas preparações. Se algumas tarefas estiverem especialmente atrasadas, talvez se tenha de abrir mão das economias das preparações a fim de que se possa cumprir os compromissos de data de vencimento dos clientes.

Uma vez que as decisões de seqüenciamento são, cada vez mais, parte integrante de sistemas computadorizados de programação, os procedimentos de seqüenciamento devem ser formalizados e programados em computadores.

A pesquisa continua a explorar métodos matemáticos para obter soluções ótimas para esses problemas de seqüenciamento complexos. A teoria da fila, simulação por computador e algoritmos de busca computadorizados têm sido usados para estudar problemas de seqüenciamento.

PROBLEMAS DE DESIGNAÇÃO

Quando chegam às job shops muitas tarefas que precisam ser atribuídas a centros de trabalho ou a máquinas dentro de centros de trabalho, a determinação de quais tarefas devem ser atribuídas a quais centros de trabalho ou máquinas é uma parte importante da atividade de programação. Esses problemas comumente são chamados **problemas de designação**.

Isso conclui nossa discussão a respeito do planejamento e controle de chão de fábrica em job shops. Voltemo-nos agora ao estudo do planejamento de chão de fábrica em fábricas focalizadas no produto.

PROGRAMANDO A MANUFATURA FOCALIZADA NO PRODUTO

Há dois tipos gerais de produção focalizada no produto: em lote e contínua. A **produção em lote** muitas vezes é chamada **flow shop**, porque os produtos fluem ao longo de roteiros lineares diretos. Lotes grandes de diversos produtos padronizados são produzidos no mesmo sistema de produção. Uma vez que os produtos são produzidos em lotes, o sistema de produção deve ser modificado quando um produto diferente deve ser produzido. Muitos fabricantes de produtos discretos[1] utilizam esse tipo de produção. Na **produção contínua**, alguns produtos altamente padronizados são produzidos continuamente em volumes muito grandes, e são raras as preparações de máquinas. Os produtos podem ser discretos, como, por exemplo, produtos moldados em plástico, ou podem ser contínuos[2], como, por exemplo, gasolina.

A Tabela 11.2 relaciona algumas características da manufatura focalizada no produto e suas implicações para a programação.

---

[1] *Discrete-product:* produto discreto, no sentido de contável, enumerável. (N. do R.T.)
[2] *Continuous product:* produto contínuo, no sentido de não enumerável. (N. do R.T.)

TABELA 11.2 — MANUFATURA FOCALIZADA NO PRODUTO: CARACTERÍSTICAS E SUAS IMPLICAÇÕES PARA A PROGRAMAÇÃO

Características	Implicações para a Programação
Os produtos têm projeto padrão. As peças e matérias-primas, passos de processamento necessários e seqüência de operações são conhecidos	É necessário pouco planejamento, pré-produção referente ao roteiro de fabricação, instruções de tarefa, planos de processamento e projetos do produto.
Produtos podem ser produzidos para estoque em vez de serem produzidos sob encomenda do cliente.	Os programas podem basear-se em lotes econômicos de produção para produtos que não sofrem pressão de entrega aos clientes.
Os passos de produção são reunidos de acordo com layouts de produto.	A produção é programada de uma maneira muito semelhante a uma adutora (pipeline[3]), concentrando-se em programas de entrada de matérias-primas (MRP) e em programas de saída (MPS).
As taxas de produção são maiores do que as taxas de demanda para os produtos.	As principais preocupações referentes à programação são o momento (timing) de se fazer preparação da linha de produção e os tamanhos de lote de produção.
Uma vez que operações são reunidas, atrasos no suprimento de materiais, quebras de equipamentos, sucata e outros fatores que podem fazer com que uma operação se torne ociosa também farão com que as operações a jusante se interrompam.	Os programas de produção devem ter fatores de segurança incorporados para levar em conta certo tempo ocioso periodicamente, devem ter um programa de manutenção preventiva e, além disso, devem ter programas de controle da qualidade eficientes.
A natureza adutora da linha de produção resulta na fluição contínua de materiais, de operação em operação, até serem retirados no final da linha de produção.	O controle da produção pode não precisar manter registros complexos da movimentação de materiais em processo, autorizar movimento de materiais em em processo ou, de outra forma, planejar o momento (timing) de fazer movimentação de materiais em processo ao longo da linha de produção. As atividades fundamentais de planejamento e autorização de movimento de materiais estão voltadas para o suprimento de materiais à linha e a retirada de unidades acabadas da linha.

Estas são as decisões de programação mais comuns para essas fábricas:

1. Se os produtos forem produzidos em lotes e múltiplos produtos forem produzidos nas mesmas linhas de produção, quão grande deve ser o tamanho do lote de produção para cada produto e quando devem ser programadas preparações de máquinas?
2. Se produtos forem produzidos de acordo com um programa de entrega específico, em qual ponto do tempo quantos produtos devem ter passado em cada operação de produção a montante se entregas futuras precisarem estar no programa?

Desenvolveremos a seguir algumas técnicas para ajudar gerentes a resolver esses problemas relacionados à programação — programação em lote, e programar e controlar a produção para programas de entrega.

---

[3] *Pipeline:* (literalmente) encanamento; canal ou rota de processamento.

Programação em Lote

Em sistemas focalizados no produto que produzem em lotes, uma questão fundamental é o tamanho dos lotes. Duas abordagens a essa questão serão discutidas aqui: LEC para lotes de produção e o método do esgotamento (*run-out*).

LEC para Lotes de Produção No Capítulo 9 discutimos o conceito de lote econômico de compra (LEC) para lotes de produção. Imagine-se num departamento de produção olhando para o armazém de produtos acabados. Quantas unidades de um produto você deve incluir em cada lote de produção de um produto para minimizar os custos de manutenção em estoque e os custos anuais de pedido (inclusive custos de preparação de máquinas na produção)? O problema do tamanho de lote econômico de fabricação é resolvido usando-se a seguinte fórmula:

$$LEC = \sqrt{(2DS/C)[p/(p-d)]}$$

A Tabela 9.3 no Capítulo 9 contém as suposições, definições de variáveis e derivação da fórmula. Quando usam essa fórmula para determinar o número de produtos para produzir um lote, os gerentes podem ter a certeza de que o custo anual de manutenção de estoques de itens em processo se iguala ao custo anual de preparação para produzir os lotes. Embora seja atraente, essa abordagem para definir o tamanho de lote não leva em consideração a capacidade de produção.

Método do Esgotamento (Run-Out) A fórmula do LEC discutida acima é usada para determinar ou o tamanho de um lote de produção, ou o lote de um único produto. Como técnica de programação abrangente para programar por lotes, entretanto, o LEC não é inteiramente satisfatório, porque deixa de levar em conta estes fatos:

1. Somente a capacidade de produção suficiente está disponível em cada semana, e os produtos compartilham da mesma capacidade de produção escassa. Os tamanhos dos lotes de produção, portanto, devem ser determinados simultaneamente para todos os produtos dentro das restrições de capacidade para cada semana.
2. As decisões sobre tamanhos de lote de produção devem basear-se na informação mais atual sobre taxas de produção e taxas de demanda, e não somente em estimativas de demanda aproximadas, como no LEC.

Essas deficiências do LEC para planejar tamanhos de lote de produção levaram ao desenvolvimento do **método do esgotamento** (run-out) em operações de produção com restrições quanto à capacidade quando lotes de produtos são produzidos nas mesmas linhas de produção. *Esse método tenta usar a capacidade total de produção disponível em cada intervalo de tempo para produzir apenas o suficiente de cada produto a fim de que, se toda a produção parar, o estoque de itens acabados de cada produto se esgote ao mesmo tempo.*

O Exemplo 11.5 usa o método do esgotamento para desenvolver um programa de produção para cinco produtos de uma empresa produtora de pasta para calafetar madeira. Observe nesse exemplo que o método do esgotamento é deficiente sob um aspecto: ele não tenta definir tamanhos de lote econômicos de produção para produtos. Mas o método do esgotamento não supera uma fragilidade fundamental do LEC como método para determinar o tamanho de lotes de produção: ele reconhece que os produtos compartilham da capacidade de produção e aloca a capacidade disponível entre produtos. Nesse exemplo, todas as 1.600 horas de tempo de trabalho de extrusão por semana são alocadas entre os cinco produtos a fim de que, se a demanda semanal prevista realmente acontecer, a empresa fique sem cada um dos cinco produtos exatamente ao mesmo tempo.

Exemplo 11.5

Método do Esgotamento de Programação da Produção

A Rock-Hard Wood Putty Company planeja sua produção para a próxima semana. Todos os produtos de calafetação de madeira na Rock-Hard devem ser processados através de 20 misturadores-extrusores em sua fábrica de Peoria, Illinois. A Rock-Hard tem uma capacidade total de produção igual a 1.600 horas de extrusor por semana, baseando-se em seu plano agregado de seis meses. O departamento de programação da Rock-Hard está revendo os níveis de estoque, horas-máquinas necessárias por 1.000 libras e a utilização prevista para seus cinco produtos principais. Desenvolva um programa de produção para os extrusores usando o método do esgotamento.

Solução

1. Primeiro, converta o estoque disponível e as previsões em horas de extrusor:

(1) Produto	(2) Estoque de Produtos Acabados (000 libras)	(3) Tempo de Extrusor Necessário (horas por 000 libras)	(4) Demanda Prevista para a Próxima Semana (000 libras)	(5) Estoque em Horas de Extrusor [(2) × (3)]	(6) Demanda Prevista para Semana Seguinte em Horas de Extrusor [(4) × (3)]
A	160,0	1,0	100,0	160,00	100,00
B	210,0	2,0	200,0	420,00	400,00
C	200,5	2,5	200,0	501,25	500,00
D	150,6	1,5	160,0	225,90	240,00
E	170,2	1,5	100,0	255,30	150,00
			Totais	1.562,45	1.390,00

2. Em seguida, compute o tempo de esgotamento agregado (em semanas). Esse valor representa a quantidade de tempo que a última unidade de um item permaneceria em estoque *além da semana que está sendo planejada, supondo-se que as demandas semanais futuras sejam as mesmas que a demanda prevista para a próxima semana*. Esse valor é computado dividindo-se o equilíbrio de estoque no final da semana que está sendo planejada (a qual é o numerador da fração que se segue) pela demanda por semana:

$$\text{Tempo de esgotamento agregado} = \frac{\begin{bmatrix}\text{(5) Estoque total}\\\text{disponível (em}\\\text{horas de extrusor)}\end{bmatrix} + \begin{bmatrix}\text{Horas de}\\\text{extrusor totais}\\\text{disponíveis por}\\\text{semana}\end{bmatrix} - \begin{bmatrix}\text{(6) Demanda prevista}\\\text{para a próxima semana}\\\text{(em horas de extrusor)}\end{bmatrix}}{\begin{bmatrix}\text{(6) Demanda prevista}\\\text{para a próxima semana}\\\text{(em horas de extrusor)}\end{bmatrix}}$$

$$= \frac{1.562,45 + 1.600,00 - 1.390,00}{1.390,00} = 1,275 \text{ semana}$$

3. Em seguida, desenvolva um programa de produção semanal que use as 1.600 horas de tempo de extrusor:

	(7)	(8)	(9)	(10)
Produto	Estoque Final Desejado no Final da Próxima Semana (000 libras) [(4) × 1,275]	Estoque Final Desejado e Previsto (000 libras) [(7) + (4)]	Produção Necessária (000 libras) [(8) − (2)]	Horas de Extrusor Alocadas aos Produtos [(9) × (3)]
A	127,5	227,5	67,5	67,50
B	255,0	455,0	245,0	490,00
C	255,0	455,0	254,5	636,25
D	204,0	364,0	213,4	320,10
E	127,5	227,5	57,3	85,95
			Total	1.599,80

Programas de Entrega: Método da Linha de Balanceamento

Alguns sistemas de produção muitas vezes se comprometem com programas de entrega de seus produtos que estipulam quantos produtos devem ser entregues aos clientes em cada semana futura. Se for importante que as efetivas entregas de produto coincidam com o programa de entrega, deve-se idealizar um sistema que programe e controle todos os passos da produção. Muito freqüentemente, a produção do pedido de um cliente parece estar no prazo, porque as entregas estão e estiveram no prazo. Mas certas coisas podem estar acontecendo na produção que resultarão em entregas atrasadas no futuro. E ações corretivas podem se tornar impossíveis depois que as entregas estiverem atrasadas, porque a adutora de produção pode ter se esvaziado. Nesses casos, uma **linha de balanceamento (LOB)** tem sido usada para programar e controlar as operações antecedentes da produção. O Exemplo 11.6 ilustra como uma empresa usa a análise linha de balanceamento para estabelecer e controlar um plano de entrega a um cliente.

Exemplo 11.6

Linha de Balanceamento na Snowball Snowblower Company

A Snowball Snowblower Company produz tratores limpa-neve em sua fábrica. A Snowball assinou há pouco um contrato para que toda a sua produção seja vendida a uma grande cadeia de lojas a varejo. Uma das determinações do contrato seria um programa de entrega rígido:

Mês	Unidades a Serem Entregues	Mês	Unidades a Serem Entregues	Mês	Unidades a Serem Entregues
Janeiro	1.000	Maio	1.000	Setembro	2.000
Fevereiro	1.000	Junho	2.000	Outubro	2.000
Março	1.000	Julho	2.000	Novembro	2.000
Abril	1.000	Agosto	2.000	Dezembro	2.000

Os passos de processamento da produção, as relações entre os passos e os lead times são mostrados no seguinte fluxograma:

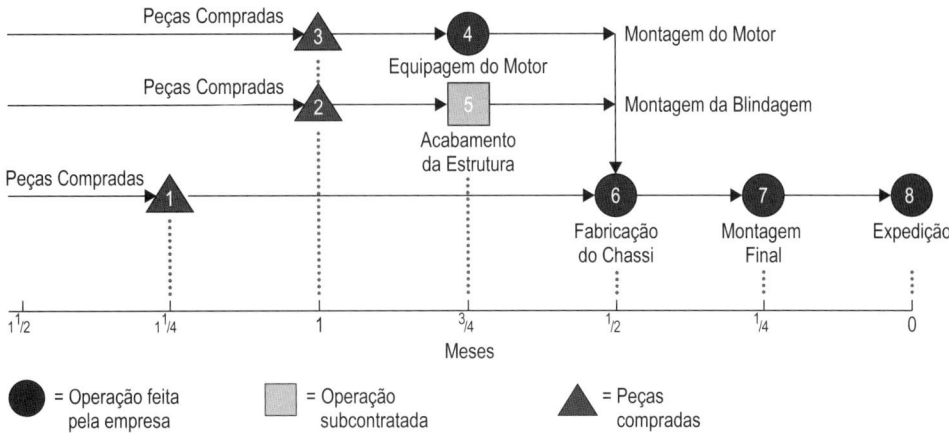

Depois de oito meses a partir do início do programa de embarque, essas quantidades cumulativas de unidades haviam passado por esses passos de processamento no processo de produção:

Passo de Processamento	Quantidade Cumulativa de Produção	Passo de Processamento	Quantidade Cumulativa de Produção
⑧ Expedição	11.000	④ Teste do motor	12.000
⑦ Montagem final	11.000	▲3 Receber peças compradas	12.000
⑥ Fabricação do chassi	11.500	▲2 Receber peças compradas	14.000
⑤ Acabamento da estrutura	12.000	▲1 Receber peças compradas	15.000

Desenvolva um gráfico de linha de balanceamento e avalie a situação da produção em cada passo do processamento.

SOLUÇÃO

1. Primeiro, construa um programa cumulativo de entrega, como mostra a Figura 11.3.
2. Em seguida, localize o ponto de revisão no programa cumulativo de entrega na Figura 11.3. O ponto de revisão está em oito meses. Prossiga verticalmente para cima até que a curva do programa cumulativo de entrega seja alcançada; avance horizontalmente para a direita até que o último passo do processamento, ⑧, no gráfico de progresso, seja alcançado. Desenhe uma linha horizontal curta de lado a lado na coluna Passo de Processamento ⑧ nesse nível: essa é a *linha de balanceamento* para o Passo de Processamento ⑧. Para localizar a linha de balanceamento para o Passo ⑦, siga *adiante* (para a direita) 1/4 de mês a partir do ponto de revisão anterior no programa cumulativo de entrega até 8¼ meses e repita o procedimento. Por que seguir adiante num programa 1/4 de mês quando o Passo ⑦ está lá atrás a montante no processo de produção? Porque as unidades que estão no Passo de Processamento ⑦ devem ser embarcadas 1/4 de mês (a quantidade de lead time entre os Passos ⑦ e ⑧) a partir de agora, ou 8¼ meses no programa. Essa linha de balanceamento é desenhada de maneira similar para todos os passos de processamento.
3. Em seguida, desenhe uma barra vertical para cada passo de processamento no gráfico de progresso, para indicar o número cumulativo de unidades que percorreram cada passo.

FIGURA 11.3   GRÁFICOS DE LINHA DE BALANCEAMENTO: SNOWBALL SNOWBLOWER COMPANY

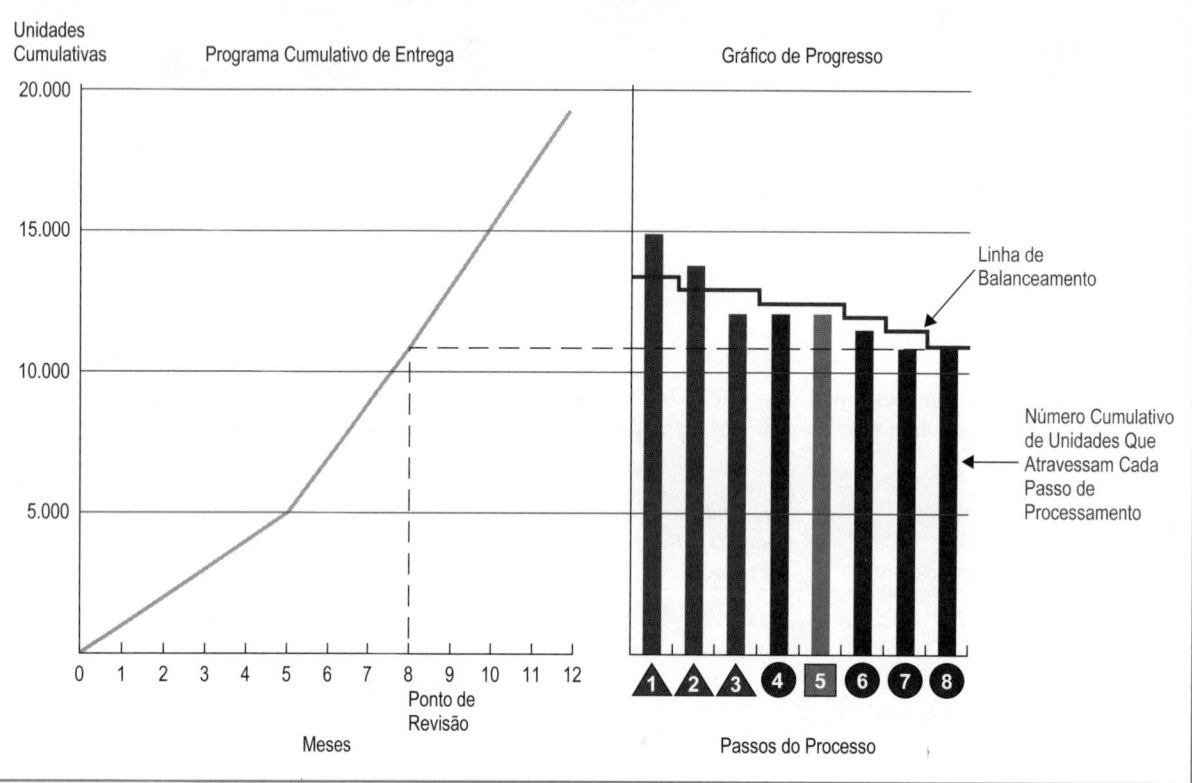

4. Em seguida, avalie o gráfico de progresso: (a) A Snowball está em seu prazo de entrega; a barra vertical correspondente às unidades expedidas ⑧ encontra exatamente a linha de balanceamento. Entretanto, surgem problemas à frente. (b) Os Passos de Processamento ② e ① são no prazo ou à frente no programa; ou seja, suas barras ou encontram ou ultrapassam a linha de balanceamento. (c) Os Passos de Processamento ⑦, montagem final, e ⑥, fabricação do chassi, estão ambos 500 unidades atrasados no programa, provavelmente devido a deficiências nas montagens do motor e montagens da blindagem. (d) O Passo de Processamento ⑤, acabamento subcontratado da estrutura, está 500 unidades atrasado no programa. A falha é do subcontratante, não de peças compradas. (e) Os Passos de Processamento ④ e ③, montagens do motor, estão 500 e 1.000 unidades atrasados no programa, respectivamente. Peças compradas está atrasando a operação de teste do motor.

Essa avaliação sugere que a administração deve pôr em prática imediatamente ações corretivas para acelerar os passos de compra de motores, teste de motores e processamento subcontratado de acabamento da estrutura. As entregas terão uma insuficiência de 500 unidades, e durante o período de revisão seguinte (1/4 de mês). A menos que sejam feitos progressos para acelerar os Passos ③ e ⑤, problemas mais sérios poderão ser esperados nos períodos vindouros.

Periodicamente, uma nova linha de balanceamento é desenhada no gráfico de progresso, e barras verticais são estendidas para refletir as unidades adicionais que atravessam cada passo de produção desde a última revisão. Desse modo, um instantâneo fotográfico da avaliação de cada passo da produção é tirado a intervalos regulares. Essas avaliações periódicas fornecem informações aos gerentes de produção sobre o desempenho de cada passo em relação ao programa. Essas informações são conhecidas antes que quaisquer dificuldades de produção afetem os programas de entrega. Portanto, ações corretivas podem ser postas em prática para evitar entregas atrasadas. A linha de balanceamento obtém seus maiores benefícios quando produtos ou serviços são produzidos para programas de entrega específicos, quando a produção envolve muitos passos de produção e quando os lead times de produção são longos.

Os pacotes de computador para programação estão crescendo em termos de número e freqüência de aplicação nos sistemas de produção atuais.

SISTEMAS COMPUTADORIZADOS DE PROGRAMAÇÃO

Pacotes de software de computador estão disponíveis para ajudar as empresas a desenvolver programas detalhados para cada centro de trabalho, e macroprogramas ajudam a coordenar todas as tarefas a serem produzidas. Cada vez mais esses programas de produção fazem parte integrante de sistemas de software de planejamento da manufatura mais abrangentes, como o *WinMagi* (**www.magimfg.com**) e o *Macola* (**www.macola.com**), ou mesmo sistemas maiores de planejamento dos recursos empresariais (ERP). Três exemplos populares desses sistemas de software ERP são o *SAP's R/3* (**www.sap.com**), o *Baan* (**www.baan.com**) e o *Peoplesoft* (**www.peoplesoft.com**). Não se pode negar que esses pacotes de computador são atraentes, mas não conclua que eles podem ser adaptados a um sistema de produção em particular rápida ou facilmente simplesmente porque os programas já estão escritos e depurados. Várias empresas descobriram, com muito desapontamento, que muitas vezes são necessários anos para implementar efetivamente os sistemas de informação.

Outros pacotes de computador de escopo menos ambicioso são projetados principalmente para fornecer informações de controle da programação ou do chão de fábrica. O *OrderLinks* (**www.pritsker.com**), comercializado pela divisão Advanced Planning & Scheduling da Symix (ex-Pritsker Corp.), é um exemplo. Independentemente do escopo desses pacotes, os programas de produção devem executar estas funções:

1. Desenvolver programas detalhados diários para cada centro de trabalho que indiquem os tempos de início e de encerramento de cada pedido.
2. Desenvolver programas departamentais diários e semanais detalhados que sejam usados para coordenar centros de trabalho.
3. Gerar programas modificados quando surgirem informações sobre novos clientes ou sobre o progresso de centros de trabalho.

Antes que esses programas possam ser usados, regras de prioridade para determinar a seqüência das tarefas nos centros de trabalho devem ser desenvolvidas, o necessário conjunto de regras para determinar quais tarefas serão atribuídas a quais centros de trabalho deve ser estabelecido, e deve ser desenvolvido um sistema de seguimento (*follow-up*) e retorno (feedback) dentro da instalação para modificar programas. Essas não são tarefas fáceis. Quando sistemas computadorizados são instalados, os gerentes não podem fazer as coisas sem prestar atenção às conseqüências no que diz respeito a suas decisões de planejamento. Uma das queixas mais comuns dos programadores é que os gerentes sempre parecem mudar as regras para se livrar das chamadas telefônicas do cliente cujo pedido está mais atrasado. Os programadores parecem se sentir derrotados diante das ordens mutáveis que recebem de cima referentes a quais são as tarefas "quentes" no período atual. Sistemas computadorizados impõem que regras coerentes devem ser desenvolvidas e seguidas, abordagens racionais ao roteiro e produção devem ser planejadas, e programas devem ser seguidos, se é que pretendemos obter informações significativas sobre planejamento da produção.

Essas exigências muitas vezes são impostas a alguns gerentes pela necessidade de instalação de um sistema computadorizado de programação. Em suma, *uma estrutura é imposta às decisões relativas à programação quando computadores são usados para desenvolver programas detalhados*. Melhorias substanciais no serviço ao cliente e na eficiência operacional interna serão possíveis nesses sistemas de produção somente se regras de seqüenciamento, roteiros e outras entradas forem realistas e se programas forem seguidos.

Alguns sistemas computadorizados de programação se concentram em administrar os gargalos dos programas de operações. Com essa abordagem, todos os programas de centros de trabalho são controlados pelos programas das operações gargalo. Eli Goldratt popularizou essa abordagem, chamada **teoria**

das restrições (discutida no Capítulo 8). Outros dão a essa abordagem o nome de **manufatura síncrona**, ou abordagem **tambor-pulmão-corda**. O software original de Goldratt, o *Optimized Production Technology* (*OPT*), é atualmente mantido e comercializado pela Scheduling Technology Ltd. (**www.stg.co.uk**). Outro software que utiliza essa abordagem é o *Resonance* da Thru-Put Technologies (**www.thru-put.com**). O Instantâneo da Indústria 11.1 descreve a experiência de uma empresa com o software OPT. Esses e tipos similares de software de programação provavelmente são mais apropriados para o ambiente de programação complexo encontrado em grandes job shops.

INSTANTÂNEO DA INDÚSTRIA 11.1

EXPERIÊNCIA DE UMA EMPRESA COM O SOFTWARE OPT

A Guest & Chrimes Ltd. é a principal fabricante de válvulas hidráulicas no Reino Unido. Seu processo de manufatura introduz sucata e ferro-gusa numa fundição numa extremidade da operação e por fim produz válvulas acabadas na outra extremidade. Ela emprega 400 pessoas em sua fábrica de 56.000 metros quadrados, e vende anualmente cerca de 100.000 válvulas de tamanhos e valores diversos.

Num esforço para melhorar os níveis de serviço ao cliente e assegurar um contínuo crescimento dos lucros no futuro, a Guest & Chrimes decidiu adotar e implementar a Optimized Production Technology (OPT), da Scheduling Technology Group Ltd. A implementação inteira foi concluída em seis meses.

Hoje, programas de trabalho são executados uma vez por semana. Além disso, muitas simulações são realizadas para propósitos gerais de previsão, bem como para medir o efeito de se manusear pedidos urgentes ou subcontratar certos processos. Dessa maneira, é mantido um estreito controle de toda a operação para minimizar a presença de pedidos em atraso. Tipicamente, a execução de uma simulação toma somente alguns minutos.

Stuart Wilson, diretor de produção da Guest & Chrimes, fala claramente sobre os resultados até agora: "Os benefícios do projeto têm sido enormes para a Guest & Chrimes. Os lead times foram reduzidos para 6 semanas na maioria de nossos produtos, sendo que alguns caíram de 36 semanas. Os níveis de Serviço ao Cliente melhoraram, sendo que o backlog de pedidos foi reduzido de 3 a 4 semanas para 2 ou 3 dias, o que é um feito fantástico se considerarmos que o rendimento (throughput) cresceu enquanto isso.

Houve uma elevação global de 20% no movimento das vendas e nos níveis de lucro, enquanto os custos com empregados permaneceram estáveis. A companhia inteira se beneficiou dessa melhoria em função de nosso Value Added Bonus melhorar de 8% para mais de 13% — uma medida verdadeira de nossa lucratividade".

Fonte: Brochura informativa sobre o software OPT. Scheduling Technology Group Ltd., Hounslow, Reino Unido.

RESUMO FINAL

O QUE OS FABRICANTES DE CLASSE MUNDIAL ESTÃO FAZENDO

A natureza das decisões relativas à programação varia de acordo com os tipos de sistema de produção. Em fábricas focalizadas no processo, prioridades devem ser definidas para cada pedido em cada centro de trabalho, pedidos devem ser atribuídos a máquinas dentro de centros de trabalho, e controle de chão de fábrica deve ser aplicado a pedidos. O planejamento e o controle de chão de fábrica em fábricas focalizadas no processo incluem definir prioridades para pedidos, emitir listas de remessa para centros de trabalho, manter atualizado o trabalho em processo (WIP), fornecer controle de entrada e saída para centros de trabalho, e medir e registrar o desempenho de centros de trabalho. Nesse tipo de produção, os fabricantes de classe mundial têm sistemas MRP II eficientes em vigor que fornecem informações em tempo real para as empresas, seus fornecedores e seus clientes a respeito da situação dos pedidos. Esses sistemas têm sido continuamente aprimorados a fim de que as promessas de entrega aos clientes sejam cumpridas, a carga das job shops esteja próxima de um nível ótimo, os custos de produção sejam baixos e a qualidade do produto seja elevada.

Ao programar fábricas focalizadas no produto, são problemas de programação importantes os tamanhos de lote de produção, o momento (timing) de realizar a preparação de máquina, e o planejamento e controle de produção para programas de entrega. Os tamanhos de lote de produção podem ser determinados pelo LEC, mas nos fabricantes de classe mundial, o LEC é definido para que caiba em contêineres de peças padrões, e o custo de preparação, S, é computado. Então, estudos do chão de fábrica são realizados para se obter esse nível de S. Dessa maneira, os tamanhos de lote são drasticamente reduzidos, os estoques em processo são diminuídos, e a receptividade do cliente é grandemente melhorada.

Nos fabricantes de classe mundial, as informações sobre programação e as decisões quanto à programação fazem parte de um sistema computadorizado de informação. *SAP's R/3, Macola, OrderLinks* e outros sistemas computadorizados de informação impõem uma estrutura às decisões relativas à programação. Dessa maneira, os tempos de entrega são mais previsíveis e o desempenho da produção é mais uniforme. Esses sistemas não somente podem fornecer informações sobre a situação dos pedidos, mas também podem responder a perguntas do tipo "o que acontecerá se" sobre pedidos de clientes e fornecedores.

QUESTÕES DE REVISÃO E DISCUSSÃO

1. Explique a relação entre planejamento das necessidades de materiais e decisões referentes à programação. De onde, no MRP, vêm as informações para que se possa tomar decisões relativas à programação de chão de fábrica?
2. Descreva uma fábrica focalizada no processo. Quais são as implicações das características dessa fábrica para as decisões relativas à programação?
3. Cite dois problemas fundamentais de programação nas job shops.
4. Explique como um gerente de operações escolheria e usaria uma regra de seqüenciamento na prática.
5. Defina estes termos: a) *carga infinita,* b) *carga finita,* c) *programação progressiva* e d) *programação regressiva.*
6. Explique as vantagens da programação regressiva sobre a programação progressiva.
7. Qual é o objetivo da regra de Johnson? Sob quais condições ela seria usada?
8. Quais decisões de programação os gerentes de operações devem resolver em fábricas focalizadas no produto?
9. Avalie o LEC como método para definir tamanhos de lote de produção. Quais são suas potencialidades e fragilidades?
10. Explique como o método do esgotamento (run-out) é melhorado no LEC. Quais são suas desvantagens?
11. O que é análise de entrada e saída? Quais informações ela fornece aos gerentes de operações? Qual é seu principal propósito?
12. Explique o que os fabricantes de classe mundial estão fazendo em suas programações de produção.

TAREFAS NA INTERNET

1. Visite e explore o site da Macola Software (**www.macola.com**) na Internet. Sob o título Macola's manufacturing software (software de manufatura da Macola), encontre seu módulo Shop Floor Control e descreva seus recursos.
2. Procure na Internet por uma empresa de consultoria que ofereça serviços que auxiliem as empresas em termos de controle de chão de fábrica ou controle de produção. Descreva os serviços que são oferecidos e forneça o site da empresa.
3. Visite uma livraria on-line e encontre dois livros recentes sobre programação na manu-fatura. Forneça as citações bibliográficas completas.
4. Procure na Internet por um fornecedor de software de controle de chão de fábrica. Descreva os recursos desse software e forneça o site da empresa.

PROBLEMAS

1. Dado este relatório de entrada e saída no final da Semana 4:
    a) Quais dificuldades de produção o relatório indica?
    b) Quais ações corretivas você recomendaria?

	Semana				
	−1	1	2	3	4
Entrada planejada (horas de trabalho)		100	50	20	100
Entrada real (horas de trabalho)		150	75	30	120
Desvio cumulativo		50	75	85	105
Saída planejada (horas de trabalho)		100	50	20	100
Saída real (horas de trabalho)		90	50	15	100
Desvio cumulativo		−10	−10	−15	−15
Estoque em Processo Final Planejado (horas de trabalho)		20	30	20	20
Estoque em Processo Final Real (horas de trabalho)	70	130	155	170	190

2. A Bill's Machining faz usinagem personalizada baseando-se em 8 horas de trabalho por dia, 5 dias por semana. Um programa de produção está sendo preparado agora para a próxima semana. As tarefas, os tempos estimados de produção, os tempos estimados de preparação e o progresso na quarta-feira ao meio-dia são mostrados a seguir:

Centro de Trabalho	Tempo de Produção da Tarefa (horas)					Tempo de Preparação (horas)	Progresso na Quarta-Feira [horas adiantadas ou atrasadas]
	A	B	C	D	E		
Torneamento	—	—	16	16	10	2	—
Usinagem	—	12	10	16	8	1	(1)
Tratamento térmico	8	8	8	8	8	3	1
Acabamento	8	8	8	8	8	1	½

A empresa acaba de encerrar uma semana de férias; portanto, centros de trabalho serão introduzidos gradualmente conforme necessário. As tarefas serão seqüenciadas nesta ordem: A-B-C-D-E. Prepare um gráfico de Gantt para a empresa que exiba os programas de semana para os centros de trabalho.

3. Seis tarefas estão aguardando para ser processadas numa estação de trabalho. Seus códigos de tarefa, tempos estimados de produção e tempos de entrega prometidos são apresentados na tabela seguinte.

Código da Tarefa	Tempo de Produção (horas)	Tempo para a Entrega Prometida (horas)
161	3,8	6,0
162	2,1	3,0
163	4,5	14,0
164	3,0	10,0
165	4,2	20,0
166	2,9	19,0

Determine a seqüência de produção das tarefas usando as seguintes regras:
a) Regra do menor tempo de processamento
b) Regra da menor folga
c) Regra da razão crítica

4. Sete tarefas estão aguardando para ser processadas numa estação de trabalho. Seus códigos de tarefa, tempos estimados de produção e os tempos de entrega prometidos são apresentados a seguir.

Código da Tarefa	Tempo de Produção (horas)	Tempo para a Entrega Prometida (horas)
241	2,4	31,0
242	3,7	12,0
243	5,2	19,0
244	3,3	14,0
245	5,6	10,0
246	6,1	27,0
247	4,0	24,0

Determine a seqüência de produção das tarefas usando as seguintes regras:
a) Regra do menor tempo de processamento
b) Regra da menor folga
c) Regra da razão crítica

5. Um planejador da produção deve decidir-se a respeito da seqüência na qual produzir quatro pedidos de clientes.

Pedido do Cliente	Tempo Estimado de Produção (dias)	Tempo para a Entrega Prometida (dias)	Seqüência de Pedido: Primeiro a Entrar, Primeiro a Ser Atendido	Tempo de Fluxo (dias)	Atraso (dias)
A	10	15	1	10	0
B	21	30	2	31	1
C	26	60	3	57	0
D	19	77	4	76	1

Classifique as regras de seqüenciamento "primeiro a entrar, primeiro a ser atendido", "menor tempo de processamento" e "razão crítica" em três critérios de avaliação: tempo médio de fluxo, número de tarefas no sistema e atraso médio da tarefa.

6. Uma empresa faz trabalhos de tratamento térmico (recozimento, cementação, imersão em óleo etc.) para clientes. Cada trabalho geralmente requer uma preparação diferente, e essas preparações têm diferentes custos. Hoje a empresa deve decidir-se a respeito da seqüência de tarefa para cinco trabalhos para minimizar os custos de preparação. Mostramos a seguir os custos de preparação entre tarefas.

Tarefas Que Precedem

Tarefas Que Sucedem	A	B	C	D	E
A	—	$ 75	$ 90	$ 60	$ 42
B	$ 85	—	79	97	45
C	62	91	—	87	75
D	95	85	55	—	65
E	55	85	65	95	—

a) Use essa regra para desenvolver uma seqüência de tarefas: primeiro, escolha o menor custo de preparação dentre todas as possibilidades; isso define a primeira e a segunda tarefa. A tarefa seguinte a ser escolhida terá o menor custo de preparação entre as tarefas restantes que sucedem a tarefa anteriormente escolhida.
b) Qual é o custo total de preparação para todas as cinco tarefas?

7. Um programador de produção deve determinar a seqüência na qual processar quatro pedidos de clientes. Cada um dos pedidos deve passar por duas operações principais: inserção e soldagem. O programador desenvolveu estas estimativas do tempo de produção para os quatro pedidos:

Numeração do Pedido do Cliente	Inserção do Componente (horas)	Solda a Fluxo (horas)
A	6,9	5,9
B	7,3	6,1
C	5,7	4,9
D	2,6	3,6

Se as operações não necessitarem de preparações para novas tarefas simultaneamente:
a) Use a regra de Johnson para definir a seqüência de produção dos pedidos nas duas operações.
b) Quantas horas serão necessárias para produzir todos os pedidos por meio de ambas as operações?

8. Um fabricante produz diversas montagens eletrônicas em base de produção para estoque. A demanda anual, custos de preparação ou de pedido, custos de manutenção em estoque, índices de demanda e taxas de produção para as montagens são mostrados a seguir.

Montagem	Demanda Anual (000 unidades)	Custo de Preparação ou Pedido ($/lote)	Custo de Manutenção em Estoque ($/unidade.ano)	Índice de Demanda (unidades/dia)	Taxa de Produção (unidades/dia)
A	10	$ 1.500	$ 8	100	300
B	12	900	6	300	500
C	8	2.000	10	100	200
D	5	1.200	5	200	400

a) Usando o LEC, compute o tamanho do lote de produção de cada montagem.
b) Qual porcentagem do lote de montagens A é usada durante a produção?
c) Para a montagem A, quanto tempo transcorrerá entre as preparações?

9. A Bell Computer Company produz cinco modelos de computador de mesa. A demanda anual, os custos de preparação ou de pedido, custos de manutenção em estoque, índices de demanda e taxas de produção para a montagem final dos computadores são apresentados a seguir:

Modelo de Computador	Demanda Anual (computadores)	Custo de Preparação ou de Pedido ($/computador.lote)	Custo de Manutenção em Estoque ($/computador.ano)	Índice de Demanda (computador/dia)	Taxa de Produção (computadores/dia)
PC1	25.000	$ 5.000	$ 120,50	100	250
PC2	20.000	4.000	166,25	80	200
PC3	15.000	4.000	191,25	60	200
PC4	10.000	5.000	223,50	40	200
PC5	5.000	5.000	353,00	20	150

a) Usando o LEC, compute o tamanho do lote de produção para cada modelo de computador.
b) Supondo que haja 300 dias úteis por ano e que o departamento de montagem final produza somente esses modelos de computador, qual porcentagem da capacidade anual é necessária para o modelo PC1?

10. A Bell Computer Company produz cinco modelos de computador de mesa. Agora é 15 de junho e a Bell está planejando seu programa do departamento de montagem final para o outono. O estoque disponível, as horas de montagem final necessárias por computador e a demanda prevista são mostrados na tabela seguinte.

(1) Modelo de Computador	(2) Estoque Disponível ou em Produção (computadores)	(3) Tempo Necessário para Montagem Final (horas/computador)	(4) Demanda Prevista para o Trimestre do Outono (computadores)
PC1	2.500	0,040	8.000
PC2	3.000	0,050	6.000
PC3	1.000	0,060	5.000
PC4	500	0,070	5.000
PC5	1.000	0,090	3.000

A previsão da demanda para o trimestre do inverno é a mesma que para o trimestre do outono. Se houver 1.400 horas de montagem final disponíveis em cada trimestre, use o método do esgotamento (run-out) para desenvolver um programa de produção de montagem final para o trimestre do outono.

11. Uma empresa tem um programa de entrega contratual para seus produtos. O programa de entrega exige que 10 mil produtos sejam entregues semanalmente durante 30 semanas. O processo de produção dos produtos tem os lead times mostrados na ilustração seguinte. Dez semanas depois do início do programa de entrega, os registros de produção indicam que essas quantidades cumulativas passaram pelos passos de produção:

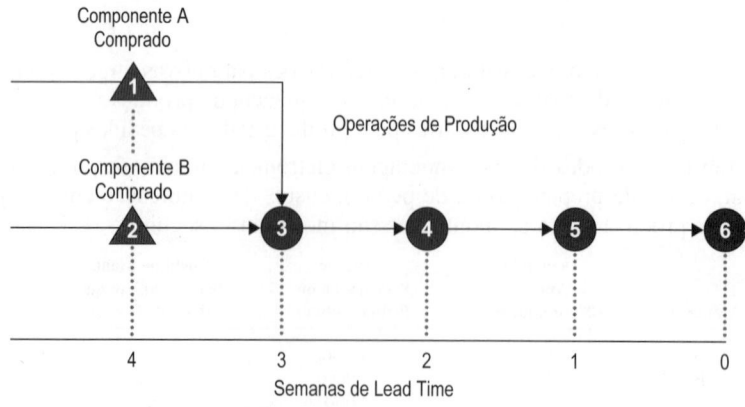

Passo de Processamento	Produção Cumulativa (produtos)	Passo de Processamento	Produção Cumulativa (produtos)
1	120.000	4	120.000
2	150.000	5	115.000
3	120.000	6	105.000

a) Prepare um gráfico de programa de entrega cumulativo, um gráfico de progresso e uma linha de balanceamento.
b) Avalie as perspectivas de entregas futuras. Parece haver qualquer dificuldade de entrega no futuro?

Estudo de Caso

Integrated Products Corporation

A Integrated Products Corporation (IPC) foi contratada para fornecer a unidade T40 da IPC a um cliente de acordo com um programa estrito de entrega. O programa acordado é mostrado a seguir:

Mês	Unidades a serem entregues	Mês	Unidades a serem entregues
Janeiro	2.000	Abril	3.000
Fevereiro	2.000	Maio	3.000
Março	2.000	Junho	3.000

Os passos de processamento da produção, as relações entre os passos e os lead times são mostrados no fluxograma a seguir:

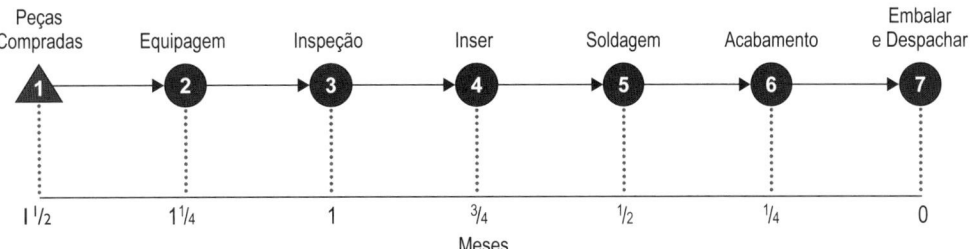

No final de março, essas quantidades de unidades cumulativas haviam passado por estes passos de processamento da produção:

Passo de Processamento	Unidades Cumulativas	Passo de Processamento	Unidades Cumulativas
1. Peças Compradas	9.000	5. Soldagem	6.500
2. Equipagem	9.000	6. Acabamento	5.250
3. Inspeção	9.000	7. Embalar e Despachar	5.000
4. Inserção	9.000		

Tarefas

1. Construa um gráfico de embarque cumulativo, um gráfico de progresso e uma linha de balanceamento para o final de março.
2. Qual é a situação do progresso da IPC até o presente?
3. Qual provavelmente será a situação futura do progresso da IPC? Quais ações corretivas provavelmente serão exigidas pelos gerentes de operações da IPC se eles quiserem cumprir seus programas de entrega?
4. Discuta a utilidade da linha de balanceamento para planejar e controlar as remessas da IPC. Como um sistema MRP se compara à linha de balanceamento nessa aplicação? Defenda sua resposta.

capítulo 12

PLANEJAMENTO E PROGRAMAÇÃO DE OPERAÇÕES DE SERVIÇO

Introdução
   A Natureza dos Serviços Revisitada
   Estratégias de Operações para o Setor de Serviços
   Tipos de Operações de Serviço
   Desafios na Atividade de Programação no Setor de Serviços
      Lidando com uma Demanda Não Uniforme

Programação de Operações de Serviço de Quase-Manufatura
   Operações Focalizadas no Produto
   Operações Focalizadas no Processo
   Programação de Turnos de Trabalho em Operações de Serviço

Programação de Operações de Serviço Tendo o Cliente como Participante
   Natureza dessas Operações
   Filas de Espera nas Operações de Serviço
      Características das Filas de Espera • Terminologia e Estruturas dos Sistemas de Filas de Espera • Quatro Modelos de Filas e Suas Fórmulas • Uma Avaliação da Análise das Filas de Espera na APO

Programação de Operações de Serviço Tendo o Cliente como Produto
   Natureza dessas Operações
   Usando Simulação Computadorizada em Operações de Serviço
   Características dos Problemas Que São Apropriados para Simulação Computadorizada • Procedimentos da Simulação Computadorizada • Uma Avaliação da Simulação Computadorizada

Resumo Final: O Que os Fabricantes de Classe Mundial Estão Fazendo

Questões de Revisão e Discussão

Tarefas na Internet

Problemas

Estudo de Caso
   Operações de Transporte em Caminhão na Computer Products Corporation

PROGRAMAÇÃO DE EMPREGADOS NA TEXAS GROCERY

A loja Texas Grocery, localizada a noroeste de Houston, Texas, emprega um total de 235 pessoas para garantir um serviço de 24 horas a seus clientes. A Texas Grocery é uma superloja completa, com departamentos que variam de produtos de padaria a itens de farmácia e produtos não alimentícios. Há pessoal designado para operar caixas registradoras nos balcões de pagamento, empacotar mantimentos, colocar estoques nas prateleiras, dirigir empilhadeiras no armazém, controlar estoques, aviar receitas de produtos farmacêuticos, receber clientes, entregar compras dos clientes, limpeza, manutenção, departamentos de administração, contabilidade, trabalho em projetos especiais, padaria e outras obrigações.

A programação do pessoal para turnos de trabalho durante a semana é complicada por dois fatores principais: demanda não uniforme e preferências de empregados. O volume de trânsito de clientes não é uniforme. A demanda varia conforme o dia da semana, ou mesmo o dia do mês, e tende a ser mais pesada nos dias que se aproximam de feriados, nas sextas-feiras, sábados e domingos, e mais leve nas quartas-feiras. O horário em torno das 8 horas da manhã e 4 horas da tarde tende a ser o mais pesado durante a semana, e o meio da manhã, a hora do almoço e o início da tarde tendem a ser os mais pesados nos finais de semana.

A empresa tem diversas políticas que afetam a programação de turnos do pessoal. (1) Cada empregado deverá trabalhar em cinco turnos de 8 horas durante cada semana. (2) Cada empregado terá dois dias consecutivos de folga durante cada semana. (3) Cada empregado girará em turnos do dia para a tarde e para a noite em base mensal. (4) A preferência por turnos da parte dos empregados será respeitada. Se ocorrerem conflitos, será usada uma grade de pagamento e de tempo para alocar turnos preferidos.

Considerando a demanda não uniforme e as políticas da empresa, o gerente da loja e o gerente adjunto devem desenvolver programas de turno de trabalho para os 235 empregados para o próximo mês.

O relato precedente ilustra parte da complexidade presente na programação de operações de serviço. Nos capítulos anteriores estudamos as operações de serviço ao longo da manufatura, quando examinamos uma variedade de tópicos e decisões na APO. Tomamos essa abordagem porque ela é considerada a melhor maneira de entendermos as similaridades e diferenças da manufatura e dos serviços. Neste capítulo, entretanto, confinamos nosso estudo ao planejamento, programação e controle das operações de serviço. Ao nos concentrar nas operações de serviço, proporcionamos um entendimento mais profundo das propriedades únicas do gerenciamento de operações de serviço.

A NATUREZA DOS SERVIÇOS REVISITADA

Antes de estudarmos o planejamento e controle das operações de serviço, vamos resumir parte daquilo que aprendemos sobre os serviços. Isso nos permitirá entender melhor a natureza da programação dessas operações diversas.

Na Tabela 2.8 do Capítulo 2, a natureza dos serviços foi resumida e comparada com a manufatura. Os serviços foram descritos como operações com:

- Produtos intangíveis que não podem ser guardados em estoque.
- Estreito contato com o cliente.
- Lead times curtos.
- Custos de mão-de-obra elevados em relação aos custos de capital, ou seja, uso intensivo de mão-de-obra.
- Qualidade determinada subjetivamente.

A discussão em torno da Tabela 2.8 enfatizou que, embora o resumo seja acurado para muitos serviços, a grande diversidade entre os serviços torna-o enganoso. O que é pior, esse resumo pode levar a concepções errôneas sobre os serviços. A Tabela 12.1 relaciona algumas idéias erradas sobre os serviços.

Algumas das maiores corporações nos Estados Unidos são negócios de serviços. A AT&T, Wal-Mart, Citicorp, State Farm, Prudential e Sears, Roebuck & Company, para citarmos alguns, se classificam entre as 20 maiores corporações americanas. Estas empresas enormes, globais e de capital aberto abrangem o espectro dos negócios de serviços — empresas aéreas, serviços bancários, vendas a varejo, atendimento à saúde, transporte rodoviário, entretenimento, seguros, setor imobiliário, serviços públicos etc. As indústrias de serviços exportam mais de US$ 150 bilhões em serviços anualmente, com um crescente superávit

TABELA 12.1	ALGUMAS IDÉIAS ERRADAS SOBRE OS SERVIÇOS
	• Os negócios de serviços são negócios de um único proprietário envolvendo a vizinhança da mamãe e do papai. • Os negócios de serviços são *drive-ins* de venda a varejo ou de fast-food. • Os serviços usam mão-de-obra intensivamente e exigem pouco investimento de capital. • A automação e novas tecnologias não afetam os serviços tanto quanto a manufatura. • Os empregados do setor de serviços preparam hambúrgueres, limpam mesas ou servem clientes, e ganham o salário mínimo. • Os empregados que trabalham em serviços precisam ser agradáveis e precisam de treinamento somente em vendas e em relações interpessoais. • Poucos engenheiros, cientistas e outras pessoas tecnicamente treinadas trabalham em serviços. • O setor de serviços nos Estados Unidos é altamente lucrativo, e o *downsizing* e cortes de funcionários praticados na década de 1990 não foram experimentados nos serviços.

comercial anual de aproximadamente US$ 50 bilhões. Bem, você captou a cena: elas são grandes, globais e diversificadas. E muitas delas são de capital intensivo e usam automação e alta tecnologia extensivamente. Na realidade, o investimento de capital por empregado para trabalhadores de escritório agora ultrapassa o dos trabalhadores na manufatura. E muitos empregados do setor de serviços têm um salário elevado e são altamente treinados tecnicamente; mais da metade dos empregados do setor de serviços tem empregos de escritório. Com 3,5 vezes mais empregados do que na manufatura, o salário médio por hora dos empregados de serviços é somente 13% inferior aos da manufatura. O pagamento horário no setor de transportes e serviços públicos é de US$ 13,42, no comércio atacadista é de US$ 11,35, e nos serviços de saúde é de US$ 11,28, ao passo que o pagamento horário na manufatura é de US$ 11,40. A única exceção é no setor varejista, responsável por 29% dos empregos nos serviços; os salários médios por hora dos trabalhadores do setor varejista são somente 2/3 dos da manufatura. A natureza de alta tecnologia de negócios de serviços como as telecomunicações, empresas aéreas e serviços públicos cria a necessidade da presença de engenheiros, cientistas e outros empregados tecnicamente treinados.

Algumas coisas que você deve ter em mente quando pensar nos negócios de serviços:

- Há uma enorme diversidade entre os serviços.
- Os negócios de serviços podem ser enormes, minúsculos, ou qualquer coisa entre esses dois extremos, exatamente como na manufatura.
- Há mais do que o dobro de negócios de serviços não varejistas do que de negócios de serviços varejistas.
- Não obstante as capacidades de relações interpessoais serem importantes nos serviços (e na manufatura), o fato é que treinamento técnico, computadores, automação e tecnologia desempenham um papel importante na maioria dos serviços.
- A maioria dos trabalhadores no setor de serviços é bem paga em relação aos da manufatura.
- Os negócios de serviços necessitam de um melhor planejamento, controle e administração para superar a competição para poder sobreviver e prosperar.

Não há uma linha clara, visível, separando manufatura e serviços. O serviço ao cliente domina parte dos negócios de manufatura, e alguns negócios de serviços se comportam e são administrados exatamente como na manufatura. Todo negócio, seja da manufatura ou do setor de serviços, tem uma mescla de serviço ao cliente de um lado e materiais, transporte, armazenamento, tecnologia e produção do outro. Portanto a manufatura tem um bocado a aprender de serviços que se destacam no serviço ao cliente, e o setor de serviços tem um bocado a aprender de fabricantes que se sobressaem na produção.

A linha que divide a manufatura e os serviços é tênue em muitos casos. Se pretendemos planejar, controlar e administrar melhor os serviços, é importante que desenvolvamos paradigmas lógicos, diretrizes que estruturem a maneira pela qual raciocinamos a respeito dessas operações de serviço diversas. As operações focalizadas no produto e focalizadas no processo da manufatura se combinam com operações de serviço de quase-manufatura[1], que têm o cliente como participante e que têm o cliente como produto para

---

[1] Do original *quasi-manufacturing*, com o sentido de semelhante à manufatura. (N. do R.T.)

formar um paradigma útil para planejar e controlar operações de produção. Se o setor de serviços nos Estados Unidos pretende prosperar, como a manufatura, ele deve continuar a melhorar a qualidade, o custo e o serviço ao cliente. O planejamento e o controle diário das operações são cruciais para essa melhoria.

Tendo como pano de fundo essa discussão a respeito da natureza dos serviços, revisemos agora a estratégia de operações no setor de serviços, porque é a estratégia que direciona o planejamento e o controle diário das operações.

ESTRATÉGIAS DE OPERAÇÕES PARA O SETOR DE SERVIÇOS

No Capítulo 2 discutimos as estratégias de posicionamento para os serviços, aqueles planos de longo prazo para captar fatias de mercado. As estratégias de posicionamento para os serviços contêm dois elementos: tipo de projeto (design) de serviço e tipo de processo de produção.

1. **Tipo de projeto de serviço**, com três dimensões — padrão ou personalizado, quantidade de contato com o cliente, e a combinação de bens físicos e serviços intangíveis.
2. **Tipo de processo de produção** — quase-manufatura, cliente como participante e cliente como produto.

A estratégia de negócios de uma empresa determina o tipo de projeto de serviço, e o tipo de projeto de serviço determina o tipo de processo de produção. A maneira como uma empresa planeja, programa e controla as operações de serviços depende do tipo de processo de produção. Portanto, a discussão a respeito da programação das operações de serviço neste capítulo gira em torno desses tipos de operações de serviço.

TIPOS DE OPERAÇÕES DE SERVIÇO

Há três tipos de operações de serviço — quase-manufatura, cliente como participante e cliente como produto.

1. **Quase-manufatura.** Neste tipo de operação de serviço a produção ocorre de uma maneira muito similar à da manufatura. A ênfase reside nos custos de produção, tecnologia, materiais e produtos físicos, qualidade de produto e pronta-entrega. Os bens físicos são predominantes sobre os serviços intangíveis, os produtos podem ser padrões ou personalizados, e há pouco contato ou envolvimento com o cliente. As operações de apoio (back-room) em bancos, serviços industriais de tratamento térmico e operações de manutenção de aeronaves são exemplos deste tipo de operação de serviço.
2. **Cliente como participante.** Há um grau elevado de envolvimento do cliente nesse tipo de operação de serviço. Os bens físicos podem ser ou não uma parte significativa do serviço, e os serviços podem ser personalizados ou padrões. A venda a varejo é um exemplo desse tipo de operação de serviço.
3. **Cliente como produto.** Nesse tipo de operação de serviço clientes são tão envolvidos que o serviço é realizado de fato no cliente. Bens físicos podem ser ou não uma parte significativa do serviço, e os serviços geralmente são personalizados. Exemplos desse tipo de operação de serviço são os salões de cabeleireiros, clínicas médicas e hospitais, e alfaiates.

É importante entender que essas classificações das operações de serviços não são mutuamente exclusivas. Não é incomum encontrarmos todos os três tipos de operações dentro de uma empresa. Por exemplo, o McDonald's terá uma operação de quase-manufatura no apoio e uma operação tendo o cliente como participante no balcão. Bancos, corretoras de valores, restaurantes, bibliotecas, oficinas mecânicas e lavanderias também têm balcões que são operações de serviço que têm o cliente como participante e apoios que são operações de serviço de quase-manufatura. Da mesma forma que um negócio de manufatura pode ter uma operação focalizada no produto e uma operação focalizada no processo funcionando lado a lado, um ou mais desses tipos de operações de serviço também podem ser encontrados dentro dos negócios de manufatura.

A ocorrência desses tipos de operações de serviço está tão difundida que o aprendizado de como planejar e controlar melhor essas operações pode ter um grande impacto.

DESAFIOS NA ATIVIDADE DE PROGRAMAÇÃO NO SETOR DE SERVIÇOS

Duas características predominantes das operações de serviços tornam desafiadoras as atividades diárias de planejamento e controle:

1. Os serviços são produzidos e entregues por pessoas — homens, mulheres, adolescentes, indivíduos, trabalhadores, empregados, pessoal, ou recursos humanos, seja qual for o termo que você prefira.
2. O padrão de demanda para os serviços não é uniforme.

Uma vez que a demanda por serviços varia de hora em hora, de dia a dia, e de semana a semana ao longo do ano, o principal desafio é variar a capacidade de produção para satisfazer esse padrão mutante de demanda. Para a maioria dos negócios de serviços, variar o tamanho da força de trabalho é a melhor a maneira de mudar rapidamente a capacidade de produção. Os gerentes de operações lutam para variar o tamanho da força de trabalho para atender uma demanda não uniforme a fim de que haja um equilíbrio razoável entre os custos de produção e a satisfação do cliente. Se um número muito grande de empregados for programado para trabalhar durante qualquer intervalo de tempo, os custos serão muito elevados. Se muito poucos empregados forem programados, a satisfação do cliente sofrerá.

Lidando com uma Demanda Não Uniforme Uma vez que os serviços geralmente não podem ser guardados em estoque durante períodos de baixa demanda para ser usados em períodos de demanda de pico, as operações de serviços desenvolveram outras táticas para lidar com a demanda não uniforme. Eis algumas dessas abordagens:

- Desenvolver ações de preempção que tentem tornar a demanda mais uniforme.
- Usar táticas que tornem as operações de serviço mais flexíveis a fim de que a capacidade de produção possa ser aumentada ou diminuída rapidamente conforme a demanda variar.
- Antecipar padrões de demanda e programar o número de empregados durante cada intervalo de tempo para satisfazer a demanda antecipada.
- Permitir que se formem filas de espera quando a demanda do cliente ultrapassar a capacidade de produção. Nessa abordagem as filas de espera nivelam a demanda e permitem que a capacidade de um sistema seja relativamente uniforme.

Diversas táticas têm sido usadas para manipular a demanda para torná-la mais uniforme. Entre elas estão os incentivos para horários fora de pico (*off-peak*), programas de hora marcada e programas fixos. Incentivos para horários fora de pico são oferecidos para motivar os clientes a mudarem sua demanda por serviços de horários de pico para horários fora de pico. Por exemplo, as companhias telefônicas oferecem tarifas reduzidas para chamadas feitas depois dos horários de trabalho durante a semana e tarifas ainda menores são cobradas para chamadas feitas em finais de semana. Médicos, dentistas, advogados e professores exigem que os clientes marquem consultas antecipadamente para receber seus serviços. Determina-se uma tabela de horários para os clientes com o duplo objetivo de reduzir os tempos de espera dos clientes e para ajudar o serviço a manter uma capacidade de produção uniforme. Outras operações de serviço, como as empresas aéreas, têm horários de partida fixos. Os clientes organizam seus padrões de demanda para se encaixar nos horários, ou não voarão pela empresa aérea. Todas essas táticas para tornar a demanda por serviços mais uniforme têm sido apenas parcialmente bem-sucedidas; a demanda é menos volátil, mas, apesar disso, ainda não uniforme. Finalmente, todas essas operações de serviço devem desenvolver maneiras de lidar com a demanda não uniforme.

Há maneiras de tornar os sistemas de serviço mais flexíveis a fim de que a capacidade de produção possa ser aumentada ou reduzida rapidamente conforme as demandas do cliente por serviços variam. Uma maneira é usar pessoal em tempo parcial, subcontratados e instalações de reserva (standby) internamente na empresa para aumentar a capacidade de produção durante períodos de demanda de pico. Similarmente, o pessoal em geral designado a uma obrigação pode ser designado a outras mais críticas durante demandas de pico. Por exemplo, trabalhadores que comumente colocam estoques em prateleiras numa mercearia poderiam empacotar e entregar mantimentos durante períodos de demanda de pico. Uma tática similar tam-

FIGURA 12.1   HORÁRIOS DAS EQUIPES DO CORPO DE BOMBEIROS DA CALIFÓRNIA

JULHO	D	S	T	Q	Q	S	S	D	S	T	Q	Q	S	S	D	S	T	Q	Q	S	S	D	S	T	Q	Q	S	S	D	S	T
	1	2	3	4	5	6	7	8	9	10	11	12	13	14	15	16	17	18	19	20	21	22	23	24	25	26	27	28	29	30	31
Equipe A																															
Equipe B																															
Equipe C																															

Observação: Os quadrados sombreados indicam um turno de 24 horas.

bém é usada em operações de serviços de emergência, como, por exemplo, serviços de ambulância e de combate a incêndios. Equipes inteiras são programadas para turnos de 24 horas a fim de que estejam à disposição durante emergências. Então, as equipes executam trabalhos que não são de emergência durante períodos de baixa demanda. Um exemplo dessa abordagem é ilustrado na Figura 12.1 e na Tabela 12.2. O Corpo de Bombeiros da Califórnia tem cinco postos nos quais trabalham um total de 21 pessoas no combate a incêndios, oferecendo proteção contra incêndios 24 horas por dia. A Figura 12.1 mostra como essas três equipes, A, B e C, são programadas para trabalhar em turnos de 24 horas. Durante períodos de baixa demanda, os bombeiros são programados para realizar tarefas que não são de emergência. A Tabela 12.2 mostra a programação de algumas tarefas que não são de emergência em cada turno de 24 horas.

Apesar das tentativas de manipular a demanda do cliente para tornar a demanda mais uniforme, a demanda não uniforme persiste na maioria das operações de serviço. Para lidar com essa situação, muitas operações de serviço tentam planejar programas de turno de trabalho que coincidam aproximadamente com a demanda de hora em hora durante o horário comercial. E muitas empresas permitem que filas de espera se formem quando a demanda ultrapassa a capacidade de produção. Discutiremos adiante quais empresas usam essas abordagens.

Encaminharemos agora a atividade de programação desses tipos de operações de serviços — quase-manufatura, cliente como participante e cliente como produto.

PROGRAMAÇÃO DE OPERAÇÕES DE SERVIÇO DE QUASE-MANUFATURA

O que há nessas operações que as torna diferentes de outras operações de serviço é que não há nenhum envolvimento de clientes na produção. Por esse motivo, as operações de serviço de quase-manufatura, para todos os fins práticos, são operações de manufatura. Elas são projetadas, planejadas, controladas, analisadas, programadas e administradas da mesma maneira que as operações de manufatura. Esse tipo de operação de serviço pode ser ou uma operação focalizada no produto ou focalizada no processo.

OPERAÇÕES FOCALIZADAS NO PRODUTO

Algumas operações de serviço se assemelham às linhas de produção focalizadas no produto existentes na manufatura. Por exemplo, imagine as operações de apoio num restaurante da rede McDonald's. O prédio, as máquinas e os postos de trabalho são projetados, e seu layout é traçado como numa operação de manufatura. A linha de montagem é balanceada exatamente como na manufatura. As questões de automação e tecnologia são consideradas e avaliadas exatamente como na manufatura. A demanda do cliente é prevista, e as decisões sobre a capacidade de produção são tomadas exatamente como na manufatura. Empregados são contratados, treinados e supervisionados exatamente como na manufatura. Caixas de papelão, produtos agrícolas, pães de hambúrguer e outros materiais são comprados, pedidos para entrega e guardados enquanto custos e padrões de demanda são considerados, exatamente como na manufatura. Volumes elevados de produtos padronizados são produzidos rotineiramente numa base combinada de produção para estoque e produção sob encomenda. Os objetivos da administração são idênticos aos da manufatura — controle dos custos do produto, qualidade do produto e pronta entrega de bens físicos. E o progresso rumo à obtenção desses objetivos pode ser medido e avaliado exatamente como na manufatura. As principais preocupações da atividade de programação são a obtenção da quantidade certa de materiais e pessoal para produzir suficientes produtos que satisfaçam a demanda do cliente que é altamente variável de hora em hora. No Capítulo 10 analisamos as políticas de atendimento de pedidos para essas operações.

TABELA 12.2   CRONOGRAMA MENSAL DE ATIVIDADES DO CORPO DE BOMBEIROS DA CALIFÓRNIA — JULHO

Dia	Comandante.	Turno	Posto 1 Manhã	Posto 1 Tarde	Posto 2 Manhã	Posto 2 Tarde	Posto 3 Manhã	Posto 3 Tarde	Posto 4 Manhã	Posto 4 Tarde	Posto 5 Manhã	Posto 5 Tarde
Domingo 01	C2	B	SM	SM	SM	SM	SM	SM	SM	SM	SM	FB
Segunda-feira 02	C5	A	FM	FM	FM	FM	FM	FM	FM	FM	FM	FM
Terça-feira 03	C2	B	HM	HM	HM	HM	HM	HM	HM	HM	HM	HM
Quarta-feira 04	C3	C	PC	PC	PC	PC	PC	PC	PC	PC	PC	PC
Quinta-feira 05	C2	B	FP	FP	FP	FP	FP	FP	FP	FP	FP	FP
Sexta-feira 06	C3	C	DS	DS	CD	CD	DS	DS	FP	FP	FP	FP
Sábado 07	C2	B	EM	EM	EM	EM	EM	EM	EM	EM	EM	FB
Domingo 08	C3	C	SD	SM	SD	SM	SD	SM	SD	SM	FB	SM
Segunda-feira 09	C5	A	FP	FP	FP	FP	FP	FP	FP	FP	FP	FP
Terça-feira 10	C3	C	FP	FP	DS	DS	CD	CD	DS	DS	CD	CD
Quarta-feira 11	C5	A	SM	SM	SM	SM	SM	SM	SM	SM	SM	SM
Quinta-feira 12	C2	B	FP	FP	FP	FP	HM	HM	HM	HM	FP	FP
Sexta-feira 13	C5	A	SD	SD	HM	HM	SD	SD	CD	CD	SD	SD
Sábado 14	C2	B	PC	PC	PC	PC	PC	PC	PC	PC	PC	PC
Domingo 15	C5	A	CD	CD	SD	SD	CD	CD	SD	SD	FB	FB
Segunda-feira 16	C2	B	PC	PC	PC	PC	PC	PC	PC	PC	PC	PC
Terça-feira 17	C3	C	HM	HM	FP	FP	HM	HM	HM	HM	DS	DS
Quarta-feira 18	C2	B	EM	EM	EM	EM	EM	EM	EM	EM	DS	DS
Quinta-feira 19	C3	C	SD	SD	SD	SD	SD	SD	SD	SD	SD	SD
Sexta-feira 20	C5	A	HM	HM	CD	CD	EM	EM	EM	EM	CD	CD
Sábado 21	C3	C	PC	PC	EM	EM	EM	EM	PC	PC	PC	PC
Domingo 22	C5	A	SD	SM	SD	SM	SD	SM	SD	SM	FB	SM
Segunda-feira 23	C3	C	FP	FP	FP	FP	FP	FP	FP	FP	FP	FP
Terça-feira 24	C5	A	CD	CD	FB	FB	CD	CD	HM	HM	HM	HM
Quarta-feira 25	C2	B	FP	FP	FP	FP	FP	CD	FP	CD	FP	FP
Quinta-feira 26	C5	A	FP	FP	FP	FP	HM	HM	HM	HM	FP	FP
Sexta-feira 27	C2	B	DS	DS	SD	SD	HM	HM	DS	DS	SD	SD
Sábado 28	C3	C	EM	EM	EM	EM	EM	EM	EM	EM	EM	EM
Domingo 29	C2	B	SM	SM	SM	SM	SM	SM	SM	SM	SM	FB
Segunda-feira 30	C3	C	CD	CD	CD	CD	CD	CD	CD	CD	CD	CD
Terça-feira 31	C2	B	SD	SD	DS	DS	DS	DS	SD	SD	SD	SD

AD — Responsabilidades administrativas
CD — A critério do capitão
DS — Treinamento físico no local
FB — Treinamento e manutenção de barco de combate a incêndio
FH — Hidrante de incêndio
HT — Mangueira de incêndio
PC — A critério do comandante do pelotão
PP — Planos de prevenção contra incêndios (*prefire*)[2]
RT — Treinamento da reserva
ST — Treinamento de simulação

AM — Manutenção do aparato — mensal
CR — Treinamento/teste para certificação
EM — Manutenção do equipamento
FP — Prevenção de incêndios
HM — Manutenção/serviço de hidrantes
PH — Pintar/usar código de cores em hidrantes
PI — Inspeção do plano de prevenção contra incêndios
PT — Teste das bombas
SD — Exercícios físicos da equipe do posto
SM — Manutenção do posto/área

Outras operações de serviço também são operações de serviço de quase-manufatura focalizada no produto. Por exemplo, considere o processo de preenchimento de apólices de seguro de vida na sede comercial de uma companhia de seguros. A solicitação de uma apólice de seguro de vida feita por um cliente é encaminhada a diversas estações de trabalho na empresa, onde o pagamento é registrado, dados são introduzidos no sistema de computador, o exame e o histórico médicos são verificados, as aprovações são obtidas, uma apólice é preparada, e finalmente a apólice é enviada pelo correio. Quando comparada com o exemplo do apoio do McDonald's, essa operação de serviço de escritório envolve um número menor de bens físicos e mais trabalho de escritório. Mas o planejamento, análise, controle, programação e administração da operação são tão familiares à manufatura que a maioria daquilo que aprendemos a respeito da manufatura também se aplica aqui.

---

[2] *Prefire:* plano específico de prevenção contra incêndios que mostra ruas, plantas de prédios, saídas de emergência, localização de materiais perigosos, painéis de controle de alarmes, elevadores, hidrantes etc. (N. do T.)

OPERAÇÕES FOCALIZADAS NO PROCESSO

Assim como a maioria das operações de manufatura é do tipo focalizado no processo, o mesmo acontece com a maioria das operações de serviço de quase-manufatura. Considere, por exemplo, uma empresa de serviços metalúrgicos que receba produtos de clientes e submeta os produtos a testes, tratamentos e procedimentos metalúrgicos. Uma variedade de procedimentos está disponível — têmpera profunda, têmpera superficial, recozimento, alívio de tensão, testes radiológicos, análise de rachadura superficial, análises metalúrgicas etc. Cada pedido de cliente especifica a natureza do serviço solicitado. Baseando-se no pedido do cliente, a tarefa é encaminhada aos departamentos apropriados dentro da empresa até que seja finalizada. As tarefas são então empacotadas e remetidas de volta ao cliente.

As operações de serviço de quase-manufatura focalizadas no processo como esta são tão assemelhadas às do tipo job shops que são planejadas, controladas, analisadas, programadas e administradas exatamente como as job shops na manufatura. Elas usam previsões para projetar estrategicamente as operações quanto à capacidade de produção, flexibilidade, tecnologia avançada e qualidade do produto. As decisões quanto ao layout das instalações se baseiam nas abordagens discutidas no Capítulo 7; os princípios de manuseio de materiais e equipamentos de manuseio de materiais, o uso de gabaritos e modelos físicos para desenvolver planos do piso de prédios e o uso de análise da seqüência de operações, análise de distância da carga e análise de layouts com computadores são especialmente relevantes.

As decisões quanto à emissão de pedidos são tomadas de acordo com as discussões nos Capítulos 9 e 10. E elas usam os mesmos métodos de programação discutidos no Capítulo 11:

1. O controle de entrada e saída é importante para balancear a capacidade entre as operações. Isso é obtido analisando-se relatórios de entrada e saída.
2. Gráficos de Gantt são usados para coordenar fluxos de tarefas dentro de e entre departamentos.
3. Um seqüenciamento eficaz de tarefas em centros de trabalho é obtido considerando-se regras de seqüenciamento, custos de preparação e tempos de fluxo.

Todas as operações de produção, seja de manufatura ou qualquer tipo de operação de serviço, devem programar o pessoal para trabalhar em turnos.

PROGRAMAÇÃO DE TURNOS DE TRABALHO EM OPERAÇÕES DE SERVIÇO

Uma coisa que todas as operações de serviço têm em comum é que o meio principal de executar serviços é através de pessoal. Três dificuldades podem ser encontradas na programação de pessoal no setor de serviços: variabilidade da demanda, variabilidade do tempo de serviço e disponibilidade de pessoal quando necessário. Considere, por exemplo, quantos atendentes você programaria para trabalhar durante cada horário de cada dia da semana numa academia de ginástica. A Figura 12.2 ilustra que o número de membros no clube varia drasticamente tanto ao longo do dia como ao longo da semana e que o padrão horário dos membros no clube varia entre os dias da semana. Se for preciso que os atendentes auxiliem os membros em seus exercícios, ofereçam orientação em seus programas de exercícios, distribuam suprimentos e executem outras obrigações, o número de atendentes necessário em cada horário da semana dependerá do número de membros no clube.

Devido aos altos e baixos na demanda do cliente, os gerentes de operações muitas vezes usam duas táticas para desenvolver programas de trabalho para os empregados. A primeira abordagem é usar somente empregados em tempo integral. Com esse arranjo, a programação de um staff excessivo resultará em tempo ocioso dos empregados em períodos de baixa demanda. Em períodos de demanda elevada, a programação de staff insuficiente exigirá a utilização de trabalho em horas extras para aumentar a capacidade. Esses períodos de programação de staff excessivo e staff insuficiente resultam da incapacidade que os gerentes têm para desenvolver programas de trabalho que coincidam exatamente com a demanda prevista.

Quando empregados em tempo integral querem programas de trabalho baseados em cinco dias consecutivos e oito horas consecutivas por dia, essas situações podem surgir.

A outra abordagem para desenvolver programas de trabalho para sistemas de serviço é usar alguns empregados em tempo integral para formar uma base e empregados adicionais em tempo parcial para compor o pessoal do sistema durante períodos de demanda de pico. Se os empregados em tempo parcial puderem ser convocados para trabalhar em curto prazo, tanto melhor. Essa abordagem evita grande parte do excesso de staff e staff insuficiente nos programas de trabalho, e o uso de empregados em tempo parcial evita a utilização de trabalho em horas extras e filas de espera durante períodos de demanda de pico. Porém, as empresas geralmente enfrentam uma rotatividade mais elevada de empregados em tempo parcial; desse modo, mais esforço e despesas são necessários para contratar e treinar novos empregados.

Em alguns serviços, o uso de programas de hora marcada e outros esforços para nivelar a demanda não são inteiramente viáveis; de fato, em alguns casos eles podem ser indesejáveis. Não obstante ser verdadeiro que o nivelamento da demanda simplifica a programação de pessoal, a natureza do serviço pode determinar o quanto a demanda do cliente pode ou deve ser controlada.

No Exemplo 12.1, a academia de ginástica é usada para ilustrar como os programas de hora marcada podem ser usados para fazer a demanda do cliente coincidir com padrões que sejam mais condutivos à programação de pessoal, mesmo que o padrão de demanda resultante não seja totalmente uniforme. Nesse exemplo remodelamos a demanda do cliente para um padrão mais manejável através de programas de hora marcada; em seguida, determinamos o número de atendentes necessário em cada dia da semana; e depois programamos trabalhadores individuais para turnos de trabalho.

EXEMPLO 12.1

PROGRAMAÇÃO DE EMPREGADOS

José Ferdinand está estudando os registros de freqüência de associados na Figura 12.2 tendo em vista programar seus atendentes para trabalharem em turnos de trabalho no Fitness Health Club. Os associados votaram recentemente para que se estabeleça um sistema de horas marcadas no clube, para evitar excesso de pessoas durante certos horários da semana e evitar o custo de horas extras dos atendentes, que anteriormente eram usadas excessivamente na empresa. José sabe que o número de membros no clube ao longo do dia tende a ser baixo na parte da manhã e mais elevado de tarde.

Apesar desse padrão que se modifica de hora em hora, José acredita que a carga de trabalho para os atendentes geralmente é uniforme ao longo do dia, porque os membros que freqüentam o clube na parte da manhã tendem a participar de programas de exercício formais e a exigir mais assistência. Os membros que freqüentam na parte da tarde tendem a participar de atividades recreativas e a exigir menos assistência. Portanto a carga de trabalho horária para os assistentes é mais ou menos uniforme.

José agora deve desenvolver programas de hora marcada e turnos de trabalho para os atendentes.

SOLUÇÃO

1. Primeiro José converte a informação sobre o uso do clube contida na Figura 12.2 para o número de atendentes necessários diariamente. Essa transformação é mostrada na Figura 12.3 de duas maneiras: sem horas marcadas e com horas marcadas.
2. Em seguida, José desenvolve o número necessário de atendentes diariamente com o sistema de horas marcadas:

Segunda-Feira	Terça-Feira	Quarta-Feira	Quinta-Feira	Sexta-Feira	Sábado	Domingo	Turnos de Trabalho Semanais para os Atendentes
6	6	6	6	10	10	10	54

Capítulo 12 – Planejamento e Programação de Operações de Serviço

FIGURA 12.2   PADRÕES DE DEMANDA DO CLIENTE PARA UMA ACADEMIA DE GINÁSTICA

FIGURA 12.3   NECESSIDADE DE ATENDENTES NO FITNESS HEALTH CLUB

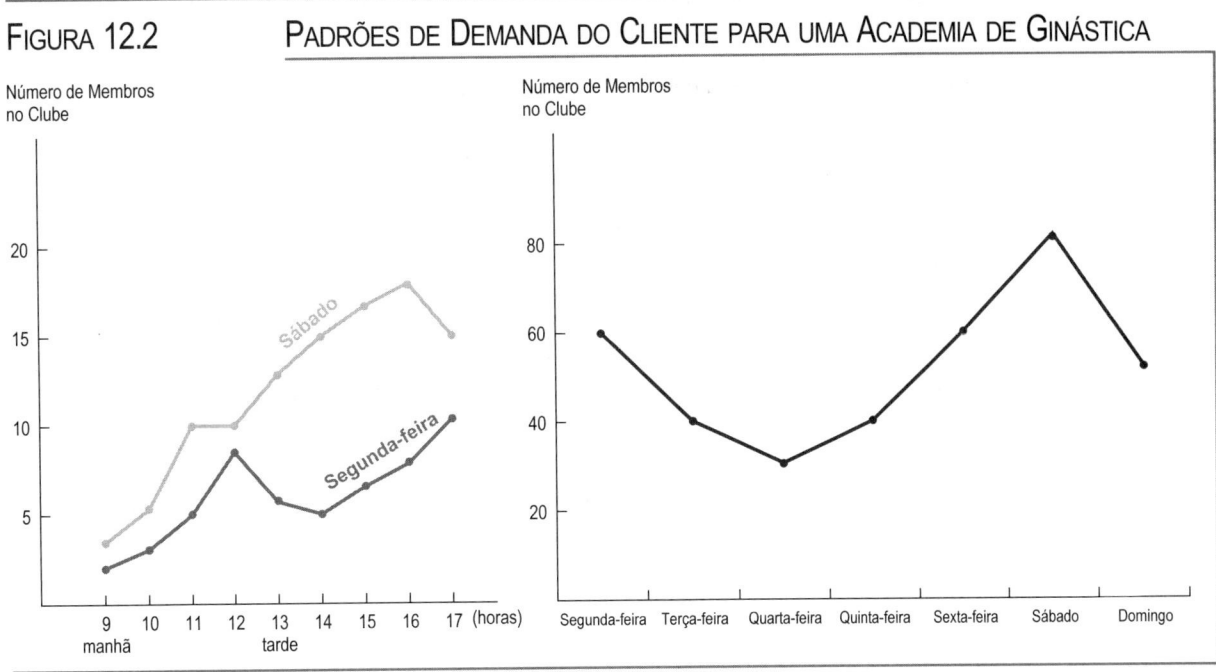

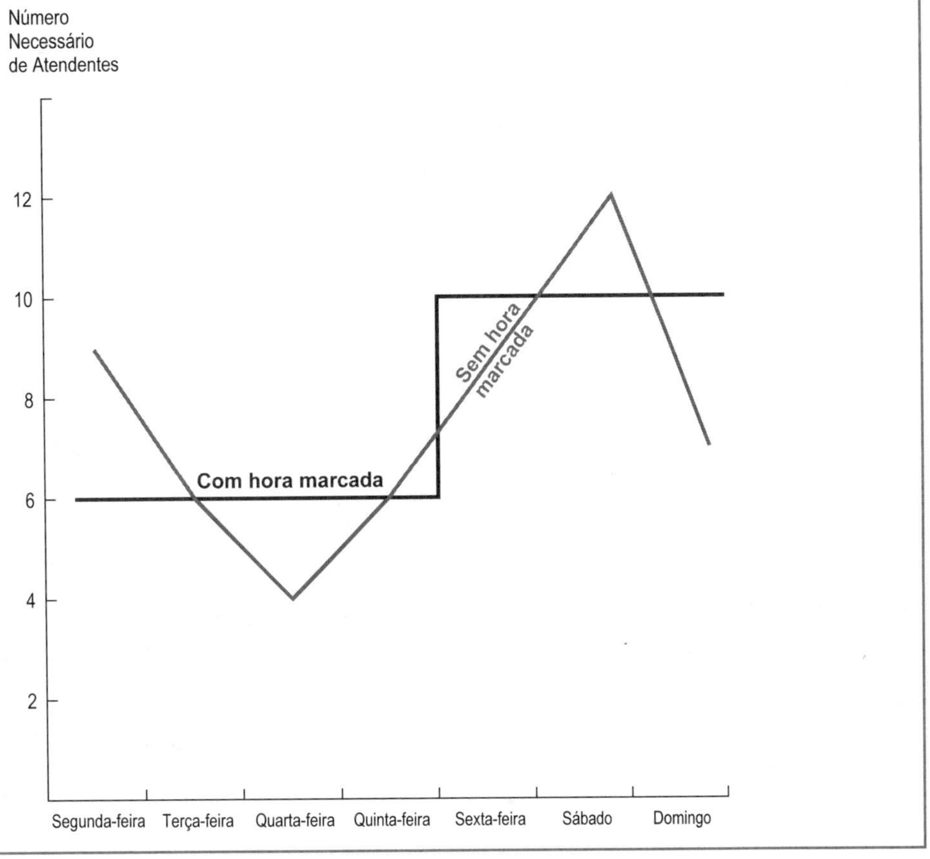

A partir dessa informação, José sabe que se cada atendente trabalhar em cinco turnos de trabalho por semana, ele precisará de um mínimo de 11 atendentes. *Mínimo* significa que o número pode não ser realmente obtido na prática devido à restrição dos cinco dias de trabalho consecutivos, dois dias de folga consecutivos e oito horas de trabalho consecutivas por dia:

$$\text{Número mínimo de atendentes} = \frac{\text{Número total de turnos de trabalho dos assistentes por semana}}{\text{Número de turnos de trabalho por semana por atendente}}$$

$$= 54/5 = 10,8, \text{ ou } 11 \text{ atendentes}$$

3. Em seguida, José desenvolve um programa de turnos de trabalho para os atendentes. A Figura 12.4 mostra o procedimento usado para desenvolver o programa de turnos de trabalho. Esse procedimento utiliza a *regra heurística do turno de trabalho* para determinar os dias de folga para cada trabalhador:

Regra heurística do turno de trabalho: *Escolha dois dias consecutivos que tenham o menor número total de turnos de trabalho necessários. No caso de ligações, escolha arbitrariamente um par e prossiga.*

O número de turnos de trabalho de atendentes necessários em cada dia quando o programa do Atendente n. 1 é planejado foi tomado da Figura 12.3. Um turno de trabalho é subtraído dos turnos de trabalho do Atendente n. 1 (quarta-feira – domingo) para produzir os turnos de trabalho restantes por atendente necessários quando o programa do Atendente n. 2 for planejado. Esse processo é repetido para cada programa de atendente até que dois zeros consecutivos estejam marcados com um círculo e todos os números da linha sejam ou 1 ou 0.

FIGURA 12.4   **PROCEDIMENTO HEURÍSTICO PARA PROGRAMAR TURNOS DE TRABALHO DE ATENDENTES NO FITNESS HEALTH CLUB**

Atendentes	Número de Turnos de Trabalho para os Atendentes						
	Segunda-feira	Terça-feira	Quarta-feira	Quinta-feira	Sexta-feira	Sábado	Domingo
1	(6	6*)	6	6	10	10	10
2	6	6	(5	5*)	9	9	9
3	(5	5*)	5	5	8	8	8
4	5	5	(4	4*)	7	7	7
5	(4	4*)	4	4	6	6	6
6	4	4	(3	3*)	5	5	5
7	(3	3*)	3	3	4	4	4
8	3	3	(2	2*)	3	3	3
9	(2	2*)	2	2	2	2	2
10	2	2	(1	1*)	1	1	1
11	1	1	1	1	(0	0*)	0**

*Os pares de dias que estão marcados com um círculo indicam os dois dias consecutivos de folga para um atendente.

**Esse dia terá um atendente extra. Esse é um afrouxamento inevitável, porque optamos por usar todos os empregados em tempo integral e somente 54 turnos de trabalho são necessários, mas 55 turnos de trabalho resultam de se empregar 11 atendentes.

4. Em seguida, a partir da Figura 12.4, José agora pode determinar os turnos em que cada atendente será programado para trabalhar durante cada semana:

Atendente	Dias de Trabalho	Dias de Folga	Atendente	Dias de Trabalho	Dias de Folga
1	Quarta–Domingo	Segunda–Terça	7	Quarta–Domingo	Segunda–Terça
2	Sexta–Terça	Quarta–Quinta	8	Sexta–Terça	Quarta–Quinta
3	Quarta–Domingo	Segunda–Terça	9	Quarta–Domingo	Segunda–Terça
4	Sexta–Terça	Quarta–Quinta	10	Sexta–Terça	Quarta–Quinta
5	Quarta–Domingo	Segunda–Terça	11	Domingo–Quinta	Sexta–Sábado
6	Sexta–Terça	Quarta–Quinta			

Consideremos agora a programação de outro tipo de operação de serviço.

PROGRAMAÇÃO DE OPERAÇÕES DE SERVIÇO TENDO O CLIENTE COMO PARTICIPANTE

Nesse tipo de operação de serviço há um grau elevado de envolvimento do cliente. Uma vez que os clientes participam de fato das operações, o projeto, planejamento, controle, análise e administração dessas operações são drasticamente afetados.

NATUREZA DESSAS OPERAÇÕES

A venda a varejo, em que os clientes compram, escolhem, pagam e levam consigo bens físicos, é um exemplo desse tipo de operação de serviço. Uma vez que os clientes participam dessas operações, o projeto (design) das instalações deve necessariamente acomodar as necessidades dos clientes. Por exemplo, a esses recursos geralmente são oferecidos:

- Fácil acesso a partir de avenidas e ruas movimentadas.
- Estacionamentos grandes, bem organizados e amplamente iluminados.
- Corredores amplos e bem projetados, entradas facilmente localizáveis, projetadas para receber um grande número de clientes nos horários de pico.
- Portas automáticas e escadas rolantes para minimizar o esforço físico de abrir portas e subir escadas quando grandes quantidades de mercadorias precisam ser transportadas.
- Saguões ou outras áreas de recepção ou de guardar volumes e filas de espera para clientes.
- Bebedouros, sanitários, departamentos de crédito, postos de devolução de mercadorias e balcões de informação.
- Balcões de serviço, caixas registradoras e estações de trabalho de empregados.
- Exposições de mercadorias, corredores e decoração e iluminação atraentes.

O grau em que esses recursos devem ser oferecidos varia de acordo com a quantidade de envolvimento dos clientes nas operações. Considere, por exemplo, as operações de um banco onde a instalação inteira deve ser projetada tendo em vista os clientes — estacionamento, entrada e saída fáceis, áreas de espera agradáveis, filas de espera para atendimento padronizado ao cliente, guichês de atendimento e caixas, e áreas individualizadas para atendimento a clientes. As operações de balcão de um restaurante McDonald's e lojas de departamentos de venda a varejo como a Wal-Mart, Foley's e Dillard's são exemplos de operações de serviço que têm o cliente como participante.

O layout e a administração dessas operações exigem uma estreita cooperação e combinação das operações e funções de marketing. O planejamento e controle de estoques, qualidade de produto de bens físicos, programação de pessoal, planejamento de filas de espera, manutenção de instalações, armazenagem, embarque, compra e administração de materiais são o domínio dos gerentes de operações. E aquilo que aprendemos sobre planejamento, controle, análise, programação e administração de operações de manufatura se aplica diretamente aqui. Mas essas questões são crucialmente afetadas pelas estratégias e táticas de comercialização. Por exemplo, o layout dessas operações deve exibir produtos de forma que os clientes possam localizá-los facilmente e ser motivados a comprá-los. A utilização de corredores angulares para chamar a atenção do cliente para itens localizados fora das alas principais, direcionamento do fluxo de pessoas em forma de diamante ou circulares, colocação de itens mais lucrativos em prateleiras do perímetro do piso da loja, colocação de itens de grande saída nos finais dos corredores, e outras táticas de comercialização são usadas para promover a venda dos produtos da organização. Além disso, políticas de preço competitivas, propaganda local e fora do local, compra e outras facetas do setor de venda a varejo são necessariamente o domínio da área de marketing e merchandising. A administração de operações e o merchandising são entrelaçados no planejamento, controle e administração dessas operações de serviço.

Os objetivos dessas operações são predominantemente a satisfação do cliente e a qualidade do produto. Todas as facetas da administração de operações são seriamente afetadas. A atividade de realização de previsões, layout das instalações, avaliação da automação e computadores nas operações, planejamento da capacidade, pedido de estoques, políticas de manutenção de estoques e programação de pessoal são todos impulsionados pela necessidade de maximizar a satisfação do cliente. E, desde que essas operações geralmente têm um forte elemento de bens físicos, uma superior qualidade de produto é extremamente importante.

Uma vez que os serviços ocorrem em encontros cara a cara entre empregados e clientes, o desempenho do empregado é crucial para se obter satisfação do cliente. Uma cuidadosa seleção, contratação, treinamento, supervisão, avaliação e recompensa de pessoal são, talvez, o fator número um para se manter ou aumentar a fatia de mercado por meio da aumentada satisfação do cliente. Discutiremos mais sobre a importância do pessoal na obtenção de satisfação do cliente posteriormente neste capítulo.

Nessas operações de serviço que têm o cliente como participante, as filas de espera de clientes são uma preocupação importante tanto para os gerentes de operações como para os clientes.

Filas de Espera nas Operações de Serviço

Como cliente, você sabe quão irritante é ficar parado em longas filas de espera. Com a proliferação das operações de serviços nos últimos anos, as filas de espera de clientes se tornaram tão comuns que ficamos imaginando se longas filas de espera são uma parte necessária dos serviços.

Fundamentalmente, longas filas de espera de clientes se formam porque os gerentes não providenciaram suficiente capacidade de produção para evitá-las. Não foi fornecido pessoal ou equipamentos suficientes para prover imediatamente serviços ao cliente quando necessário. Capacidade excessiva poderia ser fornecida na forma de uma abundância de pessoal, instalações e equipamentos, mas os custos operacionais se elevariam abruptamente. Por outro lado, se não for fornecida capacidade de produção suficiente e os clientes esperarem demasiadamente, eles poderão não retornar a uma loja em particular, que deixaria assim de lucrar. Os gerentes de operações geralmente tentam buscar um equilíbrio entre oferecer pessoal e equipamentos suficientes para manter as filas de espera relativamente curtas para que a satisfação do cliente seja elevada, mas não tão curtas a ponto de os custos operacionais serem excessivos.

A análise das filas de espera se desenvolveu para auxiliar os gerentes a responder questões como estas:

- Quantos canais de serviço ao cliente devem ser providos de pessoal durante cada horário do dia?
- Quanto tempo os clientes esperarão em média se provermos de pessoal seis canais de serviço ao cliente durante cada horário do dia?
- Quantos clientes estarão nas filas de espera, em média, se provermos de pessoal seis canais de serviço ao cliente durante cada horário do dia?
- Quantos metros quadrados de espaço de piso serão necessários para as filas de espera se provermos de pessoal seis canais de serviço ao cliente?

Filas de espera podem se formar em muitos tipos diferentes de operações: tarefas de impressão em computador aguardam para ser processadas numa impressora a laser em cores. Trabalhadores aguardam para "bater o ponto" na entrada da empresa. Clientes aguardam para ser atendidos no caixa do banco. Peças aguardam para ser processadas numa operação de manufatura. Máquinas aguardam para ser consertadas numa oficina de manutenção. Clientes aguardam para comprar passagens num balcão de venda de passagens aéreas. Caminhões aguardam para descarregar suas cargas numa doca de descarga. O que leva as filas de espera a se formar? Quando clientes, peças, máquinas, tarefas de impressão ou caminhões chegam a centros de serviço irregularmente, e a capacidade dos centros de serviço não pode ser ampliada ou reduzida para atender de maneira exata as necessidades dessas chegadas, sempre se formam filas de espera. Mesmo que os gerentes *pudessem* ampliar rapidamente as capacidades de centros de serviço, o padrão de demanda sempre é tão imprevisível que os gerentes não conseguem reagir de maneira suficientemente rápida para ampliar as capacidades dos centros de serviço; portanto, filas de espera se formam.

Para complicar ainda mais a análise das filas de espera, geralmente não sabemos com certeza quanto tempo será necessário para atender cada chegada. Nos bancos, por exemplo, alguns clientes necessitam de somente cerca de um minuto para ser atendidos, talvez para um saque de pequeno valor ou um depósito. Outros clientes necessitam de 15 a 20 minutos para ser atendidos, especialmente se tiverem uma pasta cheia de transações comerciais para serem realizadas.

Características das Filas de Espera   As filas de espera tipicamente têm estas características:

1. Os padrões de chegada são irregulares ou aleatórios. Não obstante podermos saber qual é o número médio de chegadas por hora que devem permanecer à espera, não sabemos com certeza qual é o número de chegadas em qualquer horário específico.
2. Os tempos de atendimento variam entre as chegadas. Não obstante sabermos qual é o tempo médio necessário para atender uma chegada, não sabemos antecipadamente quanto tempo será necessário para atender cada chegada.

Alguns gerentes planejam as capacidades dos centros de serviço para que atendam a condição média mais uma margem de segurança. Por exemplo, se um gerente de banco souber que, em média, cerca de 50 clientes por hora deverão ser atendidos nos guichês, um número suficiente de guichês, de dinheiro, de suprimentos e áreas de espera devem ser garantidos para atender uma média de aproximadamente 70 clientes por hora. Essa abordagem da margem de segurança baseia-se no fato de que, não obstante 50 clientes por hora chegarem, em média, de 20 a 90 clientes poderão chegar em qualquer horário de maneira simplesmente casual. Uma vez que os padrões de chegada são irregulares e aleatórios, 20 minutos podem se passar sem que *qualquer* cliente apareça, e então 15 clientes podem irromper pelas portas.

Não obstante a abordagem da margem de segurança acima descrita ser observada na prática, foram desenvolvidas técnicas de análise mais precisas que fornecem aos gerentes melhores informações para que possam planejar as capacidades dos centros de serviço em termos de filas de espera. O segundo estudo sistemático relatado das filas de espera foi realizado por A. K. Erlang, um matemático dinamarquês da Copenhagen Telephone Company, em 1917. O trabalho inicial de Erlang foi ampliado, e hoje muito já se sabe sobre o comportamento das filas de espera.

Terminologia e Estruturas dos Sistemas de Filas de Espera   Esse conjunto de conhecimentos sobre as filas de espera muitas vezes é chamado **teoria das filas**, e as filas de espera são chamadas **filas**. Antes de examinarmos os conceitos da teoria das filas e suas técnicas de análise, estude a terminologia das filas na Tabela 12.3. A Figura 12.5 mostra quatro estruturas comuns do sistema de filas.

Qual informação os gerentes comumente precisam saber a respeito das filas de espera?

1. Dado que um sistema de serviço foi projetado para atender certo número de chegadas por hora, em média:
    a) Qual é o número médio de unidades na fila de espera?
    b) Qual é o tempo médio que cada unidade gasta esperando?
    c) Qual é o número médio de unidades na fila de espera e que estão sendo atendidas — em outras palavras, qual é o número de unidades no sistema?
    d) Qual é o tempo médio que cada unidade gasta no sistema?
    e) Qual é a porcentagem de tempo que o sistema permanece vazio?
    f) Qual é a probabilidade de que n unidades estejam no sistema?

TABELA 12.3 — TERMINOLOGIA DAS FILAS

Chegada — Uma unidade da distribuição da taxa de chegada. Ocorre quando uma pessoa, máquina, peça etc. chega e necessita de atendimento. Cada unidade pode continuar a ser chamada chegada enquanto permanecer no sistema de serviço.

Taxa de chegada (λ) — A taxa em que coisas ou pessoas chegam, em chegadas por unidade de tempo (por exemplo, pessoas por hora). A taxa de chegada geralmente tem uma distribuição normal ou de Poisson.

Canais — O número de filas de espera num sistema de serviço. Um sistema de canal único tem somente uma fila, e um sistema de múltiplos canais tem duas ou mais filas.

Fila — Uma fila de espera.

Disciplina de fila — As regras que determinam a ordem na qual as chegadas são seqüenciadas através de sistemas de serviço. Algumas disciplinas de fila comuns são: primeiro a entrar, primeiro a ser atendido, o menor tempo de processamento, razão crítica e os clientes mais valorizados são atendidos primeiro.

Tamanho da fila — O número de chegadas (pessoas ou serviços) que esperam para ser atendidas.

Fases do serviço — O número de passos no atendimento das chegadas. Um sistema de serviço de fase única tem somente uma fase de atendimento, enquanto um sistema de múltiplas fases tem dois ou mais passos.

Taxa de atendimento (μ) — A razão em que as chegadas (pessoas ou serviços) são atendidas, em chegadas por unidade de tempo (horas, dias etc.). A taxa de atendimento é usualmente uma distribuição uniforme, normal ou de Poisson.

Taxa de serviço ($1/\mu$) — O tempo necessário para atender uma chegada, expresso em minutos (ou horas, dias etc.) por chegada. A medida não inclui o tempo de espera.

Tempo no sistema — O tempo total que as chegadas gastam no sistema, incluindo tanto o tempo de espera como o de atendimento.

Utilização (P_n) — O grau em que qualquer parte de um sistema de serviço é ocupada por uma chegada. Geralmente é expressa como a probabilidade de que n chegadas estejam no sistema.

Tempo de espera — A quantidade de tempo que uma chegada gasta na fila.

---

2. Ou, dado que a administração define políticas que limitam o número médio de unidades na fila de espera, o número médio de unidades no sistema, o tempo médio que cada unidade permanece na fila de espera, o tempo médio que cada unidade permanece no sistema ou a porcentagem de tempo que o sistema permanece vazio, qual capacidade do centro de serviço é necessária para que sejam cumpridas essas políticas da administração?

Quatro Modelos de Filas e Suas Fórmulas Apresentamos aqui quatro modelos que têm sido usados para estudar filas em particular. As Tabelas 12.4 e 12.5 mostram as definições de variáveis, as características desses sistemas de filas e as fórmulas para analisá-las.

Modelo 1: Canal Único e Fase Única As filas de espera que são do tipo canal único e fase única geralmente podem ser analisadas pelo Modelo 1. Quando a taxa de chegada (λ) e a taxa de serviço (μ) são conhecidas, o número médio de chegadas na fila ($\bar{n}_l$), o número médio de chegadas no sistema ($\bar{n}_s$), o tempo médio que cada chegada permanece na fila de espera ($\bar{t}_l$), o tempo médio que cada chegada permanece no sistema ($\bar{t}_s$) e a probabilidade de que exatamente n chegadas estejam no sistema (P_n), todos podem ser computados. O Exemplo 12.2 demonstra como as fórmulas desse modelo são aplicadas.

TABELA 12.4 — DEFINIÇÕES DE VARIÁVEIS PARA MODELOS DE FILAS

λ = taxa de chegada — número médio de chegadas por unidade de tempo

μ = taxa de serviço — número médio de chegadas que podem ser atendidas por unidade de tempo por canal

n = número de chegadas no sistema

$\bar{n}_l$ = número médio de chegadas que estão na fila de espera

$\bar{n}_s$ = número médio de chegadas no sistema

N = número de canais num sistema de múltiplos canais

P_n = probabilidade de que haja exatamente n chegadas no sistema

Q = número máximo de chegadas que podem estar no sistema (soma das chegadas que são atendidas e que estão na fila de espera)

$\bar{t}_l$ = tempo médio que as chegadas esperam

$\bar{t}_s$ = tempo médio que as chegadas permanecem no sistema

Capítulo 12 – Planejamento e Programação de Operações de Serviço

FIGURA 12.5   ESTRUTURAS DOS SISTEMAS DE FILAS

Fase Única
1. Canal Único

S_1

2. Múltiplos Canais

S_{11}
S_{21}
S_{31}

Múltiplas Fases
3. Canal Único

S_{11} S_{12}

4. Múltiplos Canais

S_{11} S_{12}
S_{21} S_{22}
S_{31} S_{32}

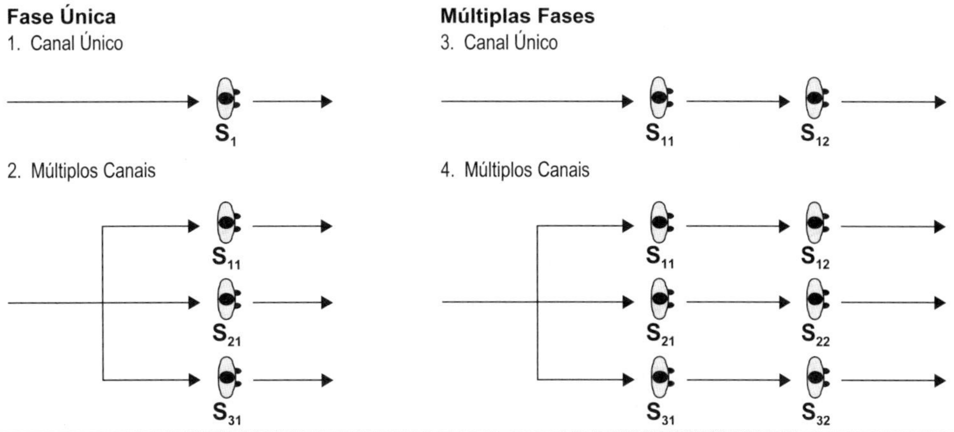

TABELA 12.5   QUATRO MODELOS DE FILAS E SUAS FÓRMULAS

	Características dos Sistemas de Filas				
Número do Modelo	Número de Canais	Distribuição da Taxa de Serviço	Tamanho Máximo da Fila	Exemplos	Fórmulas
1	Único	Poisson	Ilimitado	Vendas de ingressos para teatro num único guichê, oficina de conserto e manutenção	$\bar{n}_l = \dfrac{\lambda^2}{\mu(\mu - \lambda)}$ $\bar{t}_l = \dfrac{\lambda}{\mu(\mu - \lambda)}$ $\bar{n}_s = \dfrac{\lambda}{\mu - \lambda}$ $\bar{t}_s = \dfrac{1}{\mu - \lambda}$ $P_n = [1 - (\lambda/\mu)](\lambda/\mu)^n$
2	Único	Constante	Ilimitado	Operação de manufatura controlada mecanicamente, lava-rápido	$\bar{n}_l = \dfrac{\lambda^2}{2\mu(\mu - \lambda)}$ $\bar{t}_l = \dfrac{\lambda}{2\mu(\mu - \lambda)}$ $\bar{n}_s = \bar{n}_l + \dfrac{\lambda}{\mu}$ $\bar{t}_s = \bar{t}_l + \dfrac{1}{\mu}$
3	Único	Poisson	Limitado	Posto bancário drive-in, operação de manufatura com estoques em processo, estacionamento de loja varejista, oficina de conserto e manutenção	$\bar{n}_l = \left(\dfrac{\lambda}{\mu}\right)^2 \left[\dfrac{1 - Q(\lambda/\mu)^{Q-1} + (Q - 1)(\lambda/\mu)^Q}{[1 - (\lambda/\mu)][1 - (\lambda/\mu)^Q]}\right]$ $\bar{n}_s = \left(\dfrac{\lambda}{\mu}\right)\left[\dfrac{1 - (Q + 1)(\lambda/\mu)^Q + Q(\lambda/\mu)^{Q+1}}{[1 - (\lambda/\mu)][1 - (\lambda/\mu)^{Q+1}]}\right]$ $P_n = \left[\dfrac{1 - (\lambda/\mu)}{1 - (\lambda/\mu)^{Q+1}}\right](\lambda/\mu)^n$
4	Múltiplo	Poisson	Ilimitado	Guichê de pagamento de pedágio rodoviário, guichê bancário, oficina de conserto e manutenção	$P_0 = \dfrac{1}{\sum\limits_{n=0}^{N-1}\left[\dfrac{(\lambda/\mu)^n}{n!}\right] + \dfrac{(\lambda/\mu)^N}{N!\left(1 - \dfrac{\lambda}{\mu(N)}\right)}}$ $\bar{n}_l = P_0\left[\dfrac{\lambda\mu(\lambda/\mu)^N}{(N - 1)!(N\mu - \lambda)^2}\right]$ $\bar{t}_l = \left(\dfrac{\lambda}{\mu}\right)^N\left[\dfrac{P_0}{\mu N(N!)\left(1 - \dfrac{\lambda}{\mu N}\right)^2}\right]$ $\bar{n}_s = \bar{n}_l + (\lambda/\mu)$ $\bar{t}_s = \bar{t}_l + (1/\mu)$

Observação: Todos os quatro modelos têm serviços de fase única e distribuições de Poisson de taxa de chegada.

EXEMPLO 12.2

ANALISANDO FILAS DE ESPERA NO DMV EXPRESS

O Oregon Department of Motor Vehicles (DMV) tem um posto DMV Express no Valley River Mall[3], em Eugene, Oregon. O DMV Express tem somente um guichê de atendimento ao cliente e oferece um único serviço: renovação de carteiras de motorista no Oregon. Esta informação sobre chegadas de clientes e atendimento ao cliente é conhecida:

λ = Chegam 50 clientes por hora, em média
μ = Em média, 75 clientes por hora podem ser atendidos

Considera-se que as taxas de chegada e de serviço têm uma distribuição de Poisson, o sistema tem uma única fase e um único canal, e o tamanho máximo da fila é ilimitado. **a)** Compute o tamanho médio da fila. **b)** Compute o número médio de clientes no sistema de serviço. **c)** Compute o tempo médio que os clientes esperam. **d)** Compute o tempo médio que os clientes permanecem no sistema. **e)** Compute a probabilidade de que um ou mais clientes estejam no sistema.

SOLUÇÃO

a) Compute o tamanho médio da fila (use a fórmula para o Modelo 1):

$$\bar{n}_l = \frac{\lambda^2}{\mu(\mu - \lambda)} = \frac{(50)^2}{75(75 - 50)} = \frac{2.500}{75(25)} = \frac{2.500}{1.875} = 1{,}33 \text{ cliente}$$

b) Compute o número médio de clientes no sistema:

$$\bar{n}_s = \frac{\lambda}{(\mu - \lambda)} = \frac{50}{75 - 50} = \frac{50}{25} = 2{,}00 \text{ clientes}$$

c) Compute o tempo médio que os clientes permanecem na fila de espera:

$$\bar{t}_l = \frac{\lambda}{\mu(\mu - \lambda)} = \frac{50}{75(75 - 50)} = \frac{50}{75(25)} = \frac{50}{1.875} = 0{,}0267 \text{ minuto} = 1{,}6 \text{ minuto}$$

d) Compute o tempo médio que os clientes permanecem no sistema:

$$\bar{t}_s = \frac{1}{(\mu - \lambda)} = \frac{1}{75 - 50} = \frac{1}{25} = 0{,}040 \text{ hora} = 2{,}4 \text{ minutos}$$

e) Compute a probabilidade de que um ou mais clientes estejam no sistema.

Primeiro, compute a probabilidade de o sistema estar vazio:

$$P_n = \left(1 - \frac{\lambda}{\mu}\right)\left(\frac{\lambda}{\mu}\right)^n, \text{ onde } n = 0$$

$$P_0 = \left(1 - \frac{50}{75}\right)\left(\frac{50}{75}\right)^0 = \left(1 - \frac{50}{75}\right)(1) = 1 - \frac{50}{75} = 1 - 0{,}667 = 0{,}333$$

Em seguida, desde que P_0 é a probabilidade de que o sistema esteja vazio, $1 - P_0$ é a probabilidade de que um ou mais clientes estejam no sistema:

$$1 - P_0 = 1 - 0{,}333 = 0{,}667$$

---

[3] *Mall:* shopping center; centro comercial; "calçadão". (N. do T.)

Capítulo 12 – Planejamento e Programação de Operações de Serviço

Modelo 2: Canal Único, Fase Única e Tempos de Serviço Constantes Quando as filas de espera de canal único e fase única têm tempos de atendimento constantes, como no caso de um lava-rápido automático, uma máquina de café automática num prédio de escritórios ou uma operação de manufatura controlada mecanicamente, o Modelo 2 geralmente é apropriado para estudar esses sistemas. As medidas $\bar{n}_l$, $\bar{n}_s$, $\bar{t}_l$ e $\bar{t}_s$ também são computadas a partir das fórmulas desse modelo. Observe que esses valores sempre são inferiores aos do Modelo 1. Portanto, tempos de serviço constantes sempre são preferidos a tempos de serviço aleatórios.

O Exemplo 12.3 demonstra o uso de fórmulas do Modelo 2.

EXEMPLO 12.3

MUDANDO O DMV EXPRESS PARA UMA TAXA DE SERVIÇO CONSTANTE

O DMV Express do Exemplo 12.2 é a primeira empresa a fornecer uma máquina automatizada de renovação de carteiras de motorista. O cliente insere na máquina, juntamente com um cartão de crédito, sua carteira de motorista atual, que contém uma faixa magnética no verso. A máquina troca então informações com um computador central em Salem, Oregon, e com a empresa de cartões de crédito do cliente. Se o cliente não tiver violado nenhuma lei de trânsito, não tiver decretada sua prisão e a empresa de cartões de crédito aprovar a cobrança, então a faixa magnética na carteira de motorista é atualizada e a carteira, o cartão de crédito e o recibo são devolvidos ao cliente. As demonstrações mostraram que o processamento total leva exatamente 48 segundos para cada cliente, de forma que 75 clientes por hora podem ser atendidos.

Use o Modelo 2 de filas para computar: **a)** o tamanho médio da fila, **b)** o número médio de clientes no sistema, **c)** o tempo médio que os clientes permanecem na fila de espera e **d)** o tempo médio que os clientes permanecem no sistema.

SOLUÇÃO

a) Compute o tamanho médio da fila:

$$\bar{n}_l = \frac{\lambda^2}{2\mu(\mu - \lambda)} = \frac{(50)^2}{2(75)(75 - 50)} = \frac{2.500}{3.750} = 0,667 \text{ cliente}$$

b) Compute o número médio de clientes no sistema:

$$\bar{n}_s = \bar{n}_l + \frac{\lambda}{\mu} = \frac{\lambda^2}{2\mu(\mu - \lambda)} + \frac{\lambda}{\mu} = \frac{(50)^2}{2(75)(75 - 50)} + \frac{50}{75} = \frac{2.500}{3.750} + \frac{50}{75} = 0,6667 + 0,6667$$

$$= 1,333 \text{ cliente}$$

c) Compute o tempo médio que os clientes esperam na fila:

$$\bar{t}_l = \frac{\lambda}{2\mu(\mu - \lambda)} = \frac{50}{2(75)(75 - 50)} = \frac{50}{3.750} = 0,0133 \text{ hora} = 0,8 \text{ minuto}$$

d) Compute o tempo médio que os clientes permanecem no sistema:

$$\bar{t}_s = \bar{t}_l + \frac{1}{\mu} = \frac{\lambda}{2\mu(\mu - \lambda)} + \frac{1}{\mu} = \frac{50}{2(75)(75 - 50)} + \frac{1}{75} = \frac{50}{3.750} + \frac{1}{75} = 0,01333 + 0,01333$$

$$= 0,0267 \text{ hora} = 1,6 \text{ minuto}$$

Modelo 3: Canal Único, Fase Única e Comprimento Limitado de Fila de Espera Quando as filas de espera de canal único e fase única são limitadas quanto ao comprimento máximo que podem ter, o Modelo 3 geralmente pode ser usado. Comprimentos de filas de espera podem ser limitados por fatores como área da sala de espera, vagas no estacionamento e tamanho das esteiras rolantes que conduzem peças que esperam para ser processadas em operações de manufatura.

O Exemplo 12.4 demonstra como as fórmulas desse modelo são usadas.

EXEMPLO 12.4

A SHINY CAR WASH

A Shiny Car Wash oferece uma variedade de serviços para automóveis. Chegam aproximadamente seis carros por hora ao lava-rápido, e os empregados podem atender cerca de oito carros por hora. Se o prédio e o estacionamento particular permitem um máximo de somente quatro carros, compute: **a)** $\bar{n}_l$, **b)** $\bar{n}_s$ e **c)** a probabilidade de o lava-rápido e seu estacionamento estarem cheios.

SOLUÇÃO

a) Compute $\bar{n}_l$:

$$\bar{n}_l = \left(\frac{\lambda}{\mu}\right)^2 \left[\frac{1 - Q(\lambda/\mu)^{Q-1} + (Q-1)(\lambda/\mu)^Q}{[1 - (\lambda/\mu)][1 - (\lambda/\mu)^Q]}\right]$$

$$= \left(\frac{6}{8}\right)^2 \left[\frac{1 - 4(6/8)^{4-1} + (4-1)(6/8)^4}{[1 - (6/8)][1 - (6/8)^4]}\right]$$

$$= \left(\frac{6}{8}\right)^2 \left[\frac{1 - 4(6/8)^3 + (3)(6/8)^4}{[1 - (6/8)][1 - (6/8)^4]}\right] = 0{,}5625 \left[\frac{1 - 1{,}6875 + 0{,}9492}{0{,}25(0{,}6836)}\right]$$

$$= 0{,}5625 \left(\frac{0{,}2617}{0{,}1709}\right) = 0{,}861$$

b) Compute $\bar{n}_s$:

$$\bar{n}_s = \left(\frac{\lambda}{\mu}\right) \left[\frac{1 - (Q+1)(\lambda/\mu)^Q + Q(\lambda/\mu)^{Q+1}}{[1 - (\lambda/\mu)][1 - (\lambda/\mu)^{Q+1}]}\right]$$

$$= \left(\frac{6}{8}\right) \left[\frac{1 - (4+1)(6/8)^4 + 4(6/8)^{4+1}}{[1 - (6/8)][1 - (6/8)^{4+1}]}\right]$$

$$= \left(\frac{6}{8}\right) \left[\frac{1 - (5)(6/8)^4 + 4(6/8)^5}{[1 - (6/8)][1 - (6/8)^5]}\right] = 0{,}75 \left[\frac{1 - 1{,}5820 + 0{,}9492}{0{,}25(0{,}7627)}\right]$$

$$= 0{,}75 \left(\frac{0{,}3672}{0{,}1907}\right) = 1{,}444$$

c) Compute a probabilidade de o lava-rápido e seu estacionamento estarem cheios:

$$P_n = \left[\frac{1 - (\lambda/\mu)}{1 - (\lambda/\mu)^{Q+1}}\right] (\lambda/\mu)^n$$

$$P_4 = \left[\frac{1 - (6/8)}{1 - (6/8)^{4+1}}\right] (6/8)^4 = \left[\frac{1 - (6/8)}{1 - (6/8)^5}\right] (6/8)^4 = \left(\frac{0{,}25}{0{,}7627}\right) 0{,}3164 = 0{,}104$$

Modelo 4: Múltiplos Canais e Fase Única Quando mais de uma fila de espera é usada e os serviços têm uma única fase, geralmente o Modelo 4 pode ser usado para fornecer informações sobre esses sistemas aos gerentes. Como no Modelo 3, entretanto, as fórmulas do Modelo 4 também são mais complexas de usar e aplicar. Programas de computador como os da *POM Computer Library* simplificaram muito a aplicação desse modelo. Analistas abastecem o computador com dados sobre taxas de chegada, taxas de serviço e número de filas de espera. O computador executa então os cálculos necessários para fornecer aos analistas os valores P_n, $\bar{n}_l$, $\bar{n}_s$, $\bar{t}_l$ e $\bar{t}_s$.

O Exemplo 12.5 ilustra a aplicação desse modelo.

Exemplo 12.5

A Shiny Car Wash Se Expande

A Shiny Car Wash do Exemplo 12.4 tem recebido numerosas reclamações de seus clientes de que não conseguem receber atendimento porque o lava-rápido está cheio. O proprietário do lava-rápido pode comprar a propriedade vizinha e ampliá-lo duplicando suas instalações atuais. Aproximadamente seis carros por hora ainda esperariam para chegar ao lava-rápido, e os empregados poderiam atender cerca de oito carros por hora em cada um dos dois lava-rápidos.

O proprietário da Shiny reflete sobre como o número médio de carros que estão na fila de espera e no sistema se modificaria e qual seria a probabilidade de as duas instalações se esvaziarem.

Solução

a) Primeiro, compute P_0, a probabilidade de que o sistema se esvazie:

$$P_0 = \frac{1}{\sum_{n=0}^{N-1}\left[\frac{(\lambda/\mu)^n}{n!}\right] + \frac{(\lambda/\mu)^N}{N!\left(1 - \frac{\lambda}{\mu(N)}\right)}} = \frac{1}{\sum_{n=0}^{1}\left[\frac{(6/8)^n}{n!}\right] + \frac{(6/8)^2}{2!\left[1 - \frac{6}{8(2)}\right]}}$$

$$= \frac{1}{\left[\frac{(6/8)^0}{0!} + \frac{(6/8)^1}{1!}\right] + \frac{0.5625}{2[1 - (6/16)]}} = \frac{1}{\left[\frac{1}{1} + \frac{6/8}{1}\right] + \frac{0,5625}{2(0,625)}}$$

$$= \frac{1}{(1 + 0,75 + 0,45)} = \frac{1}{2,2} = 0,4545$$

b) Compute $\bar{n}_l$:

$$\bar{n}_l = P_0\left[\frac{\lambda\mu(\lambda/\mu)^N}{(N-1)!(N\mu - \lambda)^2}\right] = 0,4545\left[\frac{(6)(8)(6/8)^2}{(2-1)![(2)(8) - 6]^2}\right]$$

$$= 0,4545\left[\frac{27}{1(100)}\right] = 0,4545(0,27) = 0,1227$$

c) Compute $\bar{n}_s$:

$$\bar{n}_s = \bar{n}_l + (\lambda/\mu) = 0,1227 + (6/8) = 0,1227 + 0,75 = 0,8727$$

Uma Avaliação da Análise das Filas de Espera na APO Um importante benefício de se entender os modelos apresentados na Tabela 12.5 é a percepção que se tem do comportamento das filas de espera, obtida através da utilização desses modelos relativamente simples. Por exemplo, veja a fórmula para $\bar{n}_l$ no Modelo 1. O que acontece com o tamanho da fila de espera quando a taxa de chegada (λ) se aproxima da taxa de serviço (μ)? A resposta é que a fila de espera se torna muito grande. A implicação dessa descoberta para os gerentes de operações é que as capacidades do centro de serviço (taxas de serviço) sempre devem ser bem maiores, numa margem de segurança, do que os níveis de demanda do cliente (taxas de chegada). Essa descoberta bastante simplista está no centro de um novo paradigma na APO. Tradicionalmente, os gerentes de operações tentavam manter a capacidade de produção o mais baixo possível, a fim de que uma elevada utilização de pessoal e instalações pudessem ser obtidas. Pensava-se que essa abordagem era mais eficiente, uma vez que menos capacidade era usada para produzir mais bens e serviços. Agora, entretanto, *com o novo paradigma de competição baseada no tempo (TBC — time-based competition), os gerentes de operações vêem a importância de terem capacidade extra a fim de que as filas de espera para produtos e serviços sejam abreviadas e a produção ocorra mais rapidamente. Esse novo paradigma é visto como a maneira fundamental de se obter maior satisfação do cliente.* Discutiremos mais sobre esse importante conceito no Capítulo 13.

A utilização desses modelos é limitada pelos seguintes fatores:

1. Serviços de múltiplas fases podem não ser analisados pelo uso dessas fórmulas.
2. Taxas de chegada de serviço que não sejam de distribuições de Poisson infinitas podem não ser analisadas por essas fórmulas.
3. Presume-se que a disciplina de fila seja a de primeiro a entrar, primeiro a ser atendido. Outras disciplinas conhecidas como freqüentemente usadas na prática são o menor tempo de processamento, razão crítica e os clientes mais valorizados atendidos primeiro.
4. Mudança de filas não é permitido em sistemas de múltiplos canais.

Embora essas suposições pareçam restritivas, não se assuste. É reconfortante saber que um número surpreendente de sistemas de filas de fase única ocorre nas operações, que muitas pesquisas têm verificado que a maioria das taxas de chegada e de serviço são distribuições de Poisson, e que a disciplina de fila primeiro a entrar, primeiro a ser atendido prevalece nos serviços e em muitas operações de manufatura.

Digamos que um gerente de operações use esses modelos para compor o staff e projetar um sistema de fila de espera que cumpra a política de não se ter mais de dez clientes esperando em média. O que pode ser feito se as filas de espera crescerem além de dez clientes? Nem tudo está perdido. Os modelos de filas podem ajudar no projeto de sistemas de filas, mas cabe ao gerente de operações *administrar* o sistema de filas no dia-a-dia. Como vimos, trabalhadores que costumeiramente executam outras obrigações podem ser chamados para ativar canais adicionais ou agilizar canais operacionais que tenham filas excessivamente longas. Trabalhadores em tempo parcial que ficam em prontidão, equipamentos de reserva e outras medidas de contingência para evitar filas de espera excessivamente longas também são comumente usados nos serviços.

Filas de espera podem ocorrer em todos os tipos de operações de serviço e manufatura. Continuemos nossa discussão a respeito das operações de serviço examinando operações de serviço que têm o cliente como produto.

PROGRAMAÇÃO DE OPERAÇÕES DE SERVIÇO TENDO O CLIENTE COMO PRODUTO

Nas operações de serviço que têm o cliente como produto, os clientes tornam-se tão envolvidos nas operações que o serviço é realizado de fato *no* cliente — o cliente se torna o produto. Exemplos desse tipo de operação de serviço são os salões de cabeleireiro, clínicas, hospitais e alfaiates.

NATUREZA DESSAS OPERAÇÕES

Uma ampla faixa de complexidade está representada nessa classe de operações de serviço. Um exemplo de operação menos complexa de serviço que tem o cliente como produto é um salão de cabeleireiro. Os clientes entram no sistema, sentam-se na área de espera e começam a ler uma revista. Depois de esperar, recebem diversas opções de serviços — xampu e penteado, tratamentos condicionadores, cortes de cabelo, permanentes, manicure e outros serviços. Depois de receber o serviço, pagam e saem do sistema. Cada faceta dessas operações de serviço é projetada tendo em vista o cliente. Essas operações são projetadas, planejadas, controladas, analisadas e administradas com um objetivo particular supremo — clientes satisfeitos.

Muitos fatores combinam-se para criar clientes satisfeitos. Alguns desses fatores são:

- Qualidade extrínseca dos serviços. A extensão em que o próprio serviço atinge os resultados esperados pelo cliente.
- As instalações. O conforto, conveniência e clima criados pela instalação.
- A química entre o cliente e o pessoal no sistema de serviço. A amizade e cortesia do pessoal e outros clientes.
- A habilidade, competência e profissionalismo do pessoal.
- O valor do serviço. O custo dos serviços em relação à quantidade de benefícios recebidos.

Em sistemas de serviço que têm o cliente como produto, como, por exemplo, salões de cabeleireiros, o principal meio de satisfazer os clientes é através do pessoal. Eles são contratados, treinados, supervisionados e recompensados com cuidado. Obter retorno (*feedback*) dos clientes a respeito da qualidade percebida dos serviços é importante para que a força de trabalho possa ter níveis elevados de serviço ao cliente. Empresas aéreas, hotéis, restaurantes e outros serviços rotineiramente oferecem aos clientes questionários que devem ser preenchidos e devolvidos às empresas. A partir desse retorno, dois objetivos são atingidos. Primeiro, os clientes sentem que a empresa se importa com o que eles pensam e quer clientes satisfeitos. Segundo, informações valiosas são fornecidas para que se possa obter melhoria contínua das operações. *Se você pudesse escolher um fator do qual dependessem o sucesso e a sobrevivência dessas operações estratégicas, uma força de trabalho altamente treinada, motivada e eficiente seria o número um.* Evidentemente, as instalações, a qualidade dos materiais usados, os preços, rápido atendimento e outros fatores também afetam a satisfação do cliente.

A análise das filas de espera pode ser útil para determinar o número apropriado de pessoal a ser programado durante cada horário do dia nessas operações. Em outras operações, mais complexas, métodos de planejamento e programação mais abrangentes são necessários. Um exemplo de operação mais complexa de serviço que tem o cliente como produto é um hospital. Embora os hospitais tomem providências para receber pacientes, ajustar contas e liberar pacientes, a consideração preponderante ao projetar, planejar, controlar, analisar e administrar essas operações de serviço é a aplicação de conhecimentos e tecnologias médicas. Uma vez que os casos dos pacientes são muito diferentes, os hospitais devem ser flexíveis o suficiente para acomodar uma grande variedade de tipos e seqüências de tratamentos. Por esse motivo, os departamentos de cirurgia, radiologia, laboratório e exames, fisioterapia, tratamento intensivo, sala de emergência, consultórios médicos, quartos de pacientes, postos de enfermagem, lanchonete, farmácia, administração e outros departamentos são organizados de acordo com um layout de processo. A maquinaria, áreas de trabalho humano e departamentos médicos dos hospitais são agrupados e localizados de acordo com suas tecnologias de processamento, de uma maneira muito similar àquela em que uma oficina mecânica personalizada disporia suas máquinas e postos de trabalho. As instalações são projetadas para acomodar uma variedade de padrões de fluxo de pacientes que passam pelas instalações, ao mesmo tempo que agrupam habilidades de empregados e a maquinaria de uma maneira lógica de acordo com os processos técnicos executados.

Embora os hospitais tenham objetivos de eficiência de custo, relações amigáveis e de cortesia com os pacientes, entre outros, a meta principal dos hospitais é oferecer tratamentos e procedimentos médicos eficientes para os pacientes, que devem levar a uma maior satisfação do cliente. Quando hospitais são projetados, portanto, o foco principal é a eficiência tecnológica médica. Uma vez que os hospitais e outras operações de serviço complexas que têm o cliente como produto usam layouts de processo, as técnicas apropriadas discutidas no Capítulo 8 podem ser aplicadas. A análise da seqüência de operações, a análise de diagrama de blocos e a análise de distância da carga podem ser usadas ao planejar seus layouts. Essa abordagem poderia tentar minimizar a distância total percorrida mensalmente por pacientes, clientes ou materiais entre os departamentos ou o custo mensal de manuseio de materiais entre os departamentos. Em muitos serviços, as razões para se ter departamentos próximos entre si são mais complexas do que esta e muitas vezes elas têm objetivos múltiplos e são subjetivas. Num hospital, por exemplo, gostaríamos que a radiologia estivesse próximo à sala de emergência para permitir um rápido diagnóstico dos casos de emergência, e que a farmácia estivesse perto dos quartos dos pacientes para permitir uma pronta distribuição de medicamentos aos pacientes. Similarmente, usar o mesmo equipamento ou pessoal, facilidade de comunicação, movimento lógico de clientes, rapidez, segurança, contaminação ou outros fatores poderiam ser razões legítimas para querer dois departamentos próximos ou distantes um do outro. Nesses casos, são usadas **classificações de proximidade** para refletir a conveniência de se ter um departamento próximo do outro.

Quando se trata de programar operações de serviço que têm o cliente como produto e layouts de processo, as abordagens apropriadas do Capítulo 11 podem ser usadas. Controle de entrada e saída, gráficos de Gantt, regras de seqüenciamento de pedidos, custos de preparação e abordagens de minimização do tempo de fluxo podem ser especialmente úteis. Você é capaz de perceber as similaridades na programação de um hospital e na programação de uma job shop? Por exemplo, considere que a definição de prioridades entre pacientes num hospital e a definição de prioridades entre tarefas numa oficina mecânica, ainda que evidentemente baseadas em diferentes critérios, seguem o mesmo procedimento geral. As job shops poderiam usar o critério do primeiro a entrar, primeiro a ser atendido, ao passo que um hospital poderia usar o critério da necessidade mais crítica.

Encontramos extremos de sofisticação na programação desses serviços. Pequenos serviços, como, por exemplo, consultórios médicos, podem não usar quaisquer sistemas formais de programação. Aliás, dispositivos como consultas com hora marcada, sistemas de utilização de senhas ou regras do primeiro a entrar, primeiro a ser atendido freqüentemente são usados para atribuir prioridades entre clientes. Trabalhadores em tempo parcial, equipamentos de reserva e encaminhamento de pacientes a outros profissionais também são usados durante períodos de demanda de pico. No outro extremo, alguns sistemas de serviço, como, por exemplo, os hospitais, desenvolveram sistemas de programação que freqüentemente superam a sofisticação de programação na manufatura que se utiliza de job shops. Uma vez que esses serviços são sistemas de produção sob encomenda sem qualquer estoque de bens acabados, as capacidades devem ser variáveis para satisfazer amplas variações nos níveis de demanda do cliente. Uma vez que a demanda do cliente é altamente variável de semana a semana, e desde que os serviços médicos muitas vezes devem ser oferecidos em curto prazo, esses sistemas de programação tendem a funcionar num horizonte de planejamento bastante curto; não é incomum observarmos programas nesses sistemas para somente uma semana no futuro.

Em operações de serviço complexas, simulação computadorizada é uma ferramenta útil para programar pessoal e outros recursos.

Usando Simulação Computadorizada em Operações de Serviço

O Instantâneo da Indústria 12.1 ilustra o uso de simulação computadorizada para ajudar a tomar decisões quanto à composição do staff e programação em restaurantes de fast-food. A flexibilidade da simulação computadorizada para analisar uma variedade de problemas APO é, talvez, sua maior virtude. Esses problemas diversos compartilham certas características.

Características dos Problemas Que São Apropriados para Simulação Computadorizada A Tabela 12.6 relaciona seis dessas importantes características. Quando esses atributos estão presentes, a simulação computadorizada pode ser uma ferramenta eficaz para sustentar a tomada de decisões na APO.

TABELA 12.6 — **Características dos Problemas APO Que São Apropriados à Análise por Simulação Computadorizada**

1. Experimentação com o sistema real é impossível, pouco prático e não econômico.

2. O sistema que é analisado é tão complexo que fórmulas matemáticas não podem ser desenvolvidas.

3. O problema sob consideração geralmente envolve a passagem do tempo. Por exemplo, políticas são estabelecidas e depois elas são executadas com o passar do tempo. Não obstante essa característica não ser absolutamente obrigatória, geralmente ela está presente.

4. Os valores das variáveis do problema são conhecidos com certeza; aliás, seus valores variam aleatoriamente, ao acaso. Podemos conhecer seus valores médios e o grau de sua variação, mas seus valores exatos em qualquer ponto não são conhecidos antecipadamente.

5. A gravidade do problema justifica a despesa da análise baseada em computador.

6. O tempo disponível para análise é suficientemente longo para permitir a análise baseada em computador.

TABELA 12.7   PROCEDIMENTOS DA SIMULAÇÃO COMPUTADORIZADA

1. Defina cuidadosamente o problema que está em consideração — sua natureza, escopo e importância.
2. Construa um modelo matemático do problema. Isso geralmente envolve estas atividades:
   a) Identificar as variáveis e parâmetros.
   b) Especificar as regras de decisão.
   c) Compilar dados a fim de que valores realistas possam ser atribuídos às variáveis e parâmetros.
   d) Especificar as distribuições de probabilidade para cada variável e o valor dos parâmetros.
   e) Especificar os procedimentos de incremento de tempo.
   f) Especificar um procedimento para resumir os resultados da simulação.
3. Escrever um programa de computador do modelo e um resumo dos procedimentos.
4. Processar o programa no computador.
5. Avaliar os resultados da simulação computadorizada, modificar valores de programa e reexecutar o programa até que uma ampla margem de valores de parâmetros tenha sido avaliada.
6. Recomendar um curso de ação administrativa para o problema.

Para demonstrar a utilização da simulação computadorizada, identificaremos os passos fundamentais na execução dessa simulação, trabalharemos um *case study*[4] de uma análise de simulação manual e finalmente avaliaremos a utilidade da técnica na APO.

Procedimentos da Simulação Computadorizada A realização de uma simulação computadorizada geralmente não é complexa do ponto de vista matemático. A Tabela 12.7 relaciona os procedimentos para de-

INSTANTÂNEO DA INDÚSTRIA 12.1

A TACO BELL USA SIMULAÇÃO PARA DESENVOLVER PROGRAMAÇÕES DE EMPREGADOS

Na competitiva indústria do fast-food, qualquer meio de melhorar as operações para obter menores custos operacionais e melhor serviço ao cliente é altamente procurado. Num esforço para utilizar melhor seus empregados e assegurar que seus clientes não tenham de esperar em filas mais longas do que três a cinco minutos, a Taco Bell Corporation desenvolveu seu próprio software de apoio a decisões. Seu SMART (Scheduling Management And Restaurant Tool) Labor Management System consiste em três modelos: um modelo de previsão, um modelo de simulação e um modelo de programação inteira.

O modelo de previsão da Taco Bell é usado para prever o número de chegadas de clientes em diferentes momentos ao longo do dia. Uma vez que a demanda aumenta em certos momentos do dia, especialmente das 11:30 da manhã às 12:30, previsões são feitas para cada intervalo de 15 minutos durante o dia.

Essas previsões de chegada de clientes são então introduzidas numa simulação computadorizada. O modelo de simulação é usado para analisar quantos empregados serão necessários em diferentes momentos durante o dia. Além das previsões de chegada de clientes, a simulação computadorizada leva em consideração o tamanho e a configuração de um restaurante Taco Bell em especial (por exemplo, se há um guichê de drive-through), a variedade de itens de menu oferecidos, e o tempo de preparação dos alimentos.

Usando os resultados do modelo de simulação computadorizada, um modelo de programação inteira desenvolve então programações de empregados que cobrem as necessidades de atendimento ao cliente ao mesmo tempo que minimizam o custo de mão-de-obra. Esse modelo de programação leva em consideração o número de empregados necessários ao longo do dia, as diferentes responsabilidades relacionadas a serviço ao cliente (de preparar alimentos a conferir o pedido do cliente e devolver o troco) e outras tarefas como limpeza, manutenção, pagamento de vales e contabilidade de caixa.

O software SMART Labor Management System é usado em todas as lojas da Taco Bell e na maioria das lojas franquiadas. O retorno (feedback) dos empregados tem sido positivo, e outros concorrentes do ramo de fast-food gostariam de seguir o caminho da Taco Bell.

Fonte: Bistritz, Nancy. "Taco Bell Finds Recipe for Success". *OR/MS Today.* Outubro de 1997.

---

[4] *Case study:* análise intensiva de determinada unidade (pessoa, grupo social, instituição etc.) para determinação de problemas, necessidades etc. (N. do T.)

senvolver a análise de uma simulação computadorizada. Depois que o problema que está sob consideração foi definido, a atividade principal da simulação é executada: construir o modelo matemático. A construção do modelo inicia-se com a determinação de quais variáveis e parâmetros do problema são importantes para sua solução. Os elementos sujeitos a variação quando o sistema real opera podem assumir valores que variam aleatoriamente no modelo, e são chamados variáveis. Aos elementos que são constantes na operação do sistema real (ou devido a políticas da administração ou por motivos tecnológicos) são designados valores constantes, e são chamados parâmetros. Na maioria das simulações, a meta da análise é produzir um bom conjunto de valores de parâmetro (políticas administrativas) quando o modelo simular a operação do sistema real.

Em seguida, as regras de decisão do modelo são especificadas. Essas regras respondem a questões como: Se isso acontecer, o que fazer? Por exemplo, se uma entrada entrar num sistema de filas de múltiplos canais, para qual fila ela deve ir: a mais curta, a que se move mais rápido ou a mais próxima? Essas regras de decisão orientam a operação de modelos e permitem que eles simulem quão real é a operação do sistema.

A coleta de dados permite que os analistas especifiquem as distribuições de freqüência das variáveis e os valores constantes dos parâmetros. Em seguida, vem uma parte fundamental do modelo, especificando os procedimentos de incremento de tempo. Uma análise de simulação é uma série (em geral uma série longa) de instantâneos (geralmente mil, ou mais) do modelo operando à medida que o tempo transcorre entre a tomada dos instantâneos. O procedimento de incremento de tempo define o intervalo de tempo entre esses instantâneos e as regras gerais para determinar quando um instantâneo será tomado. Em cada instantâneo um valor é atribuído aleatoriamente a uma variável, as regras de decisão são seguidas, e os resultados são registrados. O modelo é concluído depois que um método de resumo dos resultados de todos os instantâneos é especificado.

Quando o modelo é escrito numa linguagem como a *Visual Basic* (**www.microsoft.com**) ou numa linguagem de simulação computadorizada especial como a *AweSim!* (**www.pritsker.com**), *MODSIM III* (**www.cacisl.com**) ou *Work Flow Analyzer* (**www.metasoftware.com**) e depois processado num computador, os resultados são avaliados. Se outros valores dos parâmetros precisarem ser analisados, um novo conjunto de parâmetros será estabelecido, a simulação será executada novamente, e seus resultados serão reavaliados. Quando uma variedade completa de valores de parâmetros tiver sido avaliada, o melhor conjunto — aqueles valores que são políticas administrativas recomendadas para resolver o problema — será escolhido. O Exemplo 12.6 ilustra esses procedimentos numa simulação computadorizada de uma clínica ambulatorial.

Exemplo 12.6

Simulação Computadorizada de uma Clínica Ambulatorial

Uma clínica ambulatorial atende pacientes que chegam aleatoriamente. O número de pacientes que chegam varia entre 6 e 10 por hora. O horário de atendimento da clínica é das 8 da manhã às 5 da tarde. Quaisquer pacientes que estejam esperando atendimento médico dentro da clínica são atendidos antes que a clínica se feche. Cada consulta leva entre 6 e 30 minutos, dependendo da natureza do problema do paciente.

Dois médicos servem atualmente no staff da clínica. Mas, ultimamente, tanto médicos como pacientes estão se queixando do serviço. Os pacientes se queixam dos excessivos tempos de espera antes de serem atendidos, e os médicos se queixam da sobrecarga de trabalho, de não terem qualquer tempo entre o atendimento dos pacientes para descansar ou executar outras obrigações, como traçar diagramas, e não podem sair do trabalho exatamente às 5 da tarde. O diretor da clínica pondera a respeito de quanto tempo de espera da parte dos pacientes e quanto tempo livre da parte dos médicos estão sendo experimentados agora e o quanto as coisas melhorariam se um terceiro médico fosse acrescentado ao staff.

Uma simulação está sendo desenvolvida agora para analisar o problema de composição do staff médico.

DEFINA O PROBLEMA

O que o diretor da clínica precisa saber a fim de resolver o problema? Ele precisa saber quanto tempo de espera da parte dos pacientes e quanto tempo livre da parte dos médicos resultarão quando dois ou três médicos estiverem na clínica. Então, o diretor poderá decidir-se a respeito de qual disposição de staff será a melhor.

CONSTRUA UM MODELO

Um modelo matemático da clínica é desenvolvido por meio dos seguintes procedimentos do Passo 2 da Tabela 12.7.

Identifique as Variáveis e Parâmetros

As variáveis-chaves do modelo são o número de pacientes que chegam a cada hora, o número de minutos necessários para que um médico atenda cada paciente, o tempo que os pacientes devem esperar para ser atendidos e o tempo livre que os médicos têm. O parâmetro-chave é o número de médicos no staff da clínica.

Especifique as Regras de Decisão

Estas regras orientarão nossa simulação:

1. Presume-se que os pacientes cheguem uniformemente ao longo de cada hora. (Os pacientes não esperam e os médicos não têm tempo livre devido às chegadas irregulares *dentro* de cada hora.)
2. Presume-se que os médicos atendam os pacientes em base do primeiro a chegar, primeiro a ser atendido. Quaisquer pacientes remanescentes de períodos anteriores são atendidos antes que pacientes recém-chegados sejam atendidos.
3. Presume-se que os padrões de chegada dos pacientes sejam aproximadamente os mesmos para todas as horas do dia.
4. O tempo de espera dos pacientes e o tempo livre dos médicos é computado de hora em hora a partir desta fórmula:

$$T_n = t_i - (60N - W_{n-1})$$

Em que:

T_n = Tempo de espera do paciente ou tempo livre do médico no intervalo de tempo n (se T_n for positivo, ele representará o tempo de espera do paciente; se T_n for negativo, ele representará o tempo livre do médico)

t_i = Tempo de atendimento correspondente ao i-ésimo paciente que chega no intervalo de tempo n

N = Número de médicos no staff

W_{n-1} = Tempo de espera no último período ou intervalo de tempo $n - 1$

Colete Dados e Especifique Variáveis e Parâmetros

A simulação comparará dois arranjos de composição do staff: $N = 2$ e $N = 3$, o número de médicos no staff. Os registros no balcão de recepção da clínica produzem as informações históricas sobre chegadas de pacientes e tempos de atendimento encontrados na Figura 12.6.

Especifique os Procedimentos de Incremento de Tempo

Cada incremento de tempo será de uma hora, e intervalos de tempo suficientes serão simulados para cobrir um dia de operação das 8 horas da manhã às 5 da tarde.

FIGURA 12.6 — DADOS HISTÓRICOS CORRESPONDENTES ÀS CHEGADAS POR HORA E TEMPOS DE ATENDIMENTO

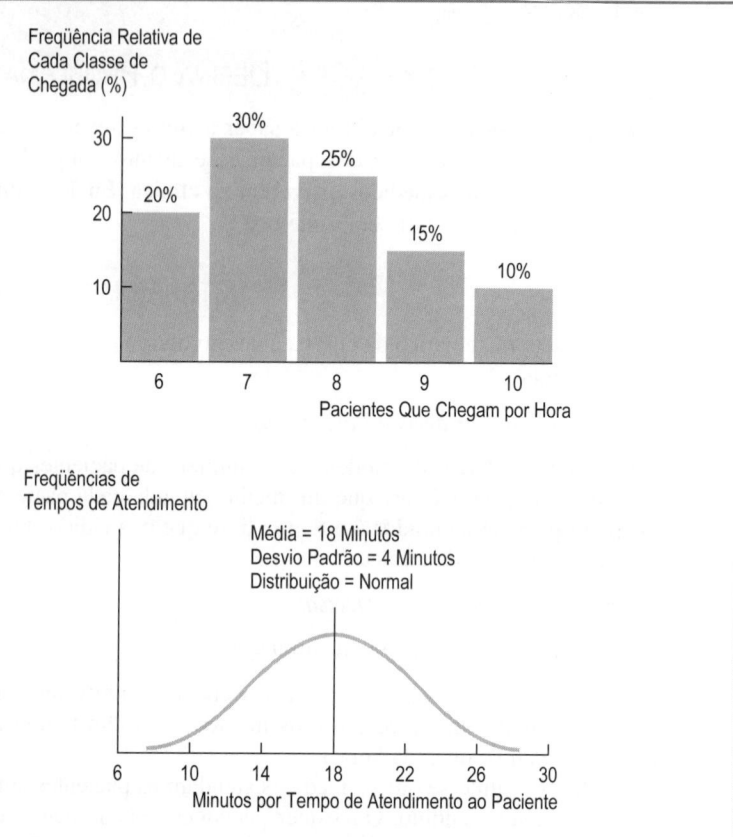

Especifique Procedimentos de Realização do Resumo

O tempo de espera do paciente e o tempo livre do médico serão totalizados ao longo de todos os intervalos de tempo da simulação. Médias serão então computadas para o tempo de atendimento ao paciente, tempo de espera do paciente e tempo livre do médico.

PROCESSE A SIMULAÇÃO

Uma vez que esse exemplo de simulação será processado manualmente, nenhum programa de computador precisará ser escrito, como geralmente acontece. O que se segue nesta seção será o resultado desse programa de computador. Os elementos essenciais dessa simulação determinam quantos pacientes chegam em cada hora e quantos minutos são necessários para atender cada paciente.

Chegadas Monte Carlo

Monte Carlo é uma técnica para gerar valores aleatórios a partir de distribuições discretas, como, por exemplo, a distribuição discreta de pacientes que chegam por hora na primeira parte da Figura 12.6. A técnica Monte Carlo usa números aleatórios uniformes (*uniforme* significa que cada número tem uma chance igual de ser retirado) para escolher aleatoriamente o número de pacientes que chegam durante cada hora. Primeiro, na Tabela 12.8, definimos faixas de números aleatórios que correspondem à freqüência relativa de cada classe da distribuição de chegadas de pacientes.

TABELA 12.8 ESTABELECENDO FAIXAS DE NÚMEROS ALEATÓRIOS PARA CADA CLASSE DA DISTRIBUIÇÃO DISCRETA DE CHEGADA MONTE CARLO

Pacientes Que Chegam por Hora	Freqüência Relativa (porcentagem)	Faixa de Números Aleatórios	Pacientes Que Chegam por Hora	Freqüência Relativa (porcentagem)	Faixa de Números Aleatórios
6	20%	0–19	9	15%	75–89
7	30	20–49	10	10	90–99
8	25	50–74			

Sob esse esquema, a faixa de números aleatórios alocada a cada classe se iguala exatamente à freqüência relativa dessa classe. Dessa forma, 100 números aleatórios de dois dígitos (zero a 99) são usados para selecionar da distribuição uma das classes de pacientes que chegam por hora.

A Tabela 12.9 é uma tabela de números aleatórios uniformemente distribuídos. Isso significa que qualquer um dos dígitos de 0 a 9 ocorre com igual freqüência. Eles não são arranjados em qualquer ordem e, dessa forma, são aleatórios. Para usar a tabela para selecionar números aleatórios de 0 a 99, como queremos fazer aqui, simplesmente pegue um ponto de partida em qualquer lugar da tabela. Para nossos objetivos, inicie na Linha 8 e leia da esquerda para a direita: 00, 28, 80, 40, 79, 86, 55, 59 e 14 são nove números aleatórios (NA) que serão usados para estabelecer o número de chegadas de pacientes durante as 9 horas de operação diárias de nossa simulação.

A Tabela 12.10 usa esses números aleatórios para definir o número de chegadas de pacientes por hora da simulação. O primeiro NA = 00 situa-se na faixa 0-19 dos números aleatórios da Tabela 12.8; isso define seis chegadas para a primeira hora. NA = 28 situa-se na faixa 20-49 para sete chegadas; NA = 80 situa-se na faixa 75-89 de números para nove chegadas; e assim por diante. Esse procedimento é usado para definir o número de chegadas em todas as nove horas da simulação. Lembre-se de que você pode ler números aleatoriamente distribuídos da Tabela 12.9 em qualquer seqüência a partir de qualquer ponto inicial na tabela: para cima, para baixo, para a direita ou para a esquerda — mas seja coerente.

Tempos de Atendimento Normalmente Distribuídos

Agora precisamos definir os tempos de atendimento para nossos pacientes. Mas não podemos usar a técnica Monte Carlo porque nossos tempos de atendimento da Figura 12.6 estão normalmente distribuídos com uma média de 18 minutos e um desvio padrão de 4 minutos. A Tabela 12.11 é uma tabela de números aleatórios normalmente distribuídos que são **pontuações Z** — o número de desvios padrões a partir da média. Esta fórmula é usada para computar o tempo de atendimento para cada paciente:

$$t_i = \mu + Z_i(\sigma) \quad \text{ou} \quad t_i = 18 + Z_i(4)$$

Z é determinado para cada paciente escolhendo-se qualquer ponto de partida na Tabela 12.11. Para nossos objetivos, vamos iniciar no canto superior esquerdo e ler da esquerda para a direita: 1,21, −1,31, −1,12, 1,32, 0,86 e 0,31 são nossas pontuações Z para os seis pacientes na primeira hora de nossa simulação. Portanto podemos computar agora os tempos de atendimento para esses pacientes:

$t_1 = 18 + 1,21(4) = 22,84$ minutos $\quad t_4 = 18 + 1,32(4) = 23,28$ minutos

$t_2 = 18 - 1,31(4) = 12,76$ minutos $\quad t_5 = 18 + 0,86(4) = 21,44$ minutos

$t_3 = 18 - 1,12(4) = 13,52$ minutos $\quad t_6 = 18 + 0,31(4) = \underline{19,24 \text{ minutos}}$

$$\text{Total} \quad 113,08 \text{ minutos}$$

Repetindo esse procedimento podemos computar os tempos de atendimento para todos os pacientes e totalizar esses tempos de atendimento para cada hora da simulação: 113,1, 135,1, 160,6, 112,8, 197,1, 180,3, 154,7, 159,2 e 98,8. Usar uma planilha eletrônica como o *Excel* da Microsoft simplifica essa tarefa.

TABELA 12.9 — TABELA DE NÚMEROS ALEATÓRIOS UNIFORMEMENTE DISTRIBUÍDOS

6351	8348	2924	2414	8168	7280	0164	5466
1322	8739	0532	4546	2482	3980	1543	3442
6763	9603	6748	4061	3636	5266	8868	5817
5091	8188	3314	6192	7322	8207	3347	6218
7182	7128	8132	4638	4643	6119	4925	4476
2533	4910	6664	5793	4777	6530	6187	8349
4415	1347	8346	7957	2627	4151	1266	0237
0028	8040	7986	5559	1479	8844	9750	8901
5661	3854	2177	8376	0663	8592	5586	6187
6844	5383	0699	5749	8201	7467	0991	8737
3509	2418	2928	5803	8471	8598	5349	4714
0141	8418	9238	9667	4857	2140	9129	5517
0939	5977	7415	0690	7409	8244	2783	2502
9969	7295	4053	8663	5499	5024	0652	8698
6321	9644	0971	9037	5476	1527	9879	5530
4268	5837	6611	7137	3323	5702	4309	4533
8417	9699	2447	7390	2312	7368	3398	4075
3869	6536	4393	7533	5664	6182	6118	1073
1377	8599	9206	7842	4198	4608	9864	7713
7495	5559	5896	5344	8997	5889	4361	3166
9744	9971	2129	3036	9055	7011	0568	0312
6759	7744	5634	4107	3940	6674	4587	7455
3451	3612	0610	1156	1445	8261	6565	5042
1163	1599	9134	0409	0248	7807	4608	7382
2822	0493	7563	0939	7569	6966	3677	9366
3100	4307	7942	8883	1821	0982	9504	8185
3570	7757	4412	6664	0271	1656	7491	0047
2857	6721	4616	7207	1696	5314	6621	1898
1800	3717	6102	3159	4036	5780	8360	8142
3607	8366	7733	1108	7052	2340	0569	2354
9008	2860	6091	0800	9986	2712	6403	4006
6416	2438	6883	9360	4209	1018	8223	0181
7079	0844	1351	0508	0886	0747	6502	2293
5241	0807	7674	8782	3627	2728	3727	7805
3291	9499	7374	8751	6143	8100	3308	6951
1928	9013	6726	9241	4907	6275	3487	4448
5310	1826	3163	2545	6803	7911	6237	6225
1215	1270	6680	8651	1790	2881	1176	1130
6195	6999	6240	4452	0552	3239	4469	7658
5731	5461	1187	7973	7158	1193	2734	5666

TABELA 12.10 — USANDO A TÉCNICA MONTE CARLO PARA DETERMINAR O NÚMERO DE CHEGADAS DE PACIENTES PARA CADA HORA DA SIMULAÇÃO

Hora	Número Aleatório Uniforme (NA)	Chegadas de Pacientes	Hora	Número Aleatório Uniforme (NA)	Chegadas de Pacientes	Hora	Número Aleatório Uniforme (NA)	Chegadas de Pacientes
1	00	6	4	40	7	7	55	8
2	28	7	5	79	9	8	59	8
3	80	9	6	86	9	9	14	6

Observação: O número de chegadas é determinado encaixando-se NA numa das faixas de números aleatórios da Tabela 12.8.

Tabela 12.11   Classificações Z Normalmente Distribuídas

1,21	−1,31	−1,12	1,32	0,86	0,31	−0,77	1,90
0,40	−0,11	−1,63	−0,75	0,92	−0,81	−1,12	1,28
1,40	−0,49	0,56	0,10	−1,05	0,48	1,00	−0,35
−0,04	1,21	1,80	−0,21	−1,58	0,15	−2,75	0,45
0,47	−0,28	2,02	3,00	1,14	−0,54	1,72	0,60
0,11	0,77	1,14	0,46	1,01	0,04	−1,05	−0,11
0,22	1,94	−0,11	1,02	−0,79	−0,24	0,52	1,66
−1,80	0,97	−0,76	0,31	1,27	0,81	−0,17	−0,28
0,09	−0,60	−0,63	0,56	0,09	1,08	−0,60	2,10
1,66	−2,26	0,10	1,66	−0,85	−0,34	0,02	0,73

Observação: Esses números não estão em qualquer ordem e estão normalmente distribuídos nas proximidades de uma média igual a zero.

Executando a Simulação

Agora estamos preparados para executar a simulação. A Tabela 12.12 relaciona o número de pacientes que chegam e totaliza o tempo de atendimento para cada hora da simulação. O tempo de espera dos pacientes e o tempo livre dos médicos são computados para cada hora correspondente aos dois arranjos de composição do staff. Por exemplo, na Hora 4:

Dois médicos:

$$T_n = t_i - (60N - W_{n-1}) \qquad T_4 = 112,8 - (120 - 55,7) = 112,8 - 64,3 = 48,5$$

Uma vez que T_4 é positivo, ele representa o tempo de espera dos pacientes.

Três médicos:

$$T_n = t_i - (60N - W_{n-1}) \qquad T_4 = 112,8 - (180 - 0) = -67,2$$

Uma vez que T_4 é negativo, ele representa o tempo livre dos médicos.

Tabela 12.12   Resumo da Simulação para a Clínica Ambulatorial

Hora	Número de Pacientes Que Chegam	Tempo Total de Atendimento (minutos)	Staff de Dois Médicos — Tempo de Espera dos Pacientes (minutos)	Staff de Dois Médicos — Tempo Livre dos Médicos (minutos)	Staff de Três Médicos — Tempo de Espera dos Pacientes (minutos)	Staff de Três Médicos — Tempo Livre dos Médicos (minutos)
1	6	113,1	0	6,9	0	66,9
2	7	135,1	15,1	0	0	44,9
3	9	160,6	55,7	0	0	19,4
4	7	112,8	48,5	0	0	67,2
5	9	197,1	125,6	0	17,1	0
6	9	180,3	185,9	0	17,4	0
7	8	154,7	220,6	0	0	7,9
8	8	159,2	259,8	0	0	20,8
9	6	98,8	238,6	0	0	81,2
Totais 69		1.311,7	1.149,8	6,9	34,5	308,3
Média por Paciente		19,0	16,7	0,1	0,5	4,5

> Depois que todos os tempos de espera dos pacientes e tempos livres dos médicos tiverem sido computados para todas as horas da simulação, os totais e as médias são computados. Resultam estas informações resumidas:
>
> | | Dois Médicos | Três Médicos |
> |---|---|---|
> | Tempo de atendimento médio por paciente | 19,0 minutos | 19,0 minutos |
> | Tempo de espera médio por paciente | 16,7 minutos | 0,5 minuto |
> | Tempo livre médio dos médicos entre o atendimento dos pacientes | 0,1 minuto | 4,5 minutos |
>
> O diretor concorda tanto com os pacientes quanto com os médicos. Um staff de três médicos amenizaria o problema de ambas as partes, mas isso teria um custo.

O Exemplo 12.6 demonstra os passos fundamentais no desenvolvimento de uma simulação computadorizada sem sobrecarregá-lo com cálculos complexos. Entretanto, você deve perceber que esse exemplo é simples em comparação com a maioria das simulações computadorizadas pelo menos em três pontos: (1) a maioria dos sistemas simulados é bem mais complexa do que a clínica ambulatorial de dois ou três médicos. (2) As regras de decisão raramente são tão simples como as desse exemplo. (3) O número de variáveis aleatórias e seus padrões de casualidade geralmente são mais extensos. Distribuições de Poisson, exponenciais e outras freqüentemente devem ser representadas, além das distribuições discretas e normais desse exemplo. Mas, apesar da simplicidade de nosso exemplo, na maioria dos aspectos seus procedimentos são similares a suas contrapartes do mundo real.

Uma Avaliação da Simulação Computadorizada A simulação computadorizada merece nossa atenção pelo menos nestes três pontos:

1. Talvez ela seja uma das ferramentas analíticas mais flexíveis em termos de que pode ser aplicada a uma variedade de problemas APO.
2. Ela é freqüentemente utilizada na indústria. Desse modo, a probabilidade de encontrá-la em seu emprego futuro é relativamente elevada.
3. Ela não é altamente matemática e complexa; ao contrário, ela usa uma abordagem experimental relativamente simples para analisar problemas.

A simulação computadorizada nem sempre produz as melhores, ou ótimas, respostas, mas boas soluções trabalháveis podem ser desenvolvidas comparando-se políticas administrativas alternativas. Não obstante ser verdadeiro que a técnica exige especialistas bem treinados na equipe e um sistema de computador eficiente, presume-se cada vez mais a existência desses elementos na maioria das organizações atuais.

Resumo Final

O Que os Fabricantes de Classe Mundial Estão Fazendo

A administração de negócios de serviços pode apresentar muitos desafios. O fato de sua produção não poder ser guardada em estoques, o envolvimento de clientes nas operações, lead times curtos, qualidade determinada de maneira subjetiva e demanda não uniforme criam dificuldades. Mas algumas das maiores e mais bem-sucedidas corporações americanas são negócios de serviços; sendo assim, essas dificuldades podem ser superadas. Empresas como a AT&T, Wal-Mart, Citicorp, American Airlines e American Express, do setor de telecomunicações, mercado de consumo, serviços bancários, transporte aéreo e serviços financeiros têm feito duas coisas fundamentais para administrar de maneira bem-sucedida suas operações:

1. Quando apropriado, elas têm adaptado abordagens avançadas e conhecidas de planejamento, análise e controle que foram desenvolvidas primeiramente na manufatura.
2. Elas reconheceram as propriedades únicas das operações de serviços e desenvolveram novas abordagens administrativas para essas operações.

Isso é facilitado classificando-se as operações de serviço nestes tipos: quase-manufatura, cliente como participante e cliente como produto. As propriedades desses tipos de operações de serviço constituem uma estrutura analítica para analisar abordagens existentes e desenvolver novas abordagens para essas operações.

Quase todo negócio de serviços tem um ou mais departamentos, grupos de departamentos ou operações inteiras que são quase-manufatura. Para todos os fins, essas operações são administradas da mesma maneira que na manufatura. Atividades como realização de previsões, projeto de processos de produção, seleção e administração da tecnologia de produção, planejamento da capacidade, layout das instalações, compras, planejamento de estoques e programação são realizadas como na manufatura. Embora se possa dizer que essas operações sejam impulsionadas mais pela necessidade de se garantir a satisfação do cliente do que na manufatura, os fabricantes de classe mundial discordariam.

As operações de serviço que têm o cliente como participante são, talvez, mais bem expressas pelo setor varejista. Aqui, no piso da loja, a administração de operações e a administração mercadológica são mescladas para se obter a administração eficaz das operações — obter uma maior fatia de mercado e lucratividade através do aumento da satisfação do cliente. Embora todos os elementos das operações afetem a satisfação do cliente, o encontro entre o pessoal e o cliente quando os serviços são oferecidos é crucial. Por esse motivo, empregados são selecionados, contratados, treinados, supervisionados, avaliados e recompensados, tendo a satisfação do cliente como meta suprema.

As operações de serviço que têm o cliente como produto têm um contato ainda mais estreito entre o cliente e o pessoal de operações porque o serviço é realizado de fato *no* cliente. Quando se reconhece a complexidade da criação de satisfação do cliente nesse ambiente, os empregados tornam-se um meio crítico para se obter uma maior fatia de mercado e lucratividade.

Para muitas empresas, a programação eficaz dessas operações de serviço é obtida através da programação do pessoal. Técnicas como programação de turnos de trabalho, análise de filas de espera e simulação computadorizada são usadas para planejar e controlar essas operações de serviço.

Questões de Revisão e Discussão

1. Cite e explique quatro propriedades dos serviços.
2. Quais são algumas das concepções errôneas a respeito dos serviços?
3. Cite e explique cinco coisas que descrevam a natureza dos serviços.
4. Cite e descreva três tipos de operações de serviços. Dê um exemplo de cada uma.
5. Quais características dos serviços tornam sua programação difícil?
6. Quais são quatro abordagens para lidar com a demanda não uniforme para os serviços?
7. Descreva uma operação de serviço de quase-manufatura e dê um exemplo.
8. Descreva como as operações de serviço de quase-manufatura são planejadas, controladas, programadas e administradas.
9. Explique e descreva brevemente a programação de turnos de trabalho nas operações de serviço.
10. Descreva uma operação de serviço que tem o cliente como participante e dê um exemplo.
11. Descreva como as operações de serviço que têm o cliente como participante são planejadas, controladas, analisadas, programadas e administradas.
12. Explique e descreva brevemente a análise das filas de espera nas operações de serviço.
13. Dê cinco exemplos de filas de espera em sistemas de produção.
14. Explique por que se formam filas de espera.
15. Quais são as suposições destes modelos de filas: a) Modelo 1, b) Modelo 2, c) Modelo 3 e d) Modelo 4?
16. Descreva algumas maneiras pelas quais os gerentes podem variar as capacidades de produção para evitar filas de espera excessivas.
17. Descreva uma operação de serviço que tem o cliente como produto e dê um exemplo.
18. Descreva como as operações de serviço que têm o

cliente como produto são planejadas, controladas, analisadas, programadas e administradas.
19. Explique e descreva brevemente a simulação computadorizada nas operações de serviço.
20. Cite seis características de problemas apropriados à análise de simulação computadorizada.
21. Cite seus passos principais na simulação computadorizada.
22. Cite seis atividades principais na criação de um modelo para simulação computadorizada.
23. Defina *Monte Carlo*.
24. Defina *números aleatórios uniformemente distribuídos*.
25. Defina *números aleatórios normalmente distribuídos*.

TAREFAS NA INTERNET

1. Visite e explore o site da CACI Products Company (**www.cacisl.com**). Localize as páginas da Web do software de simulação *MODSIM III* (ou a versão mais recente do *MODSIM*) e descreva brevemente seus recursos. Localize as páginas da Web que descrevem a utilização desse software em empresas em particular. Escolha uma empresa e descreva as operações ou processos que a ela simulou, analisados com o *MODSIM III*.
2. Procure na Internet por uma empresa que produza software para programação de staff. Descreva o software e seus recursos para programação de staff. Forneça o site da empresa.
3. Procure na Internet por uma empresa que produza software para programação de pacientes em hospitais ou centros de saúde. Descreva o software e seus recursos com respeito a programação de pacientes. Forneça o site da empresa.
4. Visite uma livraria on-line e encontre um livro sobre administração de restaurantes, hotéis ou operações de serviço de alimentação. Apresente a citação/informação bibliográfica do livro.

PROBLEMAS

1. Um banco tem caixas que trabalham oito horas por dia, de segunda a sábado. O número necessário de turnos de trabalho diários para os caixas é:

	Segunda	**Terça**	**Quarta**	**Quinta**	**Sexta**	**Sábado**	**Total**
Turnos de trabalho dos caixas	10	8	6	7	8	10	49

   Todos os caixas são empregados em tempo integral e, de acordo com a política da empresa, eles devem ter quatro dias consecutivos de trabalho e dois dias consecutivos de folga por semana.

   a) Qual é o número mínimo necessário de caixas?
   b) Use o procedimento heurístico de turno de trabalho para desenvolver programas de trabalho.
   c) Quantos caixas por turno estarão de folga na semana em sua programação proposta? Como essa folga poderia ser evitada? Seus programas são ótimos?

2. Se clientes chegarem a um único guichê de drive-in de um banco local, um a cada seis minutos, em média, e se você puder atender os clientes em quatro minutos em média:

   a) Quanto tempo os clientes devem esperar permanecer nas instalações do banco, em média?
   b) Quantos carros esperaríamos que estivessem nas instalações do drive-in, em média? (Suponhamos um cliente por carro.)
   c) Qual é a probabilidade de que três ou mais carros estejam nas instalações do drive-in?

3. O departamento de atletismo de uma universidade recebeu ordens para verificar a identificação dos estudantes antes de vender-lhes ingressos no quiosque. Espera-se que o índice médio de chegada de estudantes à fila de espera única permaneça em 30 estudantes por hora, mas espera-se que o tempo médio necessário para receber o pagamento e entregar os ingressos se eleve de 0,5 minuto para 1,4

minuto no quiosque único de venda de ingressos. Se a área da fila de espera for suficiente para acomodar os estudantes adicionais, quais mudanças essa modificação causará no número médio de estudantes na fila e a proporção de tempo que o staff estará no guichê?

4. Billy White é proprietário e opera a White's Automatic Car Wash. O mecanismo automático de lavagem toma exatamente 12 minutos para lavar cada carro. Durante os dias da semana o índice médio de chegada é de 3 carros por hora, e nos finais de semana o índice é de 4,5 carros por hora. Cada carro ocupa aproximadamente 6 metros de extensão de estacionamento.

   a) Quanta extensão de estacionamento será necessária em média para os carros que esperam para ser lavados?
   b) Durante quanto tempo cada cliente permanecerá no lava-rápido, em média?

5. Um fabricante estuda uma proposta para instalar um dispositivo automático em uma de suas operações de produção. O dispositivo executaria a operação em exatamente 0,5 minuto. O índice de chegada é de 50 produtos por hora, e o índice de atendimento atual da operação manual de canal único é de 60 produtos por hora. Se o dispositivo custar $ 10.000, 1.500 produtos forem produzidos por ano, e cada minuto economizado por produto na operação valer $ 2, deverá o dispositivo ser instalado?

6. O Financial Aid Center da Rhode Island State University gostaria de melhorar sua receptividade a estudantes que vão ao centro em busca de ajuda. Uma idéia é contratar consultores financeiros adicionais. Um estudo recente de estudantes que usam o Financial Aid Center descobriu que uma média de 17 estudantes vai ao centro em cada hora. O estudo descobriu também que cada um dos três consultores financeiros do centro atende 4 estudantes por hora, em média. Determine quantos conselheiros seriam necessários a fim de que o tempo de espera médio para os estudantes antes que eles se encontrem com os conselheiros seja inferior a 10 minutos.

7. Bubba Jones, o proprietário do Big Bubba's Bar, comprou recentemente seis máquinas de videopôquer. As novas máquinas têm sido muito populares e alguns clientes têm se queixado de que o Big Bubba precisa de mais máquinas. Durante as últimas noites, o sr. Jones tem observado estreitamente o uso das máquinas de videopôquer. Ele descobriu que uma média de 30 clientes por hora se levanta para jogar videopôquer. Se todas as máquinas estiverem em uso, a maioria dos clientes esperará até 2 minutos por uma máquina livre antes de se afastar. Quando os clientes começam a jogar videopôquer, eles permanecem na máquina uma média de 12 minutos. O sr. Jones gostaria de possuir máquinas suficientes a fim de que o tempo de espera médio por cliente fosse inferior a 1 minuto. Determine quantas máquinas de videopôquer adicionais ele deve comprar.

8. Um professor atende em sua sala entre as 10 horas da manhã e o meio-dia um dia por semana. O número de estudantes que o procuram durante esses períodos é dado nesta distribuição de freqüência relativa:

Número de Estudantes (n)	Freqüência Relativa F(n) (%)	Número de Estudantes (n)	Freqüência Relativa F(n) (%)
3	10%	5	40%
4	30	6	20

A quantidade de tempo por estudante é aproximada por uma distribuição normal com uma média de 10 minutos e um desvio padrão de 2 minutos. Use esses números aleatórios com distribuição uniforme para estabelecer o número de estudantes que chegam em 5 períodos em que o professor atende em sua sala: 5, 1, 3, 9 e 7. Use os dados da Tabela 12.11 de distribuição normal para estabelecer tempos de atendimento por estudante. (Inicie no canto superior esquerdo da tabela e leia horizontalmente ao longo da primeira linha, retorne à margem esquerda, desça para a linha seguinte e repita até haver concluído.) Siga os procedimentos do caso da clínica ambulatorial apresentado neste capítulo para determinar:

   a) O número de estudantes que chegam em cada período de atendimento no escritório durante 5 períodos.
   b) O número total de minutos necessários para ajudar os estudantes durante cada um dos 5 períodos de atendimento no escritório.

Estudo de Caso

Operações de Transporte em Caminhão na Computer Products Corporation

Cenário n. 1

A fábrica da Computer Products Corporation (CPC) em Atlanta entrega computadores pessoais e para pequenos negócios com caminhões da empresa a armazéns regionais no meio-leste dos Estados Unidos. Os caminhões retornam dos armazéns para a fabrica para carregar uma média de quatro vezes por dia de trabalho de oito horas. A fábrica usa uma equipe de carregamento no departamento de expedição que monta os pedidos de computadores pessoais e de pequenos negócios dos clientes e carrega os pedidos que saem nos caminhões. A equipe de carregamento trabalha no armazém quando não há nenhum caminhão de saída na fábrica e carrega os caminhões que saem em base do primeiro a chegar, primeiro a ser atendido. A equipe de carregamento pode carregar seis caminhões, em média, por dia de trabalho de oito horas. Cada caminhão ocupa cerca de 18,58 metros quadrados de espaço de estacionamento, cada motorista de caminhão recebe $ 20 por hora incluindo benefícios adicionais, e a equipe de carregamento recebe um total de $ 150 por hora incluindo benefícios adicionais. O contrato sindical da CPC com seus motoristas de caminhão não permite que os motoristas ajudem a carregar ou descarregar caminhões.

a) Em média, quanto espaço de estacionamento será necessário para os caminhões que esperam para ser carregados?

b) Quanto a cláusula do contrato sindical que impede os motoristas de fazerem trabalho de carga e descarga custa à CPC por ano se a fábrica de Atlanta trabalha 250 dias por ano e fizermos a pressuposição de que o tempo livre dos motoristas poderia ser utilizado de uma maneira que teria um valor igual ao que eles ganham atualmente?

Cenário n. 2

O gerente de armazéns da fábrica da CPC em Atlanta estabeleceu uma política que exige que os motoristas de caminhão levem seus caminhões para revisão no centro de manutenção da fábrica se um caminhão estiver esperando para ser carregado, mas cada caminhão pode ser revisado no máximo uma vez por viagem. Suponhamos que os caminhões revisados não afetem o índice de chegada de quatro caminhões por dia de trabalho de oito horas e que o terminal de carga de caminhões opere de uma maneira muito similar à de um sistema de fila de espera de canal único e com tamanho de fila limitado. Se cada caminhão fizer uma viagem a cada 10 dias em média, quão freqüentemente os caminhões serão revisados?

Cenário n. 3

O terminal de carga de caminhões acima descrito tem esta distribuição de chegada:

(1) Caminhões que chegam num dia de trabalho de 8 horas	(2) Minutos entre a chegada dos caminhões [1/(1) × 480]	(3) Freqüência relativa (porcentagem)
1	480	5%
2	240	15
3	160	20
4	120	30
5	96	20
6	80	10

O tempo necessário para que uma única equipe de carregamento carregue os caminhões é normalmente distribuído, com uma média de 80 minutos e um desvio padrão de 20 minutos. Use estes números aleatórios com distribuição uniforme para estabelecer o número de caminhões que chegam em dias de trabalho de 10 horas: 73, 52, 51, 45, 41, 51, 82, 08, 60 e 00. Use a Tabela 12.11 de distribuição normal para estabelecer tempos de carga para cada caminhão. (Inicie no canto inferior direito da tabela e leia horizontalmente para a esquerda ao longo da última linha, retorne à margem direita, suba para a linha seguinte e leia horizontalmente para a esquerda ao longo da linha. Repita o procedimento até haver concluído.) Siga os procedimentos do caso da clínica ambulatorial do Exemplo 12.6 para determinar:

a) O número de caminhões que chegam a cada dia durante 10 dias.
b) O número de minutos necessário para carregar os caminhões a cada dia e o total para os 10 dias.
c) O número de minutos de tempo livre dos motoristas a cada dia e o total para os 10 dias.
d) A quantidade de tempo livre da equipe de carregamento a cada dia e o total para os 10 dias.

Cenário n. 4

Em virtude do grande aumento nas vendas, o CPC duplicou o número de caminhões que transportam computadores pessoais e de pequenos negócios para os armazéns regionais. Os caminhões agora chegam à taxa de oito caminhões por dia de trabalho de oito horas, em média. Uma segunda equipe de carregamento foi acrescentada, as duas equipes trabalham em terminais de carga separados, e cada uma pode carregar seis caminhões por dia de trabalho, em média. Com os caminhões extras, os motoristas agora devem esperar passar mais tempo na fábrica do que antes?

capítulo 13

MANUFATURA JUST-IN-TIME

Introdução

A Filosofia da Manufatura Just-in-Time

Pré-Requisitos da Manufatura JIT

Elementos da Manufatura JIT
Eliminando o Desperdício
Solução Forçada de Problemas e Melhoria Contínua
São as Pessoas Que Fazem o JIT Funcionar
Administração da Qualidade Total
Processamento Paralelo
Controle de Produção Kanban
Atividade de Compras JIT
Reduzindo Estoques Através da Redução da Preparação
Trabalhando Rumo à Manufatura Repetitiva

Benefícios da Manufatura JIT

Sucesso e Manufatura JIT

Resumo Final: O Que os Fabricantes de Classe Mundial Estão Fazendo

Questões de Revisão e Discussão

Tarefas na Internet

Problemas

Estudo de Caso
The Superior Manufacturing Company

A IPS Adota o JIT

Localizada em Everett, Washington, a Intermec Printing Systems (IPS) fabrica impressoras de código de barras, uma indústria que está crescendo rapidamente, com um aumento de volume igual a 30% ao ano. Com o crescimento que a empresa tem experimentado e com mais projetos de novas impressoras em andamento, a empresa estava ficando sem espaço de manufatura. Além disso, freqüente retrabalho nas impressoras para acomodar configurações especiais, excessivos estoques de bens acabados e baixa resposta à demanda do cliente eram resultantes da abordagem da empresa à produção.

Para melhorar sua competitividade e lucratividade, e para restabelecer-se como líder mundial no negócio de impressão de código de barras, a administração da IPS decidiu adotar as técnicas da manufatura JIT. Com a ajuda de consultores, a IPS iniciou a implantação de um programa para criar um lead time curto, baixo estoque, elevada qualidade de produto e um sistema de produção de rápida resposta.

Depois de enviar todos os seus funcionários a seminários de treinamento, a IPS compilou dados e analisou cuidadosamente cada processo de produção necessário para produzir suas impressoras. Em vez de usar uma linha de produção separada para cada modelo de impressora, a IPS criou uma linha de produção única, de modelo misto, para produzir todos os seus modelos de impressora. A seqüência de produção de seus diferentes modelos, o tamanho de lote de cada modelo e o número de cartões Kanban necessários foram então determinados. Empregados receberam treinamento interfuncional para múltiplas tarefas, permitindo que eles se "flexibilizem" entre estações de trabalho quando isso é exigido pelo fluxo de produtos, e permitindo também que a administração mude dinamicamente a capacidade ao longo da linha de produção. Os salários dos empregados baseavam-se em parte no número de tarefas para as quais eles haviam sido treinados.

Empregados também foram treinados para executar inspeções da qualidade em cada processo, limitando o número de defeitos que passavam pela linha de produção. Áreas de armazenamento de matérias-primas foram criadas em múltiplas localizações próximo à linha de produção, de forma que os materiais necessários em cada estação de trabalho estivessem localizados perto dessa estação. Essas áreas de armazenamento são reabastecidas freqüentemente a partir do armazém principal por manuseadores de materiais que usam um sistema Kanban de duas gavetas.

Os resultados foram dramáticos. A IPS experimentou uma redução de 40% no espaço de manufatura, mesmo depois que dois novos modelos foram introduzidos. O estoque de bens acabados foi substancialmente reduzido, com a meta de trabalharem rumo a um estoque zero de bens acabados, com todos os produtos produzidos sob encomenda. O retrabalho para configurações especiais foi efetivamente eliminado, uma vez que impressoras pedidas de forma personalizada são construídas inicialmente conforme a encomenda. As matérias-primas nos armazéns foram reduzidas, uma vez que a IPS tem trabalhado para padronizar as matérias-primas usadas, tem trabalhado com seus fornecedores para melhorar a qualidade das matérias-primas e tem entregas mais freqüentes de pedidos menores. A IPS agora está dedicada à melhoria contínua de suas operações.

Como o relato anterior ilustra, muitas empresas estão entusiasmadas com a manufatura just-in-time (JIT). Neste capítulo estudaremos a filosofia do JIT, quando podemos usar o JIT, o funcionamento interno do JIT e seus benefícios. O *APICS Dictionary* define **JIT** como se segue:

> *"Uma filosofia de manufatura que se baseia na eliminação planejada de todo desperdício e na melhoria contínua da produtividade. Ela envolve a execução bem-sucedida de todas as atividades de manufatura necessárias para produzir um produto final, da engenharia de projetos à entrega e inclusão de todos os estados de transformação da matéria-prima em diante. Os elementos principais do just-in-time são a manutenção somente dos estoques necessários quando preciso; melhorar a qualidade até atingir um nível zero de defeitos; reduzir lead times ao reduzir os tempos de preparação, comprimentos de fila e tamanhos de lote; revisar incrementalmente as próprias operações; e realizar essas coisas a um custo mínimo. Num sentido amplo, aplica-se a todas as formas de manufatura, job shops e processos, bem como à manufatura repetitiva".*

Nem todas as empresas usam o termo *JIT*. A IBM usa o termo *manufatura de fluxo contínuo*, a Hewlett-Packard o chama tanto *produção sem estoques* como *sistema de manufatura repetitiva*, a GE o denomina *administração através da visão*, a Boeing o chama *manufatura limpa*, a Motorola usa a expressão *manufatura de ciclo breve*, e diversas empresas japonesas simplesmente referem-se a ele como *Sistema Toyota*. Algumas empresas estão usando a expressão *competição baseada no tempo* (*TBC*).

A Filosofia da Manufatura Just-in-Time

Os fabricantes americanos estão geograficamente localizados no meio do mercado mais lucrativo do mundo. Essa vantagem deveria permitir-lhes superar a concorrência respondendo rapidamente às necessidades dos clientes. O sucesso de empresas estrangeiras em mercados americanos impulsiona as empresas dos Estados Unidos a reorganizar suas idéias empresariais para enfatizar a rápida resposta aos clientes como uma arma-chave para conquistarem uma aumentada fatia de mercado. As empresas americanas também querem encontrar maneiras de fazer as coisas mais rápido, a fim de poderem ser bem-sucedidas em mercados estrangeiros atraentes em que elas estejam em desvantagem geográfica. Durante muitos anos as empresas manufatureiras nos Estados Unidos procuraram oferecer produtos com o maior valor pelo menor custo. Agora, as empresas de ponta oferecem produtos com o maior valor pelo menor custo com o menor tempo de resposta. Uma resposta rápida às demandas de mercado constitui uma vantagem competitiva poderosa e sustentável. De fato, o tempo tem se destacado como a dimensão predominante da competição global, mudando fundamentalmente a maneira pela qual as organizações competem. Não basta mais que as empresas sejam produtoras de alta qualidade e baixo custo. Para serem bem-sucedidas hoje, elas também devem ser as primeiras a levar produtos e serviços aos clientes rapidamente.

Empresas como a Northern Telecom, Xerox, Hewlett-Packard, Motorola, General Electric, Honda, Toyota, Sony e Canon estão usando o JIT como uma arma para acelerar a capacidade de resposta ao mercado. Para competir nesse novo ambiente, o **ciclo do pedido à entrega** (o tempo transcorrido entre o momento em que um cliente faz um pedido até que ele o receba) deve ser drasticamente reduzido.

A Figura 13.1 ilustra esse importante conceito. O JIT é a arma pela qual se deve optar hoje para reduzir o tempo transcorrido desse ciclo.

Na visão tradicional da manufatura, um objetivo fundamental era utilizar totalmente a capacidade de produção a fim de que mais produtos fossem produzidos com um número menor de trabalhadores e máquinas. Esse tipo de pensamento levava a grandes filas de estoque em processo de espera em centros de trabalho no setor de manufatura. Filas grandes significavam que máquinas e trabalhadores jamais tinham de esperar que produtos parcialmente acabados chegassem até eles; portanto, a utilização da capacidade era muito elevada e os custos de produção eram baixos. Infelizmente, filas grandes de estoque em processo também significavam que os produtos gastavam a maior parte de seu tempo na manufatura simplesmente esperando. Com esse arranjo, as empresas estariam mal equipadas para competir na concorrência atual, baseada no tempo.

FIGURA 13.1   O Ciclo do Pedido até a Entrega

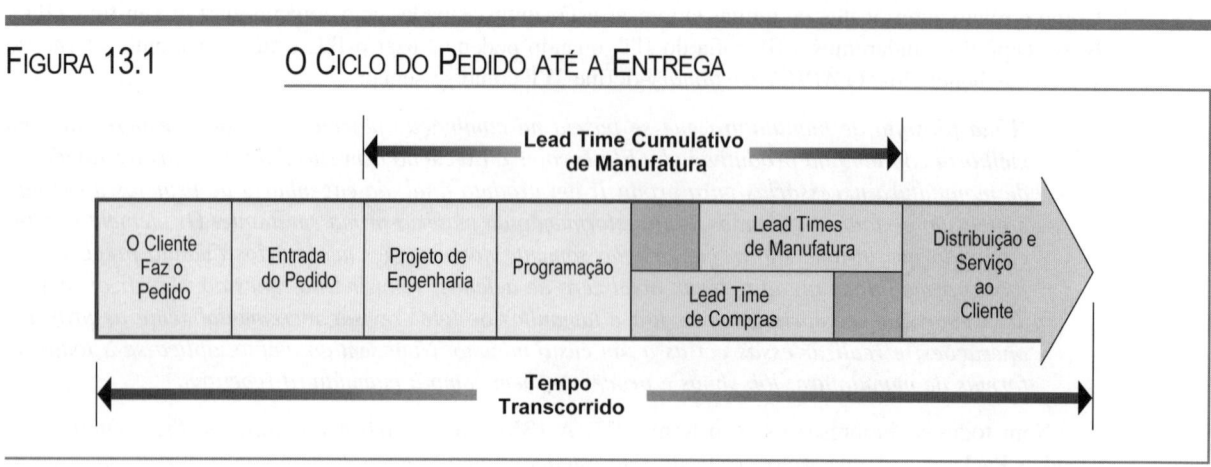

| FIGURA 13.2 | UTILIZAÇÃO DE ALTA CAPACIDADE: O INIMIGO DA COMPETIÇÃO BASEADA NO TEMPO |

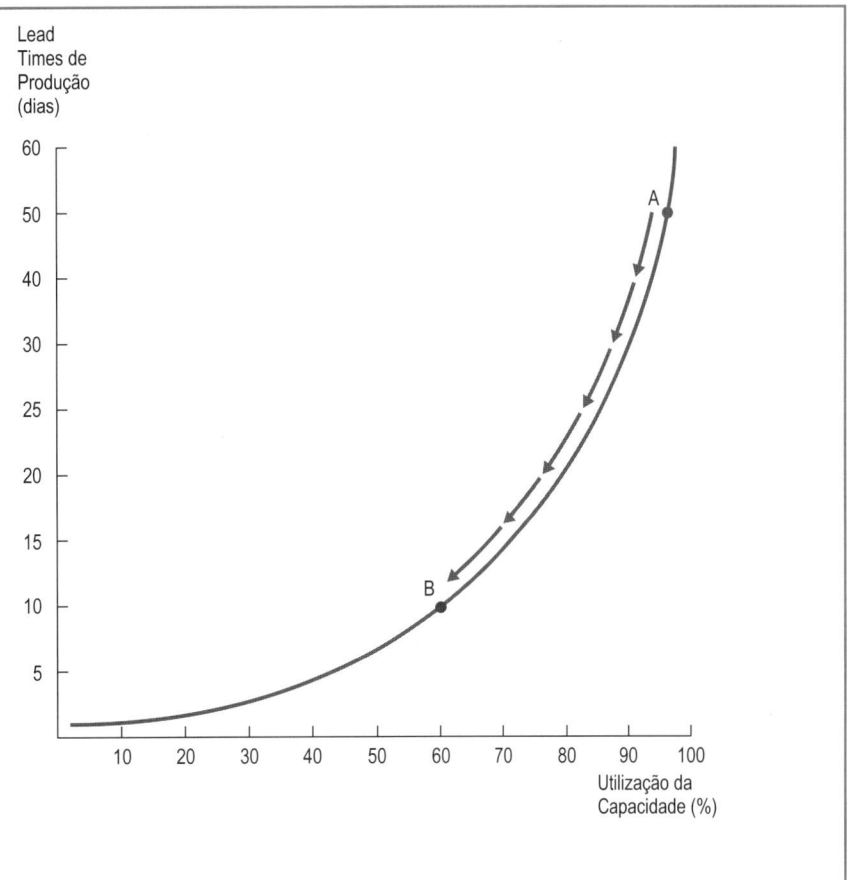

A Figura 13.2 ilustra que esse tipo de pensamento tradicional pode ser fatal para empresas que queiram usar a velocidade como arma. Nessa figura, digamos que uma empresa esteja operando no Ponto A, com uma utilização da capacidade igual a 96% e um lead time de manufatura de 50 dias. Um modo de reduzir os lead times de manufatura é encontrar maneiras de aumentar a capacidade de produção. Estudando as operações e a capacidade de produção da empresa, esta foi capaz de mover-se para o Ponto B, com um lead time de manufatura de somente 10 dias e uma utilização da capacidade igual a 60%. Para abreviar os lead times de produção, 100% da utilização da capacidade não deve ser o objetivo predominante. *Na manufatura JIT, reduzir drasticamente o tempo transcorrido do ciclo do pedido até a entrega substituiu o objetivo de utilização de 100% da capacidade de produção na manufatura tradicional.*

Há muitas oportunidades para agilizar cada passo do ciclo de pedido até a entrega. Discutiremos diversas dessas oportunidades neste capítulo. Uma maneira importante de reduzirmos os lead times de manufatura é reduzirmos os tamanhos de fila e os tempos de espera de produtos parcialmente acabados em centros de trabalho do setor de manufatura.

O Exemplo 13.1 mostra como o objetivo de se ter reduzidos lead times pode ser obtido usando-se a teoria das filas para analisar problemas de produção com filas de espera. Além disso, o Exemplo 13.1 ilustra que uma drástica redução dos lead times de manufatura e de estoques de produtos em processo muitas vezes pode ser obtida somente com ligeiros aumentos da capacidade de produção. Essa é uma percepção importante que devemos ter quando estudamos as maneiras de posicionar as empresas para que sobrevivam no ambiente atual de competição baseada no tempo.

Exemplo 13.1

Aumentar a Capacidade de Produção Reduz Lead Times de Manufatura

Uma operação de manufatura quer reduzir seu lead time de manufatura de 12 para 4 dias. Se as tarefas chegam a uma taxa média de 12 por dia e a operação pode produzir uma média de 12,083 tarefas por dia, qual nova taxa de produção permitiria um lead time de somente 4 dias? Qual seria a redução do estoque de trabalho em processo com a nova taxa de produção?

Solução

1. Use a fórmula para $\bar{t}_s$ do Modelo 1 na Tabela 12.5 do Capítulo 12:

$$\bar{t}_s = \frac{1}{(\mu - \lambda)}$$

2. Use os valores de $\lambda = 12,000$ tarefas por dia e $\mu = 12,083$ tarefas por dia para verificar se o lead time na operação é de fato 12 dias:

$$\bar{t}_s = \frac{1}{(\mu - \lambda)} = \frac{1}{(12,083 - 12,0)} = \frac{1}{0,083} = 12 \text{ dias}$$

3. Em seguida, admita que $\bar{t}_s = 4$ dias e $\lambda = 12$ tarefas por dia e resolva para um novo valor de μ:

$$\bar{t}_s = \frac{1}{(\mu - \lambda)} = \frac{1}{(\mu - 12,0)} = 4$$

$$4(\mu - 12,0) = 1$$

$$4\mu - 48 = 1$$

$$4\mu = 1 + 48 = 49$$

$$\mu = 49/4 = 12,25 \text{ tarefas por dia}$$

Aumentando-se a taxa de produção de 12,083 tarefas por dia para 12,25 tarefas por dia, o lead time é reduzido de 12 dias para somente 4 dias.

4. Compute $\bar{n}_s$ para $\mu = 12,083$ e para $\mu = 12,25$:

$$\bar{n}_{s_1} = \frac{\lambda}{(\mu_1 - \lambda)} = \frac{12}{(12,083 - 12,0)} = \frac{12}{0,083} = 144,6 \text{ tarefas}$$

$$\bar{n}_{s_2} = \frac{\lambda}{(\mu_2 - \lambda)} = \frac{12}{(12,25 - 12,0)} = \frac{12}{0,25} = 48,0 \text{ tarefas}$$

Redução em $\bar{n}_s = 144,6 - 48,0 = 96,6$ tarefas

Aumentando-se a taxa de produção de 12,083 tarefas por dia para 12,25 tarefas por dia, o estoque de produtos em processo é reduzido de 144,6 tarefas para 48 tarefas, ou seja uma redução de 96,6 tarefas.

Hoje o JIT comumente é visto como uma inovação japonesa, porque a Toyota popularizou essa abordagem duas décadas atrás. Entretanto, você pode achar interessante que a maioria das idéias incorporadas pelo JIT tenha sido combinada e implementada de maneira bem-sucedida por uma empresa americana 50 anos antes. A Ford Motor Company implementou essa abordagem em sua fábrica de Dearborn, Michigan, que produzia Fords Modelo T. Em seu livro de 1926 intitulado *Today and Tomorrow*, Henry Ford apresenta sua abordagem à produção, a qual é supreendentemente similar à JIT. Ford descreve como o minério de ferro era descarregado de um navio, transformado em aço, convertido em automóveis acabados e embarcado para o cliente num espaço inferior a 48 horas. Independentemente da origem do JIT, essa abordagem à produção consiste em um conjunto de idéias úteis que pode ajudar as empresas a se tornarem mais competitivas.

Consideremos agora os requisitos indispensáveis para a manufatura JIT.

Pré-Requisitos da Manufatura JIT

A idéia básica do JIT é bastante simples — reduzir drasticamente estoques de produtos em processo ao longo do sistema de produção. Dessa maneira, os produtos fluirão dos fornecedores para a produção e para os clientes com pouco ou nenhum atraso ou interrupções além da quantidade de tempo que gastaram para ser produzidos em centros de trabalho de manufatura. O objetivo principal do JIT é reduzir os lead times de manufatura, e isso é obtido principalmente por meio de reduções drásticas dos produtos em processo. O resultado é um fluxo uniforme, ininterrupto, de pequenos lotes de produtos ao longo da produção.

A maioria das aplicações JIT bem-sucedidas tem sido na manufatura repetitiva, operações em que lotes de produtos padrões são produzidos em alta velocidade e em volumes elevados com matérias-primas que se movem num fluxo contínuo. As fábricas de automóveis Toyota, onde a noção de JIT pode ter se iniciado, são talvez o melhor exemplo de uso do JIT na manufatura repetitiva. Nessas fábricas, o fluxo contínuo de produtos torna o planejamento e o controle bastante simples, e o JIT funciona melhor nessas situações de chão de fábrica. A utilização bem-sucedida do JIT é rara em job shops grandes e altamente complexas, onde o planejamento e o controle são extremamente complicados. Job shops menores, menos complexas, têm utilizado o JIT, mas essas empresas deram muitos passos para mudar operações a fim de que elas se comportem como a manufatura repetitiva. Discutiremos mais sobre isso na próxima seção.

O JIT não vem de graça — certas mudanças na fábrica e na maneira como ela é administrada podem ocorrer antes que os benefícios possam ser percebidos. Entre essas mudanças estão:

1. Estabilizar programas de produção.
2. Tornar as fábricas mais focalizadas.
3. Melhorar as capacidades de produção de centros de trabalho de manufatura.
4. Melhorar a qualidade do produto.
5. Fazer treinamento interfuncional de trabalhadores a fim de que eles tenham múltiplas habilidades e sejam competentes em diversas tarefas.
6. Reduzir quebras de equipamentos por meio de manutenção preventiva.
7. Desenvolver relações de longo prazo com os fornecedores para que sejam evitadas interrupções nos fluxos de materiais.

Na Toyota, por exemplo, há tanto **programas de produção estáveis** como **nivelados**. O programa mestre de produção (MPS) é congelado para o primeiro mês, e o MPS inteiro cobre um ano. O programa de produção é exatamente o mesmo para cada dia do mês. Isso significa que os mesmos produtos são produzidos nas mesmas quantidades na mesma seqüência todos os dias do mês. A Toyota divide o número total de cada modelo de automóvel a ser manufaturado durante um mês pelo número de dias de trabalho no mês para obter o número desse modelo a ser produzido diariamente. Mesmo que somente alguns veículos de um modelo em particular fossem necessários num mês, alguns seriam montados em cada dia do mês. Isso fornece o mesmo programa de produção diário ao longo do mês. Essa abordagem ao MPS simplifica explosões de peças, fluxos de materiais e atribuições de tarefas a trabalhadores. Se o JIT pretende funcionar, programas de produção estáveis e nivelados são necessários.

Outro pré-requisito indispensável da manufatura JIT é a necessidade de se ter *fábricas mais focalizadas*. Fábricas especializadas são mais fáceis de administrar, e o JIT depende da simplicidade dessas fábricas focalizadas.

Um requisito fundamental do JIT é *aumentar a capacidade de produção* dos centros de trabalho de manufatura. A Figura 13.2 ilustrou que, aumentando-se as capacidades de produção, os lead times de manufatura são reduzidos. As capacidades de produção geralmente são aumentadas de duas maneiras: aumentando-se as taxas de produção e reduzindo-se os tempos de preparação nos centros de trabalho. O Exemplo 13.1 ilustrou que pequenos aumentos nas taxas de produção dos centros de trabalho podem resultar numa drástica redução dos lead times de manufatura. A capacidade de produção também pode ser aumentada reduzindo-se os tempos de preparação nos centros de trabalho. Tempo de preparação é o tempo necessário para ajustar as configurações de máquina, substituir materiais, trocar ferramentas e fazer tudo o que é necessário para mudar da produção de um produto para a produção de um novo em um centro de trabalho. Uma vez que a produção nos centros de trabalho é interrompida enquanto os centros de trabalho estão sendo modificados, a redução dos tempos de preparação reduzirá o tempo e aumentará a capacidade de produção. Como ilustrou a Figura 13.2, aumentar as capacidades de produção resultará num fluxo mais rápido e mais contínuo de produtos através da manufatura.

Ao melhorar a qualidade do produto, dar treinamento interfuncional aos trabalhadores, reduzir quebras de equipamentos por meio da manutenção preventiva e estabelecer fluxos de material confiáveis desde os fornecedores, as interrupções na produção serão minimizadas. Estudaremos como melhorar a qualidade de produto nos Capítulos 16 e 17. E estudaremos sobre o treinamento interfuncional de trabalhadores no Capítulo 15. Uma vez que os trabalhadores são treinados em diversas tarefas, eles podem ser deslocados para outras tarefas quando necessário para compensar qualquer desequilíbrio nos fluxos de trabalho que possam ser causados ou por problemas de qualidade, ou por quebras de máquinas.

Com esses fatores presentes na manufatura, o sucesso final do JIT é enormemente aumentado.

ELEMENTOS DA MANUFATURA JIT

Discutiremos o JIT examinando seus componentes importantes: as suposições subjacentes, suas abordagens, seu método de planejamento e controle da produção, e diversas de suas atividades.

ELIMINANDO O DESPERDÍCIO

Eliminar desperdício de todos os tipos é a ideologia fundamental que há por trás do JIT. Shigeo Shingo, uma autoridade em JIT na Toyota, identificou sete desperdícios na produção que devem ser eliminados.

A Tabela 13.1 lista e descreve esses desperdícios.

SOLUÇÃO FORÇADA DE PROBLEMAS E MELHORIA CONTÍNUA

Na manufatura tradicional, estoques em processo permitem que a produção prossiga mesmo que ocorram problemas de produção; dessa forma, é obtida uma elevada utilização de máquina e de trabalhadores. Se produtos defeituosos forem encontrados e se mau funcionamento de máquinas ou stockouts de materiais ocorrerem, estoques em processo poderão ser usados para abastecer aquilo que, de outro modo, seriam trabalhadores e máquinas ociosos. Como a Figura 13.3 ilustra, o estoque em processo encobre problemas de produção na manufatura tradicional. Por trás do JIT há o impulso contínuo para melhorar processos e métodos de produção. Com essa finalidade, o JIT luta para reduzir estoques, porque níveis elevados de estoque são considerados como algo que encobre problemas de produção. Quando os estoques em processo são reduzidos drasticamente, vêm a tona problemas de produção, e a produção é interrompida até que as causas desses problemas sejam resolvidas. Somente quando a máquina é consertada, o problema de controle da qualidade é resolvido, ou a causa que há por trás do stockout é descoberta ou corrigida — somente então a produção pode ter início novamente.

O JIT é realmente um sistema de solução forçada de problemas. Há alguns fatores de segurança no JIT. Espera-se que todo material cumpra os padrões de qualidade, espera-se que toda peça chegue exatamente no tempo prometido e exatamente no lugar que se espera que ela esteja, espera-se que todo trabalhador trabalhe produtivamente, e espera-se que toda máquina funcione como se pretende, sem que-

TABELA 13.1 — RUMO À ELIMINAÇÃO DO DESPERDÍCIO NA MANUFATURA

1. **Superprodução.** Faça somente aquilo que é necessário agora.
2. **Espera.** Coordene os fluxos entre as operações e equilibre cargas desequilibradas por meio de trabalhadores e equipamentos flexíveis.
3. **Transporte.** Projete layouts de instalações que reduzam ou eliminem o manuseio e embarque de materiais.
4. **Produção desnecessária.** Elimine todos os passos de produção desnecessários.
5. **Estoques de trabalho em processo.** Elimine-os, reduzindo tempos de preparação, aumentando taxas de produção e fazendo uma melhor coordenação de taxas de produção entre centros de trabalho.
6. **Movimento e esforço.** Melhore a produtividade e a qualidade eliminando movimentos humanos desnecessários, torne os movimentos necessários mais eficientes, mecanize e depois automatize.
7. **Produtos defeituosos.** Elimine defeitos e inspeções. Faça produtos perfeitos.

Fonte: R. Hall, *Attaining Manufacturing Excellence*, p. 26. Homewood, IL: Dow Jones-Irwin, 1987.

bras. Os gerentes na manufatura JIT têm uma escolha. Eles podem fazer um grande esforço para encontrar e resolver as causas de problemas de produção, ou podem conviver com um nível intolerável de interrupções na produção. Uma das abordagens para implementar um programa JIT é reduzir os estoques em processo incrementalmente em pequenos passos. Em cada passo, diferentes problemas de produção são descobertos, e os trabalhadores e seus gerentes trabalham para eliminá-los. Então, quando não há quase nenhum estoque em processo, as causas da maioria dos problemas de produção foram removidas.

FIGURA 13.3 — DESVENDANDO PROBLEMAS DE PRODUÇÃO AO REDUZIR ESTOQUES

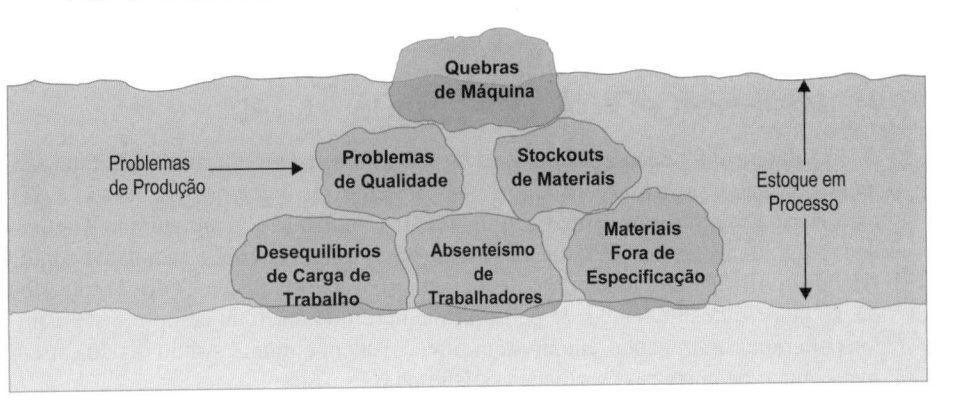

Mas a tarefa de eliminar problemas de produção não se encerrou. É necessário manter vigilância para continuar a estudar áreas de problemas potenciais para assegurar a melhoria contínua. Os fabricantes japoneses praticam há muito tempo aquilo que eles chamam *kaizen*, a meta da melhoria contínua em todas as fases da manufatura. Os gerentes podem encorajar os trabalhadores a reduzirem estoques em processo um passo a mais para ver se algum problema de produção poderá ocorrer, identificando assim um alvo para os trabalhadores eliminarem. Preparações de máquina podem ser estudadas, com trabalhadores e gerentes trabalhando para eliminar a gordura a fim de que as preparações sejam quase instantâneas. Os fabricantes japoneses usam há muito tempo o termo SMED, acrônimo de *single minute exchange of dies* (troca de moldes num único minuto), significando que a meta deles é fazer com que todas as preparações tomem menos de 1 minuto.

A melhoria contínua é fundamental para a filosofia JIT e é uma razão-chave para seu sucesso.

São as Pessoas Que Fazem o JIT Funcionar

Em última análise, os negócios obtêm sucesso ou fracassam por causa de seu pessoal. O JIT não é exceção a essa regra. Uma vez que o JIT é um sistema de solução forçada de problemas, ter uma força de trabalho dedicada, comprometida em trabalhar em conjunto para resolver problemas de produção, é fundamental. A manufatura JIT, portanto, tem um forte elemento de treinamento e envolvimento dos trabalhadores em todas as fases da manufatura.

Antes e acima de tudo, uma cultura de confiança mútua e trabalho em equipe deve ser desenvolvida numa organização. Gerentes e trabalhadores devem se ver como colaboradores comprometidos com o sucesso da empresa. Equipes de trabalho são encorajadas a se reunir para buscar soluções de longo prazo para as causas dos problemas de produção. Trabalhadores também são encorajados a sugerir maneiras melhores de fazer as coisas, de pequenas sugestões a questões estratégicas. Juntamente com uma cultura organizacional aberta e confiante, uma atitude de lealdade para com a equipe e autodisciplina também devem ser desenvolvidas. Uma vez que os trabalhadores estão comprometidos com o sucesso da empresa, a equipe de trabalho — em vez do trabalhador individual — torna-se o foco. Os trabalhadores não estão livres para seguir seu próprio rumo e experimentarem qualquer método de fazer seu trabalho de acordo com qualquer padrão de sua preferência; ao contrário, os métodos e padrões com os quais a equipe concordou devem prevalecer.

Outro fator importante que é crucial para o sucesso do JIT é a *delegação de poderes* (*empowerment*) *aos trabalhadores*. Isso significa que é dada aos trabalhadores autoridade para tomar a iniciativa de resolver problemas de produção. Em vez de esperar orientação vinda de cima, os trabalhadores têm autoridade para interromper a produção em qualquer momento devido a coisas como problemas de qualidade, mau funcionamento de máquinas ou questões de segurança. Grupos de trabalhadores são encorajados a trabalhar juntos para colocar rapidamente a produção em movimento novamente. Assim que os trabalhadores tiverem identificado problemas, eles são encorajados a se encontrar antes, durante os intervalos do trabalho, ou depois do trabalho, para discutir os problemas enquanto tentam encontrar soluções para suas causas. Ter trabalhadores ativamente envolvidos na resolução de problemas é o objetivo do empowerment de trabalhadores.

O pessoal, fornecedores, trabalhadores, gerentes e clientes devem estar motivados e comprometidos com o trabalho em equipe para que a manufatura JIT seja eficaz.

Administração da Qualidade Total

A manufatura JIT depende de um sistema de administração da qualidade total (TQM) (a qual estudaremos no Capítulo 16) estar em vigor. Não obstante ser tentador discutirmos a TQM agora, é suficiente para nosso entendimento da manufatura JIT dizermos que a manufatura JIT bem-sucedida anda de mãos dadas com uma cultura TQM que envolva a organização inteira. Exatamente como todos têm de estar envolvidos no JIT, assim também todos devem estar envolvidos na TQM. O total compromisso com a produção de produtos de qualidade perfeita o tempo todo e o total compromisso com a produção de produtos para rápida entrega aos clientes têm uma coisa em comum. Ambos estão estreitamente focalizados na meta global da obtenção de clientes satisfeitos.

Processamento Paralelo

Uma parte importante da manufatura JIT é explorarmos um processamento paralelo sempre que possível. Quaisquer operações que sejam executadas em série (uma depois da outra) e que possam ser executadas em paralelo (simultaneamente) podem consumir uma grande parcela dos lead times de manufatura. Esse conceito é similar à engenharia simultânea apresentada do Capítulo 4. Quando se faz projeto de produtos e projeto de processos simultaneamente, o tempo para introduzir novos produtos no mercado é reduzido. A mesma abordagem é assumida em empresas que querem engajar-se em competição baseada no tempo através do JIT. Muitas operações podem se tornar paralelas simplesmente através da programação, quando a produção é programada para ocorrer ao mesmo tempo que uma ou mais operações. Em outros casos, redesenho de layout e redesenho de produto podem ser necessários para se obter processamento paralelo. Mas os custos individuais geralmente podem ser mais do que compensados pelas significativas reduções dos lead times de manufatura.

CONTROLE DE PRODUÇÃO KANBAN

A manufatura JIT foi descrita no Capítulo 9 como um **sistema puxar (pull)** de planejamento e controle da produção. Num **sistema empurrar (push)**, como por exemplo um sistema MRP, examinamos o programa para determinar o que produzir em seguida. Num sistema puxar examinamos a etapa de produção seguinte para determinar o que é necessário, e depois produzimos somente isso. Dessa forma, lotes de produtos partem diretamente das fases antecedentes para as fases conseqüentes sem ser armazenados em estoque. Como afirma Robert Hall: "Não é possível se fazer algo e *enviá-lo* a lugar nenhum. Alguém terá de vir pegá-lo".

No âmago da manufatura JIT na Toyota está o Kanban, um sistema surpreendentemente simples de planejamento e controle da produção. Usaremos as Figuras 13.4 e 13.5 para ilustrar como o Kanban planeja e controla a produção entre dois centros de trabalho adjacentes.

Kanban, em japonês, significa cartão ou cartaz, como os que existem na frente de um cinema ou teatro. No contexto do JIT, Kanban é o meio de sinalizar para a estação de trabalho antecedente que a estação de trabalho seguinte está preparada para que a estação anterior produza outro lote de peças. Num ambiente de job shop simples com um ou somente alguns produtos, sinais como um engradado vazio, um lugar vazio designado no piso (marcado com fita ou pintado) ou uma bola de golfe colorida rolada por um tubo de plástico têm sido usados por algumas empresas. O sinal mais comum, entretanto, é um cartão Kanban. Muito mais comunicação pode ser transmitida por um cartão do que por um sinal que não seja em papel.

Há dois tipos de cartão Kanban: um cartão de transferência (Kanban-C) e um cartão de produção (Kanban-P). A Figura 13.4 mostra exemplos desses tipos de cartão. Basicamente esses cartões substituem a maioria das outras formas em papel de controle da produção no chão de fábrica. É importante observar que com programas de produção estáveis e nivelados, decisões a respeito da prioridade (quais pedidos são liberados a cada dia, quando pedidos são liberados e a seqüência dos pedidos) são rotineiras; desse modo, o planejamento e o controle do chão de fábrica são reduzidos ao planejamento e controle do movimento dos pedidos entre centros de trabalho. Nessas situações de programação simples, sinais visuais e Kanbans são os únicos dispositivos necessários.

A Figura 13.5 ilustra como o Kanban opera. Quando um trabalhador no chão de fábrica no Centro de Trabalho n. 2 seguinte necessita de um recipiente de peças para sua operação, ele faz o seguinte:

1. Ele localiza o Kanban-C na bolsa no lado direito do recipiente que acaba de ser esvaziado em seu centro de trabalho; esse cartão é sua autorização para substituir o recipiente vazio por um cheio existente no depósito.
2. Em seguida ele pega o Kanban-C e localiza um recipiente cheio das peças necessárias no depósito.
3. Então ele coloca o Kanban-C no recipiente cheio.
4. Em seguida ele retira o Kanban-P do recipiente cheio e coloca-o num poste ou painel de avisos no Centro de Trabalho n. 1 antecedente; esse Kanban-P é a autorização para que o Centro de Trabalho n. 1 produza outro recipiente das peças.
5. Finalmente, ele leva o recipiente cheio de peças com o Kanban-C para o Centro de Trabalho n. 2 seguinte.

Nenhuma peça pode ser produzida ou movida sem um cartão Kanban. O Kanban baseia-se na simples idéia de substituição de recipientes de peças, um por vez. Um recipiente não é movido para uma operação de produção seguinte até que seja necessário, e um recipiente de peças não é produzido até que seja preciso. Esses recipientes são reservados para peças específicas, são propositadamente mantidos pequenos, e sempre contêm o mesmo número padrão de peças para cada número de peça.

Na Toyota, os recipientes não devem conter mais do que aproximadamente 10% das necessidades de um dia. Há um mínimo de dois recipientes para cada numeração de peças, um no centro de trabalho produtor antecedente e um no centro de trabalho usuário seguinte.

O Exemplo 13.2 ilustra como o número de recipientes entre dois centros de trabalho adjacentes é calculado.

FIGURA 13.4 — CARTÕES KANBAN

Cartão Kanban de Transferência

Numeração da peça a ser produzida: M471-36

Descrição da peça: gabinete de válvula

Tamanho de lote necessário: 40

Tipo de recipiente: engradado RED

Número do cartão: 2 de 5

Local de armazenamento de recuperação: NW53D

Do centro de trabalho: 22

Para o centro de trabalho: 35

Cartão Kanban de Produção

Numeração da peça a ser produzida: M471-36

Descrição da peça: gabinete de válvula

Tamanho de lote necessário: 40

Tipo de recipiente: engradado RED

Número do cartão: 4 de 5

Local de armazenamento de peças concluídas: NW53D

Do centro de trabalho: 22

Para o centro de trabalho: 35

Requisição de Materiais:
    Material n. 744B   Local de armazenamento: NW48C
    Peça n. B238-5   Local de armazenamento: NW47B

FIGURA 13.5 — FLUXO DE CARTÕES KANBAN E RECIPIENTES ENTRE DOIS CENTROS DE TRABALHO

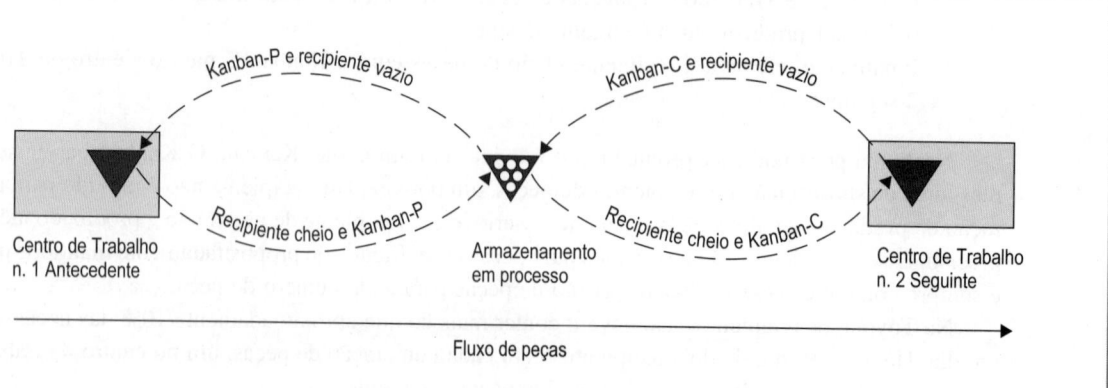

Exemplo 13.2

Calculando o Número de Contêineres entre Centros de Trabalho

Há dois centros de trabalho adjacentes, um centro de trabalho seguinte (usuário) e um centro de trabalho antecedente (produtor). A taxa de produção do centro de trabalho usuário é de 175 peças por hora. Cada contêiner Kanban padrão contém 100 peças. É necessária uma média de 1,10 hora para que um contêiner conclua o ciclo inteiro desde o momento em que ele sai cheio do centro de trabalho antecedente até que retorne vazio, seja cheio de produtos da produção e saia novamente. Compute o número de contêineres necessário se o sistema Kanban tiver uma classificação P igual a 0,25.

Solução

1. A fórmula e as definições de variáveis usadas para esse cálculo são:

$$N = \frac{UT(1 + P)}{C}, \text{ em que}$$

   N = número total de contêineres necessários entre os dois centros de trabalho.
   U = índice de utilização do centro de trabalho seguinte, geralmente peças por hora.
   T = tempo médio transcorrido necessário para que um contêiner conclua o ciclo inteiro desde o momento em que ele sai do centro de trabalho antecedente, é devolvido, é cheio novamente com produtos da produção e sai novamente. Medido nas mesmas unidades de tempo que U.
   P = variável de política que indica a eficiência do sistema. P pode assumir valores de 0 a 1. Um 0 indicaria eficiência perfeita, um 1,0 indicaria ineficiência total.
   C = capacidade do contêiner padrão, número de peças.

2. Use a fórmula para calcular N, o número de contêineres:

$$N = \frac{UT(1 + P)}{C} = \frac{175(1,1)(1 + 0,25)}{100}$$

$$= \frac{240,6}{100} = 2,4, \text{ ou } 3,0 \text{ contêineres}$$

Observe que ao arredondarmos 2,4 para 3,0 certa folga (*slack*[1]) ou estoque de segurança é introduzido no sistema, mas isso geralmente é preferível a termos um número demasiadamente pequeno de contêineres.

Pode ser usado mais do que o número mínimo de contêineres entre dois centros de trabalho, porque o centro de trabalho antecedente pode não ser capaz de preencher o contêiner imediatamente. Esses atrasos podem ocorrer porque outros Kanban-P chegaram lá primeiro e suas peças precisam ser produzidas antes, além de outras complexidades. Os trabalhadores produzem exatamente a quantidade relacionada nos cartões Kanban de reciclagem; nem mais, nem menos. Produzir uma peça a mais do que a quantidade padrão para o contêiner seria considerado tão ruim quanto produzir uma peça a menos. Produzir uma peça a mais do que o necessário seria esbanjador, porque mão-de-obra, materiais e capacidade de máquina seriam gastos para produzir a peça extra que não é necessária agora.

---

[1] *Slack:* a quantidade de tempo que uma atividade pode desviar-se do programa sem provocar um atraso na conclusão do projeto. (N. do T.)

Existem algumas variações entre os sistemas Kanban. Por exemplo, na fábrica de motores de motocicleta Kawasaki no Japão, os trabalhadores se comunicam por meio de bolas de golfe pintadas que rolam por tubos. Em algumas fábricas japonesas, os trabalhadores se comunicam por meio de luzes que piscam, sistema chamado *andon*. Uma luz verde significa que não há problemas, uma luz âmbar significa que a produção está se atrasando, e uma luz vermelha significa que há um problema sério. Trabalhadores e supervisores podem comunicar a situação da produção a centros de trabalho adjacentes simplesmente olhando para as luzes. Independentemente da variação dos sistemas Kanban, os trabalhadores devem ter atitudes cooperativas para que eles funcionem. Similarmente, programas para obter excelência na manutenção preventiva, qualidade de produto e confiança mútua com os fornecedores são uma necessidade.

O Kanban e o MRP podem coexistir? Sim, podem, pelo menos num grau limitado. O MRP pode ser usado na manufatura JIT para se obter explosões de peças e para pedir materiais e peças de fornecedores, mas há pouca influência do MRP dentro da manufatura. Os fornecedores usam os programas MRP como um plano global para a produção e para determinar a seqüência de pedidos de peças, mas a produção real se desenvolve seguindo o sistema Kanban do cliente. Semelhantemente, o controle de produção dentro da operação de manufatura do cliente é feito com o Kanban. Os estoques em processo excessivos que podem resultar da abordagem empurrar do MRP são, desse modo, evitados tanto na fábrica do fornecedor como na do cliente.

Essas versões de sistemas puxar reduzem muito o estoque em processo de peças entre centros de trabalho no chão de fábrica, mas o JIT também tem como meta reduzir estoques de matérias-primas.

ATIVIDADE DE COMPRAS JIT

O mesmo tipo de abordagem puxar no JIT é aplicado na atividade de compras de remessas de peças dos fornecedores. Na atividade de compras JIT, os fornecedores usam o princípio da substituição do Kanban utilizando contêineres pequenos, de tamanho padrão, e fazem remessas diárias para cada cliente. Se o Kanban for usado por um fornecedor, cartões Kanban autorizarão a movimentação de contêineres de peças entre a job shop do fornecedor e o cliente. Nesses arranjos, os fornecedores comumente estão localizados perto de seus clientes. Portanto o JIT não somente reduz os estoques em processo ao usar o Kanban, mas os estoques de matérias-primas também são reduzidos aplicando-se os mesmos princípios aos fornecedores.

Os elementos fundamentais da atividade de compras JIT são os seguintes:

1. O **desenvolvimento de fornecedores** ou as **relações com o fornecedor** sofrem mudanças fundamentais. A natureza das relações entre clientes e fornecedores deixa de ser adversária e passa a ser cooperativa. Os japoneses denominam essas relações **redes de fornecedores** e referem-se aos fornecedores como **parceiros**. Informações suscetíveis, ajuda para reduzir os custos e melhorar a qualidade e até mesmo financiamento muitas vezes são compartilhados por clientes e fornecedores.
2. Os departamentos de compra desenvolvem relações de longo prazo com os fornecedores. Como resultado disso obtêm contratos de suprimento de longo prazo com alguns fornecedores em vez de contratos de suprimento de curto prazo com muitos fornecedores. A repetição de negócios é a recompensa para os mesmos fornecedores, e licitações públicas geralmente se limitam a novas peças.
3. Não obstante o preço ser importante, prazos de entrega, qualidade de produto, confiança mútua e cooperação tornam-se a base principal para a escolha de fornecedores.
4. Os fornecedores são encorajados a estender os métodos JIT a seus próprios fornecedores.
5. Os fornecedores comumente estão localizados perto da fábrica da empresa compradora, ou se estiverem a certa distância da fábrica, geralmente estão agrupados. Isso faz com que os lead times sejam mais breves e mais confiáveis.
6. As remessas são entregues diretamente na linha de produção do cliente. Uma vez que os fornecedores são encorajados a produzir e a fornecer peças a uma taxa constante que coincida com a taxa de utilização da empresa compradora, um meio de transporte de propriedade da empresa tende a ser preferido.
7. As peças são entregues em contêineres pequenos, de tamanho padrão, com um mínimo de burocracia e em quantidades exatas.

8. O material entregue tem qualidade quase perfeita. Uma vez que os fornecedores têm uma relação de longo prazo com as empresas compradoras, e desde que as peças são entregues em tamanhos de lote pequenos, a qualidade dos materiais comprados tende a ser maior.

O Instantâneo da Indústria 13.1 ilustra como as empresas americanas estão obtendo sucesso com a atividade de compras JIT. As empresas americanas parecem estar adotando muitas das práticas de compras JIT, mas se elas podem adotar totalmente esses métodos é algo sobre o qual há dúvidas. Não obstante o pacote de compras JIT inteiro talvez ainda não ser aceito pelos fabricantes americanos, suas práticas de compra estão sendo afetadas pelo JIT, e parece estar se desenvolvendo um JIT híbrido americano que se enquadra no ambiente de compras único americano. Por exemplo, a operação *joint venture* da General Motors e Toyota em Fremont, Califórnia, faz pedidos diários de materiais a fornecedores do meio-oeste. Esses fornecedores embarcam seus materiais para uma área de redistribuição num pátio ferroviário no meio-oeste. Lá, os materiais são carregados em trens, na seqüência em que serão usados na produção, para entrega da noite para o dia (*overnight*) na fábrica.

REDUZINDO ESTOQUES ATRAVÉS DA REDUÇÃO DA PREPARAÇÃO

Se custa muito preparar uma máquina para produzir uma peça, faz sentido produzir muitas unidades da peça. Há muito tempo os fabricantes americanos têm seguido essa sabedoria convencional e têm se descuidado de trabalhar para reduzir os tempos de preparação e reduzir os tamanhos de lote de produção. É fundamental para o JIT um programa contínuo voltado à redução dos tamanhos de lote de produção a fim de que os níveis de estoque sejam reduzidos. Mas não parece que tamanhos de lote de produção muito

INSTANTÂNEO DA INDÚSTRIA 13.1

ATIVIDADE DE COMPRAS JIT NA WATERVILLE TG, INC.

Uma vez que muitas fábricas de automóveis têm assumido a abordagem à manufatura JIT, uma pressão cada vez maior tem sido feita sobre os fornecedores de automóveis para que garantam entregas freqüentes e confiáveis. Isso, por sua vez, exige que os fornecedores de automóveis trabalhem estreitamente com seus fornecedores de matérias-primas para garantir entregas confiáveis. A Waterville TG, Inc. (WTG), localizada em Waterville, Quebec, é especializada em projetar e manufaturar guarnições para carros. Sua linha de produtos inclui aproximadamente 500 diferentes modelos de guarnições, as quais ela fornece a cerca de uma dúzia de fabricantes de automóveis.

Para melhorar seu desempenho de compra, a WTG realizou um esforço para integrar seu sistema MRP com um sistema de programação de vendedores do tipo Kanban. O programa mestre de produção baseia-se em liberações programadas de pedidos fornecidas pelos clientes e que, tipicamente, cobrem um horizonte de 8 a 16 semanas. Os pedidos dos clientes são firmados semanalmente para a primeira semana até 10 dias. O sistema MRP da WTG computa então o número de cartões Kanban necessários para cobrir a demanda. Toda segunda-feira a WTG envia um fax a cada um de seus fornecedores sobre suas necessidades brutas para as próximas 12 semanas. Atualizações são enviadas diariamente a seus fornecedores. Uma quantidade Kanban padrão é estabelecida para cada material comprado dos clientes, e cada semana a WTG envia por fax um pedido a cada fornecedor referente a quantos Kanbans serão necessários para renovar seus estoques.

Para ajudar a implementar entregas menores e mais freqüentes dos fornecedores, a WTG estabeleceu um programa de transporte diário do tipo "entrega matinal de leite" entre suas fábricas, seu armazém de itens acabados e 8 de 12 de seus fornecedores de matérias-primas localizados na região.

Os resultados dessas ações têm sido impressionantes. Os estoques totais foram reduzidos de um suprimento de 28 para 8,4 dias. Os lead times médios de compra foram reduzidos de 2 semanas para 1 a 2 dias. O tempo médio para reagir às mudanças foi reduzido de 4 para 1 dia. E a redução de situações de emergência (stockouts iminentes) foi da ordem de 41 para 31 ocorrências anuais.

Fonte: Landry, Sylvain, Claude R. Duguay, Sylvain Chaussé e Jean-Luc Themens. "Integrating MRP, Kanban and Bar-Coding Systems to Achieve JIT Procurement". *Production and Inventory Management Journal* 38, n. 1, 1997.

FIGURA 13.6   EFEITO DA REDUÇÃO DOS TEMPOS DE PREPARAÇÃO SOBRE O TAMANHO DE LOTE DE PRODUÇÃO

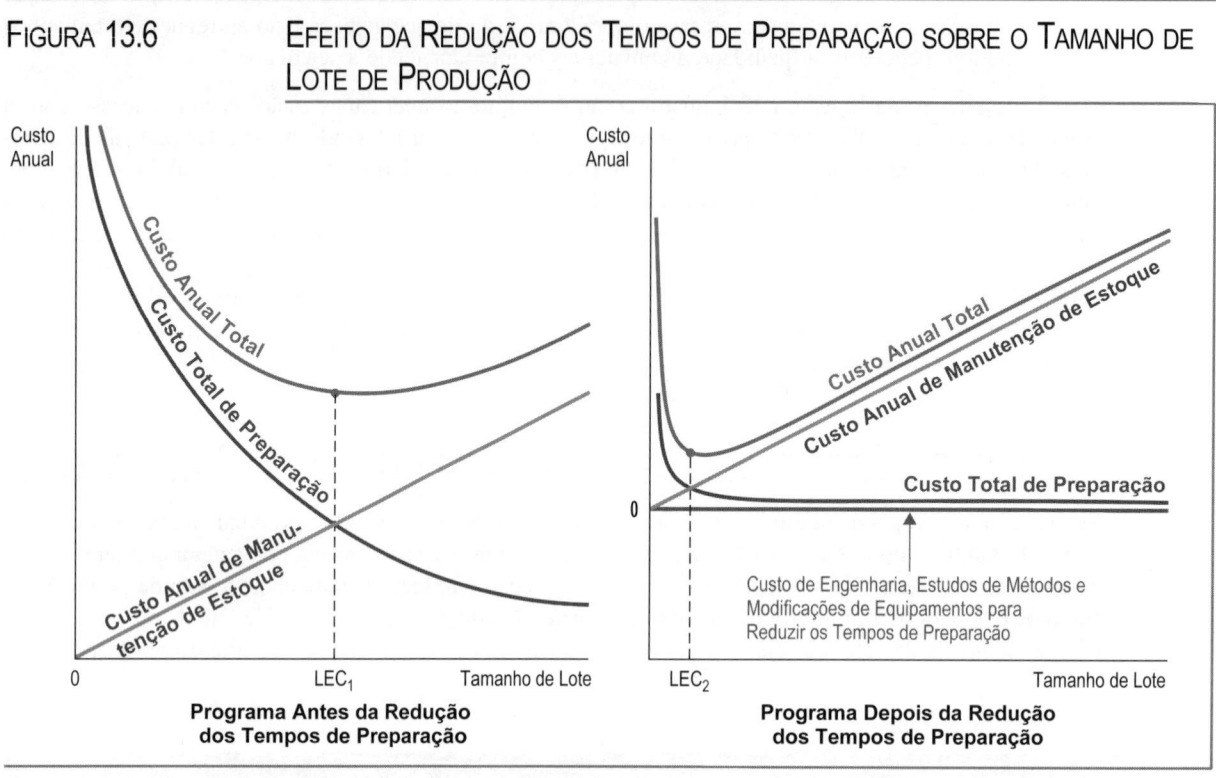

pequenos resultariam em demasiadas preparações de máquina, aumentados custos de produção e capacidade perdida devido à existência de máquinas ociosas durante as preparações? Os sistemas JIT gastam grandes somas de dinheiro para reduzir os tempos de preparação para evitar essas conseqüências negativas dos tamanhos de lote pequenos. Engenheiros estudam as configurações, dispositivos automáticos são anexados às máquinas, trabalhadores são treinados em métodos de trabalho mais eficientes, e o resultado são tempos de preparação muito curtos. Em alguns casos, controles computadorizados podem fazer as novas configurações de máquina instantaneamente, com o resultado de que o tempo de preparação entre diferentes peças se aproxima de zero. A Figura 13.6 mostra que os tamanhos de lote padrão (LEC) se aproximam de zero quando os custos de preparação se aproximam de zero. As empresas JIT usam a mesma fórmula LEC para analisar tamanhos de lote, mas dão a ela um outro sentido. Elas tratam um tamanho de lote LEC muito pequeno como um dado e depois resolvem o custo de preparação. Dessa maneira, os tamanhos de lote de produção podem ser fixados muito baixos, e os tempos de preparação resultantes podem ser usados como alvos quando os engenheiros desenvolvem programas para reduzir os tempos de preparação. O Exemplo 13.3 computa o tempo de preparação necessário para se acomodar um tamanho de lote de produção JIT pequeno. Esses tipos de computações poderiam ser usados num programa envolvendo a fábrica inteira para reduzir os custos de preparação.

EXEMPLO 13.3

COMPUTANDO O TEMPO DE PREPARAÇÃO QUANDO É DADO UM TAMANHO DE LOTE DE PRODUÇÃO JIT PEQUENO

Como parte de um programa JIT envolvendo toda a fábrica para reduzir os tempos de preparação a fim de que os tamanhos de lote de produção possam ser menores, uma empresa quer determinar qual deve ser a duração da preparação de uma operação de manufatura a fim de fornecer um lote econômico de produção (LEC) de 20 unidades de uma peça. Um analista de produção desenvolveu estes dados para a operação:

- D = demanda anual de 20.000 unidades
- d = taxa de demanda diária de 80 unidades
- p = taxa de produção diária de 200 unidades
- LEC = tamanho de lote de 20 unidades para cada rodada de produção
- C = $ 15 de custo de manutenção em estoque por unidade por ano
- S = custo por preparação, o qual é desconhecido — para ser determinado a partir da fórmula LEC para lotes de produção

Se o preço da mão-de-obra para a operação for $ 10 por hora, qual tempo de preparação resultará num tamanho de lote econômico de produção de 20 unidades?

Solução

$$LEC = \sqrt{\frac{2DS}{C}\left(\frac{p}{p-d}\right)}$$

$$LEC^2 = \frac{2DS}{C}\left(\frac{p}{p-d}\right)$$

$$S = \frac{C(LEC)^2}{2D}\left(\frac{p-d}{p}\right) = \frac{\$\,5(20)}{2(20.000)}\left(\frac{200-80}{200}\right) = \$\,0{,}09$$

$$\text{Tempo de preparação} = \frac{S}{\text{Taxa de trabalho}} = \frac{\$\,0{,}09}{\$\,10/\text{hora}}$$

$$= 0{,}009 \text{ hora, ou } 0{,}54 \text{ minuto, ou } 32{,}4 \text{ segundos}$$

A redução da preparação é um processo contínuo num ambiente JIT, e é importante envolver os trabalhadores de cada estação de trabalho no processo. As melhores idéias para redução do tempo de preparação freqüentemente vêm das pessoas que estão mais familiarizadas com a maquinaria e o equipamento — os usuários. Com estímulo dos gerentes, os trabalhadores muitas vezes podem surgir com idéias criativas e baratas para a redução da preparação. Um exemplo de melhoria de baixo custo da preparação é executar algumas das tarefas de preparação antecipadamente, enquanto a última parte do lote anterior ainda está sendo processada na máquina. Dependendo dos requisitos tecnológicos envolvidos, o trabalhador talvez seja capaz de ajuntar todas as ferramentas, calibres, gabaritos e a primeira parte do lote seguinte ao lado da máquina, prontos para serem usados. Ele poderia até mesmo ser capaz de montar a primeira peça no novo gabarito que será colocado na máquina quando esta estiver livre. Essas ações poderiam reduzir substancialmente o tempo em que a máquina permanece improdutiva, durante a preparação, com pouco custo adicional.

Percepções úteis sobre reduções de tempos de preparação podem ser obtidas através das empresas que têm implementado programas formais de redução de tempo de preparação. Num desses estudos, John Leschke, da Universidade de Virgínia, analisou os programas de redução da preparação de cinco empresas, programas que variavam em duração de 2 meses a 5 anos. Numa série de dois artigos, Leschke apresenta detalhes sobre os programas de redução da preparação das empresas e compara diferentes abordagens para alocar investimentos para as atividades de redução da preparação a fim de obter o máximo benefício. Não somente os custos de preparação grandemente reduzidos resultam em baixos níveis de estoque, mas também a fábrica começa a agir de uma maneira muito similar a um sistema de manufatura repetitiva.

Trabalhando Rumo à Manufatura Repetitiva

O *APICS Dictionary* define essa forma de produção como "produção de unidades discretas, planejadas e executadas como um programa, geralmente em velocidades e volumes relativamente elevados. Os materiais tendem a mover-se num fluxo contínuo durante a produção, mas diferentes itens podem ser produzidos seqüencialmente dentro desse fluxo". Essa é uma produção focalizada no produto de lotes de produtos padronizados. Esses são sistemas nos quais os produtos fluem continuamente ao longo de um roteiro direto até ser finalizados, e no qual há pouco estoque em processo e as peças raramente param de se mover. Manufatura repetitiva evidentemente não se refere à produção focalizada no processo de produtos personalizados que ocorre nas job shops. Os proponentes do JIT argumentariam que se pode fazer com que até mesmo job shops se comportem de uma maneira mais assemelhada à manufatura repetitiva.

Algumas empresas têm trabalhado arduamente para fazer suas fábricas se comportarem de uma maneira mais similar à manufatura repetitiva. Entre as coisas que podem ser feitas para modificar uma fábrica para que se torne mais repetitiva em sua produção estão:

- Reduzir os tempos de preparação e os tamanhos de lote de produção.
- Mudar o layout da fábrica para permitir fluxos ininterruptos de produto através da instalação.
- Transformar grupos de máquinas dentro de layouts focalizados no processo em centros de manufatura celular (MC) ou células. Na MC, grupos de máquinas funcionam como ilhas focalizadas no produto dentro do layout mais amplo.
- Instalar sistemas de manufatura flexíveis (FMS). Esses grupos de máquinas podem acomodar uma variedade de produtos sem a necessidade de preparações de máquina executadas por trabalhadores.
- Padronizar projetos de peças para reduzir o número de peças e o número de preparações.
- Treinar trabalhadores para diversas tarefas. Esses trabalhadores flexíveis podem mover-se de um centro de trabalho para outro quando necessário para equilibrar a carga de trabalho na fábrica.
- Instalar programas de manutenção preventiva a fim de que quebras de máquina não interrompam os fluxos de produto.
- Instalar programas de controle da qualidade a fim de que produtos defeituosos não interrompam os fluxos de produção.
- Desenvolver uma eficiente rede de fornecedores a fim de que os materiais fluam na fábrica de maneira harmoniosa para sustentar programas de produção in-house, permitindo assim uma produção ininterrupta.

Mesmo que uma empresa não possa transformar todas as suas operações em manufatura repetitiva, algumas partes do sistema podem ser repetitivas. Por exemplo, mesmo que muitos produtos projetados de forma personalizada estejam irregularmente programados na montagem final, seus projetos de peças componentes poderiam ser padronizados, programas de produção de peças componentes poderiam se tornar estáveis e nivelados, e as peças componentes poderiam ser produzidas por meio de manufatura repetitiva.

Com mudanças como essas, muito mais fábricas que não são puramente de manufatura repetitiva poderiam ser capazes de implementar sistemas de manufatura JIT e desfrutar dos mesmos benefícios.

BENEFÍCIOS DA MANUFATURA JIT

Alguns dos benefícios reivindicados para os sistemas JIT são:

- Os níveis de estoque são drasticamente reduzidos.
- O tempo necessário para que os produtos percorram a fábrica é grandemente reduzido, possibilitando assim que as fábricas se envolvam na competição baseada no tempo, usando a velocidade como uma arma para captar fatias de mercado.
- A qualidade do produto é melhorada, e o custo da produção de sucata é reduzido. A qualidade do produto é melhorada devido ao envolvimento do trabalhador na solução das causas dos problemas de produção; e com lotes menores, peças defeituosas são descobertas mais cedo.
- Com menos estoque em processo, menos espaço é ocupado com estoques e equipamentos de manuseio de materiais. Os trabalhadores permanecem mais próximos, de forma que eles podem se ver mutuamente, se comunicar mais facilmente, trabalhar os problemas mais eficientemente, aprender as tarefas um do outro e comutar tarefas quando necessário. Isso promove o trabalho de equipe entre os trabalhadores e maior flexibilidade nas atribuições de trabalho.
- Uma vez que o foco na manufatura está em descobrir e corrigir as causas de problemas de produção, as operações de manufatura são aceleradas e livres de problemas.

Como ilustra o Instantâneo da Indústria 13.2, empresas como a Sharp, Sanyo, Honda, Toyota, Hewlett-Packard, Kawasaki, Motorola, Matsushita, Sony, Black & Decker, General Motors, Ford, Chrysler, General Electric, Goodyear, Rolm e IBM adotaram de maneira bem-sucedida a manufatura JIT. Para conseguir os benefícios do JIT, entretanto, essas empresas tiveram de investir fortemente em estudos de engenharia e modificações de equipamentos para obter tempos de preparação drasticamente reduzidos, estabelecer programas de treinamento que treinam trabalhadores para diversas tarefas, e desenvolver diferentes estratégias empresariais com linhas de produto mais estreitas que permitem programas de produção estáveis e nivelados. A menos que os fabricantes estejam dispostos a se comprometer com esse novo preço, em vez do preço antigo dos níveis de estoque elevados e baixa receptividade do cliente, eles não poderão esperar colher os benefícios do JIT.

À medida que prosseguirmos no restante deste livro, o JIT será novamente discutido em relação a seu efeito sobre aspectos particulares da produção: administração de materiais e atividade de compras, administração da qualidade e controle, e administração da manutenção.

INSTANTÂNEO DA INDÚSTRIA 13.2

Sucessos da Manufatura JIT

Empresas como a Corning, Eaton, General Electric, Motorola e Rubbermaid reduziram estoques implementando sistemas just-in-time (JIT) de planejamento e controle da produção. Esses sistemas reduzem os níveis de estoque ao longo do processo de produção. Nem todos os fabricantes têm adotado o JIT, mas, mesmo aqueles que não o adotaram aprenderam a conviver com menos estoques. As taxas de juros mais elevadas da década de 1980, bem como outros custos de manutenção de estoques, tornaram a existência de estoques mais enxutos uma necessidade.

Além disso, estoques menores tendem a melhorar a qualidade do produto, os custos de produção e a receptividade às necessidades do cliente. Robert W. Hall, professor de negócios da Universidade de Indiana, prevê que as empresas na década de 1990 que não estão adotando a administração de estoques "simplesmente não permanecerão no negócio. Se você estiver competindo num mercado internacional e não fizer isso, não será capaz de competir". Práticas de estoque ruins, acrescenta ele, são "um fator que contribui bastante para muitas bancarrotas".

Na década de 1970, a Chrysler Corp. utilizava capacidade nivelada com estoques (produção para estoque). Ela estocava veículos para manter as fábricas funcionando harmoniosamente apesar das variações nos pedidos. Quando a demanda repentinamente se desacelerou, a Chrysler ficou com milhares de seus carros parados nos pátios da empresa. Desde então a Chrysler fez significativas melhorias. Ela mudou para planos agregados da capacidade que usam capacidade nivelada com backlog (produção sob encomenda). Agora, ela constrói carros mediante solicitação de distribuidores ou clientes.

Em sua fábrica de Belvidere, Illinois, os estoques de peças se esgotam, em média, a cada 2,5 dias de trabalho, um desempenho que se compara com o dos melhores fabricantes de automóveis, que ainda precisam de aproximadamente 2 semanas para fazer um carro assim que recebem um pedido, mais do que o dobro do tempo necessário no Japão.

Na Corning, o programa JIT iniciou-se com o slogan "estoque é mau". Ao obter um entendimento daquilo que provoca a existência de estoques, as causas fundamentais de muitos dos problemas de produção da Corning foram desvendadas. Eles descobriram que apenas 6% de seus estoques estavam de fato "vivos", ou em uso num momento qualquer. Na fábrica da Corning em Erwin, Nova Iorque, os estoques ocupavam quase tanto espaço de piso quanto seis campos de futebol, e agora já reduziram cerca de dois terços do estoque na fábrica. Hoje os serviços são mais ágeis e os contatos com os clientes, mais estreitos. As causas dos problemas de produção são encontradas por uma equipe de 16 pessoas, incluindo 12 trabalhadores horistas, a qual estuda problemas de qualidade e estoques. As previsões foram melhoradas, e isso tem auxiliado nas relações de trabalho, porque a força de trabalho não tem de ser escalada tão freqüentemente para trabalhar o estoque excessivo durante períodos de baixa de mercado.

Fonte: "Firms' Newfound Skill in Managing Inventory May Soften Downturn". *Wall Street Journal,* 19 de novembro de 1990.

SUCESSO E MANUFATURA JIT

Parte do sucesso das empresas que utilizam a manufatura JIT não pode ser atribuída somente ao JIT. As empresas bem-sucedidas também têm:

- Estratégias de negócios baseadas em produzir produtos padronizados que podem ser confeccionados maciçamente tanto a baixo custo como com uma notável qualidade de produto.
- A tecnologia de produção mais recente, inclusive robótica, sistemas de manufatura flexíveis (FMS), tecnologia de grupo (GT), sistemas automáticos de armazenamento e recuperação (ASRS), código de barras, projeto auxiliado por computador/manufatura auxiliada por computador (CAD/CAM) e manufatura integrada por computador (CIM).
- Fábricas focalizadas que são especializadas em tecnologias ou produtos particulares. Essas fábricas são menores, mais compactas e exigem menos investimento de capital.
- Programas mestres de produção que são estáveis e nivelados. Não somente eles variam em termos de nível de carga de mês a mês como também congelam a primeira parte de programas de produção.
- Economias dos tempos de preparação. Menos trabalho é utilizado para fazer as preparações, e máquinas não permanecem ociosas durante esse período. Isso pode contribuir para um menor custo de mão-de-obra e, sob certas condições, para uma mais elevada utilização da capacidade de máquina.
- Trabalhadores treinados em muitas tarefas. Eles podem mudar de uma tarefa para outra quando necessário para equilibrar a carga de trabalho, o que contribui para uma elevada utilização de trabalhadores e menores custos de mão-de-obra. Em algumas empresas, trabalhadores não sindicalizados não são inibidos pelas restritivas regras sindicais.
- Programas de segurança no trabalho para seus trabalhadores. Menos rotatividade de empregados resulta numa força de trabalho mais bem treinada e reduzidos custos de contratação e treinamento.
- Uma força de trabalho mais jovem. Os custos de atendimento à saúde e aposentadoria são menores.
- Programas de administração da qualidade total (TQM). Todo trabalhador é envolvido e motivado a tornar a empresa um sucesso através da qualidade de produto perfeita.
- Redes de fornecedores construídas sobre relações de confiança entre clientes e fornecedores. Essas disposições de longo prazo têm resultado em constância no suprimento, melhorada qualidade dos materiais fornecidos e, a longo prazo, reduzido custo de materiais.
- Estilos de administração participativa. A atitude dos gerentes em relação aos trabalhadores e políticas de pessoal benevolentes tendem a desenvolver cooperação entre os trabalhadores e a administração. Os proponentes desses estilos de administração afirmam que esses fatores têm resultado em trabalhadores mais comprometidos.

Provavelmente, jamais saberemos quais desses fatores ou combinação de fatores são responsáveis pelo sucesso dos negócios atualmente, porque todos têm sido mesclados e integrados com o JIT pelos fabricantes, e é impossível separá-los. Por fim, o JIT e os outros fatores relacionados acima compreendem um sistema e filosofia de manufatura globais, e é o todo, não as partes, o responsável pelo sucesso.

Se a maioria das empresas americanas adotará a manufatura JIT ainda é uma pergunta sem resposta. Para algumas das empresas americanas, o principal meio de competirem não é através de tempos de entrega curtos. Para essas empresas, o custo e a agitação de implementarem o JIT podem não ser justificáveis.

Podem ser necessários muitos meses e até mesmo muitos anos para que se modifique a cultura fundamental de uma empresa para uma que esteja equipada para engajar-se numa competição baseada no tempo. O comprometimento da empresa de cima para baixo é enorme, e esses programas não podem ser realizados levianamente, com a idéia de tentar outra nova "onda" da imprensa comercial. Até que tamanhos de lote pequenos sejam realizados através de programas que envolvam toda a fábrica para reduzir os tempos de preparação, o JIT simplesmente não funcionará. Além disso, a menos que as linhas de produto sejam estreitadas através de diferentes estratégias de negócios, a natureza não repetitiva nos processos de produção trabalhará contra o JIT.

Não obstante o MRP manipular extremamente bem uma grande variedade de produtos, o JIT simplesmente não funcionará sob essas condições. Em seu entusiasmo para ganhar os benefícios da manufatura JIT, os fabricantes americanos não deveriam abrir mão dos recursos positivos de seus sistemas de produção sem garantias de que novos métodos obterão melhores resultados. Atualmente, alguns fabricantes americanos aceitam estoques elevados como o preço que devem pagar para conseguir elevada utilização de trabalhadores e máquinas. Não obstante os fabricantes JIT terem obtido elevada utilização de trabalhadores e máquinas sem estoques elevados, eles estão pagando um preço diferente — investir fortemente em estudos de engenharia e modificações de equipamentos para obter tempos de preparação drasticamente reduzidos, estabelecer programas de treinamento que treinam os trabalhadores para diversas tarefas, pagar enormes somas de dinheiro para maquinaria de produção automatizada de alta tecnologia, e desenvolver diferentes estratégias de negócios com linhas de produto mais estreitas que permitem programas de produção estáveis e nivelados. A menos que os fabricantes americanos estejam dispostos a comprometer-se com esse novo preço em vez do preço antigo dos níveis de estoque elevados, eles não poderão esperar colher os benefícios do JIT.

Resumo Final

O Que os Fabricantes de Classe Mundial Estão Fazendo

Para muitas empresas atualmente, o nome do jogo é competição baseada no tempo. Para elas, o meio principal de captarem fatia de mercado é encontrando maneiras de encurtar o ciclo do pedido à entrega. A manufatura just-in-time (JIT) é um sistema que agiliza de tal forma a produção de produtos que nenhuma outra forma de produção é capaz de competir. Na manufatura JIT, a cultura fundamental da organização deve modificar-se de uma cultura que enfatiza a utilização de mão-de-obra e máquinas para uma que se concentre na velocidade. E velocidade de produção é obtida reduzindo-se drasticamente os lead times de manufatura.

Certos pré-requisitos devem estar presentes antes que o JIT tenha a oportunidade de obter sucesso. A produção deve ser do tipo manufatura repetitiva, ou a produção deve ser modificada de tal maneira que se comporte como a manufatura repetitiva. Os produtos devem mover-se entre a produção num fluxo contínuo sem esperar em nenhum passo. Os programas devem ser estabilizados e nivelados, e as fábricas devem tornar-se mais especializadas e focalizadas. Essas mudanças tornam o planejamento e o controle da produção simples o bastante para permitir que o JIT funcione. E programas dispendiosos devem ser implementados para aumentar a capacidade de produção ao aumentar as taxas de produção e reduzir os tempos de preparação. Adicionalmente, programas devem eliminar defeitos de produtos e quebras de máquinas como fontes de interrupção da produção. Para lidar com eventos inesperados, os trabalhadores devem receber treinamento interfuncional a fim de que possam realizar diversas tarefas.

Todos os elementos do JIT são fundamentais — eliminar o desperdício, solução forçada de problemas, criação de trabalho em equipe, administração da qualidade total, processamento paralelo, controle Kanban da produção, atividade de compras JIT e programas permanentes que reduzem estoques e produzam manufatura repetitiva.

Para as empresas que podem implementar um sistema de manufatura JIT bem-sucedido, as recompensas são enormes. Os estoques serão drasticamente reduzidos, e o tempo da emissão do pedido até a entrega será grandemente reduzido, permitindo que elas usem a velocidade como uma arma para captar fatias de mercado. A qualidade do produto é melhorada, e o custo de produção de sucata é reduzido. Trabalho em equipe e flexibilidade organizacional permitem que essas empresas reajam a todos os tipos de necessidades dos clientes. E, desde que o JIT se concentra na resolução de problemas na produção, as operações de manufatura são aceleradas e isentas de problemas.

Um grande número de fábricas japonesas e americanas mudou suas operações para o JIT. Mas elas tiveram de investir fortemente em estudos de engenharia e modificações de equipamentos para reduzir drasticamente os tempos de preparação, em programas de treinamento para diversas tarefas, e em novas estratégias de negócios com linhas de produto mais estreitas que permitem programas de produção estáveis e nivelados. A menos que os fabricantes estejam dispostos a assumir esse tipo de compromisso organizacional, não poderão esperar colher os benefícios do JIT.

As empresas que têm em operação programas JIT bem-sucedidos estão preparadas para engajar-se na competição baseada no tempo. Muitos acreditam que no JIT temos um relance do futuro, em que a velocidade será o fator fundamental para a conquista de fatias de mercado em mercados globais. Muitas empresas mudaram para o JIT sem prestar atenção.

Questões de Revisão e Discussão

1. Relacione alguns outros nomes para a manufatura just-in-time.
2. Explique o significado de *competição baseada no tempo*.
3. O que é *ciclo do pedido à entrega*? Quais são seus componentes?
4. Compare e contraste a filosofia da manufatura tradicional e o JIT. Quais são seus objetivos? Como eles os obtêm?
5. Explique a relação entre utilização da capacidade e lead times de manufatura da Figura 13.2.
6. Relacione e explique os pré-requisitos da manufatura JIT. Explique brevemente por que cada um é um pré-requisito.
7. Quem é Shigeo Shingo? Quais suas contribuições para a manufatura JIT?
8. Explique o significado da Figura 13.3.
9. Explique o papel das pessoas no JIT. Qual é o significado de *delegação de poderes* (empowerment) *aos trabalhadores*?
10. Por que a administração da qualidade total (TQM) é importante no JIT?
11. O que é *processamento paralelo*? Por que ele é desejável no JIT?
12. Explique brevemente como o Kanban funciona no chão de fábrica. O que são *cartões Kanban*? Como eles são usados no Kanban?
13. Relacione e explique os componentes da atividade de compras JIT. Quais são alguns dos obstáculos para sua plena adoção pelas empresas americanas? Quais são algumas das maneiras de superar esses obstáculos?
14. Explique o que as empresas podem fazer para reduzir estoques.
15. Explique algumas das coisas que as empresas podem fazer para que suas operações se comportem mais como manufatura repetitiva.
16. Relacione e explique os benefícios da manufatura JIT.
17. Explique a dificuldade de identificar as razões para o sucesso das empresas que usam a manufatura JIT.
18. As empresas que querem competir no mercado global devem adotar a manufatura JIT? Por quê?

Tarefas na Internet

1. Visite uma livraria on-line e encontre dois livros recentes sobre questões relacionadas com a manufatura just-in-time. Forneça a citação bibliográfica de cada livro.
2. Use a Internet para encontrar um artigo de pesquisa recente sobre Kanban na manufatura JIT. Apresente a citação bibliográfica do artigo.
3. Use a Internet para encontrar um artigo de pesquisa recente sobre reduções da preparação (redução do tempo ou custo de preparação). Apresente a citação bibliográfica do artigo.

Problemas

1. Uma operação de produção é um sistema de fila de canal único, fase única e tamanho de fila ilimitado. Os produtos chegam à operação a uma taxa média de 25 unidades por hora, e a taxa média de produção atual é de 27 produtos por hora. A administração quer que os produtos estejam na operação a uma média de somente 0,2 hora. Qual é a nova taxa média de produção na operação?

2. Uma operação de produção é um sistema de fila de canal único, fase única e tamanho de fila ilimitado. Os produtos chegam à operação a uma taxa média de 50 unidades por hora, e a operação automatizada produz produtos a uma taxa constante de 55 produtos por hora. A engenharia pode modificar a maquinaria na operação para aumentar a capacidade de produção para uma taxa constante de 60 produtos por hora. Em quanto o lead time médio deveria ser reduzido?

3. No Problema 2, quanto o estoque em processo médio deveria ser reduzido com a melhoria no lead time?

4. Há dois centros de trabalho adjacentes: um centro de trabalho seguinte (usuário) e um centro de trabalho antecedente (produtor). A taxa de produção do centro de trabalho usuário é de 200 peças por hora. Cada contêiner Kanban padrão contém 100 peças. É necessário uma média de 0,95 hora para que um contêiner percorra o ciclo inteiro desde o momento em que sai do centro de trabalho antecedente até ser devolvido, cheio com os produtos da produção, e saia novamente.
a) Compute o número de contêineres necessário se o sistema Kanban for classificado em um P igual a 0,30.
b) C comumente seria arredondado para cima ou para baixo? Por quê?

5. Se U = 500 peças por hora, T = 10 minutos, C = 50 e há atualmente quatro recipientes entre as operações adjacentes:
   a) Qual é o valor de P?
   b) O que o valor de P indica sobre quão eficientemente o sistema Kanban está funcionando?
   c) Explique por que esse valor de P poderia ser apropriado.

6. Um analista de produção e um engenheiro industrial estão investigando reduções potenciais de tempo de preparação em sua fábrica para ajudar a tornar os processos de produção mais eficientes. Uma máquina de estampagem hidráulica requer 25 minutos para que seu operador conclua uma preparação entre diferentes tipos de peças. Cada peça requer 2,75 minutos para o processo de estampagem. As peças são produzidas atualmente em lotes de 30 unidades. O preço da mão-de-obra é de $ 15,75 por hora.
   a) Qual é o custo médio atual da mão-de-obra por peça, incluindo as preparações?
   b) Se o tempo de preparação pudesse ser reduzido para 10 minutos, quanto custo de mão-de-obra por peça seria economizado usando-se o tamanho de lote atual de 30 unidades?
   c) Se o tempo de preparação pudesse ser reduzido para 10 minutos, em quanto o tamanho do lote poderia ser reduzido a fim de se obter o custo médio atual da mão-de-obra por unidade?

7. Uma equipe de implementação JIT está avaliando tamanhos de lote e tempos de preparação em toda a fábrica. A primeira máquina a ser avaliada atualmente requer aproximadamente 20 minutos para que seu operador conclua uma preparação entre diferentes tipos de peças. Cada peça requer 1,2 minuto para o processamento. As peças são produzidas atualmente em lotes de 60 unidades. O preço da mão-de-obra é de $ 14,50 por hora.
   a) Qual é o custo médio atual da mão-de-obra por peça, incluindo as preparações?
   b) Se o tempo de preparação pudesse ser reduzido para 10 minutos, quanto custo de mão-de-obra por peça seria economizado usando-se o tamanho de lote atual de 60 unidades?
   c) Se o tempo de preparação pudesse ser reduzido para 10 minutos, em quanto o tamanho do lote poderia ser reduzido a fim de se obter o custo médio atual da mão-de-obra por unidade?
   d) Quanto tempo de preparação seria necessário para se ter uma produção em lotes de 15 unidades e para se obter o custo médio atual da mão-de-obra por peça?

Estudo de Caso

The Superior Manufacturing Company

A The Superior Manufacturing Company produz produtos de metal laminado e usinado. A empresa está implementando um sistema de manufatura JIT e está se esforçando para reduzir os lead times em toda a produção. O centro de trabalho RTD agora está realizando um intenso escrutínio, porque ele é a operação gargalo atual da fábrica inteira. Isso significa que a taxa de produção na operação RTD é a taxa de produção mais lenta na fábrica e que a operação RTD controla a taxa de produção da fábrica. A efetiva capacidade de produção da operação RTD é aproximadamente 10% inferior à operação que tem a segunda capacidade de produção mais baixa. Desse modo, melhorias na operação RTD resultarão em melhorias na fábrica inteira.

O centro de trabalho RTD é composto de até seis máquinas idênticas que trabalham numa disposição em paralelo. As peças chegam ao centro de trabalho a uma taxa média de 100 peças por hora e fluem para a máquina com a fila de espera mais curta. Cada máquina pode processar uma média de 18 peças por hora.

Duas propostas estão sendo estudadas para acelerar o fluxo de peças através da operação RTD. A Proposta n. 1 instalaria novos controladores de velocidade variável em todas as máquinas, as taxas de produção médias seriam aumentadas para 20 peças por hora, e o custo seria igual a US$ 40.000. A Proposta n. 2 acrescentaria outra máquina idêntica às máquinas atuais, e o custo seria igual a US$ 60.000. Responda às perguntas que se seguem.

Tarefas

1. Qual é o lead time médio na operação RTD agora?
2. Qual seria o lead time médio na operação RTD sob a Proposta n. 1?
3. Qual seria o lead time médio na operação RTD sob a Proposta n. 2?
4. Avalie as duas propostas. Qual delas você recomendaria? Por quê?

CAPÍTULO 14

ADMINISTRAÇÃO DA CADEIA DE SUPRIMENTOS

Introdução

Administração da Cadeia de Suprimentos

Atividade de Compras
  Importância da Atividade de Compras Hoje
  Missão do Departamento de Compras
  O Que os Gerentes de Compras Fazem
  Departamentos de Compras nas Organizações
  Processos de Compra
    Instrumentos Básicos de Compra
  Compradores e Suas Obrigações
  Análise do Comprar Versus Fabricar
  Ética em Compras
  Atividade de Compras: A Emergente Fronteira Internacional

Atividade de Compras Just-in-Time

Logística
  Controle da Produção: Movimento de Materiais Dentro das Fábricas
  Remessas para as Fábricas e das Fábricas
  Administração da Distribuição • Planejamento das Necessidades de Distribuição
  Inovações na Logística

Armazenamento
  Operações de Armazenamento
  Métodos de Contabilidade de Estoques
  Desenvolvimentos Contemporâneos no Setor de Armazenamento

Agilização

Benchmarking do Desempenho de Gerentes de Materiais

Terceirização de Provedores de Administração da Logística

Resumo Final: O Que os Fabricantes de Classe Mundial Estão Fazendo

Questões de Revisão e Discussão

Tarefas na Internet

Problemas

Estudo de Caso
  Star Clothing Manufacturing

Administração Centralizada da Cadeia de Suprimentos na Motoarc

A Motoarc é uma empresa de produtos eletrônicos, aeroespaciais, maquinaria elétrica, semicondutores e produtos de computador. Suas vendas anuais são de US$ 5,4 bilhões, tem fábricas em 17 estados e 12 países, e emprega 284 mil pessoas em todo o mundo. Embora as operações da Motoarc tenham se expandido, suas atividades de compras, armazenamento e funções de expedição haviam ficado para trás de suas outras unidades empresariais em termos de eficiência. Não obstante um sistema JIT ter sido instalado, os problemas com materiais permaneciam, porque ninguém parecia ser responsável quando surgiam dificuldades. Por exemplo, um pedido recente de um fornecedor chegou atrasado na fábrica da Motoarc em Indianápolis. O departamento de compras culpou o pessoal do armazém e da expedição. O pessoal do armazém culpou o controle de produção. O controle de produção culpou o pessoal do armazém e de compras. O pessoal da expedição afirmou que a transportadora perdera o pedido por diversos dias em Chicago, atrasando assim a entrega. Cada função apontava um dedo acusador para outras funções. Devido a essas dificuldades, a Motoarc reorganizou recentemente todas as funções de administração de materiais sob uma vice-presidência de materiais que é responsável por todas as compras, logística, armazenamento e expedição de materiais em todas as divisões. Agora, o "bode" pára na escrivaninha do vice-presidente de materiais quando surgem quaisquer dificuldades relacionadas a materiais em qualquer divisão da companhia.

Como o relato precedente ilustra, algumas empresas estão reorganizando suas funções de administração de materiais sob um executivo de alto nível que é responsável por todas as atividades relacionadas com o fluxo de materiais pela companhia. Essas mudanças organizacionais concentram a atenção da administração nessa função e salientam a importância de se administrar o fluxo de materiais.

Materiais são quaisquer *commodities*[1] usadas direta ou indiretamente na produção de um produto ou serviço, como matérias-primas, peças componentes, montagens e suprimentos. *A administração de materiais na maioria das empresas é crucial para seu sucesso porque o custo para comprar, armazenar, movimentar e despachar materiais é responsável por mais da metade do custo de um produto. Produtividade basicamente significa impulsionar para baixo o custo de fazer negócios, e realizar melhor a tarefa de administração de materiais é cada vez mais vista como a chave para uma produtividade mais elevada em muitas empresas atualmente.* Os gerentes de operações estão trabalhando muito para desenvolver melhores maneiras de administrar materiais a fim de que entregas no tempo certo, qualidade e custos possam ser melhorados para que suas empresas possam sobreviver num mundo cada vez mais competitivo.

Administração da Cadeia de Suprimentos

Considere como os materiais poderiam fluir dos fornecedores de uma empresa, passar pelas operações da empresa e depois seguir até seus clientes. Uma perspectiva cada vez mais popular atualmente é ver o fluxo de materiais que sai dos fornecedores e percorre todo o caminho até os clientes como um sistema a ser administrado. Essa perspectiva comumente é chamada *administração da cadeia de suprimentos*.

Em seu sentido mais amplo, uma **cadeia de suprimentos** refere-se à maneira pela qual os materiais fluem através de diferentes organizações, iniciando com as matérias-primas e encerrando com produtos acabados entregues ao consumidor final. Por exemplo, considere o aço usado numa porta de automóvel. Uma companhia mineradora escava o solo que contém minério de ferro e depois extrai somente o ferro da terra. O minério de ferro é então vendido a uma usina siderúrgica, onde ele é processado com outros materiais para formar grandes lingotes de aço. Os lingotes de aço são vendidos a outra empresa siderúrgica, onde são fundidos, laminados em lâminas longas e finas e temperados. Esses rolos de metal são então vendidos a um fornecedor do setor automobilístico especializado em fazer portas. O metal laminado é recortado e estampado, e usado com outros materiais para compor uma porta de carro completa. A porta

---

[1] *Commodities*: artigos; mercadorias. (Nas relações comerciais internacionais, o termo designa um tipo particular de mercadoria em estado bruto ou produto primário de importância comercial, como o ferro, grãos, café etc.) (N. do T.)

FIGURA 14.1 — CADEIA DE SUPRIMENTOS PARA O AÇO UTILIZADO NUMA PORTA DE AUTOMÓVEL

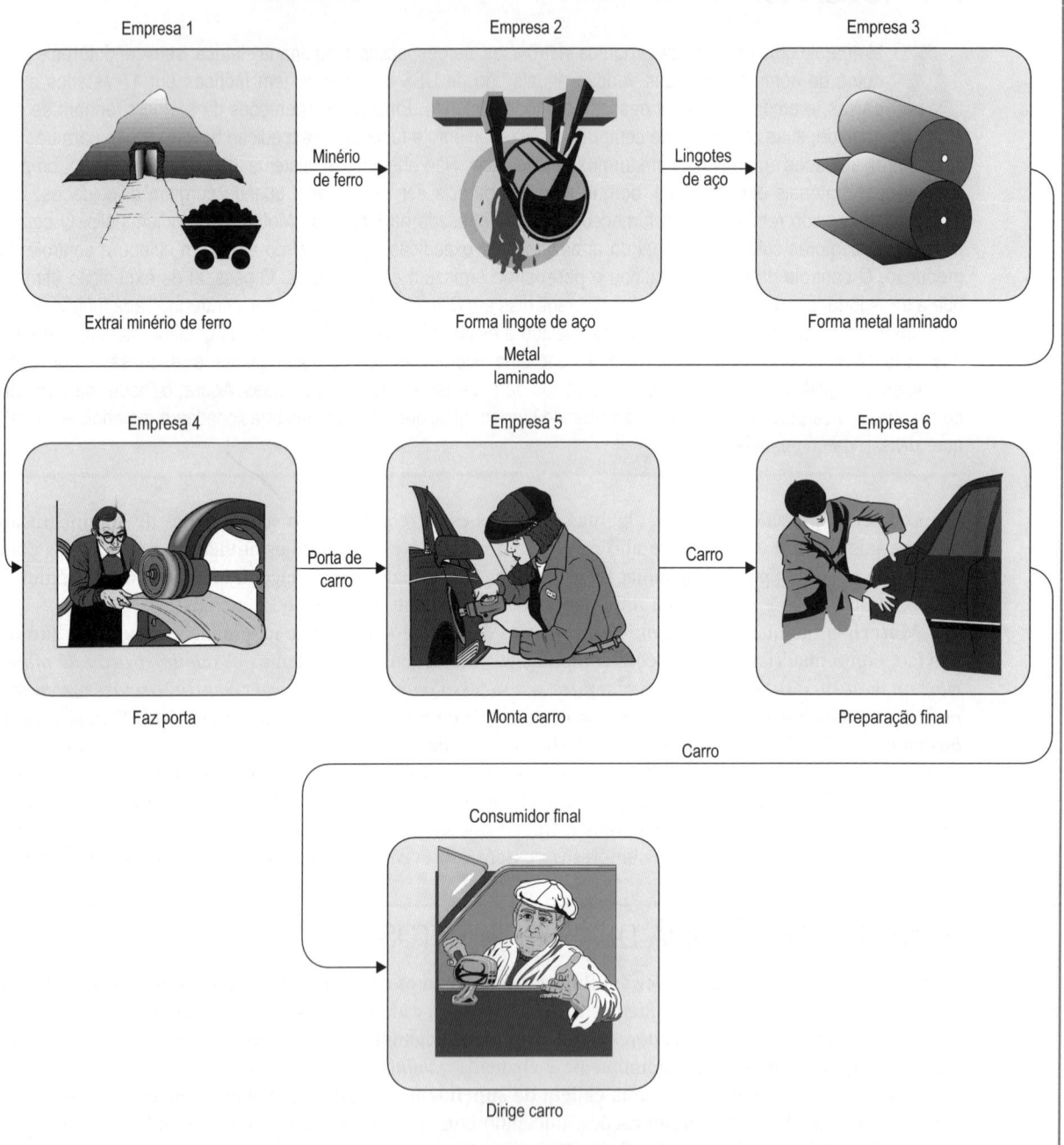

é então vendida ao fabricante de automóveis, onde é montada com outros componentes para produzir um automóvel completo. O automóvel é então vendido a uma revendedora, que executa algum trabalho de preparação final, como, por exemplo, acrescentar frisos nas laterais do carro. O consumidor final compra então o automóvel do revendedor, o elo final na cadeia de suprimentos. A Figura 14.1 ilustra essa cadeia de suprimentos completa.

Cadeias de suprimentos podem formar redes complexas que envolvem muitas empresas e materiais. Uma matéria-prima pode ser usada em muitos produtos acabados diferentes produzidos por várias em-

FIGURA 14.2 — ADMINISTRAÇÃO DA CADEIA DE SUPRIMENTOS NA MANUFATURA

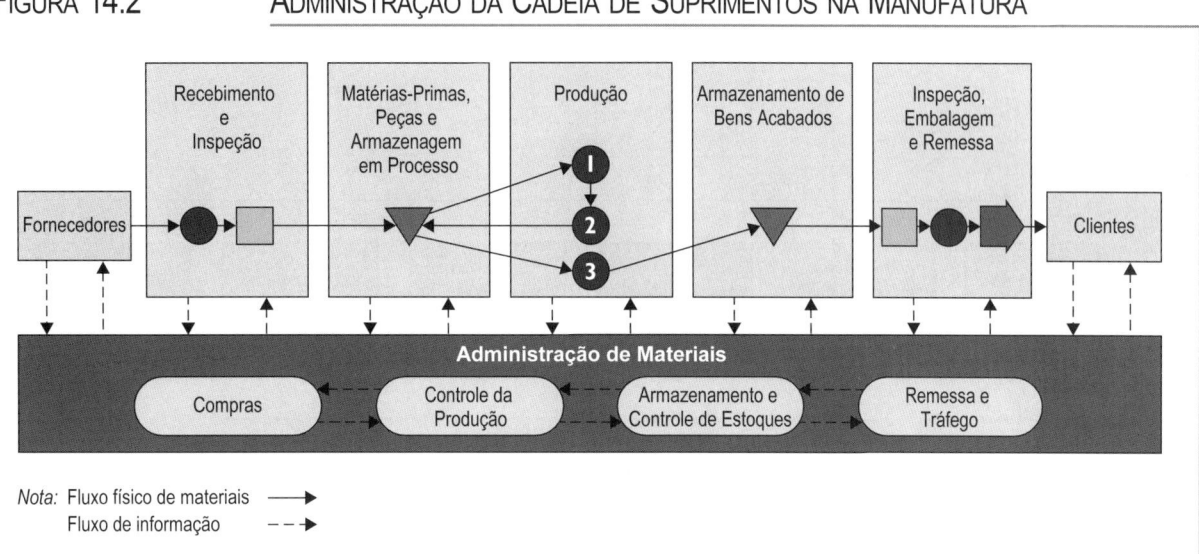

presas, e um produto acabado geralmente é feito de muitas matérias-primas diferentes de diversos fornecedores. Da perspectiva da administração de operações de uma empresa em particular que esteja no meio de uma cadeia de suprimentos, somente uma parte da cadeia de suprimentos interessa e deve ser administrada pela empresa. Desse modo, para a maioria das empresas, **administração da cadeia de suprimentos** refere-se a todas as funções administrativas relacionadas com o fluxo de materiais dos fornecedores diretos da empresa até seus clientes diretos, inclusive os departamentos de compras, armazenagem, inspeção, produção, manuseio de materiais e expedição e distribuição. A Figura 14.2 ilustra as atividades de administração da cadeia de suprimentos numa fábrica.

Estudar os fluxos de materiais — aquisição, armazenagem, movimento e processamento de matérias-primas, componentes, montagens e suprimentos — é uma boa maneira de entender a manufatura. Além disso, serviços como venda a varejo, armazenamento e empresas de transporte podem ser vistos como sistemas de fluxos de material. Nesses sistemas, todas as funções organizacionais são criticamente afetadas pelo planejamento e controle do sistema de materiais.

A **administração de materiais** e a **administração logística** são dois nomes alternativos usados para referir-se à administração da cadeia de suprimentos. A Figura 14.3 ilustra como a função de administração de materiais se enquadra em muitas organizações atualmente. Algumas organizações centralizaram suas diversas funções de administração de materiais sob um departamento dirigido por um **gerente de materiais** ou um **vice-presidente de materiais**. Esse posto executivo coordena todas as atividades de administração da cadeia de suprimentos e assume total responsabilidade pelo suprimento de baixo custo de materiais e pela qualidade especificada quando e onde os departamentos operacionais e clientes o exigirem. A responsabilidade do gerente de materiais é imensa, realidade salientada pelos salários tipicamente elevados, os quais se classificam entre aqueles dos mais altos postos da indústria.

É importante reconhecer a relação entre a administração de materiais e o planejamento e controle da produção. A Figura 14.4 ilustra os vínculos entre MPS, MRP, CRP, JIT e atividades de administração de materiais. Observe as diferenças em relação a como a administração de materiais é realizada entre o MRP e o JIT.

Nos sistemas MRP, o documento-chave é o relatório de programação de pedidos, o qual é um programa de quando pedidos de materiais devem ser enviados a fornecedores e quando pedidos de produção de peças e montagens devem ser enviados a departamentos de produção internos da empresa (in-house).

Figura 14.3 — Organograma da Administração de Materiais

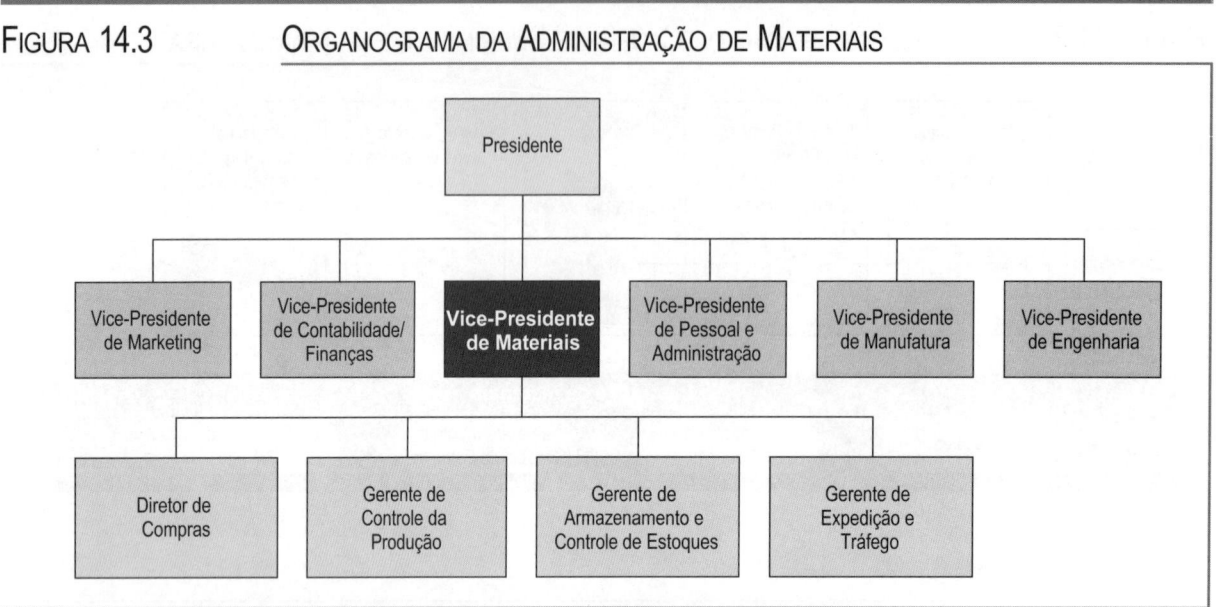

Os relatórios constituem um programa para que:

1. O *departamento de compras* peça e receba materiais dos fornecedores.
2. O *departamento de expedição* despache pedidos para os clientes e receba pedidos dos fornecedores.
3. O *controle de produção* planeje a movimentação de pedidos entre centros de trabalho na produção. Bilhetes de movimentação autorizam a movimentação de pedidos de acordo com os roteiros.

Em sistemas JIT, o relatório de programação de pedidos JIT dos fornecedores fornece ao departamento de compras, ao departamento de expedição e aos fornecedores uma programação aproximada de quando pedidos serão necessários e a **seqüência de construção** para o cliente, que é a seqüência na qual os pedidos serão necessários na instalação do cliente. O momento das remessas reais dos pedidos será determinado pelas comunicações diárias entre o cliente e os fornecedores.

No JIT, um sistema Kanban controla a produção e a movimentação de contêineres entre centros de trabalho.

Quatro atividades importantes na administração de materiais, ou administração da cadeia de suprimentos, são: compra, logística, armazenamento e agilização. Essas atividades formam a estrutura para estudarmos a natureza e o escopo da administração de materiais.

Atividade de Compras

Os **departamentos de compra** compram as matérias-primas, peças adquiridas, maquinaria, suprimentos e todos os outros bens e serviços usados em sistemas de produção — de clipes de papel a computadores.

Importância da Atividade de Compras Hoje

Diversos fatores estão aumentando a importância da atividade de compras atualmente: o enorme impacto dos custos de materiais sobre os lucros, a crescente importância da manufatura automatizada, a popularidade da manufatura JIT e a crescente competição global.

Em média, cerca de 60% do dinheiro de vendas das fábricas é pago a fornecedores por materiais comprados. Por exemplo, os fabricantes de automóveis gastam cerca de 60% de suas receitas em compras de

Capítulo 14 – Administração da Cadeia de Suprimentos

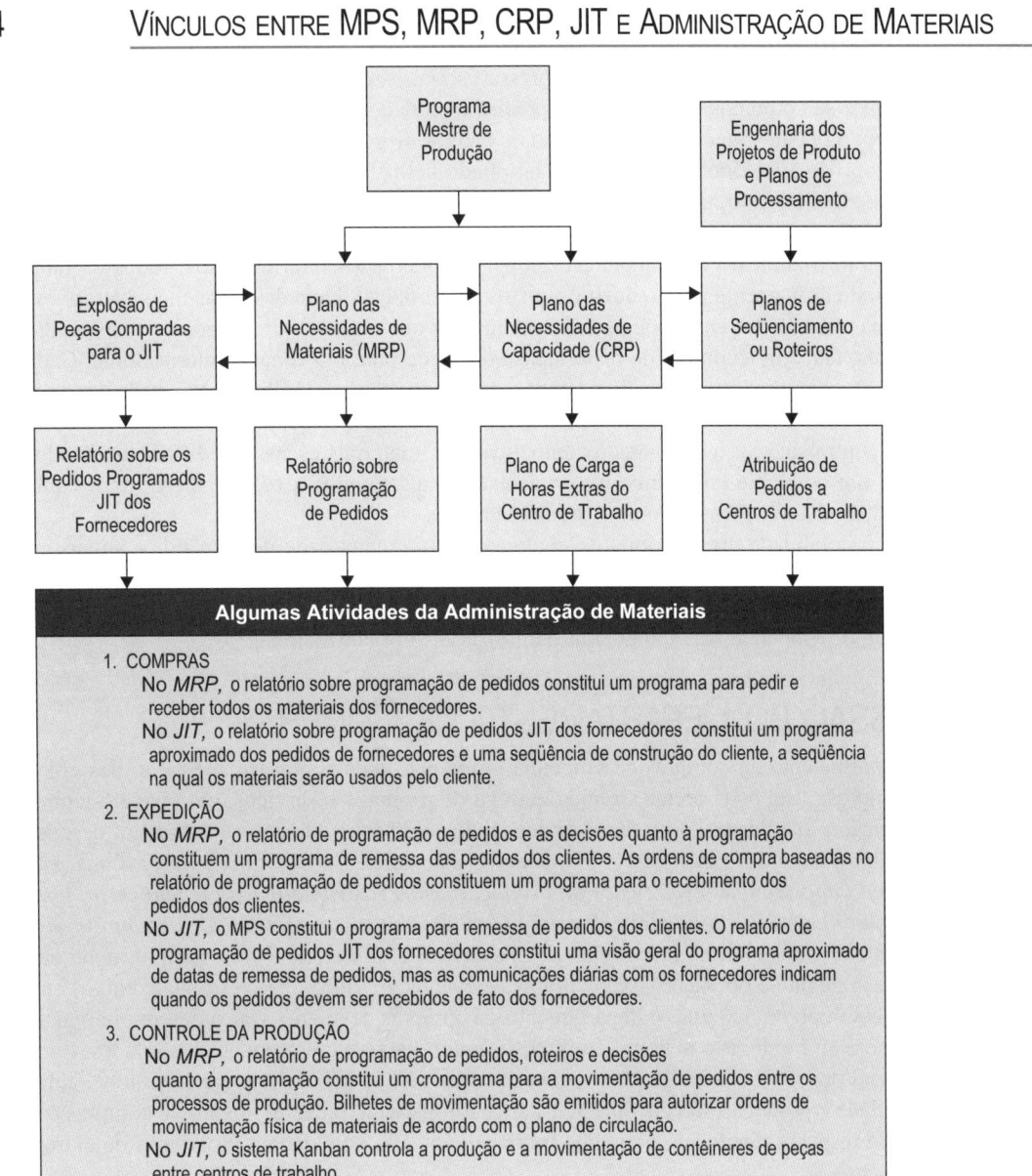

FIGURA 14.4 — VÍNCULOS ENTRE MPS, MRP, CRP, JIT E ADMINISTRAÇÃO DE MATERIAIS

materiais, os fabricantes de implementos agrícolas gastam cerca de 65%, os processadores de alimentos gastam cerca de 70%, e as refinarias de petróleo gastam cerca de 80%. E essas porcentagens estão subindo.

À medida que a automação da manufatura prossegue, dois desenvolvimentos aumentam a importância da atividade de compras. Primeiro, estima-se que os custos da mão-de-obra representam somente cerca de 10% a 15% dos custos da produção em muitas indústrias de produtos de consumo atualmente. Alguns observadores estimam que os custos de mão-de-obra declinarão para aproximadamente 5% dos custos de produção no futuro próximo. Considera-se, portanto, que em algumas indústrias os custos de materiais se tornarão o foco central no controle dos custos de produção. Em segundo lugar, a automação requer um rígido controle do projeto, programas de entrega e qualidade dos materiais adquiridos. Nesse ambiente, a atividade de compras deve estabelecer e manter relações com o fornecedor para garantir que materiais com o projeto certo e a qualidade certa sejam entregues nas quantidades certas nos tempos certos. A atividade de compras poderia ser uma função organizacional-chave que afeta o sucesso da manufatura automatizada.

Com a popularidade da manufatura JIT, materiais devem ser recebidos dos fornecedores exatamente na hora, em remessas pequenas e freqüentes, nas quantidades exatas e com qualidade perfeita. Essas exigências do JIT exercem uma grande pressão sobre os departamentos de compra para que planejem, controlem e se comuniquem de maneira precisa e cuidadosa com os fornecedores. A manufatura JIT tornou os departamentos de compra participantes-chaves no sucesso das empresas manufatureiras. Não somente o escopo da atividade de compras foi ampliado pelo JIT, mas o espaço para erros foi reduzido a praticamente zero. Discutiremos posteriormente como a avaliação e a recompensa de gerentes e pessoal de compras estão se modificando devido aos sistemas JIT.

Com o aumento da competição global por mercados internacionais, todos os fabricantes estão trabalhando arduamente para reduzir os custos de produção. Uma das áreas mais lucrativas para esse esforço está na redução dos custos de materiais. Uma vez que o escopo dos negócios se expandiu para proporções globais, também a compra de materiais se deslocou para um cenário internacional. Cada vez mais, materiais são comprados internacionalmente, transportados para fábricas no país ou no exterior e depois despachados para mercados no mundo inteiro. Essa cadeia de suprimentos estendida tornou-se necessária para contrabalançar a aumentada competição por materiais escassos. Mas o aumentado escopo da oferta criou um ambiente em que os materiais estão mais sujeitos a oferta incerta. Isso também elevou a importância das funções de compra atualmente.

Na totalidade da economia de qualquer país, a quantidade de dispêndios anuais em materiais comprados é, de fato, enorme. Contudo, os empregados dos departamentos de compras representam menos de 1% dos empregos totais da organizações. Você pode imaginar um grupo de empregados mais influente cujo desempenho seja tão crucial para o sucesso organizacional?

MISSÃO DO DEPARTAMENTO DE COMPRAS

O departamento de compras desempenha um papel fundamental na realização dos objetivos estratégicos da empresa. Ele pode afetar a rápida entrega de produtos e serviços, entregas no tempo certo, custos de produção e qualidade de produto/serviço, todos elementos-chaves na estratégia de operações. *A missão do departamento de compras é perceber as prioridades competitivas necessárias para cada produto/ serviço importante (baixos custos de produção, entregas rápidas e no tempo certo, produtos/serviços de alta qualidade e flexibilidade) e desenvolver planos de compra para cada produto/serviço importante que sejam coerentes com as estratégias de operações.* Um material, por exemplo, pode entrar num produto cuja estratégia de operações exija volumes elevados, produção para estoque e baixos custos de produção. Para esse tipo de material, o departamento de compras deve enfatizar o desenvolvimento de fornecedores que possam produzir o material a um custo muito baixo e em grandes quantidades. Por outro lado, outro material pode entrar num produto cuja estratégia de operações exija baixo volume, entregas rápidas, alta qualidade e produção sob encomenda. Para esse material, o departamento de compras deve enfatizar tempos de resposta rápidos da parte dos fornecedores, alta qualidade e programas de entrega confiáveis.

O QUE OS GERENTES DE COMPRAS FAZEM

O departamento de compras envolve-se nestas atividades quando compra materiais:

1. **Manter um banco de dados de fornecedores disponíveis.** Esse banco de dados inclui informações sobre os tipos de produtos que os fornecedores produzem ou são capazes de produzir, informações sobre a qualidade de seus produtos e informações sobre seus custos e preços. Um aspecto importante da manutenção desse banco de dados é a necessidade de executar pesquisas periódicas de fornecedores. Essas pesquisas podem incluir visitas à instalação para avaliar a capacidade que o fornecedor tem de cumprir exigências de entrega no tempo certo, quantidade, qualidade e custo.
2. **Selecionar fornecedores para suprir cada material.** Essa seleção geralmente se baseia em diversos critérios. O preço é importante, é claro, mas a qualidade, a quantidade e a pontualidade das entregas podem ter uma importância igual ou maior.
3. **Negociar contratos de suprimento com fornecedores.** Essa atividade estabelece as condições específicas que os fornecedores devem seguir quanto aos materiais fornecidos. Coisas como pre-

ços, pagamento de encargos de fretes, programa de entrega, padrões de qualidade, especificações do produto ou padrões de desempenho e termos de pagamento geralmente são incluídos nesses contratos.
4. **Agir como intermediário entre a empresa e seus fornecedores.** Quando o pessoal da produção, engenharia, contabilidade, controle da produção ou controle da qualidade precisar comunicar-se com um fornecedor, essas comunicações geralmente deverão passar pelo pessoal do departamento de compras. Similarmente, todos os fornecedores comunicam-se com a empresa por meio do departamento de compras.

O departamento de compras envolve-se nessas atividades na maioria das organizações, mas a localização do departamento de compras nas organizações varia extensamente.

Departamentos de Compras nas Organizações

O **gerente de compras** ou o **agente de compras** pode se reportar ao presidente, ao vice-presidente de materiais, ao vice-presidente de operações, ao gerente de fábrica, ao gerente de materiais ou a qualquer um dentre eles. É difícil generalizar acerca de onde na organização o departamento de compras será localizado, exceto dizer que seu nível de hierarquia em geral está diretamente relacionado com a importância de sua missão. Em outras palavras, se a atividade de compras é crucial para o sucesso de uma organização, então esperaríamos que o departamento de compras se reportasse a um vice-presidente de materiais, vice-presidente de operações ou mesmo ao presidente. Na General Motors, o vice-presidente de compras globais se reporta ao CEO[2].

As organizações tendem a atravessar ciclos de descentralização e centralização, e o departamento de compras tem sido pego nesses ciclos. A tendência atual rumo à centralização dos departamentos de compras provavelmente é estimulada pelos avanços tanto nas comunicações entre as instalações e divisões das empresas como na capacidade dos computadores para processar informações. Entre as vantagens da centralização estão:

- Comprar em quantidades maiores, o que pode significar preços melhores.
- Mais influência junto aos fornecedores quando materiais estiverem escassos, pedidos estiverem atrasados ou outras dificuldades de suprimento forem encontradas. Essa influência se traduz em maior continuidade de oferta.
- Departamentos de compra maiores que podem permitir maior especialização dos empregados. Por exemplo, um comprador pode especializar-se em comprar somente cobre. Isso pode levar a uma maior competência de compra e menores custos de materiais.
- Combinar pedidos pequenos e assim reduzir a duplicação de pedidos, o que pode reduzir os custos.
- Redução dos custos de transporte ao combinar pedidos e despachar quantidades maiores.
- Melhor controle global e coerência das transações financeiras.

Independentemente de sua localização organizacional, o departamento de compras segue certos processos para adquirir materiais.

Processos de Compra

A Figura 14.5 ilustra o processo de aquisição de materiais em sistemas de produção. A figura enfatiza a interação dos departamentos de produção, departamentos de compra e fornecedores. Existe certa variação desses procedimentos entre as organizações e entre diferentes tipos de produtos.

Instrumentos Básicos de Compra O material de trabalho diário dos departamentos de compra consiste em especificações de materiais, requisições de compra, pedidos de cotações e ordens de compra. Esses instrumentos são fundamentais para os processos de compra.

Para todo bem a ser comprado, o departamento de compras deve ter uma descrição detalhada desse material. Essa descrição detalhada é chamada **especificação de material**. Esses instrumentos podem in-

---
[2] *CEO — Chief Executive Officer:* principal executivo da empresa. (N. do R.T.)

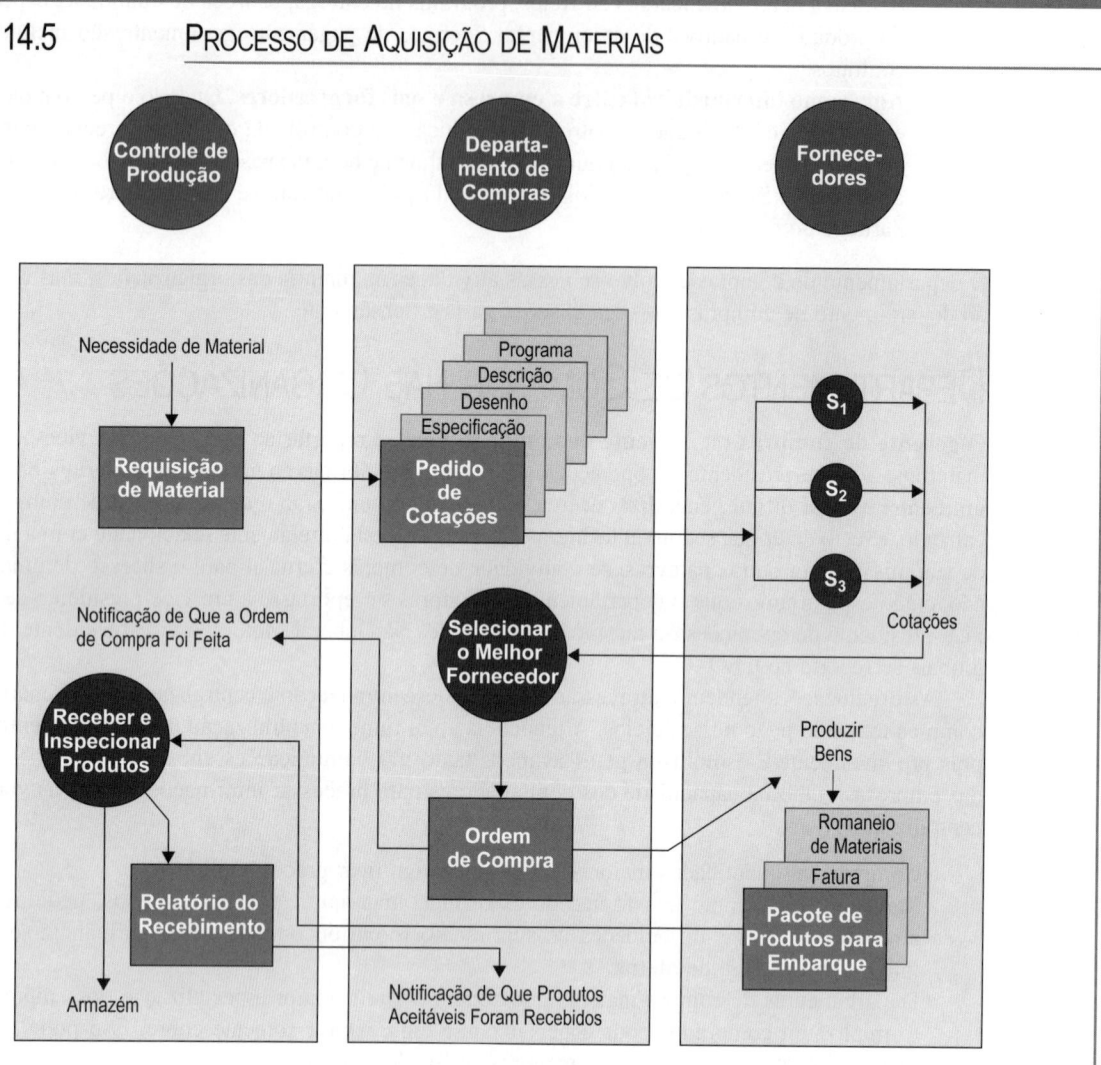

FIGURA 14.5 — PROCESSO DE AQUISIÇÃO DE MATERIAIS

cluir descrições como desenhos de engenharia, análises químicas, características físicas e outros detalhes sobre a natureza do material. Uma especificação de material se origina com o departamento que solicita o material em suas operações. As especificações de materiais são o meio fundamental de comunicar o que a produção quer que o departamento de compras compre e aquilo que o departamento de compras autoriza os fornecedores a fornecerem.

Requisições de compras se originam com os departamentos que usarão os materiais. Elas autorizam o departamento de compras a comprar os produtos e serviços. As requisições geralmente incluem uma identificação daquilo que deve ser comprado, a quantidade a ser comprada, a data ou programa de entrega solicitado, de quem o custo da compra deve ser cobrado, onde os produtos ou serviços comprados devem ser entregues, e a aprovação do gerente que possui autoridade para aprovar a compra.

Pedidos de cotação são preparados pelos departamentos de compras e enviados a fornecedores capazes de cumprir os requisitos de custo, qualidade e planificação dos departamentos solicitantes. Esses instrumentos convidam fornecedores em perspectiva a apresentar cotações para os produtos e serviços. Geralmente incluem especificações de materiais, quantidade de compra, data e programa de entrega desejados, onde os bens ou serviços deverão ser entregues, e a data em que a escolha do fornecedor será concluída. Os pedidos de cotações geralmente solicitam o seguinte de cada fornecedor em perspectiva: preço por unidade e preço total, informações sobre se o fornecedor pagará os encargos de frete, descontos para pagamento à vista e outros termos de pagamento, data ou programa de entrega, e quaisquer condições especiais do fornecedor.

Ordens de compra são os mais importantes instrumentos de compra. Elas são a base da autoridade dos fornecedores para produzirem os produtos ou serviços, e representam a obrigação dos compradores de pagar pelos itens. Um compromisso legal da parte do comprador está presente quando uma ordem de compra é emitida em resposta a uma cotação do fornecedor. Quando uma ordem de compra é emitida na ausência de um pedido de cotação, existe um compromisso legal quando o fornecedor reconhece a aceitação da ordem de compra. Essas formas geralmente são idealizadas para atender os padrões desenvolvidos pela National Association of Purchasing Managers e pela Division of Simplified Practice, do National Bureau of Standards. Os formulários de ordem de compra geralmente incluem o número da ordem de compra, a quantidade dos produtos ou serviços, especificações de materiais, data e local de entrega, instruções para remessa e faturamento, preço por unidade e preço total, descontos para pagamento à vista ou outros termos de pagamento, e quaisquer termos especiais da compra.

Esses instrumentos — especificações, requisições, pedidos de cotação e ordens de compra — formam a estrutura para comprar bens ou serviços.

COMPRADORES E SUAS OBRIGAÇÕES

Compradores, como o nome implica, fazem as compras nos departamentos de compra. Tipicamente, eles são especializados de acordo com certas commodities. Por exemplo, um comprador pode comprar todos os metais ferrosos, outro pode comprar todos os metais não ferrosos, e outro ainda pode comprar toda a maquinaria e ferramentas. Essa especialização permite que os compradores se tornem especialistas (*experts*) em comprar suas commodities particulares. Para serem eficazes, os compradores devem conhecer tanto os processos de manufatura de suas próprias empresas como os das empresas de seus fornecedores. Isso tipicamente é possível somente através da especialização de acordo com commodities. Os compradores devem conhecer seus mercados — os preços atuais das commodities e a disponibilidade das mesmas. Adicionalmente, eles devem ter consciência do custo e do valor, e serem fortes negociadores que buscam constantemente os mais baixos preços possíveis de seus fornecedores. Conhecimento da legislação que rege suas áreas de responsabilidade nas compras também é uma obrigação. Leis contratuais, má representação e fraude, violação de direitos de patente, reivindicações por danos contra fornecedores e regulamentações de embarque são somente algumas das áreas em que as leis e regulamentações devem ser entendidas pelos compradores. Compradores processam requisições de compra e pedidos de cotação, fazem seleção de fornecedores, emitem ordens de compra e dão seguimento a ordens de compra. Adicionalmente, negociam preços e condições de venda em ordens de compra em aberto, confirmam ordens de compra, fazem ajustes em ordens de compra e fazem todos os outros contratos de compra.

ANÁLISE DO COMPRAR *VERSUS* FABRICAR

Nem todas as requisições de matérias-primas e peças que são recebidas pelos departamentos de compra são automaticamente pedidas aos fornecedores. Os departamentos de produção freqüentemente fazem peças internamente na empresa (in-house) a um custo mais baixo, com qualidade mais elevada, e com entregas mais rápidas do que aquilo que seria possível se as comprassem de fornecedores. Por outro lado, uma vez que os fornecedores podem especializar-se em certos tipos de produção, algumas peças podem ser compradas desses fornecedores a um custo mais baixo, com qualidade mais elevada e com tempos de entrega mais rápidos do que aquilo que seria possível se a empresa as fizesse *internamente*. Compradores dos departamentos de compras, com assistência dos departamentos de produção, executam rotineiramente análises da conveniência de fabricar ou comprar (*make-or-buy*) para as matérias-primas e peças que entram nos produtos existentes. Nesses casos, eles devem decidir-se entre as alternativas de fazer uma peça internamente ou comprar as peças de fornecedores externos. O Exemplo 14.1 ilustra uma análise da conveniência de fabricar ou comprar na qual um gerente de operações deve decidir-se entre dois diferentes processos de produção internos e comprar a peça de um fornecedor. Esse exemplo serve somente a um propósito — determinar se o custo de compra de um fornecedor é menor do que o custo de produção se a peça fosse feita internamente. Na prática, essas análises devem ser acompanhadas de outras considerações. Por exemplo, qual alternativa oferece a melhor combinação de custo, qualidade de produto e entregas no tempo certo para a peça? Adicionalmente, há questões estratégicas envolvidas no *outsourcing*[3]. Por exemplo: Qual grau de integração vertical é desejável? Competências essenciais devem ser incluídas no outsourcing?

---

[3] *Outsourcing:* fonte externa; o ato de dirigir-se a fontes externas; sistema usado por grandes empresas que consiste em contratar subempreiteiros para executar tarefas específicas em seu lugar. (N. do T.)

EXEMPLO 14.1

UMA DECISÃO REFERENTE À CONVENIÊNCIA DE FABRICAR OU COMPRAR

A Drasco é uma fábrica de tamanho médio de bombas de campos petrolíferos. A empresa desenvolveu um novo modelo de bomba de purificação de alta pressão e recuperação secundária com desempenho melhorado. Bonnie Nelson, gerente de engenharia de processos, está tentando decidir se a Drasco deve fabricar ou comprar a válvula de entrada eletronicamente controlada para a nova bomba. Seus engenheiros desenvolveram as seguintes estimativas:

	Fabricar (Processo A)	Fabricar (Processo B)	Comprar
Volume anual	10.000 unidades	10.000 unidades	10.000 unidades
Custo fixo/ano	$ 100.000	$ 300.000	—
Custo variável/unidade	$ 75	$ 70	$ 80

a) A Drasco deve fabricar a válvula usando o Processo A, fabricar a válvula usando o Processo B ou comprar a válvula? **b)** Em qual volume anual a Drasco deve trocar a opção de comprar para fabricar a válvula usando o Processo A? **c)** Em qual volume anual a Drasco deve mudar do Processo A para o Processo B?

SOLUÇÃO

a) Desenvolva o custo anual de cada alternativa:

$$\text{Custos anuais totais} = \text{Custos fixos} + \text{Volume (custo variável)}$$
$$\text{Processo A} = \$\,100.000 + 10.000\,(\$\,75) = \$\,850.000$$
$$\text{Processo B} = \$\,300.000 + 10.000\,(\$\,70) = \$\,1.000.000$$
$$\text{Comprar} = \$\,0 + 10.000\,(\$\,80) = \$\,800.000$$

Se o volume for estimado como estável em 10.000 unidades, a Drasco deverá comprar a válvula.

b) Em qual volume anual a Drasco deve trocar a alternativa de comprar para fazer a válvula usando o Processo A (Q = volume)?

$$\text{O custo anual total} = \text{Custo anual total para comprar}$$
$$\$\,100.000 + Q(\$\,75) = Q(\$\,80)$$
$$\$\,5Q = \$\,100.000$$
$$Q = 20.000 \text{ unidades}$$

A Drasco deve mudar quando o volume anual for maior do que 20.000 unidades.

c) Em qual volume anual a Drasco deve mudar do Processo A para o Processo B (Q = volume anual, CT = custos anuais totais)?

$$CT_A = CT_B$$
$$\$\,100.000 + Q(\$\,75) = \$\,300.000 + Q(\$\,70)$$
$$\$\,5Q = \$\,200.000$$
$$Q = 40.000 \text{ unidades}$$

A Drasco deve mudar quando o volume anual for maior do que 40.000 unidades.

ÉTICA EM COMPRAS

Uma questão importante dentro dos departamentos de compras é a da ética em compras. O pessoal de vendas inunda os compradores com ofertas de almoços grátis, bebidas grátis, entradas grátis para jogos de futebol, noites grátis na cidade, fins de semana grátis em estâncias climáticas e, ocasionalmente, até mesmo casas de verão grátis na praia. Essas tentativas de oferecer presentes aos compradores levantam questões éticas. Até que ponto dar presentes aos compradores é antiético ou mesmo ilegal? Os compradores detêm grande poder, às vezes, até mesmo sobre a carreira do pessoal de vendas e suas organizações. Além disso, os compradores nem sempre são compensados por suas responsabilidades. Todos os ingredientes estão presentes para que haja tentação.

Algumas empresas estabelecem códigos de conduta estritos para os compradores. Absolutamente nenhum presente para os compradores, não mais do que três garrafas de bebida no Natal, nenhum presente que custe mais do que $ 25 por comprador por ano vindo de qualquer fonte, nenhum presente particular que ultrapasse $ 25 são exemplos dessas normas de conduta. Políticas que cubram a doação de presentes a empregados da empresa, sejam compradores ou não, certamente parecem aconselháveis. Talvez o mais importante, porém, seja a comunicação entre os departamentos de compras em relação a o que constitui **comportamento ético**. A preocupação real aqui é que os compradores podem se sentir devedores de uma obrigação para com o pessoal de vendas que lhes deu presentes e podem não agir no melhor interesse de suas organizações. O Instantâneo da Indústria 14.1 mostra que esse é um problema intricado que pode começar pequeno e desenvolver-se até atingir proporções gigantescas. Não existe outra solução além de diligência em manter abertos os canais de comunicação e manter-se no controle dos problemas para eliminar tendências indesejáveis antes que os problemas tornem-se irreversíveis. Geralmente, a maioria das empresas luta para eliminar propinas, subornos e presentes excessivos, os quais são cuidadosamente definidos. Outra prática interessante é o uso de auditorias internas para assegurar um contínuo controle organizacional da função de compra.

Outras atividades de compra antiéticas, ilegais ou questionáveis incluem tirar proveito de erros evidentes de escrita ou de computação nas cotações, na fixação de preços, conspiração entre licitantes, privilegiar favoritos entre fornecedores ao aceitar pedidos, deixar de cumprir obrigações pessoais e apresen-

---

INSTANTÂNEO DA INDÚSTRIA 14.1

ALEGAÇÕES DE COMPORTAMENTO IMPRÓPRIO DA PARTE DE COMPRADORES

A New York Telephone Company revelou que concluíra uma investigação interna sobre as práticas de compra de seu departamento de construções.

Como resultado da investigação, acusações criminais foram feitas contra alguns empregados, diversos empregados foram demitidos, e alguns empregados receberam penalidades mais bradas.

Os empregados foram acusados de:

1. Em troca de dinheiro ou presentes, permitir que fornecedores armazenassem ferramentas e estacionassem veículos na propriedade da empresa e premiar fornecedores com contratos sem licitação.
2. Aceitar presentes como bebidas alcoólicas e outros.
3. Fraude em licitações, aceitar subornos, roubo e evasão fiscal, e aceitar grandes somas de dinheiro de cinco empresas em troca de recompensá-las com contratos superfaturados.[a]

E, na Penney's, um alto funcionário do departamento de compras confessou que aceitou entre US$ 800.000 e US$ 1,5 milhão em subornos e propinas de fornecedores entre 1988 e 1992.[b]

Embora acusações como essas estejam sujeitas ao devido processo, vigilância organizacional é necessária para evitar as práticas antiéticas e ilegais mostradas.

Fontes:
[a] Adaptado de "28 Workers Depart New York Telephone". *New York Times*, 16 de novembro de 1990; e "Inquiry Caused 15 to Depart at New York Telephone". *New York Times*, 2 de novembro de 1990.
[b] "Ex-Penney's Rep Admits to Bribery". *San Antonio Express-News*, 18 de dezembro de 1994.

tar uma versão melhorada de amostras de produtos com a intenção de fornecer produtos de grau inferior. Para auxiliar empregados de departamentos de compras a terem um comportamento ético, a National Association of Purchasing Managers (NAPM) oferece um conjunto de princípios e padrões de prática de compras, como é ilustrado no Instantâneo da Indústria 14.2.

Instantâneo da Indústria 14.2

Diretrizes para Se Ter um Comportamento Ético na Atividade de Compras

A National Association of Purchasing Managers (NAPM) desenvolveu um conjunto de três princípios e 12 padrões para auxiliar na obtenção de um comportamento ético na atividade de compras. São estes os princípios:

1. Lealdade a sua organização.
2. Justiça para com aqueles com quem você lida.
3. Fé em sua profissão.

Desses princípios derivam os padrões NAPM para a prática de compras (domésticas e internacionais).

1. Evite a tentação de prática antiética nas relações, nas ações e nas comunicações.
2. Demonstre lealdade ao empregador seguindo diligentemente suas instruções legais, e utilizando somente a autoridade que lhe foi concedida.
3. Abstenha-se de quaisquer negócios pessoais ou atividade profissional que crie conflito entre interesses pessoais e os interesses do empregador.
4. Abstenha-se de solicitar ou aceitar dinheiro, empréstimos, créditos ou descontos discriminatórios, e de aceitar presentes, diversões, favores ou serviços de fornecedores atuais ou potenciais que possam influir, ou parecer influir, nas decisões de compra.
5. Manipule informações de empregadores ou fornecedores com o devido cuidado e consideração apropriada a respeito das ramificações éticas e legais e regulamentações governamentais.
6. Promova relações positivas com o fornecedor através de cortesia e imparcialidade em todas as fases do ciclo de compra.
7. Abstenha-se de acordos recíprocos que restrinjam a competição.
8. Conheça e obedeça a letra e o espírito das leis que regem a função de compra e permaneça alerta quanto às ramificações legais das decisões de compra.
9. Encoraje todos os segmentos da sociedade para que participem, demonstrando apoio por empresas pequenas, em desvantagem comercial ou ainda pertencentes a minorias étnicas.
10. Desencoraje o envolvimento do departamento de compras em programas de compras pessoais patrocinados pelos empregados que não estejam relacionados com o negócio.
11. Aumente a proficiência e a estatura da profissão de compras adquirindo e mantendo um conhecimento técnico atualizado e os mais elevados padrões de comportamento ético.
12. Realize compras internacionais de acordo com as leis, costumes e práticas dos países estrangeiros, coerentes com as leis dos Estados Unidos, suas políticas organizacionais e esses Padrões e Diretrizes Éticos.

Fonte: **www.napm.org/indexedfiles/member/ethics.html**. Reimpresso com autorização do editor, a National Association of Purchasing Management, *Principles & Standards of Purchasing Practice*, adotado em janeiro de 1992.

Atividade de Compras: A Emergente Fronteira Internacional

Cada vez mais, adquirir materiais significa comprar materiais em mercados internacionais. Por exemplo, os fabricantes americanos da indústria eletrônica e de computadores compram materiais de todas as partes do mundo. Isso significa que agentes de compras devem engajar-se em negociações com empresas de outros países. A legislação dos países estrangeiros, taxas de câmbio, diferenças culturais e uma grande quantidade de outros fatores afetam essas compras. Além disso, agentes de compras e outras pessoas viajam rotineiramente para países estrangeiros no processo de selecionar distribuidores e assinar contratos de suprimento. Uma vez que essas compras são complexas, e desde que muita coisa depende do sucesso dessas atividades, as organizações devem selecionar, desenvolver e recompensar o pessoal de compras de maneira adequada.

Esses e outros desenvolvimentos tornam o campo da atividade de compras uma área desafiadora para que os gerentes profissionais a considerem para empregos futuros.

ATIVIDADE DE COMPRAS JUST-IN-TIME

No Capítulo 13 discutimos a manufatura just-in-time (JIT). A atividade de compras JIT é uma parte importante desses problemas. Vamos resumir nossa discussão da atividade de compras JIT a partir do Capítulo 13. Os elementos-chaves da atividade de compras JIT são:

1. O **desenvolvimento de distribuidores** e as **relações com o distribuidor** sofrem mudanças fundamentais. A natureza das relações entre clientes e fornecedores deixa de ser adversária e passa a ser cooperativa.
2. Os departamentos de compras desenvolvem relações de longo prazo com os fornecedores, com uma tendência para poucos fornecedores.
3. Não obstante o preço ser importante, os prazos de entrega, qualidade de produto e confiança e cooperação mútuas tornam-se a base principal para escolha dos fornecedores.
4. Os fornecedores são encorajados a estender métodos JIT a seus próprios fornecedores.
5. Os fornecedores geralmente estão localizados próximo à fábrica da empresa compradora, ou, se estiverem a certa distância da fábrica, geralmente estão agrupados.
6. As remessas são entregues diretamente na linha de produção do cliente.
7. As peças são entregues em contêineres pequenos, de tamanho padrão, com um mínimo de burocracia e em quantidades exatas.
8. O material entregue tem uma qualidade quase perfeita.

Assim que os materiais são comprados, os gerentes de materiais devem decidir-se a respeito do método de embarque menos caro e mais eficiente para suas organizações. Similarmente, a maneira pela qual embarcar produtos acabados aos clientes é uma questão crítica. Essas questões são fundamentais para a importante atividade de administração de materiais da logística.

LOGÍSTICA

Ainda que às vezes seja definida de maneira mais ampla, a logística geralmente se refere à administração do movimento de materiais dentro da fábrica, ao embarque de materiais que chegam dos fornecedores e ao embarque de produtos que saem para os clientes.

CONTROLE DA PRODUÇÃO: MOVIMENTO DE MATERIAIS DENTRO DAS FÁBRICAS

O controle da produção inclui funções como designar datas de vencimento de entregas para pedidos, programa mestre de produção, planejamento e controle do chão de fábrica e programação detalhada da produção. Embora esses e outros tópicos relacionados sejam elementos essenciais da administração de materiais, eles foram discutidos com algum detalhe nos capítulos anteriores deste livro e, dessa forma, não serão discutidos aqui. O controle da produção também inclui o movimento de materiais dentro das fábricas, o qual consiste nas seguintes atividades:

1. Retirar materiais dos veículos que chegam e colocá-los no terminal de recebimento.
2. Deslocar materiais do terminal de recebimento para a inspeção.
3. Deslocar materiais da inspeção para o armazém e armazená-los até quando necessário.
4. Recuperar materiais do armazém e entregá-los às operações de produção quando necessário.
5. Deslocar materiais entre operações de produção.
6. Deslocar produtos acabados da montagem final e armazená-los no armazém de produtos acabados.

7. Retirar produtos acabados do armazém de produtos acabados e entregá-los para empacotamento e embarque.
8. Deslocar produtos acabados para o terminal de embarque.
9. Levar produtos acabados para os veículos que saem no terminal de embarque.

O transporte de materiais nos serviços inclui os movimentos descritos nos itens 1 a 5 acima, mas normalmente não inclui os movimentos descritos nos itens 6 a 9. Os materiais são transportados com todos os tipos de equipamento, de cestas manuais a carrinhos de mão, correias transportadoras, empilhadeiras e transportadores robóticos, conhecidos como sistemas de veículos automatizados (AGVS).

A administração do movimento de materiais dentro da fábrica pode envolver decisões a respeito de como determinar o roteiro de lotes de materiais entre departamentos. Todos esses movimentos de materiais são coordenados pelo controle de produção e são cruciais para a efetiva administração de operações.

REMESSAS PARA AS FÁBRICAS E DAS FÁBRICAS

Os **departamentos de trânsito** nas organizações examinam rotineiramente os programas de remessa e escolhem métodos de remessa, horários e maneiras de agilizar as entregas. Os custos de embarque atualmente representam para as organizações uma proporção tão grande dos custos que as fábricas, armazéns e outras instalações são localizadas tendo um pensamento predominante em mente: minimizar os custos de embarque de produtos que chegam e que saem. Apesar desses esforços, somente os custos de embarque são responsáveis por 50% ou mais dos preços de vendas de alguns itens manufaturados.

Tendo isso em mente muitas organizações estão preenchendo os departamentos de trânsito com gerentes e analistas de operações profissionais que buscam continuamente melhores técnicas de embarque. Adicionalmente, muitas empresas entraram no negócio de transportes (às vezes chamado **integração vertical regressiva e integração progressiva**) para reduzir suas contas de fretes.

A **administração de tráfego** é um campo especializado que requer intenso treinamento técnico quanto aos regulamentos e taxas de frete. Esses **regulamentos e taxas** constituem as restrições complexas com as quais os especialistas em logística devem trabalhar para atacar os custos de embarque. Eles devem conhecer as complexidades desse campo mutável.

Administração da Distribuição A **distribuição**, às vezes chamada distribuição física, consiste na remessa de produtos acabados através do sistema de distribuição aos clientes. Um **sistema de distribuição** é a rede de pontos de embarque e recebimento que se inicia com a fábrica e se encerra com os clientes. Os embarques de produtos através de sistemas de distribuição podem estar ou não sob controle direto de um gerente de materiais. Em algumas companhias, a responsabilidade pela administração do sistema de distribuição permanece com a função de marketing.

Planejamento das Necessidades de Distribuição O **planejamento das necessidades de distribuição (DRP)** é o planejamento da renovação de estoques de armazéns regionais usando uma lógica do tipo MRP para converter as necessidades do armazém em necessidades do centro de distribuição principal, as quais são então convertidas em necessidades brutas no MPS na fábrica. O Exemplo 14.2 ilustra a lógica do planejamento das necessidades de distribuição.

EXEMPLO 14.2

PLANEJAMENTO DAS NECESSIDADES DE DISTRIBUIÇÃO (DRP)

Uma companhia tem dois armazéns regionais que recebem produtos de um centro de distribuição principal na fábrica. Os registros de ponto de pedido DRP mostrados a seguir ilustram como as programações de pedidos do centro de distribuição para a fábrica tornam-se as necessidades brutas no programa mestre de produção (MPS) da fábrica.

Armazém Regional n. 1
O tempo de atendimento (lead time) para remessa de produtos do centro de distribuição principal na fábrica para o Armazém n. 1 é de 1 semana, o lote padrão de embarque é de 50 unidades, e o estoque de segurança é de 10 unidades.

	Semana					
	−1	1	2	3	4	5
Demanda prevista (unidades)		30	40	30	40	40
Recebimentos programados		50				
Estoque final projetado	60	80	40	10	20	30
Recebimento programado de remessas					50	50
Pedidos programados para remessa				50	50	

Armazém Regional n. 2

O tempo de atendimento (lead time) para remessa de produtos do centro de distribuição principal na fábrica para o Armazém n. 2 é de 2 semanas, o lote padrão de embarque é de 60 unidades, e o estoque de segurança é de 15 unidades.

	Semana					
	−1	1	2	3	4	5
Demanda prevista (unidades)		70	80	50	60	50
Recebimentos programados		60				
Estoque final projetado	110	100	20	30	30	40
Recebimento programado de remessas				60	60	60
Pedidos programados para remessa		60	60	60		

Centro de Distribuição Principal na Fábrica

O tempo de atendimento (lead time) para a montagem final de produtos e seu deslocamento para o centro de distribuição principal é de 1 semana, o lote padrão de produção é de 200 unidades, e o estoque de segurança é de 40 unidades.

	Semana					
	−1	1	2	3	4	5
Demanda prevista (unidades)		60	60	110	50	
Recebimentos programados						
Estoque final projetado	110	50	190	80	230	230
Recebimento programado de remessas			200		200	
Pedidos programados para remessa		200		200		

O **planejamento dos recursos de distribuição** amplia o planejamento das necessidades de distribuição a fim de que os recursos-chaves do espaço de armazém, o número de trabalhadores, o capital e os veículos de transporte sejam supridos nas quantidades certas e quando necessário para satisfazer as demandas dos clientes.

INOVAÇÕES NA LOGÍSTICA

Novos desenvolvimentos afetam continuamente a logística. Embarques de carretas em vagões-plataforma, reboques de caminhão em navios e outros métodos de embarque são exemplos de sistemas híbridos que têm resultado em grandes economias de fretes. Contêineres de embarque mais leves, cargas unitizadas, embarques por prancha levadiça (*drop shipping*), tarifas *in-transit*, embarques consolidados, desregulamentação das indústrias de transporte por caminhões e fretes aéreos, bem como flutuação nos custos dos combustíveis, são exemplos de desenvolvimentos que estão afetando a logística atualmente, e novos desenvolvimentos surgem a cada dia. O Instantâneo da Indústria 14.3 discute alguns novos conceitos interessantes sobre embarque. Graças aos computadores, informações recentes estão disponíveis sobre a situação de cada embarque. Adicionalmente, em problemas de distribuição complexos, o computador pode ser usado para planejar melhores métodos de embarque. O Instantâneo da Indústria 14.4 discute um software que está auxiliando as empresas na administração da cadeia de suprimentos.

Fundamental para a logística são os métodos de armazenamento de materiais e produtos assim que são recebidos dos fornecedores e antes que sejam embarcados para os clientes.

> ## INSTANTÂNEO DA INDÚSTRIA 14.3
>
> ### INOVAÇÃO NOS MÉTODOS DE EMBARQUE
>
> As empresas ferroviárias americanas empregam 240.000 pessoas e embarcam enormes quantidades de produtos. Eis as porcentagens de algumas commodities que são embarcadas por ferrovias: carvão 60%, automóveis 67%, papel 68%, madeira 53%, produtos químicos 53%, alimentos 45%, e materiais de construção 32%.[a] E as ferrovias estão desenvolvendo novos serviços para seus clientes. O *embarque intermodal*, que é o embarque de reboques de caminhão em vagões ferroviários, não é novo. Mas se espera que uma inovação amplie suas aplicações: empresas como a J. B. Hunt, Schneider National e KLLM Transport Services estão usando novos reboques de caminhão que podem ser usados em rodovias e empilhados duplamente em vagões ferroviários. Companhias ferroviárias como a Santa Fé Pacific, Union Pacific, Conrail, Norfolk Southern e Consolidated Rail estão redesenhando vagões ferroviários para que acomodem os novos reboques de caminhão. As ferrovias estão construindo novos pátios intermodais perto de Chicago, Dallas e Los Angeles, e alguns estados e o governo federal estão modificando túneis e pontes para permitir a passagem de vagões ferroviários maiores. Essa abordagem promete reduzir os custos de embarque em mais de 30% em comparação com o transporte em caminhões feito por rodovias. Não somente os custos de embarque são reduzidos, mas a escassez de motoristas de caminhão é amenizada no processo. E deslocar o tráfego das estradas para as ferrovias implica menos consumo de combustíveis, menos poluição e menos desgastes.[b]
>
> Outra inovação no setor de embarque é o desenvolvimento de aeroportos *all-freight*. Denver, Fort Worth e Huntsville (Alabama) já os têm. Localizações em Kentucky, Carolina do Norte, Nebraska, Geórgia, Washington, Arkansas, Nova Iorque, Ohio e Flórida estão considerando propostas para a construção de parques industriais *all air-freight*. O conceito é inovador, ou melhor, definitivamente revolucionário. No centro desses parques haverá fábricas, e muitas delas precisarão de suprimentos — e rápido — devido ao surgimento da manufatura just-in-time (JIT). As fábricas serão circundadas por trilhos e corredores de veículos eletrônicos ligando-as a um aeroporto com longas pistas — o caminho de entrada das fábricas para mercados globais. Esse arranjo será a síntese da manufatura JIT, em que correias transportadoras transportam peças do avião para o chão de fábrica e produtos acabados de volta para os compartimentos de carga dos aviões.[c]
>
> *Fontes:*
> [a]"Shipping by Rail". *Bryan-College Station Eagle,* 17 de abril de 1991.
> [b]"Shippers Prepare to Jump on Rail-Truck Combinations". *Wall Street Journal,* 29 de dezembro de 1992.
> [c]"All-Freight Airports, Touted as Way to Lure Firms". *Wall Street Journal,* 2 de dezembro de 1992.

ARMAZENAMENTO

Armazenamento (*warehousing*) é a administração de materiais enquanto eles ainda estão armazenados. Inclui as atividades de armazenamento, distribuição, pedido e contabilidade de todos os materiais e produtos acabados desde o início até o final do processo de produção. As instalações de armazenamento podem variar de pequenos depósitos a grandes instalações de armazenagem altamente mecanizadas.

OPERAÇÕES DE ARMAZENAMENTO

A atividade de armazenamento lida com materiais que sustentam de maneira direta as operações. Os primeiros problemas que devem ser encaminhados são: quando fazer um pedido de cada material e quanto pedir. Os pedidos são feitos e as remessas aparecem por fim no departamento de recebimento, geralmente por meio de reboques de caminhão ou de vagões ferroviários.

Materiais são rotineiramente descarregados de veículos de entrega e mantidos em áreas de armazenamento temporário até que o controle da qualidade os examine, confirme sua aceitabilidade para

INSTANTÂNEO DA INDÚSTRIA 14.4

SOFTWARE *TOP-SELLING* DE ADMINISTRAÇÃO DA CADEIA DE SUPRIMENTOS

Dirigir uma fábrica moderna exige decisões complexas baseadas em centenas de variáveis. Os preços das matérias-primas podem estar instáveis. A demanda de clientes pode desviar-se de uma linha de produtos para outra.

Na década de 1980, um jovem engenheiro de Dallas chamado Sanjiv Sidhu viu uma oportunidade comercial na observação científica de que até mesmo as pessoas mais inteligentes podem lidar com somente até nove variáveis quando tomam decisões. Com isso em mente, ele desenvolveu um software de computador baseado em modelos de inteligência artificial e simulação avançada para gerentes de chão de fábrica. Fundada em 1982, a i2 Technologies Inc. desenvolve softwares para que as fábricas administrem a entrega de componentes e o embarque de produtos. Hoje, a empresa do sr. Sidhu é a líder de mercado numa indústria rapidamente crescente para softwares de administração da cadeia de suprimentos, e sua participação de 54% na companhia vale US$ 772 milhões.

No ano passado, a i2 Technologies reivindicava 19% do mercado de softwares de administração da cadeia de suprimentos, sendo que sua rival mais próxima, a Manugistics Group Inc., reivindicava 15%. Mas, recentemente, a gigante alemã dos softwares, SAP, anunciou que lançaria em breve um módulo de administração da cadeia de suprimentos. Os analistas esperam que outros fornecedores de software, inclusive a Oracle e a Baan, se juntem também nessa empreitada.

Ao todo a i2 tem mais de 200 clientes mundialmente, numa ampla variedade de indústrias. Seu software *Rhythm* é empregado pela Ford Motor Co., U.S. Steel, Whirlpool, Coca-Cola, Black and Decker, IBM, Hewlett-Packard, Compaq, Dell Computer Corp. e Texas Instruments. O software auxilia as empresas a administrar melhor estoques e capacidades de manufatura usando modelos de simulação em vez dos princípios básicos que eram tradicionalmente aplicados ao gerenciamento de fábricas.

Uma fábrica típica que movimenta US$ 1 bilhão por ano e que mantém US$ 250 milhões em estoques pode, confortavelmente, reduzir estoques para menos de US$ 100 milhões ao realizar uma melhor administração da cadeia de suprimentos, afirma o sr. Sidhu. As economias são um resultado da reduzida tomada de empréstimos, menores custos de armazenagem e reduzido risco de dano ou obsolescência. As empresas poderão então reinvestir grande parte do dinheiro em desenvolvimento de produtos ou na criação de eficiências. Gene Ramirez, analista da Southwest Securities de Dallas que acompanha a i2, disse: "O software oferece às empresas um fenomenal retorno sobre seus investimentos".

Fonte: Goldstein, Alan. "Assembling Wealth: i2 Founder's Factory Software Fills High-Demand Niche". *Dallas Morning News*, 6 de outubro de 1997.

---

utilização nas operações e os libere. Equipamentos de manuseio de materiais como empilhadeiras, esteiras transportadoras, paletizadores e dutos acionados por bomba de compressão são usados para colocar os materiais no **estoque de matérias-primas**. Esse estoque é armazenado em paletes (uma pequena estrutura básica sobre a qual sacos e caixas de materiais são armazenados), em altas pilhas, em tanques de armazenamento ou em outros meios de guardar matérias-primas.

Em algumas empresas, como, por exemplo, fábricas de processamento de produtos químicos, materiais em grandes quantidades são usados pelos departamentos de operações quando necessário, sem pedirem para o setor de armazenamento (warehousing). Em outras instalações, entretanto, uma **requisição ao estoque** é preparada pelo controle de produção e encaminhada para o setor de armazenamento, solicitando que materiais sejam entregues em locais específicos dentro dos departamentos de produção. Em sistemas de produção que usam layouts de processo, em que os materiais se movem intermitentemente pelas instalações, geralmente são mantidos **estoques em processo**. Esses produtos parcialmente concluídos que estão entre processos são localizados em vários locais designados ao longo do sistema de produção.

O armazenamento pode ou não ser responsável pela contabilidade desses estoques em processo, administrar seu movimento, recebê-los e distribuí-los, e controlar quais materiais entram e quais são retirados. Se o tempo de permanência desses materiais no estoque em processo for curto, geralmente a produção retém o controle. Se esse tempo for longo, ou se existirem outras razões, como segurança, regulamentação governamental etc., o departamento de armazenamento se encarrega e mantém os estoques em subalmoxarifados em vários pontos do sistema de produção.

Em sistemas que usam layout de produto, em que os materiais se movem continuamente ao longo das instalações, o armazenamento de estoques em processo é raro, e portanto a produção mantém o controle dos materiais em processo até que eles se tornem produtos acabados. Nesse ponto, depois que os materiais foram transformados em estoque de bens acabados, eles são entregues ao armazém de bens acabados.

A manutenção de registros dentro do setor de armazenamento requer um **registro de estoque** de cada item mantido em estoque. O item individual é chamado **unidade de manutenção de estoque (SKU)**. Registros de estoque são contas ativas que mostram o saldo atual, recebimentos, desembolsos e quaisquer outras mudanças que realmente afetem o saldo atual útil de cada SKU. Adicionalmente, os registros de estoque podem mostrar recebimentos esperados, promessas ou alocações de SKUs, não obstante elas ainda estarem em estoque. Os computadores permitiram aos gerentes melhorar a precisão desses registros, afixar mudanças nos registros mais freqüentemente quando elas ocorrem, e ter informações sobre saldos atuais instantaneamente.

Métodos de Contabilidade de Estoques

Durante centenas de anos a contabilidade de estoques baseou-se em **sistemas de contabilidade periódica de estoques** (também conhecidos por inventários periódicos), ou atualização periódica de registros de estoque manuais, e **contagens físicas do estoque**. Os registros de estoques eram atualizados introduzindo-se periodicamente (em geral, no final de todo dia de trabalho), à mão, em cartões arquivados em fichários, o número de unidades acrescentadas e retiradas do estoque. Se alguém quisesse saber o número de unidades disponíveis de um material em particular em estoque, deveria dirigir-se ao fichário, pegar o cartão de registro de estoque do material e ver o saldo do estoque em sua última atualização. A precisão desse sistema dependia de quão freqüentemente os registros de estoque eram atualizados e de quão freqüentemente a informação contida nos registros de estoque era verificada ou corrigida por meio de contagens físicas do estoque. Quanto mais freqüente a correção e a atualização dos registros de estoque, mais acurada era a informação sobre os registros de estoque. As contagens físicas de estoque anuais ou "de final de ano", nas quais todos os materiais dos armazéns eram contados fisicamente, eram tradicionais em muitas indústrias. Algumas empresas usam atualmente esse tipo de contabilidade de estoques porque ele é ou mais econômico ou a única maneira viável de fazer a contabilidade do estoque.

Cada vez mais, entretanto, as empresas estão usando **sistemas de contabilidade contínua de estoques** (também conhecidos por inventários contínuos ou permanentes), nos quais registros de estoques são mantidos em computadores. Nesses sistemas, os registros de estoque, em vez de serem atualizados periodicamente, são atualizados no momento em que os materiais são recebidos ou retirados do estoque. O hiato entre a última atualização dos registros de estoque e o momento em que os registros são acessados para determinar o saldo do estoque é praticamente eliminado. Esses registros, no entanto, também estão sujeitos a erro, e também devem ser verificados ou corrigidos. Costuma-se usar atualmente uma contagem cíclica para manter a precisão do registro em sistemas de contabilidade contínua de estoques.

A **contagem cíclica** é um esforço contínuo para contar fisicamente o número de unidades de cada material em estoque, comparar esse número com o saldo mostrado nos registros de estoque e reconciliar a diferença. O duplo propósito da contagem cíclica é corrigir os registros de estoque e, o mais importante, identificar deficiências em todas as áreas do sistema de estoque e iniciar ações corretivas. Na contagem cíclica, *quando* um material é contado é determinado por um programa de contagem desse material. Um material pode ser contado quando atinge seu ponto de re-pedido, quando uma remessa do material é recebida, ou num intervalo de tempo particular.

Materiais de valor elevado e de rápido movimento tendem a ser contados mais freqüentemente. *Mas a freqüência com que contamos um item de estoque (mensalmente, trimestralmente) depende de dois fatores: a história de imprecisões nas contagens do item e as dificuldades decorrentes de contagens imprecisas.* Um item que tem uma história de contagens imprecisas e um que causará grandes problemas de produção se as contagens forem imprecisas devem ser contados mais freqüentemente. Itens que se movem rapidamente e que tenham contagens imprecisas geralmente causam grandes dificuldades na produção porque aparecem nos programas de produção mais freqüentemente. E quando aparecem, a imprecisão pode causar grandes mudanças nos programas mestres de produção, na agilização, dividir pedidos,

Capítulo 14 – Administração da Cadeia de Suprimentos

provocar pânico nos procedimentos de embarque, custos extras de transporte e produção e confusão no chão de fábrica.

Na contagem cíclica, uma equipe de trabalhadores especialmente treinada conta certos materiais todo dia útil, e os registros de estoque são verificados ou corrigidos em base contínua. A meta definitiva da contagem cíclica é reduzir a imprecisão dos registros de estoque a uma porcentagem muito pequena. Desde que se estima que os sistemas MRP exigem registros de estoque que tenham uma precisão dentro de ±0,5%, a contagem cíclica é uma parte importante dos sistemas MRP. O Exemplo 14.3 ilustra uma situação comum associada com a contagem cíclica.

EXEMPLO 14.3

PESSOAL NECESSÁRIO NA CONTAGEM CÍCLICA

Uma empresa quer melhorar a precisão dos registros de estoque usados em seu sistema MRP. Um consultor recomendou que todos os materiais Classe A sejam contados uma média de 24 vezes por ano, que todos os materiais Classe B sejam contados uma média de 6 vezes por ano, e que todos os materiais Classe C sejam contados uma média de 2 vezes por ano. O consultor estima que um contador experiente e bem treinado pode contar uma média de 20 materiais a cada dia. Uma empresa trabalha 260 dias por ano e determinou que possui 1.000 materiais A, 3.000 materiais B e 6.000 materiais C. Quantos trabalhadores seriam necessários para realizar a contagem cíclica (ou permanente)?

SOLUÇÃO

Classe de Materiais	Número de Materiais por Classe	Número de Contagens de Materiais por Ano	Contagens Totais por Ano
A	1.000	24	24.000
B	3.000	6	18.000
C	6.000	2	12.000
		Total	54.000

$$\text{Número de materiais contados por dia} = \frac{\text{Contagens totais por ano}}{\text{Número de dias de trabalho por ano}}$$

$$= \frac{54.000}{260} = 207,7$$

$$\text{Número necessário de contadores} = \frac{\text{Número de materiais contados por dia}}{\text{Número de materiais por dia por contador}}$$

$$= \frac{207,7}{20} = 10,4, \text{ ou 11 contadores}$$

DESENVOLVIMENTOS CONTEMPORÂNEOS NO SETOR DE ARMAZENAMENTO

Novos desenvolvimentos modificam continuamente a administração dos sistemas de armazenamento (warehousing). Progressos nos sistemas de computação estão permitindo transações instantâneas de manutenção de registros. A utilização de sistemas de código de barras é cada vez mais comum à medida que as empresas tentam minimizar os erros de entrada de dados em registros de estoques. O registro automático de produtos e preços em supermercados é um exemplo desses desenvolvimentos. Os estoques são ajustados automaticamente à medida que produtos são comprados. Os gerentes podem consultar a distância o sistema de computação para obter saldos instantâneos de estoque. A Motorola, a Honeywell, a Westinghouse e outras empresas já possuem sistemas on-line similares para manter registros de estoque para todos as SKUs. A Ralston Purina e a Westinghouse removeram quase completamente o elemento humano do armazenamento de materiais em algumas de suas localizações mais novas. Esses sistemas automatizados de armazenamento e recuperação (ASRS) removem materiais do estoque de matérias-primas, compõem lotes de pedidos de materiais completos e os entregam nos pontos apropriados dentro do sistema de produção, tudo sem contato de mãos humanas. Outros sistemas automatizados montam similarmente pedidos de embarque e os movimentam para as áreas de embarque. Esses e outros desenvolvimentos prometem tornar o setor de armazenamento ainda mais eficiente no futuro para atender as necessidades de quantidade e programação dos clientes e departamentos de operações.

Apesar dos avanços da informática, do estabelecimento de postos de gerentes de materiais e da centralização de funções de administração de materiais para se obter maior controle, ainda ocorrem falhas administrativas ocasionais. Materiais não estão onde deveriam estar quando necessário, ocorrem esgotamentos de estoque (stockouts), ou stockouts são antecipados. Quando essas ou outras situações similares ocorrerem, *e elas sempre ocorrem em todos os sistemas*, materiais devem ser agilizados.

AGILIZAÇÃO

Agilização (*expediting*) é a concentração da atenção de uma ou mais pessoas em um pedido ou lote de materiais em particular com a finalidade de agilizar o pedido ao longo de toda cadeia de suprimentos. **"Desagilização"** (*de-expediting*) significa desacelerar o movimento de um pedido. A agilização ou a "desagilização" geralmente é necessária, porque eventos imprevistos podem fazer com que um pedido de materiais ou produtos atrase ou adiante. São exemplos desses eventos:

- Um cliente aumentou a quantidade de produtos pedida. A quantidade ampliada do pedido agora ultrapassa o estoque de bens acabados, e produtos adicionais devem ser produzidos rapidamente.
- Um fornecedor deixa de remeter um pedido de materiais na data prometida. Procedimentos de embarque de emergência devem ser empregados a fim de que as peças cheguem à empresa no tempo certo para evitar um stockout ou interrupção dos processos de produção.
- Peças que são processadas por tratamento térmico encontraram dificuldades técnicas. O lote deve ser transferido rapidamente à frente de outros materiais se o processo de recozimento não precisar ser atrasado.

A agilização muitas vezes é necessária devido a incertezas presentes nos sistemas de produção; demanda do cliente, tempos de entrega de materiais e tempos de processamento in-house são apenas algumas dessas incertezas. A administração de materiais deve ser flexível o bastante para acomodar essas incertezas, reagindo rapidamente quando o inesperado acontecer. A agilização é executada periodicamente por todos os empregados do setor de administração de materiais, e essa atividade ajuda a tornar flexíveis as cadeias de suprimentos.

Alguns gerentes e suas organizações operam rotineiramente por meio da administração da crise. *Toda atividade é agilizada.* Essa abordagem à administração é uma desculpa para o mau planejamento, para procedimentos ruins e para má administração em geral. Quando a agilização se torna a atividade predominante na administração de materiais, alguma coisa está errada. Todas as pessoas e todo sistema de produção cometem erros, e esses erros podem criar a necessidade de agilização quando gerentes de materiais, compradores, gerentes de armazenamento (warehousing), o pessoal da logística ou outros da cadeia de suprimentos falham. Mas a agilização deve ser a exceção à regra, não a regra.

A agilização completa o ciclo de materiais que parte da aquisição de materiais até a entrega dos produtos acabados nas mãos dos clientes. Ao mudar procedimentos, anular políticas, fazer chamadas telefônicas e cobrar favores passados, idealizar soluções rápidas e adotar outras táticas de agilização, os gerentes fazem os sistemas de materiais funcionar efetivamente e obtêm a quantidade certa do material certo no lugar certo e na hora certa.

Benchmarking do Desempenho de Gerentes de Materiais

Dada a importância dos gerentes de materiais atualmente, como as organizações medem quão bem eles estão se saindo em suas funções? A Tabela 14.1 apresenta diversos critérios, de acordo com sua ordem de importância, que as empresas tradicionalmente têm usado para avaliar os gerentes de materiais. Esses critérios têm sido e, sem dúvida, permanecerão importantes, mas o movimento rumo a mercados globais, a competição baseada no tempo e a administração da qualidade total estão fazendo com que outros critérios importantes venham à tona. A Tabela 14.2 relaciona outros fatores que são usados pelas empresas atualmente para avaliar suas funções de administração de materiais.

TABELA 14.1 CLASSIFICAÇÃO TRADICIONAL DOS CRITÉRIOS DE DESEMPENHO NA ADMINISTRAÇÃO DE MATERIAIS

Classificação	Critérios de Desempenho
1	O nível e o valor dos estoques na empresa.
2	A porcentagem de pedidos que são entregues aos clientes no tempo certo.
3	O número e gravidade dos casos de não atendimento (stockouts) nos estoques da empresa.
4	Os custos anuais de materiais comprados dos fornecedores.
5	Os custos anuais de transporte de materiais dos fornecedores e de produtos para os clientes.
6	Os custos anuais de operação dos armazéns.
7	O número de reclamações dos clientes.
8	Outros fatores, como, por exemplo, lucratividade e custos de manutenção.

TABELA 14.2 DESEMPENHO DA ADMINISTRAÇÃO DE MATERIAIS EM FABRICANTES DE CLASSE MUNDIAL

Critérios de Desempenho	Todas as Empresas	Fabricantes de Classe Mundial
Número de fornecedores para cada agente de compra	34	5
Número de agentes de compra por $ 100 milhões de compras	5,4	2,2
Custo da atividade de compra como porcentagem das compras	3,3%	0,8%
Tempo necessário para realizar uma avaliação de um fornecedor	3 semanas	0,4 semana
Tempo necessário para fazer um pedido aos fornecedores	6 semanas	2,4 minutos
Porcentagem de entregas atrasadas	33%	2%
Porcentagem de defeitos	1,5%	0,0001%
Número de casos de não-atendimento de estoque (stockouts) de materiais por ano	400	4

Fonte: Business Week, 30 de novembro de 1992.

Terceirização de Provedores de Administração da Logística

Uma crescente tendência entre os fabricantes de classe mundial é a confiança em provedores independentes de administração da logística. Uma vez que elas tentam se concentrar mais em suas competências essenciais, muitas companhias estão terceirizando certas funções, como, por exemplo, armazenamento e distribuição. Empresas como a Caliber Logistics e a United Parcel Service oferecem uma variedade de serviços e conhecimento logísticos a outras empresas. Como um exemplo, a Dell Computer Corporation contratou recentemente a Caliber Logistics para operar seu armazém de produtos acabados e seu sistema de distribuição próximo a Austin, Texas.

Um grande número de benefícios pode ser obtido do uso de empresas independentes de administração da logística. Essas empresas podem fornecer o que há de mais moderno em sistemas de informação logística, menores preços negociados para transportadores e espaço de armazenamento, e pessoal de logística altamente treinado. E também podem ajudar a projetar um sistema logístico mais eficiente para uma companhia em particular.

RESUMO FINAL

O QUE OS FABRICANTES DE CLASSE MUNDIAL ESTÃO FAZENDO

Os fabricantes de classe mundial vêem a administração da cadeia de suprimentos como um elemento-chave para o aumento de fatias de mercados internacionais. Eles deram aos executivos encarregados novas e ampliadas responsabilidades. Esses gerentes da cadeia de suprimentos planejam e controlam todas as atividades relacionadas com os materiais que se movimentam dos fornecedores, passam pelos processos de produção e chegam aos clientes. A autoridade para que o sistema de materiais resida numa única função organizacional dá o foco e evita a situação anterior na qual todos culpavam todos os demais quando surgiam dificuldades relacionadas a materiais. Quer os fabricantes de classe mundial centralizem ou não a administração de materiais, a maneira pela qual os materiais são administrados se modificou.

Os fabricantes de classe mundial estão formando parcerias com fornecedores para produzirem produtos rapidamente com qualidade quase perfeita exatamente quando forem necessários e com pouco estoque. Prover os fornecedores de informações sobre quando pedidos dos clientes são necessários e treiná-los em técnicas de controle da qualidade e manufatura estão se tornando mais comuns. Fornecedores são selecionados e desenvolvidos tendo-se uma visão de longo prazo para melhorar a qualidade do produto, entregas rápidas e receptividade às necessidades dos clientes. Não obstante o preço ser importante, ser capaz de entregar materiais suficientes quando necessário, produzir materiais de qualidade excepcional e ser digno de confiança e cooperativo são ainda mais importantes. Contratos de longo prazo e de múltiplos anos são usados para garantir a segurança dos fornecedores e fornecer incentivos para desenvolver confiança e colaboração.

Fornecedores das vizinhanças são preferidos. Mesmo que os fornecedores estejam localizados a grandes distâncias, muitas vezes eles estão agrupados para realizar embarques combinados ou são capazes de idealizar outras maneiras de entregar materiais em base just-in-time. Isso pode exigir certa imaginação devido às grandes distâncias geográficas, mas a recompensa é encontrada em lead times mais breves e mais confiáveis e em estoques reduzidos.

Todos os materiais do sistema são preparados para ser produzidos e chegar exatamente quando a produção necessitar deles, a fim de que os produtos possam ser entregues exatamente quando os clientes precisarem deles. Equipamentos de embarque de propriedade da própria empresa tendem a ser preferíveis devido à grande confiabilidade, a qual leva a lead times mais curtos. Os fornecedores são até mesmo encorajados a estender seus métodos JIT a *seus* fornecedores.

Os fabricantes de classe mundial usam computadores extensivamente para determinar os roteiros mais eficientes para os caminhões, para encontrar a melhor maneira de carregar e descarregar caminhões, e para fornecer estreitas comunicações entre motoristas e os escritórios centrais. Essa utilização de computadores não somente mantém baixos os custos, mas também, de não menos importância, possibilita que a administração saiba onde cada pedido está no sistema inteiro e quando se espera que ele chegue a seu destino. Os fabricantes de classe mundial usam modelos computadorizados para desenvolver planos de embarque para operações de manufatura e de serviços. De especial valor é a programação linear. Com essa técnica, os custos de embarque entre muitas origens e muitos destinos podem ser minimizados com o desenvolvimento de planos que exigem menos viagens.

Alguns fabricantes de classe mundial estão começando a recorrer a empresas independentes de administração da logística, quando terceirizam algumas de suas funções de negócios para se tornar mais focalizados em suas competências essenciais.

QUESTÕES DE REVISÃO E DISCUSSÃO

1. Defina estes termos: *material, cadeia de suprimentos, administração da cadeia de suprimentos.*
2. Qual é a missão do departamento de compras? Quais fatores estão tornando a atividade de compras mais importante atualmente? Explique. Em quais atividades o departamento de compras se envolve?
3. Explique a relação entre MRP e a administração de materiais. Qual é a ligação entre a atividade de compras e o MRP? Qual é a ligação entre o controle de produção e o MRP? Qual é a ligação entre os departamentos de trânsito e o MRP?
4. Defina estes termos: *especificação de material, requisição de compra, pedido de cotação, ordem de compra.*
5. O que é integração vertical? Defina *análise do comprar* versus *fabricar.*
6. O que é atividade de compras just-in-time (JIT)? Quais são os elementos da atividade de compras JIT?
7. Quais práticas dos departamentos de compras são consideradas antiéticas? Como as empresas podem evitar ou controlar práticas de compra antiéticas?
8. Defina estes termos: *logística, administração da distribuição, planejamento das necessidades de distribuição.*
9. Relacione as atividades incluídas na logística dentro de uma fábrica.
10. Defina estes termos: *registro de estoque, armazenamento (warehousing), estoque de matérias-primas, requisição ao estoque, estoque em processo, unidade de manutenção de estoque.*
11. Descreva dois métodos de contabilidade de estoques. Defina *contagem cíclica* e explique sua finalidade. Quais fatores justificariam a contagem de um material mais freqüentemente?
12. Por que as empresas ocasionalmente têm de agilizar pedidos de materiais? A agilização ocorre somente quando os gerentes de materiais falham?
13. Quais são os critérios importantes usados na avaliação dos gerentes de materiais?
14. Quais benefícios podem ser obtidos ao se usar empresas independentes de administração da logística?

TAREFAS NA INTERNET

1. Visite o site da Caliber Logistics (**www.caliberlogistics.com**). Descreva alguns dos serviços oferecidos por esse provedor de logística.
2. A Varsity Logistics (**www.varsitynet.com**) oferece softwares para auxiliar as empresas a administrarem melhor suas logísticas. Visite e explore o site da empresa e descreva alguns dos softwares oferecidos.
3. A i2 Technologies (**www.i2.com**) fornece softwares de planejamento e programação para administração global da cadeia de suprimentos. Visite e explore o site da i2 e descreva alguns dos recursos de seus softwares.
4. Procure na Internet por uma companhia de armazéns. Descreva suas instalações e os serviços de armazenamento que ela oferece. Forneça o site da empresa.
5. Procure na Internet por uma companhia ferroviária que ofereça transporte de fretes. Descreva suas instalações e os serviços de frete que ela oferece. Forneça o site da companhia.

PROBLEMAS

1. Uma companhia está planejando um novo produto que requer uma operação chamada *deep drawing*. Um comprador do departamento de compras está tentando decidir se deve comprar o serviço de deep drawing de um fornecedor ou recomendar que o departamento de produção da empresa se ponha a fazer seu próprio deep drawing internamente. O comprador desenvolveu as seguintes estimativas:

	Fazer o Deep Draw Internamente na Empresa	Comprar o Serviço de *Deep Draw*
Número de peças necessárias por ano	15.000	15.000
Custo fixo por ano	$ 55.000	0
Custo variável por peça	$ 29,20	$ 33,50

Se a qualidade de produto e o desempenho de entrega forem aproximadamente os mesmos para as alternativas de fazer ou comprar (make-or-buy), a empresa deve comprar o serviço de deep-drawing?

2. O diretor de administração de materiais da AC Corporation está revisando os planos do próximo ano para o suprimento de um componente hoje comprado da Diamond Ltd., uma empresa da Coréia do Sul. O componente é o módulo de memória T1000, usado em muitos produtos da AC. O diretor pondera se poderiam economizar dinheiro desenvolvendo outro fornecedor para esse componente ou se a empresa deve manufaturar o T1000 dentro de uma das fábricas da AC. A equipe de análise de compras do diretor desenvolveu as seguintes estimativas:

Fonte de Suprimento do T1000	Descrição do Custo	Custo Fixo Anual	Custo Variável por Unidade
Diamond Ltd.	Usinagem anual	$ 20.000	
	Inspeção e retrabalho		$ 0,26
	Embarque		3,95
	Preço de compra		21,88
Chicago West	Usinagem anual	$ 55.000	
	Inspeção e retrabalho		$ 2,05
	Embarque		1,55
	Preço de Compra		18,59
In-house	Usinagem anual	$ 45.000	
	Inspeção e retrabalho		$ 0,95
	Embarque		0,75
	Custos de produção	5.000	20,50

O grupo de análise de compras descobriu que a empresa precisará de aproximadamente 50.000 unidades de T1000 no próximo ano.

a) Qual fonte de suprimento apresenta o menor custo para o próximo ano?
b) Quantas unidades de T1000 teriam de ser compradas no próximo ano para que cada uma das fontes seja a fonte de menor custo?

3. Neil Brockley, gerente de compras da Agrifoods Processing Company, deve decidir-se por uma estratégia de compras para o processamento de brócolis para este ano. A estação de colheita regional não se iniciará antes de cinco meses, e Neil se defronta com três estratégias alternativas de compras. Uma estratégia é que a Agrifoods espere até que a colheita se inicie antes de tentar comprar brócolis. Muitos pequenos agricultores esperarão o tempo da colheita para vender seus produtos. Outra estratégia é esperar três meses até que a maioria dos agricultores tenha plantado suas lavouras de brócolis. Nesse momento, a Agrifoods poderia negociar contratos com diversos agricultores de porte médio para comprar suas safras. A terceira estratégia de compras é negociar imediatamente um contrato com a Northern California Growers Cooperative. Neil estimou os seguintes custos por libra e associou probabilidades a cada estratégia de compra:

	Probabilidade	Custo por Libra
Pequenos agricultores	0,20	0,45
	0,25	0,60
	0,35	0,75
	0,20	0,95
Agricultores de porte médio	0,25	0,55
	0,40	0,75
	0,35	0,85
Cooperativa	0,40	0,70
	0,60	0,75

a) Use uma árvore de decisões para analisar as alternativas de decisão. (*Dica*: Reveja o Exemplo 6.1.)
b) Como a Agrifoods deve comprar brócolis?
c) Qual será o custo esperado por libra para os brócolis se a Agrifoods seguir suas recomendações?
d) Quais outros fatores devem ser considerados nessa decisão de compra?

4. Yoshinori Otake é agente de compra da MicroAir, uma fábrica de fornos de microondas. A MicroAir está prestes a mudar sua produção para uma abordagem JIT, e o sr. Otake foi solicitado a reavaliar seus fornecedores potenciais de um módulo de mostrador (*display*) digital. Depois de avaliar o provável desempenho dos três fornecedores potenciais quanto a fatores importantes, o sr. Otake preparou as seguintes informações:

Fator de Desempenho	Peso do Fator	Classificação		
		Sumsing	Parkasenic	Hatchui
Preço	0,20	$ 13,60	$ 14,30	$ 13,20
Prazo de entrega	0,20	0,8	0,7	0,9
Confiabilidade de entrega	0,25	0,8	0,6	0,7
Qualidade	0,20	0,6	0,8	0,6
Capacidade de produção	0,10	0,5	0,6	0,8
Receptividade	0,05	0,6	0,7	0,5

Qual fornecedor você recomendaria? Por quê? (*Dica*: Veja as Tabelas 5.4 e 6.7.) Quais outros fatores seriam importantes nessa decisão?

5. Produtos são embarcados do centro de distribuição principal de uma companhia (adjacente à fábrica) para dois armazéns regionais. Os registros de DRP a seguir indicam a demanda prevista, os recebimentos programados e o estoque final projetado do último período (em unidades) para um único produto. As programações de pedidos à fábrica tornam-se as necessidades brutas no programa mestre de produção (MPS) da fábrica.
a) Preencha os registros de DRP que se seguem.
b) A partir desses registros, quais necessidades brutas apareceriam no MPS da fábrica?

Armazém Regional n. 1
O tempo de atendimento (lead time) para embarcar produtos do centro de distribuição principal na fábrica para o Armazém n. 1 é de 1 semana, o lote padrão de embarque é de 200 unidades, e o estoque de segurança é de 100 unidades.

		Semana				
	−1	1	2	3	4	5
Demanda prevista		100	150	180	90	120
Recebimentos programados		200				
Estoque final projetado	300					
Recebimento programado de remessas						
Pedidos programados para embarque						

Armazém Regional n. 2
O tempo de atendimento (lead time) para embarcar produtos do centro de distribuição principal na fábrica para o Armazém n. 2 é de 2 semanas, o lote padrão de embarque é de 300 unidades, e o estoque de segurança é de 200 unidades.

		Semana				
	−1	1	2	3	4	5
Demanda prevista		150	250	200	240	200
Recebimentos programados		300				
Estoque final projetado	350					
Recebimento programado de remessas						
Pedidos programados para embarque						

Centro de Distribuição Principal na Fábrica
O tempo de atendimento (lead time) para montagem final de produtos e para deslocá-los para o centro de distribuição principal é de 1 semana, o lote padrão de produção é de 500 unidades, e o estoque de segurança é de 200 unidades.

	Semana					
	−1	1	2	3	4	5
Necessidades brutas (unidades)						
Recebimentos programados		500				
Estoque final projetado	250					
Recebimento programado de pedidos						
Pedidos programados para embarque						

6. Produtos são embarcados do armazém de fábrica de uma companhia para dois armazéns regionais. Os registros de DRP a seguir indicam a demanda prevista, os recebimentos programados e o estoque final projetado do último período em unidades para um único produto. As programações de pedidos à fábrica tornam-se as necessidades brutas no programa mestre de produção (MPS) da fábrica.
   a) Preencha os registros de DRP que se seguem.
   b) A partir desses registros, quais necessidades brutas apareceriam no MPS da fábrica?

Armazém Regional A
O tempo de atendimento (lead time) para embarcar produtos do armazém na fábrica para o Armazém A é de 2 semanas, o lote padrão de embarque é de 250 unidades, e o estoque de segurança é de 150 unidades.

	Semana					
	−1	1	2	3	4	5
Demanda prevista		130	190	280	150	310
Recebimentos programados		250				
Estoque final projetado	230					
Recebimento programado de remessas						
Pedidos programados para embarque						

Armazém Regional B
O tempo de atendimento (lead time) para embarcar produtos do armazém na fábrica para o Armazém B é de 1 semana, o lote padrão de embarque é de 150 unidades, e o estoque de segurança é de 80 unidades.

	Semana					
	−1	1	2	3	4	5
Demanda prevista		210	140	180	150	140
Recebimentos programados		150				
Estoque final projetado	180					
Recebimento programado de remessas						
Pedidos programados para embarque						

Armazém na Fábrica
O tempo de atendimento (lead time) para montagem final de produtos e para deslocá-los para o armazém na fábrica é de 1 semana, o lote padrão de produção é de 500 unidades, e o estoque de segurança é de 150 unidades.

	Semana					
	−1	1	2	3	4	5
Demanda prevista						
Recebimentos programados				500		
Estoque final projetado	100					
Recebimento programado de remessas						
Pedidos programados para embarque						

7. Uma companhia está implementando um sistema de contagem cíclica. Os itens Classe A seriam contados mensalmente, os itens Classe B seriam contados trimestralmente, e os itens Classe C seriam contados anualmente. Dos itens de produção da empresa, 65% são Classe C, 25% são Classe B, e 10% são Classe A. Se a empresa tiver 20.000 diferentes materiais e numerações de peças, quantos itens precisarão ser contados diariamente se houver 250 dias de trabalho por ano?

8. Para melhorar o programa de contagem cíclica, o gerente de armazéns e estoques propõe duplicar a freqüência de contagem das classes de materiais B e C. A situação atual é:

Classe de Material	Porcentagem de Itens na Classe de Material	Freqüência de Contagem
A	5%	Mensal
B	25	Trimestral
C	75	Anual

A companhia tinha 50.000 materiais de todos os tipos. Se um trabalhador que faz a contagem cíclica custa $ 25.000 por ano, pode contar uma média de 20 itens por dia e trabalha 250 dias por ano:
a) Quantos contadores o sistema atual requer?
b) Quanto a equipe atual de contadores custa por ano?
c) Quantos contadores o novo sistema exigiria?
d) Quanto a mais a melhorada precisão custará por ano?

ESTUDO DE CASO

STAR CLOTHING MANUFACTURING

A Star Clothing Manufacturing fabrica roupas em três fábricas no México. As caixas de roupas são despachadas para quatro armazéns regionais. A tabela seguinte mostra o custo de transporte por caixa de cada fábrica até cada armazém regional, as necessidades mensais mínimas de armazenamento e as capacidades mensais máximas de cada fábrica. A companhia deseja embarcar caixas de vestuário de suas fábricas para seus armazéns regionais a fim de que o custo mensal total de transporte seja minimizado.

Origem	Los Angeles	Dallas	Chicago	Atlanta	Capacidade Máxima da Fábrica (caixas)
Tijuana	$ 2,90	$ 5,25	$ 9,10	$ 9,50	35.500
Juarez	3,85	4,15	6,20	7,60	22.500
Matamoros	5,20	3,65	6,10	5,90	12.750
Capacidade mensal mínima de armazenamento (caixas)	20.500	15.750	16.500	18.500	

Tarefas
1. Formule a informação sobre esse caso no formato de programação linear. Defina as variáveis de decisão, escreva a função objetivo e escreva as funções de restrição. Resolva o modelo.
2. Interprete plenamente o significado da solução que obteve no n. 1. Em outras palavras, o que a administração da Star Clothing deve fazer? Explique em detalhes o significado do resultado.
3. Se você pudesse adicionar capacidade a uma das fábricas, qual delas você escolheria? Quanto você aceitaria pagar por caixa para a capacidade adicional da fábrica?
4. Toda a capacidade da fábrica é embarcada? Quanta capacidade não é embarcada? Se toda a capacidade da fábrica fosse embarcada, em quanto custo adicional se incorreria?

PARTE IV

DECISÕES QUANTO AO CONTROLE
PLANEJANDO E CONTROLANDO OPERAÇÕES PARA OBTER PRODUTIVIDADE, QUALIDADE E CONFIABILIDADE

CAPÍTULO 15
Produtividade, Trabalho em Equipe e Empowerment: Comportamento, Métodos de Trabalho e Medida do Trabalho

CAPÍTULO 16
Administração da Qualidade

CAPÍTULO 17
Controle da Qualidade

CAPÍTULO 18
Planejando e Controlando Projetos

A Parte IV deste livro preocupa-se com muitas decisões do dia-a-dia que os gerentes de operações devem tomar. Mas, por sua própria natureza, há um senso de urgência a respeito dessas decisões, porque elas têm um impacto imediato sobre o desempenho de curto prazo das operações. Por outro lado, as *questões discutidas nesta parte do livro também são de importância estratégica, porque a sobrevivência a longo prazo dos negócios na competição global depende da capacidade que as empresas têm de se superar para entregar produtos da mais alta qualidade, realizar entregas rápidas e no tempo certo, com a meta global de clientes satisfeitos.* E tanto é assim que os tópicos deste livro desempenham dois papéis: o de planejamento e controle de curto prazo, mas, desde que a competição global elevou esses tópicos à importância estratégica, eles também detêm a chave para a sobrevivência a longo prazo. Os gerentes de operações, portanto, são atores fundamentais no campo da competição global.

Eis algumas das coisas pelas quais os gerentes de operações são responsáveis:

- Produzir produtos rapidamente e cumprir as promessas de entrega aos clientes.
- Elevada produtividade e baixos custos de produção.
- Segurança dos trabalhadores.
- Produzir produtos da mais alta qualidade.
- Manter elevada a satisfação do cliente.

Mais do que qualquer outro fator, o pessoal — os empregados dos sistemas de produção — afeta diretamente os custos, a produção no tempo certo, a qualidade e a satisfação do cliente. Devido ao grande impacto dos empregados, seu trabalho deve ser cuidadosamente planejado, eles devem trabalhar juntos e devem ter poderes para assumir papéis mais ativos. Os empregados têm muitas das respostas às perguntas sobre como melhorar a produtividade, e os gerentes de operações devem lançar mão dessas idéias e ajudar os empregados a implementá-las.

Programas de administração da qualidade total (TQM) e a implementação dos programas para obter elevada qualidade de produto são cruciais para a sobrevivência a longo prazo. E o controle da qualidade no dia-a-dia deve ser administrado de forma que a organização produza produtos ou serviços que cumpram seus padrões de qualidade predeterminados e melhorem continuamente. Definir esses padrões, inspecionar saídas, comparar as características reais do produto ou serviço com esses padrões e pôr em prática ações corretivas quando necessário são aspectos importantes do trabalho diário dos gerentes de operações.

A manutenção das máquinas de produção é outro aspecto importante de controle dos custos e da qualidade. Conhecer os conceitos e técnicas da manutenção preventiva e os assuntos relacionados ajuda a garantir aos gerentes de operações que as máquinas não interferirão em seus objetivos de custo, produção no tempo certo e qualidade.

Se nossas indústrias pretendem sobreviver a longo prazo à concorrência estrangeira, elas devem melhorar a maneira pela qual estão planejando e controlando suas operações diárias. O que isso significa para nós é que os temas da Parte IV — produtividade e empregados, administração da qualidade, controle da qualidade, e planejamento e controle de projetos —, quando tomados em conjunto, são cruciais para o sucesso e sobrevivência de nossos sistemas de produção.

capítulo 15

Produtividade, Trabalho em Equipe e Empowerment
Comportamento, Métodos de Trabalho e Medida do Trabalho

Introdução

Produtividade e Comportamento Humano
   Abordagem de Múltiplos Fatores à Medição da Produtividade
   Produtividade de Mão-de-Obra

Projetando Trabalhos dos Trabalhadores

Empowerment dos Empregados

Análise de Métodos de Trabalho
   Princípios da Economia de Movimentos
   Como Fazer Análise de Métodos
      Diagramas e Gráficos

Medida do Trabalho
   Padrões de Mão-de-Obra
      Sistemas de Pagamento de Incentivo
   Estudo do Tempo
   Amostragem do Trabalho
   Padrões de Tempo Predeterminados

Saúde e Segurança dos Empregados

Resumo Final: O Que os Fabricantes de Classe Mundial Estão Fazendo

Questões de Revisão e Discussão

Tarefas na Internet

Problemas

Estudo de Caso
   Integrated Products Corporation

Introdução

EMPRESAS AMERICANAS SE CONCENTRAM NA PRODUTIVIDADE

Quando o presidente do Federal Reserve, Alan Greenspan, discursou no Congresso americano no início de 1998, ele destacou duas áreas de importância fundamental para as empresas americanas: produtividade e comércio exterior. Em nível nacional, o comércio exterior afeta o déficit comercial americano, e os ganhos de produtividade ajudam a manter um delicado equilíbrio entre crescimento econômico e inflação. Mas, em nível empresarial, os ganhos de produtividade são importantes quando as empresas lutam para reduzir custos e se tornar mais competitivas.

Nos Estados Unidos inteiro, gerentes estão queimando a pestana para calcular como espremer mais ganhos de produtividade de seus negócios. Uma vez que o desemprego nos Estados Unidos está baixo há um quarto de século, os salários estão em ascensão. Mas, em contrapartida, as companhias não podem dar-se ao luxo de elevar os preços de seus produtos, devido a uma rígida competição. Essa situação faz as potenciais melhorias de produtividade do trabalhador parecerem muito atraentes. De acordo com Greenspan, "a ameaça de elevação dos custos em mercados de mão-de-obra estrita tem provocado um substancial impulso em busca de esforços para tirar proveito de possíveis eficiências".

Tendo em vista ganhos de produtividade, as empresas americanas continuam a investir fortemente em tecnologia. Muitas companhias estão especialmente interessadas em novos sistemas de informação computadorizados, com a meta de substituir capital humano por capital de tecnologia da informação. Por exemplo, a St. Paul Co., uma grande companhia de seguros sediada em Minnesota, tem como meta ganhos de produtividade de 5% anualmente aumentando seus dispêndios em tecnologia da informação em cerca de 10% a 15% ao ano.

Além de investir em tecnologia, o aumento da produtividade em geral vem simplesmente de se pensar um pouco mais inteligentemente. Na Southland Corp, sediada em Dallas, matriz da cadeia de lojas de conveniência 7-Eleven, um recente aumento do salário mínimo combinado com um mercado de mão-de-obra estrita obrigou a empresa a pensar criativamente para melhorar a produtividade. Para utilizar melhor seus empregados, a Southland desenvolveu uma planilha eletrônica para gerentes de loja para ajudá-los a fazer a correspondência de tarefas, como colocação de estoques nas prateleiras, com as horas trabalhadas pelos empregados.

As empresas descobriram outra fonte de melhorias da produtividade através do aumentado treinamento dos empregados. A Allied Signal tem como meta ganhos de produtividade de 6% ao ano treinando todos os seus empregados da manufatura em princípios de controle da qualidade e administração da qualidade. Um menor número de erros ao longo do processo de produção significa melhor produtividade por empregado.

Como indica o relato precedente, a atenção das empresas americanas está concentrada em melhorar a produtividade. O crescimento da produtividade nos Estados Unidos é uma crescente preocupação nacional.

Os empregados têm tanto uma importância tática como estratégica quando as empresas americanas lutam por fatias de mercado internacional. Conforme mencionamos no Capítulo 2, os principais fatores que determinam quanto mercado pode ser captado pelas empresas americanas atualmente são a produtividade, custo e qualidade, e os empregados têm um impacto direto sobre esses fatores. De maneira semelhante, a implementação de métodos de produção high-tech tem de ser realizada pelos empregados. Realmente, *todas as iniciativas estratégicas que as companhias americanas precisam pôr em prática para ser mais competitivas devem ser realizadas por seus empregados. Então, quanto a isso, os empregados representam um ativo de importância estratégica.* E ainda, empregados são administrados diariamente para que os pedidos dos clientes sejam despachados e, desse modo, as ações dos empregados têm impacto de curto prazo. Dessa forma, uma discussão do impacto de curto prazo da parte dos empregados situa-se nesta seção do livro sobre planejamento e controle de operações para se obter produtividade, qualidade e confiabilidade.

Neste capítulo desenvolveremos primeiro uma compreensão do que é produtividade e como o comportamento humano está relacionado com ela. Em seguida estudaremos como os gerentes de operações projetam as funções dos empregados de forma que eles possam ser mais produtivos. Finalmente examinaremos os métodos para medir o trabalho dos empregados tendo em vista alguns padrões de trabalho. O propósito geral deste capítulo é explorarmos o cenário no qual os gerentes de operações atuais devem alcançar produtividade e desenvolvermos algumas técnicas que podem ser usadas para melhorá-la.

Produtividade e Comportamento Humano

Produtividade significa a quantidade de produtos ou serviços produzidos com os recursos utilizados. A produtividade num intervalo de tempo geralmente é medida com esta fórmula:

$$\text{Produtividade} = \frac{\text{Quantidade de produtos ou serviços produzidos}}{\text{Quantidade de recursos utilizados}}$$

Observe que há dois lados na equação da produtividade: a quantidade de produção e a quantidade de recursos utilizados. A produtividade varia com a quantidade de produção em relação à quantidade de recursos utilizados. A produtividade pode ser aumentada de diversas maneiras:

- Aumentar a produção utilizando a mesma quantidade ou quantidades menores de recursos.
- Reduzir a quantidade de recursos utilizados enquanto a mesma produção é mantida ou aumentada.
- Permitir que a quantidade de recursos utilizados se eleve contanto que a produção se eleve mais.
- Permitir que a produção decresça contanto que a quantidade de recursos utilizados decresça mais.

Observe que a fórmula da produtividade acima não inclui provisões para os preços dos produtos ou serviços ou os custos dos recursos. Há, entretanto, importantes implicações nessa fórmula quanto aos preços e custos. Podemos observar a partir da fórmula que quando o custo de um recurso se eleva, se os lucros tiverem de se manter os mesmos, deve ocorrer alguma combinação de aumentada produção, diminuída quantidade de recursos utilizados, ou elevações de preços dos produtos ou serviços. Por exemplo, quando os índices salariais se elevam, ou mais produção deve ser realizada em cada hora de trabalho, ou os preços de produtos e serviços devem se elevar para que os lucros não caiam.

A proporção da população americana que trabalha no campo caiu de 39% em 1900 para 30% em 1920, para 23% em 1940, para 8% em 1960, para 3% em 1980 e para menos de 2% em 1995. Mas a produção agrícola nos Estados Unidos nunca decresceu. Essa transformação da agricultura americana ocorreu graças à produtividade crescente da mão-de-obra resultante da mecanização das fazendas, produtos químicos agrícolas, melhoradas variedades de produtos agrícolas e melhorados métodos de cultivo. Uma transformação similar está ocorrendo na manufatura — a força de trabalho está se encolhendo, a produção está crescendo continuamente, e a produtividade está se elevando. Realmente, a manufatura americana se assemelha um bocado com a agricultura americana, com somente uma pequena força de trabalho produzindo de 25% a 30% do PIB.

A substituição da mão-de-obra na manufatura estava em curso havia muitas décadas. Então, na década de 1980, houve uma dramática mudança para a automação na manufatura e nos serviços. Essa mudança para a automação em muitas indústrias atualmente está modificando drasticamente a combinação de seus custos. Para algumas empresas, os trabalhadores da produção, ou **mão-de-obra direta**, representam uma parte tão pequena de seus custos totais que a qualidade do produto, estoques, engenharia, materiais, embarque, melhorias técnicas e outros custos gerais mantêm mais promessa de reduzir os custos e aumentar a produtividade. Deixar de reconhecer esse fato pode ser uma grande armadilha em programas de melhoria da produtividade. Os fabricantes americanos impulsionam a produtividade há muitas décadas, em grande parte fechando fábricas antigas e demitindo trabalhadores. Mas algumas companhias americanas se concentram muito em investimentos de capital como uma maneira de reduzir a mão-de-obra — ignorando os enormes benefícios a serem obtidos da qualidade melhorada, estoques reduzidos e mais rápida introdução de novos produtos. Para a maioria dos negócios americanos atualmente, o quadro da produtividade é ainda mais brilhante. Avançados sistemas de computação, CAD/ CAM, manufatura integrada por computador (CIM), todos os tipos de sistemas automatizados, projetos de produto inovadores e avanços na qualidade de produto estão modificando profundamente a natureza das operações tanto na manufatura como nos serviços.

O resultado é um número menor de empregados de assessoria, gerentes de nível médio, trabalhadores do setor de operações, enquanto as organizações se tornam menores, mais flexíveis, mais enxutas e mais produtivas.

ABORDAGEM DE MÚLTIPLOS FATORES À MEDIÇÃO DA PRODUTIVIDADE

A produtividade de um recurso é a quantidade de produtos ou serviços produzidos num intervalo de tempo dividido pela quantidade necessária desse recurso. A produtividade de cada recurso pode e deve ser medida. Por exemplo, medidas como as que se seguem poderiam ser usadas para determinar a produtividade num intervalo de tempo:

- **Capital:** Número de produtos produzidos dividido pelo valor do ativo.
- **Materiais:** Número de produtos produzidos dividido pelo dinheiro gasto em materiais.
- **Mão-de-obra direta:** Número de produtos produzidos dividido pelas horas de mão-de-obra direta.
- **Gastos gerais:** Número de produtos produzidos dividido pelo dinheiro despendido com gastos gerais.

Essas medidas não são perfeitas. Por exemplo, a medida para a produtividade de materiais inclui preço. Isso geralmente é indesejável, mas não há outra maneira prática de combinar as muitas unidades de medição diferentes para os diversos materiais utilizados na produção. Não obstante essas medidas da produtividade terem suas deficiências, elas constituem um ponto de partida para rastrear a produtividade a fim de que os gerentes possam estar cientes de suas tendências. Nas últimas décadas, quando o custo da mão-de-obra era o custo predominante da produção, a produtividade era medida pela produção por hora da mão-de-obra direta. Hoje, entretanto, há necessidade de se olhar além dos custos da mão-de-obra direta e desenvolver uma perspectiva de múltiplos fatores.

O problema com a focalização na produtividade de somente um tipo de recurso, ou fator, é que a produtividade desse recurso pode ser aumentada simplesmente substituindo-se parte desse recurso por um tipo diferente de recurso. Por exemplo, considere uma fábrica de automóveis que anteriormente comprava os componentes de uma bomba-d'água e os montava numa bomba-d'água completa para um carro. Suponhamos que eles decidam agora comprar bombas-d'água pré-montadas, reduzindo assim o número de empregados e equipamentos necessários internamente. Considere o que acontece à produtividade de diferentes fatores devido a essa mudança. O rendimento da produção permanece constante, mas o tipo de recurso usado se modifica. A produtividade da mão-de-obra direta se eleva, porque um número menor de empregados é necessário para a montagem interna. A produtividade do capital se eleva, porque os equipamentos e máquinas de montagem não mais são necessários e podem ser vendidos. Entretanto, a produtividade dos materiais decresce, porque o custo de compra de bombas-d'água pré-montadas é mais elevado do que o custo de componentes de bomba-d'água. Esse exemplo ilustra a importância de se examinar a produtividade de múltiplos fatores ao se avaliar a eficiência de um sistema de produção. O Bureau of Labor Statistics (**http://stats.bls.gov**) publica estatísticas sobre produtividade de múltiplos fatores, as quais são uma medida composta de trabalho, capital, energia e recursos de materiais.

Para entender a situação atual da produtividade do trabalho nos Estados Unidos, devemos examinar dois conceitos: produtividade do trabalho e taxa de mudança de produtividade. Consideremos primeiro a produtividade do trabalho, o nível absoluto de produtividade de mão-de-obra nos Estados Unidos.

O Bureau of Labor Statistics publica estatísticas sobre produtividade do trabalho que são computadas dividindo-se o valor real em dólares de todos os bens e serviços produzidos nos Estados Unidos em determinado ano pelas horas de mão-de-obra direta usadas para produzir esses bens e serviços. Durante muitas décadas, os Estados Unidos foram os líderes mundiais de produtividade. Outra medida que reflete as diferenças de produtividade entre os países é o produto interno bruto por pessoa empregada. A Tabela 15.1 mostra essa comparação correspondente a 14 países ao longo de duas décadas, com o valor para cada país sendo mostrado como uma porcentagem do valor americano. Não obstante seus parceiros comerciais internacionais estarem atrás dos Estados Unidos nessa medida, a Tabela 15.1 mostra que muitos os estão alcançando.

Em seguida consideremos o segundo conceito: a taxa de mudança da produtividade de mão-de-obra. Essa medida também é comumente chamada taxa de crescimento da produtividade do trabalho, o que implica que a produtividade do trabalho está crescendo. O Bureau of Labor Statistics também publica estatísticas sobre a taxa de crescimento da produtividade do trabalho nos Estados Unidos, a porcentagem de mudança a partir do ano anterior. Nas décadas de 1960, 1970 e 1980, a taxa de crescimento da produtivi-

TABELA 15.1	PRODUTO INTERNO BRUTO REAL POR PESSOA EMPREGADA, POR PAÍS				
	1976	1981	1986	1991	1996
Estados Unidos	100,0	100,0	100,0	100,0	100,0
Canadá	81,0	80,3	81,6	81,2	80,2
Japão	57,8	65,5	69,0	77,5	76,4
Coréia do Sul	21,7	25,4	33,3	42,4	50,2
Áustria	71,2	76,5	79,0	85,2	86,7
Bélgica	85,9	92,3	93,5	99,9	99,6
Dinamarca	67,7	68,7	71,2	74,3	77,7
França	76,2	83,2	85,8	92,1	90,6
Alemanha	77,7	81,3	82,8	89,3	91,4
Itália	n/a	81,8	83,8	90,7	94,4
Holanda	80,5	77,8	77,8	79,3	78,8
Noruega	68,0	72,2	76,1	81,9	83,0
Suécia	63,3	63,1	64,4	65,4	70,6
Reino Unido	63,0	66,2	70,6	71,0	69,7

Observação: O PIB de cada país por valor de pessoa empregada é mostrado como uma porcentagem do valor correspondente aos Estados Unidos nesse ano.
Fonte: O relatório do Bureau of Labor Statistics "Comparative Real Gross Domestic Product Per Capita and Per Employed Person", fevereiro de 1998 (**http://stats.bls.gov**).

dade do trabalho nos Estados Unidos se elevou de acordo com estas taxas médias: 2,5%, 1,2% e 1,0%. Ao longo do mesmo período, a taxa de crescimento da produtividade do trabalho no Reino Unido, Canadá, França, Itália, Alemanha Ocidental e Japão foi muito mais elevada do que nos Estados Unidos. Realmente, a taxa de crescimento da produtividade de mão-de-obra no Japão esteve na faixa dos dois dígitos. Com a globalização dos negócios, era de esperar que os competidores estrangeiros começassem a alcançar os Estados Unidos em termos de produtividade de mão-de-obra.

Como uma nota positiva para as companhias americanas, parece que o crescimento da produtividade do trabalho pode estar se elevando. De acordo com os números do Bureau of Labor Statistics, o crescimento da produtividade em 1996-1997 foi 1,9% para o setor de negócios da economia e 1,7% para o setor não agrícola de negócios. Mas para a manufatura o crescimento da produtividade foi de 4,4%, incluindo 5,7% para a manufatura de bens duráveis e 3,2% para manufatura de bens não duráveis.

Se os negócios americanos quiserem manter-se como o número 1 em termos de produtividade do trabalho, devem renovar seus esforços para aumentar a taxa de crescimento da produtividade do trabalho. E nossa visão da produtividade atualmente deve voltar-se para a melhoria da produtividade de todos os fatores da produção — mão-de-obra, capital, materiais e gastos gerais.

Muitas empresas atualmente estão se esforçando para melhorar seus índices de produtividade de mão-de-obra. O Instantâneo da Indústria 15.1 fornece uma descrição daquilo que a Ford Motor Company e a Toyota estão fazendo. Pode chegar o dia em que a produtividade da mão-de-obra direta receberá somente uma discussão superficial em livros didáticos como este, mas esse dia ainda não chegou. Para muitas companhias americanas, o custo da mão-de-obra direta permanece um custo significativo. Algumas operações de manufatura ainda não estão automatizadas e jamais o serão, porque ou não são eficientes quanto ao custo, ou capital suficiente não está disponível. Além disso, muitos serviços continuam exigindo mão-de-obra direta intensiva. Por esses motivos, o custo da mão-de-obra e a necessidade de melhorar a produtividade do trabalho continuam a receber atenção da administração. No restante deste capítulo, portanto, nos concentraremos na produtividade de mão-de-obra.

PRODUTIVIDADE DE MÃO-DE-OBRA

O que faz com que os empregados sejam mais produtivos? A Figura 15.1 mostra os principais fatores que afetam a produtividade do trabalho. Essa ilustração demonstra uma importante verdade: as causas da produtividade são muitas. Nós ainda não desenvolvemos um conjunto de fórmulas que descreva de maneira

INSTANTÂNEO DA INDÚSTRIA 15.1

MELHORIAS DE PRODUTIVIDADE NA FORD MOTOR COMPANY E TOYOTA

Para descobrir o segredo do sucesso da Ford Motor Company na década de 1980 não é preciso olhar para outra coisa a não ser o amplo complexo de montagem de Wixom, Michigan, que produz luxuosos Lincolns e US$ 1 bilhão de lucros por ano. Em 1979, Wixom construía 640 carros por dia com 5.420 trabalhadores. Em 1990, construía 768 carros por dia com 1.700 trabalhadores a menos. Este ganho de produtividade de mão-de-obra igual a 43% tipifica o desempenho da Ford. Esses formidáveis ganhos de produtividade foram obtidos através da utilização máxima das instalações existentes, aplicação de modernas tecnologias, forte ênfase em projetos de carros fáceis de construir e uso imediato de programas cooperativos com o United Auto Workers (UAW). Ao todo, a Ford elevou sua produção americana de veículos em 11,5% durante a década de 1980, enquanto reduzia sua força de trabalho em 21%. E os ganhos envolveram a companhia inteira.[a]

A Ford Motor Company saiu da década de 1980 com o maior aumento de produtividade entre as Três Grandes fábricas de automóveis do país. A Ford exibia um ganho de 31%, a Chrysler Corporation tinha um ganho de 17%, e a General Motors Corporation tinha um ganho de 5%. Entre as 37 fábricas pesquisadas pela Harbour & Associates, as da Ford mantinham as três posições mais altas e as da GM mantinham as três inferiores. A fábrica mais bem classificada foi a do Taurus e Sable da Ford, em Atlanta, onde 2,72 trabalhadores eram necessários para construir um carro. A fábrica menos eficiente era a da GM em Detroit, que fazia Cadillacs Eldorado e Sevilles e Buick Rivieras e Toronados, onde 7,85 trabalhadores eram necessários para construir um carro. Todas as Três Grandes fábricas de automóveis têm em andamento programas de melhoria da produtividade.[b]

Em 1992, a Ford podia produzir aproximadamente a mesma quantidade de veículos que produzia na década de 1970 nos Estados Unidos, mas com a metade dos trabalhadores. Como eles realizaram esse feito? Duas importantes razões contribuíram para isso:

- Projetar carros com um número menor de peças. O pára-choque do Taurus tinha somente 10 peças, em comparação com mais de 100 peças do pára-choque do concorrente, o Pontiac Grand Prix da GM.
- Aumentada cooperação de sua força de trabalho. A Ford convenceu seus empregados a trabalharem mais arduamente de maneira mais inteligente, e a ajudar a administração a descobrir maneiras de cortar custos.

Essas e outras melhorias permitiram que a Ford usasse um terço a menos de horas de trabalho para construir seus carros do que a GM, dando à Ford uma vantagem de custo de US$ 795 por veículo.[c]

A Toyota anunciou recentemente uma inovação no projeto de motores que aumentará sua produtividade. O motor de 120 cavalos do Corolla 1998 usa 25% menos peças do que seu predecessor, tornando-o 10% mais leve, 10% mais eficiente na utilização de combustível e significativamente mais barato para fabricar.

A Toyota não publicou todos os detalhes, mas diversos suportes foram eliminados moldando-os no bloco do motor, e diversos sensores eletrônicos foram consolidados.[d]

Fontes:
[a] Lippert, John, Knight-Ridder Newspapers. "Ford Auto Plant Has Productivity Down to Science". *Houston Chronicle*, 7 de janeiro de 1990.
[b] "Ford Tops Productivity Survey". *Houston Chronicle*, 3 de janeiro de 1990.
[c] "A Decisive Response to Crisis Brought Ford Enhanced Productivity". *Wall Street Journal*, 15 de dezembro de 1992.
[d] Taylor, Alex, III. "How Toyota Defies Gravity". *Fortune*, 8 de dezembro de 1997.

---

precisa o comportamento humano em geral e a produtividade em particular. Porém, começamos a entender o bastante acerca do comportamento dos empregados para removermos parte da incerteza sobre por que os empregados são produtivos.

Três fatores importantes afetam a produtividade da mão-de-obra: desempenho do empregado no trabalho; tecnologia, máquinas, ferramentas e métodos de trabalho que sustentam e auxiliam o trabalho deles; e qualidade de produto. Grupos de assessoria, como, por exemplo, da engenharia industrial, de processos, de produtos e de sistemas, lutam para desenvolver uma melhor automação, máquinas, ferramentas e métodos de trabalho para aumentar a produtividade. Aumentar a produtividade através de desenvolvimentos tecnológicos é, no mínimo, tão importante quanto o desempenho do empregado no trabalho para aumentar a produtividade. E reduzir defeitos, sucata e retrabalho aumenta diretamente a produtividade de todos os fatores de produção.

Figura 15.1 Variáveis Que Afetam a Produtividade de Mão-de-Obra

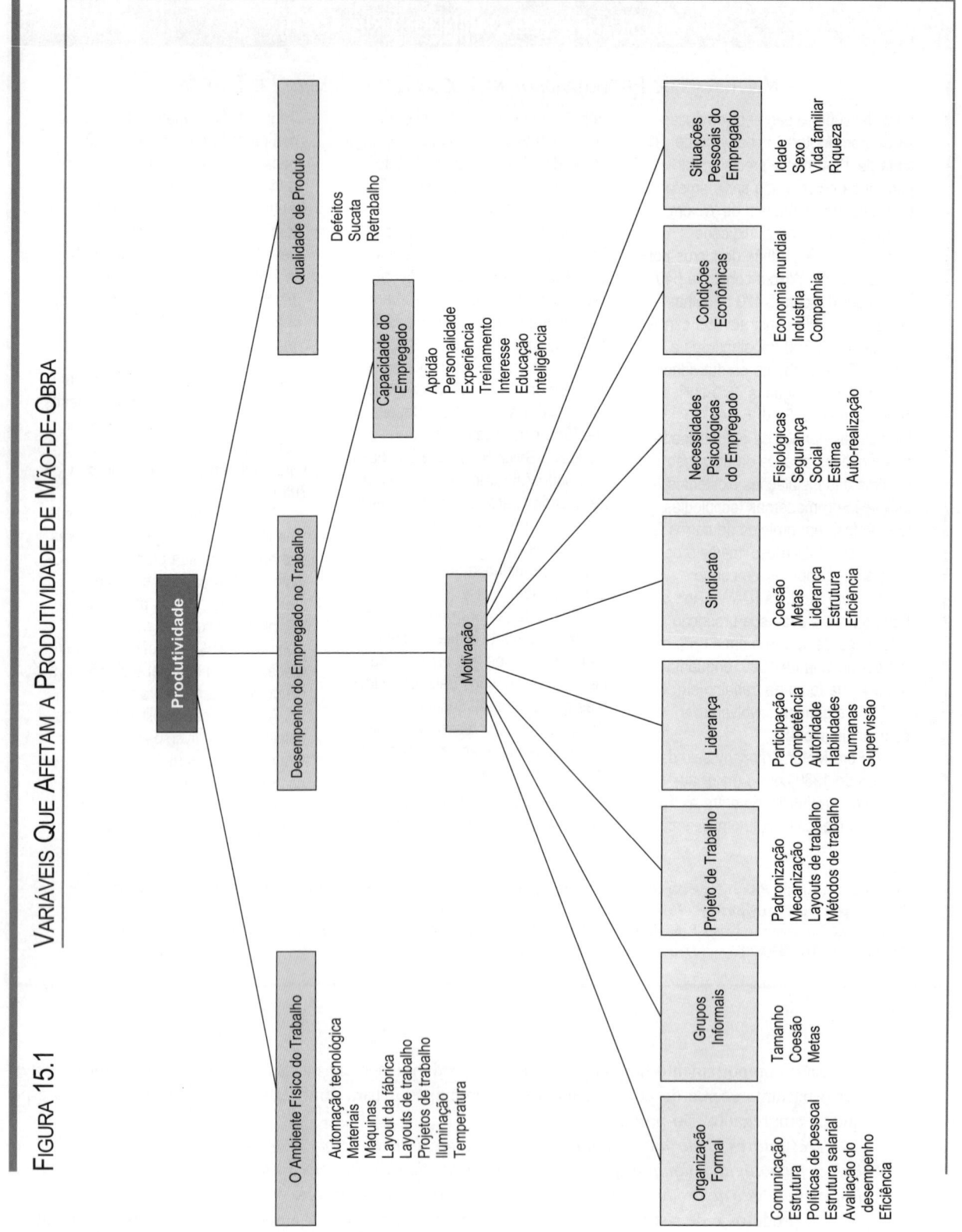

INSTANTÂNEO DA INDÚSTRIA 15.2

EMPREGADOS MAIS HÁBEIS E MAIS BEM TREINADOS

A Northeast Tool & Manufacturing Co., Carolina do Norte, exige que todos os seus 43 empregados façam exames de aptidão que medem tudo, de habilidades matemáticas e mecânicas a liderança e adaptabilidade. Os resultados dos exames são analisados pelo North Carolina Labor Department, em Raleigh, e devolvidos à Northeast Tool com uma prescrição para cada trabalhador. Baseando-se nos resultados, a empresa desenvolve um treinamento personalizado para cada trabalhador. Alguns se matricularão num colégio público dos arredores. Outros farão cursos a distância através de computadores instalados na fábrica. Alguns freqüentarão aulas à tarde com professores trazidos diretamente às instalações da fábrica.

A tendência rumo à manufatura de alta habilidade iniciou-se em meados da década de 1980, quando muitas companhias começaram a substituir o trabalho de linha de montagem de baixa habilidade por equipamentos controlados por computador que exigiam trabalhadores com habilidade e agilidade para pensar enquanto trabalhavam.

Na década de 1990, as empresas aprenderam a lição de que os investimentos em treinamento elevam a produtividade, muitas vezes com um custo menor do que os investimentos de capital.

Agora, até mesmo os pequenos fabricantes, como a Northeast Tool, vêem a alta habilidade como essencial para permanecer competitivos.

De acordo com as pesquisas que o Center for Effective Organizations da Universidade da Califórnia fez sobre as grandes companhias, o número de empresas que fez com que a maioria de seus trabalhadores passasse por diferentes tipos de treinamento se duplicou ou triplicou na última década.

Entre 1985 e 1995 a porcentagem de trabalhadores da manufatura com pelo menos alguma educação colegial se elevou de 33% para 44%.

"Há um crescimento real na disposição das empresas para investir em suas forças de trabalho", diz Pamela J. Tate, presidente do Council for Adult & Experiential Learning, um grupo de consultoria de Chicago.

Fonte: "Special Report: The New Factory Worker". *Business Week*, 30 de setembro de 1996.

O desempenho do empregado no trabalho é um tema complexo, porque todas as pessoas são diferentes. Capacidade, personalidade, interesses, ambições, níveis de energia, educação, treinamento e experiência variam muito. É importante que os gerentes de operações considerem essas diferenças, porque abordagens gerais ou universais para melhorar o desempenho no trabalho podem não ser eficazes para todos os empregados. Os departamentos de pessoal reconhecem essas diferenças e tentam selecionar empregados que tenham as capacidades desejadas para desenvolver programas de treinamento para melhorar as habilidades dos empregados.

O Instantâneo da Indústria 15.2 discute a crescente importância do treinamento e educação dos empregados.

Motivação talvez seja a variável mais complexa na equação da produtividade. Motivação é aquilo que motiva uma pessoa a agir de determinada maneira. Maslow identificou cinco níveis de necessidades que motivam as pessoas a agir: fisiológicas, segurança, sociais, estima e auto-realização. Essas necessidades são organizadas numa hierarquia, de psicológicas no nível mais baixo, a auto-realização no nível mais elevado. Somente necessidades não satisfeitas são **motivadores**, ou fazem com que as pessoas ajam, e à medida que cada necessidade de nível mais baixo torna-se relativamente satisfeita, necessidades de nível mais elevado surgem como motivadores. Hoje muitas necessidades de nível mais baixo dos empregados (fisiológicas e segurança) são, na maioria das vezes, levadas em consideração pelos programas de incentivo no trabalho. As necessidades de nível mais elevado (sociais, estima e auto-realização) podem representar uma promessa maior para os gerentes em suas tentativas de motivar os empregados.

Como a compreensão a respeito das necessidades dos empregados nos ajuda a projetar um ambiente de trabalho que encoraje a produtividade? Se pudermos determinar qual classe de necessidades é importante para nossos empregados, poderemos aplicar essa estrutura. *Se a produtividade for vista pelos empregados como um meio de satisfazer suas necessidades, é provável que isso resulte em elevada produtividade. Assim que os empregados tiverem suas necessidades satisfeitas através de recompensas condicionadas à produtividade, é provável que o processo se repita.* A Figura 15.2 ilustra esse conceito.

| FIGURA 15.2 | O CAMINHO DA PRODUTIVIDADE PARA SATISFAZER AS NECESSIDADES DOS TRABALHADORES |

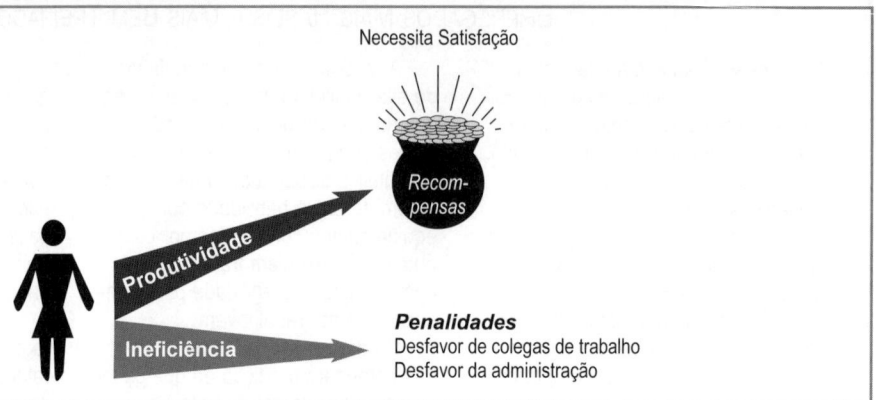

Os sindicatos de trabalhadores e grupos de trabalho podem influenciar os empregados para que sejam produtivos ou improdutivos. Se os empregados acharem que seus grupos de trabalho os tratam como párias porque têm sido produtivos, eles podem não cooperar com a administração nesse ciclo de produtividade-recompensa-produtividade. Os gerentes de operações devem reconhecer a influência que os grupos de trabalho têm sobre a produtividade da mão-de-obra e desenvolver grupos de trabalho cooperativos selecionando empregados cuidadosamente para esses grupos e influenciando normas grupais através da efetiva cooperação e comunicação.

Por que se preocupar com a satisfação das necessidades dos empregados? O que ganha a organização? A resposta evidente é uma melhoria da produtividade, conforme discutimos. Outra resposta igualmente importante é que empregados satisfeitos têm menos probabilidade de se ausentar do trabalho, menos probabilidade de sair de seus empregos para entrar em outros, e mais probabilidade de produzir produtos e serviços de alta qualidade. No ambiente de trabalho de hoje, em que o absenteísmo, a rotatividade e a baixa qualidade de produtos e serviços são problemas que se sobrepõem, essa razão sozinha parece ser suficiente para que os gerentes de operações se interessem em projetar funções de trabalho de uma maneira que envolva uma faixa mais ampla de satisfação das necessidades dos empregados.

PROJETANDO FUNÇÕES DOS TRABALHADORES

Alguns cientistas do comportamento argumentam que as funções da linha de montagem são cansativas e monótonas e que os trabalhadores não satisfazem suas necessidades de socialização, auto-estima e auto-realização nesses trabalhos. Os elevados índices de absenteísmo e rotatividade entre nossos trabalhadores parecem validar esses argumentos. Essa crítica das funções da linha de montagem tem como alvo o elevado grau de especialização nesses empregos. **Especialização da mão-de-obra** refere-se ao número de tarefas que um trabalhador executa. Um trabalho altamente especializado é aquele em que o trabalhador executa repetitivamente somente uma estreita variedade de atividades, como, por exemplo, dobrar uma folha de papel e colocá-la num envelope. Por outro lado, um trabalho que não é muito especializado seria aquele em que o trabalhador faz uma variedade de tarefas durante o dia. A Tabela 15.2 relaciona algumas vantagens e desvantagens da especialização da mão-de-obra.

Diversas propostas para modificar trabalhos especializados para que abranjam uma faixa maior de satisfação de necessidades são:

- **Treinamento multifuncional** — Treinar trabalhadores para que executem diversas funções a fim de que eles possam ser transferidos de um trabalho para outro quando necessário.
- **Ampliação do trabalho** — Adicionar tarefas similares ao trabalho dos trabalhadores; isto é chamado *ampliação horizontal do trabalho.*
- **Enriquecimento do trabalho** — Acrescentar mais planejamento, inspeção e outras funções administrativas ao trabalho dos trabalhadores; isto é chamado *ampliação vertical do trabalho.*

TABELA 15.2 — ALGUMAS VANTAGENS E DESVANTAGENS DA ESPECIALIZAÇÃO DE MÃO-DE-OBRA

Vantagens

1. Devido ao trabalho repetitivo, os índices de produção são elevados.

2. Uma vez que as necessidades de habilidade para as tarefas são baixas:
   a) As taxas salariais são baixas.
   b) Trabalhadores podem ser treinados rapidamente.
   c) Trabalhadores podem ser recrutados facilmente.

Desvantagens

1. A insatisfação do trabalhador pode fazer com que os custos totais sejam excessivos devido aos elevados índices de rotatividade.

2. A qualidade da produção pode ser baixa porque:
   a) Os trabalhadores não são motivados para produzir produtos de alta qualidade.
   b) Uma vez que os trabalhadores fazem somente uma pequena parte de um produto, nenhum trabalhador particular é responsável pela qualidade do produto inteiro.

- **Produção em equipe** — Organizar trabalhadores em equipes de trabalho; selecionar trabalhadores e treiná-los para trabalhar em equipes; atribuir alguma responsabilidade pela administração da produção às equipes.

Criar equipes de trabalho eficientes significa mais do que apenas reunir trabalhadores. Formar equipes exige treinamento em eficiência de equipe, resolução de conflitos, medição do desempenho da equipe e sistemas de motivação. Uma característica poderosa das equipes de trabalho eficientes é que elas podem concentrar-se em processos em vez de departamentos.

Por exemplo, se uma equipe precisar projetar e desenvolver um novo produto, ela poderá concentrar-se no processo de projetar e desenvolver o novo produto sem ser restringida por fronteiras e responsabilidades departamentais. Esses remédios têm sido aplicados com graus variáveis de sucesso e fracasso.

Permanece um questão: *Podemos dar aos trabalhadores a satisfação que eles querem em seus trabalhos e, ao mesmo tempo, dar à organização a produtividade e a eficiência de que ela necessita para sobreviver economicamente?* Essa é uma combinação possível? Como devemos projetar as funções dos trabalhadores de forma a integrar as necessidades de elevada produtividade da organização com as necessidades de trabalho interessante, autocontrole, socialização, participação e realização da parte dos empregados? Existem diretrizes práticas que engenheiros e outros especialistas técnicos que projetam funções dos trabalhadores possam seguir para atingir ambas essas metas necessárias e válidas? A Tabela 15.3 sugere diversas dessas diretrizes para projetar tarefas para os trabalhadores, cenários de trabalho imediatos dos trabalhadores e o ambiente de trabalho mais amplo.

A Tabela 15.3 foi desenvolvida com o pressuposto de que as tarefas do trabalhador individual foram projetadas primeiro para ser tecnicamente eficientes e produtivas. Essas sugestões para modificar tarefas dos trabalhadores têm sido aplicadas de maneira prática em organizações do mundo real para dar a eles a oportunidade de autocontrole, autodireção e socialização. O restante dessa tabela apresenta outras sugestões para modificar de maneira positiva tanto o cenário de trabalho imediato como o ambiente de trabalho mais amplo.

Os sindicatos de trabalhadores são uma força em termos de afetar as atitudes dos trabalhadores em relação ao trabalho. Os sindicatos têm visto com reserva as ações das administrações para tornar o trabalho mais satisfatório; desse modo, trabalhadores e sindicatos geralmente não têm cooperado na implementação das propostas de modificação do desenho do trabalho. Além disso, ao longo dos anos, os sindicatos têm negociado acordos trabalhistas que contêm regras trabalhistas restritivas. Essas regras controlam coisas como pagamento, horas de trabalho, horas extras, precedência para quem tem mais tempo de serviço (*seniority*) para preenchimento de vagas, escopo do trabalho, pagamento de incentivos, procedimentos de demissão e reconvocação, e transferência entre empregos. Uma regra trabalhista comum impede que um trabalhador que faz parte de uma classificação de trabalho faça um trabalho em outra classificação; por exem-

TABELA 15.3 — ALGUMAS DIRETRIZES PRÁTICAS PARA PROJETAR FUNÇÕES DOS TRABALHADORES E AMBIENTES DE TRABALHO QUE ACOMODEM AS NECESSIDADES DOS TRABALHADORES

Elementos das Funções dos Trabalhadores	Diretrizes de Projeto Sugeridas	Necessidades Afetadas dos Trabalhadores
Tarefas no trabalho dos trabalhadores (o próprio trabalho — disposição de máquinas, layouts do espaço de trabalho, métodos de trabalho e seqüência de tarefas no trabalho)	1. Evite determinar o ritmo das máquinas dos trabalhadores. Os trabalhadores devem determinar, quando possível, taxas de produção.	Autocontrole
	2. Quando for prático, combine as tarefas de inspeção com as funções a fim de que os trabalhadores inspecionem sua própria produção.	Autocontrole
	3. Projete áreas de trabalho que permitam uma comunicação aberta e contato visual com outros trabalhadores em operações adjacentes.	Socialização, criação de equipes
	4. Quando economicamente viável e geralmente desejado pelos trabalhadores, combine preparação de máquinas, novos layouts de trabalho, preparações e outros elementos de planejamento de funções imediatas no trabalho dos trabalhadores.	Autodireção/controle
	5. Substitua trabalhadores por equipamentos automatizados em trabalhos repetitivos, desconfortáveis e inseguros.	Insatisfação
Cenário de trabalho imediato (as políticas e procedimentos administrativos que recaem diretamente sobre os empregos dos trabalhadores)	1. Gire trabalhadores, quando for prático, entre tarefas que sejam repetitivas, monótonas, cansativas e de ciclo breve.	Variedade e alívio do cansaço e monotonia
	2. Designe novos trabalhadores a tarefas indesejáveis por períodos de tempo fixos e depois os transfira para funções mais desejáveis.	Igualdade
	3. Recrute pessoas portadoras de deficiências físicas, desempregados em situação difícil ou outras pessoas desprivilegiadas para trabalhos com elevado absenteísmo e elevada rotatividade.	Trabalho interessante e necessidades básicas
	4. Para aliviar a monotonia, conceda aos trabalhadores intervalos de descanso longe de tarefas repetitivas.	Alívio do cansaço e socialização
	5. Fixe índices de pagamento mais elevados para trabalhos indesejáveis.	Segurança psicológica, igualdade e realização
Ambiente de trabalho mais amplo (políticas abrangendo a organização inteira, clima, filosofia administrativa, estrutura, instalações e programas)	1. Selecione e treine supervisores que se comuniquem abertamente sobre a maioria das questões que afetam os trabalhadores.	Reconhecimento e socialização
	2. Desenvolva supervisores que se sintam à vontade num ambiente de equipe participativo, tanto em relação a seus superiores como com outros trabalhadores.	Participação, reconhecimento, socialização e realização
	3. Remova barreiras entre a administração e outros empregados, como, por exemplo, instalações de refeitórios e banheiros separados.	Igualdade e reconhecimento
	4. Crie um clima organizacional e uma filosofia administrativa que reconheça os trabalhadores e equipes de trabalho como elementos importantes da organização. Isso tende a dar aos trabalhadores um senso de valor pessoal.	Reconhecimento e realização
	5. Desenvolva canais de comunicação formais e informais entre os trabalhadores, equipes de trabalho e todos os níveis de administração. Esses canais funcionam melhor quando usados freqüentemente, em todas as direções, e numa ampla variedade de tópicos.	Participação, autocontrole e reconhecimento

plo, quando um trabalhador da produção não tem permissão para fazer qualquer trabalho de manutenção. Essas regras restringem a flexibilidade administrativa e reduzem a produtividade.

Nos últimos anos, entretanto, a perda de empregos sindicalizados devido à competição estrangeira tem exercido uma grande pressão sobre os sindicatos para modificarem regras trabalhistas restritivas nos contratos sindicais. Essas mudanças incluíram eliminar trabalhos desnecessários, mais flexibilidade para deslocar trabalhadores de um trabalho para outro, modificar regras de tempo de serviço e modificar a estrutura de equipe para ser mais apropriada para equipamentos de produção de alta tecnologia. Essas modificações melhoraram a produtividade em muitas indústrias. As mudanças nas regras trabalhistas não somente melhoram a produtividade ao eliminar desperdícios, mas também permitem a formação de equipes de trabalho motivadas, o que anteriormente era impossível.

Não obstante existirem obstáculos para projetar funções dos trabalhadores que sejam tanto eficientes como satisfatórias, a experiência mostra que esses obstáculos podem ser superados através da educação, cooperação e persistência.

EMPOWERMENT DOS TRABALHADORES

Para que as empresas americanas sobrevivam na competição global, é obrigatório que elas recorram e apliquem toda a capacidade e energia de seus empregados. Conforme discutimos em diversos lugares neste livro, a melhoria contínua dos custos de produção, qualidade de produto, tempos de entrega e satisfação do cliente são os meios pelos quais as empresas atuais ganharão fatias de mercado. Os empregados — trabalhadores do setor de produção, trabalhadores de escritório, gerentes, engenheiros e cientistas, todos juntos — formam o recurso central que é a força para se obter excelência na produção e para ganhar fatias de mercado.

Como as empresas recorrem e aplicam esse poderoso recurso para obter excelência? As diretrizes para mudança sugeridas na Tabela 15.3 representam conceitos básicos importantes; porém, mais coisas precisam ser feitas. Quando as empresas empreendem programas de melhoria contínua da administração da qualidade total (TQM), manufatura just-in-time (JIT) e outros programas de excelência radicalmente diferentes, os empregados devem dar um passo adiante e aceitar responsabilidade por todas as facetas da produção. Há algum tempo os gerentes perceberam que não podem controlar tudo na produção; são os empregados que têm controle e conhecem a maior parte dos detalhes da produção. Como os gerentes fazem com que os empregados aceitem essa responsabilidade? *Os gerentes devem, primeiramente, dar aos empregados autoridade para agir.*

O processo de transmitir autoridade da administração para os trabalhadores é denominado **empowerment dos empregados**. Para ver como o empowerment funciona, digamos que um gerente diga a seus trabalhadores que eles têm autoridade para parar as linhas de produção se virem que a qualidade do produto está começando a deteriorar-se. Segurança do trabalhador, problemas de manutenção, escassez de materiais e outras ocorrências podem provocar a necessidade de que a produção seja interrompida. Dar aos trabalhadores a autoridade para parar a produção por esses e outros motivos é talvez a mais visível concessão de autoridade. Os trabalhadores que aceitam a responsabilidade pela produção podem levar àquilo que é chamado **propriedade interna**, em que os trabalhadores sentem que a linha de produção pertence a eles, e eles são responsáveis por tudo o que acontece na produção. Mas a chave para se obter propriedade interna é dar primeiro aos trabalhadores autoridade para agir.

O empowerment dos trabalhadores é a maneira pela qual a administração libera uma força poderosa para trabalhar continuamente rumo à excelência na produção. E excelência na produção é algo de que as companhias necessitam se quiserem obter sucesso na competição global.

ANÁLISE DOS MÉTODOS DE TRABALHO

Na Figura 15.1 podemos ver que as máquinas, ferramentas, materiais e métodos de trabalho usados pelos trabalhadores afetam diretamente a produtividade da mão-de-obra. Como efetuar a melhoria dos métodos de trabalho? Uma boa idéia é iniciarmos com os próprios trabalhadores. Eles fazem seus trabalhos diariamente e, em algumas coisas relacionadas a seu trabalho, eles são especialistas. Além de apresentar algumas sugestões valiosas, os trabalhadores aos quais foi concedido empowerment para melhorar suas próprias funções terão mais probabilidade de fazer e aceitar mudanças.

Comumente, o objetivo de melhorar os métodos de trabalho é aumentar a produtividade aumentando a capacidade de produção de uma operação ou grupo de operações, reduzir os custos das operações, ou melhorar a qualidade do produto.

A chave para a análise de métodos bem-sucedida é o desenvolvimento de uma atitude de questionamento a respeito de cada faceta do trabalho que é estudado. Cada parte do trabalho é necessária? Por que ela é feita dessa maneira? Quem poderia fazê-la melhor? Questões como essas garantem que os analistas não aceitem nada como sagrado numa operação; tudo a respeito do trabalho será escrutado. Quando essa atitude de questionamento for combinada com os princípios da economia de movimentos, os analistas poderão desenvolver melhores métodos de trabalho.

PRINCÍPIOS DA ECONOMIA DE MOVIMENTOS

Na era da administração científica, como vimos no Capítulo 1, pessoas como Frank e Lillian Gilbreth e Frederick Taylor desenvolveram certos princípios a serem seguidos quando se projeta métodos de trabalho. A Tabela 15.4 relaciona alguns dos princípios da economia de movimentos aplicados ao uso do corpo hu-

Tabela 15.4	Princípios da Economia de Movimentos: Uso do Corpo Humano

1. As duas mãos devem iniciar, bem como concluir, seus movimentos ao mesmo tempo.
2. As duas mãos não devem permanecer ociosas ao mesmo tempo, exceto durante períodos de repouso.
3. Os movimentos dos braços devem ser feitos em direções opostas e simétricas, e devem ser feitos simultaneamente.
4. Os movimentos das mãos devem limitar-se à mais baixa classificação com a qual é possível executar o trabalho satisfatoriamente.
5. Impulso deve ser empregado para auxiliar o trabalho sempre que possível, e ele deve ser reduzido a um mínimo se precisar ser superado por esforço muscular.
6. Movimentos contínuos uniformes das mãos são preferíveis a movimentos em ziguezague ou movimentos em linha direta que envolvam mudanças repentinas e abruptas de direção.
7. Movimentos balísticos são mais rápidos, mais fáceis e mais acurados do que movimentos de restrição (fixação) ou controlados.
8. Ritmo é essencial para o desempenho harmonioso e automático de uma operação, e o trabalho deve ser organizado de forma a permitir um ritmo rápido e natural sempre que possível.

Fonte: Barnes, Ralph M., *Motion and Time Study*, 4. ed., p. 214, Nova Iorque, Wiley, 1958.

mano; existem outras categorias como a organização do espaço de trabalho e o projeto de ferramentas e equipamentos, não incluídos aqui. Esses princípios foram desenvolvidos de forma que os trabalhadores pudessem fazer seu trabalho rapidamente e com pouco esforço a fim de que os custos e a fadiga fossem mínimos.

Como Fazer Análise de Métodos

Como realizar a análise dos métodos de trabalho? A Tabela 15.5 relaciona 10 passos que geralmente são seguidos pelos analistas de métodos. Ao realizar análise de métodos, certos diagramas e gráficos podem ser usados.

Tabela 15.5	Procedimentos da Análise de Métodos

1. Faça uma investigação inicial da operação em consideração.
2. Decida qual nível de análise é apropriado.
3. Converse com trabalhadores, supervisores e outros que tenham familiaridade com a operação. Obtenha suas sugestões quanto a maneiras melhores de fazer o trabalho.
4. Estude o método atual. Use cartas de processo, estudo do tempo e outras técnicas de análise apropriadas. (Essas técnicas serão discutidas posteriormente nesta seção.) Descreva e avalie cuidadosamente o método atual.
5. Aplique a atitude de questionamento, os princípios da economia de movimentos e as sugestões de outras pessoas. Idealize um novo método proposto usando cartas de processo e outras técnicas de análise apropriadas.
6. Use estudo do tempo, se necessário. Compare métodos novos e propostos. Obtenha aprovação dos supervisores para prosseguir.
7. Modifique o método proposto quando necessário depois de revisar os detalhes com trabalhadores e supervisores.
8. Treine um ou mais trabalhadores para executar o método proposto experimentalmente. Avalie o método proposto. Modifique o método, quando necessário.
9. Treine trabalhadores e instale o método proposto.
10. Faça verificações periodicamente para assegurar que as economias esperadas estão sendo realizadas.

Diagramas e Gráficos Os **fluxogramas** e as **cartas de processo** são talvez as técnicas mais versáteis disponíveis para analisar métodos de trabalho. Geralmente eles são usados juntos para eliminar ou reduzir atrasos, eliminar ou combinar tarefas, ou reduzir tempo de viagem ou distância. Na Federal Express, fluxograma e cartas de processo eram usados para reduzir o tempo necessário para atender as reivindicações dos clientes de seis semanas em média para somente um dia. O Exemplo 15.1 ilustra como uma grande companhia de seguros usa fluxogramas e cartas de processo para melhorar os métodos de trabalho de funcionários que preparam repetitivamente certo tipo de formulário. Leia o exemplo e observe que primeiramente o método atual é estudado, depois um novo e melhorado método é desenvolvido, os dois métodos são comparados, e o melhor é selecionado.

EXEMPLO 15.1

ANÁLISE DE MÉTODOS NA AMERICAN INSURANCE COMPANY

O trabalho se avolumava no departamento de reclamações de seguros na American Insurance Company, porque muitos formulários de autorização para investigar tinham de ser processados. Considerou-se que a carga de trabalho poderia ser reduzida se os métodos de processamento dos formulários pudessem ser modernizados.

SOLUÇÃO

1. Prepare um fluxograma e uma carta de processo do método atual (veja a Figura 15.3).
2. Desenvolva um método melhorado e prepare um fluxograma e uma carta de processo do novo método proposto (veja a Figura 15.4).
3. Compare os dois métodos e escolha o melhor. Quais são as principais melhorias no novo método (veja a Tabela 15.6)?

Quais são as principais melhorias do método proposto?

1. Ele elimina recuperações de arquivos de clientes ao anexar ao pedido o formulário de reclamações do departamento de reclamações. Toda a informação necessária sobre o cliente está contida nesse formulário previamente preenchido.
2. Ele elimina a necessidade de funcionários para obter a aprovação do diretor da seção ao utilizar o serviço de correspondência existente entre escritórios.

Há diversas formas de **cartas de atividades múltiplas**, mas todas têm uma coisa em comum: mostram como um ou mais trabalhadores trabalham juntos e/ou com máquinas. Uma **carta homem-máquina**, por exemplo, poderia mostrar como um funcionário de uma mercearia trabalha com um cliente e com uma máquina de moagem de café para produzir café em pó para o cliente. Essas cartas são úteis para minimizar atrasos de trabalhador e máquina e determinar o número ótimo de máquinas por trabalhador.

Não obstante a análise de métodos ser um elemento importante para se obter elevada produtividade de mão-de-obra, a medida do trabalho também é útil.

MEDIDA DO TRABALHO

Quais unidades de medida devemos usar para medir o trabalho humano? Libras/pé, calorias por minuto e outras unidades têm sido usadas nas ciências físicas para medir o trabalho. Mas, nas operações, deve ser usada uma unidade de trabalho que seja tanto facilmente medida como facilmente entendida. A unidade de medida que se desenvolveu foi a **minutos-trabalhador por unidade de produção**. Em outras palavras, quantos minutos geralmente são necessários para que um trabalhador bem treinado, em média, produza

FIGURA 15.3 FLUXOGRAMA E CARTA DE PROCESSO: MÉTODO ATUAL PARA PREENCHER FORMULÁRIOS DE AUTORIZAÇÃO PARA INVESTIGAR

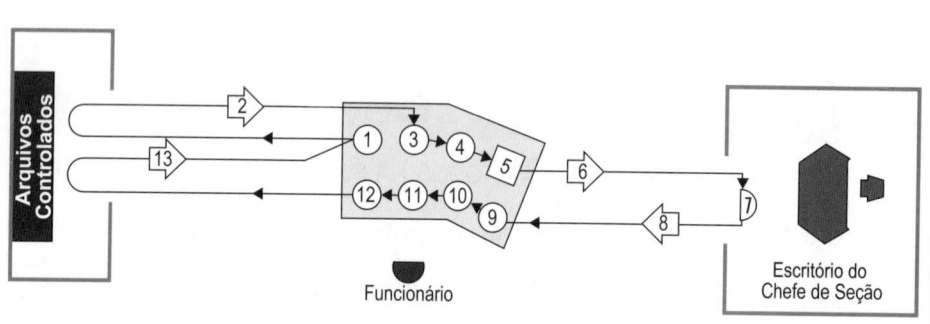

Capítulo 15 – Produtividade, Trabalho em Equipe e Empowerment

FIGURA 15.4 FLUXOGRAMA E CARTA DE PROCESSO: MÉTODO PROPOSTO PARA PREENCHER FORMULÁRIOS DE AUTORIZAÇÃO PARA INVESTIGAR

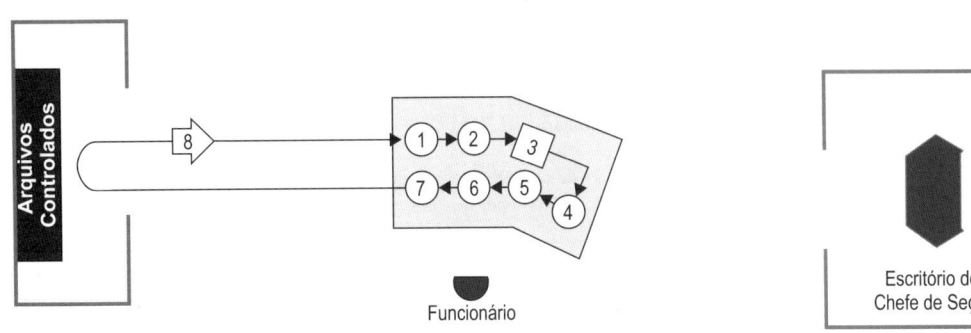

N.	Distância Deslocada (pés)	Tempo de Trabalhador (Min.)	Símbolos	Descrição
1		0,200		Retirar do cesto o pedido do Departamento de Reclamações com o formulário de reclamação do cliente anexado.
2		4,750		Digitar informações sobre autorização no formulário de investigação.
3		0,500		Formulário de inspeção.
4		0,100		Anexar lista de circulação ao formulário preenchido e colocar na cesta de correspondência na escrivaninha.
5		0,200		Retirar formulário aprovado da cesta e e dispô-lo em folhas separadas.
6		1,750		Preparar cópia do investigador regional para enviar pelo correio e colocar na cesta de correspondência na escrivaninha.
7		1,500		Preparar cópia do Departamento de Reclamações para encaminhar e colocar na cesta de correspondência na escrivaninha.
8	55	3,250		Dirigir-se à área de arquivamento, rearquivar e voltar à escrivaninha.

Operação: Preencher autorização
Produto: Formulário para investigar
Deptos.: Perda de propriedade
Desenho n. ___ **Peça n.** ___
Quantidade: Um formulário em triplicata
Atual ___ **Proposto** ✓

Folha 1 **de** 1 **Folhas**
Preparado por: João Torres
Data: 20/9
Aprovado por: Marcos Gonçalves
Data: 21/9

Resumo
- Operação: 6
- Transporte: 1
- Inspeção: 1
- Atraso: —
- Armazenar: —
- Distância vertical: —
- Distância horizontal: 55 pés
- Tempo (horas): 12,250

Tabela 15.6 — Comparação de Métodos Atuais e Propostos para Preencher Formulários de Autorização para Investigar — Departamento de Perda de Propriedade

Fator de Comparação	Método de Comparação	Método Proposto	Economias Estimadas
Distância percorrida pelo formulário (em pés)	180	55	125
Número de operações por formulário	7	6	1
Número de inspeções por formulário	1	1	—
Número de atrasos por formulário	1	—	1
Minutos por formulário	16,000	12,250	3,750
Formulário de custos de mão-de-obra ($ 10 por hora)	$ 2,667	$ 2,042	$ 0,624
Custo anual de mão-de-obra (300.000 por mês por ano)	$ 799.800	$ 612.600	$ 187.200

um componente, submontagem, produto ou serviço? Portanto, **medida do trabalho** refere-se ao processo de estimar a quantidade de tempo de trabalhador necessário para gerar uma unidade de produção. A meta final da medida do trabalho geralmente é desenvolver padrões de mão-de-obra que sejam usados para planejar e controlar operações, obtendo-se assim elevada produtividade de mão-de-obra.

PADRÕES DE MÃO-DE-OBRA

Um **padrão de mão-de-obra** é o número de minutos por trabalhador necessário para concluir um elemento, operação ou produto sob condições operacionais comuns. O termo **condições operacionais comuns** refere-se a uma situação *média* hipotética — capacidade dos trabalhadores, velocidade de trabalho, condição das máquinas, suprimento de materiais, disponibilidade de informações, presença de estresse físico ou psicológico, e todos os outros aspectos das funções dos trabalhadores.

Padrões de trabalho são usados para planejar e controlar operações. Por exemplo, quando conhecemos a quantidade de minutos por trabalhador necessária para cada produto, podemos estimar o número de trabalhadores necessários num departamento de produção. Além disso, padrões de trabalho podem ser usados para determinar se a mão-de-obra de um departamento de produção está apresentando um desempenho acima, abaixo ou dentro do padrão. Além disso, padrões de mão-de-obra são usados para desenvolver padrões de custo de mão-de-obra contábeis. Esses padrões de custo são especialmente úteis nas estimativas de custo, relatórios da variância do custo de mão-de-obra e no estabelecimento de preços de novos produtos. Os padrões de mão-de-obra também são usados nos sistemas de pagamento de incentivo.

Sistemas de Pagamento de Incentivo Um **sistema de pagamento de incentivo** condiciona o valor do pagamento aos trabalhadores ao desempenho no trabalho. Por exemplo, com um plano de pagamento por peça produzida um trabalhador receberia uma quantia específica por unidade produzida. Alternativamente, com um pagamento de participação nos ganhos, o valor do pagamento seria ajustado proporcionalmente ao desempenho. Os bônus de participação nos lucros são uma outra forma de pagamento de incentivo.

Não obstante os sistemas de pagamento de incentivo terem diminuído em popularidade nos Estados Unidos, seu uso ainda é comum, especialmente em empresas e indústrias em que a tradição determina pagamentos de incentivo. Em empresas japonesas como a Toyota, os cheques de pagamento dos trabalhadores são afetados por "tolerâncias de produção". Essas "tolerâncias" se baseiam na produção da equipe de trabalho durante um mês. Nos Estados Unidos existe uma enorme variedade de sistemas de pagamento de incentivo, e, à medida que as negociações de contrato entre sindicatos e administrações se desenvolvem, o mesmo acontece com esses sistemas. Cada vez mais as empresas estão usando sistemas de pagamento de incentivo baseados na equipe. Esses sistemas destacam o trabalho em equipe ao recompensar indivíduos baseando-se na contribuição que eles dão para as metas da equipe através de revisões dos colegas.

Essas abordagens são usadas para definir padrões de mão-de-obra: estudo do tempo, amostragem do trabalho e métodos de tempo predeterminado.

TABELA 15.7 — Passos para Determinar Padrões de Mão-de-Obra a Partir de Estudos do Tempo

1. Certifique-se de que o método correto está sendo usado para executar a operação que é estudada.

2. Determine quantos ciclos cronometrar. Um **ciclo** é um conjunto completo de tarefas elementares incluído na operação. Geralmente, mais ciclos devem ser cronometrados quando os tempos de ciclo são breves, quando os tempos de ciclo são altamente variáveis, e quando a produção anual do produto é elevada.

3. Divida a operação em tarefas básicas, também chamadas **elementos** (pegar a peça, prendê-la contra a esmerilhadeira, ajustar a máquina etc.).

4. Observe a operação e use um cronômetro para registrar o tempo transcorrido para cada elemento durante o número de ciclos necessários. Os **tempos observados do elemento** são registrados em minutos.

5. Para cada tarefa elementar, estime o ritmo em que o trabalhador está trabalhando. Um **ritmo igual** a 1,00 indica que o trabalhador está trabalhando a uma velocidade normal, que é a velocidade na qual um trabalhador bem treinado trabalharia sob condições operacionais comuns. Um ritmo igual a 1,20 indica uma velocidade 20% maior do que a normal, e um ritmo igual a 0,80 indica uma velocidade 20% menor do que a normal.

6. Compute um **fator de tolerância** para a operação. O fator de tolerância é a fração do tempo na qual os trabalhadores não podem trabalhar sem que isso seja uma falha deles. Por exemplo, se os trabalhadores não puderem trabalhar 15% do tempo devido ao trabalho de limpeza, intervalos de descanso, reuniões da companhia etc., o fator de tolerância será 0,15.

7. Determine o **tempo médio observado** para cada elemento dividindo a soma dos tempos normais pelo número de ciclos cronometrados.

8. Compute o **tempo normal** para cada elemento:

$$\text{Tempo normal} = \text{Tempo médio observado} \times \text{Ritmo}$$

9. Compute o **tempo normal total** para a operação inteira somando os tempos normais para todos os elementos.

10. Compute o **padrão de mão-de-obra** ou **tempo padrão** para a operação:

$$\text{Padrão de mão-de-obra} = \text{Tempo normal} \div (1 - \text{Fator de tolerância})$$

Estudo do Tempo

No **estudo do tempo**, os analistas cronometram a operação que é executada pelos trabalhadores. Esses tempos observados são então convertidos em padrões de mão-de-obra que são expressos em minutos por unidade de produção para a operação.

A Tabela 15.7 relaciona os passos empregados pelos analistas para determinar padrões de mão-de-obra baseados no estudo do tempo.

O Exemplo 15.2 demonstra os passos para computar um padrão de mão-de-obra a partir de um estudo do tempo.

Não obstante o estudo do tempo fornecer precisão para se determinar padrões de mão-de-obra, na maioria das situações ele requer uma equipe de analistas competente. Outra dificuldade é que o padrão de mão-de-obra não pode ser determinado antes que a operação seja realizada de fato. Essas desvantagens levaram ao desenvolvimento de outras técnicas de medida do trabalho.

Exemplo 15.2

Definindo Padrões de Mão-de-Obra com o Estudo do Tempo

Um novo *Manual de Inscrição,* a ser distribuído a todos os estudantes, é proposto para a Metro University. O reitor pondera qual seria o custo de mão-de-obra para 30.000 dos folhetos de 12 páginas.

O reitor pediu a um estudante de administração para investigar o problema e relatar os resultados. O estudante achou que uma boa maneira de estimar o custo de mão-de-obra seria:

1. Treinar um trabalhador para fazer a intercalação dos folhetos.
2. Realizar um estudo do tempo do trabalhador enquanto alguns dos folhetos eram intercalados.
3. Usar os resultados de estudo do tempo para computar um padrão de trabalho para a intercalação dos folhetos.
4. Usar o padrão de mão-de-obra para estimar o custo de mão-de-obra do projeto inteiro.

Solução

O estudante seguiu os passos da Tabela 15.7 e realizou um estudo do tempo do trabalhador enquanto os folhetos eram intercalados. Os resultados do estudo do tempo são encontrados na Figura 15.5. A partir do estudo do tempo, o estudante soube que cada folheto exigiria 0,4482 minuto do tempo de um trabalhador. Além disso, o custo de mão-de-obra dos trabalhadores na bancada de trabalho é $ 5 por hora, e cerca de 15% do tempo de cada trabalhador é gasto em limpeza da área da bancada de trabalho, tempo pessoal, atrasos inevitáveis e outras atividades não produtivas.

1. Compute o custo de mão-de-obra por folheto:

Custo de mão-de-obra por unidade = Padrão de mão-de-obra × Custo de mão-de-obra por minuto
= 0,4482 minuto × ($ 5 por hora ÷ 60 minutos por hora)
= $ 0,03735 por folheto

2. Compute o custo total de mão-de-obra para o projeto:

Custo de mão-de-obra total para o projeto = Número de folhetos × Custo de mão-de-obra por unidade
= 30.000 × $ 0,03735 = $ 1.120,50

Amostragem do Trabalho

Amostragem do trabalho é uma técnica de medida do trabalho que colhe aleatoriamente amostras do trabalho de um ou mais empregados em intervalos periódicos para determinar a proporção da operação total que é considerada numa atividade em particular. Esses estudos freqüentemente são usados para estimar a porcentagem do tempo dos empregados gasto em atividades como estas: atrasos inevitáveis, comumente chamados estudos da razão-atraso; reparo de produtos acabados de uma operação; ou fornecimento de material a uma operação. Os resultados desses estudos comumente são utilizados para definir as tolerâncias usadas para computar padrões de mão-de-obra, para estimar custos de certas atividades e para investigar métodos de trabalho.

Amostragem do trabalho também é usada para definir padrões de mão-de-obra. O Exemplo 15.3 usa um estudo de amostragem do trabalho para definir um padrão de mão-de-obra para que o pessoal do faturamento realize verificações de crédito de possíveis clientes. Nesse caso, o propósito do padrão de mão-de-obra é estimar o número de pessoal do faturamento que seria necessário se um novo departamento de verificação de crédito fosse estabelecido.

Capítulo 15 – Produtividade, Trabalho em Equipe e Empowerment

FIGURA 15.5 — O ESTUDO PARA INTERCALAR FOLHETOS

Estudo do Tempo

Operação: Intercalar Materiais para Folhetos Universitários			
Departamento: Pool de Trabalho Universitário	Início: 12:10	Data: 8/15	Operadora: Suzanne Ogden
Peça:	Parada: 12:14	Turno: 2	H. M. ✓
Tamanho: Folheto de 8,5" x 11"	Diferença (tempo transcorrido): 4 minutos	Estudo: 1	Analista: Mary Delaney
	Produção: 10 folhetos	Folha: 1	
	Tempo estimado: 0,400 minuto por folheto		
Observações: 12 pilhas são organizadas em duas fileiras de 6 pilhas cada uma numa mesa larga			

Elementos	Ciclos																Resumo			
	1	2	3	4	5	6	7	8	9	10	11	12	13	14	15	Soma	Média	Ritmo	Normal
1. Intercalar Fila n. 1	0,10	0,09	0,09	0,08	0,08	0,09	0,07	0,10	0,08	0,09						0,87	0,087	1,00	0,087
2. Bater folheto para ajustar as margens	0,04	0,03	0,04	0,05	0,03	0,04	0,04	0,04	0,03	0,05						0,39	0,039	0,90	0,035
3. Intercalar Fila n. 2																			
4. Bater folheto para ajustar as margens	0,12	0,09	0,10	0,09	0,10	0,10	0,09	0,08	0,11	0,10						0,98	0,098	1,00	0,098
5. Grampear folheto	0,04	0,02	0,03	0,05	0,03	0,04	0,04	0,03	0,05	0,04						0,37	0,037	0,90	0,033
6. Pôr ao lado																			
7. Elementos diversos	0,06	0,06	0,07	0,05	0,07	0,06	0,06	0,06	0,08	0,05						0,62	0,062	1,10	0,068
a) Aplicar "adesivo" aos dedos	0,02	0,03	0,04	0,04	0,03	0,03	0,03	0,04	0,04	0,03						0,33	0,033	1,00	0,033
b) Endireitar pilhas						0,06										0,06	0,006	1,00	0,006
								0,21								0,21	0,021	1,00	0,021
																		Total	0,381

Padrão de mão-de-obra = Tempo Total Normal ÷ (1 – Fator de tolerância) = 0,381 ÷ (1 – 0,15) = 0,4482 minuto por folheto

---

EXEMPLO 15.3

DEFININDO PADRÕES DE MÃO-DE-OBRA COM AMOSTRAGEM DO TRABALHO

O departamento de faturamento da Gasco, a empresa de serviços públicos que fornece gás natural para a região metropolitana de Los Angeles, Califórnia, tem funcionários que executam estas atividades: (1) examinar as contas dos clientes, (2) fazer correções nas contas dos clientes e (3) executar verificações de crédito de possíveis clientes. A Gasco cresceu tão rapidamente nos últimos anos que a carga de trabalho de verificação de créditos está aumentando rapidamente. O gerente do departamento de faturamento prevê que 150 mil verificações de crédito terão de ser feitas pelo departamento no próximo ano e deseja saber quantos funcionários serão necessários para realizar essas verificações. Um analista é designado para a tarefa de estimar o número de funcionários que seriam necessários. Este procedimento deve ser seguido na investigação:

1. Execute um estudo da amostragem do trabalho para determinar a proporção de tempo que um funcionário necessita para fazer verificações de crédito.
2. Compute um padrão de trabalho para cada verificação de crédito baseando-se no estudo da amostragem do trabalho.
3. Compute o número de funcionários necessários para realizar verificações de crédito no próximo ano.

Solução

1. Determine quantas observações de amostragem do trabalho são necessárias: O pessoal do departamento estimou que as verificações de crédito representaram cerca de 25% das tarefas dos funcionários. O analista consultou a Tabela 15.8 e determinou que um intervalo de confiança de 95% e um erro absoluto de ±3% exigiriam 833 observações de amostragem do trabalho. Isso significa que o analista teria 95% de confiança de que um valor entre 22% e 28% do trabalho de um funcionário seria dedicado a verificações de crédito.
2. Determine o intervalo de tempo entre as observações de amostragem do trabalho e o tempo total do estudo: O analista planejou estudar um único funcionário durante 2,5 horas, tirando instantâneos da amostragem do trabalho a cada 10 segundos, para um total de 900 observações (6/minuto × 60 minutos/hora × 2,5 horas = 900). Em cada instantâneo, o analista registrava se o funcionário estava fazendo verificações de crédito.
3. Execute o estudo de amostragem do trabalho e compute o padrão de mão-de-obra para a verificação de crédito:

Tipo de Dados	Dados
Tempo de estudo transcorrido (2,5 × 60 minutos/hora)	150 minutos
Número total de observações durante o estudo	0,900
Número de observações de verificações de crédito durante o estudo	0,211
Proporção do trabalho dos funcionários que foi dedicada a verificações de crédito	0,234
Número de verificações de crédito concluídas durante o estudo	10
Classificação do desempenho do funcionário	1,10
Fator de tolerância	0,20

$$\text{Tempo para verificação de crédito} = \left(\text{Tempo de estudo transcorrido}\right) \times \left(\text{Proporção do trabalho que foi dedicado a verificações}\right) \div \left(\text{Número de verificações de crédito concluídas}\right)$$

$$= 150 \times 0{,}234 \div 10 = 3{,}51$$

Tempo normal total = Tempo por verificação de crédito × Ritmo
= 3,51 × 1,10 = 3,861 minutos

Padrão de mão-de-obra = (Tempo normal total) ÷ (1 − Fator de tolerância)
= 3,861 ÷ (1 − 0,20)
= 4,82625 minutos por verificação de crédito

4. Compute o número de funcionários necessários por verificações de crédito no próximo ano:

$$\text{Número de funcionários por ano} = \left(\text{Número de verificações previstas para o próximo ano}\right) \times \left(\text{Padrão de mão-de-obra para verificações de crédito}\right) \div \left(\text{Minutos/ano que os funcionários trabalham}\right)$$

= (150.000 × 4,82625) ÷ (50 semanas/ano × 2.400 minutos/semana)
= 6,03, ou ligeiramente mais do que 6 funcionários

A amostragem do trabalho é menos dispendiosa do que o estudo do tempo, mas geralmente fornece menos precisão. A amostragem do trabalho geralmente é preferida quando muitos trabalhadores executam uma única operação que se espalha por uma grande região geográfica. Nesses casos, um único analista poderia observar todos os trabalhadores em intervalos de tempo fixos; digamos, tomando um instantâneo a cada 10 segundos. Essa "amostragem" das atividades dos empregados permite que os analistas dividam uma operação em elementos e registrem qual elemento cada empregado está executando quando o instantâneo de amostragem do trabalho é tomado. O número de vezes que cada elemento é executado num turno de oito horas torna-se a base para o padrão de mão-de-obra.

Padrões de Tempo Predeterminados

Quando padrões de mão-de-obra precisam ser determinados antes de se executar uma operação, **padrões de tempo predeterminados** podem ser usados. Esses padrões utilizam dados que foram desenvolvidos historicamente para movimentos corporais básicos, elementos de operações e operações inteiras. Quando estimativas de custo ou informações sobre preços são necessárias para novas operações ou novos produtos, esses padrões comumente são usados.

TABELA 15.8 — UM GUIA PARA O NÚMERO MÍNIMO DE OBSERVAÇÕES DE AMOSTRAGEM DO TRABALHO

Porcentagem da Atividade [p ou (1 − p)]	Erro Absoluto ±1%	±2%	±3%
1 ou 99	396	99	44
5 ou 95	1.900	475	211
10 ou 90	3.600	900	400
15 ou 85	5.100	1.275	567
20 ou 80	6.400	1.600	711
25 ou 75	7.500	1.875	833
30 ou 70	8.400	2.100	933
35 ou 65	9.100	2.275	1.011
40 ou 60	9.600	2.400	1.067
45 ou 55	9.900	2.475	1.099
50	10.000	2.500	1.111

Observação: Essa tabela se baseia num intervalo de confiança de 95%. Erro absoluto significa a faixa de observações reais de p, que é a porcentagem do trabalho total dedicado a uma atividade em particular. Por exemplo, se $p = 25\%$ e a coluna de $\pm 2\%$ fosse usada, poderíamos dizer que tínhamos 95% de confiança de que p variasse entre 23% e 27%. Erros absolutos menores exigem números maiores de observações de amostragem do trabalho.

Muitos sistemas de padrões de tempo predeterminados são usados atualmente — sistema fatores-trabalho, método MTM de medida de tempo, sistema para estudo de tempos por movimentos básicos (BMT), e uma enorme quantidade de sistemas projetados de forma personalizada para companhias individuais.

Para demonstrar o uso desses sistemas, examinamos o desenvolvimento de padrões MTM no Exemplo 15.4. Nesse exemplo, um gerente deve estimar o custo da mão-de-obra para uma operação de inspeção e limpeza de diodos elétricos determinada recentemente.

O MTM é uma excelente opção quando um trabalho de montagem ultraleve deve ser executado numa área pequena e quando padrões de mão-de-obra rápidos, acurados e de baixo custo são necessários.

EXEMPLO 15.4

DESENVOLVENDO PADRÕES DE MÃO-DE-OBRA COM O MTM

Carlos Sanchez, superintendente de produção da Diocom, que manufatura diodos para a indústria eletrônica, solicitou há pouco uma estimativa dos custos de mão-de-obra adicionais se o diodo XG1500 da companhia tivesse de ser inspecionado e limpo. Essa solicitação resultou de algumas falhas de componentes em campo. Amanda Jones, engenheira de produção, recebeu um relatório sobre como a nova operação de inspeção seria executada. Ela diz a Carlos que obterá uma estimativa em uma hora.

Amanda Jones sabe que não obstante o pessoal da Diocom jamais haver executado a operação de inspeção e limpeza, uma boa estimativa de mão-de-obra poderia ser desenvolvida usando-se o método MTM de medida de tempo. Ela pegou seu manual MTM, anotou as atividades para a mão direita e para a mão esquerda, estimou as distâncias a serem percorridas, descreveu a natureza dos movimentos das mãos e examinou as TMUs (unidades de tempo de medição) para cada atividade. Uma TMU é igual a 1/100.000 de uma hora. Os resultados dessa análise se encontram na Tabela 15.9.

Uma vez que Amanda estima que 80 minutos por turno serão inevitavelmente improdutivos, ela calcula o seguinte:

TABELA 15.9   CÁLCULO DO PADRÃO DE MÃO-DE-OBRA MTM PARA A OPERAÇÃO DE INSPEÇÃO E LIMPEZA DO DIODO XG1500

Mão esquerda	Código MTM	TMU (1/100.000 hora)	Código MTM	Mão direita
1. Alcance a caixa de componentes elétricos.	R10C	12,9		
2. Pegue o componente a ser testado.	G4B	9,1		
3. Mova o componente até o terminal exposto do medidor de inspeção (10 polegadas).	M10A*	11,3		
4. Posicione o componente no medidor de teste.	P2SS	19,7		
5. Observe a luz de continuidade elétrica.	EF	7,3		
6. Transfira o componente para a outra mão.	G3	5,6	G3	Pegue o componente.
		9,2	M5C	7. Mova o componente até a roda de abrasão.
		19,7	P2SS	8. Posicione o componente na roda de abrasão.
		8,0	M5B	9. Mova o componente até a caixa.
		2,0	RL1	10. Solte o componente.

Total TMU = 104,8 unidades
= 104,8 ÷ 100.000 = 0,001048 hora
= 0,001048 × 60 = 0,0629 minuto

*Examine essa TMU na Tabela 15.10.

Fator de tolerância = (Minutos de tolerância) ÷ Minutos por turno
= 80 minutos ÷ 480 minutos = 0,1667

Padrão de mão-de-obra = Tempo normal ÷ (1 − Fator de tolerância)
= 0,0629 minuto ÷ (1 − 0,1667) = 0,0755 minuto por diodo XG1500

Custo padrão = Padrão de mão-de-obra × Custo de mão-de-obra por minuto
= 0,0755 minuto × $ 0,129 por minuto = $ 0,0097 por diodo XG1500

Amanda retornou à reunião e contou a Carlos os resultados de sua análise MTM: o padrão de mão-de-obra estimado para a operação de inspeção e limpeza era 0,0755 minuto por diodo, e o custo de mão-de-obra estimado era $ 0,0097 por diodo. Ela pegou a tabela para a ação básica *Movimento* (Tabela 15.10) para demonstrar como o padrão fora estimado. Amanda explicou a terceira atividade da mão esquerda, M10A. Para encontrar isso, examine a distância movimentada de 10 polegadas, percorra a Coluna A e leia a TMU — 11,3, que está na faixa de 100.000-ésimos de uma hora. Isso é convertido para horas e minutos dividindo-se por 100.000 e multiplicando-se o resultado por 60.

Padrões de trabalho também podem ser estimados subjetivamente. Por exemplo, **padrões de mão-de-obra históricos** são determinados usando-se dados históricos do desempenho real da operação. Não obstante esse procedimento ser de baixo custo, rápido e fácil de entender, ele tem uma falha fundamental. Uma vez que nenhuma tentativa de melhorar os métodos de trabalho está envolvida, o uso de padrões de mão-de-obra provavelmente perpetuará métodos de trabalho malfeitos. **Padrões de tamanho da equipe** são determinados estimando-se o número total de trabalhadores necessários para produzir a demanda necessária por turno. Esse número total de trabalhadores-minuto por turno é então dividido pela demanda necessária por turno. **Estimativas de supervisores** também são usadas ocasionalmente. Esses padrões se baseiam no íntimo conhecimento que os supervisores têm das operações pelas quais eles são responsáveis.

TABELA 15.10   MTM — TMUs PARA MOVIMENTAR OBJETOS COM MÃOS E BRAÇOS (MOVIMENTO — M)

Distância Movimentada (polegadas)	Tempo TMU				Tolerância de Peso			Caso e Descrição
	A	B	C	Mão em Movimento B	Peso (libras) Até	Fator Dinâmico	TMU Estática Constante	
–	2,0	2,0	2,0	1,7				
1	2,5	2,9	3,4	2,3	2,5	1,00	0	A. Mova o objeto para a outra mão ou contra o terminal.
2	3,6	4,6	5,2	2,9				
3	4,9	5,7	6,7	3,6	7,5	1,06	2,2	
4	6,1	6,9	8,0	4,3				
5	7,3	8,0	9,2	5,0	12,5	1,11	3,9	
6	8,1	8,9	10,3	5,7				
7	8,9	9,7	11,1	6,5	17,5	1,17	5,6	B. Mova o objeto para aproximar ou para uma localização indefinida.
8	9,7	10,6	11,8	7,2				
9	10,5	11,5	12,7	7,9	22,5	1,22	7,4	
10	11,3	12,2	13,5	8,6				
12	12,9	13,4	15,2	10,0	27,5	1,28	9,1	
14	14,4	14,6	16,9	11,4				
16	16,0	15,8	18,7	12,8	32,5	1,33	10,8	
18	17,6	17,0	20,4	14,2				
20	19,2	18,2	22,1	15,6	37,5	1,39	12,5	C. Mova o objeto para o local exato.
22	20,8	19,4	23,8	17,0				
24	22,4	20,6	25,5	18,4	42,5	1,44	14,3	
26	24,0	21,8	27,3	19,8				
28	25,5	23,1	29,0	21,2	47,5	1,50	16,0	
30	27,1	24,3	30,7	22,7				
Adicional	0,8	0,6	0,85		TMU por polegada ao longo de 30 polegadas			

Fonte: © MTM Association for Standards and Research.

Esses e outros padrões de trabalho estimados subjetivamente são famosos por ser usados na indústria. Entretanto, o uso dos mesmos se limita àquelas situações em que técnicas mais dispendiosas podem não ser economicamente justificáveis.

Estudo do tempo, amostragem do trabalho, padrões de tempo predeterminados e padrões de mão-de-obra fixados subjetivamente podem ser todos técnicas apropriadas de medida do trabalho, dependendo da natureza do trabalho considerado.

A Tabela 15.11 descreve algumas funções para as quais cada uma dessas técnicas é apropriada. Independentemente das técnicas de medida do trabalho empregadas para desenvolver padrões de mão-de-obra, suas metas finais são as mesmas:

1. Fixar marcos ou padrões em relação aos quais medir o desempenho real das operações. O objetivo é melhorar a produtividade.
2. Estabelecer estimativas do conteúdo de mão-de-obra nas operações como um auxílio de planejamento para os gerentes de operações. Essas estimativas podem ser usadas para comparar métodos de produção, fazer estimativas de custo, determinar preços de produtos e definir taxas de pagamento de incentivo.

TABELA 15.11	TÉCNICAS APROPRIADAS DE MEDIDA DO TRABALHO PARA ALGUMAS FUNÇÕES
Função	**Técnica Apropriada de Medida do Trabalho**
1. Uma função desempenhada por um único trabalhador num local fixo. O trabalho envolve ciclos breves repetitivos e se espera que ela permaneça imutável por longos períodos enquanto produz grandes quantidades de produto. Os padrões de mão-de-obra resultantes devem ser muito acurados.	Estudo do tempo
2. Uma função desempenhada por um único trabalhador num local fixo. O trabalho envolve ciclos breves repetitivos e eles serão modificados periodicamente à medida que pedidos de quantidades relativamente pequenas de produtos se modificarem. Os padrões de mão-de-obra são usados para contabilizar padrões de custo, análises de preços e planejamento da produção.	Padrões de tempo predeterminados
3. Uma função desempenhada por muitos trabalhadores numa área compacta. As tarefas podem envolver pouca repetição; mas, se forem repetitivas, os ciclos geralmente serão muito longos. Os trabalhadores devem ser observados por um único analista. Não obstante um grau moderado de precisão nos padrões de mão-de-obra ser desejado, um estudo do tempo seria demasiadamente custoso. Somente grandes elementos de trabalho precisam ser observados; pouco detalhe é necessário para definir os padrões de mão-de-obra.	Amostragem do trabalho
4. Qualquer trabalho ou grupo de trabalho no qual padrões de mão-de-obra muito precisos não sejam necessários ou nos quais o custo de um estudo do tempo, padrões de tempo predeterminados e amostragem do trabalho seja proibitivo.	Padrões de mão-de-obra fixados subjetivamente

Os padrões de mão-de-obra são dinâmicos e devem modificar-se à medida que as condições de trabalho se modificam. A natureza dinâmica dos padrões de mão-de-obra é importante, porque, à medida que as empresas lutam pela melhoria contínua, os padrões devem ajustar-se aos novos e melhorados métodos de trabalho. Um tipo de mudança que afeta todos os empregos é que os trabalhadores aprendem, e à medida que eles aprendem os tempos de produção se diminuem.

SAÚDE E SEGURANÇA DOS EMPREGADOS

Riscos são inerentes à maioria dos empregos. Empregados podem cair em pisos escorregadios; cair de escadas; contundir-se; ter partes de suas roupas ou do corpo presas em correias, engrenagens, ferramentas de corte e prensas de perfurar; ser atingidos por fragmentos arremessados por rodas esmerilhadeiras e lascas de metal de tornos etc. Poços de elevador, degraus, sacadas, equipamentos pesados em movimento, caminhões, incêndios, explosões, eletricidade de alta voltagem, metais fundidos, produtos químicos tóxicos, vapores nocivos, poeira e ruído — tudo constitui perigo para os empregados. Esses e outros riscos sempre estão à volta. Eles não são novos. O que talvez seja novo é o crescente conjunto de leis e regulamentos governamentais que pretendem garantir aos empregados condições de trabalho seguras em todas as indústrias.

A administração tem se preocupado com a segurança e saúde dos empregados. Essa preocupação se tornou evidente no estabelecimento de departamentos de segurança e prevenção de acidentes no início do século XX, antes que as leis forçassem rigidamente os empregadores a cumprir padrões de segurança impostos pelo governo. O movimento da administração de pessoal no início de 1900 e o movimento das relações humanas na década de 1940 contribuíram, ambos, para esse desenvolvimento. Esses movimentos enfatizaram a necessidade de se proteger os empregados no emprego e contribuíram diretamente para o número crescente de programas formais de segurança no governo e na indústria.

Nos Estados Unidos, dois conjuntos de leis afetaram criticamente a saúde e a segurança dos empregados: as **leis de compensação do trabalhador** e a Occupational Safety and Health Administration Act (OSHA). Durante o início dos anos 1900, o Estado gradativamente aprovou **leis de compensação do trabalhador**, que cuidavam dos valores de compensação aos empregados por vários tipos de danos sofridos no trabalho. Os empregados não mais necessitavam mover ações judiciais e provar negligência dos empregadores. Adicionalmente, os empregadores eram protegidos pela limitação máxima dessas disposições, e o número de ações judiciais foi reduzido.

Não obstante as leis de compensação ao trabalhador terem avançado muito em termos de compensar os empregados depois que eles se feriam no trabalho, três fatos depreciavam sua eficácia para garantir condições de trabalho seguras:

1. Uma vez que as leis variavam grandemente entre estados e indústrias, essa colcha de retalhos de regulamentações criou grandes falhas na cobertura e variações extremas na compensação por danos similares.
2. A inflação e a enorme elevação do custo de atendimento à saúde tornaram os valores de compensação da maioria dessas leis inadequados.
3. As leis não vão diretamente ao cerne do problema da saúde e segurança dos trabalhadores — criar um ambiente de trabalho seguro para os empregados.

Essas e outras deficiências das leis de compensação do trabalhador e outros desenvolvimentos contemporâneos levaram à aprovação, em 1971, da **Occupational Safety and Health Administration Act (OSHA)**. A OSHA estabeleceu uma agência federal cujas funções principais eram definir padrões de segurança para todas as áreas do ambiente de trabalho para todas as indústrias e impor esses padrões através de um sistema de inspeção e reportagem. Essa lei reconheceu oficialmente, talvez pela primeira vez, o direito básico de todos os empregados a um ambiente de trabalho seguro, independentemente do estado, indústria ou empresa em que ele trabalhasse.

Nenhuma companhia americana está fora do alcance da OSHA. Seus inspetores convocam rotineiramente empregadores, realizam inspeções, identificam condições de trabalho inseguras ou violações dos padrões da OSHA, exigem ações corretivas dos empregadores, e a lei pode forçar o cumprimento através dos tribunais com multas e até mesmo processo criminal. A OSHA é, de fato, uma força potencial com a qual a administração deve lidar. Mas a OSHA não está isenta de críticas. Com somente 1.200 inspetores, a OSHA tenta proteger a segurança e a saúde de 55 milhões de trabalhadores em 3,6 milhões de locais de trabalho. A OSHA tem 40 empregados para pesquisar e redigir normas de saúde e segurança.

Na história da OSHA, ela emitiu apenas 60 regulamentos, ou instruções normativas. Cada norma, em média, passa por um período de gestação de sete anos. Tudo o que a OSHA propõe está sujeito a análise e revisão detalhadas pelo White House Office of Management and Budget (*Departamento de Administração e Orçamento da Casa Branca*). Seu orçamento no início da década de 1990 era US$ 294 milhões. O orçamento administrativo do presidente é quase igual a esse valor, e o Fish and Wildlife Service (Serviço de Pesca e Vida Selvagem) recebe quase o dobro do orçamento da OSHA. Há seis vezes mais inspetores de pesca e caça do que reguladores de segurança no trabalho. Os acidentes no trabalho matam até 80.000 trabalhadores americanos anualmente. Os críticos da OSHA acreditam que os esforços federais para melhorar a saúde e a segurança do trabalhador precisam ser intensificados.

Nos Estados Unidos, cidades, comarcas e estados também participam da regulamentação e/ou inspeção das condições de segurança no trabalho das operações. Na Califórnia, por exemplo, uma fábrica pode esperar inspeções freqüentes referentes a risco de incêndio destas fontes:

1. inspetores da própria fábrica,
2. inspetores de divisão e corporativos,
3. oficial do corpo de bombeiros municipal,
4. oficial do corpo de bombeiros da comarca,
5. oficial do corpo de bombeiros do estado,
6. OSHA,
7. agentes de seguros e
8. inspetores sindicais.

Essas e outras fontes de regulamentação de operações formam uma rede de proteção da segurança do trabalhador que deve apresentar uma diligência contínua para projetar trabalhos que sejam seguros para os empregados.

Gerentes experientes sabem, entretanto, que empregados ainda podem se ferir e ter sua saúde prejudicada. Portanto os gerentes estabelecem **departamentos de segurança e prevenção de acidentes**. Esses departamentos não somente intermedeiam todas as fontes de inspeções de segurança, mas também projetam dispositivos de segurança e procedimentos voltados a proteger os empregados, elevar seu nível de consciência e projetar programas publicitários para minimizar os danos resultantes de erro humano. Essas e outras atividades são realizadas não apenas porque é a lei, mas também porque isso é certo e ético. E, além disso, é um bom negócio. Quando as condições de trabalho são seguras, o moral do empregado e aprodutividade da mão-de-obra tendem a ser mais elevados, e os custos diretos de acidentes tendem a ser mais baixos. Portanto, a administração tem muito em jogo ao manter um ambiente de trabalho seguro para os empregados.

Resumo Final

O Que os Fabricantes de Classe Mundial Estão Fazendo

À medida que lutam para captar mercados internacionais, os fabricantes de classe mundial reconhecem que seus empregados têm uma importância tanto estratégica como tática. Os empregados têm importância estratégica porque afetam diretamente os custos do produto, a qualidade do produto, a satisfação do cliente e a implementação bem-sucedida de iniciativas estratégicas, como a instalação de sistemas de produção high-tech, JIT e TQM. De fato, as estratégias empresariais são executadas *pelos* empregados. Mas os empregados também têm importância tática: as atividades diárias de despachar pedidos dos clientes no tempo certo dentro do custo e dos padrões de qualidade devem ser feitas pelos empregados.

A produção em massa tradicionalmente significava que os trabalhadores da produção faziam minúsculas partes de um trabalho que era tão especializado que pouca capacidade mental ou treinamento era necessário.

Durante muito tempo o sistema de produção em massa funcionou: os custos eram baixos e a qualidade, aceitável. Mas esses sistemas eram tão inflexíveis que os clientes eram negligenciados e as atitudes do trabalhador se deterioravam até que os custos disparavam e a qualidade do produto já não era suficientemente boa.

Os fabricantes de classe mundial assumiram uma abordagem diferente. Agora são contratados trabalhadores que têm capacidade de resolver problemas. Eles recebem treinamento multifuncional e lhes são delegados poderes a fim de que possam trabalhar em equipes para resolver problemas de produção e estar preparados para mudar as coisas para responder às necessidades dos clientes. Essas empresas podem aplicar de 5% a 10% de seus dispêndios totais em mão-de-obra para treinar e educar empregados. Adicionalmente, são desenvolvidos uma estrutura e um clima organizacionais que encorajam a utilização plena dos empregados. A recompensa é a aumentada produtividade, melhorada qualidade de produto e aumentada receptividade às necessidades do cliente — o que é essencial para empresas que aspiram a ser fabricantes de classe mundial.

Para obter melhorias significativas na produtividade de mão-de-obra é necessário mais que trabalhadores motivados. A qualidade deve ser melhorada, e eles devem ter as máquinas, ferramentas e tecnologia de produção mais recentes com as quais trabalhar. Além disso, os produtos devem ser projetados de forma a terem manufaturabilidade. Os fabricantes de classe mundial têm investido fortemente em tecnologia de manufatura de última geração. Os empregados são a chave para a introdução bem-sucedida dessa tecnologia avançada, e suas habilidades e educação devem ser atualizadas se estes sistemas de produção avançados quiserem ser eficientes. Isso salienta a necessidade de treinamento, de comunicação e da criação de um clima organizacional cooperativo no qual a iniciativa individual e grupal seja encorajada. Dessa maneira, a tecnologia de produção avançada cria a necessidade de maneiras inovadoras de desenvolvimento e administração dos empregados.

Para os fabricantes de classe mundial, informação é a chave da administração. Toda ação administrativa inteligente baseia-se na informação. Padrões de trabalho cientificamente desenvolvidos são usados com grande vantagem quando a produção é planejada e controlada, os custos são estimados, a contabilidade de padrões de trabalho é definida e os preços de produtos são estabelecidos. Em sua cruzada para melhorar continuamente suas operações, os fabricantes de classe mundial utilizam padrões de mão-de-obra acurados como um dos marcos de referência para calibrar seu progresso.

QUESTÕES DE REVISÃO E DISCUSSÃO

1. Descreva as atitudes gerais dos empregados na indústria em relação ao trabalho. Qual explicação você pode dar para essas atitudes?
2. Defina *produtividade*. Como devemos medir a produtividade? Por que as empresas atuais devem estar especialmente preocupadas com a produtividade?
3. Dada a composição dos custos de produção para os fabricantes americanos hoje, quais recursos devem receber o foco dos programas de melhoria da produtividade? Por quê?
4. Explique por que é necessário uma abordagem de múltiplos fatores para medir a produtividade.
5. Quais três variáveis afetam a produtividade de mão-de-obra? Sob quais condições devemos esperar que empregados cujas necessidades são satisfeitas sejam produtivos?
6. Descreva a hierarquia de necessidades de Maslow. Qual significado a hierarquia tem para os gerentes de operações de hoje?
7. Dê três sugestões para cada uma dessas proposições:
   a) Modificar tarefas das funções dos empregados para melhorar necessidades de autocontrole.
   b) Modificar o cenário de trabalho dos empregados para tornar os empregos mais satisfatórios.
   c) Modificar ambientes de trabalho mais amplos dos empregados para tornar os empregos mais satisfatórios.
8. Defina *design de trabalho*.
9. Quais dois critérios devem ser usados para avaliar propostas para remediar designs de trabalho?
10. Cite três obstáculos fundamentais para se obter a integração das necessidades dos funcionários com produtividade no design de trabalho.
11. O que são normas de trabalho sindicais? Cite exemplos de normas de trabalho e explique como elas afetam a produtividade.
12. O que é *empowerment do trabalhador*? O que é *propriedade interna*? Que papel esses dois conceitos desempenham nos fabricantes de classe mundial atualmente?
13. Defina e explique a atitude de questionamento da análise de métodos.
14. Cite cinco princípios da economia de movimentos relativos ao uso do corpo humano.
15. Cite quatro técnicas de análise de métodos.
16. Defina *medida do trabalho*. Qual é a unidade universal de medida no ambiente de trabalho? Cite cinco causas de tolerâncias.
17. Cite três usos da amostragem do trabalho.
18. Discuta o papel do estudo do tempo, amostragem do trabalho e outras técnicas para projetar funções de trabalho.
19. À medida que o número de aeronaves se duplica em lotes de produção, o que acontece às horas de trabalho por unidade?

TAREFAS NA INTERNET

1. Visite e explore o site do Bureau of Labor Statistics na Internet (**http://stats.bls.gov**). Encontre e discuta as taxas de crescimento da produtividade trimestrais e anuais para diferentes setores da economia americana.
2. Durante muitas décadas, o Massachusetts Institute of Technology (MIT) operou o Laboratory for Manufacturing and Productivity (LMP). Uma área de pesquisa dentro desse laboratório é o Design and Operation of Manufacturing Systems. Visite e explore o site do MIT correspondente a seu LMP (**http://web.mit.edu/lmp/www/**). Descreva brevemente um dos projetos de pesquisa desenvolvidos atualmente na área de pesquisa do Design and Operation of Manufacturing Systems.
3. Fundada em 1977, a American Productivity & Quality Center (APQC) é uma organização educacional e de pesquisa sem fins lucrativos patrocinada por centenas de organizações. Seu propósito é auxiliar as empresas a administrar mudanças, melhorar processos, alavancar o conhecimento e aumentar o desempenho tornando-as mais ágeis, criativas e competitivas. Visite e explore o site da APQC na Internet (**www.apqc.org**). Relacione diversas grandes empresas que sejam membros/patrocinadores da APQC. Explique como o benchmarking poderia ajudar as empresas a aumentar sua produtividade.
4. Visite o site da Occupational Safety and Health Administration (OSHA) na Internet em **www.osha.gov**. Descubra e resuma a missão da OSHA. Localize e explore informações sobre a OSHA Act de 1970, emendada em 1990. Quantas seções há nesse ato ou lei do Congresso americano?

PROBLEMAS

1. Bill Bonnet é o gerente de vendas da Bratz Agricultural Chemical para a região sul. Vinte e dois vendedores apresentam relatórios a Bill e vendem produtos químicos a negociantes de 12 estados do sul. Durante os últimos cinco anos, Bill montou uma equipe de vendedores que é insuperável em sua capacidade de colaborar. Esses vendedores parecem estar satisfeitos com seus empregos em todos os sentidos, inclusive salários, supervisão, atitude em relação à companhia e moral. Bill acha que tem tudo sob controle para tornar feliz cada vendedor de seu grupo com seu emprego em particular.

   Nos últimos meses, as vendas da Bratz na região sul decresceram 10% quando comparadas com períodos anteriores. Bill quebrou a cabeça para descobrir algum motivo, como o declínio na economia global ou a atividade dos concorrentes, para explicar o declínio das vendas. Depois de muito pensar, entretanto, Bill concluiu que houvera uma queda abrupta de produtividade entre os vendedores devido à falta de motivação.

   a) Use a teoria da motivação para explicar como empregados que estão satisfeitos com seus empregos podem ser improdutivos.
   b) O que Bill estava fazendo errado?
   c) O que Bill deveria fazer para corrigir a situação? Forneça os passos específicos que ele seguiria para melhorar a produtividade da equipe de vendas para a região sul.

2. Mary Margret Tack administra uma fábrica de artigos de vestuário em El Paso, Texas. Rotatividade e absenteísmo dos trabalhadores infestaram sua operação nesses dois anos em que ela é gerente da fábrica. O custo para contratar novos trabalhadores e ter trabalhadores de reserva para ocupar o espaço de trabalhadores ausentes é excessivo. Com a ajuda de alguns integrantes do departamento de pessoal e pessoas do departamento de engenharia do escritório central em Oklahoma City, foram feitas as seguintes estimativas de economias de custo e elevações de custo a partir de soluções de projeto de emprego alternativas:

Soluções de Projeto de Emprego	Elevação do Custo Médio por Unidade Devido a Reduzida Eficiência Técnica	Economias de Custo Médio por Unidade Devido a Reduzida Rotatividade e Absenteísmo
Rotação de emprego	$ 0,059	$ 0,085
Enriquecimento do cargo	0,092	0,129
Tempo fora do emprego	0,065	0,055
Treinamento de supervisores	0,057	0,090

   a) Se somente uma das propostas puder ser aceita, classifique as soluções em ordem de desejabilidade.
   b) Mary Margret deve transferir seus engenheiros de produção a outra fábrica porque os estudos do tempo não mais serão necessários?
   c) As soluções acima são mutuamente exclusivas, ou seja, na prática somente uma pode ser aplicada por vez? Quais são algumas combinações prováveis?

3. Prepare um fluxograma e carta de processo para fazer um bule de café em sua cozinha.

4. Dirija-se à biblioteca de sua escola. Estude o procedimento para confirmar livros no balcão principal. Prepare uma carta de processo para o método atual e uma outra para um método melhorado. Quais são as economias estimadas do método melhorado em relação ao método atual em termos de dinheiro economizado de trabalho e tempo do cliente?

Estudo do Tempo

5. Num estudo do tempo de uma fábrica, o tempo médio para concluir um produto era 36,5 minutos, o ritmo era 1,20, e as tolerâncias eram 60 minutos por turno de oito horas.
   a) Compute um padrão de trabalho para a operação.
   b) Quantos produtos por turno de oito horas se esperaria que um operador experiente produzisse sob condições operacionais comuns?
   c) Se o preço de mão-de-obra for $ 15 por hora, o que o departamento de contabilidade deve usar como custo de mão-de-obra padrão por produto?

6. Um estudo do tempo é executado para uma operação, resultando nos dados que se seguem (em minutos).

Elemento	Ciclo								Ritmo
	1	2	3	4	5	6	7	8	
1. Pegar e posicionar unidade	0,08	0,10	0,11	0,15	0,06	0,12	0,11	0,12	1,15
2. Realizar calibragem	2,50	2,90	2,60	2,80	2,70	2,90	3,00	3,10	1,25
3. Realizar testes padrões	3,90	3,85	4,19	3,50	3,50	3,72	3,60	4,21	0,95
4. Atualizar placa e remover unidade	0,60	0,50	0,90	0,80	0,70	0,60	0,60	0,50	1,00

Tolerância por Turno de Oito Horas:

Troca de roupas	10 minutos
Atrasos inevitáveis	30
Almoço	30
Banho e troca de roupas	30
Total	100 minutos

   a) Compute um tempo médio observado para cada elemento em minutos.
   b) Compute o tempo normal para cada elemento e o tempo normal total em minutos.
   c) Compute o fator de tolerância para a operação.
   d) Compute o padrão de trabalho para a operação.

Amostragem do Trabalho

7. Atualmente, uma operação de produção tem 108 minutos de tolerância durante cada turno de 12 horas. Um estudo de amostragem do trabalho deve ser realizado para as operações. Se um intervalo de confiança igual a 95% e um erro absoluto de ±2% forem aceitáveis, quantas observações de amostragem do trabalho serão necessárias?

8. Um analista está executando um estudo do tempo e sabe que 75 minutos normalmente são dedicados a intervalos de descanso e almoço, mas uma tolerância por atrasos inevitáveis deve ser estimada. Um estudo de amostragem do trabalho com proporção de atraso foi realizado, com os seguintes resultados:

Atividade	Número de Observações
Atraso inevitável	29
Atraso evitável	59
Outros	387

Qual fator de tolerância deve ser usado para definir o padrão de mão-de-obra se as tolerâncias incluírem atrasos inevitáveis, almoço e intervalos de descanso? Suponhamos 480 minutos por turno.

9. Um estudo de amostragem do trabalho foi realizado para uma operação de produção ao longo de uma semana de 40 horas. Durante o estudo o operador concluiu 560 produtos acabados e recebeu uma avaliação de ritmo igual a 1,10 enquanto trabalhava. Os resultados do estudo foram:

Atividade	Número de Observações
Produção	425
Atraso evitável*	50
Intervalos de descanso*	25

*Incluído nas tolerâncias.

a) Determine o tempo normal total por produto.
b) Determine o padrão de mão-de-obra por produto.

Sistemas de Pagamento de Incentivo

10. Um empregado num plano de incentivo acaba de completar um período de pagamento de uma semana. A informação em seu cartão de ponto é:

$$\text{Total de horas trabalhadas} = 45$$
$$\text{Produção total} = 250$$
$$\text{Padrão de trabalho por unidade} = 10,575$$
$$\text{Pagamento horário básico} = \$\,9,75 \text{ por hora}$$

Se a companhia usar a seguinte fórmula para computar o pagamento horário real, qual será o pagamento do empregado pelo período?

$$\text{Pagamento horário real} = \frac{(\text{Pagamento horário básico})(\text{Unidades produzidas})(\text{Padrão de mão-de-obra})}{\text{Minutos trabalhados}}$$

11. Uma oficina mecânica instalou um sistema de pagamento de incentivo por peça trabalhada para seus empregados. Um período de pagamento de duas semanas acaba de findar-se, e um operadora de máquina estimou seu pagamento para o período a partir desta informação:

$$\text{Produção total} = 200 \text{ unidades}$$
$$\text{Padrão de trabalho por unidade} = 34,50 \text{ minutos}$$
$$\text{Pagamento horário básico} = \$\,15,501 \text{ por hora}$$

a) Compute o preço da peça feita pela operadora para esse produto.
b) Compute seu pagamento para o período.

12. Um trabalhador da produção concluiu uma semana de montagem de produtos numa fábrica. A operação que ele executa está incluída num plano de compensação por peças produzidas. Ele preencheu há pouco seu registro de produção e tempo a ser devolvido para seu supervisor e quer determinar qual será seu pagamento para essa semana. Seu registro de produção e tempo inclui esta informação:

$$\text{Produção por semana} = 595 \text{ produtos}$$
$$\text{Padrão de mão-de-obra por produto} = 5,52 \text{ minutos}$$
$$\text{Pagamento horário básico} = \$\,15 \text{ por hora}$$

a) Calcule o preço da peça feita pelo empregado para esse produto.
b) Calcule o pagamento do trabalhador para a semana.

Capítulo 15 – Produtividade, Trabalho em Equipe e Empowerment

Estudo de Caso

Integrated Products Corporation

Um analista da produção da Integrated Products Corporation (IPC) concluiu há pouco um estudo do tempo de um teste de controle da qualidade. Eis os resultados do estudo (em minutos):

Elemento	Ciclo 1	2	3	4	5	6	Ritmo
1. Pegar e colocar	0,25	0,19	0,18	0,21	0,24	0,20	1,20
2. Conectar testes	0,40	0,45	0,36	0,34	0,41	0,43	1,10
3. Teste computadorizado	3,50	3,50	3,50	3,50	3,50	3,50	1,00
4. Gravar resultados	0,70	0,69	0,69	0,65	0,68	0,66	0,90

O analista determinou que para um turno de oito horas o tempo improdutivo para a operação será igual a 20 minutos para atrasos inevitáveis, 15 minutos para iniciar a operação no início do turno, e 15 minutos para limpeza e arrumação em torno da operação.

Tarefas

1. Compute o padrão de mão-de-obra para a operação.
2. Quantos testes um trabalhador experiente executaria num turno de oito horas sob condições operacionais comuns?
3. Se fosse o gerente de operações encarregado dessa operação e os trabalhadores que realizam o teste fizessem menos testes por turno do que sua resposta à questão 2, o que você faria?
4. Como os conceitos de "velocidade normal" e "condições operacionais comuns" são usados nos estudos do tempo? Como eles afetariam o padrão de mão-de-obra desenvolvido na questão 1?
5. O que há nos estudos do tempo que deixa trabalhadores e até mesmo estudantes de administração com um sentimento ruim? O que você, como gerente de operações, faria para ajudar a aliviar esse sentimento?

capítulo 16
GERÊNCIA DA QUALIDADE

Introdução

Natureza da Qualidade
Dimensões da Qualidade
Determinantes da Qualidade
Custos da Qualidade

Gerência da Qualidade Tradicional

Gerência da Qualidade Moderna
Gurus da Qualidade
A Qualidade Impulsiona a Produtividade
Outros Aspectos do Quadro da Qualidade

Padrões Emergentes da Qualidade
O Prêmio Nacional da Qualidade Malcolm Baldrige
O Prêmio Deming
Os Padrões ISO 9000

Programas de Gestão da Qualidade Total
Compromisso e Envolvimento da Alta Administração
Envolvimento do Cliente
Projetando Produtos Voltados para a Qualidade
  Projetando Produtos Voltados para a Robustez •
  Projetando Produtos Voltados para a Produção •
  Projetando para a Confiabilidade
Projetando e Controlando Processos de Produção
Cultivando Parcerias com Fornecedores
Atendimento ao Cliente, Distribuição e Instalação
Criando Equipes de Funcionários com Mais Poder
  Programas de Treinamento de Funcionários •
  Equipes de Trabalho e Poder • Qualidade na Fonte •
  Círculos da Qualidade
O Benchmarking e a Melhoria Contínua

Gerência da Qualidade no Setor de Serviços

Resumo Final: O Que os Fabricantes de Classe Mundial Estão Fazendo

Questões de Revisão e Discussão

Tarefas na Internet

Estudo de Caso
A Confiabilidade do Produto na Valvco Inc.

GERÊNCIA DA QUALIDADE NA KFC

Administrar a qualidade das operações de prestação de serviços é tão importante quanto administrar a qualidade das operações de produção. Assim, nas organizações prestadoras de serviços, não é importante apenas a qualidade dos serviços e produtos fornecidos, mas também a qualidade da forma como os serviços são prestados.

A Kentucky Fried Chicken é uma grande cadeia de restaurantes de fast-food de propriedade da Pepsico, com mais de 5.000 franqueados ou restaurantes de propriedade da empresa. Reconhecendo a importância de administrar a qualidade dos alimentos e serviços em seus restaurantes, a KFC adotou um programa de gerência da qualidade abrangendo toda a empresa na esperança de melhorar a produtividade e a qualidade. Seu programa de gerência da qualidade continha dois componentes para medir a qualidade: (1) um programa da qualidade, serviço e limpeza (QSC) para julgar a qualidade dos serviços e alimentos fornecidos do ponto de vista do cliente e (2) um programa de revisão das operações (OFR) para medir o desempenho de um restaurante em termos de implantação de um processo em relação às especificações de processo da KFC.

Como parte do programa QSC, "falsos compradores" contratados pela KFC avaliam a qualidade, o serviço e a limpeza de certos restaurantes duas vezes por mês. Eles preenchem um formulário padrão KFC avaliando cada um dos restaurantes para que as avaliações sejam objetivas, precisas e coerentes. Além disso, utilizam-se de pesquisas com clientes e fichas de reclamações para ajudar a avaliar a qualidade em determinados restaurantes.

O objetivo do programa OFR é ajudar a KFC a assegurar a consistência de produtos e serviços de alta qualidade que os clientes aprenderam a esperar dos restaurantes KFC. O programa de avaliação OFR mede o desempenho operacional de um restaurante em relação aos padrões operacionais da KFC. O gerente geral em cada um dos restaurantes preenche semanalmente um formulário OFR padrão. Os gerentes também precisam oferecer programas de treinamento para os funcionários do restaurante e manter as instalações, os equipamentos e as premissas de acordo com os padrões operacionais da KFC. Além dos programas QSC e OFR, outros instrumentos de controle da qualidade, como gráficos de Pareto, gráficos espinha de peixe e gráficos de controle, são usados para ajudar a melhorar a qualidade de certos processos. Na verdade, o programa da qualidade da gerência do KFC resultou em várias melhorias nos processos, e essas idéias de melhoria foram disseminadas para todos os seus restaurantes.

A gerência da qualidade é tão importante para as organizações prestadoras de serviços quanto para as organizações manufatureiras. Para a maioria das empresas, a qualidade superior é o centro de sua estratégia de negócios. Para elas, obter um produto de qualidade quase perfeita é visto como o meio principal de conquistar uma parcela maior do mercado na concorrência internacional. A proeminência da qualidade do produto na estratégia de negócios para várias empresas vem da amarga consciência de que *você pode perder negócios para produtos com preços mais baixos, mas você os recupera com uma qualidade superior de produto*. Obter qualidade superior de produto dentro de um negócio requer um processo de longo prazo de mudar a cultura fundamental da organização. Este capítulo discute gerência da qualidade, que é o processo de redirecionar as culturas da organização na direção da qualidade superior do produto.

NATUREZA DA QUALIDADE

O que é qualidade? Basicamente, a qualidade dos produtos e serviços não é definida ou determinada pelas empresas produtoras. Ela é determinada pelos clientes. *A qualidade de um produto ou serviço é a percepção do cliente do grau que o produto ou serviço atende a suas expectativas*. Para entender melhor a natureza da qualidade, vamos discutir as dimensões, os determinantes e os custos da qualidade.

DIMENSÕES DA QUALIDADE

Ao avaliar a qualidade os clientes levam em consideração vários aspectos diferentes dos produtos e serviços. A Tabela 16.1 descreve algumas das dimensões de qualidade que os clientes utilizam para avaliar a qualidade. Essas dimensões da qualidade têm implicações importantes. As empresas têm de procurar os clientes para definir os padrões de medida da qualidade. As pesquisas e sugestões de clientes podem ser

TABELA 16.1	ALGUMAS DIMENSÕES DA QUALIDADE DO PRODUTO
	• **Desempenho:** Quão bem o produto ou serviço desempenha o uso esperado pelo cliente. Por exemplo, a velocidade de uma impressora a laser. • **Características:** As características especiais que atraem os clientes. Por exemplo, assentos ajustáveis por comandos elétricos de um carro. • **Confiabilidade:** A probabilidade de quebra, mau funcionamento ou a necessidade de conserto. • **Utilidade:** A velocidade, o custo e a conveniência de consertos e manutenção. • **Durabilidade:** O tempo ou o uso necessário antes de ser preciso efetuar um conserto ou substituição. • **Aparência:** Os efeitos nos sentidos humanos — visão, tato, paladar, olfato e audição. • **Atendimento ao Cliente:** Como os clientes são tratados antes, durante e depois da venda. • **Segurança:** Quanto o produto protege os usuários antes, durante e depois do uso.

usadas como dados dos clientes a respeito da qualidade. As expectativas dos clientes em relação à qualidade são afetadas por vários fatores, incluindo produtos dos concorrentes, e mudam com o decorrer do tempo. Os produtos e serviços devem, portanto, ser melhorados com o tempo para atender às mudanças nas expectativas dos clientes.

As expectativas de qualidade dos clientes não são as mesmas para produtos de **níveis** ou **classes** diferentes. Por exemplo, os clientes normalmente não esperam que os pregos de uma construção sejam obras-primas projetadas e produzidas com os mesmos padrões de exatidão de um Rolls-Royce. Mas os pregos devem fazer o que se espera que façam e ser melhores do que os concorrentes. Esse ponto é importante. Hoje a meta de várias empresas é se tornar o que chamamos de **empresa de classe mundial**. *Ser uma empresa de classe mundial em termos de qualidade significa que cada um de seus produtos e serviços é considerado o melhor em sua categoria pelos clientes.* A melhor qualidade em sua categoria significa ser o melhor produto ou serviço em uma determinada categoria de produto ou serviço.

DETERMINANTES DA QUALIDADE

Uma questão-chave é como obter a qualidade. São necessárias várias atividades ou realizações:

- **Qualidade do projeto.** Depois de identificar quem são seus clientes, uma empresa tem de determinar o que seus clientes querem de seus produtos e serviços. Depois seus produtos e serviços são elaborados para exibir os atributos necessários para atender às expectativas dos clientes.
- **Capabilidade[1] dos processos de produção.** Os processos de produção têm de ser elaborados e desenvolvidos para ter capacidade de produzir produtos com os atributos desejados pelos clientes.
- **Qualidade de conformidade.** Os locais de produção devem então ser dirigidos para produzir produtos e serviços que atendem às especificações de projeto e desempenho voltadas para as expectativas de qualidade dos clientes.
- **Qualidade do atendimento ao cliente.** Todos os contatos entre os clientes e as empresas têm de ser administrados de forma que os clientes sintam que foram tratados de forma justa e educada, com suas necessidades sendo atendidas imediatamente e com interesse.
- **Cultura de qualidade da empresa.** Toda empresa tem de trabalhar com afinco para fazer o que é necessário para projetar, produzir e dar assistência técnica aos produtos e serviços que atendam às expectativas dos clientes. Deve-se ativar mecanismos para melhorar constantemente cada uma das facetas da organização com o intuito de criar um grau cada vez maior de satisfação dos clientes.

CUSTOS DA QUALIDADE

Há custos associados com a qualidade do produto e do serviço. Alguns desses custos estão associados com evitar má qualidade e outros surgem depois da má qualidade ocorrer. Entre esses custos estão:

- **Sucata e retrabalho.** Quando os produtos se revelam defeituosos ainda na fase de produção, eles têm de ser sucateados ou consertados. Entre esses custos estão o de produzir os itens sucateados; o

---

[1] A expressão "capabilidade do processo" já está incorporada ao linguajar do pessoal envolvido com o controle da qualidade. (N. do R.T.)

custo de consertar, retrabalhar e retestar produtos defeituosos; e todos os custos de atrasos, papelada, reprogramação e outros aborrecimentos causados pelos produtos defeituosos.
- **Produtos defeituosos nas mãos dos clientes.** Quando os produtos são enviados aos clientes, os custos podem ser enormes e difíceis de medir. Entre esses custos podem estar custos de garantia, processos ou acordos de responsabilidade pelo produto e os custos de devolução ou recolhimento e perda de negócio e freguesia.
- **Detectar defeitos.** O custo de todas as atividades que visam produtos e serviços que não estão de acordo com as especificações antes de esses serem enviados para os clientes. Ele inclui o custo de inspecionar, testar e outras atividades de controle da qualidade.
- **Evitar defeitos.** O custo de treinar, representar graficamente o desempenho da qualidade para estudar tendências, revisar projetos de produtos, fazer mudanças nos processos de produção, trabalhar com os fornecedores e outras atividades que visem melhorar a qualidade e evitar defeitos.

Cada um desses custos pode ser alto, mas é fato aceito que o custo de encontrar e lidar com produtos defeituosos pode representar até 25% do custo de venda em várias empresas. Enfatizar as atividades de encontrar e lidar com defeitos tem sido a abordagem tradicional da gerência da qualidade.

GERÊNCIA DA QUALIDADE TRADICIONAL

Um dos fatores que impedem as empresas americanas de ultrapassar seus concorrentes estrangeiros é sua visão tradicional do controle da qualidade. De acordo com essa visão, a maneira de assegurar que os clientes receberão produtos e serviços de qualidade é ter um sistema rigoroso de inspeção. O conceito é de que se houver inspeção suficiente, os produtos defeituosos serão identificados e descartados, ficando só os produtos bons para serem enviados aos clientes. Nessa abordagem, a decisão principal é quantos produtos inspecionar, e essa decisão é em grande parte uma questão econômica. A Figura 16.1 demons-

FIGURA 16.1 VISÃO TRADICIONAL DE QUANTO INSPECIONAR

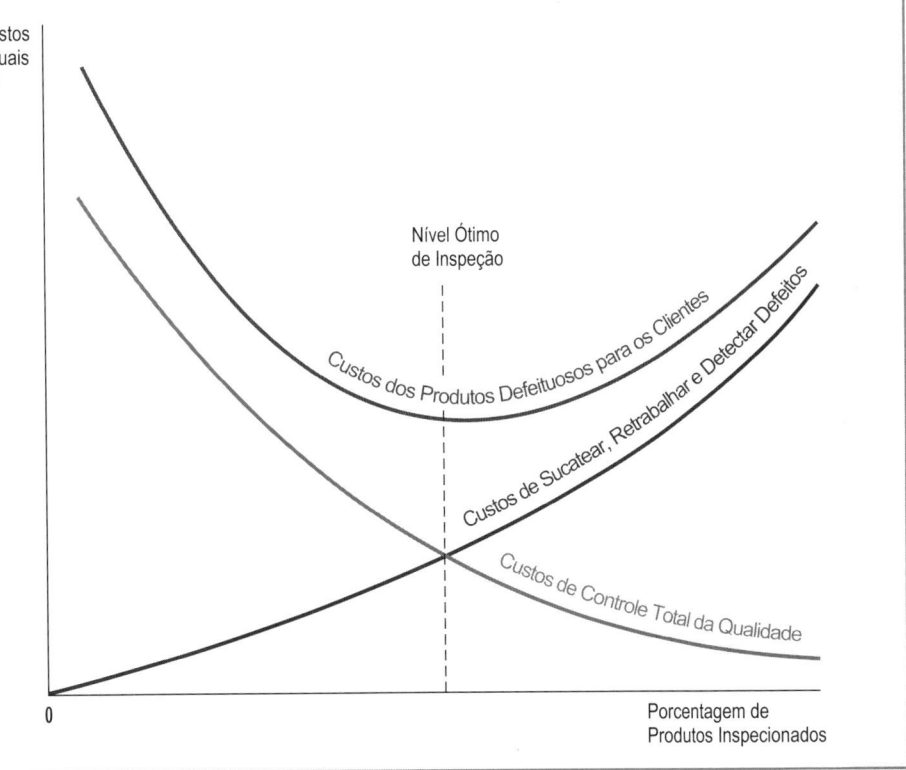

tra esta visão tradicional: à medida que mais produtos vão sendo inspecionados, os custos de sucatear, retrabalhar e detectar defeitos aumentam, enquanto os custos dos produtos defeituosos diminuem. A uma certa altura da inspeção, consegue-se um equilíbrio ótimo no ponto onde se minimizam os custos do controle da qualidade total. Os gerentes de operações devem de certa forma equilibrar esses custos quando decidem quantos produtos inspecionar.

O que está basicamente errado com essa visão tradicional de gerência da qualidade é que ela supõe que a qualidade pode ser inspecionada no produto. Em outras palavras, uma qualidade de produto aceitável pode ser obtida descartando-se produtos defeituosos encontrados na inspeção enquanto se continua produzindo produtos de qualidade inferior com práticas inadequadas de produção. Os gerentes de operações mais esclarecidos sabem que uma qualidade superior de produto não pode ser obtida com mais inspeção. Eles sabem que os fabricantes têm de voltar à produção e efetuar mudanças básicas na maneira como projetam e fabricam produtos e *fazer certo da primeira vez*. Dessa forma, produtos de qualidade superior sairão do setor de produção, e o trabalho de inspeção mudará de se descartar produtos ruins para evitar defeitos e dar feedback de como o setor de produção pode continuar melhorando a qualidade do produto.

Além disso, uma inspeção rigorosa não garante que só bons produtos e serviços irão para os clientes. Há uma história sobre a fragilidade humana dos inspetores que é sempre contada. Um supervisor queria verificar as habilidades de inspeção de seus inspetores e colocou propositadamente 100 peças defeituosas em um lote sem contar aos inspetores. Os inspetores encontraram somente 68 peças defeituosas da primeira vez. Convencido de que os inspetores deveriam ser capazes de encontrar todas as peças defeituosas, o supervisor colocou novamente o lote com as 32 peças defeituosas para ser inspecionado. Dessa vez os inspetores encontraram várias das peças, mas não todas. Depois de esse processo ser repetido pela terceira, quarta e quinta vez, foram encontradas 98 peças defeituosas. As outras duas peças defeituosas nunca foram encontradas. Elas foram para um cliente. Uma outra versão dessa mesma história diz que os inspetores encontraram 110 peças defeituosas. As empresas americanas estão cada vez mais abandonando essa visão tradicional de gerência da qualidade e adotando uma abordagem diferente.

GERÊNCIA DA QUALIDADE MODERNA

O enfoque moderno da qualidade está refletido nas discussões de gurus da qualidade que se seguem, no conceito de que a qualidade aciona a máquina da produtividade, em outros aspectos do quadro da qualidade e nos padrões emergentes da qualidade.

GURUS DA QUALIDADE

A era moderna de gerência da qualidade foi anunciada por alguns novos pensadores. Entre eles merecem destaque Deming, Crosby, Feigenbaum, Ishikawa, Juran e Taguchi. Esses educadores, autores e consultores trabalharam com indústrias para ajudar as empresas em sua trilha para a elaboração de programas de melhoria da qualidade.

W. Edwards Deming, professor da Universidade de Nova Iorque, viajou para o Japão depois da Segunda Guerra Mundial a pedido do governo japonês para ajudar suas indústrias a melhorar sua produtividade e qualidade. O dr. Deming, um estatístico e consultor, foi tão bem-sucedido em sua missão que em 1951 o governo japonês criou o **Prêmio Deming** para inovação na gerência da qualidade para ser concedido anualmente para a empresa que se destacasse no setor de programas de gerência da qualidade. O Instantâneo da Indústria 16.1 discute a abordagem de qualidade Deming. Na década de 1980 as empresas americanas correram em bando para Deming buscando sua assistência para estabelecer programas de melhoria da qualidade em suas fábricas.

Philip B. Crosby, em seu livro de 1979, estabeleceu conceitos tradicionais sobre "o grau aceitável de defeitos" que gostaria de ouvir. Crosby argumentou que qualquer nível de defeito é alto demais, e as empresas deveriam trabalhar com programas que lhes levassem cada vez mais em direção à meta de **zero defeito**. A idéia principal por detrás da qualidade grátis é que a idéia do equilíbrio entre os custos de melhorar a qualidade e os custos da má qualidade está errada. Os custos da má qualidade deveriam incluir todos os custos de não executar o trabalho corretamente desde a primeira vez: sucata, retrabalho, horas perdidas de mão-de-obra e máquinas, os custos ocultos da má vontade do cliente e vendas perdidas e custos de garantia. Ele afirma que o custo da má qualidade é tão mal avaliado que quantias ilimitadas podem ser gastas lucrativamente na melhoria da qualidade.

INSTANTÂNEO DA INDÚSTRIA 16.1

Os Princípios de Deming

W. Edwards Deming é conhecido como o pai do controle da qualidade no Japão, mas seu reconhecimento em seu próprio país, os Estados Unidos, levou muito tempo para chegar. Ele ensinou aos japoneses que mais qualidade significava menos custo, mas esse conceito estava tão distante dos gerentes americanos que eles só o ouviram quando era quase tarde demais. Deming disse aos gerentes americanos que eles precisavam:

1. Criar constância da meta de qualidade do produto.
2. Recusar-se a permitir a ocorrência de níveis normalmente aceitos de atrasos devido a erros, material defeituoso e acabamento defeituoso.
3. Cessar a dependência da inspeção para obter qualidade.
4. Reduzir a quantidade de fornecedores. Comprar baseando-se nas evidências estatísticas e não no preço.
5. Instalar programas para melhoria contínua dos custos, qualidade, serviços e produtividade.
6. Instituir treinamento para utilização total de todos os funcionários.
7. Concentrar a supervisão em ajudar as pessoas a fazer um trabalho melhor. Fornecer as ferramentas e técnicas para que as pessoas se orgulhem do seu trabalho.
8. Eliminar o medo. Estimular uma comunicação de via dupla.
9. Eliminar as barreiras entre os departamentos. Incentivar a solução de problemas através de trabalho de equipe.
10. Eliminar a utilização de metas numéricas, slogans e pôsteres para a mão-de-obra.
11. Utilizar métodos estatísticos para melhoria contínua da qualidade e produtividade e eliminar todos os padrões que prescrevem cotas numéricas.
12. Remover as barreiras ao orgulho do trabalho.
13. Instituir um programa vigoroso de educação e treinamento para manter as pessoas a par dos avanços em termos de material, métodos e tecnologias.
14. Definir claramente o compromisso permanente da alta administração com a qualidade e a produtividade.[a]

Permeando esses pontos está uma filosofia baseada na crença do desejo do trabalhador de fazer um bom trabalho e a necessidade de fazer o poder sair da diretoria e levar a tomada de decisões para a fábrica. Os trabalhadores da fábrica aprenderam estatística para poder controlar gráficos de seu progresso em termos de melhorar a qualidade. Todos na organização, desde os membros da diretoria até os porteiros, receberiam treinamento em conceitos de controle da qualidade e estatísticas, e todos estudariam a organização e sugeririam maneiras de melhorá-la. Os trabalhadores, portanto, não só trabalham, mas também ajudam a melhorar o sistema.[b]

Fontes:
[a] Tribus, Myron, diretor da AKT Systems and Energy Company, fundador e diretor do American Quality and Productivity Institute; "Os Princípios de Deming", *Mechanical Engineering*, janeiro de 1988.
[b] Ed Deming Wants Big Changes, and He Wants Them Fast. *Smithsonian*, agosto de 1990.

Armand V. Feigenbaum desenvolveu o conceito de **controle da qualidade total (TQC)** em seu livro de 1983. Feigenbaum argumentou que a responsabilidade pela qualidade deveria ficar com as pessoas que executam o trabalho. Esse conceito é denominado **qualidade na fonte** e significa que todo trabalhador, secretária, engenheiro e vendedor devem ser responsáveis por executar seu trabalho com qualidade perfeita. No TQC, onde um produto de qualidade é mais importante do que os índices de produção, os trabalhadores recebem a autoridade de parar a produção sempre que ocorrerem problemas de qualidade.

Kaoru Ishikawa não só teve um impacto direto na melhoria da qualidade em seu trabalho com indústrias, mas seu livro *Guide to Quality Control* (Guia do Controle de Qualidade) pode também ter influenciado os gurus da qualidade. Atribui-se a ele o conceito de **círculos da qualidade**, que discutiremos posteriormente neste capítulo. Ele também sugeriu o uso de **diagramas espinha de peixe**, que são utilizados para localizar reclamações dos clientes. A Figura 16.2 é um diagrama espinha de peixe utilizado para descobrir as causas de bolhas na banda de rodagem nos pneus de carros. Ishikawa argumenta que a responsabilidade das empresas americanas pela qualidade dos produtos e serviços é delegada a uns poucos funcionários, mas que os gerentes japoneses estão totalmente comprometidos com a qualidade.

FIGURA 16.2 — Diagrama Espinha de Peixe para Bolhas na Banda de Rodagem em Pneus de Automóveis

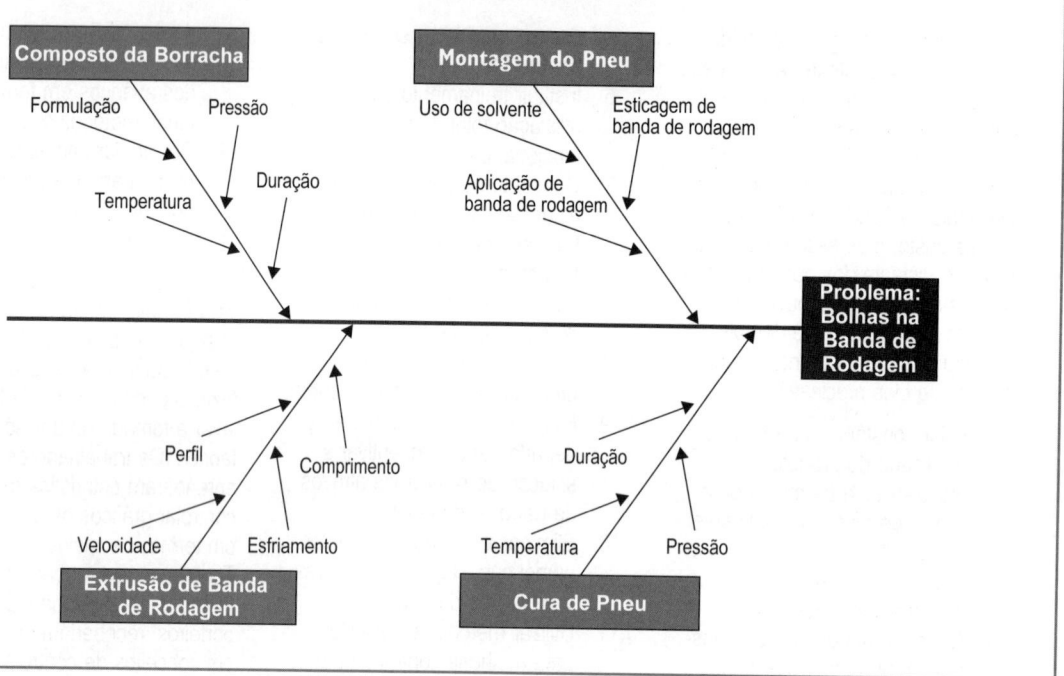

Joseph M. Juran, como Deming, foi descoberto tardiamente pelas empresas americanas. Juran teve um papel importante na tarefa de ensinar os fabricantes japoneses como melhorar a qualidade de seu produto. Juran defende o compromisso da alta administração com uma melhoria na qualidade do produto, no planejamento da qualidade, nas estatísticas para identificar discrepâncias e melhoria contínua em todos os aspectos da qualidade do produto.

Genichi Taguchi prestou consultoria a empresas importantes como a Ford e a IBM para ajudá-las a elaborar um melhor controle estatístico de seus processos de produção. Taguchi defende a idéia de que um ajuste constante das máquinas de produção para obter qualidade constante de produto não é eficaz e que, em vez disso, os produtos deveriam ser elaborados de forma que fossem suficientemente robustos para funcionar de forma satisfatória apesar das variações na linha de produção ou no campo.

As idéias desses gurus da qualidade influenciaram separada e coletivamente de forma permanente a gerência da qualidade dos produtos e serviços americanos.

A Qualidade Impulsiona a Produtividade

A visão tradicional de controle da qualidade era de que custa mais obter um produto de maior qualidade. Mas atualmente não é essa a visão que predomina. Atribui-se aos fabricantes japoneses a popularização de que *a qualidade impulsiona a produtividade*. Isso significa que se o setor de produção fizer certo da primeira vez e produzir produtos e serviços sem defeitos, elimina-se o desperdício e reduz-se os custos. Nessa nova maneira de pensar, quando os gerentes de operação trabalham para eliminar os defeitos, a qualidade dos produtos e serviços melhora e a produtividade também. Os custos diminuem à medida que a qualidade do produto aumenta, porque perdem-se menos produtos para sucata, devolve-se menos produtos para serviços dentro da garantia e há menos interrupções na produção. Calcula-se que 20% a 25% do custo geral dos produtos vendidos nos Estados Unidos são gastos na busca e na correção de erros. Os programas de gerência da qualidade são, portanto, considerados por muitas empresas como programas para melhorar a produtividade.

OUTROS ASPECTOS DO QUADRO DA QUALIDADE

Outros fatores também contribuíram para a melhoria da qualidade de produtos e serviços:

- **A fabricação just-in-time (JIT).** O JIT tem sido chamado de sistema de solução de problemas. Pelo fato de os estoques dos produtos em processo de fabricação serem reduzidos drasticamente, diminuindo-se o tamanho dos lotes, qualquer interrupção faz com que a produção pare até que o problema que provocou a interrupção seja resolvido. Isso tende a melhorar a qualidade do produto de várias maneiras. Como somente algumas poucas peças são estoque de produtos em processo de fabricação, se ocorrer um problema de qualidade serão produzidas menos peças defeituosas antes de serem descobertas, e, como a produção pára até o problema ser corrigido, a atenção de todos se voltará para solucionar o problema da qualidade para que ele não se repita. Além disso, a equipe de trabalho necessária para o JIT contribuiu para um maior orgulho em relação à qualidade do produto e um melhor desempenho na questão da qualidade.
- **Padronização do produto.** Com menos projetos de produto e menos produção repetitiva, produz-se os mesmos produtos padronizados todos os dias, as tarefas do trabalhador são bem entendidas, os trabalhadores estão familiarizados com suas tarefas, e a qualidade do produto pode ser melhorada.
- **Equipamento automatizado.** A utilização de equipamento automatizado, como robôs, pode ter um papel importante na obtenção de uma qualidade superior de produto. Essas máquinas produzem constante e previsivelmente peças dentro dos padrões de qualidade. Os robôs instalados na fábrica de caminhões da Ford Motor Company em Norfolk, Virgínia, melhoraram a qualidade do produto e permitiram menos mão-de-obra. "A robótica é uma das tecnologias mais importantes, porque a constância do robô garante que a qualidade projetada para o produto estará presente no mesmo", diz Robert S. Rennard, gerente de operações da fábrica de carrocerias e montagem da Ford.
- **Manutenção preventiva.** Os programas de manutenção preventiva minimizam os consertos de máquinas. Isso resulta em máquinas ajustadas e que produzem peças dentro dos padrões de qualidades.

Cada um desses fatores pode ser encontrado em várias empresas como parte de programas abrangentes para melhorar a qualidade dos produtos e serviços.

PADRÕES EMERGENTES DA QUALIDADE

O crescimento vertiginoso de interesse na qualidade dos produtos e serviços tornou necessário criar padrões internacionais de qualidade geralmente aceitos. Três eventos têm contribuído para esse fenômeno: o Prêmio Nacional de Qualidade Malcolm Baldrige[2], o Prêmio Deming e os padrões ISO 9000.

O PRÊMIO NACIONAL DA QUALIDADE MALCOLM BALDRIGE

Há um grande apoio para uma melhor qualidade dos produtos e serviços, não só entre os consumidores mas também entre e dentro das empresas. Talvez nada reflita mais o desejo recém-adquirido de melhor qualidade nos produtos e serviços nos Estados Unidos do que o Prêmio Nacional de Qualidade Malcolm Baldrige. Ele é administrado pelo Instituto Nacional de Padrões e Tecnologia e só empresas americanas podem concorrer a ele (**www.quality.nist.gov**).

O Instantâneo da Indústria 16.2 discute esse prêmio. A satisfação do cliente é o fator de maior peso. A lista de vencedores desse prestigioso prêmio é como um quem é quem na indústria americana.

A Tabela 16.2 mostra todos os antigos vencedores de cada categoria. Todos os candidatos recebem um resumo escrito dos resultados dos examinadores, incluindo os pontos fortes e fracos dos programas de qualidade e sugestões de como melhorar, para que ganhar não seja o maior benefício da tentativa de receber o prêmio. Os participantes dizem que passar pelo processo de candidatura força a empresa a exa-

---

[2] O correspondente no Brasil é o Prêmio Nacional da Qualidade e Produtividade. (N. do R.T.)

> ### INSTANTÂNEO DA INDÚSTRIA 16.2
>
> #### O Prêmio Nacional da Qualidade Malcolm Baldrige
>
> O Prêmio Nacional da Qualidade Malcolm Baldrige foi criado em 1987 e recebeu seu nome em homenagem a um ex-secretário de Comércio Exterior. Seu objetivo é reconhecer empresas americanas que conseguem obter liderança, incentivar outras empresas a melhorar seus programas da qualidade, desenvolver e publicar critérios que sirvam como diretrizes para melhorar a qualidade e divulgar informações não exclusivas sobre as estratégias dos recebedores do prêmio. São dados até dois prêmios por ano em três categorias: grandes fabricantes, grandes prestadoras de serviço e pequenos negócios. Para poder concorrer, a empresa tem de estar estabelecida e localizada nos Estados Unidos e apresentar uma proposta com 75 páginas. Um comitê de examinadores revisa e avalia as solicitações de candidatura. As solicitações com as pontuações mais altas recebem visitas no local. Os critérios para seleção são:
>
> 1. **Liderança.** O sistema de liderança, os valores, as expectativas e as responsabilidades públicas da empresa.
> 2. **Planejamento estratégico.** A eficácia do planejamento estratégico e de negócios e o desdobramento dos planos, concentrando-se nos requisitos do cliente e no desempenho operacional.
> 3. **Concentração no cliente e no mercado.** Como a empresa determina os requisitos e as expectativas do cliente e de mercado, amplia seus relacionamentos com os clientes e determina a satisfação dos mesmos.
> 4. **Informação e análise.** A eficácia da coleta de informações e da análise para dar suporte ao desempenho voltado para o cliente e êxito no mercado.
> 5. **Concentração nos recursos humanos.** O êxito dos esforços para realizar o potencial total da mão-de-obra para criar uma organização de ótimo desempenho.
> 6. **Gerência de processo.** A eficácia dos sistemas e processos para garantir a qualidade dos produtos e serviços.
> 7. **Resultados comerciais.** Os resultados de desempenho, as tendências e comparações com os concorrentes em áreas-chaves — satisfação do cliente, financeira e mercado, recursos humanos, fornecedores e parceiros e operações.
>
> *Fonte:* 1998 *Criteria for Performance Excellence, Malcolm Baldrige National Quality Award,* U.S. Department of Commerce, National Institute of Standards and Technology (**www.quality.nist.gov**).

minar o papel da qualidade do serviço ou produto em seus negócios e a determinar como se pode mudar as coisas para melhorar. Embora a IBM tenha perdido em 1989, ela efetuou mudanças que fizeram com que ela ganhasse em 1990. Esse prêmio tem grande significado em si, mas talvez mais importante do que isso seja o fato de ele refletir o compromisso cada vez maior nos Estados Unidos para com a qualidade dos produtos e serviços.

E a maioria dos estados americanos está entrando nessa jogada. Mais de 40 estados têm hoje seus próprios programas de prêmio da qualidade, que seguem o modelo do programa do Prêmio Baldrige da Qualidade.

À medida que mais empresas vão concorrendo a esse valioso prêmio, nossa consciência coletiva da qualidade aumenta, e, em alguns casos, são feitos grandes progressos no sentido de se obter produtos e serviços de qualidade superior. E o critério para receber esses prêmios está ficando gravado em nossas mentes como padrão de excelência no setor de gerência da qualidade.

O PRÊMIO DEMING

O *Prêmio Deming,* cujo nome homenageia W. Edwards Deming, foi concedido pela primeira vez em 1951. Esse prêmio é concedido pelo Sindicato Japonês de Cientistas e Engenheiros a empresas que apresentaram programas bem-sucedidos de melhoria da qualidade (**www.deming.org/deminghtml/demingprize.html**). Embora todas as empresas possam se candidatar, a primeira empresa não japonesa a se candidatar foi a

TABELA 16.2 — GANHADORES DO PRÊMIO NACIONAL DA QUALIDADE MALCOLM BALDRIGE

Produção
- Divisão de Produtos Dentários da 3M (1997)
- Solectrom Corporation (1997)
- Laboratórios ADAC (1996)
- Armstrong World Industries Building Products Operation (1995)
- Divisão de Produtos de Telecomunicações da Corning Incorporated (1995)
- Eastman Chemical Company (1993)
- Sistemas de Defesa & Artigos Eletrônicos da Texas Instruments Incorporated (1992) (atual Raytheon Systems Company)
- AT&T Network Systems Group Transmission Systems Business Unit (hoje parte da Lucent Technologies, Inc., Optical Networking Group)
- Solectrom Corporation (1991)
- Zytec Corporation (1991) (atual Artesyn Technologies)
- IBM Rochester, Divisão AS/400 (1990)
- Cadillac Motor Car Company (1990)
- Millilken & Company (1989)
- Xerox Corporation Business Products and Systems (1989)
- Motorola, Inc. (1988)
- Divisão de Combustível Nuclear Comercial da Westinghouse Electric Corporation (1988)

Serviços
- Merrill Lynch Credit Corporation (1997)
- Xerox Business Services (1997)
- Dana Commercial Credit Corporation (1996)
- GTE Directories Corporation (1994)
- AT&T Consumer Communications Services (1994) (hoje parte da Divisão de Mercados de Consumidores da AT&T)
- The Ritz-Carlton Hotel Company (1992)
- AT&T Universal Card Services (1992)
- Federal Express Corporation (1990)

Pequenos Negócios
- Custom Research Inc. (1996)
- Trident Precision Manufacturing, Inc. (1996)
- Wainwright Industries, Inc. (1994)
- Ames Rubber Corporation (1993)
- Granite Rock Company (1992)
- Marlow Industries, Inc. (1991)
- Wallace Company, Inc. (1990)
- Globe Metallurgical Inc. (1988)

Florida Power and Light, em 1991. Entre as empresas famosas que ganharam o prêmio estão a Toyota Motors, a NEC e a Kansai Electric Power. A ênfase do prêmio tem sido tradicionalmente o controle estatístico da qualidade como meio de melhorar a qualidade. Mas a maioria dos ganhadores também tem programas bem divulgados e detalhados que estabeleceram metas da qualidade a se atingir daqui a vários anos. O compromisso e o envolvimento da alta administração no programa é enfatizado. Reconhecem-se quatro atividades da alta administração: atividades da gerência sênior, atividade de satisfação do cliente, atividade de envolvimento do funcionário e atividade de treinamento.

Esse prêmio reconheceu muito cedo o movimento internacional de recompensar e incentivar a evolução no sentido de melhorar a qualidade dos produtos e serviços. Como tal, ele foi muito importante no movimento de elevar a excelência na qualidade ao nível estratégico nas organizações.

OS PADRÕES ISO 9000

A Organização Internacional de Padronização (**www.iso.ch**) em Genebra, Suíça, emitiu as diretrizes da qualidade aceitas pela Comunidade Européia. Os padrões abrangem a fabricação e a inspeção pré-venda de produtos e assistência técnica pós-venda. Esses padrões determinam em grande parte que produtos podem ser vendidos para e dentro do mercado unificado europeu. As empresas americanas que fazem negócios na Europa têm de revisar as operações para ficar de acordo com esses padrões.

Os padrões são agrupados em cinco classes:

- **ISO 9000.** Uma visão geral e introdução a outros padrões da série, incluindo definições de termos e conceitos ligados à qualidade.
- **ISO 9001.** Padrão geral abrangente de garantia de qualidade em projeto, desenvolvimento, manufatura, instalação e serviços.
- **ISO 9002.** Padrão mais detalhado concentrando-se especificamente na fabricação e instalação de produtos.
- **ISO 9003.** Padrão mais detalhado cobrindo a inspeção final e teste dos produtos concluídos.
- **ISO 9004.** Diretrizes para gerência de um sistema de controle da qualidade. Mais detalhes sobre sistemas de gerência da qualidade necessários em outros padrões. Elaborado para ser utilizado na auditoria de sistemas da qualidade.

Os padrões especificam o que é exigido, mas não como fazê-lo. Abrangendo as áreas de projeto, controle de processo, compras, assistência técnica, inspeção e testes, e treinamento, os padrões foram escritos para transações entre duas partes. Um comprador especifica os padrões como parte do contrato de compra. Os fornecedores então dão garantia de que obedecerão esses padrões. O processo de conformidade consome tempo e é caro. A Du Pont estima que custa US$ 250.000 para certificar uma fábrica que empregue 300 trabalhadores. A American Society for Quality (**www.asq.org**) criou uma comissão de credenciamento tentando definir algumas diretrizes para credenciar empresas americanas na ISO 9000. Ela indica que os padrões ISO agora estão sendo usados não só na Europa mas no mundo todo.

À medida que nossa consciência da qualidade vai aumentando, é inevitável que a necessidade de padrões de qualidade de aceitação geral também cresça. Isso deveria trazer mais empresas para a nova era de enfatizar a importância estratégica da qualidade do produto e do serviço.

PROGRAMAS DE GESTÃO DA QUALIDADE TOTAL

Muitos fabricantes americanos revisaram a estrutura de suas organizações, mudaram o clima e redirecionaram seus programas de qualidade do produto para se tornar líderes mundiais em qualidade. Esses esforços geralmente são chamados de gestão da qualidade total (TQM). Na Motorola são chamados de *Seis Sigmas*; na Xerox, *Liderança através da Qualidade*; na Intel, *Qualidade Perfeita do Projeto* (PDQ); e na Hewlett-Packard, *Controle da qualidade Total*. A Tabela 16.3 relaciona os elementos importantes da TQM. Nesta seção vamos estudar esses elementos.

O objetivo dos programas de TQM é criar uma organização que produza produtos e serviços que sejam considerados de primeira classe por seus clientes. Isso significa que para obter excelência em qualidade, todo negócio deve ser feito da maneira correta da primeira vez e ser continuamente melhorado.

COMPROMISSO E ENVOLVIMENTO DA ALTA ADMINISTRAÇÃO

A TQM começa com o compromisso e o envolvimento da alta administração. Se não houver um apoio genuíno da alta administração, os programas de TQM serão vistos apenas como um outro modismo que cairá no esquecimento como outros slogans e abreviaturas. Criar um produto de qualidade superior na estratégia de negócios é a base para uma organização atingir a TQM. Se quisermos que a TQM seja bem-sucedida, precisamos fazer mudanças fundamentais na cultura das organizações. O envolvimento do cliente, basear o projeto dos produtos e os processos de produção nas necessidades do cliente, transformar os fornecedores em parceiros, criar equipes de funcionários com mais poder e benchmarking são conceitos revolucionários para a maioria das organizações. Essas mudanças não são fáceis, mas são impossíveis sem o compromisso e o envolvimento da alta administração.

ENVOLVIMENTO DO CLIENTE

É preciso encontrar mecanismos que envolvam os clientes nas organizações. *Os **grupos focalizados** são grupos de clientes que se reúnem para discutir e avaliar a qualidade com os executivos e engenheiros da empresa.* Esses grupos podem ser úteis para aprender o que os clientes querem dos produtos antes que

TABELA 16.3 — OS ELEMENTOS DA GESTÃO DA QUALIDADE TOTAL (TQM)

- **Compromisso e envolvimento da alta administração.** A alta administração se envolve e continua envolvida desde a definição da estratégia de negócios baseada na utilização da qualidade do produto como uma arma para conquistar uma parcela do mercado internacional até a recompensa dos funcionários por atingirem excelência em qualidade de produto.

- **Envolvimento do cliente.** Os desejos dos clientes impulsionam o sistema TQM. As características que eles valorizam são colocadas nos produtos desde o projeto até o serviço pós-venda.

- **Projeto voltado para a qualidade.** O que os clientes querem define os atributos básicos do projeto de produto. A excelência no desempenho, nas características, na confiabilidade, utilidade, durabilidade, aparência e assistência técnica é extremamente afetada pelo projeto.

- **Projeto de processos de produção voltado para a qualidade.** O maquinário de produção e os trabalhadores formam um sistema de produção que deve ser criado para produzir produtos com as dimensões da qualidade que os clientes querem.

- **Controle dos processos produtivos voltado para a qualidade.** À medida que os produtos e serviços vão sendo produzidos, o desempenho da produção em termos de qualidade é controlado e administrado de forma a garantir que só serão produzidos produtos e serviços de qualidade superior.

- **Desenvolvimento de parcerias com os fornecedores.** Selecionar e cultivar fornecedores que se encaixem no sistema TQM é uma prioridade importante. Os relacionamentos de longo prazo são cultivados de forma que os fornecedores entreguem peças de qualidade perfeita.

- **Atendimento ao cliente, distribuição e instalação.** A embalagem, remessa, instalação e o atendimento ao cliente podem ser extremamente importantes para a percepção de qualidade do cliente.

- **Empowerment dos funcionários.** Fazer a TQM funcionar, no final, está nas mãos dos funcionários. Eles têm de ser treinados, organizados, motivados e têm de ter poder para produzir produtos e prestar serviços de qualidade perfeita.

- **Benchmarking e melhoria contínua.** Os padrões utilizados para medir o progresso são tirados do desempenho de outras empresas de classe mundial. Depois esses padrões se tornam a base para melhorias contínuas de longo prazo.

---

eles sejam criados. As pesquisas de mercado, os questionários dos clientes e os programas de pesquisa de mercado também podem fornecer informações valiosas. Quando os fabricantes de automóveis mandaram os funcionários da linha de montagem para as revendedoras para conversar com os clientes sobre os defeitos dos carros, eles levaram de volta informações valiosas sobre as necessidades e os desejos dos clientes para as empresas. Como os clientes da TQM direcionam grande parte dos esforços para atingir a qualidade, é preciso encontrar meios específicos, práticos e tangíveis de fazer com que os clientes se envolvam.

O desdobramento da função qualidade (QFD) é um sistema formal para identificar os desejos dos clientes e eliminar características de produtos e atividades que não contribuem em nada. O QFD tem suas origens na Bridgestone Tire Corporation e na Mitsubishi Heavy Industries Ltd. no final da década de 1960. O professor Yoji Akao da Universidade Tamagawa e Shigeru Mizuno no final da década de 1970 deram ao QFD seu nome e popularizaram o conceito de formalizar a inclusão dos requisitos do cliente no projeto do produto. No QFD todas as expectativas possíveis do cliente em relação ao produto são listadas. Essas são então desdobradas em características cada vez mais específicas. Por exemplo, se o cliente quiser um lápis que é fácil de segurar, isso pode ser desdobrado em características como comprimento, diâmetro, peso, acabamento da superfície e outras características funcionais.

O QFD também atribui pesos às demandas do cliente e uma classificação das características funcionais do produto em relação às dos produtos dos concorrentes. O objetivo do QFD é identificar características do produto que precisam ser melhoradas. O processo QFD é repetido até a satisfação do cliente com o projeto dos produtos não conseguir mais identificar características que possam ser melhoradas.

PROJETANDO PRODUTOS VOLTADOS PARA A QUALIDADE

Se os produtos e serviços precisam ser de qualidade superior, tudo começa com o projeto. Três aspectos do projeto são particularmente importantes: projeto robusto, projeto para a produção e projeto para a confiabilidade.

Projetando Produtos Voltados para a Robustez Não é suficiente que os produtos apresentem o desempenho desejado quando eles são produzidos e utilizados sob condições ideais. Os clientes querem que os produtos tenham um desempenho satisfatório quando utilizados em todos os tipos de condições de campo. E é um fato da vida que as condições de produção nunca são ideais, sempre acontece alguma coisa fora do comum. Um *projeto robusto é aquele que apresenta o desempenho desejado mesmo se ocorrerem condições indesejáveis na produção ou no campo*. A robustez pode ser colocada nos produtos pressupondo-se condições de campo menos do que desejáveis levando em consideração elementos como calor, frio, umidade, natureza do uso e outras condições. Da mesma maneira, pressupondo condições de produção menos do que ideais, a especialização dos funcionários, as características e especificações dos materiais e a capacidade das máquinas podem levar ao projeto de um produto mais robusto.

Genichi Taguchi enfatizou a importância dos projetos robustos. Em sua abordagem ele destacava o **parâmetro de projeto** determinando especificações de produtos e ajustes de processo de produção que permitam um desempenho satisfatório do produto apesar das condições indesejáveis de produção e campo. Nessa abordagem é fundamental identificar os **fatores controláveis** e os **fatores não controláveis** na produção e depois definir os melhores níveis de fatores controláveis.

Projetando Produtos Voltados para a Produção No Capítulo 4 o Instantâneo da Indústria 4.2 ilustrou que a qualidade do produto pode ser melhorada criando-se produtos fáceis de ser produzidos. E no Capítulo 5 discutimos os princípios de se criar produtos para montagem automatizada. Quando os produtos são criados da maneira certa, eles geralmente têm menos peças e podem ser montados rápida e facilmente. Projetar produtos que possam ser produzidos reduz muito as fontes de erros e melhoram a qualidade geral do produto.

Projetando para a Confiabilidade Cada peça do produto é criada para um dado nível de *confiabilidade do componente — a probabilidade de um tipo de peça não falhar dentro de um dado período ou determinada quantidade de testes sob condições normais de uso*. A confiabilidade do componente em geral é medida por: confiabilidade (CR), razão de falha (FR e FRn) e tempo médio entre as falhas (MTBF):

$$CR = (1 - FR)$$

onde:

$$FR = \frac{\text{Quantidade de falhas}}{\text{Quantidade de testes}}$$

$$FR_n = \frac{\text{Quantidade de falhas}}{\text{Horas de operação}}$$

$$MTBF = \frac{\text{Horas de operação}}{\text{Quantidade de falhas}}, \text{ ou } \frac{1}{FR_n}$$

Por exemplo, para um tipo específico de pneu de automóvel com uma expectativa de vida de 30.000 milhas, se somente 1% dos pneus falhar dentro dessas 30.000 milhas diremos que o pneu tem um grau de confiabilidade de 0,99.

*Quando se combina peças componentes para formar um produto, a confiabilidade combinada de todos os componentes forma a base para a **confiabilidade do produto ou do sistema (SR)**.* Quando se combina componentes essenciais independentes — aqueles que podem fazer diretamente o produto falhar — para formar um produto, determina-se a confiabilidade do sistema multiplicando-se as confiabilidades de todos os componentes essenciais que interagem. Por exemplo, quatro pneus de um automóvel, cada um com a confiabilidade de 0,99, teriam uma confiabilidade de sistema de:

$$SR = CR_1 \times CR_2 \times CR_3 \times CR_4 = 0,99 \times 0,99 \times 0,99 \times 0,99 = 0,961$$

FIGURA 16.3   CONFIABILIDADE DO SISTEMA COMO FUNÇÃO DA CONFIABILIDADE DA PEÇA COMPONENTE E DA QUANTIDADE DE PEÇAS COMPONENTES

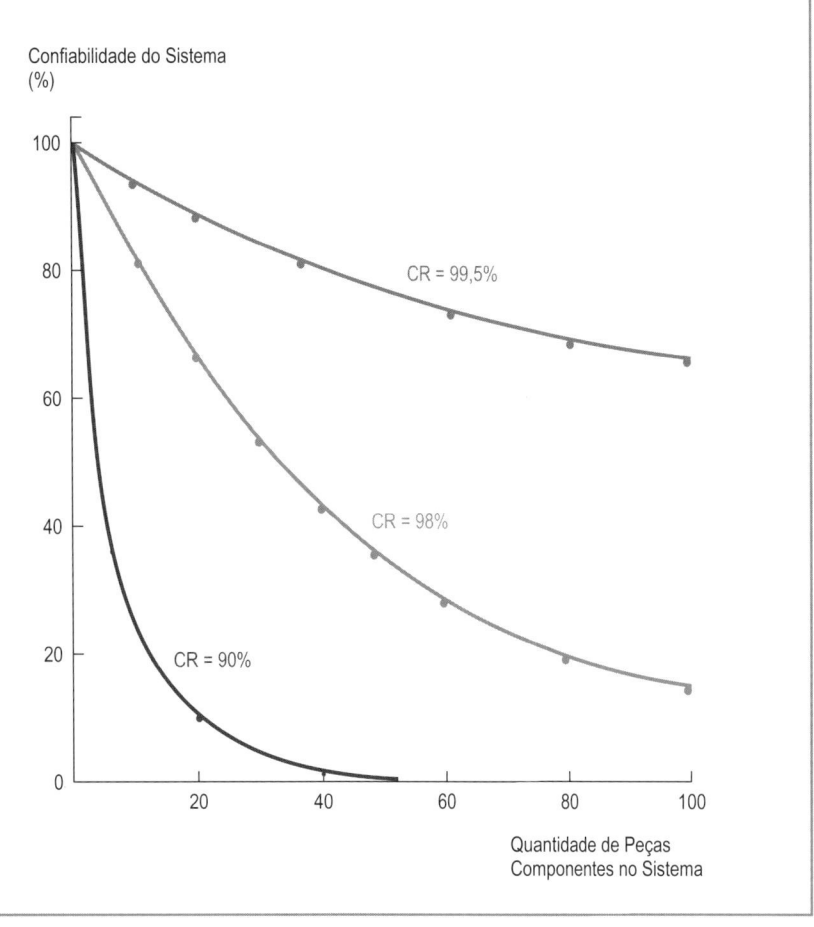

O conceito de confiabilidade do sistema é demonstrado na Figura 16.3. Se os componentes essenciais de um sistema tiverem uma confiabilidade de 90%, a confiabilidade do sistema é quase zero se houver mais de 50 peças componentes essenciais. Da mesma maneira, quando as peças componentes têm uma confiabilidade de 99,5%, a confiabilidade do sistema cai para 60,6% quando houver 100 peças componentes essenciais.

Levando em consideração o conceito de confiabilidade de sistema, quais são algumas das maneiras de os gerentes de operação aumentarem a confiabilidade dos produtos? Existem três maneiras práticas. Primeira: excesso de cautela no projeto das peças componentes para aumentar a confiabilidade pode ser uma estratégia viável para manter a confiabilidade do produto em níveis aceitáveis. *Excesso de cautela significa ampliar um projeto para evitar um determinado tipo de falha.* Assim, se uma peça tem tendência à corrosão, excesso de cautela pode significar usinar a peça de aço inoxidável para reduzir a corrosão. Ou se uma peça tende a se desgastar com o tempo, fazer a peça de aço forjado endurecido pode melhorar sua qualidade em termos de desgaste. Da mesma maneira, fabricar as peças com tolerâncias próximas pode melhorar o encaixe das peças durante a montagem e reduzir a probabilidade de acavalamento inadequado das peças durante o uso.

Quando os produtos são relativamente simples (possuem somente algumas poucas peças componentes que interagem), o excesso de cautela pode ser uma alternativa razoável para melhorar a confiabilidade do sistema. Mas quando os produtos são complexos (têm muitas peças componentes essenciais), o excesso de cautela no projeto das peças componentes pode não melhorar de forma significativa a confiabilidade do sistema. Mesmo se o excesso de cautela no projeto de peças componentes essenciais merecer consideração, o custo de projetar, testar e produzir peças superdimensionadas pode ser exorbitante. Portanto muitas vezes é preciso levar outras alternativas em consideração.

Segunda: *simplificação do projeto*; a redução da quantidade de peças que interagem em um produto normalmente aumenta a confiabilidade do sistema. Dois exemplos dessa abordagem dos anos 1980 são bem conhecidos. Na IBM Proprinter, a quantidade de peças foi reduzida à metade. Da mesma maneira, a quantidade de peças nos carros Ford Taurus e Mercury Sable foi reduzida em cerca de um terço. Um dos motivos principais para essas simplificações de projeto é melhorar a confiabilidade conjunta dos produtos.

Terceira: uma outra maneira prática de melhorar a confiabilidade do produto é fornecer **componentes redundantes**. Nessa abordagem, *um componente de baixa confiabilidade pode ter um backup colocado no sistema. Conseqüentemente, se o primeiro componente falhar, seu backup automaticamente o substitui*. A indústria de artigos eletrônicos geralmente adota essa abordagem.

O Exemplo 16.1 ilustra as abordagens do excesso de cautela e redundância para aumentar a confiabilidade do produto.

Exemplo 16.1

Aumentando a Confiabilidade do Produto com Excesso de Cautela e Redundância

A Tennessee Component Systems (TCS) estava apresentando uma quantidade excessiva de falhas em uma placa de circuito eletrônico. Duzentos dos componentes essenciais da placa de circuito foram submetidos a testes simulados de operações aceleradas. Esses testes se revelaram como correspondendo a 2.500 horas de operação normal, que é vida esperada anunciada pela propaganda de seus componentes.

Esses testes forneceram os seguintes dados:

Componente	(1) Quantidade de Falhas	(2) FR [(1)/200]	(3) CR (1 − FR) [1 − (2)]	(4) FR_n [(1)/(200 × 2.500)]	(5) MTBF $1/FR_n$ [1/(4)]
155	2	0,010	0,990	0,0000040	250.000
175	1	0,005	0,995	0,0000020	500.000
205	22	0,110	0,890	0,0000440	22.727
315	4	0,020	0,980	0,0000080	125.000

A confiabilidade do sistema da placa de circuito é calculada da seguinte maneira:

$$SR = CR_{155} \times CR_{175} \times CR_{205} \times CR_{315}$$
$$= 0,990 \times 0,995 \times 0,890 \times 0,980$$
$$= 0,8592$$

Ficou evidente para os gerentes da TCS que era preciso fazer alguma coisa para aumentar a confiabilidade do sistema da placa de circuito aumentando a confiabilidade do componente 205. Foram sugeridas duas alternativas:

- Reprojetar, desenvolver e testar uma nova configuração superdimensionada do componente 205 a um custo estimado de $ 50.000. Acreditava-se que esse projeto resultaria em uma confiabilidade de cerca de 0,960 do componente 205.
- Modificar a placa de circuito de forma que fosse automaticamente colocado em ação um backup do componente 205 se o primeiro falhasse. Estimou-se que o uso da redundância no projeto custaria somente $ 10.000, mas a TCS estava se perguntando qual seria a confiabilidade da placa de circuito com essa alternativa.

Calcule a confiabilidade do sistema das alternativas e recomende uma atitude para a TCS.

> ### Solução
>
> 1. Calcule a confiabilidade do sistema da alternativa de superdimensionamento (SR_o):
>
> $$SR_o = CR_{155} \times CR_{175} \times CR_{205} \times CR_{315}$$
> $$= 0,990 \times 0,995 \times 0,960 \times 0,980$$
> $$= 0,9267$$
>
> 2. Calcule a confiabilidade do componente 205 na alternativa de redundância. Qual é a confiabilidade combinada dos dois componentes trabalhando juntos?
>
> $$CR_{205} = \begin{pmatrix} \text{Probabilidade de} \\ \text{o componente} \\ \text{original} \\ \text{funcionar} \end{pmatrix} + \begin{pmatrix} \text{Probabilidade de} \\ \text{o componente} \\ \text{backup} \\ \text{funcionar} \end{pmatrix} \times \begin{pmatrix} \text{Probabilidade de} \\ \text{necessitar do} \\ \text{componente} \\ \text{backup} \end{pmatrix}$$
>
> $$= 0,890 + [0,890 \times (1 - 0,890)]$$
> $$= 0,9879$$
>
> 3. Calcule a confiabilidade da alternativa da redundância (SR_r):
>
> $$SR_r = CR_{155} \times CR_{175} \times CR_{205} \times CR_{315}$$
> $$= 0,990 \times 0,995 \times 0,9879 \times 0,980$$
> $$= 0,9537$$
>
> 4. Pelo fato de a confiabilidade do sistema aumentar mais com a alternativa da redundância e a um preço mais baixo, essa é a alternativa mais recomendável.

Muitos fabricantes americanos traçaram as metas de produzir produtos de qualidade quase perfeita. Os conceitos de simplificação, excesso de cautela e redundância são particularmente importantes para que essas metas sejam atingidas. Nosso conhecimento de confiabilidade do sistema também é útil em outras áreas da APO.

Projetando e Controlando Processos de Produção

Discutimos o projeto e a elaboração de processos de produção no Capítulo 4. Como indica a Tabela 16.3, os processos de produção precisam ser elaborados tendo o cliente em mente, porque eles devem ser capazes de produzir produtos com as características que o cliente quer. Uma vez colocados em prática, os processos precisam ser operados de forma que os produtos estejam de acordo com os requisitos do cliente. As organizações que fabricam produtos devem estar totalmente comprometidas a oferecer produtos e serviços de perfeita qualidade. Mas, mais do que isso, é preciso que elas se comprometam a tentar implacavelmente melhorar a qualidade do produto. O conceito de qualidade perfeita deve se aplicar a todas as facetas do sistema de produção, desde cada uma das matérias-primas nos fornecedores, passando por cada um dos funcionários do setor de produção, até cada um dos funcionários do depósito. A responsabilidade de *produzir* produtos de alta qualidade não é do pessoal de controle da qualidade. Ao contrário, são as pessoas que produzem o produto que são responsáveis. Espera-se que cada trabalhador passe para a operação seguinte produtos que sejam de perfeita qualidade. Nesse sentido, a próxima operação de produção deve ser considerada um **cliente interno**.

As variações do produto podem ser um obstáculo para a produção de produtos aceitáveis para os clientes. Dois tipos de fatores podem provocar variações nos processos de produção: fatores controláveis e fatores incontroláveis. *Os efeitos dos **fatores controláveis**, como mau funcionamento das máquinas, material ruim e métodos de trabalho incorretos, podem ser reduzidos com a diligência dos trabalhadores e da gerência. Os efeitos dos **fatores incontroláveis**, como temperatura, atrito, vibração, variação ocasional e outras causas naturais, só podem ser reduzidos redesenhando-se ou substituindo-se os proces-*

sos de produção existentes. Todo processo de produção tem um conjunto de fatores incontroláveis que causam variação no produto, e, se essa variação for muito grande, a qualidade resultante do produto pode não corresponder às expectativas do cliente.

A **capabilidade do processo** *é a capacidade do processo produtivo de fabricar produtos dentro das expectativas dos clientes.* O **índice de capabilidade do processo (Cp)** é útil para se determinar se um processo de produção é capaz de produzir produtos à altura das expectativas dos clientes. Se supusermos que a variação do processo devido a fatores incontroláveis seja distribuída normalmente:

$$Cp = \frac{LSC - LIC}{6\sigma}, \text{ onde}$$

LSC = o limite superior da característica de um produto que pode ser incluída nas expectativas do cliente
LIC = o limite inferior da característica de um produto que pode ser incluída nas expectativas do cliente
σ = o desvio padrão da característica de um produto de um processo de produção, uma medida de variação de longo prazo da característica de um produto dentro do processo de produção

Enquanto por um lado o Cp pode assumir qualquer valor positivo, estes valores de Cp têm os seguintes significados:

$Cp \geq 1,00$ o processo de produção tem capacidade de produzir produtos que atendem às expectativas do cliente

$Cp < 1,00$ o processo de produção não tem capacidade de produzir produtos que atendem às expectativas do cliente

A Figura 16.4 ilustra como o Cp pode ser utilizado para determinar se o processo de produção é capaz de produzir produtos que atendam às expectativas do cliente. Se esse não for capaz de fazê-lo, ele precisará ser reprojetado, modificado ou substituído por um com menor variabilidade no produto (σ).

Quando colocamos em prática processos que consigam atender às expectativas do cliente, esses devem ser operados de forma que produzam produtos que atendam às expectativas do cliente. Isso significa que os fatores controláveis têm de ser administrados. No Capítulo 17 exploraremos as maneiras como podemos garantir que os produtos estarão de acordo com as expectativas do cliente. Utilizam-se gráficos de controle, capabilidade do processo e amostragem para atingir esse objetivo.

Cultivando Parcerias com Fornecedores

No Capítulo 14 discutimos a abordagem moderna de selecionar e cultivar fornecedores. Para assegurar que os materiais dos fornecedores serão da mais alta qualidade, os fornecedores devem ser incluídos no programa de TQM da empresa. A Ford Motor Company é um bom exemplo de como isso deveria funcionar. Na Ford, a seleção inicial de fornecedores se baseia em como os fornecedores podem fazer interface com seu programa de TQM. A Ford tem cerca de 300 fornecedores em sua lista de Q-1, uma lista de fornecedores com os quais a Ford está disposta a ter contratos de fornecimento de longo prazo (geralmente de 3 anos) para obter a melhor qualidade a custos competitivos. Como os fornecedores Q-1 participam do projeto dos novos produtos Ford, esse projeto reflete a capacidade dos fornecedores de produzir materiais de alta qualidade. E os fornecedores participam dos programas de treinamento da Ford; conseqüentemente, os funcionários dos fornecedores são capazes de fazer a TQM funcionar nas organizações dos fornecedores.

Atendimento ao Cliente, Distribuição e Instalação

A embalagem, expedição e instalação devem se incluídas na TQM, porque os consumidores associam um desempenho ruim do produto a um produto de má qualidade, mesmo que o produto tenha sido danificado no transporte ou instalado de maneira inadequada. Isso significa que as funções de armazenagem e marketing também têm de buscar a qualidade perfeita. E todos os contatos entre as empresas, seus produtos e clientes devem ser planejados e administrados de forma a satisfazer os clientes.

FIGURA 16.4 — TRÊS EXEMPLOS DE ÍNDICE DE CAPABILIDADE DO PROCESSO

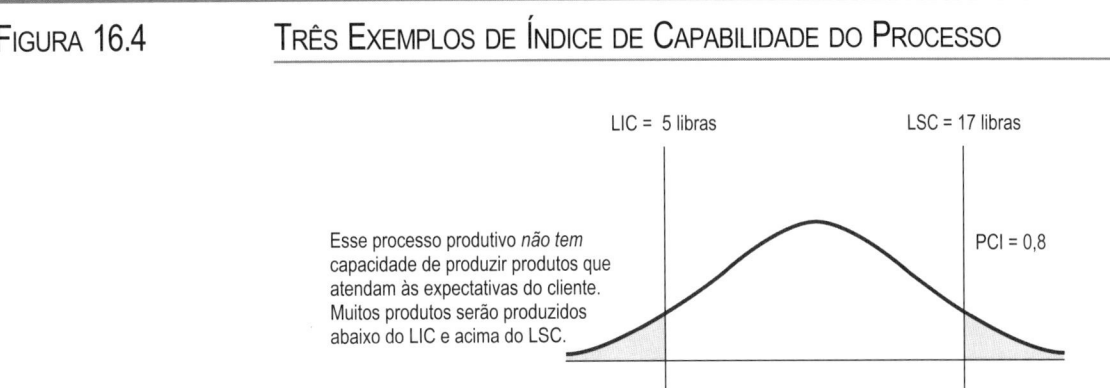

CRIANDO EQUIPES DE FUNCIONÁRIOS COM MAIS PODER

Existem vários aspectos na criação de equipes com mais poder: treinamento de funcionários, equipes de trabalho e poder, qualidade na fonte e círculos da qualidade.

Programas de Treinamento de Funcionários Quando se visa implantar a filosofia TQM, todos os funcionários — desde a fábrica até a diretoria —, bem como fornecedores e clientes, têm de participar de um programa de treinamento abrangente.

Na Ford Motor Company, por exemplo, mais de 6.000 pessoas freqüentaram 59 cursos diferentes num período de dois anos e mais de 1.000 fornecedores enviaram seus funcionários para a Ford para participarem de programas de treinamento em métodos de controle da qua lidade.

Embora muitas empresas façam seu próprio treinamento, uma quantidade cada vez maior de empresas está prestando consultoria no planejamento e execução de programas de TQM. Eis algumas delas: Philip Crosby Associates, Juran Institute, Ernst & Young, Qualtec, Guneson Group, ODI e Walker Customer Satisfaction. Existem disponíveis materiais de treinamento e educacional das seguintes empresas de controle da qualidade: The American Society for Quality and Participation, The Quality & Productivity Management Association e The American Productivity & Quality Center.

Equipes de Trabalho e Poder No Capítulo 15 discutimos a importância de criar equipes de trabalho. Para as empresas americanas conseguirem uma qualidade superior do produto, é obrigatório que elas extraiam e apliquem toda a habilidade e energia de seus funcionários. Os funcionários — operários, pessoal de escritório, gerentes, engenheiros e cientistas — compõem o recurso principal, que é o poder de atingir a excelência em termos de qualidade superior de produto. Os funcionários têm de aceitar a responsabilidade por todas as facetas da produção. Mas primeiro os gerentes têm de dar aos funcionários autoridade para agir, que é, em suma, a definição de dar poder ao trabalhador.

Dar poder aos trabalhadores é a maneira que a gerência tem de liberar uma força poderosa para trabalhar constantemente na busca da excelência na qualidade dos produtos e serviços. O Instantâneo da Indústria 16.3 ilustra o poder das equipes de trabalho na Square D Corporation.

Qualidade na Fonte O conceito de qualidade visa colocar o trabalhador do setor de produção no comando do controle da qualidade do produto. Na tentativa de atingir a meta de cada trabalhador produzir peças de qualidade perfeita, a qualidade na fonte segue os seguintes princípios:

- O trabalho de cada trabalhador se torna uma estação de controle da qualidade. Os trabalhadores são responsáveis pela inspeção de seu próprio trabalho, pela identificação de qualquer defeito, pela tarefa de retrabalhar as peças até ficarem sem nenhum defeito e pela correção das causas de qualquer defeito.
- Utilizam-se técnicas de controle estatístico da qualidade para monitorar a qualidade das peças fabricadas em cada uma das estações de trabalho e gráficos de fácil entendimento para informar o progresso aos trabalhadores e gerentes.
- Cada trabalhador tem o direito de parar a linha de produção para evitar a produção de peças defeituosas.
- Os trabalhadores e gerentes são organizados em **círculos da qualidade** ou **círculos CQ** — pequenos grupos de funcionários que analisam problemas da qualidade, trabalham para solucionar os problemas e implantar programas para melhorar a qualidade do produto.

Esse conjunto de arranjos faz quatro coisas: 1) atribui a responsabilidade pela qualidade do produto aos trabalhadores do setor e à função de produção, que é seu lugar; 2) ele pode levar os trabalhadores do setor de produção a serem mais comprometidos com uma alta qualidade do produto; 3) em vez de inspecionar os outros, o pessoal de controle da qualidade pode realizar um trabalho que tem impacto direto na fabricação de produtos de alta qualidade: trabalhar com o pessoal de produção para eliminar as causas do defeito, treinar os trabalhadores em controle da qualidade e trabalhar com os fornecedores para melhorar a qualidade de seu produto; 4) elimina um obstáculo à colaboração entre o pessoal de controle da qualidade e os trabalhadores do setor de produção para que eles possam trabalhar melhor juntos para obter um produto com mais qualidade.

INSTANTÂNEO DA INDÚSTRIA 16.3

EQUIPES DE TRABALHO COM PODER NA SQUARE D CORPORATION

Na fábrica de Lexington, Kentucky, da Square D Corporation, cerca de 800 trabalhadores se reorganizaram em equipes de trabalho de 20 a 30 membros para montar painéis de controle elétrico, interruptores e transformadores. Antes da formação dessas equipes de trabalho, os funcionários passavam o dia todo trabalhando várias vezes numa única peça sem nunca ver o produto final. Agora a fábrica está com um novo layout com cada equipe operando uma fábrica-dentro-de-uma-fábrica. Cada equipe trabalha um produto do começo ao fim e trabalha como se estivesse operando seu próprio negócio. A empresa costumava gastar mais na pintura de prédios do que em treinamento, mas agora gasta cerca de 4% em custos da folha de pagamento em treinamento. Os gerentes também deram aos trabalhadores autoridade para tomar decisões sobre todas as fases da produção na oficina. Os empregados são treinados para trabalhar como uma equipe para consertar as máquinas quando essas quebram. Eles trabalham juntos para tomar decisões sobre como solucionar problemas de produção quando esses ocorrem. Eles também são treinados para melhorar a qualidade do produto, e está dando certo. Os funcionários se encontram no início de cada turno e examinam seu desempenho em termos da qualidade. Cada funcionário representa graficamente sua precisão a cada 30 minutos. A quantidade de defeitos diminuiu em 75%, e o tempo para aprontar os pedidos dos clientes diminuiu de seis semanas para três dias.

Fonte: Jennings, Peter e Linda Patillo. "ABC Evening News", 24 de fevereiro de 1993.

FIGURA 16.5   COMO OS CÍRCULOS CQ FUNCIONAM

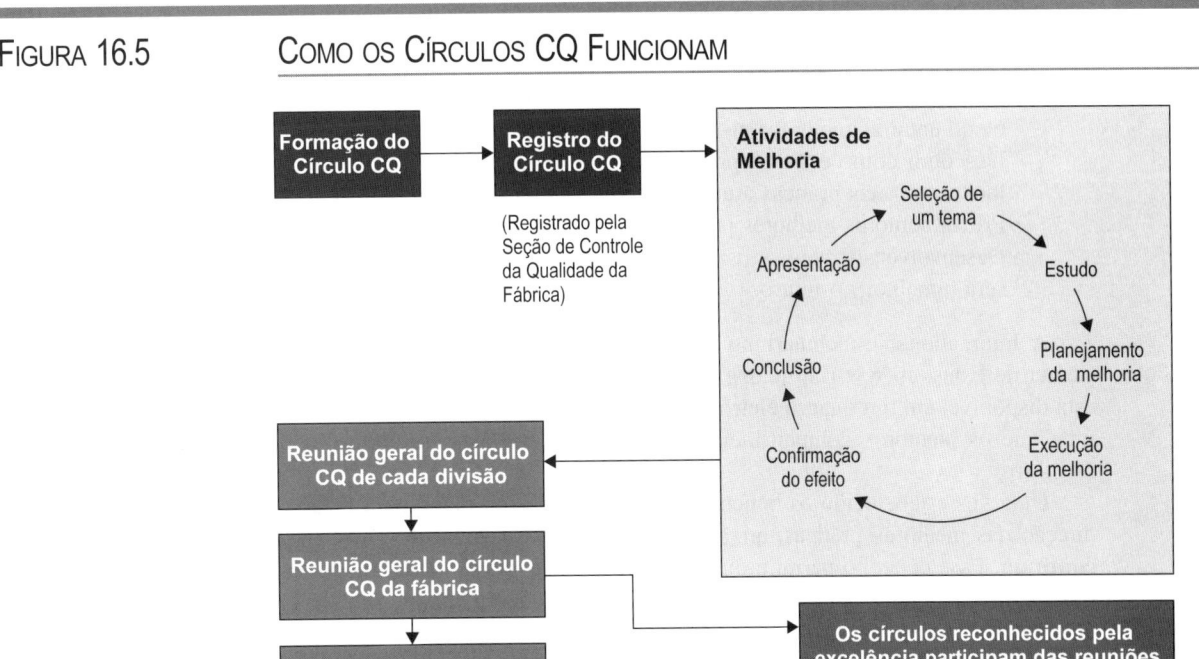

Círculos da Qualidade   Um círculo da qualidade ou círculo CQ é um pequeno grupo de funcionários — em média, nove — que se reúne regular e voluntariamente para empreender projetos relacionados ao trabalho desenvolvido para fazer a empresa avançar, melhorar as condições de trabalho e estimular o autodesenvolvimento mútuo, tudo utilizando conceitos de controle da qualidade. Os círculos CQ são incentivados pelas empresas japonesas e recebem um treinamento considerável sobre os conceitos e as técnicas de controle da qualidade. Eles tendem a selecionar seus próprios projetos para serem investigados e normalmente contam com o apoio da gerência na implantação de suas recomendações.

Há vários tipos de projeto, e podem ir além da qualidade para áreas como produtividade, projeto de ferramentas, segurança, manutenção e proteção ambiental. Fazer parte dos círculos CQ é um ato voluntário e não existem incentivos diretos em espécie. Seus membros dizem que entre os principais motivos que os levam a fazer parte desses grupos estão a satisfação pessoal de atingir um objetivo e o reconhecimento. Seu uso está se ampliando para os Estados Unidos, Inglaterra, Brasil, Indonésia, Coréia do Sul e outros países.

A Figura 16.5 mostra como esses círculos funcionam.

Apesar das diferenças culturais entre Japão e Estados Unidos, foram organizados círculos CQ em empresas como a Motorola, Minnesota Mining and Manufacturing (3M), NationsBank e Schulumberger. Para que esses programas sejam bem-sucedidos, é preciso que exista confiança e lealdade entre os trabalhadores e a gerência. Cada vez mais empresas americanas estão reconhecendo a importância de atrair seus trabalhadores para a tendência atual de seus programas de gerência da qualidade. Esse esforço certamente contribuirá para uma elevação geral da gerência da qualidade na consciência dos trabalhadores, resultando em soluções únicas e inovadoras para os problemas da qualidade, e para aumentar a probabilidade de os trabalhadores colaborarem na implantação dos programas para melhorar a qualidade do produto.

O BENCHMARKING E A MELHORIA CONTÍNUA

Empresas como a AT&T, Digital Equipment, Ford, IBM, Motorola, Milliken & Company, Texas Instruments e Xerox Corporation se envolvem em **benchmarking**, *a prática de estabelecer padrões internos de desempenho examinando como as empresas de classe mundial dirigem seus negócios.*

Fazer o benchmarking da empresa A em uma área como atendimento ao cliente envolveria as seguintes atividades:

- Examinar empresas como L. L. Bean, Federal Express e Xerox. Elas são consideradas como estando entre as melhores na obtenção de satisfação do cliente.
- Descobrir como essas empresas realizam o atendimento ao cliente. Isso inclui os mínimos detalhes sobre suas práticas atuais em termos de atendimento ao cliente.
- Prever como as melhores práticas de atendimento ao cliente mudarão no futuro.
- Desenvolver estratégias para mudar as práticas atuais da empresa A para o que provavelmente será o melhor no futuro.

A International Benchmarking Clearinghouse (IBC), sediada no American Productivity & Quality Center de Houston (**www.apqc.org**), criou um banco de dados das melhores práticas. O banco de dados está disponível em um quadro eletrônico que pode ser acessado pelos membros da IBC. Esse quadro permite que os membros compartilhem informações e solicitem informações de benchmarking de outros membros.

Uma vez estabelecido os benchmarks e elaborado um plano para fazer as empresas caminharem na direção das melhores práticas, ativa-se um elemento essencial da TQM — a necessidade de **melhoria contínua**. Esse conceito permite que as empresas aceitem começos modestos e façam pequenas melhorias na direção da excelência. Essa abordagem apresenta diversas vantagens. Primeiro, como os resultados iniciais tendem a ser na melhor das hipóteses modestos, evita-se frustração e abandono. Além disso, o progresso gradativo e contínuo na direção de melhorias significa que as empresas não podem nunca aceitar que o que são é o melhor que podem ser.

A prática da empresa, portanto, nunca é suficientemente boa. Isso faz com que as empresas, mesmo as de classe mundial, lutem por níveis de desempenho cada vez mais elevados. Isso é essencial para todo aquele que quer entrar na concorrência internacional.

GERÊNCIA DA QUALIDADE NO SETOR DE SERVIÇOS

A ex-chanceler da Universidade de Wisconsin, Donna Shalala, nomeada para o gabinete do governo Clinton, afirmou na televisão que as abordagens de TQM seriam aplicadas aos órgãos do governo americano. Ela disse que o que as universidades aprenderam da TQM sobre como melhorar o atendimento ao cliente, produtividade e eficiência em termos de custo poderia ser utilizado de forma lucrativa no governo. É evidente que cada tipo de organização pode se beneficiar com as abordagens de TQM, mesmo os órgãos governamentais.

Aplicar a TQM ao setor de serviços apresenta suas dificuldades. Muitos serviços são intangíveis e, devido sua própria natureza, é difícil determinar sua qualidade. Pegue, por exemplo, o problema que as companhias aéreas enfrentam quando tentam determinar a qualidade do desempenho dos comissários de bordo. Os elementos do desempenho de um comissário de bordo que afetam a percepção da qualidade do cliente são difíceis de se identificar e medir, e, na maioria dos casos, os padrões para medir o desempenho simplesmente não existem. Em vez disso os clientes criam seus próprios padrões, comparando o serviço que recebem com o serviço que desejariam receber.

Um outro fator que complica essa situação é que a qualidade percebida de alguns serviços é afetada por aquilo que a cerca. Uma música suave e tranqüila, uma decoração agradável, móveis confortáveis, estacionamento fácil, atendentes cordiais, limpeza das instalações e outras características podem determinar a qualidade percebida dos serviços mais do que a qualidade efetiva dos mesmos. Os hospitais, bancos e restaurantes, por exemplo, investem pesadamente na tarefa de projetar e manter instalações que despertem determinadas sensações em seus clientes e lhes causem impressões específicas.

Como vários serviços tendem a ser intensivos em termos de mão-de-obra e os trabalhadores tendem a ter contato direto com os clientes, o desempenho dos funcionários do setor de prestação de serviços determina em grande parte a qualidade dos serviços. No entanto, como os serviços tendem a ser extremamente descentralizados e geograficamente dispersos, muitas organizações prestadoras de serviços elaboram um programa intensivo de educação contínua e treinamento para seus funcionários na base de sua gerência da qualidade. O McDonald's e o Holiday Inn's University são exemplos disso.

Capítulo 16 – Gerência da Qualidade

As dificuldades de se definir programas de gerência da qualidade para serviços não são obstáculos intransponíveis. As organizações prestadoras de serviços elaboram programas sofisticados de controle da qualidade, e algumas de suas características são muito semelhantes às das organizações manufatureiras. Outros aspectos de seus programas, no entanto, são drasticamente diferentes.

O Instantâneo da Indústria 16.4 discute uma abordagem que está sendo utilizada para melhorar a qualidade dos serviços.

Os programas de controle da qualidade têm amplo impacto na gerência das empresas. Para a maioria dos serviços, a arma competitiva escolhida é a qualidade percebida do serviço, porque preço, flexibilidade e rapidez de entrega podem não ser muito diferentes do oferecido pela concorrência. A qualidade do serviço, portanto, se torna o foco principal da estratégia operacional.

Um elemento importante de vários programas da qualidade no setor de serviços é a utilização de **pesquisas de clientes**. Essa técnica permite que os clientes respondam questionários ou participem de entrevistas que visam determinar suas percepções sobre várias questões ligadas à qualidade.

Uma outra maneira de estimar a qualidade dos serviços é utilizar **"falsos compradores"** — funcionários que fingem ser clientes mas na verdade monitoram a qualidade dos serviços. Por exemplo, na

INSTANTÂNEO DA INDÚSTRIA 16.4

PRESTANDO SERVIÇOS DE QUALIDADE

O que faz com que um serviço tenha qualidade? Zeithaml, Parasuraman e Berry identificaram as seguintes dimensões da qualidade de serviço:

- **Tangibilidade**: A aparência das instalações físicas, equipamentos, pessoal e materiais de comunicação.
- **Confiabilidade**: A capacidade de oferecer o serviço prometido de maneira confiável e precisa.
- **Presteza**: A disposição de ajudar os clientes e prestar serviço imediatamente.
- **Garantia**: O conhecimento e a cortesia dos funcionários e sua capacidade de inspirar confiança.
- **Empatia**: A preocupação e atenção individualizada que a empresa dá a seus clientes.

Os clientes sempre classificam a confiabilidade como a dimensão mais importante, e a tangibilidade como a menos importante. A mensagem é clara: tenha boa aparência, seja prestativo, dê garantias, tenha empatia, mas, acima de tudo, seja confiável. Faça o que diz que vai fazer.

Zeithaml, Parasuraman e Berry identificaram algumas barreiras significativas à qualidade do serviço:

1. **A lacuna entre as expectativas do cliente e a percepção da gerência.** Existe uma lacuna entre o que a gerência acha que os clientes esperam e o que eles realmente esperam das empresas prestadoras de serviços.
2. **A lacuna entre a percepção da gerência e a especificação da qualidade do serviço.** A gerência estabelece especificações ou padrões da qualidade que estão aquém das expectativas dos clientes.
3. **A lacuna entre as especificações da qualidade e o serviço prestado.** A qualidade do serviço prestado está aquém das especificações de serviço estabelecidas pela gerência.
4. **A lacuna entre a prestação de serviço e as comunicações externas.** As expectativas do cliente foram elevadas pela propaganda na mídia, apresentações de venda e outras comunicações a níveis além da capacidade da empresa.
5. **A lacuna entre a expectativa e a percepção dos clientes.** Existe uma lacuna entre o que o cliente espera e o que cliente acha que recebeu. Essa é a principal lacuna.

Zeithaml, Parasuraman e Berry criaram uma abordagem de melhoria contínua da qualidade do serviço.

O processo de melhoria da qualidade começa com uma avaliação externa das deficiências da qualidade percebidas pelo cliente (lacuna 5), seguida de uma avaliação interna das causas principais das deficiências da organização (lacunas 1-4).

Fonte: Zeithaml, Valerie A., A. Parasuraman e Leonardo L. Berry. *Delivering Quality Service: Balancing Customer Perceptions and Expectations*, Nova Iorque, Free Press, 1990.

American Express cerca de 250 funcionários de controle da qualidade monitoram a qualidade dos serviços no mundo todo, e um elemento importante desse programa é a utilização de "falsos compradores". Além disso, como nas outras organizações prestadoras de serviços, a American Express utiliza **gráficos de controle estatístico** para monitorar elementos como o tempo necessário para processar a requisição de um cartão American Express pelo cliente. Da mesma maneira, utilizam-se gráficos de controle estatístico, usando os dados coletados a partir das pesquisas de cliente para identificar várias medidas de satisfação do cliente.

A diversidade dessas medidas enfatiza a flexibilidade dos gráficos de controle no controle da qualidade dos serviços, bem como o custo e outras dimensões do desempenho da organização. Estudaremos mais sobre controle estatístico da qualidade e gráficos de controle no Capítulo 17.

RESUMO FINAL

O QUE OS FABRICANTES DE CLASSE MUNDIAL ESTÃO FAZENDO

A qualidade do produto ou do serviço começa quando se formula a estratégia de negócios. Cria-se um plano para cada produto ou serviço com o objetivo de fazer com que ele se destaque do oferecido pelo concorrente.

Hoje a qualidade é a arma escolhida para que vários produtos e serviços conquistem mercados mundiais. A competência número 1 pela qual os fabricantes de classe mundial batalham é uma qualidade preeminente de produto ou serviço.

Os fabricantes de classe mundial não diferenciam entre melhoria da produtividade e melhoria da qualidade. Para eles, são a mesma coisa. Para esses fabricantes a qualidade aciona a máquina da produtividade.

Talvez o mais importante de tudo, os fabricantes de classe mundial pararam de depender da inspeção para identificar defeitos. Em vez disso eles estão concentrando todos os seus esforços em fazer tudo certo desde a primeira vez. Eles estão tentando encontrar e solucionar seus problemas da qualidade em vez de adotar programas de inspeção que visem identificar defeitos enquanto métodos ruins de produção continuam sendo utilizados. E os fabricantes de classe mundial adotam fabricação just-in-time, padronização de produtos, equipamentos automatizados e manutenção preventiva não só para reduzir custos mas também devido a seu impacto na qualidade e no atendimento ao cliente.

As empresas de classe mundial estão comprometendo enormes recursos para colocar em prática programas de gestão da qualidade total que visam a melhoria contínua da qualidade.

Na Motorola é o Seis Sigmas, na Xerox é o Liderança através da Qualidade, na Intel é o PQD, e na Hewlett-Packard é o Controle da Qualidade Total. Quais empresas aspiram o status de fabricantes de classe mundial? Uma maneira de responder a essa pergunta é observar quais empresas se candidatam ao Prêmio Nacional Malcolm Baldrige de Qualidade e ao Prêmio Deming e se qualificam para os padrões ISO 9000.

Os programas de gestão da qualidade total normalmente contêm os seguintes elementos:

- Compromisso e envolvimento da alta administração
- Envolvimento do cliente
- Criação de produtos de qualidade
- Criação de processos de produção de qualidade
- Controle da qualidade dos processos de produção
- Cultivo de parcerias com os fornecedores
- Atendimento ao cliente, distribuição e instalação
- Trabalho em equipe
- Benchmarking e melhorias contínuas

Uma quantidade cada vez maior de universidades, bancos, companhias de seguros, escritórios de advocacia, hospitais e outros negócios de prestação de serviços vem adotando programas de administração da qualidade total.

E há relatórios animadores de uma quantidade cada vez maior de programas bem-sucedidos de TQM no setor de fabricação. Mas algumas empresas fracassaram na tentativa de TQM porque seus programas são vagos demais e pouco específicos, tentam fazer muitas coisas ao mesmo tempo e não envolvem o cliente ou uma quantidade suficiente de funcionários, e seus gerentes seniores não são recompensados por seu desempenho na área da qualidade.

QUESTÕES DE REVISÃO E DISCUSSÃO

1. Explique o papel da qualidade do produto e do serviço na estratégia de negócios.
2. Enumere e dê uma breve descrição das *dimensões da qualidade*.
3. Enumere e dê uma breve descrição dos determinantes da qualidade e das atividades necessárias para se obter produtos e serviços de qualidade.
4. Quais são os custos da qualidade? Dê uma breve explicação de cada um deles.
5. A visão tradicional de controle da qualidade é fazer inspeções rigorosas para se encontrar e descartar peças defeituosas de forma que só produtos sem defeito saiam da inspeção. O que está basicamente errado com essa abordagem? Explique o significado desta afirmação: "Não se pode inspecionar a qualidade dos produtos".
6. Explique o significado desta afirmação: "A qualidade aciona a máquina da produtividade".
7. Resuma as contribuições destas pessoas para a gestão da qualidade: (a) W. Edwards Deming, (b) Phillip B. Crosby, (c) Armand V. Feigenbaum, (d) Kaoru Ishikawa, (e) Joseph M. Juran e (f) Genichi Taguchi.
8. Defina, descreva e explique o uso de diagramas *espinha de peixe*.
9. Explique como estes fatores afetam a qualidade do produto: (a) fabricação just-in-time (JIT), (b) manutenção preventiva.
10. Descreva o Prêmio Deming. Explique seu significado para a gerência da qualidade.
11. O que são os padrões ISO 9000? Explique seu significado.
12. Defina um *programa de gestão da qualidade total (TQM)*. Quais são alguns dos nomes utilizados pelas empresas para seus programas de gestão da qualidade total?
13. Quais são os elementos importantes da gestão da qualidade total (TQM)? Explique como cada um deles contribui para produtos e serviços de qualidade superior.
14. Explique o significado de: (a) *projetos robustos*, (b) *projetos voltados para a produção* e (c) *projeto voltado para a confiabilidade*.
15. Qual o significado da expressão *qualidade na fonte*?
16. Qual é a finalidade dos *círculos da qualidade*? Como eles funcionam? Que fatores precisam estar presentes para que esses cículos sejam bem-sucedidos? Quais são os benefícios que eles proporcionam às empresas?
17. O que faz com que um serviço tenha qualidade? Quais são as barreiras para esse serviço?
18. Discuta a gerência da qualidade no setor de serviços. Que fatores tornaram a gerência da qualidade mais difícil no setor de serviços do que no setor de fabricação? Que abordagens foram criadas para atenuar os efeitos dessas dificuldades? Que estratégia de gerência da qualidade os sistemas de serviços desenvolveram para lidar com o fato de o setor de serviços tender a ser intensivo em termos de mão-de-obra e geograficamente disperso?
19. Descreve uma TQM para estes negócios de prestação de serviços: (a) banco, (b) hospital, (c) universidade, (d) escritório de advocacia e (e) companhia de seguros.

TAREFAS NA INTERNET

1. Visite e explore o site da American Society for Quality (ASQ) (**www.asq.org**). Localize informações sobre QS-9000. Explique o que é QS-9000 e o que ele envolve.
2. Visite e explore o site da Organização Internacional de Padronização (ISO) (**www.iso.ch**). Qual foi o primeiro padrão publicado pela ISO e quando? Discuta se a Organização Internacional de Padronização emite certificados de acordo com os padrões ISO 9000.
3. Visite e explore o site do Prêmio Nacional Malcolm Baldrige de Qualidade (**www.quality.nist.gov**). Resuma o histórico desse prêmio descrevendo suas finalidades. Que empresas receberam o prêmio o ano passado?
4. Busque na Internet uma empresa de consultoria especializada em ajudar as empresas na gestão da qualidade total ou TQM. Descreva os serviços relevantes oferecidos por ela. Dê o site da empresa na Internet.
5. Visite e explore o site do Prêmio Shingo (**www.usu.edu/~shingo/**). Descreva em poucas palavras o histórico e o objetivo do Prêmio Shingo. Que organizações receberam o prêmio no ano passado?

Estudo de Caso

A Confiabilidade do Produto na Valvco Inc.

A NASA está prestes a dar um contrato de válvula hidráulica para a Valvco Inc., de Atlanta. Mas surgiu um obstáculo nas negociações contratuais. A NASA exige uma confiabilidade de pelo menos 0,990 para essa válvula. A Valvco está estudando os dados de seus testes para definir se há uma maneira prática de seu produto preencher os requisitos da NASA. A válvula tem quatro peças componentes que interagem de acordo com os seguintes dados de testes:

Peça Componente	Quantidade de Peças Testadas	Quantidade de Horas de Testes	Quantidade de Falhas
Z24	200	5.000	1
T19	190	3.000	0
A5	1.290	2.000	2
S113	323	1.000	3

Tarefas

1. Qual é a confiabilidade atual do sistema da válvula? A válvula preenche os requisitos de confiabilidade de sistema da NASA?
2. A NASA sugeriu redundância no projeto da válvula. Determine a confiabilidade da válvula com cada componente como candidato a redundância. A sugestão da NASA pode fazer o sistema atender aos requisitos de confiabilidade do sistema?
3. Um dos engenheiros da Valvco sugeriu que a NASA comprasse a válvula da Valvco como ela é no momento e utilizasse duas válvulas paralelamente, uma como a principal e a outra como reserva. Avalie essa proposta como um meio de atender aos requisitos de confiabilidade do sistema da NASA.
4. Que alternativas você recomendaria para atender aos requisitos de confiabilidade do sistema da NASA? Por quê?
5. Discuta o conceito de redundância dos componentes como um meio prático de aumentar a confiabilidade do sistema. Quais são as vantagens e desvantagens dessa abordagem?

capítulo 17

CONTROLE DA QUALIDADE

Introdução

Conceitos Estatísticos no Controle da Qualidade
Amostragem
Teorema do Limite Central e Controle da Qualidade

Gráficos de Controle
Gráficos de Controle por Atributos
Gráficos de Controle por Variáveis

Computadores no Controle da Qualidade

O Controle da Qualidade no Setor de Serviços

Resumo Final: O Que os Fabricantes de Classe Mundial Estão Fazendo

Questões de Revisão e Discussão

Tarefas na Internet

Problemas

Estudo de Caso
Integrated Products Corporation

O Controle da Qualidade na Texas Telecom

A Texas Telecom produz uma série de caixas de conversor de TV para as indústrias de TV a cabo ou por satélite. Fundada no final dos anos 1980, a Texas Telecom no início se concentrava em produtos de baixo custo. Mas, nos últimos anos, a empresa redirecionou suas operações para poder oferecer produtos confiáveis de alto desempenho. No esforço de se concentrar em produtos finais de qualidade mais elevada, a Texas Telecom implantou um programa de gestão da qualidade total (TQM) e ficou satisfeita com os resultados. Um aspecto da TQM particularmente útil no sentido de melhorar a qualidade do produto e fechar novos negócios foi o uso de gráficos de controle.

Antes de esses gráficos serem utilizados, muitos dos produtos da empresa não estavam de acordo com as especificações do cliente. Embora os produtos tenham sido elaborados para ser superiores, havia muita variação no desempenho do produto. Para solucionar esse problema, a gerente de produção, Mary Boone, introduziu gráficos de controle em todo o processo de produção. Os elementos-chaves dessa iniciativa eram o autocontrole pelos trabalhadores, reuniões de pequenos grupos para analisar o controle da qualidade e o reconhecimento dos desempenhos de alta qualidade pela gerência. As equipes de trabalho se reúnem no início de cada turno para revisar os gráficos mais recentes do período de oito horas, detectar qualquer tendência indesejável e discutir qualquer correção necessária nos processos de produção. Depois, durante seu turno, cada trabalhador plota a medida da qualidade dos produtos de sua operação a cada 30 minutos. Qualquer tendência que o trabalhador ache que esteja ficando fora de controle é imediatamente comunicada ao líder da equipe. Se for suficientemente grave, a produção é interrompida até o problema ser corrigido.

O treinamento do funcionário era parte fundamental do programa de gráfico de controle da Texas Telecom. Antes de utilizar o gráfico de controle, cada trabalhador passava por duas semanas de treinamento sobre os elementos básicos da gerência da qualidade e dos gráficos de controle. Com a ajuda dos gráficos de controle, o desempenho do produto atualmente está em níveis extremamente elevados. Os índices de defeito (produtos fora da especificação) são de apenas 0,01%, ou cerca de 1 defeito em cada 10.000 unidades — um décimo da média da indústria.

O relato acima descreve um programa para melhorar a conformidade da qualidade do produto com as especificações do cliente. É disso que este capítulo basicamente trata: a elaboração de programas de gráficos de controle para monitorar o desempenho dos processos de produção para corresponder às expectativas do cliente, e os planos de aceitação para situações especiais onde eles possam ser adequados.

Como discutido no Capítulo 16, os clientes determinam a qualidade dos produtos e serviços. As expectativas dos clientes são a base para determinar se os produtos e serviços são de qualidade superior. A Tabela 17.1 relaciona alguns produtos e serviços e as expectativas dos clientes. São as expectativas dos clientes que devem ser traduzidas em padrões de controle da qualidade dos bens e serviços que estão sendo produzidos.

Porém o controle da qualidade começa muito antes de os produtos e serviços serem entregues aos clientes. Como mostra a Figura 17.1, logo no início do sistema de produção as matérias-primas, peças e suprimentos devem ser de alta qualidade antes de ser utilizados. Os materiais são examinados para garantir que estão de acordo com as especificações adequadas — força, tamanho, cor, acabamento, aparência, conteúdo químico, peso e outras características. À medida que os materiais vão indo adiante na produção, analisa-se a qualidade dos produtos parcialmente concluídos, para determinar se os processos de produção estão operando de acordo com o desejado. Esse monitoramento visa melhorar a qualidade do produto e identificar tendências indesejáveis que indicam medidas corretivas que precisam ser tomadas. Depois estudam-se os produtos e serviços acabados para determinar se eles estão de acordo com as expectativas do cliente. O controle da qualidade inclui atividades dos fornecedores, através da produção e para os clientes.

Conceitos Estatísticos no Controle da Qualidade

Os fundamentos das práticas atuais de controle da qualidade vêm do trabalho de Shewhart, Dodge e Roming e dos Laboratórios da Bell Telephone na década de 1920, época em que esses homens criaram métodos de amostragem, gráficos de controle e planos de aceitação.

TABELA 17.1 — ALGUNS PRODUTOS E SERVIÇOS E AS EXPECTATIVAS DOS CLIENTES

Empresa Produtora/ Prestadora de Serviços	Expectativas dos Clientes
Fabricante de fertilizante químico	O produto contém a quantidade certa de cada um dos elementos químicos? A embalagem evita a absorção de excesso de umidade sob condições normais de uso? O tamanho das partículas é o correto?
Hospital	Os pacientes são tratados educadamente por todo o pessoal do hospital? Todos os pacientes recebem os tratamentos corretos nas horas certas? Todos os tratamentos são administrados com precisão? O ambiente hospitalar apóia a recuperação do paciente?
Universidade	Todos os alunos cursam os cursos previstos? Todos os alunos estão atingido um desempenho aceitável nos cursos? Todos os professores estão contribuindo para o crescimento e desenvolvimento dos alunos?
Fabricante de automóveis	O carro apresenta o desempenho desejado? Todas as peças do carro estão dentro dos limites de tolerância de fabricação? O projeto é de operação segura? O carro oferece a confiabilidade desejada? O gasto de gasolina por quilômetro, o controle de poluição e o equipamento de segurança estão dentro das normas governamentais?
Banco	Os clientes são tratados com cortesia? As transações dos clientes são concluídas com precisão? Os extratos dos clientes refletem precisamente suas transações? O banco opera de acordo com as as normas governamentais? O ambiente físico é agradável para os clientes?
Serraria	A madeira é classificada adequadamente? A madeira está dentro dos limites de tolerância de conteúdo de umidade? Há excesso de rachaduras, manchas na superfície e outros tipos de defeitos? A madeira é embalada adequadamente para remessa? A madeira está de acordo com as especificações de resistência?

FIGURA 17.1 — CONTROLE DA QUALIDADE NOS SISTEMAS DE PRODUÇÃO

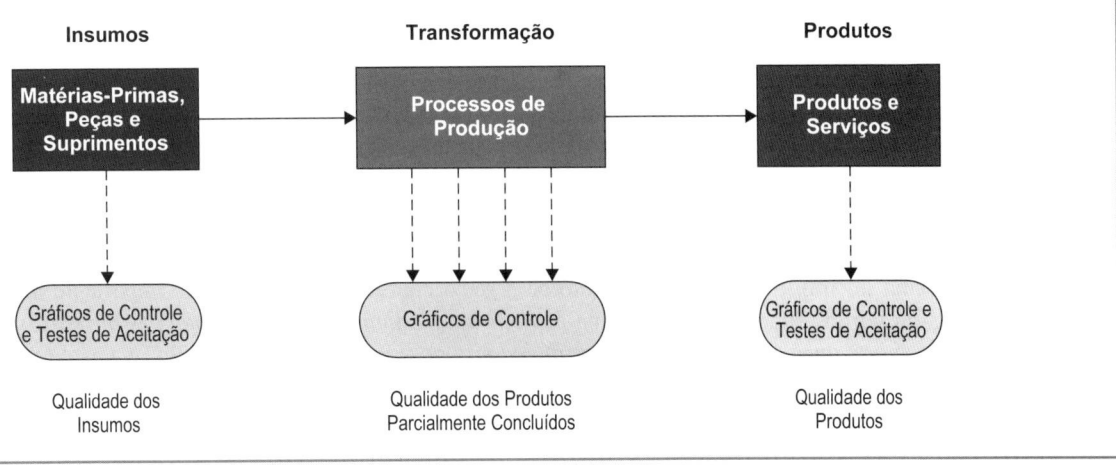

AMOSTRAGEM

O fluxo de produtos é dividido em **lotes** discretos. Um lote de controle da qualidade é produzido sob as mesmas condições operacionais. Pegam-se amostras de lotes de materiais, montagens e produtos para determinar se eles estão de acordo com os padrões de qualidade. **Amostras aleatórias** são retiradas desses lotes e medidas novamente em relação a determinados padrões. *Uma amostra aleatória é uma amostra onde todas as unidades do lote têm a mesma chance de ser incluídas na amostra*; portanto a amostra tem probabilidade de ser **representativa** do lote. Pode-se medir atributos ou variáveis e compará-los aos padrões.

Atributos são características que são classificadas em uma de duas categorias. No controle da qualidade, as duas categorias geralmente são **defeituosas** e **não defeituosas**. Por exemplo, a lâmpada ou acende ou não acende quando ligada à corrente elétrica. **Variáveis** são características que podem ser medidas em uma escala contínua. Os funcionários que inspecionam variáveis têm de medir uma característica presente e depois determinar se ela está dentro dos limites aceitáveis. Por exemplo, o diâmetro de um eixo de motor pode ser medido em milésimos de polegadas.

Que porcentagem dos lotes deveria ser incluída nas amostras? Em outras palavras, qual deveria ser o tamanho e a freqüência das amostras? Normalmente um dos argumentos é que à medida que se aumenta a porcentagem dos lotes nas amostras, provoca-se dois efeitos: (1) os custos de amostragem e teste aumentam e (2) a qualidade dos produtos que vão para os clientes aumenta. Os custos de amostragem e teste aumentam à medida que a porcentagem dos lotes amostrados e testados aumenta. E se só os bons produtos sobreviverem aos testes, a qualidade dos produtos que irão para os clientes aumentará quando aumentar a porcentagem dos lotes que estão sendo amostrados e testados. Numa era de empresas que estão tentando ser de primeira classe em termos de qualidade do produto, podemos concluir que deveríamos incluir grandes porcentagens dos lotes nas amostras. Isso é verdade para muitos produtos e certamente verdade para a maioria dos produtos que têm de ser muito confiáveis. Por exemplo, um fabricante de computador inspeciona, testa e compara todos os computadores com os padrões de qualidade. Para evitar os custos extremamente altos de testar uma porcentagem de sua produção, os testes foram totalmente automatizados. *Para as empresas que aspiram ser a primeira em sua classe em termos de qualidade do produto, parece ser uma boa tática, para alguns produtos, aumentar a qualidade reduzindo os custos de amostragem e teste de forma que quase todos os produtos possam ser testados de forma econômica.*

Para outros produtos, porcentagens relativamente pequenas dos lotes são amostradas e testadas, porque os custos de testar não podem ser significativamente reduzidos. Nesses casos, amostras muito grandes são muito caras e evitadas, e amostras extremamente pequenas podem sofrer de imprecisão estatística e também ser evitadas. Entre os dois extremos, normalmente são utilizadas amostras maiores para identificar atributos do que as usadas para identificar variáveis. Os tamanhos das amostras para identificar atributos normalmente têm de ser suficientemente grandes para detectar uma média de pelo menos um artigo defeituoso. Por exemplo, se um lote tivesse 2% de artigos defeituosos, precisaríamos de uma amostra de pelo menos 50 para identificar pelo menos uma média de 1 artigo defeituoso. Os tamanhos das amostras para identificar variáveis geralmente estão na faixa de 4 a 20.

O momento de inspecionar durante os processos produtvos normalmente pode ser determinado seguindo-se estes princípios: (1) inspecionar depois das operações que poderiam produzir itens defeituosos, (2) inspecionar antes de operações caras, (3) inspecionar antes das operações que cobrem os defeitos, (4) inspecionar antes das operações de montagem que não podem ser desfeitas, (5) nas máquinas automáticas, inspecionar as primeiras e últimas peças mas poucas peças intermediárias e (6) inspecionar os produtos acabados. Os motivos por trás desses princípios são em grande parte econômicos.

Um conceito importante na inspeção é o teorema do limite central.

TEOREMA DO LIMITE CENTRAL E CONTROLE DA QUALIDADE

O **teorema do limite central** pode muito bem ser o conceito estatístico mais importante na APO. Expresso em termos simples, esse teorema é: *Pode-se presumir que as distribuições amostrais estão distribuídas normalmente mesmo que a distribuição da população não seja normal*. A única exceção desse teorema ocorre quando os tamanhos das amostras são extremamente pequenos. Estudos computadorizados mostram que em alguns casos até mesmo quando o tamanho da amostra é de cinco unidades suas **distribuições amostrais** são muito próximas da distribuição normal.

FIGURA 17.2   COMPARAÇÃO DE POPULAÇÕES E DISTRIBUIÇÕES AMOSTRAIS

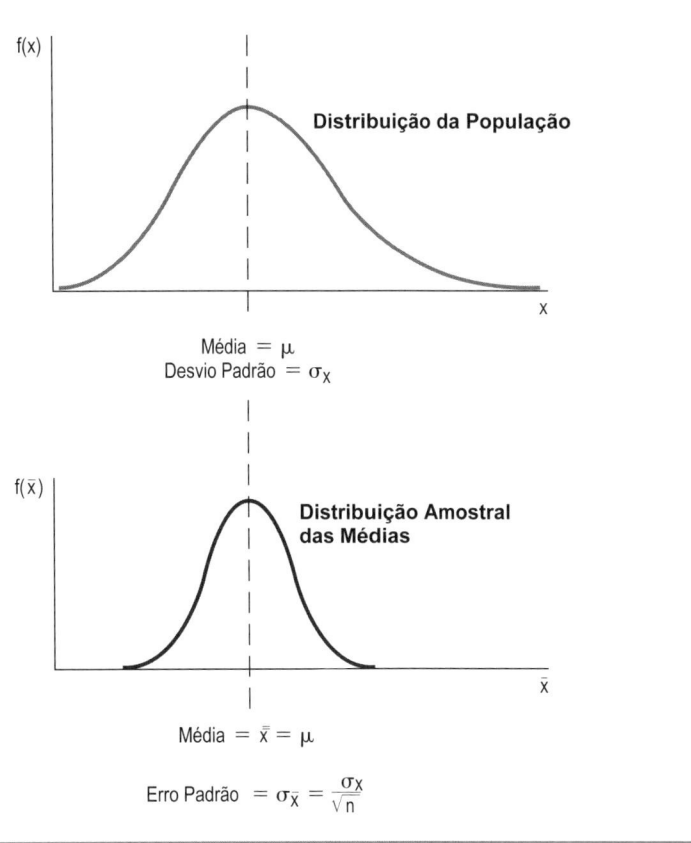

A Figura 17.2 compara a distribuição da população com a distribuição da média amostral. Essa distribuição amostral inclui todas as medidas das médias de amostra possíveis ($\bar{x}$). Pode-se fazer as seguintes generalizações sobre a distribuição amostral:

1. Pode-se considerar a distribuição amostral como sendo normal, a menos que o tamanho da amostra (n) seja extremamente pequeno.
2. A média da distribuição amostral ($\bar{\bar{x}}$) é igual à média da população (μ).
3. O desvio padrão da distribuição amostral ($\sigma_{\bar{x}}$) é menor do que o desvio padrão da população (σ_x) por um fator de $1/\sqrt{n}$.

O poder do teorema do limite central no controle da qualidade está em sua capacidade de utilizar a distribuição normal para estabelecer facilmente limites para os gráficos de controle e planos de aceitação de atributos e variáveis.

GRÁFICOS DE CONTROLE

Para a melhoria contínua da qualidade do produto, é fundamental estudar detalhadamente a qualidade dos produtos que vêm de cada operação de produção. Os gráficos de controle ajudam a atingir essa meta. Os dados periódicos de amostras de cada operação de controle são colocados em um gráfico de controle e comparados com os padrões. Se os dados da amostra estiverem próximos dos padrões, a operação está sob controle e não é preciso tomar nenhuma atitude. Porém, se os dados estiverem distantes dos padrões ou se se notar a presença de tendências inesperadas, a operação tem de ser investigada. *O objetivo principal dos* **gráficos de controle** *é indicar quando os processos de produção podem ter mudado o suficiente* *para afetar a qualidade do produto. É feita então uma investigação das causas da mudança. Se a indicação for de que a qualidade do produto se deteriorou ou pode se deteriorar no futuro, o problema é corrigido tomando-se medidas como substituir ferramentas desgastadas, fazer ajustes nas máquinas ou treinar e instruir os trabalhadores. Se a indicação for de que a qualidade é melhor do que a esperada, é importante descobrir por quê, para que a alta qualidade possa ser mantida.* A investigação dos problemas de qualidade pode revelar que não é necessário nenhuma medida corretiva, que a variação dos dados foi somente uma anormalidade. A beleza dos gráficos de controle é que os gerentes e trabalhadores podem dar uma olhada rápida neles e determinar se os padrões da qualidade estão sendo obedecidos ou se é preciso investigar tendências fora do comum. Devido à flexibilidade da aplicação dessas ferramentas, os gráficos de controle são usados em todos os tipos de negócios e organizações governamentais. A utilização dos gráficos de controle geralmente é chamada de **controle estatístico de processos (CEP)**.

Gráficos de Controle por Atributos

A elaboração de gráficos de controle envolve a determinação de três coisas: (1) a linha central, (2) o limite superior de controle e (3) o limite inferior de controle. Uma vez estabelecidos esses três valores, eles se tornam os padrões ou benchmarks com os quais serão feitas as comparações no futuro. A Figura 17.3 é um gráfico p utilizado para plotar a porcentagem de peças defeituosas nas amostras diárias no mês de março. O limite superior de controle é um pouco acima de 10%, a linha central é de 5%, e o limite inferior de controle é de 0%. À medida que a porcentagem de peças defeituosas da amostra diária vai sendo plotada nesse gráfico de controle, podemos ver que todos os pontos estão dentro dos limites superior e inferior de controle e que não há presença de tendências fora do comum. Portanto não se investiga a qualidade do produto dessa operação nesse momento.

| Figura 17.3 | Gráfico p para Controlar a Porcentagem de Peças Defeituosas nas Amostras |

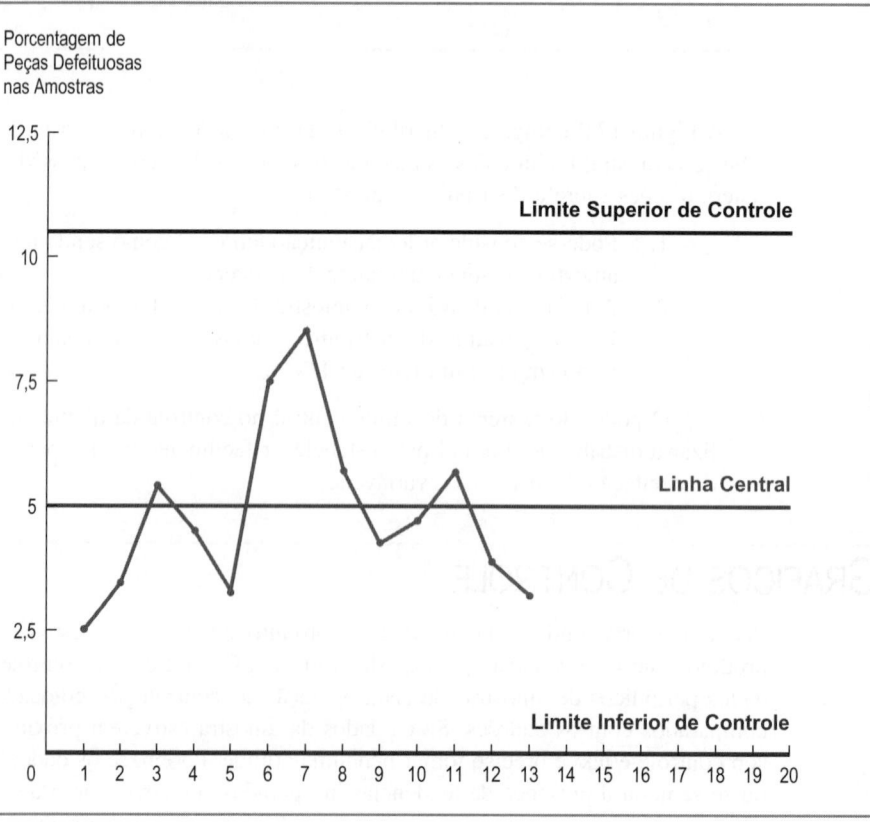

Capítulo 17 – Controle da Qualidade

TABELA 17.2 — Fórmulas e Definições de Variáveis para Calcular os Limites 3σ de Controle dos Gráficos de Controle

Tipo de Gráfico de Controle	Linha Central	Limite 3σ Inferior de Controle	Limite 3σ Superior de Controle
p	$\bar{p}$	$\bar{p} - 3\sqrt{\bar{p}(100 - \bar{p})/n}$	$\bar{p} + 3\sqrt{\bar{p}(100 - \bar{p})/n}$
$\bar{x}$	$\bar{\bar{x}}$	$\bar{\bar{x}} - A\bar{R}$	$\bar{\bar{x}} + A\bar{R}$
R	$\bar{R}$	$D_1\bar{R}$	$D_2\bar{R}$

p = porcentagens de peças defeituosas numa amostra
$\bar{p}$ = porcentagem média de peças defeituosas de várias amostras
n = tamanho da amostra — quantidade de observações numa amostra
$\bar{x}$ = média de uma amostra
$\bar{\bar{x}}$ = média das médias de várias amostras
R = amplitude da amostra
$\bar{R}$ = média das amplitudes de várias amostras
A, D_1, D_2 = fatores da Tabela 17.3

A Tabela 17.2 mostra as fórmulas e as definições de variáveis para os cálculos necessários nos gráficos de controle.

O Exemplo 17.1 apresenta a preparação de um gráfico p para monitorar a porcentagem de peças defeituosas dos condensadores produzidos pelos operadores das máquinas. A linha central de um gráfico de controle idealmente é determinada a partir da observação da capabilidade do processo. Mas em alguns casos, principalmente nos processos novos, as linhas centrais podem ser determinadas a partir do conhecimento de um supervisor, uma meta que se deseja atingir, a média de um período de experiência ou as especificações sobre a capabilidade da máquina, fornecidas por seu fabricante.

EXEMPLO 17.1

ELABORANDO GRÁFICOS DE CONTROLE DE ATRIBUTO

Pedro Reyes opera uma máquina que produz condensadores. A empresa de Pedro está implantando um programa de autocontrole e ele quer começar a acompanhar a porcentagem de peças defeituosas em sua operação. Ele sabe que, com esse tipo de processo, eles esperam cerca de 4% de peças defeituosas mais ou menos alguma variação ocasional.

Pedro inicialmente quer fazer um gráfico p com limites de controle de três desvios padrões e preparou 10 amostras diárias com 100 condensadores cada.

Nº da amostra	Porcentagem de peças defeituosas	Nº da amostra	Porcentagem de peças defeituosas	Nº da amostra	Porcentagem de peças defeituosas
1	4	5	1	8	12
2	3	6	9	9	4
3	3	7	5	10	3
4	6				

SOLUÇÃO

1. Calcule os limites 3σ de controle de p.

   Primeiro observe os limites de controle dos gráficos p da Tabela 17.2:

$$\text{Limite superior de controle} = \bar{p} + 3\sqrt{\bar{p}(100 - \bar{p})/n} = 4 + 3\sqrt{4(96)/100} = 4 + 3(1,9596)$$
$$= 4 + 5,8788 = 9,88\%$$

$$\text{Limite inferior de controle} = \bar{p} + 3\sqrt{\bar{p}(100 - \bar{p})/n} = 4 - 3\sqrt{4(96)/100} = 4 - 3(1,9596)$$
$$= 4 - 5,8788 = -1,88\%, \text{ ou } 0\%$$

2. Crie um gráfico p e plote os dados que Pedro obteve:

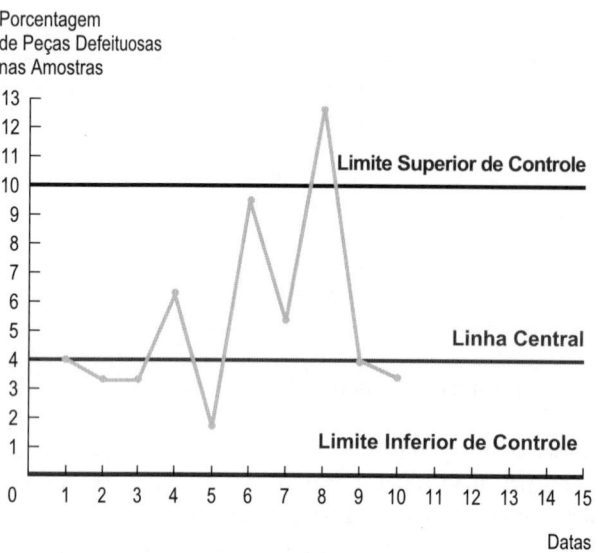

3. Embora a maioria das amostras esteja dentro dos limites de controle, Pedro pretende investigar as condições que cercam as amostras 6 e 8.

Os limites de controle da Tabela 17.2 são limites 3σ de controle. Isso significa que os limites de controle são três desvios padrões da linha central. Os gráficos de controle são realmente distribuições amostrais, porque estamos plotando estatísticas de amostras, e do teorema de limite central sabemos que as distribuições amostrais estão distribuídas normalmente. Nas distribuições normais, os três desvios padrões de qualquer lado da média incluem 99,7% das observações totais. Portanto existe 99,7% de probabilidade de pontos amostrais estarem dentro dos limites 3σ de controle dos gráficos de controle se a linha central do processo que está sendo monitorado não mudou. Quando os pontos tendem a ficar fora dos limites de controle, o processo básico está mudando e é preciso que a gerência faça uma investigação. Os limites de controle por atributos também poderiam ser estabelecidos em 95%, 90% ou qualquer outro intervalo de confiança substituindo os valores de Z adequados da distribuição normal pelos 3 nas fórmulas dos gráficos p na Tabela 17.2. Por exemplo, 95% fornece Z = 1,96, 90%, Z = 1,64 e assim por diante.

Como o limite inferior de controle do Exemplo 17.1 é negativo, estabelecemos o limite de 0% de peças defeituosas. Os limites inferiores de controle não precisam ser negativos ou zero. Eles podem também ser valores positivos. Se a porcentagem de peças defeituosas for menor do que o limite inferior de um gráfico de controle, o que isso indica? Indica somente que as amostras contêm menos peças defeituosas do que esperado. Isso não quer dizer que há algo de errado, mas indica que algo pode ter mudado no setor de produção, e portanto vamos querer investigar para descobrir o porquê e assim continuar produzindo um produto de tão alta qualidade. Por quê? Porque um dos objetivos principais da utilização dos gráficos de controle é *melhorar* a qualidade.

TABELA 17.3 — FATORES DO GRÁFICO 3σ DE CONTROLE DAS VARIÁVEIS

Tamanho da Amostra n	Fator de Limite de Controle da Média das Amostras A	Fator de Limite de Controle da Variação da Média	
		D_1	D_2
2	1,880	0	3,267
3	1,023	0	2,575
4	0,729	0	2,282
5	0,577	0	2,116
10	0,308	0,223	1,777
15	0,223	0,348	1,652
20	0,180	0,414	1,586
25	0,153	0,459	1,541
Acima de 25	$0,75(1/\sqrt{n})$*	$0,45 + 0,001(n)$*	$1,55 - 0,0015(n)$*

*Esses valores são aproximações lineares para uso dos alunos na elaboração de gráficos de controle.

Fonte: Economics Control of Manufactured Products. Nova Iorque, Litton Educational Publishing. Van Nostrand Reinhold Co., 1931. Copyright 1931, Bell Telephone Laboratories.

GRÁFICOS DE CONTROLE POR VARIÁVEIS

Os gráficos de controle são elaborados para monitorar as variáveis $\bar{x}$ e R. Os gráficos $\bar{x}$ e R geralmente são utilizados para monitorar a qualidade dos produtos e serviços.

O gráfico $\bar{x}$ monitora o valor médio da variável que está sendo medida.

O gráfico R monitora a amplitude entre os itens nas amostras. Esse monitoramento duplo, portanto, controla os valores médios e a variação dos valores de suas médias. Pegue, por exemplo, os pesos das caixas de flocos de milho de uma linha de produção.

Um gráfico $\bar{x}$ pode indicar que as médias amostrais estão dentro da meta, mas, sem um gráfico R para monitorar a amplitude, os pesos da caixa poderiam variar de 0 a 10 libras (supondo que uma caixa comportasse tudo isso) nas amostras. Esse exemplo demonstra que geralmente não podemos concluir que um processo está sob controle somente monitorando as médias das amostras e que é preciso também monitorar suas amplitudes.

A Tabela 17.3 lista os fatores A, D_1 e D_2 dos gráficos de controle de variáveis.

O Exemplo 17.2, que demonstra a elaboração dos gráficos $\bar{x}$ e R no monitoramento dos pesos das caixas de flocos de milho, ilustra uma verdade importante na interpretação das informações fornecidas pelos gráficos de controle.

Às vezes, as tendências dos dados são mais importantes do que seus valores absolutos. Tendências desfavoráveis podem indicar a necessidade de uma medida corretiva *antes* de se produzir produtos e serviços de qualidade. E tendências favoráveis podem indicar que é preciso fazer mudanças no setor de produção para incorporar a melhor qualidade do produto.

Portanto gerentes e trabalhadores monitoram cuidadosamente as tendências dos gráficos de controle com o objetivo de fazer mudanças nos processos de produção que resultarão em melhoria contínua da qualidade do produto.

Exemplo 17.2

Criando Gráficos de Controle para Variáveis

Como parte do programa de autocotrole em sua empresa, Joe Wilson quer criar gráficos $\bar{x}$ e R na operação de encher caixas de 16 onças do produto flocos de milho. Os engenheiros estudaram essa operação e determinaram que, quando a operação corre bem, as caixas apresentam uma média de 16,1 onças, e amostras horárias de 20 caixas cada apresentam amplitudes com média de 2,22 onças. Eis os dados das 12 amostras horárias que Joe pegou.

Amostra Nº	Média da Amostra (onças)	Amplitude da Amostra (onças)	Amostra Nº	Média da Amostra (onças)	Amplitude da Amostra (onças)
1	16,2	2,0	7	16,0	2,9
2	15,9	2,1	8	16,1	1,8
3	16,3	1,8	9	16,3	1,5
4	16,4	3,0	10	16,3	1,0
5	15,8	3,5	11	16,4	1,0
6	15,9	3,1	12	16,5	0,9

Solução

1. Calcule os limites superior e inferior de controle dos gráficos $\bar{x}$ e R:

   Em primeiro lugar observe os limites de controle de um gráfico $\bar{x}$ ($\bar{\bar{x}}$ é a linha central e é igual a 16,1 onças; A se encontra na Tabela 17.3, A = 0,180 quando n = 20):

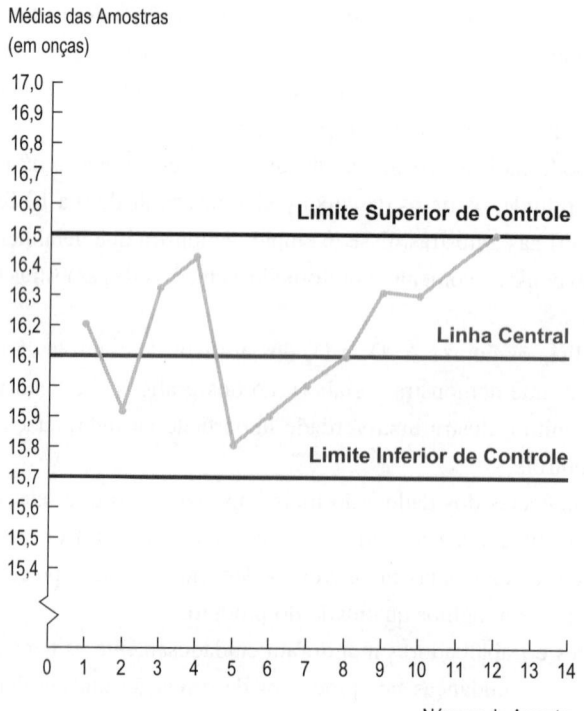

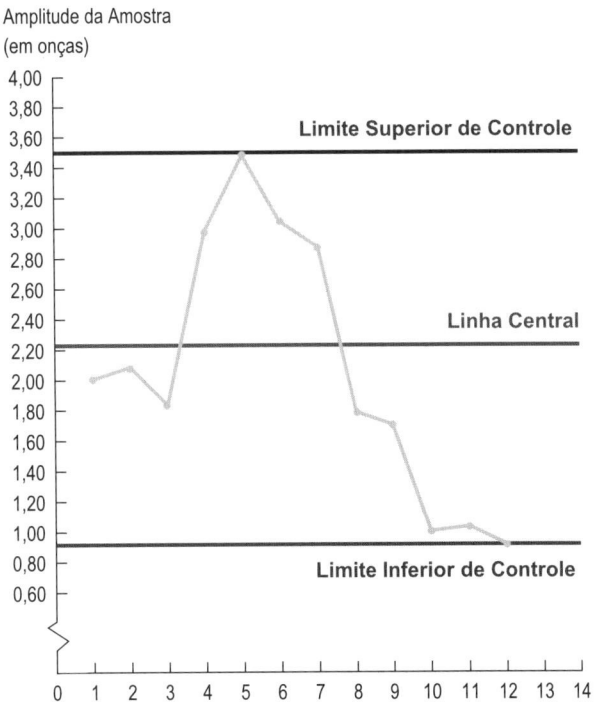

Limite superior de controle = $\bar{x} + A\bar{R}$ = 16,1 + 0,180(2,22) = 16,1 + 0,400 = 16,500 libras

Limite inferior de controle = $\bar{r} - A\bar{R}$ = 16,1 − 0,180(2,22) = 16,1 − 0,400 = 15,700 libras

Depois observe os limites de controle de um gráfico R da Tabela 17.2 (D_2 se encontra na Tabela 17.3, D_2 = 1,586 quando n = 20; D_1 se encontra na Tabela 17.3, D_1 = 0,414 quando n = 20):

Limite superior de controle $D_2\bar{R}$ = 1,586(2,22) = 3,521 libras

Limite inferior de controle $D_1\bar{R}$ = 0,414(2.22) = 0,919 libra

2. Plote as mesmas médias e amplitudes nos gráficos de controle $\bar{x}$ e R.
3. O que Joe pode concluir sobre a operação de enchimento das caixas?

Embora nenhuma das médias das amostras tenha excedido os limites de controle, a tendência das últimas oito horas indica uma situação definitivamente fora de controle. A menos que essa tendência seja revertida por uma medida corretiva, teremos uma quantidade excessiva de caixas demasiadamente cheias. O gráfico R indica que as amplitudes das amostras não estão excedendo os limites de controle. Porém, curiosamente, as amplitudes das amostras nas últimas oito horas diminuíram. Essa tendência poderia ser associada a uma situação fora de controle das médias das amostras e deve ser investigada.

COMPUTADORES NO CONTROLE DA QUALIDADE

É grande o uso de computadores no controle da qualidade. As normas governamentais americanas exigem que as indústrias como a automobilística, farmacêutica, de alimentos e de produtos químicos especiais sejam capazes de detectar defeitos em todos os sistemas de produção e distribuição. Mesmo se uma indústria não é controlada por órgãos governamentais, esses registros são mantidos em ordem, para o caso de um processo de responsabilidade pelo produto. Além disso, é um bom negócio para a empresa acompanhar seus produtos desde sua produção até o momento em que é utilizado pelo consumidor, e esse acompanhamento se tornou viável economicamente com o uso de computadores. Programas amplamente divulgados de recolhimento de produtos são uma prova da importância desses sistemas computadorizados. Esses programas exigem que os fabricantes (1) saibam os números de lote das matérias-primas, montagens e peças que são responsáveis por possíveis defeitos; (2) tenham um sistema de armazenamento de informações que possa ligar os números de lote das matérias-primas, montagens e peças suspeitas aos números dos modelos dos produtos finais e (3) tenham um sistema de informações que possa identificar os números dos modelos dos produtos finais aos clientes.

Os computadores também fornecem informações mais constantes e econômicas sobre a qualidade dos produtos e serviços aos gerentes. Pelo fato de os gráficos de controle poderem ser preparados rapidamente, reduz-se o espaço de tempo entre o momento em que as matérias-primas, montagens e peças são inspecionadas e o momento em que os resultados são colocados nos gráficos de controle. *Os programas de computador também são usados nas decisões de aceitação dos lotes. Com a automação, a inspeção e os testes podem ser tão baratos e rápidos que as empresas podem aumentar os tamanhos dos lotes e a freqüência das amostras, obtendo assim mais precisão nos gráficos de controle e nos planos de aceitação.* Em alguns casos, os planos de aceitação podem ser totalmente abandonados e substituídos por 100% de inspeção e testes. Por exemplo, na Garret Pneumatic Systems em Phoenix, os computadores são utilizados para testar produtos à medida que eles vão saindo da linha de montagem. Esses testes são tão rápidos que 100% de inspeção agora é econômico. Além disso, os testes são tão completos que todas as funções do produto podem ser testadas rapidamente.

Além das inspeções automáticas, nas quais se utilizam computadores para checar a qualidade dos produtos *depois* de eles serem feitos, os computadores também estão sendo utilizados para controlar diretamente a qualidade dos produtos *enquanto* eles estão sendo feitos. Como discutimos no Capítulo 5, os controles de processo automatizados medem o desempenho dos processos de produção durante a produção e corrigem automaticamente os parâmetros do processo para evitar produzir produtos com defeito.

Os sistemas de serviços também devem se preocupar com a qualidade de seus serviços.

O Controle da Qualidade no Setor de Serviços

No Capítulo 16 discutimos a TQM no setor de serviços. Sabemos que a TQM é aplicada, por exemplo, em bancos, hospitais, universidades, escritórios de advocacia e companhias de seguro. Em todas essas aplicações há uma necessidade constante de monitorar a evolução em termos da qualidade. Os gráficos de controle são ideais para isso. Um exemplo do Capítulo 16 explicava como a American Express, uma empresa de serviços financeiros, utiliza os gráficos de controle para monitorar coisas como o tempo necessário para processar uma requisição de cartão de crédito American Express. Devido a sua flexibilidade, os gráficos de controle são muito utilizados no setor de serviços.

Resumo Final

O Que os Fabricantes de Classe Mundial Estão Fazendo

Os fabricantes de classe mundial entendem que a gerência da qualidade dos produtos e serviços é muito mais ampla do que o controle da qualidade. Essas empresas têm programas proativos abrangentes de gestão da qualidade total (TQM) com projetos específicos que visam melhorar a qualidade do produto para que ele atenda às expectativas do cliente. Mas isso não significa que elas abandonaram o controle da qualidade. Uma vez criados e desenvolvidos os processos de produção capazes de produzir produtos que atendam às expectativas do cliente,

esses processos precisam ser operados de forma que consigam produzir de acordo com a qualidade especificada. E o controle da qualidade é a maneira de fazer a qualidade do produto ficar de acordo com as expectativas do cliente.

Várias técnicas ajudam a obter um eficaz controle da qualidade. Os gráficos de controle estatístico são muito usados para dar a todos um feedback sobre o desempenho em termos da qualidade. Esses gráficos podem ser preparados pelos próprios trabalhadores, portanto eles podem assumir a responsabilidade pela qualidade do produto na produção. Sendo tão flexíveis, os gráficos de controle podem ser usados para quase toda aplicação (desde a fabricação automatizada até as operações de serviços) que se baseie em serviço pessoal. E em certas situações especiais onde é impraticável inspecionar e testar 100% dos produtos, pode-se utilizar planos de aceitação para determinar se os lotes de produto irão corresponder às expectativas dos clientes. Automatizar a inspeção e os testes tornou essa abordagem eficaz e econômica.

Questões de Revisão e Discussão

1. Explique a relação entre a gestão da qualidade total (TQM) e o controle da qualidade.
2. Quais são as expectativas dos clientes em relação a estas organizações: (a) fabricante de fertilizante, (b) hospital, (c) universidade, (d) fabricante de automóvel, (e) banco e (f) serraria?
3. Defina estes termos: (a) *amostra aleatória*, (b) *atributo*, (c) *variável* e (d) *amostra única*.
4. p, x e R são variáveis ou atributos?
5. Qual é o *teorema do limite central*? Qual é sua importância para o controle da qualidade?
6. Qual é a finalidade dos controles da qualidade? Explique como se atinge esse objetivo.
7. O que é controle estatístico de processo (CEP)?
8. Por que os gráficos $\bar{x}$ e R são usados juntos?
9. Discuta o papel dos computadores no controle da qualidade.
10. Discuta o controle da qualidade no setor de serviços.
11. Que fatores tornam a gerência da qualidade mais difícil no setor de serviços do que no setor de produtos? Que abordagens foram criadas para atenuar os efeitos dessas dificuldades?

Tarefas na Internet

1. Procure na Internet uma empresa que produza software de CEP. Descreva algumas das características do software de CEP. Dê o endereço do site da empresa.
2. Procure na Internet uma empresa de consultoria que preste serviços de consultoria ligados ao controle da qualidade. Descreva os tipos de serviços relacionados que a empresa oferece. Dê o endereço do site da empresa.
3. Procure na Internet um título de jornal ou revista sobre gráficos de controle (que forneça pelo menos um resumo). Explique em poucas palavras do que trata o artigo e dê uma bibliografia completa do mesmo.
4. Visite uma livraria on-line e encontre dois livros recentes sobre CEP ou controle da qualidade. Dê uma bibliografia completa.

Problemas

Gráficos de Controle

1. Um processo de produção automatizado consiste na montagem de quatro componentes para fazer um fusível de 5 ampères. A cada duas horas coleta-se uma amostra de 75 fusíveis, e cada um deles é testado. Normalmente no passado uma média de 1,8 fusível não passava no teste. Calcule os limites 3σ de controle de um gráfico p.

2. Uma soldadora robótica solda um suporte a ponto em uma estrutura de metal. A solda deve ser capaz de suportar 350 libras aplicadas ao suporte. A cada duas horas pega-se uma amostra de 50 estruturas soldadas e coloca-se um peso de 350 libras no suporte. Normalmente no passado uma média de 2,2 suportes se soltava da estrutura quando se aplicava o teste do peso. Se fôssemos usar um gráfico de controle para monitorar a constância do processo de solda, que limites de controle deveriam ser usados?

3. Numa operação de fabricação, a porcentagem de peças defeituosas é, em média, 2,5%, e o tamanho da amostra é de 200 peças.
   a) Calcule a linha central do gráfico p.
   b) Calcule os limites 3σ de controle do gráfico.
   c) Plote esses dados recentes coletados das amostras diárias e decida se a operação está sob controle; quantidade de peças defeituosas por amostra = 2, 9, 7, 5, 0, 3, 8, 7, 2, 5, 3, 2.

4. O programa de gráfico de controle da operação de solda especificou um tamanho de amostra de 300 unidades, uma meta de 1,0% de peças defeituosas e limites 2σ de controle. As amostras recentes tinham a seguinte quantidade de peças defeituosas: 1, 0, 4, 3, 6, 2, 0, 5, 7, 3.
   a) Calcule a linha central e os limites superior e inferior de controle do gráfico.
   b) Plote os dados das 10 amostras e decida se a operação de solda está sob controle.

5. Uma companhia de seguro acompanha o absenteísmo por meio de amostras aleatórias. A empresa espera que falte uma média de 250 funcionários de seu quadro de pessoal de 5.000. Foram registrados os seguintes tamanhos de amostras e quantidade de faltas:

Número da Amostra	Tamanho da Amostra	Quantidade de Faltas	Número da Amostra	Tamanho da Amostra	Quantidade de Faltas
1	100	5	6	100	7
2	120	6	7	110	8
3	90	6	8	90	10
4	95	7	9	130	11
5	110	7	10	120	10

   a) Crie um gráfico 3σ de controle para p e plote os dados das amostras. (*Dica:* Os limites superior e inferior de controle variam com o tamanho da amostra.)
   b) Houve mudança na taxa de absenteísmo?

6. Se $\bar{\bar{x}} = 12$ polegadas, $\bar{R} = 3$ polegadas, e $n = 20$:
   a) Calcule os limites 3σ de controle de x.
   b) Plote essas médias de amostras nos gráficos de controle para $\bar{x}$: 12,1, 12,5, 12,7, 12,2, 12,8, 12,7, 12,1, 11,8, 11,7, 12,0.
   c) Esse processo está sob controle?

7. Uma empresa de transporte de mercadorias por caminhão recebeu muitas reclamações de atraso nas entregas. A empresa tenta entregar todos os seus fretes numa média de 12 horas. Foram pegas amostras semanais de 25 clientes e observou-se uma amplitude média de 2,5 horas. A empresa acha que isso está certo.
   a) Calcule os limites 3σ de controle para $\bar{x}$.
   b) Plote essas médias amostrais nos gráficos 3σ de controle para $\bar{x}$: 11,4, 12,2, 12,0, 11,9, 12,6, 12,4, 12,1, 11,8, 11,5 e 12,4.
   c) A meta da gerência de uma média de 12 horas para entrega está sendo atingida?

Estudo de Caso

Integrated Products Corporation

A Integrated Products Corporation (IPC) fabrica resinas. A empresa instalou o que ela chama de gestão da qualidade total (TQM) no ano passado. O objetivo do novo programa era envolver todos, desde o gerente até os trabalhadores da fábrica, em atingir uma ótima qualidade do produto. Esse programa apresentaria conceitos de *qualidade na fonte* e *círculos da qualidade*. Foi criada uma nova resina, e o departamento de controle da qualidade agora está desenvolvendo um plano da qualidade para o novo produto. É de especial importância um plano de aceitação para a resina acabada antes de ela ser enviada para os clientes da IPC. A característica-chave de desempenho da resina é sua "vida de reator" — o tempo que a resina leva para ser convertida para sua forma final depois de ser misturada com plastificantes. A "vida de reator" nominal da resina é de 2,5 minutos à temperatura ambiente com um desvio padrão de 0,2 minuto. A embalagem padrão da resina é um saco de 10 libras, e o plano da qualidade requer amostras aleatórias de 200 sacos tirados de lotes de 10.000 sacos de produto acabado.

Tarefas

1. O que significa gestão da qualidade total (TQM)? Quais são os elementos principais da TQM? Quais são os principais benefícios da TQM?
2. Explique o significado de qualidade na fonte. Em que princípios ela se baseia? Quais são seus principais benefícios?
3. Descreva os círculos da qualidade. Quais são seus principais benefícios?
4. Se a TQM visa a qualidade perfeita do produto, por que seria necessário um plano de aceitação para a nova resina? Isso não viola um princípio básico da TQM — produzir produtos de alta qualidade e tentar não inspecionar a qualidade do produto depois? Qual é o papel adequado da amostragem de aceitação em um ambiente TQM?

capítulo 18

PLANEJANDO E CONTROLANDO PROJETOS

Introdução

Gerência de Projeto

Técnicas de Planejamento e Controle de Projeto
Gráficos de Programação e Controle
O Método do Caminho Crítico
Técnica de Avaliação e Revisão de Programa
Sistemas de Controle de Custos do Projeto
CPM/PERT na Prática
   Folga Meta x Folga do Projeto •
   Relações Custo x Tempo das Atividades

Software para Gerência de Projetos

Uma Avaliação do CPM/PERT

Resumo Final: O Que os Fabricantes de Classe Mundial Estão Fazendo

Questões de Revisão e Discussão

Tarefas na Internet

Problemas

Estudo de Caso
Maxwell Construction Company

Introdução

GERENCIANDO O PROJETO RATS

Bill Williams, gerente da fábrica da Power em Marion, Illinois, recebeu uma ligação de Ivor Kaney, vice-presidente de marketing do escritório central. Ivor perguntou se Bill queria apresentar uma proposta para um novo produto que poderia mais do que dobrar as vendas anuais na fábrica, de US$ 9,5 milhões para US$ 20,6 milhões.

O novo produto, chamado Rocket Aerial Target System (RATS), era um alvo aéreo expansível, de baixo custo, movido a foguete, que seria abatido pelas artilharias militares americanas por mísseis em busca de calor. O projeto exigiria: elaborar uma proposta técnica, apresentar uma proposta de orçamento, construir dez foguetes protótipos e dirigir três foguetes para o exército americano. E tudo isso teria de ser feito em 4 meses e meio. Depois de uma reunião com o pessoal de marketing da divisão e representantes do exército americano, Bill decidiu formar uma equipe de projeto em sua fábrica para responder à proposta e ao projeto de desenvolvimento. Bill designou um gerente de projeto para a equipe, um engenheiro de vôo, um especialista em projetos de sistema, um engenheiro de produção, um agente de segurança e um analista de custos. Essas pessoas estavam entre as melhores de seu quadro de pessoal dos vários departamentos da fábrica. Os membros do projeto seriam designados para a equipe pela duração do projeto, que se esperava que fosse levar no máximo 5 meses. O gerente de projeto se reportaria diretamente ao gerente da fábrica e seria responsável pelo desempenho da equipe no sentido de ficar dentro do orçamento, cumprir os prazos e atingir os objetivos da equipe de projeto. Esta teve de criar rapidamente um plano para concluir as atividades do projeto e depois executar o plano.

Geralmente é preciso formar equipes de projeto para atingir iniciativas-chaves da organização. Projetos como os de desenvolver de um novo produto, automatizar as atividades de produção, implantar uma fabricação just-in-time (JIT) e começar um programa de gestão da qualidade total (TQM) são fundamentais para o sucesso na concorrência internacional. E todas essas atividades requerem que os funcionários trabalhem como uma equipe.

É provável que você tenha chance de trabalhar numa dessas equipes no início de sua carreira. Você vai ver que trabalhar em equipe é um desafio porque geralmente as equipes têm de trabalhar com prazos apertados e orçamentos limitados. Enquanto algumas pessoas trabalham no projeto, o restante da organização tem de continuar produzindo os outros produtos da empresa. Devido à dificuldade de gerenciar esses projetos e ao mesmo tempo continuar produzindo os produtos e serviços da organização, foram desenvolvidas novas abordagens de planejamento e controle de projetos.

GERÊNCIA DE PROJETO

Foram criadas novas formas de organização para garantir a continuidade do sistema de produção em suas atividades diárias e a conclusão bem-sucedida dos projetos. A mais importante entre essas novas formas de organização é a **organização baseada em projetos**. A Figura 18.1 mostra que as equipes de projeto são tiradas dos departamentos das organizações e designadas temporariamente, em meio período ou em tempo integral, para as equipes de projeto.

Geralmente designa-se um gerente de projeto para comandar a equipe, coordenar suas atividades e as de outros departamentos no projeto. Esse profissional deve se reportar diretamente ao topo da organização. Essa exposição da gerência executiva dá ao projeto alta visibilidade dentro da organização, garante a atenção dos departamentos para o projeto e incentiva a colaboração entre a equipe de projeto e as outras unidades organizacionais.

A organização baseada em projetos geralmente é constituída bem antes do início dos projetos para que se possa elaborar o plano de projeto. A Figura 18.2 mostra as inter-relações entre as funções de planejamento, programação e controle do projeto. Observe que o plano de projeto é definido antes do início das atividades de projeto e se modifica à medida que as condições vão mudando durante o projeto. O plano é a planta do projeto e guia geral para se conseguir uma conclusão bem-sucedida do mesmo.

As funções de programação e controle do projeto ocorrem à medida que o projeto vai evoluindo. Essas funções garantem o desempenho oportuno das atividades do projeto dentro dos padrões de custo e qualidade.

FIGURA 18.1   ORGANIZAÇÃO BASEADA EM PROJETOS

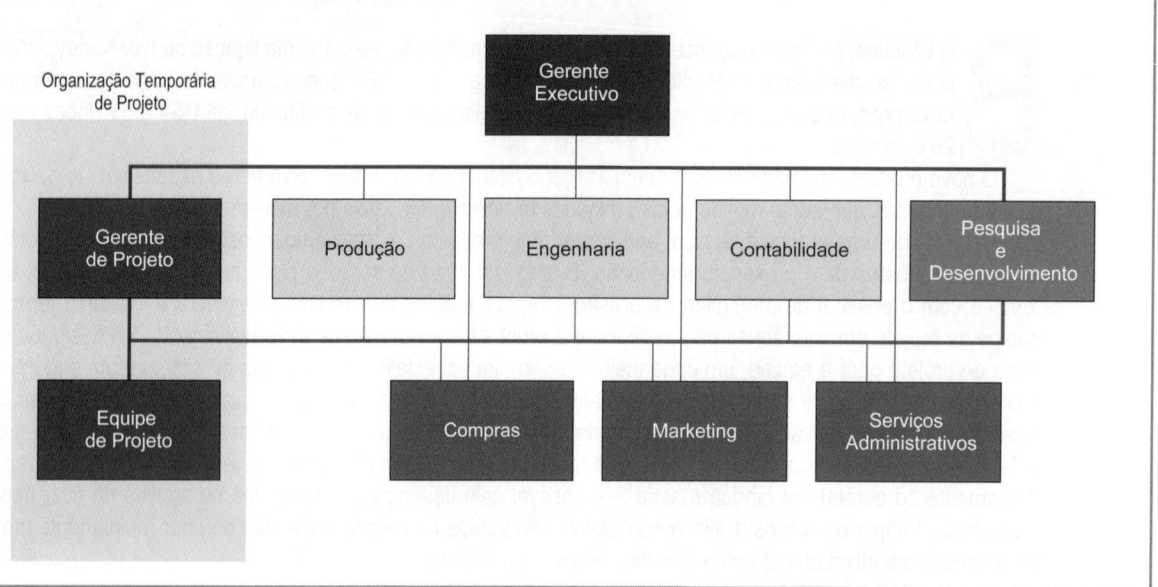

FIGURA 18.2   PLANEJAMENTO, PROGRAMAÇÃO E CONTROLE

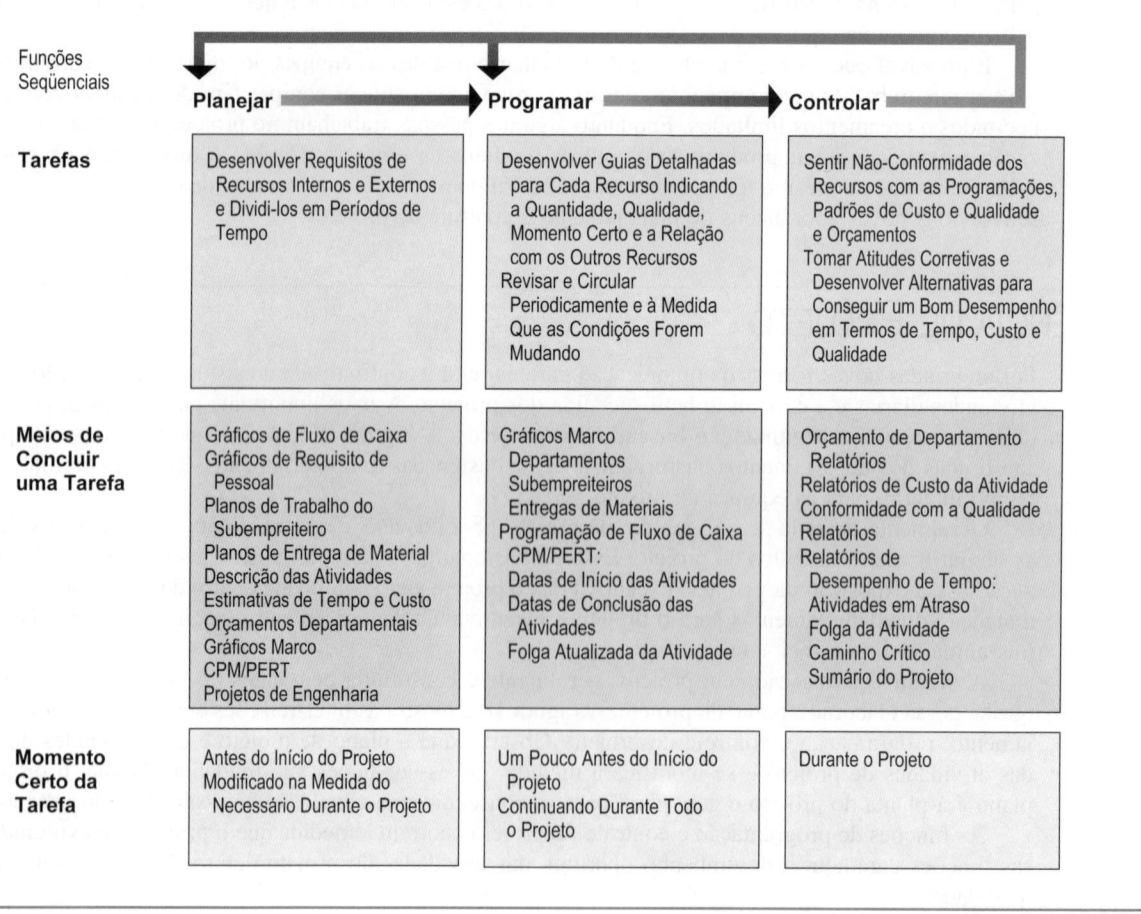

FIGURA 18.3 — PROGRAMANDO E CONTROLANDO PROJETOS COM EQUIPES DE PROJETO

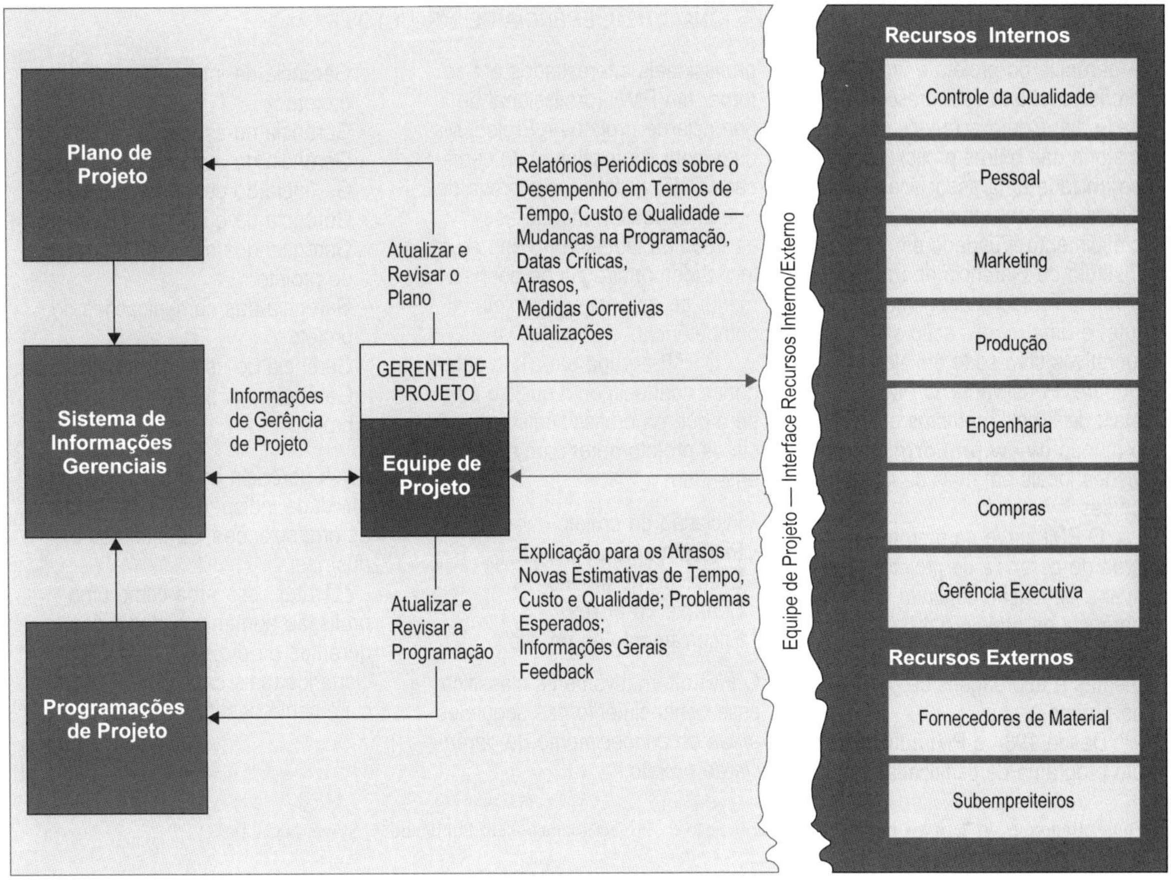

A geração periódica de gráficos, relatórios e programações atualizados mantém todas as partes do projeto informadas sobre seu trabalho específico, quando cada atividade tem de ser executada, as medidas corretivas necessárias e os problemas específicos para os quais elas precisam ficar atentas.

O ingrediente-chave da programação e controle do projeto é a equipe de projeto. A Figura 18.3 mostra que a equipe de projeto é o centro ao redor do qual o projeto gira. A equipe de projeto fornece mudanças atualizadas para o plano e as programações do projeto através do sistema de informações da gerência. A equipe de projeto envia relatórios de desempenho em termos de tempo, custo e qualidade para os recursos internos e externos. A equipe de projeto recebe de volta informações sobre a evolução do projeto. Esse processo continua durante todo o projeto.

Um desenvolvimento bastante interessante diz respeito à institucionalização permanente nas organizações baseadas em processos que dependem predominantemente de produtos mais bem administrados como projetos. As empresas aeroespaciais, de construção, de computação e outras vêm utilizando projetos há tanto tempo que eles já se tornaram parte permanente de sua estrutura organizacional. Os gerentes de projeto, os membros da equipe de projeto e o sistema de informações da gerência de projetos continuam mudando e se adaptando a novas tarefas de projeto. O Instantâneo da Indústria 18.1 discute a área de gerência de projeto como profissão.

Novas técnicas foram desenvolvidas para facilitar a conclusão das atividades de projeto dentro dos padrões de tempo, custo e qualidade do plano de projeto. Aqui apresentamos algumas das técnicas de programação e controle mais utilizadas.

INSTANTÂNEO DA INDÚSTRIA 18.1

PROFISSIONAIS DE GERÊNCIA DE PROJETOS

A gerência de projeto é um campo profissional que está crescendo a cada dia. Como acontece com a maioria das outras profissões, foi organizada uma associação profissional para dar suporte a esse crescimento. Fundado em 1969, o Instituto de Gerência de Projeto (PMI — Project Management Institute) é uma organização sem fins lucrativos com sede em Newton Square, Pensilvânia. O PMI tem mais de 30 mil membros em todo o mundo (**www.pmi.org**), com divisões locais em mais de 40 países.

O PMI serve para promover a área de gerência de projeto, incentivar a educação contínua em gerência de projeto e disseminar informações sobre as últimas ferramentas e abordagens de gerência de projeto.

Desde 1984 o PMI administra um programa de certificação para profissionais interessados em se tornar um PMP (profissional de gerência de projeto — Project Management Professional). O certificado PMP é visto como prova de que uma pessoa atende aos padrões da indústria no que se refere à demonstração de conhecimento de gerência de projeto e competência.

O PMI agrupa em cinco categorias conhecimento que se espera que os profissionais de gerência de projeto aprendam e entendam:

- Iniciação do projeto
- Planejamento do projeto
- Execução do projeto
- Controle de projeto
- Encerramento do projeto

O PMI alternativamente classifica esse conhecimento nas seguintes *áreas de conhecimento de gerência de projeto*:

- Gerência de integração de projeto
- Gerência do escopo do projeto
- Gerência da duração do projeto
- Gerência do custo do projeto
- Gerência da qualidade do projeto
- Gerência dos recursos humanos do projeto
- Gerência das comunicações do projeto
- Gerência do risco do projeto
- Gerência das aquisições do projeto

A gerência de projeto é uma atividade indispensável em todas as organizações, de todas as indústrias.

Tratar essa área como uma profissão aumenta o status dos gerentes de projeto e leva a funcionários mais capacitados, o que claramente beneficia a organização.

Fonte: Reproduzido de **www.pmi.org** com autorização da Project Management Publications, Sylva, N.C., 1998.

TÉCNICAS DE PLANEJAMENTO E CONTROLE DE PROJETO

A Tabela 18.1 apresenta definições dos termos utilizados no planejamento e controle de projeto. *Esses termos são a linguagem da gerência de projeto*. Além disso, nós os utilizamos para explicar o uso dos gráficos de programação e controle, CPM, PERT e sistemas de controle de custo do projeto.

GRÁFICOS DE PROGRAMAÇÃO E CONTROLE

Os gráficos de programação e controle são os instrumentos mais utilizados para gerenciar projetos. Cada gráfico primeiro planeja e programa uma determinada parte do projeto — o que deve ser feito e quando. Depois, à medida que o projeto evolui, cada um dos gráficos é atualizado de forma que indique quanto do plano foi concluído. Dessa forma, os gerentes de projeto podem comparar o trabalho efetivamente realizado com a evolução planejada do projeto. Esse procedimento permite mudanças racionais no uso de recursos por parte da gerência para concluir o projeto dentro das metas de tempo, custo e qualidade.

Talvez o gráfico mais utilizado seja o de barra horizontal. Esses gráficos são aplicações dos gráficos de Gantt, aplicados no Capítulo 11. A Figura 18.4 ilustra um gráfico de barra particularmente útil. Esse gráfico é preparado antes do projeto para planejar e programar as atividades do projeto. Desenha-se uma barra horizontal para cada atividade ou grupo de atividades ao longo de uma dimensão de tempo. As letras no começo de cada barra (à esquerda) indicam as atividades que precisam ser concluídas para que se possa dar início à atividade em questão.

TABELA 18.1 — TERMOS USADOS EM GERÊNCIA DE PROJETO

Atividade — Uma determinada quantidade de trabalho necessária no projeto.

Duração da atividade — Em CPM, a melhor estimativa do tempo para concluir uma atividade. Em PERT, o tempo esperado ou o tempo médio para concluir a atividade.

Atividade crítica — Uma atividade na qual não há espaço para atrasos. Se ela atrasar, toda a conclusão do projeto atrasará. Uma atividade com folga zero.

Caminho crítico — A cadeia de atividades críticas para o projeto. O caminho mais longo da rede.

Atividade fictícia — Uma atividade que não consome tempo mas tem prioridade entre as atividades.

Primeira data de término (PDT) — O mais cedo que uma atividade pode terminar, a partir do início do projeto.

Primeira data de início (PDI) — O mais cedo que uma atividade pode começar, a partir do início do projeto.

Evento — Um início, ponto de conclusão ou feito que marca o projeto. Uma atividade começa e termina com eventos.

Última data de término (UDT) — O mais tarde que uma atividade pode ser concluída, sem provocar atraso na conclusão do projeto.

Última data de início (UDI) — O mais tarde que uma atividade pode ser iniciada, sem provocar atraso na conclusão do projeto.

A duração mais provável (t_m) — A duração de uma atividade que é consensualmente considerada a melhor estimativa.

Duração otimista (t_o) — O tempo para concluir uma atividade se tudo correr bem; utilizado no PERT.

Duração pessimista (t_p) — O tempo para concluir uma atividade se algo ruim acontecer; utilizado em PERT.

Atividade antecedente — Uma atividade que tem de ocorrer antes de uma outra.

Folga — O tempo que uma atividade ou um grupo de atividades pode passar do prazo sem provocar atraso na conclusão do projeto.

Atividade subseqüente — Uma atividade que tem de ocorrer depois de uma outra.

Depois de preparado o gráfico de barra, os gerentes podem assegurar que todas as atividades do projeto serão planejadas, se levará em conta a ordem na qual as atividades devem ser executadas, serão incluídas estimativas de tempo para concluir cada atividade e, por fim, se fará uma estimava geral do tempo necessário para concluir o projeto. O gráfico de barra torna-se o plano geral do projeto.

À medida que o projeto vai evoluindo e as atividades vão sendo concluídas, registra-se o progresso efetivo sombreando as barras horizontais. Quanto da barra de atividade deve ser sombreado depende das estimativas de porcentagem de conclusão do trabalho envolvidas em cada atividade. Se estimar-se que um terço da atividade será concluído, por exemplo, então sombreia-se um terço da barra horizontal.

Periodicamente esses gráficos são atualizados e distribuídos a todos os participantes. Desenha-se uma linha vertical no gráfico correspondente à data do relatório de status. A evolução da atividade pode ser comparada com a data de status.

Na Figura 18.4, por exemplo, pode-se observar que a Atividade *g*, Modificações no Projeto do Sistema de Vôo, está dentro do prazo, porque a barra está sombreada até a linha vertical de data do status. A Atividade *j*, Custos dos Materiais e dos Componentes, está aproximadamente uma semana atrasada, porque sua barra horizontal está sombreada até um ponto cerca de uma semana depois da data de status. Da mesma forma, a Atividade *k*, Custos de Mão-de-Obra e Despesas Gerais, está aproximadamente uma semana adiantada.

Esses relatórios de status permitem ao gerente observar a evolução das atividades do projeto, identificar áreas problemáticas e elaborar medidas corretivas para fazer com que o projeto volte a ficar dentro das metas. Esses relatórios podem ser usados sozinhos ou em conjunto com outras técnicas. Quando os

FIGURA 18.4 GRÁFICO DE BARRA — PROGRAMAÇÃO DO PROJETO RATS
PLANO/RELATÓRIO DE STATUS

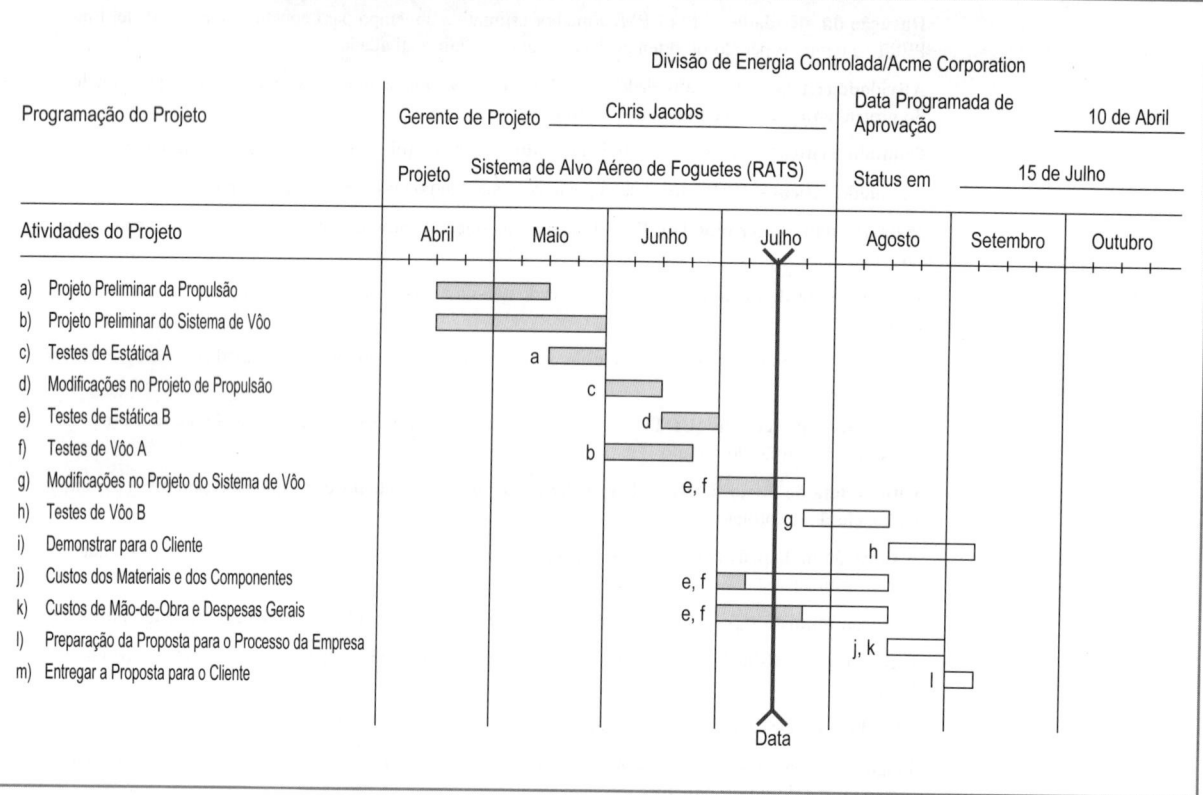

projetos não são muito complexos, caros ou de longa duração, os gráficos de barra podem ser utilizados sozinhos para planejar e controlar a conclusão em tempo do projeto.

Por outro lado, em projetos mais complexos e caros, esses gráficos podem ser usados como um resumo do status do projeto mesmo que sejam usadas outras técnicas mais detalhadas.

As principais vantagens dos gráficos de barra são o fato de serem fáceis de entender, fáceis de modificar e baratos. Suas principais desvantagens são o fato de que, nos projetos mais complexos, a quantidade de atividades envolvida pode requerer gráficos de difícil manejo ou a agregação de atividades, e os gráficos podem não indicar de maneira adequada o grau de correlação entre as atividades do projeto.

São utilizados outros gráficos para planejar e controlar a aquisição e o uso dos recursos como caixa, pessoal e materiais. A Figura 18.5 mostra um exemplo de um gráfico utilizado para planejar e controlar os gastos acumulados até junho e uma projeção de gastos no restante do projeto.

Os gerentes normalmente procuram respostas para as seguintes perguntas nos gráficos:

- Estamos dentro de nossas metas de gastos no momento?
- Estamos esperando estar dentro de nossas metas de gastos no final do projeto?
- Se não esperamos estar dentro de nossas metas de gastos no final do projeto, a gerência deveria começar a tomar uma medida corretiva para os gastos ficarem dentro da meta?

A entrega de materiais, componentes e peças subcontratadas apresenta problemas especiais de planejamento e controle para os gerentes de projeto. Em primeiro lugar, a curta duração e a característica exclusiva de não-recorrência dos projetos eliminam a fabricação de componentes e peças internamente, portanto muitos materiais, componentes e peças são comprados de fornecedores. Segundo, os projetos geralmente precisam dos materiais "para ontem", devido às grandes pressões de tempo. Terceiro, os mate-

FIGURA 18.5   GRÁFICO DE GASTOS — GASTOS DO PROJETO RATS
PLANO/RELATÓRIO DE STATUS: 30 DE JUNHO

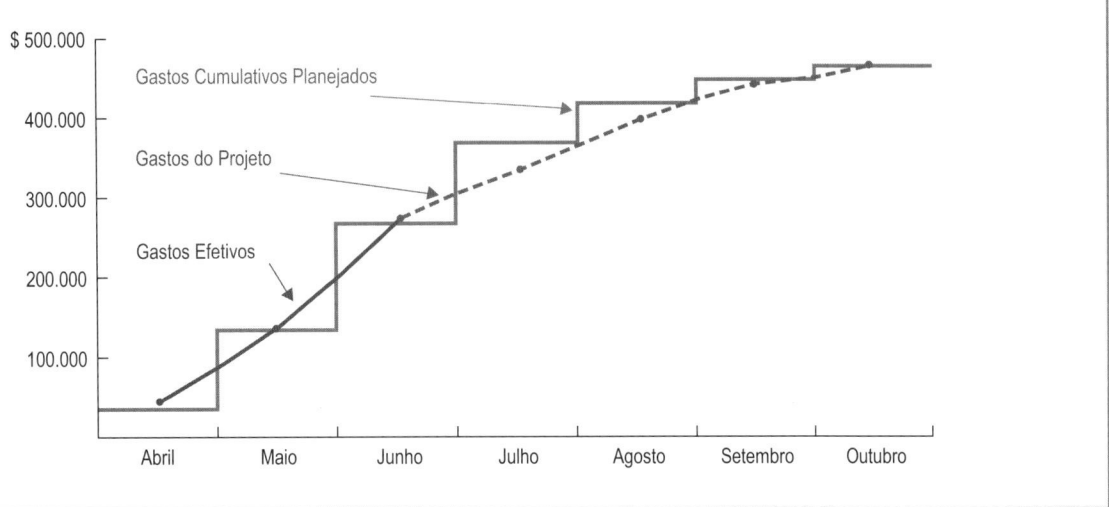

riais para projeto podem ser suficientemente diferentes dos outros materiais comprados pela organização para que os fornecedores habituais sejam preteridos em favor de novos fornecedores não experimentados anteriormente especializados nesses novos materiais.

Apesar da incerteza associada com a busca de novos fornecedores e as grandes pressões de tempo, as organizações aprenderam a administrar bem a aquisição de materiais, componentes e peças subcontratadas para os projetos. A Figura 18.6 mostra uma abordagem de planejamento e controle da aquisição de materiais para o projeto RATS. Esse gráfico de materiais, também chamado de gráfico de marco, mostra os materiais-chaves que devem ser adquiridos para o projeto, quando são feitos os pedidos (x), quando devem ser feitas as verificações das expedições (✓), quando o fornecedor está planejando processar o pedido (uma barra horizontal aberta), o andamento efetivo do processamento do fornecedor (parte cinza da barra horizontal) e as entregas planejadas (△).

Os gráficos aqui apresentados sugerem que uma vasta gama dessas ferramentas pode ser aplicada a várias situações de planejamento e controle de projetos. Na verdade essa flexibilidade é a razão principal de os gráficos serem a técnica utilizada com mais freqüência na gerência de projeto. A flexibilidade, o baixo custo e a facilidade de entendimento — tudo isso contribui para o uso quase universal dos gráficos na área de gerência de projetos.

O MÉTODO DO CAMINHO CRÍTICO

Criado em 1957 por J. E. Kelly, da Remington Rand, e M. R. Walker, da Du Pont, para ajudar a programar projetos de manutenção em fábricas de produtos químicos, o **método do caminho crítico** (CPM) é hoje uma importante técnica de planejamento e controle de projetos.

A técnica de avaliação e revisão do programa (PERT) foi desenvolvida mais ou menos na mesma época do CPM pelo Departamento de Projetos Especiais da Marinha americana em colaboração com a empresa de consultoria Booz, Allen & Hamilton para planejar e controlar o projeto e construção do submarino a energia atômica Polaris e seus sistemas de mísseis balísticos intercontinentais. A PERT e o CPM são semelhantes em muitos aspectos, exceto por uns poucos refinamentos incorporados à PERT que não encontramos no CPM. Devido à grande semelhança dos dois métodos e pelo fato de vários usuários do CPM também se referirem a seu método como PERT (os dois termos costumam ser usados de forma intercambiável), apresentaremos o CPM primeiro e tudo o que for coberto em relação ao CPM também se aplicará à PERT. Na seção seguinte cobrimos os refinamentos da PERT.

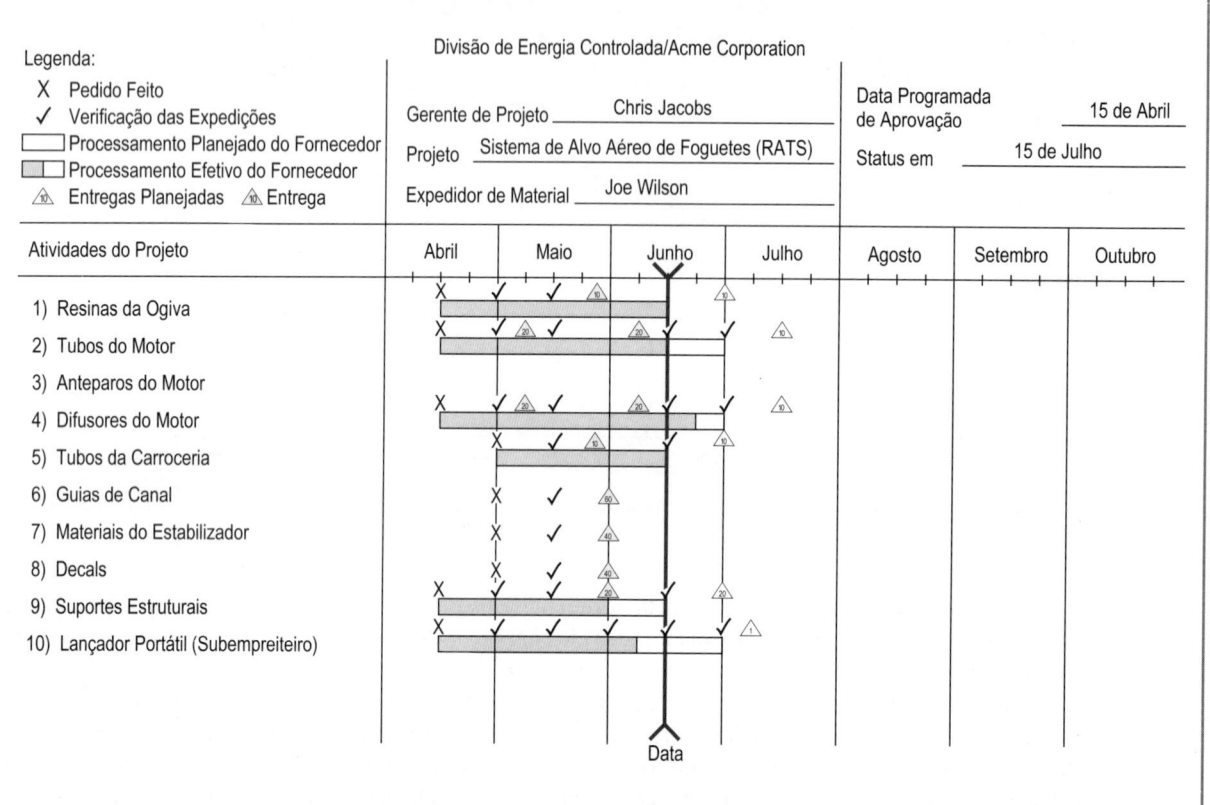

FIGURA 18.6 — GRÁFICO DE MATERIAIS — PLANO/RELATÓRIO DE STATUS DOS MATERIAIS-CHAVES DO PROJETO RATS

O CPM foi elaborado para os projetos com muitas atividades onde a conclusão no prazo é imprescindível. Onde os gráficos de planejamento e controle da seção anterior ofereciam um macrocontrole geral, o CPM foi elaborado para oferecer um intenso microcontrole.

Em sua forma original, o desempenho em termos de tempo era considerado de suma importância. Em outras palavras, o legado do uso do CPM pelo governo era a hipótese implícita de fundos ilimitados. O governo federal estava correndo para concluir o programa Polaris para evitar uma possível chantagem nuclear que os russos pudessem impor aos Estados Unidos. Sob essa grande pressão de tempo, não é de admirar que se supusesse fundos ilimitados.

O CPM hoje geralmente é combinado com outros sistemas de controle de custo de projeto como os gráficos da seção anterior. A combinação de macrocontrole dos gráficos de controle com o microcontrole do CPM dá à gerência tanto o quadro geral como um controle detalhado.

A Figura 18.7 mostra a visão do gerente sobre o CPM. Que informações eu devo dar ao CPM e que informações de gerência de projeto eu recebo em troca?

O CPM não é um sistema de programação e controle que é feito uma vez, colocado na prateleira e nunca mais é usado. Ao contrário, o sistema é dinâmico. O CPM continua fornecendo à gerência relatórios periódicos à medida que o projeto vai evoluindo.

Como mostra a Figura 18.8, os gerentes de projeto atualizam suas estimativas originais de duração para concluir cada uma das atividades à medida que o tempo vai passando e o sistema computadorizado de CPM fornece informações atuais sobre gerência de projeto: novas estimativas de duração do projeto, uma nova lista de atividades críticas, novas estimativas de atividades e relatórios de exceções (por exemplo, novas atividades em atraso e atividades comprimidas).

Capítulo 18 – Planejando e Controlando Projetos

FIGURA 18.7 UMA VISÃO DE CPM DO GERENTE

Insumos

(Que informações devem ser fornecidas ao CPM?)

- Uma lista completa das atividades do projeto
- A relação de antecedência entre as atividades
- Estimativa da duração de cada atividade

Procedimentos de processamento do CPM

Produtos

(Que informações resultam do CPM que permitem uma melhor gerência de projeto?)

- Duração estimada do projeto
- Identificação das atividades essenciais
- A folga de cada uma das atividades

FIGURA 18.8 O SISTEMA DE INFORMAÇÕES DE GERÊNCIA DO CPM

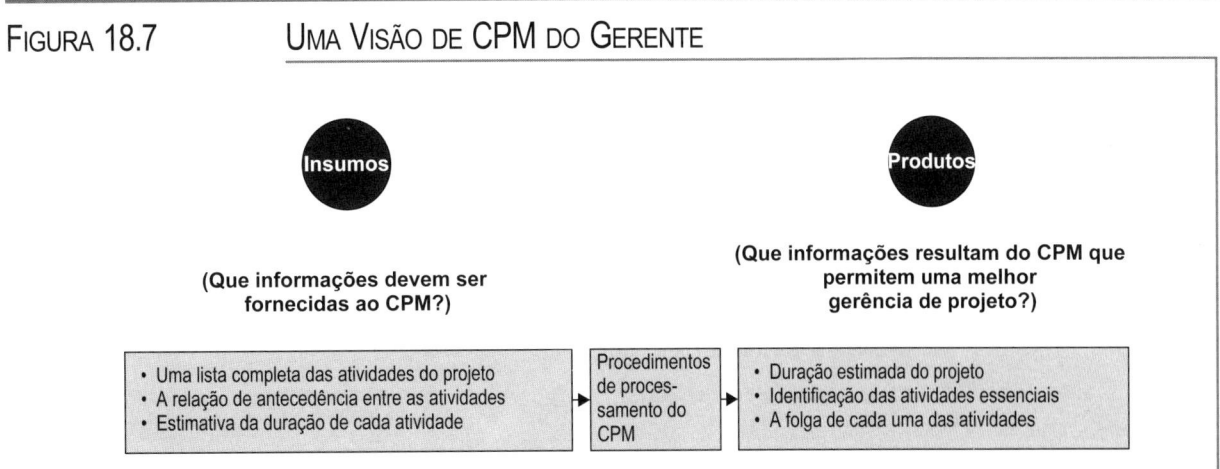

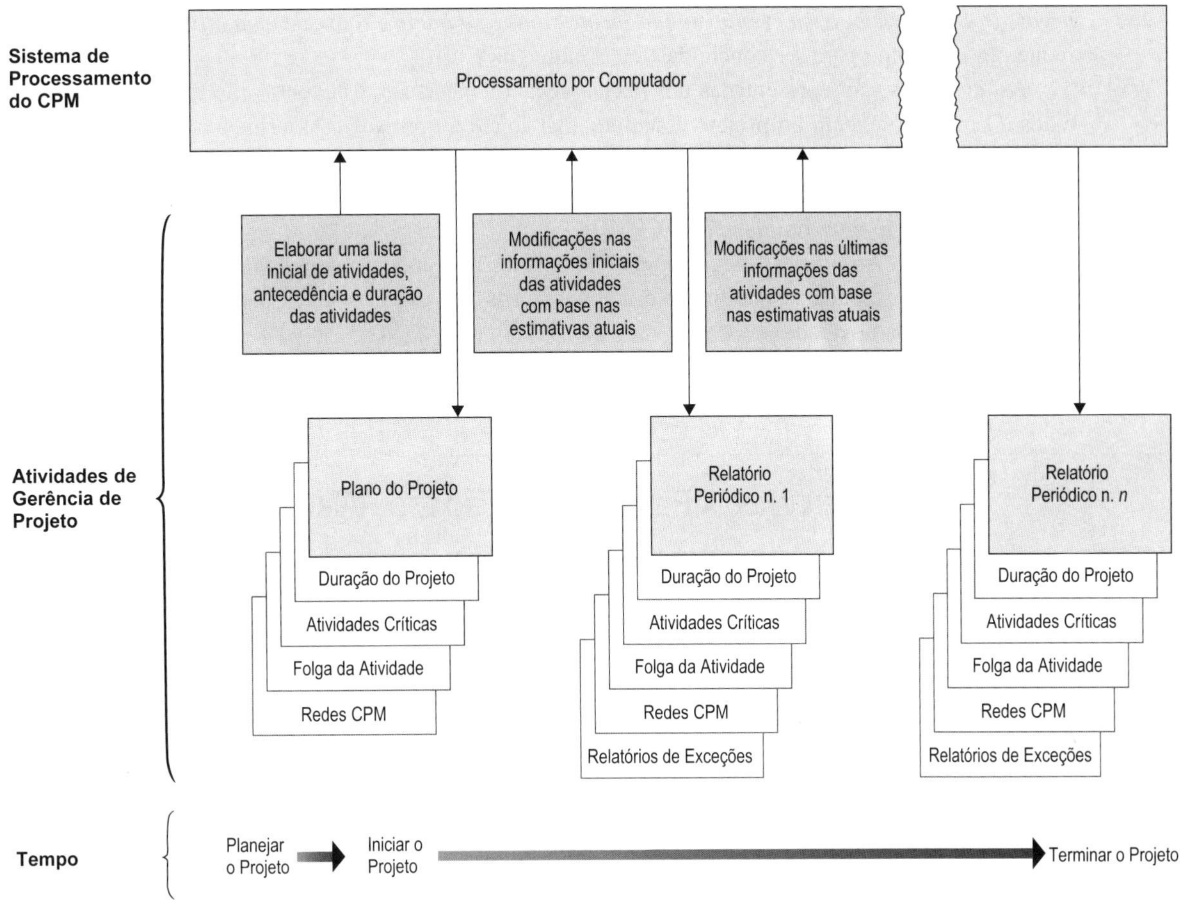

Sistema de Processamento do CPM

Processamento por Computador

Elaborar uma lista inicial de atividades, antecedência e duração das atividades

Modificações nas informações iniciais das atividades com base nas estimativas atuais

Modificações nas últimas informações das atividades com base nas estimativas atuais

Atividades de Gerência de Projeto

Plano do Projeto
- Duração do Projeto
- Atividades Críticas
- Folga da Atividade
- Redes CPM

Relatório Periódico n. 1
- Duração do Projeto
- Atividades Críticas
- Folga da Atividade
- Redes CPM
- Relatórios de Exceções

Relatório Periódico n. *n*
- Duração do Projeto
- Atividades Críticas
- Folga da Atividade
- Redes CPM
- Relatórios de Exceções

Tempo

Planejar o Projeto → Iniciar o Projeto ⟶ Terminar o Projeto

| TABELA 18.2 | ETAPAS NA ANÁLISE DO CPM |

1. Desenhe uma rede CPM. Esse diagrama proporciona uma visão gráfica das atividades incluídas no projeto e a ordem das atividades.

2. Dê uma visão geral do projeto analisando os caminhos da rede. Determine a duração de cada caminho (o tempo necessário para concluir cada caminho), identifique o caminho crítico (o caminho mais longo da rede, o caminho que determina o tempo necessário para concluir o projeto) e determine quanto tempo se espera levar para concluir o projeto.

3. Calcule a primeira data de término (PDT) de cada atividade.

4. Calcule a última data de término (UDT) de cada atividade.

5. Calcule a folga de cada atividade.

6. Calcule a primeira data de início (PDI) e a última data de início (UDI) de cada atividade.

Uma série de exemplos demonstra o funcionamento interno do CPM.
A Tabela 18.2 relaciona as etapas seguidas em uma análise de CPM.
Os Exemplos de 18.1 a 18.5 ilustram essas etapas.
No Exemplo 18.1 descrevemos o projeto RAMOV e criamos uma rede CPM para o projeto.

A Tabela 18.3 lista as atividades e os eventos do projeto, as atividades imediatamente antecedentes e a duração de cada uma delas. *Uma **atividade** é uma tarefa ou uma determinada quantidade de trabalho necessária no projeto, e um **evento** simplesmente sinaliza o início e o fim de uma atividade.* As atividades requerem um tempo para ser concluídas; os eventos, não.

As atividades são representadas por flechas retas (não curvas); os eventos são representados por círculos. O primeiro evento do projeto é sempre "dar início ao projeto". As primeiras atividades (flechas) de um projeto são sempre desenhadas a partir do primeiro evento (círculo), e as últimas atividades de um projeto são sempre desenhadas de forma que terminem no último evento. Essa convenção evita flechas pendentes no início e no fim das redes CPM.

A coluna das Atividades Imediatamente Anteriores na Tabela 18.3 indica a ordem na qual as atividades devem ser executadas. A duração das atividades é uma estimativa de quanto tempo será necessário para concluir cada atividade.

EXEMPLO 18.1

DESENHANDO A REDE CPM DO PROJETO RAMOV

Organizou-se uma equipe de projeto na Manufacturing Technology Inc. (MTI) para elaborar e desenvolver uma versão ligeiramente diferente dos robôs industriais de uma empresa. O novo robô é chamado de Robô Visão Ortogonal Móvel de Acesso Aleatório (RAMOV). Ele é móvel, tem capacidades visuais, é multiaxial e programável na oficina. Um dos clientes mais importantes da MTI, um grande fabricante de automóveis, está planejando substituir um banco de máquinas pelos novos robôs em suas linhas de montagens em cinco fábricas.

O cliente quer ver uma demonstração do robô, uma proposta técnica e uma proposta de preço em dois meses. A primeira coisa que a equipe de projeto fez foi listar e descrever as atividades do projeto, determinar a ordem das atividades e estimar quanto tempo cada atividade levaria.

Essas informações sobre as atividades e eventos do projeto são apresentadas na Tabela 18.3. Prepare um diagrama CPM a partir das informações dessa tabela.

TABELA 18.3 — ATIVIDADES E EVENTOS DO PROJETO RAMOV

Atividade	Atividades Imediatamente Anteriores	Duração das Atividades (dias)
a) Elaborar o RAMOV	—	20
b) Construir protótipos	a	10
c) Testar os protótipos	b	8
d) Estimar o custo dos materiais	a	11
e) Refinar o projeto do RAMOV	c,d	7
f) Demonstrar o RAMOV para o cliente	e	6
g) Estimar os custos da mão-de-obra	d	12
h) Preparar a proposta técnica	e	13
i) Entregar a proposta ao cliente	g,h	5

Evento

1. Dá-se início ao projeto.
2. Conclui-se o projeto do RAMOV.
3. Constrói-se os protótipos.
4. Conclui-se os testes dos protótipos.
5. Conclui-se as estimativas de custo dos materiais.
6. Conclui-se o refinamento do projeto do RAMOV.
7. Conclui-se a proposta técnica e as estimativas de custo de mão-de-obra.
8. Demonstra-se as unidades RAMOV e entrega-se a proposta ao cliente. O projeto é concluído.

SOLUÇÃO

1. Primeiro observe a Figura 18.9. Ela contém as convenções seguidas para se desenhar redes CPM.
2. Depois, comece com as informações sobre as atividades e os eventos da Tabela 18.3. As **atividades** são tarefas ou trabalhos que precisam ser feitos à medida que o projeto evolui e são representadas por flechas retas. Os eventos são o início e o fim das atividades e são representados por círculos. O projeto começa com o Evento 1, que é seguido da Atividade a. A ordem das atividades está na coluna Atividades Imediatamente Anteriores da Tabela 18.3 e indica que atividade tem de ser concluída antes de se dar início a uma outra. Por exemplo, a atividade imediatamente anterior à Atividade b é a Atividade a. Isso significa que a Atividade a tem de ser concluída para que se possa dar início à Atividade b.
3. Desenhe a rede CPM e coloque a letra de cada atividade sob sua flecha:

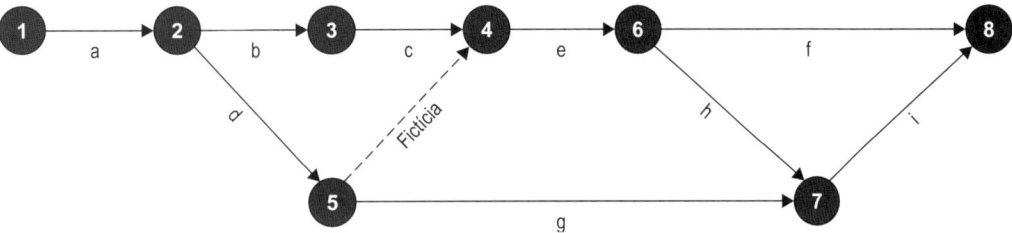

Observe que tanto a Atividade c como a d são imediatamente anteriores à Atividade e. Para mostrar que a Atividade d tem de ser concluída antes de se dar início à Atividade e, utiliza-se uma atividade fictícia. Uma **atividade fictícia** não envolve trabalho nem tempo. Ela simplesmente mostra a relação de antecedência ou a ordem das atividades.

FIGURA 18.9 — CONVENÇÕES DA REDE CPM

Representação da Rede | **Interpretação**

1. É preciso concluir a Atividade *a* antes de se poder começar a Atividade *b*.

2. As Atividades *b* e *c* têm de ocorrer simultaneamente, mas a Atividade *a* tem de ser concluída para que se possa dar início a qualquer uma das duas.

3. As Atividades *a* e *b* podem ocorrer simultaneamente, mas a Atividade *c* não pode ser iniciada antes de se concluir *a* e *b*.

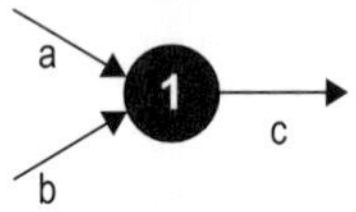

4. As Atividades *a*, *b*, *c* e *d* podem ocorrer simultaneamente, mas as Atividades *a* e *b* precisam ser concluídas para que se possa dar início à Atividade *c* ou *d*.

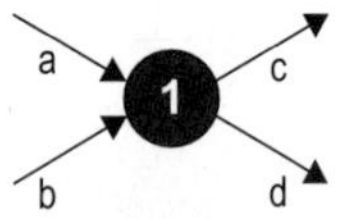

5. A Atividade *a* tem de ser concluída para que se possa dar início à Atividade *b*, e a Atividade *c* tem de ser concluída para que se possa dar início à Atividade *d*, mas o caminho a-b é independente da caminho c-d.

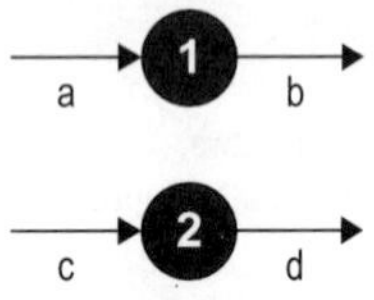

6. A Atividade *a* tem de ser concluída antes de se dar início à Atividade *b* ou *c*. As Atividades *b* e *c* têm de ser concluídas antes de se dar início à Atividade *d*. A flecha pontilhada é uma atividade fictícia. As atividades fictícias têm duração zero e mostram apenas a relação de antecedência.

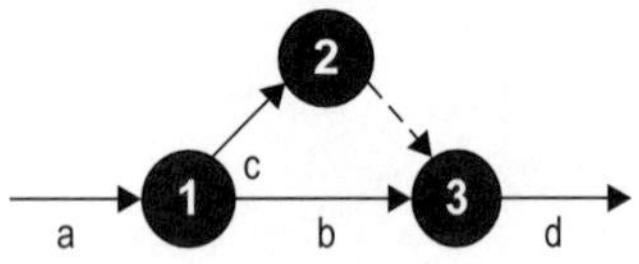

7. As Atividades *a* e *b*, *c* e *d* podem ocorrer simultaneamente, mas as Atividades *a* e *b* precisam ser concluídas para que se possa dar início à Atividade *c*, e a Atividade *b* tem de ser concluída antes de se dar início à Atividade *d*. A flecha pontilhada é uma atividade fictícia. As atividades fictícias têm duração zero e mostram apenas a relação de antecedência.

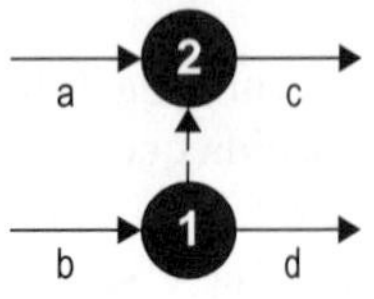

Estude primeiro as convenções para se desenhar uma rede CPM da Figura 18.9 e depois siga o Exemplo 18.1. Observe que as Convenções 6 e 7 da Figura 18.9 utilizam uma atividade fictícia. Uma atividade fictícia indica somente a presença de relações de antecedência ou a ordem em que as atividades devem ser executadas. As atividades fictícias não requerem qualquer tempo ou esforço. Tendo uma rede CPM, temos uma visão gráfica das atividades que foram concluídas no projeto, a ordem na qual as atividades têm de ser executadas e as correlações entre elas. Para desenhar esse tipo de rede, é aconselhável primeiro fazer um rascunho em uma folha de papel. Depois determine se as informações imediatamente anteriores do projeto se encaixam em seu rascunho. Se não se encaixarem, revise o rascunho e transfira-o em sua forma final para uma outra folha de papel.

O Exemplo 18.2 dá uma visão geral do projeto RAMOV fazendo uma análise dos caminhos do projeto. Nesse exemplo, as durações das atividades de cada um dos cinco caminhos são somadas para determinar quanto tempo se estima que será necessário para cada caminho. Observe que se estima que o caminho a-b-c-e-h-i leve 63 dias, e esse é o caminho mais longo ou o caminho crítico. Estima-se que todos os outros caminhos requeiram menos de 63 dias. Se o caminho crítico atrasar por qualquer motivo, o projeto também atrasará pelo mesmo período de tempo.

Exemplo 18.2

Visão Geral do Projeto RAMOV: Analisando Seus Caminhos

Elaborado o diagrama da rede para o projeto RAMOV no Exemplo 18.1, analise os caminhos dessa rede. Qual deles é o caminho crítico? Quanto tempo o projeto levará para ser concluído?

Solução

1. Primeiro escreva a duração de cada atividade sob sua flecha. Por exemplo a = 20 está escrito sob a flecha de *a*.

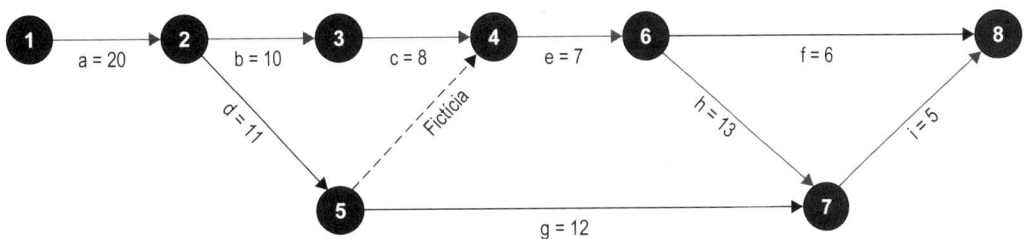

2. Depois identifique os caminhos e calcule a duração de cada um deles:

Caminhos	Duração dos Caminhos (dias)
a-b-c-e-f	20 + 10 + 8 + 7 + 6 = 51
a-b-c-e-h-i	20 + 10 + 8 + 7 + 13 + 5 = 63*
a-d-e-f	20 + 11 + 7 + 6 = 44
a-d-e-h-i	20 + 11 + 7 + 13 + 5 = 56
a-d-g-i	20 + 11 + 12 + 5 = 48

*Caminhos críticos.

O caminho mais longo leva 63 dias e é o caminho crítico. Ele determina a duração do projeto. Conseqüentemente espera-se que o projeto leve 63 dias para ser concluído.

O Exemplo 18.3 ilustra como se calculam os valores da **primeira data de término (PDT)** de cada atividade do projeto RAMOV. PDT é o menor período de tempo no qual podemos terminar uma atividade. Percorrendo a rede CPM *da esquerda para a direita*, os valores PDT são escritos na parte esquerda da caixa sobre a flecha de cada atividade. As atividades que iniciam um projeto sempre têm a PDT igual a suas durações (D). Se uma atividade tiver mais de uma atividade imediatamente anterior, sua PDT é calculada utilizando-se a maior PDT entre as atividades imediatamente anteriores. O tempo esperado de conclusão do projeto é a maior PDT de todas aquelas atividades que terminam no último evento. Essa PDT maior representa a duração do caminho crítico.

Exemplo 18.3

Calculando a Primeira Data de Término (PDT) das Atividades do Projeto RAMOV

A partir da rede do Exemplo 18.1, calcule a Primeira Data de Término (PDT) de cada atividade. Escreva a PDT de cada atividade na parte esquerda da caixa sobre sua flecha. Comece no Evento 1 e vá percorrendo a rede *da esquerda para a direita* e determine o valor da PDT de cada atividade. *A PDT representa o menor período de tempo no qual podemos concluir uma atividade. As PDTs de todas as atividades que iniciam um projeto são suas durações*. Por exemplo, a PDT da Atividade *a* é 20, que é sua duração, porque ela inicia o projeto. *Para todas as outras atividades, sua PDT é a PDT de sua atividade imediatamente anterior mais sua duração (D)*. Vamos calcular os valores PDT:

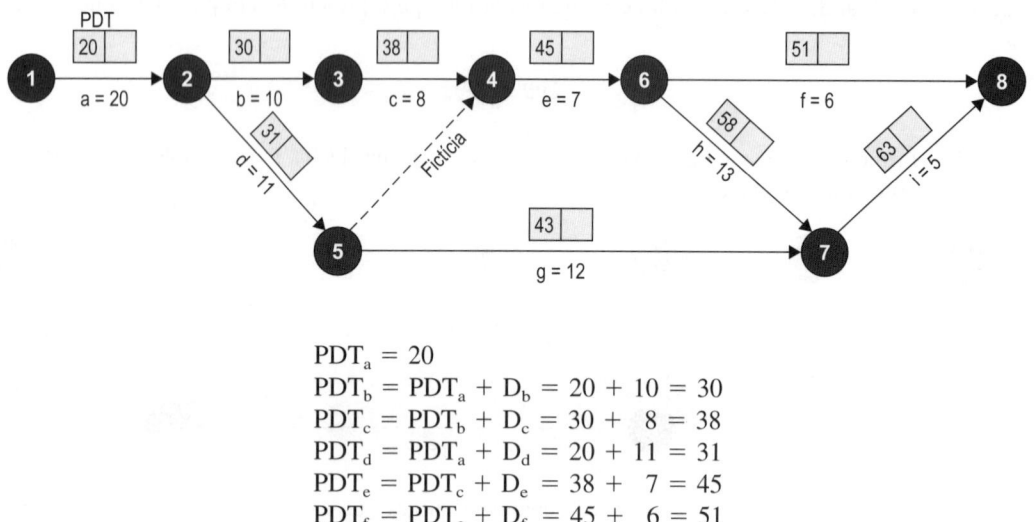

$$PDT_a = 20$$
$$PDT_b = PDT_a + D_b = 20 + 10 = 30$$
$$PDT_c = PDT_b + D_c = 30 + 8 = 38$$
$$PDT_d = PDT_a + D_d = 20 + 11 = 31$$
$$PDT_e = PDT_c + D_e = 38 + 7 = 45$$
$$PDT_f = PDT_e + D_f = 45 + 6 = 51$$
$$PDT_g = PDT_d + D_g = 31 + 12 = 43$$
$$PDT_h = PDT_e + D_h = 45 + 13 = 58$$
$$PDT_i = PDT_h + D_i = 58 + 5 = 63$$

*Observe que quando uma atividade tem duas ou mais atividades imediatamente anteriores, é preciso usar a **maior PDT** para calcular sua PDT.* Por exemplo, a Atividade *i* tem duas atividades imediatamente anteriores — *h* e *g*. Como $PDT_h = 58$ é maior do que $PDT_g = 43$, é preciso utilizar a PDT_h para calcular a PDT_i:

$$PDT_i = PDT_h + D_i = 58 + 5 = 63$$

Da mesma maneira, a Atividade *e* tem duas antecessoras — *c* e *d*. Como $PDT_c = 38$ é maior do que $PDT_d = 31$, é preciso usar PDT_c para calcular PDT_e:

$$PDT_e = PDT_c + D_e = 38 + 7 = 45$$

A maior PDT das atividades que terminam no Evento 8 representa o tempo esperado de conclusão do projeto e a duração do caminho crítico. Nesse exemplo, a maior PDT é $PDT_i = 63$, portanto espera-se que o projeto RAMOV seja concluído 63 dias depois de seu início.

O Exemplo 18.4 ilustra como são calculados os valores da **última data de término (UDT)** e das folgas (S) para cada uma das atividades do projeto RAMOV. A UDT é o maior período de tempo desde o início do projeto dentro do qual podemos terminar uma atividade sem atrasar a conclusão do projeto. Percorrendo a rede da CPM *da direita para a esquerda*, os valores UDT são escritos do lado direito da caixa sobre a flecha de cada atividade. As UDTs das atividades que terminam no último evento do projeto são sempre iguais à maior PDT entre as atividades do projeto. Se uma atividade tiver mais de uma atividade imediatamente posterior, sua UDT é a menor UDT – D entre suas atividades posteriores. O valor da **folga (S)** de uma atividade é calculado subtraindo-se sua PDT a partir de sua UDT e colocando-se o valor na parte superior da caixa sobre sua flecha.

Exemplo 18.4

Calculando a Última Data de Término (UDT) e a Folga (S) das Atividades do Projeto RAMOV

No Exemplo 18.3, percorrendo a rede da esquerda para a direita, foram concluídas as primeiras datas de término (PDT) de todas as atividades do projeto. Agora calcule a última data de término (UDT) e a folga (S) de cada atividade.

Solução

1. Calcule a UDT de cada atividade:

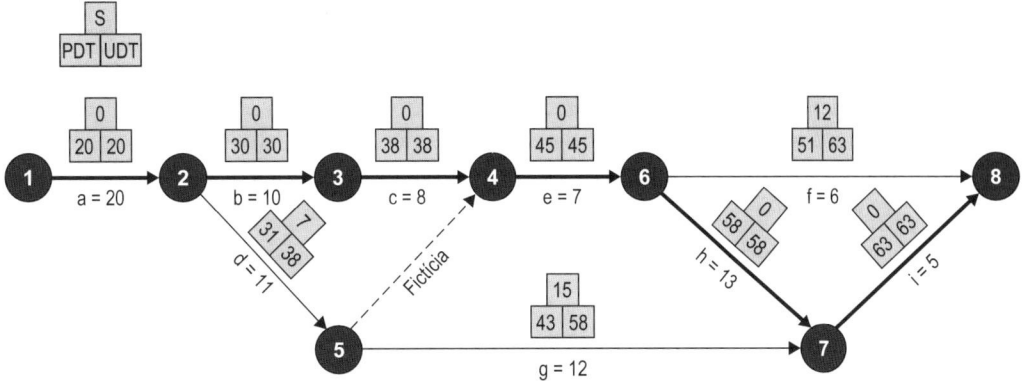

Comece no Evento 8 na ponta do lado direito e vá *da direita para a esquerda*. Escreva a UDT de cada atividade do lado direito da caixa sobre sua flecha. *A UDT representa o período máximo desde o início do projeto no qual podemos terminar uma atividade. A UDT de todas as atividades que terminem no último evento vai ser sempre a maior PDT do projeto.* A UDT das Atividades f e i é, portanto, 63 dias, o mesmo valor da PDT_j, que é a maior PDT de todas as atividades:

$$UDT_i = PDT_j = 63$$
$$UDT_f = PDT_j = 63$$

A UDT de qualquer outra atividade é calculada subtraindo-se a duração (D) da atividade imediatamente posterior (a atividade logo à direita na rede) da UDT da mesma. As últimas datas de término das atividades do projeto são calculadas da seguinte maneira:

$$UDT_h = UDT_i - D_i = 63 - 5 = 58$$
$$UDT_g = UDT_i - D_i = 63 - 5 = 58$$
$$UDT_e = UDT_h - D_h = 58 - 13 = 45*$$
$$UDT_d = UDT_e - D_e = 45 - 7 = 38*$$
$$UDT_c = UDT_e - D_e = 45 - 7 = 38$$
$$UDT_b = UDT_c - D_c = 38 - 8 = 30$$
$$UDT_a = UDT_b - D_b = 30 - 10 = 20*$$

*Note que quando uma atividade tem mais do que uma atividade imediatamente posterior (atividades logo à direita na rede), sua UDT é calculada comparando-se os valores da UDT — D para todas as Atividades imediatamente posteriores. Os **menores** valores UDT — D são então usados como sua UDT.* Por exemplo, as atividades e, d e a acima têm um asterisco (*) para indicar que elas têm mais que uma Atividade posterior. Pegue a atividade e, por exemplo: ambas as Atividades f e h sucedem a Atividade e. A UDT_e é calculada assim:

$$UDT_e = UDT_f - D_f = 63 - 6 = 57 \quad \text{ou} \quad UDT_e = UDT_h - D_h = 58 - 13 = 45$$

Portanto, $UDT_e = 45$.

2. Calcule a folga (S) de cada atividade:

   Para cada atividade S = UDT − PDT, subtraia a PDT de cada atividade de sua UDT e escreva o valor de S na parte de cima da caixa sobre sua flecha. A folga de todas as atividades da rede é calculada da seguinte maneira:

   $$S_i = UDT_i - PDT_i = 63 - 63 = 0^*$$
   $$S_h = UDT_h - PDT_h = 58 - 58 = 0^*$$
   $$S_g = UDT_g - PDT_g = 58 - 43 = 15$$
   $$S_f = UDT_f - PDT_f = 63 - 51 = 12$$
   $$S_e = UDT_e - PDT_e = 45 - 45 = 0^*$$
   $$S_d = UDT_d - PDT_d = 38 - 31 = 7$$
   $$S_c = UDT_c - PDT_c = 38 - 38 = 0^*$$
   $$S_b = UDT_b - PDT_b = 30 - 30 = 0^*$$
   $$S_a = UDT_a - PDT_a = 20 - 20 = 0^*$$

   Observe que as atividades acima com asterisco têm folga zero. Essas atividades estão no caminho a-b-c-e-h-i, que é denotado pelas flechas em negrito em toda a rede.

   As atividades adjacentes nas seções do caminho compartilham folga. Por exemplo, considere o caminho a-d-g-i na rede CPM. A Atividade *d* tem sete dias de folga, e a Atividade *g* tem 15 dias de folga. Mas a soma das durações das atividades ao longo do caminho é de 48 dias. Isso significa que há um *total* de 63 − 48 = 15 dias de folga ao longo do caminho. Portanto, as Atividades *d* e *g* compartilham 7 dias de folga.

O Exemplo 18.5 completa a análise CPM do projeto RAMOV. Nesse exemplo os valores PDT, UDT e S são transferidos da rede do Exemplo 18.4 para a tabela. Depois calcula-se os valores PDI e UDI de cada atividade utilizando-se as fórmulas a seguir, e esses valores são registrados na tabela:

$$PDI = PDT - D$$
$$UDI = UDT - D$$

A tabela do Exemplo 18.5 é típica dos produtos dos programas computadorizados de CPM. Os valores de folga (S) de cada atividade indicam o quanto uma atividade pode atrasar sem prejudicar o prazo de conclusão do projeto. *As atividades com folga zero são as atividades do **caminho crítico**. Se houver atraso em qualquer uma delas, o prazo de conclusão do projeto também sofrerá o mesmo atraso.*

Exemplo 18.5

Calculando a Primeira Data de Início (PDI) e a Última Data de Início (UDI) de Cada uma das Atividades do Projeto RAMOV

A partir da rede do Exemplo 18.4, calcule o início mais cedo (es) e o início mais remoto (ls) de cada uma das atividades.

Solução

Obtenha os valores PDT, UDT e S de cada atividade do Exemplo 18.4 e coloque-os na tabela a seguir. Depois calcule os valores PDI e UDI de cada atividade utilizando estas fórmulas:

$$PDI = PDT - D$$
$$UDI = UDT - D$$

Atividade	Duração da Atividade (D)	Primeira Data de Início (PDI)	Primeira Data de Término (PDT)	Última Data de Início (UDI)	Última Data de Término (UDT)	Folga (S)
a	20	0	20	0	20	0
b	10	20	30	20	30	0
c	8	30	38	30	38	0
d	11	20	31	27	38	7
e	7	38	45	38	45	0
f	6	45	51	57	63	12
g	12	31	43	46	58	15
h	13	45	58	45	58	0
i	5	58	63	58	63	0

Assim demonstramos como a análise CPM desenvolve informações para a gerência — duração do projeto, atividades críticas e folga das atividades. Esses cálculos são elaborados no início do projeto e modificados quando se obtém novas estimativas à medida que o projeto vai evoluindo.

A Figura 18.8 ilustrou como ocorre essa atualização do CPM. Essas atualizações resultam em novos relatórios periódicos que são enviados aos gerentes de projeto. Os Relatórios de Exceções de CPM, os Relatórios de Atividades em Atraso e os Relatórios de Atividades Comprimidas são exemplos de relatórios que dão aos gerentes informações atuais sobre os detalhes do projeto, o que conseqüentemente lhes permite fazer um controle rigoroso das atividades.

Agora que estudamos o CPM, tratemos da PERT.

TÉCNICA DE AVALIAÇÃO E REVISÃO DE PROGRAMA

A PERT é quase idêntica ao CPM no que diz respeito às funções, aos diagramas de rede, aos cálculos internos e aos relatórios de gerência de projeto resultantes. As pequenas exceções dizem respeito às estimativas das durações das atividades.[1]

No CPM a duração da atividade baseia-se em uma única estimativa de tempo. Na PERT fazem-se três estimativas de duração para cada atividade: a **duração pessimista (t_p)**, se algo sair errado; a **duração mais provável (t_m)**, a melhor estimativa por consenso; e a **duração otimista (t_o)**, se tudo correr bem. Dessas três estimativas calcula-se uma média (t_e) e uma variância (V_t) para cada atividade:

$$t_e = (t_o + 4t_m + t_p)/6 \quad e \quad V_t = [(t_p - t_o)/6]^2$$

Por que a PERT utiliza várias estimativas do tempo das atividades? Porque não temos certeza da duração das mesmas. Estimando uma duração pessimista e uma duração otimista obtém-se uma faixa provável de duração. O tempo mais provável é nossa melhor estimativa de duração. Três estimativas de tempo nos permitem elaborar uma duração média e uma variância para cada caminho da rede, o que define totalmente as distribuições das durações dos caminhos. A duração média de um caminho é igual à soma das durações médias de suas atividades, e a variância de um caminho é igual à soma das variâncias de suas atividades. Quando se supõe que a distribuição da duração do caminho seja normal e sua média e variância já foram calculadas, pode-se fazer afirmações com base em probabilidades sobre o caminho. Por exemplo: (1) há uma probabilidade de apenas 10% de que o caminho crítico seja maior do que 35 semanas; (2) há uma probabilidade de 35% de que o projeto seja concluído em menos de 50 semanas. A capacidade de fazer esse tipo de afirmação sobre as durações de um caminho é a única diferença entre o CPM e a PERT. A PERT utiliza o t_e para durações das atividades, enquanto o CPM utiliza uma única estimativa de tempo das durações das atividades. Todos os outros cálculos dos dois métodos são idênticos.

O Exemplo 18.6 ilustra como a PERT seria usada para analisar o projeto RAMOV.

---

[1] Para fins de simplificação, ultilizamos a convenção atividade-na-flecha (AOA) para o CPM e a PERT.

Exemplo 18.6

Uma Análise PERT do Projeto RAMOV

Leia a descrição do projeto RAMOV do Exemplo 18.1. Os clientes pediram à equipe de projeto que fizesse uma estimativa da probabilidade de o projeto ser concluído dentro de 65 dias. Para responder a essa pergunta, a equipe elaborou três estimativas de durações para cada uma das atividades do projeto. Faça uma análise PERT do projeto e responda à pergunta do cliente.

Solução

1. Primeiro calcule a média e a variância de cada atividade:

Atividade	Duração Otimista (t_o)	Duração Mais Provável (t_m)	Duração Pessimista (t_p)	Duração Média $t_e = (t_o + 4t_m + t_p)/6$	Variância $V_t = [(t_p - t_o)/6]^2$
a	18	20	22	20,00	0,44
b	8	10	14	10,33	1,00
c	5	8	9	7,67	0,44
d	10	11	12	11,00	0,11
e	7	7	7	7,00	0
f	4	6	7	5,83	0,25
g	10	12	14	12,00	0,44
h	12	13	15	13,17	0,25
i	5	5	5	5,00	0

2. A seguir, desenhe a rede PERT e calcule a primeira data de término (PDT), a última data de término (UDT) e a folga (S) de cada atividade. Determine o caminho crítico.

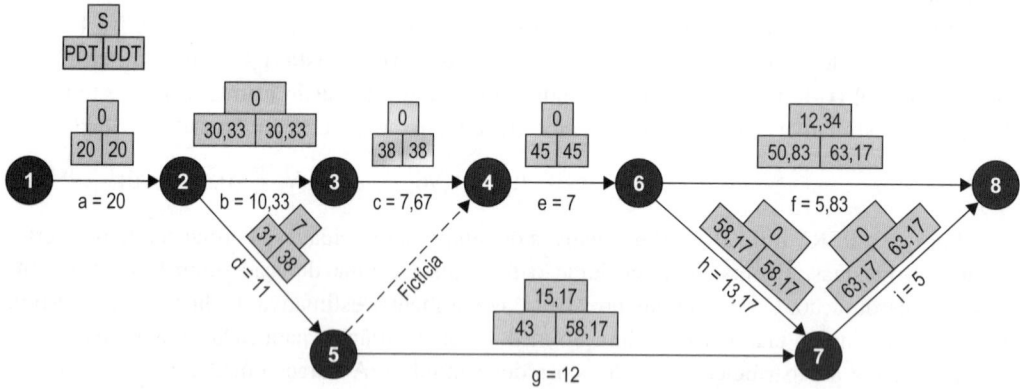

Como se pode ver da rede acima, o caminho crítico é o a-b-c-e-h-i e espera-se que ele leve 63,17 dias.

3. Depois calcule o desvio padrão do caminho crítico:

Some as variâncias das atividades ao longo do caminho crítico a-b-c-e-h-i:

$$V_{caminho} = V_a + V_b + V_c + V_e + V_h + V_i = 0,44 + 1,0 + 0,44 + 0 + 0,25 + 0 = 2,13$$

$$\sigma_{caminho} = \sqrt{\text{variância do caminho a-b-c-e-h-i}} = \sqrt{2,13} = 1,46 \text{ dia}$$

Supondo-se que a distribuição do prazo de conclusão do caminho a-b-c-e-h-i seja normal com uma média de 63,17 dias e um desvio padrão de 1,46:

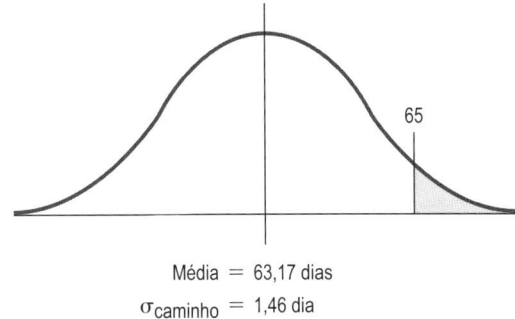

Média = 63,17 dias
$\sigma_{caminho}$ = 1,46 dia

Descubra quantos desvios padrões da média 65 dias representam:

$$Z = \frac{65 - 63,17}{\sigma_{caminho}} = \frac{65 - 63,17}{1,46} = 1,25$$

No final do livro, localize Z = 1,25 na margem esquerda da tabela. A probabilidade de o projeto ser concluído em menos de 65 dias é de 0,89435 (cerca de 89,4%), mas essa é a boa notícia. A má notícia é que há uma probabilidade de 0,10565 (cerca de 10,6%) de que o projeto leve mais do que 65 dias.

Temos de ter o mesmo cuidado ao interpretar um caminho crítico na análise PERT. O caminho crítico numa análise PERT é tão-só o caminho com a duração *esperada* mais longa. O caminho crítico no Exemplo 18.6 era o caminho a-b-c-e-h-i, com duração esperada de 63,17 dias. Poderia haver um ou mais caminhos na rede RAMOV com durações esperadas menores mas sujeitos a grandes incertezas. Esses caminhos não críticos poderiam na verdade ter uma maior probabilidade do que o caminho a-b-c-e-h-i de levar mais do que 65 dias para ser concluídos. Nesses casos, a variância do caminho crítico apresenta de forma atenuada a variância real da duração do projeto. A importância desse ponto é que, quando se utiliza a PERT, os analistas devem prestar atenção ao caminho crítico e a qualquer outro caminho com duração esperada próxima da duração do caminho crítico antes de determinar a probabilidade de ultrapassar uma determinada data de conclusão do projeto. O Exemplo 18.7 ilustra esse conceito.

Exemplo 18.7

Uma Análise Mais Detalhada dos Caminhos Críticos PERT

Dados esses dois caminhos PERT, qual deles apresenta maior probabilidade de ultrapassar a meta de 20 semanas de duração do projeto?

Caminho 1: Σt_e = 19,34 semanas, σ_t = 0,780 semana (caminho crítico)
Caminho 2: Σt_e = 19,17 semanas, σ_t = 1,170 semana (caminho não crítico)

Solução

1. Compare as distribuições das durações dos dois caminhos:

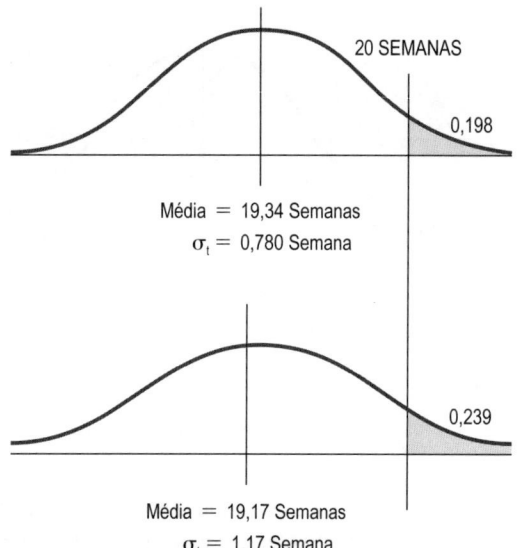

2. Calcule a probabilidade de a duração de cada caminho levar mais do que 20 semanas. Calcule o valor Z de cada caminho, utilize os valores Z e consulte a probabilidade de cada caminho levar menos de 20 semanas (ver a tabela Áreas sob a Curva Normal no final do livro) e depois calcule a probabilidade de cada caminho levar mais de 20 semanas:

$$Z_1 = (T - \Sigma t_e)/\sigma_t = (20 - 19{,}34)/0{,}780 = 0{,}846$$

Da tabela, P (D_1 < 20 semanas) = 0,80234.

$$P(D_1 > 20 \text{ semanas}) = 1 - 0{,}80234 = 0{,}198$$

$$Z_2 = (T - \Sigma t_e)/\sigma_t = (20 - 19{,}17)/1{,}170 = 0{,}709$$

Da tabela, P(D_2 < 20 semanas) = 0,76115.

$$P(D_1 > 20 \text{ semanas}) = 1 - 0{,}76115 = 0{,}239$$

3. A duração do caminho 2 (um caminho não crítico) na verdade tem maior probabilidade de ultrapassar a meta de 20 semanas do que o caminho 1 (o caminho crítico).

SISTEMAS DE CONTROLE DE CUSTOS DO PROJETO

O CPM e a PERT foram elaborados para oferecer planejamento, programação e controle aos gerentes de projeto visando apenas uma dimensão de desempenho do projeto — o desempenho em termos de tempo. A maioria das organizações, sejam elas produtoras de bens e serviços, indústrias privadas ou públicas, também tem de planejar e controlar uma outra dimensão de desempenho de projeto — custo ou gastos do projeto. PERT/Custo foi elaborada pelo Ministério da Defesa americana (DOD) e a Administração Nacional de Espaço e Aeronáutica (NASA) em 1962 para juntar o desempenho em termos de tempo e custo nos contratos do governo. O termo **PERT/Custo** é hoje utilizado como uma descrição da categoria geral dos sistemas de planejamento e controle de tempo/custo de projetos.

A Tabela 18.4 ilustra um relatório PERT/Custo comum: o Relatório de Status do Tempo/Custo do RATS. Esses relatórios computadorizados mostram periodicamente o status efetivo em termos de tempo e custos em relação ao status programado de cada atividade do projeto. Por exemplo, a Atividade *c* pode ser avaliada da seguinte maneira: (1) a atividade é concluída; (2) a duração efetiva da atividade é a mesma da duração programada; (3) uma quantia de US$ 4.500 a menos do que o custo programado foi efetivamente gasta na atividade. Da mesma maneira, a Atividade *j* pode ser assim avaliada: (1) a atividade não foi concluída; (2) a duração da atividade aumentou das seis semanas programadas para uma estimativa de sete semanas; (3) a data estimada de conclusão e a última data permissível de conclusão são as mesmas — 22 de agosto; (4) há folga zero para a atividade. Se a duração da atividade se esticar para além

TABELA 18.4 — RELATÓRIO DE STATUS DO TEMPO/CUSTO DO RATS

Atividade		Tempo (Semanas)				Custo (Milhares de Dólares)		
Atividade	Conta	Duração Programada da Atividade	Nova Duração Estimada	Data Estimada de Conclusão × Última Data Permissível	Folga	Custo Programado da Atividade	Custo Efetivo até o Momento	Custo Estimado para Concluir a Atividade
a	R-100	4	4	*		36,5	40,0	(3,5)
b	R-101	5	5	*		60,0	66,0	(6,0)
c	R-102	2	2	*		35,0	30,5	4,5
d	R-103	2	2	*		28,5	28,5	---
e	R-104	2	2	*		42,0	40,0	2,0
f	R-105	3	3	*		67,5	65,0	2,5
g	R-106	3	3	15/7 - 15/7	2	52,0	31,0	5,0
h	R-107	3	3	7/8 - 7/8	2	39,5	----	---
i	R-108	2	2	1/9 - 1/9	2	63,5	----	---
j	R-109	6	7	22/8 - 22/8	0	14,0	4,5	(4,0)
k	R-110	6	5	7/8 - 22/8	2	9,5	5,0	2,0
l	R-111	2	2	7/9 - 7/9	0	1,0	----	---
m	R-112	1	1	15/9 - 15/9	0	1,0	----	---
							Total	2,5

*A atividade foi concluída.

das sete semanas estimadas, todo o projeto se atrasará pelo mesmo período de tempo; (5) embora o custo efetivo da atividade esteja bem abaixo de seu custo programado, calcula-se que a atividade gaste US$ 4.000 a mais por ocasião da conclusão da atividade. Essas avaliações das atividades do projeto dão aos gerentes de projeto informações sobre como gerenciar melhor as mesmas. Pode-se elaborar relatórios desse tipo e outros semelhantes para que ofereçam uma mostra bem mais sofisticada dos custos. O status de custo da Tabela 18.4 poderia, por exemplo, ser dividido em mão-de-obra, materiais e despesas gerais ou qualquer outra divisão significativa dos custos de cada atividade.

Utilizamos gráficos e outros recursos visuais para avaliar simultaneamente o status do custo e do tempo dos projetos. A Figura 18.10 é um exemplo de um gráfico que resume o status real do projeto em termos de custo e tempo em comparação com a programação do projeto. Ele mostra que o projeto RATS em 15 de julho está cerca de uma semana atrasado e aproximadamente US$ 30.000 acima do orçamento. Os gastos estão projetados para ser o valor programado por ocasião da conclusão do projeto.

Independente do formato dos relatórios de tempo/custo dos projetos, os desempenhos em termos de tempo e custo são elementos de suma importância para a gerência de projetos.

CPM/PERT NA PRÁTICA

CPM/PERT é amplamente utilizado em uma série de organizações. Mas ele tende a ser utilizado em uma faixa restrita de aplicativos. O planejamento e controle de projeto é área predominante de todos os outros aplicativos, enquanto o planejamento e controle de produção e o planejamento e controle da manutenção são as outras áreas em que PERT/CPM é utilizada.

Folga Meta x Folga do Projeto O Exemplo 18.4 calcula a folga de cada atividade — a quantidade de dias que uma atividade pode atrasar sem provocar atraso na conclusão do projeto. A folga baseia-se na duração do caminho crítico, que é de 63 dias. Se o requisito do cliente fosse 65 dias, mesmo se qualquer atividade crítica atrasasse 2 dias, o requisito do cliente ainda seria atendido. Cada uma das atividades, portanto, na verdade tem 2 dias adicionais de folga, se o padrão for o requisito do cliente. Algumas organizações acrescentam essa semana adicional de folga à folga do projeto para cada atividade. Portanto a folga das atividades baseia-se em uma duração meta do objetivo e não na duração do caminho crítico.

FIGURA 18.10   PLANO DE TEMPO/CUSTO DO PROJETO RATS x GRÁFICO DO DESEMPENHO REAL

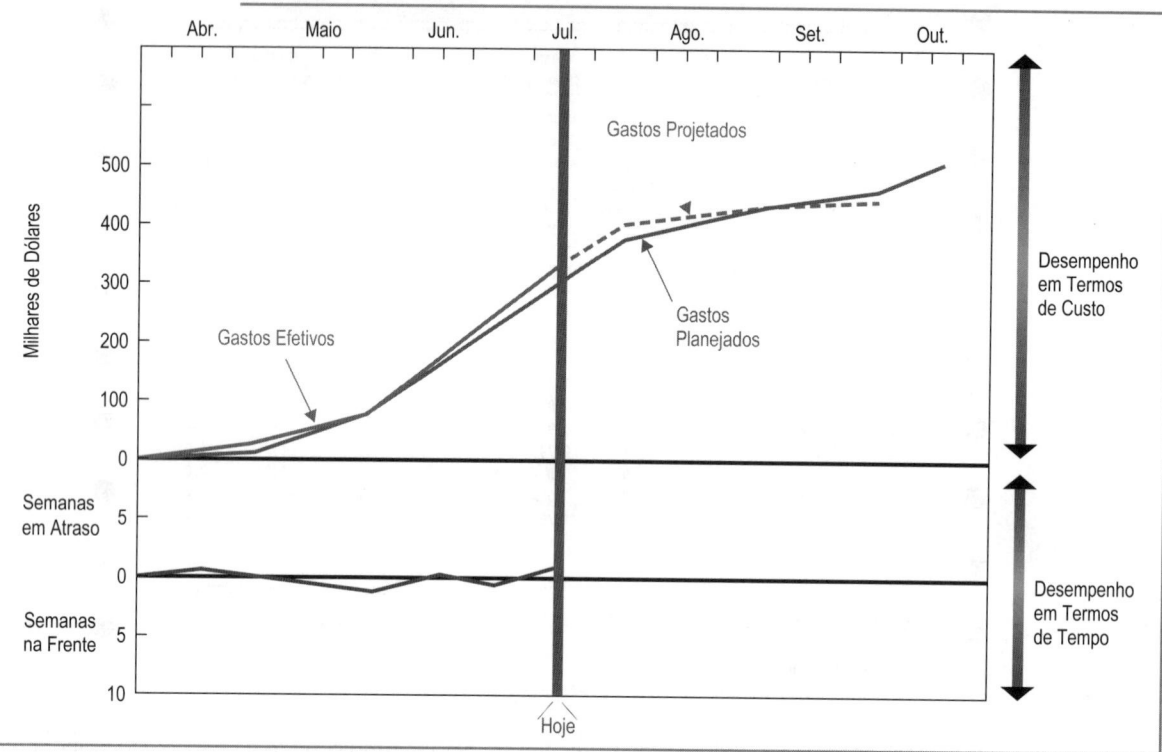

Relações Custo x Tempo das Atividades   Os gerentes de projeto de vez em quando podem ter a opção de **intensificar ou acelerar as atividades** — gastar dinheiro extra para comprimir a duração de uma atividade utilizando horas extras, subcontratação, expedição de materiais e assim por diante. Se os projetos correm o risco de ultrapassar a duração permissível do projeto, os gerentes geralmente encaram a intensificação como uma alternativa viável.

Como os gerentes têm várias atividades que podem ser intensificadas ou aceleradas no projeto, como se decidem quais atividades não intensificar, quais intensificar e em que ordem? As regras gerais são:

1. Intensificar somente as atividades críticas — as atividades do caminho crítico, as atividades com folga zero.
2. Intensificar primeiro atividades com o menor custo de intensificação por unidade de tempo até se obter a duração de projeto desejada.
3. Quando existirem caminhos críticos paralelos, cada um deles deve ser comprimido. Acelerar somente um dos caminhos não reduzirá a duração do projeto.

O Exemplo 18.8 ilustra a aplicação desses princípios no projeto RAMOV.

EXEMPLO 18.8

RELAÇÕES CUSTO x TEMPO DO PROJETO RAMOV

O cliente da MTI dos Exemplos 18.1 até 18.5 quer encurtar a conclusão do projeto RAMOV. O cliente indicou disposição de discutir pagar à MTI pelos custos adicionais para encurtar a duração do projeto. A equipe do projeto RAMOV sabe que se pode utilizar horas extras e outros meios para acelerar algumas das atividades. Preparando-se para essas discussões, a equipe do projeto RAMOV elaborou estas relações custo x tempo:

Atividade	Duração Presente (dias)	Duração Acelerada (dias)	Custo Presente	Custo Acelerado
a	20	18	$ 10.000	$ 14.000
b	10	5	12.000	16.500
c	8	3	6.000	11.000
d	11	9	4.000	5.600
e	7*	—	—	—
f	6*	—	—	—
g	12	9	9.000	11.000
h	13	12	12.000	13.500
i	5*	—	—	—

*Essas atividades não podem ser aceleradas.

Se a meta é reduzir o máximo possível o tempo de conclusão do projeto, em que ordem e em quanto você aceleraria as atividades do projeto RAMOV e qual seria o custo de acelerar as atividades?

Solução

1. Primeiro crie uma rede CPM para o projeto sem acelerar qualquer atividade. Esta rede CPM foi elaborada no Exemplo 18.4:

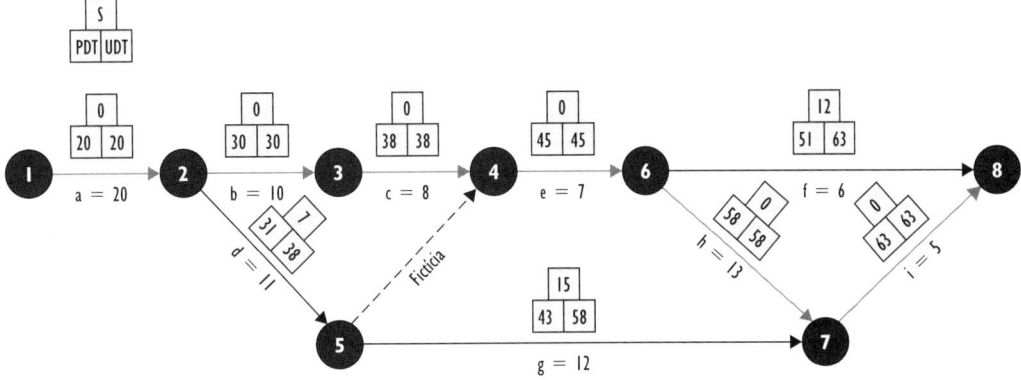

2. A seguir calcule o custo diário de acelerar todas as atividades que podem ser aceleradas.

(1) Atividade	(2) Quantidade Máxima de Aceleração (dias)	(3) Custo Adicional da Aceleração	(4) Custo da Aceleração por Dia [$/dia = (3)/(2)]
a	2	$ 4.000	$ 2.000
b	5	4.500	900
c	5	5.000	1.000
d	2	1.600	800
g	3	2.000	667
h	1	1.500	1.500

3. Depois desenvolva as etapas de aceleração do projeto. Nós supomos que a duração presente de uma atividade pode ser parcialmente acelerada em qualquer quantidade de dias, mas não pode ficar abaixo de sua "duração acelerada" mínima. Também podemos trabalhar com a hipótese simplificadora de que o custo diário da aceleração calculado acima se aplica a cada dia a mais que uma atividade é acelerada. (Na prática, algumas atividades podem custar cada vez mais por cada dia adicional que são aceleradas.)

O processo de aceleração segue as seguintes etapas:

Etapa 1. Identificar o(s) caminho(s) crítico(s).
Etapa 2. Identificar todas as combinações alternativas possíveis das atividades nos caminhos críticos que poderiam ser aceleradas em um dia e resultariam na redução em um dia da duração do projeto. Se não houver alternativas, o projeto foi acelerado o máximo possível.
Etapa 3. Calcular o custo de cada atividade ou conjunto de atividades alternativas.
Etapa 4. Selecione a alternativa menos custosa e acelere a(s) atividade(s) em um dia. Acompanhe a duração atual de cada atividade do projeto.
Etapa 5. Volte à Etapa 1 e repita todas as etapas.

A tabela a seguir resume todas as iterações do projeto de aceleração do processo.

Iteração	Caminho(s) Crítico(s) Atual(is)	Duração do Projeto (dias)	Atividades a Serem Aceleradas em um Dia	Custo Adicional da Aceleração	Novo(s) Caminho(s) Crítico(s)	Nova Duração do Projeto (dias)
1	a-b-c-e-h-i	63	b	$ 900	a-b-c-e-h-i	62
2	a-b-c-e-h-i	62	b	900	a-b-c-e-h-i	61
3	a-b-c-e-h-i	61	b	900	a-b-c-e-h-i	60
4	a-b-c-e-h-i	60	b	900	a-b-c-e-h-i	59
5	a-b-c-e-h-i	59	b	900	a-b-c-e-h-i	58
6	a-b-c-e-h-i	58	c	1.000	a-b-c-e-h-i	57
7	a-b-c-e-h-i	57	c	1.000	a-b-c-e-h-i; a-d-e-h-i	56
8	a-b-c-e-h-i; a-d-e-h-i	56	h	1.500	a-b-c-e-h-i; a-d-e-h-i	55
9	a-b-c-e-h-i; a-d-e-h-i	55	c,d	1.800	a-b-c-e-h-i; a-d-e-h-i	54
10	a-b-c-e-h-i; a-d-e-h-i	54	c,d	1.800	a-b-c-e-h-i; a-d-e-h-i	53
11	a-b-c-e-h-i; a-d-e-h-i	53	a	2.000	a-b-c-e-h-i; a-d-e-h-i	52
12	a-b-c-e-h-i; a-d-e-h-i	52	a	2.000	a-b-c-e-h-i; a-d-e-h-i	51*

*Todas as atividades do caminho crítico a-d-e-h-i foram aceleradas até sua duração acelerada mínima. Portanto o projeto foi acelerado o máximo possível.

Iteração 1

Etapa 1: O caminho crítico inicial é o a-b-c-e-h-i, e a duração inicial do projeto é de 63 dias.

Etapas 2 e 3: As atividades alternativas do caminho crítico que poderiam ser aceleradas em um dia e resultariam na redução em um dia da duração do projeto são:

Atividade	Custo Adicional da Aceleração
a	$ 2.000
b	900
c	1.000
h	1.500

Etapa 4: A Atividade *b* é a alternativa menos custosa, portanto é selecionada, e sua duração é acelerada de 10 para 9 dias a um custo adicional de $ 900. Isso resulta numa nova duração do projeto de 62 dias.

Iterações 2, 3, 4 e 5

A Atividade *b* também seria selecionada nas Iterações de 2 a 5. Depois da Iteração 5, a Atividade *b* está em sua duração acelerada mínima, a duração do projeto é de 58 dias, e o caminho crítico ainda é o a-b-c-e-h-i.

Iteração 6

Etapa 1: O caminho crítico atual é o a-b-c-e-h-i, e a duração atual do projeto é de 58 dias.

Etapas 2 e 3: As atividades alternativas do caminho crítico que não puderam ser aceleradas em um dia e resultariam na duração do projeto ser um dia mais curta são:

Atividade	Custo Adicional da Aceleração
a	$ 2.000
c	1.000
h	1.500

Etapa 4: A Atividade *c* é a alternativa mais barata, por isso é selecionada, e a duração de sua atividade é acelerada de 8 para 7 dias a um custo adicional de $ 1.000. Isso resulta numa duração de projeto de 57 dias.

Iteração 7

A Atividade *c* também é selecionada na Iteração 7, e a nova duração do projeto é de 56 dias. No entanto, agora existem dois caminhos críticos: a-b-c-e-h-i e a-d-e-h-i.

Iteração 8

Etapa 1: Os caminhos críticos atuais são a-b-c-e-h-i e a-d-e-h-i, e a duração do projeto é de 56 dias.

Etapas 2 e 3: As atividades alternativas ou combinações de atividades que poderiam ser aceleradas em um dia e que resultariam em ambos os caminhos críticos serem um dia mais curtos são:

Atividade	Custo Adicional da Aceleração
a	$ 2.000
c e d	1.800
h	1.500

Etapa 4: A Atividade *h* é a alternativa mais barata, portanto é selecionada, e a duração de sua atividade é acelerada de 13 para 12 dias a um custo adicional de $ 1.500. Isso resulta em uma nova duração de projeto de 55 dias. A Atividade *h* agora está em sua duração acelerada mínima.

Iteração 9

Etapa 1: Os caminhos críticos atuais são a-b-c-e-h-i e a-d-e-h-i.

Etapas 2 e 3: As atividades alternativas ou combinações de atividades que poderiam ser aceleradas em um dia e que resultariam em ambos os caminhos críticos serem um dia mais curtos são:

Atividade	Custo Adicional da Aceleração
a	$ 2.000
c e d	1.800

Etapa 4: As Atividades *c* e *d* juntas são a alternativa mais barata, portanto são selecionadas, e a duração de suas atividades é acelerada em um dia a um custo adicional de $ 1.800. Isso resulta em uma nova duração de projeto de 54 dias.

Iteração 10

As Atividades *c* e *d* também são selecionadas na Iteração 10. A Atividade *d* agora está em sua duração acelerada mínima, mas a Atividade *c* não está.

Iterações 11 e 12

Etapa 1: Os caminhos críticos atuais são a-b-c-e-h-i e a-d-e-h-i.

Etapas 2 e 3: A Atividade *a* é a única alternativa que encurtaria ambos os caminhos críticos. Embora a Atividade *c* ainda possa ser acelerada em mais um dia, fazer isso não encurtaria o caminho crítico a-d-e-h-i.

Depois da Iteração 12, a Atividade *a* está em sua duração acelerada mínima. Além disso, todas as atividades do caminho a-d-e-h-i foram encurtadas para sua duração acelerada mínima, portanto o projeto agora foi acelerado o máximo possível. A duração mínima do projeto resultante é de 51 dias, e o custo adicional total para acelerar o projeto de 63 para 51 dias é a soma do custo adicional da aceleração em cada iteração, ou $ 15.600.

SOFTWARE PARA GERÊNCIA DE PROJETOS

Hoje a maioria dos aplicativos de gerência de projeto usa abundantemente o computador. Embora nossos cálculos PERT/CPM neste capítulo tenham sido feitos manualmente, esses aplicativos quase nunca são calculados sem computadores.

Em alguns softwares, o usuário digita as estimativas dos tempos das atividades e outras informações e o programa calcula a folga para cada uma delas, a duração e a variância do caminho crítico e outras informações úteis para a gerência de projeto. O Instituto de Gerência de Projetos (**www.pmi.org**) mantém uma lista abrangente de produtos e vendedores de software de gerência de projetos. Alguns desses pacotes de software são:

- *Microsoft Project*, Microsoft Corp.
- *MacProject*, Claris Corp.
- *Pert Chart Expert*, Jim Spiller & Associates
- *PowerProject*, ASTA Development Inc.
- *Primavera Project Planner (P3) for Windows*, Primavera
- *Project Scheduler*, Scitor Corp.
- *Project Workbench*, ABT Corp.
- *SuperProject*, Computer Associates International Inc.
- *TurboProject*, IMSI
- *VX-1 Project Management Simulator*, Virtual Experience Corp.

A Figura 18.11 mostra um gráfico de Gantt para o projeto RAMOV gerado pelo *Microsoft Project*. A data de início especificada para o projeto foi segunda, 3 de janeiro de 2000, e supôs-se uma semana de cinco dias. A lacuna de dois dias entre a Atividade *a* e a Atividade *b* representa um sábado e um domingo (dias não úteis).

A gerência de projeto é uma atividade executada em várias organizações, e os fornecedores de software estão oferecendo uma variedade cada vez maior de pacotes para esses aplicativos.

UMA AVALIAÇÃO DO CPM/PERT

Com o aumento do uso do CPM e da PERT, apareceram críticas a essas técnicas. Entre elas estão:

1. O CPM/PERT pressupõe que as atividades do projeto são independentes. Na prática sabemos que em algumas circunstâncias a duração de uma atividade depende das dificuldades encontradas no desempenho de outras atividades relacionadas. Nesses casos, a duração de uma atividade depende da duração de uma ou mais atividades.

FIGURA 18.11 — GRÁFICO DE GANTT DO MICROSOFT PROJECT PARA O PROJETO RAMOV

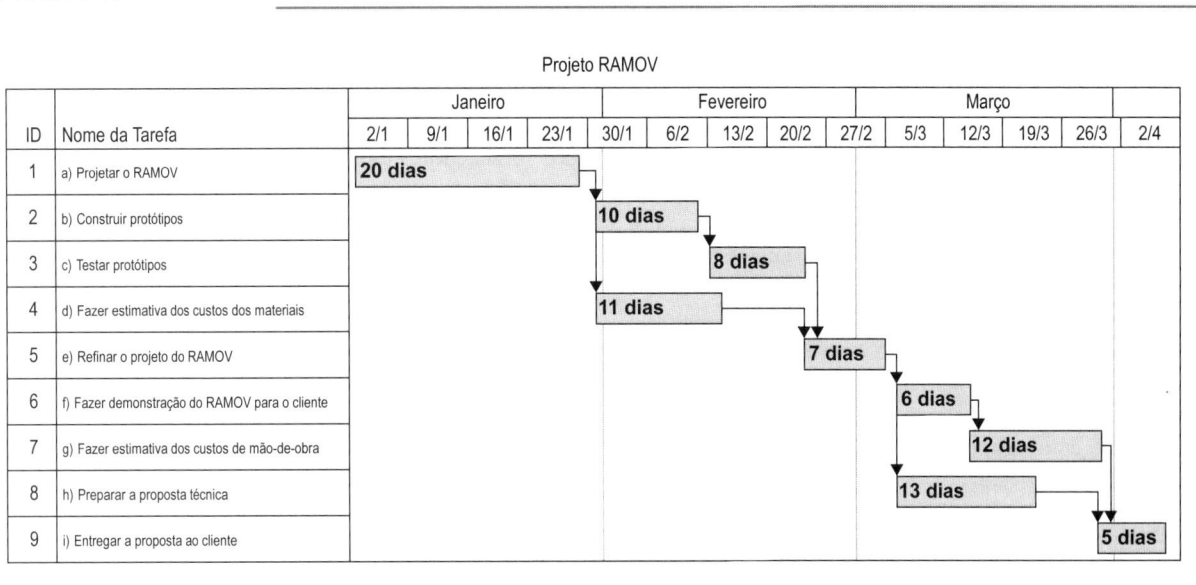

2. O CPM/PERT pressupõe que existem fronteiras precisas onde uma atividade termina e a outra começa. Na prática, uma atividade pode começar antes de uma atividade antecedente ser concluída, desde que o trabalho preparatório tenha sido feito.

3. O CPM/PERT se concentra demasiadamente no caminho crítico. Na prática uma atividade que não está no caminho crítico no início do projeto pode encontrar dificuldades e atrasos. Essa atividade pode não receber a atenção que merece até aparecer no caminho crítico, e aí pode ser tarde demais para tomar uma medida corretiva para evitar que o projeto atrase.

4. As estimativas dos tempos das atividades podem refletir questões comportamentais que podem diminuir a utilidade do CPM/PERT. Por exemplo, as pessoas que fornecem as estimativas podem ser otimistas demais, podem estimar durações de atividades longas demais, o que lhes dá um fator de amortecimento ou de ultrapassagem de limites.

5. A PERT foi muitas vezes criticada porque: (a) pode ser irreal esperar três estimativas de duração precisas do pessoal; (b) pode ser esperar demais que o pessoal entenda seus conceitos estatísticos; (c) foi demonstrado que as hipóteses da PERT no que diz respeito às distribuições de probabilidade das atividades e dos caminhos provocaram erros nos resultados PERT; (d) o custo extra da PERT em relação ao CPM não é justificado pelo valor das informações adicionais fornecidas.

6. O CPM/PERT aplica-se a uma quantidade excessiva de projetos, um legado arrasador do governo e da indústria aeroespacial. Em muitas dessas aplicações, o custo do CPM/PERT não pode ser justificado pelo valor das informações fornecidas quando comparado a outras técnicas de gerência de projetos, como gráficos de projeto.

Apesar dessas críticas, o CPM/PERT forma a família das técnicas amplamente utilizadas hoje nas organizações. Essas técnicas ajudam os gerentes de operação a estruturar projetos de forma que se entenda que atividades precisam ser executadas e quando, identifique as medidas corretivas que precisam ser tomadas, atribua responsabilidades pelas atividades, controle custos, e planeje e controle o desempenho em termos de tempo. A verdade é que elas funcionam — e funcionam bem — para os gerentes de operações, apesar de suas falhas, e é por isso que elas são tão utilizadas. O fato de haver tantos pacotes de software disponíveis hoje também favorece ainda mais seu uso contínuo.

Resumo Final

O Que os Fabricantes de Classe Mundial Estão Fazendo

Os fabricantes de classe mundial assumem a posição de tirar proveito das oportunidades de negócios globais. Eles desenvolvem formas de organização que são suficientemente flexíveis para produzir seus produtos e serviços para os mercados mundiais e ao mesmo tempo são capazes de responder agressivamente às oportunidades de negócios. As formas convencionais de organizações se baseavam somente em departamentos funcionais que não se revelaram suficientemente flexíveis para explorar oportunidades que estão rapidamente se desenvolvendo.

A mais importante entre essas novas formas é a organização por projetos. Pega-se o melhor pessoal dos departamentos e designa-se essas pessoas para projetos de forma que se possa trazer a perícia necessária para lidar com as oportunidades de negócios que estão surgindo rapidamente.

Os fabricantes de classe mundial selecionam e treinam pessoal para ser suficientemente flexíveis para ir de um departamento e de um projeto para outro na medida do necessário.

A flexibilidade é a chave para ser um fabricante de classe mundial hoje, e as equipes de projeto em uma organização por projetos fornecem parte dessa flexibilidade necessária.

A introdução de novos produtos, projetos de desenvolvimento de novos produtos, projetos de construção, investigação de novos empreendimentos, projetos de implantação de sistemas de comunicação e informação, projetos de treinamento especializado e educação, estudos de locais para instalação de fábrica, projetos de automação de fábricas, projetos de implantação de programa just-in-time, programas de melhoria dos fornecedores e programas de redução de custos são exemplos de projetos que precisam ser administrados por fabricantes de classe mundial. E quanto mais de classe mundial um fabricante for, mais intensa é a necessidade de gerenciar esses tipos de projetos. Tentar sempre ser o melhor cria a necessidade desses tipos de projetos.

A necessidade de um planejamento e controle eficaz do desempenho em termos de tempo e custo motivaram os fabricantes de classe mundial a desenvolver técnicas de gerência de projeto.

Geralmente usamos gráficos de programação e controle devido a sua simplicidade, flexibilidade, baixo custo e capacidade de serem utilizados como dispositivos eficazes de comunicação.

O CPM, a PERT e a PERT/Custo também são utilizados para fornecer um controle de planejamento computadorizado de atividade por atividade.

Relatórios periódicos de status vão para as partes interessadas com a duração atualizada do projeto, as atividades críticas, a folga das atividades, diagramas da rede e relatórios de exceções, e a partir deles se determina o que é preciso ser feito para assegurar a conclusão bem-sucedida do projeto.

Novos enfoques de planejamento e controle de projetos ainda estão sendo elaborados. Por exemplo, a técnica de avaliação gráfica e revisão (GERT) foi elaborada para acomodar necessidades como atividades que podem não ser necessárias. Algumas atividades podem falhar, e isso afeta as atividades subseqüentes, e as atividades podem voltar ao início. Esses refinamentos das técnicas existentes provavelmente continuarão sendo feitos à medida que a gerência de projetos for evoluindo.

Questões de Revisão e Discussão

1. Defina *gerência de projeto*.
2. Por que a gerência de projetos é um desafio para a maioria dos gerentes nos sistemas de produção? Como esses gerentes enfrentam esses desafios?
3. Que tarefas a equipe de projetos precisa executar antes de o projeto começar?
4. Que tarefas a equipe de projetos precisa executar à medida que o projeto vai evoluindo?

5. Por que o planejamento, a programação e o controle dos materiais, suprimentos e subempreiteiros de projetos são mais difíceis com esses recursos utilizados na produção dos produtos e serviços habituais da organização?
6. Defina estes termos: *atividade, evento, atividade crítica, caminho crítico, duração da atividade* e *folga*.
7. Defina estes termos: *atividade antecessora, atividade fictícia, primeira data de início, primeira data de término, última data de término, última data de início*.
8. Defina estes termos: *duração mais provável* (t_m), *duração otimista* (t_o) e *duração pessimista* (t_p).
9. Como a duração da atividade difere entre o CPM e a PERT?
10. Os gráficos de barra e outras técnicas de elaboração de gráficos oferecem aos gerentes de operações um macrocontrole dos projetos, enquanto o CPM e a PERT oferecem microcontrole. Explique.
11. Quais são as informações fornecidas e as informações devolvidas pelo CPM?
12. Dê o nome de três etapas do processamento CPM.
13. Quais são os três princípios de intensificação de projetos?

Tarefas na Internet

1. Visite e explore o site do Project Management Institute (Instituto de Gerência de Projetos) (PMI) (**www.pmi.org**) na Internet. O PMI mantém uma lista de vagas de empregos para cargos relacionados com gerência de projetos. Encontre dois cargos que lhe pareçam interessantes. Descreva esses cargos e suas responsabilidades.
2. Visite e explore o site do Project Management Institute (PMI) (**www.pmi.org**) na Internet. Pesquise em uma livraria on-line livros sobre gerência de projetos do PMI e encontre um livro lançado recentemente. Dê uma breve descrição do que trata o livro e forneça as citações bibliográficas.
3. Visite o site da Microsoft na Internet (**www.microsoft.com**). Localize as páginas da web referentes ao *Microsoft Project*. Encontre e resuma algumas das novas ampliações da versão mais recente do *Microsoft Project*.
4. Encontre e resuma um artigo na Internet relacionado à gerência de projeto. Dê as citações bibliográficas e o endereço na Internet.
5. Procure na Internet uma empresa de consultoria que seja especialista em gerência de projetos. Descreva os serviços que ela pode oferecer. Dê o endereço do site da empresa na Internet.

Problemas

Gráficos de Programação e Controle

1. A partir da Figura 18.12 descreva em detalhes o status do projeto de desenvolvimento de um novo produto da Stratophonic em 1º de março.

2. A partir da Figura 18.13, descreva detalhadamente o status das entregas dos materiais-chaves do projeto de desenvolvimento de novo produto da Stratophonic em 1º de março.

3. A Buildrite Construction Company está elaborando planos para construir um novo centro médico em Denver, no Colorado. A Buildrite definiu as atividades de projeto que se seguem, suas relações de antecedência e suas durações estimadas.

Figura 18.12 — Programação do Projeto — Projeto de Desenvolvimento de Novo Produto: Stratophonic Sound Inc.

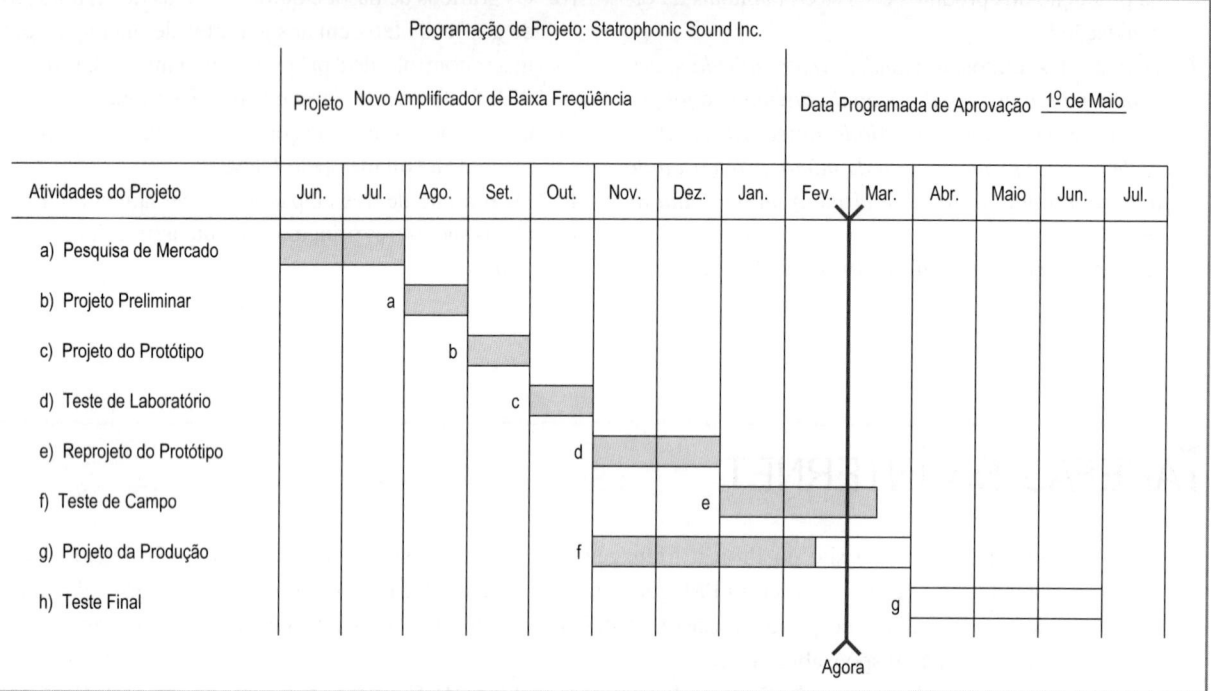

Figura 18.13 — Gráfico de Materiais — Projeto de Desenvolvimento de Novo Produto: Stratophonic Sound Inc.

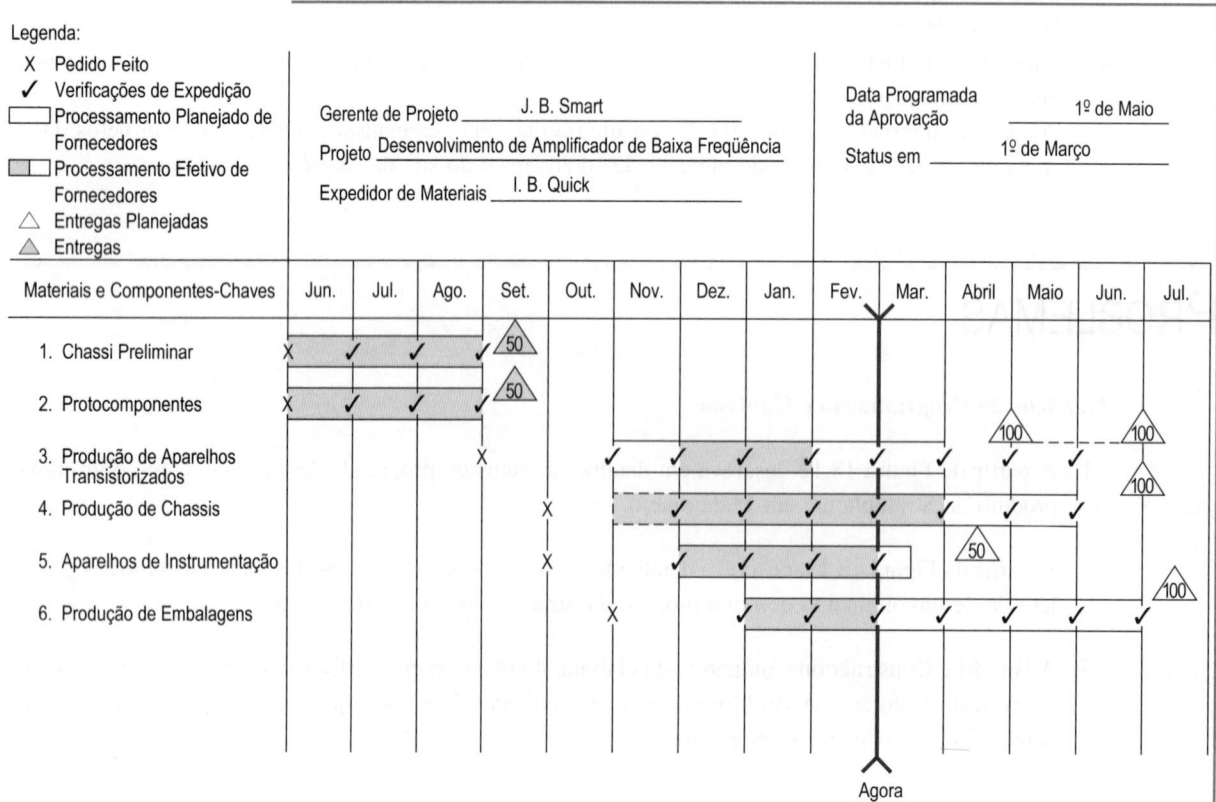

Capítulo 18 – Planejando e Controlando Projetos

Atividade	Relação de Antecedência (atividades imediatamente anteriores)	Duração Estimada das Atividades (semanas)
a) Demolição das estruturas atuais	—	4
b) Terraplanagem	a	5
c) Formação e concretagem das sapatas e do alicerce	b	5
d) Construção do esqueleto da estrutura de aço	c	6
e) Construção da estrutura de concreto	d	8
f) Construção do revestimento exterior	e	12
g) Instalação do sistema de encanamento	e	5
h) Instalação do sistema elétrico	e	3
i) Instalação do sistema de calefação/refrigeração	e	4
j) Construção das divisões interiores	g,h,i	3
k) Instalação de lustres e término da obra	j	5

Prepare um gráfico de barra para planejar a programação desse projeto de construção se as obras começarem no dia 1º de janeiro.

CPM

4. Um projeto possui as seguintes atividades, relações de antecedência e durações de atividades:

Atividade	Atividades Imediatamente Anteriores	Duração das Atividades (dias)	Atividade	Atividades Imediatamente Anteriores	Duração das Atividades (dias)
a	—	6	f	a	15
b	—	8	g	a	17
c	—	5	h	f	9
d	b	13	i	g	6
e	c	9	j	d,e	12

a) Desenhe uma rede CPM para o projeto.
b) Dê uma visão geral do projeto calculando a duração de cada caminho.
c) Qual é o caminho crítico? Qual é a duração estimada do projeto?

5. Uma empresa está prestes a começar um projeto para elaborar um processo de produção para produzir um novo produto. A gerência estimou que o projeto irá requerer 45 dias para ser concluído. A princípio 45 dias pareceu um prazo muito curto para os engenheiros de processo, mas depois de alguma discussão concluiu-se que eles provavelmente conseguiriam cumprir o prazo, porque os produtos e seus processos eram muito similares às tecnologias de processamento atualmente utilizadas na fábrica.

Os engenheiros estimaram estas atividades, suas relações de antecedência e suas durações:

Atividade	Duração das Atividades (dias)	Atividades Imediatamente Anteriores
a) Estudo inicial do projeto do produto	12	—
b) Estudo preliminar das tecnologias de processo	10	—
c) Pesquisa da capacidade dos vendedores	8	—
d) Modificação da fábrica para reprojeto do produto	14	b
e) Reprojeto intermediário da fábrica	6	c
f) Reprojeto intermediário do produto	18	b,a
g) Projeto do maquinário específico para o processo	11	d,e
h) Envolvimento e integração do vendedor	21	c
i) Instalações, produto e projeto de processo final	7	f,g

a) Desenhe uma rede CPM para o projeto.
b) Calcule a PDT, a UDT e a folga de cada atividade. Escreva os valores na rede CPM.

c) Calcule a PDI a UDI de todas as atividades. Mostre os valores da PDI, PDT, UDI, UDT e da folga em uma tabela.

d) Qual é o caminho crítico? Qual é a duração estimada do projeto?

6. Um grupo de engenharia de fábrica é responsável pela instalação de uma linha de montagem para produzir um novo produto. Os processos de produção já foram elaborados pelo grupo de engenharia de processo e os vendedores entregaram o maquinário à fábrica. Como a fábrica foi reprojetada para comportar a linha de montagem e as máquinas já estão no local, a linha de montagem deve estar pronta para um teste em um mês. O grupo de engenharia de fábrica identificou as atividades listadas a seguir, determinou suas relações de antecedência e suas durações estimadas:

Atividade	Duração das Atividades (dias)	Atividades Imediatamente Anteriores
a) Montar um pacote de projeto do processo	3	—
b) Organizar a equipe de layout de maquinário	5	—
c) Organizar a equipe de modificação da fábrica	7	b
d) Reunião com o pessoal de produção	4	b
e) Determinar as tarefas do pessoal	3	a,c
f) Colocar o maquinário no lugar	9	d
g) Conectar água e luz às máquinas	5	e,f
h) Modificar o transportador aéreo	6	d
i) Treinar pessoal	3	e,f
j) Pintar e limpar	5	g,h
k) Fazer um lote piloto dos produtos	4	i,j

a) Desenhe uma rede CPM para o projeto.
b) Calcule a PDT, UDT e a folga de cada atividade. Escreva os valores na rede CPM.
c) Calcule a PDI e a UDI de todas as atividades. Mostre os valores da PDI, PDT, UDI, UDT e da folga em uma tabela.
d) Qual é o caminho crítico? Qual é a duração estimada do projeto?

Relações Custo x Tempo

7. A partir do Problema 5:

a) Se você ainda não o fez, construa uma rede CPM para o projeto, calcule a PDT, a UDT e a folga de cada atividade e escreva seus valores em uma rede CPM. Qual é o caminho crítico e qual sua duração?

b) Dados os custos de intensificação das atividades do projeto a seguir, elabore uma análise da relação custo x tempo. Detalhe as etapas que você utilizaria para acelerar ou intensificar o projeto de forma a concluí-lo no máximo em 38 dias. Quais são os novos custos e duração do projeto?

Atividade	Duração Presente (dias)	Duração Acelerada (dias)	Custo Presente	Custo Acelerado
a	12	12*	$ 20.000	$ 20.000
b	10	8	18.000	20.000
c	8	6	20.000	24.000
d	14	9*	12.000	12.000
e	6	4	4.000	5.600
f	18	12*	19.000	19.000
g	11	10	24.000	25.500
h	21	20	34.000	34.700
i	7	6	31.000	32.800

*Essas atividades não podem ser aceleradas.

Capítulo 18 – Planejando e Controlando Projetos

Estudo de Caso

Maxwell Construction Company

A Maxwell Construction Company é uma grande empresa especializada em projetos de construção industrial e para o governo. A empresa só participa da concorrência dos maiores projetos a preços altamente compensadores e tende a obter sua parcela justa porque ela criou uma fama de fazer um trabalho extraordinário dentro dos prazos de seus contratos. A Maxwell agora está no processo de participar da concorrência de uma expansão do estádio de futebol da Western State University, um projeto de cerca de US$ 20 milhões. O único problema é que a Maxwell ganhou outros grandes contratos e não quer ter excesso de contratos e espalhar muito seus recursos. Se o projeto pudesse ser concluído em 300 dias, a empresa estaria confiante em disputar o contrato. O estimador de custos da Maxwell elaborou as estimativas das durações das atividades e suas relações de antecedência, que são mostradas a seguir.

Atividade	Relação de Antecedência (atividades imediatamente anteriores)	Duração Estimada das Atividades (semanas)
a) Demolir as estruturas existentes	—	10
b) Terraplanar	a	15
c) Concretar as sapatas do alicerce e a base de concreto	b	17
d) Instalar os encanamentos (enterrados)	b	20
e) Instalar a fiação elétrica	b	8
f) Pré-montar o esqueleto de aço do nível intermediário	b	14
g) Construir e concretar a subestrutura de concreto	c,d,e	16
h) Concretar os pisos dos níveis inferiores	g	12
i) Erigir o esqueleto de aço do nível intermediário	f,h	9
j) Erigir as colunas de concreto e as vigas transversais do nível intermediário	i	21
k) Instalar os encanamentos acima do solo da fase 2	j	18
l) Instalar a fiação elétrica acima do solo da fase 2	j	14
m) Concretar os pisos dos níveis intermediários	k,l	23
n) Pré-montar o esqueleto de aço do nível superior	i	14
o) Erigir o esqueleto de aço do nível superior	m,n	23
p) Erigir as colunas de concreto e vigas transversais do nível superior	o	36
q) Concretar os pisos do nível superior	p	37
r) Construir o complexo de cabines de imprensa	q	45
s) Erigir as luzes do campo	p	14
t) Construir banheiros	m,n	48
u) Instalar assentos	q	21
v) Pintar e dar acabamento às paredes, pisos e tetos	u	14
w) Limpar a estrutura	v	7

Tarefas

1. Desenhe um diagrama de rede de CPM do projeto.
2. Elabore um gráfico de barra que resuma o plano do projeto. Cada atividade deve ser "mapeada" nesse gráfico. Discuta como esse gráfico seria utilizado à medida que o projeto fosse evoluindo e como ele seria utilizado nas fases de planejamento do projeto.
3. Qual é a duração estimada do projeto? Que atividades estão no caminho crítico? Quanto a Atividade *u* pode atrasar sem afetar a data de conclusão do projeto?
4. Discuta como os resultados da análise CPM se comparam com seu gráfico n. 2. Quais são as vantagens e desvantagens do CPM como técnica de planejamento e controle quando comparado com o gráfico do projeto ou com o gráfico de barra?
5. A Maxwell Construction Company deveria participar na concorrência do projeto? O projeto requer mais tempo do que a Maxwell tem disponível?

APÊNDICES

Respostas de Alguns dos Problemas Propostos

Glossário

Respostas de Alguns dos Problemas Propostos

Capítulo 3

(2) a = -7,1467, b = 8,0229, Y_7 = $ 49,01 milhões. • **(3)** a = -12,110, b = 2,58825, Y_7 = $ 44,57 milhões. • **(4)** a) a = -196,412, b = 67,242, Y_9 = 247,384; b) r2 = 0,927. • **(5)** Fap = 2 = 140, Fap = 4 = 138, Fap = 6 = 138,5 auditores. • **(6)** b) 0,3; c) F_{17} = $ 0,949 • **(8)** DAM é mínimo quando a = 0,9. • **(10)** F_7 = $ 46,7 milhões. • **(13)** a) s_{yx} = 8,093; b) 616,3 e 676,3. • **(15)** a) Y_7 = $ 44,57 milhões; b) s_{yx} = 2,7606521; intervalo = $ 31,86 a $ 57,28 milhões. • **(17)** s_{yx} = 7,431 mil caixas, UL_{13} = 315.000 caixas.

Capítulo 4

(6) a) $TC_{comprar}$ = $ 2.625.000; b) Q = 304.878 peças; c) Q = 196.078 peças. • **(7)** a) Sim; b) $ 13.000 por ano; c) 75.000 peças.

Capítulo 5

(2) a) Vandine: $ 17.180, e Murcheck: $ 20.640; b) 75 classificações por ano. • **(5)** a) MC e NC: 3.928,6 unidades, e NC e FMS: 19.571 unidades; b) MC: 2.893.000 e 3.838.000, NC: 2.738.000 e 3.613.000, e FMS: 2.770.000 e 3.610.000. • **(6)** a) Máquina A: 3,389 anos, e Máquina B: 2,923 anos; b) Máquina A: $ 2.700, e Máquina B: $ 1.600. • **(8)** Gamma: 0,69 e Omega: 0,79.

Capítulo 6

(1) a) 8.044 capacetes; b) $ 796.356; c) $ 160.000; d) $ 108,34. • **(3)** b) Construir fábrica grande; c) $ 10 milhões; $ 5 milhões; ou $ 3 milhões. • **(5)** Pagamento = 13,6 anos, alugar o prédio. • **(7)** a) San Antonio no ano 1, Dallas no ano 3 e além; b) San Antonio, 0 - 6.500, e Dallas 6.500 +.

Capítulo 7

(4) Layout I: 221,65 mil metros por ano, Layout II: 222,32 mil metros por ano. • **(8)** Trocar de lugar B e F.

Capítulo 8

(1) T_{1t} = 84 empregados, T_{1mi} = 74, T_{1r} = 30, T_{1tot} = 188; T_{2t} = 90, T_{2mi} = 70, T_{2r} = 20, T_{2tot} = 180; T_{3t} = 104, T_{3mi} = 100, T_{3r} = 40, T_{3tot} = 244; T_{4t} = 80, T_{4mi} = 70, T_{4r} = 20, T_{4tot} = 170. • **(2)** a) T_1 = 22,0 mil toneladas, T_2 = 21,0, T_3 = 21,0, T_4 = 31,0; b) T_1 = 110 mil horas, T_2 = 105, T_3 = 105, T_4 = 155; c) T_1 = 211,5 empregados, T_2 = 201,9, T_3 = 201,9, T_4 = 298,1. • **(3)** Plano 2, $ 395.000 contra $ 396.000. • **(4)** Plano nivelado, $ 206.250 contra $ 258.000. • **(6)** Custos do plano de horas extras $ 337.500; custos do plano de subcontratação $ 300.000. • **(8)** a) Carga total = 109.250 horas, capacidade total = 120.000 horas; b) sim, mas existe subcarga nas semanas 1, 2, 5 e existe sobrecarga nas semanas 3, 4, 6; c) mudar parte da produção das semanas 3, 4, 6 para as semanas 1, 2, 5. • **(10)** A: 5.000 nas semanas 1, 3 e 6; B: 8.000 nas semanas 1, 3, 4, 7 e 8, e 8.600 na semana 6; C: 2.000 nas semanas 1, 3, 4 e 7.

Capítulo 9

(1) a) 5.200,52; b) $ 11.441,16; c) $ 117,17. • (2) a) $ 1.286.953,80; b) $ 102.956,30; c) 13,4 dias. • (4) a) 51.639,778 barris; b) $ 145.236,88; c) 10,3 dias; d) 25.819,89 barris. • (5) a) $ 2.063.174,80; b) 1.275,93 janelas; c) 9,3 dias. • (7) a) 812.5992 caixas; b) $ 220.959,68; c) 707, 27682; d) $ 219.156,86; e) sim, economias = $ 1.802,82 por ano. • (8) a) 96 rolamentos; b) 17,46. • (13) a) 8504,85 g; b) VEIP = $ 3.600. • (14) $ 400.000.

Capítulo 10

(1) 0, 400, 300, 800, 1.000, 500. • (4) a) Liberações planejadas de encomendas — 500: 400 na Semana 3, 500 na Semana 4; 10: 350 na Semana 2, 500 na Semana 3; 20: 150 na Semana 2, 500 na Semana 3; 30: 550 na Semana 2, 1.000 na Semana 3; 11: 500 na Semana 1, 900 na Semana 2; 12: 500 nas Semanas 1 e 2; 21: 1.000 na Semana 1; 22: 1.000 nas Semanas 1 e 2. • (7) a) LFL: custo = $ 48.000; b) LEC: lotes de 5.586 nas Semanas 1, 5 e 8, custo = $ 32.780; c) POQ: lotes de 5.000 e 7.000 nas Semanas 1 e 5, custo = $ 24.115,39. • (8) a) Mão-de-obra: 58, 87, 115, 87, 87 e 58%; máquina: 60, 90, 120, 90, 90 e 60%.

Capítulo 11

(3) a) 162, 166, 164, 161, 165, 163; b) 162, 161, 164, 163, 165, 166; c) 162, 161, 163, 164, 165, 166. • (6) a) E-A-C-D-B; b) $ 256. • (8) a) LEC_1 = 2.371,7, LEC_2 = 3.000,0, LEC3 = 2.529,8, LEC_4 = 2.190,9 unidades; b) 33%; c) 23,7 dias. • (10) Tempo de esgotamento agregado = 0,192 trimestre, horas de montagem final para cada brinquedo — 1: 281,4, 2: 207,6, 3: 297,6, 4: 382,2, 5: 231,8. • (11) b) Todos os passos estão no programa, exceto 1 e 3; a entrega do componente A parece ser a causa da dificuldade.

Capítulo 12

(1) a) 12,25 ou 13 funcionários; c) sim, o programa é ótimo, 13 funcionários são necessários, há três turnos com um funcionário extra. • (3) Atual: 0,083 estudante na fila, 0,167 minuto e 0,250; proposto: 1,63 estudante na fila, 3,27 minutos, e 0,700. • (5) As economias anuais são $ 7.981,50 por ano, as economias podem pagar pelo dispositivo em 1,25 ano, comprar o dispositivo. • (6) N = 4: instável; N = 5: 0,2182 hora, ou 13,09 minutos; N = 6: 0,0499 hora, ou 2,994 minutos. • (8) a) número de estudantes que chegam em 5 períodos: 5, 4, 4, 6, 5; b) número de minutos necessários para atender os clientes em 5 períodos: 51,92, 43,68, 36,86, 61,64, 50,36.

Capítulo 13

(1) 30 produtos por hora. • (2) O LT seria reduzido de 6,545 para 3,50 minutos, ou 3,045 minutos. • (5) a) P = 0,80; b) P é muito elevado, o sistema Kanban não é muito eficiente.

Capítulo 14

(1) Fazer; $TC_{comprar}$ = $ 502.500; TC_{fazer} = $ 493.000. • (2) a) Fazer in-house, $ 1.160.000; b) Diamond Ltd.: 0–43.694,90 unidades, Chicago West: 43.694,90–49.797,2 unidades. Fazer in-house: 49.797,2 unidades ou mais. • (4) Pontuação da Sumsing = 0,754, pontuação da Parkasenic = 0,730, pontuação da Hatchui = 0,780; Hatchui é a fornecedora preferida. • (6) b) 500 unidades na semana 1 e semana 2. • (8) a) 23,5, ou 24 contadores; b) $ 600.000; c) 41 contadores; d) $ 425.000.

Respostas de Alguns dos Problemas Propostos

Capítulo 15

(2) a) Classificação das soluções nesta ordem: treinamento de supervisores, rotação de emprego, enriquecimento do cargo e tempo fora do emprego. • **(6)** a) 1: 0,10625 minuto, 2: 2,8125, 3: 3,80875, 4: 0,65000; b) 1: 0,12219 minuto, 2: 3,51563, 3: 3.61831, 4: 0,65000; c: 0,2083; d) 9,986 minutos. • **(8)** 0,2173. • **(9)** a) 4,007 minutos por produto; b) 4,714 minutos por produto. • **(11)** a) $ 8,913 por unidade; b) $ 1.782,62.

Capítulo 17

(1) 0 e 7,70%. • **(3)** a) 2,5%; b) 0 e 5,812%. • **(6)** a) 11,46 e 12,54 polegadas; c) não, o meio de amostragem em polegadas é errático e o processo está fora de controle na parte superior. • **(7)** a) 11,617 e 12,383 horas; c) sim, o processo parece estar sob controle; embora algumas amostras estejam além dos limites, nenhuma situação fora do controle parece existir.

Capítulo 18

(1) A atividade F, teste em campo, foi concluída, e está adiantada 2 semanas no programa; a atividade G, projeto de produção, está 2 semanas atrasada no programa. • **(2)** A produção dos aparelhos transistorizados foi iniciada com 1 mês de atraso, está aproximadamente 1 mês atrasada no programa e há a projeção de que os aparelhos sejam entregues com 2 meses de atraso. A produção dos chassis foi iniciada com 1 mês de antecipação, está 1 mês adiantada no programa e há a projeção de que os chassis serão entregues no prazo. • **(5)** d) caminho b-d-g-i, 42 dias. • **(6)** d) caminho b-d-f-g-j-k, 32 dias.

Glossário

A

Administração científica Aplicação de princípios científicos à administração de sistemas de produção.

Administração da demanda Reconhecer e administrar todas as demandas de produtos e serviços para garantir que o programa mestre tenha ciência delas.

Administração da produção e operações (APO) Administração do sistema de produção de uma organização cuja função principal é transformar entradas nas saídas, que são os produtos ou serviços da organização.

Administração da qualidade total (TQM) *Veja* Gestão da qualidade total.

Administração de materiais Administração de todas as funções relacionadas com o ciclo completo de fluxos de materiais, inclusive a compra e o controle interno de materiais, o planejamento e o controle de processos de trabalho, e o armazenamento, embarque e distribuição de itens finais.

Administração de projetos Administração de todas as funções relativas a um conjunto específico de atividades que resultarão num projeto acabado único.

Agilização Agilizar um pedido através de todo ou parte do sistema de materiais.

Alavancagem operacional Medida da relação entre os custos anuais de uma empresa e suas vendas anuais.

Amostra aleatória Amostra de um produto na qual cada unidade do lote de produto tem uma chance igual de ser incluída na amostra.

Amostragem de trabalho Técnica de medição do trabalho que toma amostras aleatoriamente do trabalho de uma ou mais pessoas em intervalos periódicos para determinar a proporção da operação total que é responsável por uma atividade em particular.

Análise da árvore de decisões Auxílio gráfico para tomar decisões de múltiplas etapas que mostra a seqüência e a interdependência das decisões.

Análise da distância da carga Técnica para planejar layouts de instalações que compara layouts alternativos para identificar aquele que tem a menor distância percorrida pelo produto ou material por intervalo de tempo.

Análise da seqüência de operações Técnica de análise gráfica para planejar layouts de instalações que desenvolve um esquema para a disposição de departamentos.

Análise de break-even Processo de determinação do volume de produção necessário para igualar receita e custos.

Análise de diagrama de blocos Técnica para planejar layouts de instalações que define a forma geral e as dimensões de um prédio e a localização das fronteiras organizacionais internas.

Análise de regressão Modelo de previsão de longo prazo que desenvolve uma linha de tendência através de dados passados e a projeta para intervalos de tempo futuros.

Análise de regressão linear Modelo de previsão que estabelece uma relação entre uma variável dependente e uma ou mais variáveis independentes.

Análise de regressão multilinear Modelo de previsão usado quando há duas ou mais variáveis independentes.

Análise do valor atual Processo de determinação da quantidade de dinheiro que deve ser investida agora, à taxa de juros atual, para se acumular até certo valor no futuro.

Análise econômica Análise baseada no desenvolvimento de funções de custo para a alternativa de processamento e a comparação dessas funções.

Análise do fabricar *versus* comprar Análise que determina se um material ou uma peça devem ser feitos in-house ou comprados de um fornecedor.

Análise marginal Técnica que computa a probabilidade de que o custo de longo prazo esperado se iguale ao custo de curto prazo esperado para qualquer DDLT.

Anexos de máquina Complementos para máquinas que reduzem a quantidade de esforço humano e tempo necessário para executar uma operação.

Aparência O efeito sobre os sentidos humanos — a visão, o tato, o paladar, o olfato ou a audição.

Armazenamento (warehousing) Administração de materiais enquanto eles estão em estoque.

Arquivo lista de materiais Lista completa de todos os produtos acabados, quantidade de cada material em cada produto e a estrutura de todos os produtos; também pode ser chamado lista estruturada de peças.

Arquivo situação do estoque Arquivo computadorizado com um registro completo de cada material mantido em estoque.

Atendimento ao cliente O tratamento recebido pelos clientes antes, durante e depois de uma venda.

Atividade Na administração de projetos, uma tarefa ou certa quantidade de trabalho necessário num projeto.

Atividade crítica Na administração de projetos, uma atividade que não tem espaço para não-cumprimento do programa; uma atividade com folga nula.

Atividade de compra Processo de comprar as matérias-primas, peças adquiridas, maquinaria, suprimentos e todos os outros bens e serviços usados num sistema de produção.

Atividade fictícia Na administração de projetos, um dispositivo de rede CPM que simplesmente indica relações de precedência.

Atividade predecessora Na administração de projetos, uma atividade que deve ocorrer antes de outra.

Atividade sucessora Na administração de projetos, uma atividade que deve ocorrer depois de outra.

Atributos No controle da qualidade, características de produto que são classificadas numa de duas categorias: defeituosos ou não defeituosos.

Automação Integrar uma ampla variedade de avançadas descobertas científicas e de engenharia em processos de produção para propósitos estratégicos.

Automação flexível Uso de máquinas de automação acionadas por computador que são facilmente reprogramáveis para outros produtos.

Automação rígida Uso de maquinaria automática que é difícil de modificar para outros produtos.

B

Backlogging de pedidos Guardar pedidos para embarque posterior.

Benchmarking A prática de estabelecer padrões internos de desempenho observando como empresas de classe mundial dirigem seus negócios.

Bens de consumo duráveis Produtos que são usados diretamente pelos consumidores e que se espera que durem pelo menos três anos.

Bucket Unidade principal de medição do tempo num sistema de planejamento das necessidades de materiais; geralmente, uma semana.

C

CAD/CAM Projeto auxiliado por computador e manufatura auxiliada por computador.

Caminho crítico Na administração de projetos, uma cadeia de atividades críticas de um projeto; o caminho mais longo através de uma rede.

Canais O número de filas de espera num sistema de serviço. Um sistema de canal único tem somente uma fila, e um sistema de múltiplos canais tem duas ou mais filas.

Canal Fila de espera num sistema de serviço.

Capacidade da produção Taxa de produção máxima de uma organização.

Capacidade da taxa de entrada Medida que permite que taxas de várias entradas sejam convertidas para uma unidade comum de medida de entrada.

Capacidade de processo Capacidade do processo de produção para produzir produtos dentro das expectativas dos clientes.

Capital intensivo Que depende de capital em vez de mão-de-obra como recurso predominante numa operação.

Chegada Uma unidade da distribuição do índice de chegada. Ocorre quando uma pessoa, máquina, peça etc. chega e necessita de atendimento. Cada unidade pode continuar a ser chamada chegada enquanto está no sistema de serviço.

Ciclo de estoque Atividades de sentir a necessidade de um material, fazer um pedido, esperar que o material seja entregue, receber o material e usá-lo.

Ciclo do pedido até a entrega O tempo transcorrido entre o momento em que um cliente faz um pedido até o momento em que ele o recebe.

Círculo da qualidade (círculo QC) Pequeno grupo de empregados que se reúnem voluntária e regularmente para analisar e resolver problemas de produção e qualidade.

Classificações de proximidade Usadas para refletir a conveniência de se ter um departamento próximo do outro.

Cliente como participante Há um grau elevado de envolvimento do cliente nesse tipo de operação de serviço. Bens físicos podem ser ou não uma parte significativa do serviço, e os serviços podem ser personalizados ou padrões. A venda a varejo é um exemplo desse tipo de operação de serviço.

Cliente como produto Nesse tipo de operação, os clientes estão tão envolvidos que o serviço é realizado de fato no cliente. Bens físicos podem ser ou não uma parte significativa do serviço, e os serviços geralmente são personalizados. Exemplos desse tipo de operação de serviço são os salões de cabeleireiro, as clínicas médicas, os hospitais e os alfaiates.

Cliente interno A operação de produção seguinte.

Codificação de baixo nível Codificação de um material no nível mais baixo em que o material aparece em qualquer estrutura de produto.

Coeficiente de correlação Medida que explica a importância relativa das relações entre duas variáveis distintas.

Coeficiente de determinação Medida da precisão esperada de uma previsão que explica a quantidade de variação numa variável que é explicada por outra variável.

Coeficientes de administração Técnica de planejamento da capacidade que descreve os processos de decisão de gerentes individuais.

Companhia internacional Companhia que se empenha em compartilhamento da produção e vende seus produtos em mercados internacionais.

Compartilhamento da produção Participação de diversas companhias de vários países no projeto, financiamento, produção, montagem, embarque e venda de um produto.

Compensação pelo lead time Contabilidade do tempo necessário para produzir um lote de produção in-house ou para receber um lote comprado de um fornecedor. Uma necessidade num intervalo de tempo exigirá a liberação do pedido em algum intervalo de tempo anterior; o número de intervalos entre a necessidade e a liberação é a compensação, e é igual ao lead time.

Componente   Peça que entra numa montagem.

Componente redundante   Componente de reserva incorporado a uma máquina ou produto.

Confiabilidade   Capacidade de um produto para se comportar conforme o esperado em condições normais sem freqüência excessiva de falhas.

Confiabilidade do componente   Probabilidade de que um tipo de peça não falhará num determinado intervalo de tempo ou numa série de experiências sob condições comuns de uso.

Confiabilidade do sistema (SR)   Confiabilidade combinada de todos os componentes de uma máquina que interagem.

Contabilidade permanente de estoques   Sistema no qual registros de estoque são continuamente atualizados quando materiais são recebidos ou retirados de estoque.

Contagem cíclica   Verificar a precisão dos registros de estoque contando periodicamente o número de unidades de cada material em estoque.

Controle estatístico do processo (CEP)   Utilização de gráficos de controle para determinar se os padrões da qualidade são cumpridos.

Co-produtores   Maneira pela qual os japoneses chamam os fornecedores.

Crash   Acelerar uma atividade acrescentando recursos; reduzir o tempo necessário para um projeto.

Curva característica operacional (OC)   No controle da qualidade, um gráfico do desempenho de um plano de aceitação.

Curva de aprendizagem   Curva que ilustra a relação entre o número de unidades produzidas e a quantidade de trabalho necessário por unidade.

Custo anual da aquisição   O custo total para comprar ou produzir um material durante o ano inteiro. Calculado multiplicando-se a demanda anual pelo custo de aquisição por unidade.

Custo anual de manutenção de estoque   O custo total de provimento de estoques para o ano inteiro. Calculado para um material multiplicando-se o nível de estoque médio pelo custo de manutenção em estoque por unidade por ano.

Custo anual de obtenção (ou de pedido)   Custo total de aquisição de renovações de estoque para o ano inteiro. Calculado para um material multiplicando-se o número de pedidos por ano pelo custo de emissão do pedido.

Custo da aquisição   Custo para comprar ou produzir uma unidade de um material ou produto.

Custo de manutenção em estoque   Custo total para manter um material em estoque; expresso em $ por unidade por ano.

Custo de oportunidade   Custo na forma de lucros não auferidos.

Custo de preparação   Custo para transformar um passo do processamento num sistema de processamento de um produto para outro.

Custo de realização do pedido   Custo médio de cada renovação de estoque; inclui custos como o processamento de requisições de compra, pedido de compra, preparações de máquinas, postagem, chamadas telefônicas, inspeções da qualidade e recebimento.

Custo de stockout   Inclui custos como lucros não auferidos através de vendas perdidas, custo de clientes desapontados que reclamam, agilização especial, manuseio especial de pedidos em reserva (backlogged) e custos de produção adicionais.

Custo total anual de estocagem (CTE)   O custo total de manutenção de um material em estoque durante um ano. Inclui o custo anual de manutenção em estoque e o custo anual de realização de pedidos, mas não o custo anual de aquisição.

Custo total anual de um material (CTM)   O total do custo anual de aquisição e o custo total anual para estocar um material.

D

Decisão de controle   Decisão de curto prazo relativamente simples sobre o planejamento e controle das operações do dia-a-dia.

Decisão estratégica   Decisão complexa, de longo prazo e tomada uma única vez sobre um produto, processo ou instalação.

Decisão operacional   Decisão de curto prazo ou de prazo intermediário sobre como planejar a produção para atender a demanda.

Decisões quanto ao tamanho de lote   Dado um programa de necessidades líquidas, decisões sobre como agrupar essas necessidades em lotes de produção ou lotes de compra. As decisões geralmente incluem tanto o tamanho como o tempo de ocorrência dos lotes.

Definição da promessa de um pedido   Definir uma data na qual um produto deve ser entregue ao cliente.

Demanda anual (D)   Estimativa da demanda por ano do número de unidades de um material.

Demanda dependente   Demanda de um item que depende das demandas de outros itens do estoque.

Demanda durante o lead time (DDLT)   Número de unidades de um material necessário durante o processo ou lead time de renovação de estoque.

Demanda esperada durante o lead time (DEDLT)   Demanda média por dia multiplicada pelo lead time médio.

Demanda independente Demanda para um item que é independente da demanda correspondente a qualquer outro item mantido em estoque.

Demanda instável Demanda por um material que tem padrão irregular de intervalo a intervalo.

Deming Prize (Prêmio Deming) Criado em 1951 para inovações na administração da qualidade, é concedido anualmente a uma empresa que se tenha distinguido em programas de administração da qualidade.

Departamento de trânsito Divisão de uma organização que examina rotineiramente os programas de embarque e escolhe métodos de embarque, tabelas de horário e maneiras de agilizar as entregas.

Desconto por quantidade Diminuição no preço por unidade quando quantidades maiores são pedidas.

Desdobramento da função qualidade (QFD) Um sistema formal para identificar a vontade dos clientes e eliminar recursos e atividades que não contribuem em nada.

Deseconomias de escala Aumento do custo unitário causado por volume adicional de saídas além do ponto de melhor nível operacional para uma instalação.

Desembolso Ato de remover fisicamente um material do estoque.

Desempenho Quão bem o produto ou serviço desempenha o uso pretendido pelo cliente. Por exemplo, a velocidade de uma impressora a laser.

Desvio absoluto médio (DAM) Medida da precisão do modelo de previsão; soma dos valores absolutos de erros de previsão ao longo de uma série de períodos divididos pelo número de períodos.

Determinação do tamanho de lote Determinar quantas unidades de um produto devem ser produzidas para minimizar o custo por unidade.

Diagrama de fluxo (ou fluxograma) Diagrama do fluxo dos trabalhadores, equipamentos ou materiais através do processo.

Diagrama espinha de peixe Diagrama usado para rastrear a queixa de um cliente sobre um problema de qualidade até a operação de produção responsável.

Disciplina de fila As regras que determinam a ordem na qual as chegadas são dispostas em seqüência em sistemas de serviço. Algumas disciplinas de fila comuns são: primeiro a entrar, primeiro a ser atendido, o mais breve tempo de processamento, razão crítica e os clientes mais valorizados atendidos primeiro.

Durabilidade A extensão de tempo ou quantidade de uso de um bem antes de necessitar ser reparado ou substituído.

E

Economias de escala Redução do custo unitário à medida que os custos fixos se dispersam de maneira crescente por mais unidades.

Economias de escopo Produção de muitos modelos de produto numa instalação de produção altamente flexível de maneira mais barata do que em instalações de produção separadas.

Empresa de classe mundial Cada produto e serviço seria considerado "o melhor da classe" por seus clientes.

Empresa de montagem sob encomenda Empresa que monta, a partir de algumas montagens ou componentes relativamente importantes, itens finais pedidos pelos clientes que têm muitas opções.

Engenharia simultânea Conceito de projeto de produto/serviço que se desenvolve ao mesmo tempo que o projeto do processo, com interação contínua entre os dois.

Entrada de pedido Aceitação de um pedido no programa mestre de produção; inclui verificação da data de entrega, atribuição de slots de produção no MPS, e comunicação da data prometida ao cliente.

Entradas Qualquer matéria-prima, pessoal, capital, utilidades ou informações introduzida num sistema de transformação.

Especificação Descrição detalhada de um material, peça ou produto que apresenta todas as medidas físicas necessárias para seu projeto.

Especificação de material Descrição detalhada de um bem a ser comprado; pode incluir desenhos de engenharia, análise química e uma lista de características físicas.

Estimativa do supervisor Padrão de mão-de-obra baseado no conhecimento íntimo que um supervisor tem das operações pelas quais ele é responsável.

Estoque à mão A quantidade de um material realmente em estoque. Pode incluir estoque de segurança e materiais alocados para outros usos, mas não pode incluir materiais sob encomenda.

Estoque alocado Materiais que estão em estoque ou sob encomenda, mas foram designados a pedidos de produção específicos no futuro. Esses materiais não estão, portanto, disponíveis para ser usados em outros pedidos.

Estoque cíclico A parte do estoque que se esgota gradualmente e é renovada ciclicamente quando pedidos são recebidos.

Estoque de bens acabados Depósito de itens ou produtos finais mantidos para demanda do cliente.

Estoque de matérias-primas O depósito de matérias-primas guardado em armazéns até que sejam necessários na produção.

Estoque de reserva Estoque de produtos acabados que pode ser usado quando a demanda for maior do que o previsto ou quando a oferta for menor do que o esperado.

Estoque de segurança Quantidade de um material mantido em estoque para ser usado em intervalos de tempo em que a demanda é maior do que a esperada e quando a oferta é menor do que a esperada.

Estoque disponível Materiais que estão em estoque ou sob encomenda que não são estoque de segurança ou alocados para outros usos.

Estoque em processo Estoque de produtos parcialmente concluídos que há entre etapas de processamento.

Estratégia de negócios Plano de longo prazo de uma organização e os métodos a serem usados para atingir seus objetivos corporativos.

Estratégia de operações Plano para atingir o objetivo das operações de uma grande linha de produtos.

Estratégia de posicionamento Estratégia de manufatura que inclui uma política de estoque, tipo de projeto de produto e tipo de processo de produção.

Estudo do tempo Método de estabelecimento de padrões de tempo que cronometra as operações executadas por trabalhadores.

Evento Na administração de projetos, um sinal de que uma atividade iniciou ou encerrou.

F

Fábrica focalizada ou dedicada Fábrica que é especializada de alguma maneira; por exemplo, uma que se concentra numa estreita combinação de produtos para um mercado particular.

Fábricas do futuro Termo usado na década de 1980 para designar fábricas nas quais computadores seriam a base para métodos de produção high-tech.

Falsos compradores Empregados que fingem ser clientes mas que, na realidade, monitoram a qualidade dos serviços mundialmente.

Fases de serviço O número de etapas para atender as chegadas. Um sistema de serviço de fase única tem somente uma etapa de serviço, ao passo que um sistema de múltiplas fases tem duas ou mais etapas de serviço.

Fatores controláveis Mau funcionamento de máquinas, máquinas ruins e métodos de trabalho incorretos.

Fatores incontroláveis Temperatura, fricção, vibração, variação casual, causas naturais.

Fila Fila de espera.

Flexibilidade de produto Capacidade do sistema de produção para mudar-se rapidamente da produção de um produto/serviço para a produção de outro.

Flexibilidade de volume Capacidade para aumentar ou reduzir rapidamente o volume de produtos/serviços produzidos.

Flow shop Tipo de fábrica focalizada no produto no qual grandes lotes de produtos padronizados são produzidos no mesmo sistema de produção.

Folga Na administração de projetos, uma quantidade de tempo que uma atividade ou grupo de atividades pode desviar-se do programa sem provocar atraso na conclusão do projeto.

Força de trabalho flexível Grupo de trabalhadores e que receberam treinamento multifuncional em diversos tipos de funções.

Função objetivo Função matemática que descreve um objetivo; maximizar lucros ou minimizar custos são funções objetivos comuns.

Funcionalidade Grau em que um produto executa sua função pretendida.

G

Garantia da qualidade Sistemas para assegurar o controle da qualidade em todas as operações.

Gestão da qualidade total (TQM) Sistema de produção de produtos e serviços que obtém elevada qualidade já na primeira vez, em vez de depender de detecção posterior de defeitos através de inspeção. Também conhecida como administração da qualidade total.

Gráfico de controle Gráfico que monitora continuamente uma operação de produção para determinar se suas saídas cumprem padrões de qualidade.

Gráfico de Gantt Gráfico que coordena programas de centros de trabalho mostrando o progresso de cada tarefa em relação à data de conclusão programada.

Gráfico de montagem Gráfico de macrovisão que relaciona todos os materiais, componentes importantes, operações de submontagens e inspeções de um produto.

Gráfico de múltiplas atividades Gráfico que mostra como um ou mais trabalhadores trabalham juntos e/ou com máquinas.

Gráfico de operação Tipo de gráfico de processo que examina os movimentos coordenados das mãos de um trabalhador.

Gráfico de processo Documentação gráfica dos passos elementares numa das diversas operações para produzir um produto.

Gráficos de controle estatístico Utilizados para rastrear diversas medidas da satisfação do cliente usando-se dados coletados de pesquisas de clientes.

H

Horizonte de planejamento Número de intervalos incluídos no programa de planejamento da produção.

I

Índice da capacidade de processo (PCI) Determina se um processo de produção tem a capacidade de produzir produtos dentro das expectativas dos clientes.

Índice de chegada O índice em que coisas ou pessoas chegam, em chegadas por unidade de tempo (por exemplo, pessoas por hora). O índice de chegada geralmente tem uma distribuição normal ou de Poisson.

Informação e análise A coleta e a análise de informações da companhia relacionadas a melhoria da qualidade e planejamento.

Integração progressiva Expansão da propriedade da cadeia de produção e distribuição de uma companhia para a frente, rumo ao mercado.

Integração reversa Expansão da propriedade da cadeia de produção e distribuição de uma empresa para trás rumo a fontes de suprimento.

Integração vertical Quantidade da cadeia de produção e distribuição sob a propriedade de uma companhia.

Intervalo ótimo de pedido Tempo, em frações de um ano, entre as revisões da situação de um material que equilibra exatamente os custos anuais de realização de pedidos com os custos anuais de manutenção em estoque num sistema de estoques do intervalo padrão.

Item final Produto, serviço ou outra saída que tem uma demanda independente das demandas de outros componentes ou itens finais.

J

Job shop Fábrica cujos departamentos de centros de trabalho são organizados em torno de tipos particulares de equipamentos ou operações; os produtos fluem através dos departamentos em lotes que correspondem a pedidos do estoque ou pedidos do cliente.

K

Kanban Sistema de produção baseado em cartões de transferência e produção que determinam o movimento de pedidos de produção entre estações de trabalho.

L

Layout da instalação Plano para a localização de todas as máquinas e utilidades e para a disposição física dentro das instalações de todos os processos de manufatura e suas funções de suporte.

Layout de posição fixa Layout que localiza o produto numa posição fixa e transporta trabalhadores, materiais, máquinas e subcontratados até o produto e a partir do produto.

Layout híbrido Layout que usa uma combinação de tipos de layout, como uma linha de montagem combinada com um layout de processo.

Layout por processo Layout para a produção de uma variedade de produtos não padrões em lotes relativamente pequenos, como numa oficina mecânica personalizada.

Layout por produto Layout projetado para acomodar somente alguns projetos de produto, como na produção focalizada no produto.

Lead time (LT) Extensão de tempo necessário para renovar o estoque de um material a partir do momento em que a necessidade de um material adicional é sentida, até que o novo pedido do material esteja em estoque e pronto para uso.

Lead time cumulativo de item final Quantidade de tempo necessário para se obter materiais de fornecedores, produzir e montar todas as partes de um produto e entregar o produto ao cliente.

Leis de compensação de trabalhadores Leis que determinam valores de compensação específicos a serem pagos aos empregados por vários tipos de danos incorridos no trabalho.

Liberação de pedido programado Quantidade de material a ser pedida em cada intervalo de tempo do horizonte de planejamento.

Liderança Sucesso na criação e manutenção de uma cultura de qualidade clara e visível.

Limite de qualidade média de saída (AOQL) Máxima qualidade média de saída que pode ocorrer à medida que a porcentagem real dos itens defeituosos varia.

Linha automatizada de fluxo Linha de produção que inclui diversas máquinas automatizadas ligadas por máquinas de transferência e manuseio de peças; projetada para produzir um tipo de componente ou produto.

Linha de balanceamento (LOB) Método de programação e controle das operações antecedentes de produção para assegurar as entregas aos clientes.

Lista de materiais Lista de materiais e suas quantidades necessárias para produzir uma unidade de um produto ou item final.

Lista modular de materiais Em empresas que fazem montagem sob encomenda, uma lista de materiais que relaciona a porcentagem prevista de pedidos de clientes que exigem cada opção junto com o kit de peças comuns a todos os pedidos de clientes.

Lista Q-1 Lista de fornecedores com a qual a Ford deseja ter contratos de suprimento de longo prazo (geralmente três anos) a fim de atingir a mais elevada qualidade a custos competitivos.

Logística Administração do movimento de materiais dentro de uma fábrica, embarque de materiais que chegam de fornecedores, e embarque de produtos que saem para os clientes.

Lote Grupo discreto de produtos que foram produzidos sob as mesmas condições.

Lote de produção Uma quantidade de material produzido, armazenado em estoque e depois enviado para a etapa de produção seguinte ou embarcado para os clientes.

Lote econômico de compra (LEC) Quantidade de pedido ótima que minimiza os custos anuais totais de estoque.

Lote econômico padrão viável Em problemas de desconto por quantidades, uma LEC computada é viável se a LEC puder ser comprada ao custo de aquisição usado para se computar a LEC.

M

Manufatura auxiliada por computador (CAM) Utilização de computadores para planejar e programar equipamentos de produção na produção de itens manufaturados.

Manufatura celular (MC) Agrupamento de máquinas em células que funcionam como uma ilha de layout de produto dentro de uma job shop ou layout de processo maior.

Manufatura de unidade discreta Manufaturar produtos distintos ou separados, como automóveis e máquinas de lavar pratos.

Manufatura integrada por computador (CIM) Integração total de todas as funções comerciais associadas com a produção através de sistemas de computador.

Manufatura síncrona Sistema de planejamento e controle da produção no qual todas as partes de uma organização trabalham juntas para atingir a meta da organização.

Manutenção preventiva (PM) Atividades, como ajustes de máquinas, lubrificação, limpeza, troca de peças, pintura e reparos e vistorias, que são executadas antes que ocorra mau funcionamento das instalações ou das máquinas.

Manutenibilidade Facilidade para realizar a manutenção de um produto.

Mão-de-obra direta Mão-de-obra despendida por trabalhadores na produção.

Mão-de-obra intensiva Que depende de mão-de-obra em vez de capital como recurso predominante numa operação.

Máquinas de controle numérico (NC) Máquinas programadas através de fita magnética ou microcomputadores para executar um ciclo de operações repetidamente.

Materiais Quaisquer commodities usadas direta ou indiretamente para produzir um produto ou serviço, como matérias-primas, partes, componentes, montagens e suprimentos.

Máxima capacidade prática Produção obtida dentro do programa operacional normal de turnos por dia e dias por semana enquanto entra em instalações ineficientes de alto custo.

Medida de trabalho Processo para estimar a quantidade de tempo de trabalho necessária para gerar uma unidade de produto.

Melhoria contínua Permite que as empresas aceitem inícios mais modestos e façam pequenas melhorias incrementais rumo à excelência.

Método da designação Método de solução de programação linear usado para atribuir funções ou pessoal a máquinas ou departamentos.

Método da média móvel Método de previsão de curto prazo que tira a média dos dados a partir de alguns períodos passados recentes para formar a previsão para o período seguinte.

Método de transporte Solução de programação linear usada para encontrar o custo mínimo de embarque de produtos de diversas fontes até diversos destinos.

Método Delphi Método de previsão qualitativo usado para se obter consenso dentro de uma comissão.

Método do caminho crítico (CPM) Administração de projetos baseada em rede usada inicialmente em projetos de manutenção e defesa; quase idêntico a PERT.

Método do esgotamento (run-out) Método para planejar programas de produção e entrega que aloca capacidade de produção a produtos em proporção com sua demanda e seus níveis de estoque.

Método simplex Método de resolução da programação linear que fornece soluções precisas para problemas complexos que têm muitas variáveis e restrições.

Modelo de Box-Jenkins Modelo de previsão que encaixa uma função matemática em pontos de dados históricos reais, com essa função se tornando então o modelo de previsão para estimativas futuras.

Modelo de previsão causal Modelo que desenvolve previsões depois de estabelecer e medir uma associação entre a variável dependente e uma ou mais variáveis independentes; usado para prever pontos decisivos nas vendas.

Modificações nos pedidos programados Relatórios que mostram como os programas de pedidos programados devem ser modificados para entrega anterior ou posterior, para cancelamento ou para mudança de quantidade.

Monte Carlo Na simulação computadorizada, uma técnica para gerar valores aleatórios a partir de distribuições discretas.

Movimento das relações humanas Desenvolvimento de uma filosofia entre gerentes no início do século XX, segundo a qual trabalhadores são seres humanos e devem ser tratados com dignidade no ambiente de trabalho.

MRP de loop fechado Sistema construído em torno do planejamento das necessidades de materiais e que também inclui planejamento da produção, programa mestre de produção, planejamento das necessidades de capacidade e várias funções de execução.

MRP I (planejamento dos recursos de manufatura) Forma primitiva de planejamento das necessidades de materiais que simplesmente explodia o MPS nos materiais necessários.

MRP II Processo de planejamento dos recursos de uma empresa, incluindo planejamento dos negócios, planejamento da produção, programa mestre da produção, planejamento das necessidades de materiais e planejamento das necessidades de capacidade.

N

Necessidade líquida A quantidade e o tempo de ocorrência (timing) da necessidade de um material que deve ser satisfeita através de produção ou compra. Ela é calculada subtraindo-se o material disponível das necessidades brutas.

Necessidades brutas A quantidade e tempo de ocorrência das necessidades totais de um material em particular, sem considerar quaisquer disponibilidades do material em estoque ou recebimentos programados.

Níveis de estrutura do produto Estratos da hierarquia da estrutura de produto. O Nível 0, por exemplo, seriam os itens finais em montagem final, o Nível 1 seriam os componentes que entram na montagem final e o Nível 2 seriam todos os componentes que entram nos componentes do Nível 1.

Nível aceitável de qualidade (AQL) No controle da qualidade, nível usado para definir lotes bons.

Nível de estoque Quantidade de materiais que estão realmente à mão no estoque que está disponível para uso. Inclui tanto o estoque cíclico como o de segurança.

Nível de serviço Probabilidade de que ocorrerá uma falta de estoque durante o lead time.

O

O menor tempo de processamento (MTP) Regra de seqüenciamento na qual a tarefa seguinte a ser processada é aquela que tem a menor duração de processamento entre as tarefas à espera.

O melhor da classe Ser o melhor produto ou serviço numa classe de produtos ou serviços em particular.

O menor custo de preparação Regra de seqüenciamento pela qual a seqüência inteira de tarefas que estão à espera é determinada analisando-se o custo total de realização de todas as preparações de máquina entre as tarefas.

Operação de entrada Primeira operação de produção numa linha de produção.

Operação gargalo Operação de produção que tem a menor capacidade para um produto.

P

Padrão de mão-de-obra Número de minutos de trabalhador necessário para concluir um elemento, operação ou produto sob condições operacionais comuns.

Padrão histórico de mão-de-obra Padrão de trabalho determinado usando-se dados históricos do desempenho real da operação que é estudada.

Padrões de tempo predeterminados Técnica de medição do trabalho que usa dados desenvolvidos historicamente para determinar padrões de mão-de-obra antes que uma operação seja executada.

Padronização Redução da variedade entre um grupo de produtos ou peças.

Pai Termo que descreve uma relação de superioridade numa estrutura de produto; por exemplo, uma peça (componente) que entra numa montagem (pai).

Peças de serviço Materiais que são necessários como itens finais quando pedidos por centros de serviço para ser usados para consertar outros itens finais. Esses materiais geralmente têm demandas dependentes quando são montados em outros componentes de nível mais alto.

Pedido de cotação Formulário que convida possíveis fornecedores a licitarem ou cotarem um bem ou serviço.

Percentual tolerável de defeitos no lote (LTPD) No controle da qualidade, expressão usada para definir lotes ruins; se os lotes forem maiores do que o LTPD, eles serão considerados ruins.

Pesquisa operacional (PO) Termo usado na Segunda Guerra Mundial para investigações científicas; tinha em vista substituir a tomada de decisões intuitiva por uma abordagem analítica, sistemática e interdisciplinar.

Pesquisas dos clientes Permite que os clientes preencham questionários de pesquisa ou participem de entrevistas que se destinam a determinar sua percepção a respeito de diversas questões relacionadas à qualidade.

Planejamento agregado Processo de prover um esquema de capacidade de produção com horizonte de médio prazo para sustentar a previsão de vendas de um produto.

Planejamento da distribuição de recursos Planejar para a provisão de recursos-chaves de espaço de armazém — número de trabalhadores, dinheiro, veículos de embarque etc. — nas quantidades certas e quando necessário.

Planejamento das instalações Determinação de quando e de quanta capacidade de produção de longo prazo é necessária, onde as facilidades de produção devem ser localizadas, e o layout e as características dessas facilidades.

Planejamento das necessidades de capacidade (CRP) Processo de reconciliação do programa mestre de produção com as capacidades de mão-de-obra e de máquinas de um departamento de produção.

Planejamento das necessidades de distribuição (DRP) Planejar para a renovação de estoques de armazéns regionais.

Planejamento das necessidades de materiais (MRP) Sistema computadorizado que determina quanto de um material deve ser comprado ou produzido em cada intervalo de tempo futuro.

Planejamento das necessidades de recursos Determinação da quantidade e tempo de ocorrência (timing) de todos os recursos de produção necessários para produzir os itens finais num programa mestre de produção.

Planejamento de capacidade de médio prazo (RCCP) Verificação preliminar do programa mestre de produção que identifica qualquer semana no MPS em que ocorra subcarga ou sobrecarga da capacidade de produção e depois revisa o MPS quando necessário.

Planejamento do estoque Todas as atividades de administração que resultam em estocar a quantidade certa de cada material. As principais preocupações são as quantidades dos pedidos, pontos de pedido e períodos de pedido.

Planejamento do processo Determinação dos passos do processo tecnológico específico e a seqüência dos mesmos que possibilitará que o sistema de produção produza os produtos/serviços com a qualidade desejada e dentro do custo orçado.

Planejamento dos recursos de manufatura Veja MRP II.

Planejamento estratégico da qualidade A integração das necessidades de qualidade em planos comerciais.

Planejamento sistemático de layout (SLP) Técnica para planejar layouts de instalações que traça a importância relativa dos vários departamentos, colocando-os alternadamente próximos entre si.

Plano de aceitação No controle da qualidade, o esquema global para aceitar ou rejeitar um lote de produto baseando-se em informações colhidas de amostras.

Plano de amostragem seqüencial No controle da qualidade, um plano de amostragem da aceitação no qual cada vez que uma unidade é testada, é tomada uma decisão de aceitar, rejeitar ou prosseguir a amostragem.

Plano de amostragem simples No controle da qualidade, um plano de amostragem da aceitação no qual uma decisão de aceitar ou rejeitar é tomada depois de se tomar somente uma amostra de um lote.

Plano de capacidade nivelada Plano agregado de produção que tem uma capacidade uniforme por dia de intervalo a intervalo de tempo.

Plano de demanda coincidente Plano agregado de produção no qual a capacidade de produção em cada intervalo de tempo é variada para que coincida exatamente com a demanda agregada nesse intervalo de tempo.

Plano de dupla amostragem No controle da qualidade, um plano de amostragem da aceitação no qual uma decisão de aceitar ou rejeitar pode ser tomada na primeira amostra tirada, mas, se não for, uma segunda amostra será tirada, e uma segunda decisão será tomada baseando-se nas amostras combinadas.

Plano de roteiros Rede de centros de trabalho através da qual um pedido deve passar antes de ser concluído.

Ponto de pedido (PP) Ponto em que é feita um pedido de um material num sistema de estoque do intervalo padrão; demanda esperada durante o lead time mais o estoque de segurança.

Porcentagem de utilização da capacidade Medida que relaciona a medida da produção com as entradas disponíveis.

Previsão Estimar a demanda futura para produtos/serviços e os recursos necessários para produzi-los.

Primeira data de término (PDT) Na administração de projetos, o prazo mais breve em que uma atividade pode se encerrar.

Primeira data de vencimento Regra de seqüenciamento na qual a tarefa seguinte a ser processada é aquela que tem a primeira data de vencimento entre as tarefas à espera.

Primeiro a entrar, primeiro a ser atendio (PEPS) Regra de seqüenciamento na qual a tarefa a ser processada é aquela que chega primeiro entre as tarefas que estão à espera.

Produção contínua Produção focalizada no produto na qual alguns produtos altamente personalizados são produzidos continuamente em volumes muito grandes.

Produção de fluxo de linha Produção na qual produtos/serviços seguem caminhos lineares diretos sem recuos ou desvios.

Produção em lote Produção focalizada na produção na qual grandes lotes de produtos padronizados seguem rotas lineares diretas no mesmo sistema de produção.

Produção focalizada Conceito segundo o qual cada instalação de produção deve ser especializada de alguma maneira para torná-la menos vulnerável à competição.

Produção focalizada no processo Operação de fábrica que produz muitos produtos únicos em lotes relativamente pequenos que fluem ao longo de diferentes caminhos através da fábrica e exigem freqüentes preparações de máquina; também chamada job shop.

Produção focalizada no produto Operação de fábrica ou de serviço na qual há somente alguns projetos de produto/serviço padronizados, os produtos/serviços geralmente são produzidos para estoque de bens acabados e as taxas de produção de produtos e serviços individuais geralmente são maiores do que seus índices de demanda.

Produção intermitente Produção executada em produtos em base de início e parada.

Produção nivelada Níveis de saída de produção estabilizados de intervalo a intervalo de tempo.

Produção para estoque Produzir produtos antecipadamente e colocá-los em estoque até que os clientes necessitem deles.

Produção sob encomenda Produzir produtos somente depois que se tem em mãos os pedidos dos clientes.

Produtividade Quantidade de produtos ou serviços produzidos com os recursos usados.

Produtividade do trabalhador Valor em dinheiro de todos os bens e serviços produzidos em determinado ano, dividido pelas horas de trabalho diretas usadas na produção desses bens e serviços.

Produto padronizado Produto produzido continuamente ou em lotes muito grandes; implica somente alguns projetos do produto.

Produto personalizado Produto projetado para atender as necessidades de clientes individuais.

Programa de montagem final (PMF) Programa para montar produtos únicos pedidos por clientes.

Programa mestre de produção (MPS) Programa da quantidade e tempo de ocorrência (timing) de todos os itens finais ao longo de um horizonte de planejamento específico.

Programa mestre de produção aberto Parte de um MPS na qual toda a capacidade de produção foi alocada e na qual novos pedidos são reservados.

Programa mestre de produção com mudança líquida MPS que mostra somente as modificações no último MPS.

Programa mestre de produção congelado Primeiros períodos do programa mestre de produção que não estão sujeitos a mudança.

Programa mestre de produção da empresa Parte de um programa mestre de produção na qual mudanças podem ocorrer, mas somente em casos excepcionais.

Programa mestre de produção pleno Parte de um programa mestre de produção na qual toda a capacidade de produção disponível foi alocada.

Programa MRP de computador Um programa de computador que é o processador central de informações MRP. Ele recebe entradas do MPS, do arquivo de situação do estoque e do arquivo lista de materiais. O programa produz estas saídas principais: pedido programado, liberações de pedidos programados e mudanças em pedidos programados. Adicionalmente, o programa fornece dados sobre transações ao arquivo situação de estoque e registros secundários para os gerentes de operações.

Programação da carga Comparação das horas de mão-de-obra e máquinas necessárias para produzir o programa mestre de produção com as horas de mão-de-obra e máquinas realmente disponíveis em cada semana.

Programação de pedidos Programa de liberações de pedidos futuros programados ao longo de todo o horizonte de planejamento.

Programação linear (PL) Técnica para aplicar otimamente recursos escassos a demandas concorrentes.

Projeto auxiliado por computador (CAD) Processo computadorizado para projetar novos produtos e modificar produtos existentes.

Projeto de trabalho Descrição do conteúdo de um trabalho e especificação das habilidades e treinamento necessários para executar esse trabalho.

Projeto parâmetro Determinar especificações do produto e definições do processo de produção que permitirão um desempenho satisfatório do produto apesar de condições de produção e de campo indesejáveis.

Projeto protótipo Projeto de produto inicial que exibe as características básicas da forma, encaixe e função de um produto que serão exigidos do projeto final.

Projeto robusto Projeto que se comportará conforme o esperado mesmo que ocorram condições indesejáveis na produção ou em campo.

Q

Qualidade média de saída (AOQ) Porcentagem média de itens defeituosos em lotes que saem de um posto de inspeção.

Qualidade na fonte Atribuição de responsabilidade pela qualidade do produto a trabalhadores da produção, dos quais se espera que produzam peças de qualidade perfeita antes que essas peças sejam passadas para a operação de produção seguinte.

Quantidade pedida Quantidade de um material pedida a cada vez que o estoque é renovado.

Quase-manufatura Nesse tipo de operação de serviço, a produção ocorre de uma maneira muito similar à manufatura. A ênfase é colocada nos custos de produção, tecnologia, materiais físicos e produtos, qualidade do produto e pronta-entrega. Os bens físicos são dominantes sobre serviços intangíveis, os produtos podem ser ou padrão ou personalizados, e há pouco contato ou envolvimento com o cliente. Operações de apoio em bancos são exemplos desse tipo de operação de serviço.

R

Razão crítica Regra de seqüenciamento pela qual a tarefa seguinte a ser processada é aquela que tem a menor relação (tempo até a data de vencimento dividido pelo tempo restante total) entre tarefas à espera.

Recebimento de pedido programado Quantidade de material a ser recebida em cada intervalo de tempo do horizonte de planejamento.

Recebimentos programados Materiais que estão sob encomenda de um fornecedor e programados para ser recebidos num período específico.

Recursos As características especiais que atraem clientes.

Redes de subcontratados e fornecedores Arranjos nos quais um fabricante desenvolve relações de contrato de longo prazo com diversos fornecedores de peças, componentes ou submontagens.

Registro de estoque Exibição de todas as transações de estoque que afetaram um material.

Regra da decisão linear Função matemática de custo para um sistema de produção em particular que trabalha com um número de unidades de saída a serem produzidas e o tamanho da força de trabalho em cada intervalo de tempo.

Regra heurística Regra ou orientação simples para ação.

Regra heurística da tarefa de mais longa duração (LTT) Adicionar tarefas a uma estação de trabalho, uma por vez, na ordem de precedência.

Regra heurística da utilização incremental (IU) Adicionar tarefas a uma estação de trabalho, uma a cada vez, em ordem de precedência até que a utilização do trabalho seja ou 100% ou se observe uma queda, repetindo-se então o processo para as tarefas restantes.

Relatório de controle de entrada e saída Relatório que detalha como as tarefas estão fluindo entre os centros de trabalho de forma que os gerentes possam determinar se a capacidade do centro de trabalho está se desenvolvendo conforme o previsto.

Renovação O processo de adicionar materiais ao estoque. Inclui sentir a necessidade de um pedido de materiais, fazer o pedido e recebê-lo.

Reprodutibilidade Capacidade de um sistema de produção para produzir produtos coerentemente com a qualidade e quantidade desejadas.

Requisição de compra Autorização para comprar um bem ou serviço.

Reserva de capacidade Quantidade adicional de capacidade de produção adicionada à demanda esperada.

Resposta ao impulso Em previsão, a velocidade na qual as previsões refletem as mudanças nos dados subjacentes.

Resultados da garantia da qualidade Realização e melhoria da qualidade demonstradas através de medidas quantitativas.

Revolução dos serviços Evolução do setor de serviços como setor predominante da economia mundial.

Revolução Industrial Substituição generalizada da força humana e da água pela força mecanizada e o estabelecimento do sistema fabril.

Risco do consumidor No controle da qualidade, a probabilidade de aceitação de um lote ruim.

Risco do produtor No controle da qualidade, a probabilidade de rejeição de um lote bom.

Robô Manipulador reprogramável, multifuncional, projetado para mover materiais, peças, ferramentas ou dispositivos especializados por meio de movimentos variáveis programados para o desempenho de uma variedade de tarefas.

S

Saída Produto final ou serviço de um sistema de produção.

Satisfação do cliente Determinação das necessidades do cliente e demonstrado sucesso em atendê-las.

Sazonalidade Padrões sazonais que são flutuações, geralmente dentro de um ano, e que tendem a se repetir anualmente.

Série temporal Conjunto de valores observados, geralmente de vendas, medido ao longo de sucessivos intervalos de tempo.

Serviçabilidade A velocidade, custo e conveniência de reparos e manutenção.

Serviço padrão Serviço que é uniforme para a maioria dos clientes.

Serviço personalizado Serviço projetado para atender as necessidades de clientes individuais.

Simplificação Eliminação de recursos complexos num produto ou serviço a fim de que os custos sejam reduzidos e a qualidade seja melhorada.

Simplificação de projeto Na confiabilidade de produto e máquina, a redução do número de peças que interagem numa máquina ou produto.

Sinal de rastreamento Medida que mostra se uma previsão tem qualquer inclinação incorporada ao longo de um intervalo de tempo.

Sistema automático de identificação (AIS) Sistema que usa códigos de barras, freqüências de rádio, tarjas magnéticas, reconhecimento ótico de caracteres e visão de máquina para "sentir" e introduzir dados em computadores.

Sistema automatizado de armazenamento e recuperação (ASRS) Sistema para receber pedidos de materiais, coletar os materiais e entregá-los às estações de trabalho nas operações.

Sistema automatizado de inspeção do controle da qualidade Sistema que utiliza máquinas que foram integradas à inspeção de produtos para fins de controle da qualidade.

Sistema automatizado de montagem Sistema de máquinas de montagem automatizadas ligadas por equipamentos automatizados de manuseio de materiais; usado para produzir montagens ou produtos acabados.

Sistema de canal único, fase única Sistema de fila no qual há somente uma fila de espera ou canal, e o serviço é executado em somente um passo, ou fase.

Sistema de distribuição Rede de pontos de embarque e recebimento que iniciam na fábrica e encerram com o cliente.

Sistema de duas gavetas Sistema de controle de estoques do lote padrão que usa duas gavetas para manter um material em estoque; pedidos são disparados quando uma gaveta se torna vazia, e ambas as gavetas são preenchidas quando o estoque é renovado.

Sistema de estoque básico Sistema simples de planejamento de estoques que renova estoques somente na quantidade de cada retirada, mantendo assim o estoque num nível constante.

Sistema de manufatura flexível (FMS) Sistema no qual grupos de máquinas de produção são ligados seqüencialmente por máquinas automatizadas de manuseio e transferência de materiais e integrados num sistema computadorizado.

Sistema de manuseio de materiais Rede de transporte inteira que recebe, classifica, movimenta e entrega materiais dentro de uma instalação de produção.

Sistema de materiais Rede de todos os tipos de fluxos de materiais dentro de um sistema de produção.

Sistema de múltiplas fases Sistema de fila no qual há diversas filas de espera e o serviço é executado em mais de uma etapa.

Sistema de pagamento de incentivo Sistema de pagamento que torna o valor do pagamento dos trabalhadores condicional ao desempenho no trabalho.

Sistema de planejamento das necessidades de materiais com mudança líquida Sistema MRP no qual as modificações no programa mestre de produção iniciam uma atualização somente dos registros de estoque afetados.

Sistema de produção Sistema cuja função é transformar um conjunto de entradas num conjunto de saídas desejadas.

Sistema de produção (Shop System) Abordagem sistemática para melhorar a eficiência da mão-de-obra, introduzida por Frederick Winslow Taylor no final do século XIX.

Sistema de renovação opcional Sistema de planejamento que revisa os níveis de estoque em intervalos de tempo fixos, mas substitui o estoque somente se os níveis tiverem caído abaixo de certo nível mínimo.

Sistema de transformação Subsistema de um sistema de produção mais amplo no qual entradas são transformadas em saídas.

Sistema de veículos automatizados (AGVS) Sistema que usa transportadores mecânicos e controlados por computador, como, por exemplo, trens não tripulados, paletes e transportadores de carga unitizada para entregar pedidos em estações de trabalho nas operações.

Sistema do intervalo padrão Sistema de planejamento de estoques que realiza contagens fixas dos materiais em estoque em intervalos de tempo fixos.

Sistema do lote padrão Sistema de planejamento de estoques que faz pedidos de quantidades fixas de um material quando o nível de estoque cai a um nível crítico predeterminado.

Sistema empurrar (push) Sistema de planejamento e controle da produção no qual produtos são movidos para a frente ao longo da produção pelo passo precedente no processo.

Sistema just-in-time (JIT) Sistema de controle de produção e estoque baseado em tamanhos de lote pequenos, programas de produção estáveis e nivelados, e fábricas focalizadas; sistema de resolução forçada de problemas.

Sistema MRP regenerativo Sistema de planejamento das necessidades de materiais no qual um MRP completo é processado periodicamente, resultando num novo MPS, um arquivo situação do estoque e um arquivo lista de materiais atualizado que gera um conjunto completo de saídas no programa de computador MRP.

Sistema multicanal Sistema de fila no qual há duas ou mais filas de espera.

Sistema puxar (pull) Sistema de planejamento e controle da produção no qual se olha para a etapa de produção seguinte, determina-se o que é necessário, e somente isso é produzido.

Sistemas automatizados de controles de processo Sistema que usa sensores para obter medidas do desempenho de processos industriais, compará-los com padrões predeterminados e depois sinalizar mudanças automaticamente nas configurações desses processos.

Stockout Redução a zero do nível de estoque usável de um material.

Suavização exponencial Modelo de previsão de curto prazo que toma a previsão correspondente ao período precedente e adiciona um ajuste para obter a previsão para o período seguinte.

Subsistema de controle Subsistema de um sistema de produção mais amplo no qual uma parte das saídas é monitorada quanto a sinais de feedback para fornecer ações corretivas, se necessário.

Superdimensionamento no projeto Ampliação do projeto de uma máquina para evitar um tipo de falha em particular durante a produção.

T

Tabela de compensação Na tomada de decisões, uma tabela que mostra os custos esperados de cada alternativa para atender diferentes níveis de demanda.

Tabelas de Dodge-Roming No controle da qualidade, planos de aceitação de atributos que definem tamanho de amostra e número máximo de itens defeituosos numa amostra para aceitar o lote.

Tamanho de fila O número de chegadas que esperam para ser atendidas.

Tamanho do lote de produção O número de unidades produzidas de um produto em determinada etapa do processo de produção, entre preparações de máquinas.

Tamanho padrão de equipe Padrão de mão-de-obra determinado estimando-se o número total de trabalhadores necessários para produzir a saída necessária por turno.

Taxa de demanda Número de unidades de que clientes ou departamentos de produção necessitam por unidade de tempo; também chamada taxa de uso.

Taxa de serviço A taxa em que as chegadas são atendidas, em chegadas por unidade de tempo (por exemplo, por hora). A taxa de serviço geralmente tem uma distribuição constante, normal ou de Poisson.

Taxa de suprimento (p) Número de unidades de um material fornecido para estoque por unidade de tempo se ele for entregue gradativamente; também chamada taxa de produção.

Técnica computadorizada de busca Método de planejamento da capacidade que usa regras pré-programadas que controlam a maneira pela qual recursos são combinados para selecionar um plano de capacidade de baixo custo durante um intervalo de tempo.

Técnica de avaliação e revisão de programa (PERT) Método de planejamento de projeto que usa múltiplas estimativas de duração de atividade.

Tecnologia de grupo/manufatura celular (GT/CM) Forma de produção baseada num sistema de codificação de peças que permite que famílias de peças sejam designadas a células de manufatura para produção.

Tecnologia de produção otimizada (OPT) Um sistema de informação de planejamento e controle da produção que localiza os gargalos num processo de produção.

Tempo de atendimento O tempo necessário para atender uma chegada, expresso em minutos (horas, dias etc.) por chegada. A medida não inclui filas de espera.

Tempo de espera A quantidade de tempo que uma chegada gasta na fila.

Tempo no sistema O tempo total que as unidades que chegam permanecem no sistema, incluindo tanto o tempo de espera como o de atendimento.

Teorema do limite central Teorema que estabelece a suposição de que as distribuições de amostragens são normalmente distribuídas não obstante as distribuições da população não serem normais.

Teoria das filas Conjunto de conhecimentos sobre filas de espera.

Throughput Taxa em que capital é gerado pela venda de produtos.

Tolerância Especificação de cada dimensão de um produto físico numa faixa que varia de mínimo a máximo.

Última data de término (UDT) Na administração de projetos, a última data a partir do início do projeto em que uma atividade pode ser finalizada.

Unidade agregada de capacidade Medida que permite que taxas de produção de vários produtos sejam convertidas para uma unidade comum de medida de produção.

Unidade de manutenção de estoque (SKU) Qualquer item que seja mantido em estoque.

Utilização O grau em que qualquer parte de um sistema de serviço é ocupada por uma chegada. Geralmente expressa como a probabilidade de que n chegadas estejam no sistema.

Utilização de recursos humanos Utilização do potencial total da força de trabalho para se obter qualidade.

Variáveis No controle da qualidade, características de produto que podem ser medidas numa escala contínua.

ÍNDICE ANALÍTICO

A

À espera, 411
A menor folga, 347
ABC – classificação de materiais, 298
Abordagem
    da escala de classificação, 161
    da escala ponderada de classificação, 162
    dos sistemas totais, 12
Aceleração, 550
Ackoff, Russell L., 14
Acordo de Livre Comércio da América do Norte (NAFTA), 25, 38
Acordo Geral de Tarifas e Comércio (GATT), 25
Administração
    científica, 9-11
    da cadeia de suprimentos, 427
        definição, 427
        fabricantes de classe mundial e, 448
        na Motoarc, 427
    da demanda, 255
    da distribuição, 440
    da produção e operações (APO)
        abordagens de estudo para, 14
        algumas ocupações, 6
        decisões para, 16
        definição de, 5
        evolução de, 7
        fatores atuais, 14
        marcos históricos da, 7
        tomada de decisões na, 16
    da qualidade
        visão moderna da, 492
        visão tradicional da, 491
    da qualidade total (TQM)
        atendimento ao cliente e, 504
        benchmarking e, 507
        compromisso e envolvimento da alta administração na, 498
        desenvolvimento de parcerias com o fornecedor e, 504
        distribuição e, 504
        empowerment do trabalhador e, 467
        envolvimento do cliente e, 498
        fabricantes de classe mundial e, 510
        manufatura just-in-time e, 412
        melhoria contínua e, 507
        nos serviços, 508
        programas para, 498
        qualidade de produto e, 500
    de materiais
        armazenamento e, 442
        compras e, 430
        critérios de desempenho na, 448
        definição de, 429
        desempenho em empresas de classe internacional, 448
        embarques para/de fábricas, 440
        gráfico organizacional, 430
        logística e, 439
    de projetos, 529
        fabricantes de classe mundial e, 556
        profissionais, 532
        sistemas de controle de custos do projeto e, 548
        software de computador para, 554
        técnica de avaliação e revisão de programa para, 545
        termos usados na, 533
    do tráfego, 440
Agente de compras, 433
Agilização, 446
AGVS (sistemas de veículos automatizados), 150
Airco Division, 269
AIS (sistemas automáticos de identificação), 146
Alavancagem operacional, 120
Aldeia global, 25
ALDEP (programas automatizados de projeto de layout), 209
Alemanha, taxas de câmbio da moeda, 29
Alianças estratégicas, 27
All-freight, aeroportos, 442
Alocação
    computadorizada relativa de instalações (CRAFT), 209
    de recursos para alternativas estratégicas, 43
Alta administração, na administração da qualidade total, 498
Alta precisão, 57
Alta tecnologia (high-tech), 155
    sistemas de produção, 33
    tecnologia de produção, 143
Alternativas de processamento
    funções de custo de, 119
    decidindo entre, 117
Ambientes de trabalho, projeto de, 466
American Insurance Company, 469
American Production and Inventory Control Society (APICS), 255
Amostra representativa, 516
Amostragem, 516
    de trabalho, para definir padrões de mão-de-obra, 474
Amostras aleatórias, 516
Ampliação de trabalho, 464
Análise
    computadorizada, de layouts de instalações, 209
    convencional de custos, 187
    da árvore de decisões, 176
    da distância da carga, 207
    da seqüência de operações, 204
    de break-even, 121, 176
    de diagrama de blocos, 205
    de métodos de trabalho, 467
    de regressão, 58
        linear, 58, 60
        múltipla, 66
        múltipla não linear, 66
    de regressão linear simples, 60
        exemplo de, 61
        definições e fórmulas de variáveis, 61
    de valor, 100
    do comprar *versus* fabricar, 435
    do valor presente, 176
    econômica
        das decisões de automação, 160
        de projetos de processo, 118
    financeira, de alternativas de projeto de processo, 123
Analista
    de estoques, descrição/ obrigações de trabalho de, 6
    de produção, descrição de trabalho/obrigações do, 6
Analogia histórica, 56
Andrews, Bruce H., 69
APICS (American Production and Inventory Control Society), 255
    Dictionary, 405, 419
APO. Veja Administração da produção e operações (APO)
Armazenamento (warehousing)
    definição de, 442
    desenvolvimentos contemporâneos no, 445
    métodos de contabilidade de estoques para, 444
    operações de, 442
Arntzen Bruce C., 181
Arquivo
    estrutura analítica do produto, 314
    lista de materiais, 314
    situação do estoque, 315
ASRS (sistemas automatizados de armazenamento e recuperação), 150
AT&T, 27, 35, 507
Atendimento de pedidos, 134
Atenuação de ruído, 71
Atitudes do consumidor, 35
Atividade, 533, 539
    crítica, 533
    de compras
        administração de materiais e, 430
        análise do comprar *versus* fabricar, 435
        antecedente, 533
        emergente fronteira internacional, 438
        importância atual da, 430
        manufatura just-in-time e, 416, 439
        missão da, 432
        processos de, 433
        subseqüente, 533
Atributos
    gráficos de controle por, 518
    na amostragem, 516
Automação
    abordagem da escala de classificação para, 161

abordagem da escala ponderada de classificação para, 162
alternativas para, 160, 163
análise econômica da, 160
dedicada, 147, 157
demissão de trabalhadores e, 160
fixa, 147
flexibilidade da atividade de manufatura e, 157
flexível, 157
grau de, 105
importância da atividade de compras e, 430
nível tecnológico e, 155
nos serviços, 153
projetos, justificação da, 158
questões da, 155
tipos de, 144
uso corrente do termo, 143
Avaliação econômica do projeto protótipo, 98

B

Backlog de pedidos (carteira de pedidos), 113
Baixa resposta ao impulso, 71
Baixa tecnologia, 155
Balanceamento de linha
 com a regra heurística de utilização incremental, 211, 212
 com a regra heurística da tarefa de mais longa duração, 214, 215
 de modelo misto, 218
 planejando layouts de produto e, 209
 questões de, 217
 regra heurística e, 211
Bancos, automação nos, 153
Barnard, Chester, 11
Barnes, Ralph M., 468
Barth, Carl G., 9
Behaviorismo, 11
Behavioristas, 11
Belton, Beth, 145
Benchmarking, 499, 507
Bens (produtos)
 físicos, combinação e serviços intangíveis, 102
 intangíveis, 44
 tangíveis, 15, 44
Bistritz, Nancy, 391
Boeing Company, 204
Bowman, E. H., 249
Brown, Gerald G., 181
Bryan-College Station Eagle, 442
Bucket, 315
Bureau of Labor Statistics, 459
Business Week, 29, 36, 80, 98, 106, 303, 447, 463

C

CAD (projeto auxiliado por computador), 33, 151
CAD/CAM (projeto auxiliado por computador/manufatura auxiliada por computador), 151
Cadeia de suprimentos, 427
Cadências variáveis de produção, 158
Caixas eletrônicos, 155
Caliber Logistics, 448
CAM (manufatura auxiliada por computador), 33, 151
Caminhões, para manuseio de materiais, 199
Canais, 382
Capacidade
 das instalações
  incremental, aumento da, 175
  utilização, escalonamento de produtos no tempo, 173
 de armazenamento, sistemas automatizados de armazenamento e recuperação e, 150
 de longo prazo
  decisões, fabricantes de classe mundial e, 189
  mudando, 172
  planejando, 170
 demanda por, previsão da, 171
 de produção
  definição, 170
  dimensões de, 237
  escalonamento para cima e para baixo, 238
  lead times de manufatura e, 408
  médio prazo, fontes de, 238
  mudando, 172
  previsão, 171
 do processo, 504
 excessiva, 158
 mudando, 172
 nivelada
  com backlog, 241, 243
  com estoque, 240, 241
  com horas extras, 241, 245, 246
  com subcontratação, 241, 245, 246
 planos de instalações e, 170
 prática sustentável, 170
Capital, 459
 -intensivas, 105, 182
Carga
 finita, 345
 infinita, 345
Carrier Corporation, 35
Carros, 28
Carteira de pedidos, 113
Cartões
 de movimentação, 343
 de produção (Kanban P), 413
 de transferência (Kanban C), 413
 Kanban, 413, 414
Células de manufatura, 201
Cenário de trabalho, 466
Centro de distribuição regional, passeio pelas instalações de, 133
Centros de trabalho
 balanceamento de linha e, 209
 contêineres entre, calculando o número de, 415
 regras de prioridade para, sistemas computadorizados de programação e, 361
seqüenciamento de tarefas através, 352
Chaussé, Sylvain, 417
Chegada, 382
Ciclo(s), 58, 473
 do pedido à entrega, 406
 de estoque, 272
 de vida do processo, 117
 de vida do produto
  abreviado, 42
  capacidade de produção e, 171
  etapas, 42
 do tempo do pedido à entrega, 406
CIM (manufatura integrada por computador), 152
Círculos da qualidade (círculos QC), 493, 506, 507
Clairol, 35
Classes de produtos, 490
Classificação do desempenho, 473
Classificações de proximidade
 definição de, 222
 localizações departamentais e, 389
 para desenvolver layouts de instalações de serviços, 223
Clean Air Act de 1990, 36
Cliente interno, 503
Clientes, serviços e, 30
Coca-Cola Company, 27
Código do material, 315
Coeficiente
 de correlação, 60
 múltiplo, 66
 parcial, 66
 de determinação, 64
Cohen, Stephen, 34
Communications Oriented Production Information and Control Systems (COPICS), 257, 258
Compaq Computer Corporation, 35, 37, 54, 116
Compartilhamento da produção, 27
Compensação para lead times, 332
Compensar
 com estoque, 240
 com pedidos em carteira (backlog), 241, 243
 com tempo parcial, 241
 com trabalho em horas extras, 241, 245
 com subcontratação, 241, 245
Competências essenciais, 39
Competição
 baseada no tempo
  análise de filas de espera e, 384
  utilização de alta capacidade e, 407
 fabricantes americanos e, 49
 global, 25
Componentes, 318
 redundantes, 502
Comportamento
 ético
  ao comprar, 437
  definição, 437
 humano, produtividade e, 458
Compradores
 comportamento impróprio, 437

da equipe de compras, descrição de trabalho/obrigações do, 6
obrigações dos, 435
Computadores
em sistemas automatizados de armazenamento e recuperação, 150
no controle da qualidade, 523
para decisões relativas a estoques, 315
planejamento de estoques e, 300
programas. *Veja* Software
Conceitos estatísticos no controle da qualidade, 514
Condições
dos negócios globais, 24
financeiras internacionais, flutuação das, 28
Confiabilidade, 500
do componente, 500
do sistema, 500
Conformidade, capacidade da qualidade de, 490
Consenso do comitê executivo, 56
Conservação ambiental, 36
Constante de amortecimento, 74
Contagem
cíclica, 444
física do estoque, 444
Contato com o cliente, equipamento automatizado e, 154
Contêineres
de embarque, 299
para manipulação de materiais, 199
Controlador de produção, descrições de trabalho/obrigações de, 6
Controlando o projeto na administração de projetos, 531
Controle
automatizado de processo, 147
da qualidade
computadores no, 523
conceitos estatísticos no, 514
em sistemas de produção, 515
fabricantes de classe mundial e, 524
gráficos de controle e, 517
nos serviços, 524
sistemas automatizados de inspeção para, 146
teorema do limite central e, 516
da qualidade total (TQC), 493
de entrada e saída, 344
de produção, 439
numérico
computadorizado, 144
direto, 144
Cook, Nathan H., 149
Cooke, Morris L., 9
COPICS (Communications Oriented Production Information and Control Systems), 257, 258
Corda, 262
CORELAP (planejamento computadorizado do layout das relações), 209
Corpo humano, economia de movimentos e, 467
Corporações sem pátria, 27

Correio dos Estados Unidos, 23
Correlação
coeficiente de, 65
regressão linear e, 60
Corte de bobinas de papel (slitting), 132
CPM. *Veja* Método do caminho crítico (CPM)
CRAFT (alocação computadorizada relativa de instalações), 209
CRP. *Veja* Planejamento das necessidades de capacidade (CRP)
Cultura da qualidade na organização, 490
Curvas CTM (custo anual total de materiais), 281
Custo(s)
anual
da aquisição, 277
de emissão de pedidos, 273
de estocagem, 273
de manutenção em estoque, 273
total de estocagem, 274
da aquisição, 270
da atividade, 550
da capacidade reduzida, estoques e, 271
da demissão de empregados, 245
da mão-de-obra
reduzindo, 32
sistemas automatizados de armazenamento e recuperação e, 150
da oportunidade, 295
da preparação, 347, 350, 351
da qualidade de lotes grandes, estoques e, 271
da qualidade inicial, 270
da receptividade ao cliente, estoques e, 270
de contratação, 245
de emissão do pedido, 269
de manutenção em estoque, 270, 273
balanceados contra os custos de pedido, 269
de pedido, equilibrando com os custos de manutenção em estoque, 269
de produção, fabricantes americanos e, 30
do retorno sobre o investimento (ROI), 271
do stockout, 270
mínimo da conversão, 347
Cox, James, 26
Cox, Jeff, 262
Crosby, Philip B., 492
Cunningham, Shawn M., 69

D

Dallas Morning News, 29, 36, 443
DAM (desvio absoluto médio), 71
Data de vencimento mais breve, 347
DDLT. *Veja* Demanda durante o lead time (DDLT)
Decisão(ões)
de meio-termo (*trade-off*), 179
de controle, 19
estratégicas, 20
multifásicas, 176
operacionais, 20
quanto à comunidade, para localização de instalações, 179

quanto à formação de células, 200
quanto à região, para localização de instalações, 179
quanto ao planejamento da capacidade, 176
DEDLT. *Veja* Demanda esperada durante o lead time (DEDLT)
Definição do tamanho de lote
com demandas instáveis, 323
decisões quanto à, 323
em empresas de produção sob encomenda e produção para estoque, 256
no planejamento das necessidades de materiais, 323
Dell Computer Corporation, 23, 448
Demanda
de caixa real *versus* previsões de média móvel, 74
durante o lead time (DDLT)
distribuições contínuas, 286
definição de, 279
distribuições discretas, 286
esperada durante o lead time (DEDLT), 290
porcentagem de, 290
raiz quadrada de, 291
instável, 323
não uniforme, na programação de serviços, 372
por dia, 282
por produto/serviço, natureza da, 104
Deming, Prêmio, 492, 496
Deming, W. Edwards, 492
Demissão de trabalhadores, 32, 160
Departamento(s)
da função de produção, 18
de compra, 430, 433
de recebimento, 131
de trânsito, 440
Desagilização, 446
Descontos por quantidade, 277
Deseconomias de escala, 174
Desenvolvimento de distribuidores, 416, 439
Despesas operacionais, 262
Desvio
absoluto médio (DAM), 71
padrão da previsão, 76
Determinação, coeficiente de, 64, 65
Diagrama(s)
de fluxos, 469
espinha de peixe, 493, 494
Dickson, W. J., 11
Digital Equipment Corporation (DEC), 29
Disciplina das filas, 382
Dispositivos automáticos de transferência, 199
Distribuição(ões)
administração da qualidade total e, 504
amostrais, 516
DDLT
contínua, 282, 286
discreta, 282, 286
definição de, 440
de lead-time, parâmetros, 282
LT (lead time), parâmetros, 282

populacional, *versus* distribuição da amostragem, 516
qualidade e, 504
Divisão do trabalho, 7
Downsizing, 31
DRP (planejamento das necessidades de distribuição), 440
Drucker, Peter, 11
Duguay, Claude R., 417
DuPont, 27, 36
Duração da atividade, 533

E

Economia
 de escala, 172
 de escopo, 176
 de movimentos, 467
 de produção, de fábricas do futuro, 153
 de serviços, 34
Eficácia operacional, 24
Eficiência, 11
Elevada resposta ao impulso, 71
Elevadores, para manuseio de materiais, 199
Eliminação do desperdício na manufatura, 410
Embalagem padrão, 299
Embarque, 132
Emerson, Harrington, 9
Empowerment
 de empregados, criação de equipes para, 499
 de trabalhadores, 467
 equipes de trabalho e, 505
Empregado(s)
 construção de equipes de, 505
 empowerment dos, 467
 produtividade e, 460
 projetando funções de, 464
 qualidade e, 505
 treinamento para obter margem competitiva, 463
Empresas
 de classe mundial, 490
 internacionais, 26
 -mãe, país de origem de, 28
 representantes, 13
Empresas de montagem sob encomenda, planejamento das necessidades de materiais e, 327
Engenharia
 concorrente, 100
 simultânea, 100, 103
Engenheiros
 da eficiência, 9
 de produção, 9
Enriquecimento do trabalho, 464
Entrega de pedidos de clientes, de fábricas do futuro, 153
Environmental Protection Agency (EPA), 36
EPA (Environmental Protection Agency), 36
EQM (erro quadrático médio), 71

Equipamento automatizado
 de manuseio de materiais, 199
Equipes interdisciplinares, 12
Erro
 de previsão, 57, 66
 padrão da previsão, 66
 quadrático médio (EQM), 71
Escalonamento de tempo de produtos, utilização da capacidade das instalações e, 173
Especialista
 em eficiência, 9
 em qualidade, descrição de trabalho/obrigações do, 6
Especialização de mão-de-obra, 7, 464
Especificação, 101
 de materiais, 433
Estação de trabalho, 209, 210
Estados Unidos
 crescimento das exportações nos, 26
 leis antitruste, 28
 produtividade da mão-de-obra, 460
 taxas de câmbio da moeda, 28
Estimativas
 da demanda, 256
 do supervisor, 478
Estoque
 capacidade de produção de médio prazo e, 238
 com demanda independente, 272
 de matérias-primas, 312, 443
 demanda dependente *versus* demanda independente, 272
 de segurança
  definição de, 270
  definindo, nos níveis de serviço
   para lead time constante e demanda normalmente distribuída por dia, 289
   para distribuição DDLT discreta, 286
   para DDLT normalmente distribuída, 288
  definindo pontos de pedido e, 290
  planejamento das necessidades de materiais e, 326
 determinando quantidades pedidas, 274
 de trabalho em processo, 411
 em processo, 443
 enxuto, 301
 manufatura just-in-time, 261
 manufatura síncrona e, 261
 manutenção
  fundamento lógico contrário a, 270
  fundamento lógico a favor, 269
 modelos de estoque de período único de, 294
 modelos híbridos de, 294
 natureza do, 272
 pontos de pedido, determinação de, 279
 sistemas
  de controle para, duas gavetas, 273
  do intervalo padrão, 292
  do lote padrão, 272
 visões opostas do, 269
Estratégia(s)
 de marketing, 47

 de mercado, vinculando à estratégia de posicionamento, 47
 de negócios, 38, 126
 de operações, 38
  alocação de recursos para alternativas estratégicas, 43
  definição de, 39
  elementos de, 40
  formando, 45
  nos serviços, 43
  planos de instalações, capacidade, localização e layout, 43
  planos de produto/serviço e, 42
  planos tecnológicos e, 43
  processo de produção e 43
  variedade de, 47
  vinculando à estratégia de marketing, 47
 de posicionamento
  evolução da, 46
  mistas, 47
  puras, 47
  vinculando à estratégia de marketing, 47
Estrutura organizacional das fábricas do futuro, 153
Estudo(s)
 da viabilidade técnica e econômica, 98
 de Hawthorne, 11
 do tempo, para medição do trabalho, 473
Etapa(s)
 de crescimento do ciclo de vida, 42
 de declínio do ciclo de vida, 42
 de introdução do ciclo de vida, 42
 de maturidade do ciclo de vida, 42
 de serviço, 382
Evento, 533
Expansão, capacidade de longo prazo e, 171
Expectativas do cliente, 515
Exponencial móvel dupla, 75

F

Fábrica dedicada, passeio pelas instalações de uma, 124
Fabricantes
 de classe mundial
  administração da cadeia de suprimentos e, 448
  administração da produção e operações e, 20
  administração da qualidade total e, 510
  administração de operações de serviço e, 398
  administração de projetos e, 556
  controle da qualidade e, 524
  decisões quanto à capacidade de longo prazo, 189
  decisões quanto à localização das instalações e, 189
  estratégias de operações e, 50
  layouts das instalações e, 225
  manufatura just-in-time e, 423

planejamento e projeto do processo de produção, 136
previsão e, 86
produtividade e, 482
sistemas de controle de estoques e, 301
sistemas de planejamento das necessidades de recursos e, 333
tecnologia de produção avançada e, 163
japoneses
abordagem da capacidade nivelada e, 243
círculos da qualidade e, 507
de automóveis, 28
Fábricas
do futuro, 153
dos Estados Unidos
atendimento ao cliente e, 30
competitividade, 49
custos da produção e, 30
qualidade de produto e, 30
embarques para, e de, 440
focalizadas, 41
movimento nas, 439
Família de peças, 109, 200
Family Leave Act de 1993, 36
Fatores
controláveis, 503
econômicos, nas decisões de automação, 161
incontroláveis, 503
Feigenbaum, Armand V., 493
Fila, 381
Filas
análise das, 176
avaliação na APO e, 388
canal único
fase única e tempos de serviço constantes (modelo 2), 385
fase única e tamanho limitado da fila de espera (modelo 3), 386
fase única (modelo 1), 382
características das, 381
em operações de serviço, 380
multicanal, fase única (modelo 4), 387
sistemas de fila, terminologia e estrutura dos, 381
Folga, 533, 543, 549
Flexibilidade
decisões quanto à automação e, 160
de fábricas do futuro, 153
de manufatura, 157
de produção, 105
de produto, 105
de volume, 105
Flow shops, 354
Flutuação aleatória, 58
Fluxo de produto, 129
FMS (sistemas de manufatura flexível), 148
Foco nos recursos humanos, 496
Fontes
de informação para carreiras de administração de produção e operações, 6

de inovação de produto, 97
Força de trabalho
diversidade de, 32
mecanizada, 7
programação, previsão e, 55
Ford, Henry, 10, 409
Ford Motor Company, 10, 461
Fortune 500, lista da, 13
Fortune, 303, 461
Frazier, Gregory V., 201
Fronteira Estados Unidos-México, 38

G

Gaither, Norman, 201, 324
Gantt, Henry L., 9
Gastos gerais, 459
General Motors, 31
Geoffrion, A. M., 187
Gerente(s)
de compras, 432
responsabilidades dos, 432
de materiais, 429, 447
de operações, 5
atividades de planejamento da produção dos, 236
na APO, 5
na função financeira, 5
na função de marketing, 5
Gilbreth, Frank B., 9
Gilbreth, Lillian M., 9
Goldratt, Eliyahu M., 262
Goldstein, Alan, 443
Graduações de produtos, 490
Gráfico(s)
da mão direita, 477
da mão esquerda, 447
de atividades múltiplas, 469
de balanceamento, 82
de barras, 534
de controle, 517
estatístico, 510
fórmulas e definições para, 517
para atributos, 518
para controlar o percentual de defeitos em amostras, 518
para variáveis, 521
de Gantt, 345, 346
de montagem, 124, 125
de processo, 124, 126, 469
gozinto, 124
homem-máquina, 469
Grau de padronização do serviço, 101
Graves, G. W., 187
Green Thumb Water Sprinkler Company, 316
Groff, G. K., 324
Gross, Neil, 98
Grupos de trabalho, 464
GT/CM (tecnologia de grupo/manufatura celular), 108
GTE, 13
Guindastes, para manuseio de materiais, 199
Gurus da qualidade, 492

H

Halberstam, David., 10
Hall, Robert W., 411, 413
Harrison, Terry P., 181
Harvard Business Review, 151
Hayes, R. H., 46
Herzberg, Frederick, 11
Heurística, regras, de utilização incremental (IU), 212
Hewlett-Packard, 421, 443
Hierarquia do planejamento da produção, 235
Holt, Charles C., 249
Horizontes de planejamento, 257
Houston Chronicle, 28, 29, 35, 36, 151, 173, 186, 461
Hyundai Electronics Industries, 27

I

IBC (International Benchmarking Clearinghouse), 508
Impacto
ambiental, 37
sobre os empregados, 38
Implementação de automação, 161
Incentivos, localização de instalações e, 184
Incerteza, LEC e, 299
Indicador de antecipação, 66
Índice
crítico, 388
de capabilidade do processo, 504
zero defeito, 492
Industrial Engineering, 151
Indústria(s)
aeronáuticas, automação na, 153
automobilística, 31
de atendimento à saúde, automação na, 153
de caixas econômicas, automação na, 153
de serviços, 13
financeiros, automação na, 153
de venda a varejo e no atacado, automação nas, 153
Informação e análise, 496
Inspeção, visão tradicional da, 491
Instalação(ões)
administração da qualidade total e, 498, 504
de manufatura leves, localização de, 183
de venda a varejo, localizações para, 185
passeios por, 124
qualidade e, 504
Instrumentos de compra, 433
Insumo(s), 14
de pedidos, 255
de materiais, processo de aquisição para, 434
de mercado, 15
externos, 14

Integração vertical, 104
    regressiva e progressiva, 440
Intel Corporation, 84
Intercalação, 132, 475
Interesse próprio, 36
International Benchmarking Clearinghouse (IBC), 508
International Business Machines (IBM), 257
Intervalo
    de pedido ótimo, 293
    de previsão, 66
    de previsões de séries temporais, 66
Ishikawa, Kaoru, 493
ISO 9000, padrões, 497
Item final, 314

J

Jennings, Peter, 506
Job shops
    definição de, 108
    focalizadas no processo, 108
    manufatura just-in-time e, 261
    metalurgia, 109
    programando a manufatura focalizada no processo e, 341
    versus manufatura celular e, 108
Johnson, S. M., 352
Joint ventures, alianças estratégicas, 27
Juran, Joseph M., 494
Justificação de processos de automação, 158

K

Kanban, 413
Keiretsu, 28
Kentucky Fried Chicken (KFC), 489
Kim, Jay S., 49
Kuttner, Robert, 27

L

Landry, Sylvian, 417
Lawrence Livermore National Laboratory, 28
Layouts
    de instalações
        analisando, 222
        análise computadorizada de, 209
        análise da distância da carga, 207
        análise de, 203
        análise de diagrama de blocos, 205
        definição de, 197
        desenvolvendo, classificações de proximidade, 222
    de serviço, 221
    de processo, 199
    de produtos, 200
        definição de, 200
        planejamento, 209
    funcionais. Veja Layouts de processo
    híbridos, 201, 202
    modernos, 201
    novas tendências de, 201
    objetivos dos, 198
    para instalações de manufatura, 197
    para manufatura celular, 200
    para operações de serviço, 221
    posição fixa, 201, 202
    tipos de, 221
    tradicionais versus modernos, 203
LDR (regra de decisão linear), 249
Lead time (LT), 282
    constante e demanda normalmente distribuída por dia, 289
    cumulativo de item final, 257
    de manufatura, elevando capacidades de produção e, 408
LEC. Veja Lote econômico de compra (LEC)
Leschke, John P., 419
LFL (lote por lote), 256
Liberação de pedidos programados, 330
Liderança, 496
Linha(s)
    automatizada de fluxo, 147
    de balanceamento (LOB), para programas de entrega, 358
    de montagem, 107
    de produção
        análise, terminologia para, 210
        balanceamento de linha, 209
        em forma de U, 203
Lippert, John, 461
Lista(s)
    de materiais, 314, 318
    de remessa, 344
    estruturada de materiais, 314, 318
    modulada de materiais, 327
    Q-1, 504
L. L. Bean, 69
LOB (linha de balanceamento), 358
Localização das instalações
    análise da
        decisão para, 180
        fatores de determinação para, 179
        para operações industriais, 187
        para operações de venda a varejo e serviços, 185
    dados para, 184
    doméstica, 179
    dominante, para diferentes tipos de instalações, 181
    fatores qualitativos, 188
    fatores quantitativos, 188
    importância relativa da, 183
    incentivos e, 184
    política e, 184
    problemas com, 187
    tática de preempção e, 184
Logística
    administração de materiais e, 429, 440
    controle de produção, 439
    inovações na, 441
Lote(s), 516
    de produção, 271, 276, 356
    econômico de compra (LEC), 272
        definição de, 272
    incerteza e, 299
    modelo I, 274
    modelo II, 276
    modelo III, 277, 280
    modelo IV, 292
    tamanhos de lote de produção, 276, 356
    por lote (LFL), 256
LP. Veja Programação linear (LP)

M

Malcolm Baldrige, Prêmio Nacional da Qualidade, 495
Maney, Kevin, 157
Manufatura
    auxiliada por computador (CAM), 33, 151
    celular
        definição, 108
        layouts, 200
        planejamento da, 218
        repetitiva e, 420
        versus job shops, 109
    flexibilidade de, 157
    integrada por computador (CIM), 152
    de fábricas do futuro, 153
    JIT. Veja Manufatura just-in-time (manufatura JIT)
    just-in-time (manufatura JIT), 32, 261
        administração da qualidade total e, 412
        benefícios da, 420
        compras e, 416, 439
        controle de produção Kanban e, 413
        eliminação do desperdício e, 410
        fabricantes de classe mundial e, 423
        filosofia da, 406
        manufatura repetitiva e, 419
        na IPS, 405
        operações bem-sucedidas
            fatores em, 422
            pessoal e, 412
        processamento paralelo e, 412
        qualidade e, 495
        redução de estoques e, 411, 417
        requisito indispensável para, 409
        sistemas puxar e, 260
    objetivos do layout de operações para, 201
    por processo, 107
    repetitiva, sistema, 419
    síncrona, 261, 362
Manuseio de materiais
    equipamento para, 199
    sistemas, 198
Manutenção preventiva, qualidade e, 495
Mão-de-obra
    direta, 459
    especialização ou divisão da, 7
Máquina(s)
    anexos de, 144
    com flexibilidade de manufatura, 157
    de armazenamento e recuperação (máquina S/R), 150

de controle numérico (máquinas NC), 144
de dobrar e perfurar, 130
de dosagem da mistura de ignição, 130
de enrolar tubos, 128
de preenchimento, 129
NC (máquinas de controle numérico), 144
para misturar produtos químicos, 126, 128
S/R (máquina de armazenamento e recuperação), 150
Markland, R. E., 187
Maslow, A. H., 463
Maslow, Abraham, 11
Materiais
　classificação ABC de, 298
　com demanda irregular, 299
　com lead times irregulares, 299
　com vida mais breve na prateleira, 459
　críticos para a produção, 299
　definição de, 427
　grandes e volumosos, 299
　medições da produtividade e, 459
　movimento com fábricas, 439
　sujeitos a roubo, 299
Mayo, Elton, 11
McDonald's, 13, 36, 186
McGregor, Douglas, 11
Meal, H. C., 324
Mechanical Engineering, 493
Média
　móvel exponencialmente ponderada, 75
　tecnologia, 155
Medição do trabalho
　padrões de mão-de-obra e, 469
　métodos de, 467
Medida(s)
　absolutas, 176
　de tempo, 477
　relativas, 176
Melhoria contínua
　administração da qualidade total e, 508
　na manufatura just-in-time, 410
Mercadorias
　que chegam, 134
　que saem, 135
Método(s)
　da média móvel, 58, 72
　da média ponderada móvel, 58, 74
　de embarque, inovações nos, 442
　Delphi, 56
　de previsão qualitativos, 55, 57
　de previsão quantitativos, 57
　do caminho crítico (CPM), 535
　　avaliação do, 554
　　etapas no, 538
　　rede para o, 538
　　sistema de administração da informação para, 537
　　visão que os gerentes têm do, 537
　do esgotamento (run-out), de programação da produção, 356, 357
　do intervalo padrão (método POQ), 324
　do lote por lote, 323

heurístico, para balanceamento de linha, 211
POQ (método do intervalo padrão), 324
Miller, Jeffrey G., 49
Minutos-trabalhador por unidade de produção, 469
Mitrofanov, S. P., 108
Modelo(s), 203
　de estoque, 294
　　básico, 294
　　de período único, 294
　de filas
　　canal único, fase única, 382
　　definições de variáveis para, 382
　　fórmulas para, 382, 383
　　terminologia e estrutura dos, 381
　de previsão causais, 60
　do centro de gravidade, 186
　matemáticos, para o planejamento agregado, 248
　opcional de renovação de estoque, 294
Modificações em pedidos programados, 315
Modigliani, Franco, 249
Motivação, 463
Motivadores, 463
Motoarc, 427
Motor a vapor, 7
Motorola, 99, 507
Movimento
　das relações humanas, 11
　e esforço, 411
MPS. *Veja* Programa mestre de produção (MPS)
MRP
　I (planejamento dos recursos de manufatura), 327
　II (planejamento dos recursos de manufatura), 327
　regenerativo, 326
　Veja também Planejamento das necessidades de materiais (MRP)
MTBF (tempo médio entre as falhas), 500
MTM (medida de tempo), 477
Mudança tecnológica, administrando, 159
Muth, John F., 249

N

NAFTA (Acordo de Livre Comércio da América do Norte), 25, 38
National Association of Purchasing Managers (NAPM), 438
National Institute of Standards and Technology, 496
National Semiconductor Corporation, 29
Necessidades
　brutas, 322
　de capital
　　para automação, 161
　　para projetos de processo, 118
　de tempo, para decisões quanto à implementação da automação, 161
Negócios globais, natureza mutável dos, 25
New Generation Computers (NGC), 235
New York Times, 29, 116, 437
NGC (New Generation Computers), 235

Nível(is)
　de estrutura de produto, 319
　de serviço
　　estoque de segurança e, 286
　　definindo pontos de pedido e, 285
　　ótimo de estoque de segurança, 282
Novos empreendimentos, previsão em, 85
Número
　de estações de trabalho em funcionamento, 210
　de produtos a programar, 256
　médio de tarefas no sistema, 347
　mínimo de estações de trabalho, 210
　real de estações de trabalho na análise da linha de produção, 210

O

O melhor
　da classe, 490
　nível operacional, 172
Occupational Safety & Health Administration Act (OSHA), 36
Olin Corporation, 83
Operação(ões)
　com mão-de-obra intensiva, 32
　de armazém, layouts das instalações de, 204
　de entrada (gateway), 238
　de preparo de chapas de impressão, 131
　de prova de chapas de impressão, 131
　de serviços
　　automação em, 155
　　controle de qualidade para, 523
　　de quase-manufatura, 371, 373
　　　descrição de, 114
　　　focalizadas no processo, 375
　　　focalizadas no produto, 373
　　　programação, 373
　　　programação do turno de trabalho nas, 375
　　estratégias de operações para, 371
　　estratégias de posicionamento para, 45
　　gargalo, 237, 261
　　instalações de operações, localizações para, 185
　　layouts de instalações, objetivos, 198
　　natureza das, 369
　　novas, projetando e desenvolvendo, 98, 101
　　passeio pelas instalações, 130
　　planos agregados para, 245
　　prioridades competitivas para, 45
　　programação
　　　demanda não uniforme e, 372
　　　desafios da, 372
　　　filas de espera em, 380
　　　tipos de, 371
　　projetando e desenvolvendo, 97
　　projeto de processo em, 114
　　que têm o cliente como participante
　　　descrições de, 115, 371
　　　filas de espera nas, 380
　　　natureza das, 379
　　　programação nas, 372, 379

que têm o cliente como produto
  descrição das, 116, 371
  natureza das, 388
  programação para, 388
  simulação computadorizada nas, 390
Ordens de compra, 435
Organização de projeto, 529, 530
Orlicky, Joseph, 324,
Outsourcing estratégico, 105

P

P&D (pesquisa e desenvolvimento), 181
Padrões
  de demanda do cliente, 377
  de mão-de-obra
    definição, 472
      com medidas de tempo, 477
      com estudo do tempo, 473
      com amostragem do trabalho, 474
      históricos, 478
  de tamanho da equipe, 478
  de tempo predeterminados, 476
  sazonais, 66
Padronização, 101
  de produto, qualidade e, 495
Parâmetros, em simulação computadorizada, 391
Parcerias com o fornecedor, desenvolvimento de, qualidade e, 504
Parceiros, 416
Passeio pelas instalações
  de uma fábrica dedicada, 124
  de uma fábrica focalizada no processo, 130
  de operações de serviço, 133
Patillo, Linda, 506
PDQ (Projeto de Qualidade Perfeita, Pretty Darn Quick), 498
Peças intercambiáveis, 8
Pedidos, 134
  de cotação, 434
  programados, mudanças em, 315
PEPS (primeiro a entrar, primeiro a ser atendido), 347
Pequenos negócios, previsão em, 85
Percepção e avaliação de mercado, 98
Período(s)
  de congelamento, 250
  pós-Gerra Civil, 8
PERT. *Veja* Técnica de avaliação e revisão de programa (PERT)
PERT/CPM, 12
PERT/Custo, 548
Pesquisa(s)
  aplicada, 98
  básica, 98
  da equipe de vendas, 56
  de clientes, 56,
  de mercado, 56
  e desenvolvimento (P&D), 181
  operacional, 11
Pessoal. *Veja também* Empregado(s)
  com trabalho em tempo parcial, 391
Planejamento

agregado
  compensando com estoque e, 240
  compensando com pedidos em carteira (backlog) e, 243
  critérios de seleção para, 245
  demanda agregada e, 237
  dimensões da capacidade de produção e, 237
  fontes de capacidade de produção de médio prazo e, 238
  modelos matemáticos de, 248
  na Quick Cargo Air Freight Company, 247
  nível de capacidade, 240
  nível de capacidade com trabalho em horas extras ou subcontratação e, 241, 245, 246
  para a Sherman-Brown Chemical Company, 237, 238, 242
  para serviços, 245
  passos no, 237
  táticas de preempção para, 249
  tradicional, 239
computadorizado do layout da relação (CORELAP), 209
da pré-produção, 113, 342
  atividades dos gerentes de operações para, 236
  curto prazo, 236
  longo prazo, 236
  médio prazo, 236
das instalações, 169
  para capacidade de produção de longo prazo, 43
  previsão e, 55
das necessidades de capacidade (CRP), 330
  administração de materiais e, 429
  definição de, 330
  hierarquia da capacidade de carga, 333
  job shops e, 341
  processo de, 329
  programas de carga e, 330
das necessidades de distribuição (DRP), 440
das necessidades de materiais (MRP)
  adaptações a mudanças, 328
  avaliação do, 329
  características do sistema de produção para, 329
  definição do tamanho de lote no, 323
  efeito do carregamento sobre as capacidades do centro de trabalho, 332
  elementos do sistema, 313
  em empresas de montagem sob encomenda, 327
  estoque de segurança e, 326
  exemplo de, 316
  filosofia do, 403
  implementação de, 329
  job shops e, 341
  loop fechado, 327
  mudança líquida *versus* regenerativo, 326
  níveis de estoque de matérias-primas *versus* lote padrão e ponto de pedido 312

níveis reduzidos de estoque e, 309
objetivos do, 312
programa de computador para, 315
programa para, 321
questões no, 325
saídas do, 315
tipo I, 327
tipo II, 327
de estoques
  computadores e, 300
  dinâmica do, 299
  fatores no, 300
  sob incerteza, 282
de loop fechado das necessidades de materiais, 327
do processo, 103
dos recursos de distribuição, 441
dos recursos de manufatura (MRPI e MRPII), 328
dos recursos empresariais (ERP), 152, 328
e controle do chão de fábrica, 343
  carga finita e, 345
  gráficos de Gantt e, 345
  programação progressiva e, 346
  programação retrógrada e, 346
estratégico da qualidade, 496
layouts de manufatura celular, 218
Plano(s)
  de demanda coincidente, 239
  de determinação do roteiro, 330, 342
  de pagamento de incentivo grupal, 472
  de produto/serviço, 42
  mestre, para automação, 159
  tecnológicos, 43
Plataformas giratórias, para manuseio de materiais, 199
PM. *Veja* Manutenção preventiva
Polaroid, 35
Política(s)
  de estoques
    pontos de vista conflitantes da, 269
    projeto de processo e, 113
    projeto de produto e, 113
  localização de instalações e, 184
Ponderação de dados passados, na exponencial móvel, 80
Ponto(s)
  de coleta, 150
  de depósito, 150
  de pedido
    definição de, 272
    definindo nos níveis de serviço, 285
    determinação de, 279
    princípios básicos para, 290
  viragem, 60
Pontuações Z, 395
Porcentagem
  de demanda esperada
    durante o lead time, 290
  de utilização da capacidade, 171
Porter, Michael E., 24
Posicionando o sistema de produção, 40
PP. *Veja* Pontos de pedido
Precedência de tarefa, 210

Índice Analítico

Precisão da previsão, 57
Preços
   com desconto, 249
   de pico, 249
Prensas de impressão, 131
Prevendo a demanda por capacidade, 171
Previsão(ões)
   atenuação de ruído e, 82
   chamadas telefônicas, na L. L. Bean, 69
   custos e, 81
   dados disponíveis e, 81
   de amortecimento exponencial
      com tendência, 58, 75
      exemplo de, 75
      fórmulas e definições de variáveis para, 75
      versus demanda real de capital, 74
   de curto prazo, 68
      amortecimento exponencial e, 74
      definição de, 68
      ingênuas, 72
      intervalo de tempo para, 82
      medidas da precisão, 71
      método da média móvel para, 72
      método da média ponderada móvel para, 74
      modelos para, avaliando o desempenho de, 68
   definição de, 54
   de longo prazo, 55
      ciclos e, 59
      decisões em, 56
      fabricantes de classe mundial e, 86
      intervalo de tempo para, 59
      intervalos, 66
      padrões de dados em, 59
      regressão linear e correlações para, 60
      sazonalidade e, 59
      tendências e, 59
   de médio prazo, 55
   de série temporal, sazonalidade, 66
   de vendas, 54
   de vendas de sinalizadores na Olin Corporation, 82, 83
   do foco, 83
   em empresas de produção para estoque, 256
   em novos empreendimentos, 85
   em pequenos negócios, 85
   ineficaz, razões para, 81
   ingênuas, 72
   intervalo de tempo e, 82
   métodos qualitativos, 55
   métodos, seleção de, 81
   modelos de, monitorando e controlando, 82
   modelos quantitativos, 57
   natureza de produtos/serviços e, 82
   no planejamento dos negócios, 54
   precisão da, 81
   resposta ao impulso e, 82
   sistemas bem-sucedidos para, 81
   software e, 85
Primeira data de início, 533, 544
Primeira data de término, 533, 541

Primeiro a entrar, primeiro a ser atendido (PEPS), 347, 350
Principles & Standards of Purchasing Practice, 438
Prioridades competitivas, 343
   de produção, 39
   em empresas americanas em futuras estratégias de negócios, 49
   estratégia de posicionamento e, 45
   para serviços, 45
Problema(s)
   de designação, 354
   de produção
      custos de, estoques e, 271
      desvendando, ao reduzir estoques, 411
   de seqüenciamento de pedidos, 347
      controlando custos de preparação, 350
      minimizando o tempo total de produção, 352
      seqüenciando tarefas através de dois centros de trabalho, 352
   de transbordo, 187
   de transporte, 187
   do jornaleiro, 294
Processamento paralelo, manufatura just-in-time e, 412
Processo(s)
   de banho de cera, 130
   de planejamento, layouts de armazém e, 204
   de produção
      capacidade de qualidade dos, 490
      controlando, para obter qualidade, 500, 503
      exemplos, 103
      projetando, para obter qualidade, 503
      projeto de, qualidade e, 500
      software, 554
      tipos de, 371
   de secagem de papel, 131
Produção
   como função organizacional, 16
   como sistema, 14
   contínua, 107, 354
   custo da coordenação de, estoques e, 271
   definição de, 5
   desnecessária, 411
   de unidades discretas, 107
   em equipe, 465
   em lote, 354
   em massa, 11
   fluxo de linha de, 41, 107
   focalizada, 175
   focalizada no processo
      características da, 341
      descrição da, 108
      estratégia operacional e, 41
      passeio pelas instalações de, 130
      programação para, 341
      quase-manufatura e, 375
      sistema do estoque de reserva e, 259
   focalizada no produto
      características da, 354
      decisões quanto à programação, 354
      descrição da, 41, 107
      implicações da programação de, 354

      operações de semimanufatura, 373
   foco da, 41
   prioridades competitivas de, 39
   projeto de produto para, 500
Produtividade
   comportamento humano e, 458
   definição de, 458
   fabricantes de classe mundial, 482
   mão-de-obra, 460
      variáveis na, 462
   medição da, abordagem de múltiplos fatores à, 459
   melhoria na Ford Motor Company, 461
   necessidades dos empregados e, 463, 464
   qualidade e, 494
Produto(s), 15
   colocando mais rapidamente no mercado, 99
   defeituosos
      controle da qualidade e, 516
      detecção de, 491
      eliminação de desperdício e, 410
      em mãos dos clientes, 491
      em amostras, gráfico de controle para, 518
   diretos, 15
   indiretos, 15
   intangíveis, 15
   interno bruto, 25, 460
   manufaturados
      características dos, 43
      serviços e, 43
   não defeituoso, 516
   novo, desenvolvimento de, 97
   padrões, 40
   padronizados, 40
   perfeito e qualidade de serviço, 30
   personalizados, 40
   projetando e desenvolvendo, 97
Programa(s)
   automatizado de projeto de layout (ALDEP), 209
   de benefício aos empregados, 38
   de carga, 330
   de entrega, método da linha de balanceamento, 358
   de entregas de pedidos aos clientes, das fábricas do futuro, 153
   de montagem final, 327
   de produção estáveis, 409
   de produção nivelada, 409
   de reciclagem, 36
   de treinamento de funcionários, 505
   de treinamento, para mudança de cargo de trabalhadores, 160
   mestre de produção (MPS)
      administração da demanda e, 255
      atualização semanal do, 255
      computadorizado, 257
      congelado, 250
      da empresa, 250
      definição de, 235, 249, 313
      em empresas de produção para estoque, 256
      em empresa de produção sob encomenda, 256

estimativas da demanda e, 256
exemplo de, 318
extensão de horizontes de planejamento de, 257
objetivos do, 250
planejamento das necessdades de materiais e, 310
procedimentos de desenvolvimento, 250
tempos de congelamento e, 250
Programação
de manufatura focalizada no processo, 341
de manufatura focalizada no produto, 354
de pedidos, 315, 322, 323
desafios de, nos serviços, 372
do turno de trabalho, em operações de serviço de quase-manufatura, 375
em lote, 356
em operações focalizadas no processo, 342
em operações que têm o cliente como participante, 379
gráficos de controle e, 532
linear inteira, 352
linear (LP), 352
problemas de seqüenciamento de pedidos, 347
programas de entrega, 358
progressiva, 346
regressiva, 346
serviços com operação que tem o cliente como produto, 388
sistemas computadorizados de programação, 361
Projeto(s)
auxiliado por computador (CAD), 33, 151
de funções, 464
de processo
alternativas
análise de break-even de, 121
análise financeira do, 123
alavancagem operacional e, 120
focalizado no produto, 107
gráficos de montagem e, 124, 125
gráficos de processo e, 124
análise econômica do, 118
decisões, 104
necessidades de capital para, 118
nos serviços, 114
política de estoques e, 113
projeto de produto e, 113
tipos de, 107
de produção, 98
de produto
existente, melhoria de, 100
padrão, 113
para obter qualidade, 102
para facilidade de produção, 101
política de estoque e, 113
simplificação, 101
sistema automatizado de montagem para, 148

parâmetro de, 500
protótipo, 98
qualidade de, 490
RATS (Rocket Aerial Target System), 534, 535
robusto, 500
Promessa de entrega do pedido, 255
Propriedade interna, 467
Provedores de administração da logística de terceiros, 447
Pulmão (armazenamento temporário), 262

Q

QFD (desdobramento da função da qualidade), 499
Qualidade
adequada, 30
custos da, 490
de produto
decisões quanto à automação e, 150
de fábricas do futuro, 153
fábricas americanas e, 30
sistemas automatizados de armazenamento e recuperação e, 150
determinantes da, 490
desdobramento da função (QFD), 499
dimensões da, 489
equipamentos automatizados e, 495
manutenção preventiva e, 495
na fonte, 493
natureza da, 489
padrões, emergentes, 495
padronização de produto e, 495
produtividade e, 494
produto/serviço, 106
projeto de produto para, 102
Quantidades pedidas, 272, 274
Questões de responsabilidade social
impacto sobre os empregados, 38
impacto ambiental, 37
Quick Cargo Air Freight Company, 247

R

Raiz quadrada da EDDLT, 291
RAMOV, projeto
administração do, 538
análise da técnica de avaliação e revisão de programa, 545
Reciclagem
de papel, 36
de plástico, 36
Recursos
de produção
capacidade de. *Veja* Capacidade de produção
disponibilidade de, 237
escassez de, 34
primários, 15
Redes
de subcontratados, 175, 416
de subcontratados e fornecedores, 175
Redução
capacidade de longo prazo, 172

da preparação, reduzindo estoques através da, 417
Reengenharia de processo, 117
Reequilibrando uma linha de balanceamento, 209
Reestruturação de empregos, 32
Registro
de estoque, 273, 444
de materiais, 315
Regra(s)
de decisão linear (LDR), 249
de seqüenciamento, 347
avaliação de, 347
comparação de, 347
critérios de avaliação para, 347
heurística do turno de trabalho, 378
Regressão passo a passo, 66
Regulamentação governamental, 36
Regulamentos e taxas, 440
Relações, com o fornecedor, 416
Relatório(s)
da situação de estoque, 319
de controle de entrada e saída, 344
de exceção, 316
de planejamento, 316
sobre o desempenho, 316
Renovação de estoque, 294
Requisição
ao estoque, 443
de compra, 434
Reserva de capacidade, 171
Resolução de problemas, imposição de, 410
Resposta ao impulso e atenuação de ruído, 82
Restrições (TOC), teoria das, 261
Retornos, 159
Retrabalho, 490
Retreinamento de trabalhadores, 32, 160
Revolução
dos serviços, 12
Industrial, 7
Reynolds Metals, 35
Riqueza das nações, A, 7
Risco de stockouts, 282
Robôs, 144
Robótica, 144
Roethlisberger, F. J., 11
R. R. Donnelley & Sons, 130
ROI (custo do retorno sobre o investimento), 271
Ruído, 58, 71

S

Safety Products Corporation, passeio pelas instalações, 124
San Antonio Express-News, 437
Satisfação do cliente
administração da qualidade total e, 504
capacidade de qualidade da, 490
fabricantes americanos e, 30
qualidade e, 504
Sazonalidade, 58
SC Corporation, 309
Scheduling Technology Group Ltd., 262, 362

Índice Analítico

Scientific American, 149
Sematech, 28
Sensores
 de proximidade, 146
 de visão de máquina, 146
 óticos, 146
 táteis, 146
Seqüência
 de construção, 430
 de tarefa, custos de preparação e, 351
Série temporal, 57
Setor de serviços, crescimento contínuo do, 34
Sherman-Brown Chemical Company
 capacidade nivelada, 242, 244
 planejamento agregado, capacidade nivelada com horas extras ou subcontratação, 246
 plano agregado com demanda coincidente da, 239
Shostack, G. Lynn, 116
Silver, Edward, 324
Simon, Herbert A., 249
Simplificação
 de projeto, 502
 de projeto de produtos, 101
Simulação computadorizada, 176
 avaliação da, 398
 exemplo de, 392
 problemas, características de, 390
 procedimentos de, 391
Sinal de rastreamento, 84
Sindicatos trabalhistas, 465
Sistema(s). *Veja também* Sistemas específicos
 automáticos de identificação (AIS), 146
 automatizados
  de armazenamento e recuperação (ASRS), 150
  de inspeção do controle da qualidade, 146
  de manipulação e entrega de materiais, 150
  de montagem, 148
  de veículos (AGVS), 150
  razões para instalar, 150
 caseiro, 7
 computadorizados de programação, 361
 de armazenamento e recuperação em armazéns, 150
 de canal único e fase única, 382
 de codificação, para tecnologia de grupo, 109
 de comunicação, em sistemas automatizados de armazenamento e recuperação, 150
 de controle
  da produção, 257
  de custo do programas, 548
  de distribuição, 440
  de duas gavetas, 273
 de estoque
  do intervalo padrão, 292
  do lote padrão, 272
  definição, 14

de informação de assuntos administrativos, para administração do caminho crítico, 547
de inventário
 permanente de estoques, 273, 444
 periódico de estoques, 444
de manufatura
 fixa, 157
 flexível (FMS), 148
de montagem, automatizados, 149
de múltiplas fases, 382
de pagamento de incentivo, 472
de partes intercambiáveis, 101
de planejamento
 da produção, 257
 das necessidades de capacidade, 330
 das necessidades de materiais com mudança líquida (MRP), 326
 das necessidades de recursos, fluxo grama para, 311
 e projeto de processo, 103
de planejamento e controle da produção focalizados em gargalos, 261
 tipos de
  sistemas do estoque de reserva, 259
  sistemas puxar, 260
  sistemas empurrar, 259
de produção, 9
 automatizados, 147
 com flexibilidade de manufatura, 157
 definição de, 14
 diversidade, 16
 exemplos, 33
 modelo de, 15
 posicionamento de, 40
 típico, 17
de produção para estoque
 estratégia de posicionamento e, 45
 fluxograma de, 112
 política de, 41
 programa mestre de produção e, 256
de produção sob encomenda
 estratégia de posicionamento e, 45
 fluxograma de, 115
 política de, 41
 programa mestre de produção e, 256
 tipos de montagem sob encomenda de, 327
do intervalo padrão, 292
do lote padrão, 272
empurrar, 259
especialista de previsão, usando na Xerox Corporation, 80
fabril, 7
multicanal, 382
produção como um, 14
puxar, 260, 413
transportador/classificador, 135
Skinner, Wickham, 41
SKU (unidade de manutenção de estoque), 444
Smith, Adam, 7
Smith, Bernard, 83
Smithsonian, 493

Software
 administração da cadeia de suprimentos, 443
 localização de pontos, para o McDonald's, 186
 para previsão, 85
 planejamento das necessidades de materiais, 315
Soldagem com robótica, 146
Stockout, 281
Subcarga, 253
Subcontratação, 239
Subsistema
 de controle, 15
 de transformação, 15, 17
Sucata, 490
Superprodução, 411
Supervisão de produção, descrição de trabalho/obrigações de, 6

T

Tabela(s)
 de custos esperados, 282, 295
 de números aleatórios, 396
Taco Bell, 391
Taguchi, Genichi, 494
Tamanho(s)
 da fila, 382
 de lote
  decisões quanto a, 324
  definição de, 272
  de produção, 271
  em empresas de produção para estoque, 256
  grandes, vantagens de, 323
  mínimos, 323
  pequenos, vantagens de, 323
  variedade de produto e, 117
Tamanho do veículo, 299
Tambor, 262
 -pulmão-corda, 362
Tapando e dobrando tubos, 128
Tarefas, 210
Táticas de preempção, 184, 249
Taxa(s)
 de câmbio da moeda, 28
 de câmbio japonesas, 29
 de chegada, 382
 de serviço, 382
 de suprimento (p), 276
Taylor, Alex, III, 461
Taylor, Frederick Winslow, 8
TBC. *Veja* Competição baseada no tempo (TBC)
TCQ (controle da qualidade total), 633
Técnica(s)
 de avaliação e revisão de programa (PERT), 545
  na prática, 549
 de busca computadorizada, 249
 de planejamento e controle de projeto, 532
 matemáticas complexas, 12
Tecnologia

de grupo, 108
de grupo/manufatura celular (GT/CM), 108
de produção
  avançada, 32
  otimizada (OPT), 262
Tempo(s)
  de ciclo, 210
  de elemento observados, 473
  de espera, 382
  de preparação, manufatura just-in-time e, 418
  de processamento mais breve, 347, 350
  de serviço, 382
  de tarefa, 210
  mais provável, 545
  médio de fluxo, 347
  médio observado, 473
  médio entre as falhas (MTBF), 500
  no sistema, 382
  normal do elemento, 473
  otimista (para), 545
  pessimista, 545
  produtivo por hora, 210
  total de produção, minimização do, 352
  total normal, 473
Tendências, 58
Teorema do limite central, controle da qualidade e, 516
Teoria
  das filas, 381
  das restrições (TOC), 261, 361
Testes de mercado, 57
The Goal: A Process of Ongoing Improvement, 262
Themens, Jean-Luc, 417
Throughput, 262
Toffler, Alvim, 27
Tolerâncias, 101
Tomada de decisões, na APO, 16

Toyota, 461
TQM (administração da qualidade total), 498
Trabalhadores. *Veja* Empregado(s)
Trabalho
  em horas extras, 239
  em horas normais, 239
Trafton, Linda L., 181
Transportadores para manuseio de materiais, 199
Transporte
  decisões quanto à localização das instalações e, 179
  de materiais nos serviços, 439
  eliminação do desperdício na manufatura e, 410
Treinamento multifuncional, 464
3M, 35
Tribus, Myron, 493
Tubulações, para manuseio de materiais, 199

U

UAW (United Auto Workers), 461
UE (União Européia), 25
Última data de início, 533, 544
Última data de término, 533, 543
União Européia (UE), 25
Unidade
  agregada de capacidade, 170
  de manutenção de estoque (SKU), 444
Union Carbide, 35
United Auto Workers (UAW), 461
USA Today, 26, 36, 145, 157, 173
Utilização
  alta capacidade, competição baseada no tempo e, 407
  em filas, 382
  na análise da linha de produção, 210

V

Valor esperado, como critério de decisão, 176
Variação
  da variável dependente, 64
  explicada, 64
  não explicada, 64
  total, 64
Variáveis
  definição de, 516
  gráficos de controle para, 521
Variedade de produto, tamanho de lote e, 117
Vice-presidente de materiais, 429
Visão de máquina e sensores óticos, 146

W

Wagner, H. M., 324
Wagner, Harvey, 187
Wall Street Journal, 27, 29, 35, 300, 421, 442, 461
Wal-Mart, 27, 133
Watt, James, 7
Wei, J. C., 201
Wheelwright, Steven C., 46
Whitehead, T. N., 11
Whitin, T. M., 324
Whitney, Eli, 8
Whyco Chromium, 35
Wight, Oliver, 327
W. R. Grace, 35

X

Xerox Corporation, 36, 80, 508

Z

Zeithaml, Valarie A., 509
Zysman, John, 34

TABELAS

Áreas sob a Curva Normal

Distribuição de Probabilidades *t* de Student

TABELA 1 — ÁREAS SOB A CURVA NORMAL

Z	00	0,01	0,02	0,03	0,04	0,05	0,06	0,07	0,08	0,09
0,0	0,50000	0,50399	0,50798	0,51197	0,51595	0,51994	0,52392	0,52790	0,53188	0,53586
0,1	0,53983	0,54380	0,54776	0,55172	0,55567	0,55962	0,56356	0,56749	0,57142	0,57535
0,2	0,57926	0,58317	0,58706	0,59095	0,59483	0,59871	0,60257	0,60642	0,61026	0,61409
0,3	0,61791	0,62172	0,62552	0,62930	0,63307	0,63683	0,64058	0,64431	0,64803	0,65173
0,4	0,65542	0,65910	0,66276	0,66640	0,67003	0,67364	0,67724	0,68082	0,68439	0,68793
0,5	0,69146	0,69497	0,69847	0,70194	0,70540	0,70884	0,71226	0,71566	0,71904	0,72240
0,6	0,72575	0,72907	0,73237	0,73536	0,73891	0,74215	0,74537	0,74857	0,75175	0,75490
0,7	0,75804	0,76115	0,76424	0,76730	0,77035	0,77337	0,77637	0,77935	0,78230	0,78524
0,8	0,78814	0,79103	0,79389	0,79673	0,79955	0,80234	0,80511	0,80785	0,81057	0,81327
0,9	0,81594	0,81859	0,82121	0,82381	0,82639	0,82894	0,83147	0,83398	0,83646	0,83891
1,0	0,84134	0,84375	0,84614	0,84849	0,85083	0,85314	0,85543	0,85769	0,85993	0,86214
1,1	0,86433	0,86650	0,86864	0,87076	0,87286	0,87493	0,87698	0,87900	0,88100	0,88298
1,2	0,88493	0,88686	0,88877	0,89065	0,89251	0,89435	0,89617	0,89796	0,88973	0,90147
1,3	0,90320	0,90490	0,90658	0,90824	0,90988	0,91149	0,91309	0,91466	0,91621	0,91774
1,4	0,91924	0,92073	0,92220	0,92364	0,92507	0,92647	0,92785	0,92922	0,93056	0,93189
1,5	0,93319	0,93448	0,93574	0,93699	0,93822	0,93943	0,94062	0,94179	0,94295	0,94408
1,6	0,94520	0,94630	0,94738	0,94845	0,94950	0,95053	0,95154	0,95254	0,95352	0,95449
1,7	0,95543	0,95637	0,95728	0,95818	0,95907	0,95994	0,96080	0,96164	0,96246	0,96327
1,8	0,96407	0,96485	0,96562	0,96638	0,96712	0,96784	0,96856	0,96926	0,96995	0,97062
1,9	0,97128	0,97193	0,97257	0,97320	0,97381	0,97441	0,97500	0,97558	0,97615	0,97670
2,0	0,97725	0,97784	0,97831	0,97882	0,97932	0,97982	0,98030	0,98077	0,98124	0,98169
2,1	0,98214	0,98257	0,98300	0,98341	0,98382	0,98422	0,98461	0,98500	0,98537	0,98574
2,2	0,98610	0,98645	0,98679	0,98713	0,98745	0,98778	0,98809	0,98840	0,98870	0,98899
2,3	0,98928	0,98956	0,98983	0,99010	0,99036	0,99061	0,99086	0,99111	0,99134	0,99158
2,4	0,99180	0,99202	0,99224	0,99245	0,99266	0,99286	0,99305	0,99324	0,99343	0,99361
2,5	0,99379	0,99396	0,99413	0,99430	0,99446	0,99461	0,99477	0,99492	0,99506	0,99520
2,6	0,99534	0,99547	0,99560	0,99573	0,99585	0,99598	0,99606	0,99621	0,99632	0,99643
2,7	0,99653	0,99664	0,99674	0,99683	0,99693	0,99702	0,99711	0,99720	0,99728	0,99736
2,8	0,99744	0,99752	0,99760	0,99767	0,99774	0,99781	0,99788	0,99795	0,99801	0,99807
2,9	0,99813	0,99819	0,99825	0,99831	0,99836	0,99841	0,99846	0,99851	0,99856	0,99861
3,0	0,99865	0,99869	0,99874	0,99878	0,99882	0,99886	0,99889	0,99893	0,99896	0,99900
3,1	0,99903	0,99906	0,99910	0,99913	0,99916	0,99918	0,99921	0,99924	0,99926	0,99929
3,2	0,99931	0,99934	0,99936	0,99938	0,99940	0,99942	0,99944	0,99946	0,99948	0,99950
3,3	0,99952	0,99953	0,99955	0,99957	0,99958	0,99960	0,99961	0,99962	0,99964	0,99965
3,4	0,99966	0,99968	0,99969	0,99970	0,99971	0,99972	0,99973	0,99974	0,99975	0,99976
3,5	0,99977	0,99978	0,99978	0,99979	0,99980	0,99981	0,99981	0,99982	0,99983	0,99983
3,6	0,99984	0,99985	0,99985	0,99986	0,99986	0,99987	0,99987	0,99988	0,99988	0,99989
3,7	0,99989	0,99990	0,99990	0,99990	0,99991	0,99991	0,99992	0,99992	0,99992	0,99992
3,8	0,99993	0,99993	0,99993	0,99994	0,99994	0,99994	0,99994	0,99995	0,99995	0,99995
3,9	0,99995	0,99995	0,99996	0,99996	0,99996	0,99996	0,99996	0,99996	0,99997	0,99997

TABELA 2

DISTRIBUIÇÃO DE PROBABILIDADES t DE STUDENT

d.f.	0,9	0,8	0,7	0,6	0,5	0,4	0,3	0,2	0,1	0,05	0,02	0,01	0,001
1	0,158	0,325	0,510	0,727	1,000	1,376	1,963	3,078	6,314	12,706	31,821	63,657	636,619
2	0,142	0,289	0,445	0,617	0,816	1,061	1,386	1,886	2,910	4,303	6,965	9,925	31,598
3	0,137	0,277	0,424	0,584	0,765	0,978	1,250	1,638	2,353	30,182	4,541	5,841	12,941
4	0,134	0,271	0,414	0,569	0,741	0,941	1,190	1,533	2,132	2,776	3,747	4,604	8,610
5	0,132	0,267	0,408	0,559	0,727	0,920	1,156	1,476	2,015	2,571	3,365	4,032	6,859
6	0,131	0,265	0,404	0,553	0,718	0,906	1,134	1,440	1,943	2,447	3,143	3,707	5,959
7	0,130	0,263	0,402	0,549	0,711	0,896	1,119	1,415	1,895	2,365	2,998	3,499	5,405
8	0,130	0,262	0,399	0,546	0,706	0,889	1,108	1,397	1,860	2,306	2,896	3,355	5,041
9	0,129	0,261	0,398	0,543	0,703	0,883	1,100	1,383	1,833	2,262	2,821	3,250	4,781
10	0,129	0,260	0,397	0,542	0,700	0,879	1,093	1,372	1,812	2,228	2,764	3,169	4,587
11	0,129	0,260	0,396	0,540	0,697	0,876	1,088	1,363	1,796	2,201	2,718	3,106	4,437
12	0,128	0,259	0,395	0,539	0,695	0,873	1,083	1,356	1,782	2,179	2,681	3,055	4,318
13	0,128	0,259	0,394	0,538	0,694	0,870	1,079	1,350	1,771	2,160	2,650	3,012	4,221
14	0,128	0,258	0,393	0,537	0,692	0,868	1,076	1,345	1,761	2,145	2,624	2,977	4,140
15	0,128	0,258	0,393	0,536	0,691	0,866	1,074	1,341	1,753	2,131	2,602	2,947	4,073
16	0,128	0,258	0,392	0,535	0,690	0,865	1,071	1,337	1,746	2,120	2,583	2,921	4,015
17	0,128	0,257	0,392	0,534	0,689	0,863	1,069	1,333	1,740	2,110	2,567	2,898	3,965
18	0,127	0,257	0,392	0,534	0,688	0,862	1,067	1,330	1,734	2,101	2,552	2,878	3,922
19	0,127	0,257	0,391	0,533	0,688	0,861	1,066	1,328	1,729	2,093	2,539	2,861	3,883
20	0,127	0,257	0,391	0,533	0,687	0,860	1,064	1,325	1,725	2,086	2,528	2,845	3,850
21	0,127	0,257	0,391	0,532	0,686	0,859	1,063	1,323	1,721	2,080	2,518	2,831	3,819
22	0,127	0,256	0,390	0,532	0,686	0,858	1,061	1,321	1,717	2,074	2,508	2,819	3,792
23	0,127	0,256	0,390	0,532	0,685	0,858	1,060	1,319	1,714	2,069	2,500	2,807	3,767
24	0,127	0,256	0,390	0,531	0,685	0,857	1,059	1,318	1,711	2,064	2,492	2,797	3,745
25	0,127	0,256	0,390	0,531	0,684	0,856	1,058	1,316	1,708	2,060	2,485	2,787	3,725
26	0,127	0,256	0,390	0,531	0,684	0,856	1,058	1,315	1,706	2,056	2,479	2,779	3,707
27	0,127	0,256	0,389	0,531	0,684	0,855	1,057	1,314	1,703	2,052	2,473	2,771	3,690
28	0,127	0,256	0,389	0,530	0,683	0,855	1,056	1,313	1,701	2,048	2,467	2,763	3,674
29	0,127	0,256	0,389	0,530	0,683	0,854	1,055	1,311	1,699	2,045	2,462	2,756	3,659
30	0,127	0,256	0,389	0,530	0,683	0,854	1,055	1,310	1,697	2,042	2,457	2,750	3,646
40	0,126	0,255	0,388	0,529	0,681	0,851	1,050	1,303	1,684	2,021	2,423	2,704	3,551
60	0,126	0,254	0,387	0,527	0,679	0,848	1,046	1,296	1,671	2,000	2,390	2,660	3,460
128	0,126	0,254	0,386	0,526	0,677	0,845	1,041	1,289	1,658	1,980	2,358	2,617	3,373
∞	0,126	0,253	0,385	0,524	0,674	0,842	1,036	1,282	1,645	1,960	2,326	2,576	3,291

Fonte: Fisher e Yates: *Statistical Tables for Biological, Agricultural and Medical Research*, Longman Group Ltd., londres.

Community Redevelopment Agency of the City of Los Angeles (CRA L.A.), 220
Configurations, theatre, 9–11, 96–97
 overhead and rigging and, 98–99, 101
Connectors, 137
Consultants, theatre, 88–90, 105
Continental seating, 112
Control booth, 58, 107–108, 151
Conversion, 61, 131
 cost of, 54–55, 146, 152
Cooling, 122–123, 126, 146. See also Air conditioning
 energy efficiency and, 142–143
Cooperative costume shops, 136
Cornices, 50
Corporations, funding and, 75
Corridors, 159
 inspection of, 50
 means of egress and, 174
Costs
 of electrical installations, 140
 operational, 68
 of renovations. See Renovations, cost of
Costume Collection, The, 126, 136, 221
Costume shop, 19–20, 133
 checklist for, 126
Counterweight systems, 103–104
County Assessors (Chicago), 231
Courthouses, 38–39
Cowell Theater (San Francisco), 60–61, 64

D

Dead load, 160
Demand charges, 143
Department of Business Services Retention and Relocation Program (NYC), 221
Department of Buildings (Chicago), 230
Department of Buildings (NYC), 158, 226
 plans for, 190, 196
Department of Cultural Affairs, City of New York (DCA), 115, 134, 222

Department of Cultural Affairs, Cultural Development Division (Chicago), 219
Department of Finance (Atlanta), 228
Department of Finance (Chicago), 231
Department of Finance (NYC), 227
Department of Fire (Chicago), 231
Department of General Services (Chicago), 231
Department of General Services (NYC), 228
Department of General Services Salvage Section (Los Angeles), 233
Department of Planning (Chicago), 231
Department of Planning (NYC), 227
Department of Revenue (Chicago), 231
Department of the Tax Collector (San Francisco), 234
Department of Transportation Highway (New York City), 227
Department of Zoning (Chicago), 231
Department stores, 36
Depth and width of space, 24
Disabled people
 access for, building codes, 204, 206, 208, 210, 212
 permit requirements and, 199
 rest rooms for, 14, 109
 seating for, 14, 115–116
Division of Electrical Inspection (Atlanta), 228
Division of Facilities and Technical Services (New York City), 227
Dollar-per-square-foot value, 53, 67
Donations, 134
Doors, 50
 means of egress and, 164, 174
Double decking, 22
Double Image Theatre (NYC), 118
Down payment, 69
Dressing rooms, 59, 109, 120, 122–124, 132–133
 electrical code, 178
 fire code and, 182
 size requirements, 14
Drinking fountains, 175

E

Earthquake regulations, 209

Economic Development Corporation (EDC; New York City), 74, 222–223
Egress. See Means of egress
Electrical installations, 139–140
Electrical Code, NYC, 178–180
Electricity, energy efficiency and, 143
Electric shop, 125
Elevators, 50–51, 108, 115
Emergency lighting
 in audience space, 118
 building codes and, 203, 205, 208
  new code, 174
  old code, 165
 Electrical Code, 178–179
Emergency systems, 52
End stage, 10, 97, 120
 overhead and rigging for, 101
Energy efficiency, 52, 142–143
Energy management plan, 143
Ensemble Studio Theatre (NYC), 12, 54, 128
Entrances, 50
Equipment. See Materials and equipment
Erdman, Jean, 145
ETA Creative Arts Foundation (Chicago), 22, 24
Eureka Theatre (San Francisco), 63, 69
Eustis, Oscar, 63
Evaluating space, 48–55
 bringing building up to code and, 52–53
 building inspection, 49–52
 neighborhood, 48
 noise, 49
 profile, 56–64
 renovation and conversion costs, 54–55
 rent, 53–54
 transportation and accessibility, 49
Executive Service Corps, 219
Exit lighting, building classification and, 210
 new code, 174
 old code, 165
Exits, 51–52, 160. See also Means of egress
 building codes and, 164, 174, 203, 205, 207–208, 210, 212
 distance between, 164, 174
 fire code and, 182
Exit stairs, 164, 174
Extinguishers, fire, 181

F

Federal Rehabilitation Act of 1973, 115
Fees
  broker's, 70
  lawyer's, 70
  for permits and licenses, 190, 196, 199
  of real estate agents, 45
Filing procedures, 204, 206–207, 209–212
Finances, 7–8. See also Budget; Funding
Fine Arts Center Studio Theatre (University of Oklahoma), 103
Fire Department (Boston), 230
Fire Department (NYC), 227
Fire escapes, 50
Firehouses, 38, 131
Fire inspections, 155
Fire prevention, 52
Fire Prevention Bureau (Los Angeles), 233
Fire prevention code, NYC, 181–188
  flameproofing and, 182
  inspection checklist and, 181–182
  log book and, 182
  permits and, 182
Fireproofing, 125
Fire protection and finish materials in new code, 176
Fire-resistance rating, 160
Fire-retardant
  definition of, 160
  in old code, 166
Fire Safety Department (Atlanta), 229
First story, 160
Fixed grid system, 98–101
Flameproofing
  building codes and, 118, 203, 205
  old code, 166
  definition of, 160
  fire code and, 182
Flame-spread rating, 160
Flexible and multiform theatre, 11
Floors
  inspection of, 50
  stage, 91–95, 107, 111
Fort Mason complex (San Francisco), 38, 60–61, 63–64
42nd Street Development Corporation, 75–76, 78–83
Foundation Center, 84, 214

Foundations, 61, 75, 84, 148
Foyer. See Lobby
Free-span without columns, 24
Fulton County Arts Council (Atlanta), 216
Fulton County Reference Library (Atlanta), 229
Fund for the City of New York, 223
Funding, 72–86, 147–148
  campaign organization for, 86
  corporate, 75
  foundations, 61, 75, 84, 148
  government, 72–75
    federal, 72–74, 86
    local, 74–75
    state, 74
  individuals, 84, 86
  loans, 84
  service organizations and. See Service organizations
  for Theatre Row, 81–82
  of Vineyard Theatre, 86

G

Garages, 38
General Services (Los Angeles), 233
General Services Administration, U.S., 47, 135
George Street Playhouse (New Brunswick, New Jersey), 36
Goodman Theatre (Chicago), 104
Government Documents (Boston), 230
Government funding, 72–75
  federal, 72–74, 86
  local, 71, 74–75
  state, 74
Grade, 160
Granville-Barker, Harley, 56
Ground-floor space, advantages of, 26
Grounding, 179

H

Handicapped people. See Disabled people
Handrails, 164
Harlem Children's Theatre (NYC), 76, 82
Harold Clurman Theatre (NYC), 83
Heating, 51, 122–123, 126, 140, 146

energy efficiency and, 142–143
Height of space, 22, 24
Herbst Pavilion, 60–61, 64
Hogan, Polly, 105, 107
Horizon Theatre (Atlanta), 126
Horton Plaza Lyceum Theatre (San Diego, California), 39
House lights, 118, 178
Housing developments, 33
Huntington Theatre Company (Boston), 39, 41, 104
HVAC. See Air conditioning; Heating; Ventilation

I

Illinois Arts Council (IAC), 219
Improvements, 67–68
Index Publishing Corporation (Chicago), 231
Individuals, funding by, 84, 86
Industrial and commercial incentive programs, 75
Industrial Development Agency (IDA), 222
Industrial revenue bonds, 74
Inspections
  of building, 49–52
  building codes and, 204, 209, 212
  fire, 181–182
  routine on-site, 154–155
Inspection Services Department (Boston), 229
Insurance, 69
INTAR (NYC), 26, 76
Interart Theatre (NYC), 51, 54, 71, 128
Intersection for the Arts (San Francisco), 36

J

Jails, 38–39
Jean Cocteau Repertory Theatre (NYC), 32
Jeter, Richard, 105
Jewish Theatre of New England (Newton, Massachusetts), 33
Joint Purchasing Corporation (JPC), 135
Judith Anderson Theatre (NYC), 26, 82
Julian Theatre (San Francisco), 36

K

Kasky, Marc, 63–64
Kresge Foundation, 84
Krieger, Barbara Zinn, 86
Kurtz, Mitchell, 146

L

Labor, cost of, 55
Lamps, 137
Landlord, 68
Landmark buildings, 39, 47
Landmarks Preservation Commission (New York City), 228
Latino Chicago Theatre Company (LCTC), 38, 131
Lavatories. *See* Rest rooms
Lawyer's fees, 70
League of Chicago Theatres, 219
Leases
  commercial, 61, 67–69, 108
  net, 68
Legal assistance, 70
Licenses. *See* Application procedures, New York City
Life on the Water (San Francisco), 60, 63
Lighting, 58, 109, 118, 124, 126, 150–151. *See also* Emergency lighting; Exit lighting
  buying materials and equipment for, 136–137
  in dressing rooms, 122
  Electrical Code, 178–180
  energy efficiency and, 142–143
  overhead and rigging and, 97–102
Lion Theatre (NYC), 28–29, 76, 82
Live load, 204
  definition of, 160
  in new code, 175
  in old code, 164–165
Load-bearing walls and columns, 51, 160
Loans, 84
Lobby, 58, 129, 150
  building codes and, 203, 205, 208
  size requirements, 16
Local development corporations (LDCs), 75, 78–83
Loft space, 26, 32
Log book, theatre, 182
Los Angeles
  agencies, 232–233
  building code, 209–211
  energy efficiency in, 52
  service organizations, 213
Los Angeles Cultural Affairs Department, 220
Los Angeles Historic Theatre Foundation, 47
Los Angeles Theatre Center, 32
Lounge/bar, 17, 36, 38, 129
Lyric Stage Company (Boston), 15–16, 45, 105–109

M

Magic Theatre (San Francisco), 12, 22, 63–64
Majestic Theatre (Boston), 44
Management, energy plan and, 143
Manhattan Borough Superintendent (NYC), 226
Manhattan Theatre Club (MTC; New York City), 12, 75
Manufacturing buildings, 26, 32
Maps and Publications (NYC), 227
Marina Music Hall (San Francisco), 60
Masonry, 50
Massachusetts Cultural Alliance, 217
Massachusetts Cultural Council Space Program, 217
Massachusetts Health and Educational Facilities Authority, 217–218
Massachusetts Industrial Finance Agency, 218
Materials and equipment
  cost of, 55
  installations, 137–140
  sources of, 134–137
Materials for the Arts (MFA), 134
Mayor's Office for People (NYC), 228
Mayor's Office of Consumer Affairs and Licensing (Boston), 230
Means of egress, 160. *See also* Exits
  building codes and, 50, 204, 206, 208, 210, 212
  new code, 168–174
  old code, 163–164
Mechanical Bureau (Los Angeles), 232
Metheny, Russell, 149–150, 152
Metropolitan Atlanta Community Foundation, Inc. (Metro Atlanta), 216
MIDI, 139
Minimum live loads, building codes and, 204, 206, 208, 210, 212
Mixers, 139
Mortgage, 57, 70
Mortuaries, 36
Moss, Robert, 76
Movie theatres, 32–33
Municipal Reference and Research Center (New York City), 227
Municipal Reference Library (Chicago), 231
Municipal Reference Library (Los Angeles), 233

N

Nat Horne Theatre Company (NYC), 76
National Endowment for the Arts (NEA), 72–73, 86
National/State/County Partnership, The, 220
National Trust for Historic Preservation, 47, 72–74
Neighborhood, evaluating space and, 48
Neighborhood assistance, 70–71
New code requirements, 166–176
  for building classification, 167–168
  for emergency lighting, 174
  for exit lighting, 174
  for fire protection and finish materials, 176
  for live load, 175
  for means of egress, 168–174
  plumbing and sanitary, 175
  for seat and row spacing, 175
  for sprinklers, 176
  for steps, 175
  for ventilation, 174–175
Newspapers, space listings and, 44–45
New York City, 154–201. *See also* Application procedures, New York City; Building Code, New York City; Fire prevention code, NYC
  agencies, 226–228
  disabled people and, 115–116

Electrical Code of, 178–180
materials and equipment in, 134–136
service organizations, 214–215, 221–224
zoning in, 154, 156–158
New York Landmarks Conservancy, 39, 47, 223
New York Landmarks Commission, 47
New York Shakespeare Festival, 39
New York State Council on the Arts (NYSCA), 74, 223–224
New York State Preservation Trust, 39
New York State Urban Development Corporation, 74, 78–80
Nightclubs, 36, 38
Noise, 49
Nondisturbance agreement, 68
Non-Profit Performing Arts Loan Program, 224

O

Occupancy
 definition of, 160
 occupancy classification, new code, 166–167
 in old code vs. new code, 161–162
Office of Economic Development, New York City, 45, 47, 78
Office space, 6, 58, 62, 130, 152
 double-decked, 22
 size requirements, 18
Off-stage spaces, 58
 size requirements for, 12–13
Old code requirements, 162–166
 for building classification, 162–163
 for emergency lighting, 165
 for fire-retardant and flameproof, 166
 for lighting, 165
 for live load, 164–165
 for means of egress, 163
 plumbing and sanitary, 165–166
 for sear and row spacing, 164
 for sprinklers, 166
 for ventilation, 165
Open Eye Theatre (NYC), 144–148
Open or thrust stage (three-sided arena), 10, 58, 105, 107
 access to, 96–97
 overhead and rigging for, 98–99
Option to buy, 69
Overhead and rigging, 97–104
 catwalks, 102
 counterweight systems, 103–104
 fixed grid system, 98–101
 for flown scenery, 102–103
 parallel system of pipes, 101–102
 rolling scaffold, genie tower, or A-frame ladder, 97
 tension-wire grid, 102

P

Packaged lighting systems, 137
Panic bars, 140
Papert, Fred, 76
Parallel pipe system, 101–102
Parking, 49, 156–157
Pass-along and escalation charges, 68
Pearl Theatre Company (NYC), 12, 32
Performing Arts Services (PASS), 224–225
Permanent equipment, Electrical Code, 178
Permits. See Application procedures, New York City
 fire code and, 182
Permits requirements. See also Application procedures, New York City
 building codes and, 204
Pertalion, Albert, 56
Place of assembly permit, 160
 application for, 196
Planning Department (Los Angeles), 232
Planning Department (San Francisco), 234
Playwright's Horizon (NYC), 12, 76, 82–83, 124
Plumbing and sanitary requirements, 52
 in new code, 175
 in old code, 165–166
 permits for, 199
Points, 70
Police department, 135
Police locks, 140
Police stations, 38–39
Portable equipment, Electrical Code, 178–179

Post Office, U.S., 135
Production requirements, 6
Production Values, Inc. (PVI), 126, 136, 216
Professional assistance, cost of, 55
Program, 134
Properties, surplus, 38–39, 47, 135
Property values, 44
Prop shop, 125
Proscenium stage, 9, 97, 105, 107
 overhead and rigging for, 102–103
Public development corporations (PDCs), 75
Public Theatre, 49
Pubs, 36, 38
Puerto Rican Traveling Theatre (NYC), 38

R

Ramirez, Juan, 131
Ramps, 115
 building codes and, 204, 206, 210, 212
Real estate agents, 45
Real estate taxes, 66–67
Real Property Department (Boston), 230
Reel-to-reel tape decks, 139
Rehearsal space, 6–7, 126–128
 size requirements, 17
Renewal options, 68
Renovations, 108
 cost of, 58–59
 estimating, 54
 of Lyric Stage, 105–109
Rent (renting), 41, 44, 61, 66–69, 108, 147
 commercial leases and, 67–69
 evaluation of, 53–54
 of materials and equipment, 136
 real estate taxes and, 66–67
 on two adjacent floors, 26
Repairs, 67–68
Restaurants, 36, 38
Rest rooms
 for actors, 14–15, 123
 for disabled people, 109
 public, 14, 109
Revolving Loan Fund (RLF), 223
Rewiring, 140
Rigging. See Overhead and rigging
Ritchell, Ron, 105

Roof, 50
Rows, curved, 112, 114

S

Safe area, 160
St. Clements (NYC), 33
Salvage yards, 136
Samuel Beckett Theatre (NYC), 76
San Diego Repertory Theatre, 39
San Francisco
  agencies, 233–234
    building code, 211–212
    service organizations, 214–215, 224–225
San Francisco Arts Commission, 225
San Francisco Costume Bank, 126, 225
San Francisco Opera House, 103
Sashes, 51
Scavenging, 134–135
Scenery, flown, rigging system, 102–103
Scenery and construction shop, 132
  checklist for, 124–125
  size requirements, 18–19
Scenic Central, 124, 224
Scheduling, 6–7
Schools, 33
Search for space, 3–64, 105. *See also* Evaluating space
  guidelines in, 4–8
  how to find it, 42–47
    gathering information, 44–47
    where to look, 42–44
  shape and size requirements, 9–21
  what to look for in, 22–41
    general characteristics, 22–26
    types of buildings, 26–41
Seating (seats), 58, 105, 109, 150
  building codes, 203, 205, 207, 209–212
  commercial modular platforms for, 113–114
  continental, 112
  for the disabled, 14
  for disabled people, 115–116
  fixed vs. movable, 114
  layout of, 112–116
  movable platform modules for, 112–113
  in new code, 175
  in old code, 164
  sightlines and, 110–112
  size requirements, 13–14
  staggered, 112
  temporary, 113
  types of, 114–115
Second Stage Theatre (NYC), 143
Security, 52
Security systems, installation of, 140
Service organizations, 86
  Atlanta, 213, 215–216
  Boston, 214–218
  Chicago, 213–215, 218–219
  Los Angeles, 213–215, 219–221
  national, 213–215
  New York City, 214–215, 221–224
  San Francisco, 214–215, 224–225
Settling of building, 49
Seven Stages (Atlanta), 33
Shubert Organization, 115, 146
Sightlines, 110–112, 151
Sign permits, application for, 196
Sills, Paul, 56
Size requirements, 11–21
  necessary areas, 11–16
  optional areas, 11, 16–20, 21
  for stage, 96
  total square footage estimates and, 20
Smoking, fire code and, 182
Soundproofing, 118
Sound systems, installation of, 137–138
Southern Building Code International, 202
South Street Theatre (NYC), 76, 82
Space, theatre, search for. *See* Search for space
Space referral banks, 45, 47
Speakers, location of, 139
Sprinklers, 108, 125, 146
  building codes and, 206, 208, 210, 212
  fire code and, 182
  in new code, 176
  in old code, 166
Square footage estimates, 20, 67
  renovations costs and, 54
  value and, 53
Stables, 38
Stage lighting, equipment and installations, 178–179
StageSource: The Alliance of Theatre Artists and Producers, 218
Stage space, 91–104
  access to, 96–97
  building codes, 204, 206, 208, 210, 212
  configurations, 9–11
  floors, 91–95, 107, 111
  lighting equipment for, 136–137
  means of egress and, 174
  overhead and rigging for. *See* Overhead and rigging
  size of, 96
  size requirements, 11–12
  walls, 95
StageWest (Springfield, Massachusetts), 39
Stahl Associates, 105
Stairs, 119, 164
  access, 159
  building codes, 204, 206, 208, 210, 212
  exit, 174
  inspection of, 50
  lighting on, 174
Standard Building Code (SBC), 202
Standards (Los Angeles), 233
State Bookstore (Boston), 230
Steppenwolf Theatre (Chicago), 132
Steps in new code, 175
Stoops, 50
Storage space, 6, 20, 58, 126
Storefront space, 24, 32, 58
Studio Theatre (University of Oklahoma), 117
Studio Theatre (Washington, D.C.), 38, 112, 144, 149–152
Subleasing, 69
Superintendent (San Francisco), 234
Supermarkets, 38
Support Services for the Arts (SSA), 225
Support spaces. *See also* Box office; Dressing rooms; Lobby; Lounge/bar; Office space
  design and planning of, 121–130
Surplus properties, 38–39, 47, 135

T

Tax Assessor's Office (Los Angeles), 233
Tax Collection Division (NYC), 227
Tax Collection (Los Angeles), 233

Index

Taxes
  real estate, 66–67
  unpaid, 67
Technical control space, 15–16, 121–130
Tension-wire grid, 102
Theatre Artaud (San Francisco), 26
Theatre Bay Area, 225
Theatre Company (Chicago), 33
Theatre Development Fund (TDF), 214
Theatre-in-the-round (four-sided arena), 10
  overhead and rigging for, 98
Theatre League Alliance (Theatre L.A.), 220–221
Theatre Off Park (NYC), 12
Theatre Row Project, 74, 78–83
Theatre Row Theatre (NYC), 83
Thrift shops, 136
Thrust stage, 10, 58, 105, 107
  access to, 96–97
  overhead and rigging for, 98–99
Ticket Central, 129
Ticket system, 6, 58–59, 128–129, 152
Title search, 70
Trade-offs, rent and, 53–54
Transportation, 49
Triangle Theatre (Boston), 69

U

Uniform Building Code (UBC), 13, 202
United States Institute for Theatre Technology (USITT), 214–215
Unit width of egress, 160
Upper floor spaces, 164
Urban development corporations (UDCs), 74, 78–80
Urban renewal areas, 44
Use groups, 42
Utility bills, 68

V

Vacancy, extended, 68
Variance zoning, 157–158
Ventilation, 51, 109, 122–123, 125–126, 140
  energy efficiency and, 142–143
  in new code, 174–175
  in old code, 165
Victory Gardens Theater (VG; Chicago), 56, 128–129
Victory Theatre (Burbank, California), 32
Vineyard Theatre (NYC), 39, 75, 86
Violations, 67
Vivian Beaumont Theatre (NYC), 96
Voluntary Arts Contribution Fund Grants for the Arts, The, 225
Volunteer Consulting Group (VCG), 224
Volunteer Lawyers for the Arts (VLA), 70, 215

W

Wagner, Daniel McLean, 150
Walking the streets to find space, 45
Walls, 51
  load-bearing, 51, 160
  stage, 95
Warehouses, 26, 32, 38
West Side Arts Theatre (NYC), 33
Wharves, 38
Width and depth of space, 24
Windows, 51
  gates and shutters for, 140
Wisdom Bridge Theatre (Chicago), 123
Work lights, 118, 178
Workshop spaces, 18–20
Writers Theatre (NYC), 12

Y

York Theatre Company (NYC), 12
Young Performers Theatre (San Francisco), 60, 63

Z

Zeckendorf, William, 86
Zinoman, Joy, 144
Zoning, 42–44
  checklist for, 177
  codes and, 154
  commercial leases and, 67
  maps, 157, 189
  neighborhood assistance and, 70–71
  use groups and, 42, 156–157
  variance and, 157–158
Zoning (Atlanta), 228
Zoning Board of Appeals (Chicago), 231

About The Alliance of Resident Theatres/New York

The Alliance of Resident Theatres/New York (A.R.T./New York) is the not-for-profit service organization for New York City's not-for-profit Off- and Off-Off-Broadway theatres. It seeks to ensure the continued survival and vitality of the nonprofit theatre in New York City by fostering communication among theatre companies; supporting managerial strength through special programs and services; identifying and addressing long-term artistic, financial and administrative problems and opportunities that face the field; and promoting the value of New York's not-for-profit theatre to the public, press, government, and funders.

Founded in 1972 by a group of New York City not-for-profit theatres, A.R.T./New York's constituents include over 130 not-for-profit Off- and Off-Off-Broadway theatres of diverse artistic missions, organizational goals, and budget sizes located throughout New York City. A.R.T./New York's constituents comprise a $100 million industry producing over 14,000 performances of 600 plays annually for an audience of over 3 million people.

A.R.T./New York is publishing this handbook in response to the chronic need for more effective, centralized guidance in space acquisition, design, planning, financing and code compliance.

About ACA

Founded in 1960, the American Council for the Arts (ACA) is a national organization whose purpose is to define issues and promote public policies that advance the contributions of the arts and the artist to American life. To accomplish its mission, ACA conducts research, sponsors conferences and public forums, publishes books, reports, and periodicals, advocates before Congress for legislation that benefits the arts, and maintains a 15,000-volume specialized library. ACA is one of the nation's primary sources of legislative news affecting all of the arts and serves as a leading advisor to arts administrators, individual artists, educators, elected officials, arts patrons and the general public.

BOARD OF DIRECTORS

Chairman
Mrs. Jack Blanton, Sr.

President and CEO
Milton Rhodes

Vice Chairmen
Donald R. Greene
Howard S. Kelberg
Patrick W. Kenny
Elton B. Stephens

Secretary
Fred Lazarus IV

Treasurer
John A. Koten

Past Chairmen
Gerald D. Blatherwick
Eugene C. Dorsey
Donald G. Conrad
Marshall S. Cogan
Louis Harris
David Rockefeller, Jr.
George M. Irwin

Members
John G. Avrett
Judith F. Baca
John Paul Batiste
Harry Belafonte
Madeleine Berman
Theodore Bikel
Cheryl McClenney-Brooker
Marie Bosca
Willard Boyd
Ernest L. Boyer
John Brademas
Mrs. Martin Brown
Nedda Casei
Terri Childs
Donald G. Conrad
Elizabeth Christopherson
Mrs. Howard Stephen Cowan
Stephanie French
Sonnai Frock-Rohrbeck
John Galvin
Jack Golodner
Richard S. Gurin
Mrs. John R. Hall
Eldridge C. Hanes
Mrs. Joan W. Harris
Daniel Herrick
Linda L. Hoeschler
Rosario Holguin
A. William Holmberg
Richard Hunt
Alexander Julian
John Kilpatrick
Allan S. Kushen
Steven David Lavine
John J. Mahlmann
Bruce Marks
Mrs. Peter W. Mauger
Timothy J. McClimon
Lee Kimche McGrath
Charles K. McWhorter
Mrs. Michael A. Miles
Jackie Millan
Henry Moran
Velma V. Morrison
Sondra G. Myers
Adolfo V. Nodal
Paul M. Ostergard
Gerald Reiser
Mrs. Richard S. Reynolds III
Dr. W. Ann Reynolds
James M. Rosser
Mrs. LeRoy Rubin
John Rubinstein
Scott Sanders
Mrs. Paul Schorr III
Gerard Schwarz
Mrs. Alfred R. Shands
Mrs. David E. Skinner
Steven D. Spiess
John Straus
Dr. Billy Taylor
Esther Wachtell
Sheila E. Weisman
Mrs. Gerald H. Westby
Masaru Yokouchi

Special Counsel
Jack S. Duncan

Members Emeriti
Eugene C. Dorsey
Louis Harris
Irma Lazarus